PSYCHOLOGY

PSYCHOLOGY

John P. Dworetzky

Department of Psychology
Glendale College, Arizona

West Publishing Company   St. Paul   New York   Los Angeles   San Francisco

A study guide has been developed to assist you in mastering the concepts presented in this text. The study guide clarifies concepts by presenting them in concise, condensed form. It reinforces your understanding of terms, concepts, and individuals and also provides a programmed review and self-test questions. The study guide is available from your local bookstore under the title Study Guide to Accompany Psychology, prepared by Stephen Cooper and Richard Rees.

If you cannot locate it in the bookstore, ask your bookstore manager to order it for you.

Library of Congress Cataloging in Publication Data
Dworetzky, John.
   Psychology.

   Bibliography: p.
   Includes index.
   1. Psychology.   I. Title.
BF121.D96   150   82–1956
ISBN 0–314–63168–2   AACR2

Copy editing: Carol Henderson
Design: Janet Bollow
Technical illustrations: Ayxa Art Studio
Anatomical illustrations: Barbara Hack
Cartoons: Tom Barnett
Cover art: Christa Keiffer
Production coordination: Janet Bollow Associates
Composition: Typothetae

ACKNOWLEDGEMENTS

Page 38, Figure 2.4. From "The Neuron," by Charles F. Stevens. Copyright © 1979 by Scientific American, Inc. All rights reserved.
Color Section, Figure 2.9. From "The Organization of the Brain," by Walle J. H. Nauta and Michael Feirtag. Copyright © 1979 by Scientific American, Inc. All rights reserved.
Page 47, Figure 2.11. From "The Brain," by David H. Hubel. Copyright © 1979 by Scientific American, Inc. All rights reserved.
Page 49, Figure 2.13. From "Specializations of the Human Brain," by Norman Geschwind. Copyright © 1979 by Scientific American, Inc. All rights reserved.
Page 55, Figure 2.15. From "Emotions are Expressed More Intensely on the Left Side of the Face," by H. A. Sackeim, R. C. Gur, & M. C. Saucy. In *Science*, 1978, *202*, 434–436. Copyright 1978 by the American Association for the Advancement of Science.
Page 67, Figure 2.19. From "Genetic Differences in Maze Learning in Rats," by R. C. Tryon. In *Yearbook of the National Society for Studies in Education*, 1940, *39*, 111–119. Reprinted by permission of the National Society for the Study of Education.
Page 86, Figure 3.14. From "Adaptation to Spatial Stimuli," by C. Blakemore and F. W. Campbell. In *Journal of Physiology*, 1968, *200*, 11P–13P. Reprinted by permission of Cambridge University Press and Colin Blakemore.
Page 89, Figure 3.19. From *Seeing: Illusion, Brain and Mind*, John P. Frisby, Oxford University Press, Inc., © 1979, reprinted with permission of Roxby Press Ltd.
Page 90, Figure 3.20. Reprinted by permission from Beiser, Arthur, PHYSICS, Menlo Park, California, The Benjamin/Cummings Publishing Company, Inc., fig. 13–26, p. 305.
Page 93, Figure 3.22. From George Nicholson/DISCOVER Magazine © 1981 Time Inc.
Page 130, Figure 4.21. Reproduced, with permission, from the *Annual Review of Psychology* Volume 31. © 1980 by Annual Reviews, Inc.
Page 138, Figure 5.1. From *The Brain* by J. Fincher. Used with permission of U.S. News & World Report Books.
Page 151, Figure 5.6. From "The Brain as a Dream State Generator," by J. A. Hobson & R. W. McCarley. In *American Journal of Psychiatry*, 1977, *134*, 1335–1348. Copyright 1977, the American Psychiatric Association. Reprinted by permission.
Page 153, Table 5.2. Copyrighted, Stanford University, 1962, and used by permission.
Page 180, Figure 6.4. From "Thorndike and the Problem of Animal Intelligence," by M. E. Bitterman. In *American Psychologist*, 1969, *24*, 444–453. Copyright 1969 by the American Psychological Association. Reprinted by permission of the publisher and author.

(continued following Subject Index)

CONTENTS IN BRIEF

CONTENTS

CHAPTER 4

Perception   103

CHAPTER 5

States of Consciousness   135

UNIT TWO
Interacting with the Environment   167

CHAPTER 6
Learning and Conditioning   169

CHAPTER 7

Memory and Information Processing   203

FOCUS ON AN APPLICATION:
WHY CHILDREN STOP BELIEVING IN
SANTA CLAUS   353

FOCUS ON THE FUTURE:
WHY DO WE GROW OLD, AND CAN
AGING BE PREVENTED?   365

CHAPTER 12

Intelligence and Individual Differences   371

FOCUS ON A CONTROVERSY:
THE HERITABILITY OF INTELLECTUAL
CAPACITY   382

FOCUS ON AN APPLICATION:
MEETING THE NEEDS OF
EXCEPTIONAL PEOPLE   390

CHAPTER 15
Abnormal Behavior 453

CHAPTER 16
Therapy   499

Psychology is the study of ourselves, our behavior, our thoughts, our feelings, our lives. We have learned much about human behavior and we are learning more. The amount of information psychologists have gathered doubles every seven years. Some day, perhaps in the not too distant future, psychologists will be able to apply their knowledge to reshape the world. Some of the first great breakthroughs may come with our increasing knowledge of the brain and its chemistry, or in our understanding of aggression and war, or perhaps through a greater understanding of what factors motivate us or control our feelings. This textbook contains an introduction to the research and knowledge psychologists and others have gathered to date.

There are 18 chapters in this text, divided into five major divisions. While the text is designed to be used as an introduction to psychology for undergraduates, it has a strong research base and a strong emphasis on reporting the most recent and important research. Although the text material is extensive and sometimes detailed, great efforts were taken to make certain that every aspect was written in a way that is clear and easy for a beginner in psychology to understand. This does not mean that material has been made simple, but just that it is understandable. I do not credit myself for this, but rather give thanks to the many students who have provided me with invaluable feedback in the more than 50 introductory psychology classes I have taught.

The text is comprehensive, but as must be with all introductory psychology textbooks, the research presented is selective rather than inclusive. Contained within the text material are focus sections in which a particular discussion appears in depth. The focus sections present biographies, selected research, applications, controversies, and possible effects that research may have on our future. Almost every chapter opens with a dramatization of a classic experiment, written as though the reader were present. In this way the reader may feel more like a participant than a bystander. And each chapter ends with an epilogue that demonstrates how material in the chapter directly affected the life of just one person.

To better serve the reader, a running glossary is provided in the margin. Whenever a new important term is presented it appears in boldface. Even though it may be defined in text, it is also defined in the running glossary to help students review and reinforce their learning. In this way important terms are emphasized and readers may become more familiar with them. Every boldface term also appears in a glossary at the back of the book. At the end of each chapter are suggestions for further reading. The selections have been chosen for students who are interested in pursuing a particular area. They will provide more information at a level suitable for the introductory student.

The text follows the style suggested by the American Psychological Association in that each important piece of research is referenced. These references generally appear at the end of the sentence to which they pertain and are contained within parentheses. To find the original source of the research or statement, students may look up each reference in the reference section at the back of the text. By going to the original sources, students may examine particular research in greater detail.

There are also a number of important supplements to the textbook. A study guide for *Psychology* was prepared by two of my colleagues, Stephen S. Cooper and Richard D. Rees, and has been developed to assist students in making full use of the textbook. An instructor's manual, containing suggestions for class and lecture, has also been developed by Professors Cooper and Rees, and myself. A comprehensive test item bank is also included, along with film suggestions, capsule summaries for each chapter, and behavioral objectives.

No work of this size could ever be accomplished alone, and I owe a great debt to many others. I wish to express thanks to the following members of our academic community who reviewed these chapters and provided comments, suggestions, and critiques.

Ellen B. Barker
Bloomsburg State College, Pennsylvania

Ronald K. Barrett
Loyola Marymount University, California

D. Thompson Bond
Thomas Nelson Community College, Virginia

Arthur Brody
Lehigh University, Pennsylvania

Dennis Coon
Santa Barbara City College, California

Donald Elman
Kent State University, Ohio

Robert B. Graham
East Carolina State University, North Carolina

Charles G. Halcomb
Texas Tech University

A. Christine Harris
Chaffey College, California

Courtland Holdgrafer
Santa Ana College, California

Ellen C. Huft
Glendale College, Arizona

Max W. Lewis
University of Arkansas

Svenn Lindskold
Ohio University

Spencer A. McWilliams
University of Arizona

Robert R. Pagano
University of Washington

John N. Park
Mankato State University, Minnesota

Robert J. Pellegrini
San Jose State University, California

Janet D. Proctor
Auburn University, Alabama

Duane Reeder
Glendale College, Arizona

Robert P. Robison
Everett Community College, Washington

Susan A. Shodahl
San Bernardino Valley College, California

Lee Springer
Glendale College, Arizona

Stanley E. Taylor
Marquette University, Wisconsin

Joe M. Tinnin
Richland College, Texas

David Wilson
Texas A & M University

Carol Woodward
California State University, Northridge

I also wish to thank Professors Duane Reeder, Lee Springer, Ellen Huft, Elizabeth Cooper, Carl Samuels, Curt Pechtel, and all my colleagues at Glendale College for their comments and advice.

I especially wish to thank Professors Stephen Cooper and Richard Rees for their support, encouragement, advice, and friendship.

I am most grateful to Janet Bollow for the beautiful design of this textbook, and especially for her endless good humor, friendship, talent, and limitless energy. I also wish to thank Christa Keiffer for the fine cover, all the members of Typothetae for their excellent composition and typesetting, and especially Carol Henderson, whose exceptional copyediting and knowledge of psychology never ceased to impress me. And finally, I wish to thank Clyde Perlee, Editor-in-Chief of West's College Division, for his encouragement, support, friendship, and professionalism; without him this book would never have been written.

JOHN P. DWORETZKY

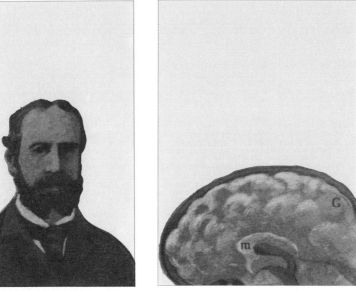

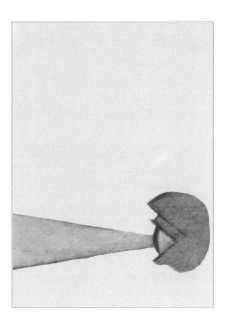

UNIT ONE

Psychological Foundations: The Mind and the Body

CONTENTS

CHAPTER 1

History, Systems, and Research Methods

You are a human being. You must be, because no other creature on earth could be reading this sentence. Human beings are the most complex of all living things. We alone seek knowledge for its own sake. And we alone have broken our terrestrial bonds to explore beyond our world. Some have said that outer space is the final frontier, but it isn't. Even if we should conquer the vastness of space there will be one frontier remaining— ourselves. Although we've gazed at the stars and looked outward for centuries, it's been only in the last hundred years that we've begun a systematic exploration inward. Inner space is the final frontier, and psychology has begun the exploration. As you take the journey inward you will encounter many worlds that may at first seem familiar to you. Among these are memories, senses, emotions, thoughts, and motivations—all of them a part of you and of every human being. As you take a closer look, however, you may discover that things are not as you have assumed. Instead, you may find a new understanding of yourself and those around you.

An Introduction to Psychology

■ In a university laboratory an experimenter makes a tiny incision in a selected part of an anesthetized rat's brain. When the rat recovers from the surgery it appears perfectly normal, except that it no longer seems to know when to stop eating.

■ A researcher working for NASA asks astronauts to respond to emergency lights on a control board as quickly as possible. When green and red lights are flashed the astronauts have trouble telling them apart using their peripheral vision. When the researcher tries yellow and blue lights instead, the astronauts' errors decrease significantly.

■ In a laboratory, an investigator stays awake all night observing sleeping subjects who are attached to sensors and measuring devices. By watching the sensors she can tell when the sleepers begin to dream, when they become restless, or when sleep disturbances start. She is trying to find patterns that may help explain why some people have difficulty sleeping.

■ At a large metropolitan zoo, a scientist places a series of small steel rails along the ground throughout the mountain lion compound. From time to time a mechanical rabbit runs along one of the rails starting from a tunnel. When a lion catches a rabbit, meat is automatically dispensed from a hopper at the far end of the enclosure. The scientist structures the situation so that the lions quickly learn what to do. The curator of the zoo notes that the big cats are healthier and more active now that they are getting exercise and hunting "game."

■ An investigator observes a three-month-old infant who is watching a rolling ball. The moment the ball rolls behind a couch the infant loses all interest in the object and acts as though it never existed. The investigator repeats the process with an older infant. When the ball disappears the older infant leans to one side and tries to see where the ball went. The investigator wonders if young infants understand that objects still exist even though they are out of sight.

■ A therapist in a city hospital interviews a young woman who wants to go home. Five weeks earlier the woman had suffered a deep depression and had tried to stab her husband and take her own life. The therapist interviews her carefully, calling on all his skill in order to make a decision that will represent his best professional judgment. He doesn't want to detain her without cause, but he also doesn't want her to return to a situation she cannot handle.

■ An investigator leaves self-addressed unsealed envelopes containing money in church pews all over the city just before the congregations assemble. She leaves similar envelopes in nonreligious halls just before meetings begin. The envelopes are secretly marked so that they can be distinguished later. The investigator then waits at home to see if church-goers are more likely to return the money.

All of the professionals in the above examples have one thing in common: They are psychologists. **Psychology** is the study of the behavior of organisms. Whether studying a rat with a brain lesion, an astronaut reacting to an emergency, a sleeping person, a hungry mountain lion, a three-month-old baby, a depressed woman in a hospital, or the honesty of churchgoers, each of the psychologists was studying behavior.

Look at the Table of Contents and you will begin to appreciate how

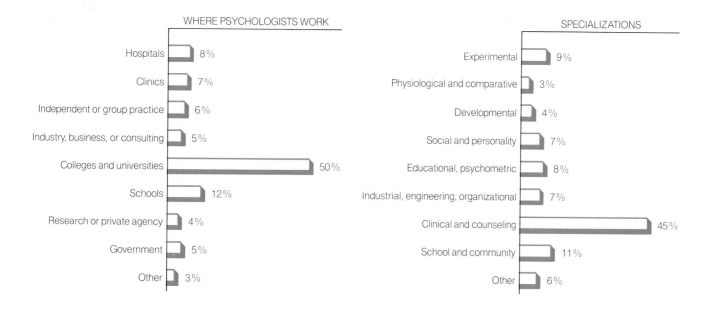

WHERE PSYCHOLOGISTS WORK

- Hospitals 8%
- Clinics 7%
- Independent or group practice 6%
- Industry, business, or consulting 5%
- Colleges and universities 50%
- Schools 12%
- Research or private agency 4%
- Government 5%
- Other 3%

SPECIALIZATIONS

- Experimental 9%
- Physiological and comparative 3%
- Developmental 4%
- Social and personality 7%
- Educational, psychometric 8%
- Industrial, engineering, organizational 7%
- Clinical and counseling 45%
- School and community 11%
- Other 6%

diversified and encompassing psychology is. If you were to become a psychologist, you might spend your career working within an area described by just one of these chapters, or perhaps by just one of the paragraphs within one of the chapters. Psychologists are interested in every aspect of behavior.

Figure 1.1 *Places and spheres of work in psychology (Data from survey of over 30,000 psychologists, as reported in Boneau & Cuca, 1974)*

BECOMING A PSYCHOLOGIST

Psychologists receive a doctoral degree (Ph.D., Psy.D., or Ed.D.) after three to six years of postgraduate training. At this point they are properly called doctor, although they are not physicians. Some states require that psychologists be licensed before they are permitted to administer psychological tests or to engage in psychological therapy and treatment of clients. Clinical psychologists who work at hospitals or clinics may be required to complete an additional year of psychological internship as part of their training. Some psychologists have a masters degree (M.A. or M.S.) instead of a doctorate, indicating that they have completed one to three years of postgraduate training. Increasingly, however, a doctoral degree is required for employment as a psychotherapist or research psychologist. Figure 1.1 shows the places in which psychologists work and their specializations. As you can see, a large proportion of psychologists are employed by colleges and universities to conduct research and teach.

AREAS OF SPECIALIZATION

There are many different areas of specialization in psychology. This is one of the reasons psychology is so appealing; it offers something for everybody. If you consider the divisions of the American Psychological Association (APA) shown in the following list, you will further appreciate the broad scope and diversification of psychology.

General Psychology
Teaching of Psychology
Experimental Psychology
Evaluation and Measurement
Physiological and Comparative
  Psychology
Developmental Psychology
Personality and Social Psychology
Society for the Psychological Study
  of Social Issues
Psychology and the Arts
Clinical Psychology
Consulting Psychology
Industrial and Organizational
  Psychology
Educational Psychology
School Psychology
Counseling Psychology
Psychologists in Public Service
Military Psychology
Adult Development and Aging
Society of Engineering
  Psychologists

Rehabilitation Psychology
Consumer Psychology
Philosophical Psychology
Experimental Analysis of Behavior
History of Psychology
Community Psychology
Psychopharmacology
Psychotherapy
Psychological Hypnosis
State Psychological Association
  Affairs
Humanistic Psychology
Mental Retardation
Population and Environmental
  Psychology
Psychology of Women
Psychologists Interested in
  Religious Issues
Child and Youth Services
Health Psychology
Psychoanalysis
Clinical Neuropsychology
Psychology and Law

These divisions represent areas of mutual interest among groups of psychologists. It is not uncommon for a psychologist to belong to more than one division at a time, especially if the divisions have similar interests. In the following paragraphs, we will describe some of the different kinds of psychologists and the interests they share.

Experimental psychologists, like most psychologists, rely on scientific methods and experiments to examine the fundamental processes that govern behavior. Very often their research is conducted in a laboratory. They investigate areas such as sensation, perception, learning, memory, and motivation in both humans and lower animals.

Physiological and comparative psychologists are interested in biological factors and their effect on behavior. Physiological psychologists study the brain, nervous system, genes, and drugs in relation to behavior. Comparative psychologists are interested in behavioral differences and similarities between species.

Developmental psychologists study the way in which common human behaviors develop and change during a life span. Special areas of interest include the development of language, social attachments, emotions, thinking, and perception.

Social psychologists use scientific techniques to examine the effects that people have on each other. They are interested in topics such as altruism, cooperation, aggression, affection, and group pressure.

Clinical psychologists focus their efforts on understanding, diagnosing, and treating abnormal or deviant behaviors.

Industrial or organizational psychologists work with business. They are concerned with improving working conditions, raising production rates, and developing decision-making abilities.

Industrial psychologists, using time-motion studies, helped to organize workers' efforts to improve productivity. Such techniques were incorporated by the Ford Motor Company when they developed the first mass assembly line.

Educational psychologists study educational systems, methods of teaching, different curricula, and other factors influencing the learning process. Their goal is to improve education and make learning easier and more efficient.

Counseling psychologists are trained to help individuals solve personal, academic, or vocational problems that do not stem from serious mental disorders. Counseling and clinical psychologists often have similar training.

As you can see from the APA list, we could describe many other kinds of psychologists as well. Some of the more specialized areas may be new to you. When I was first introduced to psychology, for instance, I felt as though I had walked into a strange town where I didn't know anyone and where the buildings, streets, and landmarks were all unfamiliar. Of course, a town isn't strange to the people who have lived there all their lives. They can remember when this building was built, or when that street was named, and they know who lives where and which children belong to which parents. It's easy for long-time residents to make sense of a place; they saw it take shape from the beginning. In the same way, the complex community of psychological interests would no doubt be more familiar to you had you been there from the start. You would know why certain structures had been created, why certain roads had been paved, and which ideas were the offspring of which psychological families. The place to begin, then, is in a laboratory in Leipzig, Germany, a little over a century ago.

The History of Psychology

Psychology was born of two parents, philosophy and physiology. For centuries philosophers had asked questions about human emotions, thoughts, and behavior. They had tried to deduce answers to their questions by applying logic and common-sense reasoning, but they were not always successful. For example, the great philosopher Aristotle believed that thinking

Wilhelm Wundt, the father of experimental psychology (1832–1920).

occurred in the heart, while the brain only served to help cool the blood. The famous physician Hippocrates believed that emotions resulted from different combinations or levels of four bodily humors—black bile, yellow bile, blood, and phlegm. Aristotle's and Hippocrates' ideas about the body and behavior were accepted as fact for almost 2,000 years before they were finally challenged by physiologists during the Renaissance.

Physiologists were especially influential in providing a new understanding of the brain and the nervous system and the way in which they affect behavior. Formerly, the common belief had been that a person's muscular responses occurred the instant they were desired. But by a series of careful scientific analyses physiologists were able to demonstrate that nerve impulses take time to travel from their place of origin in the brain or spine to the muscles. In addition to the brain and the nerves, physiologists also explored the senses and the rest of the body. It was the union between the questions asked by the philosophers and the careful scientific analysis of the physiologists that led to the field of study we call psychology.

STRUCTURALISM

Psychology hasn't always been concerned with mental illness, animal behavior, unconscious thoughts, dreams, IQ tests, personality, or childhood. At the beginning, its objective was to analyze the structure of *conscious experience*. This interest in analyzing conscious experience began when Wilhelm Wundt (1832–1920), whom many consider to be the father of psychology, became curious about an effect that could be produced by a metronome. A metronome is a pendulum-like device that ticks at a steady rate and is used in music training to help maintain a tempo. If you happen to have a metronome you might listen to it and see if you notice the same thing that Wundt did. Each tick of a metronome should sound the same as the last one, but Wundt noticed that people listening to a metronome began to perceive a pattern in the sound. Some would hear tick-tock. Others would hear TICK-tick-TICK-tick or, like a waltz, TICK-tick-tick, TICK-tick-tick. The listeners' conscious minds seemed to *structure* what they heard. Wundt wondered about this apparent tendency of the mind. He set up a laboratory in Leipzig, Germany, in order to carry out a systematic analysis of the structure of the conscious adult mind. By first breaking down consciousness into elements and then discovering how the elements interacted with one another, Wundt hoped to establish a field of psychological research that would follow in the footsteps of physics and chemistry.

The best way to analyze the structure of the mind, Wundt decided, was to rely on self-observation, a technique known as **introspection.** Trained self-observers, or introspectionists, tried to break down the content of their conscious experiences into its basic parts. According to Wundt, only persons skilled in the techniques of introspection could provide an objective description of conscious experience because only they were trained to describe their immediate perception of an event without adding conclusions drawn from memory or knowledge. For example, if you as an untrained observer saw a white sheet of paper placed in a dimly lit corner of a room and you were then asked, "What color is that paper?", you would most likely reply, "White." A trained introspectionist, even knowing that the paper was white, would rely only on the immediate conscious experience and would say, "Light gray."

This kind of psychology, which became known as **structuralism,** was brought to the United States by Edward B. Titchener (1867–1927), who had studied in Wundt's laboratory. Titchener began a psychology laboratory at Cornell University in 1892.

The structural approach taken by Wundt and Titchener might have remained a powerful force in psychology, had it not been for a few critical flaws. The worst of these flaws was the introspective method itself. Have you ever applied introspection to your own conscious experience? For instance, have you ever tried to stop in the middle of a daydream and pay attention to your thoughts or sensations? Observing what you are experiencing changes the experience. Psychologists began to discover that the very act of introspection altered the conscious experience they wanted to examine. But even more devastating was the discovery that different researchers independently using the introspective method were getting different results. Nothing could be done to resolve the problem of a disagreement between trained observers. After all, each was describing a personal experience, and who could say which observer was correct? By the 1930s researchers had begun to abandon structuralism. Psychologists working with animals were finding exciting results without introspection, European psychoanalysts were examining the influence of *unconscious processes* in maladjustment, and many American psychologists were searching for practical solutions to everyday problems.

Still, all psychology owes a debt to the structural movement for three reasons: First, it provided psychology with a strong scientific and research impetus. Second, it gave the introspective method a thorough test, which was worthwhile since most psychologists are now in agreement that introspection has severe limitations. Third, it served as a foundation against which new schools of psychological thought could rebel.

FUNCTIONALISM

Functionalism was the first completely American psychology. Its founder was William James (1842–1910), who is still regarded by many as the greatest American psychologist. James received an M.D. from Harvard and was a professor of anatomy. He became interested in psychological inquiry in 1875 and published his famous two-volume work, *Principles of Psychology*, in 1890. It still makes for fascinating reading. James wasn't an experimentalist, but he had a way of brilliantly synthesizing psychological principles and getting to the heart of difficult problems. His functionalism began as a rebellion against the structural approach, which he considered narrow, artificial, and pointless. He rejected the idea that the conscious mind had a permanent structure or "blueprint." To him, conscious experience was more like a river that was always changing and flowing. He coined his famous term **stream of consciousness** in order to express this property.

James was greatly influenced by the work of Charles Darwin, who stated that, because of the process of **natural selection,** characteristics in animals that served a valuable function would be favored and carried over from one generation to the next. For example, Darwin argued that sex was pleasurable because only those species that found it so would have survived. A species that didn't like sex would not last more than a generation. Physical characteristics as well, such as eyes, ears, hands, paws, and claws, had all been favored by natural selection because they served a useful function.

William James (1842–1910).

G. Stanley Hall (1844–1924).

With this in mind, James concluded that human consciousness must also have a function, or why would it have evolved? He believed that the conscious mind enabled people to make rational choices which in turn helped them to survive generation after generation. James considered consciousness to be like "an organ added for the sake of steering a nervous system grown too complex to regulate itself" (James, 1890, p. 144).

Because of this philosophical emphasis, other functionalists who followed in James' footsteps were concerned with *why* a thought or behavior occurred rather than *what* a thought or behavior was. This was the major distinction between functionalism and structuralism, and it opened the door to many new areas of psychological study.

G. Stanley Hall (1844–1924) was perhaps William James' most illustrious student. Hall was the first to receive a Ph.D. in psychology; he was also the founder of the American Psychological Association. Hall's interest in the development of human beings during childhood and adolescence and his systematic investigations were the beginnings of developmental psychology. John Dewey (1859–1952), another functional psychologist and educator, became interested in the problem-solving ability of the conscious mind as a factor in our species' survival (Dewey, 1910). Dewey's interest in problem solving and in ways of improving teaching contributed to the establishment of another new discipline, educational psychology. And, since animals are capable of learning and their behavior too can serve a purpose or function, the study of animal psychology was born. Industrial psychology came into being when researchers began making time-motion studies of the value and function of each movement of workers on assembly lines with the goal of improving efficiency by eliminating wasteful motions. All of these psychologies shared the functional philosophy.

Functionalism is no longer a distinct psychological system. Even at its peak early in this century, it was a diversified and informal system, a collection of new fields that were linked by a common philosophy. Today, the fields of psychology to which functionalism gave birth have matured and developed in their own right.

BEHAVIORISM

Early in this century an American psychologist, John B. Watson (1878–1958), developed an objective system of psychology he called **behaviorism.** Behaviorism has since become one of the most influential and controversial schools of American psychology.

Watson had been trained as a functional psychologist and was especially interested in the purpose and functions of animal behavior. Like psychologists who investigated humans, researchers who studied animal subjects were careful to be scientific in their work. They objectively observed and recorded everything they could. But to Watson's way of thinking, human psychology still had a serious fault: There was no way to objectively observe the conscious mind. Watson felt that functionalism hadn't gone far enough in its rebellion against structuralism. No matter how you looked at it, if you wanted to know what people thought, you had to ask them. They alone could tell you. To Watson, this was introspectionism again. He felt that if a purely objective experimental science of psychology was to be developed, psychologists must reject all subjective methods and rely

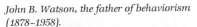

John B. Watson, the father of behaviorism (1878–1958).

A METRONOME, A HOROPTER CHART, AND A FROG-WHIRLING DEVICE

As you read this text you will find that psychologists are in disagreement over some important issues. Some of these controversies have been settled through painstaking research and experimentation, while others remain to be decided. Some arguments die hard, and from time to time resurface. The following controversy is undoubtedly one of the oldest in psychology since it involves psychology's very beginnings. To be sure, there are other more important debates in psychology, but why not join in on this one and decide for yourself how much importance to give to a metronome, a horopter chart, and a frog-whirling device.

In 1979, the American Psychological Association celebrated 100 years of psychology since the founding of Wilhelm Wundt's laboratory in 1879. No sooner had the announcement been made than a number of champions arose for what, after all these years, may seem an odd cause. They argued that William James had been the first to begin a psychology lab, and that he did so in 1874, or was it 1876? Perhaps it was 1878.

Anyway, it was before Wundt in 1879. Thus the stage was set for the "battle of the labs."

Supporters of James cited evidence from his biographer R. B. Perry. According to Perry, James had set up a laboratory for himself at Harvard "in two rooms of the Scientific School Building" in "1874–5, or 1876" (Perry, 1926, p. 179), and he had offered a graduate course on the relationship between physiology and psychology and "made the class take part in experiments which he arranged in a room in the Lawrence Scientific School building" (Perry, 1926, p. 224). James' champions also noted G. Stanley Hall's comment that James had a lab "in a tiny room under the stairway of the Agassiz Museum" where James "had a metronome, a device for whirling a frog,* a horopter chart, and one or two bits of apparatus" (Perry, 1936, p. 15).

But then Edmund Jacobson, a man who had actually been a student of

*This device was used to test the reflexes and perceptual abilities of dizzy frogs—why else would you whirl one?

William James, added his recollection that James had once said to him, "Why don't you experimental psychologists study the whole man?" (Jacobson, 1979). If James did not think of himself as an experimental psychologist, how could anyone argue that he was the founder of the first experimental psychology lab? Others added that James' experiments in class in 1874 (or was it 1876?) were only demonstrations, not the endeavors of a full-blown psychology lab like Wundt's.

Then a letter written by James to G. Stanley Hall on October 12, 1895, turned up in which James stated that his lectures in 1878 on the brain and the mind had been "exclusively experimental." What can you say about a man who had a small lab under a staircase containing psychological equipment and whose lectures were "exclusively experimental" in 1878? Was he first, and Wundt second? But then again, Wundt had the same kind of informal laboratory in Heidelberg in 1865 (Bringmann, 1979).

---

solely on what could be objectively observed and recorded. In 1929 he wrote that

> [psychology] made a false start under Wundt . . . because it would not bury its past. It tried to hang on to tradition with one hand and push forward as a science with the other. Before progress could be made in astronomy, it had to bury astrology; neurology had to bury phrenology; and chemistry had to bury alchemy. But the social sciences, psychology, sociology, political science, and economics, will not bury their "medicine men." (Watson, 1929, p. 3)

Watson took a tremendous philosophical step in rejecting the study of conscious thought and mental activity because they were unobservable. Instead he emphasized observable environmental stimuli (e.g., a loud noise,

BEHAVIORISM
The school of psychology that views learning as the most important aspect of an organism's development. Behaviorists objectively measure behavior and the way in which stimulus-response relationships are formed.

Max Wertheimer (1880–1943).

a red stoplight, a candy bar, praise from a friend) and the observable behaviors or responses that occurred in the presence of such stimuli. For this reason behaviorism is known as *S–R psychology* (for stimulus-response). It is also referred to as "black box" psychology because Watson considered the mind to be like a mysterious black box that could never be examined objectively.

Behaviorism remains a powerful force in modern psychology, and has been of great value in demonstrating that much of our behavior is the product of our immediate environment. Behaviorists have shown that the associations we experience, the pleasant or unpleasant consequences following our actions, and our observations of the actions of those around us often determine our responses. Through behavioral technology, problems such as aggression, phobias, shyness, and poor study habits can often be corrected. In addition, behavioral psychologists have emphasized the need to define terms carefully, run controlled experiments, and in general make psychology more of a science. Ironically, this effort has provoked some of the strongest criticism of behaviorism. It has been argued that behaviorists often ignore important but unobservable aspects of human behavior, such as emotion, thought, and unconscious processes, and that they discredit feelings or ideas that don't readily lend themselves to controlled experimentation.

GESTALT PSYCHOLOGY

At about the same time that behaviorism was becoming the dominant force in American psychology, a different reaction to structuralism was developing in Germany, the *Gestalt* view. In a strange way, **Gestalt psychology*** owes its inception largely to the motion picture projector. Structuralists, who wished to break down conscious experience into its simplest elements, had a difficult time trying to explain how a series of still pictures, shown one after another, could seem to move (which is, of course, how a motion picture projector works). The structuralists reasoned that if sensations are elemental, then each picture might be expected to be a separate sensation. But that's not what happens. Someone viewing a movie sees one picture that appears to be moving. This false perception of motion is known as the **phi phenomenon.**

In 1912, Max Wertheimer (1880–1943) presented a paper in which he, Wolfgang Köhler (1887–1967), and Kurt Koffka (1886–1941) argued that the phi phenomenon needed no explanation. Rather, it was a real phenomenon in its own right, and any attempt to reduce it to simpler sensations would destroy it. At first glance, this argument may not seem revolutionary, but it was. It rejected a fundamental tenet of structuralism, that all experience can be broken down into elementary parts in order to understand it better. Wertheimer, Köhler, and Koffka argued that the whole experience (in German, the *Gestalt*) was not just the sum of its parts; it was more, it was itself. For example, the color white is created by an equal mixture of red, green, and blue. Gestalt psychologists point out that the experience of white is more than the sum of its parts. Certainly it is red plus green plus blue, but it is also itself; it is white. Experiencing red, then experiencing green, and finally experiencing blue is obviously not the same as experiencing white, all at once.

---

*Not to be confused with a more recent innovation, Gestalt therapy.

Interestingly, the Gestalt psychologists weren't the first to rebel against the idea of reducing consciousness to its supposed constituent parts. Twenty-two years before the beginning of Gestalt psychology, William James, whose brilliant mind seemed to be everywhere at once, stated, "The traditional psychologist [structuralist] talks like one who would say a river consists of nothing but pailsful, spoonsful, quartpotsful, barrelsful, and other moulded forms of water. Even were the pails and the pots all actually standing in the same stream, still between them the free water would continue to flow" (James, 1890, p. 279). Had James pursued this line of reasoning a little further he might have founded Gestalt psychology as well as functionalism!

Gestalt psychology argues that conscious sensations can be examined but that the whole experience must be taken for what it is. Moreover, the use of specially trained self-observers is unnecessary. To the Gestaltists, the laws of psychology are the laws of systems, not parts. Gestalt psychology is still an active force in the areas of perception and learning, and we will present some of its experiments and discoveries when we cover these topics in detail in later chapters.

PSYCHOANALYSIS

Psychoanalysis has probably been the most widely publicized of the psychological systems, especially among nonpsychologists. Psychoanalytic theory was developed by a Viennese physician, Sigmund Freud (1856–1939). From its beginning in 1895, psychoanalysis created a storm of controversy. Some of its principles and concepts were so shocking that many people regarded them as entirely new. Nonetheless, like all important ideas, it too had its antecedents (Sulloway, 1979).

Psychoanalytic theory did not develop as a reaction against structuralism, but instead traces its roots to neurology and medicine. Its goal was to treat and understand abnormal behavior. Freud presented, as one of the major tenets of psychoanalysis, the concept of the unconscious mind. He argued that the mind was like an iceberg in that most of it was hidden beneath the surface. He stated that human beings are not controlled primarily by rational and conscious processes, but rather by drives and urges hidden within the unconscious. To some critics, this was the last of three great blows to human pride. The first was given when Copernicus demonstrated that the earth was not the center of the universe; the second, when Darwin stated that humans had evolved from lower species. Now Freud was arguing that we were not even the conscious masters of our behavior.

Freud believed that abnormal behavior and, for that matter, all personality could be explained by analyzing the motives and drives of the unconscious. Like the functionalists, Freud had been influenced by Darwin, and he maintained that the unconscious served a function, which was to keep unacceptable thoughts or desires repressed or hidden from the conscious mind. Because of this, he argued that the unconscious mind would be reluctant to give up its knowledge and that special techniques would be needed in order to probe its secrets. Among the techniques Freud used were hypnosis, **free association** (in which the patient is asked to say whatever first comes to mind, regardless of how foolish it may seem), dream interpretation, and analysis of slips of the tongue. In the last technique, for example, a psychoanalyst might conclude that a patient was exhibiting a repressed sexual desire if she answered the question "What is your

Sigmund Freud, the founder of psycho-analysis (1856–1939). Freud is shown in this rare photograph celebrating his seventy-fifth birthday by taking an airplane ride.

HUMANISTIC PSYCHOLOGY
A school of psychology that emphasizes
the uniqueness of the individual and
the search for self-actualization.

SELF-ACTUALIZATION
Maslow's term for the process of an
individual's constant striving to realize
full potential.

COGNITIVE PSYCHOLOGY
The school of psychology that concen-
trates primarily on the development of
human thought processes.

SCIENTIFIC METHOD
The principles and processes used
to conduct scientific investigations,
including hypotheses formation, observation, and experimentation.

religion?" by stating, "I'm a prostitute, I mean, protestant." Freud believed that analysis could help resolve unconscious conflicts and correct arrested personality or abnormal behavior.

Psychoanalysis has been severely criticized for its lack of scientific con-
trol and careful experimentation. Many modern psychologists, although agreeing that psychoanalysis is colorful, argue that as a psychology it is unscientific. "The unfortunate truth is that the *analysts' statements are so general that they can explain whatever behavior occurs. A genuine scientific explanation cannot do this*" (Marx & Hillix, 1963, p. 231). Others point out that psychoanalysis relies on techniques that have never been validated. For instance, no one has found a way to discover whether dreams have important meanings or are simply the brain's attempt to make sense of random electrical activity that occurs during sleep. And yet many conclusions drawn by psychoanalysts rest heavily on dream interpretation.

At the same time, the historical importance of psychoanalysis cannot be denied. Freud's work made a great contribution to psychology because the interest it stimulated in many hitherto neglected areas—the workings of the unconscious mind, sexuality, emotionality, abnormal behavior, conflict, childhood—did prove fruitful.

HUMANISTIC PSYCHOLOGY

Humanistic psychology has often been called the third force in psychology. The psychoanalytic and behavioral viewpoints constitute the first two forces. Abraham Maslow (1908–1970) and the contemporary psychologist Carl Rogers have been the leading proponents of the humanistic theory.

Humanistic psychologists view behavior very differently from psycho-
analysts or behaviorists. Humanists don't believe that behavior is governed either by unconscious drives and motives or by external stimuli and rewards in the environment. Instead, they argue that people are free agents, having free will, and that they are conscious, creative, and born with an inner motivation to fulfill their potential. Maslow referred to this as **self-actualization.** The humanists view self-actualization as a lifelong process rather than as a final goal that one eventually reaches.

Humanists argue that behavior can only be understood by examining each individual's unique self-perception. In this view, the world is different for all of us because we all perceive it differently. Some humanistic psychologists, like Maslow, have developed a concept of personality based on these ideas. Others, like Carl Rogers, have developed therapies to help in de-
veloping individual potential. These aspects of humanistic psychology are examined in greater detail in Chapters 13 and 16.

Abraham Maslow (1908–1970).

MODERN TRENDS AND THE EMERGENCE OF SCIENTIFIC PSYCHOLOGY

Psychology continues to be influenced by new ideas and philosophical forces. Advanced techniques in physiology and biochemistry have enabled psychologists to explore the brain and the sensory system in more detail than ever before. Research into genetics has stimulated interest in inheritance and its influence on behavior. The rapid growth of the computer industry and knowledge about computers has drawn attention to human abilities to process, store, recall, and integrate information, and similarities

and differences between human thought and computer operation. Some of the original systems of psychology, too, matured and changed. For example, behaviorism has expanded and given birth to clinical therapies, social and other learning theories, and theories of motivation. Psychoanalysis has become more diversified and now includes many variations of Freud's original therapeutic treatments. And **cognitive psychology,** which is concerned with thinking and conscious processes, has grown in strength thanks mainly to the brilliant clinical work of the Swiss psychologist Jean Piaget.

Research Methods

Although hundreds of pages could be written about the different psychological groups, subgroups, and offshoots, this doesn't mean that psychology has become a loose amalgam of splinter groups, all going in different directions. All psychologists who rely on the special techniques of the **scientific method** are, philosophically, on common ground; they are scientific psychologists. It doesn't matter that one may be a physiological psychologist studying a hormone's effects on behavior and another a school psychologist testing a child's academic ability. If both are using scientific methods for research, or relying on information obtained by scientific methods, they share a common ground.

All scientific research is based on systematic and objective methods of observing, recording, and describing events. Table 1.1 outlines the six dimensions of psychological research. All of the research discussed in this text (and for that matter, all psychological research) will fall into one of

Table 1.1   Dimensions of research

DIMENSIONS OF RESEARCH	DESCRIPTION
Descriptive vs. explanatory	Descriptive research describes *what* has occurred, while explanatory research attempts to explain *why* something has occurred. (As many scientists have discovered, it is often unwise to be prematurely explanatory.)
Naturalistic vs. manipulative	When conducting naturalistic research, researchers refrain from interacting with the variables they are observing. In manipulative research, they purposely manipulate variables in order to observe the effects of their manipulations.
Historical vs. ahistorical	If research is fundamentally dependent on past events it is considered historical research; if not, it is called ahistorical.
Theoretical vs. serendipitous	Research designed to investigate a particular theory is called theoretical research. Research designed simply to investigate phenomena is called serendipitous, or sometimes atheoretical.
Basic vs. applied	Basic research advances knowledge; applied research advances technology. Or, as one scientist pleading for more funding for basic research put it, basic research created the polio vaccine; applied research would have built a better iron lung.
Single subject vs. group	In single-subject research, the behavior and behavioral changes of one person at a time are of interest. In group research, researchers consider group averages, ignoring whether these averages accurately reflect the behavioral patterns of any given individual within the group.

EXPERIMENT
A test made to demonstrate the validity of a hypothesis or to determine the predictability of a theory. Variables are manipulated and changes are contrasted with a control that has not been exposed to the variables of interest.

CATHARSIS
In psychoanalytic theory, elimination of a complex by bringing it to consciousness and allowing it to express itself. Any emotional release resulting from a buildup of internal tensions.

SOCIAL LEARNING THEORY
A theory developed by Albert Bandura and others that stresses learning by observing and imitating others. Social learning is sometimes called observational learning or vicarious conditioning.

SAMPLE
A group of subjects who should normally be representative of the population about which an inference is made.

INTEROBSERVER RELIABILITY
The degree of disagreement or agreement between two or more observers who simultaneously observe a single event.

these categories. If you become familiar with these dimensions, it will be easier for you to understand the research described in the following chapters.

DESIGNING EXPERIMENTS

The scientific **experiment** is one of the most powerful research tools that psychologists possess. Perhaps the best way to learn how to conduct an experiment, and how not to conduct one, is to try it yourself. So, for the next few pages, let's work on one together.

First, we need an issue that is testable. Some issues are not testable, as, for instance, the following:

Are dreams meaningful?

How did prehistoric man raise children?

What will the world be like in 20 years?

Is there life on Neptune?

Tests cannot be devised for these questions because no one has access to concrete observable information about them. We would need a soil sample from Neptune, for example, or child-rearing advice carved in stone by prehistoric people before we could design experiments to explore these subjects. Instead, let's examine an issue that can be tested: Do violent programs on television cause aggressive behavior in children who view them?

Sigmund Freud believed that the desire to be violent was instinctive and that viewing violence might satisfy an instinctive urge, acting as a release or a **catharsis.** As a result, the viewer's desire to be violent would be reduced. On the other hand, the contemporary psychologist Albert Bandura has developed a **social learning theory** (which stems from behaviorism) that contradicts Freud's catharsis prediction. Bandura predicts that viewing violence will increase the probability that the viewer will imitate the violence. Clearly we have a disagreement—and one that can be tested.

To begin our experiment we need some children and some violent programs. We also need some observers to watch the children's behavior and to record what happens when the children are exposed to the shows.

Selecting Subjects   In selecting the children, we should probably call on children of many ages and backgrounds, since it is always risky to generalize beyond a particular **sample.** If you conduct a study on little boys, for instance, you must be very cautious about applying your findings to little girls. (And unless you have a sound reason for doing so, you shouldn't even attempt such a generalization.) Psychologists, like all scientists, should not go beyond their data unless they specifically state that they are speculating.

Now that we've assembled the children, let's show them some of those violent Saturday morning cartoons and see what happens. But first we must solve a problem: How can we tell which cartoons are violent? Moreover, after showing the cartoons, how will we decide whether the children are being aggressive?

Defining Terms   In France there used to be a platinum-iridium rod that was kept inside a sealed glass case that had been emptied of air. The rod was exactly one meter in length. Whenever a physicist needed to be certain that her meter stick was a meter long, she could compare it with the rod. The rod was the standard. Nowadays physicists use an even more precise standard for length. The point is that everyone agrees on the definition of a meter, but do we all agree on what *aggression* is? Is a good salesman aggressive? Are all murderers aggressive? Is it good for a football player to be aggressive? Obviously, aggression has come to mean many different things, and before we can study it, and perhaps conclude that watching TV violence causes aggression, we must be able to define it. If aggression means something different to everyone who reads our findings, we will only have succeeded in confusing the issue.

If a tree falls in the forest, and no one is there to hear it, does it make a noise? You may have heard this famous philosophical question before, but do you know the answer? It depends totally on how you define *noise*. If you define noise as the production of sound waves, the answer to the question will be yes. If you define noise as the perception of sound waves by a living creature, the answer will be no. The only reason that such a question can cause an argument in the first place is that people are often unaware of using different definitions.

How shall we define *aggression* in order to avoid confusion in our experiment? One definition is "any act committed with the intention of damaging property or injuring another person." Since this description fits most people's idea of aggression, let's try it even though intentions aren't easy to observe. We must also agree on a definition of violent cartoons. Once we have defined both terms, we can begin the experiment. It will be your job to watch a particular child after the child has viewed a violent cartoon. You will note if aggression occurs and how often. Can you be trusted to be accurate in your observations?

Interobserver Reliability   You might consider something to be an aggressive act according to our definition that another observer applying the same definition would not consider aggressive. This could be a serious problem, since it would mean that different observers had described the same behavior as both aggressive and nonaggressive. To avoid this problem, we will use two or more people who will *independently* observe the same child over the same period of time. The observations can then be compared and, if they are in fairly good agreement, we can conclude that we have a reliable means of observing and recording the behavior in question. This technique yields what is known as **interobserver reliability** (see Table 1.2); it is a way of testing the adequacy of our definitions. If our interobserver reliability turns out to be low, we will have to define aggression more carefully.

The Control   Now that we have used interobserver reliability to assure that we agree on definitions of aggression and violent cartoons, shall we show a violent cartoon to the children and observe their behavior? If the children are aggressive after viewing the cartoon, how will we know that it was the violence in the cartoon that provoked the aggression? For that matter, how can we be sure that the children wouldn't have been even more aggressive had they not watched the cartoon? If you ask someone who won the baseball game and all they tell you is that the Yankees scored five runs, you won't know whether the Yankees won or lost. To know, you will need the other team's score as a comparison. It's the same with an experiment.

Table 1.2 Interobserver reliability in observations of a child's behavior in a 5-minute period

		AGGRESSIVE RESPONSE			
Time	*Yes*	*No*	*Unsure*	*No Observation*	
Independent Observer I					
Start 0–30 sec	X	_____	_____	_____	(1)
30 sec–1 min	X	_____	_____	_____	(2)
1–1.5 min	_____	X	_____	_____	(3)
1.5–2 min	_____	X	_____	_____	(4)
2–2.5 min	_____	X	_____	_____	(5)
2.5–3 min	_____	_____	_____	X	(6)
3–3.5 min	_____	X	_____	_____	(7)
3.5–4 min	_____	X	_____	_____	(8)
4–4.5 min	X	_____	_____	_____	(9)
4.5–5 min	X	_____	_____	_____	(10)
Independent Observer II					
Start 0–30 sec	X	_____	_____	_____	(1)
30 sec–1 min	X	_____	_____	_____	(2)
1–1.5 min	_____	X	_____	_____	(3)
1.5–2 min	_____	X	_____	_____	(4)
2–2.5 min	_____	X	_____	_____	(5)
2.5–3 min	_____	X	_____	_____	(6)
3–3.5 min	_____	X	_____	_____	(7)
3.5–4 min	X	_____	_____	_____	(8)
4–4.5 min	X	_____	_____	_____	(9)
4.5–5 min	X	_____	_____	_____	(10)

NOTE: The observers disagreed only on observation (8). On observation (6), Observer I failed to notice the child's behavior. Interobserver reliability in this case appears to be high.

You will need a comparison, a similar group of children who do not see the violent cartoon. This second group of children is the **control.** In fact, it is the use of a control that defines an experiment.

The best way to obtain a second group of children who are similar to the first is simply to divide the original group of children in half. Then, in all probability, the two groups will be alike. You must divide the groups randomly, however. *Randomly* means that each child has an equal chance of being placed in either group. For example, you might divide the children into an experimental and a control group by flipping a coin.

The control and experimental groups *must be treated exactly the same* except for the one variable you wish to measure, in this case, violence. If you show the control group no cartoon at all, you fail to control for the effects of simply watching a cartoon. Thus while the experimental group is watching a violent cartoon, the control group should see a nonviolent cartoon of the same length. In this way the effect of violence is isolated from all other effects. Everything that happens to the experimental group is controlled for if it also happens to the control group. In our case everything is controlled except viewing violence, which happens to the experimental group. If the amount of aggression observed in both groups of children is similar before they see the cartoon but different afterwards, we have isolated the effect of watching violence and nothing else. In this way psychologists are able to separate variables and to observe their effects one at a time.

To reiterate, since both groups shared all of the variables but one, and since both groups were similar to each other at the beginning of the experiment, any difference between the groups at the end of the experiment can be attributed to the one variable the groups didn't share. Remember, variables shared by both groups are controlled. If it starts to rain on the experimental group, your experiment won't be disrupted as long as it starts to rain on the control group, too. The variable that is manipulated, in our case how much and what kind of TV violence we showed, is called the **independent variable.** The variable that may be influenced by the manipulations, in our case the amount of aggression, is called the **dependent variable.***

Observer and Subject Bias   Before continuing the experiment we need to examine other problems that might arise. Among these are observer and subject bias. Consider the outcome of one particular experiment in which 25 elementary or special-education teachers were asked by researchers to record the kinds of behavior they would expect to see while observing a normal fourth-grade boy. When they were finished, the teachers were shown a videotape of a normal fourth-grade boy and were asked to describe the behavior displayed by the child. When the two reports were compared, it was clear that the behavior the teachers actually saw was very similar to the behavior they had expected to see.

Later, another group of 25 teachers similar to the first group was assembled. These teachers were asked to describe the kinds of behavior they would expect to see in a fourth-grade boy with a learning disability. Then they viewed a videotape of a learning-disabled fourth-grade boy and recorded the behavior they observed. Once again, what the teachers saw was very similar to what they had expected to see.

A third group of 25 teachers, much like the first two groups, was gathered. These teachers were asked to write down the kinds of behavior they might expect to see in an emotionally disturbed fourth-grade boy. They were then shown a videotape of an emotionally disturbed boy and, as with the other groups, what they actually observed closely matched their expectations.

A fourth and final group of 25 teachers followed the same procedure. They were asked to observe a mentally retarded fourth-grade boy. Once again the teachers were accurate—actually observing the severe disturbances that they had expected to see.

Perhaps the accuracy of the observing teachers doesn't surprise you. After all, they were professional teachers, who might be expected to be aware of typical behavior in normal, learning-disabled, emotionally disturbed, and mentally retarded children. What might surprise you, though, is that all 100 teachers, regardless of the group to which they were assigned, had seen the same videotape—one of a normal fourth-grade boy! Although professionals, the teachers responded to the label that the experimenters placed on the child and, from that point on, they saw in the child what they expected to see (Foster & Ysseldyke, 1976). This is an example of **observer bias,** since the observers were biased by their expectations.

The subjects in experiments can also be biased. Workers at the Western Electric Company's Hawthorne Plant once participated in an experiment

CONTROL
Deliberate arrangement of experimental or research conditions so that observed effects can be directly traced to a known variable or variables.

INDEPENDENT VARIABLE
In an experiment, the variable that is manipulated or treated to see what effect differences in it will have on the variables considered to be dependent on it.

DEPENDENT VARIABLE
In an experiment, the variable that may change as a result of changes in the independent variable.

OBSERVER BIAS
An error in observation caused by the expectations of the observer.

---

*If you have trouble recalling which variable is which, just think of freedom and independence. The variable that the experimenter is *free* to manipulate is the *independent* variable.

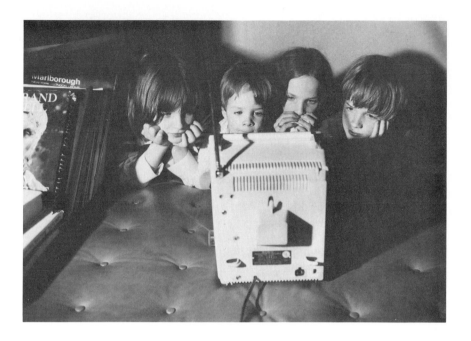

Television can be a significant force in shaping the behavior of young viewers.

designed to measure the effect of lighting intensity on work output. Whether the lighting was made brighter or dimmer, output increased. As it turned out, the workers were aware that they were being tested and they responded by doing what they believed was expected of them (Roethlisberger & Dickson, 1940). This type of **subject bias** has come to be called the **Hawthorne effect.** It is well-known among developmental psychologists, who may want to visit a child's home in order to observe the environment firsthand. Upon entering they are greeted by formally dressed parents, a spotless home, the scent of Lemon Pledge in the air, and a well-scrubbed child with slicked-down hair approaching timidly to attempt a handshake. Subjects can act differently simply because they know they are being observed.

In our experiment, we have used a control group and an experimental group and treated each the same except for showing violence to the latter. We probably don't have to worry about subject bias, since the effects of any biases would have been controlled. But what about you and your colleagues? You may be susceptible to an observer bias similar to that of the teachers who viewed the fourth-grade boy in the videotape. Suppose that you are scornful of Freud's theories and certain that Bandura's predictions are accurate. You might all be hoping to see more aggression in the experimental group. Though working independently, you might all consider certain behavior aggressive if it is exhibited by a child from the experimental group, while you might consider the same behavior nonaggressive if you observed it in a child from the control group. In this way your observations could be badly biased even though interobserver reliability might remain high.

Even careful observers can't always avoid such mistakes, since it is very hard not to see what you expect to see. For years students in psychology labs have been sent by "sly" professors to observe "bright" rats and "dull" rats running mazes. Even the most careful students have tended to report that the bright rats do better than the dull ones, although the rats have been labeled bright or dull simply by the flip of a coin.

We can easily avoid any observer bias in our experiment. The observers must not know whether the children they are watching are from the experimental or the control group (someone else can keep track of that). This will prevent the observers from unconsciously leaning toward one group or the other, because they won't know which is which. Since the children too are unaware of which group they are in, our study can now be called a **double-blind controlled experiment.** That is, neither the subjects nor the observers know who is in which group. Double-blind controlled experiments are extremely effective as a research tool, since they allow us to examine variables one at a time while they eliminate human biases.

The Results of Our Experiments Once we have observed the levels of aggression in the children from both groups, we will statistically analyze the data in order to determine whether there is a significant difference in observed aggression between the control and experimental group.* Let's assume that the results of our hypothetical experiment are similar to those obtained by researchers who have conducted actual experiments examining the effects of TV violence on children. Like them, we will find that the experimental group was significantly more aggressive (Hanratty, 1969; Savitsky, Rogers, Izard, & Liebert, 1971; Hanratty, O'Neal, & Sulzer, 1972). Our conclusion: Viewing cartoon violence increases the probability of aggression in grade-school children immediately after they have watched the program. In addition, we may note that Albert Bandura's theory fits our observations well while Sigmund Freud's does not. After we have carried our experiment a bit further, we may even suggest that cartoon violence on children's television be toned down or eliminated.

Replication and Expansion At the finish of our double-blind controlled experiment, we might want to consider two other valuable procedures, **replication** and **expansion.** An old rule in research states, "If it hasn't happened twice, it hasn't happened." For this reason it would be a good idea to have someone else, perhaps at another institution, replicate (duplicate) our study to see if the same results are obtained. If they are, we will feel more confident about our own findings. Such confirmation is important, since there may have been something unusual about our particular sample of children or an important event, unknown to us, that interfered with the treatment or testing.

We may also wish to exapnd upon our research. For instance, what would happen if we used live actors instead of cartoons? Would adults become aggressive in the way that children do? How long does the aggression last? Obviously, the answer in an experiment can generate many new questions, all of which may be worth pursuing.

Recalling the division of research methods given in table 1.1, we can define the dimensions of our own experiment as follows:

Explanatory. We concluded that watching violence was *why* aggression occurred.

Manipulative. We altered the situation so that the children were exposed to the variables that we wanted them to see.

Ahistorical. We were unconcerned with the children's history.

SUBJECT BIAS
Unwanted changes in a subject's behavior owing to knowledge about the experiment or awareness of being observed.

HAWTHORNE EFFECT
A type of bias that may arise when a research subject is aware of being studied, and changes his or her behavior to match perceived expectations.

DOUBLE-BLIND
A research technique in which neither the subjects nor the experimenters know which subjects have been exposed to the independent variable. It is used for controlling biases that may be introduced by either the subjects or the researchers.

REPLICATION
Repeating an experiment in order to affirm the reliability of the results.

EXPANSION
An enlargement or extension of initial research efforts.

---

*The kinds of statistical analyses used by psychologists are outlined in the Statistics Appendix.

Theoretical. We were deciding between Freud's theoretical prediction and Bandura's.

Basic. We were advancing our knowledge rather than attempting to change the technology of the cartoon industry (although that may eventually be a result of our research).

Group. We worked with groups of children instead of concentrating on a single subject.

Single-Subject Experiments   You may wonder about the practicability of conducting an experiment with only one subject, since you would obviously have no control group. But it can be done. In **single-subject experiments** we use time as the control. That is, we create a certain condition and note the response, then we observe whether the response continues as long as the condition is maintained. Examine Figure 1.2, the record of an experiment to find the effect of a drug on memory. Since time has been used as a control, we can feel confident that the drug has indeed reduced the subject's ability to recall a list of items. First, the drug was administered and recall ability declined (condition A). Then, in condition B, the effect of the drug wore off and recall improved. To be sure that this result was not just a coincidence, the drug was administered a second time, and once again recall ability decreased (a return to condition A). Since recall ability again diminished when the drug was given, the experimenters could assert with more confidence that the drug was causing a recall deficiency. It seems that by giving the drug, withholding it, and giving it again the researchers were controlling the subject's ability to recall. This is called an **A-B-A single-subject experimental design.** It can be taken one step further, by measuring recall once more after the drug has worn off. An A-B-A-B design will thus be created, demonstrating once again the expected behavioral change in the B condition and lending support to the conviction that a cause-effect relationship exists between the administration of the drug and the subsequent decline in recall ability. Be cautious, however, about assuming that what you have discovered about one subject will explain the behavior of any other subject; it may not.

NONEXPERIMENTAL METHODS

The Correlational Method   A **correlation** is defined as the relationship between two variables. For example, there is a strong correlation between height and weight. The taller one is, the heavier one tends to be, and vice versa.

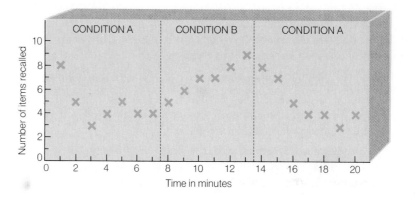

Figure 1.2 *Example of a single-subject A-B-A experimental design. The purpose of this experiment was to test a drug's effect on immediate recall (memory) by introducing and withholding the drug. In condition A, the drug is active; in condition B it has worn off.*

By the late 1800s army physicians were aware that the best way to stop a malaria outbreak was to move everyone to high, dry ground. Although these physicians were unaware that the disease was carried by mosquitoes, they knew that malaria was well correlated with altitude and moisture. Without knowing the cause of the disease, they were still able to predict the chances of an outbreak.

Sometimes psychologists are unable to conduct experiments or, like the army doctors, they may not know which experiments to conduct. They may then be forced to rely on correlational data. Such data are valuable because they allow predictions to be made. Frequently, too, correlations are scientists' first clue in the path of an important discovery. As you can imagine, doctors soon wondered what it was about damp, warm lowlands that related to malaria.

Nonetheless, when dealing with a correlation you must be extremely careful not to assume that a **cause-effect relationship** exists simply because two variables go together. For example, if you were to tell me that ice cream sales in Detroit had increased, I would be able to predict that the number of drownings would also increase—and I'd be correct. But this does not mean that eating ice cream makes you drown or, conversely, that drowning makes you want ice cream! If true, this would be an example of cause and effect. The reason for the correlation between ice cream and drownings is, of course, that in summer both swimming and ice cream sales increase. Although no one is likely to make this particular cause-effect connection, the difference between a correlation and an apparent cause-effect relationship is not always so clear.

Suppose you are watching children at play who are being supervised by their parents. You notice that the children whose parents discipline them by yelling at them are more aggressive. What would you conclude? Would you decide that parents who are verbally harsh *cause* their children to act out and be aggressive? If you did you would be making a mistake, since only a correlation exists. Parental yelling *coincides* with the aggressive behavior in the children. Perhaps the children were aggressive to start with, or perhaps their aggression even drove their parents to yelling. To examine cause and effect you have to create an experiment in which you manipulate the variables involved. Until then you only know that one variable is correlated with the other.

Suppose you walk into a large college classroom and make a survey of more than a hundred students. You learn that the only ones who have become parents before the age of 20 have red hair. In such a case, you should go to another classroom and replicate your observation before you even consider the possibility of a cause-effect relationship. Sometimes things go together (and are well correlated) by accident. When you flip a coin, you may get ten heads in a row, but this doesn't necessarily mean that the coin is weighted. Even results from an experiment may be only a coincidence. If there is a reason for early parenthood and red hair to be correlated, you should continue to obtain the same results as you sample different groups of students. But if your finding was only a chance event, it probably won't happen again. Whenever you discover something very unexpected, you would be well advised to replicate your study a few times.

Naturalistic Observation As you will recall from Table 1.1, researchers conducting **naturalistic observations** refrain from directly interacting with

SINGLE-SUBJECT EXPERIMENT
An experiment in which only one subject participates. Time is normally used as the control, that is, the subject's behavior changes over time in relation to the presentation and withdrawal of the independent variable.

A-B-A SINGLE-SUBJECT EXPERIMENTAL DESIGN
An experimental design in which time is used as a control and only one subject is monitored. The independent variable is given in condition A and withdrawn in condition B. The dependent variable is the subject's behavioral change over time as the independent variable is presented, withdrawn, and finally presented again.

CORRELATION
The relationship between two variables.

CAUSE-EFFECT RELATIONSHIP
A relationship whereby one act, of necessity, regularly brings about a particular result.

NATURALISTIC OBSERVATIONS
Observations in which researchers refrain from directly interacting with the variables being observed.

the variables they are observing. Naturalistic observations can be carried out in an informal or a structured way. The more informal the observations, though, the greater the chance that bias or inaccurate observations will affect the outcome. Part of our experiment with children and TV violence could have been a naturalistic study. Suppose we had simply wanted to observe aggression in a group of children. If we had just watched the children, perhaps from behind one-way glass, and had carefully recorded incidences of aggression (for example, by using the interobserver reliability technique), we would have been performing a naturalistic observation. But once we decided to manipulate variables by showing violent and nonviolent films to randomly chosen experimental and control groups, our study became a manipulative experiment.

Naturalistic observation is most often used to investigate behavior in the natural environment outside of the laboratory. A *natural environment* is defined as any environment that the researcher has not purposely manipulated. The incidence of aggression among gorillas in their natural habitat, the amount of overt affection displayed in a college cafeteria, or the frequency with which vehicles on a particular road exceed the speed limit could all be subjects for naturalistic observation. When collecting data of this kind, observers should be as unobtrusive as possible in order not to change the behavior of those being observed. As you might imagine, information about the incidence of highway speeding might not be too accurate if you collected it from inside a marked, clearly visible police car.

Case Studies   In a **case study,** researchers report or analyze the behavior, emotions, beliefs, or life history of a single individual in more depth than is usually possible with groups of subjects. The rigorous controls common to single-subject experimental design are not applied in case studies. Still, careful observation of a subject and scrupulous recording of what is observed can yield valuable information.

Sometimes a case study is the only option available because, for one reason or another, it is impossible for a psychologist to conduct an experiment or observe a correlation in order to gather data. It would not be ethically proper, for example, to remove part of a healthy individual's brain just to see what would happen afterward. But sometimes such information becomes available through a case study, as in the incredible case of Phineas Gage, a work-crew foreman for the railroad in 1848. Part of Gage's job was to tamp dynamite with a 13-pound steel rod into holes bored into rock. One unfortunate day the dynamite charge detonated while Gage was tamping it with the rod. The explosion sent the rod through Gage's face and out the top of his skull (see Figure 1.3), taking with it the front matter of his brain. Incredibly, he survived, but not without undergoing some profound personality changes. As Dr. J. M. Harlow, who reported this case study, stated:

> His physical health is good, and I am inclined to say that he has recovered. Has no pain in head, but says it has a queer feeling which he is not able to describe. Applied for his situation as foreman, but is undecided whether to work or travel. His contractors, who regarded him as the most efficient and capable foreman in their employ previous to his injury, considered the change in his mind so marked that they could not give him his place again. The equilibrium or balance, so to speak, between his intellectual faculties and animal propensities, seems to have been destroyed. He is fitful, irreverent, indulging at times in the grossest profanity (which was not previously his custom), manifesting but little deference for his fellows, impatient of restraint or advice when it conflicts with his desires, at times

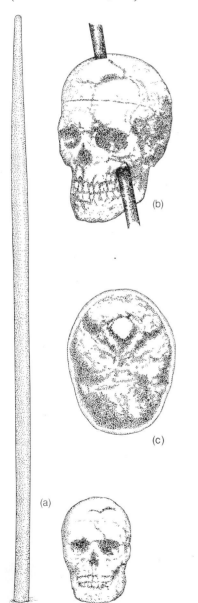

Figure 1.3 *Harlow's illustrations of the case of Phineas Gage*
(a) *comparison of the relative sizes of the tamping iron and Gage's skull*
(b) *view depicting the trajectory of the iron through Gage's cranium*
(c) *upward view of the cranium showing the location and diameter of the hole*
(SOURCE: *From Harlow, 1868*)

pertinaciously obstinate, yet capricious and vacillating, devising many plans of future operations, which are no sooner arranged than they are abandoned in turn for others . . . his mind is radically changed, so decidedly that his friends and acquaintances said he was "no longer Gage." (1868, pp. 339–40)

While such case studies provide valuable data, they cannot by themselves be the basis for solid conclusions. In the Gage case, for instance, it would be impossible to know without further scientific evidence whether Gage's personality changes were due to the loss of brain matter or to the severe shock and facial disfigurement he had suffered.

Surveys   When direct observation is impossible, psychologists must sometimes rely on **survey** techniques such as conducting interviews or administering a questionnaire. Among the best-known national surveys are the Gallup and Roper political polls, the Nielsen television survey, and the U.S. Census. Surveys are difficult to conduct properly and to interpret. They are subject to a number of problems. When people answer questions they often report what they wish were true or recall things differently from the way they actually happened. For example, married couples asked to report how often they engage in sexual relations per month have a tendency to overestimate. The wording of the questions can influence the results as well. For example, subjects who viewed a traffic accident were more likely to answer yes to the question "Did you see *the* broken headlight?" than they were to the question "Did you see *a* broken headlight?" Also, surveys are often susceptible to sampling error. The classic case is the 1936 political poll in which a random sample was picked from the telephone book and asked, "For whom will you vote in the presidential election, Landon or Roosevelt?" The majority chose Landon and the pollsters predicted Landon the winner. Unfortunately for the pollsters, in 1936 only rich people had phones—and Roosevelt won easily.

Testing   Tests are valuable research instruments. Psychologists use them to measure many aptitudes and abilities. Tests make it possible to measure these aspects in large groups of individuals at one time. For this reason, group tests have an important place in education and industry. Tests may also be administered to individuals singly, often for the purpose of clinical or personality assessment.

Test use and construction are not simple matters. Psychological tests must be given only by individuals who are trained to understand their limits and value. Unfortunately, the general public has come to believe that many psychological tests are far more authoritative and accurate than they really are (Snyder, Shenkel, & Lowery, 1977). In Chapters 12 and 13 we will examine some of the problems encountered in developing and interpreting tests as well as the benefits that can be derived from their proper use.

EXPLANATION, PREDICTION, AND CONTROL

All of the efforts of scientific psychology are aimed at a common goal, to explain, to predict, and eventually to control behavior. Psychologists make **deductions** based on their observations of human behavior during research, much as Sherlock Holmes deduced the identity of criminals from the clues he had gathered ("Elementary, my dear Watson."). From their deductions, psychologists are able to derive explanations and predictions of behavior.

CASE STUDY
An intensive study of a single case, with all available data, test results, and opinions about that individual. Usually done in more depth than studies of groups of individuals.

SURVEY
A method of collecting data through the use of interviews and questionnaires.

DEDUCTION
A logical conclusion derived by reasoning from stated premises.

To learn how this process works, let's examine a familiar prediction: Water when heated to 212° F at sea level will boil. To make this prediction, you must first consider what are known as **antecedent conditions.** The antecedent conditions in this example are:

1. Water is present.
2. The water is at sea level.
3. The water's temperature is 212° F.

For years scientists have observed that when these antecedent conditions are fulfilled at the same time, the result is boiling water. From their observations they have derived the rule: Water at 212° F at sea level will boil. When you apply this rule in the presence of the previously listed antecedent conditions, you are making a **prediction:** The water will boil. In a **theory** (defined as a system of rules or assumptions used to predict or explain phenomena), antecedent conditions are described, rules are applied, and, through deduction, predictions are derived.

Of course, sometimes the predictions are inaccurate and the expected outcomes don't occur. This may happen because antecedent conditions haven't been carefully observed or because some have been overlooked. Perhaps a faulty rule has been applied. Many things can be wrong. The trick is to develop a theory that yields accurate predictions most of the time and then to keep refining it so that future predictions become more and more reliable. All theories are tentative, and revisions are to be expected.

Many philosophers consider an **explanation** to be derived in exactly the same manner as a prediction. In making a prediction, antecedent conditions are observed, a rule is applied, and a prediction is made. However, if you predict an event *after* it has occurred, you are said to be giving an explanation, not making a prediction. For instance, suppose that the water from the previous example is already boiling and you want to know why. The explanation would be that:

1. It is water.
2. We are at sea level.
3. The water is being heated to 212° F.

These are the antecedent conditions. Furthermore, it is known that water at sea level when heated to 212° F will boil (rule). And this is why it's boiling (explanation). If you had asked what was going to happen *before* the water had boiled, the same logic would have been applied, only the end result would have been a prediction.

If this reasoning doesn't seem to have produced a very satisfactory explanation of why water boils, perhaps you would like to ask a chemist. He would describe many antecedent conditions concerning molecules, and he'd apply chemical rules. But eventually you might ask why hydrogen and oxygen molecules behave the way they do, and he would have to send you to a physicist. She would probably describe antecedent conditions concerning atomic forces, and she'd apply physical rules, but finally you would wonder why atomic forces act the way they do.

The ultimate answer to the question "Why does water boil?" is, and probably always will be, "Beats me!" (You will hear this response a lot while pursuing ultimate answers.) Predictions or explanations are never absolute; they are only useful (satisfactory) or not useful (unsatisfactory). Chasing after an ultimate answer in the way that we just did with the boiling water is an example of **reductionism.** Sometimes reducing your predictions

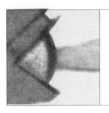

ETHICS AND PSYCHOLOGICAL RESEARCH

Sometimes a professional group will outline or describe behavior that they consider moral and appropriate for dealing with the specific issues faced by the profession. Such "professional morals" are called **ethics**. Throughout this text experiments will be discussed and issues examined that raise questions about ethical procedures and practices.

In order to deal with the kinds of ethical problems that may arise when researchers conduct experiments, the American Psychological Association has published guidelines for psychological research. The following is a summary of the major points.

1. All safeguards for the protection of each human research participant must be maintained. The researcher should protect participants from physical or mental discomfort, harm, or danger.
2. Researchers are ultimately responsible for their own ethical practices as well as for those of others who may assist in their research.
3. All research subjects must be informed of any aspect of the research that may be likely to affect their willingness to participate.
4. Subjects should be fully debriefed following any concealment or deception.
5. Subjects must be allowed to decline or terminate participation in research at any time.
6. The investigator must honor all promises and commitments.
7. All information obtained about participants during research is confidential.

Read the following accounts of experiments. Do you feel there have been breaches in ethical conduct on the part of the researchers?

Social psychologists once designed and carried out an experiment in order to measure the invasion of personal space and the tension it created. They placed a hidden periscope overlooking the men's room so that the men who used the urinals could be secretly observed. The researchers wanted to find out whether it would take longer for a subject to begin urinating if someone else were using the adjacent urinal than if the subject were alone. The results of the study showed that it took subjects longer to begin urination if someone else was nearby (Middlemist, Knowles, & Matter, 1976). The subjects were never informed that they were being observed. Was this a breach of ethics?

In 1973, psychologist Philip Zimbardo conducted a mock prison study at Stanford University in which students acted out the roles of guards or prisoners within a prison-like setting. The study had to be terminated early, however, because some of the "guards" became so sadistic that four of the "prisoners" had acute psychological reactions ranging from fear and rage to crying. One "prisoner" begged for hours to be released from the experiment (Zimbardo, Haney, & Banks, 1973). Zimbardo himself became so wrapped up in his role as prison warden that he admitted he may have failed to respond quickly enough to the seriousness of the problem. Was this a breach of ethics?

---

or explanations to a more molecular level of discourse is very satisfactory, sometimes not so satisfactory. Imagine trying to describe a mob riot with formulas from atomic physics!

In psychology, the goal is not to find ultimate answers—which are probably unobtainable anyway—but rather to predict and explain human behavior as accurately as possible. Psychologists hope to discover rules they can apply when certain antecedent conditions are present and, by applying these rules, to be able to predict behavior (or explain behavior that has already occurred) in a way that is useful to them and to everyone else. This is a very powerful technique because it allows people to predict the future, and to know the future is to have great power. If you like what is about to occur, you simply let it happen; if you don't like it, you can try to avoid or change it. This is what is meant by *control*. Whether you are watching water boil or a person behave, the logic and the deductive process you apply to predict, explain, and control the outcome of a situation are the same.

Summary

- Psychology is the study of the behavior of organisms.
- There are many different areas of specialization or interest within psychology. Among them are experimental, physiological, comparative, developmental, social, clinical, industrial, organizational, educational, and counseling psychology.
- Psychology was born of two parents, philosophy and physiology. It was the union of the philosophers' questions and the physiologists' careful scientific analysis that led to psychological research, which began in a laboratory in Leipzig, Germany, in 1879.
- The first experimental psychology laboratory was started by Wilhelm Wundt, who was interested in analyzing the structure of the conscious mind. This system of psychology, known as structuralism, relied on the technique of introspection. Introspection failed, and by the 1930s structuralism had begun to be abandoned.
- Functionalism was the first completely American psychology. Its founder was William James. Functionalists, influenced by Charles Darwin, believed human consciousness and behavior must serve a function. Functionalism gave birth to many modern areas of psychological interest.
- Early in this century an American psychologist, John B. Watson, developed an objective system of psychology he called behaviorism. Behaviorism remains a powerful force in modern psychology and has been of great value in demonstrating that much of our behavior is determined by our immediate environment.
- At about the same time that behaviorism was becoming the dominant force in American psychology, a different reaction to structuralism was developing in Germany, the Gestalt view. Gestalt psychologists argue that conscious sensations can be examined but that the whole experience must be taken for what it is.
- Psychoanalytic theory was developed by a Viennese physician, Sigmund Freud. It did not develop as a reaction against structuralism but rather has its roots in neurology and medicine. Psychoanalysis has been severely criticized for its lack of scientific control and careful experimentation.
- Humanistic psychology has often been called the third force in psychology. Humanists do not believe that people are governed by stimuli or unconscious motives and drives. Rather, they believe that people have free will and a need to achieve self-actualization.
- All scientific research relies on systematic and objective methods of observing, recording, and describing events. The scientific experiment is one of the most powerful research tools that psychologists possess.
- A good experiment requires the use of proper procedures for selecting subjects, defining terms, maintaining control, and eliminating biases.
- Single-subject experiments use time as the control.
- A correlation is defined as the relationship between two variables. Data from correlations are valuable because predictions can be made from them. However, cause-effect relationships cannot be assumed merely because a correlation exists.
- In naturalistic observations, researchers refrain from directly interacting with the variables being observed. Naturalistic observation is most often used to investigate behavior in natural environments, those in which the researcher refrains from purposeful manipulation.

- Other research tools used by psychologists include case studies, surveys, and testing.
- All of the efforts of scientific psychology are aimed at a common goal, to predict, to explain, and eventually to control behavior. Psychologists make deductions based on their observations of human behavior during research. From their deductions, they are able to derive explanations and predictions of behavior.

EPILOGUE: SCIENCE AND THE SPIRIT WORLD

There is an epilogue at the end of each chapter in this text. These epilogues are not intended to be chapter summaries; they simply illustrate the way in which one individual's life was affected by some aspect of the material discussed in the chapter. In this first epilogue you will see how the scientific method influenced the thinking and behavior of one researcher.

Clark Hull (1884–1952) loved scientific experiments. Early in his career he earned a reputation because of his rigorously controlled experiments on smoking and hypnosis. He eventually applied his scientific efforts toward the creation of a system of theorems and postulates that he hoped would result in a behaviorism as exact as Euclidean geometry. So it came as a surprise to his family and colleagues when he announced one day that he planned to attend a seance in order to make contact with his dead sister. Hull said that he had heard about a medium who could reach the spirit world and he wanted to try it.

At the seance Hull took a seat and joined hands with the medium and other members of the group. He explained what he wanted and the medium said she would do her best. The lights dimmed and the medium appeared to enter a trance.

She called on the spirit world and suddenly a different voice seemed to come from her throat. "Clark, Clark, it's your sister," the voice said. Hull asked his sister how she was and what the spirit world was like. His sister said that her spirit was at rest and that all was well. She added that someday they would be together and until then she would keep a protective watch over him. She told him not to worry, that she was all right. Hull began to ask specific questions but suddenly the lights came on again and the medium awoke from her trance. "I'm sorry," she said, "I can only maintain contact for a short time; the strain is too great." Hull was smiling. The medium said, "I see you are happy that you could talk to your sister." Hull's smile became a grin. "I never had a sister," he said. Yes, Clark Hull loved scientific experiments.

Suggestions for Further Reading

1. American Psychological Association. *Careers in Psychology.* Washington, D.C.: American Psychological Association, 1976.
2. Deese, J. *Psychology as science and art.* New York: Harcourt Brace Jovanovich, 1972.

3. Kimble, G. A. *How to use (and misuse) statistics.* Englewood Cliffs: Prentice-Hall, 1978.

4. Marx, M. H., & Hillix, W. A. *Systems and theories in psychology* (2nd ed.). New York: McGraw-Hill, 1973.

5. McCain, G., & Segal, E. M. *The game of science* (2nd ed.). Monterey, Calif.: Brooks/Cole, 1973.

6. Wertheimer, M. *A brief history of psychology.* New York: Holt, Rinehart and Winston, 1970.

CHAPTER 2

The Biological Bases of Behavior

PROLOGUE

You are standing in the laboratory and Professor James Olds has just handed you a rat. "Here, you can have this one," he says. "We had an accident and put the electrode in the wrong place, but you may as well test him anyway." You look at the electrode. It's a small, short metal rod, and it's sticking directly out of the rat's head. A few days ago you and the other graduate assistants had watched as the electrodes were inserted into the brains of the anesthetized rats. Their skulls were opened and the electrodes were pushed into the brains. The bone was then resealed with dental cement. When the rats recovered, the electrodes were attached to small transformers so that a mild electric current could be sent into their brains.

Professor Olds is pursuing work begun by Hebb at McGill University and Delgado, Roberts, and Miller at Yale. They had used the same kinds of electrodes, placing them in the lower section of the midline system of rats' brains. They discovered that mild electrical stimulation to the midline caused the rats to avoid from then on whatever they had been doing when they received the electric impulse. Apparently the

mild current was painful or noxious in some way, and now Professor Olds is investigating further.

Unfortunately, in the rat you're supposed to test, the surgeon missed the midline system entirely, and the electrode ended up along a nerve pathway coming from a section of the brain called the rhinencephalon. Although other students are having good results obtaining the avoidance response from the rats that have electrodes in the right place, you doubt that you'll be successful. You place your rat in the test area, a large empty box with corners labeled A, B, C, and D. When the rat goes to one of the corners you will electrically stimulate his brain through the electrode. You will note whether he avoids that corner from then on. The rat goes to corner A. You press a button, administering electrical stimulation to the brain (ESB). The rat moves away from corner A. Is he avoiding that corner? Or did he just happen to walk away? No, it's not working; he's back in corner A. Better give him another ESB. He sniffs around a bit, moves off, and then returns to corner A. You give him more ESB. For the better part of an hour the rat stays in corner A, even though

31

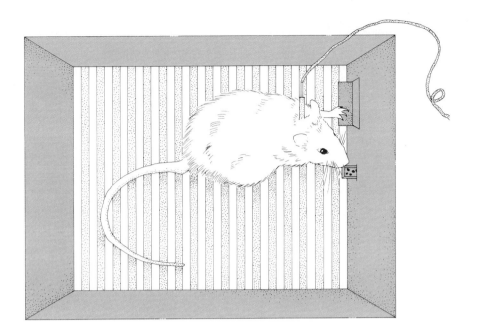

you keep giving him ESB. Finally, the rat moves to another corner to sleep.

When your rat wakes he immediately goes to corner A. You tell Professor Olds that there is something unusual happening; your rat almost acts as if he likes the ESB. Everyone comes over to watch. The animal won't leave corner A. "Are you sure you're giving him ESB?" Professor Olds asks. "Is your transformer working?" You answer yes, you had checked that. Olds says, "We can test whether he really likes the ESB by using a technique and apparatus devised by the behaviorist B. F. Skinner."

By the end of the day the apparatus is ready. A lever has been mounted in the rat's box. The lever is set up so that whenever the rat presses it he will close an electrical circuit and administer ESB to himself. Earlier, while Professor Olds was still connecting the wiring, you trained the rat to work the lever by giving him food whenever he pressed it. Now the lever is connected to the electrode. Everyone gathers around. The rat presses

the lever, but this time, instead of receiving food, he receives ESB.

Your rat appears excited. He presses the lever again. Soon he is pressing the lever at a rate of 200 times per hour. Is it possible that the misguided electrode has revealed a "pleasure center" in the brain? Could there actually be a specific place in the brain where good feelings register? If there is such an area, how sensitive is it?

Professor Olds wonders whether your rat's electrode is square in the middle of this pleasure center or only near it. In order to find out, he has more rats implanted with electrodes. Each electrode is placed in the same general area as the electrode in your rat but in a slightly different spot.

Some of the new rats, whose electrodes are closer to their brains' midlines, begin to respond. You sit there hour after hour, watching as the rats press the lever over 30 times per minute for 24 hours, without stopping, until they finally collapse from exhaustion and you feel like joining them. What must it be like? How could anything feel that good?

The next day you let the rats go hungry. On the day after that you give them a choice—freely available food or the lever. They ignore the food and run straight to the levers.

It has been known for many years that specific places in the brain are concerned with the senses and with the movement of different parts of the body. But until that day in Professor Olds' laboratory in 1956, no one had presumed that pleasure was to be found in a particular place. Since then, many special centers in the brain have been postulated. Some appear to control hunger or thirst, others to control memory or emotions or

other aspects of a person's psychology. Even other pleasure centers have been discovered. Many of these areas seem to share control with one another. Yet the brain remains a largely unknown and uncharted territory, like darkest Africa two centuries ago.

In this chapter you will learn about your brain. It already knows a great deal, so why not give it a chance to learn something about itself? You will also find out how your nervous system works and how the genes you have inherited from your parents may be influencing your behavior.

NERVES
Bundles of neural fibers that carry impulses from one point in the body to another.

Why Psychologists Study the Brain, the Nervous System, and Genetics

All human behavior has its roots in the nervous system, of which the brain is an integral part. In studying behavior, psychologists are concerned with sensations, perception, consciousness, learning, memory, thinking, motivation, emotion, intelligence, personality, conflict, love, and abnormal behavior, to mention a few of the most prominent interests. Every one of these areas of study can be based on neurophysical principles. The nervous system itself develops according to orders provided by inherited genetic material.

Among physiological psychologists, who study the biological bases of behavior, are many who believe that knowledge of the brain and nervous system will eventually be so complete that the physiological approach will be the predominant means of understanding, predicting, and controlling behavior. Other psychologists, however, argue that reducing all psychological discourse to the physiological level may be centuries away, if not impossible. They maintain that the brain is so complex that it seems to defy understanding, and that even thinking about abandoning other psychological approaches is premature. But the work has begun.

The Divisions of the Nervous System

Moving, sensing, feeling, thinking, remembering—none of these would be possible without a nervous system. In fact, your entire life, and all of your behavior, depends on the functioning of your nervous system. **Nerves** transmit messages throughout your body, telling you to inhale and exhale and your heart to beat. Nerves can bring stored memories to your attention or help you follow a bird in flight. The nervous system is perhaps the most complex system in the human body.

Although the entire nervous system is interrelated, it is often described in parts in order to make it more comprehensible. Figure 2.1 shows the nervous system broken down into its component parts. As you can see, the first division is between the central nervous system and the peripheral nervous system. The **central nervous system** is centrally located and comprises all of the nerves that are encased within bone. It includes the **brain** and the **spinal cord** (see Figure 2.2). The **peripheral nervous system** is a complex system of nerves that carry information to and from the central nervous system. The peripheral nervous system is divided into the somatic and the autonomic nervous systems.

The **somatic nervous system** carries messages inward from the sense organs and outward to the muscles of the skeleton. Nerves that carry messages inward to the central nervous system are called **afferent nerves;** nerves that carry messages outward from the central nervous system are called **efferent nerves.** These two sets of nerves interact to form one of the simplest arrangements in the nervous system—the **reflex arc.** In a reflex arc an afferent sensory message travels to the spinal cord and an efferent motor message immediately returns to the muscles. The quick response provided by the reflex arc can be very helpful, for instance, if you should place your hand on a hot stove. If you had to wait for the sensory message to travel all the way up your spine to your brain, as most sensory messages do, you'd waste valuable time while your hand cooked. Thanks to the reflex arc your hand will be off the stove before your brain knows why.

The **autonomic nervous system** carries information to and from organs, glands, and other muscles within the body. Among the muscles controlled by the autonomic nervous system are those responsible for digestion and heart beat. This system is called autonomic (as in automatic) because the glands, internal organs, and muscles it affects are not usually considered to be under voluntary control. The autonomic nervous system is divided into sympathetic and parasympathetic systems.

Figure 2.1 *The divisions of the human nervous system*

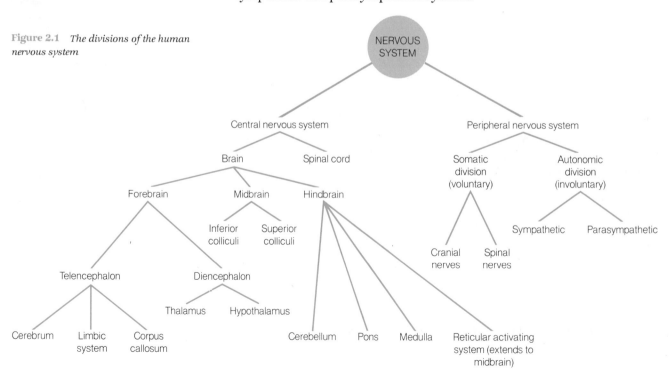

The **sympathetic nervous system** is sometimes referred to as the fight-or-flight system. If you became angry enough to fight or frightened enough to run, the sympathetic nervous system would be especially active (see Figure 2.3). The functions controlled by the sympathetic nervous system are helpful in preparing you to fight or run. When you become excited, your pupils dilate, allowing more light to enter. Your heart rate speeds up, causing more oxygen to be sent to the muscles. Digestion is inhibited, which allows more blood to flow to the muscles. Finally, the sympathetic nervous system orders the release of adrenaline. In a frightening or provoking situation you will know that the sympathetic nervous system has been engaged when your heart starts to pound, you begin to sweat, your mouth becomes dry, and you feel a fluttering in your stomach.

Once the sympathetic nervous system has become active, there must be

REFLEX ARC
The pathway a sensory message travels from a receptor to the spinal cord and back to an effector (the bodily organ that responds to the stimulation) in order to produce a reflex.

AUTONOMIC NERVOUS SYSTEM
The portion of the peripheral nervous system that carries information to and from organs, glands, and muscles within the body.

SYMPATHETIC NERVOUS SYSTEM
The portion of the autonomic nervous system that is primarily concerned with emergencies and emotional states.

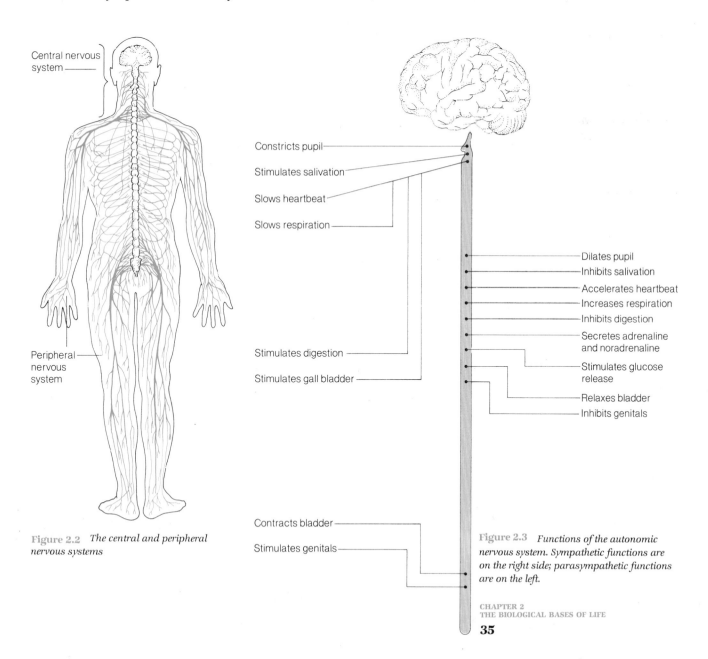

Figure 2.2 *The central and peripheral nervous systems*

Figure 2.3 *Functions of the autonomic nervous system. Sympathetic functions are on the right side; parasympathetic functions are on the left.*

PARASYMPATHETIC NERVOUS SYSTEM
The portion of the autonomic nervous system that is most active during the body's quiescent states.

NEURONS
Specialized cells that transmit electrical impulses from one part of the body to another.

SOMA
The cell body.

DENDRITES
The short, branched processes of a neuron that receive impulses from other neurons and conduct them toward the cell body.

AXON
The long process of a neuron that transmits impulses away from the cell body to the synapse.

NUCLEUS
A central body within a living cell that contains the cell's hereditary material and controls its metabolism, growth, and reproduction.

a counterbalance in order to return the organism to its original state. The **parasympathetic nervous system** helps bring about this change. It causes the pupils to constrict, stimulates salivation, inhibits the heart rate, and in a sense undoes the stimulation resulting from the activation of the sympathetic nervous system (see Figure 2.3). However, these two systems are not always antagonistic. For example, during sexual arousal both systems are stimulated.

A helpful way to summarize the different divisions and functions of the nervous system is to imagine that you're traveling down the highway at a good speed and just a little too close to the person ahead. Suddenly, the car in front of you brakes. Afferent nerves of the somatic system (part of the peripheral system) send messages to the brain (part of the central nervous system) about the glow of the brake lights and the apparent increasing size of the other vehicle as you rapidly approach it. The brain has to analyze and decide on a response. The response is then sent from the brain to the spinal cord and out along somatic efferent nerves, which stimulate the muscles necessary for you to turn the wheel or step on the brake. At the same time the autonomic nervous system has been active. Its sympathetic division has caused your heart rate to increase, adrenaline to be secreted, your pupils to dilate, and your mouth to become dry. After more information has passed from the somatic system into the brain telling you that the accident has been avoided and that you are safely stopped on the side of the road, the brain sends a message down the spinal cord to the somatic system telling it to relax; this is your signal to release your grip on the steering wheel. Simultaneously, the parasympathetic part of the autonomic system begins to fulfill its role of calming you down by slowing the heart rate, making salivation resume, and constricting the pupils. But since it may take a while for the effects of the secreted adrenaline to wear off, you may remain somewhat shaky for 20 or 30 minutes.

Neurons and the Body's Electrochemical System

As you examine the nervous system and all its parts, you may think that it looks something like a wiring diagram. It looks almost as if your body were wired so that electrical messages could constantly travel between one place and another. But nerves are distinctly unlike wires. A wire is a single entity stretching a particular length, but nerves are not single entities. They are made up of thousands upon thousands of individual nerve cells called **neurons,** which, except in rare circumstances, never touch each other at the point of transmission.

If you broke a wire into thousands of pieces, it's unlikely that a signal would be able to pass through its entire length. Similarly, electrical signals cannot usually pass unaided from neuron to neuron because of the gap between the neurons at the point of transmission. Instead, an electrical signal is sent the length of the neuron and when it reaches the end, a liquid chemical is secreted by the neuron which affects neighboring neurons. The chemical message may stimulate another electrical message to be sent the length of another neuron, and so on. In this way *electrochemical* messages are transmitted throughout the body. Your body is an electrochemical system, not strictly an electrical system. Electrical systems are dry (you wouldn't, for instance, pour water into a television set), but electrochemical systems of necessity are wet. Your brain, spinal column, and all of the other parts of your nervous system are soaked in a water-based fluid.

NEURON STRUCTURE

The neuron is one of the many individual cells (bone cells, blood cells, skin cells, muscle cells, etc.) that make up your body. No one knows exactly how many cells there are in the average human body, but a rough estimate would be in the neighborhood of 60 trillion (60,000,000,000,000, or 6×10^{13}). The neuron is the basic unit of the brain and the rest of the nervous system, and most neurons are located in the brain. No one knows how many neurons are in the average brain. The standard estimate is about 10 billion (10,000,000,000, or 10^{10}) cells. However, other estimates range as high as 1 trillion (Nauta & Feirtag, 1979).

One reason estimates are so difficult to make is that we cannot simply count the number of neurons in a part of the brain and then extrapolate to the whole brain. The brain differs greatly in the kinds of neurons that are present and in their concentrations from one place to the next. Since each neuron may receive messages from or give messages to over a thousand other neurons, an attempt to comprehend the neurocircuitry in the brain is likely to make you want to turn to something simple-minded like nuclear physics. For this reason, much of our information about neurons has come from studying individual neurons rather than neural systems. In the following pages, we will examine a typical neuron and learn how it functions. Although it may not be apparent at first, the way in which the neuron responds to electrical stimulation and the kinds of chemicals it secretes have a great bearing on every aspect of your psychology.

Neurons come in many sizes and shapes, and they often appear to serve unique and specialized functions. In Figure 2.4 you will see a typical neuron. Keep in mind, though, that exceptions to the general description abound. The typical neuron has three distinct structural features: the **soma,** or cell body, the **dendrites,** and the **axon.** The soma contains the **nucleus** of the cell and manufactures enzymes and molecules essential for the maintenance of the cell's life. The dendrites generally receive nerve impulses from surrounding neurons. The axon is the mechanism by which the neuron transmits its own nerve impulses. Messages traveling down the axon may eventually stimulate other neurons, muscles, or glands. Some axons are very short, while others are as long as 3 feet—a formidable length given the microscopic size of the neuron.

Surrounding the entire neuron is a thin skin or membrane. The structure and properties of the membrane directly affect the function and action of the cell. The membrane acts as a kind of skin, permitting the cell to maintain an internal fluid that is markedly different from the fluid surrounding the cell. This difference is most striking in the concentrations of two particular ions, sodium (Na^+) and potassium (K^+). When the neuron is at rest, that is, when it is not sending a message, there is about ten times more potassium within the cell's axon than sodium. Conversely, the medium surrounding the axon contains about ten times more sodium than potassium. Both the sodium and the potassium tend to leak through openings or channels along the axon membrane. Because of this, sodium-potassium "pumps" must work continuously to maintain the different ion concentra-

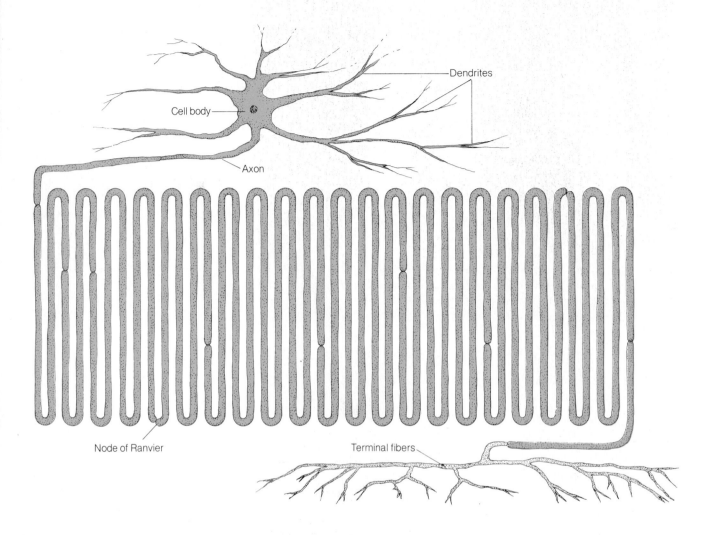

Labels in figure: Dendrites, Cell body, Axon, Node of Ranvier, Terminal fibers

Figure 2.4 *Typical neuron of a vertebrate animal can carry nerve impulses for a considerable distance. The neuron depicted here, with its various parts drawn to scale, is enlarged 250 times. The nerve impulses originate in the cell body and are propagated along the axon, which may have one or more branches. This axon, which is folded for diagrammatic purposes, would be a centimeter long at actual size. Some axons are more than a meter long. The axon's terminal branches form synapses with as many as 1,000 other neurons. Most synapses join the axon terminals of one neuron with the dendrites forming a "tree" around the cell body of another neuron. Thus the dendrites surrounding the neuron in the diagram might receive incoming signals from tens, hundreds or even thousands of other neurons. Many axons, such as this one, are insulated by a myelin sheath interrupted at intervals by the regions known as nodes of Ranvier.* (SOURCE: *Stevens, 1979, p. 55*)

tions within and without the axon. The average small neuron might contain approximately 1 million sodium-potassium pumps. These differing concentrations of sodium and potassium ions give the neuron the ability to transmit signals along its entire length.

NEURAL TRANSMISSIONS

When a neuron's dendrites are stimulated by neighboring neurons, an electrical change is initiated within the soma. If the soma changes enough, a reaction will occur at the beginning of the axon, causing the neuron to fire and to send its own message the length of the axon. Figure 2.5 illustrates this process. The dendrites of a neuron can receive messages from hundreds of other neurons simultaneously, or from only one other neuron.

The messages that affect a particular neuron's dendrites are received in the form of chemicals secreted by nearby neurons. These secreted chemicals are called **neurotransmitters.** They excite the receiving neuron, causing channels in the dendrites and soma membrane to open through which positively charged ions can enter. Originally, the soma's interior was negative with respect to the charge surrounding the cell. But as the positive ions

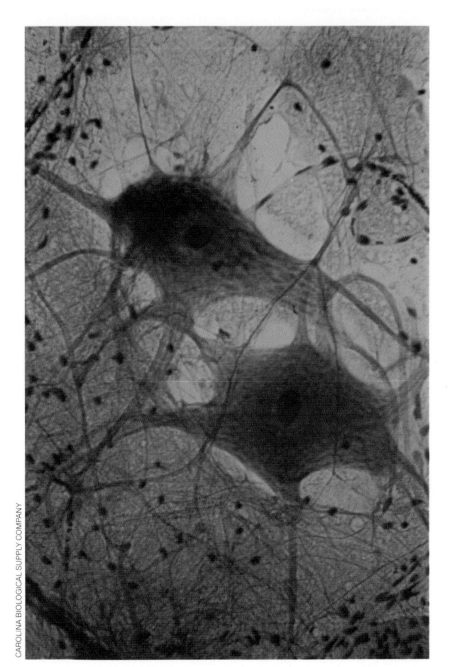

Figure 2.8 For reasons that are unknown, the Golgi stain, apparently at random, completely stains about 5 percent of the neurons in any one group. The dark bodies are the neural somas, and the spidery threads are the axons.

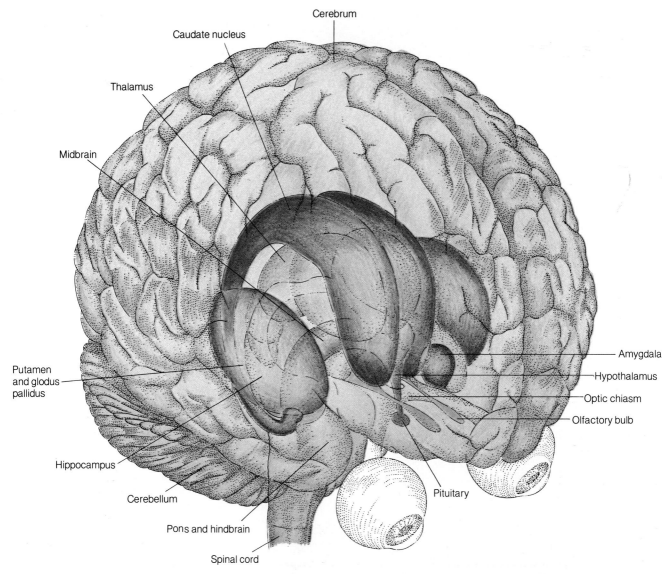

Cerebrum

Caudate nucleus

Thalamus

Midbrain

Putamen
and glodus
pallidus

Hippocampus

Cerebellum

Pons and hindbrain

Spinal cord

Amygdala

Hypothalamus

Optic chiasm

Olfactory bulb

Pituitary

Figure 2.9 The brain and spinal cord of human beings and other mammals can be subdivided into smaller regions according to gross appearance, embryology, or cellular organization. A human brain has been drawn so that its internal structures are visible through "transparent" outer layers of the cerebrum. A generalized mammalian brain is shown in a highly schematic view. Corresponding structures in the realistic and schematic models are the same color.

The most general way of dividing the brain is into hindbrain, midbrain, and forebrain. The hindbrain includes the cerebellum. The midbrain includes the two elevations known as the inferior and superior colliculi. The forebrain is more complex. Its outer part is the cerebral hemisphere, the surface of which is the convoluted sheet of the cerebral cortex. The rest of the forebrain is the diencephalon, the upper two-thirds comprising the thalamus (which has numerous subdivisions) and the lower third the hypothalamus (which connects to the pituitary complex). Some structures depicted in this drawing have not been mentioned in the text because they are beyond the scope of our discussion. They have been included here, however, to show that each major structure has a name. (SOURCE: Nauta & Feirtag, 1979, p. 102)

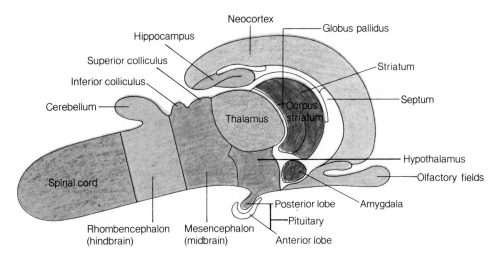

Neocortex

Hippocampus

Superior colliculus

Inferior colliculus

Cerebellum

Globus pallidus

Striatum

Septum

Corpus striatum

Thalamus

Spinal cord

Hypothalamus

Olfactory fields

Amygdala

Posterior lobe
Pituitary
Anterior lobe

Rhombencephalon
(hindbrain)

Mesencephalon
(midbrain)

Figure 12.9, continued   Schematic drawing of a generalized mammalian brain.

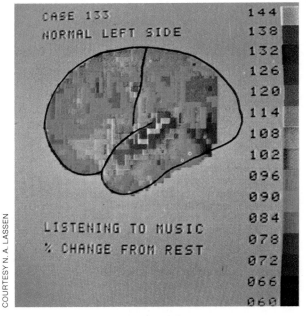

CASE 133
NORMAL LEFT SIDE

144
138
132
126
120
114
108
102
096
090
084
078
072
066
060

LISTENING TO MUSIC
% CHANGE FROM REST

In this brain scan the subject is listening to music.   The lighter colors depict areas of higher activity, in this case the temporal lobes.   This brain scan was obtained using a technique similar to that incorporated in the PET scan.   A radioactive substance was injected to measure blood flow.

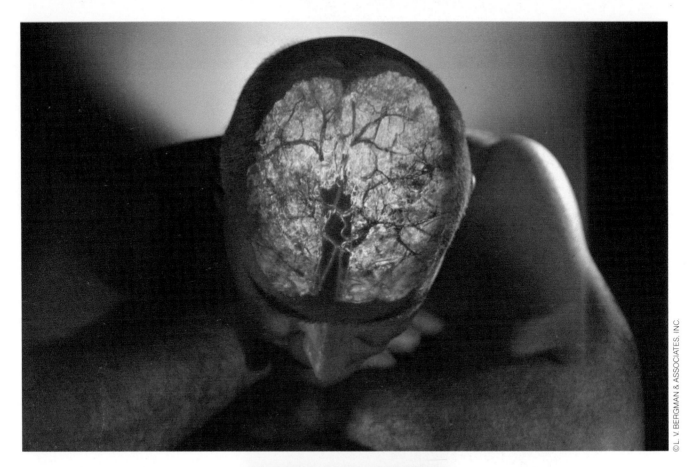

Figure 2.10   The human brain. When viewed from this angle, only the cebral cortex is visible. The cerebral cortex is the largest part of the human brain and contains 70 percent of the neurons in the nervous system.

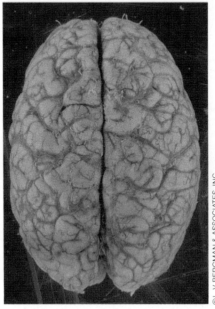

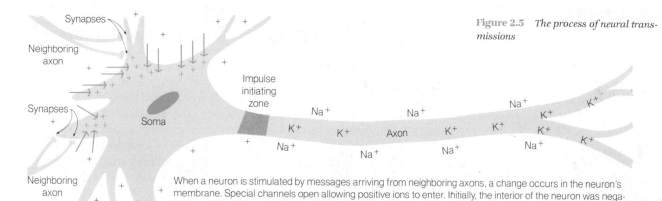

Figure 2.5 *The process of neural transmissions*

When a neuron is stimulated by messages arriving from neighboring axons, a change occurs in the neuron's membrane. Special channels open allowing positive ions to enter. Initially, the interior of the neuron was negative in relation to the exterior. As positive ions enter, the interior becomes more positive. If enough positive ions enter, the impulse initiating zone will be sufficiently stimulated to reach action potential. This begins the process that will send a nerve impulse, or spike, the length of the axon. The spike is represented by the shaded area.

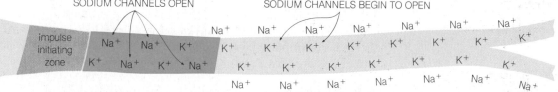

When action potential has been reached, a change occurs in the membrane at the beginning of the axon. Sodium channels open so that the positive ion sodium (Na^+) can enter. Before action potential was reached, the interior of the axon at this spot was −70 millivolts relative to the exterior. Now, for the instant, the interior becomes exceedingly positive.

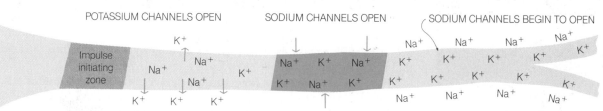

Next, potassium channels open at the beginning of the axon through which potassium (K^+) can exit, reducing the positive charge within. Sodium now enters open sodium channels farther down the axon causing the spike to continue its passage. Each time, the spike causes sodium channels farther along the axon's membrane to open.

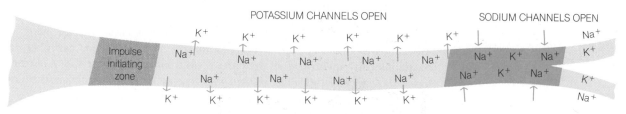

As the nerve impulse, or spike, continues propagating, it alters each successive portion of the axon membrane until it reaches the end of the axon.

flow into the soma, the difference in electrical charge between the inside and the outside of the cell diminishes. If the interior of the soma becomes positive enough, the **impulse initiating zone** will be stimulated. This is the point at which the sodium and potassium ions in and around the axon play their role.

The inside of the axon, with its greater concentration of potassium, is electrically different from the outside of the axon, measuring about 70

NEUROTRANSMITTERS
Chemicals secreted by neurons into the synapse which have an effect on adjacent neurons, muscles, or glands.

IMPULSE INITIATING ZONE
The area at the beginning of an axon that, when sufficiently stimulated, initiates a nerve impulse, or spike.

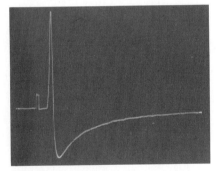

Figure 2.6 *A nerve impulse registers on an oscilloscope as a spike. If an auditory amplifier is attached to the oscilloscope a click can be heard each time an impulse occurs.*

millivolts (70/1000ths of a volt) negative relative to the surrounding medium. Because of this, the neuron is said to have a value of −70 millivolts when at rest. This is known as the **resting potential.** By making use of the difference in voltage across the membrane, the neuron can generate a **nerve impulse** down the length of its axon. When the impulse initiating zone has been sufficiently stimulated, the membrane at the *beginning* of the axon undergoes a dramatic change. As with the dendrites and the soma, special channels open in the membrane allowing ions to rush in—in this case, sodium ions. This causes the front part of the axon to become more positive relative to the external medium. Next, other channels in the immediate vicinity open so that the potassium ions can rush out, thereby restoring the original resting potential of −70 millivolts. While this ion exchange is occurring at the beginning of the axon, it will affect the adjacent portion of the axon membrane, causing the entire process to repeat itself—only this time a little farther down the axon. This reaction will in turn affect the next part of the axon, and so on. The rapid ion exchange races down the length of the axon like a flame following a line of black powder. The sudden shift from negative to positive and back to negative as the nerve impulse passes along the axon shows up on an oscilloscope as a sharp **spike** (see Figure 2.6). If an auditory amplifier is attached to the oscilloscope, this spike can be heard as a click. Whenever enough sodium and potassium are exchanged to cause a nerve impulse to extend the length of the axon, the neuron is said to have reached its **action potential.**

Nerve impulses produced in this way travel relatively long distances without any loss of strength. The action potential is an all-or-nothing proposition. For the neuron to fire, the impulse initiating zone at the head of the axon must be sufficiently stimulated. Otherwise, although some positive ions may flow into the neural soma, not enough will enter to cause action potential to be reached. As an analogy, you might think of a fuse that is singed rather than lighted.

You may be wondering how you can feel a great range of intensities of such things as light, sound, and pressure if a neuron can fire at only one strength. Furthermore, how can you have such a range of motor responses? You can pick something up gently or with a tight grip. These different intensities are achieved in several ways. To express weak intensities, it may be enough for only a few neurons to fire. Strong intensities, on the other hand, may require that thousands upon thousands of neurons fire. Although the strength of each individual impulse is constant, the firing of thousands of neurons can have a cumulative effect. Neurons can also indicate intensity by how often they fire. A mild intensity may cause a neuron to fire only once or twice in a second, whereas an extremely intense stimulation may cause the neuron to fire as often as 1,000 times per second.

Action potentials are not the only way in which a neuron can transmit information. Ions flowing into the dendrites and soma that do not stimulate the axon's impulse initiating zone sufficiently to cause firing may nonetheless enable the cell to pass electrical information to nearby neurons. The electrical gradations between the resting potential and the action potential are called **graded potentials.** Graded potentials encompass the whole range of electrical ion exchanges that are insufficient to cause action potential or generate a spike but greater than those found at resting potential. Unlike action potentials, graded potentials rapidly lose their electrical strength over a distance as their energy dissipates. For this reason action potentials are required for long-distance transmission, while graded potentials are useful for local communication. Neurons that rely heavily on graded potentials in order to exchange information are often called **silent cells** because they do not generate the sudden burst of energy associated with the clicking sound of a spike. Although messages from silent cells can travel down axons, many silent neurons don't even have axons. Such neurons communicate from one cell to the next and from their dendrites to another cell's axon, or from their dendrites to those of another neuron, by means of changes in membrane permeability that allow limited amounts of ions to flow between the neurons. These ion flows, which can alter graded potentials, can be a source of information exchange between neurons. In fact, according to some estimates the major part of neural communication in the brain may occur between silent cells ("Silent Cells," 1977).

SYNAPTIC TRANSMISSIONS

Years ago it was debated whether an electric spark actually jumped the gap between neurons. We now know that the secretion of neurotransmitters is responsible for neurons' ability to communicate with one another. The space between neurons in which they communicate is called the **synapse.** Synapses are generally no more than 5 millionths of an inch across. When an electrical spike traveling down an axon reaches its end, the spike typically causes neurotransmitters to be secreted into the synapse. If you follow the trunk of a tree downward into the earth you discover that it divides again and again into many individual roots. Similarly, if you follow an axon to its end you will find that it divides and subdivides into perhaps 1,000 **end buttons** or **synaptic knobs.** Figure 2.7 is an enlargement of a synaptic knob. When a spike reaches a synaptic knob, a change occurs in the knob's membrane. Channels in the membrane open, allowing the positive ion calcium (Ca^+) to enter. The calcium, acting in a way that is not fully understood, attracts the small vesicles that float within the synaptic knob so that they are attracted to the **presynaptic surface.** The vesicles carry droplets of neurotransmitter which they spill from the presynaptic membrane into the synapse. Across the synapse, receptors on the **postsynaptic**

SILENT CELLS
Neurons that communicate via graded potentials and that are called silent because they do not create a clicking sound when monitored by an oscilloscope that will register an auditory click when action potential is reached. Silent cells generally communicate over short distances and only with cells in their immediate vicinity.

SYNAPSE
The small space between neurons in which they communicate.

END BUTTONS
See SYNAPTIC KNOBS

SYNAPTIC KNOBS
The extreme ends of an axon in which neurotransmitter is stored.

PRESYNAPTIC SURFACE
The cell surface from which neurotransmitter is secreted into the synapse.

POSTSYNAPTIC SURFACE
The cell surface receiving neurotransmitter secreted into the synapse.

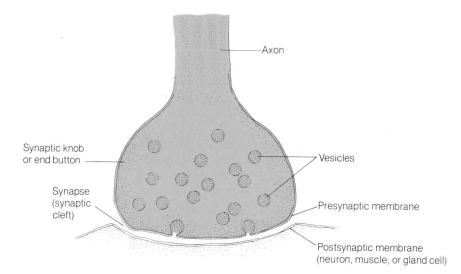

Synaptic knob or end button

Synapse (synaptic cleft)

Axon

Vesicles

Presynaptic membrane

Postsynaptic membrane (neuron, muscle, or gland cell)

Figure 2.7 *When a neural impulse reaches the synaptic knobs at the end of the axon, neurotransmitters carried in the vesicles may be released from the presynaptic surface into the synapse. The neurotransmitter affects receptors on the postsynaptic surface.*

EXCITATORY SYNAPSES
Synapses associated with depolarization of the receiving cell once neurotransmitter is secreted. If the receiving cell is a neuron it will become more likely to fire or may even reach action potential.

INHIBITORY SYNAPSES
A synapse associated with hyperpolarization of the receiving cell once neurotransmitter is secreted. If the receiving cell is a neuron it will become harder to fire.

GOLGI STAIN
A stain used to make neurons visible for inspection under a microscope. The stain is accepted by about 5 percent of any given group of neurons.

BRAIN MAPPING
A technique neurosurgeons use to pinpoint the functions of different areas in the brain so that they don't destroy something vital during brain surgery.

SULCI
The narrow fissures separating adjacent cerebral convolutions.

GYRI
The prominent rounded and elevated convolutions at the surfaces of the cerebral hemispheres.

surface react to the neurotransmitter. If the postsynaptic membrane is the surface of a gland, the neurotransmitter may interact with the receptors and cause the gland to secrete. If the postsynaptic membrane is the surface of a muscle, the neurotransmitter may cause the muscle to contract.

If the postsynaptic surface belongs to another neuron, the neurotransmitter may excite the second neuron, causing an increased graded potential within its soma. Of course, if the graded potential is increased enough, the neuron may reach action potential. Once the neurotransmitter has affected the receptors on the postsynaptic membrane it is either recaptured by the presynaptic membrane, broken down by enzymes, or left to diffuse.

Excitatory Synapses   There are two kinds of synapses, excitatory and inhibitory. So far we have discussed **excitatory synapses,** in which a message from one neuron causes a second neuron to become excited, or more likely to fire. However, it would be dismal if one neuron in the brain passed on a message stimulating thousands of other neurons, which in turn passed on a stimulating message to thousands more. In short order all or a large portion of the neurons would be firing and the brain would be out of control. This unfortunate event is prevented by the existence of **inhibitory synapses.**

Inhibitory Synapses   In an inhibitory synaptic transmission between two neurons a neurotransmitter is also secreted from the presynaptic membrane into the synapse, but this time different ion channels in the postsynaptic membrane open that allow only *negative* ions to flow in. This produces a negative potential which is even greater than the resting potential. In effect, the neural message from the first neuron has made the second neuron less likely to fire than it was before it was stimulated. In some areas of the brain inhibitory synapses outnumber excitatory synapses.

The Structure of the Brain

Imagine you're looking at a slide under a microscope. On the slide is a tiny speck, a piece of brain. What do you see? The piece of brain resembles a small translucent blob. Within the blob are thousands of extremely tiny, black, spider-like specks that have long streaks emanating from them. The spider-like specks and streaks appear to meander in a crazy, tangled pattern.

What you are viewing are neurons that have been stained. The medium was **Golgi stain,** which causes certain neurons to stand out (see Figure 2.8, in color section). The Golgi stain affects only about 5 percent of the neurons in any particular sample, so that most of the neurons in the speck you are viewing are clear and invisible to your eye. The Golgi stain colors the entire body and axon of the neurons that accept it. No one knows why the stain works or why it should stain, apparently at random, only 5 percent of the neurons it comes in contact with. The thousands of spider-like specks you see are the somas and dendrites, and the streaks are the axons. In the background there seems to be a black haze, caused by the microscope's inability to accommodate the whole depth of the speck at one focus setting. As you turn the focus the neurons you were looking at become blurry and the haze that was in the background shows up as more neurons. Beneath are even more neurons, thousands of them, and millions of synapses—and all of this in one small speck of brain.

The idea of exploring the brain at this microscopic level and tracing all of its neurochemical circuits is far beyond the present capacity of our science. The experience of viewing just one small speck can be overwhelming. Even professionals familiar with the brain and its workings sometimes find themselves overcome by a sense of awe. Consider a certain neurosurgeon who was mapping the brain of a patient. **Brain mapping** is a technique neurosurgeons use in order to make certain that they don't cut through or destroy something vital during brain surgery. Throughout the brain-mapping procedure the patient is alert and awake. The skull has been opened and the brain exposed, but because of local anesthetics the patient does not feel pain. As the neurosurgeon touches different places on the surface of the brain with a small electrode through which a tiny current is passed, the patient reports what he senses. For example, when one point on the brain is stimulated the patient may report that he feels a tingling on his gums; at another point he may report a ringing in his ears; at another point the little finger on his left hand may twitch. The surgeon then places tiny numbered paper tags directly on the brain at each point identified and records the function of the point. The neurosurgeon of our example was discussing with his patient the different sensations that the electric probe was causing when, for a moment, he just stood there staring at her brain. After surgery the resident who had assisted asked what he had been thinking during that moment. "I'm not sure," the surgeon replied. "It's just that it suddenly occurred to me that I was talking to a body organ and it was answering back!"

When you look at a human brain (shown in Figure 2.9, in color section), there are three features that are likely to catch your attention immediately. First, the brain appears to be rippled, filled with crevices and folds. Second, a long fissure running the length of the brain appears to separate it into a left and a right half. Finally, some portions of the brain seem to be lighter or darker in color than other portions, the white and gray matter.*

Why is the brain convoluted and rippled? One good reason is to save space. If you flattened the brain out it would take up an area of about 2 feet by 2 feet. Perhaps our brains could have evolved in the shape of a great circuit board, instead of the way they did, but the skull shape necessary to contain such a form would certainly have been unusual, and it would probably have presented aerodynamic problems on a windy day! The best way, then, of fitting a large brain into a reasonably shaped skull is to crumple it up. If you crumple a piece of paper into a ball, you will see that you have created fissures and convolutions. In the brain the fissures are called **sulci** and the convolutions **gyri.**

The long fissure running the length of the brain does in fact divide it in half, except for a few important connections. As you will see, it may be more accurate to consider the brain to be two brains, joined and sharing information and controlling different things, different aspects of your behavior.

---

*Actually, the white and gray matter have a pinkish-red hue because of the blood flowing to the brain.

MYELIN

A white fatty covering on neural fibers that serves to channel impulses along fibers and increase their speed.

CEREBRUM

The large rounded structure of the brain occupying most of the cranial cavity, divided into two cerebral hemispheres by a deep fissure and joined at the bottom by the corpus callosum.

CEREBRAL CORTEX

The extensive outer layer of convoluted gray tissue of the cerebral hemispheres which is largely responsible for higher nervous functions, including intellectual processes; also called the *neocortex*.

NEOCORTEX

See CEREBRAL CORTEX

HINDBRAIN

The posterior section of the brain which includes the cerebellum, pons, and medulla.

MIDBRAIN

The middle section of the brain which contains the inferior and superior colliculi, the structures responsible for processing and relaying visual and auditory information.

FOREBRAIN

The top portion of the brain which includes the thalamus, hypothalamus, corpus callosum, limbic system, and cerebrum.

MEDULLA

The oblong structure at the top of the spinal cord that is responsible for many vital life-support functions, including breathing and heart beat.

PONS

Part of the brain stem lying just above the medulla and regulating motor messages traveling from the higher brain downward through the pons to the cerebellum. It also regulates sensory information.

CEREBELLUM

A portion of the hindbrain situated just beneath the posterior portion of the cerebrum. Its function is to coordinate muscle tone and fine motor control.

When Agatha Christie's master detective, Hercule Poirot, was deep in thought, he would often tap his forehead and refer to the "little gray cells." These gray cells are neurons without myelin. **Myelin** is a white fatty sheath that coats the axons of some neurons. It insulates and provides nourishment to the neuron. Myelinated neurons are able to transmit messages faster than nonmyelinated neurons. Billions of nonmyelinated neurons give the appearance of a grayish mass within the brain—the gray matter. Billions of myelinated neurons create a white glistening sheen—the white matter—because of the white of their myelin sheaths.

The largest part of the brain, and the part you usually think of when you picture the brain, is the **cerebrum** (see Figure 2.10 in color section). No fewer than 70 percent of all the neurons in the central nervous system are contained in the cerebrum (Nauta & Feirtag, 1979). The outer layer of the cerebrum is called the **cerebral cortex.** *Cortex* in Latin means "bark," and, in a way, the sulci and gyri of the cortex do resemble the bark of a tree. The cerebral cortex is also known as the **neocortex,** meaning new cortex, because in evolution it is the most recent development. You can trace the evolutionary history and development of your brain by following the lower structures upward to the neocortex. The structures that are deeper and lower in the brain are evolutionarily older. For convenience, the brain may be divided into the **hindbrain,** the **midbrain,** and the **forebrain,** and each area may be subdivided (see Figures 2.9 and 2.10, in color section).

THE HINDBRAIN

The major components of the hindbrain are the **medulla,** the **pons,** and the **cerebellum.** In evolutionary terms, these portions of the brain are very old. Humans share these brain structures with older and less complex species such as reptiles. In fact, the hindbrain in humans is often referred to as the "reptilian brain."

The Medulla   As the spinal column enters the stem of the hindbrain it begins to widen. This is the location, deep and low within the brain, of the medulla, a small, narrow concentration of millions of neurons perhaps 1½ inches in length. The medulla controls many vital life-support functions, including breathing and heart beat. The slightest damage to it can result in death.

The Pons   Just above the medulla, in the front portion of the brain stem, is the pons. Many important ascending and descending nerve fibers run through the pons. The pons regulates motor messages traveling from the higher brain downward through the pons to the cerebellum. It also regulates some sensory information. Cells involved with vision have been found in the pons (Glickstein & Gibson, 1976). In addition, nuclei (densely packed concentrations of neural dendrites and somas) associated with respiratory regulation have been found in the pons.

The Cerebellum   At about the same level as the pons, but in the rear portion of the brain stem, is the cerebellum. In Greek *cerebellum* means "little chamber." Like the neocortex, it has sulci and gyri. The function of the cerebellum appears to be pretty much the same for reptiles, fishes, birds, and mammals, including humans. It coordinates muscle tone and fine motor control. Although the commands for motor movements may originate in higher areas of the brain, it is the cerebellum that controls and fine-tunes the movements. Damage to the cerebellum causes awkward and uncontrolled movements.

The Reticular Activating System   Running upward from the hindbrain toward the midbrain is a complex network of neurons known collectively as the **reticular activating system.** This system is made up of relatively few neurons which seem to monitor the general level of activity in the hindbrain, maintaining a state of arousal. Wakefulness and sleeping are regulated in part by this portion of the brain. Sleeping animals whose reticular systems are stimulated by electrodes will usually awaken. If the reticular system is severely damaged, a permanent state of sleep may result. The reticular system also seems to be important in helping to focus attention or make an organism alert. As you can see, the evolutionarily old hindbrain contains structures vital to the survival of all animals.

THE MIDBRAIN

The upper portions of the reticular formation are found in the midbrain along with the **superior colliculi** and the **inferior colliculi.** There are four colliculi altogether, an inferior and a superior colliculus on either side of the midbrain in front of the cerebellum (see Figure 2.9, in color section). These four small knobs are sensory processing and relay areas. The superior colliculi are involved in controlling and regulating eye movement as well as in processing and relaying visual information. The inferior colliculi relay and process auditory information.

THE FOREBRAIN

The forebrain is divided into two structures, the **diencephalon** and the **telencephalon.** The diencephalon consists of the thalamus and the hypothalamus, and the telencephalon of the corpus callosum, the limbic system, and the cerebrum.

The Thalamus   Buried beneath the neocortex on top of the brain stem are two structures lying on either side of the brain and shaped something like large eggs. These are the left and right halves of the **thalamus.** We know of two important functions that are served by the millions, or perhaps billions, of neurons that make up the thalamus. Like the reticular activating system, the thalamus seems to be involved in wakefulness and sleep. But, perhaps more importantly, the thalamus is also a relay center for sensory information. Before continuing on to higher brain structures, information from the senses passes through the thalamus. There is one exception, however, and that is the sense of smell. Olfactory messages from the nose bypass the thalamus, traveling direct to the area known as the **olfactory bulb.** The sense of smell may be a very old sense and may have evolved in its own direction, while the newer senses have taken advantage of the relatively newer areas of the brain and become involved with them (Nauta & Feirtag, 1979). It is assumed that sensory information other than olfactory must be processed by passing it through the synaptic connections in the thalamus in order for the messages to be understood at the higher brain levels.

RETICULAR ACTIVATING SYSTEM
A complex network of neurons that monitors the general level of activity in the hindbrain, maintaining a state of arousal.

SUPERIOR COLLICULI
Small knoblike processes in the midbrain that are primarily involved in controlling and regulating eye movement and processing and relaying visual information.

INFERIOR COLLICULI
Small knoblike processes in the midbrain that are primarily involved in relaying and processing auditory information.

DIENCEPHALON
A division of the forebrain that contains the thalamus and the hypothalamus.

TELENCEPHALON
A division of the forebrain that contains the corpus callosum, the limbic system, and the cerebrum.

THALAMUS
Part of the forebrain that relays sensory information and is involved in wakefulness and sleep.

OLFACTORY BULB
A mass of cells in the forebrain associated with the sense of smell into which the olfactory nerve fibers enter and form a tract leading farther into the brain.

The Hypothalamus The **hypothalamus** is an elongated structure located in front of and between the thalamus orbs. Although it is a relatively small structure in the brain, it has been the focus of intense interest because it appears to play a role in a large number of important brain functions and behaviors. If the hypothalamus is destroyed, death is almost certain. For this reason, neurosurgeons who must work near it are extremely careful not even to bump it.

The hypothalamus apparently controls an entire range of autonomic functions. It takes part in regulating sleep and wakefulness and in controlling body temperature, hunger, and thirst. Blood pressure and metabolism are also related to activities within the hypothalamus. At the lower tip of the hypothalamus is the **pituitary gland,** which controls many hormonal secretions. **Hormones** are substances that travel throughout the body and have wide-ranging effects on behavior. Many of the pituitary gland's orders, and some of its hormones, come from the hypothalamus. The pituitary gland has often been called the master gland because it appears to control other glands all over the body. Since the hypothalamus is related to the endocrine (hormonal) system, it has been implicated in the control of sexual behavior and reproductive cycles as well as aggression and reactions to stress. We'll discuss the function of glands and the endocrine system later.

The Corpus Callosum The **corpus callosum** in the telencephalon is the most important interconnection between the two hemispheres of the brain. The left and right hemispheres, though separate and distinct, share information by passing neural messages back and forth. *Corpus callosum* means "hard or calloused body." If you were to insert your fingers between the two soft hemispheres and press down, you would feel the corpus callosum as a hard surface in the surrounding tissue. Certain forms of severe epilepsy can be controlled by cutting the corpus callosum, thereby severing the two hemispheres and literally creating two independent brains. Patients with such split brains show some amazing qualities, which we will investigate later in this chapter.

The Limbic System The **limbic system** is located in the telencephalon beneath the cerebral cortex. It is not a single structure but an aggregation of structures, its two major components being the **hippocampus** and the **amygdala.** The limbic system is believed to represent one of the first evolutionary steps toward breaking away from fixed, instinctive behavioral patterns. While animals such as reptiles flee, fight, or eat in very stereotypical and repetitive ways, animals with limbic systems are often able to modify inherited responses in order to meet new demands.

The hippocampus, a small area at the back of the telencephalon, is known to be important in the memory process. Damage to the hippocampus can cause certain memories to be disrupted. The amygdala is a small bulb located in the front of the brain. It sends most of its neural information to the neocortex. The amygdala is associated with emotion. In monkeys, if a lesion or cut is made on one portion of the amygdala, the animal may go into a blind rage, attacking everything within sight. If another part of the amygdala is cut, the animal may respond to attacks against it without any emotional expression, remaining passive, as if nothing were happening.

The Cerebrum   As mentioned earlier, the cerebrum in humans contains fully 70 percent of all of the neurons in the central nervous system; it is a massive portion of the brain. Throughout evolution the cerebrum has grown and become the brain's most prominent aspect (see Figure 2.11).

The folds and shapes of the cerebral cortex lend themselves to a division into four main lobes. These four lobes, appearing in both left and right hemispheres, are the **frontal,** the **parietal,** the **occipital,** and the **tem-**

Figure 2.11   *The progressive increase in the size of the cerebrum in vertebrates is evident in these drawings, which show a representative selection of vertebrate brains, all drawn to the same scale. In vertebrates lower than mammals the cerebrum is small. In carnivores, and particularly in primates, it increases dramatically in both size and complexity.* (SOURCE: *Hubel, 1979, pp. 46–47*)

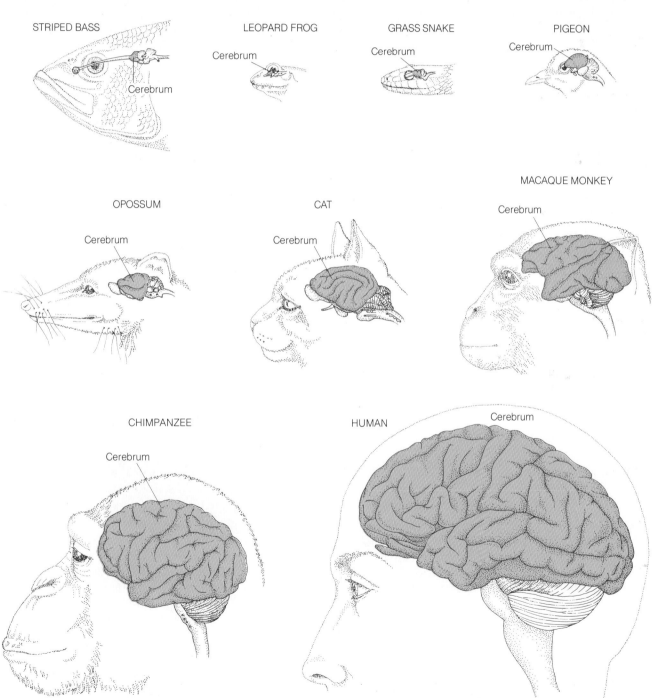

STRIPED BASS

Cerebrum

LEOPARD FROG

Cerebrum

GRASS SNAKE

Cerebrum

PIGEON

Cerebrum

OPOSSUM

Cerebrum

CAT

Cerebrum

MACAQUE MONKEY

Cerebrum

CHIMPANZEE

Cerebrum

HUMAN

Cerebrum

TEMPORAL LOBES

TEMPORAL LOBES
The portions of the cerebrum on either side of the head near the temples. The temporal lobes contain the primary auditory areas, as well as association areas. They have to do with emotion, vision, and language.

CENTRAL SULCUS
A major fissure in the brain, also known as the fissure of Rolando, which separates the frontal from the parietal lobes.

MOTOR AREA
An area located in front of the brain's central fissure that controls body movement.

SOMATOSENSORY AREA
An area in the brain located behind the central fissure at the start of the parietal lobe and which controls sensation.

VISUAL CORTEX
An area in the brain located in the occipital lobes through which most visual information is processed.

ASSOCIATION AREAS
The parts of the cerebral cortex, other than the sensory and motor areas, that appear to be linked with language, thinking, and memory.

poral lobes (see Figure 2.12). More than any other part of the brain, our large and complex cerebrum is probably responsible for the unique qualities that we as humans share. It is believed to give us our great capacities for thought, language, memory, and comprehension.

In 1870, Gustav Fritsch and Eduard Hitzig were making the first attempt at brain mapping when they discovered that applying a weak electric current to an area of the neocortex immediately in front of the **central sulcus,** a major fold, caused twitches in muscles on the side of the body *opposite* the brain hemisphere being stimulated. It has since been discovered that, as neural fibers from one side of the body ascend through the spinal column, they cross to the opposite side at the hindbrain. As a result, the left hemisphere of the brain controls the right side of the body, and the right hemisphere controls the left side of the body. If an individual suffers a stroke that leaves the left side of the body paralyzed, the neurosurgeon knows that the stroke must have occurred in the right cerebral hemisphere, and vice versa.

Further experiments along this line have revealed areas along the cerebral cortex that are responsible for both sensory and motor stimulation. At the back of the frontal lobe, just in front of the central fissure, lies the **motor area** that controls the body's movement. Electrical stimulation anywhere in this area can produce contractions in particular skeletal muscles. Figure 2.13 shows which muscles are controlled by the different portions of the motor area. As you can see, much of the motor area is reserved for the control of the hands, which in our species are extremely important. Another large area is given over to the control of the lips and the mouth. Speech is also an important aspect of our species. If you had less brain to

Figure 2.12 *The four lobes of the cerebral cortex*

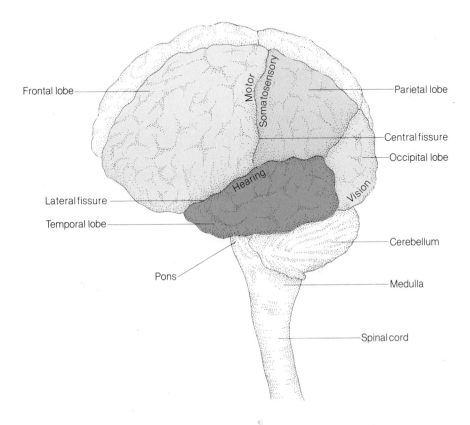

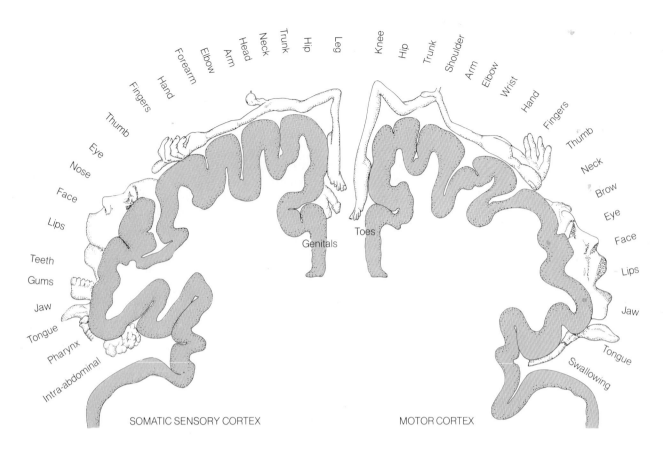

Labels on the left (Somatic Sensory Cortex), from top going around: Trunk, Neck, Head, Arm, Elbow, Forearm, Hand, Fingers, Thumb, Eye, Nose, Face, Lips, Teeth, Gums, Jaw, Tongue, Pharynx, Intra-abdominal, Hip, Leg

Labels at top center: Hip, Leg, Knee

Labels in middle: Genitals, Toes

Labels on the right (Motor Cortex), from top going around: Hip, Trunk, Shoulder, Arm, Elbow, Wrist, Hand, Fingers, Thumb, Neck, Brow, Eye, Face, Lips, Jaw, Tongue, Swallowing, Knee

SOMATIC SENSORY CORTEX

MOTOR CORTEX

control these functions you might find it impossible to be articulate, that is, to make the sounds necessary for language. Similarly, if you had less brain available for hand control you might find you were clumsy in using your hands and less able to make delicate movements.

Directly behind the central fissure at the start of the parietal lobe is a section known as the **somatosensory area.** If this area is electrically stimulated, a sensation will be perceived as though a message had been received by the brain from a place on the body. For instance, a subject may feel a tingling on her finger, or pressure on her lips. Again, a large part of this area is concerned with the hands, mouth, lips, and tongue (see Figure 2.13).

The occipital lobes form the **visual cortex.** Most visual information is sent, or as physiologists say, *projected*, to the occipital lobes. (However, some aspects of peripheral vision are projected to the temporal lobes.) Since the cells in the occipital lobes respond to visual information, if you should be struck on the back of the head and the shock causes visual neurons to fire, you will see stars. Or, more exactly, firing will cause you to perceive little points of light. These same points of light can be created by touching the visual cortex with an electrode carrying a mild current.

The temporal lobes receive auditory messages arriving from the ears. If the temporal lobes are electrically stimulated, sounds are perceived.

The parts of the cerebral cortex other than the sensory and motor areas are known collectively as association areas. **Association areas** appear to be linked with language, thinking, and memory, and may even be specialized to realize certain scientific or artistic abilities.

Figure 2.13 *Somatic sensory and motor regions of the cerebral cortex are specialized in the sense that every site in these regions can be associated with some part of the body. In other words, most of the body can be mapped onto the cortex, yielding two distorted homunculi. The distortions come about because the area of the cortex dedicated to a part of the body is proportional not to that part's actual size but to the precision with which it must be controlled. In man the motor and somatic sensory regions given over to the face and to the hands are greatly exaggerated. Only half of each cortical region is shown: the left somatic sensory area (which receives sensations primarily from the right side of the body) and the right motor cortex (which exercises control over movement in the left half of the body). (SOURCE: Geschwind, 1979, p. 182)*

The Brain and Behavior

Scientists and psychologists have known for years that the way in which the brain functions directly affects behavior. We have learned much of what we know about the relationship between specific parts of the brain and specific behaviors by studying brain injury or disease. The first comprehensive studies of this kind were conducted on patients who had received brain injuries during World War I. It was discovered, of course, that damage to the left side of the brain brought about changes on the right side of the body, and vice versa. It was also found that damage to the frontal lobes could effect personality changes (as was the case with Phineas Gage, as recounted in Chapter 1). Damage to the occipital lobe often affected sight, and damage to the temporal lobes often affected hearing. A further discovery was that damage to the left side of the brain more often affected language ability than did damage to the right side of the brain. Since that time, we have learned that most adults have specific centers for language in the left side of the brain. In some individuals, however, this organization is reversed. Whatever the case, the halves of the brain are not identical.

SPECIALIZED AREAS IN THE BRAIN

To show you how specialized certain portions of the brain are, we will examine some of the findings that have come about as a result of brain injuries, disease, or accidents, beginning with the case of Charles Whitman in Texas. One morning in 1966 Whitman, a young man with no previous history of violence, awoke, picked up a rifle and a pistol, and shot and killed his wife and mother. He calmly gathered up his weapons, food, and water, and went to a university campus, where he climbed to the top of a bell tower, took out his rifle, and proceeded to shoot 38 people. It took police many hours to corner him; he died in a shoot-out.

We've all heard of cases of unexplained violence and aggression, in which someone seems to explode and murders innocent people. In the case of Charles Whitman, however, there may be some hint to the sudden and horrible change in his behavior. During an autopsy of his brain, a malignant

Charles Whitman as he appeared at his wedding in 1962. Four years later in an uncontrollable rage, probably due to a brain tumor, Whitman climbed a tower and began sniping at students at the University of Texas.

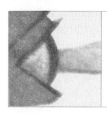

THE PET SCAN

Always structure, never function, that's been the problem. Whenever psychologists or neurologists looked at the brain, they saw structure. If they opened the skull they could see the structure. If they cut sections of the brain and put them under slides they could see the structure, and if they scanned the brain with X rays they could see the structure. But never the function, never what was going on inside the brain—at least not with much detail. But now for the first time it's possible to trace the functions, and psychologists and other scientists are seeing the brain in a completely new light. The breakthrough is the **PET** scan, which stands for **positron emission tomography. Positrons** are atomic particles which are emitted by some radioactive substances. If a radioactive substance that emits positrons is placed in the body, sensors can monitor the positrons when they are radiated. With this in mind, scientists have begun injecting people who are to undergo the PET scan with positron-emitting substances.

The brain runs on sugar. It doesn't burn fat or protein. As the different parts of the brain become active, they demand more sugar. Consequently, a substance used for the PET scan is a kind of radioactive sugar that emits positrons. When one part of the brain becomes active the radioactive sugar races to that location, and the machine scanning the brain registers high

positron emissions coming from that area of the brain.

A patient who is undergoing a PET scan must insert his head into a circular scanning device. Positrons are not easy to produce, and expensive equipment is necessary. For safety reasons, radioactive substances are used that quickly lose their strength; researchers must therefore rush to inject the patient before the positron-emitting substance finishes radiating. Once the substance is in the body and on its way to the brain, the functioning of the brain can be observed. If the patient is instructed to lift his left arm, a colored composite picture of the brain that is displayed by the scanner suddenly shows the right motor cortex beginning to glow. If the patient is shown a photograph, the occipital lobes begin to brighten. If the patient listens to music, the temporal lobes light up (Landis, 1980) (see color section).

Thanks to the PET scan, we are learning that some areas of the brain perform functions we never suspected. The scan should prove an invaluable tool for mapping the brain. The PET scan can also be used for diagnosis (Ter-Pogossian, Raichle, & Sobel, 1980) (see Chapter 15). It can locate brain tumors and the sites of epileptic seizures, and it can be used to scan the heart and other organs for defects and improper functioning.

To psychologists, however, the PET

scan's most exciting potential is in the diagnosis and investigation of mental illness. Although research results are tentative, early evidence from PET scans indicates that the brains of patients with certain forms of mental illness are clearly and consistently different from normal brains. Among the disorders that show a clear pattern in the PET scan is schizophrenia. Schizophrenic patients have bizarre thoughts, hallucinations, strange emotions, and disorganized speech. So far PET scans have consistently shown poor sugar use by the frontal lobes in schizophrenic patients. The frontal lobes are responsible, in part, for emotional control. In a normal brain the frontal lobes show activity during the scan, but in a schizophrenic brain the frontal lobes remain dark and cool (Landis, 1980).

The PET scan has also shown different and consistent findings with other forms of mental illness (see Chapter 15). Dr. Tibor Farkas, a psychiatrist working with the PET scan, has said:

By the year 2000, this will be the standard method of psychiatric evaluation. Today, if a man complains to his physician of chest pains, he is routinely sent to have an electrocardiogram. In 20 years, if a man complains to his psychiatrist of hallucinations or delusions, he will routinely be sent for diagnosis by the PET scan. (Landis, 1980, p. 28)

tumor was discovered pressing against the amygdala, which, as you may recall, is part of the limbic system. This cancerous tumor would eventually have caused Whitman's death. It had been undetected until the autopsy and, because of its deep location beneath the cerebral cortex, it could not have been operated on even if detected. Was his act the first symptom of the tumor's existence? It is known that the amygdala and the limbic system are involved in emotional response. If this area is stimulated in cats, they react with tremendous rage, arching their backs, spitting and hissing, fighting with anything that comes near. Could Charles Whitman's act have been a rage response that he could not comprehend or contain? The rest of his brain was working normally. He was able to think of a plan by which to express his rage, and he had the motor coordination necessary to carry it out. But had something interfered with the portion of his brain that normally enabled him to maintain emotional control? We may never know the answers to these questions, but the autopsy has given us a hint as to what may have set off Whitman's rampage.

In our earlier discussion of the hippocampus, we mentioned that part of its function related to memory. The first indication of this relationship came about 30 years ago when a neurosurgeon named Milner performed a radical surgical procedure on a patient that required much of the hippocampus and several associated areas in both temporal lobes to be destroyed (Geschwind, 1979). After the operation the patient's memory seemed to be intact, and he was still able to attend to ongoing events. However, it soon became obvious that he was unable to remember any of these new events. Psychologists have long been aware of two types of memory, short-term and long-term. Short-term memory holds information for about 30 seconds, and enables you to recall such things as an unfamiliar telephone number long enough to dial it. Long-term memory contains information that you've retained for a long time and are not likely to forget. In the case of Milner's patient, the operation had apparently destroyed his long-term memory capacity for acquiring new information, while his short-term memory was unaffected. Consequently, information that had been logged in the long-term memory prior to the operation was intact, but no new information could be stored. If someone came into the room and was introduced to the patient, the patient would reach out, shake hands, introduce himself, and learn the individual's name. The entire introduction would seem completely normal. But if this individual left the room for a couple of minutes and then reentered, the patient would not be able to recall anything about the previous introduction, and he would act as though he were meeting the person for the first time. Horribly, the man must now live from moment to moment, unable to learn his new address or to remember the location of even the simplest everyday object.

On the underside of both occipital lobes is a part of the brain that has a very special purpose—the recognition of faces. In normal individuals the ability to recognize people by their faces is truly remarkable. Our brains are well organized to attend to unique features such as head shape, eye shape, nose and mouth shape, the sharpness or softness of features. We know about the function of this area of the brain because of what happens to people when the area is damaged. They can no longer recognize faces, a disorder known as **prosoagnosia.** This disorder is accompanied by almost no other neurological or physiological symptoms. Occasionally there is some loss of vision, but the individual continues to be able to perform most tasks, including those that require information processing, without difficulty. The one thing a person with prosoagnosia cannot do is look at another person's face and put a name to it. Even spouses and children may be unfamiliar. It is not that individuals suffering from this disorder don't know who their wives, husbands, or children are; they simply cannot match faces with identities. For instance, a person may not realize that the child she can plainly see is her child until she hears the child's voice. Although she can see and describe the face in fine detail, and even match the face with a photograph, she's unable to form the associations between that particular face and a particular identity (Geschwind, 1979).

In the left side of the brain are a number of areas that are involved in the production and organization of language. **Broca's area** is one of them. Damage to Broca's area following a stroke or other condition may result in **aphasia,** the absence of speech or severe difficulty in speaking. That the problem is with speech itself, and not with the muscles involved in speaking, is evident since individuals with damage to Broca's area can sing without difficulty!

The brain has also been found to be somewhat plastic or flexible. It has been known for a long time that if some areas of the brain were damaged, other areas might take over their functions. For instance, in an individual who has suffered a stroke that has left the language center in the left cerebral hemisphere damaged, the lost language ability can sometimes be regained through the use of nearby portions of the brain. Such plasticity is most apparent in young children, especially under the age of six or seven. If the language center in the left cerebral hemisphere of a young child is destroyed, the right cerebral hemisphere may take over and provide all of the lost language function.

No discussion of the brain and behavior would be complete without examining at least three other important areas of research. One involves what is known as split-brain research, research with subjects who have had the corpus callosum severed and whose left and right hemispheres are now functioning independently. A second area of interest has to do with the neurotransmitters secreted into the synapses by the neurons. The third area deals with the endocrine system of hormone-secreting glands and their various effects on behavior.

THE SPLIT BRAIN

Occasionally, when a person suffers from a severe form of **epilepsy** and cannot be treated in any other way, the corpus callosum connecting the two hemispheres of the brain is severed. This prevents the spreading of the epileptic seizure from one hemisphere to the other (Bogen, Fisher, & Vogel, 1965).

In the early 1950s, R. E. Myers and R. W. Sperry made a startling discovery when examining cats whose corpora callosa had been cut. They found that the right hemisphere could learn something while the left hemisphere remained ignorant of what had been learned, and vice versa. For the next three decades Sperry, working at the California Institute of Technology, and M. S. Gazzaniga, working at Cornell University Medical College, have added to our knowledge about the divided hemispheres. They have found evidence in human patients with split brains not only that the two hemispheres of the brain function independently of one another but also that each hemisphere has capabilities, which sometimes differ from those of the other.

Interestingly, if you were to meet a patient with a split brain you would not notice anything unusual about him or her. To find a difference you would have to conduct some tests, for instance, of the seeing process (Gazzaniga, 1970). Look at Figure 2.14 and you will see that the seeing process is much the same in both a split-brain and a normal person. The

PROSOAGNOSIA
A disorder in which the subject can no longer recognize faces. It is usually accompanied by almost no other neurological or physiological symptoms.

BROCA'S AREA
An area in the frontal lobe of the cerebral hemisphere that plays an important role in speech production.

APHASIA
The loss of the ability to understand or to use speech, which is usually the result of brain damage.

EPILEPSY
A neural disorder characterized by recurring attacks of motor, sensory, or psychic malfunction with or without unconsciousness or convulsive movements.

Figure 2.14 *Both the left and right eyes send messages to both hemispheres because of the crossover at the optic chiasma. However, the back right halves of both eyes send messages only to the right hemisphere, while the back left halves send messages only to the left hemisphere.*

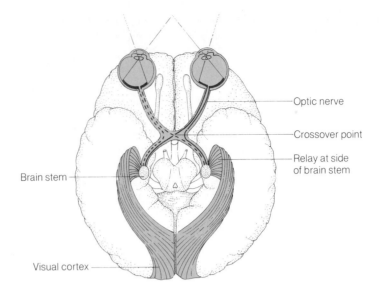

Optic nerve

Crossover point

Relay at side of brain stem

Brain stem

Visual cortex

left half of each retina sends messages to the left hemisphere; the right half sends messages to the right hemisphere. Something quickly glimpsed out of the corner of the eyes will be projected onto only the opposite half of each retina (from right to left and vice versa) and from there sent to the corresponding hemisphere (left to left, right to right). In a normal person, the message will be relayed to the other hemisphere via the corpus callosum. In a split-brain person, the other hemisphere will never receive the information.

A split-brain person has no trouble interpreting such visual messages when they are sent to the left hemisphere. Whatever object or photograph has been presented, he can tell you what it was. However, if an image is presented off to the left, so that it strikes only the back right half of both eyes and is sent only to the right hemisphere, the split-brain person will be unable to tell you what he has seen. This is because the right hemisphere has very poor language and speech ability compared with the left hemisphere. In most people the left hemisphere can speak and describe what it has seen, but the right hemisphere, although it too can see, cannot say what it has seen. We know this to be true because of the following experiment: A number of objects, such as a spoon, a block, a ball, a toy car, are hidden behind a cloth barrier so that the split-brain patient cannot see them. Then a photograph of one of the objects is shown to the left so that the right hemisphere registers it and the left brain is ignorant of what has been seen. The split-brain patient will say that he does not know what the picture is. In an individual whose corpus callosum has not been severed, the right brain would send the visual information over to the left brain and the left brain could say what had been seen. But although the split-brain patient can't articulate what his right brain saw, he can find the object by reaching behind the curtain with his *left* hand and feeling for it! This is because the right brain, which controls the left hand, knows what the object is and what it should feel like, even though it cannot put this knowledge into words.

Just as the left brain appears to be specialized—for language and speech—the right brain appears to be specialized for spatial orientation, that is, the ability to recognize shapes and objects in space. Some people have argued that the left brain is more logical and analytical and the right brain more musical and artistic. While it is unlikely that the brain can be completely explained by such a neat dichotomy, there may be a tendency toward this kind of orientation. For instance, although the majority of music and art majors are right-handed, a much larger percentage than would be expected are left-handed, and being left-handed may be an indication that the right brain is playing a more dominant role (Peterson, 1979).

What other differences may exist between the right and left hemispheres? Emotionality may be one. It appears that the left hemisphere may not be as emotional as the right hemisphere. Researchers have tested this possibility by having subjects wear special contact lenses and, through them, directing viewed material to either the left or the right hemisphere. The subjects were shown several short films and asked to rate each as pleasant, horrific, humorous, or unpleasant. A control group watched the films without the special lenses, exposing both hemispheres to the images simultaneously. Subjects who could see the films only with their left hemisphere reported ratings similar to those of the control group. However, those who saw the films only with their right hemisphere rated the films as significantly more unpleasant and horrific (Dimond, Farrington, & Johnson, 1976).

Further evidence that the right hemisphere may be more emotional has been gathered by researchers at the University of Pennsylvania. Look at the three photographs in Figure 2.15. Frames (a), (b), and (c) are of the same person. But which expression shows the most disgust? If you picked frame (a), you're in the majority, since most people tested felt that the expression in frame (a) showed the most disgust. What's interesting is that frame (a) is a composite mirror image of the left halves of the individual's face. Frame (b) is his normal face, and frame (c) is a mirror composite of the right halves of his face. Fourteen different composite faces were shown to 86 subjects, and they were asked to rate them on a 7-point scale of intensity. Regardless of the emotion pictured (happiness, fear, anger, sadness, surprise), the left

Figure 2.15 *Which face expresses the most disgust?* (SOURCE: *Sackeim, Gur, & Saucy, 1978, p. 434*)

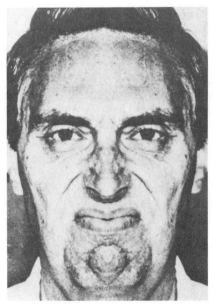

(a)

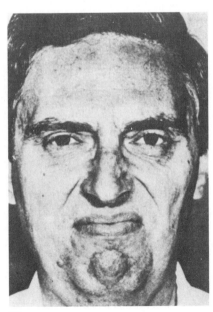

(b)

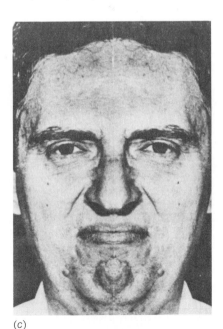

(c)

side of the face seemed more expressive (Sackeim, Gur, & Saucy, 1978). The researchers concluded, "In light of these findings, our results point to greater right hemispheric involvement with the production of emotional expression." Remember, it is the right hemisphere that controls the left side of the face.

There are other differences between the hemispheres. For instance, the right brain seems to be more sensitive to alcohol than the left brain (Chandler & Parsons, 1977). Damage to the right brain is more likely to affect our ability to attend to things than is damage to the left brain. There is even evidence that some retarded children who fail tests measuring left-brain skills may have right-brain abilities that are normal or above average (Mesulam & Geschwind, 1978; Musick, 1977).

All of these findings seem to imply that we have two brains instead of one, and in a sense this is true. Research has even shown that you can give one half of your brain too much to do. In one experiment, the subjects were asked to balance a long rod on their index fingertips, first with one hand and then with the other. The researchers timed the balancing act, in this way obtaining an average of how long a person was able to balance a rod with either hand. Then the subjects were asked to try again, only this time they were required to recite material as they balanced the rod. When they used the left hand their scores did not differ appreciably from their scores when they weren't reciting. However, balancing the rod with the right hand was much more difficult while reciting, and the scores were appreciably lower (Johnson & Kozma, 1977). Why should this happen? We all know it's easier to concentrate on one thing at a time, and maybe that's what the individual hemispheres of the brain are telling us. As you'll recall, only the left hemisphere can recite complex material, and if that hemisphere must balance a rod, that is, in the right hand, and speak, too, then it has *two* tasks to perform, and the difficulty increases. However, if the right hemisphere balances the rod, in the left hand, while the subject is reciting, the right hemisphere is no more busy than before since the left hemisphere is doing the speaking. Consequently, there is no change in score.

The left brain has been called the dominant brain because most people are right-handed. Furthermore, in right-handed people the occipital and parietal lobes are wider in the left than in the right hemisphere, and the left hemisphere is generally a little larger. But what about left-handed people? For years it was believed that the functions of the brain hemispheres were reversed in left-handed people. That is, they were thought to be right-brain dominant, and to have the language and speech centers in their right brain and the centers of spatial perception in their left brain. But discoveries made during the 1970s showed that in fact most left-handed people are still left-brain dominant and have their centers of language, speech, and space perception in the same place as right-handed people. Nonetheless, a minority of left-handed people are reversed, and there is an easy way to identify these people. Watch a left-handed person writing, and note the placement of the hand (see Figure 2.16). Is the writing done with a hooked hand? Approximately two-thirds of left-handers write with a hooked hand. For decades it was assumed that people who were left-handed wrote in this manner because they had somehow learned to. But tests now indicate that 99 percent of these individuals are left-brain dominant (Levy & Reid, 1976). Left-handers who really are reversed will write with their hand unhooked. Although the Latin word for left is *sinister* and there are many myths claiming that left-handers are somehow inferior, no

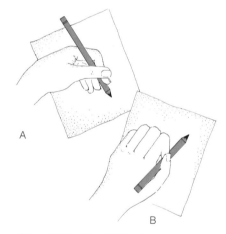

Figure 2.16 *Most left-handed persons who are also left-brain dominant write with a hooked hand (A). One-third of left-handers are right-brain dominant. They write unhooked (B).*

defects, physical or mental, have ever been associated with being left-handed (Hardyck, Petrinovich, & Goldman, 1976).

In some people the right and left hemispheres show some striking differences. These people are said to be highly **lateralized** in terms of brain organization. Other individuals are not very lateralized. In these latter individuals the right brain may be only slightly inferior to the left brain in language capability, and the left brain may show some spatial skills. Interestingly, men tend to be more lateralized than women. This sexual difference in lateralization is especially marked among children. Lateralization is often quite evident in boys by the age of six, but in girls it's hard to find any kind of spatial and linguistic lateralization until adolescence (Witelson, 1976). Some researchers believe that these differences may be related to the fact that males often outperform females on some tests of spatial abilities.

Neither half of the brain is really complete in itself. Except in split-brain persons, the two halves function together and complement each other. Research has definitely shattered the old idea that the two hemispheres must be alike simply because they look alike.

THE WORLD OF NEUROTRANSMITTERS

A neurotransmitter is a chemical that travels across the synaptic gap between two cells and affects specific receptor sites on the postsynaptic membrane. In 1979 at least 30 different substances in the brain were known or suspected to be neurotransmitters (Iversen, 1979). These substances are not found randomly in all parts of the brain but tend to be localized in specific groups of neurons whose axons send messages to specific areas within the brain. Some neurotransmitters are more concentrated in the right hemisphere than in the left, and vice versa (Oke, Keller, Mefford, & Adams, 1978). Psychologists are interested in neurotransmitters because their effects are directly related to behavior. For example, close examination of concentrations of the neurotransmitter norepinephrine has led researchers to believe that it may be involved in arousal, dream sleep, and mood regulation. It may also be active in one of the brain's suspected pleasure centers; the amount of norepinephrine secreted may determine how rewarding we find a particular experience. A further reason for studying neurotransmitters is that many drugs are known to have their effects because of their ability to modify or disrupt neural transmissions between brain cells. There is also evidence that certain kinds of mental illness may be directly related to dysfunctions in certain transmitters.

Monoamines and Amino Acids   The two main kinds of neurotransmitters are the **monoamines** and the **amino acids.** The chemicals found in each group are:

MONOAMINES	AMINO ACIDS
Acetylcholine	Aspartic acid
Dopamine	Gamma-aminobutyric acid (GABA)
Histamine	Glutamic acid
Norepinephrine	Glycine
Serotonin	Taurine

Each of these neurotransmitters has a characteristic inhibitory or excitatory effect on nearby neurons. Some transmitters may be excitatory in one part

LATERALIZED (LATERALIZATION)
The degree to which the right and left cerebral hemispheres differ in specific functions.

MONOAMINES
A group of neurotransmitters that are related because they all contain one amine group (a specific kind of organic molecule). Among these are dopamine, norepinephrine, and serotonin.

AMINO ACIDS
The basic building blocks of proteins. All animal life makes use of the same 20 amino acids. Some amino acids have been discovered to be neurotransmitters as well. Among these are aspartic acid, glycine, and taurine.

of the brain and inhibitory in another part. The general rule is that only one kind of transmitter is found in each axon, but there are exceptions (Iversen, 1979).

Neurons containing the monoamine transmitter dopamine are found in greatest concentration in the midbrain. The axons of these neurons extend to the forebrain and are thought to be involved with the regulation of emotions. Bizarre emotional responses are associated with a number of forms of mental illness, and it is believed, for example, that dopamine may play an important role in the onset of schizophrenia. This theory is known as the **dopamine hypothesis** and will be investigated in detail in Chapter 15. Dopamine is also concentrated in the areas of the brain that control complex movement. If dopamine fibers in this area degenerate, the result may be **Parkinson's disease,** in which muscular rigidity and tremors occur. One of the great breakthroughs in medicine occurred in the 1970s when a form of dopamine called L-dopa was found to help prevent and control the symptoms of Parkinson's disease. L-dopa can be taken by mouth, in the form of a pill, and the chemical finds its way into the brain and substitutes for the missing dopamine. Individuals with Parkinson's disease who are unable even to button a shirt, within minutes of taking L-dopa can perform such tasks easily and appear to have normal motor and muscular control.

The monoamine transmitter serotonin is concentrated in the brain stem. The axons of neurons containing serotonin project to the thalamus, hypothalamus, and other brain regions. Serotonin is thought to be involved in bringing on sleep, temperature regulation, and sensory perception.

Amino acids are the basic building blocks of proteins, but they also appear to act as neurotransmitters. Aspartic acid and glutamic acid, which typically have an excitatory effect on most neurons, are thought to be the commonest excitatory transmitters in the brain. Glycine, the simplest of all amino acids, functions as an inhibitory transmitter within the spine. Within the brain, gamma-aminobutyric acid (GABA) is the most common of the inhibitory transmitters. It is believed that one-third of the synapses in the brain employ GABA.

Among the most interesting findings in the last decade is that many drugs seem to have their effect because they mimic neurotransmitters. Hallucinogenic drugs such as mescaline, psilocybin, and LSD may work in this way. Their chemical structure strongly resembles that of the monoamine transmitters.

Neuropeptides   In the last decade a whole new class of chemical messengers has been discovered—the **neuropeptides.** By 1982 over 2,000 of these biochemicals had been isolated. The chemicals in this group include the following:

NEUROPEPTIDES

ACTH (corticotropin)	Luteinizing-hormone releasing hormone (LHRH)
Angiotensin II	Met-enkephalin
Beta endorphin	Neurotensin
Bombesin	Oxytocin
Carnosine	Somatostatin
Cholecystokinin-like	Substance P
peptide	Thyrotropin releasing hormone (TRH)
Dynorphin	Vasoactive intestinal polypeptide (VIP)
Leu-enkephalin	Vasopressin

Neuropeptides a. ...iolecules made from short chains of amino acids. Their effects on behavior are wide-ranging. Let's take a look at one of them, beta endorphin. The story begins with a man named Avram Goldstein, who in the early 1970s was working with drugs derived from opium such as morphine. In 1971 he discovered that when opium was ingested it tended to concentrate in three areas of the brain: in the medial thalamus and the **periaqueductal gray matter,** which are associated with the perception of pain, and in the limbic system, which is associated with emotion. This made sense to Goldstein because morphine is known to be a strong pain reliever, and it gives the user a good feeling, a sense of emotional well-being. Goldstein went one step further; he wondered why human beings and animals respond to opium, which is an extract from a poppy plant. What connection could there be between a human brain and a plant?

Goldstein hypothesized that opiates such as heroin, morphine, and codeine work because they mimic some natural brain substance that is meant to bind with the receptors that heroin, morphine, and codeine bind with. In other words, a natural heroin or morphine must exist in the brain. In late 1975 a natural body substance chemically very similar to heroin was discovered independently by John Hughes and Hans Kosterlitz in Scotland and Solomon Schneider and Rabi Simantov at Johns Hopkins. It was a chain of five simple amino acids they called **enkephalin.** The problem was that enkephalin was rapidly broken down by enzymes in the body, its effects lasting for only 2 seconds, whereas morphine was known to be unaffected by these enzymes, and capable of lasting for hours. The researchers therefore knew that they were close but that they hadn't found what they were looking for yet. The breakthrough was Avram Goldstein's discovery that enkephalin was only the tail of the kite, so to speak, of a much larger molecule located in the pituitary gland, called **beta endorphin** (the "morphine within"). Immediately following Goldstein's discovery Choh Hao Li demonstrated that a compound found in the pituitary 11 years earlier, and not understood at that time, was the large precursor of both enkephalin and beta endorphin. Li began to synthesize the natural body substance, beta endorphin, and in June of 1977 he was able to manufacture a small amount.

Meanwhile, the medical community was pondering over something completely different—the Chinese technique of **acupuncture.** By inserting thin needles into particular places on a person's body and rotating the needles back and forth, an anesthetic reaction could be induced so that the person could even undergo surgery without feeling any pain. Nothing was injected through the needles. Western medical authorities were highly skeptical, but evidence of acupuncture's effectiveness continued to mount. At about this time Bruce Pomeranz and his colleagues at the University of Toronto began to wonder whether there could be a link between the anesthesia of acupuncture and the body's natural morphine, beta endorphin. With this in mind, Pomeranz began a series of experiments.

Pomeranz placed a **microelectrode** capable of monitoring a single neuron into a particular area of a cat's brain. After the skull had healed, he was able to monitor arriving pain messages caused by sticking the cat in the toe with a pin. Pomeranz then gave the cat acupuncture, and after a short time he found that the pain messages were no longer being received by the pain-sensing neuron that he was monitoring. Something had blocked the message. Pomeranz speculated that acupuncture needles might somehow stimulate the pituitary to secrete beta endorphin, which should be a

DOPAMINE HYPOTHESIS
A proposal that an excess of dopamine or dopamine receptors may be responsible for some forms of schizophrenia.

PARKINSON'S DISEASE
A progressive nervous disease characterized by muscle tremor, slowing of movement, peculiarity of gait and posture, and weakness. It is a direct result of dopamine deficiency and can be treated with a dopaminelike drug, L-dopa.

NEUROPEPTIDES
Extremely small chemical messengers made from short chains of amino acids. Among the neuropeptides are beta endorphin and vasopressin.

PERIAQUEDUCTAL GRAY MATTER
A small area within the cerebrum associated with the reception of pain.

ENKEPHALIN
A chemical constituent of beta endorphin, known to be involved in the brain's pleasure and pain systems.

BETA ENDORPHIN
A powerful natural neuropeptide. It means "the morphine within" and is so named because it has properties similar to those of heroin and morphine. It is a powerful painkiller and mood elevator.

ACUPUNCTURE
A traditional Chinese therapeutic technique whereby the body is punctured with fine needles. Usually used as an anesthetic or to relieve pain.

MICROELECTRODE
An extremely small electric probe capable of monitoring a single cell.

NALOXONE
A heroin antagonist. Naloxone binds with and essentially neutralizes heroin. Naloxone has the same effect on morphine and beta endorphin.

PLACEBO
An inert substance often given to control subjects in place of the drug given the subjects in the experimental group.

DYNORPHIN
A neuropeptide similar to beta endorphin but which appears to be about 50 times more powerful.

EXOCRINE GLANDS
Glands that secrete fluids through a duct to the outside of the body or to a specific organ.

ENDOCRINE SYSTEM
A system of ductless glands that pour their secretions directly into the bloodstream. The hormones secreted by the endocrine glands are important regulators of many body activities.

ADRENAL GLANDS
Endocrine glands located above the kidneys that secrete the hormones adrenaline, noradrenaline, and steroids. These hormones influence metabolism and the body's reaction to stressful situations.

GONADS
The sex glands that regulate sex drive and the physiological changes that accompany physical maturity. These glands are the ovaries in the female and the testes in the male.

powerful natural painkiller. To test this, Pomeranz once again tried acupuncture, but this time on cats whose pituitary gland had been removed. Incredibly, he found what he had hoped: Acupuncture didn't work when the pituitary gland had been removed (Pomeranz, Cheng, & Law, 1977). Since it's impossible to run such an experiment on humans (you're not likely to get many volunteers), another approach was taken. **Naloxone** is a drug that has been found to counter the effects of beta endorphin. In experiments with human subjects it was learned that acupuncture does not work after naloxone has been injected.

But there was more. For years, psychologists have known that when people who are in pain are given a **placebo** and told to expect relief, approximately one-third of them will report that their pain has lessened. These people are called *placebo reactors*. The placebo may be a sugar pill, an injection of water, or a magic incantation—nothing that would usually be expected to relieve pain. Why should this power of suggestion work? Research now indicates that placebo reactors in some unconscious way may be activating their body's natural pain suppression system and causing the release of beta endorphin. It had always been thought that placebo reactors changed their perception of pain psychologically, but now there is strong evidence that their decrease in pain has a physiological basis. Researchers from the University of California investigated 50 patients who were recovering from wisdom tooth extractions. In a double-blind experiment some of the patients received morphine as a postoperative treatment while others received a placebo injection. The patients then rated their changes in pain on a 10-point scale, ranging from "no pain" to "the worst pain ever." As was expected, a significant reduction in pain was reported by approximately one-third of the patients who received placebos. Some of the placebo reactors were then injected with naloxone, and all of them reported that their pain was now back up to its original level. Naloxone by itself has never been known to cause pain. Yet it could have blocked any beta endorphin that the placebo reactors were secreting. Apparently, it was the beta endorphin all along that was reducing their pain (Levine, Gordon, & Fields, 1978).

Beta endorphin seems to be involved in more than just pain suppression. John Liebeskind of UCLA and Floyd Bloom of the Salk Institute wondered why beta endorphin appears in such concentrated levels in the limbic system, since the limbic system is associated with emotion rather than pain. These researchers now believe that beta endorphin may be the body's own "tonic against disappointment." They have also discovered that the famous pleasure center found years ago by Professor Olds is loaded with enkephalin (Gerner, Catlin, Gorelick, Hui, & Li, 1980).

In 1981 Dr. Lee S. Berk of Loma Linda University Medical Center in California discovered what he believes to be a reason for the "addiction" that many people have for regular strenuous exercise. Berk and his colleagues found an important difference between those who exercise regularly (run four to five miles four to five times a week for over a year) and those who are usually sedentary. While testing six men and six women on a treadmill he discovered that those who exercised produced far more beta endorphin and produced it sooner than those who were sedentary. After exercise the rates returned to normal for both groups. The high levels of beta endorphin produced by those who exercised regularly may explain the high associated with regular vigorous activity. Beta endorphin is also known to produce vasodilation, which in turn helps to lower blood pressure, a result often associated with regular exercise (Berk, 1981).

The neuropeptides have been implicated in other areas besides pleasure and pain. Research has indicated that excess endorphin may lead to overeating (Margules, 1979), and met-enkephalin and vasopressin have been found to boost memory significantly (Bohus, 1977). Without question, these chemical substances are opening a new chapter in physiological psychology, and the surprises have only just begun. One interesting addition to the class of neuropeptides—dynorphin—was discovered as recently as December 1979 by Avram Goldstein. He called it **dynorphin** after the Greek *dynamus*, meaning "power." Though work with dynorphin is just beginning, it appears to be 50 times more powerful than beta endorphin and 200 times more powerful than morphine. Moreover, there is evidence that dynorphin may be created from a larger, as yet undiscovered, brain molecule (Goldstein, Tachiban, Lowney, Hunkapil, & Hood, 1979).

HORMONES AND THE ENDOCRINE SYSTEM

There are two kinds of glands found throughout the body. The **exocrine glands** secrete onto the surface of the body; they include tear and sweat glands. The endocrine glands, on the other hand, which make up the **endocrine system,** secrete hormones directly into the bloodstream (see Figure 2.17). Chief among these glands are the pituitary gland, the **adrenal glands,** and the **gonads.** Hormones are messengers, but unlike neurotransmitters, they are carried throughout the body by the bloodstream. Some substances, such as norepinephrine, do double duty, acting as hormones in some cases and neurotransmitters in others.

Endocrine glands secrete hormones in response to neural messages or as

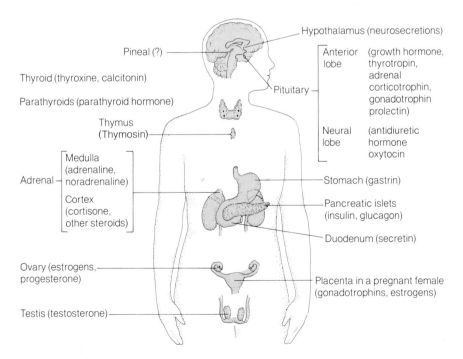

Hypothalamus (neurosecretions)

Pineal (?)

Thyroid (thyroxine, calcitonin)

Parathyroids (parathyroid hormone)

Thymus (Thymosin)

Pituitary

Anterior lobe (growth hormone, thyrotropin, adrenal corticotrophin, gonadotrophin prolactin)

Neural lobe (antidiuretic hormone oxytocin)

Adrenal — Medulla (adrenaline, noradrenaline)

Cortex (cortisone, other steroids)

Stomach (gastrin)

Pancreatic islets (insulin, glucagon)

Duodenum (secretin)

Ovary (estrogens, progesterone)

Placenta in a pregnant female (gonadotrophins, estrogens)

Testis (testosterone)

Figure 2.17 *The glands of the endocrine system, and some of the hormones they secrete. Where a question mark appears after a gland, we don't know the hormone secreted.*

a reaction to changes in body chemistry. Since hormones are carried in the bloodstream, they can affect parts of the body distant from the gland or many different parts of the body at once. A neurotransmitter, on the other hand, is limited because it can only affect the postsynaptic surface across the synapse. Hormones are known to have a vital function in physical growth and sexual development. They are also involved in changes of mood, reactions to stress, and levels of activity.

The pituitary gland is located just below the hypothalamus. The posterior or rear part of the pituitary gland can be more accurately described as a continuation of the brain's nervous system. Hormones released in the posterior pituitary are created in the hypothalamus and delivered to the pituitary by axons extending from the hypothalamus. Some of the hormones released by glands or by the hypothalamus are called **executive hormones** because they in turn can bring about the release of other hormones in the endocrine system. Some hormones serve more than one function. For instance, thyrotropin releasing hormone (TRH), a hormone released by the hypothalamus, has been found in the skin, the pancreas, and the retina, and in each place it appears to be serving a different function (Martino, Seo, Lernmark, & Rafetoff, 1980).

The anterior or front end of the pituitary is also controlled by the hypothalamus. The anterior pituitary releases its hormones when it receives executive hormones from the hypothalamus, in this case carried by a system of small capillaries. Orders from the hypothalamus tell the anterior pituitary how much growth hormone to secrete. If an individual receives too little or too much of this hormone his or her growth can be dramatically affected, creating either a dwarf or a giant.

The adrenal glands are located on the adrenal cortex just above both kidneys. They secrete **adrenaline** and **noradrenaline** (also called, respectively, epinephrine and norepinephrine). Both hormones have much to do with the action of the sympathetic nervous system. They help to prepare an organism for an emergency or a stressful situation. Adrenaline causes the heart to beat faster and blood vessels to constrict within the stomach and intestines. Noradrenaline is an executive hormone. When it reaches the pituitary, it stimulates the release of other executive hormones which, acting on the adrenal glands, cause them to secrete steroids. **Steroids** are a class of hormones that cause the liver to release stored sugar so that energy is available for emergency action.

The gonads, which secrete sex hormones, will be discussed in Chapter 18.

Although **endocrinologists,** who study the endocrine system, and psychologists know that hormones can have a direct influence on behavior and physical development, they do not understand exactly how hormones achieve their results. Complicating the issue is the presence in the blood of many other substances that are mediated by, or themselves mediate, hormones. For example, it has been discovered that growth hormone alone will not induce growth. Accompanying the growth hormone there must be a small peptide mediator made from amino acids, called somatomedins (Silberner, 1980). Sometimes, too, new hormones are discovered, such as endoxin, which appears to regulate the amount of salt excreted by the body and which may be linked with hypertension (Gruber, Whitaker, & Buckalew, 1980). Endocrinology is a complex and rewarding field of study. In the future, its role in helping us to understand human behavior is likely to grow larger.

Genetics and Behavior

CHROMOSOMES

When a certain colored stain is applied to the nucleus of a cell, small bodies within the nucleus absorb the stain and become visible. These small bodies are called **chromosomes.** In fact, the word *chromosome* means "colored body."

In a human body cell there are 23 pairs of chromosomes, 46 chromosomes in all. The number of chromosomes varies from one plant or animal to another. It may range from as few as 2 to as many as 127 pairs (Sinott, Dunn, & Dobzhansky, 1958). The 23 pairs of chromosomes that you have in your body cells put you between toads and potatoes, which have 22 and 24 pairs, respectively. You inherit 23 chromosomes from your father, and 23 from your mother. On the chromosomes of each cell lie the genes, which contain the genetic code and building instructions for your entire body.

Chromosomes that have been made visible by staining can be photographed. The individual chromosomes can be cut from the finished picture, arranged in pairs, and placed in rows for easy inspection. Such an arrangement is called a **karyotype** (see Figure 2.18). The first 22 pairs are called the **autosomes.** The 23rd pair is labeled separately from the others; these two chromosomes are known as **sex chromosomes.**

Sperm or egg cells, called **gametes,** contain only 23 chromosomes each, rather than 23 pairs. During the creation of the sex cells, a special process known as **meiosis** creates gametes with half the usual number of chromosomes. In this way, when a sperm and egg unite at fertilization, the next generation will have 46 chromosomes in its body cells, too. Like the autosomes, the sex chromosomes carry many genetic codes. The sex chromosomes are different, however, in that they also carry the genetic codes that determine your sex. Interestingly, these chromosomes are shaped differ-

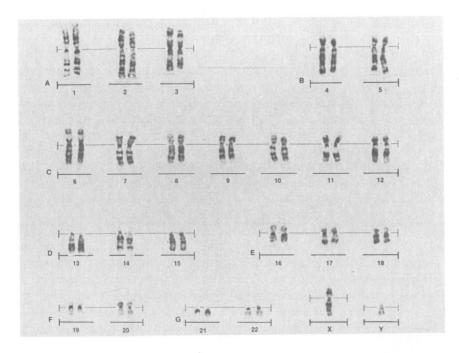

Figure 2.18 *A karyotype of human chromosomes showing the 22 pairs of autosomes and the one pair of sex chromosomes. This person is male because his sex chromosome pair is XY.*

ently depending on which sex is being carried. Sex chromosomes carrying the genetic code for a girl are shaped like an X, while those carrying the code for a boy are shaped like a Y. These chromosomes are, in fact, referred to as X and Y chromosomes. As you can see, the 23rd pair in the karyotype picture in Figure 2.18 contains both an X and a Y chromosome. In this case the individual would be male. Males have an XY 23rd pair, while females have an XX 23rd pair. Since females are XX, they have no Y chromosomes in their cells. A woman's **ovum,** or egg, created during meiosis can only contain X sex chromosomes. Therefore, *both* boys and girls will receive one X chromosome from their mothers. Since men are XY, their sperm cells, also created by meiosis, may contain either an X or a Y sex chromosome. The child will inherit one or the other, which will then determine the child's sex. If a **sperm** carrying an X chromosome fertilizes the mother's ovum, a girl will be produced, and if a sperm carrying a Y chromosome fertilizes the mother's ovum, the child will be a boy.

Through mechanisms of inheritance, characteristics are transmitted from one generation to the next.

Since only the male can contribute a Y chromosome, the sex of the offspring is determined by the father's sperm. Perhaps someone should have told King Henry VIII about this, before he had Anne Boleyn executed for not having borne him a son. Still, in the 16th century, no one knew about the genetic mechanisms of inheritance. These mechanisms were first discovered in the mid-1800s, when Gregor Mendel, an obscure Austrian monk, discovered the fundamental laws that govern inheritance. Mendel spent many years carefully crossing garden-variety pea plants with one another and cataloging the results. He watched as a number of traits, such as wrinkled or smooth seeds, tall or short stalks, and yellow or green seeds appeared, disappeared, and reappeared from one generation to the next. Although Mendel didn't actually discover genes, he did see the way genes worked by indirectly observing how they affected the expression of various traits. Mendel discovered that a number of simple traits in offspring would occur at particular ratios depending on the kinds of traits possessed by the parents (even peas have parents). This kind of simple inheritance is also found in human beings. Such things as hair shape, whether kinky or straight, eye color, or blood type are inherited according to the simple laws first discovered by Gregor Mendel. Inheritance is no simple matter, however. Qualities such as personality, intelligence, or emotion do not follow the simple rules associated with the inheritance of features such as eye color, although genetics probably plays a role in their development.

EVOLUTION AND NATURAL SELECTION

No organisms are exactly the same, nor are there any that have exactly the same abilities. Many of the differences between organisms are due to their genetically inherited biological attributes and predispositions. For billions of years, biological attributes carried within the genes and expressed by the organisms that inherited them have been naturally favored or selected by forces within the environment over inferior attributes or traits that did not help the species to live and reproduce. While learning and experience are extremely important factors in determining your behavior, you—your brain, your body, and perhaps certain behavioral predispositions—are also the product of billions of years of **evolution** and natural selection. Some simple behaviors in human beings are obviously inherited. They are found in all healthy members of the species. Sneezing, coughing, blinking, and swallowing are just a few of these. More complex behaviors, however, such as operating a typewriter or driving a car must be learned. But genetics may play a role even in learning to operate a typewriter or drive a car. Our superior inherited brains make it possible for us to handle the amount of learning necessary to operate a typewriter or a car. We may be predisposed to find it easy to learn these skills because millions of years ago our predecessors who were most successful at using tools were the ones most likely to survive and pass on their genetic predispositions to their offspring. Such genetic predispositions are apparent when we consider how much easier it is to teach a pigeon to peck at something than it is to teach the same thing to a pig. This is the phenomenon of **canalization.*** A behavior is said to be canalized not by whether it is

OVUM
The female reproductive cell of animals; also called an *egg*.

SPERM
The male reproductive cell of animals, which fertilizes the ovum to produce a zygote (the cell formed by the union of sperm and ovum).

EVOLUTION
The theory, first proposed by Charles Darwin, that organisms may change in time depending on whether they have characteristics favored by the environment.

CANALIZATION
The process by which behaviors, due to genetic predisposition, are learned extremely easily, almost inevitably. The more canalized a behavior is, the more difficult it is to change or alter.

---

*Some researchers prefer to use the term *preparedness* (Seligman, 1970).

learned or inherited, but by the fact that there is an inherited predisposition
to learn the behavior easily, almost with certainty. Washburn and Hamburg
(1965) described the phenomenon as follows:

> What is inherited is ease of learning rather than fixed instinctive patterns. The
> species easily, almost inevitably learns the essential behaviors for its survival.
> So, although it is true that monkeys learn to be social, they are so constructed
> that under normal circumstances this learning always takes place. Similarly,
> human beings learn to talk, but they inherit structures that make this inevitable,
> except under the most peculiar circumstances.

Not only are highly canalized behaviors almost inevitable, they are also
highly resistant to the effects of the environment. Conversely, weakly canalized behaviors are highly susceptible to environmental influences.

In a classic experiment that demonstrated the phenomenon of canalization J. Garcia and R. A. Koelling (1966) allowed thirsty rats to drink
saccharine-flavored water from a tube. Whenever the rats drank the
water, lights were turned on and a tone sounded. In the first part of the
experiment, the rats were exposed to a strong dose of X rays before they
drank. Because of the X rays the rats became nauseous about an hour after
they had consumed the liquid. Garcia and Koelling discovered that the
nausea taught the rats to avoid the sweetened water, but it did *not* teach
them to fear or avoid the lights and tone. In the second part of the experiment an electric shock, instead of X rays, was administered to different rats
when they drank. Under the new circumstances the rats learned to fear the
lights and tone, but their desire to drink the sweetened water wasn't noticeably affected. It was as though drinking and nausea were naturally paired,
while the lights and sound went naturally with the shock.

Perhaps you've had a similar experience. If you accidentally burned your
tongue while eating sauerbraten (a German dish), the experience probably

*Rats whose parents were excellent maze
runners are generally excellent maze runners
themselves.*

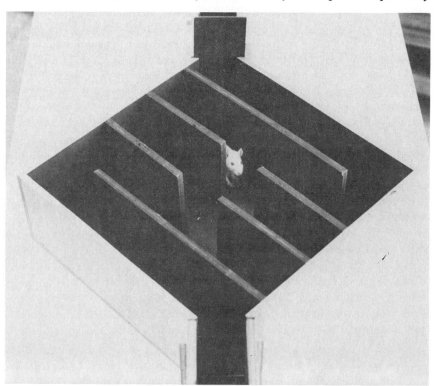

wouldn't affect your fondness for that food even if the burn was very pain-ful. If, however, you ate sauerbraten and coincidentally caught the flu, which caused you to become extremely sick to your stomach, your desire for that dish might be gone forever, and it probably wouldn't help much to realize that the food didn't cause the nausea. From an evolutionary stand-point, such a built-in or canalized tendency would make sense. If an animal was startled while eating a certain food, there would be no survival benefit in thereafter avoiding that food. But if the animal became sick after eating a certain food, there would be a good reason to avoid that food in the future.

Other genetic predispositions may exist in our species as well. There may be special times during our development when a particular influence is most likely to have an effect because we are biologically predisposed to react to that influence at that particular time (Hinde, 1966). This is known as a **sensitive period.** For example, young children seem to pick up lan-guages with greater speed and ease than adults do. Is this because young children are biologically primed to learn languages more easily, while adults have more difficulty because the sensitive period for language ac-quisition has passed? Or consider sexual roles and preferences, which have been given much attention lately. How are they formed? They seem to develop early. In a study of people who desired sex-change operations, most felt that they had been "trapped in the wrong sexed body" for as long as they could remember (Stoller, 1976). Is this because there is a genetically programmed sensitive period during which a child is extremely influenced by various sexual stimuli? In the chapter on learning we'll take a closer look at the possibility of sensitive periods in humans and see how they may in-fluence behavior.

In order to examine complicated kinds of behavioral inheritance psychol-ogists have sometimes tried to produce particular behaviors in animals through **selective breeding.** In an early experiment, a researcher (Tryon, 1940) mated rats that had been fairly successful at running a maze; these were the "maze-bright" rats. At the same time he mated "maze-dull" rats, which were not good runners. He continued this process for a number of generations until, in the final generation, the dullest of the maze-bright rats was superior in maze running to the brightest of the maze-dull rats (see Figure 2.19). This result indicates that the ability to run a maze (or perhaps the desire to) could be bred into or out of a particular species.

Many hundreds of selective-breeding studies have been conducted with animals over the last two decades, and much valuable information has been gathered from them. Psychologists can't very well conduct selective-breeding studies with human beings, but we can study the role of inheri-tance in intelligence and other characteristics by examining people who are related to one another. Relatives share many of the same genes. As you will see when we discuss intelligence in a later chapter, the closer individ-uals are in terms of their genetic relationship, the more likely they are to have similar IQs. This indicates that genetics may play an important role. However, data from studies about close relatives are often difficult to in-terpret because close relatives usually share the same environments, and environments can affect intelligence. These kinds of difficulties are known as **nature-nurture questions.** How much of a particular behavior or attri-bute is owed to nature (the genes that have been inherited) and how much to nurture (a person's learning and experience) is the focus of the problem. As you will learn, nature and nurture considerations may be important in almost every area of psychology.

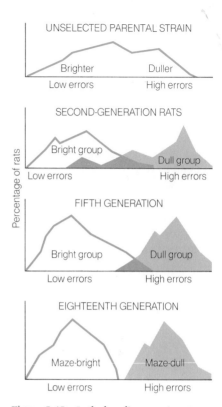

Figure 2.19 *In the breeding experiment with maze-bright and maze-dull rats the differences between the two groups, in terms of errors made while running a maze, be-came greater each generation. Since each new generation initially had no experience with running mazes, the difference between the bright and dull groups was considered due to breeding and genetic inheritance.* (SOURCE: Yearbook of the National Society for the Study of Education, *1940)*

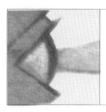

EUGENICS: SELECTIVELY BREEDING HUMAN BEINGS

In 1883 Sir Francis Galton, a cousin of Charles Darwin, coined the term **eugenics** and attempted to begin a scientific movement concerned with the selective breeding of human beings. According to this new science, selected human beings would be mated with each other in an attempt to obtain certain traits in their offspring, much the way that animal breeders work with champion stock. The eventual goal of eugenics was to create a better human race.

Galton believed that intelligence was inherited, along with many "civilized" behavioral patterns. He felt that the upper class of his day best represented these "inherited" traits, and although his hope was to improve the lot of the common man, the thrust of his argument seemed centered on the idea that the English upper class was truly better-bred. Such a concept was well accepted by English aristocracy. The idea that learning and experience might play the most important role in determining the behavioral patterns of upper, middle, or lower class seemed ridiculous. Nineteenth century England simply wasn't ready for such democratic notions. In fact, in 1912, when George Bernard Shaw wrote the play *Pygmalion* (later rewritten as *My Fair Lady*), it was quite revolutionary, since the plot

was about a professor of language *teaching* a street urchin to pass as a lady of royalty. For numerous scientific, political, and social reasons, Galton's eugenics movement never attracted a strong following.

Although the term eugenics was coined by Galton, the concept was not new. The Greek philosopher Plato argued that babies should only be born to those who possessed the most desirable characteristics. In the Greek city-state of Sparta, the soldiers offered their wives to the strongest and most powerful warriors in order that their women might bear children who would become as strong and fierce as their fathers (Sussman, 1976). Two hundred years ago Frederick the Great attempted to breed tall palace guards by having tall soldiers and robust peasant girls mate. We don't know the results of the breeding, however (Johnson & Medinnus, 1969).

From time to time various groups and sects have incorporated selective breeding into their social doctrine. For example, a 19th century commune at Oneida, New York, begun by John Humphrey Noyes, tried some specific breeding with humans, but the commune's efforts were not well documented (Sussman, 1976). Perhaps the most organized, and horrifying, efforts to carry out a eugenics program

were made in Germany during World War II.

There have been recent attempts to create eugenics programs. Eugenics is currently being practiced in the United States and elsewhere. To understand the issues clearly, it is perhaps best to divide the subject into two categories: negative eugenics and positive eugenics.

Negative Eugenics

Negative eugenics is a process of elimination, not necessarily by murder, as Hitler had ordered, but possibly by compulsory sterilization or by controlling the right to reproduce. Many argue that since the state has the right to quarantine in order to prevent the spread of infectious diseases, the state should also have the right to prevent the spread of defective genes.

Ordinarily, you might expect the process of natural selection eventually to take care of the spread of defective genes. But since medical science can now keep healthy many who would ordinarily have been unable to reproduce, and since we are exposed to more mutation-causing events than ever before, our gene pool (the genes currently in existence) is becoming more and more "polluted" with genetic errors. Assuming an increase in survival of 8 percent per century of

EUGENICS
The science concerned with improving animals by controlling hereditary factors.

Summary

■ All human behavior has its roots in the nervous system, of which the brain is an integral part. Psychologists are concerned with all aspects of behavior. The psychologists who study the biological bases of behavior are called physiological psychologists.

■ The nervous system can be divided into a number of interrelated component parts: the central nervous system, which includes the brain and

those who would normally die from genetic disease, the eminent biogeneticist Theodosius Dobzhansky has estimated that the majority of the world's population will be seriously genetically defective in only six hundred years (Packard, 1977).

While it seems frightening that someone should be able to decide who should be sterilized and who should be allowed to have children, such measures perhaps are necessary. As a citizen of this country and, in a sense, of the world, you may be the one to decide. The following facts are offered without comment:

In Denmark, women who have an IQ score below 75 are required by law to be sterilized (Packard, 1977).

1. IQ tests measure only limited aspects of a person's ability.
2. Approximately 80 percent of those with IQ scores below 75 are physically normal and have no history of brain or nerve damage (Liebert, Poulos, & Marmor, 1977).
3. IQ scores may change or vary by as much as 40 points or more during one's lifetime (Skeels, Updegraff, Wellman, & Williams, 1938).

During the last 30 years, thousands of people in North Carolina have been sterilized by law because they were examined and found to be mentally defective by the North Carolina State Eugenics Board (Coburn, 1974).

1. During the 1960s, 63 percent of those sterilized in North Carolina were black, although blacks only con-stituted 24 percent of North Carolina's population.
2. Black children tend to score 10 to 15 points lower on IQ tests than white children (Kennedy, 1969).
3. Many IQ tests have been criticized for asking ''white'' questions, that is, questions that are easier for white children to answer because of their cultural background (Kagan, 1973).
4. Black children raised in white homes tend to score about as well on IQ tests as white children do (Scarr & Weinberg, 1976).

Twenty-six states have statutes that allow eugenic measures for controlling the incidence of defects.

1. A few years ago the Illinois state legislature considered a proposal to disallow marriage licenses to Illinois citizens who are carriers of genetic disorders or diseases that could lead to birth defects (Packard, 1977).
2. Robert Todd Lincoln, the American Secretary of War from 1881 to 1885, might never have been born had such a law been in effect during the 19th century because his father, a citizen of Illinois, apparently suffered from **Marfan's syndrome**, a serious and slowly debilitating disease of the body's connective tissue, which results in elongated fingers, toes, and a generally ugly appearance. But then some people are able to endure in spite of their genetic hardships, as did Robert Todd Lincoln's father, Abraham Lincoln, the 16th president of the United States (Schwartz, 1978).

Positive Eugenics

Positive eugenics places the emphasis on creative rather than weeding-out processes. With positive eugenics, selected women would be fertilized with the best sperm. But who should decide which sperm or egg is best? That's the catch. What kind of man or woman represents the best—Mr. Universe, Miss America, a Nobel Prize winner, a movie star? J. J. Thompson, a Nobel Prize winner, had a mother who couldn't find her way from her home to the railway station, a distance of about two blocks! Who would have selected her ova? Or, if the best seed were to refer to the most socially respectable people what about ex-convicts such as Cervantes, Thoreau, Gandhi, and Martin Luther King?

Chauncey Depew, a wealthy American capitalist, stated in 1922 that the fittest were those who rose to the top of the New York financial world. Around 1929, opinions seemed to change (Hardin, 1959).

It's interesting to study people's reaction to eugenics programs. A psychologist, Roger McIntire, once proposed that anyone who couldn't pass a community college course in being a parent should be injected with a substance that would prevent reproduction. The antidote was to be given only after both parents-to-be passed the course. McIntire received hundreds of letters which, as he noted, ranged from ''right-on'' to ''Sieg Heil'' (Packard, 1977). What do you think?

the spinal column, and the peripheral nervous system, which includes the somatic and autonomic nervous systems.
- A nerve is made up of thousands upon thousands of individual nerve cells called neurons. Neurons communicate by using electrical impulses and secreting chemicals. The nervous system is therefore considered to be an electrochemical system.
- The typical neuron has three distinct structural features: the soma, the dendrites, and the axon. Messages are generally received by the den-

MARFAN'S SYNDROME
An inherited disorder associated with elongated fingers and toes, and degeneration of connective tissue; the result of a defective gene.

drites and transmitted by the axon. Neurons can communicate with other neurons, glands, or muscles when they are stimulated to action potential and discharge an impulse, called a spike, that runs the length of the axon. Silent neurons are cells that communicate with each other by means of graded potentials, but only over short distances.

■ Messages are carried from a neuron to adjacent cells when neurotransmitters are secreted into the synapse between the cells. Some synapses are excitatory, others are inhibitory.

■ The brain is extremely complex and much of its functioning remains a mystery. Through the use of such techniques as brain mapping and the PET scan, the complexities of the brain's functions are being unraveled. The brain may be conveniently divided into three areas: the hindbrain, the midbrain, and the forebrain.

■ A massive portion of the forebrain is the cerebrum. The cortex of the cerebrum can be divided into four lobes: frontal, parietal, occipital, and temporal.

■ We have gathered many clues to the way in which the brain functions by studying brain damage and disease. For example, damage to the limbic system may cause emotional disturbances, and damage to the hippocampus may impair memory functioning.

■ Research with split-brain patients (in whom the corpus callosum has been severed) indicates that the brain might best be considered two distinct entities, the left and right hemispheres. In most individuals the left hemisphere controls language and analytical functions, and the right hemisphere is associated with spatial and artistic capabilities.

■ Neurotransmitters, neuropeptides, and hormones may have dramatic and wide-ranging effects on a great many aspects of human behavior. For instance, beta endorphin, a neuropeptide, has been implicated in pain and pleasure control.

■ Many drugs that affect behavior appear to mimic or alter the functions of natural body substances.

■ Chromosomes are found in the cells of every living creature. They carry the genetic codes that determine the organism's inheritance. Human beings have 23 pairs of chromosomes.

■ While simple genetic mechanisms may help explain the heritability of eye color or blood type, more complex mechanisms are required to explain the inherited components of such things as intelligence and personality.

■ Canalized behaviors and sensitive periods may be inherited predispositions that can influence behavior.

This is an account of how one man, among thousands, has directly benefited from the research described in this chapter.

When Charles Niethold walked into the dentist's office, he wasn't particularly worried about receiving an injection of novocaine or having his tooth filled. Niethold told his dentist that he preferred to have the tooth filled without novocaine. His dentist cautioned him that there might be pain, but Niethold said, "No, it won't hurt." With this comment Niethold pulled a small radio transmitter from his pocket, extended the aerial, held the transmitter above his chest a distance of about a foot, and pressed a button. He then closed the antenna and put the transmitter back in his pocket, and said, "OK, doc, go ahead. It won't hurt now." The dentist wasn't sure whether Mr. Niethold needed a psychologist, or whether he had been taken in by some quack pushing a piece of phony equipment that was supposed to relieve pain. But the dentist, not wanting to embarrass his patient, proceeded, trying as he filled the tooth not to touch the sensitive nerve. A couple of times, though, he was sure he had hurt his patient. But while he waited for a reaction, Mr. Niethold appeared calm, collected, and even somewhat happy.

After the filling the patient said, "See, I told you it wouldn't hurt." The dentist finally broke down and asked for an explanation, and Charles Niethold told him the following story.

In 1975 Mr. Niethold had seriously injured his back for the sec-ond time in a fall at work. After three operations he was still in chronic pain in his lower extremities. His case was brought to the attention of the University of California Medical Center at San Francisco, and specifically, to neurosurgeon Yoshiro Hosobuchi. Dr. Hosobuchi operated, but not on Niethold's back, where the injury had occurred, or on his lower extremities, where he felt the pain. Instead, the neurosurgeon operated on Niethold's chest and brain. He placed a radio receiver within the chest cavity and ran wires up through the neck to the brain where he implanted small electrodes in the periaqueductal gray matter. The radio receiver in the chest could be operated by holding a small transmitter close to it and pressing the button on the transmitter. The receiver would then send an electrical message to the electrodes implanted in the brain. Dr. Hosobuchi discovered that when this area of the brain is stimulated the level of beta endorphin in the central nervous system becomes two to seven times greater (Hosobuchi, Rossier, Bloom, & Guillemin, 1979). Now whenever Mr. Niethold feels pain from his accident, he takes out his transmitter, presses the button, and the pain goes away almost magically for hours and sometimes days. Of course, not worrying about the dentist is a bonus.

Suggestions for Further Reading

1. *The brain*. San Francisco: W. H. Freeman, 1979. (A book edition of the September 1979 issue of *Scientifiic American*)
2. Eccles, J. C. *The understanding of the brain* (2nd ed.). New York: McGraw-Hill, 1977.
3. Gazzaniga, M. S. *The bisected brain*. New York: Appleton, Century, Crofts, 1970.
4. Stevens, L. A. *Explorers of the brain*. New York: Knopf, 1971.

CONTENTS

C H A P T E R 3

Sensation

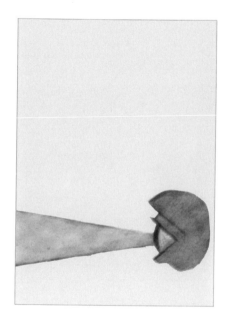

PROLOGUE

You are a neurophysiologist, and you know that there are many different kinds of sensory neurons responsive to many different stimuli. When you were a child, your teachers and your parents told you that there were only five senses—vision, hearing, taste, smell, and touch. That, you now know, was a simplistic description of a range of distinct sensory capabilities that may number in the hundreds or even thousands. In the eye alone are neurons that are sensitive to different areas of the spectrum; neurons that sense motion upward and downward and from left to right and right to left (Cynader & Regan, 1978); neurons that sense brightness and darkness; neurons that sense sudden changes in observed size (Regan & Cynader, 1979). There even appear to be neurons sensitive to vertical and horizontal edges, and to orientations in between (Marr, 1976). Each one of these capabilities represents a different sense, all of them forming vision.

In the last few decades, there's been a growing interest in your field in the apparent tendency of some sensory neurons to atrophy or die if they are not stimulated during certain critical periods early in an

organism's development. Your experiment with the cats is an attempt to verify this phenomenon.

The three kittens are almost grown now, but you started the experiment when they were born. You raised all three in total darkness until they were three weeks old, and then you exposed them to light in a special room for only an hour a day until they were 14 weeks old. The room was painted with vertical stripes so that the cats could see only vertical lines or edges. They were not allowed any experience of horizontal edges. This was a critical period early in the cats' development, and you were testing whether it was possible to stimulate only one kind of visual neuron, the vertical-edge detectors, while permitting the visual neurons sensitive to nonvertical orientations to atrophy from disuse. When the cats reached 14 weeks, you exposed them to normal surroundings. But they were never normal. Your guess had been correct; none of the cats was ever able to detect nonvertical edges.

Although the cats may seem normal to a visitor at first, they are not. They can easily walk around table or chair legs, but they can't jump onto a chair or a couch be-

cause they can't detect the horizontal edge of the chair or the couch seat. They can easily negotiate the corners of the room, but they are completely unable to climb or descend the stairs. They bump their noses into the step in front of them, unable to see where the edge is. No amount of experience during their adult lives will ever undo the loss of those nonvertical detector cells (Blakemore & Cooper, 1970).

In this chapter we will examine the senses, your contact with the world around you. You're likely to discover some surprising things about them.

Why Psychologists Study Sensation

What would it be like to be sitting on top of a hydrogen bomb when it exploded? Most people say that whatever the feeling, it would be over with quickly. Perhaps a very bright light and a tremendous noise and then nothing. Perhaps a sense of searing heat and of being hurled away. Or perhaps all of that at once, contained within a great roaring explosion, lasting (from your point of view) just a fraction of a second. Obviously, no one could experience this and live to describe it. But we know the answer anyway. Imagine yourself sitting on top of a hydrogen bomb, waiting for it to detonate. You would be looking over your notebook, ready to write down your experiences, feeling the steel casing beneath you, and perhaps listening to the countdown over the speakers broadcasting from the block house miles away. And then suddenly—there would be nothing. There would be no light, no sound, no feeling of heat. You would not have sensed a thing. How can we be sure? We know because neural messages have to be translated into electrochemical impulses before they are sent to the brain. Consequently, long before your brain had received any of the messages from your nervous system you would have been vaporized. In fact, the odds are that you would have been vaporized long before visual, auditory, heat, or pressure neurons had a chance to fire.

This ridiculous, but perhaps memorable, example emphasizes the fact that our senses are our only contact with the world outside our bodies. Before we can know the world outside, we must wait until sensory messages reach their destinations inside. Without messages from the senses there can be no experience of external reality, and without such experience there would be little in the way of organized behavior.

The senses are not perfect. They are filters. There are many loud sounds that our species cannot hear, many bright lights that we cannot see, and many impacts that we cannot feel. There are also many substances we cannot taste and many odors we cannot smell. Our way of organizing and responding to the world depends a great deal on the way in which our senses filter the stimuli and information around us. We come to know our world primarily through our senses and what we sense often affects our behavior. This is the reason psychologists study the senses.

Sensory Thresholds

Our senses inform us of the presence of stimuli or of any change in a stimulus. But before energy such as sound or light can be sensed, it must satisfy two conditions. First, it must be energy to which our senses are tuned. No matter how bright an X ray is, we cannot see it. Second, the energy must be strong enough to stimulate our senses. Although delicate instruments might be able to sense the light from a match struck on a mountaintop 50 miles away on a dark night, your eyes would not. The amount of energy required to create a noticeable sensation is called the **absolute threshold.** If the match had been struck at a distance of 30 miles on a dark night under the most ideal conditions you might have been able to detect it, but just barely. This amount of energy would have been within your absolute threshold. The term is misleading, however, because the absolute threshold for any given stimulus can change depending on your physical condition or motivation.

Just as a certain amount of energy is required before you can detect a stimulus, so must the existing energy fluctuate a certain amount before you can detect a change in a stimulus. This minimum amount of energy fluctuation is known as the **difference threshold.** Psychologists often refer to difference thresholds as *just noticeable differences*, or JNDs. Difference thresholds can also change depending on physical condition, motivation, or the qualities of the stimulus being tested.

An interesting aspect of just noticeable differences is that they tend to be fairly constant fractions of the stimulus intensity. For example, if you picked up a 1-pound weight and got used to the feel of it, about half an ounce could be added or subtracted from that weight before you would feel a just noticeable difference. Then, if you became accustomed to a 2-pound weight instead of the 1-pound weight, the just noticeable difference would be close to 1 ounce instead of half an ounce. Thus, as the weight you held was doubled, the just noticeable difference also doubled, that is, the ratio stayed the same. This relationship was first described by Ernst Weber in 1834 and has come to be known as **Weber's law** (see Table 3.1). Weber's law might better have been called "Weber's best guess," however, because although these fractions hold up for a fairly wide range of stimulations, they change quite drastically when the intensity of the stimulus becomes very great or very small (Carlson, Drury, & Webber, 1977).

Vision

Is the human eye like a camera? Both the eye and a camera have a lens through which light passes, and which focuses light. A camera has light-sensitive film, the eye has a light-sensitive area, the **retina.** In addition, the eye has a pupil that opens and closes allowing more or less light to enter. But then again, most expensive cameras have a mechanical "pupil."

ABSOLUTE THRESHOLD
The minimum intensity a stimulus must have in order to produce a sensation.

DIFFERENCE THRESHOLD
The minimum change that a stimulus must undergo before the change can be reliably detected; also called *just noticeable difference*.

WEBER'S LAW
The rule that the larger or stronger a stimulus, the larger the change required for an observer to notice a difference. The smallest difference in intensity between two stimuli that can be reliably detected is a constant fraction of the original stimulus.

RETINA
The delicate multilayer, light-sensitive membrane lining the inner eyeball. It consists of layers of ganglion and bipolar cells and photoreceptor cells called rods and cones.

Table 3.1   Selected applications of Weber's law

SENSE	WEBER FRACTION	PERCENTAGE CHANGE NEEDED FOR JUST NOTICEABLE DIFFERENCE
Brightness of light	1/61	1.6
Tone pitch	1/333	0.3
Pressure on skin surface	1/7	14.3
Taste (salty water)	1/5	20.0
Smell (of rubber)	1/10	10.0
Lifted weight	1/51	2.0

CORNEA
The transparent outer bulge in the front of the eye through which light waves pass.

PUPIL
The dark circular aperture in the center of the iris of the eye, which helps regulate the amount of light entering the eye.

LENS
The transparent biconvex structure of the eye which covers the iris and pupil and focuses light rays entering through the pupil to form an image on the retina.

GANGLION CELLS
Nerve cells of the first layer of the retina which receive impulses from rods and cones via the bipolar cells and transmit these impulses to the brain.

BIPOLAR CELLS
Nerve cells that receive impulses from the rods and cones in the retina and transmit these impulses to the ganglion cells.

RODS
Specialized photoreceptor cells in the retina that are primarily responsive to changes in the intensity of light waves and are therefore important in peripheral vision and night vision.

CONES
Specialized photoreceptor cells in the retina that are primarily responsive to different wavelengths of light and are therefore important in color vision; also associated with high visual acuity.

We have two retinas, one at the back of each eye, and each is filled with thousands of receptive visual cells. In a sense, the retina works like film. In fact, light-sensitive chemicals taken from the retina of rabbits have been used on film in cameras and found to work! Once light strikes the retina, neural messages are sent farther into the brain where cells are either stimulated or not stimulated depending on which parts of the retina were excited by the light. Film is developed in much the same way. A picture emerges because certain parts of the film have been stimulated by light while others haven't. When an image enters a camera it is projected through the lens onto the film upside down. When an image enters the eye it is also projected onto the retina upside down (see Figure 3.1). On the surface, then, the camera and the eye seem to be very similar.

Actually, nothing could be further from the truth. Although the "camera theory" of vision is very popular among the general public, it provides an extremely limited understanding of vision. There may be many parallels between the camera and the eye, but the two are actually more different than alike. The visual system, unlike a camera, sees things that aren't there and alters things that are there, and in doing so, affects our understanding of the world. Its abilities are strange and awesome.

Let's reconsider the camera for a moment. Have you ever seen a newsreel of a dramatic event during which the cameraman who was filming the action had to begin running? What happens to the camera's view of the world when the person who is holding it begins to run? The picture starts to shake violently. It looks as if an earthquake were in progress, and it's almost impossible to see what's happening. To make good movies you must hold the camera steady, so that light entering strikes the film in roughly the same place for each frame. If you move the camera violently, the light image striking the film will also move violently, and when the film is projected onto a screen everything will seem to be moving and jerking in all directions at once. If the same thing happened to the visual system, everyone would be walking about as gently as they could in order to avoid quaking motions in their view of the surrounding world. But this is not the case. You can run down a street and, although the world about you may seem to be moving, it will not be moving with the agitation that you would see had you been taking movies as you ran. The difference lies in the fact that the retina is not a piece of film; instead, it functions as if it were a piece of brain. While a piece of film passively records what it "sees," the brain interacts with the light.

Figure 3.1 *Visual images received by the eye are projected onto the retina upside down.*

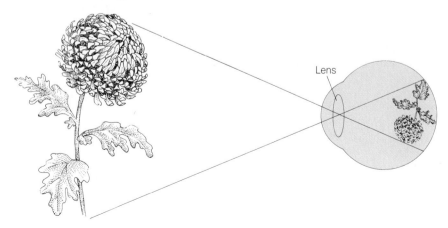

Lens

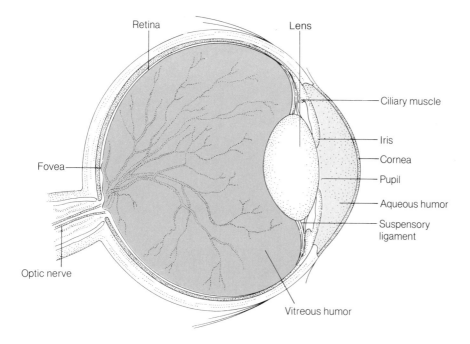

Figure 3.2   *The human eye*

Retina

Lens

Ciliary muscle

Iris

Cornea

Pupil

Aqueous humor

Suspensory
ligament

Fovea

Optic nerve

Vitreous humor

THE RETINA

Figure 3.2 shows the major parts of the human eye. Light entering the eye passes through the transparent **cornea** and hits the **pupil,** which regulates the amount of light entering and passing through the **lens.** The lens focuses the light onto the retina.

The retina consists of three layers. The first layer contains the **ganglion cells** whose axons form the optic nerve. In the second layer are the **bipolar cells** which connect with the third layer. The third layer is made up of photoreceptors called **rods** and **cones** which are sensitive to light (see Figure 3.3). When the rods and cones are stimulated by light, their neural messages travel first to the bipolar cells, then to the ganglion cells, and then down the optic nerve to higher parts of the brain, much as people in a bucket brigade pass buckets of water from one person to the next in order to help put out a fire. In the last few years, however, evidence has been found of lateral "crosstalk" between neighboring receptors within the same layer of the retina (MacLeod, 1978). For instance, cone cells that have been stimulated may directly affect other cone cells that have not been stimulated (Baylor, Fuortes, & O'Bryan, 1971), or cone cells that have been stimulated may affect rod cells (Raviola, 1976). The reason for this kind of lateral circuitry in the retina is not known (Fain, Gold, & Dowling, 1976; Lamb & Simon, 1976). It may be that these lateral connections help rectify the image and eliminate visual errors in processing. Whatever is going on, the same thing certainly doesn't happen in a camera!

The Fovea   If you stare at a bright white wall or a rich blue sky you can often see outlines of blood vessels layered within the eye. In addition, many people by their late 20s notice floating, blurry black specks, sometimes with little streamers, that seem to pass through their visual field. These are known as vitreous floaters, and they are in fact small objects floating in the vitreous humor. But how is it possible to see something that is inside of your

Figure 3.3 *The photoreceptors of the retina. The rods and cones are embedded in the pigmented layer. Receptors pass on their messages to the bipolar cells. The axons of the ganglion cells form the optic nerve. Notice that before light strikes the rods and cones it must pass through the other layers of the retina.*

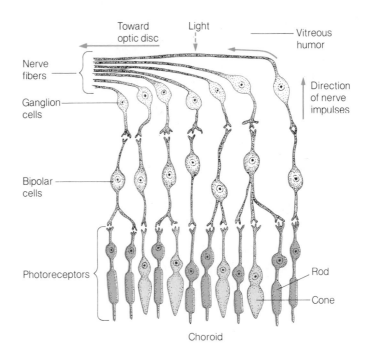

own eye? The answer is that these blood vessels or floating specks interfere with the light image as it passes through the lens on its way to the retina, and if the light is sufficiently bright and the background is homogeneous, the shadow the objects cast onto the retina becomes noticeable. Since the objects are inside the eye and cannot be brought into focus by the lens, they are perceived only as a shadow cast onto the back of the retina. In terms of normal daylight vision the most sensitive portion of the eye, and the part onto which these shadows are cast, is the **fovea.** The clarity and acuity of human vision depend a great deal on this area.

Look at a single word on this page. That one word, which will be projecting directly onto the fovea, will be very clear, while the words around it, which will be projecting onto peripheral portions of the retina, are indistinct. If you try to read the nearby words without removing your glance from the first word, you'll find you will be unable to recognize other words only a short distance away. To see something clearly you need to focus directly on that object. Then it will be projected back onto the fovea.

The Blind Spot One portion of the peripheral retina contains no photoreceptors because it is here that the **optic nerve** passes through the retina on its way to the brain. Because it has no photoreceptors, this area is unable to sense light and is known as the **blind spot.** You can locate your own blind spot by following the directions in Figure 3.4. As you will see, the white circle completely vanishes. Look at the figure again, but this time, while keeping your eye on the cross, notice what replaces the white spot when it disappears. You should see bricks and mortar. How can this be? The white spot cannot be seen because there are no photoreceptor cells on the portion of the retina onto which the spot is projected. But without photoreceptors how can you see bricks and mortar where the spot had been? The answer is that our brain is lying to us and, unlike the camera, is telling us that there is something where there is nothing. These blind spots in each eye are always with us, but rather than let us go through life with two holes in our vision, the brain takes the surrounding material, copies it, and fills in the blind spots with similar material. It may be a lie, but it makes life, at least our visual understanding of it, a little nicer.

Photoreceptor Cells   The photoreceptors in the retina are the first neurons activated by the incoming light. They are the first step in the process by which the brain interprets what it sees. The way in which these receptors work is the key to several interesting phenomena.

The two main types of photoreceptive neurons are the rods and the cones. As their names imply, the rods have a cylindrical shape while the cones are more pear-shaped or conical. Each retina contains more than 100 million rods and 6 million cones. These are afferent sensory neurons that are sensitive to light waves.

Light travels in waves and the distance between waves, called the **wavelength,** determines the kind of light. Figure 3.5 (see color section) shows the **electromagnetic spectrum.** The human eye is sensitive to only a small portion of this spectrum, known as the **visible spectrum.** X rays and radio waves, which you may not have thought of as light, are found on the spectrum and are in fact light. Within the visible spectrum a long wavelength appears red; as the wavelength shortens, the color changes. The middle wavelengths appear green, and the shorter wavelengths blue.

Different rods and cones are stimulated by different wavelengths within the visible light range. The rods are sensitive to all of the light within the visual spectrum except for red. The cones are not uniform in their response to light. Some are red-sensitive, some are green-sensitive, and some are blue-sensitive (see Figure 3.6). Rods and cones are also different in two other important ways—sensitivity and acuity. Rods are far more sensitive to light. Cones are typically active only during daylight or in indoor light. The rods function best under reduced illumination; they give us our ability to see when there is little light. The cones have greater acuity. The fovea has no rods, only cones. This explains the clarity with which we see images striking the fovea. Rods and cones together make up the periphery of the retina.

The eye has a second blind spot, associated with the concentration of cones in the fovea. If you look directly at a dim star on a very dark night, the star may seem to disappear. But if you shift your glance a little to one side of the star, it may reappear. This is because the light from the star,

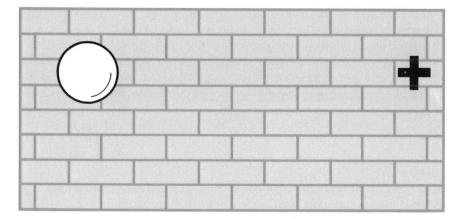

Figure 3.4   *The blind spot. With your right eye closed look at the cross in the upper right-hand corner. Hold the book up and slowly move it back and forth until the circle disappears (about a foot from your eye).*

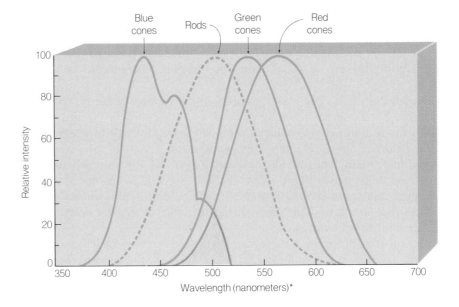

when you look directly at it, shines on the fovea, which contains only cones, and the cones are not sensitive enough to see it. When you look to the side, however, the light from the star strikes the periphery of the retina. Rods in the periphery are able to be stimulated by the dim illumination, and the star reappears. This blind spot is distinctly different from the other blind spot, which is the result of the optic nerve's exit through the retina in a location where there are no photoreceptors at all.

Contrary Neurons Although the rods and cones are neurons, they do not behave like most neurons. Visual neurons rely on graded potentials rather than action potentials. Moreover, a stimulated visual neuron exhibits a different ion flow across the membrane. When light is absorbed by a rod or a cone the interior of the neuron becomes more negative than it was before. Rather than becoming **depolarized** when stimulated, as most other neurons do, visual neurons become **hyperpolarized** when light strikes them (Penn & Hagins, 1972; Davson, 1976; MacLeod, 1978). Rods and cones are also contrary in secreting transmitter when they are *not* stimulated by light, and in decreasing the amount of transmitter secreted when more light strikes them (Ripps, Shakib, & MacDonald, 1976).

Hyperpolarity and reduced secretion of neurotransmitter in response to stimulation may be just as good as depolarization and an increase in neurotransmitter secretion. There may be no reason for the differences between the two systems. Nonetheless, one researcher has suggested that the visual system evolved to be more excited by dark objects against a lighter background, the appearance something would take if it suddenly moved between you and the brighter sky in the background. This response may have helped organisms to better sense predators and other dangers (Hodgkin, 1971). Whatever the reason, visual neurons certainly are unusual.

DARK ADAPTATION

We've all had the experience of going from a lighted room into a dark one. At first you can't see anything, and it's difficult to make out forms or shapes. You're likely to trip over objects or bump into them. Gradually, however, you adapt to the dark. After about 40 minutes, assuming there's a little light, perhaps moonlight or other dim glow, you're able to see the shapes of objects.

The ability to see in the dark is due mainly to the functioning of the rods. As you'll recall, the rods are extremely sensitive to small amounts of illumination. Thirty or forty minutes after you enter the darkness the rods have reached full sensitivity; they have become **dark adapted.** This dark adaptation is due to a slow chemical change in the rods. To reverse your dark adaptation you need only turn on a bright light; the rods will quickly lose their dark adaptation. If you've been in the light for a few minutes, and become **light adapted,** and then turn out the lights again, the rods will have to become dark adapted again, and this will take some time. Since you have two retinas, you can use a trick to keep your dark adaptation. When you have to turn on a light after you've become dark adapted, tightly close one eye, or even put your hand over it, so that only the uncovered eye is exposed to the bright light. Use the open eye to work in the light. Of course, when you turn out the lights again you won't be able to see anything in the eye that you've been using because of its light adaptation. This is the time to take your hand off of the closed eye and open it. You will see that this eye has remained dark adapted and that you can use it to see your way around in the dark.

Once your eyes have become dark adapted, a brief exposure to a bright light will not necessarily cause you to lose your entire dark adaptation. Perhaps you've noticed this while driving at night. If you look at the oncoming headlights of a car briefly, the glare may disrupt your night vision but only for about 20 seconds. However, if you look at the headlights for a long time, the time you need to recover from the glare will be longer, and may even be dangerous. Glare recovery time is lengthened by ingestion of alcohol. After only a few drinks it may take 30 to 50 percent longer for the rods to recover their dark adaptation following exposure to the glare of oncoming headlights. This may be one of the many reasons driving accidents occur at a higher rate among drinkers.

Vitamin A deficiency is also associated with poor night vision, that is, the poor ability of rods to adapt to the dark. Vitamin A is an integral part of the chemistry of rods. Women are two or three times more sensitive to light during ovulation than on other days. It is speculated that this change results from the larger amounts of vitamin A and other hormones present in the blood at this time ("Seeing Stars," 1978). Eating carrots has long been associated with seeing better in the dark. Although eating a lot of carrots won't improve your night vision, not having enough vitamin A, which is found in carrots, can inhibit the dark adaptation. The B vitamins have also been found to be essential for proper visual functioning (Masland & Mills, 1980).

COLOR VISION

Why does a bull charge at a red cape? Whatever the reason, it's certainly not because the cape is red. Bulls do not have color vision, and wouldn't know a red cape from a green one. In fact, most animals are totally color-blind and can see only blacks, whites, and grays. Color vision is rare in mammals, and the primates (humans, apes, monkeys) are among the few mammals that have it. Color vision is much more common among birds, fish, insects, and reptiles.

DEPOLARIZED
A decrease in the internal negativity of a nerve cell.

HYPERPOLARIZED
An increase in the internal negativity of a nerve cell.

DARK ADAPTED
The process by which the eyes become more sensitive to light in dim illumination.

LIGHT ADAPTED
The process by which the eyes become less sensitive to light in bright illumination.

Your faithful dog may be able to tell a red ball from a yellow one because the red ball looks darker to him, but it won't be because of color. Dogs can't see color. Cats, on the other hand, present a strange case. Cats can see an object in color as long as the object projects an image onto the retina that covers an area larger than 20 degrees. Thus a cat can see large objects in color or objects that are very close in color, but small objects seen at a distance appear to be black and white (Loop & Bruce, 1978).

In humans, the most sensitive cone cells respond to yellowish-green wavelengths. The weakest colors that can effectively stimulate cones are found at these wavelengths. Yellow green is the color to use if you are trying to attract the eye in dim illumination by means of color. This is the reason some fire departments have painted their trucks a kind of dayglow yellow green. This color can still be perceived in dimly lighted surroundings when others may appear to be gray or black and white. In order to see reds or blues more light is necessary.

Rod cells cannot sense color alone, but they are quite sensitive to green-blue. This does not mean that a sensation of green-blue is created when rods are struck by green-blue light waves; rather, a very dim green-blue light might be sensed by the rods when an equally dim yellow light could not be. Of course, the rods are not sensitive to red no matter how bright it is.

The Young-Helmholtz Theory   Color vision is a complicated phenomenon, and there are a number of theories to explain how it operates in humans. A popular theory of color vision developed during the 19th century is known as the **Young-Helmholtz theory.** It is based on the work of Thomas Young, an English physicist, and on the additional work, half a century later, of Hermann von Helmholtz, a German physiologist. It derives from the fact that all colors in the spectrum can be produced from three **primary colors,** red, green, and blue.* Color television works essentially on this principle. All of the colors in a color picture can be created from the three primaries.

If someone gave you buckets of red, green, and blue paint, claiming that you could mix any color from them, you would have difficulty. But if someone gave you red, green, and blue beams of light and asked you to mix all colors from them, you could easily do so. In the case of the paints, you would be attempting what is called **subtractive mixing,** and it's impossible to create all possible colors by this process. But combining beams of light would be **additive mixing,** and by this process it is possible to create all colors. Paint pigments absorb as well as reflect light, and the more pigments you mix together, the more light is absorbed or subtracted. However, beams of light generate their own color and become added together. If you mixed red, green, and blue light in equal intensities, you would see white (see Figure 3.7, in color section). Black, on the other hand, is the absence of all color. Objects that appear black have absorbed all of the wavelengths of light that shine on them; nothing is reflected off. In fact, black objects would be invisible if they were not surrounded by objects that are reflecting light.

---

*Scientists used to think the primary colors were red, *yellow*, and blue. A painter's palette will usually contain red, yellow, and blue because in pigment form, these three colors are the basis for all others.

The Young-Helmholtz theory proposes that there are three kinds of color receptors in the eye, one for receiving each of the primary colors. Modern physiological data have supported this hypothesis, and three different kinds of cones have been discovered—one kind sensitive to red, one to green, and one to blue light (MacNichol, 1964). The Young-Helmholtz view seems fairly straightforward. When you look at a red object, the red cones are stimulated to send a message to the brain, and you sense redness. You respond to green and blue objects in the same way. When you look at something white, all red, green, and blue cones are stimulated, producing the sensation of white, and when you look at something black, none of the cones is stimulated, and you sense black. According to this theory, any color might be sensed, depending on how much each of the individual receptor cones is stimulated.

The Young-Helmholtz theory seems like a good description of the way in which we see color. Look at the yellow circle in Figure 3.8 (color section). Stare at the center of this circle under bright light for about a minute. Then glance at a white wall or sheet of paper and blink your eyes a few times. A blue circle should suddenly appear. This is known as a **negative afterimage.** Afterimages occur because visual cells become fatigued when they have been stimulated for a long time. If you stare uninterruptedly at a speck on the wall minute after minute, the cells in your eye will tire and cease to respond to the visual information. Whole portions of the wall and even of the room may seem to disappear. The only way to prevent this from happening is to glance about from time to time, changing the light that is being taken in so that it strikes different parts of the retina. According to the Young-Helmholtz view, a negative afterimage arose when you stared at the yellow spot because the green and red cones which were receiving the yellow light became tired (yellow is a mixture of red and green). Then, when you looked at a white surface, which should have stimulated the blue, green, and red cones all together, only the blue cones responded because the red and green cones were too tired.

A more interesting example of a negative afterimage can be studied in Figure 3.9 (color section). It shows an American flag of unusual color, black and green stripes with black stars on a yellow field. Stare at the speck in the center of the flag for about a minute under bright light, then look at a white wall or sheet of paper and blink your eyes a few times. You'll see the negative afterimage displaying the flag in its proper red, white, and blue colors.

The Opponent-Process Theory The three-color Young-Helmholtz theory was challenged around 1870. Researcher Ewald Hering had noticed that certain kinds of **color blindness** were not well explained by the Young-Helmholtz view. Hering was aware that the most common kind of color blindness was red-green color blindness, which is found in about 8 percent of all males and about 0.5 percent of females. People with red-green color blindness find it difficult to sense red or green, and in severe cases they cannot tell the difference between red and green at all (see Figure 3.10, in color section). But interestingly, people with red-green color blindness have no trouble whatsoever seeing yellow! This fact doesn't agree with the Young-Helmholtz theory, which implies that since yellow is a mixture of red and green, a weakness in red and green receptors should impair the ability to see yellow as well. Consequently, Hering argued that yellow was

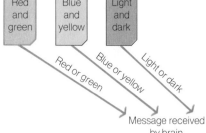

Sensory receptors receiving stimulus

Red and green | Blue and yellow | Light and dark

Red or green | Blue or yellow | Light or dark

Message received by brain

Figure 3.11 *The visual receptor system as Hering believed it might be. Today there is evidence that the cones are receptive to red, green, and blue (MacNichol, 1964) and not red-green, blue-yellow, and light-dark as Hering thought. However, an opponent-process system somewhat as Hering envisioned does operate at levels higher than the first layer of the retina.*

just as much a primary color as red or green or blue. He referred to these four colors as **psychological primaries.**

Hering believed with Young and Helmholtz that there were three kinds of receptors, but he did not agree that they responded to red, green, and blue. Instead, Hering thought that the first receptor responded only to brightness; it was a dark-light receptor. The second receptor was on a red-green continuum, and the third was on a yellow-blue continuum (see Figure 3.11). Hering felt, for example, that if receptors along the red-green continuum were at rest, no color in that continuum would be sensed, but that either red or green would be sensed should the receptors be depolarized in one direction or hyperpolarized in the other. He referred to these conditions as the **anabolic** (building up) phase and the **catabolic** (tearing down) phase. This theory, Hering believed, explained afterimages more accurately. When a red-green sensitive receptor is looking at red, red is the message that is sent to the brain. When the red message is turned off, the cell leaves the anabolic phase and shifts to the catabolic phase, producing a green afterimage. Hering envisioned the same process for blue-yellow receptors. Hering also noted that the existence of blue-yellow color blindness, which is much rarer than red-green, supported his view. Hering's theory became known as the **opponent-process theory.**

Which theory is correct? Modern theories of color vision include aspects of both. The three-color Young-Helmholtz theory seems a good description of the first stage of visual processing on the retina, since cones have been found to be sensitive to red, green, and blue, rather than to red-green and blue-yellow. But the opponent-process theory seems to be a better explanation of color vision at higher levels within the brain.

The Retinex Theory A third theory of color vision, known as the **retinex theory,** has been proposed by Edwin Land, the inventor of the Polaroid camera. Through his work with black and white images, Land discovered that under certain conditions the full color spectrum could be perceived from combinations of black, white and red alone. He suggested that the most important determinants in the discrimination of color were brightness discrepancies among the rods and the three kinds of cones. Figure 3.12 describes Land's experiment (Land, 1977), and Figure 3.13 illustrates his theory of color vision. Other researchers have also discovered that, contrary to the prevailing view, the rod cells can contribute to the perception of color images (McKee, McCann, & Benton, 1977).

To date none of the three theories has been found to completely explain all that we know about color vision, and all three theories have merit based on different experimental evidence. Many psychologists feel that each theory may explain a part of what is happening when we sense colors. Color sensing, like all visual sensing, does not seem to take place in one location only. The retina is only the beginning of a long processing system that continues throughout the brain.

SPECIALIZED DETECTORS

The human visual system has many kinds of specialized detectors. Some detectors are sensitive to high contrasts such as those found along vertical or horizontal edges, or gradations (diagonals) in between. You can test the existence of these edge detectors by following the directions in Figure 3.14.

Figure 3.12 *The two black and white photographs shown here are identical except that the one on the left was photographed through a red filter while the one on the right was photographed through a green filter. For this reason, red or near-red objects appear bright in the photo on the left (the oranges look like ostrich eggs!) and dark in the photo on the right. Conversely, green or near-green objects appear light in the photo on the right but dark in the photo on the left. In Land's experiment, the two slides are projected so that they overlap to form one image. The photo taken through the green filter is projected normally. Since the white light in this black and white photo is a mixture of red, green, and blue (as is all white light) all of the photo-receptors in the eye "see" this photo. The slide taken through the red filter, however, is projected through a red filter; only the red-sensitive cones can "see" this photo. The red photocells in the visual system send a message to the brain that the oranges are bright while other photocells send messages that the oranges are dark. This brightness discrepancy is interpreted by the brain and a sensation of color is created. A fairly full range of colors can be created from the brightness discrepancies that result when the slides are overlapped.*

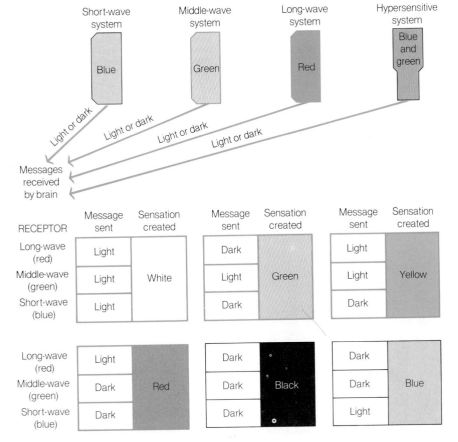

Figure 3.13 *According to Land, receptors in the retina do not send color messages to the brain (as the Young-Helmholtz three-color theory suggests), but rather messages of light or dark (a brightness continuum). Different-colored stimuli, however, will cause different cells to send bright or dark messages. Once these brightness discrepancies reach the cortex an understanding of color is created. In this theory, the rods (the hypersensitive system) can contribute to color as well as the cones.*

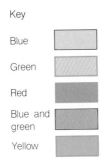

85

Effects brought on by fatigue in visual receptors at higher levels in the visual system. Negative aftereffects, unlike negative afterimages, transfer from one eye to another.

Aftereffects Other detectors are sensitive to motion. Have you ever watched a waterfall for a long time? If you stare at it long enough and then look to one side, perhaps at the cliffs alongside the waterfall, the stationary cliff wall may appear to move upward, in the opposite direction to the water's movement. This is known as a **negative aftereffect.** It appears that there are motion detectors in the visual system that monitor downward and upward motion, and motion from left to right and right to left. Apparently, if an object is stationary, all of the detectors send a signal and cancel each other out. In the waterfall example, the downward-motion detectors appear to become fatigued, and only the upward-motion detectors respond when you look at the stationary wall, creating the illusion that the wall is moving up (see Figure 3.15). Similarly, if you stand on the deck of a moving ship and look overboard at the ocean as it rushes by, and then look down at the deck, the deck may appear to be flowing in the other direction.

Aftereffects are different from afterimages in an important way. Aftereffects can transfer from one eye to the other (though the transer effect may be quite weak). You will recall the afterimage experiment with the American flag. If you look at the flag again, but this time with the left eye only,

Figure 3.14 *Testing for edge detectors. Brace your book in an upright position so that it stands freely and you can walk away from it. Continue to back away until you can just barely see the rain falling on the man. Look at the high-contrast adapation grading in the upper left. Stare at it for 30 seconds to 1 minute, keep moving your gaze around within the circle. As you do this you'll fatigue the vertical-edge detectors. Then look at the man for an instant and the rain should disappear. Looking at the other test gradings, which have either horizontal lines or a different distance between the vertical lines, will not produce this effect. The effect is very short-lived, and you have to be quick. You can fatigue horizontal- and diagonal-edge detectors in the same way.* (SOURCE: *Blakemore & Campbell, 1968, p. 120*)

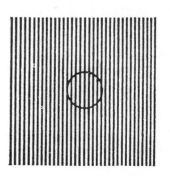

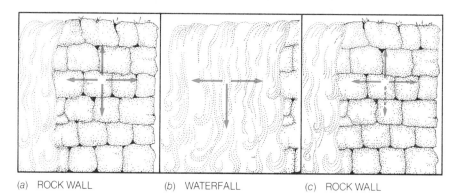

(a) ROCK WALL   (b) WATERFALL   (c) ROCK WALL

Figure 3.15 *Testing for motion detectors. When you look at a stationary object, such as a rock wall (a), firing occurs in detectors sensitive to upward and downward motion and motion from right to left and left to right, and these responses cancel each other out. If you look at an adjacent waterfall (b), the downward motion detectors dominate, while left to right and right to left again cancel each other out. If you watch the waterfall for a long time the downward detectors become fatigued. This becomes evident if you again look at the rock wall (c). All detectors should fire, canceling each other out, but this time the upward detectors dominate because the downward ones are fatigued. The result is that the rock wall appears to drift upward.*

and then search for the afterimage with your right eye, you'll see that it doesn't work. This kind of color-image phenomenon occurs at the retinal level, and information can't be transferred from one eye to the other at that level. However, if you look at a spiral, as in Figure 3.16, while it is spinning and then continue to stare at it when it has stopped spinning, you'll see it turning in the opposite direction, and this aftereffect will transfer from one eye to the other. We can infer that the detectors that were fatigued by the spinning spiral are not in the retina, but are located at a higher level, either in the superior colliculus or in the visual cortex (see Figure 3.17) (Favreau & Corballis, 1976).

Figure 3.16 *The aftereffect created when the spiral stops spinning transfers from one eye to the other. Afterimages are not transferred.*

Spatial Frequency Detectors   There may also be detectors in the brain tuned to different spatial frequencies. High-frequency spatial detectors, it is argued, are tuned to respond to many changes in contrast or to intricacies in edge pattern or contours within a very small space, such as you would see in work that contained fine detail. Low-frequency detectors, on the other hand, are said to be responsive to limited changes in detail within larger spaces (Enroth-Cugell & Robson, 1966). There is evidence that these two kinds of detectors compete with each other when we view objects, suggesting that each has a role to play while neither is fully in command (Harmon & Julesz, 1973).

You can test the existence of these detectors by looking at the photographs in Figure 3.18. It is very difficult to tell what they are. The reason is that they contain high-frequency spatial data (fine detail) in the form of blocks, while the identifiable portions—faces—are made from low-frequency spatial data (gross detail). The faces will emerge, however, if you give control to your low-frequency spatial detectors by "shutting off" your high-frequency spatial detectors and preventing their unwanted competition. Simply blur your vision by crossing your eyes slightly, so that you lose fine detail (the high-frequency spatial data). Paradoxically, as your

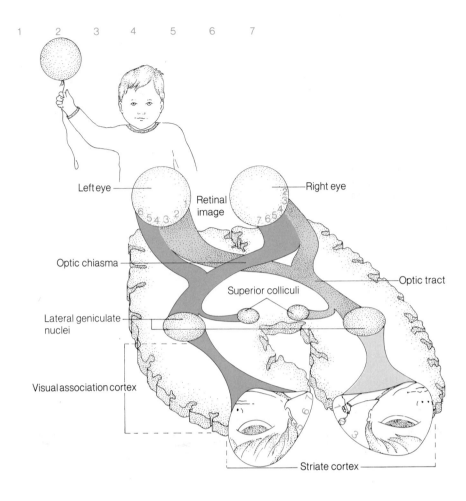

1 2 3 4 5 6 7

Left eye

Retinal image

Right eye

Optic chiasma

Optic tract

Superior colliculi

Lateral geniculate nuclei

Visual association cortex

Striate cortex

Figure 3.17 *Visual processing continues beyond the retina. In this figure you can see how the images from each eye converge at the optic chiasma. Images from the right halves of each retina go to the right hemisphere, and images from the left halves go to the left hemisphere. The lateral geniculate nuclei and superior colliculi are important way stations enroute to the occipital lobes where a distorted visual sensation is processed into a whole and meaningful perception.*

PITCH
The relative position of a tone in a scale, which is determined by the frequency of the sound. Higher frequencies yield higher pitches.

FREQUENCY
The number of cycles per unit of time in a periodic vibration. Determines the pitch of a sound.

AMPLITUDE
A measurement of the amount of energy carried by a wave, shown in the height of the oscillation.

LOUDNESS
A measurement of sound intensity which corresponds to the amplitude of the sound waves.

vision gets blurrier the photographs become clearer because the activity of the low-frequency spatial detectors enables you to concentrate on the gross detail. The same effect can be obtained by viewing the photographs from across a room because you will be too far away to see the high-frequency spatial detail of the boxes, and only low-frequency spatial detail will be apparent.

Hearing

HOW SOUND IS CREATED

While your eyes are sensitive to a limited range of the electromagnetic spectrum, your ears are sensitive to a limited range of frequencies caused by the compression and rarefaction of air, which creates waves (see Figure 3.19). In order for something to make a sound it must disturb the surrounding air, creating air waves that radiate from it and reach your ear. Although light can travel in a vacuum, sound cannot, since sound depends on air, which is not present in a vacuum. Hollywood movies notwithstanding, real spaceships that went zipping by you in outer space would pass in total silence, without the familiar accompanying whoosh of things rushing by in an atmosphere. The moon has no atmosphere, for instance, and everything that happens on the moon happens in complete silence.

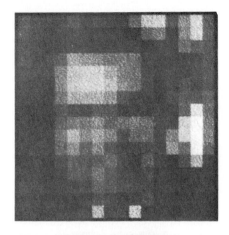
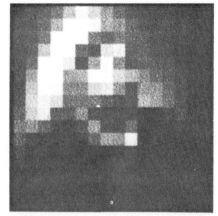
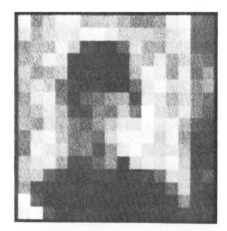

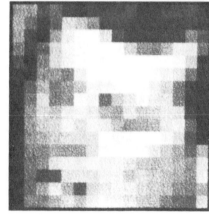
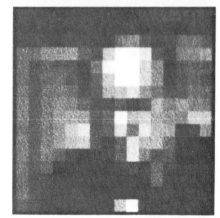

Figure 3.18 *High-frequency spatial detail shows only squares. Low-frequency spatial detail, however, contains faces. By blurring your vision you can eliminate the high-* *frequency interference and, paradoxically, make the picture clearer. (The answers are printed upside down.)*

FROM LEFT TO RIGHT: Richard Nixon, Queen Victoria, Charlie Chaplin, Groucho Marx, John Kennedy, Winston Churchill

When astronauts spoke to each other on the moon, they spoke by means of radio waves, a form of light. Radio waves reaching the astronauts' helmets were converted into sound waves by speakers that caused impacts and compressions within the atmosphere inside the helmets. Had the astronauts removed their helmets and tried to speak to each other, they wouldn't have heard a thing.

Air waves travel out from the source of a sound in much the same way that waves on a pond ripple outward after a rock has been dropped into the water. Sound waves are generated in all directions and, like light waves, they have measurable wavelengths. Wavelength in hearing corresponds to **pitch,** while wavelength in vision corresponds to hue. Long sound wavelengths are heard as very low pitches. Short wavelengths are heard as very high pitches. The human ear can perceive a range between approximately 20 cycles, or waves passing, per second and about 20,000 cycles per second (corresponding to wavelengths of between 17 meters and 17 millimeters). The number of sound waves per second is known as the **frequency.** The **amplitude,** or height, of the wave determines the **loudness** (see Figure 3.20). If you could switch your eyes and ears around in some bizarre way, you might imagine that a bright blue light would sound like a loud high-pitched tone or that a soft low-pitched tone would look like a dim red light.

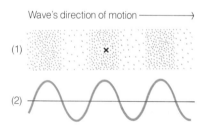

Figure 3.19 *A sound wave. The wave consists of a pulse of compressed air (X) followed by an area of low density.*

DECIBEL SCALE FOR SOUNDS FROM HARMFUL TO FAINT

140	Physical damage
120	Painful
100	Deafening
80	Very loud
60	Loud
40	Moderate
20	Faint
0	

Figure 3.20 *Loudness is measured by decibels (db). Ten db is 10 times louder than 0 db (which is the faintest sound that can be heard). Twenty db is 100 times louder than 0 db and 10 times louder than 10 db. Interestingly, the average loud conversation (60 db) is 1 million times louder than the faintest sound that can be heard.* (SOURCE: *Beiser, 1978, p. 305*)

Some animals are capable of hearing frequencies higher than humans can distinguish. Dogs, for example, can hear up to 30,000 or 40,000 cycles per second. Dog whistles work in this range. Dogs trained to respond to these whistles can be summoned from blocks away by a very loud blast on the whistle which neither you nor anyone else around can hear. Although your ear cannot pick up such high frequencies, the sound is in fact very loud.

THE STRUCTURE OF THE EAR

Figure 3.21 shows a schematic breakdown of the human ear. The **pinna,** or outer ear, helps capture sound waves that enter through the external auditory canal and strike the **tympanic membrane,** or eardrum. A subtle vibration of the eardrum sets in motion the three extremely small bones of the middle ear—the **malleus,** the **incus,** and the **stapes.** These bones in turn generate an identical vibration which passes into the inner ear. Within the inner ear are approximately 15,000 **cilia,** or hair cells, which respond to different frequencies of sound waves. When the cilia are bent, they trigger nerve impulses that are sent by the **auditory nerve** to the brain.

In a sense, the ear functions much as a phonograph does. On a phonograph record a set of waves or oscillations are embossed into the plastic. The record revolves on a turntable at a certain speed, and in this way the frequency can be controlled. Like the malleus, which rides on the tympanic membrane, the stylus of the phonograph needle rides on the grooves of the record. With each jostle and oscillation the message is sent from the needle to the speakers. The speakers oscillate in exact synchrony with the grooves on the record, just as the stapes rocks back and forth in exact synchrony with the tympanic membrane. With the record player, waves are sent out from the speaker; with the ear, waves are sent from the stapes into the **cochlea.** A phonograph, then, can be thought of as nothing more than a means of repeating again and again a particular series of wave oscillations and frequencies, which explains why you hear the same thing each time you play a particular record.

THEORIES OF HEARING

The inner ear is smaller than a marble, and yet it allows us to discriminate among thousands of incredibly complex tones. How is this possible? A number of theories have been developed to explain how hearing works. The cilia within the **organ of Corti** are moved by the vibrations of the eardrum hitting against the oval window at the entrance to the inner ear. It is generally agreed that loudness is determined by the total number of nerves that fire and by the activation of **high-threshold fibers.** The cilia associated with high-threshold fibers are very difficult to bend, and it is only when they are bent by the considerable force of a loud noise that the nerves associated with these cilia fire and you become aware of a loud noise.

Pitch discrimination is a far more complicated matter. The perception of high-range and middle-range tones appears to be determined by the *place* within the organ of Corti where cilia are stimulated. Very high-pitched tones stimulate cilia near the oval window, while intermediate-range tones stimulate cilia farther within the cochlea. This is known as the **place theory.** The place theory would be adequate by itself to explain hearing, except that low tones, those below 4,000 cycles per second, tend to stimulate cilia through the entire organ of Corti.

Frequency theory has been advanced to explain the sensation of tones between 1,000 cycles and 20 cycles (the lowest that can be registered by the human ear). Since auditory neurons, like many other neurons, can fire up to 1,000 times per second, it is thought that auditory neurons may modify their firing rates in order to respond to a range of frequencies. It has been discovered that frequencies between 20 cycles and 1,000 cycles per second are fairly well correlated with neural firing. Neurons stimulated by very low-frequency sounds within the range of 20 to 1,000 cycles per second fire roughly an equivalent number of times per second, while neurons stimulated by sounds near 1,000 cycles per second fire at their maximum of 1,000 times per second. But this fact still leaves the range between 1,000 and 4,000 cycles per second unexplained. A proposal that may help fill the gap is the **volley theory.** Although 4,000 firings per second would be impossible for one neuron, four neurons firing together in volleys could generate 4,000 pulses per second.

Like the theories about color vision, the theories about hearing help explain phenomena that have been observed but that in time may require clarification or redefinition. If each theory proves to be accurate for the frequency range it attempts to explain, hearing might more accurately be described as three different mechanisms, one for each of three different sound ranges. We might even have to acknowledge a fourth mechanism if we consider loudness a separate kind of hearing. In this case there would be (1) a sensation of loudness generated by high-threshold fibers and an accumulative index of the total number of cells firing, (2) perception of sounds between 4,000 and 20,000 cycles per second as a result of the stimulation of cilia located at specific places within the organ of Corti, (3) perception of sounds between 20 cycles and 1,000 cycles per second as a result of neurons firing at rates corresponding to these frequencies, and (4) perception of sounds between 1,000 and 4,000 cycles per second as a result of volleys of neurons firing.

PINNA
The visible external portion of the ear.

TYMPANIC MEMBRANE
The thin, semitransparent membrane separating the middle ear from the external ear; also called the *eardrum.*

MALLEUS
The largest of the three small bones in the middle ear; also called the *hammer.*

INCUS
One of the three small bones in the middle ear; also called the *anvil.*

STAPES
One of the three small bones in the middle ear; also called the *stirrup.*

CILIA
Microscopic, hairlike processes extending from a cell surface.

AUDITORY NERVE
The nerve leading from the cochlea; transmits sound impulses to the brain.

COCHLEA
A spiral tube in the inner ear resembling a snail shell which contains nerve endings essential for hearing.

ORGAN OF CORTI
The organ containing hair cells which are hearing receptors. It is located on the basilar membrane in the cochlea.

HIGH-THRESHOLD FIBERS
Cilia in the inner ear that are difficult to bend and respond only to loud noises or sounds.

PLACE THEORY
The theory of hearing that attempts to explain the reception of sound waves between 4,000 and 20,000 cycles per second. Different frequencies stimulate cilia at different places within the cochlea. High frequencies stimulate cilia near the oval window while low frequencies stimulate cilia farther from the oval window.

FREQUENCY THEORY
A theory of hearing that attempts to explain the reception of sound waves between 20 and 1,000 cycles per second. According to this theory, auditory neurons fire at rates well correlated with the frequency of the sound.

VOLLEY THEORY
A theory of hearing that attempts to explain the reception of sound waves between 1,000 and 4,000 cycles per second. According to this theory, auditory neurons fire in volleys that are well correlated with the frequency of the sound.

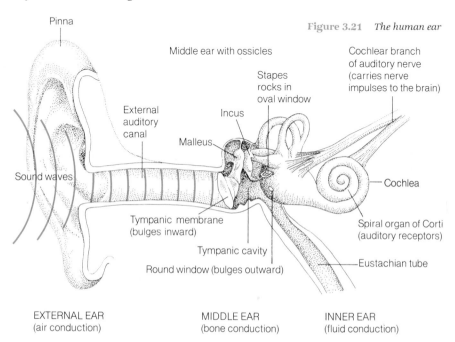

Figure 3.21   *The human ear*

Pinna

Middle ear with ossicles

Stapes rocks in oval window

Cochlear branch of auditory nerve (carries nerve impulses to the brain)

External auditory canal

Incus

Malleus

Sound waves

Tympanic membrane (bulges inward)

Tympanic cavity

Round window (bulges outward)

Cochlea

Spiral organ of Corti (auditory receptors)

Eustachian tube

EXTERNAL EAR
(air conduction)

MIDDLE EAR
(bone conduction)

INNER EAR
(fluid conduction)

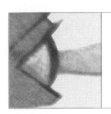

THE ARTIFICIAL EAR

Donald Eddington is a bioengineer. He makes artificial human ears from machine parts in his laboratory at the University of Utah in Salt Lake City. For the last several years he has been working with a man, let's call him George, who has been totally deaf. Until George was 27 he was able to hear perfectly well. Then one day he had a bad attack of dizziness and nausea. A few months after that, when George was sitting in a barber chair, he noticed that when the barber spoke to him from the right side his voice seemed to fade away. Shortly after that he went completely deaf in his right ear. Then, one morning George awoke and his wife seemed to be talking to him hysterically, but he couldn't hear a thing she was saying. He realized that he had lost hearing in his left ear, too, and was now completely deaf.

George was a victim of **Ménière's disease**. Ménière's disease can destroy the thousands of fragile cilia which line the inner ear, causing total and permanent deafness. George was now confined to a life of silence, along with 2 million other Americans who have suffered diseases that destroy the cilia. Hearing aids, which amplify sound entering the ear, are useless without the cilia to turn the sound amplified by the hearing aid into auditory nerve signals. And once the cilia are gone surgery is of no use.

George is now in his late 40s, and after spending 20 years in silence, he is able to hear again. There's a small plug about the size of a dime protruding from behind his left ear. He can hook a thin cable into the plug and listen to speech that he can understand. The voice he hears is Donald Eddington's, the designer and builder of the implant.

What Eddington did was run six tiny platinum electrodes into different points along the cochlea's inner surface. In this way Eddington electrically tapped into the auditory nerve. Eddington said, "The implant actually bypasses the damaged ear interior. Our electrodes simply stimulate the nerves directly, not with vibrations, but with minute electrical shocks. The system mimics the electrical patterns received by the brain as speech" (Weintraub, 1980, p. 50). The cable that George connects to the plug behind his left ear runs through a computer to a microphone. The microphone picks up sounds and sends them to the computer, which breaks them down depending on their frequencies. The computer then stimulates the six electrodes inside of the cochlea according to the frequencies that have been received (see Figure 3.22). In this way the auditory nerve is tricked into responding to the implants as if they were cilia, and sends messages to the brain based on the stimulation it receives.

Although six implants can hardly replace 15,000 cilia, George is able to discriminate crude sounds such as slamming doors or ringing bells. Eddington has been able to get his patients to recognize such tunes as "Mary had a little lamb" and "Twinkle, twinkle, little star." With his patients' help Eddington has been able to pin-

---

MÉNIÈRE'S DISEASE
A disease that can destroy the cilia lining the inner ear, causing total and permanent deafness.

TASTE BUDS
Groups of cells distributed over the tongue that constitute the end organs of the sense of taste.

Taste

Taste is a fairly limited sense. Most of what we consider taste is really smell. If you were blindfolded so that you could not see what you were eating and then had your nose plugged, you could not tell the difference between a piece of raw apple, a piece of raw potato, or a piece of raw onion. Although the three foods smell different, they taste alike. Think of how hard it is to "taste" foods when you have a cold; it's actually the sense of smell that's being hindered.

The major taste senses are sweet, sour, salty, and bitter. The taste receptors are located primarily on the tongue, and a few are found in the throat. **Taste buds** are replaced about every seven days, so that destroying some by burning your tongue is not likely to do any long-term damage. In a human adult there are approximately 10,000 taste buds. Some taste

point which locations are responsive to which frequencies and pitches.

With the aid of the computer to sort through and clarify frequencies, George can now understand about 75 percent of the words on a list that includes such sounds as bit, bat, bite, and boat (Weintraub, 1980). George is pleased with the results. He says, ''I never expected to hear so well so quickly'' (Weintraub, 1980, p. 51).

Eddington is now working on an implant that will have 18 electrodes, which should dramatically boost the patient's ability to discriminate sounds. As computers become more miniaturized and more is learned about the relationship between places within the inner ear and the kinds of sounds created when these places are stimulated, the artificial ear will be improved. Researchers are now imagining a pocket-sized computer that could filter incoming sounds and send messages to an artificial ear containing over 5,000 platinum implants throughout the inner ear. Perhaps within a decade individuals who had thought they would be deaf for life will be listening to Beethoven's Fifth and hearing it as clearly as they would have if their ears had never been damaged.

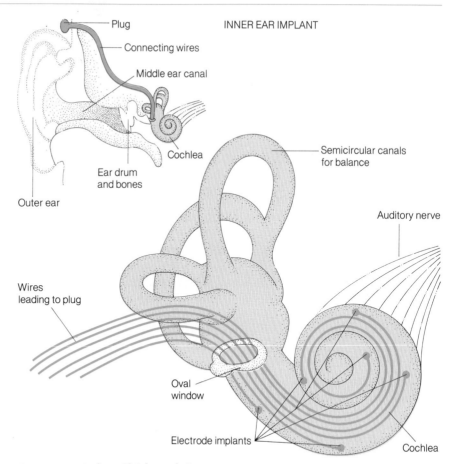

Figure 3.22 *In the artificial ear, platinum electrode implants replace the destroyed cilia. The implants stimulate the auditory nerve by generating small electric shocks in response to different frequencies of sound.* (SOURCE: *Weintraub, 1980, p. 51*)

buds are sensitive to only one quality, for instance, sweet. Others react to combinations of qualities and some individual taste buds respond to all four qualities (Arvidson & Friberg, 1980). Most of the taste buds that respond to sweet are found at the tip of the tongue, salty on the sides and at the tip, sour on the sides, and bitter toward the back.

Taste senses are quite active early in life. Newborns readily respond to sugar, salt, lemon juice and quinine, which stimulate the sweet, salty, sour, and bitter senses. Newborns like sweet, but dislike salt, sour, and bitter in that order. By adulthood many people have acquired a liking for salty and sour, but few people ever acquire a liking for bitter. This probably doesn't surprise you. Most people like sweet candy, salty peanuts, or even sour pickles, but very few like the bitter taste of dissolving aspirin.

It has been argued that the senses of taste evolved because of the purposes they served. We may wonder, for example, why cats have no taste buds sensitive to sweet, while dogs and human beings do. The reason may be that cats, unlike dogs and human beings, have never needed these taste buds. Wild dogs eat meat, roots, or berries, and human beings in the wild eat the same. Since bitter and sour roots and berries are more likely to be poisonous than sweet roots or berries, the sense of sweet may have evolved as a protective measure. Animals attracted to sweet would be less likely to be poisoned, and they would pass on their affinity for sweet to their off-spring. Cats, on the other hand, are carnivores (meat eaters) in the wild; an affinity for sweet would serve no purpose for them.

Smell

Smell may be one of the oldest of the senses, and scent messages, unlike information from the other senses, are not relayed through the thalamus but pass to lower, evolutionarily older areas of the brain. The receptors for smell are contained in the **olfactory epithelium** high up within the nose. Receptors in the olfactory epithelium are thought to function according to the lock and key principle. According to this view, substances have different odors because they have different molecular shapes. Molecules that are shaped alike will fit into receptors that are responsive to them just as keys of the same cut will fit into a particular lock. Therefore, molecules of similar shape have the same or similar odors. The olfactory epithelium contains hundreds of different kinds of receptors. Odors result from the firing of individual receptors or combinations of different kinds of receptors. Some molecules, such as carbon dioxide, have a shape that will not stimulate receptors in the olfactory epithelium, and they are therefore odorless.

Many animals have a better sense of smell than humans. Dogs, for instance, are capable of detecting odors 1,000 times weaker than would be necessary for detection by a human nose. The sense of smell helps animals recognize objects, locations, and food. In many animals it is especially important for sexual communication. Sexually active substances, called **pheromones,** may be secreted by an animal and carried downwind where their reception in the olfactory epithelium of another animal arouses sexual interest. For instance, when dogs in heat secrete pheromones, they can attract male dogs that are downwind even at a distance of one or two miles. But what about human beings? Do we use our sense of smell for sexual identification? Recent discoveries in this area have led to an increased interest in the olfactory sense and to some further, surprising discoveries both of a sexual and nonsexual nature.

In 1977 Michael Russell reported a study he had conducted at San Francisco State University. A colleague of Russell's named Genevieve was gathering information about the onset of different women's menstrual cycles, and after several months she noticed something peculiar. The menstrual cycles of women with whom she had personal contact appeared to alter so that they became more and more like Genevieve's cycle in terms of when they began and ended. Genevieve's cycle seemed to be dominating the cycles of the other women. Russell wondered if olfaction could be responsible. Since some of the most potent scent glands in human beings are on the underarms, Russell had Genevieve wear cotton pads under her arms for several days in order to collect the perspiration. Then he ran an experiment in which volunteer women had a substance painted on their upper lip three times a week for four months. Half the applicants received alcohol. The other half received a combination of alcohol and Genevieve's underarm perspiration. The menstrual cycles of the first group did not change, and their cycle starting dates averaged about 9.3 days apart. Incredibly, the women receiving "eau de Genevieve" showed a startling change; within four months their menstrual cycles were all only 3.4 days apart. Apparently some substance secreted by Genevieve was influencing the menstrual cycles of the other women, and it was obviously happening through the olfactory sense ("Olfactory Synchrony," 1977). Why there should be such a secretion and what value it may have is not known. Russell suspects that the mystery may have something to do with estrogen, a female hormone.

There may be other odors given off by humans that can affect other humans. An experiment done by researchers at Brooklyn College is intriguing. It has been known for some time that among mice, the odor of a male's urine can bring out aggression in other males. But because mice are so little and they're always running around, it's terribly difficult to collect a decent amount of mouse urine. So, out of frustration the researchers at Brooklyn College decided to use urine from human males. They found that when they painted a mouse with urine from a human male and set it loose among other mice, the males would become aggressive. Urine from human women, boys or girls, had no effect (Hopson, 1979).

Another scent study was conducted at the Hatfield Polytechnic Institute in Hertfordshire, in which British psychology students were asked to assess the leadership of six candidates running for student body secretary. Researcher J. J. Cowley and his co-workers had the students wear surgical masks under the pretense of hiding their facial expressions when they reviewed the different candidates. Actually, the surgical masks contained three different scents. One group of masks was saturated with vaginal acids from human females, the second group was saturated with boar scent from wild pigs, and the third group was saturated with men's perspiration. Those wearing the boar-tainted masks were used as a control group. The men students' judgments were unaffected, but among the women students there were obvious differences. Women wearing masks containing female scent approved of the more shy and retiring candidates and disliked the assertive candidates, while women wearing the masks with the male scent preferred the assertive candidates over the retiring candidates. Women in the control group showed no particular preference for either kind of candidate (Hopson, 1979). This study indicates that olfaction may affect emotion and judgment, even though the process may be subliminal.

There is also an interesting relationship between scent and memory. Researchers Trygg Engen and Bruce Ross demonstrated that memory for odors is very different from memory for sights or sounds. Subjects who were shown a photograph were able after short periods of time to pick it out from among photographs they had not seen with almost 100 percent accuracy. But after three months the accuracy level fell to only about 50 percent of the time. With smells, the record is different. Subjects can remember smells to which they have been exposed with about 80 percent accuracy over short periods. However, the accuracy levels do not change even after a year. Another finding of the study was that individuals may have a very good memory for smells, but they have a very hard time remembering the name of a particular smell. The implication is that odor

OLFACTORY EPITHELIUM
Nasal membranes containing receptor cells sensitive to odors.

PHEROMONES
Sexually active substances that, when secreted, attract receptive organisms via olfactory perception.

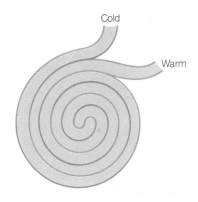

Cold

Warm

Figure 3.23 *A subject placing a hand on top of these concentric pipes, which contain cold and warm water, will report a strong sensation of heat.*

recognition may occur at a level in the brain that is preverbal, a more primitive, noncognitive level.

Many neuroscientists believe that olfaction may be closely tied to emotion in ways that are not yet understood. Their belief rests on the fact that many nerve fibers leaving the olfactory epithelium detour through the limbic system before traveling to other locations. The limbic system, as you'll recall, is a center of emotionality. Perhaps during the next decade some of the more subtle effects of smell will come to be understood.

Touch

There are many senses of touch. Different sensory systems measure pressure, light touch, vibration, aching pain, sharp pain, cold, warmth, and heat. In addition, there are complex interactions among the touch receptors. Although some receptors are specifically organized to respond to hot, simultaneous stimulation of cold and warm receptors will also produce the sensation of hot (see Figure 3.23).

Touch receptors on the skin are not evenly distributed. For example, the lips and the fingertips are far more sensitive than the back. If someone places two sharp pencils side by side, holding them so that their tips are only about a millimeter apart, and then touches them to your fingertip while your eyes are closed, you will find it easy to tell whether you're being touched with one point or two. This two-point discrimination is simple on the fingertip because of the high concentration of touch receptors there. On the back, however, where there is a lower concentration of touch receptors, pencil points sometimes have to be placed as far as 2½ inches apart before the person being touched can tell whether one or two points are being used.

Like the sense of smell, the sense of touch may also hold some interesting surprises. It may have a direct effect on emotions and judgments in some very subtle ways. One experimenter demonstrated such a possibility in some conditions by having a librarian lightly touch individuals on the hand as she returned their library cards and in other conditions having her refrain from touching the subjects. The librarian said the same thing and maintained the same expression whether or not she touched the individual checking out the book. As the people who had checked out books were leaving the library they were stopped and asked by the researcher to rate the library in terms of how pleasurable they found it. A significant number of the individuals who had been lightly touched rated the library as more enjoyable, although the majority of those who had been touched were unaware that the touching had occurred ("Nova," 1980).

Kinesthetic and Equilibratory Senses

You may always have considered vision, hearing, smell, taste, and touch to be "the senses," but there are other senses that in many ways are very important. The kinesthetic sense is one of these. **Kinesthesis** is the sense that informs us of the position of our body and limbs at any given time. From the feedback we receive when we move or reach for objects, we learn to interpret the weight and pressure on our muscles and joints and to use this information to ascertain our body's orientation in space.

The kinesthetic sense can be altered to some degree, and an interesting experiment demonstrates this. If you put on a pair of prism goggles that displaced everything 15 degrees to the right, at first it would be very difficult to function. If an object was directly in front of you, you would reach for it only to find your hand 15 degrees right of where it should be, since the object would have appeared to you to be 15 degrees to the right of its actual position. If you kept the goggles on and continued to reach for the object until your hand finally located it, and you did this many times, pretty soon your kinesthetic sense would become adjusted to the 15-degree displacement. After that you would have no trouble reaching for objects even if you continued to wear the goggles that displaced everything 15 degrees to the right. But if you took off the goggles the world would immediately become a strange place again. There you would be with your goggles off and you would think everything was normal. You'd see an object directly in front and you'd reach for it, relying on your kinesthetic sense to tell you where to move your hand. Amazingly, your hand would shoot off to the *left*, 15 degrees from where it should be. Again, a period of adjustment would be required until you learned kinesthetically to position your arms in space. In one fascinating experiment, it was demonstrated that the kinesthetic sense could be tricked by producing certain kinds of vibrations in the wrist tendons. Subjects in the experiment were amazed because the vibrations caused them to experience impossible limb positions or the sense of having multiple forearms (Craske, 1977).

The **equilibratory sense** is the sense of balance. It tells you the direction in which the force of gravity is operating. The equilibratory sense arises from the functioning of the inner ear where the **semicircular canals** and **vestibular sacs** are located. The three semicircular canals are roughly perpendicular to each other and lie on three planes so that body rotation can be monitored in all three directions (see Figure 3.22). When cilia within the canals are displaced by moving fluid, you know that you have changed position in relation to the field of gravity. In this way you can sense that you are lying down or standing up at any given moment, even with your eyes shut. If the fluid is disturbed to a great degree it's difficult to maintain balance. If you ever got on a wound-up swing as a child and spun around and around, you'll recall what it was like to finally step off and find it absolutely impossible to maintain your balance. The fluid in the semicircular canals continued to move, and it wasn't until the fluid became still again that you regained your orientation. Similarly, diseases or injury to the inner ear can cause an immediate loss of balance.

Magnetic Senses

The study of human sensation is ongoing, and there may be more surprises in store. Recently, bacteria and birds have been found to have a magnetic sense, a sense that may also exist in humans. A magnetic sense is a sense of direction in response to the magnetic field of the earth. When the swallows return every year to the mission in San Juan Capistrano, they are responding to magnetism (Presti & Pettigrew, 1980).

Researchers have wondered for years exactly how homing pigeons are able to home and how other birds are able to find distant migratory locations at different times of the year. Now researchers David Presti and

KINESTHESIS
An inclusive term for the muscle, tendon, and joint senses that yield information about the position and movement of various parts of the body.

EQUILIBRATORY SENSE
The sense that keeps an organism in proper balance.

SEMICIRCULAR CANALS
Three small liquid-filled canals located in the inner ear containing receptors sensitive to changes in orientation.

VESTIBULAR SACS
Two baglike structures at the base of the semicircular canals containing receptors for the sense of balance.

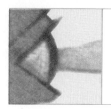

EXTRASENSORY PERCEPTION

We have words describing extra senses or powers: *clairvoyance,* the ability to sense events at a distance unhindered by normal physical barriers. *Telepathy,* sending thought messages from one person to another. *Precognition,* seeing the future before it happens. *Psychokinesis,* moving solid objects with pure mind power. Although we have words for these senses and powers, does anyone really have any of these faculties? How can we tell? The only way, of course, is to conduct very carefully controlled experiments examining the different powers and senses that individuals claim to possess.

Most researchers feel that no *extrasensory* perception has ever been demonstrated under carefully controlled conditions in a manner that could not be explained as chance. Nonetheless, a number of cases have been intriguing. These positive findings may confirm the existence of a weak, but real, phenomenon that is difficult to demonstrate. On the other hand, they may simply confirm that scientists are among the easiest people to fool, especially if an expert magician tries to fool them. People can make a lot of money by claiming they have certain powers of prediction, and it's difficult, even under what seem to be controlled conditions, to uncover the gimmick they are using to create the illusion of unusual powers.

These days most scientists, when confronted with discussions of extrasensory perception, reincarnation, UFOs, the Bermuda triangle, or Jeanne Dixon, just throw up their hands in disgust and refuse to talk about it. But this is a poor attitude because any strange or claimed phenomenon probably merits investigation. With this in mind a committee has been formed to investigate unusual phenomena, including extrasensory perception. Among its over 40 members are B. F. Skinner, Carl Sagan, and a magician, the Great Randi. Randi's there to help show up the tricksters.

Uri Geller was one such trickster. Geller claimed to have a number of extraordinary powers, and he convinced Edgar Mitchell, a scientist and one of the astronauts who walked on the moon, that his powers were real. Mitchell accompanied Geller on a number of talk shows asserting that Geller's powers were genuine. Geller claimed to be able to bend nails and spoons with the power of his mind, and to be able to start watches all over the country whenever he desired, even when the watches were broken. However, without fail, the Great Randi was able to duplicate every one of Geller's tricks. Geller had no real powers. Randi describes the tricks Geller used to fool the scientists in his book *The Magic of Uri Geller.*

More recently, Randi investigated a gentleman who claimed to have the power of psychokinesis. The man stated that he could turn the pages of a phone book placed on a table by kneeling down to eye level with the table and concentrating. The pages certainly did begin to turn, and viewers were amazed. Randi wasn't. He surrounded the book with styrofoam balls and asked the fellow to try again. This time the power mysteriously failed him. Randi explained that the "psychokinesis" in this case was really a fine jet of air expelled between the lips in pulses in a very subtle way that required some practice. Had the man tried to turn the pages the second time he would have blown the styrofoam balls all over the place and his trick would have been obvious (Rucker, 1981).

Still, even the most fantastic claims merit examination. And some researchers have found pretty ingenious ways to investigate them. For instance, one researcher placed $5,000 in a sealed box, along with a slip of paper on which he had written a name of his own choosing, first, middle, and last. He invited any psychic who makes a living by such "powers" simply to state the name on the slip of paper in the box and to collect the $5,000. To date—no takers.

Uri Geller "bends a spoon" with his "mind power."

John D. Pettigrew have discovered magnetic material in the joints of birds, bees, and other animals. This magnetic material, a kind of lodestone, is apparently attracted to positions within the muscle near joints. The magnetic material is pulled by the earth's magnetic field, just as a magnetic needle on a compass is pulled toward the north or south. This pull exerts a very fine pressure on the muscles, making them sensitive to the magnetic field. This magnetic muscular sense is especially prominent among homing pigeons and migratory white-crowned sparrows, which have been found to have a high degree of magnetic material in their heads and necks. These birds were dissected with glass knives in order to prevent contamination by metallic knives. The magnetism associated with the birds' heads seems to be spread over the entire skull. The spindle fibers of the muscles, where the lodestone resides, are very sensitive to stretching. Changes in the magnetic field produce a torque effect in the magnets within the muscles, so that the bird actually feels the geomagnetic field on its muscles.

This magnetic sense may be quite widespread in the animal kingdom, and it has also been discovered in common bacteria (Thomsen, 1980). Research is under way to investigate the possibility of a magnetic sense in human beings. Presti and Pettigrew point out an interesting prospect in the use of the **divining rod.** Diviners, or as they are sometimes called, dowsers, are individuals who supposedly are able to find water by walking about with a divining rod. The divining rod is a three-pronged object. The single prong on one side is pointed outward as though it were pointing in a direction, and the other two prongs are held in a very tight flex. Any slight change in the muscle tension of the diviner will cause the extended prong to point downward. Water will supposedly be found under the tip. Of course, modern scientists consider this to be nothing more than superstition since science knows of no way in which an individual could succeed in finding water by such a method. But Presti and Pettigrew point out that the geomagnetic field changes considerably in the presence of underground water. They wonder whether, with the rod held under such tension, very slight changes in the geomagnetic field could affect minute amounts of lodestone within spindle fibers in the muscles, thereby causing the diviner's rod to dip. There are a lot of people who swear by divining rods, but then again, there are a lot of people who swear by rain dances. But suppose, just suppose. . . .

DIVINING ROD
A forked branch or stick that allegedly indicates subterranean water or minerals by bending downward when held over the source; also called a *dowsing rod.*

Summary

- Our way of organizing the world and responding to it depends a great deal on the way in which our senses filter the stimuli and information around us. We come to know our world primarily through our senses, and what we sense often affects our behavior.
- The amount of energy required to create a noticeable sensation is called the absolute threshold. The minimum amount of energy difference necessary before a change in stimulation can be detected is known as the difference threshold.
- Although there are many parallels between the camera and the eye, the two are actually more different than alike.
- The retina is composed of three layers, containing the ganglion cells, the bipolar cells, and the photoreceptors, called rods and cones.

- In normal daylight vision the most sensitive portion of the eye is the fovea.
- One portion of the peripheral retina contains no photoreceptors because it is here that the optic nerve passes through the retina on its way to the brain. This area is known as the blind spot.
- Different neural receptors are stimulated by different wavelengths within the visible light range. The rods are sensitive to all light except red. The cones are specialized, some responding to red, some to green, and some to blue wavelengths.
- The fovea is made up exclusively of cones. For this reason the fovea is not sensitive to extremely dim illumination.
- Visual neurons function differently from most other neurons. Visual neurons rely on graded potentials, and when stimulated become hyperpolarized and secrete less neurotransmitter.
- After 30 or 40 minutes in the dark the rods reach their full sensitivity, a stage called dark adaptation.
- All colors in the spectrum can be produced from three primary colors, red, green, and blue. Using beams of light, all colors can be created by additive mixing (as opposed to subtractive mixing, the process by which pigments are combined).
- There are several theories that attempt to explain color vision. Among these are the Young-Helmholtz theory, the Hering opponent-process theory, and Land's retinex theory. To date no one theory has adequately explained all of the aspects of color vision.
- Aftereffects differ from afterimages. Aftereffects transfer from one eye to the other.
- There are many detectors in the visual system aside from color. Among them are motion detectors and spatial frequency detectors.
- While the eyes are sensitive to a limited range of the electromagnetic spectrum, the ears are sensitive to a limited range of frequencies caused by the compression and rarefaction of air.
- The pitch of a sound is determined by the frequency of the sound wave, and the loudness of a sound is determined by the amplitude of the sound wave.
- Three theories of hearing have been proposed to explain the range of the human auditory system. These are the place theory, the frequency theory, and the volley theory.
- Bioengineers are engaged in producing an artificial ear. Platinum implants replace damaged cilia and stimulate the auditory nerve by generating small electric shocks in response to different frequencies.
- Taste is a fairly limited sense. Taste buds respond to sweet, sour, salt, and bitter.
- Smell is one of the oldest senses. The sense of smell works according to the lock and key principle, in which molecules of a particular shape fit into receptors that are responsive to them, allowing a particular odor to be perceived.
- In many animals the olfactory sense is especially important for sexual communication. Olfaction may also affect emotion and judgment. Olfactory memories are long-lasting and resistant to change.
- There are many senses of touch. Different systems measure pressure, light touch, vibration, aching pain, sharp pain, cold, warmth, and heat.
- The kinesthetic sense informs us of the position of our body and limbs at any given time.

- The equilibratory sense helps us keep our balance.
- A magnetic sense has been discovered in some animals and may exist in human beings.
- Most researchers feel that no extrasensory perception has ever been demonstrated in a manner that could not be explained as chance.

EPILOGUE: THE READY ROOM

Psychologists who study sensation generally focus on the structure and function of human sensory systems. From this study they often gain insights that can be applied to the everyday world. The following is an account of how one psychologist used his knowledge of sensation to help the Allied cause in World War II.

In 1940 Hitler launched his Luftwaffe against the British coast. Hitler had one goal in mind, to totally destroy the Royal Air Force and gain complete command over the English Channel in preparation for Operation Sea Lion, the invasion of Britain. On the other side of the channel facing this aerial onslaught were a few Royal Air Force pilots manning fighter planes. Seriously outnumbered, they took off at all hours of the night to meet the oncoming enemy. Many of them never returned.

Since the pilots had to rush to their planes at a moment's notice in the predawn light, they had to keep their eyes dark adapted. They were never sure when they would be called into the air, and so they had to avoid light from about sunset on, waiting in pitch-black rooms. They couldn't play cards, read books, or even see each other's faces. They simply waited, hour after hour in complete darkness, until a call came to take to the air. The loneliness and fear in those ready rooms must have been terrible. Fear has a way of making hours pass very slowly.

In the United States a psychologist named Walter R. Miles, who was a renowned researcher in sensory systems, heard about the plight of the British pilots. Miles understood that the fighter pilots had to maintain dark adaptation, but he also realized that it was absolutely unnecessary for them to sit in the dark. Miles knew that the rod photoreceptors, those required for night vision, were not sensitive to the red end of the spectrum, and that red light could therefore not bleach the rods. He informed the Royal Air Force of this fact, and red lights were placed in the fighter pilots' ready rooms. Thereafter, pilots waiting for their flights were able to see each other's faces as they played cards or read books. They could pass the time sharing each other's company (Miller, 1980).

Ever since that time in 1940 it has been the practice of the military to use red light in submarines at night in case the ship has to surface, or in aircraft at night so that the pilots can see when they look out into the dark. Work can go on because the red-sensitive cones are stimulated by the red light, and dark adaptation is maintained because the rods don't react to the light.

Suggestions for Further Reading

1. Frisby, J. P. *Seeing.* Oxford, England: Oxford University Press, 1980.
2. Goldstein, E. B. *Sensation and perception.* Belmont, California: Wadsworth, 1980.
3. Ludel, J. *Introduction to sensory processes.* San Francisco: W. H. Freeman, 1978.
4. McBurney, D., & Collings, V. *Introduction to sensation and perception.* Englewood Cliffs, New Jersey: Prentice-Hall, 1977.

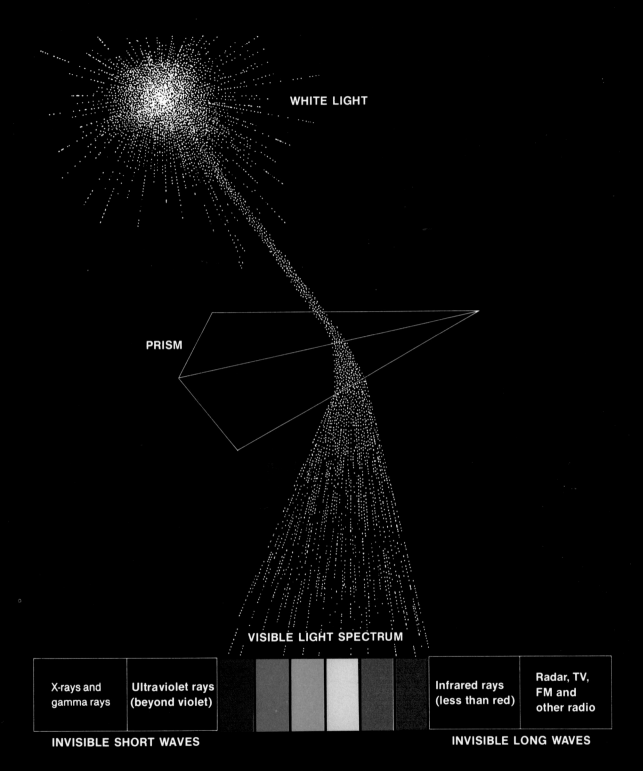

WHITE LIGHT

PRISM

VISIBLE LIGHT SPECTRUM

| X-rays and gamma rays | Ultraviolet rays (beyond violet) | | | | | | Infrared rays (less than red) | Radar, TV, FM and other radio |

INVISIBLE SHORT WAVES

INVISIBLE LONG WAVES

When a white light is directed through a prism,
the visible light spectrum results.

Figure 3.5   The electromagnetic spectrum.

Figure 3.7 Additive mixing—combining beams of light—can create all possible colors, because beams of light generate their own color. When equal intensities of red, green, and blue are combined, they produce white.

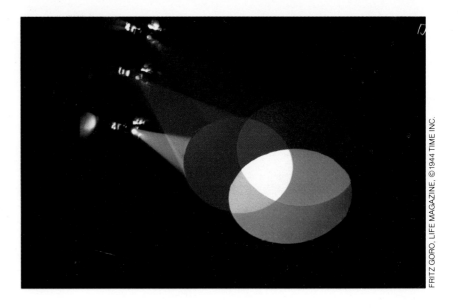

Figure 3.8 To experience negative after-image, stare at the yellow circle for about a minute. Then glance at a white sheet of paper or a white wall and blink your eyes a few times. A blue circle should appear.

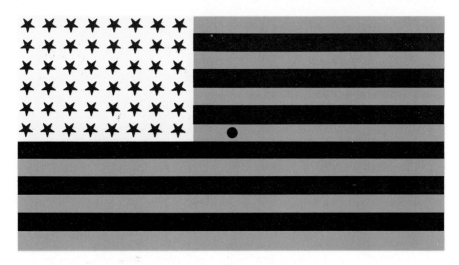

Figure 3.9 Another example of negative afterimage. Look at the dot in the middle of the flag for 30 seconds or more. Then look at the dot in the white space below. An American flag in its usual colors should appear.

ARE YOU COLOR BLIND?

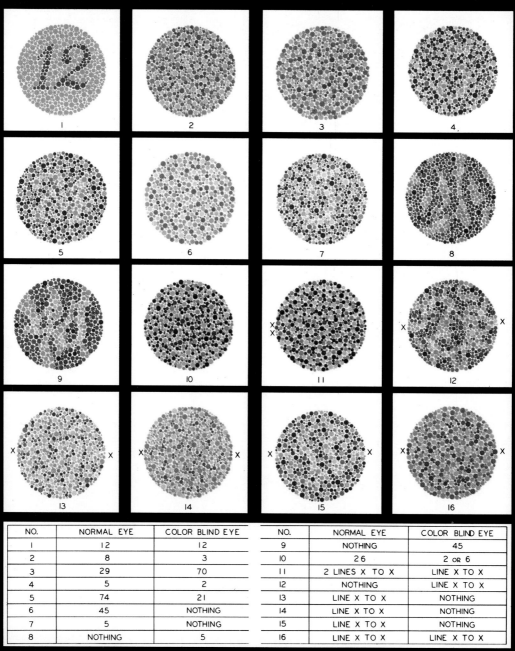

NO.	NORMAL EYE	COLOR BLIND EYE	NO.	NORMAL EYE	COLOR BLIND EYE
1	12	12	9	NOTHING	45
2	8	3	10	26	2 OR 6
3	29	70	11	2 LINES X TO X	LINE X TO X
4	5	2	12	NOTHING	LINE X TO X
5	74	21	13	LINE X TO X	NOTHING
6	45	NOTHING	14	LINE X TO X	NOTHING
7	5	NOTHING	15	LINE X TO X	NOTHING
8	NOTHING	5	16	LINE X TO X	LINE X TO X

Figure 3.10   A test for color blindness.

CONTENTS

CHAPTER 4

Perception

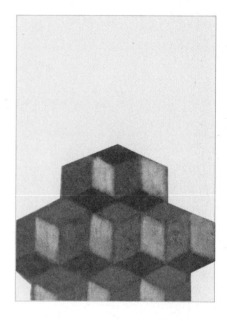

You are driving through the dense rain forest of the Congo river valley. You are in a jeep with a native pygmy named Kenge and anthropologist Colin Turnbull. You and Turnbull have been collecting anthropological data, and the native has offered to assist you. The pygmy has never ridden in a jeep before. He's having a good time. He and his tribe roam exclusively within the rain forest, and this will be the first time he's ventured beyond it. After a few hours of driving you reach the crest of a great hill where the rain forest ends. Beyond is the wide expanse of the African plain. Visibility is almost 70 miles. In the rain forest the foliage was so dense it was hard to see more than 100 yards.

Far away on the plain, in the direction you are traveling, is a herd of water buffalo. You point them out to Turnbull and Kenge. The pygmy laughs and says, "No, they're insects." Turnbull repeats that they're buffalo far away. Kenge tells you both to stop telling such stupid lies; he seems insulted. He continues to insist that the water buffalo are obviously insects. Since you are traveling toward the animals, it seems that the argument will be settled in short order. As the distance lessens, the buffalo seem to grow larger and larger until finally it's apparent that what you have been looking at is indeed a large herd of water buffalo.

The pygmy looks shocked and confused and frightened. He doesn't say any more and refuses to leave the jeep. It's then that you realize that he is totally unfamiliar with great vistas, since he's spent his life in the rain forest. His perception was different from yours because he never learned that objects appear to be very small when they are far away. Seeing the tiny buffalo, he assumed that they were close at hand and must be insects. On the plain, without a tree or some other measure, Kenge is totally unable to judge distance. Later that day, you show him Lake Edward, so large that its opposite shore can't be seen. Kenge can't comprehend this expanse of water, which seems to be a river without banks. Far out on the lake is a wooden boat filled with people. When you tell Kenge what it is, he's amazed. He thought it was a nearby piece of driftwood. It is too much; he wants to go back to the rain forest (Turnbull, 1961).

In this chapter we will examine the way in which you organize your senses in order to form perceptions of the world around you. Two important theories of perception will be presented and the merits of each will be discussed. Along the way you'll learn how moviemakers create special effects, how three-dimensional vision works, what illusions are, and how your biology helps you organize the complexities of your environment.

103

Why Psychologists Study Perception

Perception refers to the way in which we interpret messages from our senses. By understanding perception, we can better understand how people are organized to deal with their environment and, in turn, why they behave as they do. First we must distinguish between sensation and perception. Look at Figure 4.1. You will see a spiral curving downward until it reaches the apex. If this were a staircase and you began at the top, you would eventually reach the bottom by walking round and round. At least that's what your brain tells you. But put your finger at any point on the curves of the design and begin to move down the spiral staircase with your fingertip, and see how far you get! Trace very carefully. As you can see, there's no spiral at all, only concentric circles, one inside the other.

This design is known as Fraser's spiral. The spiral that you see is an **illusion;** it doesn't exist. Your senses—your eyes—have told you the truth, that there is no spiral. Your brain, however, has interpreted what it sensed based on some organization, and you *perceived* a spiral. The illusion is so strong that people tracing the spiral sometimes begin to move inward from one circle to the next, but as long as you trace carefully you'll always come back to your starting point. This example clearly shows the difference between sensation and perception. Sensation occurs when the sense organs are stimulated; perception is an active interpretation of sensory information.

Theories of Perception

Psychologists have puzzled over perceptual problems for decades, but in the last few years there has been an explosion of perceptual research. This has been due in part to the development of new technology. Such tools as

Figure 4.1 *Fraser's spiral*

computer-controlled equipment, the PET scan, and modern electronic devices for examining the senses have opened up a number of new possibilities. Among the many theories of visual perception the two that have received the most attention are the **image and cue theory** and the **direct-perception theory.** Both of these theories attempt to explain our ability to make perceptual sense out of the formidable amount of sensation that we receive.

If you think about it, just understanding the information necessary to negotiate traffic is an impressive accomplishment. How can you make sense of such a complex world? How can you tell whether something is far away or nearby, whether it's large or small, whether it's moving, or whether you're moving? How do you know when you are about to step off a ledge or walk into a wall? Why are you able to extend your hand just the right distance to grasp something that is directly in front of you? You will probably respond that the reason you can do all these things is that you can see. If you really think about it, though, you will realize that seeing (sensing) isn't enough. Not only must you be able to see things, you must also understand what you see—you must perceive. The question is, How do you go about doing this? Both the image and cue theory and the direct-perception theory attempt to answer this question.

IMAGE AND CUE THEORY

When you're sitting in a room and you're looking at things, you can tell how far away they are or how close they are with a fair degree of accuracy. This is called **depth perception.**

Monocular Cues   You may have heard that depth perception is a function of using both eyes and that people who are blind in one eye lose their depth perception. But is this true? Close one eye and look around the room. It may seem that your depth perception is a little impaired, but you can still tell which objects are closest and which are farthest away without much difficulty. Even if you went to a neighbor's house with a patch over one eye and sat in a room you've never been in before, you could still judge whether a lamp was closer than a particular chair, the chair was closer than a particular couch, the couch was closer than a particular wall, and the trees were outside the house. You'd still have depth perception.

Researchers working in the last century and early in this century wondered how it was possible to make three-dimensional sense out of an image that must be two-dimensional when it strikes the retina. Because of the work of such early researchers as Berkeley, Helmholtz, Wundt, and Boring, interest in this question began to grow. The basic research that has ensued has expanded our knowledge of the brain's organization. It has also given us information that has been applied in many interesting ways, from architecture to special effects in film. Researchers working in this area have developed what is known as the image and cue model, or image and cue theory of perception. They believe that visual perception is learned. According to their theory, the only way the brain can make sense of a two-dimensional retinal image is through learning and experience. Certain cues come to mean certain things, and by recognizing these cues we come to understand our immediate environment.

Consider the plight of special-effects expert Willis H. O'Brien. In 1930 film producers came to him with an interesting plot for a movie. An expedi-

MONOCULAR CUES
Cues seen in two dimensions that give
rise to a perception of depth. These cues
include an object's height on a plane,
linear perspective, overlap, relative size,
gradient of texture, aerial perspective,
and relative motion.

HEIGHT ON A PLANE
A monocular depth cue. Objects higher
on a plane are perceived as being farther
away.

LINEAR PERSPECTIVE
A monocular depth cue. Parallel lines
appear to converge in the distance.

OVERLAP
A monocular depth cue. Objects that are
behind (overlapped by) other objects are
farther away.

RELATIVE SIZE
A monocular depth cue. Given objects
of identical size, those that are closer appear larger than those that are distant.

tion would be made to a place called Skull Island in order to capture a huge ape named King Kong and to bring him back to New York, where Kong would escape, kidnap a woman, and climb the Empire State Building, there to be killed by fighter planes. Believe it or not, the producers described this as essentially a love story, with the 50-foot-tall ape in love with the blonde heroine. They said that they would supply the actors. All they wanted from O'Brien was a 50-foot ape, various extinct dinosaurs, and Skull Island—all on film. A lesser man might have run screaming from the room, but O'Brien sat back and wondered. How could you make a film like *King Kong* when no such gorilla or island existed and fool the audience into perceiving the situation as real? The only way, of course, was to manipulate the cues that people use in their day-to-day lives to gauge such things as size, distance, and motion. O'Brien knew that image and cue theorists had been trying to determine exactly which cues in the two-dimensional image formed on the retina give rise to depth perception. He knew that quite a number of cues had been isolated. The more O'Brien thought about it, the more it seemed that it might be possible to make people believe in the reality of King Kong.

Some of the cues O'Brien made use of will probably be familiar to you even though you may not know their names. Whether you are conscious of it or not, you've used them all of your life in order to judge depth (see Table 4.1).

The first of these **monocular cues, height on a plane,** indicates that objects that from our point of view are higher on a plane are farther away than objects lower on the plane. Inside a room, objects that are closer to you will always appear to be lower on the plane.

The second depth cue, **linear perspective,** refers to the fact that parallel lines appear to converge on the horizon. Linear perspective is one of the earliest tricks that any artist learns in order to make a two-dimensional canvas appear three-dimensional. If you look at the railroad tracks in Figure 4.2 you can see the effect of linear perspective and the depth it appears to create on a flat page.

Overlap is another important cue. We know that if one object appears to overlap another, the object that is overlapped is behind the first object and therefore must be farther away (see Figure 4.3). **Relative size** is a factor in depth perception when we know how large particular objects are. We can then judge their distance by how large they appear relative to each other. If you look overhead and see two jetliners that you know are the same size,

Table 4.1   Monocular depth cues (cues that can be perceived with only one eye).

CUE	LEARNED MEANING
Height on a plane	Objects higher on a plane are farther away.
Linear perspective	Parallel lines appear to converge in the distance and to diverge nearby.
Overlap	Overlapped objects are farther away.
Relative size	Comparing objects of known size reveals which is closer (closer objects appear larger).
Gradient of texture	Objects that are closer have greater detail.
Aerial perspective	Closer objects are bright and sharp. Distant objects are pastel and hazy.
Relative motion	When moving from side to side, nearby objects appear to move more than distant objects.

Figure 4.2 *An example of linear perspective: parallel lines converging at the horizon*

Figure 4.3 *Objects that are overlapped appear farther away than objects that are not.*

and one appears to be much larger than the other, you will immediately assume, because of your knowledge of relative size, that the smaller jetliner is higher in altitude and farther away.

Gradient of texture has to do with differences in detail. Look around you. Regardless of the objects you focus on, you'll be able to see more detail in those that are closer and less detail in those that are distant. If you're sitting on a huge lawn, you see the grass that's close to you as individual blades, but on the horizon you see a smooth, uninterrupted green. At intermediate distances, you can't see individual blades of grass, but the green may appear to be somewhat patchy rather than uniform in color.

If you're out-of-doors and viewing objects over a considerable distance, **aerial perspective** lends a sense of depth because, as distance increases, dust and haze in the air tend to reduce clarity. Consequently, the colors and outlines of distant objects appear pastel, while nearby objects appear sharp and bright. On very clear days, things at a distance may stand out so sharply that they appear to have moved closer.

O'Brien was unable to use the last depth cue, **relative motion,** because it will not work with a two-dimensional image such as a motion picture screen. For relative motion to make an impression, a three-dimensional scene is necessary. The idea of relative motion is simple. If you move your head from side to side, you'll immediately notice that nearby objects seem to move a great distance while distant objects hardly seem to move at all.

Before we find out how these cues were exploited in making *King Kong*, review the three drawings in Figure 4.4 and see whether you could use the cues they contain in order to land an airplane. It should be possible to make a safe landing even if you use only one eye. In the topmost photograph you can see the runway. But should you touch down yet? The runway is higher on the plane than the trees; this means that the trees are closer to you than the runway and that you have not yet passed them. The linear perspective and texture gradient in the first picture also indicate that it's too early to touch down. Aerial haze offers another hint. At the very bottom, and a little bit to the left, you can see that one tree is overlapping another tree. This means that the first tree is closer. You can also use your knowledge of relative size to judge which trees are closer and which are farther away. If you touch down in frame *A*, you'll go right into the trees.

In frame *B*, you're much closer to the runway, as indicated by the texture gradient. You can distinguish individual landing lights and the stripes on the runway. You're past the trees now; they no longer appear between you and the aircraft. Nonetheless, the feature nearest to you, that is, lowest on the plane and clearest in terms of gradient texture, is the ground, not the runway. So it's still too soon to touch down.

In frame *C*, you know it's time to touch down. The runway is at the very bottom of the view, that is, low on the plane, and it's dead center in the picture. Your angle, texture gradient, and especially linear perspective tell you that you're making a proper approach. In fact, most pilots do not consider lining up and knowing when the airplane is over the runway a difficult part of their job. The problem is judging the right altitude for touchdown. This takes practice. In frame *C*, you can see the stripes within the squares on the runway. Experienced pilots know that when these stripes are a particular size, they are just the right height from the runway for touchdown. If the stripes appear too small, the airplane is too high.

Knowing how close the runway should be for the wheels to touch down

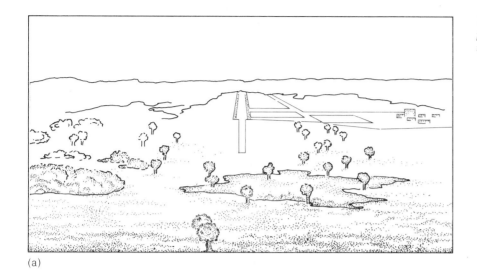
(a)

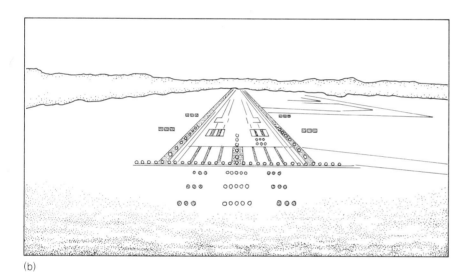
(b)

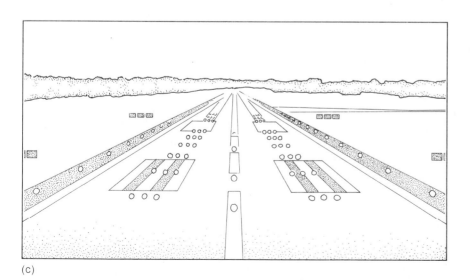
(c)

Figure 4.4 *Although these pictures are perfectly flat (two-dimensional), they contain many three-dimensional cues.*

was a disadvantage for pilots learning to fly the first jumbo jets. They had gained their experience on standard-sized jets, and they could not get used to being 60 feet off the ground in the pilot's seat when the wheels of the jumbo touched down. Many pilots on training flights got too close to the runway, hitting the ground so hard that they knocked the nose wheel of the jet up into the fuselage. Passengers don't like it when pilots do things like that. Consequently, pilots of jumbo jets had to make many practice landings to relearn the perceptual cues that enabled them to touch down at the appropriate height. As you learned in examining the three drawings in Figure 4.4, a two-dimensional image is all that's needed to land an airplane. For this reason, a person who lost sight in one eye would still have depth perception and be able to fly an airplane. Now that you have your feet back on the ground, however, how are you going to make King Kong believable?

O'Brien took his knowledge of pictorial depth cues and proceeded to build a model of King Kong which stood about 2½ feet high. He then built models of Skull Island, dinosaurs, and familiar objects such as trees. In the famous scene in which King Kong first grabs actress Fay Wray, he appears to be his full 50 feet in height. Look at Figure 4.5 and identify the cues O'Brien relied on. Relative size is one. We know how tall the woman should

Figure 4.5 *King Kong holding Fay Wray. What cues did O'Brien make use of to create the impression of great size?*

be, and King Kong towers above her. Furthermore, his hand overlaps her, which means that his hand must be closer to us than she is, which adds to the illusion of size. O'Brien used overlap effectively in many instances. In another scene King Kong is again standing on a cliff, and in a corner of the screen we see very small birds (made from India-ink sketches) flying by. The birds appear to be quite far away because of their small size, but as they pass King Kong they fly *in front of him*. This overlap gives the impression of a very large ape some distance away. Using a small model and the appropriate cues, O'Brien was able to trick the audience into believing King Kong to be much larger than he actually was.

All of these examples depend on our experience with different cues in the environment. This is the essence of the image and cue theory. A two-dimensional image on the retina is understood as a three-dimensional perception because of your learning and experience with objects and cues in the world around you.

The Moon Illusion   Have you ever looked at the full moon when it's just coming over the horizon? It looks huge. But the same full moon doesn't appear to be so large once it's high in the sky. Have you ever wondered why this is so?

In 1962, in a series of classic experiments, Kaufman and Rock demonstrated that the moon illusion was due to learned cues, particularly relative size (Kaufman & Rock, 1962). They observed that when the moon is directly overhead it's difficult to judge how large it is. Among the cues for depth perception that you've learned, consider whether any of them would help you determine the size of an object high in the sky. Linear perspective is of no use. Relative size doesn't help much, either, because there is no basis of comparison. Overlap is ineffectual because nothing appears between you and the moon. There is no texture-gradient cue, since nothing between you and the moon can show a change in detail. Aerial perspective may give you some clue; if the moon looks fairly hazy, you may realize that it's more than 20 or 30 miles away! Height on the plane is no help because there is no plane in your line of sight to the moon. There's simply darkness, pinpoints of light which are the stars, and the round moon.

The situation is different when the moon is first rising. Kaufman and Rock noticed that the moon illusion was especially pronounced if a large number of objects separated the observer and the rising moon. For instance, if the moon is rising behind the lights and buildings of a city, the depth cues that have been learned have an immediate effect. One of the most powerful is overlap. The fact that the city is in *front* of the moon means that the moon is farther away. Another cue is relative size. By experience we know that buildings or hills and mountains are fairly large, and yet they are specks compared with the moon globe that is rising behind them. Height on the plane is also informative. Because the moon is highest on the plane that extends from you along the surface of the earth to the moon, it is obviously farther away than anything else on that plane. All of these cues together tell the viewer that the moon coming over the horizon is huge. Since we are not used to dealing with objects bigger than entire cities or the mountains that surround them, the illusion created when the moon rises above the horizon is one of awesome size. This perspective, as well as an appreciation of its true size—3,000 miles in diameter—is totally lost when the moon is seen directly overhead, without any cues to indicate size.

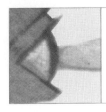

ATTENTION AND PERCEPTION

How we perceive a particular image depends on how we attend to and organize the cues within that image. The same image seen in different circumstances may appear to be totally different from our original perception of it. In the early 1900s Gustave Verbeek, a cartoonist working for the Sunday *New York Herald*, composed a comic strip made of six panels, the standard format of the time. Verbeek wanted to have a longer comic strip, but he couldn't obtain the space. Undaunted, he found an imaginative way of putting a 12-panel comic strip into six panels. Figure 4.6 shows his six-panel comic strip, entitled ''The Upside-Downs of Little Lady Lovekins and Old Man Muffaroo.'' In the first six panels Old Man Muffaroo has some serious problems with a swordfish. But the story doesn't end there. Six more panels can be created by turning the cartoon upside down! In the second half of the strip, a story emerges in which a Roc, a large mythical bird, captures Little

Lady Lovekins. Panel 5, which is also panel 8, affords an ideal example of how the switch was accomplished. In panel 5 you see the old man in the canoe with a large fish; next to them is an island topped by a couple of trees. When you reverse the panel, you see Lady Lovekins as a captive of the giant Roc. The information striking the retina was the same in both cases. But we attended to the different cues and adjusted our perception to match what we were told in the story—a clear example of how attention and perception can go hand in hand (Frisby, 1980). In the same way, you and I may share the same sensations and still have totally different perceptions.

In Verbeek's comic strip the narration served to focus your attention on certain aspects of the stimulus. This in turn influenced your perception of each panel. Similarly, advertisers use techniques to focus attention, and thereby affect your perception of what you see and hear. The following are

among the most effective techniques for attracting attention in television commercials:

1. *Sudden change.* You are looking at a printed page describing the merits of a certain car when suddenly the car bursts through the page at high speed. You immediately realize that you had been looking at a very large page mounted as a barrier for the car to drive through. The sudden change has attracted your attention.
2. *Novelty.* This is one of the most frequently used devices.
3. *Complexity.* Advertisers often show many scenes in a very brief time, creating the effect of complexity. Commercials using this device usually bombard you with rapid action before showing the product.
4. *Intensity.* Television ads often use higher volume and try to obtain as bright and colorful a picture as possible.
5. *Repetition.* The product name is repeated again and again while jingles

---

BINOCULAR VISION
Visual perception based on information obtained from the use of two retinas (both eyes) simultaneously. *See also* RETINAL DISPARITY.

PERCEPTUAL CONSTANCIES
The learned perception that an object remains the same in size, shape, and brightness even though the retina conveys a sensory message of a changing size, shape, brightness

Now that you've filmed King Kong, landed an airplane, and learned why the moon rising above the horizon is so large, you might expect to proceed to the direct-perception theory. As a prelude to examining the direct-perception theory, however, let's look at two important aspects of perception—**binocular vision** and **perceptual constancies.**

BINOCULAR VISION

All of the perceptual cues that we have discussed so far have been monocular cues. That is, they are cues that can be sensed with only one eye. As you may have gathered, you can perceive depth more accurately with two eyes than with one. According to image and cue theorists, this is because of additional cues called **binocular cues** which can be sensed by both eyes together but not by each eye individually. One such binocular cue is **convergence.** When you look at an object that is closer than approximately 25 feet, your eyes must converge on the object in order to perceive

In the canoe is an enormous fish that Lovekins and Muffaroo have caught.

Lovekins takes the fish on shore while Muffaroo pushes off in the canoe to see if he can catch another.

Unluckily he hooks a sword fish, and there is trouble right away. The old man fights bravely. The sword fish dives.

Then he comes up again, and this time he thrusts his sharp snout right through the bottom of the canoe. Muffaroo tries to get the sinking boat to the nearest shore.

Just as he reaches a small grassy point of land, another fish attacks him, lashing furiously with his tail.

The canoe sinks in the sea which has now become choppy, but Muffaroo jumps ashore, safe and sound, and starts back across the point to rejoin Lovekins.

are sung over and over. Within limits repetition attracts attention. These techniques also have application outside the world of advertising. How does the siren on a police car get your attention, and why does a police car have flashing lights instead of steady ones? These techniques will attract your attention in many circumstances.

Figure 4.6 *If you attend to the cues, you can read this story in two ways—an example of how attention and perception go hand in hand.*

it as a single object clearly in focus. Figure 4.7 gives an example of convergence. It's an easy thing to test for yourself. Look at a distant object, and while keeping that object clearly in focus, hold your finger in front of your face. As long as you are looking at the distant object you'll see two fingers with blurry outlines. Now look at your finger. You will see a single image clearly in focus. By converging your eyes upon your finger, you created tension on the muscles required for this kind of eye movement. Image and cue theorists argue that through your learning and experience you come to understand that a certain amount of muscular tension means that a particular object is a certain distance away. If you must make a very strong effort to converge or cross your eyes in order to look at a nearby object (such as a fly on the tip of your nose), the muscular feedback lets you know that the object must be very close.

Convergence is not a factor when you are looking at objects farther away than 25 feet. In this case the eyes do not converge. As perceptual psychologists say, they focus at infinity instead.

BINOCULAR CUES
Depth cues that arise only when both eyes are used. Examples include convergence and retinal disparity.

CONVERGENCE
A binocular depth cue. The eyes tend to turn toward each other in focusing on nearby objects, and tend to focus at infinity when viewing objects farther away.

RETINAL DISPARITY

A binocular depth cue. Because the eyes are set apart, objects closer than 25 feet are sensed on significantly different locations on the left and right retinas. At close distances retinal disparity, more than any other cue, gives a strong perception of depth.

HOLOGRAPHIC PHOTOGRAPHY

A method by which a picture can be created through the use of coherent light (light that is reflected in only one direction). Such a picture produces retinal disparity regardless of the viewing angle, and the part of the picture that is seen depends on the viewer's location. The result is an illusion of a real three-dimensional object suspended in space.

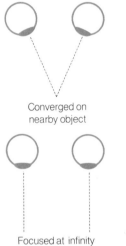

Converged on
nearby object

Focused at infinity

Figure 4.7 *When the eyes focus on a nearby object they converge. When they focus on a distant object they do not.*

Figure 4.8 *Viewing objects at a distance creates little retinal disparity, while viewing objects that are close causes considerable retinal disparity.*

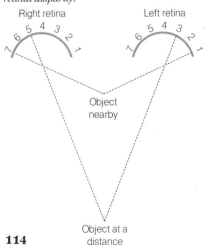

Another very powerful binocular cue is **retinal disparity.** Because the eyes are set a certain distance apart in the head, objects closer than 25 feet are sensed on significantly different locations on each retina. Figure 4.8 demonstrates this phenomenon. Retinal disparity is also easy for you to demonstrate. Simply hold the index finger of one hand close to your face and the index finger of the other farther away. Line them up. Now look at them with your left eye and then with your right eye, and then with your left again, and keep switching back and forth from one eye to the other. The near finger will seem to leap back and forth a considerable distance while the other finger will seem to move only slightly. As Figure 4.8 shows, an object directly in front of your nose is seen on the far right side of the right retina and on the far left side of the left retina, while an object that is far away is seen on almost the same place on both retinas. Another way of saying this is that objects that are extremely close create great retinal disparity while objects that are far away produce almost no disparity. At close distance retinal disparity, perhaps more than any other cue, gives you a strong perception of depth.

Beginning in the 1950s a number of films were made in 3D, or three dimensions. Of course, it's impossible to create real three-dimensional images on a flat two-dimensional screen. However, by using retinal disparity filmmakers were able to create 3D movies that were so realistic that the action sometimes seemed to be taking place right in the audience. Two copies of the movie were projected onto the screen at the same time—a red copy and a blue copy. But the two copies did not overlap exactly. A viewer looking at the movie with the naked eye would see a double image, one red, one blue. With the special glasses that were provided, however, in which one lens was red and one blue, the viewer saw only one film—each eye seeing the film separately. The blue film was seen through the red lens and the red through the blue. The illusion of depth was created by manipulating the double image: When the images were moved farther apart, greater retinal disparity was created and the objects on the screen would appear to be closer to the audience. Modern 3D movies make use of different polarized light, and don't require colored lenses in the glasses.

PERCEPTUAL CONSTANCIES

Mastering the cues in your environment and understanding their meaning is essential for survival. If you were to examine the world solely on the basis of the image projected on the retina, you'd quickly see that familiar objects would be constantly changing in size and shape depending on the angle from which they were viewed. Yet in spite of these constant alterations, produced by viewing objects from different distances and different angles, we still recognize familiar objects as familiar. This is one of the primary functions of perception. For example, when you look at your parked car as you are walking away from it your visual sensory system sends a message to your brain. First, the image of the car is projected onto the retina. If you continue looking at your car, the image projected onto the retina gets smaller and smaller as you move farther away. When this happens do you gasp in horror and cry out, "My car is shrinking!"? No, you aren't upset at all. Although the sensory image of your car is shrinking rapidly, you don't *perceive* that your car is changing size. Instead, you perceive that your car is becoming more distant. You know that the size

THE TELEVISION OF TOMORROW

A television picture doesn't look real. It's flat, or two-dimensional, and the light coming from the screen has a glow that isn't apparent on most of the objects around us. The screen produces its own light, while objects around us typically reflect light. Nonetheless, because the shapes and colors of television objects are similar to those we see in real life, and because these objects have the correct size relative to each other, we perceive the television picture as real enough, and we are able to make sense of it. But no one would mistake what they saw on television for an image of a real object. When you look at an actor's face on the screen, you know that you are not looking at an actor sitting in your living room. A number of different cues confirm this. One is that the actor's features are contained within the boundaries of the television screen. Then, the face appears to be glowing, and there are scan lines across it. Perhaps most powerful, there is no three-dimensional effect. If you walked behind the television set, you would not expect to see the back of the actor's head! Moreover, if you move your head from side to side, the picture on the screen does not change as it would if you were watching a real, three-dimensional object. That is, you perceive no relative motion. You can't walk around objects on the television screen and view them from different angles as you could real objects. At least, you never could before.

A new technological development may change all of this. It's called **holographic photography**. If you look at a regular photograph the photograph will look the same whether you view it from the left side or the right side. If you walk behind the photograph you will see nothing but the back of the paper. A holographic photograph is different. It is made by scanning objects with laser beams. Laser light is coherent light which travels in only one direction. In a holographic picture, the light reflecting from the photograph, unlike light reflecting from a normal picture, does not travel in all directions, so that the picture looks about the same from all angles. Instead, it is beamed in different directions depending on the observer's position. In other words, if I had a holographic picture of a house, only the person standing right in front of the picture could see the front of the house, because information about the front of the house would be carried exclusively by the light traveling toward that observer. Individuals standing behind the picture would see only the back of the house! In fact, a holographic picture of a house carries all of the information put out by a normal house. You can walk around the picture and see the house from every angle. You can even look down on top of the picture and see the roof. The picture is not printed on paper but is projected into space, and appears to be suspended there. Retinal disparity is created no matter where an individual stands; different light from the picture will strike the left and right eyes. As a result it appears that a solid, three-dimensional house is hanging in space directly in front of you. The house doesn't look completely real, however, because it has the ghostly white color of most holograms.

Today holograms are being investigated for use in the entertainment media. Motion picture holograms have been developed, and it may be possible to use holograms for television. Imagine what it might be like if the holographic technique could be perfected. Suppose the exact kinds of light reflected from normal objects could be produced and beamed in particular directions depending on where viewers were situated. Imagine arriving at a friend's house and finding three or four people you don't know standing in the living room having a discussion. Your friend is sitting in a chair watching them. Surprised to see he has guests, you walk forward and extend your hand to introduce yourself. Your friend laughs and says, "Oh no, it's just the television." And then, with a flick of a switch, the people who were standing there disappear! Your friend had been watching a talk show being projected into the center of the living room.

A television projection set like this would take a little getting used to, especially if you decided to watch "The Invasion of the Giant Spiders from Mars." Would it be possible to get used to "false objects" that were perceived as real objects? Should young children be exposed to westerns in which "real" cowboys blast away at each other in your living room? How would adults react to X-rated movies? What would it be like to have such a television set?

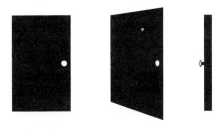

Figure 4.9 *Although the shapes of a door's image cast upon the retina can change drastically, the door is not perceived to have changed shape. Instead, it is perceived to be a rectangular door that is opening.*

Figure 4.10   *The Ames room*

remains the same. Even when you are five blocks from your car and it seems no larger than your fingernail, you perceive that it is still your car and it is still the same size. This learned perception is known as **size constancy.** It is one of a number of such perceptual constancies.

Some people fail to learn size constancy. Mr. S.B. was a 53-year-old cataract patient who had been blind since birth. When his sight was restored by surgery, he had a difficult time adjusting to all the new sensory inputs. One day he was found trying to crawl out of his hospital window in order to get a better look at the traffic that he believed was close enough to touch. The trouble was that his window was on the fourth floor (Gregory, 1970).

Even people who have been able to see all their lives may have a limited understanding of size constancy as a result of their particular experience. The pygmy whom you met at the beginning of the chapter was such an individual. Because of his limited experience, his perception of size constancy did not extend to objects at great distances.

Other constancies also develop through an individual's experience. **Shape constancy** is demonstrated in Figure 4.9. As you can see, objects are perceived to remain constant even though the shape projected onto the retina may change. A door may appear to be rectangular when viewed straight on, or trapezoidal when it is partially opened, but we do not perceive that the door is changing shape from a rectangle to a trapezoid. Instead we perceive that the door is opening.

Another of the perceptual constancies is known as **brightness constancy.** Brightness constancy refers to the fact that objects appear to have the same brightness independent of the light in which they are seen. For example, although gray paper in the sun is brighter than white paper in the shade, the white paper appears brighter. We perceive white as bright and gray as dark regardless of the amount of reflected light actually coming from the surface.

A perceptual psychologist named Ames demonstrated the power of these perceptual constancies by creating what he called the **Ames room** (see Figure 4.10). Strange things seem to happen in the Ames room. People

standing on one side of the room appear to be giants, and people on the other side appear to be dwarfs (see Figure 4.11). Individuals crossing the Ames room appear to steadily grow or shrink depending on the direction in which they are walking. The illusion of the Ames room depends on our use of size and shape constancy. Anyone looking at the Ames room will *sense* the truth. Their senses will report that one window is much larger than the other, that the windows are shaped like trapezoids, that the floor is uneven so that one end of the room is higher on the plane than the other, and that the floor tiles are diamond-shaped and of different sizes. But because we have not experienced this kind of bizarre arrangement our perceptual constancies try to make different sense of the room. Thus we perceive both windows as equal in size and rectangular. The room seems to be level and the floor to be made of square tiles. Our desire to perceive the room according to our experience is so strong that when an individual walks from one end to the other, our brain prefers to perceive that person as growing or shrinking rather than give up the idea that the room is regular in shape and size.

DIRECT-PERCEPTION THEORY

Is our perceptual understanding of the world learned, as image and cue theorists suggest? Is the image that shines on the retina filled with cues that we must come to understand? Must we establish certain relationships in order to find our way around in this complex world? Or are we already organized by our genetics and biology in such a way that we can make sense of the world without relying primarily on learning? Many years ago William James argued that the infant's world was a "blooming buzzing confusion" and that until the infant had experience with the world he could make no sense of it. In the last 20 years, however, a number of arguments have been put forth suggesting that we are biologically organized to perceive our world directly and that experience, while somewhat important, plays a far smaller role than had been believed.

Figure 4.11 *People in an Ames room seem to come in different sizes.*

Direct-perception theorists argue that, to a great degree, perception comes to us naturally as a result of our physical organization. Studies have shown surprising perceptual capabilities in infants. Furthermore, physiological investigations have demonstrated the presence of cells in the brain that are specifically organized to make immediate perceptual sense of certain sensations. In the occipital lobe, for instance, there are cells that respond only to binocular disparity and never to information from only the left or the right eye (Bishop, 1973; Cynader & Regan, 1978; Regan & Cynader, 1979). These findings support the idea of direct perceptions (De Valois & De Valois, 1980).

In his book *The Perception of the Visual World* (1950), J. J. Gibson established himself as perhaps the most influential proponent of the direct-perception theory. Gibson made a number of masterful arguments against the image and cue position. The image and cue theory, as you will recall, assumes that whenever you look at something, a two-dimensional image rests on the retina like a picture, and that from this two-dimensional picture the brain perceives a three-dimensional world based on what it knows about cues. It was this concept of a static retinal image that Gibson first attacked. He argued that the eye simply didn't work that way, and that the "eye is like a camera" analogy had been taken too far. Gibson pointed out that when an image is received by the retina, only the center portion of the image, which strikes the fovea, is clear and crisp, while all of the material that strikes the periphery is blurred. He also pointed out that the eyes don't stay still. They wobble back and forth in a series of very subtle, but constant, motions.

If you try to hold your eyes still for any length of time, staring at a particular spot, the cells become fatigued and vision begins to break down so that entire areas in your sight become blank. This particular failure of vision never happens unless you go out of your way to make it happen, because your eyes are always moving. Gibson argued that we perceive our world in this way, not as one static image falling on the retina, from which we have to respond to cues that we have learned, but as a whole series of partially clear, partially blurry images falling on the retina, one after another, shifting rapidly as the eyes move about. Gibson believed that this kind of *motion* is extremely important to perception.

Gibson also believed that enough information falls on just one retina to give some understanding of depth, even if the individual has had no experience with the world. Gradient of texture, he argued, is one example. When objects are close there is more texture; when the same object is at a distance there is less texture. Gibson asserted that it wasn't necessary to have experience with objects for the eyes to make sense of this ratio. The brain could know this at birth, the first time the eyes took something in, before any cues were learned. Anything that appeared to have more texture or grain would be "understood" by the brain to be closer.

Other direct-perception theorists have made similar arguments. For instance, Gunnar Johansson of the University of Uppsala in Sweden has maintained that there are decoding principles within each organism and that these decoding principles may be located in the neural system, working in a "blind mechanical way" (Johansson, 1970).

According to direct-perception theorists, therefore, built-in or prewired perceptual mechanisms exist in our species and in others. They argue that the discovery of cells in the brain specifically tuned to respond to movement, size, or retinal disparity is evidence of this fact. Learning may be important in perception, but our biological organization is preset to make full use of our experiences. This is why, these theorists argue, such things as size, shape, and brightness constancies are acquired by the time infants are three months old.

Motion Perception   Since Gibson's work deemphasized the concept of a static image on the retina, interest in motion and the perception of motion has developed. Direct-perception theorists have shown that the neurology involved in the perception of movement implies a predetermined biological arrangement or organization of motion detection. In fact, Gibson and his colleagues have argued that either the motion of objects, or the motion of our own bodies or eyes, are the foundations upon which perception of a three-dimensional world can be built.

One of the more unusual problems of motion perception is the following. When you sense motion, how can you know whether an object has moved or you have moved? If a baseball player is running back for a long fly ball, what lets him know the amount of motion to attribute to the ball and the amount of motion to attribute to his own body? Is his knowledge based exclusively on learning? New physiological evidence indicates that there are neural mechanisms that allow us to judge the different degrees of motion whenever we perceive motion occurring in our visual field. The physiological mechanism involved is **peripheral vision,** an area too long ignored by researchers. It seems that the fovea of the retina is tuned to respond to local changes in the visual field, that is, objects moving within the visual field. But the periphery of the retina responds to global changes in the visual field, the kind that occur whenever we move.

If you turn your head from side to side, or get up and walk, you'll notice that there is a tremendous amount of motion in the periphery, which you see out of the corner of your eyes. Motion within the fovea leads us to perceive the motion of an object, while motion in the periphery leads us to perceive our own motion (Johansson, von Hofsten, & Jansson, 1980). You can demonstrate this phenomenon in a rotary-drum room, a very small room contained within a large cylinder. The walls are covered with vertical stripes, and the subject sits on a chair in the middle of the room. While the chair and floor remain stationary, the walls of the room begin to rotate so that the vertical stripes pass rapidly in a horizontal direction in front of your eyes. The walls are so close that the spinning surface fills your entire visual field. Because of this, you sense motion in your peripheral vision. It's a sickening feeling, and after about 10 seconds you grab your chair swearing that the walls aren't turning but that the chair you are sitting on is spinning! Subjects are often afraid to get up off the chair because they think they'll be thrown to the ground. They sometimes lean as though they are accelerating or they yell for help, but all the time the chair is still and only the cylinder walls are rotating.

The reason subjects in the rotary-drum room think they are in motion is that their peripheral vision is totally involved (Brandt, Wist, & Dichgans, 1975; Wong & Frost, 1978). This peripheral-foveal distinction argues that there is a physiological organization to help us perceive motion. In fact, while most of the neurons from the foveal region are projected to the occipital lobes, neural messages from the periphery tend to be projected to the temporal lobes (Dichgans & Brandt, 1978). Additionally, neural messages

PERIPHERAL VISION
All visual experiences outside of the immediate line of sight, that is, other than those derived from light focused on the fovea. The photoreceptor field on the retina surrounding the fovea gives rise to peripheral vision. Peripheral vision is especially important for determining motion.

from the semicircular canals, which provide us with a sense of balance and orientation, are projected to areas of the temporal lobes very close to those receiving information from the peripheral vision. It may be that the messages from the semicircular canals function with messages from the peripheral vision to help us maintain our balance, head position, and motion in relation to the world around us.

These two visual systems, the foveal and peripheral, also seem to be related to hand-eye coordination. We use peripheral vision when moving an arm or a hand toward an object, and foveal vision when feeling carefully for and grasping an object. Motion and reaching are thus controlled by peripheral vision, while fine object manipulation is controlled by foveal vision (Brinkman & Kuypers, 1972; Paillard & Beaubaton, 1976). We know that young infants will reach for objects months before they are capable of grasping them. We also know that peripheral vision in young infants develops before foveal vision. There may be a relationship, then, between the development of foveal vision and the infant's ability to grasp an object (Field, 1977; von Hofsten & Lindhagen, 1979).

Blindsight   The fact that vision is projected to the temporal lobes as well as the occipital lobes may help explain the puzzling phenomenon of **blindsight.** Blindsight was first discovered by two British researchers, Larry Weiskrantz and Elizabeth Warrington. They observed the phenomenon in a 34-year-old patient, Mr. D.B., who had recently recovered from brain surgery. The surgery had damaged his occipital lobes, and Mr. D.B. couldn't see anything in the left visual field of either eye. That is, when he looked straight ahead he was blind to everything on his left side.

The researchers were startled to discover, however, that D.B. could somehow sense things in his left visual field in spite of his blindness. If the researchers flashed a point of light off to the left while D.B. looked straight ahead he was aware of the light, and if they presented the letters X or O on his left side he could tell one from the other. To Weiskrantz, "the interesting thing about the tests is that D.B. insisted that he was 'just guessing'; that he could not see the objects" (Lewin, 1981, p. 42). Other cases of blindsight have been discovered in France, Germany, and the United States.

Blindsight may have to do with the fact that peripheral and foveal vision (sometimes called ambient and focal vision) project to different areas of the brain. Roger Lewin has stated that

> The two visual systems work very much in tandem, but it appears that the brain's primary mode of sight, focal vision, is registered in our conscious mind. Ambient vision, what we see from the corner of the eye, takes place in our unconscious. The first route travels through the more advanced, evolutionarily younger areas of the brain and eventually meets the visual cortex on the surface of the brain at the rear of the head. In a sense it is in the visual cortex that we "see": Damage the cortex and you lose part of your vision. The second route, which apparently controls orientation and muscular coordination, plunges deep into the more primitive "reptilian brain." This visual pathway evidently remains intact in most people who have suffered damage to the visual cortex. It is probably here that blindsight functions, too deep to rise into our conscious minds. (Lewin, 1981, p. 42)

The Visual Cliff   Does the discovery of physiological mechanisms related to different perceptual abilities prove that learning may not always be necessary for perception to occur? Do we have any way of finding out whether certain perceptual abilities are **innate,** that is, inborn and independent of experience?

Most animals will avoid a sharp drop-off or cliff, and this tendency can be used to examine aspects of innate perception. Over 20 years ago Gibson and Walk (1960) constructed a device known as the **visual cliff,** a table with a glass surface marked to simulate a deep drop-off on one side and a shallow drop-off on the other (see Figure 4.12). Infant animals, including humans, may be placed at the center between the shallow and deep sides. Because of the glass, the subject cannot actually fall off the cliff.

Babies of many species were tested on the cliff, and the results demonstrated that they possessed an innate ability to avoid a drop-off, called *cliff avoidance.* Newborn chicks, whose first visual experience was on the cliff, refused to cross over to the deep side. Kittens, puppies, piglets, and various other infant animals also refused to venture onto the deep end. Baby mountain goats (a species that would have an exceptional reason for avoiding cliffs) similarly refused to cross to the deep side, and if pushed in that direction, collapsed their front legs. Gibson and Walk, and many other researchers, also demonstrated that human infants were much more easily coaxed onto the shallow side than the deep side, although some infants were willing to crawl onto the deep side. But does this mean that cliff avoidance is innate in humans? Unfortunately, the research conducted on humans was not as clear-cut as the research conducted on other species.

Unlike baby chicks, kittens, or mountain goats, human infants aren't precocious in terms of motor development. They are usually not able to

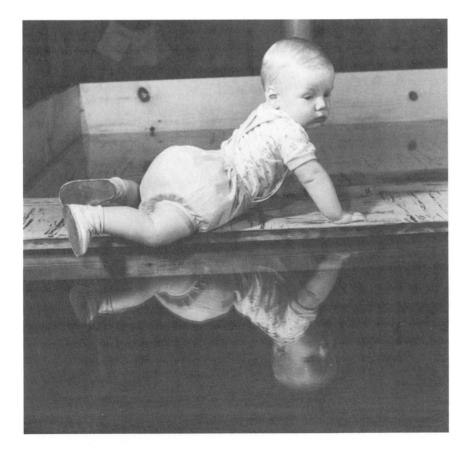

Figure 4.12 *The visual cliff*

NEARNESS
A Gestalt principle of perceptual organization stating that things near to each other appear to be grouped together.

SIMILARITY
A Gestalt principle of perceptual organization stating that similar things appear to be grouped together.

CONTINUITY
A Gestalt principle of perceptual organization stating that points or lines that form straight or gently curving lines when connected will be seen to belong together, and that lines will be seen to follow the smoothest path.

SIMPLICITY
A Gestalt principle of perceptual organization stating that every stimulus pattern is perceived in such a way that the resulting structure is as simple as possible.

NATIVIST
One who considers that behavior stems from biological and genetic forces.

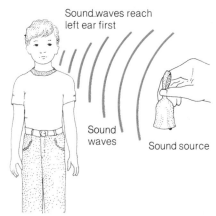

Sound waves reach left ear first

Sound waves

Sound source

Figure 4.13 *Although this single sound is sensed twice, you hear, or perceive it only once, but off to one side.*

crawl until they are about six months old, and independent movement is a prerequisite for testing cliff avoidance. Consequently, by the time they can be tested on the cliff, human infants may already have *learned* to avoid drop-offs. This possibility has been suggested (Campos, Hiatt, Ramsay, Henderson, & Svejda, 1978). Campos and his colleagues observed that pre-crawling infants of two, three and a half, and five months of age showed only a decelerated heart rate when placed on the glass over the deep side. Heart rate deceleration is generally taken to be a sign of interest, not fear. The implication is that the infants had not yet come to fear the cliff edge and that they would probably learn such avoidance behavior later.

Another researcher (Rader, 1979) has argued that cliff avoidance is a genetically inherited predisposition but one that doesn't express itself until it is triggered at about the age of six months.

Auditory Perception Although visual perception dominates the research field, many studies of auditory perception or perception involving the minor senses have also been conducted for the purpose of examining possible innate perceptual mechanisms in humans. When you hear a sound, you actually sense it twice, once in each ear, unless its source is equidistant from both ears. It takes sound slightly less time to reach the ear closer to the origin of the sound than to reach the ear farther away (see Figure 4.13). But we are organized so that we perceive the sound as occurring only once, and we use the two sounds to localize the source. In other words, although your senses send two messages to the brain at different times, you perceive only one sound, but perhaps off to one side. Is this perceptual ability inborn? There's only one way to find out. Make a sound off to the side of a newborn and note whether he or she attempts to respond in the direction of the sound. This is what Michael Wertheimer did in 1961. He tested a newborn girl in a delivery room by sounding a clicker to her right side and then to her left side. The baby responded by turning to the right when the clicker sound came from that side, and to the left when the sound came from that side. Wertheimer was surprised to discover that the infant also looked in the direction of the sound, as though she expected to see something. Just seconds after birth, a newborn's visual and auditory perceptual abilities were already integrated.

THE GESTALT VIEW OF PERCEPTION

Much of the interest in the psychology of perception can trace its roots to the work of Gestalt psychologists. In the course of their research, they observed that people tended to organize perceptions in certain ways. The Gestaltists stated a number of principles that expressed this organization, among them **nearness, similarity, continuity,** and **simplicity.** Figure 4.14 illustrates each of these perceptual principles.

How did the Gestalt psychologists resolve the conflict between image and cue theorists and direct-perception theorists? Did they assume a **nativist** position, that is, did they agree with the direct-perception theorists that biological variables determined perceptual responses? Or did they assume, with the image and cue theorists, that learning and past experience were the most important determinants of perception? Most Gestalt psychologists didn't care one way or the other (Kohler, 1925/1938). They were primarily interested in demonstrating that the structuralist approach of breaking

SIMILARITY

Similar things appear to be grouped together:

```
X X X X X X        X X X X X X
X X X X X X        O O O O O O
X X X X X X        X X X X X X
X X X X X X        O O O O O O
X X X X X X        X X X X X X
X X X X X X        O O O O O O
```

Can be seen as either horizontal *or* vertical rows of X's

Is usually seen as horizontal rows of X's and O's. The similar objects are grouped together.

NEARNESS

Things that are near to each other appear to be grouped together:

```
X X X X X X        XOXOXOXOXOXO
X X X X X X        XOXOXOXOXOXO
X X X X X X        XOXOXOXOXOXO
X X X X X X        XOXOXOXOXOXO
X X X X X X        XOXOXOXOXOXO
X X X X X X        XOXOXOXOXOXO
```

Can be seen as either horizontal *or* vertical rows of X's

Is usually seen as horizontal rows, even though the X's and O's are dissimilar figures.

CONTINUITY

Points or lines that when connected result in straight or gently curving lines are seen as belonging together, and lines tend to be seen as following the smoothest path:

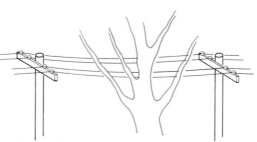

The power lines are seen as *continuous*, despite the fact that they have been segmented by the tree branches.

SIMPLICITY

Every stimulus pattern is perceived in such a way that the resulting structure is as simple as possible:

Is viewed as a triangle and a circle:

And not in a more complicated fashion, as in:

 or

Figure 4.14 *Principles of organization set forth by Gestalt psychologists*

conscious perceptions into component parts was an ineffective way of understanding perception because humans often organize perception into units.
As you read in Chapter 1, Gestaltists often stated that "the whole is greater
than the sum of the parts." Certainly the examples in Figure 4.14 indicate
that the organization of the parts can give rise to different perceptions or
"wholes."

Major arguments about the extent to which perception was learned or
attributable to biological organization did not arise until after World War II,
when our understanding of learning and biology began to increase greatly.
This nature-nurture issue has not been settled. In some cases, as in the
perception of illusions, the debate is still raging.

Illusions

Figure 4.15 contains a number of illusions. Before you look at them, you
might want to get a ruler because some of them are so eerie that you'll want
to measure them to see for yourself that the captions are correct.

Since our three-dimensional world is so complicated, many perceptual
researchers have turned to examining simple two-dimensional illusions.
The idea was to find and understand perceptual effects at the simplest level
before trying to understand them at more complex levels.

The Müller-Lyer illusion is a good one to examine in detail. It's been the
focus of a lot of controversy. Most people looking at this illusion perceive the
horizontal line bordered by the inward-turned arrowheads as shorter than
the horizontal line bordered by the outward-turned arrowheads. If you measure the horizontal lines, however, you'll find that they are the same length.
Why does the illusion occur?

Knowing that you're being tricked doesn't make much difference; the
effect remains. Researchers know that the illusion doesn't take place in the
retina. They resolved this issue by an ingenious method. A subject's head
and eyes were held very still in an apparatus while the horizontal lines of
the Müller-Lyer illusion were flashed into the left eye and the arrowheads
were flashed into the right eye. When the subject interpreted the combined
sensations in his brain, the illusion was still apparent (Gillam, 1980). This
outcome proved that the illusion must be happening at a higher level than
the retina. Could the illusion have something to do with the movement of
the eyes? As you recall, J. J. Gibson argued that most of our perception is
due to motion effects rather than to static effects. However, if the illusion is
flashed so briefly that there isn't time for the eye to scan or move, the
illusion is still seen (Gillam, 1980).

These are just a few examples of the kinds of experiments perceptual
psychologists conduct in order to eliminate the different variables that may
be responsible for the creation of an illusion. Although many explanations
have been advanced, no one really knows why illusions occur. The major
theoretical arguments continue to be between image and cue theorists and
direct-perception theorists. The latter theorists argue that the Müller-Lyer
illusion is caused by competition between different edge detectors or different spatial frequency detectors at higher levels in the brain. They attempt
to explain the illusion as the result of our biological and genetic organization.

What explanation of the Müller-Lyer illusion could an image and cue
theorist offer? How could you have learned the illusion? You probably had

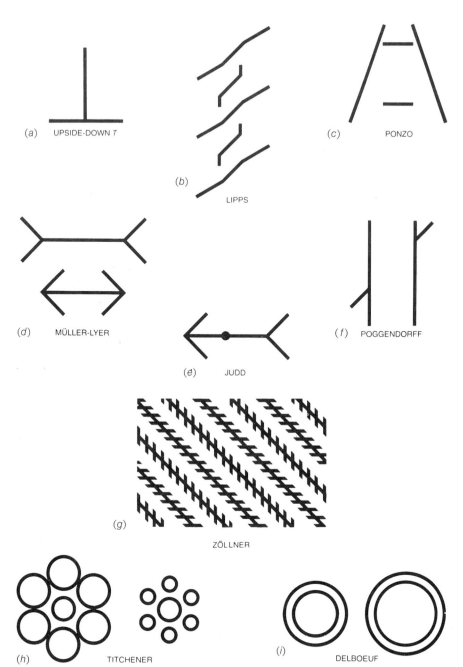

Figure 4.15 *Illusions. (a) Both lines are the same length although the vertical line looks longer. (b) The middle segments of all the lines are parallel to each other. (c) Although the upper horizontal line looks longer, both horizontal lines are the same length. (d) Both horizontal lines are the same length, although the upper one looks longer. (e) A variation of Müller-Lyer. The dot is in the center of the horizontal line. (f) The diagonal lines, if continued toward each other, would join although it appears that the line on the right would be above the line on the left. (g) The long diagonal lines are parallel and do not converge. (h) The middle circles are the same size. (i) The outer circle on the left has the same diameter as the inner circle on the right.*

(a)   UPSIDE-DOWN *T*

(b)   LIPPS

(c)   PONZO

(d)   MÜLLER-LYER

(e)   JUDD

(f)   POGGENDORFF

(g)   ZÖLLNER

(h)   TITCHENER

(i)   DELBOEUF

never even seen it before you read this book. Image and cue theorists counter that in fact you have seen this illusion before, and the others shown in the figure, too. You simply haven't realized it.

In Figure 4.16 you will see the Müller-Lyer figures. Or you may think you are looking at the floor of a room, or any rectangle lying in front of you with one end more distant than the other. Notice that the horizontal edge that seems to be farther away always has the arrowheads pointing outward, while the horizontal edge that's closer always has the arrowheads pointed inward. According to image and cue theorists, when you look at the Müller-Lyer illusion the horizontal line enclosed by the inward-turned arrowheads is perceived as being closer than the line with the outward-

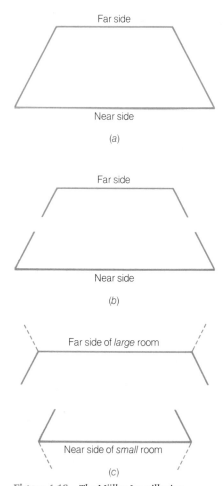

Figure 4.16 *The Müller-Lyer illusion can be explained by our experience with floors. (a) If we view a floor from one side of a room, the far side appears foreshortened, although we know that the far side is the same length as the near side. (b) By removing midsections of the floor, we begin to approximate the Müller-Lyer figures. We still assume that the far side is the same length as the near side. (c) The horizontal lines are now made equal, as in the Müller-Lyer figure. We perceive the top figure to be the long far side of a large room and the bottom figure to be the short near side of a small room. By applying our knowledge of three dimensions to a two-dimensional figure we may be making an assumption that creates the illusion.*

turned arrowheads. If two objects appear to be the same size but you know that one is closer, then you know—because of size constancy—that the one that's farther away must be bigger (see Figure 4.17). And this, the image and cue theorists argue, is what happens when you look at the Müller-Lyer illusion.

We can see the same assumption at work in the Ponzo illusion. That illusion is reproduced every time you look at railroad tracks. The upper horizontal line and the lower horizontal line in the Ponzo illusion are exactly the same length, but the upper horizontal line looks longer. Many image and cue theorists argue that this illusion is the result of size constancy. The upper horizontal line appears to be farther away, and according to experience and learning, if two objects appear to be the same size but one is farther away, then the one farther away must be bigger.

What about the Poggendorff illusion? Again, image and cue theorists might argue that our experience with three-dimensional objects and with shape constancy causes the illusion. You may never have seen the Poggendorff illusion before, but you've seen something like it, perhaps an overturned chair. The resemblance is obvious in Figure 4.18. Similarly, the Zöllner illusion is caused by shape constancy. Instead of perceiving the hatched lines as parallelograms, which they are, we perceive them as rectangles viewed from an angle, and if these rectangles angle one direction we see the long lines leaning in that direction, too. Image and cue theorists argue that this way of seeing is due to our experience with rectangles.

But what about individuals from other cultures who aren't familiar with rectangles? Suppose they come from a world where there aren't many buildings with windows. Suppose they haven't been exposed much to railroad tracks or overturned chairs. Researchers who have measured members of such cultures have reported that these illusions are *not* perceived. For instance, members of the Zulu tribe in Africa live in round huts and are not exposed to many rectangular shapes and forms. These individuals do not experience the Müller-Lyer illusion when it is shown to them (Deregowski, 1972; Gillam, 1980). Such data imply that learning and experience are extremely important factors in individual perception. However, the studies that have yielded the data have been criticized for a number of reasons, among the most important of which is the possibility that members of other cultures may not fully understand the questions being asked. It's one thing to say that the Zulu don't see an illusion in the Müller-Lyer comparisons, but it's another to contend that they fully understood the comparison you wanted them to make.

Still, there is other evidence that learning might have an important bearing on the perception of illusions. Illusions tend to diminish in effect the more you observe them. The first time you see the Müller-Lyer illusion the lines are likely to appear strikingly different, but after you've seen it many times the illusion has less impact. It has been argued that this change in our response is due to learning and experience, rather than to any arrangement in unmodifiable or unchanging neural mechanisms (Gillam, 1980).

An Interactionist View

Clearly, there is evidence to support both explanations of perception—learning and experience, and neurological organization. In fact, it isn't necessary to choose one theory over the other. They need not be mutually exclusive. Important aspects of each could easily be involved in any perceptual organization. In the last few years a number of researchers have been arguing that "the old theoretical polarity is going to fade away.... Real perception is far more than an automatic recording: it also implies intentional scanning and active search for relevant information" (Johansson, von Hofsten, & Jansson, 1980, p. 39).

CANALIZED PERCEPTUAL MECHANISMS

According to evolutionary theory, an organism's biologically organized perceptual apparatus should have been naturally selected to make the best use of the experience the organism is likely to have. An organism's biological mechanisms can therefore be said to have been formed by the kinds of experiences its ancestors had (Turvey & Shaw, 1979). This process would favor the perception of the properties in the environment that are directly relevant to survival.

It's been demonstrated, for instance, that frogs possess perceptual systems that help them perceive bugs. These "bug detectors" help frogs organize their perceptual understanding of the world in the most beneficial way. Since frogs eat bugs, there is obvious value in their perceiving the world in a fashion that makes it easier to retrieve bugs from it. Cats, on the other hand, are highly receptive to motion. They may ignore a stationary object but be immediately fascinated by it if it moves. To some degree this characteristic is also true of humans, but it's especially pronounced in the perceptual mechanisms of cats. J. J. Gibson has called the properties of the environment that relate to a particular organism's perceptual arrangement **affordances** (Gibson, 1979). Gibson's idea of an affordance implies that the properties of any sensed object are perceived by a species in a way that will help support the species' survival. In this view, how objects or actions are perceived depends on their meaning to the organism (Johansson, von Hofsten, & Jansson, 1980).

If we start with the concept of perceptual affordances and add the effects of learning and experience, we can regard perception as an interaction

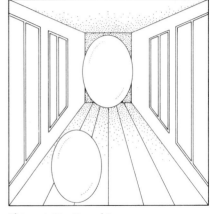

Figure 4.17 *Two objects may cast an image of the same size on the retina, as is the case with the objects in the picture, but if one is perceived to be farther away, it will also be perceived to be larger.*

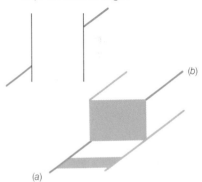

Figure 4.18 *The Poggendorff illusion in two dimensions makes sense in the three-dimensional world. If this were a real chair, lines A and B could never meet. In two dimensions, however, A and B do meet (use your ruler to prove it).*

Zulus live in a "round" world and are not exposed to the common rectangular angles of modern cities.

SIGHTLESS VISION

John M. Kennedy is a professor of psychology at the University of Toronto's Scarborough College. For the last ten years, he and his colleagues have worked with blind children and adults, many of whom have been sightless since birth. Through his research, Kennedy has gathered persuasive evidence that congenitally blind individuals can picture things in their mind's "eye," even though they've never seen them. Kennedy argues that they do this by using an internal sense of perspective.

Early in his project, Kennedy observed that when blind children, ages five to eight, were asked to point to objects from different spots in a room, they showed an understanding of perspective that would be assumed possible only in persons with sight. Kennedy stated,

In pointing to the corners of a room, they make their pointing arms converge more and more as they walk away from the corners, in pointing to the perimeter of a plate, they make their fingers describe a small circle when pointing directly from above the plate and an ellipse when pointing from a point off to one side. The ellipse becomes more eccentric as the vantage point approaches the plane of the circular plate. Hence, the keys to perspective are already present in their familiar activities— a point of view, convergence and shape transformation. (Greenberg, 1978, p. 332)

In the next phase of the project, Kennedy asked blind subjects to make drawings. He gave them a special plastic sheet on which a ball-point pen leaves a raised image, so that his subjects could feel what they had drawn. The drawings included a table, crossed fingers, a person running (with one leg foreshortened), and a boy. The crossed fingers clearly show overlap, just as they would if drawn by a sighted person. The table also has perspective, that is, a construction that takes a particular viewpoint into consideration. Kennedy stressed that his subjects "have little or no previous pictorial experience" and that "they have not been taught how to solve the mysteries of pictorial depiction. They figure out solutions on their own" (Greenberg, 1978, pp. 332–333).

Kennedy has concluded that the principles that underlie visual perception are the same principles used in touch. He argues that vision and touch, unlike hearing, are responsive to dimensions of shape and form. He points out that we do not "see" with our eyes or "feel" with our touch receptors. Instead, both sight and touch are perceptions generated by the brain based on incoming stimuli. Because of this, blind individuals, relying on a sense of touch, may organize and understand their perceptions in ways very similar to those of sighted persons.

That blind people seem to develop a perceptual understanding of form, perspective, distance, and overlap, and to extend their understanding of touch to help them comprehend the geometry of their world, was of interest between the biologically inherited perceptual mechanisms and the organization of perceptions resulting from learning and experience. This kind of interaction is easier to comprehend if you recall the concept of canalization introduced in Chapter 2. Canalized behaviors are behaviors that, because of our biological inheritance (or, if you prefer, our biological predispositions), are learned easily, almost inevitably. Following this train of thought, human beings would have been born with a preorganized perceptual apparatus ready to make particular sense of the immediate world. As we have seen, however, experience is also important for the development of perception. It may be that our perceptual affordances are canalized, making it extremely easy for certain kinds of perceptual experiences to be acquired through experience and learning.

For the researchers studying human perception by analyzing two-dimensional illusions, there may be irony in this possibility. As we mentioned earlier, it has long been thought that complex three-dimensional perceptions might eventually be understood by first examining perceptions in their simplest, or two-dimensional, form. Numerous data now suggest

to biophysicist Carter Collins and others, who set out to design a new aid for the blind. The work began with Geldard's 1957 article in which he discussed the possibility that stimulation of the skin could serve to communicate information. Paul Bach-Y-Rita and his colleagues then began developing a system based on this principle (Bach-Y-Rita, Collins, Saunders, White, & Scadden, 1969; White, Saunders, Scadden, Bach-Y-Rita, & Collins, 1970). At the Smith-Kettlewell Institute of Visual Sciences in San Francisco, Collins impresses televised pictures directly onto a person's back or chest by using a technique called **tactile sensory replacement (TSR)**. A TSR user wears a vest containing a grid upon which are hundreds of tiny points that touch the wearer. When the vest is connected to a small black and white television camera, the light and dark messages gathered by the camera can be "shined" on the person's back or chest by electrically stimulating the different points and making them vibrate. The entire device weighs only 5 pounds (see Figure 4.19). Blind persons using it have been able to quickly find objects in a room, read meters, and even use an oscilloscope.

Figure 4.19 *The TSR device, which allows blind subjects to "feel" what sighted subjects can "see."*

One blind technician wearing the device was able to assemble something as small as a microcircuit.

What does it feel like to wear the device? The following account is by a person with normal sight who tried out Collins' TSR device.

I sat blindfolded in the chair, the cones cold against my back. At first I felt only formless waves of sensation. Collins said he was just waving his hand in front of me so that I could get used to the feeling. Suddenly I felt or saw, I wasn't sure which, a black triangle in the lower left corner of a square. The sensation was hard to pinpoint. I felt vibrations on my back, but the triangle appeared in a square frame in my head. There was no color, but there was a light area and a dark area. If you close your eyes and face a light or the sun and pass an object in front of your eyes, a difference appears in the darkness. That difference is approximately what I saw. The image was fuzzy at first, but, even in my ten minutes in the chair, it became clearer. When Collins confirmed that he was holding a triangle, it was clearer still.

For me, believing that there is a difference between sensation and perception has always required an enormous leap of faith. It is hard to believe that I do not see with my eyes or hear with my ears. Although we may learn that there is a difference between sensation and perception, we rarely experience [it]. . . . At the TSR lab I experienced the difference for the first time. The sensation was on my back, the perception was in my head. Feeling is believing. (Hechinger, 1981, p. 43)

---

that we are equipped with perceptual affordances that are organized to deal with a three-dimensional world but that we are not similarly equipped to handle a two-dimensional world. In this sense, if we wanted to study "simple" perceptions we would have to examine our perceptions of three-dimensional objects rather than our sometimes questionable ability to make sense of two-dimensional pictures (see Figure 4.20).

INVESTIGATING HUMAN AFFORDANCES

If frogs possess an affordance for bugs, and cats an affordance for motion, are there affordances in humans? This possibility is being investigated in a new branch of research known as **biological motion perception** (Johansson, von Hofsten, & Jansson, 1980; Johansson, 1973). Biological motion refers to the motion of living objects. Look at Figure 4.21 and see what you can make of it. No matter how hard you try you're not likely to make any sense of it at all. It will remain a jumble of wavy lines that seem to converge on the left side of the figure and open out on the right.

TACTILE SENSORY REPLACEMENT (TSR) A device to aid the blind. A television camera is connected to a vest worn by the subject. An image is then formed on the viewer's back by means of tactile stimulation. Through practice, the wearer can obtain a perceptual understanding of the visual world.

BIOLOGICAL MOTION PERCEPTION An affordance that may exist in human beings that enables us to easily and quickly make perceptual sense of live objects in motion.

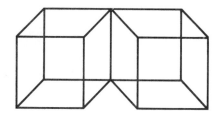

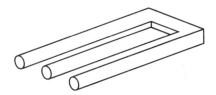

Figure 4.20 *The brain's desire to make three-dimensional sense of two-dimensional drawings that mimic the edges and facets of three-dimensional objects can lead to some strange experiences. The Necker cubes may seem to flip depending on whether your brain decides it's looking down or up at them. And let's not even discuss the three-pronged widget!*

Figure 4.21 *Tracks of light show biological motion.* (SOURCE: *Johansson, von Hofsten, & Jansson, 1980, p. 42)*

Figure 4.21 is a photographic record made by 12 individual points of light as they moved from left to right. The tracks of the points of light are uneven because the lights tended to bounce or oscillate as they moved. The lights were attached to the main joints of a person walking in darkness. If you were to sit in a dark room and watch these dots of light in motion, you would immediately perceive, without any difficulty at all, that it was a walking person approaching, even if the lights were all you could see. All of the complicated information that you see in Figure 4.21 would crystallize into an aspect so obvious that your recognition would be practically instantaneous (Johansson, 1976).

Studies such as these have been conducted primarily in order to investigate the way in which our perceptual abilities abstract information from biological patterns. The results indicate a high sensitivity to certain patterns. In fact, people are so good at making these kinds of judgments that they are often able to identify friends just by the way the lights move as they walk (Cutting & Kozlowski, 1977). Some people can even deduce the sex of the individual by estimating an invisible center of movement from the combination of lights in motion (Cutting, Proffitt, & Kozlowski, 1978; Barclay, Cutting, & Kozlowski, 1978). Is biological motion a human affordance? Are we such social creatures, so dependent on or threatened by others, that our perceptual mechanisms have evolved so that we can rapidly recognize the human form under many different circumstances? These data indicate that this appraisal may be correct.

In other experiments, researchers working in a darkened room have illuminated various parts of the human face with dots of light and have demonstrated that facial expressions too can be identified (Bassili, 1978). Facial movements are due to a combination of rigid jaw motions and the elastic motions of particular skin structures on the face, and the lights follow

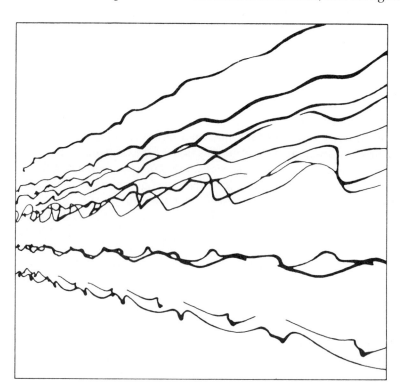

the movements in a way that makes the different expressions easy to recognize. We may be predisposed to learn easily to make quick sense of facial expressions, even in an abstract way.

Research into human perception is growing rapidly. Understanding the processes by which the brain interprets what it senses is fundamental to our knowledge of human perception. Armed with this knowledge, we will be better able to adapt our environments to our needs and to understand the limitations and requirements of our perceptual abilities.

Summary

- Perception is defined as the way in which we interpret messages from our senses.
- Among the many theories of visual perception the two that have received the most attention are the image and cue theory and the direct-perception theory.
- The image and cue theory relies on learned cues to explain such functions as depth perception. The theory argues that through learning we are able to make three-dimensional sense of a two-dimensional image projected on the retina.
- The image and cue theory has been used to explain the moon illusion.
- How we perceive a particular image depends on how we attend to and organize the cues within that image.
- In addition to monocular cues, that is, cues sensed with only one eye, there are binocular cues derived from convergence and retinal disparity.
- A three-dimensional effect on film is obtained by using retinal disparity.
- The brightness, size, and shape constancies are perceptual cues that help us make sense of the world.
- Direct-perception theorists believe that our genetic and biological organization equips us to make perceptual sense of the world without having to rely much on learning.
- The direct-perception theorist J. J. Gibson has argued that motion is essential for perception of three-dimensional space.
- Peripheral vision enables us to differentiate between our own movement and that of our surroundings.
- The phenomenon of blindsight has demonstrated that peripheral vision may function below the conscious level.
- The visual-cliff experiment indicates that the ability to perceive drop-offs is innate in some animals. Research has also been conducted into a comparable cliff-avoidance mechanism in humans.
- There appear to be innate perceptual auditory mechanisms in humans.
- Gestalt psychologists studying perception were not concerned with the nativist versus learning argument. Instead, they were interested in demonstrating that the whole was greater than the sum of the parts.
- Sightless vision is made possible by tactual feedback that helps the blind perceive the three-dimensional world.
- The debate between nativist and learning theorists became most heated following World War II, and the ongoing investigations of illusions afforded a ready battleground for the argument.
- The interactionist view considers aspects of both nativist and learning theories. The concept of canalization highlights this interpretation.

- J. J. Gibson coined the term *affordance* to imply that the properties to any sensed object are perceived by a species in a way that will help support the species' survival.
- Biological motion perception has been suggested as a possible affordance in human beings.

Psychologists who study perception have come to appreciate that we cannot always trust our brain to accurately interpret the messages of our senses. In the following account, we will see how one man's understanding of perception led him to question the perceptions of others.

In the mid-1970s a researcher named Robert Buckhout was arguing strongly that eyewitness testimony could not always be trusted and therefore should not be relied on as heavily as it was. Buckhout pointed out that such testimony had often been challenged in particular instances in the past, but as a rule it was still accepted as conclusive evidence in courtrooms. Behind this willingness, Buckhout believed, was a misconception about the way in which the eye functioned. People considered the eye to be like a camera. If an eyewitness saw someone clearly, and then later identified a suspect definitely, there could be little doubt of that individual's guilt. An eyewitness's testimony was questioned only if the opportunity to observe the suspect had been extremely poor. In cases of face-to-face contact, however, when the victim could pick out the assailant among the other people in the courtroom, eyewitness testimony was almost always accepted.

But Buckhout knew that perception did not work like photography. He knew, as you discovered in reading the comic strip about Little Lady Lovekins and Old Man Muffaroo, that individuals attend to some cues more than others and that they later rely on these cues in order to make comparisons.

When Buckhout presented his arguments (Buckhout, 1974), his intention was to demonstrate to the legal community, and to others interested in eyewitness testimony, that the way in which we attend to particular cues can affect our assumptions about the innocence or guilt of a particular individual. He supported his argument by describing, in detail, a recent case of mistaken identity.

It all began when a young man named Lawrence Berson was arrested for having committed several rapes. The victims had gotten a good look at the rapist, and they identified Berson in police lineups. Some time later, however, the police arrested a man named Richard Carbone, who confessed to the crimes, clearing Berson. Look at photographs (a) and (b) in Figure 4.22. Which cues do you think the eyewitnesses attended to, ignoring others, when they positively identified Lawrence Berson as the rapist? Carbone and Berson give several of the same cues, although they are not really doubles. You may argue that this kind of mistaken identification, made by eyewitnesses who were certain about what they had seen, cannot be common. But there was another twist to Buckhout's example. When Carbone was arrested, he not only confessed to the rape, he also confessed to a

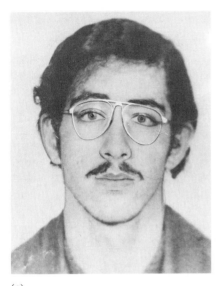

(a)

(b)

(c)

robbery. The police were surprised to hear the latter confession, too, since they had arrested George Morales for the robbery on the basis of a positive identification by eyewitnesses. Morales is shown in photograph (c) of Figure 4.22.

The eyewitnesses were amazed by their errors; they had been "so sure." Remembering this case, you may have doubts the next time you hear someone say, "That's the man! I could never forget his face!" Like Buckhout, you now know that the eye is not a camera and that recording something with your perception is not the same as recording it on film.

Figure 4.22 *From left to right, Richard Carbone, Larry Berson, and George Morales*

Suggestions for Further Reading

1. Gibson, J. J. *The senses considered as perceptual systems.* Boston: Houghton Mifflin, 1966.
2. Goldstein, E. B. *Sensation and perception.* Belmont, California: Wadsworth, 1980.
3. Gregory, R. L. "The confounded eye." In R. L. Gregory and E. H. Gombrich (eds.), *Illusion in nature and art.* London: Duckworth, 1973.
4. Gregory, R. L. *Eye and brain: The psychology of seeing* (3rd rev. ed.). New York: McGraw-Hill, 1978.

CONTENTS

States of Consciousness

PROLOGUE

You are at Harvard University working with John Pappenheimer. For weeks you've been collecting cerebral-spinal fluid from goats through two Teflon tubes surgically inserted just behind the animals' occipital lobes. As the fluid is drawn off, it is replaced with synthetic fluid so that the goats are not harmed or upset. Some of the goats have been deprived of sleep for different amounts of time; others have been allowed to rest normally. The fluid drawn from the sleepy goats looks the same as that taken from the goats who have just had a good night's sleep. You wouldn't expect any difference to be visible, though.

The fluid will be injected into rats and rabbits which Pappenheimer has prepared to take part in the experiment. An activity measure will be used as the dependent variable. Photoelectric rays have been installed in the rats and rabbits' cages; when the animals move around, the rays will be broken. The number of times the rays are broken constitutes an activity level. The more active the animals, the more often the beams will be interrupted.

Some of the rats and rabbits are given cerebral-spinal fluids from sleep-deprived goats, others are given fluid from the rested goats. As the days pass and the data are

collected, you and the others become more and more convinced that there is a sleep-promoting substance that collects in the cerebral-spinal fluid as waking time passes. The rats and rabbits injected with the fluid of sleep-deprived goats are falling asleep sooner and sleeping longer.

Pappenheimer wants your team to isolate the sleep-promoting factor itself (Pappenheimer, 1976). Can you imagine what it would be like to isolate this substance? It could lead to incredible breakthroughs. An instant and safe sleeping pill might be developed, or an inoculation might be found that would prevent sleepiness for indefinite periods. Sleep disorders might be effectively treated. Your work might even help answer an age-old question: Why do we sleep?

Whatever the sleep-promoting substance is, a tiny bit goes a long way. So far you and the team have isolated about a drop from hundreds of liters of cerebral-spinal fluid. Still, the sleep-promoting factor itself has not been completely identified. And, as you work, the same questions keep plaguing you. What is the chemistry of sleep, and why is it so elusive?

In this chapter we will examine altered states of consciousness, including sleeping and dreaming, hypnosis, meditation, and the ef-

135

fects of drugs. We'll discuss how long dreams last, how to engage in self-hypnosis, theories about why we sleep, the reasons drugs affect us as they do, and how to alter dreams by taking part in them.

Why Psychologists Study States of Consciousness

Consciousness is the state in which you are aware not only of the external environment but also of internal events such as thinking. Before people act they often consider things "internally," that is, they think about them. This fact made the study of consciousness a paramount issue when psychology began as a science. An early definition of psychology was "the description and explanation of states of consciousness and such" (Ladd, 1887). Defining consciousness is not easy, however. When George Trumbull Ladd put forth that definition in 1887, it drew a lot of humorous comment about the content of "and such."

In 1913 John Watson, in his paper "Psychology as the Behaviorist Views It," rejected the study of consciousness as too subjective to be of scientific interest. Although it appeared that objectivity could be preserved by avoiding the issue of consciousness, the concept seemed so self-apparent and central to the human experience that it was impossible to ignore for long and psychologists were drawn to study it (Hilgard, 1980).

Today, thanks to advances in scientific technology, there are some objective ways of measuring conscious states. We are able to monitor changes in conscious experience by using such instruments as the electroencephalograph and the PET scan.

Consciousness in the Waking State and the Return of Introspection

At the University of Minnesota at Morris, psychology students in Eric Klinger's class take unusual examinations. During the exams the students are required to respond to loud beeps that are occasionally emitted from a small box on the instructor's desk. They have been told to write down whatever they were thinking about just before the beep occurred. The beep is also used during class lectures; again, the students must write down exactly what was on their minds just before they heard the tone.

Klinger has been doing this work for about a decade. He says, "It's surprising how little we know about what goes on in people's heads. What I'm hoping to do is find out how much time is spent on different thoughts and how much impact these thoughts have on a person's life" (Bartusiak, 1980, p. 57). Klinger has also given student volunteers a small pocket alarm that beeps at random throughout the day, approximately once every 40 minutes. He explains that "each student is trained to fix his mind on the inner experience that occurred right before the signal, to estimate the duration, and to write down those thoughts on a special questionnaire."

During one lecture, Klinger reports, a student wrote down that at the sound of the beep he had been thinking about his church pastor, the Minnesota Vikings football team, and a station wagon. Another man had been fantasizing about being shaved by two women; someone else had been wondering whether to have ham or turkey for dinner. As you can see, Klinger's research indicates that people spend a great deal of time daydreaming about things that are irrelevant to the task at hand. Daydreaming is often considered to be undirected thought. Amazingly, it appears that the average person spends about one third of his or her waking conscious time daydreaming. (Doesn't it make you feel better to know you're not the only one?)

Klinger's technique has also been used to investigate times of intense concentration. The subjects in this case were the players in a basketball game. When the game was filled with action, some players reported that their concentration was so complete that they were thinking about nothing; they were simply watching the ball. At such times they seemed almost to be in a trance. At other, less active times, concentration was less intense, and players occasionally reported reflecting on how well their team was doing or how they might have played the last shot.

Interestingly, the percentage of daydreaming that occurs when people are awake and the percentage of night dreaming that occurs when people are asleep is about the same (Foulkes & Fleisher, 1975; Webb & Cartwright, 1978). In each case about a third of our time is involved in dreams. Why this is so is unknown.

Altered States of Consciousness

The conscious state is said to be altered any time the content or quality of conscious experience undergoes a significant change. There are many ways to alter conscious experience. Psychoactive drugs can alter your conscious state and your perceptions of the world. Sleeping and dreaming are also considered to be altered states of consciousness. Hypnosis can alter conscious experience. Other causes are sleep deprivation, religious experiences, mystical or emotional experiences, sensory overload or deprivation, a high fever, and prolonged strenuous exercise. Most of the research into altered states of consciousness has concentrated on sleep, hypnosis, and psychoactive drugs; we'll examine each of these areas individually.

SLEEP

In 1937 Loomis and his associates discovered, by means of a new device, the **electroencephalograph (EEG),** that brain waves could be recorded as electrical changes. It was observed that brain waves changed dramatically following the onset of sleep and during sleep.

After World War II electroencephalograms were routinely incorporated into sleep research. The EEG yielded some interesting findings in the late 1940s and early 1950s. One was that not everyone "drifts off to sleep." Instead, some people go abruptly from a drowsy waking state to sleeping. It was also discovered that distinctly different sleep stages occur throughout the sleeping period. Each stage is characterized by a different EEG pattern.

Stages of Sleep When you fall asleep, **alpha waves,** which are associated with a drowsy but awake state, change abruptly to **theta waves.** Theta waves are associated with the first stage of sleep. Have you ever caught yourself falling asleep? Sometimes you can, especially if you're very tired and

CONSCIOUSNESS
A state of awareness of the external environment and of internal events such as thought.

ELECTROENCEPHALOGRAPH (EEG)
An instrument that records the electrical activity of the brain.

ALPHA WAVES
A pattern of brain waves typical of the relaxed, waking state.

THETA WAVES
A pattern of brain waves typically associated with the first stage of sleep.

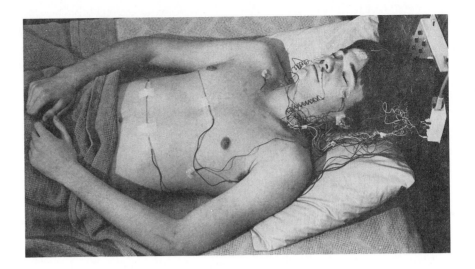

In sleep labs, researchers stay awake throughout the night in order to monitor sleepers with complex electronic sensors.

are thinking about something in particular when you fall asleep. As you shift from alpha to theta waves you might, just for an instant, realize that your thoughts have become incoherent and illogical. This can happen because a rational train of thought can be lost at the onset of theta waves.

After spending some time in stage 1, the sleeper descends to stage 2, and then to stage 3 and 4, which are associated with **delta waves.** Delta-wave sleep is sometimes known as **slow-wave sleep.** After spending time in slow-wave sleep the sleeper returns to stage 2 or 1, spends time there, and then sinks back into slow-wave sleep. This cycle may occur three or four times in a night before the sleeper finally ascends through stages 2 and stage 1 and then awakes (see Figure 5.1).

The slow-wave stages of sleep are the deepest. Waking up is more or less difficult depending on the stage of sleep. It's most difficult when sleepers are in stage 4 (Webb & Cartwright, 1978). As people grow older they often notice that they become lighter sleepers. The EEG confirms this; it is well documented that slow-wave sleep decreases with age.

Researchers have also investigated animals at sleep. Other primates—monkeys, gorillas, and orangutans—record sleep patters on the EEG that

Figure 5.1 *The sleep cycle of human beings. Sleep progressively grows less deep throughout the night, and dreams tend to lengthen and intensify. "REM" refers to rapid eye movement associated with some stage 1s.* (SOURCE: *Fincher, 1981, p. 129*)

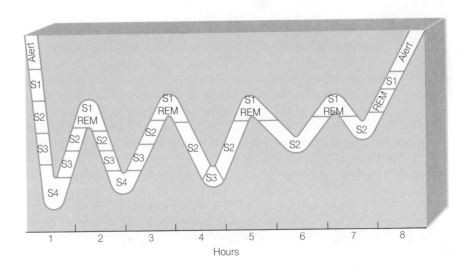

are quite similar to the human pattern (Tauber, 1974). In general, animals vary widely in their durtion of sleep. Horses, cows, and elephants usually sleep only two to four hours a day, while at the other extreme opossums and bats sleep 20 hours a day. There is even evidence that some creatures, such as Dall's porpoise and the bullfrog, don't sleep at all (Webb & Cartwright, 1978).

REM Sleep One of the most astounding discoveries in sleep research occurred in 1953 as a result of the careful observations of a graduate student named Eugene Aserinsky. While watching a subject in the laboratory whose sleep was being monitored by an EEG, Aserinsky notices that from time to time the subject's eyes appeared to move rapidly back and forth beneath his closed eyelids. After a while these rapid eye movements stopped and the subject slept soundly. A little while later they began again. Further investigation revealed that this kind of rapid eye movement occurred in all subjects. Aserinsky wondered whether **rapid eye movement, or REM,** as it is called, was related to anything in particular. By carefully examining individuals awakened from REM sleep and from periods of sleep when they were not engaging in rapid eye movement, called **NREM sleep** or **orthodox sleep,** Aserinsky and others discovered that an overwhelming number of subjects awakened from REM sleep had been dreaming. This discovery of a physiological correlate associated with dreaming excited researchers to further investigations, and the area of sleep research began to grow rapidly.

In human beings NREM and REM sleep are considered to be two distinct kinds of sleep. NREM sleep has been divided into the four stages described in Figure 5.2. REM sleep has its own characteristic EEG wave pattern. During REM sleep the sympathetic nervous system becomes quite active. Blood pressure and heart rate may increase dramatically; the body acts as though it's under attack or is responding to an alarming situation. This heightened activity level doesn't necessarily mean that a nightmare is occurring—the sleeper may be having a pleasant dream—but it may help explain why people sometimes die in their sleep from heart attack or stroke. REM sleep is sometimes referred to as **paradoxical sleep** because during REM the brain waves are similar to those of waking state.

DELTA WAVES
A pattern of brain waves associated with the deepest stages of sleep, often called slow waves because of their relatively low frequency.

SLOW-WAVE SLEEP
The deepest stages of sleep, characterized by an EEG pattern of delta waves.

RAPID EYE MOVEMENT (REM)
The eyes' rapid back-and-forth movement during sleep. Dreaming is often associated with REM.

NREM SLEEP
Non-REM sleep during which no rapid eye movement takes place. Also called *orthodox sleep.*

ORTHODOX SLEEP
All sleep except REM sleep. It is called orthodox because the EEG pattern is markedly different from the waking state. Also called *NREM sleep.*

PARADOXICAL SLEEP
REM sleep. The EEG pattern closely resembles that of a person who is awake, even though the person is still asleep. Dreaming occurs during this kind of sleep.

For all of history, people have been fascinated by dreams.

Figure 5.2 *EEG patterns clearly show the differences in states of consciousness. Each state is characterized by a different pattern. Notice how similar the patterns are during the waking state and REM sleep.*

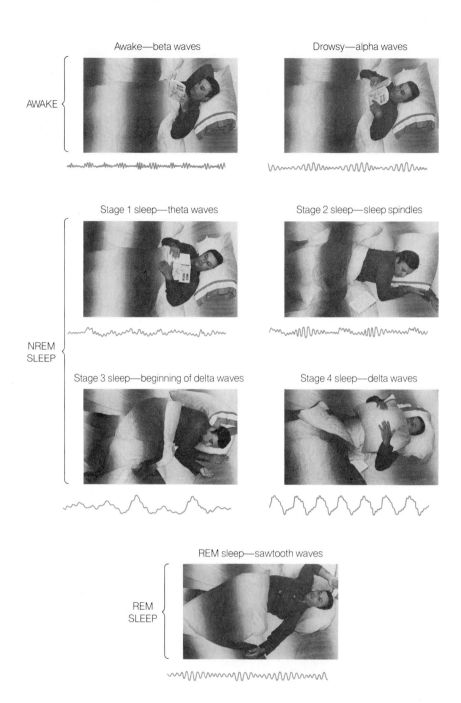

Awake—beta waves

Drowsy—alpha waves

AWAKE

Stage 1 sleep—theta waves

Stage 2 sleep—sleep spindles

NREM SLEEP

Stage 3 sleep—beginning of delta waves

Stage 4 sleep—delta waves

REM sleep—sawtooth waves

REM SLEEP

During REM sleep the body loses muscle tone, resulting in a state of semi-paralysis. Some researchers believe that this change may occur to protect sleepers from physically responding to or acting out dreams. Talking and walking during sleep have been found to occur mostly in NREM sleep, when the body is better able to move.

Individuals who are deprived of REM sleep in the laboratory often engage in **REM rebound** when they are finally given a chance to sleep undisturbed. REM rebound refers to an increase in REM sleep after a person has been deprived. Such a person will drop into REM sleep very soon after falling asleep, and will engage in more REM than usual.

The body generally tries to devote a certain portion of its sleeping time to REM sleep each night. During REM sleep people sometimes incorporate an unexpected sound into their dreams rather than allow the sound to awaken them. This tendency, which may be one way of avoiding REM-sleep disruption, is not at all uncommon. Suppose street repairs are in progress outside, and an air hammer begins to clatter while you're in REM sleep. Rather than wake up, you might dream that you are on a battlefield firing a machine gun. Some companies have tried to exploit this effect by producing records that can be played while you are sleeping and from which you can supposedly learn the material on the recording by incorporating it into your dreams. If you play German-language records while sleeping, for example, it is argued that you can learn German. The Soviets have claimed that this method of study is effective. However, no one in the United States or elsewhere has ever been able to show convincingly that complicated verbal material can be learned during sleep (Aarons, 1976).

Sleep Patterns   Many interesting phenomena have been studied in the sleep laboratory. Some people seem to have their own internal way of measuring the passage of time. If a person with that ability wants to get up at 4 o'clock in the morning to go on a fishing trip, she doesn't have to set an alarm clock; she just says to herself, "Wake up at 4:00." She lies down, goes to sleep, and sure enough, at about 4 o'clock she wakes up. Why are some people able to do this?

When people plan to get up at a particular hour, they show different sleep patterns than they normally do. There is less slow-wave sleep, less REM, and more occasional awakenings, as if they were keeping an eye on the passage of time throughout the night. They may be worrying about oversleeping. In the laboratory, the same effects can be obtained by threatening to shock a subject some time during the night while he is sleeping (the things people do for science). A subject who is worried about getting a shock will also show less REM, less slow-wave sleep, and more awakening (Bonnet & Webb, 1976).

Many things can disrupt sleep patterns. Excessive heat is one (Schmidt-Kessen & Kendel, 1973). Who hasn't had the exasperating experience of tossing and turning while trying to sleep in a hot room? As in other stressful situations, the tendency in this case is to experience less slow-wave sleep, less REM, and more occasional awakenings.

Sleep Duration   The average young adult needs between 6½ and 8½ hours of sleep a night (Tune, 1969). Of course, some people need a little more and some a little less. Some can get by on a lot less. There are individuals who are quite comfortable getting only three hours of sleep a night (Jones & Oswald, 1968)! Such individuals have been carefully monitored in sleep laboratories, and they have been shown to function very well after as few as three hours of sleep a night. During the day (and a good part of the night) they are wide-awake and feel fine. When Jones and Oswald reported these findings, they didn't know what to call these people. Should they be considered sleep-deprived? The label didn't really apply, since three hours was all they needed. Jones and Oswald finally decided to describe these individuals as **healthy insomniacs.** Some healthy insomniacs get much less than three hours of sleep a night. A woman who slept 45 minutes a night, day after day, reported that she felt absolutely fine and refreshed, and able to

REM REBOUND
An increase in REM sleep by a person who has been deprived of it.

HEALTHY INSOMNIACS
Individuals who function very well with only three hours of sleep a night or less, and who don't seem to need more than this.

do her work without difficulty (Meddis, Pearson, & Langford, 1973). The researchers referred to this as an extreme case of healthy insomnia. Most people with healthy insomnia enjoy themselves. They don't get sleepy, and they have a lot of extra time. One man said that after his usual one hour of sleep, he often gets up, leaving his wife to her additional seven hours, and spends the rest of the night reading all the books he'd ever wanted to read. He seemed to be having a fine time.

You may be wondering whether these "healthy insomniacs" eventually burn out. After all, sleep gives the body a chance to rest, which it requires— or does it? Many very large animals expend a great deal of energy but sleep only two hours a night, and do very well. Elephants have a life span fairly close to ours, and yet we spend 400 percent more time sleeping than they do. The exceptions, of course, are healthy insomniacs who like to catch up on their reading. Elephants can't catch up on their reading, but they can catch up on their eating. And this brings us to the first of two theories that attempt to explain why we sleep.

Theories about Sleep   The first theory, known as the **adaptive theory** (Meddis, 1975; Webb, 1974; 1975), argues that each species needs a certain amount of waking time in order to survive. Large herbivores (plant eaters) such as elephants and cows must consume vast amounts of vegetation in order to live. Grazing and eating takes a lot of time. If elephants slept for eight hours a day, they probably wouldn't have time for the waking activi-ties that maintain their species.

Unlike elephants, humans don't need 22 hours of waking time in order to survive. In examining the Laplanders, a modern tribe in northern Scandi-navia which still follows the herds and lives off the land in the same way that our ancestors did many thousands of years ago, we find that approxi-mately 15 to 16 hours of daily waking activity are required to sustain their lives and foster the next generation. This leaves eight hours in each day that aren't needed. Sleep may be nature's way of telling people to lie down and be quiet during the extra time. Sleep is a good protective mechanism, keeping people out of trouble. If, in your extra eight hours a day, you wandered about stirring up fights with other tribes, falling off a cliff, break-ing your leg, or using up your resources, then you would not be as likely to survive and pass on your genes to your offspring. On the other hand, it would be an adaptive advantage if you inherited a predisposition to "pass out" during your spare time. Perhaps the sleep-promoting factor introduced in the prologue was created because of the survival value of being quiet after a day's tasks had been accomplished.

The second theory, known as the **conserving-energy theory,** goes hand in hand with the adaptive theory. Two researchers (Allison & Cicchetti, 1976) observed the sleep patterns in 38 different species and reported that differences in species body weight, which is a good indication of metabo-lism, and the amount of danger faced by different species in their environ-ments, correlate well with the amount of sleep the species needs. The implication is that animals that sleep a great deal and have a high meta-bolic rate may be sleeping to conserve energy as well as to protect them-selves. Human beings, too, may have come to use sleep as a means of conserving energy. You burn fewer calories when you're sleeping than when you're awake and active. If food supplies are scarce, going into a kind of hibernation for eight hours every day would be a way of assuring that a limited food supply would be consumed less quickly. Both the adaptive theory and the conserving-energy theory have played an important role in our understanding of sleep.

Sleep Deprivation What would happen if you did not get enough sleep? In one experiment, researchers attempting to answer this question placed subjects on a three-hour-a-day sleep schedule for a week. Under controlled conditions the subjects were carefully examined and tested. It was observed that their performance on a number of simple tasks was somewhat impaired (Webb & Agnew, 1965). Nothing else of any consequence was noted. Another study restricted subjects to 5½ hours a night for approximately eight weeks and found only limited deterioration in task performance. In still another experiment, six couples were asked to reduce their sleep by a half hour a week until they felt too uncomfortable to continue. All of the subjects stopped before they reached 4½ hours a night (Johnson & Mac-Leod, 1973). No serious inability to perform different tasks occurred with the smaller amounts of sleep, but the subjects all reported discomfort.

There is no question about it: When you don't get enough sleep you get sleepy. But what happens when you not only reduce your sleep but stay awake as long as possible? The question of how long people can go without sleep has been investigated extensively, beginning with the first studies conducted in 1842 (Patrick & Gilbert, 1896). Most of us have missed one night's sleep, and maybe even two. But some individuals have stayed awake much longer. In one carefully controlled experiment, six human subjects were kept awake for a period of 205 hours straight (Kales, Tan, Kollar, Naitoh, Preston, & Malmstrom, 1970). After eight days without sleep the subjects didn't go mad or become psychotic or collapse. They did, however, become very sleepy. Beyond that there were only a few decrements in their ability to perform tasks. After about 60 hours of deprivation hallucinations and delusions occurred. Generally, however, reflexes were unimpaired. Some subjects experienced shaky hands and difficulty in controlling the motion of their eyes, and it was common for them to have reduced pain thresholds. But other functions, such as heart rate, blood pressure, respiration, and temperature, did not show much change. When the subjects were finally allowed to sleep, they slept for a few days, awoke, and felt quite good. This would seem to indicate that missing a few nights' sleep may not be harmful in the long run as long as you are healthy to begin with.

The Need for REM Sleep In the early 1960s William Dement conducted an interesting experiment (Dement, 1960). He deprived sleeping subjects in his laboratory of REM sleep only. The first REM sleep typically begins after you've been asleep for about 90 minutes. Dement watched for this in his experimental group and as soon as REM sleep began he awakened the members of this group. A control group was awakened just as often, but only during NREM sleep. Dement noticed a number of effects. Sleepers who were deprived of REM sleep seemed to be trying to get REM sleep more desperately as time passed. They would fall into REM sleep sooner after falling asleep, in some cases immediately. Dement also noticed that after extended REM deprivation, the subjects became hostile, paranoid, and aggressive. Subjects deprived of NREM sleep did not exhibit these behaviors.

Following this research it was common to hear warnings about the psychological dangers of depriving subjects of REM sleep for too long.

MICROSLEEP
Short snatches of sleep, usually occurring when a person has been sleep-deprived. The person may be totally unaware of having slept, but the EEG will have registered the brain-wave patterns typical of sleep.

ENDOGENOUS DEPRESSION
Depression triggered not by events in the environment but by internal states.

INSOMNIA
Difficulty in going to sleep or in staying asleep for the necessary amount of time.

CIRCADIAN RHYTHM
A daily 24-hour cycle. Sleep and waking cycles are considered circadian rhythms.

The belief was that sleeping must be essential because REM sleep was apparently essential; perhaps we slept solely to engage in the REM portion. This hypothesis is difficult to test, however. As in Dement's experiment, human volunteers who were selectively deprived of REM sleep would move into that phase the moment they fell asleep again. The only way to impose total deprivation would be to force subjects to stay awake day after day. But this doesn't work, either, even if someone is willing. In individuals who are forcibly kept awake for many days, a process known as **microsleep** begins. Microsleep occurs when the body catches a few seconds of sleep even though the person may be standing up and trying as hard as possible to stay awake. Electroencephalograms of people who have been awake for many hours often record microsleep, and the people are totally unaware that they have been sleeping. This is a danger that truck drivers and other people who drive long distances must keep in mind. It's possible to be awake at one moment, and asleep at the next, without realizing it at all. You don't even have to close your eyes.

Sleep researchers were not to be denied, however, and animal studies of REM deprivation began. In a particularly gruesome study, a small animal such as a rat was placed on a tiny platform over some water. The rat had to sleep standing up. As you will recall, when REM sleep begins the body loses muscle tone. Each time the rat fell into REM sleep, therefore, it toppled off the platform into the water. During NREM sleep the animal was able to maintain the muscle tone necessary to sleep standing on the small platform. In this way animals can be deprived of REM sleep exclusively for great lengths of time (Morden, Mitchell, & Dement, 1967). Contrary to expectations, this long-term REM deprivation did not seem to cause serious psychological problems (rats dunked during NREM were just as upset).

In the meantime methods have been developed for depriving human subjects of REM sleep. The means have not been so harsh as the dunking platform devised for the rats. In human experiments, REM deprivation is often effected by the use of drugs known to prevent REM sleep. Because of these studies, we now know that long-term REM deprivation in humans is not likely to cause permanent psychological harm (Vogel, 1975). Some researchers have argued, however, that long-term REM deprivation may inhibit an individual's ability to learn complex things (Greenberg & Pearlman, 1974). Individuals have also been deprived specifically of slow-wave sleep. These tests, like those of REM deprivation, have not produced any definite effects (Johnson & Naitoh, 1974).

In some cases REM deprivation may even be beneficial. It has been used to treat **endogenous depression.** This kind of depression, unlike that triggered by specific events, is a general sense of sadness that has no apparent cause. Systematic REM deprivation in the laboratory has been found in some cases to help people overcome endogenous depression (Arehart-Treichel, 1977).

SLEEP ABNORMALITIES AND PATHOLOGY

There are many sleep-related disturbances, among them insomnia, narcolepsy, and sleep apnea. All of these disorders are being investigated in the laboratory and ways of dealing with them are being developed.

If stress, an uncomfortable room, or other factors are affecting your sleep, you shouldn't feel alone. Approximately 50 million people in the

United States have sleep problems, and about 20 percent of them feel that their difficulty is serious enough to warrant at least a doctor's visit during any particular year ("The Big Sleep," 1980). Unfortunately, about 9 million people a year try to combat sleep difficulties by relying on barbiturates and other tranquilizers such as Dalmane or Librium. Laboratory studies have demonstrated that eight hours of drug-induced sleep is not equivalent to normal sleep. Tranquilizers often decrease the amount of REM sleep and alter the time spent in the different stages of sleep. Further complicating the problem, many people become used to a certain dosage and need to increase it in order to sleep, beginning a dangerous cycle. In general, it's far better to miss a few nights of sleep than to take medications against insomnia.

Researchers have also found extensive loss of REM sleep among those who drink alcohol in order to get to sleep. In fact, this kind of REM deprivation may be a factor in the delirium and hallucinations that often occur during alcohol withdrawal (Greenberg & Pearlman, 1967).

Insomnia   Individuals who have **insomnia** find it difficult to go to sleep or, once asleep, to stay asleep. The difficulty may be temporary or long-term, be mild or severe, and be accompanied by one or many symptoms. In a recent survey of over 700,000 adults from ages 30 to over 90, 6 percent of all men and 14 percent of all women reported that they had insomnia either fairly often or very often (Kripke & Simons, 1976).

People suffer insomnia for many reasons. Two major causes are depression (Kales, Caldwell, Preston, Healey, & Kales, 1976) and an irregular **circadian rhythm.** *Circadian* refers to events occurring in cycles of 24 hours. The sleep cycle, being daily, is therefore a circadian rhythm. Figure 5.3 shows a typical sleep cycle of an individual who is sleeping eight hours a night. As the circadian rhythm begins its downward trend the person becomes sleepy, and when the circadian rhythm comes back up the person awakens. During the day as the circadian rhythm nears its high point, the senses become more acute, body temperature rises, and by early evening vision, hearing, smell, and taste are at their peak. At this time the person is the most alert.

You can easily sense your own circadian rhythm by staying up all night. By 4:00 or 5:00 A.M. you feel extremely tired, and by 6:00 or 7:00 you may be quite exhausted. By 8:00 or 9:00, however, it's common to begin to wake up. This resurgence occurs because the circadian rhythm is beginning to pick up. Interestingly, after missing a night's sleep you don't need a full eight hours extra to make up for it; an additional one or two is usually enough.

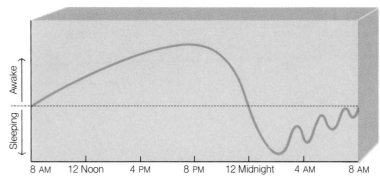

Figure 5.3   *The circadian sleep cycle of a typical person who sleeps eight hours a night and who usually awakens at 8:00 A.M.*

The circadian rhythm may also explain why oversleeping can sometimes make you feel even worse than not getting enough sleep. When you sleep longer than usual, you are sleeping when your circadian rhythm is beginning to rise, and you are out of synchrony. The circadian rhythm is also a factor in the many deaths that occur in the early morning hours. If someone is extremely ill, falling deeply asleep may be enough to cause complete collapse. In some hospitals, operating schedules have been changed from the usual early-morning hours to much later in the day for people who work the graveyard shift (midnight to 8:00 A.M.) and who typically go to bed in the morning. In this way these patients aren't undergoing surgery at exactly the time they are used to falling asleep.

But what does the circadian rhythm have to do with insomnia? Like most biological rhythms, the circadian isn't totally stable. In fact, if you tend to go to bed and get up at different times throughout the week you may have one fairly weak main rhythm and a number of ghost rhythms, as shown in Figure 5.4. This kind of confusion can lead to insomnia. To overcome insomnia in this case, the best thing to do is go to bed and arise at the same time every day for at least a three-week period. Over three weeks you can readjust your circadian rhythm to just about any cycle.

Attempting to change the circadian rhythm abruptly is the cause of **jet lag.** That sleepy uncomfortable feeling that can come after traveling great distances has nothing to do with riding in jets or the length of the trip. It has to do with readjusting yourself to new time zones. If you leave an American city and fly to Belgium, you won't experience jet lag if you continue to follow the time at home. However, if you try to adjust to Belgian time immediately, and have breakfast when you'd have been going to bed back home, you will disrupt your circadian rhythm and find it very difficult to get through the first few days.

Some people (larks) like to go to bed early and get up early, while others (owls) like to go to bed late and get up late (Ostberg, 1973). What happens to these people if they are forced by job or other commitments to follow other schedules? Insomnia or excessive sleepiness is the usual result. If this happens to you there is a way to reset your circadian rhythm (Taub & Berger, 1976). You must force yourself to go to bed at least one hour later each day. Once you go to bed you may sleep as long as you like. The next day, however, you must go to bed at least an hour later than you did the night before. When you finally find the schedule you like you can stop advancing there. By "going around the clock" in this fashion you can comfortably adjust yourself to any schedule.

Figure 5.4 *Main circadian rhythm (caused by rising at 8:00 A.M. and retiring at midnight) and ghost rhythms (caused by rising and retiring at many different hours). Individuals with such sleep schedules may find it difficult to wake up or fall asleep easily during certain times (shaded areas), since the body is not sure which circadian rhythm to follow.*

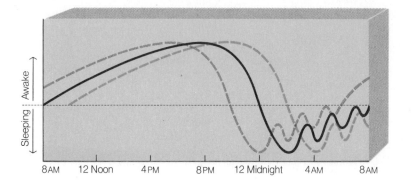

Narcolepsy **Narcolepsy** is a peculiar disorder that was poorly understood for many years. It afflicts approximately 250,000 Americans, both males and females. Although narcolepsy is sometimes called "sleep epilepsy," it appears to have little or nothing to do with actual epilepsy. Narcolepsy is an uncontrollable, recurring, and sudden onset of sleep during the daytime waking hours. The total loss of muscle control during a narcoleptic episode often causes the person to fall. Narcoleptics are most likely to sleep at moments of high anxiety or worry. The disorder appears to occur because there is a sudden onset of REM sleep during the waking state.

Narcolepsy appears to be associated with disturbances in the reticular activating system of the brain stem. The exact nature of the disturbances is unknown, but strong evidence now exists that narcolepsy is inherited. It has been noticed for many years that there was a tendency for narcolepsy to run in families. In general, people who have narcolepsy in their families are 50 times more likely to have the disorder than others. Narcolepsy has also been observed in dogs. Researcher Dement at Stanford University demonstrated that narcolepsy can be inherited by breeding narcoleptic Doberman pinschers with each other (see Figure 5.5). The number of narcoleptic puppies that resulted from this crossbreeding was strikingly

Figure 5.5 *Narcolepsy appears to be a genetic phenomenon. Here, Doberman puppies bred from narcoleptic parents fall asleep uncontrollably when the pack becomes excited at mealtime.*

high. This discovery may help researchers determine the exact biological nature of narcolepsy and provide a means of aiding people who suffer from the disease ("Genetic Basis," 1978).

Sleep Apnea   **Sleep apnea** is the cessation of breathing during sleep. It may occur for only a few seconds at a time or for minutes. Sleep patterns may be severely disturbed, and the sleeper often begins gasping or choking. In one sleep study a subject was found to have such severe apnea that he was unable to breathe and sleep at the same time. He would fall asleep, stop breathing, stay asleep for a minute or two, and then awake gasping. When he had gotten enough air, he would fall asleep again, only to stop breathing once more. This severe form of apnea is rare, but mild apnea is not uncommon.

If a person's sleep is sufficiently disrupted by apnea, he or she may experience excessive daytime sleepiness, headaches upon awakening, or other uncomfortable symptoms of insufficient air and a poor night's rest. Some individuals thought to be senile have been discovered to be actually suffering brain damage each night because of a lack of air.

Individuals suffering from apnea rarely realize that they have stopped breathing. Persons who show symptoms should ask someone to check whether they stop breathing during the night. Apnea can sometimes be controlled by placing a pillow at the nape of the neck so that the head is tilted backward during sleep. Since apnea seems to be related to throat closure, **tracheotomies** are sometimes performed in more severe cases (Arehart-Treichel, 1977).

DREAMING

Dreaming seems to be associated primarily with REM sleep. Eighty to eighty-five percent of subjects awakened from REM sleep report that they were dreaming before awakening (Berger, 1969). Occasional dreaming or dream-like experiences can also occur during NREM sleep, especially among light sleepers (Zimmerman, 1970). Typically, a person may have three or four dreams nightly, each associated with the REM period. Moreover, dreams change during the night, later dreams becoming progressively longer, more vivid, and more unrealistic than earlier dreams. No one knows what dreams are, but there are a number of theories.

Psychoanalytic Theory   The psychoanalytic interpretation of dreams, first described by Sigmund Freud (see Chapter 1), argues that dreams are disguised representations of repressed desires appearing in symbolic form. In this view, the purpose of dreams is to provide unconscious gratification so that certain desires will be satisfied and not intrude into wakefulness later. Furthermore, the argument continues, only the surface, or apparent, content of dreams is open to experimental investigation, and without an in-depth psychoanalysis the underlying purpose of the dreams would be wholly lost. Unfortunately, since this deep interpretation of underlying purpose is not open to experimental investigation, it remains conjecture whether the psychoanalytic view of the purpose of dreams is accurate.

Dreams as Expressions of Everyday Life   Other therapists believe that dreams are expressions of things that are missing in a person's life. Fritz Perls, a well-known psychotherapist, often argued this point. Still others feel that dreams are merely expressions of daily activity. For instance, re-

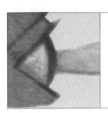

LUCID DREAMS, OR HOW TO STOP A NIGHTMARE

Almost everyone has at one time or another had a nightmare. Some of the worst nightmares are associated with physical feelings, such as the sense that you are falling or drowning or being physically attacked. Nobody likes these kinds of dreams, and it would be nice if there were a way to get rid of them. Like everyone else, Stephen LaBerge used to have nightmares, but he doesn't anymore. He has found a way of entering his dreams at will and changing their outcome. He calls this procedure *lucid dreaming*. A **lucid dream** occurs when you become aware that you're dreaming. Have you ever had a dream and said to yourself, while dreaming, "I'm just dreaming?" If you have, then you've had a lucid dream. This phenomenon has been known since the time of the ancient Greeks.

LaBerge says that during a lucid dream, "the dreamer may take an active hand in resolving the dream's conflict and in bringing the plot to a satisfactory conclusion" (LaBerge, 1981). LaBerge has learned—and so, apparently, can others—to produce lucid dreams on command. LaBerge refers to his method as *mnemonic induction of lucid dreams*, or MILD for short. Mnemonic induction is a simple way to remember something, and it will

be described in detail in Chapter 8. It works basically as follows: Suppose you want to remember to contact someone during the day. If you plan to make the contact by telephone, you might remember by looking at the telephone and picturing the person you need to call, perhaps in miniature, sitting on the phone waving at you. If your mental image is really sharp it will be hard to forget. From then on, every time you look at the telephone you may find yourself thinking about the person you have to call. This trick is a **mnemonic device**.

LaBerge used this technique to train himself to realize that he was dreaming when he was dreaming. He would lie in bed while fully awake and think for a long time that every time he dreamed he must remind himself that he was dreaming. He would say, "Next time I'm dreaming, I want to remember I'm dreaming." After practicing this for a while, he discovered that the next time he had a dream he found himself saying, "I'm only dreaming." Eventually, he was able to produce as many as four lucid dreams a night and an average of 21.5 lucid dreams a month.

This technique may be especially helpful for people who have nightmares, especially repetitive ones. If, for instance, you have a falling dream

that you would like to change, try lying down, relaxing, and thinking the dream through very carefully. As you think the dream through, say to yourself, "I'm only dreaming. I don't want to fall, and I won't fall. This is just a dream." If you say this often enough while imagining the dream, the next time you have the dream you may find that you can control it, just as LaBerge found. In the middle of what was beginning to be the familiar nightmare you will say, "This is only a dream. I'm only dreaming." The more you practice, the more lucid dreams you are likely to have. In this way you become the director. You can step in and change things whenever you want by planning ahead.

If mnemonic induction doesn't work, however, there is one more thing you can do. British psychologist Keith Herne at Hull University has developed a nightmare alarm that became available for purchase at selected stores in 1981. The alarm is a meter with a small nose-clip connection. The nose clip monitors breathing. When nightmares begin, breathing rates increase rapidly to 25 to 30 breaths a minute, a sign of stressful dreaming. The meter counts the number of breaths per minute and sounds an alarm when they reach the stressful level ("The Dream Machine," 1981).

---

searchers have found that men are more likely to dream about other men, while women are likely to dream equally about both sexes (Hall & Domhoff, 1963). Psychoanalysts might argue from the Freudian perspective that this demonstrates men's greater unconscious involvement with the male, or father figure. However, cross-cultural studies in India and Peru have shown that this kind of sex difference in dreams is highly dependent on waking social experiences and the frequency of contact between the sexes. In other words, men may be more likely to dream about men in Western culture because they are more likely to have daily contact with men (Grey & Kalsched, 1971; Urbina & Grey, 1975).

ACTIVATION-SYNTHESIS MODEL
A physiological model of dreaming
that argues that the brain synthesizes
random neural activity generated during sleep and organizes this activity
into a dream.

ANIMAL MAGNETISM
Term coined by Anton Mesmer to describe the supposed magnetic force that
people could exert on each other.

MESMERISM
A forerunner of hypnosis. In mesmerism, magnetic forces were called on to
relieve pain. Mesmerism was named
after Anton Mesmer, who claimed he
could cure the ill with magnetism.

LeVine's study of Nigerian school boys is perhaps a classic in the literature that attempts to relate daily experience to dream imagery. In studying three distinct cultural groups, LeVine discovered that knowing the social
power and achievements of each group enabled him to predict the general
level of power and achievement imagery contained in the dreams of children from each group (LeVine, 1966). Still, if dreams are only sleeping
expressions of our daily experience, we may wonder why researchers have
never succeeded in causing subjects to have particular dreams based on
occurrences during the day. In fact, when subjects were exposed to particular experiences and then told to dream about them a vast majority
dreamed about something else entirely. In one study, young men were
shown erotic movies for many hours, and then their dreams were monitored. They dreamed about all sorts of things, but nothing they dreamed
had anything to do with what they had seen in the films (Cartwright, Bernick, Borowitz, & Kling, 1969).

The Activation-Synthesis Model   One of the most interesting dream theories
has been proposed by J. Alan Hobson and Robert W. McCarley of Harvard
Medical School (1977). They based their theory on research conducted into
the brain activity of cats during REM sleep. Of course, you can't ask a cat
to tell you whether it's been dreaming, but cats do engage in REM sleep
and the electrical changes in their brain are very similar to those of dreaming human beings. Hobson and McCarley called their theory the **activation-
synthesis model** of dreams. During the activation phase a time-triggered
mechanism in the back of the brain generates neural impulses that stimulate both the oculomotor and reticular systems. *Oculomotor* refers to motor
neurons associated with eye muscles. This stimulation may be the cause of
rapid eye movement. The reticular system, as you'll recall from Chapter 2,

*Some people could make good use of a
nightmare alarm!*

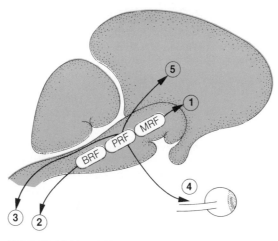

Figure 5.6 *A biological time-triggered mechanism of sleep. This physiological model of dream state generation, used the sagittal section of the cat brain and shows the bulbar (BRF), pontine (PRF), and midbrain (MRF) divisions of the reticular formation. Pontine is the adjective form of pons.* (SOURCE: *Hobson & McCarley, 1977, p. 1337*)

PROCESS ACCOUNTED FOR:

1 Activation of forebrain

2 Blockade of exteroceptive input [external stimuli]

3 Blockade of motor output [paralysis associated with REM]

4 Oculomotor activation [eye movement]

5 Provision of forebrain with internally generated information [random electrical activity generates dreams]

is involved in activating the organism. The time-triggered mechanism itself is located in the pons (see Figure 5.6). Once this pontine region has been stimulated, the midbrain and bulbar regions are activated. At this point several things happen. As you can see in the figure, midbrain stimulation activates the forebrain, and the bulbar region blocks outside input, making it more difficult to awaken the sleeper. Signals from the pons inhibit motor activity (which is associated with REM sleep) and at the same time cause oculomotor activity. Pontine signals are also projected to the forebrain. The question is: What happens to all this electrical information heading into the forebrain? How does the brain interpret it?

In the chapter on perception, you learned that the brain likes to organize incoming material, even if the material is only partial. Hobson and McCarley argue that dreaming may be nothing more than the brain's attempt to make some sense of what may amount to random electrical activity that enters the forebrain. This is the synthesis phase of the model. (McDonald, 1981).

HYPNOSIS

During the 18th century, the Austrian physician Anton Mesmer claimed that he could cure the ill with magnetism. Arguing that living things were influenced by magnetic forces, he coined the term **animal magnetism** to describe the "magnetic" force that people could exert on each other. Hundreds of Mesmer's patients claimed to be relieved of their pain through Mesmer's efforts. This kind of treatment became known as **mesmerism.**

Mesmer was a faith healer who knew how to make money. To serve the thousands who requested his services he "magnetized" inanimate objects and claimed that they could heal. The French Academy of Sciences (in consultation with Benjamin Franklin) found no evidence of any curative effects to be derived from magnetism. However, the Academy did suggest that Mesmer's personality had influenced his patients' imaginations. Or, to say it another way, Mesmer had the "power of suggestion."

What, exactly, this power of suggestion may be, or how it works, has been explored since the time of Mesmer and continues to be a subject of much interest. Today the term **hypnosis,** after Hypnos, the Greek god of sleep, is used to describe the effects of suggestion. Hypnosis is not a state of sleep, however. Although a hypnotist may say, "You are falling deeply asleep," EEG readings have shown that hypnotized subjects supposedly in a deep sleep are actually wide-awake and drowsy. You should also know that hypnosis appears not to be a single phenomenon, but is rather a single word used to describe a number of relatively separate phenomena (Barber, 1969) (see Table 5.1).

Some subjects can be hypnotized, while others cannot. The hypnotist begins a hypnosis session by getting the subject to relax. The subject is usually asked to fix her gaze on a particular place or point, and then to respond to the hypnotist. Once the subject is relaxed, the hypnotist can test for suggestibility. A scale used to measure suggestibility, or susceptibility, is shown in Table 5.2. Individuals who are highly suggestible will meet many of the criteria on this test. These people are likely to be good subjects for hypnosis. Others, especially those who are alert and curious about the hypnotic effect, and who are waiting for something to "happen to them," are likely not to be susceptible. Some subjects have failed to become hypnotized even after thousands of attempts.

Dissociation   Once the subject is prepared and showing susceptibility, the hypnotist can create a number of interesting effects. One of the most fascinating is the **dissociation** that can occur in a hypnotized state. The subject can be maneuvered to engage in two things simultaneously, and yet to remember only one clearly. **Automatic writing** is an example of this kind of dissociation. The hypnotist will ask the subject to write something, and

By the late nineteenth century the medical profession was seriously investigating hypnosis.

while the subject's hand is writing, the hypnotist will draw the subject into discussing or describing something else. Later, the subject may be surprised to learn what his hand has written. At the same time, he will clearly recall the topic under discussion while the writing was in progress. This dissociation between verbal discussion and handwriting is an interesting effect, and part of what has been called hypnosis (Hilgard, 1977).

Table 5.1   The many aspects of hypnosis

HYPNOTIC EFFECT	POSSIBLE REASONS FOR THE HYPNOTIC EFFECT
Dissociation	When conscious attention is distracted, ingrained habits may continue to function without the subject's awareness.
Memory enhancement	Anxiety that may interfere with memory retrieval is reduced.
Relief from pain or changes in the emotional state	Subject expects a change; subject reacts only to actual pain or emotional state rather than to expected pain or emotions.
"Unusual" behavior	Subject feels such behavior is expected or wishes to please hypnotist by being a "good subject" (social pressure).
Sensory or perceptual changes	Perceptual mechanisms may actually change; subject may lie, either consciously or unconsciously, in order to be a "good subject."
Disinhibition	Subject can now place responsibility for his or her acts elsewhere (on the hypnotist).
Posthypnotic suggestion	Subject unconsciously learns an association between two events so that later, when one event occurs, the second event is acted upon or is brought to mind.

Table 5.2   Stanford hypnotic susceptibility scale, form C

ITEM	CRITERION OF PASSING
0. Eye closure during induction	(Noted, but not scored)
1. Hand lowering (right hand)	Lowers at least 6 inches in 10 seconds
2. Moving hands apart	Hands 6 inches or more apart after 10 seconds
3. Mosquito hallucination	Any acknowledgment of effect
4. Taste hallucination (sweet, sour)	Both tastes experienced and one strong or with overt movements
5. Arm rigidity (right arm)	Less than 2 inches of arm bending in 10 seconds
6. Dream	Dreams well, experience comparable to a dream
7. Age regression (school fifth and second grades)	Clear change in handwriting between present and one regressed age
8. Anosmia to ammonia	Odor of ammonia denied and overt signs absent
9. Arm immobilization (left arm)	Arm rises less than 1 inch in 10 seconds
10. Hallucinated voice	Subject answers voice realistically at least once
11. Negative visual hallucination (sees two of three boxes)	Reports seeing only two boxes
12. Posthypnotic amnesia	Subject recalls three or fewer items before "Now you can remember everything"

SOURCE: Weitzenhoffer and Hilgard (1962).

NOTE: This scale is used in conjunction with a brief attempted induction of hypnosis, during which the subject is observed and rated on performance on the above 12 items. The hypnotist suggests each item and notes if the subject responds to the suggestion. The possible score is 12, and the average score is 5.19.

When students first encounter something like automatic writing, they often believe that it's a trick or that the subject was lying and really did know what he was writing. Yet most of us, through **self-hypnosis,** have had a similar dissociating experience at one time or another. It may actually be easier to be self-hypnotized than to be hypnotized by someone else (Ruch, 1975). If you are by yourself and you fix your gaze on a particular place and begin to daydream, your EEG state may be identical to that of a hypnotized subject. In fact, a very deep daydream may be a perfect example of hypnosis. Some people drive their cars in this state. They fix their gaze, perhaps on the horizon (or worse, on the hood ornament), and begin to daydream. An experience such as this can also have an element of dissociation. That is, while daydreaming you may still manage to arrive at your destination, taking the correct turns and stopping at the stoplights, without remembering a single detail about the trip. This experience, called **highway hypnosis,** is familiar to most drivers. It occurs very easily at night when there are few visual distractions and when the broken white line on the highway is going by at a steady rate. If this has ever happened to you, then you've experienced an effect of dissociation while self-hypnotized.

Memory Enhancement   Another phenomenon of hypnosis is memory enhancement. Although memory itself cannot be improved through hypnosis, hypnosis can be used to alleviate anxiety which can, in turn, affect memory. Memory can be inhibited by anxiety. The greater the anxiety, the less likely a person is to remember clearly and accurately. Hypnosis has been used effectively by police departments and other agencies to calm individuals who are trying to remember something.

Pain Relief and Changed Emotional States   Hypnosis has also been used to relieve pain and to change emotional states. The possibility that hypnosis can raise endorphin levels enough to relieve pain has excited a great deal of interest (see Chapter 2). In examinations of hypnotic procedures, however, endorphin has not been shown to be related in any way to the kind of pain relief obtained under hypnosis. Even when subjects were given naloxone, which blocks the effects of endorphin, hypnosis could still relieve pain. Hypnosis can also effectively prevent an individual from laughing in humorous situations. How can hypnosis bring about such changes? It may be that under hypnosis an individual distinguishes between *expected* and *actual* pain or humor. There is a difference. In many cultures people are taught that pain is more severe than it physically should be. Any dentist can tell you this. Some patients start screaming when the dentist touches their mouth. Many dentists have begun using hypnosis to ease such fears. Patients who expect the hypnosis to work, and who are relaxed and comfortable, may then experience only the "real" pain rather than the much worse "expected" pain. Certainly hypnosis has its limits. In cases of extreme pain no amount of hypnosis is likely to help. Nonetheless, hypnosis has occasionally been successful when anesthetics could not be used, even when general surgery was being performed. Hypnosis can be especially effective in operations requiring incisions to be made in the back, where there are few pain receptors.

Behavioral Changes   Subjects who are hypnotized frequently behave in strange ways. Following instructions, they may become amnesiac, forgetting specific things, or they may exhibit sensory changes, claiming that they see objects when the objects are not there or denying that they see objects when the objects are in front of them. In the latter case, it is not clear whether the hypnosis causes a real sensory change in the brain. Most researchers attribute this change to "social pressures," feeling that participants, in their desire to be "good" subjects, will go along with the hypnotist even to the point of lying (Sarbin, 1950). They may swear, for instance, that they see only the hypnotist although they are standing in a crowded room. There may also be sensory changes hampering the subjects' ability to sense the other people in the room, but the physiology of such changes has not been discovered.

Stage hypnotists frequently entertain their audiences by getting people to act in bizarre ways. A volunteer may begin to imitate a chicken when told that he is one. On the other hand, people who volunteer to be chickens may be a little unusual to start with. Perhaps they simply want to be on stage (Sarbin & Coe, 1972). They may also be doing what they think is expected of them. Some "hypnotists" have a bag of dirty tricks. They may hand a steel ball to a volunteer, saying, "I'm going to make you feel as though this steel ball is getting hotter and hotter." Suddenly, the volunteer cries "My hands are burning!" and drops the ball, convinced that it was hypnosis that caused the sensation. In fact, the hypnotist has used a steel ball containing two chemicals that, when mixed (when the ball was turned and handed to the subject), caused the ball to become extremely hot in reality.

Disinhibition Hypnosis can also *disinhibit* subjects, that is, remove their reluctance to do specific things. One of the misconceptions about hypnosis is that a subject will never do something while hypnotized that he or she wouldn't do while "awake" (Orne & Evans, 1965). This is not necessarily true. If a hypnotist tells Sergeant Jones to hit Colonel Brown in the face with a pie, and the sergeant is not hypnotized, the sergeant will wisely say, "No thank you, sir." Once the sergeant is hypnotized, however, and the hypnotist says, "Now hit the colonel in the face with a pie," the sergeant may do as instructed. The difference may be that the sergeant can now attribute

Once hypnotized, the subject becomes extremely susceptible to suggestion.

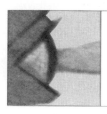

HYPNOSIS AND AGE REGRESSION

Throughout the years hypnosis has been credited with many achievements. Some have received great publicity although no substantial data are available to support them. One of the most controversial has been age regression. The hypnotist tells the subject to relax and to feel that he is moving back in time to his youth. When asked how old he is, the subject might reply ''Ten,'' despite the fact that he is obviously an adult. Then, the subject might describe what it was like when he was ten. He might even be able to recall a language that he spoke then that he can no longer speak with fluency (Fromm, 1970). The hypnotist might ask the subject to regress further back, to when he was eight, six, four, or one, or even to the time he was in the womb. At this point the adult might curl up in a fetal position. When asked what he is doing he might not be able to respond because he is too young to speak. Then the hypnotist might ask the subject to go back even further, many years before his birth, and to describe what it is like. Suddenly the adult might say that he is a shoemaker in Germany in 1853, and his name is Hans Gunwaldt. ''What is life like for you, Hans?'' asks the hypnotist, and the subject begins to describe what his earlier life was like.

What has happened here? Has the subject been sent back to another time, another life? There is no evidence to support such a notion. The adult, desiring to comply with the hypnotist's request, has apparently tried to act out what he feels may be expected of him (Sarbin & Coe, 1972). When led back to a time before birth, he will often reenact an earlier life because this has become part of the hypnosis myth.

There are ways of testing this phenomenon to see if it is real. Adults in the age-regressed state, who are supposedly only five years old, often display cognitive abilities far beyond those of a five-year-old. They answer questions that most adults wrongly believe a five-year-old could answer but that a real child of that age would never be able to answer.

Another way of showing the improbability of the prebirth phenomenon is by demonstrating that hypnotists can impose almost any previous life they wish on their subjects. In one experiment, hypnotists were each given a fabricated previous-life story to pass on to their hypnotized subjects. The subjects were then age-regressed back many years before their birth. By subtle cuing, the hypnotists were able to elicit these fake previous lives from their subjects. Each subject related almost exactly the story that had been made up ahead of time.

---

responsibility to the hypnotist, especially if the colonel has been watching the whole performance. The sergeant will know that, since he was hypnotized, no one can blame him. Furthermore, if the sergeant has always wanted to hit the colonel with a pie, this is as good a time as any. Since responsibility can be transferred to someone else, namely the hypnotist, you as a subject may therefore be willing to engage in activities that you had always wanted to but had never dared before.

Posthypnotic Suggestion Hypnotists can in many instances give **posthypnotic suggestions,** that is, tell subjects that later, when they see or hear a particular stimulus, they will get an urge to do something. The hypnotist may say, for example, "The next time you hear a car horn your shoulder will itch, and you will scratch it." Posthypnotic suggestion may work on the same principle as mnemonic association. By relaxing and thinking that a car horn goes with an itching shoulder, you may actually be cued (reminded) to scratch your shoulder the next time you hear a car horn.

Meditation, transcendental or otherwise, is a very simple technique that can be practiced by anyone. Unfortunately, this simple and helpful practice has been heralded by many as a bestower of magical powers, enabling people to walk through walls, float above the ground, and end crime. If you sit back, close your eyes, breathe deeply, relax, and concentrate on a particular sound or word (it doesn't matter which) for about 15 minutes, a number of changes will probably occur. Your heart rate will slow, your blood pressure will lower, and the amount of oxygen you consume will decrease. Body temperature at the extremities will rise. Muscles will relax. Practicing this relaxation technique perhaps twice a day can be beneficial, helping you to become calm and to think a little more clearly. It can be especially useful if you have a hectic job or one that keeps you under considerable pressure. That's all there is to meditation.

Some people can exercise great control over their bodies through years of practicing this relaxation technique. **Yogis** in India can reduce their oxygen needs, blood pressure, and heart rate considerably (Calder, 1971). This ability can be gained more rapidly through the use of **biofeedback.** In biofeedback one aspect of an individual's biology is amplified on a machine so that changes can be observed that normally would require great concentra-

POSTHYPNOTIC SUGGESTION
A suggestion made to a hypnotized subject to perform some task at a particular cue after the hypnotic session is over.

MEDITATION
Deep relaxation brought on by focusing one's attention on a particular sound or image.

YOGI
One who practices yoga, a Hindu discipline whose aim is to train consciousness to attain a state of perfect spiritual insight and tranquility. Control of bodily functions and mental states is practiced.

BIOFEEDBACK
A technique of monitoring internal processes such as heart rate, brain waves, or blood pressure in order to enable the subject to gain voluntary control over these processes.

During meditation, a yogi's heartrate, respiration, and blood pressure will decrease dramatically.

PSYCHOACTIVE DRUGS
Drugs that alter conscious awareness or perception.

STIMULANTS
Drugs that can stimulate or excite the central nervous system. Caffeine and amphetamines are examples of stimulants.

DEPRESSANTS
Drugs that can depress or slow the central nervous system. Alcohol and tranquilizers are examples of depressants.

HALLUCINOGENS
Drugs that cause excitation at synapses associated with sense perception. A person taking these drugs may perceive sensations when there is nothing real to see, hear, or feel.

AMPHETAMINES
A group of drugs that excite the central nervous system and suppress appetite, increase heart rate and blood pressure, and alter sleep patterns.

COCAINE
A habit-forming stimulant that is typically inhaled, and occasionally swallowed, smoked, or injected. It is derived from the leaves of the coca plant and used in medicine as a local anesthetic.

NARCOTIC
Any drug that dulls the senses, induces sleep, and with prolonged use becomes addictive, for example heroin, morphine, and codeine.

tion to perceive. Unlike a yogi, who must spend many years learning to be aware of changes in body temperature, you can perceive differences immediately because of the amplifier hooked to your fingertips which gives you a digital reading. Since the capillaries at the extremities dilate when you relax, you can alter the body temperature at the fingertips by making yourself relax. Conversely, if you become anxious (perhaps by thinking of your bank account, a trick that works for me), you can cause the temperature at the extremities to drop rapidly as the sympathetic nervous system becomes aroused. By practicing with biofeedback, you can become adept at changing the temperature at the surface of your skin. This technique has been found to be quite effective in alleviating migraine headaches (severe headaches that can last for hours or even days), since capillary dilation also helps to lower blood pressure. In this way you can acquire a degree of control over many aspects of the autonomic nervous system, from brain waves to heart rate (Gatchel & Proctor, 1976).

PSYCHOACTIVE DRUGS

Any drug that alters conscious awareness or perception is called psychoactive. **Psychoactive drugs** often work directly on the brain. The most commonly used psychoactive drugs—including alcohol, nicotine, and caffeine—are so familiar that we rarely think of them as drugs or consider that they have psychological effects. Psychoactive drugs can be classified according to their effects as **stimulants, depressants,** and **hallucinogens.** In this chapter we will discuss the properties and effects on the conscious state of various drugs. Alcoholism and drug abuse will be treated separately in Chapter 15, and therapy for alcoholics and drug abusers will be considered in Chapter 16.

Amphetamines **Amphetamines** are powerful stimulants originally developed by the military for soldiers who had to stay alert in combat. They are sold under names such as Dexedrine, Benzedrine, and Methedrine. On the street they are known as uppers, speed, or bennies. The way in which amphetamines work is not clearly understood, but they probably dampen the effects of inhibitory synapses in the brain. If taken in low doses for a limited time, the drugs can help overcome fatigue, the purpose for which they were developed. Sustained use, however, can result in a number of unpleasant states that can last for a long time. These include paranoia, anger, and prolonged restlessness (Snyder, 1973). Amphetamines can also decrease appetite, and they were widely prescribed as diet pills during the early 1970s. However, people who used them for this purpose over an extended period found that they became accustomed to them and, as they gradually regained their appetites, they continued to desire them. The result was an overweight person dependent on amphetamines. Consequently, the drugs have not been widely accepted as a viable means of controlling weight.

Some amphetamine abusers mainline, meaning that they inject the drug intravenously (in a vein). Intravenous injections can be extremely dangerous, rapidly creating a need for more and more of the drug in order to prevent the "crash," or deep depression, brought on by discontinuation of the drug. Amphetamine users who mainline do not have a long life expectancy, and they often compound their problems by shooting up with heroin in order to avoid or eliminate the adverse effects of a crash.

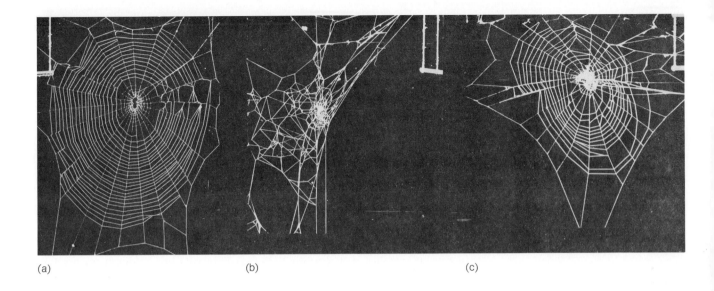

(a)   (b)   (c)

Cocaine   **Cocaine** is a stimulant. It is usually inhaled, or snorted, and occasionally injected. It may also be smoked. One of the leading experts in the study of the psychoactive effects of cocaine was Sigmund Freud (1885/1974). Freud initially argued that cocaine was relatively safe and encouraged its use. He found that it increased his alertness, made him feel invigorated, and gave him a sensation of pleasure. Later, however, after observing the visual disturbances experienced by a friend who had taken too much cocaine, he withdrew his support, realizing that the drug could have dangerous side effects.

Cocaine was an ingredient in Coca-Cola until its use in soft drinks was banned by law in 1903. In fact, the drug gave the drink its name. After the law was passed, the Coca-Cola company found that caffeine was an adequate substitute.

For years cocaine was misunderstood and generally thought to be a **narcotic,** which it is not. Medically, cocaine injected under the skin is used as a local anesthetic. Today, cocaine is widely known as a pleasure-inducing drug. Very expensive, it is sometimes called the rich man's drug.

In the past few years several dangers associated with cocaine use have come to light. The most alarming is that cocaine can apparently cause sudden death in first-time and long-term users alike. Between 1969 and 1978 it was reported that 24 persons died as a direct result of using cocaine alone. Eleven of these persons had injected the drug, seven had swallowed it, five had snorted it, and one person's method was unknown (Wetli & Wright, 1979). The deaths caused by snorting came as a particular surprise, since snorting had been widely considered to be the safest way to take the drug. The deaths were the result of convulsions which occurred without warning a few minutes to an hour after the drug was inhaled. People have different tolerances for drugs, and just as some people can die from bee stings, some people can die from taking cocaine.

Like amphetamines, cocaine is suspected of dampening the inhibitory synapses in the brain, but the exact mechanism of the drug's functioning is unknown. Although cocaine is not physically addictive, it can be extremely habit-forming. Heavy users of cocaine are excitable, likely to lose weight, and susceptible to illness.

(a) The normal web of the female spider, Araneus diadematus. The irregularity at the right side of the web was caused by the spider's rushing away when the photo was taken. (b) The same spider built this strange web after receiving a high dose of amphetamine. (c) This web, built one day after receiving the amphetamine, shows partial recovery.

CAFFEINE
A drug contained in coffee, tea, and kola nuts, which functions as a stimulant and diuretic.

DELIRIUM TREMENS
A state of delirium resulting from prolonged alcoholism and marked by extreme confusion, vivid hallucinations, and body tremors.

BENZODIAZEPINES
An important class of minor tranquilizers which, since the mid-1950s, has come to replace the more dangerous barbiturates. Usually prescribed by physicians to control anxiety and tension.

TRANQUILIZERS
Any of various drugs that are used to pacify.

HEROIN
A highly addictive narcotic drug that is derived from morphine.

HALLUCINATIONS
A false sense perception for which there is no appropriate external stimulus.

PCP
A dangerous hallucinogenic drug that can lead to aggressive or psychotic behavior. Also known as *angel dust*.

Caffeine **Caffeine** is known to function as a dampener of inhibitory synapses in the brain. The increased feeling of energy and alertness associated with caffeine use is similar to that obtained from small amounts of cocaine. Like any drug, caffeine can be abused. Individuals taking more than 0.75 of a gram of caffeine per day (approximately four to five cups of coffee) may suffer withdrawal symptoms if the caffeine is removed, including excessive urination, anxiety, and dizziness. The amount of caffeine consumed per day depends on the kind of coffee or tea consumed. Instant coffee tends to have less caffeine than ground coffee. In one study, 78 percent of heavy caffeine users were found to show signs of depression which, they reported, was alleviated by drinking coffee (Greden, Fontaine, Lubetsky, & Chamberlin, 1978).

Alcohol Alcohol is a depressant which acts on the central nervous system, slowing down its functioning. Some alcohol users swear that, in limited amounts, alcohol is a stimulant. This belief probably comes from the fact that alcohol, although a depressant even in small amounts, does cause an elevation in sex hormones, which may create greater sexual arousal. In this sense, alcohol may make you "want to more, but able to less." Alcohol can also make you less inhibited.

At concentrations as low as 0.0003 (three hundredths of 1 percent) of alcohol per total volume of blood, the user may feel relaxed or giddy. At concentrations of 0.001, after about three drinks or perhaps three beers, nervous functions in the sensory and motor systems may be impaired to a point at which driving a vehicle would be dangerous. At 0.002, the drinker would be severely incapacitated, and levels above 0.004 are often lethal. Most state laws define legal intoxication as concentrations above 0.001. Because of its widespread use by people engaged in activities requiring concentration and alertness, especially driving, alcohol has shown itself to be an extremely dangerous drug. Between 30 and 50 percent of all automobile deaths are related to drinking while driving (Zylman, 1975). Moreover, approximately 25 percent of all pedestrians killed by automobiles were drunk by legal standards when they were hit ("Drunk Walking," 1977).

Alcohol, while not classified as a hallucinogen, may, with excessive use, lead to hallucinations either while it is being consumed or during alcohol withdrawal. **Delirium tremens** is the term for the hallucinations suffered by alcoholics upon withdrawal, during which they often hallucinate about bugs or animals crawling on them.

Benzodiazepines **Benzodiazepines** are **tranquilizers,** and they are the most widely prescribed drugs in the world. They include such common names as Librium and Valium. Benzodiazepines have been found to work hand in hand with GABA (gamma-aminobutyric acid), a neurotransmitter abundant in the brain and associated with inhibitory synapses (see Chapter 2).

There appear to be natural receptors in the brain that are particularly sensitive to Valium and other benzodiazepines. GABA helps Valium bind more tightly with these receptors, causing lengthy and increased inhibition at the inhibitory synapses (Guidotti, Baraldi, Schwartz, Toffano, & Costa, 1979). The presence of these natural receptors suggests that the brain may produce its own kind of Valium, and that the drug merely mimics this natural substance. As you'll recall, this was true of heroin, which mimicked endorphin. So far, from thousands of quarts of urine, Danish researchers have been able to isolate only 2 milligrams of what appears to be the brain's own Valium. The natural substance appears to bind even more tightly than the antianxiety drugs, perhaps enabling the brain to produce a natural tranquilized state. This substance may eventually be identified and purified, and by examining it scientists may learn the exact way in which tranquilizers affect the brain. The result may be a new drug that will outclass any of the benzodiazepines, a natural antianxiety drug (Braestrup, Nielsen, Squires & Laurberg, 1978).

Heroin **Heroin** is indirectly derived from opium, as are morphine and codeine. Heroin is made from but is stronger than morphine, which in turn is stronger than codeine. Heroin is a powerful narcotic and is extremely physically addictive. As discussed in Chapter 2, heroin works by mimicking the brain's own morphine-like substance, endorphin. Heroin is an excellent painkiller and creates a great sense of well-being in the user. It is usually injected, but recently smoking heroin has become popular. Smokers refer to it as "chasing the dragon."

If they are very careful about the quality of the drug and use it under sterile conditions, heroin addicts may be able to continue taking it for some time without necessarily suffering serious detrimental effects. However, this is not usually the case. Heroin deaths are often related to overdose, the dosage being uncertain because heroin is often cut to make it go further. Sometimes the heroin is cut with deadly substances. Heroin deaths may also result from unsterile and improper injections, which may cause hepatitis or serious circulatory disorders. Malnutrition is another factor. Heroin addicts often use their money to buy the drug instead of food, and their sense of well-being as well as the painkilling properties of the drug can render them insensitive to feelings of hunger. As you'll recall from our earlier discussion, endorphin appears to be used by the brain to create a natural high when the time is right for feelings of happiness and well-being (Leff, 1978). Heroin users, however, short-circuit their natural reward system. This may explain why heroin addicts often don't care that they may be going to die, or that someone is hurt by their behavior, or that they don't eat or engage in sex. Since the endorphin system has been overridden, no external events of significance are likely to have an effect.

Hallucinogens Hallucinogens are drugs that cause excitation at synapses associated with sense perception. **Hallucinations** can result, that is, the perception of light, sound, and other forms of sensation when there is nothing "real" to see, hear, or feel. The drugs in this category include mescaline, which is derived from a cactus; psilocybin, derived from mushrooms; LSD, derived from ergot, a rye mold; and DMT, which is a synthetic but which may also be a naturally occurring neurotransmitter. As mentioned in Chapter 2, these drugs probably have their effect because they mimic neurotransmitters associated with sensation and perception. Some hallucinogens, such as DMT, last a short time, while others, such as LSD, may last for many hours.

PCP Phencyclidine hydrochloride (**PCP**), better known as angel dust, has become, unfortunately, a popular drug in the last decade. One of its effects is to cause hallucinations. It has been argued, however, that PCP represents

MARIJUANA
The dried flowers and leaves of the cannibis variety of hemp.

THC
Tetrahydrocannabinol, the active ingredient in marijuana, which causes hallucinations in high enough doses.

an entirely new class of psychoactive drug (Balster & Chait, 1976). This is because its use gives rise to many other serious disorders besides hallucinations. In many cases a complete loss of contact with reality occurs, accompanied by unpredictably aggressive behavior which can persist for weeks after the drug has been taken. Based on over 100 cases, a typical PCP reaction has been found to include three distinct phases: violent, psychotic behavior lasting approximately five days; unpredictable and restless behavior lasting about five more days; and rapid improvement and personality reintegration during the final four days. PCP use should be considered a psychiatric emergency. Even if the drug is not taken again, about one fourth of those treated after using it suffer serious behavioral disturbances later (Luisada & Brown, 1976). There is also evidence that PCP creates a strong psychological dependency (Bolster, Heminger, Martin, & Fry, 1976).

PCP may have its effect because it, too, mimics a natural substance made by the brain. While the possibility of a naturally occurring PCP is still highly uncertain, initial results indicate that it may exist. Researchers investigating the question have injected radioactive PCP into animal brains, finding receptor sites in the brain that appear to attract and bind to PCP and nothing else. Such exclusive receptors argue in favor of the existence of a naturally occurring PCP. Most of the receptors are concentrated in the hippocampus (Zukin & Zukin, 1979).

Why would the brain produce a version of what appears to be a terrible drug? Possibly it uses natural PCP in tiny amounts. Laboratory research has shown that the drug is highly desired. Monkeys have repeatedly given themselves PCP, even if they had to sacrifice food to do so (Zukin & Zukin, 1979). PCP may therefore be part of the brain's reward mechanism. It may be used to tell an organism that something should be repeated.

Marijuana **Marijuana** is classified as an hallucinogen because in sufficient dosages its active ingredient, **THC,** causes hallucinations. Along with its hallucinogenic properties, marijuana can function as both a depressant

Drug use among the young is a serious problem.

UNIT ONE
PSYCHOLOGICAL FOUNDATIONS:
THE MIND AND THE BODY

162

and a stimulant. The difference appears to be related to dosage. At higher doses it acts as a stimulant, and at lower doses it acts as a depressant (Blum, Briggs, Feinglass, Domey, & Wallace, 1977).

Small or medium doses (0.2 to 0.4 milligrams per kilogram of body weight) seem to have little effect on higher brain functions. Consequently, the effect reported by subjects who have taken small doses may be mostly a placebo reaction (Miller, Cornett, & Brightwell, 1976; Babor, Mendelson, & Kuehnle, 1976). In smoking a joint, part of the effect may come from the practice of inhaling very deeply and holding the smoke in the lungs for some time before exhaling. Even without marijuana this kind of hyperventilation may lead to dizziness or produce a "rush" simply because it brings about a change in oxygen level in the blood. At higher doses, three or four times above a mild dose, the effect becomes hallucinogenic.

Arguments over whether marijuana is dangerous continue. The amount of danger may be related to dose and use.

Summary

■ Consciousness is the state in which you are aware not only of the external environment but also of internal events such as thinking.

■ Thanks to important advances in scientific technology, there are now some objective ways to measure conscious states.

■ By monitoring the conscious state during the waking hours, researchers have found that the same percentage of time is spent daydreaming as is spent dreaming at night.

■ The conscious state is said to be altered any time the content or quality of conscious experience undergoes a significant change.

■ The electroencephalograph (EEG) records brain waves as electrical changes, and has been used to monitor states of consciousness.

■ There are four stages of sleep. Stages 3 and 4 are often referred to as slow-wave sleep. Rapid eye movement (REM) sleep has been associated with dreaming. REM sleep is sometimes referred to as paradoxical sleep because during REM the brain waves are similar to those of the waking state.

■ REM rebound is a phenomenon that occurs when there has been REM deprivation.

■ The average young adult needs between 6½ and 8½ hours of sleep a night. Some people, known as healthy insomniacs, can get by with much less.

■ Two theories attempt to explain why we sleep. The adaptive theory argues that each species requires a certain amount of waking time in order to survive and that the rest of the time is best spent in a state, such as sleeping, in which there is the least chance of danger or injury. The second theory, known as the conserving-energy theory, argues that sleep is a way of conserving energy and using fewer calories.

■ Long-term sleep deprivation has not been found to be physically detrimental as long as the subjects were healthy to begin with. The effects of such long-term deprivation are decreased performance on tasks, hallucinations, delusions, and microsleep.

■ At one point it was believed that REM was necessary, but more recent evidence indicates that total REM deprivation may not be harmful.

- There are many sleep-related disturbances, including insomnia, narcolepsy, and sleep apnea.
- The psychoanalytic interpretation of dreams argues that dreams are disguised representations of repressed desires. The activation-synthesis model of dreams argues that dreaming may be nothing more than the brain's attempt to make sense of what may amount to random electrical activity entering the forebrain.
- Hypnosis is not a state of sleep. Hypnosis encompasses a number of relatively separate phenomena.
- Among the different aspects of hypnosis are dissociation, memory enhancement, pain relief, changed emotional states, unusual behavior, sensory and perceptual changes, disinhibition, and posthypnotic suggestion.
- Meditation is a very simple phenomenon that can be practiced by anyone.
- In biofeedback one aspect of an individual's biology is amplified on a machine so that changes can be observed that would normally require great concentration to perceive.
- Any drug that alters conscious awareness or perception is called a psychoactive drug. The three major classifications of psychoactive drugs are stimulants, depressants, and hallucinogens.

EPILOGUE: 414—?

Psychologists who study consciousness know that it has many states. Behavior and even memory can be affected by these states. In the following account, a police department uses this knowledge to help solve an infamous crime.

In July 1976 in Chowchilla, California, three masked gunmen kidnapped a busload of children as they were returning from summer camp. The 26 children and the bus driver, Ed Ray, were transferred at gunpoint into a closed truck van that was then buried in a rock quarry. Eventually they managed to escape from their underground tomb.

During the ordeal, Ed Ray had looked at the license plate on the car that the gunmen had been driving. He had tried to memorize it. But now he couldn't remember all of it. All he could recall was 414. The other half of the plate was a blank.

Ed Ray was upset, frightened, and trying hard to remember. The harder he tried, the less he could

recall. The California police decided to try hypnosis. The hypnotist realized that his primary function would be to relax Mr. Ray so that he could try to recall the number without the interfering effects of intense anxiety. In slow gentle steps the hypnotist helped Ray recreate the scene as though it were a television program. He asked Ray about many things not directly related to the fearful event. Sometime during the conversation he casually asked about the number of the license plate. "That's easy," Ray said, and without any difficulty he supplied the police with the complete number. In short order the kidnappers were arrested (Ray & Herskowitz, 1976).

Suggestions for Further Reading

1. Dement, W. *Some must watch while some must sleep.* New York: Norton, 1978.
2. Goleman, D., & Davidson, R. J. *Consciousness: Brain, states of awareness, and mysticism.* New York: Harper & Row, 1979.
3. Hilgard, E. R. *Divided consciousness.* New York: Wiley, 1977.
4. Wolman, B. *Handbook of dreams: Research, theories, and applications.* New York: Van Nostrand, 1979.

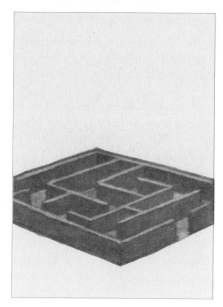

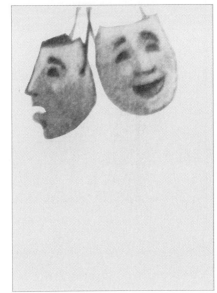

UNIT TWO

Interacting with the Environment

CONTENTS

Learning and Conditioning

PROLOGUE

You are in the southern United States with Dr. Kenneth Clark. The year is 1947. You have been watching Dr. Clark and a group of young white children. He has told them a story about a good boy and a bad boy. Never once during the story does he mention race. Now he begins the experiment that you and he had discussed. He takes two dolls from a small case, a white doll and a black doll. He holds them before the children. One by one the children are asked, "Which doll looks like you?" Almost all of the children indicate that they look like the white doll. "Now tell me which doll is the good boy and which doll is the bad boy." A large majority of the children indicate that the white doll is the good boy and the black doll is the bad boy; the white doll is nice and the black doll is dirty or ugly (Clark & Clark, 1947).

How had these southern white children learned to make these associations? During the decades of racial prejudice that had come before, darker skin had become associated with poverty and with being "inferior," not just in the South, but generally throughout the

United States. The white children had learned to attribute these characteristics to black people. Later, you realize the full scope of the problem when Dr. Clark asks black children the same questions, "Which doll looks like you?" and "Which doll is the good boy and which is the bad boy?" The black children know that the black doll looks like them, but a majority of them point to the white doll and say, "That's the good boy." Then they point to the black doll and say, "That's the bad one." The black children, having been raised in the same general environment as the white children, had learned to make the same associations. They had seen that the whites were better off and the blacks were worse off. They were suffering the worst effects of racism: They believed the lies about themselves.

During the 1960s, when the phrase "Black is beautiful" became popular, many people didn't understand its significance. It actually wasn't difficult to understand; it was simply another association, this one pairing "black" with "beautiful"—an association long

169

overdue. Today, children are far less likely to label the black doll or the white doll as particularly good or bad (Hraba & Grant, 1970).

The children Clark interviewed were not born with the attitudes and beliefs that they expressed. They had acquired them through learning. Because of the associations they had experienced, they had learned to feel a certain way about darker skin. Learning through associations is only one of the ways in which people learn. In this chapter we'll examine different ways of learning. As you'll soon discover, most of the behaviors that we consider "human" are acquired through learning and experience.

Why Psychologists Study Learning

Psychology is the study of behavior. Psychologists study learning because among humans, the vast majority of behaviors are learned. **Learning** may be defined as a relatively permanent change in behavior that results from experience. We say "relatively permanent change" in order to exclude the effects of such factors as fatigue. Fatigue, which occurs because of experience, may change behavior, but only temporarily, whereas learning implies a more lasting change. Learning is also said to be the result of experience. Not all behaviors, however, are the result of experience. Behaviors that are "built into" or inherited by an organism are called unlearned or inherited behaviors. Such behaviors have been the subject of considerable research, especially in the last 40 years or so.

The Evolution of Behavior — Instincts, Ethologists, and Ducks

You are a product of billions of years of evolution. Your body has been shaped and fashioned by the forces and stresses of those times. This process is the focal point of anthropological studies of evolutionary biology. Evolution is important in psychology as well, since behavior, or the tendency to behave in certain ways, can be inherited (McClearn, 1970). Behavior, too, has been shaped by the forces of evolution. We can cite many examples of inherited behaviors in other species. For instance, all healthy cats bathe themselves with their tongues; robins begin building nests without benefit of blueprints; and salmon return to the same stream in which they were spawned. These behaviors don't appear to be acquired through experience. Instead, they are most likely "in the genes." Just as the bodies of these creatures have evolved, so have many of their behavioral patterns. Being carried in the genes, these behaviors are passed from one generation to the next.

Throughout this century, research on inherited behavior has attracted great interest, especially in Europe. Those who specialize in this area of research are called ethologists, and their field of study is called **ethology** (Hess, 1970). Ethologists usually conduct naturalistic observations, and they are also interested in learned behavior.

Ethology traces its experimental roots to 19th century zoology. In an early ethological experiment, conducted in 1873, D. A. Spalding discovered that baby chicks tended to follow the first moving object that they saw, usually the mother hen. This tendency seemed to exist either at birth or shortly thereafter. Spalding speculated that the tendency to follow was probably **innate**, since it helped the chicks to survive by keeping the babies with the mother. Spalding wanted to be sure that the behavior was not learned, that is, acquired through experience, so he covered the chick's heads with hoods immediately after they were hatched, before they opened their eyes. When the hoods were removed a few hours later, the chicks followed the first object that crossed their field of vision, regardless of what the object was. This result demonstrated that the tendency was not learned, since experience could not have played a role.

Research in this new field began to grow significantly after Konrad Lorenz published a paper in 1937 describing the *following response*. At one time Lorenz actually made certain that he was the first moving object that some newborn ducklings saw. From that time on, the ducklings followed "Mama" Lorenz everywhere he went, even swimming. It seemed to Lorenz that the first object to move past these ducklings was "stamped into" the animal's brain as the object to be followed. Lorenz called this stamping phenomenon **imprinting.** He also observed that imprinting could occur only during a **critical period** lasting from hatching until about two days later. The most effective imprinting occurred approximately 14 hours after hatching. If the chicks were more than two days old when they saw their first moving object imprinting was not observed to occur.

Ethologists and other researchers believe that such inherited behavior must serve a function. The following response has the obvious function of keeping the chick or duckling close to its mother. Offspring that didn't stay close to the mother would have less chance of surviving and passing on genes.

Imprinting is only one example of numerous innate behaviors. Ethologists and psychologists are also interested in **fixed-response patterns.** A fixed-response pattern is a complex inherited behavior that is triggered by a particular **stimulus** (a stimulus being anything that can be sensed), called, because of its function, a **releaser** or **sign stimulus.** The reactions themselves are known as **species-specific behaviors** because they are peculiar to particular species. For example, dangling a worm above a baby robin is a releaser stimulus for the fixed-response pattern of chirping, opening the mouth, tipping back the head, and fluttering the wings. On the other hand, holding a worm in the palm of the hand beneath the baby robin's beak will not provoke this response because it is not a releaser stimulus for such a response pattern.

You may be wondering about the existence of imprinting or fixed-response patterns in humans. As far as researchers can tell, there are no imprinting phenomena in human beings that resemble those found in chicks or ducklings. Scientists are also doubtful about the existence of fixed-response patterns or **instincts** in our species. Certainly, human beings have a number of inborn behaviors, such as blinking, coughing, swallowing, hiccoughing, and sucking. But these behaviors are usually considered to be simple **reflexes** and not truly comparable with the complex fixed-response patterns found in other species.

But could human beings have a maternal instinct? Such an instinct does appear to exist in other animals, for instance in cats. All healthy female cats build some form of nest before giving birth, and after delivery they lick the afterbirth off the kittens, stimulate them, and nurse them. But human

Mama Lorenz

responses are not so fixed from one mother to another. Some mothers nurse, others don't; some mothers want their babies, others don't; some mothers cuddle their children, others are distant. In evolutionary terms, however, the idea of a human maternal instinct seems plausible. Human babies require a great deal of care before they are able to survive on their own, and it would be an advantage if the sight of a human baby were a releaser stimulus for a pattern of instinctive maternal care, comforting, and protection. Indeed, many ethologists and psychologists note that people tend to be attracted to small, cuddly, babylike animals, and believe that this babyish quality may be a releaser stimulus for a parental instinct (Lorenz, 1943) (see Figure 6.1). After all, if people didn't find their babies attractive the next generation might not survive. Other psychologists cite the general rule that the more advanced a species is on the evolutionary scale, the less its behavioral patterns seem to be rigidly fixed by the genes. Many psychologists take the further step of totally rejecting the idea of fixed-response patterns in human beings. The issue is still being vigorously debated.

Figure 6.1 *Comparison of visual features provided by morphological characteristics of infantile and adult forms of four different species: human, rabbit, dog, and bird. While the infantile characteristics release parental responses, the adult ones do not. (Adapted from Lorenz, 1943)*

The Importance of Learning

Is learning important? If we could rely on species-specific behaviors, we could inherit all valuable behaviors and act only in fixed-response patterns. Why have learning? The answer seems to be that, like fixed-response patterns, the ability to learn has a survival value. In this sense, the ability to learn has been inherited. But unlike fixed-response patterns, which are rigid and resistant to change, learning allows great flexibility in behavior. An animal that can learn is not restricted to a fixed-response pattern, but can take into account changes that occur in the immediate environment and respond to them. Obviously, creatures with this ability are more likely to survive, procreate, and pass on the tendency to learn.

Some of the simplest creatures can learn. Geneticists like to work with fruit flies (drosophila) because these flies have a relatively small number of genes that can be studied by selective breeding. A fruit fly can learn; even its larvae can learn. This was demonstrated in an experiment carried out by Efrain Aceves-Pina and William Quinn of Princeton University (1979). They put the larvae of fruit flies on both sides of a plate that had been divided in half. One side of the plate was coated with a substance known as substance O. The other side of the plate contained a substance known as substance A. Both substances had an odor that fruit-fly larvae could smell.

Electric shocks were administered to larvae on the half of the plate containing substance A. Very quickly the larvae on that side wriggled along the plate to the side that gave no shock. It was later observed that, even if no shock was given, these larvae would move away from substance A when it was placed in their presence. That is, they had learned to avoid substance A, since it was associated with a shock. As a control, another group of fruit-fly larvae were placed on a plate similarly divided and were given shocks on the side coated with substance O. Very quickly these larvae wriggled over to the other side. It was later observed that these larvae had learned to avoid substance O.

This was not the first time that learning was observed to occur in an extremely simple organism. The surprising outcome in this experiment was the discovery that four of the fruit fly larvae were *not* able to learn. Upon careful examination the researchers found that one larva could learn but simply could not respond to odors. Curious about the remaining larvae, named Dunce, Turnip, and Cabbage, the researchers bred them together and created a strain of fruit fly that was incapable of learning (Aceves-Pina & Quinn, 1979). This is strong evidence that the ability to learn, that is, the ability to respond to the environment in a flexible way, is inherited. An organism that can learn is not limited to reflexes or fixed-response patterns but can adapt to the environment. No two members of any species need adapt in exactly the same way, since different experiences can give rise to different learning.

Simple Forms of Learning

HABITUATION

Since you are a human being, and not a member of the Dunce, Turnip, or Cabbage strain of fruit fly, you are able to learn. People learn in a number of ways. One of the simplest forms of learning is **habituation,** which takes place when a person becomes accustomed to a stimulus because it has been

HABITUATION
A process whereby an organism ceases to respond reflexively to an unconditioned stimulus that is presented repeatedly.

presented repeatedly. If construction work began outside your window, the first ka-BLAM of a pile driver might startle you. This response would be natural, since being startled is an inborn, not a learned, response. The stimulus in this case would be the loud noise. If the pile driver continued to make the noise over and over, you would eventually become habituated to it; you would learn not to react any more. We can probably consider this a kind of learning, in that your behavior will have changed as a result of your experience. The only way to bring back the startle reflex would be to remove the loud noise for some time and then unexpectedly to present it again.

The trouble with applying the definition of learning to the phenomenon of habituation is that although a change has taken place owing to experience, the change is not necessarily "relatively permanent." Nonetheless, a person can be so habituated to a particular sound that the change becomes somewhat permanent. It's more important to realize that habituation occurs than to argue about whether habituation is learning. The value of habituation is that we come to ignore a stimulus that has lost its novelty or importance. Habituation frees you to attend to stimuli that are new or that appear suddenly. If you were in the woods picking berries and heard a deep throaty growl nearby, attending to that new stimulus would obviously have survival value.

SENSITIZATION

Sensitization may occur when an animal or a human being is exposed to a stimulus that is accompanied by pain of some kind. As with habituation, the effects of sensitization can last from minutes to weeks depending on the amount of training. The effect of sensitization may be opposite to that of habituation. If you become sensitized to a sound, the next time that sound occurs you may startle more easily than you would have before you were sensitized. A soft clicking sound, for example, would not ordinarily startle anyone. When associated with pain, however, it can cause sensitization, and you may react by jumping the next time you hear it. Soldiers suffering from battle fatigue often show signs of sensitization. They are jumpy and anxious; the slightest sudden noise may startle them.

BIOLOGICAL BASES

When a loud noise startles you, neurotransmitters must have been secreted from motor neurons to excite skeletal muscles, or you would not have jumped. But what happens biologically when habituation occurs? Evidence gathered in the last several years has demonstrated that as habituation proceeds, the amount of neurotransmitter secreted into synapses along the skeletal muscles becomes progressively less. Once habituation is complete, the loud noise no longer affects you because the neurotransmitter secreted by the motor neurons in response to the noise is greatly reduced (Kandel, 1979).

During sensitization, more than the usual amount of neurotransmitter is secreted. A soldier who has been traumatized by loud noises and painful associated stimuli may jump at the sound of an automobile horn that everyone else ignores because his neurotransmitters have been secreted at very high levels into synapses adjacent to the skeletal muscles (Kandel, 1979).

The biological explanations of the more complicated kinds of learning, which we will discuss later in this chapter, are far too complex to give in an introductory textbook. Furthermore, in many cases the biological explanations are completely unknown. For this reason psychologists have attempted to understand learning without relying extensively on biological principles. They have conducted experiments knowing that learning is undoubtedly based on underlying biological processes, but believing that because these biological processes are not readily observable, other ways of examining learning must be found.

Associative Learning

Aside from habituation and sensitization, there are three main ways, according to **behavioral theory,** in which we learn. The first is **associative learning,** that is, learning to associate one thing with another thing. The second is learning through rewards and punishments, or learning due to the rewarding or punishing consequences that follow a particular behavior; this kind of learning is known as instrumental learning. The third is learning through observation of what others do, usually called social learning. Regardless of the kind, all learning is still defined as a relatively permanent change in behavior brought about by practice or experience.

CLASSICAL CONDITIONING

During the 1890s the Russian physiologist Ivan Pavlov reported an experiment of an associative learning process. He had been investigating digestion in dogs and had been trying to understand why his dogs often began to salivate before they received food. This reaction seemed to occur when the dogs were led to expect food, such as when they saw someone in the laboratory open the cupboard where the dog food was kept. Other researchers had observed this phenomenon but had either considered it a nuisance or ignored it. Pavlov, however, became seriously interested in this learning process and began to investigate it systematically.

Pavlov's Experiments   In a series of well-known experiments, Pavlov decided to *pair* a stimulus (food), which would elicit an unlearned response (salivation), with a stimulus (bell), which did not elicit salivation and was therefore neutral at the beginning of the experiment. Because no learning is required to make dogs salivate when they are given meat, meat is referred to as an **unconditioned stimulus** (US), while the reflex response of salivating is referred to as an **unconditioned response** (UR). Pavlov took the stimulus that did not cause salivation in dogs (a bell) and began to pair it systematically with the presentation of food. He would ring the bell, immediately present the food (US), and observe the salivation (UR). After the bell and the food had been paired, or associated, for some time, Pavlov was able to cause salivation without giving food; it was enough to ring the bell. The dogs would begin to anticipate the food when they heard the bell, and they would salivate. The bell had new meaning; it had become a stimulus to which the dogs responded in a predictable way. For this reason, the bell is referred to as a **conditioned stimulus** (CS) (see Figure 6.2). This method, by which an unlearned response can be manipulated so as to be elicited by a new stimulus, is referred to as **classical conditioning.**

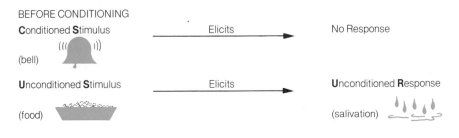

BEFORE CONDITIONING

Conditioned **S**timulus ——— Elicits ———▶ No Response

(bell)

Unconditioned **S**timulus ——— Elicits ———▶ **U**nconditioned **R**esponse

(food)   (salivation)

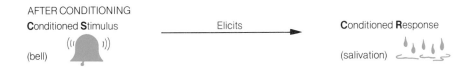

DURING CONDITIONING

Conditioned stimulus (bell) is followed by presentation of Unconditioned Stimulus (food), which elicits Uncondtioned Response (salivation).

AFTER CONDITIONING

Conditioned **S**timulus ——— Elicits ———▶ **C**onditioned **R**esponse

(bell)   (salivation)

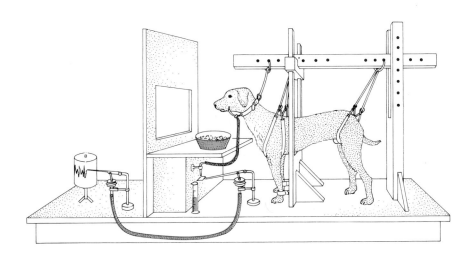

The Case of Little Albert   Classical conditioning is also demonstrable in humans. Perhaps the classic example of such conditioning is the case of Little Albert published by John Watson and Rosalie Rayner in 1920. Prior to that time, no one had clearly demonstrated classical conditioning in humans.

Watson and Rayner tested Albert B., a healthy 11-month-old boy, by systematically exposing him to a white rat, a rabbit, a dog, a monkey, various masks, cotton wool, and even a burning newspaper. As Watson noted, "at no time did this infant ever show fear in any situation." The two researchers found, however, that making a very loud noise by striking a steel rod with a hammer (US) startled baby Albert and made him cry (UR). Next, the researchers paired the loud gong with the white rat that Albert had previously seen. Whenever Albert touched the rat (CS), the loud gong would be struck (US), which would startle Albert and cause him to cry (UR) (see Figure 6.3). Eventually, Albert would start to cry as soon as he saw the rat. In Watson's words,

The instant the rat was shown, the baby began to cry. Almost instantly he turned sharply to the left, fell over on left side, raised himself on all fours and began to crawl away so rapidly that he was caught with difficulty before reaching the edge of the table. (Watson & Rayner, 1920)

In addition, Albert's fears generalized to related objects, such as a rabbit, a dog, a white cotton ball, and even a Santa Claus mask (probably because of the white beard), but not to dissimilar objects, such as blocks. This **stimulus generalization** probably occurred because Albert had associated the loud noise with characteristics possessed by the rat—white, live, legged, and furry—which he subsequently saw in some of the other objects as well.

Not all children can be conditioned as Little Albert was. Consider H. B. English's attempt in 1929 to replicate Watson and Rayner's findings. English tested a 14-month-old girl placed in a high chair. A wooden duck was presented to her and, as in the earlier experiment, a steel gong was struck from behind the child. After 50 pairings, the child remained wholly un-afraid of the duck. English wrote, "The writer must express surprise—and admiration—at the child's iron nerves." English then decided to try a 2-pound steel mallet on the gong in order to obtain the fear response, but the child remained unafraid of the duck, although other faculty members throughout the building complained of the noise (English, 1929). English knew that the child was able to hear. He also knew that she was capable of fear, because she had previously developed a fear of boots, for an unknown reason. Why, then, had the duck failed to become a conditioned stimulus?

Upon further investigation, English discovered that the little girl had three older brothers who kept up a screaming, banging racket throughout her house. Apparently, the little girl had become habituated to loud noise, and the noise no longer functioned as an unconditioned stimulus for her. As any parent with three little boys can confirm, there are times when even a 2-pound steel mallet striking a gong will go unnoticed! Then again, per-haps such older brothers make for iron-nerved little sisters.

The experiment with Little Albert had notable ethical implications. Was it ethical to create what amounted to a phobia in the child? By today's

STIMULUS GENERALIZATION
Once a stimulus has come to elicit or cue a response, similar stimuli may also elicit or cue the response, though not usually as effectively.

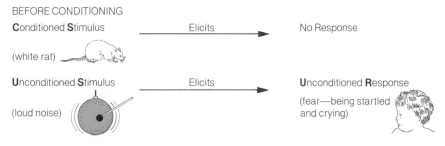

BEFORE CONDITIONING

Conditioned Stimulus — Elicits → No Response

(white rat)

Unconditioned Stimulus — Elicits → Unconditioned Response

(loud noise)   (fear—being startled and crying)

DURING CONDITIONING

Conditioned Stimulus (white rat) is followed by presentation of Unconditioned Stimulus (loud noise), which elicits Unconditioned Response (being startled and crying).

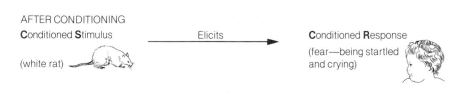

AFTER CONDITIONING

Conditioned Stimulus — Elicits → Conditioned Response

(white rat)   (fear—being startled and crying)

Figure 6.3   *The paradigm used by Watson and Rayner to condition Little Albert to fear a rat.*

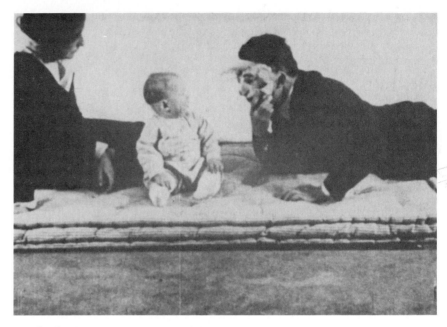

standards this experiment would clearly have violated ethical procedures. On the other hand, Watson and Rayner had discussed ways in which to cure Albert of his experimentally induced fears. They thought that by offering Albert candy or his favorite food in the presence of the white rat, they might create a positive association, and thereby **countercondition** him. Alternatively, they considered stimulating Albert's erogenous zones in the presence of the rat in order to help alter his associations. A third idea was simply to show Albert the rat again and again, without pairing it with the gong, until he finally became used to it—a process known as **extinction.***

Unfortunately, the researchers never had a chance to try any of their plans because Albert's mother moved away, taking him with her. It appears that before Watson and Rayner ever began their experiment, they knew that Albert was going to have to leave early and that they would probably never have a chance to undo any learned fear response that they might produce. Yet they went ahead and conducted the experiment anyway (Harris, 1979). Of course, Little Albert was not the only human ever to be classically conditioned; millions of children are daily conditioned in this way as they come in contact with their environment. Any pediatrician who has given a child an injection can attest to this fact. The child's screaming fit the next time he or she enters the office is a good indication that classical conditioning plays a role in fear responses.

OTHER KINDS OF ASSOCIATIVE LEARNING

In addition to classical conditioning, in which a new stimulus obtains the power to elicit a reflex, associative experiences can also lead to the formation of beliefs and attitudes. In a study by Nunnally, Duchnowski, and Parker (1965), elementary school children were asked to play a game

---

*Extinction is not the same as habituation. Extinction occurs through repeated presentation of the conditioned stimulus alone, while habituation occurs through repeated presentation of an unconditioned stimulus.

involving a spinning arrow that could end up pointing at any of three nonsense syllables (GYQ, ZOJ, and MYV). The game was arranged so that one syllable paid a 2-cent reward, another cost a 1-cent fine, and the last brought no loss or gain. These three syllables meant nothing to the children at the beginning of the experiment. After allowing the children to play the game for some time, the researchers showed them three stick figures that were identical except that one of the three nonsense syllables was placed below each figure. The children were then asked questions such as, "Which is the friendly boy?" or "Which is the mean boy?" (Sound familiar?) The stick figure associated with the positive nonsense syllable, the one that yielded a 2-cent gain, was almost always chosen as the "friendly boy," while the figure paired with the syllable that was associated with the fine was almost always identified as the "mean boy."

In another study by Staats and Staats (1958), college students were asked to look at one word while pronouncing another. Without being aware of the purpose of the experiment, the students were maneuvered into pairing pleasant words or unpleasant words with a particular name (Tom or Bill) or a certain nationality (Swedish or Dutch). In a short time, obvious differences in attitudes were obtained toward these names and nationalities, simply because they had been paired with positive or negative words.

Sometimes a single stimulus can be paired both with something positive and with something negative. If this happens, the individual for whom the associations have been made may tend to feel neutral toward the stimulus. Or, if the associations are strong ones the person may feel both learned aspects of the stimulus simultaneously, giving rise to bittersweet memories or feelings, a very apt description for the sensations encountered.

The kinds of discrimination observed by Kenneth Clark in his experiments with black children and white children and discussed in the Prologue were probably learned through associative processes. Other learning processes that we will examine may also have played a role, however.

Instrumental Learning

Instrumental behaviors are learned behaviors that serve a purpose. **Instrumental learning** helps someone to obtain a goal. As you'll recall, associative learning can result from simply pairing or associating stimuli with one another; the resulting response to the new stimulus doesn't need to be purposeful. When Pavlov's dogs salivated to the sound of a bell, for example, the salivation did not serve the purpose of helping the dogs obtain or avoid the bell; it occurred because the bell had previously been paired with food. Similarly, Little Albert cried when he saw the rat because the rat had previously been paired with a loud noise, not because the crying helped him obtain or avoid the rat. But when Little Albert rolled over on all fours and almost crawled off the table, his behavior was instrumental because its purpose was escape or avoidance.

According to some psychologists, most notably B. F. Skinner, to consider that an animal behaves with a specific purpose in mind is to attribute thoughts to the animal that are not readily observable. Instead, Skinner has argued for the use of the term **operant conditioning,** signifying the conditioning of behaviors that operate upon the environment. Skinner prefers to picture the organism as emitting a variety of responses for unknown

COUNTERCONDITIONING
A technique used by behavioral therapists to eliminate unwanted behavior through extinction or punishment, while at the same time promoting the acquisition of a new, more appropriate behavior in place of the old.

EXTINCTION
The process of eliminating associations or reinforcement in classical or instrumental conditioning, which results in failure to perform the learned response.

INSTRUMENTAL LEARNING
The process by which an organism learns to behave because of the consequences that follow the behavior. The behavior is considered purposeful since it helps the organism to approach pleasant or avoid unpleasant stimuli.

OPERANT CONDITIONING
B. F. Skinner's term for changes in behavior that occur as a result of stimulus consequences that reinforce or punish emitted responses. These responses are not considered to be purposeful but merely to operate on the environment. They may in turn be shaped by environmental experiences.

LAW OF EFFECT
Thorndike's principle that responses that are reinforced (rewarded) tend to be repeated, while those that lead to something aversive tend to be eliminated.

reasons, some of which responses are conditioned by the consequences that follow them. For the purposes of this text, however, we will consider that instrumental learning and operant conditioning are synonymous terms and that both refer to the conditioning of behaviors by the stimulus consequences following the behaviors.

THE LAW OF EFFECT

About the time that Pavlov was studying behavior in dogs, an American psychologist, E. L. Thorndike, was observing the behavior of cats. Thorndike would deprive a cat of food for some time and then place it inside a puzzle box, a container from which escape is possible if the animal happens to trip a latch that opens the door (see Figure 6.4). Food was placed outside of the box in plain view of the cat. Eventually, the cat would accidently hook a claw onto the wire loop or step on the treadle that pulled the latch, and the door to the box would open. As the cats came to appreciate this way of escaping, each time they were put into the box they released themselves sooner (see Figure 6.5).

Thorndike's observations of such trial-and-error learning led him to consider the consequences of an act to be an important factor in determining the probability that any action will occur. His thesis was that

> Any act which in a given situation produces satisfaction becomes associated with that situation, so that when the situation recurs, the act is more likely than ever before to recur also. Conversely, any act which in a given situation produces discomfort becomes disassociated from that situation, so that when the situation recurs, the act is less likely than before to recur. (Thorndike, 1905, p. 202)

Thorndike's explanation, known as the **law of effect,** is one of the cornerstones of instrumental learning. Much of what you've learned in life has been acquired through instrumental learning.

Since instrumental responses are maintained or changed depending on the consequences that follow a response, when you respond to something the response is strengthened if the consequence is pleasant and weakened if the consequence is aversive. In this way you, and hundreds of other species, learn because of the outcome of different behaviors.

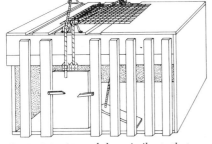

Figure 6.4 *A puzzle box similar to that used by Thorndike in 1898. (*SOURCE: *Bitterman, 1969, p. 445)*

Figure 6.5 *The graph shows the gradual decline in the amount of time necessary for one animal to release itself from the Thorndikian puzzle box in successive trials. This is one of the earliest learning curves in the experimental study of conditioning. Notice, however, that the curve is not completely smooth but has marked fluctuations. Smooth learning curves usually result when many learning curves are averaged out. (*SOURCE: *Bitterman, 1969, p. 446)*

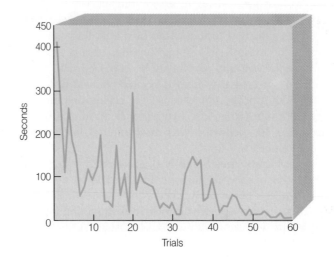

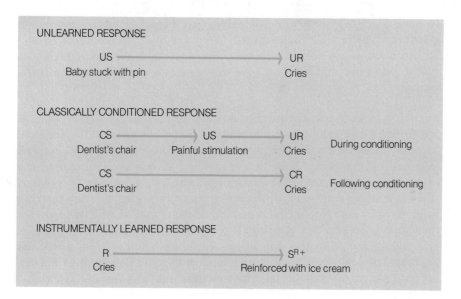

UNLEARNED RESPONSE

US ———————————————→ UR
Baby stuck with pin   Cries

CLASSICALLY CONDITIONED RESPONSE

CS ———→ US ———————→ UR
Dentist's chair   Painful stimulation   Cries   During conditioning

CS ———————————————→ CR
Dentist's chair   Cries   Following conditioning

INSTRUMENTALLY LEARNED RESPONSE

R ———————————————→ S^{R+}
Cries   Reinforced with ice cream

Figure 6.6   A short review of learning. Is crying an unlearned reflex, a classically conditioned response, or an instrumentally learned response? You've probably learned enough by now to realize that it may be any one of the three. If a baby cries (UR) when stuck with a pin (US), the crying has not been learned and is therefore considered to be a reflex. If a child cries (CR) at seeing a dentist's chair (CS), the crying may be the result of the chair's having been associated with pain in the past, and it can therefore be said to be classically conditioned. (Notice, too, that this kind of crying is not instrumental because it does not help the child obtain or avoid the chair.) Finally, if a child cries in order to get ice cream or avoid doing homework, the crying is serving a purpose and is instrumental. A reinforcing stimulus consequence is depicted as S^{R+}.

Figure 6.6 offers a short review of what you've learned about learning so far.

REINFORCEMENT

The strength of an instrumental behavior can be measured by its resistance to extinction. That is, how long does it take for the behavior to return to its original rate once the pleasant consequence following the behavior no longer occurs (see Figure 6.7). It is correct generally to say that to strengthen an instrumental response, the response should be rewarded. But rewards usually denote specific things such as money, candy, or praise, and you can't always be sure that something commonly considered a reward will strengthen an instrumental response. Suppose, for example, that you had a toothache. In this case, eating chocolate candy, something you might normally consider a reward, wouldn't be likely to strengthen your desire

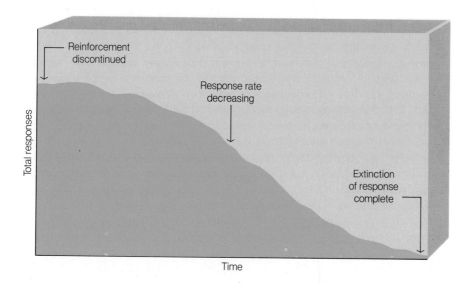

Figure 6.7   Once a response is no longer reinforced it will undergo extinction. Slowly, over time the response occurs less and less until it reaches the level it held prior to reinforcement.

Through the selective use and application of reinforcement, pigeons can be shaped to peck and discriminate written words.

to have a second piece. For this reason psychologists prefer to speak of **reinforcement** rather than reward. Reinforcement may be defined as a **stimulus consequence** that increases the strength of the emitted response that it follows or that maintains the response at a higher level than it was before.

Shaping   In instrumental learning a response must occur before it can be reinforced. Obviously, you can't reinforce a response that hasn't occurred. Have you ever seen a chicken play "Twinkle, Twinkle Little Star" by pecking the keys on a piano? If the trainer had had to wait for the first rendering of the song before reinforcing the chicken he'd still be waiting. Fortunately, there is a way to develop a behavior without requiring that the response be given in its entirety the first time. The behavior can be built up piecemeal through a process called **shaping.** If you'd like to try shaping, all you need is a willing organism that can learn. A human being will do, a dog will do, in fact almost any animal will do (except the fruit flies Dunce, Cabbage, or Turnip). In psychology laboratories rats and pigeons are often used because they are easy to work with and they learn relatively quickly. Let's use a pigeon, and let's shape it to "read."

The average undergraduate can teach a pigeon reading in about four hours. Of course, the pigeon's ability will be extremely limited; after four hours you can't expect it to complete Tolstoy's *War and Peace* (in fact, you never can). But in four hours of careful shaping, the bird should be able to respond correctly to words written on paper, such as *peck* or *turn*. When you show the word *peck*, the bird will look at it and then peck at a disk mounted inside its cage. When you hold up the word *turn*, the bird will look at it and then do a 360-degree circle. You don't have to hold up the signs in any particular order; whatever word is held up, the bird will "read" it, and then do as instructed.

People watching birds perform in this way usually want to know what the trick is. When told that there is no trick—the bird is, in a limited sense, reading—they ask how a birdbrained pigeon (as if there were other kinds) could be trained to read English words, and in only four hours. The answer is shaping. Let's look in detail at how this is done.

If you show an untrained pigeon the word *peck*, it will not usually follow the instruction. You begin the shaping process by reinforcing successive approximations toward the final goal of pecking. If the bird is hungry, birdseed will probably be a good reinforcer. If the pigeon happens to walk toward the disk when you hold up the word *peck*, you reinforce the action. Soon the pigeon learns to stay in the part of the cage where the disk is (a little closer to what you eventually want). You demand a little more. You require that the pigeon motion with his head toward the disk. The pigeon will probably make such a move eventually, and when it does, you reinforce it again. Pretty soon you will have the pigeon bobbing its head toward the disk. Then you require that it make a pecking motion, either at the disk, or in the nearby vicinity. Each time this happens you reinforce the motion. Finally, pecking the disk becomes the only response that you will accept and reinforce. In this way, you have shaped the pigeon, leading it to learn, bit by bit, what you want. When you remove the word *peck*, the pigeon will continue to peck anyhow, but you will not reinforce the pecking this time. (In technical terms, you are extinguishing the inappropriate response of pecking while the peck sign is absent.) When you replace the peck sign,

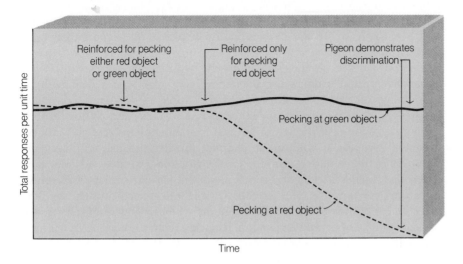

Figure 6.8 *In this example, a pigeon is initially reinforced for pecking either the red object or the green object. When it is reinforced only for pecking the red object, the pigeon begins to develop the discrimination. Eventually, pecking the green object is extinguished, while pecking the red object is maintained, and the discrimination is complete.*

the pigeon will peck and you will reinforce the action. Soon the pigeon makes what is known as a **discrimination** (see Figure 6.8). It has learned that pecking the disk will be followed by a food reward when the word *peck* is present; conversely, pecking the disk will not be followed by a food reward when the word *peck* is not present. Once the bird has learned to discriminate, it will peck the disk to attain food only when the word *peck* is presented; extinction of the unwanted response will be complete.

Next you hold up the word *turn*. What do you think the pigeon will do? It will probably peck because it has not discriminated between the words *peck* and *turn*. This lack of differentiation is known as **generalization** (see Figure 6.9). The pigeon treats the two words the same, perhaps simply "understanding" that when letters are shown, pecking pays off. So, you must now shape the bird to turn in the presence of the word *turn*. If the bird pecks when the sign says *turn*, it receives nothing. On the other hand, if it should inadvertently turn slightly to the left or the right (choose one beforehand) you immediately reinforce the action. Gradually you shape a turn. Once you get the pigeon halfway it's easy to get it the rest of the way around. Now you go back and forth between the two stimuli, reinforcing the pecking behavior when the word *peck* is present and reinforcing the

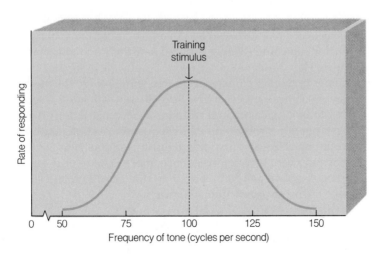

Figure 6.9 *Example of stimulus generalization. The organism is trained to respond to a tone whose frequency is 100 cycles per second. Stimulus generalization occurs when the organism responds to similar tones somewhat as it responded to the training stimulus. However, as the above gradient of generalization indicates, generalized responses are often not as strong as responses to the training stimulus.*

turning behavior when the word *turn* is present. If you are lucky, the pigeon will eventually make the discrimination between the signs and respond appropriately.

As you can see, shaping is a powerful way of teaching a complicated behavior. Animal trainers use it effectively. It also works well with human beings, as can be demonstrated by a simple experiment. A particular teacher may never lecture from the corner of a room, and so this response cannot be reinforced. But ten or so well-trained students scattered about a larger class may be able to use shaping to alter the teacher's behavior. These students should be careful to pay attention, smile, and take notes when the teacher makes any move toward a chosen corner of the room, but to appear bored or uninterested when the teacher heads in any other direction. Some instructors will change their behavior without any awareness of what's happening and end up lecturing from the corner.*

Strengthening a Response by Positive and Negative Reinforcement   Although all reinforcement, by definition, strengthens the response that it follows, a distinction is often made between positive and negative reinforcement. **Positive reinforcement** occurs when an organism is reinforced for having approached or obtained something. **Negative reinforcement** occurs when an organism is reinforced for successfully avoiding or escaping an aversive situation. This distinction is outlined below.

POSITIVE REINFORCEMENT	NEGATIVE REINFORCEMENT
Behavior helps organism obtain something pleasant.	Behavior helps organism avoid or terminate something unpleasant.
Behavior is strengthened.	Behavior is strengthened.

For example, if an animal successfully avoids a shock by pressing a lever, the lever-pressing response is strengthened, and we say the response has been negatively reinforced. Similarly, if a child cleans her room in order to avoid her parents' constant reminders, she is being negatively reinforced. Remember, when a response is negatively reinforced the response becomes *stronger*.

It should be noted that positive and negative reinforcement may occur simultaneously. A child learning to eat is an example. Since a child obtains food by using a spoon, the strengthening of spoon use is considered positive reinforcement. Since, however, the child may also be eating to avoid an uncomfortable state of hunger, the strengthening of spoon use may also be considered negative reinforcement. By using the spoon the child realizes a positive outcome (feeling full and satisfied) and simultaneously avoids a negative state (hunger).

Under certain circumstances, some stimuli have the power to strengthen responses simply by occurring immediately after the responses have been made. In fact, response and stimulus consequence don't necessarily have to be connected in a cause-and-effect sequence. If a ball player taps home plate with the tip of his bat just before hitting a home run, the plate-tapping behavior may well be reinforced. Since there is no logical connection between tapping the plate and hitting a home run, acquiring such a response is said to result from **superstitious learning.**

*Caution: The use of such a technique on your professor may be hazardous to your grade.

Weakening a Response by Punishment and Extinction **Punishment** occurs when a response is followed by an aversive stimulus that decreases the strength of the response or maintains it at a lower level than it was originally. As with reinforcement, punishment is something that affects behavior. Remember, people aren't reinforced or punished, behaviors are! The following story illustrates the meaning of this statement.

At 11 o'clock on a Wednesday morning an alert neighbor spotted a stranger breaking through the front window of the home across the street. Since the people who lived in the house were at work, the neighbor dutifully called the police. Shortly, two squad cars arrived and silently coasted to a stop. Four armed officers stepped from the vehicles, leaving their doors ajar so as to make no sound. The officers positioned themselves at the front and the back of the house. A few minutes later the unsuspecting burglar walked out of the front door lugging a color television. He was greeted by two of the officers. Assessing the potential rewards and punishments of the situation, the burglar searched for an ingenious solution to his predicament and in short order found one—he surrendered. By making fighting or running away likely to lead to unpleasant consequences, the officers had practically assured this choice.

The burglar was brought to trial and was found guilty (the jury refusing to believe that he had planned to repair his brother's TV and had entered the wrong house). The burglar listened helplessly as the judge pronounced a three-year prison sentence. Later that night the burglar awaited transportation from the city jail to the state prison. He was depressed and miserable. Pondering his hapless condition, he vowed to turn over a new leaf. He swore on everything that was dear to him that he would never again break into a house—through a front window.

In this story a behavior was punished, but not the one that society had hoped to alter. Instead of teaching the burglar not to steal, his arrest taught the burglar not to steal stupidly. As you can see, before you employ reinforcement and punishment techniques, you should ascertain which behavior will be strengthened or weakened.

Punishment can be extremely powerful, and it can control our behavior. Some researchers have argued that punishment is the most effective means of stopping a behavior (Azrin & Holz, 1966). This outcome is especially certain if the punishment is severe. Anyone who's ever tried to cook bacon while naked will tell you that the adverse consequences of that behavior diminished the probability of a repeat performance.

Although punishment can be an effective way of terminating a behavior, it can have serious drawbacks. When a behavior is punished, especially if it is punished severely, there is often a general suppression of other behaviors. The person or animal may then become withdrawn and less active. Punishment can also lead to hostility and aggression, especially if it is accompanied by pain.

Instrumental learning is essential in training seeing-eye dogs, but the trainers almost never use punishment. If a dog walks forward when it should have stayed, beating it in an attempt to punish the inappropriate move could lead to a general suppression of behaviors, and the animal might cower in a corner and no longer respond to commands. Or the dog might react aggressively and counterattack. Because of these potential

Seeing eye dogs are trained through the use of positive reinforcement, shaping, and discrimination. Punishment is rarely used.

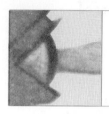

SPANKING AND BEHAVIOR CONTROL

In American culture the use of spanking to control children's behavior seems to be growing in popularity. Parents are turning away from permissive methods and relying on stricter controls (Walters & Grusec, 1977). Furthermore, many people have advocated reintroducing spanking in the schools in order to maintain discipline. Many psychologists, however, are concerned about the growing use of spanking and have voiced their concern. Why do they feel that spanking is wrong?

Based on what you have learned about learning in this chapter, you should be able to appreciate the following arguments for abolishing spanking as a technique for controlling children's behavior:

1. All too often the adult administering the spanking becomes overly emotional and inflicts severe physical damage upon the child. Such child abuse has been demonstrated among parents of all educational and income levels. Although actual torture of children is rare, most abuse begins with an intent to spank.

2. Through a process called habituation, the child sometimes becomes used to spanking, so that the adult has to be more and more severe in order to have any effect.

3. Through the process of classical conditioning, the parent becomes paired with pain, with the result that the parent comes to elicit a fear response from the child, even without inflicting punishment.

4. Through instrumental learning the child is often reinforced in such a way that he or she may avoid the parents, lie, or run away from home.

5. According to research on punishment, mild spankings usually have only a temporary effect.

6. Additional research on instrumental learning has demonstrated that many nonphysical techniques are highly successful in controlling and modifying children's behavior. Among the most frequently mentioned are time-out and reinforcement of incompatible responses. In time-out, children who behave inappropriately are immediately placed in a boring environment (usually a small room); after a few minutes they are released as long as they behaved well during their time-out. The second technique, reinforcing incompatible responses, relies on the fact that opposite behaviors can't occur at the same time. "Good" behaviors such as waiting patiently are incompatible with "bad" behaviors such as interrupting while others are talking. The behaviors are considered incompatible because they can't occur simultaneously. By reinforcing patience, that response becomes more likely to occur—which means, of course, that interrupting becomes less likely to occur. In this way interrupting can be eliminated without resorting to punishment.

7. Many well-behaved children and adults have never been spanked or hit by either of their parents (so much for spare the rod, spoil the child).

8. The last and perhaps most compelling point has to do with spanking and social learning. It appears that when parents or other adults spank a child, the child may be learning more than the adult intended. One father stated that he realized something was wrong when he said, as he spanked his five-year-old son for hitting his two-year-old brother, "This will teach you not to hit someone smaller than you." Of course, just the opposite was likely to be taught. By watching others (social learning), children who are spanked apparently learn that physical force is an appropriate response when you are frustrated with someone; that it's all right to hit people; and that spanking is something that parents are supposed to do (which may help explain why so many child abusers were themselves abused as children) (Fairchild & Erwin, 1977).

These findings, gathered by psychologists during many years of careful research, have not gone completely unheeded. One nation (Sweden) passed a law in 1979 based on a modern psychological understanding of spanking. The law made it illegal for anyone, including parents, to spank or even verbally abuse a child. Although the legislators realized that the law would be almost impossible to enforce, they felt it would alert people to the problem and impress upon them that spanking was wrong.

drawbacks, trainers use techniques other than punishment to teach the dog and to correct mistakes. If the dog walks when it shouldn't, the trainer will bring the dog back and try again. If the dog stays the next time the trainer will reinforce the dog for staying. In this way the dog learns to stay, and the inappropriate behavior is eliminated without punishment. The more the animal is taught to respond appropriately, the less chance it has to respond inappropriately.

Another way of weakening a response without punishment is based on the purposefulness of instrumental responses. Once a response no longer serves a purpose it becomes unnecessary. A child who throws a temper tantrum because his behavior is being reinforced by his parents' attention will stop throwing tantrums if the reinforcement is discontinued. This weakening or elimination of a response by the removal of a reinforcer that maintained the response is known as extinction. Even after a response has been eliminated through extinction, it may briefly reappear. It's almost as though the organism had forgotten that the response no longer served its purpose, or as though the organism were checking whether the response would work at a later time. This brief reoccurrence of a response following extinction is called **spontaneous recovery.**

Primary and Secondary Reinforcement You learn because your experiences, in conjunction with your physical needs and genetic tendencies, affect you in some meaningful way. Stimuli necessary for sustaining life can obtain the power to reinforce simply by being withheld for a time; no learning is required. The stimuli in this category include water, food, and air, as well as proper temperature and barometric pressure. Such stimuli are known as **primary reinforcers.** Other reinforcers such as money, status, attention, green traffic lights, or even bottle caps (if you would be willing to work for one) are known as **secondary** or **acquired reinforcers.** You have learned that these things are reinforcers because of their association with primary or other secondary reinforcers. In this sense, primary reinforcers are built-in, and secondary reinforcers are learned.

Certain instrumental responses are easier to learn than others because of a species' biological organization. For instance, although you can easily teach a pigeon to peck a disk, you would have trouble obtaining the same response from a pig. Or, as one badly shaken circus trainer put it, "No matter how hungry the elephant, or how many peanuts you have to offer, the double somersault is out!" Similarly, humans find some behaviors easier to learn than others. You've probably heard that once you learn to ride a bicycle you never forget. There is a great deal of truth in this claim. Motor responses that are learned, such as those required for riding a bicycle, are much longer-lasting than other kinds of learned responses. If you were to learn a list of words, you would find that your ability to recall the words would decrease rapidly over time. The fact that motor responses tend to last longer than verbal responses may have to do with our biological organization. Figure 6.10 shows the different retention rates for these two responses.

Schedules of Reinforcement We're not reinforced for everything we do, but we do receive reinforcement every once in a while. Oddly, once a behavior is learned, reinforcing it less often may actually serve to strengthen it. Remember, the strength of a response may be measured by its resistance to extinction. A strong response will persist for a long time in the absence of

SPONTANEOUS RECOVERY
The brief reoccurrence of a response following extinction.

PRIMARY REINFORCERS
Stimuli that are innately reinforcing, such as food or sleep.

SECONDARY REINFORCER
A reinforcer whose value is learned through association with primary reinforcers or other secondary reinforcers.

ACQUIRED REINFORCER
See **SECONDARY REINFORCER.**

Figure 6.10 *These curves represent the rate at which particular skills are forgotten and the percentage decrease in skills over time. Verbal knowledge (especially of meaningless nonsense syllables) is lost far more quickly than a motor skill.* (SOURCE: *Leavitt and Schlosberg, 1944, p. 412*)

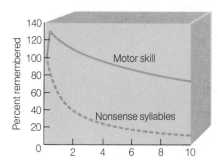

CONTINUOUS REINFORCEMENT
Reinforcing a particular response each time it occurs.

INTERMITTENT SCHEDULE
Reinforcing a particular response, but not each time the response occurs.

DISCRIMINATIVE STIMULI
Stimuli in whose presence a response is likely to occur. Discriminative stimuli function as cues enabling us to know when a response is likely to be reinforced.

STIMULUS CONTROL
From learning theory, the idea that discriminative stimuli come to control the behavior that they cue.

reinforcement, that is, it will extinguish slowly. A weak response will extinguish rapidly without reinforcement. To demonstrate this phenomenon, we can shape a hungry rat to press a lever by feeding the rat whenever it successfully presses the lever. In the beginning, the rat is reinforced for each correct press. This is known as **continuous reinforcement.** Once reinforcement is discontinued the pressing behavior will extinguish rapidly, indicating a weak response. If, however, we begin reinforcing every fifth press instead of withholding reinforcement entirely, the behavior will not extinguish rapidly. Instead, the rat will learn to persist, at least for as long as five presses. Once the rat becomes used to five presses per reinforcer, the behavior is easily maintained. If we gradually increase the number of presses required for reinforcement, the rat may eventually make as many as 500 presses in order to receive one reinforcer (a miserable, but persistent, rat). Such a schedule, in which every response is not reinforced, is called an **intermittent schedule,** and it can lead to the formation of very strong responses. For instance, if we place our rat on an extinction schedule after it has become accustomed to 500 presses per reinforcer, it might press several thousand times before it finally gave up, because it had become used to giving 500 presses. This resistance to extinction is the sign of a strong response. Figure 6.11 describes several intermittent reinforcement schedules.

DISCRIMINATION AND STIMULUS CONTROL

It would be a chaotic world if instrumental responses were likely to occur at any time or in any place. This does not happen because your learning has been such that your instrumental responses are controlled by various stimuli or cues, called **discriminative stimuli.** In the presence of a discriminative stimulus, a particular behavior is more likely to occur. Experi-

Intermittent schedules of reinforcement are a powerful means of controlling behavior. Such schedules strengthen responses by making them resistant to extinction.

FIXED RATIO
Ratio of responses to reinforcements is fixed and regular. (Example: Pigeon is reinforced after every fourth response.) Note the pause after each reinforcement, which is characteristic of fixed-ratio schedules.

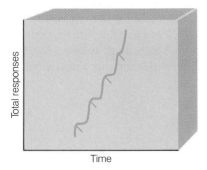

VARIABLE RATIO
Ratio of responses to reinforcements is varied. (Example: Pigeon is reinforced after four responses, eight responses, two responses, 10 responses, etc.) Note the high response rates and lack of pauses produced by this schedule.

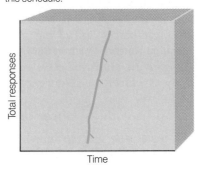

Figure 6.11 *Schedules of intermittent reinforcement. (Slash marks indicate times when the animal is reinforced.) (*SOURCE: *After Ferster and Skinner, 1957)*

FIXED INTERVAL
The delivery of reinforcement is contingent upon both the passage of time and the occurence of a response. (Example: Pigeon is reinforced after the first response following the passage of one minute, after the first response following the passage of another minute, etc.) The scalloped shape is typical of fixed-interval schedules.

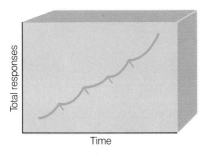

VARIABLE INTERVAL
The delivery of reinforcement is contingent upon both passage of time and occurrence of a response, but the length of time is varied rather than fixed. (Example: Pigeon is reinforced after the first response following the passage of one minute, then after the first response following the passage of three minutes, then after the first response following the passage of two minutes, etc.) Leads to very stable and uniform response rates.

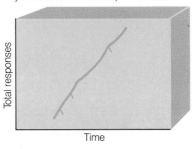

ence has taught you the meaning of these cues, and you have come to rely on them for assessing which actions or behaviors are likely to yield satisfactory results. For example, what cues should be present in order to increase the probability that you will undress? A comfortable bed, sleepiness, and a clock that reads midnight? The privacy of a bathroom and the sound of running water? Or perhaps a drumroll and a spotlight? People may discriminate stimuli differently. A stimulus that functions as a cue for you may not be a cue for someone else. Once these cues are well learned, they come to control the times and places in which certain behaviors are likely to occur. This result is known as **stimulus control.** How do red traffic lights, ringing telephones, and timepieces "control" your behavior?

Although we often think of ourselves as behaving in a relatively consistent way from one setting to another, it is often the discriminative stimuli that are governing our behavior. Consider a group of strangers exiting from an elevator. They tend to be courteous, holding the door open for each other and offering to yield. But follow these people into the parking lot, and you may see some changes after they get into their cars. The discriminative stimuli derived from their individual experiences may cue very different behaviors. The same person who politely held the door for you may be the one who will cut you off and almost cause an accident.

You do not need to be aware of discriminative stimuli for them to affect your behavior. Smokers often find themselves unconsciously lighting up at the same places and at the same times. This is probably an example of stimulus control. Furthermore, one cue can lead directly to another, creating an **operant chain** of cues, responses, and reinforcements known collectively as a **habit** (see Figure 6.12).

OPERANT CHAIN
A series of cues, responses, and reinforcers linked together in such a way that each stimulus consequence reinforces the person's response and cues the next one. Also known as a *habit*.

HABIT
See OPERANT CHAIN.

SOCIAL LEARNING
Learning by observing the actions of others. Also called *vicarious conditioning*.

MODEL
In social learning theory, anyone who demonstrates a behavior that others observe.

Social Learning—Observation and Imitation

You have seen that an individual can learn by experiencing associations between stimuli or as a result of the reinforcing or punishing consequences that may follow behaviors. Now we will investigate a third possibility—learning through observation of another's behavior, or **social learning.**

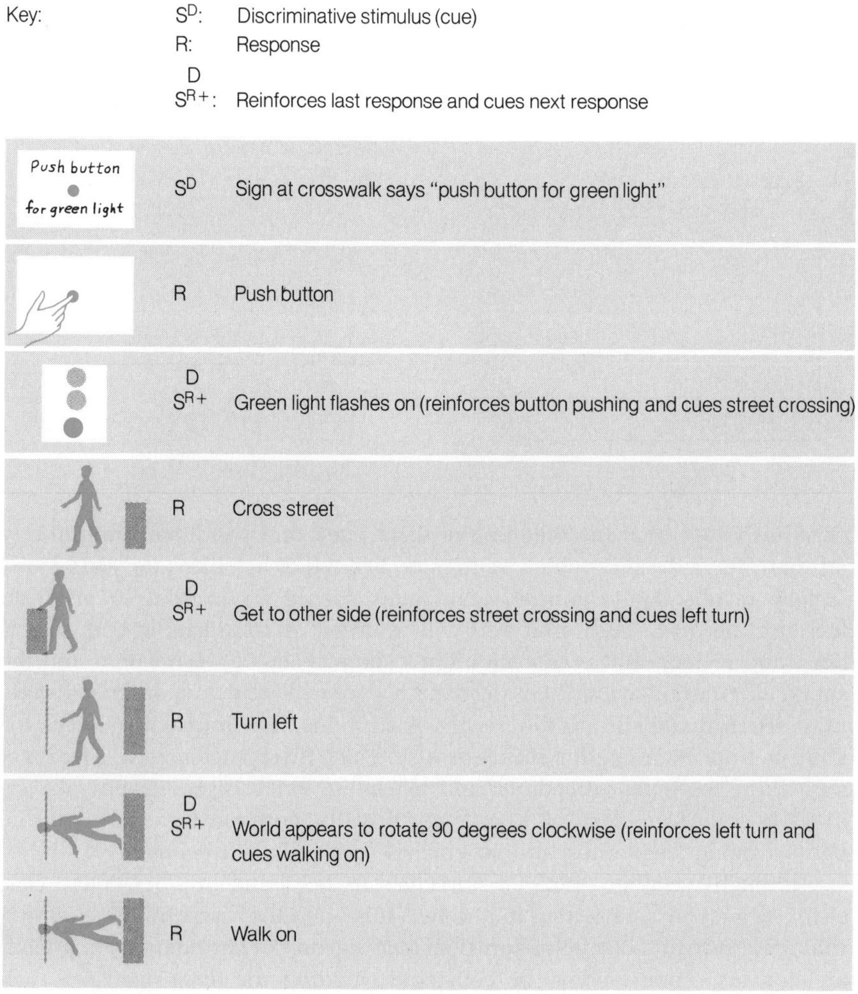

Key:
S^D: Discriminative stimulus (cue)
R: Response
S^{R+}_{D}: Reinforces last response and cues next response
Push button for green light
S^D Sign at crosswalk says "push button for green light"
R Push button
S^{R+}_{D} Green light flashes on (reinforces button pushing and cues street crossing)
R Cross street
S^{R+}_{D} Get to other side (reinforces street crossing and cues left turn)
R Turn left
S^{R+}_{D} World appears to rotate 90 degrees clockwise (reinforces left turn and cues walking on)
R Walk on

Figure 6.12 *An operant chain, or a habit, is composed of cues, responses, and reinforcements.*

Social learning through imitation may often occur without the need for direct reinforcement.

THE IMPORTANCE OF MODELS

Albert Bandura and several of his colleagues at Stanford University have argued that social learning is a distinct kind of learning that requires new principles in order to be understood. Bandura, Ross, and Ross demonstrated their thesis in 1963 in an experiment now considered by many to be a classic. They asked nursery-school children to observe an adult **model** striking a large inflated Bobo doll with a mallet. The model also hit, kicked, and sat upon the doll. During the assault, the model said a number of unusual sentences, probably unlike any the children had heard before. Neither the model nor the observing children were directly reinforced at any time during the session.

Later, after the model had gone, the children were secretly observed as they played in a toy-filled room with the Bobo doll. For comparison, other children who had not seen the model's behavior were also allowed to interact with the doll. The results of the experiment clearly demonstrated that the children who had observed the model were far more likely to be aggressive, in imitation of the model's behavior, than were the other children. Furthermore, many of the children who had observed the model also imitated the model's unusual verbal statements. These results would not have been predicted by associative or instrumental learning theories, since the imitation seemed to be occurring without reinforcement.

If you consider that learning by trial and error can be very time-consuming, and even dangerous, you will readily see the value of learning by imitating the successful behavior of another. If our learning were restricted to what we could gain through associative and instrumental learning, our ability to master our world would be severely limited. Bandura emphasizes this point in the following description of an instructor attempting to teach a driving student to operate a car strictly by using the principles of reinforcement:

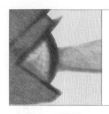

B. F. SKINNER

B. F. Skinner, born in 1904, is perhaps the best-known psychologist in America today. He is behavioral psychology's leading advocate, and his influence has helped to strengthen experimental psychology and make it into a science.

Skinner was born in Susquehanna, Pennsylvania. He graduated from Hamilton College in New York in 1926 with a degree in English, planning a literary career for himself. It has been through his works, *Walden Two*, published in 1948, and *Beyond Freedom and Dignity*, published in 1971, that the general public has come to know him best.

Considering all of the early turns in Skinner's career, it's interesting that he ended up in psychology. After graduation, it appeared that he might have a budding career as a writer. He once sent some short stories to the American poet Robert Frost wondering if he might get some helpful advice. In reply, Frost encouraged Skinner to become a writer. With this encouragement, Skinner returned to school to pursue a writing career in earnest. Unfortunately, or fortunately, Skinner

B. F. Skinner

found that he really didn't have anything to say. Next he decided to attempt a professional career. He planned to begin by acquiring a degree in biology, which seemed a reasonable academic and professional choice. Once the

decision to enter biology was made, however, he wasn't long in changing his mind. Skinner had been reading the works of the American behaviorist, John B. Watson, and had become intrigued. He decided to become a student of psychology.

Skinner earned a Ph.D. in experimental psychology in 1931 at Harvard University and continued to work there until 1936, when he left to teach at the University of Minnesota. There, in carefully controlled experiments, Skinner examined organisms' responses to various consequences following their behavior. He developed the *Skinner box*, a cage in which an animal can be isolated with a device that can count aspects of behavior, such as a lever that can be pressed or a disk that can be pecked. A feeding apparatus is included to provide reinforcement (see Figure 6.13).

With the controlled conditions available in this box, Skinner uncovered many amazing things. He discovered the effects of intermittent reinforcement. He discovered shaping, and how quickly it can be effected. He

As a first step our trainer, who has been carefully programmed to produce head nods, resonant hm-hms, and other verbal reinforcers, loads up with an ample supply of candy, chewing gum and filter-tip cigarettes. A semi-willing subject who has never observed a person driving an automobile, and a parked car complete the picture. Our trainer might have to wait a long time before the subject emits an orienting response toward the vehicle. At the moment the subject does look even in the general direction of the car, this response is immediately reinforced and gradually he begins to gaze longingly at the stationary automobile. Similarly, approach responses in the desired direction are promptly reinforced in order to bring the subject in proximity to the car. Eventually, through the skillful use of differential reinforcement, the trainer will teach the subject to open and close the car door. With perseverance he will move the subject from the back seat or any other inappropriate location chosen in this trial-and-error ramble until at length the subject is shaped up behind the steering wheel. It is unnecessary to depict the remainder of the training procedure beyond noting that it will likely prove an exceedingly tedious, not to mention an expensive and hazardous enterprise. (Bandura, 1962, pp. 212–213)

Figure 6.13 *The Skinner box. B. F. Skinner designed this device so that he could study conditioning in a controlled environment. When the rat presses the bar, a light signals the presentation of a reinforcer (food or water).*

conducted experiments on discrimination and generalization. During World War II, he worked on a number of projects for the navy. In one such project he successfully taught pigeons to fly guided missiles to enemy targets by training them to peck at the target as it appeared on a television screen display in front of them. After the war he moved to Indiana University and became the chairman of the psychology department. There he transferred his knowledge of experimental psychology to human subjects, including his own daughter.

He developed what he called the *air crib*, a soundproof, relatively germ-free enclosure made of clear glass and plastic—an enlarged Skinner box for his child. His daughter spent part of the day in the crib and comfortably explored the articles that he included in her environment. She did not have to wear diapers, as the floor of the crib was absorbent and could be rolled out and rolled back in again. His daughter enjoyed the time she spent in the air crib.

In the late 1940s Skinner returned to Harvard University as a member of the faculty. There, he improved the Skinner box so that it could be more easily used for rats and pigeons, and he began to employ statistical analysis in his experiments with different subjects. Also at this time Skinner began to advocate the use of behavior modification in order to improve teaching and help people acquire skills or eliminate problems in their lives. Modern behavior modification theory and learning tech-

nology owe a great debt of gratitude to B. F. Skinner. His understanding of environmental forces and their effect on human beings has led us to realize the power of these forces. In his book *Beyond Freedom and Dignity*, Skinner argued that the environment was so important in controlling an individual's behavior that the idea of freedom had to be reexamined. He asserted that freedom was an illusion and that we were under greater stimulus control than we could imagine.

Social learning can be observed in other species as well. Dachshund puppies will learn to pull a food cart sooner if they see other puppies doing it than if they never observe such behavior (Adler & Adler, 1977). Rats learn by observing rat leaders, the first to discover the best route through a cage door (Konopasky & Telegdy, 1977). Another study demonstrated that naive mice will learn to copulate sooner by watching other mice do it (Hayashi & Kimura, 1976). Many studies have demonstrated this kind of observational learning in other species.

PERFORMANCE VERSUS ACQUISITION

Although learning can apparently take place simply through observing another's behavior, reinforcement can be an important supplement in social learning. Consider a second experiment conducted by Bandura in 1965. On one occasion a group of young children watched as a model was re-

LATENT LEARNING
Learning that occurs in the absence of any obvious reinforcement, apparently as a result of just being exposed to stimuli.

COGNITION
Mental activity involving thinking, remembering, problem solving, or decision making.

BEHAVIOR MODIFICATION
A set of procedures for changing human behavior, especially by using behavior therapy and operant conditioning techniques.

Children who watch a live actor model violence are more likely to imitate the violence than children who have not seen the model.

warded with juice and candy for being aggressive, and on another occasion a different group of children watched as the same model was scolded for the same aggression. The results of the experiment indicated that the consequences following the model's behavior were very important in determining whether the children would imitate the model. The children who had observed the model receiving juice and candy for aggressive behavior became more aggressive. The children who had observed the model being scolded for aggressive behavior rarely imitated the aggression.

At first glance this experiment may seem to indicate that reinforcement is necessary for social learning. We can resolve this problem by distinguishing between performing a behavior and acquiring it. Reinforcing or punishing the model's behavior did affect whether the children imitated the model. Nonetheless, the children who had seen the model disciplined for aggression were quite able, when offered reinforcers for demonstrating what the model had done, to recall and demonstrate the model's behavior, even though they had not spontaneously imitated the model before. This experiment showed that children who observed a model being disciplined for aggressive behavior were unlikely to imitate (perform) the behavior, but that they did learn (acquire) the behavior, and could imitate it at a later time if the reinforcing and punishing contingencies changed.

The term **latent learning** is sometimes used to describe this kind of incidental learning, when the learning may not be apparent from an animal's or a person's behavior. This kind of learning often occurs in the absence of reward. Rats placed in a maze and allowed to wander for a time

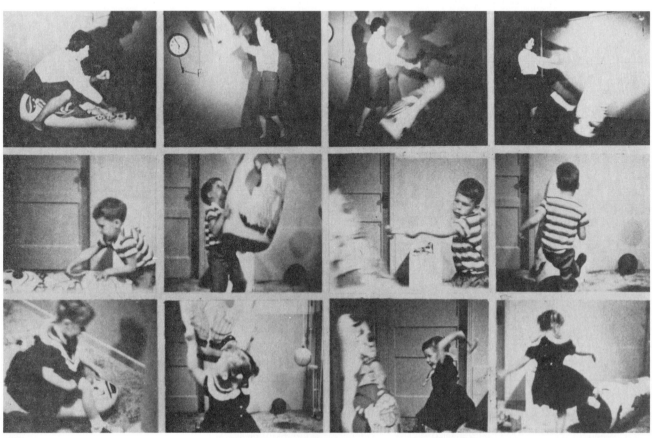

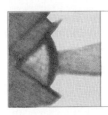

BEHAVIOR MODIFICATION

Albert Bandura and his colleagues at Stanford once placed an advertisement in a newspaper offering free aid to anyone with a snake phobia (an unrealistic fear of snakes). Many people answered the advertisement. As it turned out, the majority of respondents were men who held outdoor jobs and were deathly afraid of encountering a snake. It was hoped that a behavior modification program could help these volunteers overcome their phobia. **Behavior modification** is an offshoot of learning theory. By arranging particular associations between stimuli or particular consequences for behavior, or by modeling the behavior that is desired, it is possible to change a subject's behavior. That is, the environment and the experiences of the subject are purposely manipulated in order to change behavior.

In the first part of the behavior modification program, Bandura made certain that his volunteers did indeed have a snake phobia. He asked each subject to handle a snake, but none was willing to do so under any circumstances. Next, Bandura used models to help his subjects overcome their phobia. The models did not have a snake phobia. They approached and handled the snakes while the subjects watched. For any male subjects who so desired, Bandura even enlisted the aid of a striptease artist who worked with a boa constrictor named Squeezer. No doubt some associative learning was also involved here (Bandura, 1977). Many of the men found themselves sitting in the middle rows wanting to be close to the show but far from the snake.

The results of this experiment in behavior modification demonstrated, as have many similar experiments in the past, the power of modeling as a behavior modification technique. Within 48 hours the subjects found themselves able comfortably to handle the snake that they had so feared at the beginning of the experiment. In addition, no recurrences of phobia were reported when the subjects were interviewed a month later.

Using models as a behavior modification technique is usually incorporated into more comprehensive modification programs which often include both associative and instrumental learning. A good example of such a comprehensive program is described in the book *Toilet Training in Less than a Day* by Nathan Azrin and Richard Foxx (1974).

Toilet training doesn't have to be a three-year siege. It can be accomplished in under 24 hours using the learning principles that have been described in this chapter. To see how this is possible, let's examine some of the techniques used in the toilet training program developed by Azrin and Foxx. As you'll discover, this program takes both physical and environmental aspects into consideration.

1. The authors recommend that no attempt be made to train children much younger than 24 months. Children younger than this do not usually have the muscle development necessary for bladder and bowel control.
2. A learning environment should be created in which the child and parent are together, without distraction, for the whole day. In this way all of their energy can be devoted to learning and strengthening the new behavior.

3. The steps in the desired behavior sequence are as follows: The child will go to the potty-chair when the need arises, lower his or her training pants, urinate or defecate, wipe where appropriate, raise the training pants, remove the plastic pot from the potty-chair, empty its contents into the toilet, flush the toilet, and return the plastic pot to the potty chair.
4. The authors give a number of tips on accomplishing these behaviors more easily. They suggest, for example, using large, loose training pants because they are easier to raise and lower.
5. Instrumental learning is achieved as the child's appropriate behaviors are reinforced through lavish praise and the administration of large amounts of juice or soda. Drinking liquid makes urination more likely, giving the child more chances to learn the desired response; remember, a behavior must occur before it can be reinforced.
6. The technique of modeling is incorporated in an ingenious way by making use of a doll that wets. At the beginning of the Azrin and Foxx program, before anything else, the child is required to toilet train the doll. The child watches as the doll models the desired behavior and then sees that the doll is immediately rewarded for its good behavior with praise and juice (administered to the doll in a special baby bottle that refills its reservoir). This is an effective technique because a model, even a doll, is more likely to be imitated if the observer sees that the model's behavior is reinforced.

COGNITIVE PSYCHOLOGY
The study of behavior as it relates to thinking, remembering, problem solving, or decision making.

COGNITIVE MAP
A mental representation of one's location in relationship to other locations in a given environment.

without reinforcement will later, when reinforced, learn to find the goal box faster than will rats that are new to the maze. Latent learning had apparently occurred in the animals as they wandered about in the maze. Although no direct reinforcement was given, just the experience of walking through the maze seems to have taught them something.

Other factors besides reinforcement and punishment of a model's behavior can affect the likelihood that imitation will occur. For instance, the perceived status of the model can be very important. Some of the earliest social learning studies demonstrated that the behavior of an entire group of people can best be altered by having the individuals with the highest status (as perceived by the group) model the desired behavior, rather than by attempting to influence each group member singly (Lippitt, Polansky, & Rosen, 1952; Polansky, Lippitt, & Redl, 1950). Such prominent models can have a powerful effect, especially when presented to large numbers of observers by mass media (newspapers, movies, or television). In addition, a behavior is more likely to be imitated when the models are nurturant, aggressive, or similar to the observers. Imitation is also more likely when a person can already perform the component subskills of the behavior that has been modeled, and when the person's usual environment is similar to that in which the model was originally observed.

Of course, whether a particular model will be perceived as a person of high status, or whether a model's behavior will appear worthy of imitation, depends largely on the thoughts of the observer. For this reason social learning theorists have become very interested in the thinking process and in its role in the formation of beliefs and attitudes.

Cognitive Learning

Cognition refers to thinking. Philosophically, social learning is considered to be an interaction between environment and thought, rather than mainly a function of environmental input (Bandura, 1978). Human beings think, and social learning theory includes complex internal "self-programming" within its scope because each environmental experience can be altered by thought in a way that can affect how the next experience will be perceived. In other words, the internal rules and beliefs that you have come to hold as a result of your experience and thinking can modify the effect of future experiences. For example, one study demonstrated that viewing television violence could create aggressive thoughts and attitudes, which in turn could alter the interpretation of new environmental experiences so that they would tend to be viewed in an aggressive context (Chaffee & McLeod, 1971). This example demonstrates what social learning theorists have come to believe—that it is impossible to consider the environment completely separately from the internal thought processes of the individual who is interacting with it. As Albert Bandura stated, to exclude thinking from any theory of learning would be like attributing "Shakespeare's masterpieces to his prior instruction in the mechanics of writing" (Bandura, 1978).

Human beings think, and thinking affects behavior. Traditional behaviorists, especially in Watson's day, were unwilling to examine the mind or thought processes because they were not directly observable. Since then, learning theorists have devoted increasing effort to exploring thought processes, problem solving, and the internal understanding we have of our

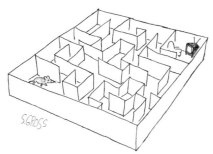

Drawing S. Gross; ©1978 The New Yorker Magazine, Inc.

world. The study of thinking and its influence on our behavior is known as **cognitive psychology.** Cognitive psychology is also concerned with learning.

COGNITIVE MAPS

Let's look at thinking a little more closely. We respond to the world, not just through our conditioned responses, but also through our knowledge of it. But does a dog do this? Do dogs think? Most people with dogs assume that they do. Suppose you come home and make a sound as you unlock the door; your dog will be waiting to greet you on the other side (assuming you have a dog). Why was your dog waiting there? Did it have a mental image of you on the other side of the door? Did it know from the sounds you made that it was *you?* Or did it simply hear a series of cues, or discriminative stimuli, and run for the door because that response in the presence of those cues had previously been reinforced? Moreover, did the dog become excited and wag its tail because it had been classically conditioned so that the sounds of the door being unlocked aroused the autonomic nervous system—a conditioned arousal? If the dog merely responded to cues and classical conditioning, then it ran for the door, became excited, and wagged its tail without having any "idea" why it acted in this way. The question whether dogs or other animals rely on mental representations of their world is debatable. All we know for sure is that humans often use mental or cognitive abilities when they interact with their environment.

A cognitive representation of the world is a valuable asset. With it you can manipulate, alter, or change things mentally in order to examine possible outcomes before you actually do anything. You use your cognitive understanding to orient yourself to particular problems or situations. A rat running a maze in search of food has to learn which turns to make in order to find the food (see Figure 6.14). After a number of trials, it learns that at a certain corner it should turn right, and at another corner it should turn right again, and soon it will come to the food. Similarly, when you enter a strange town or go to a new neighborhood, you may initially have to find your way around by trial and error, or by memorizing certain details. Eventually, however, you become oriented and you acquire what is known as a **cognitive map,** an internal understanding of the location of things in relation to each other.

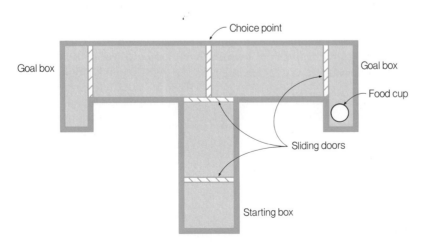

Figure 6.14 *A simple T maze used to study choice learning. Sliding doors prevent the animal from turning back once the choice is made. The food cup may be placed in either goal box.*

PLACE-LEARNING
Acquiring an understanding of one's location relative to other locations in an environment through experience with the environment.

NEGATIVE TRANSFER OF LEARNING
The process whereby learning one task makes it harder to learn another.

POSITIVE TRANSFER OF LEARNING
The process whereby learning one task makes it easier to learn another.

In the late 1940s Edward Tolman came to the conclusion that rats, too, had cognitive maps. Working with rats that had learned their way through a maze, he found that if a particular path was blocked the rats would attempt to find another path, one never used before but lying in the same general direction (Tolman, Ritchie, & Kalish, 1946). Tolman referred to this tendency as **place-learning.** Cognitive learning in animals seems to be quite limited in comparison with human cognitive capacity.

TRANSFER OF LEARNING

Figure 6.15 shows typewriter keys as they are arranged on most typewriters. If you think about it, this particular arrangement may seem foolish. Since the letter *e* is the most common letter in the English language it would seem more logical to place it beneath one of the fingers, probably the index finger of the right hand, so that it could be struck quickly. Similarly, you might expect that the other keys beneath the fingers (called home keys) would represent the most commonly used letters. Why put a semicolon on a home key?

Very early typewriters were in fact arranged in this "more logical" way, with the most frequently used letters under the fingers. Unfortunately, typists could go so fast with this arrangement that they often surpassed the capacity of the machine. They jammed the keys. As a result, Sholes and Company, the developers of the first American typewriter, purposely scrambled the letters in order to slow typists down. Nowadays electric typewriters can respond so quickly that it is impossible to type too fast. You may wonder, then, why the keyboards of modern typewriters haven't all been rearranged so that typists can build up their speed again. Or would such a switch create a nightmare for anyone who already knew how to type?

Negative Transfer of Learning Proficient typists need only look at a word and their fingers automatically "know" which letters to type. Knowing how to type might not be an advantage if you tried to learn a new keyboard. Such previously learned skills can even interfere with the ability to learn a new skill. This result is referred to as **negative transfer of learning.**

Modern keyboards for typewriters have been developed. Figure 6.16 shows the Maltron keyboard. In a study requiring the typing of 1 million words, it was discovered that typists using the usual keyboard had to leave their home keys 82,000 times while Maltron users needed to do so only 320 times ("The Case of Qwerty," 1981). Yet the Maltron keyboard has not been well accepted in spite of its greater speed and comfort. There is too much fear of negative transfer of learning which would make the typewriter almost impossible to use by anyone who knew the usual keyboard.

Figure 6.15 *The arrangement of the keys on most typewriters. The home keys are shaded.*

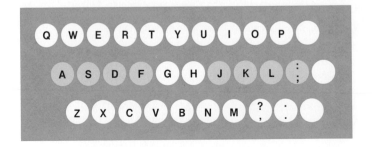

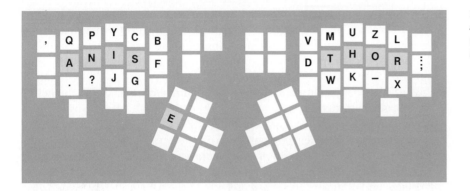

Positive Transfer of Learning and Cognitive Aspects of Motor Performance
When you write with a pen on paper you use many small muscles that require fine muscle control. In painting a wall, you generally use different and larger muscles. In each case the muscles have "learned" certain responses to different stimuli. The term *motor learning* may be a poor choice of words, however. You can't teach a muscle. Learning takes place in the nervous system, usually in the brain. If you paint your name on a wall (using gross muscle activity), your handwriting is still easily recognizable (just as though you had used fine muscle activity and written with pen on paper). This suggests a central mechanism that controls sequences of muscle activity that can easily take place in one muscle group or another.

This brings us back to typewriter keyboards. As it turns out, typists familiar with the usual keyboard can use their previous typing experience to master the Maltron keyboard ("The Case of Qwerty," 1981). When a previously learned skill helps you acquire a new skill, you are said to be demonstrating **positive transfer of learning.** The average typist used to the usual keyboard can master Maltron in about a month. A beginner takes longer than this. Learning how to type, then, is more than just learning where the keys are or learning a series of operant muscle habits. Learning to type may be better described as a detailed cognitive understanding of manual dexterity and how to apply it.

Summary

- Learning may be defined as a relatively permanent change in behavior that results from experience.
- Those who specialize in the study of inherited behavior patterns are called ethologists, and their field of study is called ethology.
- Lorenz was one of the first to observe that baby chicks will follow the first object that moves through their visual field during an early critical period of their lives. Lorenz referred to this phenomenon as imprinting.
- Imprinting is only one example of a large number of innate behavioral tendencies. Ethologists and psychologists are also interested in studying fixed-response patterns which are elicited by releaser stimuli.
- Learning is important because it has survival value. It allows greater flexibility in behavior than fixed-response patterns alone would.
- Experiments with fruit fly larvae have demonstrated that learning is probably an inherited ability.

- Habituation and sensitization are simple kinds of learning. Habituation occurs when a person becomes accustomed to a stimulus because it has been presented repeatedly. Sensitization may occur when an animal or a human being is exposed to a stimulus that is accompanied by some kind of pain.
- The effects of habituation and sensitization have been traced to the action of neurotransmitters.
- During the 1890s the Russian physiologist Pavlov reported an experiment with an associative learning process. By systematically associating the presentation of a bell with the presentation of food, Pavlov was able to classically condition dogs to respond to the bell by salivating.
- Watson and Rayner's experiment with Little Albert demonstrated that classical conditioning can also occur in humans.
- Associative experiences can also lead to the formation of beliefs and attitudes.
- In instrumental conditioning, behaviors are learned because of the reinforcing or punishing consequences that follow the behavior.
- The basic premise of instrumental learning was formulated by E. L. Thorndike at the turn of the century. It is known as the law of effect.
- Reinforcement occurs when a pleasant consequence reinforces the response that it follows.
- An instrumental behavior can occasionally be built up piecemeal through a process known as shaping. Shaping consists of reinforcing successive approximations toward the final response.
- An organism's responses can become highly selective or more general through the processes of discrimination and generalization. When an organism discriminates it responds differentially to two stimuli. When it generalizes, similar stimuli evoke the same response.
- Positive and negative reinforcement are both ways of strengthening a response. Positive reinforcement occurs when an organism is reinforced for having approached or obtained something. Negative reinforcement occurs when an organism is reinforced for successfully avoiding or escaping an aversive situation.
- Punishment and extinction are both ways of weakening a response.
- Punishment is an extremely effective way of decreasing a behavior's strength, but its use may have serious drawbacks, including withdrawal, suppression of other behaviors, hostility, or aggression.
- Stimuli necessary for sustaining life can obtain the power to reinforce simply by being withheld for a time; such stimuli are called primary reinforcers. Other stimuli, known as secondary or acquired reinforcers, are effective because of their association with primary or other secondary reinforcers.
- Instrumental behavior may be maintained by different schedules of reinforcement.
- Through learning, different stimuli come to cue specific instrumental responses. Such cues are known as discriminative stimuli.
- Learning through observation of another's behavior is called social learning.
- Albert Bandura has argued that social learning is a different kind of learning because it does not depend on reinforcement.
- Social learning theorists draw a distinction between the performance (imitation) of a behavior and its learning (acquisition). Latent learning

is the term used to describe the kind of incidental learning that may not be apparent from an animal's or a person's behavior.

- Models are most likely to be imitated if they are of high status, nurturant, aggressive, or similar to the observer.
- Cognition refers to thinking. Cognitive learning theorists believe that thought processes have an important effect on learning.
- Cognitive aspects of learning can be seen by studying cognitive maps. A cognitive map is a mental representation of the location of things in relation to each other.
- Sometimes a previously learned skill interferes with the ability to learn a new skill. This result is referred to as negative transfer of learning. When a previously learned skill helps you learn a new skill, you are said to have demonstrated positive transfer of learning.

EPILOGUE: THE NAIL BITES THE DUST

The following account should probably come under the heading "Strange but True." It describes a psychologist's use of self-administered punishment to change a socially unacceptable behavior.

I once knew a psychologist who, for reasons you will shortly discover, shall remain anonymous. For the sake of the story, let's call him Richard. Richard had a bad habit. He chewed his nails. Well, that's not actually correct; he chewed his nails off and then spit them out, usually while he was lecturing. Once in a great while this practice was called to his attention, and it always embarrassed him. He said that he wasn't aware that he was doing it. It had become such an ingrained habit that he could chew off all ten nails, spit them in all directions, and still be totally unconscious of doing it.

Richard was a respected learning theorist, and he decided that if anyone could devise a behavior modification technique to eliminate his habit, he could. The next day he arrived, all smiles, and said he had a request: If any of us should see him biting his nails, we should let him know about it. It wasn't long before someone said, "Uh, Richard, you're doing it." He stopped and looked at his nails and said, "So I

am." Then, as everyone watched, he pulled up his shirtsleeve, grabbed hold of a heavy-duty rubber band that he had wrapped around his wrist, stretched it out about a distance of 10 inches, and let it go. There was a vicious snap. He yelled, cursed, and shook his hand. Everyone looked on in amazement. Surely, learning theorists were all a little insane. "Punishment," he said. "Punishment is the answer!"

What happened to the people around Richard was interesting. Some took relish in pointing out that he was biting his nails, just to see him snap the huge rubber band against his wrist; others preferred to ignore his habit, because they couldn't stand to see him in that much pain. Happily, after two days, Richard's habit had been broken.

I asked him how he thought his program had worked. He said, "Well, if I unconsciously learned to chew my nails, then I could certainly unconsciously unlearn it. Whenever I was chewing my nails, I administered this punishment. Pretty soon my brain learned that nail chewing re-

sulted in something very unpleasant." He said that the last time he reached his hand up to his mouth (quite unconsciously), he got a terrible sinking feeling that something awful was about to happen. "It made me aware," he said. "I looked at my hand and saw that it was approaching my mouth. Somewhere deep in my brain the little gray cells were screaming, 'Don't do it'!"

It was reported that some days later Richard was wearing rubber bands around his ankles, but nobody wanted to ask why.

Suggestions for Further Reading

1. Flaherty, C. F., Hamilton, L. W., Gandelman, R. J., & Spear, N. E. *Learning and memory.* Chicago: Rand McNally, 1977.
2. Pavlov, I. *Conditioned reflexes.* Clarendon Press, 1927.
3. Powers, R. B., & Osborne, J. G. *Fundamentals of behavior.* St. Paul, Minnesota: West Publishing Company, 1976.
4. Reynolds, G. S. *A primer of operant conditioning* (2nd ed.). Glenview, Illinois: Scott Foresman, 1975.
5. Skinner, B. F. *Beyond freedom and dignity.* New York: Knopf, 1971.

CONTENTS

CHAPTER 7

Memory and Information Processing

PROLOGUE

You are working in a German laboratory in 1885. You've been at the laboratory for a couple of weeks now and have met the other workers, except for Dr. Ebbinghaus. Hermann Ebbinghaus keeps mostly to himself. Since his office is only one door down, however, you decide to drop by and make his acquaintance.

As you come to knock on his door, you notice that it's already open. Ebbinghaus is sitting in the office, looking concerned. He notices you and motions you to enter. Before you can say anything or introduce yourself, he looks at you and says, "Do you have any idea how quickly we forget?" You look perplexed and shake your head no. Ebbinghaus seems excited and beckons you over to look at some charts that he's prepared. "Look," he says. "Look at what I've done."

As you look over his shoulder, he begins to explain his current project. "I've taken consonant-vowel-consonant trigrams and turned them into nonsense syllables. See?" You look at his list of syllables: DAX, BUP, LOC, and ten others. "I

used nonsense syllables because they have no prior meaning. I taught them to myself, all 13, until I could repeat them twice without error. Then I put the list away and checked how many I could remember at various times. Then, if I had forgotten any, I recorded how long it took me to relearn the entire list twice. It took me 1,156 seconds to learn the list the first time," he says, "and only 467 seconds to relearn it, a savings of 689 seconds the second time. You see I've expressed this savings as a percentage, 64.2 percent, and I've plotted these percentages on a graph."

At this point you're sorry that you came to his office. You haven't even met the man, and he's already bombarding you with boring charts and numbers. "Look," he says, pointing to the graph. "See how quickly forgetting happens." You look at his chart (Figure 7.1) and notice that his retention dropped dramatically within only 20 minutes after he memorized the material, and that within nine hours it had dropped even further. "Isn't that

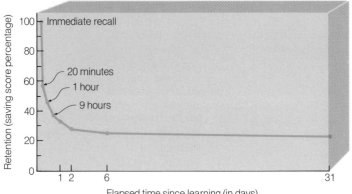

Hermann Ebbinghaus (1850–1909)

interesting?" he remarks. "A tremendous amount of what we learn is forgotten rapidly at first, and then the forgetting tapers off, although some may occur even 30 days later. If I study these syllables many, many times, I forget them less quickly, but still the initial forgetting is much greater than the later forgetting. Isn't that interesting? I always thought that forgetting happened slowly and steadily, not like this. Imagine," he continues, almost talking to himself, "it wouldn't be very good to finish studying for a test a few days before you were going to take it, would it? As a matter of fact, all those bright students who take our exams and do so well—I wonder how much they remember a week later?" Then he looks at you. "It's really interesting, eh, eh, I'm sorry, what is your name again?"

"Dr. Ebbinghaus, we've never met."

"Oh, forgive me," he says. "I thought perhaps we had met earlier but that I had just forgotten."

Unwittingly, you had witnessed the world's first memory experiment. Ebbinghaus continued to work, using mainly himself as a subject. And despite all the advances in science and technology, Ebbinghaus' original data have stood the test of time. His forgetting curve is still considered extremely accurate.

In this chapter we'll examine how your memory works—how you put information into your memory, store it, and retrieve it. We'll also examine how you can improve your memory and use it more successfully.

MEMORY
The complex mental function of recalling what has been learned or experienced.

Why Psychologists Study Memory

You rely on your **memory** every moment of the day. Without it you would have no sense of continuity, no realization of the past; and you couldn't benefit from any learning or experience. Without memory it would be impossible for you to function. All images and materials not immediately available to your senses must be drawn from your memory. Plans for the future, recollections of the past—all require a functioning memory. Your very sense of self-awareness requires that you remember you had a "self" yesterday. Without a memory you wouldn't seem human.

Yet memory is not perfect. The mind does not remember like a camera; our memories alter and change. Some memories are forgotten, others are hidden in hard-to-reach places. How well we use our memories influences our ability to think and to understand. Before we can understand human behavior and capability, we must understand how the memory works and what its limitations and potential are.

A Model of Memory

Unlike a theory, a **model** is never considered right or wrong. It is simply a picture or a depiction that is used to clarify an idea. Figure 7.2 is a model of human memory; its only purpose is to help you organize your thinking about memory. As you can see, it is composed of three major parts: the sensory memory, short-term memory, and long-term memory. We will examine each in turn.

SENSORY MEMORY

The world is filled with sights, sounds, and many other kinds of sensory stimulation, but you don't remember all of them. When you first receive a particular visual stimulus, the image is held for only a fraction of a second in what is known as the sensory memory, or sensory register. Unless you pay attention to the image and encode it successfully into the short-term memory, the image will decay and be lost. Decay can occur within just a fourth of a second after a sensation is registered in the sensory memory. In other words, if you don't pay attention to a sensation, it is lost almost immediately.

In 1960 George Sperling demonstrated the existence of sensory memory. He organized a series of experiments in which rows of numbers or letters were flashed on a screen for different fractions of a second (see Figure 7.3). When the subjects were asked to state what they had seen, the average person could remember only three or four letters or numbers. The remainder could not be remembered, even though the subjects knew they had seen them. Those memories had already decayed.

Sperling later used a tone, either high, medium, or low in pitch, to indicate the row that he wanted the subjects to remember and report. The tone was sounded immediately after the letters and numbers had been displayed. Subjects remembered rows better when the tone was sounded because it helped them focus their attention on the particular row, thus enabling them to recall the information before it decayed (see Figure 7.2). However, if the tone sounded more than a second after the display had disappeared, the subjects had a difficult time recalling the numbers and letters in the designated row. This implied that a sensory memory existed, but decayed within a second.

SHORT-TERM MEMORY

Short-term memory is the working, active memory. Using a computer model for a moment, you might think of the long-term memory as the large storage area of the computer and the short-term memory as the material that can be retrieved onto the computer's display screen at a given time.

MODEL
A mathematical, logical, or mechanical replica of a relationship or a system of events so designed that a study of the model can yield some understanding of the real thing.

SENSORY MEMORY
The first stage in the memory process. New information is held in the sensory memory for less than one second and will decay unless it is attended to, that is, encoded and placed in the short-term memory. Also called *sensory register*.

SHORT-TERM MEMORY
Memory that has a limited storage capacity and a short duration. It is often called working memory because it must call up items from long-term memory so that the items can be examined. Information encoded from the sensory memory is held in the short-term memory and will decay unless the information is rehearsed or stored in the long-term memory.

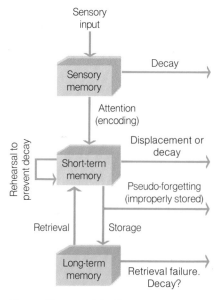

Figure 7.2 *A model of human memory. In the first stage of memory, sensory input registers in the sensory memory. Sensory memories decay within a fraction of a second unless they are attended to. Paying attention to sensory memories encodes them into the short-term memory, where they can be held by rehearsal or lost through decay and displacement. To enter the long-term memory, short-term memories must be stored. These stored long-term memories can be retrieved by the short-term memory for examination. They can also be lost through retrieval failure and perhaps through decay.*

205

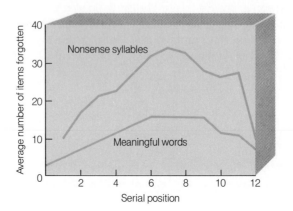

Figure 7.3 *Rows of numbers and letters similar to the arrangement used by Sperling in 1960.*

```
7  B  L  3
J  N  1  6
4  R  6  K
```

Information held in short-term memory is active information—information that you are paying attention to. But, as its name suggests, this memory is limited: If the information is new (from the sensory memory), it can be held in the short-term memory for only a brief time, and whether the information is new or old (retrieved from long-term memory), only a certain amount of it can be held at any given time. Most people's short-term memory can hold about seven "items," give or take two.

Consider what happens when you look up a new number in the telephone book. As you close the book, you must remember all seven digits in order to dial the phone. As you can see by looking at the model of human memory shown in Figure 7.2, there is only one way you can keep the information in short-term memory for longer than approximately 30 seconds. This is by using **rehearsal**—by saying the number over and over again to yourself, constantly restoring it in your short-term memory.

Has the following ever happened to you? You repeat a phone number to yourself again and again until you dial it. Now you've dialed the number and no longer need to rehearse it. But then the line is busy. Guess what? Back to the phone book to look it up again! Typically, the new information in the short-term memory was lost because it was not rehearsed or stored in the long-term memory.

Perhaps it's good that we forget new information that we need to use only once. How would you like to store everything you've ever known—every phone number, every street address, every new acquaintance's name? Interestingly, some people have a poor ability to forget information once they are exposed to it. They easily transfer any information held in their short-term memory into their long-term memory for storage. Contrary to what you might think, this is not a happy state of affairs. Such individuals find their minds cluttered with large amounts of useless information that obscure more timely and important facts (Luria, 1968).

Displacement What happens if you overload your short-term memory by trying to place 20 items into it? You are likely to remember a few of the first and a few of the last items, about seven altogether. The middle items, however, are very difficult to recall (see Figure 7.4). The first few items may be easier to recall because you may try to rehearse them, knowing that many more are on the way. But soon you become overwhelmed by the large number of items and lose most of them. When you reach the end of the list, you remember the last few because you have just recently been

Figure 7.4 *Middle items in a series, whether meaningful or not, are the most difficult to recall. This phenomenon is known as the serial position effect. (SOURCE: Adapted from Postman & Rau, 1957)*

exposed to them. This sequence of remembering is known as the **serial position effect.** The items that you lose undergo **displacement** as other items are retained.

Just as material in the sensory memory must be encoded into the short-term memory in order to be retained, material from the short-term memory must be stored in long-term memory in such a way that it can later be retrieved; otherwise the information will be lost, and lost rapidly. As you recall from the chapter Prologue, this memory loss is exactly what Ebbinghaus discovered when he tried to learn many nonsense syllables. Although he could hold onto the syllables for a short time after rehearsal, he found that he quickly forgot a great number. Students can fall into this trap without realizing it, thinking they have learned much more information than they really have. This is why it's important to go back and test yourself on material after some time has passed. In this way you can be certain that the material has settled into long-term memory, and not simply been held for a moment in short-term memory and then lost.

Chunking Here's a test of your short-term memory. Look at these four nonsense syllables. Then close the book and try to repeat them.

DAK   GIR   JOP   FID

Most people are able to repeat four nonsense syllables. Now press yourself a little further. Try these six nonsense syllables:

DIT   LON   KIF   JAT   WUB   BIP

Some people are able to remember six nonsense syllables, but most can't. It's hard to hold that much information in the short-term memory. Or is it? While you may have had some trouble repeating six nonsense syllables, you're not going to have any trouble repeating six one-syllable words:

STONE   BRIDGE   PATH   HOP   CUBE   LINE

Why are six one-word syllables easier than six nonsense syllables? It's because they have a meaning. How far can the short-term memory be pushed? Try nine one-syllable words:

SHOE   MONK   BLADE   JUMP   PLAY   HATE   RUST   SOUP   POND

It's likely that nine one-syllable words have pushed your short-term memory too far. So that's the limit of short-term memory. Or is it? How about twelve syllables contained within three words?

CANADIAN   TESTIMONY   PSYCHOLOGY

It's easy because you are holding on to three meanings rather than 12 unrelated syllables. Not too difficult. But if you try six four-syllable words you're likely to have a little trouble:

DECLARATION   MINORITY   PESSIMISTIC   CONDITIONAL
INFURIATE   AMERICAN

But if you try a 19-word sentence you may have an easier time of it:

MARTIN LUTHER KING, WINNER OF THE NOBEL PEACE PRIZE, GAVE A SPEECH AT THE LINCOLN MEMORIAL ABOUT CIVIL RIGHTS.

Short-term memory doesn't seem to have trouble with this (Anderson, 1980).

REHEARSAL
A process by which memories can be held in the short-term memory for relatively long periods. In rehearsal, an item is repeated over and over so that it is not lost. A technique that may eventually result in the storage of items in the long-term memory.

SERIAL POSITION EFFECT
A phenomenon in verbal learning. Items at the beginning or at the end of a long series are more easily remembered. Items in the middle are the hardest to recall.

DISPLACEMENT
The loss of an item of information from short-term memory because of the addition of a new item of information.

In 1956 George Miller used the term **chunk** to describe a unit of memory. He said that the short-term memory could hold approximately seven of these chunks and that chunks were determined not by the amount of material they contained, such as letters or syllables, but instead by the meanings and organization of that material (Miller, 1956).

LONG-TERM MEMORY

In order to store information for days, weeks, years, or a lifetime, we must store short-term memories in **long-term memory,** which has a virtually unlimited storage capacity. In order to examine a long-term memory, we **retrieve** it into the short-term or working memory. There, approximately seven chunks of stored long-term memories can be examined at any one time. Chunks displaced from working memory (by new chunks called up from long-term memory) return to the long-term memory storage and can be retrieved again.

Short-term memories can be stored in the long-term memory in various ways. Important or unusual experiences are easily stored; that is, they are "memorable." Rehearsing an item (such as a phone number) many times may cause it to be stored in the long-term memory. And other techniques can be mastered to facilitate both storage and retrieval. Let's take a look at some of these techniques.

Meaning and Memory   Most of us complain about our memory from time to time, but strategies can be learned to improve it. Shortly you will learn how to use your memory in a way you may never have thought possible. You will be able to memorize a 100-item shopping list in about 15 minutes, and not only will you remember every item, but also you'll be able to tell which item was number 71, which item was number 29, and so on. You *can* remember; you just need to know how your memory works and how to use it.

You have seen that the short-term memory can hold about seven chunks of information. You have also seen that the more meaning contained in a chunk, the more easily the information can be stored. Chunks without meaning, such as nonsense syllables, are difficult to recall. Chunks with meaning, such as sentences, are much easier to recall. For this reason, you might have as much trouble remembering a few nonsense syllables as a few much longer but meaningful sentences.

It seems, then, that our memories rely on meaning. After all, it's much more valuable to remember things that have meaning, such as where food and water are and how to get them, than to recall the meaningless.

All day long we're bombarded with the meaningless. The number eight means something—it means eight objects, or two units of four, or four units of two. But what does it mean when it's used in a phone number, such as 831-9011? Eight in this instance is merely a place holder. It may just as well be a nonsense syllable.

Numbers used as place holders are abstract and make no sense. How would you like to remember a list of 50 numbers? It would seem impossible, not because your memory is incapable, but only because there are no meanings attached to the numbers. With great practice and rehearsal it may be possible to learn a 50-digit sequence, but it would take a long time. For information to be stored easily, it must have meaning. Yet there is a way to give meaning to things that seem meaningless.

The method you are about to use was developed by Bruno Furst (Furst, 1948). Look at Table 7.1 and you'll see a code that's used to turn "meaningless" numbers into sounds. You'll have to memorize this table to go further, but it's a very easy table to memorize. Look at the first consonants in the "sound" row: t, n, m, r, l, j, k, f, p, and z. Each consonant goes with the number it appears next to. Whenever you think of one of these numbers, you should immediately know which consonant or sound it goes with: Three goes with an "m" sound; seven goes with a "k" sound, etc.

This table is based on the *sounds* of letters. Both "d" and "th" are included under number 1, for example, because "t," "d," and "th" all sound alike. Other sounds are listed together for the same reason. From these sounds, Furst has composed a 100-word basic list (see Table 7.2).

Memory expert Bruno Furst demonstrates his principles of memory recall.

Table 7.1   Code for turning numbers into sounds

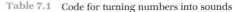

NUMBER	SOUND	AID FOR REMEMBERING
1	t (d, th)	stands on one leg
2	n	stands on two legs
3	m	stands on three legs
4	r	the word four ends in an "r" sound
5	l	L is the roman numeral for 50
6	j (sh, ch, soft g)	looks a bit like a backward 6
7	k (q, hard c, hard g, ng)	K can be made from two sevens
8	f (v, ph)	script f looks like 8 (ƒ)
9	b (p)	looks like backward upside down 9
0	z (s, soft c)	"z" sound in zero

SOURCE: Adapted from Furst, 1948.

NOTE: Each number is represented by a different sound group. Study this chart using the aids provided until you know which sound group goes with the numbers 1 through 0.

Table 7.2   Furst's 100-word basic list

1. tea	21. net	41. rat	61. chat	81. fat
2. Noah	22. nun	42. rain	62. chain	82. fan
3. May	23. name	43. ram	63. chime	83. fame
4. ray	24. Nero	44. rear	64. chair	84. fare
5. law	25. nail	45. rail	65. Chile	85. fall
6. jaw	26. niche	46. rash	66. judge	86. fish
7. key	27. neck	47. rake	67. check	87. fig
8. fee	28. navy	48. reef	68. chef	88. fife
9. bay	29. nap	49. rope	69. chip	89. fob
10. toes	30. mass	50. lace	70. case	90. base
11. tot	31. mat	51. lot	71. cat	91. bat
12. tan	32. man	52. lane	72. can	92. bean
13. tam	33. mama	53. lime	73. cam	93. beam
14. tar	34. mare	54. lair	74. car	94. bar
15. tale	35. mail	55. lily	75. coal	95. ball
16. tissue	36. match	56. lash	76. cash	96. badge
17. tack	37. mike	57. lake	77. cake	97. back
18. taffy	38. muff	58. leaf	78. cuff	98. beef
19. tap	39. map	59. lap	79. cap	99. babe
20. nose	40. race	60. chase	80. face	100. thesis

SOURCE: Furst, 1948, p. 64.

NOTE: Each word corresponds with its number by using the correct sounds from the code. Example: #1 (a "t" sound) = *tea*; #56 (an "L" and a "sh" sound) = *lash*; #100 (a "th" sound and two "s" sounds) = *thesis*, etc.

Look over all the code words in Table 7.2, then close the book. Think to yourself any of the numbers between 1 and 100, and see if you can immediately, by using the sound code of the number, recall the word. For instance, number 22 must be two n's; therefore nun is the code word. It's easy to learn these code words because the number tips you off to the sound. These code words will stay with you forever if you work with them, and you can use them over and over again to remember any list of 100 new items. To save time on this exercise, we will just use the following 20-item list. Normally, such a list would overload your memory—but not any more.

1. tower
2. star
3. orchard
4. picture
5. parade
6. violin
7. files
8. school
9. garden
10. ball
11. cigarette
12. cake
13. straw
14. honey
15. letter
16. car
17. sheet music
18. book
19. Coca-Cola
20. bone

The first word on this list of 20 is tower, and your first code word is tea. Now put them together in a visual image—an image in your mind's eye. Use an image that's meaningful to you; something that's especially memorable. You might imagine yourself at the top of a great tower, pouring tea off the tower into a tiny cup far below; or perhaps you can picture a huge teapot balancing precariously on top of a tall tower. Use any good association. It should be left to your own imagination, because the things you dream up are easier for you to remember. Then look at the next word, star. Your second code word is Noah. Somehow pair star and Noah—the more memorable the pairing, the more vivid and *meaningful* the image, the better it will be stored and recalled. The third word is orchard, and the code word is May. The fourth word is picture, and the code word is ray. I see a burglar in an art museum using the ray from his flashlight to find the picture he wants to steal. What do you imagine?

Go through this process carefully and slowly for the 20 items, and then set the book down and try to remember them. It's amazing how much you can remember if you put information into long-term memory by using meaning and bring it out by using meaning. Abstract numbers will no longer defeat you. There's something significant about them now—they're not simply place holders. What was number 4? Number 4 = "r" sound. The code word for the "r" sound = ray. Ray—ah, yes: picture. It's easy.

You can use these techniques to memorize long lists of numbers as well. Simply translate the numbers into the sounds and make words out of the sounds, and then sentences, even silly sentences (which are easier to remember).

Look at Figure 7.5. When people simply study this figure and later try to redraw it, their drawings are not very accurate. But suppose I told you that this was a midget playing a trombone in a telephone booth? As soon as I told you this, the figure would take on a meaning. Individuals who have such an image in mind are much better able to recall the item when tested later than those who simply look at it and try to memorize it (Bower, Karlin, & Dueck, 1975).

Mnemonics The memory aids we have been discussing are known collectively as **mnemonics.** A mnemonic is any kind of memory system or memory aid. There are many popular mnemonic devices. One of the oldest

Figure 7.5 *This figure is easier to remember if it's made meaningful.*

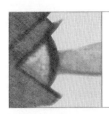

SNIFF—OH, NOW I REMEMBER!

If you turn back to Chapter 2 for a moment and take a look at the list of brain neuropeptides (p. 58), you'll notice that one of them is called **vasopressin**. In 1976, researcher David de Wied accidentally discovered something that seemed to come from the pages of science fiction—a "memory pill." He injected some rats with a vasopressin hormone and found to his surprise that they became easier to train and had better memories (de Wied, van Wimersma Greidanus, Bohus, Urban, & Gispen, 1976). Further research has shown that injections aren't necessary. Vasopressin can be put into a nasal spray and sniffed.

In 1978 a Belgian and Swiss team compared experimental and placebo groups of men between the ages of 50 and 65 who were suffering from memory loss. The experimental group received three exposures to vasopressin in nasal spray each day, and the control group received three exposures to a placebo nasal spray. The experimental group clearly did better on tests that measured attention, recognition, learning, concentration, and immediate memory (Legros, Gilot, Seron, Claessens, Adam, Moeglen, Audibert, & Berchier, 1978). Later in 1978, four amnesia patients

in Spain—three car accident victims and one suffering the effects of alcoholism—were treated with vasopressin. All four were reported to have regained their memories within five to nine days, which is much faster than would have been thought possible. Following is a brief account of one of these patients:

The third patient, a man aged 21, presented with severe **retrograde amnesia** after a car accident 6 months previously (coma for 15 days). He could remember nothing of the 3 months before the accident and the 3½ months after it. Vasopressin was given by nasal spray (5 puffs or about 13.5 I.U. daily). After 1 day the patient could recall several features of the accident, and his memory rapidly improved. By the fourth day of treatment he was even **hypermnesic**. Improvement progressed continuously, and by day 7 he had completely recovered his memory. His mood had improved, he became self-confident and slept well. When placebo was given in place of vasopressin, after 7 days, no change occurred, and his condition has remained satisfactory (Oliveros, Jandali, Timsit-Berthier, Remy, Benghezal, Audibert, & Moeglen, 1978, p. 42).

Herbert Weingartner and his colleagues at the National Institute of Mental Health went on to test vasopressin on healthy subjects. In addition, they included depressed subjects and senile subjects in their studies.

Some of the subjects received vasopressin, others were given a placebo. All took sniffs daily for two to three weeks, and every day they were tested for their ability to remember and learn. All three groups of volunteers significantly improved their learning and memory, while those who received the placebo did not (Weingartner, Gold, Bullenger, Smallberg, Summers, Rubinow, Post, & Goodwin, 1981).

How vasopressin works to help people remember is not understood. The hormone is experimental at this point and is not readily available to the public. When it is understood better, and if it is found to be safe with continued use, it may become publicly available. Then you might see a number of strange things. Classes of students, while waiting to take tests, might be snorting away on their nasal spray. People might go into drug stores saying, "I need some vasopressin. I've forgotten where I parked my car." Doctors and dentists might give complementary sprays to help patients remember appointments. But until, uh, what's it called again? becomes available, we'll just have to struggle along without it.

---

is known as the **method of loci,** which works well for lists of 10-15 items and is very easy to use. Think of a familiar pathway, perhaps the entrance to your home, and then think of 10 or 15 items that appear in a certain order along that path. Associate each item on your list with one of the familiar things along the path. If you are going grocery shopping, imagine bread in the mailbox, broken eggs on the walkway, an orange where the doorknob used to be, etc. You'll find, after you've made the associations, that it's relatively easy to recall your whole shopping list just by walking down that path again in your mind's eye and stopping at the different loci to recall the associations made at each.

Mnemonics may not be totally new to you. Did you ever have to memorize the colors of the rainbow in the right order—red, orange, yellow, green, blue, indigo, and violet? You may have been taught the mnemonic aid Roy G. Biv; and every budding musician has learned "Every Good Boy Does Fine" (EGBDF) to represent the musical staff. William James once said that there are three ways to remember things: mechanical methods, which require intensive study and repetition, such as the way children learn the alphabet; judicious methods, which are based on logic, classification, and analysis; and ingenious methods, which include the mnemonic devices we've been discussing and which give meaning to the abstract.

The Biology of Memory—Searching for the Engram

In 1917 neurophysiologist Karl Lashley began a search for what he called the brain's **engram,** the hypothesized biochemical structure that contains memories. Lashley systematically removed sections from the brains of trained rats, searching for the portion that held the elusive engram. In his book *In Search of the Engram*, published in 1950, he reported that his studies had yielded information about where the engrams didn't exist, but not about where they did. He concluded that memory was not held in one portion of the brain but was distributed equally throughout—a theory that he referred to as **equipotentiality.**

The biochemical structure of the engram, or memory trace, is still debated, as well as whether Lashley was correct about equipotentiality. Several theories suggest that memories may reside in small molecular chains or proteins. In 1960 James McConnell and his associates conditioned flatworms (planaria) to respond to light. Then the flatworms were chopped up and fed to other flatworms who had not been conditioned. McConnell reported that the second group of flatworms exhibited the same conditioned response to light that had been developed in the first group of worms (McConnell, 1977). McConnell reasoned that the biochemicals responsible for the memories were somehow transferred from the first worms to the second by ingestion. In other words, the second group of worms had eaten the engrams of the first. Others who attempted to replicate McConnell's original experiment were not always successful, however, implying that the effect is a difficult one to obtain.

For a time, McConnell and others believed that RNA might hold the key to the engram. RNA helps to relay genetic information and build proteins. It is known that **RNA** is formed as memories are created, because an animal's neurons typically contain more RNA after memories are acquired. By the 1970s, however, the experiments of Georges Ungar had led researchers to believe that it wasn't RNA itself, but rather the small proteins made by RNA, that contained memories.

Rats are nocturnal creatures and generally prefer to avoid light. Ungar trained rats to avoid the darkened corner of a maze by electrifying that portion of the floor (see Figure 7.6). After the training, he examined extracts from the rats' brains and found a new protein he called **scotophobin.** If untrained rats were injected with synthetic scotophobin (which Ungar was able to manufacture once the formula for scotophobin was obtained through chemical analysis), they avoided the darkened corner of the maze as though they, too, had received training. It seemed that Ungar might have dis-

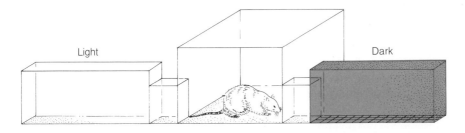

Figure 7.6 *A device similar to that used by Ungar and his colleagues to isolate scotophobin. A rat (which is nocturnal) naturally seeks the darkened box, but an electrified grid floor conditions it to avoid the dark box. Another untrained rat that is injected with scotophobin from the conditioned rat's brain also avoids the darkened box.*

covered the formula for one specific memory (Ungar, Galvan, & Clark, 1968; Ungar, Desiderio, & Parr, 1972).

Later it was discovered that only one small part of Ungar's scotophobin, a small neuropeptide, was responsible for the effect. Neuropeptides associated with other specific memories and experiences have also been isolated. Dan Tate and his colleagues taught goldfish to avoid either green or blue and were later able to isolate distinctly different neuropeptides from the brains of each group of fish (Tate, Galvan, & Ungar, 1976). Perhaps future research will uncover the exact nature and role of these neuropeptides in memory. They may be Lashley's long-sought engrams.

Theories of Memory

DUAL-CODE THEORY

One popular theory of memory, the **dual-code theory,** argues that memories contain both sensory and verbal information (Paivio, 1971). Look at Figure 7.7 for about 30 seconds (don't name the items—just look), and then close the book and see how many items you can recall. People with good visual memory will remember most or all of the items. The picture in your mind's eye after the book is closed is called an **eidetic image.** A very strong

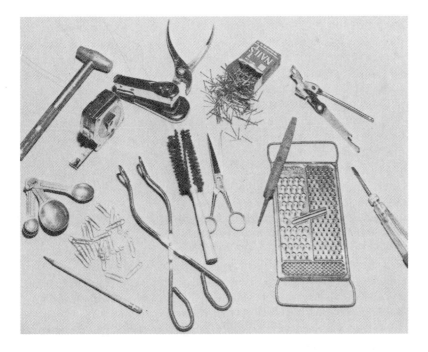

Figure 7.7 *How good is your photographic memory? Look at this photograph for 30 seconds (don't name the objects), close the book, and see how many objects you can remember.*

PHOTOGRAPHIC MEMORY
See EIDETIC IMAGE.

ACOUSTIC CODE
From the dual-code theory of memory. Sensory information may be stored directly as sounds.

PROPOSITIONS
The smallest units of information about which it makes sense to render a judgment of true or false. For example, "red apple" is not a proposition. However, "The apple is red" is a proposition, since the statement is either true or false.

PROPOSITIONAL NETWORK THEORY
The memory theory that states that sensory information and words are transformed into propositions in order to be stored in memory.

NODES
From the propositional network theory of memory, the individual parts of the proposition. Nodes serve as junctions and access points in the memory.

LINKS
From the propositional network theory of memory, links are the pathways between the nodes of the proposition. If two nodes are not directly linked, then recalling the information at one of the nodes will not lead to directly recalling the information at the other node.

eidetic image may last up to four minutes (Haber, 1969). The ability to use eidetic imagery is known informally as **photographic memory.**

According to the dual-code theory, sensory information can be stored as pictures or sounds. If you look at the following three-syllable nonsense word, you might store it as a visual image, but you are more likely to break it down into syllables and store it acoustically.

KARNOBLIK

If you stored KARNOBLIK acoustically, you probably remember it as KAR-NO-BLIK. In that case you are using an **acoustic code** as opposed to a visual or eidetic code. Dual-code theory argues that along with eidetic and acoustic codes you can also use verbal codes for storing individual words. In this way you can store information either as sensory experience or as words.

PROPOSITIONAL NETWORK THEORY

Although there is evidence that some memories may be stored as pictures, sounds, or words, it appears that much of our memory is based on a network of abstract representations that we have tied to meanings, rather than to sensory or verbal information. For example, suppose a friend of yours came up to you on the street and told you a long-winded story about what happened the day before. If someone else asked you to explain what your friend told you, what would you say? Would you repeat everything your friend said, word for word? No, you would use your own words. In such instances, your memory stores *meaning*, not words or sensations (Wanner, 1968).

The concept of a memory network is not new. The physiological foundations of such a network were described by Donald Hebb in 1949. He argued that memories must somehow be fixed directly within the nerve pathways of the brain. Hebb believed that synapses in the brain were altered by the continuous flow of electric impulses and that when the impulses died down the changes in the synapses remained, creating a network of neurons that stored specific memories. He argued that activating one or two of the neurons in the network could trigger others, thereby bringing stored memories back to mind.

The most popular theory about how meaning is represented in memory is based on **propositions** (Anderson, 1976; Anderson & Bower, 1973; Clark, 1974; Fredericksen, 1975; Kintsch, 1974; Norman & Rumelhart, 1975). The word *proposition* is borrowed from logic theory. A proposition is "the smallest unit about which it makes sense to make the judgment true or false" (Anderson, 1980, p. 102). For example, consider the following sentence: "Jack gave a new Chevrolet to Mary, who is his fiancée." This sentence can be broken into a number of simpler statements. "Jack gave the Chevrolet to Mary." "The Chevrolet was new." "Mary is Jack's fiancée." These are considered propositions, because if any of these shorter and simpler sentences were false, the entire complex sentence, "Jack gave a new Chevrolet to Mary, who is his fiancée," would be false.

Storing what something *means* rather than how it sounds or looks requires a propositional representation rather than a visual or auditory representation. **Propositional network theory** argues that if we wish to recall how something looked or sounded, we must first locate (recall) its meaning and from there reconstruct the actual sensory representation.

If the long-term memory is filled with many propositions—that is, bits of simple meaning—then there must be a way in which the bits can interact. In a propositional network, each proposition is represented by a circle that is connected to the components of the proposition by arrows. The components are called **nodes** and the arrows connecting the nodes are called **links.** Each arrow is labeled to indicate what kind of link it is. In Figure 7.8 you see the proposition "Jack gave a Chevrolet to Mary" as it might appear in the long-term memory, with the different nodes connected by links. Perhaps this arrangement approximates the biochemical organization of memory.

In Figure 7.9 are two other propositions, "The Chevrolet is new," and "Mary is Jack's fiancée." In Figure 7.10 the three propositions are joined. By starting at the node "Mary," you can travel to the nodes "fiancée," "Jack," or "recipient of Chevrolet." Once you reach the node "Chevrolet," you can travel down the links to the "new" node. If information is organized like this in your long-term memory, then thinking of Mary may remind you that she is Jack's fiancée and that she's received a Chevrolet, and thinking of Chevrolet may then trigger the recollection that the Chevrolet was new. In order to recall a particular node you may need to travel to a number of other nodes; one recollection is likely to trigger another.

But memories seem to be linked in different ways. Some nodes are very close and strongly linked to other nodes, so that if you remember one, you are likely to remember the others. Then again, some nodes may be far away from others or poorly linked, in which case remembering one node helps you very little in recalling the other ones. Digging into your memory is much like parachuting into a city. If you land near your target you can reach it quickly. Otherwise it may take you a long time, by way of a number of complex routes, to get where you want to be.

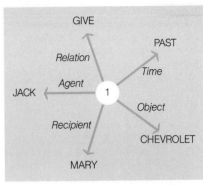

Figure 7.8 *Proposition 1. Jack gave a Chevrolet to Mary. This proposition contains five nodes. A node is an item of information. Each node is connected to the proposition by different kinds of links. (Links are italicized; nodes are in roman print.) Thinking about any of the nodes (Jack, Mary, Chevrolet, something that happened in the past, or giving) may bring to mind the entire proposition. The arrows are not meant to imply which direction thoughts must flow (links are usually two-way streets) but only to show to which propositions nodes belong when propositions are combined in a complex elaboration, as you will see later.*

Figure 7.9 *Proposition 2. The Chevrolet is new. Proposition 3. Mary is Jack's fiancée.*

Figure 7.10 *The propositions combined.*

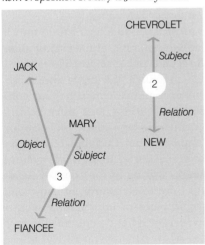

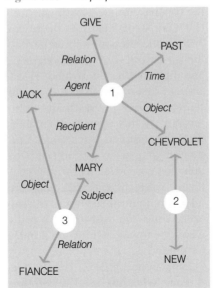

Computers with parallel access, such as RAM (random access memory), are much faster than old or inexpensive computers that have to retrieve data stored on lengths of tape.

TRACE COLUMN THEORY

At this point you may well wonder why many psychologists have come to believe that the long-term memory is filled with propositional networks, all interconnected by different kinds of links. Why does memory have to be laid out like a complex city, with streets stretching and intersecting in every direction? Why can't memory be like a videotape—one long, sequential record? If you want to recall something on a videotape recorder, you need only wind the tape forward or backward until you reach the point where the desired information is. Kurt Koffka, in his book *The Principles of Gestalt Psychology* (1935), proposed that human memory worked exactly that way— that it was not a series of associations, as propositional network theory suggests, but rather a continuous record of experiences. He called this record a **trace column,** which is analogous to a videotape. However, given the relative slowness with which neurons operate in the brain, we can conclude fairly certainly that the trace column theory is invalid.

Synaptic transmission is perhaps the most basic functional time unit in the brain, and it can function, as discussed in Chapter 2, at the rate of about one thousandth of a second, or one millisecond, per synapse. Therefore, it seems reasonable that the shortest time in which the brain could ever search out one propositional unit or item of memory would be one millisecond. At this speed, about 1,000 memory locations in a trace column could be sampled per second. But if you consider how many bits of information your brain contains, it becomes apparent that 1,000 bits of information per second is terribly slow (Wickelgren, 1981). If the trace column theory were correct, with your brain synapses firing at top speed it would take you about three hours to search the entire trace column of your brain every time you wanted to recall any single piece of information such as what day it was, where you'd parked your car, or what you planned to have for dinner.

This same problem is experienced by researchers who use computers. Anyone who has used a computer knows that information stored on a length of tape takes a very long time to retrieve. Computers using long reels of tape seem to take forever to search for information. Modern, high-speed computers have a capability that is known as **parallel access:** They can search memory banks from many different access points at once. Our memory systems must have some similar processing capacity (Fahlman, 1979). In other words, rather than being scattered along one long road, our memories are more likely to be located at "city intersections" that have many different entrances or access points. For this reason, the propositional network theory of long-term memory is rapidly becoming accepted. Another reason is that the theory helps to predict and explain many interesting things about memory, such as **interference effects.**

Interference Effects

PROACTIVE INTERFERENCE

What happens if the nodes you choose as an entry point into your memory network lead you in the wrong direction? Suppose you have a new telephone number. Whenever you want to think of your new phone number, you begin a search in the memory network for the node that holds the number. This old search pattern (looking for your phone number) has been activated so many times that the search for your new number may lead you to your old number. You know that you have a new phone number, but you can remember only the old one. What you are experiencing is **proactive interference;** that is, previously learned material is somehow interfering with your ability to learn something new. Again, think of long-term memory as a network of streets running through a city to different locations—streets that crisscross each other. If you are used to driving down three or four streets to get to a particular place but now have to get to another place by using the same streets, it's easy to take the wrong turn near the end of your route and go to the old location.

RETROACTIVE INTERFERENCE

If you practice your new number often enough and are required to recall it under many different circumstances, you will rearrange your memory network so that the new number is associated with many nodes. Eventually the links to the new number will be *stronger* than those to the old one, and you'll tend to retrieve the new number when you try to recall your phone exchange. Most interesting is that once you've thoroughly learned your new number, it's often hard to retrieve your old one again. This is known as **retroactive interference;** that is, learning something new interferes with old memories (see Figure 7.11).

TRACE COLUMN
A continuous record of memories analogous to a videotape, put forth by Kurt Koffka in 1935 as an explanation for the way memory functions. Our modern understanding of neural transmission rates in the brain has led us to reject the trace column because it would require neurons to fire much faster than they do.

PARALLEL ACCESS
A term borrowed from computer terminology and used to describe the fact that we can enter our memories at many different points and locations rather than at only one point as suggested by the trace column theory.

INTERFERENCE EFFECTS
Effects that occur any time stored memories and their associated networks interfere with the storage of new information or the retrieval of old information.

PROACTIVE INTERFERENCE
When previously learned material interferes with the ability to learn something new.

RETROACTIVE INTERFERENCE
When learning something new interferes with the ability to recall previously learned information.

A	Experimental group:	Learn A	Learn B	Test A
	Control group:	Learn A	Rest	Test A
B	Experimental group:	Learn A	Learn B	Test B
	Control group:	Rest	Learn B	Test B

Figure 7.11 *Experimental arrangements designed to test interference effects. Organization A tests for retroactive interference, while B tests for proactive interference.*

CHAPTER 7
MEMORY AND INFORMATION PROCESSING

Besides proactive and retroactive interference, other things can get in the way of long-term memory retrieval. Sometimes we can't seem to retrieve a bit of information that we're sure we have because we can't find a path through the network to the information. This frustration has been known for many years as the **tip of the tongue phenomenon.** William James described the experience in this way:

> Suppose we try to recall a forgotten name. The state of our consciousness is peculiar: There is a gap therein; but no mere gap. It is a gap that is intensively active. A sort of wraith of the name is in it, beckoning us in a given direction, making us at moments tingle with the sense of our closeness and then letting us sink back without the longed-for term. If wrong names are proposed to us, this singularly defined gap acts immediately so as to negate them. They do not fit into its mould. And the gap of one word does not feel like the gap of another, all empty of content as both might seem necessarily to be when described as gaps. (James, 1890)

The tip of the tongue experience is particularly frustrating because we feel so close to the information for which we are searching. We even seem to know things about what we can't remember. We seem to be actively searching through our long-term memory network for an association or link that will take us to the right node.

Nonetheless, you can use some specific methods to make the needed association. Suppose you can't remember the name of a particular person, but it's on the tip of your tongue. How might you find the path that leads to the correct node? One way is to travel to related nodes and see if there is a direct link from any of them to the node for which you are searching. For instance, you might reflect on a picture of that person or on the sound of that person's voice. Or you might proceed through the alphabet, sounding out letters to see if any of those sounds suddenly triggers the recall of the name. By selectively searching all the different accesses you might have to the necessary node, you are likely to eventually find a retrieval cue or direct link.

The tip-of-the-tongue experience can be frustrating.

Retrieval Cues

A **retrieval cue** can be a great help in getting at something that you can almost remember. This is why multiple choice tests are easier than tests that require strict recall; the former are loaded with retrieval cues. Let's take a look at the difference between a recall versus a recognition test.

Here is a recall question: "Who was the President after Washington?" In order to answer this question, you need to activate the "Washington" node in your memory and travel from that point to the associations that you have made with Washington. You may have many associations with Washington. But can you activate the link that will lead you to the node that holds the answer? Perhaps not. That link may be too weak, or it may have never existed.

How about a question that encompasses two points of memory access: "Was Adams the President after Washington?" Now you have two places from which to begin your search. You can go to the "Washington" node, check associations about Washington, and try to find a link that leads to Adams. Or you can start with the "Adams" node. If one of the things you know about Adams is that he came after Washington, then you can answer the question correctly.

Curiously, there seem to be a lot of one-way links in long-term memory. If you can't get from Washington to Adams, you may be able to get from Adams to Washington. By making the latter association, however, you strengthen the link from Washington to Adams, so that if you are asked again who was the next president after Washington, you'll be more likely to recall.

Many things determine whether links between nodes will be strong or weak. Shocking or surprising events, either pleasant or unpleasant, usually create very strong links. If the event is powerful enough, a strong link will be created between nearly every associated event and the event itself. Whatever the sudden news—that Pearl Harbor had been attacked, John Kennedy had been shot, or Neil Armstrong had just stepped on the moon— you can probably recall where you were standing, who and what were around you, and what people said. This effect is sometimes called **flashbulb memory** (Brown & Kulik, 1977). Flashbulb memories may be particularly vivid because the hormone ACTH is secreted at times of stress; ACTH has been found to enhance memory formation by increasing attention (Sandman, George, Nolan, Van Riezen, & Kastin, 1975).

Forgetting

You're not always able to retrieve information that you put into your long-term memory. Why not? If it's there, why can't you get to it?

DECAY AND LOSS

The first reason is a simple one: The information may no longer be in the long-term memory. Although some researchers believe that long-term memories are permanent (Anderson, 1980), others have concluded that some of them may decay and be lost (Loftus & Loftus, 1980). Perhaps they can be lost if they are not extremely important or not well rehearsed. Perhaps some of the chemistry upon which the long-term memory is based changes and breaks down. If this happens the memory is truly forgotten, and there could never be any way to retrieve it.

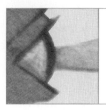

ARE LONG-TERM MEMORIES FOREVER?

In an informal survey, 169 individuals (75 of whom were psychologists) were asked to state which of the following statements best reflected their view of how human memory works:

1. Everything we learn is permanently stored in the mind, although sometimes particular details are not accessible. With hypnosis, or other special techniques, these inaccessible details could eventually be recovered.
2. Some details that we learn may be permanently lost from memory. Such details would never be able to be recovered by hypnosis, or any other special technique, because these details are simply no longer there. (Loftus & Loftus, 1980, p. 410)

The subjects were asked to elaborate briefly or give reasons for their view. Position 1 was chosen by 84 percent of the psychologists and 69 percent of

the nonpsychologists. These individuals were assuming that forgetting is not due to the loss of specific information but rather to the loss of access to information, which, once stored, stays in the memory forever. Many prominent researchers have agreed that while memories can be lost from the short-term memory, once they register and consolidate in the long-term memory, they are essentially there forever (Shiffran & Atkinson, 1969; Tulving, 1974).

These researchers support their argument by describing how a number of techniques can be used to retrieve previously forgotten memories. The techniques include psychoanalytic procedures, hypnosis, and electrical stimulation of the brain. In 1959 Wilder Penfield and his associates noticed

while conducting brain surgery that they could elicit long-forgotten memories by stimulating points on the temporal lobes with an electric probe (Penfield & Roberts, 1959). This work clearly implied that "forgotten" memories had actually been stored in various places in the brain and could be retrieved through the use of appropriate techniques.

Many people are familiar with the experience of suddenly remembering something that they thought they had forgotten long ago (Crowder, 1976). But does this necessarily mean that *all* long-term memories are permanent? Researchers Elizabeth and Geoffrey Loftus of the University of Washington have challenged this assumption, arguing that while some long-term memories may be permanent, not all

RETRIEVAL FAILURE

The second possibility is that you are no longer able to find the links in your network to the memory node that you are trying to retrieve. When you first learn something, you link together a number of associations that may lead you back to that information when you wish to retrieve it. But these associations are vulnerable to interference by newer information, so that if you have only a limited number of associations to lead you to a specific memory, you may easily lose access to the memory.

In a famous experiment conducted by Jenkins and Dallenbach in 1924, subjects' long-term memories of recently learned material were compared after intervals during which the subjects had been either awake or asleep. The subjects had learned a list of ten nonsense syllables. Jenkins and Dallenbach reasoned that sleeping subjects would have less chance to encounter new information that might interfere with their ability to remember the syllables. Their findings were striking. If the subjects slept for eight hours, they could remember 50 percent of the material when they awoke. If they stayed awake for eight hours after they had learned their list, however, they could remember only 10 percent of the material. (These subjects did not miss a night's sleep—they had memorized the material earlier in the day.) Jenkins and Dallenbach argued that the material was not

of them are. They state further that many spontaneously recalled memories from long ago are in fact recent reconstructions—based on fragments of past experience—which have little resemblance to the actual experience. As an example, consider the following:

Psychologist Jean Piaget vividly remembered an attempt to kidnap him from his baby carriage along the Champs Elysées. He recalled the gathered crowd, the scratches on the face of the heroic nurse who saved him, the policeman's white baton, the assailant running away. However vivid, Piaget's recollections were false. Years later the nurse confessed that she had made up the entire story. (Leo, 1981, p. 89).

The Loftuses point out that even in Wilder Penfield's experiment on brain stimulation, memory recovery occurred in only about 40 of 1,132 cases surveyed (Penfield, 1969, p. 154). One patient whose brain was being stimulated remembered hearing a voice from a long time ago. She heard the voice coming from an area she could see— it was a lumberyard, and yet she said she had never been in a lumberyard. This has led some researchers to argue that some patients are reconstructing an experience rather than reliving it, even during brain stimulation (Neisser, 1967).

But what about long-lost memories that can be retrieved vividly during hypnosis? Again the evidence indicates that while some memories may be retrieved this way, a lot of reconstruction and "creative remembering" can occur. Research has shown that subjects under hypnosis can confidently recall memories from the past that they believed they had forgotten, but at the same time these subjects can confidently recall memories from the future that they have not yet had (Kline, 1958; Rubenstein & Newman, 1954).

Furthermore, researchers can purposely distort a subject's memory in the laboratory by asking leading questions. In one experiment, subjects who had viewed an automobile accident were asked one of two questions: "Did you see a broken headlight?" or "Did you see the broken headlight?" Subjects who were asked the second question were more likely to recall seeing a broken headlight because the question had led them to assume that there was one. In such cases, even if the subjects are offered money for correct answers or told that they may have been manipulated to remember incorrectly, they still swear that there was a broken headlight (when there really wasn't). These kinds of studies imply that "the misleading information has irrevocably replaced the original information in the subject's brain" (Loftus & Loftus, 1980, p. 418). Think of the implications for eyewitness testimony gathered under hypnosis!

It may never be possible to prove whether or not long-term memories are permanent. But as the Loftuses and others have shown, even though many psychologists as well as laymen believe that long-term memories are forever, there is evidence that casts doubt upon this supposition.

actually forgotten but was merely not retrievable because the network that was laid down to hold the nonsense syllables was overlaid by all kinds of other associations that went on during the waking time. The sleepers, too, forgot things, perhaps because of the interference of dreams and other thought processes during sleep, but the activity to which they were exposed was less than in the waking state, and they were therefore better able to retrieve the material.

Another experiment demonstrating the same phenomenon was conducted by Grissom, Suedfeld, and Vernon in 1962. Subjects were given a passage of verse to study and were then confined in a room designed for sensory deprivation. The room was soundproof and pitch black. The subjects had to lie in bed and remain silent for 24 hours. Control subjects were allowed to continue their normal activities. The subjects in the control group forgot 12.6 percent of the verse, while the sensory-deprived subjects actually improved their performance by 1.8 percent.

This research indicates that if you're planning to study for a test and want to risk as little interference as possible, you should study on the night before the test until it's time to go to bed and then sleep until it's time to take the test. In this way you'll be most likely to retrieve the new memories that you've stored.

PSEUDO-FORGETTING

A third way of "forgetting" long-term memories isn't really forgetting; it just seems like it. In fact, we might call it **pseudo-forgetting.** Pseudo-forgetting occurs when you never had a particular memory in the first place, but you thought you did and are therefore surprised when you can't recall it. You assume forgetting has occurred. We think that our memory is fairly accurate, but just as the eye is not like a camera, memory is not like a photograph. Even familiar things may not be impressed upon memory.

Look at Figure 7.12. Nearly everybody in the United States has seen an American penny thousands of times. The penny is so ubiquitous, in fact, that foreigners are often familiar with it as well. Certainly you've placed the visual image of a penny into your long-term memory. Or have you? Psychologist Elizabeth Loftus argues that our long-term memories are filled with many errors and mistakes. Do you know which of the pennies in Figure 7.12 is the real one? A great number of people don't. If you're not sure, get a penny and check. If you were wrong, why were you wrong? Is it because you had "forgotten" what a penny looked like? Or is it that, amazingly, you never really knew? All these years you've been looking at pennies and you've never really learned what they're like. It's hard to believe that interference effects have ruined your remembrance of pennies, because you've seen them so often (rehearsal). The best explanation seems to be that you've never paid enough attention to the penny; the image you've had in your long-term memory was only of a round, copper coin with a portrait of Lincoln on the face. But which way was Lincoln facing? What did the inscriptions say? Come to think of it, which way is George Washington facing on the dollar bill?

FAILURE OF CONSOLIDATION

Long-term memories may also be lost through the failure of **consolidation.** Consolidation is a phenomenon that is not well understood, but it seems that after information is first put into the long-term memory, a certain

Figure 7.12 *Which drawing shows the real penny?* (SOURCE: *Nickerson and Adams, 1979, p. 297)*

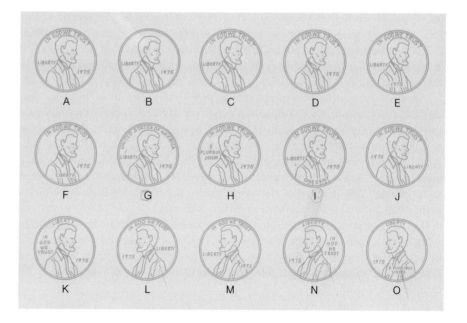

amount of time is necessary for it to consolidate or to take its place in the memory (John, 1967). That is, information new to the long-term memory is fragile, and it may take as long as a few hours before it is firmly implanted (or consolidated), and not so easily lost. Consolidation may be thought of as a time of transition from short-term to long-term memory.

A number of things can interfere with the consolidation process. For instance, cigarette smoking is known to affect it. The active agent involved appears to be nicotine (Houston, Schneider, & Jarvik, 1978). But exactly how nicotine interferes is unknown. A sudden shock or trauma can interfere with consolidation to an extensive degree, causing complete loss of very recent memories. It's not uncommon for a person who's been involved in a terrifying incident such as a severe car crash to forget everything that occurred within a half hour to an hour before the accident. Such loss of memory is known as *retrograde amnesia,* and it may be a permanent loss. If the memories were lost during the process of consolidating in the long-term memory, they may be as forgotten as if they had been lost from short-term memory. Some victims of car crashes find it particularly upsetting that they can't even remember why they were on a particular road or where they had been planning to go when the accident occurred.

MOTIVATED FORGETTING

Motivated forgetting is another way in which long-term memory can seem to be lost. This sort of forgetting is an active and purposeful one that is used to keep one from recalling threatening, painful, or embarrassing memories. Clinical psychologists often use the term **repression** when referring to the process through which memories are forced from conscious awareness. Repressed memories are not available for active recall.

Strengthening Memory Through Elaboration

Elaboration refers to the process of linking related memories in order to create greater access to stored information. In his book *Cognitive Psychology and Its Implications,* John R. Anderson has used propositional networks to demonstrate how elaboration works to improve memory. He begins his demonstration with the simple sentence "The doctor hates the lawyer." Figure 7.13 shows the sentence as a propositional network. Subject X hates subject Y. Subject X is connected by a separate link "is a" to the node "doctor." Similarly, subject Y "is a" lawyer. So we have X, who is a doctor, hating Y, who is a lawyer. This is proposition 1.

If you learn this sentence, but only this sentence, you may eventually have a hard time recalling it. But you may have an easy time if you associate this memory with others. Consider, then, proposition 2: "I studied the first proposition in the psychology laboratory one dreary morning." By adding to the first proposition the fact that you were studying it one dreary morning in the psychology laboratory, you have linked two propositions, which is the beginning of elaboration.

Now add proposition 3: "The lawyer had sued the doctor for malpractice." Add to this proposition 4: "The malpractice suit was the source of the doctor's hatred of the lawyer." Tack on the fact that all this hating and suing is unpleasant (proposition 5), and add the general knowledge that lawyers sue doctors for malpractice (proposition 6). Now you have an elaborated structure, as pictured in Figure 7.14.

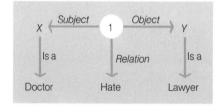

Figure 7.13 *Proposition 1. X, who is a doctor, hates Y, who is a lawyer. (*SOURCE: *Anderson, 1980, p. 195)*

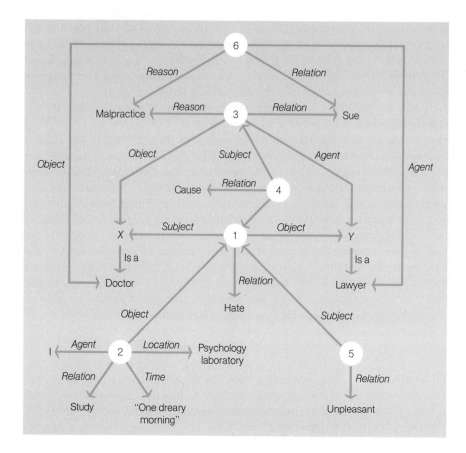

At this point your memory for the fact that the doctor hates the lawyer is greatly improved because you have many different routes for recalling that fact. For instance, suppose the link from node "X" to the rest of proposition 1 were so weak that when you thought of "X," (who is the doctor) you could not recall his relationship to "Y," (who is the lawyer). If that were the case, there would be no way at all for you to recall the relationship, since you had only one link to the rest of the proposition. However, with the kind of elaboration that appears in Figure 7.14, you could go on from "X" to recall all of proposition 1, even if the link from "X" to proposition 1 were too weak, because other routes could lead you to proposition 1.

If this doesn't seem clear to you, just think for a moment about how your memory seems to work. When you think of one thing, doesn't that often remind you of another, which in turn triggers thoughts of a third thing? Look again at Figure 7.14, the elaborated memory, and you'll see. Suppose you realize that it's a dreary morning. Suddenly that "dreary morning" node might lead you to proposition 2, and you might remember, "Oh, yes, I was studying one dreary morning in the psychology laboratory," which might lead you to proposition 1: "I was studying about the doctor hating the lawyer." That memory might lead you to proposition 5 (that it was unpleasant) or to proposition 4 (that the doctor hated the lawyer because the lawyer had sued him for malpractice), and so on. How you decide where to enter your memory in order to begin retrieving a particular piece of information is still not well understood.

Encoding Effects

The elaborated network in Figure 7.14 suggests that some very interesting things may be going on in human memory. For instance, if you were trying to recall that the doctor hated the lawyer, do you think it would be easier if you happened to be sitting in the psychology laboratory on a dreary morning, just as you were when you first studied the proposition? The familiar atmosphere might very well place you at the proper node for retrieving the information you wanted. If you were sitting on the beach on a sunny day, it might be much harder to remember that the doctor hated the lawyer!

Two researchers, Godden and Baddeley, demonstrated this phenomenon in 1975. They had people learn 40 unrelated words either on the beach or, using scuba equipment, 20 feet under the sea. Half the people in each group were then asked to switch locations before everyone tried to recall the words. Table 7.3 shows the results of the study. As you can see, individuals who learned the list on the beach were able to recall it better on the beach than beneath the water, while those who learned beneath the water could recall better under water. This indicates that during learning, elements in the environment become associated in the memory with the items to be remembered, so that reexposure to the same elements may facilitate recall of those items.

In another study conducted at the University of Michigan, students memorized paired lists of items one day in a large, windowless room with an instructor who was dressed in a suit and tie. On the second day the subjects learned paired items in a small room filled with daylight, and this time the instructor was dressed casually in jeans and a flannel shirt. In both cases the items to be learned were presented on a tape recorder. On the third day subjects were asked to recall what they had learned; some subjects were placed in one setting and some in the other. Those who had learned the list in the setting where they were tested were successful in recalling 59 percent of the list, but subjects who had learned the list in a different setting could remember only 46 percent of the list (Smith, Glenberg, & Bjork, 1978).

Figure 7.14 indicates that in addition to your surroundings, your emotional state may have an effect on your ability to remember particular items. As you see, proposition 5 is related to the node "unpleasant," reminding you

Table 7.3   Relationship between recall and environment

GROUP	LOCATION TO LEARN MATERIAL	LOCATION TO RECALL MATERIAL	MEAN RECALL SCORE
A	dry	dry	13.5
B	dry	wet	8.6
C	wet	wet	11.4
D	wet	dry	8.4

SOURCE: Adapted from Godden & Baddeley, 1975, p. 328.

NOTE: Material studied in one location is recalled better when subjects are in that same location.

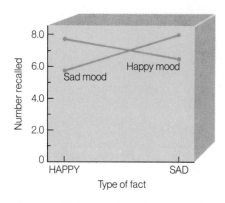

Figure 7.15 *The number of happy or sad events subjects could recall was dependent on their mood at recall.* (SOURCE: *Adapted from Bower, 1981, p. 144*)

that the doctor's hating the lawyer is an unpleasant thing. In order to reach proposition 1, "The doctor hates the lawyer," you might go through proposition 5, and to reach proposition 5, you must begin at the node "unpleasant." Does this mean that if you were in an unpleasant mood or felt that something was unpleasant, you would remember proposition 1 more easily? Evidence suggests so.

Gordon H. Bower of Stanford University has investigated the effects of mood on memory. He discovered that people who studied material while in a certain mood were better able to remember the material later if they were in the same mood. Subjects in his experiments were told happy or sad stories, or they watched happy or sad events on film. Later, when these individuals were asked to recall what they had experienced, they were first put in a happy or sad mood by hypnosis or by other aids used to generate happiness or sadness. Figure 7.15 shows the effects: Individuals in a sad mood were better able to remember events in the sad story, while individuals in a happy mood were better able to recall the happy story (Bower, 1981).

This phenomenon is called **state-dependent learning.** If people can return to the same emotional or physical state that they were in when they learned information, they find it easier to remember. In Charlie Chaplin's classic comedy *City Lights*, Chaplin plays a character he made famous, the Little Tramp. In the film, Charlie saves a drunken man from leaping to his death. As it turns out, the drunk is a millionaire and becomes Charlie's friend. The two spend the evening together, having a good time and becoming drinking buddies. However, the next day the millionaire is sober and, not recognizing Charlie, refuses even to speak to him. Later the millionaire becomes drunk once more, and the moment he sees Charlie he reacts as though he had found a long-lost friend. Interestingly, evidence for this effect exists. Individuals who learn something when they are under the influence of alcohol may find that they cannot recall what they learned when they are sober, but that they remember if they once again become drunk (Overton, 1972).

The Spacing Effect

Researcher S. A. Madigan once asked subjects to repeat as many items as they could remember from a list of 48 words that had been presented to them at the rate of one word every 1½ seconds. It took a little over one minute for the 48 words to be read, and most subjects were able to recall about 28 percent of the words. Madigan discovered, however, that if some of the words were repeated, subjects were more likely to remember those words. Specifically, he found that although the subjects could recall only 28 percent of the words that they had heard once, they could recall 47 percent of the words that they had heard twice (Madigan, 1969).

This discovery should hardly come as a surprise to anyone. After all, the more familiar you become with something, the more likely you are to remember it. But Madigan discovered something surprising in his research: Among words heard twice, a word was more likely to be remembered if the interval between the first and second presentation had been a long one. If the word had been said twice in a row, it was least likely to be remembered. Madigan's finding is known as the **spacing effect.** And, as far as anyone can tell, there seems to be no amount of spacing (additional time between first and second presentations) beyond which further improvement of memory will not occur (Anderson, 1980).

Why does the spacing effect occur? One researcher has argued that if you study something for the second time immediately after you have studied it the first time, you may think of the second study session as unnecessary and redundant and pay little attention to it. But if you study something a second time after considerable delay, you might think of it as a more valuable experience and pay stricter attention to it (Rundus, 1971).

Another possibility is that if you let enough time pass before you study something a second time, your emotional state and the context of your environment will be different on the second occasion. If the contextual variables—that is, the physical environment and your emotional state at the time you study—are important to your recall of information, then it might be valuable to study in as many different physical contexts as possible. This change of time and place provides what is known as **encoding variability,** and it helps to enlarge the elaboration network of a particular memory. In other words:

> The greater the difference between the two study contexts [the first and second time you study the same material], the greater is the probability that one of the contexts will overlap with the test context. On the other hand, at short lags the two study contexts will be more similar, and the probability of study context matching test context will be not much greater than in the single-presentation condition. (Anderson, 1980, p. 214)

The message to the student couldn't be more obvious. If you want to study, study the material, wait some time, and then restudy the material in a different context; and if possible, study it a third time, once again after a delay. This procedure is known as **spaced practice,** and it can greatly improve test scores.

Because of contextual overlap, the student who studies in the library will be more likely to recall the information during the test, unless, of course, the test is given out of doors!

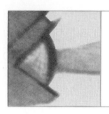

TO CRAM OR NOT TO CRAM

It's a rare and lucky student who loves to study. Most students, although they may enjoy reading assigned material, find that they must make a concentrated effort in order to recall it during a test. And, since studying can be a strenuous process, students commonly put it off until the last possible moment. Those who do so often find that they must learn a great deal of material in the few hours remaining before the examination. This concentrated learning is called **massed practice** or cramming. But is cramming the best way to study?

Of course it isn't, you say. Everybody knows it's a stupid thing to do—a sign of procrastination and poor study habits. The good student will study material regularly as it is assigned. Conversely, a bad student will cram. Therefore, it must be better not to cram. Sounds logical, doesn't it? But is it true?

You will recall that the spacing effect has shown that information will be recalled better if it is learned more than once, especially if there is a large gap in time between the first and second exposure to the material. The spacing effect, therefore, certainly argues against cramming. But why does the spacing effect work? It has been argued that if there is a significant amount of time between the first and second exposure to the same material, it's likely that the material will be learned in different contexts and moods. Thus the chances are better that the mood and physical surroundings at the time of the test will be similar to at least one of the study sessions. If you are in the same mood, feel about the same way, and have similar physical surroundings when you take your test as you did when you studied the material, you'll have more access to the memory networks containing the information.

For the same reasons, cramming *can* work well if you know exactly when you are due to take a particular test. If you cram within limits, so that you don't become excessively fatigued, there is a good chance that you will be in the same mood and mental set during studying and testing. If you study thoroughly for many hours before a test and then walk straight into the testing situation feeling much as you did while you studied, you're likely to do well (Glenberg, 1976; Anderson, 1980). If, however, you have to study at a time long in advance of the test, you're likely to be in a different mood, physical condition, and setting when you finally take the test. In that case, spaced practice is best.

Cramming has both weaknesses and strengths. If you plan to sleep the night before the test, you should study until you go to bed and then try to take the test as soon as possible after you awaken. You should remember one thing, however: Cramming is not an effective way to learn material permanently. It might get you through one test, but it's a poor way to study for long-term gain or for comprehensive examinations. For lasting comprehension spaced practice in many different moods and contexts works better. Or, as memory researcher John Anderson has stated:

Although I hate to admit this, if one's purpose is to pass an exam, concentrating a lot of study the night before the exam should be advantageous; in other words, it's best to cram. Of course, cramming will lead to poor long term retention, as frequently noted by students a year after a course. Studying throughout the term does have some benefit, though this method is just not as efficient as cramming. The strategy that will result in the best grade combines the techniques of studying during the term and cramming the night before. (Anderson, 1980, pp. 216–217)

MASSED PRACTICE
Also known as *cramming*. A study method that will not create a spacing effect and is therefore not likely to lead to long-term retention. Material is studied in a single session without any interruption.

Summary

- All of the images and sensations not immediately available to your senses must be drawn from your memory. Plans for the future, recollections of the past—all require a functioning memory.
- Memory is composed of three major parts: the sensory memory, short-term memory, and long-term memory.
- When you first receive a particular visual stimulus, the image is held for only a fraction of a second in what is known as the sensory memory, or sensory register. Unless you pay attention to the image and encode it successfully into the short-term memory, it will decay and be lost.

- Short-term memory is also known as working memory. It holds active information—information that you are paying attention to; but it can hold this information for only a brief time. Maintaining information in short-term memory for more than about 30 seconds requires rehearsal. The information can be lost through displacement or decay.
- A chunk is a unit of memory. Chunks are not determined by the numbers of things they contain, such as letters or syllables, but instead by the meaning and organization they hold. They are the items used for memory storage.
- The short-term memory is generally limited to a capacity of seven chunks, give or take two. If the short-term memory tries to acquire more chunks than it can hold, some of them (generally the middle items—those acquired neither most nor least recently) will be displaced. This displacement pattern is known as the serial position effect.
- In order to store information for days, weeks, years, or a lifetime, one must store short-term memories in long-term memory, which has a virtually unlimited storage capacity.
- Meaningful items are stored in long-term memory more easily than meaningless items.
- A mnemonic is any kind of memory system or memory aid. One of the oldest is known as the method of loci, which is the technique of remembering items by associating them in one's mind with points along a familiar pathway.
- Vasopressin is a brain neuropeptide that has the ability to improve memory.
- In 1917 Karl Lashley began a search for the brain's engram. Engrams are the hypothesized biochemical structures that contain memories.
- Researchers have been able to isolate specific brain neuropeptides found only in trained animals and then give these neuropeptides to naive animals, who proceed to exhibit the qualities of the training.
- The trace column theory of memory, which argued that memories were aligned sequentially along one pathway in the brain, has been disproven by modern understanding of the function of brain neurons.
- Today's two most prominent theories of memory are the dual-code theory, which argues that information can be stored as sensory experience or as words, and the propositional network theory, which argues that how information is stored depends on its meaning.
- In propositional network theory, the bits of information that make up the propositions are called nodes, and the connections between the nodes are called links.
- A number of interference effects can obstruct long-term memory retrieval. Among these are proactive interference, by which previously learned material interferes with the ability to learn something new, and retroactive interference, by which learning something new interferes with an old memory.
- The tip of the tongue phenomenon describes a situation in which a memory is almost, but not quite, available.
- A retrieval cue may provide access to a memory that is difficult to find. Such cues can be a great help in getting at tip of the tongue memories.
- Forgetting may occur for a number of reasons, such as decay, interference effects, pseudo-forgetting, and motivated forgetting.
- Elaboration helps to strengthen memory retrieval because it provides multiple access to specific memories.

- While most psychologists believe that long-term memories last forever, the evidence for this assumption may not be as strong as was once thought.
- Both physical location and emotional state can affect ability to memorize information. The result of these influences is known as state-dependent learning.
- The more time that passes between the first and second exposures to information, the more likely it is that the information will be remembered. This discovery is known as the spacing effect.
- The spacing effect may occur as the result of encoding variability. Encoding variability refers to the increased capacity to recall information that has been learned in different moods and environments. Changing the circumstances in which one learns can facilitate recall because it increases the chance that the recall situation will be similar to the circumstances in which the material was first learned.

EPILOGUE: THE ASSASSIN WHO COULDN'T REMEMBER

The following is an account of how one man's moods are linked to the horrible memories he carries within him.

Bernard Diamond is a forensic psychiatrist who lives in the San Francisco Bay Area. In 1968 Diamond was telephoned by the attorneys of Sirhan Sirhan, the assassin of Senator Robert F. Kennedy. A few months earlier, in a furious and agitated mood, Sirhan had shot Kennedy several times in the kitchen of the Ambassador Hotel in Los Angeles. But later, in a calm and relaxed mood, he was unable to remember anything about the event.

Diamond realized that because the event was such a traumatic one, Sirhan would probably repress his memories of it in order to protect himself from the pain of recollection. Diamond also knew that he might gain access to Sirhan's memory network if he could recreate in Sirhan the mood and feelings that

gripped him when he fired the shots. Recreating the feelings might tap an emotional node in Sirhan's memory, a node that would be linked directly to the memories of the assassination.

As Diamond worked with Sirhan, he used techniques to arouse and excite the assassin's emotions. As Sirhan became more agitated, he began to recall more and more of the incident. Finally, memories came flowing out, building up to the moment of the shooting. Remembering that moment, Sirhan actually shouted out the curses and acted out firing the shots. He even reexperienced the choking that had occurred when one of Kennedy's bodyguards grabbed him by the neck after the shooting. Interestingly, when he finally became calm, he was again unable to remember the murder (Diamond, 1969).

Suggestions for Further Reading

1. Higbee, K. L. *Your memory: How it works and how to improve it.* Englewood Cliffs, New Jersey: Prentice-Hall, 1977.
2. Kihlstrom, J., & Evans, F. *Functional disorders of memory.* Hillsdale, N.J.: Erlbaum, 1979.
3. Klatzky, R. *Human memory: Structures and processes* (2nd ed.). San Francisco: W. H. Freeman, 1980.
4. Luria, A. R. *The mind of a mnemonist.* New York: Basic Books, 1968.

CONTENTS

CHAPTER 8

Thought and Language

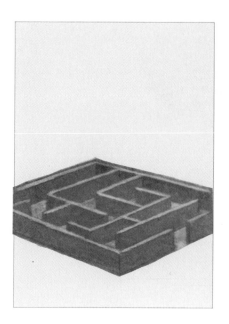

PROLOGUE

It is 1917 and the Americans have declared war on Kaiser Wilhelm of Germany, and the whole North Atlantic has become a battleground. A short time before, when you and Wolfgang Köhler left Germany to travel to America, you had stopped on Tenerife in the Canary Islands, 200 miles off the coast of North Africa. It was to have been a refueling stop, but now German U-boats and British and American men-of-war prowl the sea, and it's not safe to leave. So you are stuck here—who knows for how long.

Köhler was never one to sit around, however. He's been studying a colony of captive chimpanzees on the island, and he says it's an interesting pastime. He watches them almost every day, occasionally inviting you to join him. You finally decide that watching chimps act like chimps is more interesting than watching a wall act like a wall, so you join him.

As you soon discover, Köhler isn't just watching the chimps; he's giving them things to do. One of the chimpanzees, named Sultan, is particularly glad to see Köhler. Sultan has learned that he can often get bananas when he solves Köhler's problems. Köhler places a banana outside Sultan's cage beyond the animal's reach, but provides him with a stick. Sultan grabs the stick and reaches outside the cage, catches the edge of the banana, and begins to pull it toward him. When the banana is within reach, Sultan grabs it.

"That's interesting, isn't it?" says Köhler.

"Oh sure," you reply, looking out at the ocean, and wishing that the island were bigger than 20 square miles.

"Let's try something different," Köhler says. He puts the banana out of reach of a single stick and places two sticks inside Sultan's cage. You wonder what's going on. You notice that one stick is larger than the other and has a hollow opening into which the smaller stick can be inserted. Now you understand: Mentally you imagine the smaller stick being inserted into the larger one so that together they form one very long stick. With the long stick Sultan might be able to reach the banana.

"Has he done this one before?" you ask Köhler.

"No," he says. "I just wonder what he'll do."

"He'll probably throw them at you," you say, as you put your hands in your pockets and watch the chimp stupidly try to reach the banana with just one of the sticks.

233

Sultan used insight in order to solve the two-stick problem.

Sultan seems moody and angry; he pulls the stick back and then tries again, and puts the stick down. "I know how he feels," you say, again looking out over the ocean while trying to think of a way off the island. You're watching the ocean, Köhler is watching Sultan, and Sultan is watching the sticks. Sometimes the chimp seems to have human expressions; at the moment he looks as though he's thinking. "What are you thinking about, Sultan?" you wonder. "Why doesn't your stick work any more? Who is the strange man who keeps giving you bananas and sticks?" Suddenly Sultan's expression seems to change. He stands up and slowly approaches the sticks. He picks up the larger one in his left hand, and turns the hollow end toward him. Then he picks up the smaller stick and inserts it into the larger one to make one long stick. "I don't believe it,"

you whisper. "He seems to understand." Sultan goes to the end of the cage and extends the extra-long stick toward the banana.

"He does understand," says Köhler, as Sultan reaches the banana with the stick and pulls it toward him.

Based on this observation and a number of later ones, Köhler came to believe that chimpanzees could engage in creative problem solving by using **insight.** Insight, Köhler says, comes when you have mentally been manipulating different operations toward a goal solution. Suddenly your mental operations strike on the solution that will work. Then you approach the real situation and put your plan into effect. This, he argues, is very different from a trial-and-error ramble that might occur without thinking. In Sultan's case, the chimpanzee thought about the problem, *came up with the solution, and applied it. In other words, the animal relied on insight.*

In this chapter we'll examine thinking and problem solving and the relationship between thinking and language. We'll learn how language emerges and what language is. In addition, we'll consider whether language is unique to hu-man beings. Other topics will in-clude learning to speak foreign languages without an accent, puzzles requiring considerable mental dexterity and insight, and a look at how different areas of the brain can directly affect under-standing of language and the abil-ity to speak.

INSIGHT
In problem solving, the sudden per-ception of relationships leading to a solution. A solution arrived at in this way can be repeated promptly when the same or a similar problem is confronted again.

THINKING
The process that occurs between the sensing of a stimulus and the emergence of an overt response, and that involves the interplay of concepts, symbols, or mediating responses rather than a direct manipulation of environmental objects.

SUBVOCAL SPEECH
From learning theory, Watson's argu-ment that thinking is really a series of muscular responses.

Why Psychologists Study Thought and Language

Thought and language make us unique, perhaps more than any other aspects of our nature. Although the great apes may think, their thinking is limited, and although they may acquire the rudiments of language, they do not use it naturally. Our ability to communicate and to solve problems is the cornerstone upon which modern civilization is built. The generations before us found solutions to many problems and communicated these solu-tions to us through language. We have built on their knowledge; as we solve our own problems, we will communicate the answers to the next genera-tion. More than any other species, we may have the power to control our world and to make it a better place in which to live. Ironically, this same ability to think and communicate could be our undoing, since we have used it to develop weapons of devastating potential.

Whatever the future holds, our ability to think and communicate has placed us in a unique situation, one that is fundamentally different from the situations of all other species. Psychologists study thinking, problem solving, and language because these aspects of our psychology are the essence of the human experience.

Thinking

What is thought? **Thinking** refers to the use of mental combinations and internal representations of symbols, objects, or concepts. When you solve problems mentally or imagine something internally, you are said to be thinking. Mental manipulations of objects can occur without actually having to move or handle objects. For example, instead of moving any pieces about you might mentally picture the appearance of a room with the furniture rearranged. Such mental manipulations are independent of physical mus-cular actions.

John Watson, the father of behaviorism, argued that there was no such thing as internal mental activity (Watson, 1930). Watson said that humans didn't think; they simply emitted responses that had been conditioned to various stimuli. You might wonder how anyone could believe that humans didn't think, but Watson had an intriguing answer. He said that thinking was not a "mental" activity, but **subvocal speech,** that is, a muscular activity. In other words, people didn't think, they talked to themselves, but so quietly that it wasn't apparent. Interestingly, measurements taken of the muscles, tongue, and throat disclosed that some people did register very subtle muscular motions when they were "thinking" to themselves. Was it possible, then, that Watson was right, and that we only believe we think when we are actually engaging in subvocal speech, a muscular response? This idea appealed to behaviorists, since they wished to avoid the concept of "mind" or "mental." Watson argued that even a person who was mute might make subtle muscular responses in the form of hand signing or other gestures that would be muscular representations of what was assumed to be internal thinking.

One way to test this hypothesis might be to paralyze a subject and find out whether thinking continued while no muscle could be moved. Such a test has actually been carried out (Smith, Brown, Toman, & Goodman, 1947). The paralyzing agent was a derivative of curare, a substance used by Amazonian tribes to poison their darts. The subject—Smith—was one of the researchers. An artificial respirator was used to keep him alive, since he could no longer breathe on his own (the things people do for science!). Once injected with the curare it was impossible for him to move his body in any way. He couldn't engage in subvocal speech; he couldn't even blink. After the experiment, when Smith could move again, he reported that he had been able to understand everything that was going on around him during the time he was paralyzed. He could understand what people said to him, and easily think about what was going on. These results indicate that thinking is an internal mental activity, independent of muscular responses, and that Watson's hypothesis was wrong. Perhaps it was good to discover that Watson hadn't, as Herbert Reigl once said, "made up his voice box that he had no mind" (Anderson, 1980, p. 383). As it is, thinking is difficult enough to comprehend.

CONCEPTS AND CONCEPT FORMATION

One of the most valuable ways in which thinking can be organized is by forming concepts. A **concept** may be defined as the relationship between, or the properties shared by, the objects or ideas in a given group. If you have the concept of "boat" you can recognize something as a boat even though it may look different from all the other boats you've ever seen. A new boat can be included within the concept because it has qualities that are common to the entire class of objects we call boats. It has a hull; it floats in water; and it's used for transport. Boats belong to an even larger conceptual category, "vehicles of transportation." Possessing a concept such as "boat," "dog," or "building" is very useful. Most of the ideas and objects we come across each day belong to familiar categories, although they may appear to be different. By applying concepts, we can develop an immediate understanding of new objects or ideas because we can relate them to a general class of similar objects and ideas with which we are familiar. We know what to expect from them even though we're meeting them for the first time. In this way we save a tremendous amount of time, which would otherwise have to be spent learning what each new thing was.

We acquire concepts by learning the attributes that define each particular category. Watching concept formation in children gives us some idea as to how concepts develop. Generally, rules classifying concrete objects and ideas are more easily acquired than rules that outline more abstract qualities. A child's early concepts might include "adults," "children," "cars," "candy," and other concrete concepts. Abstract concepts are generally acquired later. For instance, if you were asked in what way an apple and a peach are alike, you could respond that they both belong to the same conceptual class—fruit. Fruit is a concrete concept. It is tangible. But if you were asked in what way a rose and a hippopotamus are alike, you would have to respond with a more abstract concept. They are alike because they are both alive.

Some concepts are very well defined, that is, the rules that classify them are stated explicitly. Among such explicit concepts are "registered voters," "diamonds," and "hours." These concepts are exclusive: You are either a registered voter or you are not. Some concepts, though, are fuzzy. Is a whale a mammal or a fish? People argued this question for years. The reason they had difficulty with the concept was that whales, depending on how you looked at them, seemed to fit both concepts. Whales swim in the water, they look like fish, they have fins, and they act like fish. In this sense they fit the concept of "fish." On the other hand, they have no gills and they breathe air, they are warm-blooded, and they suckle their young. In this sense they fit the concept of "mammal." For classification purposes, biologists have outlined specific rules for determining the conceptual class to which any animal should belong. Accordingly, whales have been classified as mammals, even though their most striking qualities are a fishlike appearance and behavior. Using the classification rules they are taught in school, most children would see much greater similarity between a whale and a shark than a whale and a cow, while biologists, applying their own conceptual classifications, find much more similarity between a whale and a cow than a whale and a shark.

Another fuzzy concept is "bird." Robins and sparrows are considered to be highly typical examples of this concept. But turkeys and chickens are not as readily accepted into the concept, especially by children, and penguins are even less likely to be considered birds (Rosch, 1977).

We develop concepts, then, by classifying objects according to their similarity to other objects. Objects and ideas that appear to be similar will tend to be classified under one conceptual heading until a difference becomes apparent. All of the concepts you have are based on your knowledge of the similarities and differences between objects. Because you possess concepts, your understanding has been expanded far beyond your own limited experience.

PROBLEM SOLVING

Human beings use their thinking ability to do a number of amazing things. Two of the most impressive, problem solving and language, are facilitated by cognitive operations such as concept formation. Problem solving is defined as a sequence of cognitive operations directed toward achieving a particular goal. If problem solving makes use of thoughts and concepts you have already acquired, it is called **routine problem solving.** If, however, you have to develop new thoughts or concepts in order to solve a problem, the process is referred to as **creative problem solving.**

You are said to be in the initial state of problem solving when you are first presented with a problem. You must then find a way to go from the initial state to the goal. Think about the steps you must go through to find a solution in the following example. Figure 8.1 shows the cheap-necklace problem. Here are the instructions:

CONCEPT
An abstract idea based on grouping objects by common properties.

ROUTINE PROBLEM SOLVING
Problem solving that requires concepts, thoughts, actions, and an understanding that are already in one's repertoire.

CREATIVE PROBLEM SOLVING
Problem solving that requires concepts, thoughts, actions, or an understanding that are not currently in one's repertoire.

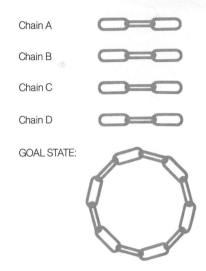

Chain A

Chain B

Chain C

Chain D

GOAL STATE:

Figure 8.1 *The cheap-necklace problem.*

You are given four separate pieces of chain that are each three links in length. It costs 2 cents to open a link, 3 cents to close a link. All links are closed at the beginning of the problem. Your goal is to join all 12 links of a chain into a single circle at a cost of no more than 15 cents. (Silveira, 1971)

You are now in the initial state. Your goal, of course, is to make the necklace cheaply, that is, for no more than 15 cents. If you approach the problem with a straightforward sequence of operations, and link each segment of chain to the next one, finally closing up the chain entirely, it would cost 20 cents, 5 cents over budget. Most people initially attack the problem in this way.

When the cheap-necklace problem was first used in an experiment, the subjects were divided into three different groups. The first group worked with the problem for half an hour; during that time 50 percent of the group was able to solve the problem. Members of the second group also worked on the problem for half an hour, but during this time they were told to take a half hour break, in which they did some unrelated activities. Interestingly, after returning, 64 percent of these subjects were able to solve the problem. A third group also worked for about half an hour on the problem, but was given a four-hour break during the work period. Eighty-five percent of the subjects in this group solved the problem upon returning. The subjects were kept busy during their breaks and didn't have a chance to think about the cheap-necklace problem. Why should a break be beneficial, the longer the better? Although subjects rarely came back after their break with the solution at hand, they often came back with a fresh approach to the problem (Silveira, 1971).

Improving your chances of solving a problem by leaving it for a while and then coming back to it is known as an **incubation effect.** However, if you're on the right track in the first place, taking a break can be disruptive rather than helpful. The most likely time to expect good incubation effects is when you start out with an inappropriate strategy. You might try the break tactic if you haven't been able to solve the cheap-necklace problem yet. Rather than looking ahead to see what the answer is, take a break and try again later. The cheap-necklace problem gives you a good opportunity to experience insight. Many subjects have reported working on the problem for up to an hour and then, suddenly, knowing what to do. All at once the answer will be clear, and you will wonder how you didn't see it before. On the other hand, if you can't stand it anymore, here is the solution:

Open all three links of chain A at a cost of 6 cents, then use the three links to connect chains B, C, and D with each other, at a cost of 9 cents. In this way you can close the entire necklace spending only 15 cents (devastatingly simple, isn't it?).

Algorithms versus Heuristics Playing checkers, backgammon, chess, or any other game of strategy requires that the player engage in problem solving. People have programmed computers to solve problems, and to play games. Computers can play chess, checkers, backgammon, and a number of other games. Have you ever played a game of chess with a computer? You might be surprised to learn that there's not a computer in the world—yet—that can consistently beat a really good human chess player.

What goes on inside the computer's "mind" when it's deciding on a move, and how is the process different from that used by human beings to solve problems? Computers generally work according to **algorithms,** while human beings attempt to solve problems by **heuristics.** An algorithm is defined as a method guaranteed to lead to a solution if one is possible. Solving a problem by algorithms requires that a systematic search be made of every possible avenue or approach to the solution. Computers can apply this method because they can calculate so quickly. A chess computer will examine, first, every possible move and, then, the possible moves that might follow any of the first possible moves. The computer will even consider very stupid moves that no experienced human player would bother to investigate. As you can imagine, this computer strategy can encompass an almost infinite number of possible moves. And even though the computer is very fast, it might take two or three days just to "think" four or five moves ahead. For this reason, an algorithm guaranteed to win any game of chess could lead to games that would take centuries to play. Since it's not practical for a chess computer to take more than a couple of hours per move when playing against a human, any algorithmic method is limited.

Human beings use heuristic methods. Heuristic methods aren't guaranteed to reach a solution, and they aren't as systematic as algorithmic methods. But sometimes they can produce solutions a lot faster. In using heuristic methods, you take the steps that seem most reasonable in order to approach the goal. For example, you might start by moving some of your major pieces toward the opponent's king (since in chess, when the opponent's king is captured, the game is won). You may not know exactly how you're going to maneuver these pieces later, but you do know that if they are in the vicinity of your opponent's king they are more likely to be useful when you need them. For this reason you may plan to control the left side of the board, or the right side, or the center, or to simply line up as many pieces against the opponent's king as possible. Later, when opportunities present themselves, you will be in a good position to take advantage of them. Unlike the computer, which will be trying out every possible solution,

Good chess players generally use more routine problem solving and less creative problem solving than beginners.

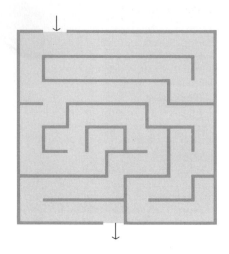

Figure 8.2 *Find your way through the maze.*

you will be working only with those that seem the most reasonable.* You don't know how the sequences may lead to the solution, you simply take the first few steps toward the apparent direction of the goal, hoping that as you get closer, you'll see the further steps that will lead you to your final goal.

People using heuristics often rely on similarity to the final goal to indicate their next step. In other words, they manipulate the situation so that it comes to look more and more like the goal state. Using similarity to the final goal as a heuristic is not always the best choice, however. Figure 8.2 shows a maze. The goal, of course, is to get to the bottom. If you are guided by similarity to the final goal, you will always choose a direction or turn that leads you closer to the goal. The reason this maze is difficult, however, is that the quickest solution requires you to make choices that sometimes lead *away* from the goal. If you rely too heavily on similarity to the final goal in deciding on each step, you may have trouble solving problems that require you to take two steps backward in order to go three ahead.

Means-End Analysis   Heuristically searching for the next right step toward the final goal can be very difficult, since the necessary move is not always obvious. Sometimes, though, it's possible to use a plan or general strategy in order to organize problem solving. Two researchers, Newell and Simon, have developed a computer planning and strategy program that they call the general problem solver, GPS (Newell & Simon, 1972). The GPS does not use an algorithm, but relies on the heuristic of **means-end analysis.** Means-end analysis is typified by the following kind of common-sense argument:

> I want to take my son to nursery school. What's the difference between what I have and what I want? One of distance. What changes distance? My automobile. My automobile won't work. What is needed to make it work? A new battery. What has new batteries? An auto repair shop. I want the repair shop to put in a new battery; but the shop doesn't know I need one. What is the difficulty? One of communication. What allows communication? A telephone . . . and so on.

> It is profitable, therefore, to try to eliminate "difficult" differences, even at the cost of introducing new differences of lesser difficulty. This process can be repeated as long as progress is being made toward eliminating the more difficult differences. (Newell & Simon, 1972, p. 416)

In this example, the major difficulty (taking your son to nursery school) can be solved only by overcoming lesser difficulties (obtaining a battery, making a phone call, etc.). In means-end analysis, you must proceed from where you are (the initial state) to where you want to be (the goal) by a series of intermediate steps. Each step is accomplished by particular means until the major goal is reached, assuming that it is reachable.

Students studying this kind of problem-solving strategy for the first time sometimes question its usefulness. If you begin to apply it, however, you may be amazed by how much it can affect your thinking. In fact, you may be surprised at how inventive you become. The following passage is an example of how means-end analysis can affect your thinking.

---

*Efforts to program computers to use heuristic methods have met with limited success. Perhaps in the future powerful heuristic programs will be developed, and computers will "think" more like humans.

Problem: People are often injured in the shower and bathtub. Your goal is to reduce or eliminate such injuries. *Question:* Why are people hurt in the shower or bathtub? They often fall. (At this point the solution may appear to be to suspend gravity or to stop people from falling, except that in posing the problem, you've made a classic error. You must always be careful in defining the problem. People are not hurt in the shower or bathtub because they fall. No one is hurt by falling. It's landing that causes the trouble. Just remember the man who fell out of a ten-story building and was heard to say as he passed each floor, "So far, so good." So let's start over.) People are hurt in the bathtub because they land on something hard when they fall. What is the difference between what you have (initial state) and what you want (end state)? Hardness. What determines hardness? The manufacturing materials. What you need, then, is soft material for a bathtub and shower stall. But soft material is porous. What's the difference between what you have and what you need? A nonporous soft material. Is there such a material? You could find out by checking in the library. If there is such a material, you are set. If not, then what is the difference between what is available and what you need, and can you develop a soft nonporous material? As it turns out there are many soft, fairly rigid, nonporous materials. And there's the answer to your problem, a soft bathtub or soft shower stall. In fact, such tubs and showers have recently been developed. They keep their form, they hold water well, and they are very comfortable. As a bonus, soft materials have a lot of friction, and they are very difficult to slip on. If a person should fall, however, the original problem of a body landing on a hard surface is eliminated.

The idea of a soft bathtub is so unusual that it might not have occurred to you had you not gone through the means-end analysis and realized that you were trying to eliminate collision with hard objects rather than falling. People who are good at this kind of general problem solving or means-end analysis may find that they are able to invent some fascinating things. Any time you have a problem, state the problem carefully and ask yourself, What is the difference between what I have now and what I want? Then break the problem down into subgoals and see where it leads you. The next good invention may be yours!

MEANS-END ANALYSIS
Problem-solving process in which the difference between the current situation and the desired situation is defined and then a series of steps is taken in order to reduce, and finally eliminate, the difference. Applicable whenever there is a clearly specifiable problem and a clearly specifiable solution.

IMPEDIMENTS TO PROBLEM SOLVING

Mental Set   In 1942 Luchins formulated a series of water jug problems. In these problems subjects were given three jugs, each having an absolute maximum capacity. They were required to use the jugs to obtain an exact amount of liquid. Table 8.1 sets out ten of these problems. In the first problem the jugs can hold 21, 127, or 3 ounces of liquid. The desired amount is 100 ounces. How could you, using only these three jugs, measure exactly 100 ounces? The answer is to fill jug B to capacity, then pour liquid into jug C, filling it once, dumping that liquid out, filling jug C again, and dumping the liquid out again. This leaves 121 ounces in jug B. If you now fill jug A once, you will be left with exactly 100 ounces in jug B.

Working on your own, solve the problems for the remaining nine groups of jugs. By the time you are finished you may have noticed something interesting. The first five problems can be solved in the same way:

Table 8.1   Luchins' water jug problems

	CAPACITY OF JUG A	CAPACITY OF JUG B	CAPACITY OF JUG C	DESIRED QUANTITY
1.	21	127	3	100
2.	14	163	25	99
3.	18	43	10	5
4.	9	42	6	21
5.	20	59	4	31
6.	23	49	3	20
7.	15	39	3	18
8.	28	76	3	25
9.	18	48	4	22
10.	14	36	8	6

Jug B − 2C jugs − jug A = desired amount. Problems 7 and 9 can be solved more simply: A + C = desired amount. Problem 8 cannot be solved by the B − 2C − A method, but by the simpler solution of A − C. Problems 6 and 10 are also solved with the more simple solution of A − C.

When Luchins conducted this experiment, he discovered that 83 percent of his subjects used the B − 2C − A method on problems 6 and 7, even though problem 6 could have been solved by the easier solution of A − C and problem 7 by the easier solution of A + C. This tendency is known as a **mental set.** After solving the first five problems by B − 2C − A, the subjects were so used to applying this formula that they used it on problems 6 and 7 as well, even though there were simpler solutions. Subjects who skipped the first five problems and began with 6 and 7 discovered the easier solutions immediately. Interestingly, in Luchins' experiment, 64 percent of the subjects failed altogether to solve problem 8, although it only required A − C; the subjects tried to apply the B − 2C − A method that they had used so successfully for the first seven problems. Unable to use a strategy they had come to rely on, a majority of these subjects said problem 8 couldn't be solved. Seventy-nine percent of the subjects in Luchins' experiment also used the B − 2C − A method to solve problems 9 and 10, which are easily solved by other means. If we use the same method to solve similar problems, we may overlook better ways. A mental set can even cause us to ignore the obvious.

Studying the effects of mental sets is important because just being aware that they exist can help you. Luchins discovered that subjects whom he had advised to pay careful attention were often able to overcome their mental set.

Examine Figure 8.3. There are nine dots. The problem is to connect the dots with only four straight lines without lifting the pen from the paper. When you try it, do you find that there is one dot left over no matter how hard you try? If so, keep working at it. It can be solved. Your difficulty may be the result of a mental set people have when looking at this figure. The nine dots are often perceived as a box, a container. Containers are perceived to have boundaries, and people searching for a solution to the nine-dot problem tend to stay within the "nine-dot boundary." The answer, however, requires that you break through your mental set of seeing the nine dots as a box, and draw lines that continue beyond the boundaries of the "box." Figure 8.4 gives the solution to the nine-dot problem. As you can see, one of the reasons we have such difficulty with creative problem solving

Figure 8.3   *The nine-dot problem. (Answer appears on page 244.)*

is that we tend to think of the things around us in a limited way according to our experience.

Functional Fixedness   We can also develop the mental set of thinking that objects that have a specific function can function only in the intended way. This inclination is known as **functional fixedness.** Recall, for a moment, the soft bathtub that you derived from means-end analysis.

The idea of a soft bathtub is so reasonable that it's hard to believe no one thought of it sooner. New inventions often seem obvious—after they've been invented. The problem with the tub is that experience has taught us to think that only hard objects are suitable containers for large amounts of water. This obviously isn't the case. When we link a particular item or material with one particular function, we may find it difficult to imagine other possibilities for it. In Figure 8.5 you'll see a table on which there are matches, a candle, and a box of tacks. The task is to use these materials to attach the candle to the door so that the candle can burn normally (Duncker, 1945). Can you think of a good way to do this? Figure 8.6 poses another problem. The two strings must be joined and tied together, but they are so far apart that one person alone can't grasp them at the same time. Suppose you are this person, and you must solve the problem with only the materials shown in the picture. What would you do (Maier, 1931)?

MENTAL SET
A tendency to continue to use a particular approach or type of solution to a problem based on previous experience or instruction.

FUNCTIONAL FIXEDNESS
A mental set in which the individual is unable to see beyond an object's customary function to its other possible uses.

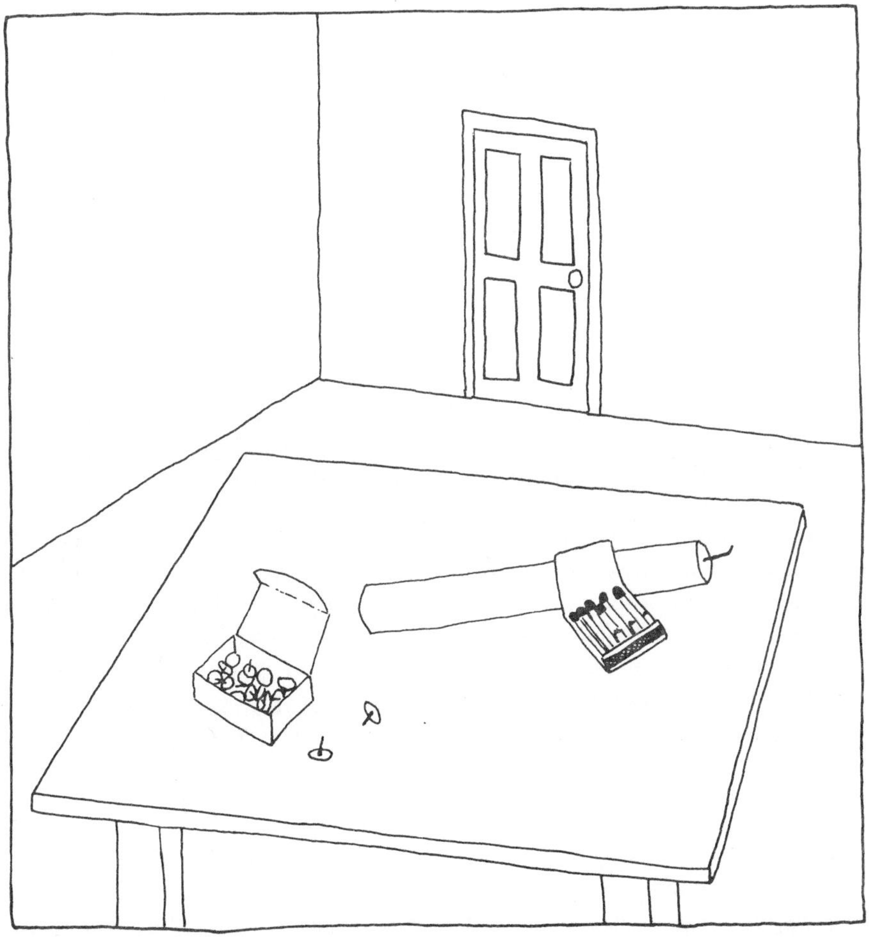

Figure 8.5   *Using only these materials, support the candle against the door so that it can burn naturally.*

Figure 8.6 *How can you tie the strings together?*

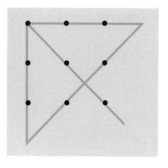

Figure 8.4 *The solution to the nine-dot problem.*

If you've had trouble with either problem, you may be suffering from functional fixedness. To solve these problems, it's necessary to use the materials differently from the way in which they're normally used. In the first problem (Figure 8.5) most people think of the box as a container for the tacks. The answer, however, is to empty the box of the tacks, affix the candle to the middle of the box by pushing a thumbtack up through the bottom, and then fasten the box to the door by pushing thumbtacks through the side of the box into the door. In this way the box becomes a platform for the candle. The matches aren't needed except to light the candle.

The solution to the second problem (Figure 8.6) requires that the pliers be used as a weight. We don't typically think of pliers as a weight, but rather as a tool. However, if you tie the pliers to one of the strings, you can start the string swinging. Then you can go over and grab the other string, come back, and retrieve the swinging string as it nears you. In this way you'll be able to hold both strings at once, bring them together, and tie them.

If you're used to using items in unique ways, or if you're aware of unique properties of particular items, functional fixedness is easier to overcome. In one study, the solution required that a screwdriver blade be used as a conductor of electricity in a circuit (Glucksberg & Danks, 1968). The subjects had a great deal of difficulty finding the solution because they were not accustomed to thinking of the screwdriver in this light. Functional fixedness had struck again. In a follow-up study, however, a researcher gave subjects practice ahead of time in classifying objects such as paper clips and crayons according to their ability to conduct electricity (Teborg, 1968). These subjects were able to transcend their functional fixedness and to realize immediately that the screwdriver blade could be used in an electric circuit. This experiment indicates that the more practice a person has solving problems, the more likely that person will be able to solve future problems.

Mental set and functional fixedness don't always interfere with problem

WHAT TO DO WHEN YOU'RE STUCK— CONSULT AN EXPERT

How many times in your life have you tried to solve a problem? Whether major or minor, there's probably been at least one problem to solve every day of your life. Sometimes you see the solution immediately, and other times you have to work at a problem to solve it. In this chapter you've learned some strategies that may help you reach a solution. But the fact remains that sometimes you end up stuck. You can't find an answer to the problem, and no strategy seems to be helpful. Means-end analysis, incubation, or even unorthodox heuristic approaches don't seem to do any good. Being stuck is a unique situation. Robert Pirsig, in his book *Zen and the Art of Motorcycle Maintenance*, may have described being stuck better than anyone else in recent literature.

Stuckness. That's what I want to talk about. A screw sticks, for example, on a side cover assembly. You check the manual to see if there might be any special cause for this screw to come off so hard, but all it says is "Remove side cover plate" in that wonderful terse technical style that never tells you what you want to know. There's no earlier procedure left undone that might cause the cover screws to stick.

If you're experienced you'd probably apply a penetrating liquid and an impact driver at this point. But suppose you're inexperienced and you attach a self-locking plier wrench to the shank of your screwdriver and really twist it hard, a procedure you've had success with in the past, but

which this time succeeds only in tearing the slot of the screw.

Your mind was already thinking ahead to what you would do when the cover plate was off, and so it takes a little time to realize that this irritating minor annoyance of a torn screw slot isn't just irritating and minor. You're stuck. Stopped. Terminated. It's absolutely stopped you from fixing the motorcycle.

This is the zero moment of consciousness. Stuck. No answer. Honked. Kaput. It's a miserable experience emotionally. You're losing time. You're incompetent. You don't know what you're doing. You should be ashamed of yourself. You should take the machine to a *real* mechanic who knows how to figure these things out.

It's normal at this point for the fear-anger syndrome to take over and make you want to hammer on that side plate with a chisel, to pound it off with a sledge if necessary. You think about it, and the more you think about it the more you're inclined to take the whole machine to a high bridge and drop it off. It's just outrageous that a tiny little slot of a screw can defeat you so totally. What you're up against is the great unknown, the void of all Western thought. You need some ideas, some hypotheses. Traditional scientific method, unfortunately, has never quite gotten around to say exactly where to pick up more of these hypotheses. Traditional scientific method has always been at the very *best*, 20-20 hindsight. It's good for seeing where you've been. It's good for testing the truth of what you think you know, but it can't tell you where you *ought* to go, unless where you ought to go is a continuation of where you were going in the past. Creativity, originality,

inventiveness, intuition, imagination—"unstuckness," in other words—are completely outside its domain. (Pirsig, 1974, pp. 279–280)

What should you do when you're stuck? You could try a number of different strategies that might or might not help you reach a solution, but your best approach would be to consult an expert. Remember, not all problem solving is creative problem solving. Some of it is routine problem solving. In other words, there is no substitute for experience. This doesn't mean that you must spend your entire life deferring to experts; after all, one way of becoming an expert yourself is by learning from others. There are ways to remove a slotless screw from a side cover plate. You may be unaware of the special tools that can be used, or of how to drill out a screw. By watching others who know how to solve this kind of problem and who do it routinely, you can learn solutions. Experts are experts because they have stored in their memory many different routine ways of solving problems.

But suppose you were the world's leading expert in a certain area, you had tried a number of techniques for solving a particular problem, and you were unable to do it. What could you do then? You would be stuck, and there would be no one more expert than you. At that point, good luck, you'd be on your own!

solving. In fact, routine problem solving is facilitated by mental sets and functional fixedness, since old methods usually work and using an object as it was intended to be used is normally good strategy. If mental set or functional fixedness does cause a problem, it's likely to be during creative problem solving when finding a solution may entail breaking away from old ideas and methods. When engaging in creative problem solving, then, be careful not to begin with too many preconceived notions or strategies.

Language

There is a difference between **language** and **communication.** Have you ever seen a dog carry its leash and drop it at its master's feet? The meaning is clear, but language isn't necessary. In this way dogs can communicate, but they don't have language. A language is based on the use of signs or symbols within a **grammar,** that is, within a structure of rules that determine how the various signs or symbols are to be arranged. Language also allows you to use signs or symbols within a grammar to create a **novel construction.**

The idea of a novel construction is easy to understand. If a myna bird says, "Candy is dandy, but liquor is quicker," you know that the bird is simply imitating someone who has been reading Ogden Nash poems aloud. Myna birds don't use English to express meaning. They only mimic the sounds they have heard. Although the sentence the myna spoke was made with English words, and was grammatically correct, the myna is not said to have language. Ogden Nash, on the other hand, as the originator of the statement (a novel construction), has proved his language capability.

THINKING AND LANGUAGE

When we think we often use abstract mental representations and symbols. We are also able to communicate our thoughts to others abstractly. Whenever we speak a language, we are communicating information in a symbolic fashion. Thinking and language seem to go together quite naturally. In thinking to ourselves, we often use the words and grammar by which we communicate with others.

It has been argued that language can influence thinking so strongly that thinking is modified and limited by the words and concepts available in the language. In other words, the fact that you speak the language you do may make it more difficult for you to have particular thoughts or ideas than if you spoke another language. In China, for instance, most scientific writing and research is done in English. This may be because many Chinese scientists were trained in the United States, and English is an international language of science; or it may be that the Chinese languages are not equipped to deal with scientific ideas. Languages such as Mandarin or Cantonese are based on characters that stand for entities. New "words" cannot be created easily, and new characters are very rarely added to the language. In English, on the other hand, it's easy to make up a new word, such as electron, or proton, or hyperspace. When we think about something like hyperspace we use the word, we don't picture it. But how would you use Chinese characters to write a word like hyperspace? There is no character for such a word. Is it possible, then, that if you spoke only Mandarin such an idea would never occur to you because the language wouldn't facilitate this kind of thinking?

Benjamin Lee Whorf in 1956 proposed an hypothesis of **linguistic relativity.** Whorf had been trained at the Massachusetts Institute of Technology as a chemical engineer and spent most of his life working for the Hartford Fire Insurance Company. As a hobby, Whorf studied North American Indian languages. It was apparent from the different languages that each tribe emphasized certain aspects of its world. Whorf noted that Eskimos had many different words for snow, depending on its condition—slushy, powdery, ice-covered, etc.—while the Hanunoo people in the Philippines had 92 names for kinds of rice. Whorf believed that language directly affected people's thoughts about and perceptions of their world. He argued that the Eskimos were much more aware of snow conditions, and the Hanunoo of the kind of rice they were eating, because they had the words available in their language to make these distinctions.

Linguistic relativity is an interesting idea. Many people who are bilingual claim that they are able to think and express certain thoughts in one language much better than they can in the other. But is it true that our thinking, viewpoint, and perceptions are directly influenced by the words we have in our language? To test this hypothesis, one researcher compared the Dani, a Stone Age agricultural people who live in New Guinea, to persons who spoke English (Rosch, 1973). In the Dani language there are just two terms for color, *mola* for bright, warm colors and *mili* for dark, cold colors. In English there are many words for colors. There are 11 short, simple words for basic colors called **focal colors:** red, green, yellow, blue, brown, purple, orange, pink, gray, white, and black. There are also a number of more complex words describing colors, for example, periwinkle and magenta. In her experiment Rosch showed subjects who spoke English the 11 focal colors. Each color was then paired with a nonsense syllable—a new word for the color. The Dani were also shown the 11 focal colors and given a new name to memorize for each color. If Whorf's suggestion was true, that words facilitated perception and understanding, a likely outcome of the experiment was that the English-speaking individuals would easily learn to discriminate between the 11 focal colors, even after being given new words for each, because of the variety of color words in English. Conversely, the Dani would not understand that the colors were different because their language distinguished between colors in only two ways. Rosch found that the English speakers were able to learn the nonsense names for focal colors quite well, and so were the Dani. Moreover, the Dani could easily tell the colors apart, even though they had no words for them in their own language. This result indicated that the Dani and the English speakers perceived color distinctions independently of the language they spoke.

If the Whorf hypothesis is wrong, it would mean that Eskimos have many different names for snow because snow is important to them. They would have observed the many different kinds of snow and *then* found words for them rather than noticing the different kinds of snow *because* they had the words. English-speaking skiers, too, who spend much time in the snow, must notice many kinds of snow, although they don't necessarily have words for the different varieties. Because they need to communicate with others, they may invent a whole new vocabulary of ski terms agreed on and shared by friends (powder, corn snow, slush, hardpack, etc.). Furthermore, young children appear to be cognitively able to manipulate objects internally before they develop language to a significant degree. It is argued that this, too, indicates that thinking can occur in the absence of extensive language ability. Still, the Whorfian hypothesis is hard to test fully, and it may well be that the kind of language people speak facilitates the ways in which they approach problems or make discriminations.

LANGUAGE ACQUISITION

The Onset of Language Newborn infants don't possess language. Of this we are sure. As infants grow, they develop language in a step-by-step sequence. Interestingly, the sequence of language acquisition is similar among children the world over.

The English language is made up of over 100,000 words, 26 letters, and

LANGUAGE
Any means of communication that uses signs, symbols, or gestures within a grammar and through which novel constructions can be created.

COMMUNICATION
The process of making one's thoughts, ideas, desires, or emotions recognizable to another.

GRAMMAR
A set of rules that determine how sounds may be put together to make words and how words may be put together to make sentences.

NOVEL CONSTRUCTION
Use of a language and its grammar in order to form new statements to which the originator had not been exposed before. One of the elements defining language.

LINGUISTIC RELATIVITY
Whorf's hypothesis that thought is structured according to the language spoken. Those who speak different languages would have different thinking patterns.

FOCAL COLORS
Basic colors, described by short, simple words. In English the focal colors are red, green, yellow, blue, brown, purple, orange, pink, gray, white, and black.

PHONEME
The most basic distinctive sounds in any given language. Phonemes are combined into words.

PHONETIC EXPANSION
The beginning of the babbling stage, when infants enlarge their repertoire to include more phonemes than they eventually will come to use.

BABBLING STAGE
One of the first stages of language development in infants, characterized by inarticulate, meaningless speech sounds.

PHONETIC CONTRACTION
The end of the babbling stage, when infants narrow their use of phonemes mainly to the ones they will be using in the language they will eventually acquire.

approximately 40 **phonemes.** Phonemes are the smallest units of speech that can be discriminated. For instance, the "m" sound in *mat* and the "b" sound in *bat* are phonemes. In English there are 14 different phonetic (phoneme) vowel sounds and 36 different phonetic consonant sounds. Some consonants can stand for more than one phonetic sound. The letter *c*, for example, can stand for the phoneme in *cat* or the phoneme in *cent*. Different languages, and different accents within languages, are based on different groups of phonemes. Some languages use more phonemes than others.

By the time human beings are six or seven months old they produce many phonetic sounds. Earlier differences between a young infant's and an adult's sounds may be due to the fact that an infant's developing skull and oral cavity are not like an adult's. Anthropologists comparing the skulls and oral cavities of adults and infants have found evidence that infants younger than six months may be physically incapable of making the sounds necessary for spoken language (Lieberman, Crelin, & Klatt, 1972).

At first, infants produce only a few phonemes, and then they include more and more phonemes in their repertoire. This process is called **phonetic expansion.** As an infant's phonetic repertoire grows, parents become aware that the infant has begun to babble. Not surprisingly, this time is referred to as the **babbling stage.** Contrary to what you might expect, infants early in this stage tend to babble just about every phoneme in existence (Jespersen, 1922). For this reason most researchers believe that babbling is a genetically triggered development independent of experience. Even babies of deaf parents, who are rarely exposed to language, will babble (Lenneberg, 1967). The hypothesis that the babbling stage is determined by genetics is further supported by the observation that babies the world over begin to babble at about the same time, and that they all produce this expanding and eventually inclusive array of phonemes (Atkinson, McWhinney, & Stoel, 1970).

At the beginning of the babbling stage no differences can be detected between the babblings of an infant who has been exposed to English and those of an infant who has been exposed to Chinese. The first noticeable differences are in tonality. Tonal languages use high-pitched or low-pitched tones to give completely different meanings to the same words; many African and Asian languages are tonal. During the latter part of the babbling stage, infants who have been exposed to a tonal language often engage in pitch modulation that gives their babbling the singsong quality of the language they are destined to master. In this sense, the acquisition of inflections may be one of the earliest language developments (Weir, 1966).

As the babbling stage comes to an end, between 9 and 14 months of age, infants narrow their use of phonemes mainly to the ones they will be using in the language they will eventually learn. This process is called **phonetic contraction.** By this time infants are also beginning to acquire the pacing and rhythm of the language. Sometimes an infant joins phonemes with a rhythm, pacing, and length that is so similar to actual language (except that real words are not spoken) that parents swear that their baby has just spoken a totally intelligible sentence. It's just that they somehow missed what the infant said (imagine their anguish when they try to get the baby to repeat the phrase).

For infants to acquire the specific phonemes of their language it appears that feedback is necessary. That is, the infants have to be able to imitate what they hear before phonetic contraction can begin. This brings up the first of many linguistic problems. If infants imitate what they hear, why don't they speak in sentences? After all, they hear language, not babbling.

The reason that infants babble rather than imitate full sentences may be due to the fact that individual words can be discriminated or recognized only after they have been associated with particular objects, actions, or circumstances. This process of recognition takes place through experience, as infants grow. Until these associations have been made—that is, until these different sounds have a meaning—any of us can discern only the phonemes. Suppose you were suddenly transported to a foreign land where everyone spoke an unfamiliar language. You wouldn't be aware of distinct words. Everything that was said would sound like jibberish to you. After a short time, though, you might become aware of some aspects of the language. Perhaps you'd become aware of the spacing—when sounds began and when they ended. You might also become aware of the rhythm and tonal changes or differences in phonetic sounds. Unfortunately, your sensitivity to these aspects of language wouldn't enable you to communicate. It wouldn't be long before you'd feel helpless, or even childlike. On the other hand, you could be learning to imitate the sounds of the language so well that you would appear to be a native speaker, although you couldn't say a single word of the language. It's easy to do; you've probably heard it done many times. Comedians like Sid Caesar and Danny Kaye are able in this way to "speak" many languages. You can usually identify the language you are hearing by listening to the phonemes alone; you don't need to be familiar with the words. French simply doesn't sound like Russian, and neither sounds like Swahili.

Learning the phonemes of a particular language, which is what infants do during phonetic contraction, is easy. Have you ever listened to someone speak with an accent? Can you imitate that person? Many people can imitate regional or foreign accents, especially if they are exposed to them for some time. If you can imitate a foreign accent, then you have learned the phonemes of that language. Interestingly, since your accent is based on the use of certain phonemes, and not on the particular words of a language, it can carry over to any other language. For example, if you can imitate a Swedish accent while speaking English, you should be able just as easily to do your Swedish accent while reading a German sentence. You would then be speaking German with a Swedish accent (Swedish phonemes, tonality, and rhythm).

You can use this same technique to eliminate an accent. Would you like to speak French like a native, that is, without a foreign accent? Then listen to someone who has a French accent while they speak English, and learn to imitate that person's French accent. Then do your new French accent while you are speaking French, and voilà!*

The First Words   A child usually speaks the first words by the age of ten months to a year. Typically, these first words relate directly to certain objects or actions within a child's experience. Although it is often difficult to generalize from an adult's experience to that of a child, you might again imagine yourself living in the foreign land we spoke of earlier. Like a child,

---

*Caution: When I tried this I made the mistake of learning my French accent from old Charles Boyer movies. Although no one in France thought I was an American, they did wonder why I was constantly imitating Charles Boyer.

you might first acquire words that you could pair directly with some tangible object or obvious action. Children seem to acquire concrete nouns and verbs first, such as mama or "wa-wa" (water); they learn more abstract words later. The first abstract words tend to be adjectives such as red, tall, or big.

The average one-year-old knows about four or five words. A child will use these words individually, rather than putting them together to form a sentence; hence this period of language acquisition is called the **one-word stage.** Children at the one-word stage may at first only repeat a word they have heard. Soon, however, it becomes obvious that they intend to communicate, if only with single words. By the time children have a vocabulary of a hundred words or more, there is logic behind their choice of words. They usually choose a word that names or points out something new. Later in the one-word stage they begin to use a chosen word to ask for things (Greenfield & Smith, as cited by Moskowitz, 1978).

Syntax and Language Comprehension   You might logically assume that children would speak their first sentence when they said two words, a noun and a verb, one following the other. But it may be that "sentences" already exist in the one-word stage, albeit not true sentences, which require a verb and a noun. Nonetheless, there have been questions about whether children in the one-word stage possess an understanding of syntax.

This would be a good place to make a short excursion into the world of linguistic terms. The **syntax** of a language refers to the rules that describe how words may be put together to form sentences. Grammar is a broader term than syntax; it includes both syntax and **phonology.** Phonology is the study of how sounds (phonemes) are put together to make words. Whether children in the one-word stage have a knowledge of syntax is difficult to establish since assessing the degree of language awareness a child has isn't a simple thing. You can't always tell the meaning just by listening to what a child says. A short conversation between Harvard professor Roger Brown and a young child furnishes a classic example:

CHILD: "Fis."

BROWN: "Fis?"

CHILD: (*Correcting Brown*) "Fis!"

BROWN: (*Confused*) "Fis?"

CHILD: "Fis!"

BROWN: "Fish?"

CHILD: "Yes, fis."

(Brown, as cited by Moskowitz, 1978)

Although the child couldn't say the word, he knew what it should have sounded like. Similarly, although children in the one-word stage are unable to demonstrate an understanding of syntactic rules by constructing sentences, some syntactic understanding is reflected in their ability to comprehend sentences addressed to them. One study has demonstrated that children in the one-word stage can understand two-word instructions. Twelve children in the one-word stage (between 16 and 24 months of age) were given orders, such as "Kiss duck," "Kiss car," "Bang duck," or "Bang car." Nonlinguistic cues were eliminated. The subjects were able to respond correctly to the instructions much of the time—even when requested to do unfamiliar or strange things, such as "Tickle book" (Sachs & Truswell, 1978).

Children in the one-word stage may also be demonstrating some early syntactic comprehension in the way in which they often "vertically" arrange the single words they speak. When we speak sentences we say the words "horizontally," that is, one word following the next (as the words would be written on a line). Single words, as spoken in the one-word stage (one word per line), may show evidence of an early attempt at syntactic structure when read vertically. Consider the following conversation between psycholinguist Ronald Scollon and Brenda, a child in the one-word stage (Scollon & Bloom, as cited by Moskowitz, 1978):

BRENDA:	"Ka. Ka. Ka. Ka." (*car*)
SCOLLON:	"What?"
BRENDA:	"Go. Go."
SCOLLON:	Undecipherable.
BRENDA:	"Baish. Baish. Baish. Baish. Baish. Baish. Baish. Baish. Baish." (*bus*)
SCOLLON:	"What? Oh, bicycle? Is that what you said?"
BRENDA:	"Na." (*not*)
SCOLLON:	"No?"
BRENDA:	"Not."
SCOLLON:	"No. I got it wrong."

Here Brenda never says more than one word at a time, which, of course, defines a child in the one-word stage. Still, can we discover an attempt to structure a sentence by reading Brenda's words vertically from top to bottom? Was Brenda saying that hearing the car reminded her that she'd been on the bus the day before and not on the bicycle? What do you think?

As recently as 15 years ago it was generally agreed that children in the one-word stage were only learning the names of various objects, actions, or concepts, but not syntactic rules. But investigation of children's responses to multiword sentences during the one-word stage, and of the way in which they order their single-word utterances, is turning up evidence that these children are already forming hypotheses about how to put words together to make sentences.

Figure 8.7 illustrates the very rapid acquisition of vocabulary in young children. Most children have mastered over 200 words by the time they begin to speak in sentences.

The Two-Word Stage   By the time children are between 18 and 20 months of age they have usually begun to utter two-word statements. During this stage (brilliantly referred to as the **two-word stage**), children rapidly learn the value of language for expressing concepts, and especially for communi-

Figure 8.7   *A typical acquisition rate of vocabulary in children. Children's average vocabulary size increases rapidly between the ages of one and a half and six and a half. The number of children tested in each sample age group is shown in color. (Data are based on work done by Madorah E. Smith of the University of Hawaii, as presented by Moskowitz, 1978.)*

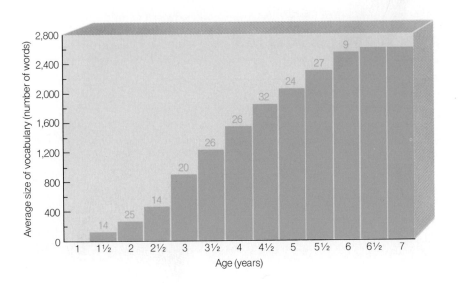

cating their desires to others. During this time it is not unusual for more than a thousand new two-word statements to appear monthly (Braine, 1963). Such two-word utterances enable children to make use of many of the descriptive forms found in language—nominative ("that house"), possessive ("Daddy book"), and action ("kitty go"). Throughout the two-word stage children have a chance to practice these language forms before attempting to expand upon them. The two-word stage is a universal phenomenon (Slobin, 1970).

Telegraphic Speech Children do not enter a three-word stage. Instead, following the two-word stage, they spend the next few years creating many short sentences. Roger Brown at Harvard University has referred to children's speech during this time as **telegraphic speech.**

Telegraphic speech is an apt term. When people send telegraphs, at so many cents per word, they want to be brief and to the point; unnecessary words are excluded. Children's telegraphic speech is quite similar. A famous example of telegraphic speech can be found in the old Tarzan films. Johnny Weismuller believed that since Tarzan was just getting the hang of English after having lived with the apes for so long, he would speak in a certain way. The speech pattern Weismuller chose in portraying Tarzan was a telegraphic one, that is, rich in important words such as nouns or verbs ("Jane go now," "Boy come soon," "Tarzan help Cheetah"). Function words are missing; there are no tenses, plurals, conjunctions, articles, prepositions, etc. This is typical of telegraphic speech.

In arranging their expressive statements, children during this stage adopt a grammar of rigid word order. They usually place the subject before the verb, its position in normal English word order. This rigid word order is necessary because without function words such as conjunctions or prepositions, many of the more subtle meanings of a language are difficult to convey. Children therefore rely heavily on word order to make sure that their meaning is clear.

Even at this early time, it is obvious that the development of grammar is closely linked with that of **semantics** (the meaning in a language). Children are trying to find a way to link the words together in order to express a meaning, and rigid word order often allows them to effectively communicate a particular meaning. For example, if your three-year-old child suddenly informs you, "Kitty follow Ann home," you know from the word order that (a) "Kitty" is the subject; (b) "follow" was the action taken; and (c) "Ann" is about to begin imploring you to keep the cat. You can demonstrate that young children use rigid word order to express meanings by performing an experiment. Explain to your three-year-old child, using a passive sentence, that "Ann was followed home by the kitty." An interesting thing will happen. A child of one and a half or two might actually have a better grasp of what you said, but a three-year-old using telegraphic speech and rigid word order will typically ignore such words as "was" or "by" and will notice only that "Ann" came first in the sentence, "follow" came second, and "kitty" came last. Children of this age hearing such passive sentences are likely to interpret them to mean that Ann is now following the cat (Slobin, 1966). Since you and I use function words, we are able to understand that "Ann was followed home by the cat" means the same as "The cat followed Ann home." Although we sometimes rely on word order to express our meaning, we don't rely on it exclusively.

TWO-WORD STAGE
The universal stage of language development in which children's expressions are limited to two-word utterances.

TELEGRAPHIC SPEECH
Pattern of speech following the two-word stage, in which children rely on a grammar of strict word order to convey their meaning and do not use conjunctions, prepositions, or other function words.

SEMANTICS
The study of meaning in language.

Table 8.2   Fourteen English suffixes and function words

FORM	MEANING	EXAMPLE
1. Present progressive: -ing	Ongoing process	He is sitt*ing* down.
2. Preposition: in	Containment	The mouse is *in* the box.
3. Preposition: on	Support	The book is *on* the table.
4. Plural: -s	Number	The dog*s* ran away.
5. Past irregular: e.g., went	Earlier in time relative to time of speaking	The boy *went* home.
6. Possessive: -'s	Possession	The girl*'s* dog is big.
7. Uncontractible copula be: e.g., are, was	Number; earlier in time	*Are* they boys or girls? *Was* that a dog?
8. Articles: the, a	Definite/indefinite	He has *a* book.
9. Past regular: -ed	Earlier in time	He jump*ed* the stream.
10. Third person regular: -s	Number; earlier in time	She run*s* fast.
11. Third person irregular: e.g., has, does	Number; earlier in time	*Does* the dog bark?
12. Uncontractible auxiliary be: e.g., is, were	Number; earlier in time; ongoing process	*Is* he running? *Were* they at home?
13. Contractible copula be: e.g., -'s, -'re	Number; earlier in time	That*'s* a spaniel.
14. Contractible auxiliary be: e.g., -'s, -'re	Number; earlier in time; ongoing process	They*'re* running very slowly.

SOURCE: Clark & Clark, 1977; based on Brown, 1973.

Figure 8.8 *An example of the "wugs" used by Berko in her study of the acquisition of language rules.* (SOURCE: *Berko, 1958, p. 154*)

THIS IS A WUG.

NOW THERE IS ANOTHER ONE.
THERE ARE TWO OF THEM.
THERE ARE TWO _____ .

Function Words Children eventually acquire the **function words** that adults use. Although research in this area is not extensive, findings indicate that children the world over acquire function words in the same general order, though at different rates (deVilliers & deVilliers, 1973). Table 8.2 shows 14 suffixes and function words used in the English language, given in the order in which children generally acquire them.

Researchers aren't certain why children learn to use function words in this order, although it may have to do with the complexity of each task. Return for a moment to that foreign land to which you were sent earlier in this chapter. Once you had acquired single words and then two words, and had begun to string them together in a clipped, telegraphic manner, you too would slowly begin to acquire function words and suffixes, but in what order? You might learn the simplest and most obvious ones first. Children may do exactly this, learning the easiest and most obvious rule first and then simply beginning to apply it. As you will notice, all 14 function words and suffixes in Table 8.2 have a semantic meaning. Each carries information. For example, when you hear the plural word *dogs* you know immediately that the speaker means more than one dog. Children learn this connection as a rule governing plurals.

That children understand the rules they are using and are not simply repeating the word *dogs*, for instance, has been demonstrated in an experiment (Berko, 1958). Children were asked to answer the question posed in Figure 8.8. They correctly answered, "Wugs," a clear demonstration that they had learned the plural rule, since they had never before heard the word wug.

Children are seldom consciously aware that they have acquired these rules. We know this because children who are able to use the new rules properly are often unable to state them. The same thing can happen to adults. Read the following two sentences carefully:

1. John is eager to please, therefore one eagerly pleases John.
2. John is easy to please, therefore one easily pleases John.

The first sentence is false, and the second is true. But do you know why? Although both sentences appear to have the same grammatical structure, your understanding of grammar and semantics alerts you to the problem in the first sentence. Ask yourself what the subject of the first sentence is. If you said John you were correct. Now, what is the subject of the second sentence? If you said John again you were wrong. The subject of the second sentence is "one" (implying you). Most people are unaware of the grammatical and semantic rules they have come to learn. While almost everyone would know that the first sentence is false and the second is true—an evaluation that of course requires an understanding of the grammar and semantics involved—very few would be able to explain how they knew.

Caretaker Speech   Whenever adults interact with children they seem to restructure their language for the child's benefit, often quite unconsciously. This restructured language is called **caretaker speech,** and it differs in a number of ways from the language generally used by adults to communicate with each other. Caretaker speech is characterized by short, simple sentences. The sentences are usually said in a higher-pitched voice and often with exaggerated inflections. The vocabulary is simple, and individual

FUNCTION WORDS
Words or word additions that help add meaning to a sentence and are acquired by children generally between the ages of two and a half and five. *In, on, went, are,* and *was* are examples of function words.

CARETAKER SPEECH
A speech pattern used in addressing others who are obviously less competent in their speech than is the speaker. Universally applied, caretaker speech is characterized by short simple sentences, simple vocabulary, a higher-pitched voice, and exaggerated inflections.

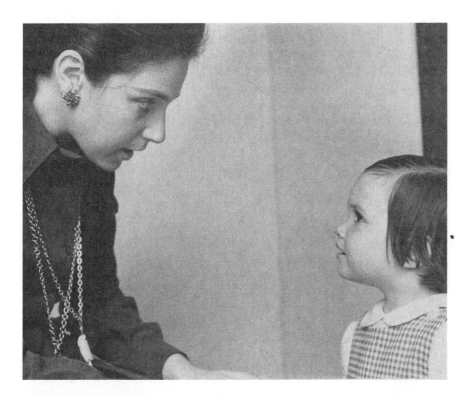

Parents generally use caretaker speech while speaking to children.

BABY TALK
The simplification of both vocabulary and individual words. Not to be confused with caretaker speech, which is a more inclusive term.

LINGUISTS
Those who specialize in and study language.

SPOONERISMS
Unintentional transpositions of sounds in a sentence, as in "people in glass houses shouldn't stow thrones," named for an English clergyman, William A. Spooner (1844-1930), who was well known for such errors.

TRANSFORMATIONAL GRAMMAR THEORY
Noam Chomsky's theory of grammar in which he argues that the semantic content of a language is more important than the grammar in helping us to understand how we come to express our meanings or grasp the meanings of others.

SURFACE STRUCTURE
A term used by linguists to denote the grammar structure within which the semantic or deep structure is carried.

DEEP STRUCTURE
A term used by linguists to describe the meaning that a person who constructs an utterance, such as a sentence, intends to convey.

words are sometimes simplified by reducing their phonetic complexity. Caretaker speech is different from **baby talk**. Baby talk refers solely to the simplification of vocabulary and individual words; the speaker might say "wa-wa" for water or reduce the number of consonants in a single grouping, for instance, from *stomach* to *tummy*. Caretaker speech is a broader category, engaged in by parents and also by older children who regularly adjust their speech to a level just slightly above that of the younger child to whom they are speaking.

Caretaker speech enables children to grasp the language more easily. Return again to the foreign country you visited earlier (I hope your travel agent is giving you a discount). You would no doubt have found it very helpful if the local people had adjusted their speech for you, so that their sentences were shorter, simpler, and less involved than those they used with their compatriots. You might readily do the same for someone who was just learning English. Even among adults who speak the same language, elaboration and simplification is common when one adult perceives that the other is at a disadvantage. In an experiment carried out in Boston, a man speaking with a Boston accent and dressed in casual clothes asked passersby the best way to get to the Boston Commons. He was typically given concise information, such as "Take the MTA" (the Boston subway system) a certain number of stops. However, if the same man wore a cowboy hat and boots and spoke with a heavy Texas accent, people would stop and answer in great detail. They would explain what the MTA was, how it was used, how much it would cost, the direction of the Commons, how long it would take to get there, and other routes that might be appropriate. Based on the appearance and accent of the man asking for information, people deduced whether he already had some knowledge of the immediate vicinity. They then elaborated on their answer or not, as appropriate (Krauss & Glucksberg, 1977).

SYNTACTIC AND SEMANTIC STRUCTURE

Once language competence is acquired, how do people learn to express themselves by means of language? Can you recall how you learned to express what you wanted to say? In fact, are you even aware of the process you currently go through in deciding how to express yourself? **Linguists** the world over examine human language in order to discover how we "decide to say what we say." As you will see, the process is not simple.

Suppose you are working in the hot sun and are becoming thirsty. How do you express a desire for a glass of water? How do you tell your friend on the job that you think it's time to take a break and get a drink? How do you express your meaning in a structured sentence? You may say simply, "Let's take a break and get a drink of water." But was it that simple? How did you come up with that sentence? Did you just string the words together? Were some words more important than others? Could you have strung them together differently?

In formulating that sentence, you probably didn't begin by searching your entire vocabulary until you struck upon the word *let*'s, which you then decided was the best first word. Although a language computer might perform in this way, choosing each word in sequence before uttering it, people don't. People sort out entire sentences before they say them. They build the syntax of a sentence so that it expresses a meaning, and they do this before they begin to speak.

Spoonerisms give us a clue to the way in which people are busy organizing their syntax in order to express their meaning. Spoonerisms are rather interesting transpositions named after William A. Spooner (1844–1930), an English clergyman well known for accidentally making such rearrangements. No doubt you've occasionally committed a spoonerism yourself. I think of a theater usher who recently baffled my friends and me when he asked, "Would you like me to sew you to your sheets?" Everyone soon realized that he had meant to say, "Would you like me to show you to your seats?" What this spoonerism demonstrates is that the usher had to have had the word *seats* in mind (the tenth word in the sentence) before he ever said *show* (the sixth word). Otherwise, how could he have gotten them confused? People work out their syntax before they say the sentence; they don't simply link one word to the next.

Noam Chomsky

Some words in a sentence are more important than others, while other words are systematically arranged around the main words in order to help express the meaning. Like children in the two-word stage, older children and adults stress nouns and verbs. Unlike children in the two-word stage, older children and adults build on the nouns and verbs. In one interesting experiment, adults were classically conditioned to salivate when they heard certain sentences. Later, the individual words of the sentence were spoken to them and the amount of salivation was recorded. Although articles, adjectives, and prepositions were as much a part of the sentence as the nouns and verbs, it was the nouns and verbs that generated the greatest salivary response (Razran, 1961).

TRANSFORMATIONAL GRAMMAR AND SEMANTICS

Psycholinguist Noam Chomsky has developed an elaborate theory called **transformational grammar theory.** Broadly, Chomsky's theory states that there is probably little value in studying grammatical usage in order to understand how we come to express our meanings or, conversely, to grasp the meanings of others. Chomsky feels that when we hear a spoken sentence, we don't retain the grammatical structure, which he calls **surface structure.** Instead, he believes, we transform the grammar into another form, which he calls **deep structure.** Chomsky believes that the meaning or semantic content of a sentence is preserved within the transformed grammar of the deep structure. Similarly, if we wish to express a meaning that we retain within the deep structure grammar, we must first transform our meaning into any of a number of grammatically acceptable surface structures. Chomsky believes that his theory helps to explain how one sentence can have two meanings. For example, the sentence "The shooting of the hunters was terrible" can mean either that the hunters were poor shots or that they were shot. One surface structure, therefore, can have two possible deep structures.

Whether the transformational grammar theory or other equally interesting theories will eventually explain language processing remains to be seen. Currently, most language research is descriptive rather than explanatory, and language theorists carry on a vigorous debate over the issues surrounding the acquisition and use of language.

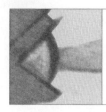

THE DEBATE BETWEEN NATIVISTS AND LEARNING THEORISTS

By the time Grace and Virginia Kennedy were of school age, their parents were well aware that something was wrong. The girls were identical twins, and although they were five years old, they hadn't learned to talk. Arrangements were made to have the twins tested. To their parents' dismay both girls were found to have IQ scores below 50—which placed them in a category known as TMR, or trainably mentally retarded. Of course, one of the reasons for their low scores was that they had not developed language. They only babbled senselessly to each other.

In January 1977 Grace and Virginia were enrolled in a school for the retarded. There, they failed to acquire language, but they did excel in other areas. The question was raised whether they belonged in a school for the retarded. Finally, they were referred to the Speech, Hearing and Neurosensory Center of the Children's Hospital of San Diego for examination, where speech pathologists discovered something surprising. They observed that the "jibberish" the twins spoke to each other seemed to have a structure. They also noticed that certain sounds the twins made seemed to relate to specific objects. Furthermore, the jibberish seemed to have the markings of a conversation. For instance, Grace would smile and say something to Virginia, and Virginia would turn and hand her an object. When the twins observed a new object, they would appear to discuss it, and then seem to agree on a name for it. They even had names for each other—Poto and Cabengo. It appeared that the

Kennedy twins had developed their own language!

To test this possibility, researchers placed Poto in a room with various objects arranged in a certain way. Poto then described the objects and their arrangement to Cabengo via an intercom using their special language. Without difficulty, Cabengo arranged identical objects in her room to match Poto's description.

Although such "twin speech" has been observed in twins up to the age of two or three, the Kennedy twins used their special language beyond the age of seven, which is quite rare. By that time their language was becoming complex. How far would they go? Language investigators from all parts of the nation began to take an interest in the Kennedy twins. Was this proof that language acquisition was inborn, or "native," to our species? If children weren't taught language, would they "instinctively" develop a rich and complex language of their own? Or was there another explanation?

One of the longest ongoing debates concerning language development centers on whether language is basically a learned phenomenon or whether we, as a species, are biogenetically "prewired" for the acquisition of language. Noam Chomsky, for instance, believes that human beings have a **language acquisition device**. Chomsky's position is therefore nativist. On the other side of the argument are learning theorists who argue that human beings do not have a language acquisition device. Rather, they are able to learn, and to learn rapidly, and

this general learning ability is applied to language as well as to many other skills. Debates about the nature of language are interesting and they sometimes become heated; let's listen in on one.

LEARNING THEORIST: There is little evidence to demonstrate that humans have evolved brains that are specifically organized for the acquisition of language. What we as a species do possess are brains that enable us to learn a great deal and to learn it very quickly.

NATIVIST: I must disagree. Language acquisition is a particularly human ability. Every human being, except under the most unusual circumstances, will acquire language. Like walking, it is maturationally part of a human being's development. Our brain has obviously been selected for language because of the survival value that exists in having the ability to communicate. How can anyone believe otherwise?

LEARNING THEORIST: I think you're making some large assumptions. You say that language comes "naturally" to us, that we all engage in it, and that *therefore* it has been naturally selected and we have evolved "language brains." Then what about reading? The ability to read couldn't have been naturally selected; there hasn't been enough time. The printing press was invented only a few hundred years ago, and very few people were exposed to writing before that. Yet hundreds of millions of people can and do easily learn to read. We use our sense of vision and our motor-tracking skills, which evolved before reading material ever came along, and combine them with our general intelligence to provide an ability that we find useful. It's much the same with ballet. We invented and refined ballet. We are the only species to engage in ballet. Obviously the muscles and skeletal structure needed for ballet evolved—but for reasons other than the ''survival benefits'' derived from dancing. Similarly, we invented language by using our powerful learning brains and by making use of our mouths and tongues, whose structure may have evolved for other reasons.

NATIVIST: Oh what nonsense! All healthy human beings do not naturally acquire reading or ballet, yet we all speak! In fact, we know now that there are specific neurological areas of the brain directly involved with language development, namely Broca's area, Wernicke's area, and the angular gyrus. Damage to any of these areas may cause severe speech disorders.

LEARNING THEORIST: Now wait a minute. Just because certain areas of the human brain are involved with language production doesn't mean that our brain evolved specifically for language acquisition—any more than the fact that parts of the brain are used for reading means that we evolved specific abilities for that skill. We simply have a powerful general intelligence and we use it.

NATIVIST: You're not serious! What about the speed at which children acquire language? Are their parents running a conditioning laboratory in their homes where each approximation of a word is reinforced promptly until the word is shaped? No. Babies are often played with and reinforced when they only babble nonsense. How could you possibly explain the speed at which children learn under the typically haphazard reinforcement conditions of

the home if they were not genetically set for language acquisition?

LEARNING THEORIST: Parents often speak to their children while showing affection. Perhaps the parents' words become secondary reinforcers by being paired with affection and other reinforcers, and then the children try to obtain these reinforcing word sounds by making them themselves. In this way children would be shaped into imitating their parents as closely as possible. This would even explain why children learn their parents' accents.

NATIVIST: Then how would you explain the fact that infants as early as one month of age can tell the difference between subtle language sounds such as ''pah'' and ''bah'' (Moffitt, 1971)? It's because, my friend, they are designed for language acquisition.

LEARNING THEORIST: Squirrels can also discriminate between subtle language sounds such as ''pah'' and ''bah''. If I'm not mistaken they don't ever speak a language! All you're telling me with your data is that infants hear well. That's one of the problems with you nativists; you're always rushing to conclusions. For example, consider the Kennedy twins. Some of you nativists were claiming that language acquisition had to be an inborn ability since these twins had invented their own language. But then look at what was discovered after some careful research. The Kennedy twins were found to be speaking only slurred English with a little German thrown in, languages they had been hearing in their home. Their language was hard to understand because they used little inflection and no auxiliary verbs, but they did follow English word-order rules. In fact, after getting used to their bizarre English, researchers were able to understand them 90 percent of the time (Newport, 1979). The twins were

actually developing syntax in a normal, though slower, order. But before that was discovered, they were on national talk shows and were heralded as examples of instinctive language ability.

NATIVIST: Well, well—speak of jumping to conclusions. It seems that you believe that if one case turns out not to be an example of natural language acquisition then all cases are not. You must admit that's not a very scientific attitude. Perhaps the Kennedy twins are not examples of native language acquisition, but there have been other cases. In 1977 Goldin-Meadow and Feldman videotaped six deaf children over a period of six to eight weeks. The children were between 17 and 49 months of age. Four were boys and two were girls, all of average intelligence. None of the children had ever been exposed to manual sign language because their parents wanted to teach them oral expression and communication. Yet these children spontaneously developed a complex sign system including a lexicon, syntax, and semantic relationships! Frankly, I can't understand how you fail to see that language acquisition is a canalized process that proceeds through a number of stages as a result of brain maturation (Lenneberg, 1966, 1967). If you don't give children language they'll develop it anyway.

LEARNING THEORIST: Oh, there you go again, jumping to conclusions. . . .

Unfortunately, because of space limitations, we have to bid our debaters a fond farewell.*

*For those who feel that the sarcasm of the debate is unrealistic or immature, I would like to point out that the last time I attended a public debate between a learning theorist and a nativist on the subject of language development, the learning theorist stormed out of the room, slamming the door behind him. The nativist continued on his own with a lecture about innate forms of hostility and aggression.

LANGUAGE ACQUISITION DEVICE
An innate biological mechanism that enables humans to acquire and use language. Postulated by Noam Chomsky.

Some theorists take an interactionist position on the subject of language, believing that both learning theorists and nativists may be partly correct. Many aspects of both viewpoints have merit, and there's no reason why we couldn't have been naturally selected for language acquisition *and* for a very powerful learning brain, and develop language as a result of both predispositions. We might test this supposition on a highly intelligent species that doesn't have natural language, applying what we know about language acquisition in an attempt to teach the species to speak. Research has already been conducted along this line, and since the late 1960s there have been nonhuman creatures roaming this planet that speak a real language—the great apes.

In the early 1950s two psychologists attempted to get a chimpanzee named Viki to speak English. After many months of trying Viki could say "cup" and "up" (and less convincingly, "mama" and "papa") (Hayes & Hayes, 1952). Many believe that the chimp's vocal apparatus is unsuited for making English phonemes. In fact, poor Viki even had to hold her own lips together with her fingers in order to make the *m* sound in "mama." But consider this: Could chimps be intelligent enough to learn language even though they're anatomically unable to form the sounds?

Sign Language   In 1966 Beatrice and Allen Gardner began to investigate this question. They speculated that chimps might be able to learn to speak if they were taught sign language, specifically the American Sign Language (ASL) used by the deaf (Gardner & Gardner, 1969). This was an ingenious idea; after all, chimps are extremely competent with their hands. They can pick up dimes, work screwdrivers, wind watches, and even thread needles.

The Gardners' first attempt was with a female chimp named Washoe (after Washoe County, Nevada, where the Gardners lived). Their experi-

Washoe

ment worked. By the age of 12 Washoe had acquired over 180 signs (Fouts, as cited by Zimbardo, 1979). She had learned syntax and could put signs together in multiword fashion. For example, when Washoe's baby doll was placed in her drinking cup, she signed "baby" (by holding her arms to her chest like a mother holding her baby and then rocking from side to side), then "in" (by placing the fingers of one hand within an opening made by cupping the other), then "my" (by pointing to herself), and finally "drink" (by placing her thumb to her lips and tipping her hand back)—"Baby in my drink"—all with perfectly good ASL signs. Washoe also made a number of novel constructions. For example, before she could be taught the sign for "duck" she spontaneously placed the signs for water and bird together. It was also clear that Washoe understood the concepts represented by her words. When she saw a door she would sign "open," and she would be let inside. You might argue that this wasn't proof that Washoe really knew the meaning of "open." Her gesture might simply have been a learned instrumental response to the sight of the door reinforced by the door being opened. Later, however, when Washoe was first exposed to a car door and a satchel (both of which look very different from a regular door), she immediately signed "open" and seemed anxious to look inside—evidence that she understood the concept of "open." Washoe was also quite aware of the abilities of those around her. When speaking to a visitor whose ASL signing was a bit rusty, Washoe would slow her signing down (caretaker speech?). Some visitors confessed to feeling embarrassed at being signed to slowly by an ape.

An even more impressive example of language acquisition among the great apes is the progress of Koko, a lowland female gorilla that was studied for over seven years by Francine Patterson, then a student at Stanford University. Koko has mastered almost 400 signs, and she understands many equivalent English words for these signs. She has developed syntax and a number of novel constructions. She has even invented her own combinations of signs for nail file, eye makeup, runny nose, and obnoxious, using the last word to express her disapproval of anyone who bothers her. She signs "obnoxious" by making a knocking sign. This indicates that she knows

1. That the sign "knock" is associated with the sound of the spoken word "knock";
2. That "knock" sounds like the spoken word "obnoxious"; and
3. That the sign "knock" can therefore be applied semantically to mean someone who is being obnoxious.

Koko has developed 20 of these novel gestures. Her hearing is excellent, and she is able to make subtle auditory language discriminations. For instance, one day during a discussion of time Koko made the sign for a fruit, specifically, a lemon. That seemed odd, but wasn't really. Since Koko's thumb is too short to make the ASL sign for "eleven," she picked a like-sounding word—"lemon" o'clock. And Koko had every reason to know about 11 o'clock, because that was the time of her morning snack!

Speaking to a gorilla is like taking a glimpse into the mind of an alien, who sees some things in a different way, sometimes a metaphorically beautiful way. Consider some of Koko's fabulous terms for objects with which we are all familiar:

OBJECT	KOKO'S SIGNS
cigarette lighter	bottle match
zebra	white tiger
hide and seek	quiet chase
pomegranate seeds	red corn drink
viewmaster	look mask
nose	false mouth
Pinocchio doll	elephant baby
mask	eye hat

Koko has used her language for numerous purposes. Once, when shown a white cloth and asked to sign the color, Koko signed "red." An argument ensued, with the researcher signing "white" and Koko persisting in signing "red." Finally, Koko pointed to a tiny red speck on the cloth, signed "red," and chuckled in the odd way that gorillas have when they seem to laugh. In short order she suckered another researcher into the white-red game with the same cloth.

Koko can also use language to express anger. When upset she once signed "red mad gorilla." She has even taken to making threats. Unlike other gorillas who might bare their teeth or take threatening postures, Koko often uses language:

KOKO: "Bite, big trouble."

FRANCINE: "What?"

KOKO: "Bite, big trouble. Give apple."

Like Washoe, Koko has an excellent memory. A month after celebrating her sixth birthday she saw a piece of birthday cake and signed "six." Another time she pointed to a door and signed "drink." It was a place she had received a drink four months earlier. She often discusses the events of the previous day. Sometimes, though, she conveniently forgets things. Koko managed to escape one day, and on the day after her escape the following conversation took place.

FRANCINE: "Remember yesterday?"

KOKO: "Koko yesterday forgot."

Koko has even lied by blaming others, claiming events that never happened, and purposely describing acts as different than they were. In terms of language capability, this is quite sophisticated behavior (Patterson, 1979).

Koko also pays close attention to the conversations around her. Once two researchers were discussing whether Koko was a juvenile or an adolescent, and Koko interrupted to inform them, "No, gorilla."

Many other great apes have also been taught language. Although their ability does not reach a human's level of complexity, they have demonstrated that they can acquire language even though the simian brain appears to lack the language areas in the neocortex that exist in our species. Perhaps apes do not naturally acquire language because they lack these areas. Both the great apes' ability to learn language and their inability to match the complexity of our own species lend support to an interactionist position that both learning ability and brain organization are important factors in the acquisition of a language.

There are hopes that apes with language may eventually sign to each other. It was hoped, for instance, that Washoe might spontaneously teach her own babies to sign, but both of her infants died shortly after birth. As the last one died, Washoe stood by signing, "My baby, my baby." Since then, Washoe has adopted a baby chimp son named Loulis. The experiment to observe whether Washoe would teach Loulis to sign began in March 1979. The experiment went well, and Washoe began signing to Loulis daily. Loulis has imitated a number of Washoe's signs, but it is not yet clear that he understands what they mean.

At the Institute for Primate Studies in Norman, Oklahoma, it was observed that chimps appeared to use signs to ask each other for things, usually food, but that generally they ignored each other (perhaps a case of "If I don't see you asking for my apple I don't have to give it to you"). Then in 1978 Savage-Rumbaugh, Rumbaugh, and Boysen at the Yerkes Center reported "the first instance of . . . symbolic communication between non-human primates." They arranged an experiment in which each chimp had to depend on the other in order to obtain containers of food filled with their favorite items, peanut butter and jelly sandwiches and orange drink. To get the food, each chimp had to choose the correct sign and flash it on a projector for the other to view. The requested item could then be passed through a hole in the glass from one chimp to the other. The chimp team was accurate between 70 and 100 percent of the time.

Arguments Against Language in Apes   Although the evidence for language acquisition in the great apes seems strong, some researchers have presented arguments that may require linguists to look long and hard at this phenomenon. After working for five years with his own chimp, Nimchimsky, psychologist Herbert S. Terrace has concluded that although chimpanzees can acquire a large vocabulary, they are not capable of producing original sentences (Terrace, 1979). Terrace argues that language production is still a phenomenon unique to human beings. He believes that the great apes have been instrumentally conditioned to make certain signs in order to get what they want and that they are often inadvertently cued by their owners to produce these signs in sequence. He contends that the apes aren't really aware of what the signs mean. In support of this position B. F. Skinner demonstrated the same kind of communication as the Rumbaughs had produced between chimps—but this time using pigeons!

Rumbaugh, however, does not accept this argument. He contends that

> The difference between a chimpanzee and a pigeon is that the chimpanzee is aware of the content of the intended message and he will seek to amplify and clarify a symbolic request by a glance, gesture or whatever other means are at his disposal. . . . If a pigeon who saw a color and pecked a key was asked, "What do you mean—green?" he would not readily amplify or restate. By contrast, when a chimpanzee asks for an M&M, he looks you directly in the eye and points to it. If a chimpanzee says, "Go outdoors" and you say, "What do you mean?" he finds a collar, puts it around his neck and leads you to the door. (Greenberg, 1980, p. 300)

THE PHYSIOLOGY OF GRAMMAR AND SEMANTICS

In Chapter 2 you learned about specialized regions in the brain that appear to be directly involved with language. Broca's area was named after Paul Broca, a French physician who during the 1860s discovered that damage to a particular region in the cerebral cortex causes aphasia, a speech disorder. Broca's area is located on the side of the frontal lobes. Broca discovered that aphasia occurs only when this area is damaged on the left side of the brain. If the same area is damaged on the right side of the brain, speech remains intact. Over the last 120 years this finding has been repeatedly confirmed. Since patients with aphasia in Broca's area have difficulty speaking, but not singing, it may be that singing is controlled by a different area in the brain.

In 1874 another kind of aphasia was identified by Carl Wernicke, a German researcher. **Wernicke's aphasia** is associated with damage to another part of the cortex also found in the left hemisphere. **Wernicke's area** is in the left temporal and parietal lobes rather than the frontal lobe, the location of Broca's area (see Figure 8.9). Wernicke's area is connected to Broca's area by a bundle of nerve fibers called the **arcuate fasciculus.**

The symptoms of **Broca's aphasia** are impaired articulation and slow and labored speech. Though their responses make sense, people with Broca's aphasia find it difficult to express themselves in a fully formed or grammatical sentence. They also have trouble with verb inflections, connective words, pronouns, and complex grammatical constructions. Halting telegraphic speech in an adult is a sign of Broca's aphasia. For instance, in referring to a visit from friends a person with Broca's aphasia might say, "Yes . . . Friday . . . No . . . Joe and Susan . . . Sunday morning . . . 8 o'clock . . . Joe . . . and Susan . . . visit . . . "

People with Wernicke's aphasia have speech that is phonetically and grammatically normal, but its semantic content is bizarre. They can string

Figure 8.9 *Major areas of the brain, including portions specialized for language.*

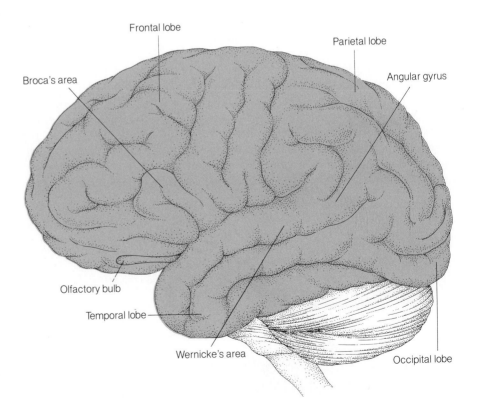

together words with the proper inflections and grammar, and yet make no sense whatsoever. It may be that semantic content is generated in Wernicke's area, but it is not structured in a suitable grammar until it has passed by way of the arcuate fasciculus to Broca's area, which provides the grammatical structure. These different specializations may explain why damage to Broca's area causes one kind of speech disruption, while damage to Wernicke's area causes another. As information travels forward from Wernicke's area through Broca's area, it passes on to the facial area of the motor cortex, which can then activate the mouth, larynx, tongue, lips, and other appropriate muscles for speech.

Wernicke's area is also important in the comprehension of reading and writing. When a sound is initially heard, it must pass through the primary auditory cortex to Wernicke's area, which is adjacent, before the message can be understood. A word that is read, however, must pass from the primary visual cortex to an area called the **angular gyrus.** The angular gyrus does an amazing thing to the visual image of the word: It transforms it into an auditory form so that it enters Wernicke's area in the same way as a spoken word does. This is why some people seem to hear the words they are reading.

If the arcuate fasciculus, which connects Wernicke's area to Broca's area, is destroyed or disconnected, speech will remain well articulated and fluent. But semantics may be lost because Broca's area is operating without receiving any information from Wernicke's area. Since other pathways into Wernicke's area are undisturbed, a patient who has had the connection destroyed will appear completely normal when trying to comprehend spoken or written words. This kind of brain damage is especially frustrating because the patient can understand everything that is being said but cannot say anything that makes sense, although the nonsense may be formulated quite grammatically.

A patient who has suffered damage to the angular gyrus may be able to understand speech, but unable to write at all. Damage to the angular gyrus does not affect the spoken word, only the written word. It may be responsible for some cases of **dyslexia,** a "difficulty in reading." Such damage may also explain the apparent limitation of the many children who are alert, intelligent, and able to understand anything as long as it's not in written form. Individuals who have difficulty with written material may be considered learning disabled. On the other hand, this assessment must be made with great caution, since many children in today's educational system are very poor at word recognition and comprehension not because of brain damage, but because they've never been adequately taught to read.

As you can see, the distinction between semantic and syntactic structure appears to have a physiological basis in the brain. While Broca's area may help formulate surface structures which are convenient carriers of information, Wernicke's area appears to control the semantic aspects of communication. The semantic aspects may then be lodged in the memory and later recalled to Wernicke's area, from there to be sent into Broca's area and put into a new surface structure for the purpose of expressing a thought. In a sense, these areas may very well constitute Chomsky's language acquisition device. As evidence of linguistic competence continues to be associated with the human neocortex, the nativist position continues to be strengthened.

WERNICKE'S APHASIA
The inability to understand spoken language because of damage to Wernicke's area. Individuals with this disorder generally speak normally in terms of phonetics and grammar content, but their speech is semantically bizarre.

WERNICKE'S AREA
An area in the temporal and parietal lobes of the brain associated with speech control.

ARCUATE FASCICULUS
The bundle of nerve fibers in the brain that connects Wernicke's area with Broca's area.

BROCA'S APHASIA
A disorder caused by damage to Broca's area. Individuals with this disorder have impaired articulation, labored speech, and difficulty in forming a grammatical sentence, but semantic content is usually clear.

ANGULAR GYRUS
A portion of the brain in the parietal lobes adjacent to Wernicke's area. The angular gyrus is involved with reading and appears to "translate" the visual word images received by the primary visual cortex into auditory form before passing the information on to Wernicke's area.

DYSLEXIA
An impairment of reading ability, in which letters or words are transposed.

Summary

■ Thought and language make us unique, perhaps more than any other aspects of our nature.

■ By definition, thinking refers to the use of mental combinations and internal representations of symbols, objects, or concepts.

■ John Watson, the father of behaviorism, argued that all mental activity was really subvocal speech (a muscular activity). But an experiment using a derivative of curare, a powerful paralyzing agent, demonstrated that the thought process can continue even when the body is fully paralyzed.

■ One of the most valuable ways in which thinking can be organized is by forming concepts. A concept is defined as the relationship between, or the properties shared by, the objects or ideas in a group. We acquire concepts by learning attributes that define each particular category.

■ Problem solving is defined as a sequence of cognitive operations directed toward achieving a particular goal.

■ Computers generally work according to algorithms, while human beings attempt to solve problems using heuristics. An algorithm is defined as a method guaranteed to lead to a solution if one is possible. Heuristic methods, while not guaranteed to reach a solution, are sometimes able to produce solutions faster. A person using heuristic methods takes the steps that seem most reasonable in order to approach a goal.

■ Means-end analysis is one way to proceed from the initial state to the goal. In means-end analysis a series of intermediate steps are accomplished by particular means until the final goal is reached.

■ A mental set is a strategy gained from previous experience that is applied to similar situations.

■ Another kind of mental set, functional fixedness, has to do with our tendency to think that objects that have a specific function can function only in the intended way.

■ Both mental sets and functional fixedness may facilitate problem solving, since old methods usually work and using an object as it was intended to be used is normally good strategy. If mental set or functional fixedness does cause a problem, it's likely to be during creative problem solving when the solution requires the application of new ideas or methods.

■ A language is based on the use of signs and symbols within a grammar. A language also allows novel constructions to be created by manipulation of the various signs and symbols within the grammatical structure.

■ Whorf's hypothesis of linguistic relativity argues that the language people use affects the way in which they think and perceive their world.

■ At about six or seven months the babbling stage begins with the onset of phonetic expansion. The onset of babbling appears to be a function of maturation.

■ By one year children have often begun to speak their first words. This is known as the one-word stage.

■ After the one-word stage, children enter the two-word stage. Both the one-word and two-word stages appear to be universal among children. During the two-word stage a child may utter over a thousand new statements every month.

■ Children don't enter a three-word stage, but instead begin to use telegraphic speech. That is, they form sentences without using function words. Function words are learned later in a specific sequence, probably dependent on the difficulty of mastering each rule.

■ Both adults and children engage in caretaker speech, which appears to be a universal way of addressing others whose language competence is less developed than one's own.

■ Chomsky's transformational grammar theory addresses the way in which sentences are structured. Chomsky distinguishes between a deep and surface structure of language that separate semantic from syntactic arrangements.

■ There are many theories of language development. Among the most debated are the nature-nurture arguments posed, on one hand, by nativists who believe that humans are prewired for language acquisition and, on the other hand, by learning theorists who feel that we use our general learning ability to invent and maintain language. Many researchers take an interactionist view.

■ In human beings there appear to be specialized regions in the brain that are directly involved with language. These include Broca's area, Wernicke's area, and the angular gyrus.

■ The symptoms of Broca's aphasia include impaired articulation and slow and labored speech. In Wernicke's aphasia, semantic content is bizarre, but speech is phonetically and grammatically normal.

EPILOGUE: THE MAN WITH THE MEANS TO REACH HIS ENDS

The following account describes a man who was especially proficient in using means-end analysis to solve problems. His efforts have touched all our lives.

Solving problems requires a particular attitude. Peter Goldmark had that attitude. He came from a family that believed if you didn't like things the way they were and wanted them to be different, then you should make them different. His uncle, Karl Goldmark, wanted opera to be different, and so he wrote his own operas. Another uncle, Joseph Goldmark, invented kitchen matches. As a child, Peter Goldmark was encouraged to create new things. When he was only 12, he built a motion picture projector from parts that he had obtained. In the 1920s he wrote away for a primitive television kit and built it, even though the picture was no larger than the size of a postage stamp, and could hardly be seen. He enjoyed making things.

In the 1930s, interested in television, he came to the United States and got a job with CBS. He liked working there, and he liked solving problems. By 1938 CBS had developed a small but practical black and white television set. Peter Goldmark and others had worked on it for many months, and it was an exciting new development that had promise for the future.

But then Peter went to see the technicolor movie, Gone with the Wind. *He was so stunned by the color and the beauty that he came away with what he described as "an inferiority feeling about television in black and white" (Manchester, 1974, p. 1192). Peter went back to his laboratory and took a look at what he had, and thought about what he wanted. He had*

Peter Goldmark

black and white television; he wanted color. He began a means-end analysis.

How could he get color light? He knew that a television screen was made up of many different lines composed of many different dots, and that the dots were white, black, and shades of gray. He wanted red, green, and blue, with which he knew he could make any color. So he built a wheel, a spinning wheel with red, green, and blue windows, which spun in front of the ray that projected on the television screen. He then synchronized the ray with the passing red, green, and blue windows. If he wanted a particular point on the screen to be green, the ray would fire only when the green window of the spinning wheel was in front of it. Three months after seeing Gone with the Wind, *Peter Goldmark had built the first color television set.*

The CBS television executives were awed. The television picture was perfect, the brightest, clearest color they had ever imagined. World War II interrupted further work on color television, and it wasn't until 1960 that the television set was advanced enough to make the color process economically feasible, and to introduce it on the market.

Peter Goldmark had not been idle in the interim. Back in 1950, he recalled, he was sitting with friends listening to a recording of Vladimir Horowitz playing Brahms on the piano, when "Suddenly there was a click. The most horrible sound man ever invented, right in the middle of the music. Somebody rushed to change records. The mood was broken. I knew right there and then I had to stop that sort of thing" (Manchester, 1974, p. 1192). Goldmark was referring to the short duration of music produced by a 78-rpm record, which was the only kind of record available then. Goldmark wanted to hear music uninterrupted. He defined the difference between what he had and what he wanted. He found out that 78-rpm records had from 85 to 100 grooves to each inch, and the number of grooves per inch determined the duration of a record. The next thing Goldmark wanted to know was whether it was possible to put more grooves per inch on a record. By proceeding carefully, breaking his steps into subgoals, he was able to get from 224 to 300 grooves per inch. The speed of play was also an important variable. Was it possible to slow the record down and maintain quality? What kinds of things happened when the record slowed down, and how could they be corrected? Bit by bit he was able to drop the speed of the record until finally he found a comfortable point, 33⅓ rpm. Peter Goldmark wouldn't have to have his music interrupted anymore. He had just invented the first long-playing record.

Goldmark continued his work, advocating the advance of cable television and satellite networks until his tragic death a few years ago in an automobile accident. His ability to solve problems was legendary, and he held well over a hundred patents. Perhaps his power as a problem solver was best expressed by William Manchester when he said about Goldmark:

Once in the late 1960s a radio interviewer asked him whether he thought mental telepathy would ever replace TV. Peter paused, adjusted his glasses, and said it was conceivable that undiscovered radiation from the brain might be used someday. He added: "But that's a long way off." There was a protracted silence in the studio. With Peter you couldn't be sure (Manchester, 1974, p. 1194).

Suggestions for Further Reading

1. Brown, R. *A first language: The early stages.* Cambridge: Harvard University Press, 1973.
2. Clark, H. H., & Clark, E. V. *Psychology and language: An introduction to psycholinguistics.* New York: Harcourt Brace Jovanovich, 1977.
3. Terrace, H. S. *Nim.* New York: Knopf, 1979.
4. Wickelgren, W. A. *How to solve problems.* San Francisco: W. H. Freeman and Company, 1974.

CONTENTS

CHAPTER 9

Motivation

You are working for Professor Harry Harlow in his monkey lab at the University of Wisconsin, helping to conduct experiments in which rhesus monkeys are subjects. When you arrived, Dr. Harlow asked you to give the monkeys in your group some of the puzzles used at the Primate Center, and observe how they behaved toward them. The puzzles are of the simple mechanical kind that two- and three-year-olds might play with. You notice that the monkeys like to take the puzzles apart. They also put them together quite readily and seem pleased when they are finished (see Figure 9.1).

Harlow wonders whether the monkeys will learn to work the puzzles faster if they are offered reinforcers for doing so. He thinks they will. So you give the monkeys raisins whenever they work with the puzzles. The monkeys love raisins, and they work harder than ever, proving Harlow's hypothesis.

Later, because you like to watch the monkeys put the puzzles together, you give them one, even though the experiment is over and you don't happen to have any

raisins. But they behave differently than they did before the experiment. They put out their hands; they want raisins—payment. They appear to become angry when they don't receive any. From that day on no matter how often the puzzles are presented to them they won't work them. You wonder how their motivation could have changed. Before raisins were offered, they liked to work the puzzles, apparently just for enjoyment. But once they knew they would be rewarded for working the puzzles, they refused to do it for nothing (Harlow, 1950). What had changed? Weren't the puzzles fun any more (deCharms, 1968)?

In this chapter we will explore the biology and learning that can influence our drives, needs, and motives. We'll examine specific areas of motivational research and investigate two theories that attempt to account for many different motives. Along the way you'll find out why you can tell when you're hungry and thirsty, why some people are motivated to succeed, and why others find a thrill in harrowing experiences.

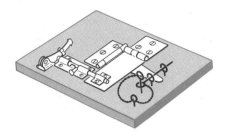

Figure 9.1 *A puzzle similar to those used by Harlow in his 1950 experiment.* (SOURCE: *Harlow, 1950, p. 290*)

Why Psychologists Study Motivation

Psychologists study motivation because they want to know *why* a behavior occurs. They want to understand the underlying processes that activate behaviors. Of course, psychologists aren't the only ones with an interest in motivation. The study of history, art, religion, theater, literature, and practically every other area of human endeavor is marked by attempts to understand the motivation behind actions. What are the forces behind love and hate? What makes some people desire power? Why do some people find it easy to share and others not? Why do some people use drugs? Which motivations are learned or taught, and which are innate? How do motives such as hunger, thirst, or sex affect our behavior?

These questions are not new to psychology or the human experience. Practically every question ever asked about a human action has, in one way or another, addressed the issue of motivation. Whenever you want to know why someone did something, you are questioning the motivation behind the action.

Biological Motives

Perhaps the most obvious kinds of motivations are those that result directly from physical needs. If your water supply were suddenly cut off, your **need** for water would eventually increase. As the need intensified and you became more thirsty, the motivation, or **drive,** to satisfy the need would grow. Your actions would increasingly be directed to filling the need. Similarly, if you went without food or sleep your motivation to satisfy these needs would increase relative to the length of time you went without them. These experiences are so common to the human condition that it seems strange to spend time discussing them. After all, who doesn't know that when you are without water and become thirsty, you are driven to get a drink? We can infer these drives or motives just by watching a person's behavior. If we watch someone searching desperately for food, we immediately assume that that person is hungry; if someone is looking for water, we assume that the person is thirsty. Actually, the only way to observe motivations is by watching the behavior that stems from them. The same thing is true of learning. We assume that learning has occurred because of changes in performance. Likewise, we assume that motivation exists because of changes in behavior.

Biological motivations such as hunger and thirst are assumed to be built-in, meaning that they exist from birth. You don't have to learn to feel thirsty or hungry. If you go without food or water for a sufficient time, the motivation to obtain it occurs automatically. You then want a certain amount of food or water until the condition is alleviated, bringing you back to your original stable point. Psychologists refer to this built-in tendency as **homeostasis.** Homeostatic mechanisms are regulatory and attempt to maintain an optimal level (Cannon, 1939). Any deviation from the optimal level will create a need (Hull, 1943). The need will usually produce a drive which is the motivational force for action.

A thermostat in a home is a homeostatic mechanism, analogous to the biological ones that exist in humans. Suppose you set the thermostat at 76 degrees. If it becomes too warm the air conditioning will turn on, cooling the house; if it becomes too cold the furnace will turn on, warming the air. In both cases the temperature of the house will be returned to an optimal level.

Eating food satisfies a primary biological need. Too little food will result in starvation; too much food will eventually result in serious obesity. The homeostatic mechanism for food intake in most people is extremely sensitive, even among those who are considerably overweight or underweight. The average person doesn't keep track of the number of calories he or she takes in during the day, thinking that to become overweight requires the ingestion of large amounts of high-calorie food. It doesn't. If you ate one apple more a day than you usually eat, and all of the calories from the apple were stored, at the end of seven years you would (theoretically) be about 70 pounds overweight! The homeostatic mechanism for food intake is so sensitive that only a slight imbalance in the mechanism will cause a tremendous change in weight.

Presumably other homeostatic mechanisms exist besides those that regulate food and water intake. Our need for an optimal temperature, for example, appears to be homeostatically controlled as well. In order for such mechanisms to work, there must be sensors in the body to detect deviations from the optimal state. Researchers have attempted to uncover these detectors and to learn how changes in detection mechanisms can alter motivation.

HUNGER

How do you know when you're hungry? It seems a simple enough question, but the more you examine it the more you will see that it's really a complicated matter. Perhaps you feel the hunger in your stomach. Your stomach may growl, or it may feel as though it has shrunk. Conversely, your stomach feels full when you have had enough to eat. It may be the pressure of the food against the walls of your stomach that signals you to stop eating. This seems a reasonable assumption—until it's tested. If a hungry person swallows a small balloon attached to a tube and the balloon is inflated so that it exerts pressure, the hunger doesn't go away. An even more striking example is provided by patients who have had their stomachs removed because of cancer or other difficulties and who continue to feel hunger and satiation. So the sensor for the homeostatic mechanisms of hunger and satiation can't be located solely in the stomach. Where then might a "hunger center" be situated?

In 1954 Stellar presented a strong argument that such a center existed in the hypothalamus of the brain. His theory became known as the **hypothalamocentric hypothesis.** Excitement grew as more data began to support the idea that the hypothalamus controlled food intake, and perhaps water intake as well (Grossman, 1972; 1975).

In one study it was found that lesions or cuts in the ventromedial hypothalamus (VMH), the underside-middle of the hypothalamus, resulted in overeating and obesity (see Figure 9.2) (Brobeck, Tepperman, & Long, 1943). If the researchers stimulated the VMH instead of destroying it, the hungry animal would stop eating immediately. It was also discovered that lesions made in an adjacent area—the dorsolateral portion of the hypothalamus—produced aphagia and adipsia. *Aphagia* means that the animal will not eat at all, *adipsia* that it will not drink. Conversely, stimulating the dorsolateral portion caused the animal to start eating immediately, even though it might have been full (Anand & Brobeck, 1951).

An animal whose VMH has been cut won't continue eating until it explodes. Instead, the homeostatic mechanism is apparently reset at a

Figure 9.2   *This rat's "weight problem" was caused by lesions in the ventromedial hypothalamus.*

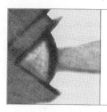

CONTROLLING OBESITY

Technically an individual is obese whose body weight is more than 20 percent above his or her ideal weight. Over the last decade researchers have found that obesity can't usually be traced to simple gluttony. Although some people gain weight because of overeating, it appears that fatness may be largely due to regulatory defects in the brain and elsewhere in the body. Yale psychologist Judith Rodin has said, ''There is not terribly good experimental evidence that obese people do eat significantly more on the average than their lean counterparts'' (Langone, 1981, p. 58).

By the late 1960s evidence was accumulating that obese individuals either did not attend properly to internal regulating mechanisms of satiation or that their internal mechanisms were defective. Stanley Schachter and his associates found that overweight subjects were more attentive to the passage of time in order to know when to eat, and that they were more excited by the taste and sight of food and the number of food cues present, than were subjects of normal weight (Nisbett, 1968; Schachter & Gross, 1968). By placing people in rooms where clocks went faster than they should, Schachter and his colleagues demonstrated that obese subjects ate more as the clock neared ''lunchtime'' than did subjects of normal weight. These studies suggested that people of normal weight attended more to internal cues to tell them when they were hungry.

For several years this internal-external dichotomy was viewed as the cornerstone of psychological research on obesity. But recently this dichotomy has been found to be overly simplistic (Rodin, 1981). It has been shown that many individuals of normal weight are externally cued and will eat more if placed in an environment with a great amount of food (Rodin & Slochower, 1976). Other evidence has found that these people are poor at regulating their intake if they must rely on internal signals alone (Jordan, 1975; Spiegel, 1973; Wooley, 1972). As one researcher has said, ''Attempts to provide simplistic explanations of obesity or descriptions of the characteristics of all obese people may often be misleading. Unfortunately, this is the state of affairs in current applications of the 'internal-external' hypothesis for obesity'' (Rodin, 1981, p. 362).

While it is not clear that the obese are controlled by different stimuli than other individuals, there are many biochemical reasons why some people may be overweight. The number of fat cells (cells able to store fat) is determined in part by inheritance and the amount of feeding that an individual receives during infancy. After infancy the number of fat cells a person has stays about the same (Faust, Johnson, & Hirsch, 1977). Overfeeding during infancy may lead to obesity later on. Obese children are three times more likely than slim ones to become obese adults.

Some obese people may actually burn as little as 80 percent of the cal-

higher optimal point. The animal will eat and gain weight until it reaches a certain level beyond its previous capacity, and then it will maintain its weight at that new point. Animals with aphagia reduced their food intake to a lower set point. Sometimes, however, that set point was so low that the animal would starve to death if not force-fed.

Further evidence that the hypothalamus was involved in food regulation was gathered by taking liquid and tissue from the hypothalamus of a food-deprived monkey and placing it in the hypothalamus of a satiated monkey. This substance caused the full monkey to become hungry immediately (Yaksh & Myers, 1972).

The idea that the hypothalamus contained centers that activated or inhibited hunger and thirst was very popular during the last decade. But there were some voices of dissent. For instance, one researcher found that lesions in *other* areas of the brain could also drastically affect eating and drinking (Morgane, as cited by deCharms & Muir, 1978). Physiologist

ories that a normal person would. This slower rate may be due to the lower number of chemical sodium-potassium pumps that many overweight people have. As you may recall from Chapter 2, the number of sodium-potassium pumps is directly related to metabolic rate. The pumps require energy; the more pumps a person has, the more calories per day will be burned. According to Dr. William James, a clinical nutritionist at Cambridge University in England, "It is not so much that these obese get fat because they eat too much, but because they eat a normal amount" (Langone, 1981, p. 58). In other words, they may eat normally, but they burn less of what they eat.

A cooler body temperature may also aggravate obesity. One good source of heat is brown fat, so-called because of its brown color. This kind of fat accumulates in small clumps around various internal organs. In mice, brown fat functions like a mini-furnace, keeping temperature high and burning excess calories. It may function the same way in humans. There is some evidence that thin people have more brown fat than obese people. The extra brown fat may keep a thin person's temperature slightly

higher, which in turn would increase the metabolic rate and help to burn calories. A cooler body may also mean a cooler hypothalamus, and cooling the hypothalamus stimulates appetite. Mice that have low levels of brown fat and correspondingly cooler bodies tend to become more obese.

Studies have been conducted of the way in which the body uses energy and the relationship between obesity and energy. Flier and his colleagues at Beth-Israel Hospital in Boston have found that obese people continue to burn calories at a slower rate even after they become thin. This finding implies that the lower metabolic rate is not a function of being fat but that it preceded the obesity. As Flier has said, "For the first time, we have evidence that obese people have a biochemical defect not caused by overeating or excess weight" (Langone, 1981, p. 60).

On the other hand, having less brown fat, a lower metabolic rate, and a tendency to store fat can be an advantage in times of famine. There is evidence that obesity-prone individuals may have inherited these predispositions. Among the Pima Indians in Arizona, a farming tribe for the last 2,000 years, the vast majority are

extremely obese. By the time they are 35, about half have diabetes. They seem to be able to store calories easily, and they have reduced sodium-potassium pump activity. It appears that through natural selection the Pimas' bodies are prepared for a famine. However, in the food-rich United States bodily preparation for a famine may not be an advantage.

Perhaps someday a "thin pill" will be developed that can boost the rate of sodium-potassium pump activity and thereby step up metabolism. Or a way may be found to trigger appetite-reducing mechanisms. The latter possibility has been investigated with a hormone called cholecystokinin (CCK). Secreted by the gastrointestinal tract, CCK apparently signals the brain to stop eating (Straus & Yalow, 1979). Researchers have found consistently that genetically obese mice have only about one fourth as much CCK in their brains as normal mice. These animals may therefore be overeating because their satiation signal is too weak. Perhaps someday CCK will be available in pill form to help the brain recognize when the stomach is full.

Elliot Valenstein and others have argued that the hypothalamus is not directly involved in eating or drinking but is simply an "activating center." Valenstein argues that most of the experimental subjects became active or inactive when the hypothalamus was stimulated, rather than hungry or thirsty. Since these subjects were primarily animals in cages that contained nothing but a food dish and a water spigot, the behavior they chose to engage in when they became active was eating or drinking. Conversely, when they were inactive, they didn't eat or drink (Valenstein, 1976; Antelman, Rowland, & Fisher, 1976).

Other criticisms followed as different researchers began to discover that organs far from the brain directly affected hunger. For example, signals from the duodenum below the stomach appear to influence food intake. Injections of glucose (sugar) into the duodenum will suppress food intake in rabbits (Novin, 1976).

The liver, too, appears to give signals of both hunger and satiation

OSMOSIS

The diffusion of fluid through a semi-permeable membrane, such as that surrounding a living cell, until the concentration of fluid on either side of the membrane is equal.

(Novin, 1976; Vanderweele & Sanderson, 1976). The liver may contain receptors for glucose that transmit information along the vagus nerve to the hypothalamus (Schmitt, 1973). Furthermore, the rate of metabolism in the liver is an extremely good predictor of how hungry an individual will be (Friedman, & Stricker, 1976). (The metabolic rate determines how quickly food or other biological matter will be broken down.) Maybe next time you tell someone you're hungry, instead of saying that your stomach feels empty you ought to say that your liver is too active!

The researchers who support the hypothalamocentric theory have not given up, however. Evidence gathered recently has indicated that the hypothalamus is not simply a center for activation, as Valenstein had suggested. Rather, it does appear to have hunger and thirst monitoring and sensing areas (Olds & Fobes, 1981). These areas seem to work in conjunction with other sensing and regulating mechanisms located elsewhere in the brain and in peripheral organs such as the stomach, the duodenum, the intestine, and the liver. One of the most difficult and challenging aspects of this kind of research is tracing the neural signals from sensor to sensor. The routes signals travel and how they are interpreted in the brain is not yet clear. Hunger is a highly complex and sophisticated system that we may have to study intensively for many more years before we fully understand it.

THIRST

Thirst, like hunger, seems to be controlled by a homeostatic mechanism. Again we might ask, How do we know when we're thirsty? A common answer is that the mouth becomes dry, but as you may have guessed, a dry mouth alone cannot account for the motivation to drink water (Fitzsimons, 1973).

The desire to drink appears to be controlled by the way in which water is distributed throughout the body, and at least two separate mechanisms appear to control the body's water balance. To begin with, the body's water is not distributed evenly. About two thirds of it is contained in the cells. About one fourth is found in the spaces between cells, and roughly one twelfth is contained in the blood. The two mechanisms that appear to be involved in thirst regulation are called intracellular and extracellular mechanisms. Intracellular mechanisms are based on sensor recordings of the amount of water within cells, while extracellular mechanisms are based on sensor recordings of the amount of fluid surrounding cells.

Several things can change intracellular and extracellular fluid levels. The two needn't be affected simultaneously. Extracellular fluid, for instance, can be directly affected by loss of blood or by diarrhea, while intracellular fluid may not be influenced by these changes at all. Cholera, which killed thousands of people in the United States until it was controlled, was accompanied by incessant diarrhea which caused a massive loss of fluid that could not be replaced quickly enough. In this sense many cholera victims died from thirst or dehydration. Blood loss also results in rapid dehydration. In battle, wounded soldiers sometimes cry out for water because of the loss of extracellular fluid.

There is neurological evidence for the existence of these two separate thirst-sensing systems. Rats in which the frontal area of the brain has been damaged will drink only when the extracellular fluid level is reduced, not when the intracellular fluid level becomes lower. This result suggests

that different control mechanisms are monitoring the water levels inside and outside the cells.

The need for water and the drive to drink are common to all animal species.

One way in which the fluid balance might be detected by the brain is through receptors that are sensitive to concentrations of sodium. Sodium does not pass into cells, but rather draws water from cells by a process known as **osmosis.** Certain brain cells, then, might be able to regulate the body's water balance by being sensitive to the amount of water being drawn from them by sodium. These receptors could then signal thirst when the volume of water within their cell walls decreased. In fact, salt solutions injected directly into the lateral hypothalamus have been found to produce drinking (Andersson, 1971). Apparently, the injections tricked the osmotic receptors at that location into believing that the cells throughout the body lacked water when in fact only those in the area of the hypothalamus were dehydrated.

Hormones produced by the pituitary gland, the liver, and the kidneys can affect the amount of water eliminated by the kidneys (Carlson, 1977). Clearly, thirst, like hunger, is controlled by the brain, hormones, and the peripheral action of organs far from the brain. Like hunger, it is complex and not fully understood.

SEX DRIVES

For a vast majority of people, sex feels good. We are biologically organized to feel this way. In fact, all species seem to like sex, and for a good reason. Can you imagine an entire species that disliked sex? It wouldn't last long; it would be gone in one generation. Nature has in this way favored animals that enjoy sex. It would seem reasonable, then, to assume that there might be a biological drive or need for sex. But unlike food and water, sex is not necessary to keep an individual alive, only to maintain the species. For this reason a drive to engage in sexual activity may not be as obvious in an individual as the drive to satisfy hunger or thirst.

Research over the last 20 years has indicated that the more physio-logically advanced the species, the less its sexual behavior appears to be governed directly by chemical and hormonal forces. But even in humans these forces may play a role. (Hormones and human sexual behavior will be discussed more fully in Chapter 18.)

The hypothalamus appears to be involved in regulating the sex drive. It has detectors that are sensitive to different levels of hormones, and these detectors also seem able to regulate hormonal output by stimulating the pituitary. How these regulatory mechanisms work and exactly how hor-mones affect sexual behavior is not clearly understood, however. For example, does an excess of the male sex hormone **testosterone** cause the sex drive to increase? S. Mitchell Harman and colleagues at the Gerontology Research Center in Baltimore have addressed this question. They found that the answer was "maybe yes, maybe no"—hardly a conclusive finding. Harman and his coworkers noted that sexual activity in healthy men tends to decrease considerably with age. However, testosterone levels do not decrease as men grow older, indicating that a declining sex drive cannot be the result of decreased levels of male hormone.

On the other hand, Harman and his coworkers discovered that among men 70 years of age or older who were sexually active, the levels of testos-terone were higher. This finding implies that sexual activity and testosterone may be linked after all. It may be that increased sexual activity can increase testosterone production, or an excess of testosterone may in some way be able to stop a sex drive from decreasing. No one is sure (Tsitoura, Martin, Harman, & Gregerman, 1979).

In lower species the data are not so inconclusive. Male dogs injected with high levels of testosterone will become more sexually active. Female dogs, too, will begin to engage in "male" sexual behaviors when injected with high levels of testosterone. As documented by researcher Frank Beach, they will mount and attempt sexual intercourse with other female dogs. Injecting human females with testosterone may cause some physiological changes, such as the development of facial hair and a shrinking of the breasts, but it will not alter sexual preference.

In lower mammals, mating occurs only during ovulation, and females typically must be receptive before they will engage in sexual intercourse with males. During these receptive periods the female often secretes a pheromone (see Chapter 3), whose smell can be picked up by males some distance away. The scent of this pheromone stimulates the males to engage in sexual behavior. As any owner of a female dog in heat can testify, every male dog in the neighborhood shows up at the front door wanting a place on her dance card.

Among primates (which includes human beings, of course) it appears that sexual receptivity in the female is not rigidly tied to a state of being in heat. Nonetheless, evidence gathered during the last several years indi-cates that primates may prefer sex during a particular time, especially when the female is ovulating, and may engage in sex partly in response to hormones secreted by the female. Researchers Richard P. Michael and R. W. Bonsall of Emory University School of Medicine, studying rhesus monkeys, have reported a preference for sex during the ovulation period of the female monkey's menstrual cycle (Michael & Bonsall, 1977). The male rhesus monkey is twice the size of the female and usually threatens assault unless the female capitulates. This makes it very difficult to tell when the female wants sexual intercourse. In their studies, Michael and Bonsall developed a unique way of testing the female monkey's desire. They used a cage divided by a door, placing the male on one side and the female on the other. The only way to open the door was by a handle on the female's side. When the male monkey was on the female's side of the partition, therefore, the experimenters could assume that the female was receptive.

As it turned out, the female rhesus let the male in primarily when she was ovulating. Blood samples taken from the female showed that her desire for sexual relations was very closely tied to the level of sex hormones in her body. An important question not answered by this research is how the female's desire for sexual intercourse stimulates the male to want to engage in sex, too. Michael and Bonsall have isolated vaginal substances from rhesus females that appear to have the properties of pheromones. These substances, which are secreted at the time of ovulation, may help stimulate the male to engage in sex. From an evolutionary standpoint, such an effect would make sense, since it would be most valuable to engage in sexual intercourse when the female was most likely to become pregnant.

You may be wondering whether these findings apply to humans. Human females appear to be receptive depending on social circumstances rather than biological triggers, and it is generally assumed that mating is likely to occur at any time during the female's menstrual cycle. But there is some evidence that women's sexual drives do fluctuate throughout their menstrual cycle. Is it possible that women secrete sexual attractants at the time of ovulation that might help to attract men? Although pheromones have not been conclusively identified in humans, in 1975 Michael and his colleagues found vaginal secretions in women that were identical to the sex attractants found in monkeys. They discovered that more of these particular acids are present at the time of ovulation than at other points during the menstrual cycle. Then, in another study, conducted by Richard L. Doty and his colleagues at the University of Pennsylvania, men were found to consider women's vaginal odors more agreeable and more intense just before and just after ovulation than at any other time during the menstrual cycle (Doty, Ford, Preti, & Huggins, 1975). These results indicate that there may be biological forces at work that fluctuate during a woman's monthly cycle and that not only influence her desire for sexual intercourse, but also encourage potential partners who are within scent range of her.

There may also be times when the desire to engage in sexual intercourse noticeably diminishes. Healthy, active human partners sometimes become sexually bored with one another. Richard Michael and his colleague Doris Zumpe have noticed similar reactions among rhesus monkeys. Adult male monkeys, after being with particular females for a significant time, appear to become bored with them. In Michael and Zumpe's studies, four adult male monkeys were paired for 2½ years with four females. After two years the males' sexual interest had decreased by two thirds, and they avoided sex twice as often. When four new females were introduced into the cages, the males' interest and intercourse rates immediately doubled, and the attempts to avoid sex were cut in half. Some time later the original four females were returned to the cages, and the males immediately showed a loss of interest. This result implies that the attraction between the sexes is not so much dependent on hormones or other biological influences but, as the researchers have said, "on the nature of the bond between partners." Of course, research in this area is incomplete since the female monkeys' responses have not been studied.

Michael and Zumpe have noted that the same kinds of behavior are

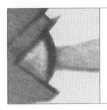

THE SOCIOBIOLOGICAL VIEW OF MOTIVATION

The ideas of **sociobiology** are disturbing and, to some, even shocking. Sociobiologists believe that children are born deceitful, that conflicts between parents and children are inevitable because of biology, and that all human acts, even the most altruistic, are ultimately selfish ways of passing on and maintaining one's genes. Morality, love, kindness, aggression, anger, and hatred—sociobiologists believe that all of these traits are rooted deeply in our genetic structure. During millions of years of evolution, they argue, we have been shaped by natural selection so that the behaviors that would help us pass on our genes are the behaviors that are most likely to occur. In this sense all life forms exist solely to serve **DNA**, the coded master molecule of life contained in the genes. British ethologist Richard Dawkins suggests in his book *The Selfish Gene* that you

consider yourself to be a throwaway container for your immortal genes, and that your genes should be thought of as a "swarm in huge colonies, safe inside gigantic lumbering robots, sealed off from the outside world, manipulating it by remote control. They are in you and me; they created us body and mind; and their preservation is the ultimate rationale for our existence . . . we are their survival machines" (Galvan, Leo, & McIntosh, 1977, p. 54).

The concept of sociobiology was developed by Harvard zoologist Edward Wilson. In 1975 he published a book entitled *Sociobiology: A New Synthesis,* in which he argued that sociobiology was the completion of a Darwinian revolution, that organisms were constantly in the process of being perfected as they competed to survive and pass on their genes, and

that this process could explain all human motivation and behavior.

To sociobiologists altruism is a selfish genetic act. They believe that a person is more willing to help relatives because relatives share many of his or her genes, and cooperation between individuals with the same genes increases the chance that some of these genes will survive. Twenty-five years ago, British biologist J. B. S. Haldane anticipated this view when he jokingly announced that he would lay down his life for two brothers or eight cousins. His reasoning was that each brother would have half of his genes, and each cousin about one eighth of his genes, which made the decision acceptable in terms of genetic survivability.

Sociobiologists argue that parents have a genetic investment in their children and will make sacrifices for them

---

DNA
Deoxyribonucleic acid. A chemical constituent of cell nuclei, consisting of two long chains of alternating phosphate and deoxyribose units twisted into a double helix and joined by bonds between the complementary bases of adenine, thymine, cytosine, and guanine. It is the substance that enables cells to copy themselves.

SOCIOBIOLOGY
A theory of motivation and behavior put forth by zoologist Edward Wilson in 1975 and stating that all human behavior is a function of an inherited biological drive to pass on one's genes. In this sense, morality, love, kindness, aggression, anger, hatred, and all other aspects of human behavior are understood in terms of their functional value for ensuring the survival of one's genes.

reported by human subjects. In drawing conclusions about humans from monkey data, Michael says that they "are frightfully, frightfully careful—we're tiptoeing on a tightrope" ("A Monkey Blueprint," 1978, p. 294). That new partners tend to renew a person's sexual interest may, in the researchers' view, have something to do with a tendency to break and remake sexual bonds. The researchers argue that maintaining sexual interest in a monogamous society may necessitate wearing alluring colognes, clothing, and hairstyles, and, particularly, refraining from sexual intercourse at times (Michael & Zumpe, 1978).

Sociobiologists, who believe that all human behavior is motivated by the underlying need to pass on genes to the next generation, find it logical that males, including human males, would become tired of their sex partner. For sociobiologists, all human motivation is a biological drive. They point out that males can fertilize many females in a lifetime; the most effective way for males to pass on their genes, therefore, is to have many partners. Females, on the other hand, can pass on their genes no more than once every nine months by becoming pregnant and giving birth. For this reason sociobiologists believe that both human and nonhuman males are driven to find as many partners as possible, and they believe, using the

in order to protect this investment. Children, on the other hand, have no such genetic investment in their parents. In this sense, it is argued, children are born selfish. Sociobiologists feel that this difference is behind the frequent conflict between parents and children. Children are selfish, and parents don't understand why.

Many people find these ideas disturbing. A young man who received the Carnegie Gold Medal for saving a drowning person wrote to Edward Wilson about how much the theory had upset him. Wilson recalled that the young man "found it difficult to grasp the notion that somehow his act was preordained through genes. I convinced him that the impulse and emotion behind his rational choice, though genetically determined, in no way detracted from the rationality and value of his altruistic act" (Galvan, Leo, & McIntosh, 1977, p. 56).

Sociobiology seems to have an explanation for virtually every human motive, and some of its explanations do seem depressing. Mother love is considered to be an investment policy for genetics. Friendship, helping, and laws are rooted in a reciprocal kind of altruism, a mathematics of self-interest. Ethnic pride might be viewed as a genetic distrust of strangers and a preference for individuals who look like us and are more likely to have similar genes. And teaching in school might be considered a forced indoctrination in reciprocal altruism.

Wilson, a specialist in entomology (the study of insects), may have been influenced by the behavior of ants, which do appear to function according to a grand sociobiological plan. Chemical and hormonal influences trigger behavior after behavior. Their sole motivation appears to be the survival of their genes. But is the same true of human beings?

Sociobiology has probably drawn more criticism and rebuttal than any other motivational viewpoint. Addressing an audience at the Massachusetts Institute of Technology, anthropologist Marvin Harris stated, "Sociobiologists tend to drastically underestimate the result to which human cultures represent an emergent novelty" (Galvan, Leo, & McIntosh, 1977, p. 56). Harris was arguing that sociobiology overlooks learning and culture and the effects that each may have.

To reject sociobiology is not to reject the work of Charles Darwin and the concept of natural selection. The opponents of sociobiology believe that the genes human beings have inherited have even more remarkable properties than the sociobiologists believe. Our inheritance, these critics argue, is not a series of tightly controlled behavioral exchanges aimed at passing on our own genes, but rather a tremendous flexibility—the ability to learn and develop a culture—which allows us generation after generation to adapt to changes, even radical ones, in the environment. If this view is correct, then our genes have evolved a "hands-off" approach to our behavior, and we have developed a psychology according to our learning and experience, relatively independent of our genetic heritage. This way we may have been even better equipped to survive and pass on our genes.

---

same logic, that females are driven to find one partner only, become pregnant, and then make a nest. This view of female sexuality is not supported by hard evidence, however. As with the rhesus monkey studies, it doesn't examine female preferences and lifestyles, which are obviously not limited to this aspiration and which are just as obviously changing as new social attitudes emerge. Many psychologists argue that the desire for more than one sexual partner, whether experienced by a male or a female, is culturally determined and that the sociobiological view only serves to give unwarranted authority to a double standard that should not be maintained.

Stimulus Motives

The biological or physiological drives such as hunger or thirst are not the only ones that do not need to be learned. In addition, both human beings and animals seem to require a certain amount of stimulation. The need to obtain sensory stimulation, to be active, and to explore and manipulate the environment produce motivations that are referred to collectively as **stimulus motives.**

STIMULUS MOTIVES
Drives or motives that appear to satisfy a need for certain amounts of sensory stimulation.

SENSORY ISOLATION
Lack of stimulus input needed for maintaining homeostasis. Prolonged reduction of external stimulation, either in intensity or variety, produces boredom, restlessness, and disturbances of thought processes. *Also called* SENSORY DEPRIVATION.

SENSORY DEPRIVATION
See SENSORY ISOLATION.

SOCIAL MOTIVATION
Learned motivational states that result from the individual's interaction with his or her social environment or culture.

HIERARCHY OF MOTIVES
A theory of motivation developed by Abraham Maslow in which more basic needs must be met first before needs of a higher order can come into play.

The motivation to experience a certain amount of stimulation appears to have evolved because of its survival value. By manipulating and exploring the environment and by actively sensing it, you, and every other organism, learn about it and learn what to expect from it. If you own pets and have ever moved to a new home, you will have observed the need to explore expressed, not just in yourself, but in your pets as well. Animals in a new environment are motivated to explore that new environment, to learn every aspect of it, to investigate its perimeters and, in general, to know which parts of the environment are safe and which are dangerous. Stimulus motives derive from the idea that it's better to know what you're dealing with than to be surprised.

The need for stimulation is apparent among subjects who have been placed in **sensory isolation** or, as it is sometimes called, **sensory deprivation.** The subjects in such experiments are put in a room in which there is no sound or light, bound so that their limbs are unable to feel very much, and generally isolated from all surrounding sensations (see Figure 9.3). People kept in these conditions for any length of time begin to hallucinate and create their own sensations, as if searching for what they have been deprived of—a certain amount of stimulation. Similarly, people in highly stimulating situations often seek quiet and solitude, as though they have had too much stimulation. Perhaps there is an optimal level of arousal somewhere between too little and too much. In fact, human beings and lower animals do appear to have an optimal level of stimulation at which they are most efficient (Yerkes & Dodson, 1908). If you're not sufficiently aroused your performance is likely to be poor. As you know, you're not at your best if you're exhausted when you have to take a complex test. But too much arousal can have the same effect: It's difficult to be efficient when in a state of terror. Yerkes and Dodson stated that organisms are most efficient at a medium level of arousal. Nonetheless, the best level of arousal depends on the difficulty of the task.

Figure 9.3 *A subject is made ready for a sensory-isolation chamber.*

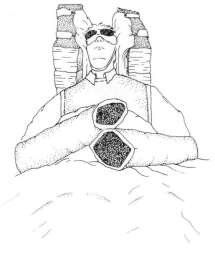

Learned Motivation

Certain motivations can be learned. No one is born desiring a Chevrolet Corvette. Learned motives can be powerful forces. They are often related to incentives, that is, particular things that we want to possess. When these incentives are present, the motivation to acquire them becomes much stronger, especially if we know what we must do in order to obtain them.

Learned motivations can imitate biological ones. For example, it's possible to learn to become hungry. One way to bring this about is through classical conditioning (see Chapter 6). Consider what happens when you eat sugar. The sugar (an unconditioned stimulus) triggers the pancreas to secrete insulin (an unconditioned response), and the insulin metabolizes the sugar. Before swallowing the sugar, however, you probably looked at the sweet food, tasted it, and noted its texture, all of which can become conditioned stimuli. If the relationship between these stimuli and the ingestion of sugar is strongly enough established, you can teach your pancreas to secrete insulin. All you need do is see or think about food (a conditioned stimulus), and the pancreas will sometimes secrete insulin (a conditioned response), although no sugar has been swallowed (see Figure 9.4). When insulin is secreted without sugar intake, blood sugar may drop, or oxidative metabolism change, which in turn can lead directly to an increase in hunger. In this way you can learn to create a genuine biological drive to eat, even when the need may not be present (Booth, 1977).

Drinking can also be affected by learning. We frequently take a drink for social reasons or other learned reasons, without really requiring the liquid. The interplay between learned motives and biological drives can be so complex that it's almost impossible to isolate the one from the other (Rodin, 1981). Some researchers have argued that, of the two kinds of motivation, learned motives are more responsible for the complex aspects of human behavior.

MASLOW'S HIERARCHY OF MOTIVES

No one (with the possible exception of sociobiologists) expects to find a homeostatic mechanism that controls a desire for power by means of "power regulatory senses" located throughout the brain and body. Instead, psychologists study the way in which people learn to want particular things. The term **social motivation** is often used to refer to motives acquired through learning and culture. Theories of social motivation attempt to account for all kinds of impulses or deliberate actions that are not the direct result of biological drives (deCharms & Muir, 1978).

In the past, "grand theories" of social motivation were popular—grand in that they attempted to explain most of human motivation. One of the most interesting and frequently cited of these theories was the **hierarchy of motives** postulated by the humanist psychologist Abraham Maslow as part of his research on self-actualization (see Chapters 1 and 13). By a hierarchy of motives, Maslow meant that some needs were more powerful than others, depending on an individual's particular circumstance. The hierarchy is shown in Figure 9.5. As you can see, physiological needs form its base. In other words, to a starving person the motivation to find food is more powerful and basic than a motivation to find love, a sense of belonging, or self-esteem. A starving person will even be motivated to find food before safety.

Maslow argued that the higher motivations can come into play only when the basic needs have been satisfied. Before a person can be free to engage in self-actualization, that is, free to continue fulfilling his or her potential, it is necessary to meet the physiological needs of safety and security, to find love and belonging, and to have self-esteem and the esteem of others. Accordingly, Maslow placed self-actualization at the top of the hierarchy. But the motivation to realize one's full potential is a fragile thing, easily interfered with by disturbances at the lower levels.

You can easily see how this hierarchy could explain many of your own motives. Imagine that you arrived in a strange town hungry and broke. According to Maslow, you would be motivated first of all to ensure a supply of food and water in order to satisfy your physiological needs. Then perhaps a job in order to obtain money for shelter and security. Only after you had a secure base of operations would you begin to make inroads in the community in order to develop a sense of belonging, perhaps by forming relationships. Once you felt that you belonged and that you shared love with others, a sense of self-esteem could develop as your loved ones and friends held you in esteem. At that point, as a fulfilled member of a community, you might begin to develop your full self-potential.

Maslow's motivational theory has not always been supported by re-

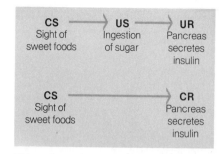

Figure 9.4 *Classical conditioning of the pancreas. After sufficient pairing between the sight of sweet foods and the ingestion of sugar, the sight of the foods alone can result in the secretion of insulin.*

Figure 9.5 *Maslow's hierarchy of motives.*

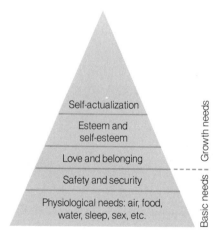

search, and many questions can be raised about it. For instance, how would you explain someone who threw himself or herself on a hand grenade in order to protect friends, or someone like Gandhi who fasted in order to attain greater self-awareness? Maslow's theory, like most grand theories of social motivation, often fails to predict the complex patterns of human behavior and motivation in unusual circumstances. Consequently, modern motivational theory has generally limited itself to highly detailed investigations of many separate areas, rather than attempting to develop one grand theory.

Some fascinating specific areas of research are developing. We'll examine a few of them here.

LEARNED HELPLESSNESS

Some people aren't motivated to help themselves when they could easily do so. When abused they may fail to protect themselves. This behavior is known as **learned helplessness.**

It's possible to teach an animal to become helpless. Rats trained to avoid a shock by jumping from one side of a box to another will soon give up jumping when the shock is applied to both sides of the box. And no wonder—there is no escape once both sides are electrified. The more interesting outcome is that the rats rarely ever try again to avoid the shock. The electric current on the far side of the box may be turned off, but the rats will simply stay where they are, suffering the shock when it comes. They never discover that the other side is now safe because they no longer try the other side. They have given up. The rats will also generalize this learned helplessness to new situations. When placed in water-filled mazes, they will stop swimming and will drown if not rescued. Rats who have not learned to be helpless will complete the swim to safety (Altenor, Kay, & Richter, 1977).

Learned helplessness has also been observed in human infants. Two researchers (Watson & Ramey, 1969; 1972) placed rotating mobiles above the heads of three groups of infants. A pressure-sensitive pillow was placed beneath the heads of the infants in the first group. By moving their heads, these infants could open and close circuits that made their mobiles turn. These infants had control over this aspect of their environment. The infants in the second group were given no control; their pillows were not connected to the mobiles. As a result, their mobiles remained stationary. The third group of infants was also given no control, but in this case, the mobiles turned randomly. (The purpose of the third variation was to ensure that the infants who learned to move their heads against their pillow were doing so because they had *control* over their environment, not simply because they were watching a turning object.) After being exposed to the mobiles for 10 minutes a day for a period of 14 weeks, the infants in the first group learned to turn their heads to make the mobiles move. This is what you might expect an infant to be able to do through simple learning. But there's more.

The most interesting aspect of these experiments was how *lack of control* affected the later behavior of the second and third group of infants. Once again researchers presented the second and third group of infants with the mobiles, but this time both groups were given control over the mobiles' movements. Even after extensive training, these infants failed to learn to operate the mobiles. Like the rats who gave up trying to escape because their earlier attempts had failed, the second and third group of infants had learned to be helpless; they had learned not to expect their behavior to have any effect on their mobiles. As a result, they never seemed to appreciate the link between their head movements and the mobiles' turning that the first group of infants had been able to make. And, as with the rats transferred to the water maze, such learned helplessness in infants can also transfer to new situations (Finkelstein & Ramey, 1977).

Not surprisingly, individuals in institutions and other situations in which they are given little opportunity to manipulate their environment, and in which things are always being done to them or for them, may quickly learn not to try. The U.S. Office of Education has reported (Coleman, Campbell, Hobson, McPartland, Mood, Weinfeld, & York, 1966) that members of minority groups who believed they were controlled by their environment rather than the other way around were more likely to fail in school. It's ironic that certain life experiences may be helping children learn not to learn.

Motivational researchers use the term **locus of control** to describe the measure of control people believe they have over their environment. If you think that the locus of control resides in the environment rather than in yourself, then this perceived lack of control may lead you to feel helpless even in situations in which you are not (Seligman, 1975). By the same token, if you feel that you can't achieve goals, then you're likely to become less and less motivated to take action, and failure in one area may easily generalize to helplessness in another (Hiroto & Seligman, 1975).

In one study (Dweck & Reppucci, 1973), a fifth-grade teacher gave a solvable problem to some students and an unsolvable problem to others. When children who had worked on the unsolvable problem were presented with a solvable one, many were not able to find the solution even though their peers who had started with a solvable problem were able to do so. This may indicate that people who are motivated to succeed have learned that they can be successful, while people who fail have learned to expect failure.

Learned helplessness doesn't usually occur all at once. Most people, perceiving that they are losing control over their environment, will attempt to regain control (Wortman & Brehm, 1975). Their immediate reaction to lack of success will be to find out what's wrong and look for ways in which to improve their performance. This tendency is known as **psychological reticence** (Roth & Bootzin, 1974). It's only after consecutive failures that learned helplessness begins to set in.

Many psychologists have been concerned with helping those who have learned to be helpless. Dweck and others have succeeded in altering this attitude in children by teaching them to attribute their failure to a lack of effort on their own part and to nothing else. This shift in the perceived locus of control, from the environment to the individual, was accomplished by a slow shaping process. In the end, the children learned that their efforts could be successful. Some researchers have called this result **learned industriousness** (Eisenberger, Park, & Frank, 1976).

THE POWER MOTIVE

During the last decade two motivational researchers, David McClelland and David Winter, have studied power as a motivation. The research began in the mid-1960s when McClelland was investigating the effects of alcohol on

LEARNED HELPLESSNESS
Giving up even though success is possible because of previous experience with situations in which success was impossible.

LOCUS OF CONTROL
Beliefs or expectations about whether desired outcomes are contingent on one's own behavior (internal locus of control) or on environmental forces (external locus of control).

PSYCHOLOGICAL RETICENCE
A common reaction to initial failure. An individual will try to discover what is wrong and look for ways in which to improve performance. After continued failure, psychological reticence may break down, and learned helplessness may begin.

LEARNED INDUSTRIOUSNESS
A technique for overcoming learned helplessness in which one is taught to take responsibility for one's own failures and in which one is exposed to success through a slow shaping process.

NEED FOR ACHIEVEMENT
A learned motivation, abbreviated
n-Ach, described by researcher David
McClelland. Those who score high in
n-Ach often behave in different ways
from those who score low in n-Ach.

ACHIEVING SOCIETY THEORY
David McClelland's theory that nations
whose members show the lowest need
for achievement also tend to have the
lowest gross national product, while
nations whose members show the highest need for achievement have the
highest gross national product.

INTRINSIC MOTIVATION
A drive to engage in a behavior for its
own sake in the absence of any obvious
external reward or reinforcer.

the production of fantasies. He found that as people drank more, they imagined and articulated more power images (McClelland, Davis, Kalin, & Wanner, 1972). McClelland wondered whether one of the reinforcing aspects of alcohol was that it helped individuals feel more powerful and achieve the power they wanted. Power in this sense is broadly defined. It is more than success, it is a need to have an impact on others, to control and influence other people. In a study of male college students, David Winter found that those who scored highest on power motivation (by producing the most power images and statements when they told a story) were the ones who most often tried to attain high status, owned prestigious objects, and engaged in sex strictly to exploit it. Winter said that the subjects in this group fit the Don Juan stereotype—the macho male who likes sports, gambling, fast cars, and women (Winter, as cited by deCharms & Muir, 1978). Winter also noticed that some individuals who had a great need for power showed a fear of using power.

McClelland, in working with other motivational measurements, concluded that there were three distinctly different kinds of individuals who had high power motivation. The first desired power but also had a need to affiliate with others. McClelland referred to this mode as the "personal enclave pattern." The second group wanted power but had a low need to affiliate with others and was fearful of using power. McClelland called this the "imperial motivation group." The third group had a great desire for power, a low need to be with others, and very little inhibition about using power—the "conquistador pattern," in McClelland's words. McClelland has discussed these people's abilities as leaders and empire builders (deCharms & Muir, 1978).

THE NEED TO ACHIEVE

Over 20 years ago David McClelland described the **need for achievement,** abbreviated as n-Ach, as a motivating force (see Figure 9.6), and used it to make predictions about motivation. By showing different photographs or drawings to subjects, McClelland was able to isolate themes that demonstrated a high need to achieve and to use these findings to make predictions. For instance, people with a high need to achieve tended to do better in school than those with a low need. McClelland attempted to generalize his findings to whole cultures and nations. He argued in a paper in 1961 that in nations in which the citizens scored low in n-Ach on his tests, the economic standards and gross national product were lower than in nations in which the citizens scored high in n-Ach. This assertion came to be known as McClelland's **achieving society theory.** However, as so often happens with motivational theories that attempt a grand scope, data gathered since 1961 have not supported McClelland's speculations (Mazur & Rosa, 1977).

INTRINSIC MOTIVATION

Many people share with each other, but sharing may not be altruistic. Altruism takes into consideration the motive behind the act. An altruistic act is not motivated by self-interest. Sometimes people share altruistically; at other times they share for reasons of self-interest (for example, to avoid punitive action or to obtain a future good). The motive of self-interest can be used to structure people's environment in a way that will ensure sharing

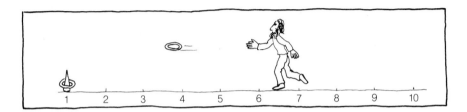

Figure 9.6 *McClelland used this ring-toss game to illustrate the way in which people are motivated to obtain an optimal level of achievement satisfaction. Most subjects preferred to stand at distance markers 6 or 7 when throwing the ring because doing so provided the greatest sense of achievement. At marker 1 it's easy to get a ringer on, but achievement satisfaction is minimized because it's too easy. At marker 10 it's too hard to succeed, and achievement satisfaction is also lowered.*

or fairness. Consider the mother whose two children constantly argued about who would get the larger "half" of the Twinkie or the larger "half" of the doughnut. Her solution was to alter the environment so that the children would share equally. She instructed the first child to divide the food in half, but allowed the second child to get first choice of a piece. From that day on, food was always divided right down the middle—unless the children were alone, in which case the older child got the whole Twinkie, unless the younger child threatened to tell. As you can see, this is not altruism. Still, many children will share when no adult is around to make them do so, just as adults, too, will sometimes share when there is nothing obvious compelling them to do so.

Psychologists are interested in altruistic behaviors because they appear to be controlled by internalized systems of self-reward and morality. Such **intrinsic motivation** has been found in many cases to be superior to extrinsic (external) motivation in creating and maintaining behavior. In one experiment an attempt was made to teach fifth graders not to litter and to clean up after others. The children were divided into two groups. The children in the first group were told each day for eight days that they should be neat and tidy, and the reasons this behavior would be good for them were explained. The children in the second group were told, for the same number of days, that they *were* neat and tidy. Littering and cleanliness were measured on the tenth and fourteenth days. The differences were considerable. The children in the first group, who were motivated extrinsically, were far less likely to have helped clean up than were the children in the second group, who had begun to think of themselves as neat and tidy and who wanted to maintain this positive attitude (intrinsic motivation) (Miller, Brickman, & Bolen, 1975).

As you recall from the Prologue to the chapter, Harlow's rhesus monkeys enjoyed working with puzzles. They found them intrinsically interesting. Their motivation changed, however, when they began to be given raisins for working the puzzles. The reward created an extrinsic motive for solving the puzzles, and the monkeys lost interest in the puzzles if they were not offered a raisin.

One of the classic studies in this area was conducted with children who were drawing (Lepper, Greene, & Nisbett, 1973). After a time the researchers gave some of the children a good-player certificate as a reward for having drawn. Interestingly, these children were less likely to draw after that than were the children who had not been rewarded. In this case the reward actually seemed to undermine the intrinsic motivation behind the drawing.

Since the Harlow experiments, many motivational theorists have become interested in discovering the circumstances under which extrinsic reinforcement will undermine behavior that is intrinsically motivated. This area of

Monkeys find manipulating these locks to be intrinsically motivating.

research is of special interest to behavioral theorists. In many schools and institutions, people who are not motivated to work are often stimulated to do so through the use of "token economies." That is, when the people behave appropriately, they are given a token that can be traded in for something of value. It has been argued that token economies, while effective, can have drawbacks, and that researchers and therapists must determine at the outset whether the behavior they want to encourage isn't already intrinsically motivated. If it is, then giving tokens as rewards may undermine the intrinsic motivation. If this happens, individuals may change so that instead of doing something because it's fun or has its own value, they'll do it only if there is something "in it for them." Imagine the poverty of a world in which no positive behaviors occurred unless obvious extrinsic reinforcement were immediately available. The internal motivations behind love, empathy, charity, and humanity would be gone; there would be no more selflessness (Greene, Sternberg, & Lepper, 1976).

Although most of the social motivation theories we have been investigating are limited to specific areas of motivation, such as learned helplessness or the need to achieve, some recent theories have once again attempted to explain human motivation on a grander scale, laying down general principles to throw light on many different behaviors. Among the modern grand theories are two that have attracted particular attention: Zimbardo's social-temporal theory and Solomon's opponent-process theory.* These theories tend to have a stronger research base than the older grand theories and, as you'll see, they provide some exciting insights into acquired motivations.

ZIMBARDO'S SOCIAL-TEMPORAL THEORY

In recent years there has been growing interest in the way a person's perception of time can affect his or her motivational state. Psychologist Philip Zimbardo's **social-temporal theory of motivation** is based on our

*Not to be confused with the opponent-process theory of color vision.

perception of time. He argues that we learn to treat time as extremely important, planning our lives about events as they occur throughout time.

Of course, only the present actually exists. There is no future except in our present plans, and no past except in our present memories. Nonetheless, our feelings about time and about organizing time can greatly influence our motivation. People who are motivated to be organized and who have a great need to achieve are very future-oriented. They think a great deal about the future, they plan events in the future, and they consider the present as a base of operations from which to launch expeditions into the future (Zimbardo, 1981).

Other people are not motivated by future aspirations, but by present considerations. This concern for the present can also be a temporary effect. Sometimes the present can seem to become expanded for us; it can seem to be the only thing for the moment. The environment can be purposely structured to create such an expanded present. In gambling casinos, for instance, it is hard to tell whether it's day or night. There are few windows, no wall clocks. The action is continuous, so that there are no obvious clues to the passage of time. The future doesn't matter. This perspective changes people's motivation. If clocks were in the room, the action slowed down early in the morning, and it was clearly dark outside, people might be motivated to do something other than gambling, a change the casino operators would not want.

People can also become basically oriented toward the present, and be motivated by immediate rather than future goals. This is often the case for individuals who do not trust in the future because it has rarely provided

SOCIAL-TEMPORAL THEORY OF MOTIVATION
A theory of motivation put forward by Philip Zimbardo in which it is argued that an individual's view of time (past, present, or future orientation) can have a profound effect on motivation and behavior.

People who are very future-oriented often miss the present in their pursuit of future goals.

ZEN MASTERS
A skilled practitioner of the Japanese religion Zen Buddhism. Zen Buddhists assert that enlightenment can be achieved through meditation and self-contemplation, rather than by reading scriptures.

OPPONENT-PROCESS THEORY OF MOTIVATION
A theory of motivation proposed by Richard Solomon in which it is argued that many acquired motives such as drug addiction, love, affection, social attachment, cravings for sensory and esthetic experiences, skydiving, jogging, sauna bathing, and even self-administered aversive stimuli seem to follow the laws of addiction.

them with security. Zimbardo has argued that the tendency to be present-oriented will be strong in anyone raised in a family in which future bargains could not be counted on, the unexpected was always happening, and satisfaction could be achieved only in the present. People of a lower socioeconomic status are particularly prone to this orientation because they have learned that their future aspirations are not likely to be met (Zimbardo, 1981).

Schools affect motivation by training children to think of time in a certain way. In African schools, education is commonly handed down from elders who give verbal reports about the past to the next generation. These cultures are exceptionally oriented toward the past. In the United States, however, the emphasis is on the future. American schools, and Western schools in general, may be training children to be motivated by future incentives.

Orientations toward time can affect motivation in a number of ways. **Zen masters** learn to expand their present experience. After many years of practice, they may still experience each sunset with awe, as though it were the first they had seen, and may still regard each flower with great pleasure, as though it were their first sight of a flower. Psychological evidence for this ability has been gathered in attempts to habituate Zen masters to particular stimuli. In general, such habituation among Zen masters is almost nonexistent, or very difficult to attain (Zimbardo, 1981).

In Western culture, individuals who perceive the expanded present as the most meaningful time will be motivated to get immediate gratification without regard to the long-term consequences. Conversely, those who consider the future to be the most meaningful time will be motivated by future gain, perhaps at the expense of present enjoyment. Zimbardo has given some examples of the changes that can occur in people's motivations when their view of time changes. He has argued that individuals living in the expanded present are less likely to think about the future or be intellectual in terms of cognitive processing. They are more likely to find drugs, sex, and music immediately gratifying and valuable experiences. These individuals have no means-end future orientation. They are more likely to engage in vandalism, which has an immediate impact on society, than to be creative, which takes time. They have little awareness of the control that outside forces exercise over their lives, since their sense of time determines their perception of social control. In other words, they are not likely to think about the future consequences of any of their acts, and are therefore less inhibited about engaging in crime.

Being excessively future-oriented has its drawbacks, too. People who are future-oriented often worry about what people will think of them, thereby depriving themselves of the fun of present experiences. Concern for the future can also make you less effective in the present. Philip Caputo, a journalist and Vietnam veteran, has said that future-oriented combat soldiers are the worst because they're always thinking about what's likely to happen to them instead of just reacting (Caputo, 1977).

A person's time orientation can be changed through hypnosis. At the University of California at Berkeley, researchers Maslach and Garber gave students a maze to solve. Seventy-five percent of the first group was successful. The members of the second group were hypnotized and told that there was no future, their life was to be experienced exclusively in the present. Only 55 percent of this group solved the maze. Those who failed were more interested in how the pencil felt on the paper and the lines

looked as they drew them. Maslach and Garber noted that this behavior was very similar to that of learning-disabled children. They wondered whether such children might be living in an expanded present, lacking motivation because they do not perceive the future as most of us have been taught to (Zimbardo, 1981).

How do you view time? Can you expand your present? Can you plan adequately for the future? If you find yourself living excessively in the present or the future, perhaps you should try to develop a strong awareness of the time frame you are lacking. If you are too future-oriented, take time to sense the present—smell the air, hear the birds, or, if more appropriate, taste the air and listen to the traffic. Either way, sense your world and concentrate on it; try to let your inhibitions go. If you are too present-oriented, write your actions in a diary and consider them day by day. Where will you be in the future based on your present behavior? With practice, you may find that the best of both worlds is available to you.

SOLOMON'S OPPONENT-PROCESS THEORY

Over the last decade researcher Richard L. Solomon of the University of Pennsylvania has developed a powerful theory that attempts to explain acquired or learned motivation on a relatively grand scale—the **opponent-process theory of motivation.** This theory addresses many of the motivational questions that we have discussed so far. Its startling central theme is that most learned motivations are in fact addictions. As Solomon has said,

> The theory attempts to account for such diverse acquired motives as drug addiction, love, affection and social attachment, and cravings for sensory and esthetic experiences (cases in which the initial reinforcers are positive) and for such acquired motives as parachuting, jogging, "marathoning," sauna bathing, and a variety of self-administered, aversive stimuli like electric shocks (cases in which the initial reinforcers are negative).

Acquired motives can be as powerful as innate ones. They can become the focus for the major behaviors of an organism, even at the expense of innate needs. A heroin addict, for example, may spend the better part of each day in

drug-seeking behavior, may ignore food, liquid, and sexual incentives, and may
abandon normal societal obligations. The heroin motive is acquired only because certain experiences have occurred; it is not innate. We tend to think of
such addictions as pathological, but they are not. . . . Most acquired motives,
such as love, social attachments, food-taste cravings, thrill seeking, and needs
for achievement, power, and affiliation, obey the empirical laws for the addictions. (Solomon, 1980, p. 691)

In other words, acquired behaviors—love, jogging, sauna bathing, parachute jumping, and so on—can be addicting. Even cravings for certain esthetic experiences can be addicting.

Consider parachute jumping. What actually happens? The first parachuting experience is usually frightening. Parachutists report that the moment
of stepping out of the airplane door is truly a terrifying one (see Figure 9.7).
Until the last second, many feel that they won't be able to jump. The
sensation of falling seems to be slight immediately after the jump but then
increases rapidly. There is a sickening feeling in the stomach. What
started as a gentle descent through the air is now a brutal plunge in which
winds between 120 and 180 miles per hour batter the sky diver. The winds
are surprisingly cold and ripping. The sense of time is distorted: It seems
that the parachute should have opened by now, which adds to the terror.
Suddenly there is the upward jerk of the parachute unfurling, and fear
recedes as the reassuring brightly colored canopy appears overhead.

Emotional Contrast   When the first-time jumpers land they usually walk
about in stony-faced silence for a while, slowly recovering from their terror.
Then an interesting thing happens, which Solomon calls affective or **emotional contrast.** The parachutists begin to smile at one another. They are
elated. They run toward each other laughing, shaking hands, and slapping
each other on the back. Jokes are made, more laughter, a sense of great
relief abounds. This intense feeling can last for several hours. You can
imagine it easily even if you haven't watched parachutists, because it is
such a natural human reaction.

Figure 9.7 *The jumpers' fear is at the
highest level just before the jump, and it
lessens significantly when the parachute
opens.* (SOURCE: *Epstein & Fenz, 1965, p. 2*)

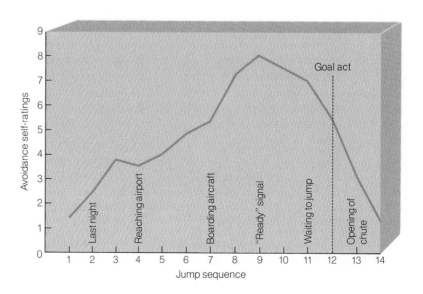

Solomon first noticed this effect when he went into a hospital where one-day-old infants were resting. The infants still had some of the amniotic fluid in their stomachs from before birth and were digesting that. They weren't hungry yet. But Solomon gave them milk to drink. They enjoyed it, drinking it readily when he placed the nipple in their mouths. Then he removed the nipple, and the babies began to cry. They had been happy without the milk before he showed up, but now they were crying. After a while the crying subsided, and the babies returned to their initial peaceful state. This, Solomon realized, was an example of emotional contrast. The import of emotional contrast is that surviving a terrifying or painful experience can, in itself, lead to exhilaration. Conversely, an exhilarating experience can lead to feelings of depression. In this way pleasure can eventually lead to sadness, and pain can eventually lead to happiness!

Solomon has examined many emotional contrasts. As you can see in Figure 9.8, there is an initial primary effect. With the parachutists it was one of terror. It peaks, remains steady for a time, and then is followed by an intense afterreaction during which the emotions swing in the opposite direction. After a time that, too, wears off, and there is a return to the middle.

In Table 9.1, Solomon has shown examples of emotional contrast in four different conditions. The first depicts shooting heroin for the first time; the second, imprinting in ducklings on their first exposure to a moving mother duck (see Chapter 6); the third, people's first experience of sauna bathing; and the fourth, military parachutists' first experience of free-fall. As you can see, there is an initial state (before). Then comes what Solomon has called the A process, or the first affective (emotional) peak (during). Then comes the B process, which is the afterreaction (after), and then a return to the resting state. If the A process is extremely stimulating, the B process is likely to be extremely stimulating in the opposite direction.

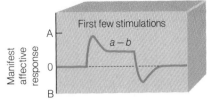

Figure 9.8 *Emotional contrast. Initially, during the first few stimulations, there is an intense affective (emotional) reaction. Then the person adapts to the reaction, and it remains steady for a time. This state is followed by a strong affective afterreaction that eventually decays, returning the person to the initial state.* (SOURCE: *Solomon, 1980, p. 700*)

Table 9.1 Emotional contrast in four conditions

I Changes in Affect Before, During, and After Each Stimulation (Self-Dosing With Opiates) for the First Few Experiences and After Many Experiences

PERIOD	FIRST FEW	AFTER MANY
Before	Resting state	Craving
During	Rush, euphoria	Contentment
After	Craving	Abstinence-agony
	Resting state	Craving

II Changes in Affect Before, During, and After Each Stimulation (Social Attachment in Ducklings) for the First Few Experiences and After Many Experiences

PERIOD	FIRST FEW	AFTER MANY
Before	Contentment	Some distress
During	Excitement	Following
After	Distress	Intense distress
	Contentment	Some distress

III Changes in Affect Before, During, and After Each Stimulation (Sauna Bathing) for the First Few Experiences and After Many Experiences

PERIOD	FIRST FEW	AFTER MANY
Before	Resting state	Resting state
During	Pain, burning	Hot, exciting
After	Relief	Exhilaration
	Resting state	Resting state

IV Changes in Affect Before, During, and After Each Stimulation (Free-Fall in Military Parachuting) for the First Few Experiences and After Many Experiences

PERIOD	FIRST FEW	AFTER MANY
Before	Anxiety	Eagerness
During	Terror	Thrill
After	Relief	Exhilaration
	Resting state	Resting state

SOURCE: Solomon, 1980, pp. 696–697.

NOTE: The emotions in the "After many" column are those associated with addictive effects.

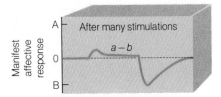

Figure 9.9 *Changes in the A and B processes after repeated emotional contrasts. The initial A state becomes weaker and the B state becomes stronger.* (SOURCE: *Solomon, 1980, p. 700*)

One of the most incredible examples of emotional contrast was described by David H. Rosen. The Golden Gate Bridge, which connects San Francisco and Sausalito, is one of the longest suspension bridges in the world, and its roadway is hundreds of feet above the strong currents of San Francisco Bay. Unfortunately, over the years the bridge has attracted many suicides, and almost 500 people have died jumping from it. Incredibly, ten people survived. This fact is remarkable because at a speed of over 120 miles per hour the water would feel like concrete at impact, and after that, assuming the person were still conscious, there would be the tremendous swim against the cold currents to reach safety. In 1976 David Rosen interviewed seven of the survivors. All of them, he found, had undergone a "spiritual rebirth." They were happy, enjoyed their lives, and felt better than they ever had. Consider these individuals in the light of Solomon's discussion of emotional contrast for a moment. Is it possible that the A process was so intense, the terror and certain realization of imminent death so overwhelming, that surviving the jump called up an opposing B process of such intense exhilaration that the individuals were left with a happier outlook even after the feeling of excitement had subsided?

Addiction　　Solomon has gone on to say that emotional contrast can lead to addictions because of two changes that take place in the A and B processes over time. He noticed that when people engage in the same kind of emotional contrast again and again the initial A state becomes less potent. People adapt to it; they get used to it. The B state, on the other hand, becomes stronger; it starts sooner and lasts longer (see Figure 9.9). Solomon postulated the *state rule* to describe this development, which is the beginning of an addiction. In his words,

> (a) If |a – b| shows a > b, then the organism is in State A, and (b) if |a – b| shows b > a, then the organism is in State B. Furthermore, if being in State A is positively reinforcing (pleasant, desirable), then being in State B will be negatively reinforcing (aversive, undesirable), and vice versa. (Solomon, 1980, p. 699)

After emotional contrast, then, a person does not always return to the original state. A weak A process, caused by repeating the experience many times, followed by a strong B process will leave the person in the B state longer. The decline in the A process will occur whether the A state is aversive or pleasant. If the B state is aversive, the urge to return to the A state will be greater, which, ironically, will lead only to a further weakening of the A state and strengthening of the B.

Take another look at Table 9.1, and you'll see the kinds of changes that occur if a particular emotional contrast is engaged in often enough. In cases I and II (heroin, mother duck) the A process during the first few exposures is pleasant. The contrasting B process that follows is aversive. At first the organism is left in a fairly neutral state, |A – B| = 0, since the A and B processes are equal in strength. After many exposures, however, the A process weakens: The heroin high is mild; the duckling follows its mother but is not excited by her. The B process simultaneously becomes stronger. This change will eventually leave the organism in the B state: |weak A – strong B | = B > A. The B state is aversive in cases I and II. The organism will strongly desire to return to the A state but in so doing will only make the A state weaker still and the B state stronger. The addiction is complete, the hook is set. This is why long-term heroin addicts don't enjoy their heroin, they simply shoot up to avoid withdrawal—and the addiction becomes worse.

In cases III and IV (sauna bathing, parachuting) the A process during the first few exposures is aversive. The people may have tried these activities at first because of military orders or social pressure. After a few times, however, the aversive A process weakens and the pleasant B process grows: $|A - B| = B > A$. As a result, the B process is sought more and more often, and the addictive process is underway.

Another important part of the opponent-process theory is the **critical decay duration** of the opponent process. If you engage in something that will produce an emotional contrast, the A process will become weaker and the B process stronger only if you engage in that behavior again and again. The changes won't happen if you wait long enough between experiences. After the critical decay duration, the addicting effect won't occur. In other words, if you wait a long enough time before skydiving again, the terror of the A process may be just as great as it was originally, and the elation of the B process no more than it was before. However, if you immediately jump again and do it a number of times, the A process will weaken and the B process will strengthen, thus beginning the addiction (Starr, 1978).

More research is needed to demonstrate the power of the opponent-process theory of motivation and to investigate the prevalence of its effect. Still, it helps explain how people can come to enjoy danger or pain, and why pleasure and happiness can be so fleeting. It might also help to answer a number of other questions. For instance, why do people who diet and who find the initial experiences painful sometimes come to enjoy being hungry? Why do soldiers initially terrified of war sometimes reenlist for combat when their enlistment time is up? Why does a job that is initially exciting sometimes become dull and tedious after a while? We may also learn from research into the opponent-process theory how to avoid these kinds of emotional shifts, perhaps by building in critical decay durations at the appropriate times. We may come to understand motivations that at first seem bizarre or unusual. And we may find a better explanation for thrill-seeking than George Mallory's statement about climbing Everest "because it's there." Data obtained in the future about this theory should be anything but dull.

CRITICAL DECAY DURATION From the opponent-process theory of motivation, a time of sufficient length between the onset of an affective A process and its repetition so that no decrease in A process intensity, or increase in B process intensity, is noted.

"Because it's there," and because $|A–B| = B > A$."

Summary

- Psychologists study motivation because they want to know why a behavior occurs.
- Biological motivations such as hunger and thirst are assumed to be built-in, meaning that they exist from birth.
- Homeostasis refers to built-in regulatory systems for maintaining the status quo. Any deviation from an optimal state creates a need that usually produces a drive that is the motivational force for action.
- The hypothalamocentric hypothesis argues that hunger and thirst centers located in the hypothalamus monitor deviations from optimal states. Lesions in the ventromedial hypothalamus result in overeating and obesity. Lesions in an adjacent area, the dorsolateral portion of the hypothalamus, result in aphagia and adipsia.

- Hunger and thirst also seem to be regulated by sensors distant from the brain.
- The homeostatic mechanism that monitors thirst appears to depend on sodium levels in the intracellular and extracellular fluids.
- Although some people gain weight because of overeating, fatness may be largely due to defects in regulators in the brain and elsewhere in the body.
- Research has indicated that the more physiologically advanced a species is, the less its sexual behavior appears to be governed directly by chemical or hormonal forces. Even in humans, though, chemical and hormonal factors may play a role.
- The sex drive in humans may have something to do with sensors in the hypothalamus that are sensitive to different levels of hormones.
- Sociobiologists argue that organisms are constantly in the process of being perfected as they compete to survive and pass on their genes and that this process explains all human motivation and behavior. They also state that behaviors such as morality, love, kindness, aggression, anger, and hatred are all rooted deeply in our genetic structure.
- Human beings and animals seem to have a need for a certain amount of stimulation. Motivations generated by these needs are referred to as stimulus motives.
- Certain motivations can be learned. Learned motives are often related to incentives, which are particular things that we want to possess.
- Learned motivations can imitate biological ones. For instance, it's possible to learn to become hungry through classical conditioning.
- In the past, grand theories of social motivation were popular. These theories attempted to explain most of human behavior. Abraham Maslow, a humanistic psychologist, developed a grand theory based on a hierarchy of motives in which some needs were more powerful than others. Modern motivational theory, however, has usually limited itself to highly detailed investigations of specific areas.
- It's possible to learn to become helpless, though this type of learning doesn't usually occur all at once. Learned helplessness has been overcome by teaching people to attribute their failure to a lack of effort on their own part and to nothing else.
- Over the last 20 years researchers have investigated the needs for power and achievement evident in some individuals. These needs are believed to be learned as the result of experience.
- In many cases intrinsic motivation has been found to be superior to extrinsic motivation in creating and maintaining behavior.
- Psychologist Philip Zimbardo has presented a social-temporal theory of motivation based on our perception of time. He argues that the way in which we understand and treat time is extremely important in helping to explain motivation.
- Richard Solomon has developed a theory of acquired motivation called the opponent-process theory. His theory explains many motivational phenomena as a function of addictions. The theory may help to explain thrill-seeking behavior. It may also explain how some people can come to enjoy danger or pain, and why pleasure and happiness can be so fleeting.

EPILOGUE: GETTING A CHARGE OUT OF LIFE

The following observation by one researcher added impetus to another researcher's investigations and eventually helped give birth to a theory of motivation.

H. B. Taussig had been interested in motivation for many years. Like all of us, she found the reasons behind people's actions interesting. In 1969 Taussig became especially curious about what some researchers were calling emotional contrast. Her curiosity stemmed from an incident involving her neighbor's son.

The young man had been playing golf when a storm began. He packed up his clubs and started to leave the golf course. Suddenly there was a tremendous flash of light. The ground seemed to rush up at him. A gigantic BOOM almost broke his eardrums. He lay there, shocked. His shorts were torn to shreds, and he was burned across his thighs. His companions realized that he had been struck by lightning. As they ran up to him, he screamed, "I'm dead. I'm dead!" (Taussig, 1969, p. 306). An ambulance was called, but by the time it arrived the young man's legs were numb and blue and he was unable to move.

They rushed him to the hospital emergency room. As he was wheeled in, he was laughing happily. In fact, he was euphoric, talking to every-one, telling them what had happened, showing them his tattered shorts, and smiling broadly from ear to ear.

The more Taussig thought about it the more incredible it seemed. The young man hadn't been that happy before the lightning hit him. What a strange way to become so elated, being slammed to the ground by over a million volts of electricity. Taussig mused about how interesting it was that terror could turn into joy.

Taussig later related this story to Richard Solomon. It convinced Solomon more than ever that such extreme emotional switches needed to be more closely investigated, and he eventually developed the opponent-process theory of motivation.

Suggestions for Further Reading

1. Arkes, H. R., & Garske, J. P. *Psychological theories of motivation.* Monterey, California: Brooks/Cole, 1977.
2. Atkinson, J. W., & Raynor, J. O. *Personality, motivation, and achievement.* Washington, D.C.: Hemisphere, 1978.
3. Jung, J. *Understanding human motivation: A cognitive approach.* New York: Macmillan, 1978.
4. Lepper, M. R., & Greene, D. (eds.). *The hidden costs of reward.* Hillsdale, N.J.: Erlbaum, 1978.
5. Petri, H. L. *Motivation: Theory and research.* Belmont, California: Wadsworth, 1981.

CONTENTS

CHAPTER 10

Emotion

PROLOGUE

You are standing in a small observation area looking through one-way glass into a darkened room at a subject seated in a chair. A microphone has been placed over his heart. A wire from the microphone runs back to a recorder. You've told the subject that you are going to monitor his heartbeat during the experiment. In front of him is a screen on which slides will be shown. The young man sits in his chair quite comfortably. He's interested in the experiment, since you've told him that he's going to be seeing slides of Playboy magazine centerfolds. You throw a switch to begin the experiment, and the first slide, Miss January, shines on the screen.

The subject says, "I think I'm going to like this." You ask him to refrain from speaking during the experiment. The sound of his heartbeat can be heard as the recorder collects the data. It's loud enough so that the subject can hear—you rigged it that way. After a time Miss February comes on the screen. The man's heartbeat accelerates and becomes louder. Then Miss March, and his heartbeat slows to its earlier rate.

You're trying not to smile or laugh, since you know the secret.

Your colleague, Stuart Valins, wanted to test the effect that thinking has on emotion, and so he designed this study. The microphone is a fake; the subject can't really hear his own heartbeat. Instead, the sound of a false heartbeat fills the room. You control the heartbeat and can make it go faster or slower by turning a dial. Before, you chose at random the playmates of the month who were going to be associated with a rapid heartbeat—Miss February, Miss August, and Miss November. The subject is now watching Miss April, so you don't touch the dial. You'll have to wait until August and then November before accelerating the heartbeat again. The whole time, the subject will think he's listening to the sound of his own heart. How will this belief affect him?

At the end of the experiment you thank the subject. He smiles and thanks you! Then you tell him that he can choose any three of the centerfold photographs to take home with him. Unbeknownst to the subject, this is the dependent variable you want to measure. You show him all 12 photographs, and watch as he picks out February, then November, and then after a little

299

thought, September. That makes 2 for 3—in statistical terms, significant (Valins, 1966).

Apparently, the subjects in this experiment thought that they had become emotionally aroused while watching particular slides. And they used the false emotional feedback to make a judgment about their preferences and feelings. Valins likes to say that even in the absence of specific physiological reactions, the cognitive or thought component of an emotion can still have an effect. In other words, how you assess your feelings is part of your emotional makeup. How many times during the day do you rely on cognitive assessments in order to know what your emotional state is,

and how many times have you been "tricked" or manipulated by circumstances, in the way that the subjects were in the experiment? How can you be sure how you really feel about things?

In this chapter we'll try to accomplish what has been to date one of the most difficult and all-consuming tasks in psychology, finding out what emotions are. Although we deal with emotions daily, and they are an integral part of human interaction and behavior, nobody really knows what they are. Still, some recent theories have brought us closer to an understanding of emotion, and the implications for our understanding of behavior are significant.

Why Psychologists Study Emotions

It has been said that our emotions are what make us seem most human. We rage, we laugh, we cry, we fear, and we love. To be without emotions is to be unfeeling, perhaps "inhuman." Having feelings is an important part of being human.

Everyone has emotions, even infants a few weeks old. Babies demonstrate striking emotional behaviors. They smile and laugh, they form loving attachments, and they show fear. Parents often report that the first smile from their baby is a magical moment that seems instantly to create a closer and more meaningful bond. As adults, we pay close attention to others in order to discern their attitudes and emotional reactions. Even in the absence of any other cues, emotional monitoring can provide vital information about the people around you. At the same time we often look to our own feelings, even at the expense of thought and logic, in order to understand why we behave in the way that we do. Emotions pervade our existence, affecting our every moment, and no study of human behavior would be complete without an attempt to understand the power and value of our emotional experiences.

Defining Emotions

What do you mean when you say you're happy, angry, sad, jealous, or disgusted? How do you know that the meaning you attach to a particular word describing an emotion is exactly the same as the meaning attributed to it by someone else? Expressing your emotions to others, or even deciding how you yourself feel, can be very confusing. For one thing, emotional states are often a mixture of both unpleasant and pleasant feelings, of both good and bad memories (Brenner, as cited by Plutchik, 1980). Soldiers may feel elated by having saved their own lives and those of their comrades by killing the enemy, and at the same time they may feel remorse and compassion for those they have killed. Someone can be thrilled by a first sexual experience and yet feel guilty, or perhaps melancholy, over a "loss of innocence." And a person may feel jubilant at graduation and ambivalent about the future. Mixed emotions or bittersweet feelings can be confusing and difficult to understand.

Perhaps this is the first thing that should be said: Emotions are complicated. Trying to tell others how we feel can be frustrating, because much of the time we're not sure how we feel. Still, the attempt is important because feelings are an integral part of life. Imagine what it would be like if you had no emotions. Life could easily lose its quality. Things would seem "flat," perhaps purposeless.

The complexity of **emotion** is sometimes, but not necessarily, reflected in language. In English, for instance, there is a wealth of words available to describe emotions. One psychologist has found over 400 (Davitz, 1969). They included anger, rage, despair, disgust, joy, pensiveness, sorrow, fear, vigilance, amazement, ecstasy, gratitude, impatience, surprise, anticipation, distraction, embarrassment, humiliation, boredom, amusement, jealousy, terror, love, adoration, reverence, grief, and loathing. Do each of these words represent a different emotion, or do some overlap, that is, share emotional elements with others? What, for instance, is the difference between sadness and melancholy? This is like asking what the difference is between scarlet and crimson—there isn't any. At the other extreme are emotions that appear to be opposites, such as love and hate. They don't seem to overlap at all, though we could always confuse the issue by saying, "You often hate the person you love and love the one you hate." But who likes to be confused?

Some languages have very few words for emotions, but this doesn't mean that the people who speak these languages are less emotional. Researchers have found that the members of these cultures are just as emotional as the members of cultures whose language includes many words for emotions. So language alone is a poor indicator of emotionality. Nonetheless, the fact that there are always words, and sometimes many words, for emotions does show us that emotions are important in one way or another to all people.

Emotions are so pervasive that it seems strange to consider them separately in one chapter while discussing different psychological aspects in other chapters as though these aspects were unaffected by emotion. In Chapter 6, for instance, the chapter on learning, we dealt with the concept of extinction. As you'll recall, extinction occurs when a reinforcer is no longer given for a particular behavior. The behavior is then engaged in less and less, since it no longer serves a purpose. This sounds dry and technical; there seems to be no feeling in it. But when you watch an animal that has been placed on an extinction schedule, you will often observe a whole series of emotional reactions. For example, a pigeon that is used to getting food as a reinforcer is likely to become emotional when deprived of it. It may flap its wings, squawk, and stomp about the cage, and it may peck angrily at parts of the cage.

Similar kinds of emotional behavior often occur in human beings during extinction. Have you ever seen someone put money in a coffee machine, watch the coffee come out, and then the cup? The person might very well stand there and go a couple of rounds with the machine, punching, kicking, and yelling at it. Just as emotional as the pigeon ever was. How would you

EMOTION
A complex feeling-state involving conscious experience and internal and overt physical responses that tend to facilitate or inhibit motivated behavior.

Emotional behavior develops early in life.

describe this response? The person is upset and angry. The machine didn't perform as expected. It cheated, broke a contract. It took the money and returned nothing, so it deserves to be punished. That's justice. Actually, that's not justice, that's emotion.

Highly emotional experiences tend to be memorable. The joy of falling in love, the anguish when a loved pet dies, the embarrassment of being called on in class when you're unprepared, and the frustration of discovering that your alarm clock didn't go off and you've missed an important appointment—not only are these likely to be memorable experiences, but even if they should happen to someone else, they can evoke an emotional response in ourselves when we hear about them. We communicate emotionally. I understand how you feel once I imagine myself in your position, and then feel what you might be feeling. It's not until I feel what you might be feeling that I can truly understand what you are going through. This ability to feel someone else's emotions is called **empathy.**

The word *feeling* is often used interchangeably with the word *emotion.* This is because we can feel, or sense, an emotion. Most people find it difficult to express exactly what they feel, since the way in which they experience emotion is very subjective. Writers sometimes try to express these subjective sensations with phrases such as "She was so happy she could walk on air," "He was so humiliated that he shrank into insignificance," "She was so angry her blood boiled," "He was so disgusted that he gagged." Such descriptions can give us clues to what people feel in certain emotional states, but, being subjective, the sensations vary from person to person.

Assessing Emotions

Subjective reports are not always totally reliable as a basis for assessing emotion. For this reason psychologists often prefer to rely on observations of overt behavior.

Observing overt behavior can be useful. We all learn to recognize different behavioral cues and their emotional content. Movie stars in silent films, unable to use language, relied heavily on body and facial cues in order to show emotion. The feeling at the time was that the audience would not pick up subtle cues, and so it was necessary to overact. Consequently, a heroine in trouble would put the back of her hand to her forehead, assume a look of horror, pant, and lean backward as though she were about to fall. (Actually, this kind of behavior is more in line with cardiac arrest than fear.) These contortions weren't really necessary, though. People are so responsive to facial expressions and body cues that the actors could have succeeded in conveying emotional states by much subtler means. Today, actors have difficulty going from the screen to the stage and vice versa. On the stage the audience is farther away, and body cues and emotional expressions must be exaggerated. On the screen, during a close-up, a very slight change in facial expression can carry a tremendous impact. For this reason many actors practice for hours with videotape equipment and mirrors in order to learn subtle changes in mood and expression.

This discussion of actors brings up a problem with relying exclusively on overt behavior in order to understand emotions. Suppose the hero in a play bares his teeth, shouts and yells, clenches his fists, makes threatening gestures, glares, and speaks in a deep and threatening voice. Is he really angry? Maybe he's happy because the play's about to end and he can get some dinner. After all, actors are trained to pretend. When you see these same behaviors in others, then, how do you know they are angry? Perhaps you look at the situation they're in and deduce that they're not acting. Of course, this requires a subjective assessment on your part based on the overt behavior you are viewing, and so subjectivity enters in once more.

Look at the picture in Figure 10.1. Is this person happy or sad? It's not hard to tell, is it? She's obviously sad. In fact, she looks as though some great tragedy has befallen her. A child may have died, or her home burned down. We know what emotions feel like, and we can usually tell by looking at others what they must be feeling. Or can we? Turn to page 306 and you will see the entire photograph.

Some tragedy! These people are participating in a joyous reunion. What you see on their faces is an intense emotional response, easy to mislabel. Emotions can be confusing. When we're extremely happy we sometimes cry, and when we're extremely distraught we sometimes laugh. Understanding emotion can be a lifelong pursuit; we all engage in it, whether or not we're psychologists.

As difficult as emotions are to understand, some methods have been developed that may help explain what emotions are or, as significantly, what they are not. The chapter Prologue hinted at this direction: There, you learned that people's perception of their own emotional states can be altered without bringing about any real physiological feelings or changes. Still, physiological change is something that is often apparent in shifting emotional states, and it's one area that's being investigated thoroughly.

Emotion and Physiological Arousal

As you recall from Chapter 2, emotional reactions are often associated with an arousal of the autonomic nervous system. The sympathetic nervous system and the parasympathetic nervous system are the two divisions of the autonomic nervous system. They usually work antagonistically but may occasionally (for instance, during sexual arousal) work in tandem. The sympathetic nervous system is activated to prepare the body for some emergency action such as fleeing or fighting, while the parasympathetic system promotes relaxation and energy conservation and helps return the body to its "normal" state. During intense emotional reactions such as fear, rage, sexual arousal, and love, the sympathetic branch of the autonomic nervous system becomes quite active. This occurrence will result in several physical changes (see Table 10.1). The heartbeat, for instance, may climb to 140 beats per minute or more, strictly as a result of emotional arousal.

EMPATHY
An insightful awareness and ability to share the emotions, thoughts, and behavior of another person.

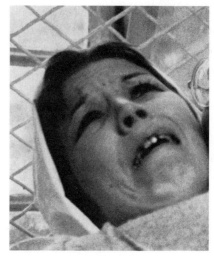

Figure 10.1   *What emotion is this person feeling?*

Table 10.1   Physiological reactions associated with emotional arousal

REACTION	DIVISION OF AUTONOMIC NERVOUS SYSTEM CONTROLLING REACTION
Pupils dilate	Sympathetic
Mouth becomes dry	Sympathetic
Heartbeat increases	Sympathetic
Tears are produced	Parasympathetic
Adrenaline is secreted	Sympathetic
Sweating increases	Sympathetic
Bladder relaxes	Sympathetic
Genitals are stimulated	Parasympathetic

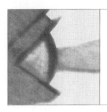

LIE DETECTION

A polygraph, also called a lie detector, is designed to measure physiological changes that occur in conjunction with emotional states. The polygraph is called a "poly"-graph because it measures several different physiological states. One "graph" monitors respiration. Another monitors heart rate, a third blood pressure, and a fourth electrical changes on the surface of the skin, known as a GSR (galvanic skin response) measuring device.

When a subject is connected to the polygraph he or she is asked questions. Many of the initial questions are routine, such as, "What is your name?" or "What is your address?" These routine questions help to establish a baseline against which to measure important emotional changes.

A person suspected of having broken into a store the night before might be asked such questions as, "Where were you the other night?" If the person answers, "I stayed home all night watching television," the fear the person feels when lying may reg-ister as a change in the physiological mechanisms measured by the polygraph. In this way the machine might be able to detect a lie.

At first glance the lie detector may seem a marvelous breakthrough in criminology because it is able to tell when someone is lying. Lie detectors, however, have become controversial because they *don't* detect lies. They do, however, detect nervousness, and there is a very important difference.

Are you the kind of person who becomes nervous when you are accused of having done something wrong, even though you are innocent? Some innocent people confess just to get the accusations over with. Individuals who tend to be nervous when questioned, especially if they are aware which questions are the serious ones, may easily register high rates of nervousness when they have done nothing wrong. Other individuals can remain absolutely calm and not be the least bit upset after committing some heinous act. For this reason many courts do not admit lie detector evidence unless both the prosecution and defense have agreed to allow its admission. But this control alone may not provide sufficient safeguards, since the vast majority of lie detector tests given in this country are not given by law enforcement agencies, but by employers to employees.

Consider the case of Linda V., who worked for the S. S. Kresge Company as a bookkeeper when she was 22 years old. She reported that $150 was missing from receipts gathered the day before. A couple of weeks later she was taken by a company security agent to a room in a local motel where she had to take a lie detector test or lose her job. After the test was over the lie detector operator said, "Linda, you've tried to deceive me. You did steal the money" (Beach, 1980, p. 44). Linda had been a good bookkeeper for six years, and she quit before she was fired. She was so traumatized by the incident that she spent much of the next few years in a suicidal depression;

POLYGRAPH

A lie detector. This device measures physiological changes regulated by the autonomic nervous system (heartbeat, blood pressure, galvanic skin response, and breathing rate). The assumption is that deliberate lying will produce detectable physical reactions.

Interestingly, the heartbeat rhythm that's produced by emotional arousal is significantly different from the rhythm that's produced by physical exercise ("Got Problems?", 1978). The fact that strong measurable physiological changes occur in direct relationship with emotional changes is the basis for the **polygraph,** or lie detector.

While it is true that arousal of the autonomic nervous system is well correlated with emotional excitement, it must be remembered that the autonomic nervous system is controlled directly by the central nervous system, mainly the brain. As you will recall from Chapter 2, different emotional behaviors can be elicited by stimulating different parts of the brain. If a certain portion of the limbic system of a cat's brain is electrically stimulated, a "rage response" will occur. The pupils dilate, the ears flatten and point back, the fur along the back and tail stands upright, the claws become unsheathed, and the cat spits and hisses. During this rage the autonomic nervous system is quite active, as adrenaline is secreted and the

she also became dependent on Valium. Even six years after the incident she was too frightened to handle books. This case has a somewhat happy ending, however, since Linda filed suit against the company and a jury that believed her story ordered the company to pay her $100,000 in damages for the distress it had put her through.

Linda V.'s case is rare; most instances of abuse go unchecked. For example, in Los Angeles a supermarket clerk was fired after failing the lie detector test on the question, "Have you ever checked out groceries at a discount to your mother?" It turned out that her mother had died five years earlier (Beach, 1980, p. 44). The opportunity for abuse is great, since businesses, especially banking and retail outlets, administer thousands of tests each year to employees and managers who are under suspicion of some kind, and as a routine personnel screening device. In the past few years many states have passed laws to help curb some of these abuses.

David Lykken, a professor of psychiatry and psychology at the University of Minnesota, has stated that the most commonly used lie detector tests are accurate no more than two thirds of the time, and that when

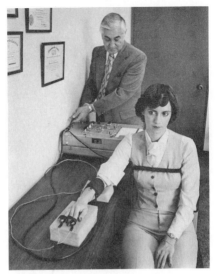

Lie detectors don't measure lies, but rather a person's physiological level of arousal or anxiety.

they do make a mistake, which is often, they are most likely to accuse an honest person of telling a lie (Lykken, 1981). Some of the problems reside with the people who administer the tests. Joseph Buckley, who heads one of the largest testing firms, has said, "Like an X ray, a polygraph records data that take a lot of expertise to interpret. In the wrong hands, it's worse than nothing" (Beach, 1980,

p. 44). Other researchers have found that even in the hands of experts, the analysis of lie detector results is often poor and subject to error (Szucko & Kleinmuntz, 1981). Yet in most states, including the two most populous, New York and California, lie detector operators don't even have to be licensed.

To make matters worse, it's quite easy to fool a lie detector. If a subject is agitated when answering the initial baseline questions, perhaps because he or she has purposely thought of something frightening or arousing, the lie detector will react strongly to *truthful* statements. The baseline then becomes very high in terms of physiological arousal, and later lies will go undetected—lost within the large baseline. Researchers have also discovered that a subject who has taken 400 milligrams of meprobamate (a common tranquilizer) before a lie detector test has only about a 1 in 5 chance of being caught in a deliberate lie (Waid, Orne, Cook, and Orne, 1981). Obviously, any machine that can be so easily tricked should not be relied on exclusively, but should be used limitedly, as the FBI often does, as an aid in following up possible leads.

heart rate increases. In Chapter 2 you also read about Charles Whitman, who climbed the tower on the Texas campus and shot several people, evidence that the same kind of rage reaction can occur in humans if a particular portion of the limbic system is stimulated (in Whitman's case, by a tumor).

Cats and other animals can react to stimulation with these kinds of emotional behaviors even if they've never seen them demonstrated. This suggests that certain emotional responses are built-in, that is, they come with the organism's biology. Human beings, too, seem to have built-in emotional responses; crying and laughing, for example, are common in all cultures.

Although the brain can control and direct emotional responses, it does so usually in response to external events rather than some internal dysfunction such as a brain tumor. Many emotional responses are influenced by learning and culture. Even a powerful and seemingly visceral emotional response such as aggression may be shaped and altered by our experiences.

Aggression and Violence

Over the years many attempts have been made to explain aggression and violence. One of the oldest (and at one time the most popular) of these explanations suggested that aggression and violence were the inevitable result of being blocked or frustrated in an attempt to achieve a desired goal (Dollard, Doob, Miller, Mowrer, & Sears, 1939). This became known as the **frustration-aggression hypothesis.**

A second theory, drawn from ethology, argues that aggression or violent behavior in humans is related to the fixed-response patterns of aggression found in lower animals. According to this theory, aggression is a natural response to specific situations rather than a learned response.

A third theory, based on physiological determinants, argues that aggression and violence result from different levels of hormones or neurotransmitters within the brain.

The final explanation derives from learning theory and argues that aggression and violence are acquired by observing aggressive models, being reinforced for aggression, and having pleasant stimuli associated with aggression.

All of these explanations have been evaluated. The frustration-aggression hypothesis has generally been rejected. Some people react to frustration by becoming aggressive, but aggression isn't an inevitable response to frustration (Berkowitz, 1965). Frustrated people have also been known to respond by trying harder, by crying, and by giving up. Reactions to frustration appear to depend on the individual and the specific situation.

As for the other theories, there may be fixed patterns of aggressive behavior in lower animals, but in humans, the evidence for such species-specific aggression in response to specific triggering stimuli is weak. And although neurochemical and hormonal imbalances are occasionally related to acts of violence, there is only tentative evidence that aggressive people are physiologically different from nonaggressive people. One correlational study, however, has shown a strong relationship between human aggression and levels of certain neurotransmitters in the brain. In research involving 26 Navy enlisted men, those individuals with high levels of norepinephrine and low levels of serotonin were found to rate up to five times higher on measures of aggression than members of the same group whose neurotransmitter levels were opposite (high serotonin, low norepinephrine) (Goodwin, 1978).

Currently, most researchers believe that human aggression is strongly influenced by learning, especially social learning (Eron, 1980). In other words, although aggression may be easy to acquire because of our biological heritage, the things that make us aggressive appear to derive mostly from experience and learning.

FRUSTRATION-AGGRESSION HYPOTHESIS The hypothesis that frustration is the necessary and sufficient condition of aggression and that all aggressive acts are the result of frustration.

Theories of Emotion

From what you've read so far, it's apparent that any theory of emotion must deal with a very complex, hard-to-define series of events and feelings. In the remainder of this chapter, we'll discuss different theories of emotion.

THE COMMON-SENSE THEORY

Common sense tells us that an emotion is the result of some specific event, and that we react to emotions once they occur. This sequence is shown in Figure 10.2. However, as you learned at the beginning of the chapter, a subjective assessment of an emotional state can influence a person's behavior even in the *absence* of any real emotional arousal. When researcher Stuart Valins played false heartbeat feedback, subjects were influenced by what they thought to be real emotional arousal, inappropriately labeled their "arousal" as sexual interest, and acted accordingly. This kind of occurrence seems to argue against our common-sense understanding, which tells us that an emotion must be *felt* before we react to it. Many years before Valins' research this idea was examined by William James, whose brilliant mind was probing psychological issues before most people had ever heard of psychology.

THE JAMES-LANGE THEORY

In 1890 James argued that the common-sense explanation of emotions— that environmental events create an emotion that in turn gives rise to responses—might be incorrect. Instead, James asserted that environmental

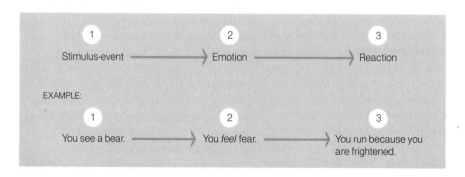

Figure 10.2   *The common-sense concept of emotion.*

Figure 10.3   *The James-Lange theory of emotion.*

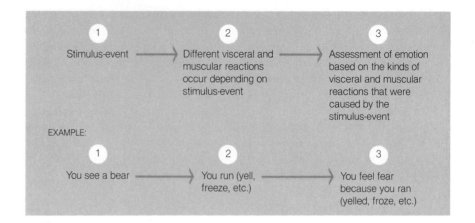

experiences give rise to different visceral and muscular responses and that these responses lead to emotional states.

According to James, the emotion *follows* the behavior, rather than producing it. James believed that encountering something dangerous, such as a bear in the woods, would immediately cause bodily changes associated with danger and you would run (or freeze, or do something to avoid the danger). Only *after* reacting would you experience the emotion. The unique body changes that trigger a behavior are not, according to James, emotion. The emotion is an assessment made after the behavior has occurred (see Figure 10.3). For example, if you are walking down the street and you trip and start to fall, immediate changes occur in the body, and you thrust out your hands in order to protect yourself. You don't label your emotional state "fear" until after you've extended your hands. James argued that behavior often occurs too fast for the emotion to be felt. A Danish researcher named Carl Lange wrote along similar lines, emphasizing the bodily changes that led to immediate responses. Ever since, the theory has been known as the **James-Lange theory of emotion** (Lange & James, 1922).

The James-Lange theory was developed toward the end of the 19th century. It was undisputed for over 30 years until it was strongly challenged by the Cannon-Bard theory.

THE CANNON-BARD THEORY

In 1927 the American physiologist Walter Cannon and his student, Phillip Bard, took issue with James and Lange's assertion that there were many different visceral and muscular responses associated with emotion-inducing stimuli. Cannon and Bard showed that the physiological arousals associated with intense anger, happiness, and sadness were quite similar (Cannon, 1927). During all of them, adrenaline was secreted, heartbeat accelerated, respiration increased, and pupils dilated. To be sure, there are some physiological differences between these emotions, but they are few while the similarities are striking. According to the **Cannon-Bard theory,** then, the body becomes physiologically aroused during intense emotion, but the differences between the kinds of physiological arousal are not significant enough to explain the rich and varied emotional life experienced by people. Cannon and Bard concluded, therefore, that different kinds of visceral and muscular arousal are not the cause of emotion, but rather that such arousal and emotion occur simultaneously (see Figure 10.4) (Bard, 1934). In general, though, the Cannon-Bard theory has not proven to be a very accurate assessment of emotion. Modern exploration of the nervous system has not uncovered evidence to support the contention that cognitive assessment and visceral-muscular reaction always occur simultaneously and independently, or that emotional input is mediated by either the thalamus or the hypothalamus.

SCHACHTER'S COGNITIVE THEORY

In 1962 psychologist Stanley Schachter developed a theory of emotion that was a refinement of the James-Lange theory. As you recall, Cannon and Bard had attacked the James-Lange contention that different muscular and visceral responses preceded each emotional state. They argued instead that most emotional states were associated with very similar arousal states. Schachter wondered if the James-Lange idea that emotion occurred *after* the behavioral response could still be correct even if only a very general visceral and muscular arousal state existed prior to the creation of the emotion. Schachter believed that the cognitive (thinking and perceptual) processes could create an emotion following behavior that occurs during a state of general arousal (see Figure 10.5).

Imagine, for example, that someone is walking through a desert and that she comes upon a 6-foot-long rattlesnake. She freezes, gasping, and her eyes open wide. How would you assess her emotional state? If you think about how you'd feel, you might call it horror or terror. As for her physiological state, her pupils would probably be dilated, her heart would be beating faster, her respiration would have increased, and her adrenaline level would be high—all indications of an aroused sympathetic nervous system. However, these signs alone wouldn't enable you to define her emotional state. She, too, might have trouble labeling her emotion if she relied only on her *general* physical arousal. Rather, she must make a mental or cognitive assessment of the situation. When she does so, she comes to the conclusion that what she feels is happiness because she has now found her lost rattlesnake Buffy, which escaped from her snake farm.

JAMES-LANGE THEORY OF EMOTION
A classical theory of emotion named for the men who independently proposed it. The theory argues that a stimulus first leads to visceral and motor responses, and that the following awareness of these responses constitutes the experience of the emotion. The theory argues, for instance, that we are sad because we cry rather than that we cry because we are sad.

CANNON-BARD THEORY OF EMOTION
The theory that environmental stimuli may set off patterns of activity in the hypothalamus and thalamus. These patterns are then relayed to the autonomic and somatic nervous systems, where they trigger the bodily changes associated with emotion, and to the cerebral cortex, where they simultaneously result in the assessment and feeling of emotion.

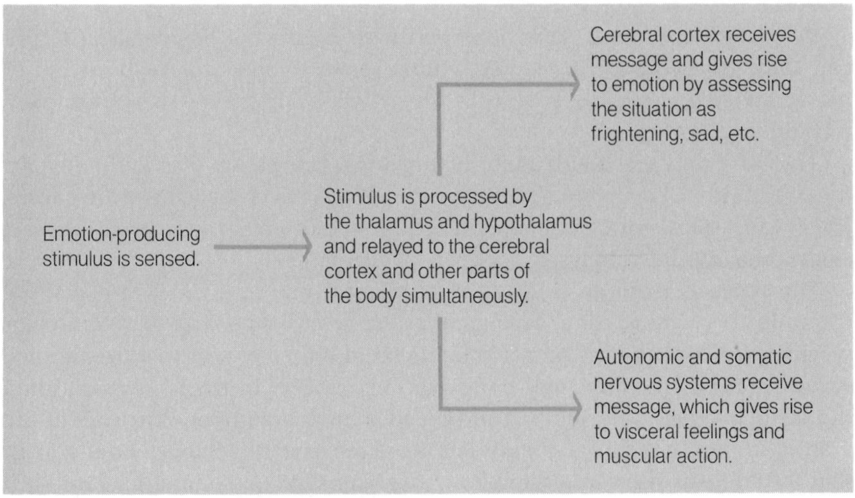

Emotion-producing stimulus is sensed. → Stimulus is processed by the thalamus and hypothalamus and relayed to the cerebral cortex and other parts of the body simultaneously. → Cerebral cortex receives message and gives rise to emotion by assessing the situation as frightening, sad, etc.

→ Autonomic and somatic nervous systems receive message, which gives rise to visceral feelings and muscular action.

Figure 10.4 *The Cannon-Bard theory of emotion. Emotions do not depend on visceral and muscular reactions; but instead, they occur simultaneously with and independently of them.*

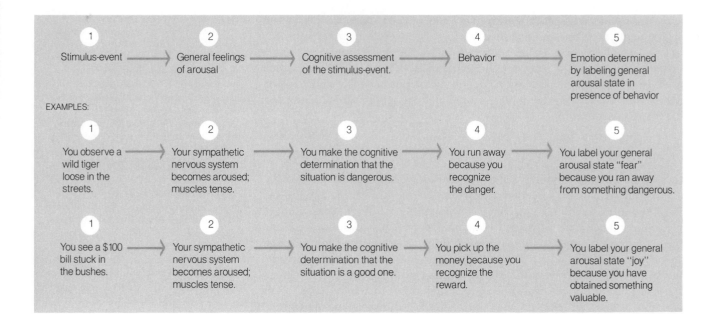

EXAMPLES:

Figure 10.5 *Schachter's theory of emotion. Different labels may be placed on similar states of arousal depending on how the situation is assessed.*

Her excitement was not due to terror, but to happy surprise, since she had just about given up the search. Yet her initial physiological reaction was the same as a tourist's would have been, had he simply wandered off the road to look for a tumbleweed and stumbled across a deadly snake by accident. In that case, though, the subjective assessment would have been that he was in big trouble and likely to be severely injured. He would have assessed his similar arousal as fear.

Schachter designed an ingenious experiment to test his theory. The subjects were secretly given a dose of adrenaline, which caused them to feel a certain amount of physiological arousal. Initially, Schachter had planned to spray the subjects' waiting room with adrenaline so that it would be inhaled, but this idea was too expensive. Instead, he invited the subjects into a room and told them that they were going to take part in a vision experiment. They were given an injection of adrenaline, believing it to be a substance that would improve their vision.

By today's standards such an experiment might not be considered ethical, since injecting an individual with a potent substance without his or her knowledge could be harmful. Nevertheless, the research results were intriguing.

The subjects were divided into two groups. One group was told to expect the symptoms they would shortly be feeling (faster heartbeat, sweating, jitters, fluttering stomach, etc.), while the second group was told to expect symptoms unrelated to the true effects of adrenaline.

The subjects from each group were placed, one at a time, in a waiting room. In the waiting room was another "subject," who was really an actor working for Schachter. The actor behaved in either one of two preplanned ways: He seemed either very happy or very angry. In the happy condition the actor laughed, told jokes, and played with a hula hoop that was in the waiting room. In the angry condition the actor became furious about a form that the subjects were asked to fill out, which asked personal questions such as "With how many men (other than your father) has your mother had extramarital relationships? Four and under ——; five to nine ——; ten and over ——.''

The subjects who had been told to expect the symptoms that they began to feel attributed their physical arousal to the injection rather than to the actor's behavior, while those who were expecting different symptoms attributed their physical arousal to an emotional reaction brought on by the actor's behavior. The second group of subjects began to believe that they were feeling what the actor was feeling, either happiness or anger. In the angry condition, for example, the actor became more and more incensed at the questions as he filled out the form, finally crumpling it up, swearing that he would never answer such personal questions, and storming out of the room. Subjects who attributed their physical arousal to emotion, rather than to the injection, were much more likely to become angry, too, in this circumstance (see Figure 10.6). This result indicates that the presence of a physiological arousal may cue a person to search for the reason behind the arousal. Then, by examining the immediate circumstances, the person may come to the conclusion that "I must be angry" or "I must be happy." The same general physical arousal, then, can lead to different emotions based on a subjective labeling of the immediate situation (Schachter & Singer, 1962).

Schachter's ideas, called the **cognitive theory of emotion,** were taken one step further by Valins, who demonstrated, as you'll recall from the chapter Prologue, that emotional assessment and related behavior could occur even in the absence of real physiological arousal. Yet our physiology plays an important role in many aspects of our emotional makeup. Emotions aren't always a strictly cognitive matter. Think especially of the facial expressions of those who are happy, angry, or sad. Are these expressions learned or part of a cognitive assessment of emotion, or are they derived from inherited patterns of behavior?

FACIAL-FEEDBACK THEORY

Are emotional facial expressions universal? Except in extreme cases, such as the reunion example, we can often tell people's moods by their expressions. If you traveled to a foreign land, Malaysia, for instance, you would be able to recognize facial expressions and know which emotion the expression was showing (Ekman, 1973; Ekman, Sorenson, & Friesen, 1969; Izard, 1971; Boucher, 1973). This ability to recognize facial expressions and the corresponding emotions is also found among tribes that have had little contact with the West or with mass media (Ekman, 1973; Ekman & Friesen, 1974).

COGNITIVE THEORY OF EMOTION
Schachter's theory that emotion stems from one's interpretation of a physiological state occurring under specific circumstances.

SUBJECTS' AWARENESS OF SYMPTOMS

	Subjects expect symptoms (attribute arousal to injection)	Subjects do not expect symptoms (attribute arousal to actor)
Actor angry	Subjects generally unaffected by actor's behavior.	Subjects became angry.
Actor happy	Subjects generally unaffected by actor's behavior.	Subjects became happy.

ACTOR'S STATE WHEN SUBJECT ENTERED ROOM

Figure 10.6 *In Schachter's experiment the subjects were placed in one of four different conditions.*

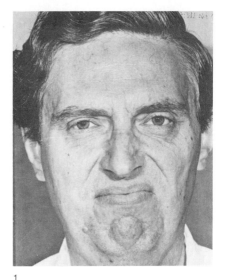

1

2

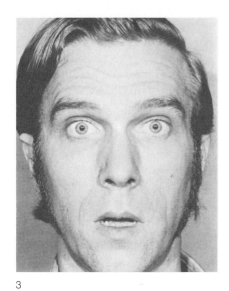

3

Figure 10.7 *The five universal facial expressions. Can you match each photograph with its proper emotion?*

(Answers: 1 disgust; 2 happiness; 3 fear-surprise; 4 anger; 5 sadness)

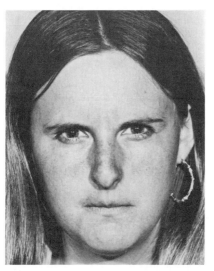

4

5

Except in cultures in which people are taught not to display certain emotional expressions, people universally show the same expressions when experiencing the same emotions (Ekman & Oster, 1979). Five different facial expressions have been found to be universal, that is, clear to most all who see them. These expressions are happiness, anger, disgust, sadness, and fear-surprise, a combination of fear and surprise (see Figure 10.7).

No one knows why certain facial muscles become active when particular emotions are being experienced. Why, for instance, should the corners of the mouth turn up when someone is happy and down when someone is sad? Many researchers feel that these expressions are tied to an innate, genetically predetermined organization that activates certain facial muscles during a particular emotional state (Redican, 1975; Eibl-Eibesfeldt, 1972). Even individuals blind since birth, who could never have seen facial expressions, tend to show them (Charlesworth & Kreutzer, 1973).

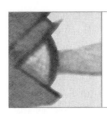

ASSESSING NONVERBAL CUES

Facial expression is not the only nonverbal indication of how someone is feeling. When we interpret a person's emotional state from **nonverbal cues**, we rely on posture and body motions as well as facial expression. Most experiments have found that observing body posture and movement is an important aid to interpreting facial expression. Facial expressions are more difficult to judge if body motion and posture are not observable (Burns & Beier, 1973; DePaulo, Rosenthal, Eisenstat, Finkelstein, & Rogers, 1978). In some instances it's even been found that another person's emotional state can be more readily understood by observing body posture and motion than by observing facial expression (Shapiro, 1972; Berman, Shulman, & Marwit, 1976).

When do we depend on nonverbal cues and when on verbal cues? On the whole, observers consider verbal cues to be more important in determining a subject's mood and feelings than even a full array of nonverbal cues. In other words, what the subject says is generally given more weight than facial expression, posture, or body movements (Cline, Atzet, & Holmes, 1972). Nonetheless, we do rely on nonverbal cues at times, especially if we perceive that the person is attempting to conceal his or her feelings or is avoiding any discussion of emotion. Then our attention to nonverbal cues may become heightened in order to discern the person's real feelings (Ekman, Friesen, O'Sullivan, & Scherer, as cited by Ekman & Oster, 1979). Furthermore, the emphasis given to nonverbal cues may depend on a person's experience and maturity. In one study, a woman smiled

Figure 10.8 *Subjects in Archer and Akert's experiment viewed videotapes and were asked to make judgments based on the video portion only (no sound). In the top photograph, the subjects were asked who was the mother of the baby, the woman on the left, the woman on the right, or neither woman. In the bottom photograph, the subjects were asked whether the two people were friends who had known each other for six months or acquaintances who had had several conversations.*

(Answers: Top: The woman on the right is the mother of the baby. Bottom: The two people are strangers.)

as she spoke negative words in a harsh voice. Children observing her judged her to be more angry and upset than adults who observed her (Bugental, Kaswan, Love, & Fox, 1970).

People's ability to judge nonverbal cues can differ greatly (Buck, 1977; Zuckerman, DeFrank, Hall, & Rosenthal, 1978). Researchers Dane Archer and Robin Akert conducted a series of experiments in which they exhibited videotaped scenes of people interacting and then asked the viewers to make judgments about the people on the tape. Figure 10.8 shows two scenes from the Archer and Akert tapes. Although this is only one portion of the videotape, you may still be able to use the nonverbal cues that are present in order to judge the answers to the questions posed. After watching the entire videotape, subjects in Archer and Akert's studies were able to assess both scenes accurately about two thirds of the time (Archer & Akert, 1977).

Researchers have also discovered that in general women are better able to read nonverbal cues than men (Hall, 1978). A possible explanation for this is that women may be trained by society and culture to be more attentive to the feelings of others. If learning is important in determining our ability to attend to and understand the emotions of others by reading nonverbal cues, then it may be possible for all of us to train ourselves to be more sensitive to the needs and feelings of others by observing them more carefully (Archer, 1980).

Of course, just because our facial expressions may be based on genetic organization doesn't mean that we can't control them. Who hasn't tried to keep a straight face when something funny happens at a time when it is inappropriate to laugh? It's like trying not to sneeze, which is possible even though sneezing is an innate behavior.

Researchers have wondered whether feedback from our own facial expressions could tell us which emotion to experience. S. S. Tomkins has argued that feedback from facial expressions may be the muscular precursors of emotion. Like James and Lange, Tomkins believes that different kinds of muscular action must precede the experience of different emotions (Tomkins, 1962; 1963).

Tomkins' critics argue that it isn't necessary for certain facial expressions to occur in order for the emotion to occur. Rather than create emotions, facial expressions appear in conjunction with them (Ekman & Oster, 1979). This view is almost a "Cannon-Bard" theory of facial expressions.

To test Tomkins' **facial-feedback theory,** researchers asked subjects to produce different facial expressions as they carried out certain tasks. They then measured the subjects' self-reported feelings afterwards. The purpose was to find out whether deliberately altering facial expressions would directly affect emotions (Laird, 1974). So far, the best evidence supporting S. S. Tomkins' facial-feedback theory has come from reports of different emotional responses to shock in conjunction with different facial expressions. Subjects reported that the electric shock was more severe when they made facial signs of pain than when they tried to avoid any outward signs of pain (Colby, Lanzetta, & Kleck, 1977).

Of course, this one study doesn't prove that different facial expressions give rise to our whole range of emotions. Its results can be interpreted in other ways, for instance, that the change in facial expression may have gone hand in hand with a change in thinking about the shock. If so, then different thought strategies about dealing with the shock may have caused an emotional change, rather than just a change in facial expression (Lanzetta, Cartwright-Smith, & Kleck, 1976). "Putting on a happy face" may make you feel happier, or it may not—no one is certain (Ekman & Oster, 1979).

PLUTCHIK'S THEORY OF THE ORIGIN OF EMOTIONS

Although much of what is considered emotional behavior may be the result of learning and cognitive processes, undoubtedly some of it is innate. The existence of similar facial expressions and emotional reactions in all members of our species is evidence of this. These expressions of emotion are conspicuous in other species as well (see Figure 10.9). The kinds of emotions that we see in our species and others may have evolved because they help ensure survival. In this sense, emotions may exist because they serve a function.

Researcher Robert Plutchik has outlined a theory of the **psychoevolutionary synthesis of emotion** (Plutchik, 1980) in which he argues that emotions are inherited behavioral patterns that have important functions and that are modifiable by experience. Plutchik's theory begins where others have left off. He defines emotion as "a complex sequence of events having elements of cognitive appraisal, feeling, impulses to action, and overt behavior—all of which are designed to deal with a stimulus that triggered the chain in the first place" (Plutchik, 1980, p. 68).

Primary Emotions   According to Plutchik, emotions can be thought of in the same terms as colors. Some are fundamental, or primary, and others are mixtures of the primaries (see Figure 10.10). Plutchik has deduced from his research that there are eight primary emotions: sadness, fear, surprise, anger, disgust, anticipation, joy, and acceptance (in the form of receptivity). He has found that these eight emotions are consistent across a wide range of situations involving emotion and personality. We may have hundreds of words for emotions, but all of them describe either one of the eight emotions or combinations of them (Plutchik, 1980).

Functional Aspects of Emotion   Plutchik's theory includes not only behavioral aspects of emotion, such as hitting, running away, crying, and laughing, but functional aspects as well. Functional aspects of emotions are those aspects which help ensure management of the environment and survival. Charles Darwin assumed that emotions evolved because of the function they

Figure 10.9   *Many species of animals display emotions. Such expressions of emotion are often very similar to those displayed by human beings.*

Figure 10.10 *Plutchik's wheel of emotion. Some emotions are primary (within wheel) while others are secondary (composites or dyads) made from two primaries (outside of wheel).* (SOURCE: *Plutchik, 1980, p. 75*)

fulfill. He published his arguments on this topic in his book *The Expression of the Emotions in Man and Animals* (Darwin, 1872/1967).

Table 10.2 outlines the eight basic behavioral patterns of animals and human beings according to Plutchik. Each category is functional, that is, it serves a purpose, which is why it was selected by the evolutionary process (see Chapter 2).

According to this view, an emotion has five components: a stimulus-event, cognition of that event, an assessment of feeling, a behavior guided by innate mechanisms and based on that assessment, and the function served by the behavior. Figure 10.11 gives examples of this kind of emotional sequence. The difference from the James-Lange theory is obvious: In this model we do run because we feel afraid. Plutchik also argues that not only do we run because we feel afraid, but we also run because running leads to

Table 10.2 Functional aspects of the eight primary emotions

PRIMARY EMOTION	FUNCTION	FUNCTIONAL DESCRIPTION
Fear	Protection	Behavior designed to avoid danger or harm, such as running away or any action that puts distance between an organism and the source of danger.
Anger	Destruction	Behavior designed to eliminate a barrier to satisfaction of an important need. This includes biting, striking, or various symbolic acts of destruction, such as cursing or theatening.
Joy	Incorporation	Behavior that involves accepting a beneficial stimulus from the outside world, as in eating, grooming, mating, or affiliation with members of one's own social group. Such actions have the effect of nurturing the individual.
Disgust	Rejection	Behavior designed to expel something harmful that has been ingested, such as vomiting or, at times, defecation. This behavior is believed to be associated with feelings of contempt and hostility and with sarcasm, all of which are essentially a rejection of other people or their ideas.
Acceptance	Reproduction	Behavior designed to provide contact with sex for the purpose of perpetuating one's gene pool. Expressions of this function include sexual signaling, courtship rituals, and sexual intercourse.
Sadness	Reintegration	Behavior associated with the loss of someone who has provided important nurturance in the past. In such circumstances, the individual sends signals that serve to encourage the return of the lost individual or to attract a substitute. Expressions of this function include crying, emission of distress signals, and "babyish" behavior.
Surprise	Orientation	Behavioral reactions to contact with a new, unfamiliar stimulus: a loud noise, a strange animal, or a new territory, for example. The organism must quickly reorient the body and stop what it is doing so that the sense organs can take in information about the novel stimulus.
Anticipation	Exploration	Behavior designed to bring the organism into contact with many aspects of its environment. Getting to know one's neighborhood permits a form of mental mapping that enables the animal to anticipate and deal with future challenges to its survival.

SOURCE: Plutchik, 1980, p. 73.

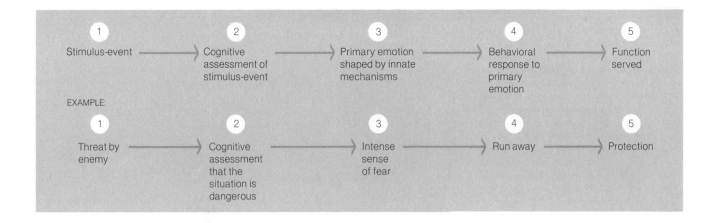

EXAMPLE:

protection (the function or value of the emotion). Running functions to ensure our survival. This model is similar to Schachter's cognitive model of emotion because the "feeling" is not labeled until a cognitive assessment is made. However, in Plutchik's theory an emotion is not just based on a cognitive assessment, it is also tied to innate mechanisms that guide our responses in order to serve a valuable function.

Plutchik has taken the interesting viewpoint that our cognitive abilities have grown and advanced largely to serve emotion! With a powerful brain that can make rapid calculations and evaluate many situations, we find it easier to interpret what our feelings mean and then to react in a way that's most functional. This idea is unusual in that many people think that emotions can get in the way of clear, rational thinking. Plutchik, on the other hand, views rational thinking as something that can help develop and perfect the emotional experience.

Emotional Intensities, Similarities, and Differences Emotions, as we all know, can vary in intensity. Compare annoyance and rage or apprehension and terror—the difference is one of intensity. Furthermore, some emotions have elements in common, such as rage and loathing, while other emotions are distinctly opposites, such as grief and ecstasy. Plutchik has developed a model that maps emotional intensities. In Figure 10.12 you see a three-dimensional figure that resembles a top. Similar emotions are placed close to one another; those that are opposites appear across from one another. The figure is shaped to represent the fact that intense emotions are more definable. Less intense emotions are more alike, which is indicated by their nearness to one another at the bottom of the figure.

It is possible to demonstrate whether emotions are similar to one another in several ways. As you'll recall from Chapter 7, information learned in one emotional state is easier to recall in the same emotional state, and more difficult to recall in the opposite emotional state (mood-dependent learning). Using Plutchik's map of emotional intensity, researcher Gordon Bower tested similarities and differences between emotions. Working with Stanford undergraduate Bret Thompson, Bower hypnotized his subjects and taught each subject four different lists of words; each list was learned in a different emotional state induced by the hypnosis. The four emotions chosen were among Plutchik's primaries: joy, sadness, fear, and anger.

Each list consisted of 16 unusual words from taxonomy related to birds, mammals, fish, or trees. Each subject, after being placed in a specific mood,

Figure 10.11 *Plutchik's psychoevolutionary synthesis of emotion. Plutchik's theory has elements of both the common-sense theory and Schachter's cognitive theory. It also incorporates Darwin's idea of adaptive function through natural selection. It is like the common-sense theory because the emotion stimulates the behavior. It resembles Schachter's theory because a cognitive assessment must be made before a primary emotion can be generated from what would be only a general state of physiological arousal. Finally, Darwin's ideas are expressed by the argument that primary emotional states exist because they serve a valuable function.*

Figure 10.12 *Plutchik's model for depicting the relative similarities and intensities of the primary emotions. Each lengthwise slice of the figure represents a primary emotion, from its most intense to its mildest expression (for example, grief-sadness-pensiveness). Emotions that most resemble each other are adjacent; those most unlike are far apart or opposite each other. All positions on the figure are plotted from ratings by subjects in a number of studies. At mild intensities the emotions aren't labelled because they are often too difficult to discriminate. The adrenaline injection used in Schachter's experiment may have created an arousal in this range, allowing subjects to more easily misinterpret their emotional state. Confusing loathing with adoration, or ecstacy with grief would be much less likely. (SOURCE: Plutchik, 1980, p. 74)*

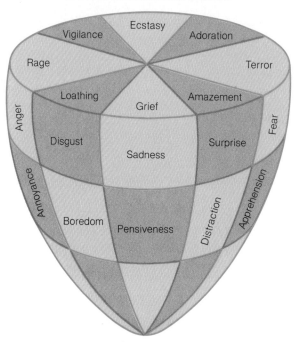

was given two chances to learn and recall one list of words. The mood was then altered hypnotically and the subject was asked to learn another list. After studying all four lists, the subjects were tested on them in the order in which they had been mastered. The subjects were cued as to which list to recall, as in "Now, recall the fish list; it was the second one you learned" (Bower, 1981, p. 137). Before recalling a list, subjects were again hypnotized into one of the four emotional states. The results confirmed Plutchik's model. Subjects were best able to recall a list if their attempt was made in the same mood as when they learned the list. Subjects did most poorly if they had learned in one mood and tried to recall in a mood on the opposite side of Plutchik's model. Subjects who learned in one mood and tried to recall material in a mood halfway around the circle had intermediate success (Bower, 1981) (see Figure 10.13). These findings support Plutchik's view that some emotions are the opposite of others, and some are tangential or complementary to others.

As you have discovered, emotion is a complex area including aspects of physiology, cognition, and innate mechanisms. No one theory of emotion has been totally accepted. No doubt, future research will help us understand emotion more fully.

Summary

- Everyone has emotions; even infants a few weeks after birth exhibit them. Emotions pervade our existence, and no study of human behavior would be complete without an attempt to understand the power and value of our emotional experiences.
- The English language has over 400 words for emotions. Some languages have very few words for emotions. But researchers have found that

members of cultures in which there are few words for emotions are just as emotional as members of cultures in which there are many.

- The word *feeling* is often used interchangeably with the word *emotion* because we feel, or sense, an emotion. Most people find it very difficult to express exactly what they feel because the experience of emotion is so subjective.

- Because subjective reports are not always a reliable guide in assessing emotion, many psychologists prefer to rely on observations of overt behavior.

- Emotional reactions are often associated with an arousal of the autonomic nervous system. During intense emotional reactions such as fear, rage, sexual arousal, and love, the sympathetic branch of the autonomic nervous system becomes quite active. The strong, measurable physiological changes that occur then is the basis on which the polygraph, or lie detector, assesses truth.

- Different kinds of emotional behaviors can be elicited by stimulating different parts of the brain. This effect suggests that certain emotional responses are built-in.

- Four theories have been developed to explain aggression and violence: the frustration-aggression hypothesis, an ethological theory, a physiological theory, and a learning theory. Currently, most researchers believe that aggression may be easy to acquire because of biological heritage, but the things that make us aggressive appear to derive mostly from experience and learning.

- Common sense tells us that an emotion is the result of a specific event and that we react to emotions once they occur.

- The James-Lange theory of emotion argues that environmental experiences give rise to different visceral and muscular responses, which in turn lead to emotional states. In this view emotion follows the behavior, rather than producing it.

- The Cannon-Bard theory takes issue with the James-Lange idea that there are many different visceral and muscular responses associated with emotion-inducing stimuli. In Cannon and Bard's view, although the body may become physiologically aroused during intense emotion, the differences between the kinds of physiological arousal are not significant enough to explain the wide range of emotions that most people feel. Visceral and muscular arousal is not considered to be the cause of emotion but rather is considered to occur simultaneously with emotion.

- Stanley Schachter developed a cognitive theory of emotion that was a refinement of the James-Lange theory. Schachter demonstrated that it was possible for the cognitive (perceptual and thinking) processes to create an emotion following behavior that occurs during a state of general arousal.

- Five different facial expressions have been found to be universal: happiness, anger, disgust, sadness, and fear-surprise. S. S. Tomkins argues that feedback from our own facial expressions tells us which emotion to experience. In a sense Tomkins' facial-feedback theory is similar to the James-Lange theory.

- Robert Plutchik's psychoevolutionary synthesis of emotion is an attempt to trace the origin of emotions. Plutchik argues that emotions are inherited behavior patterns that have important functions and that are modifiable by experience. Plutchik considers emotions to be like colors: Some are fundamental or primary, and others are mixtures of the primaries.

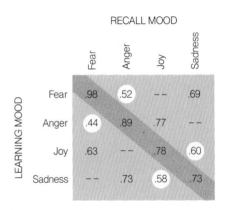

RECALL MOOD

LEARNING MOOD	Fear	Anger	Joy	Sadness
Fear	.98	.52	--	.69
Anger	.44	.89	.77	--
Joy	.63	--	.78	.60
Sadness	--	.73	.58	.73

Figure 10.13 *Percentage of correct scores for subjects who learned lists of words in Bower's experiment and then later recalled the lists. The mood in which they learned the material is read from left to right in rows, while the mood in which they recalled the material is read from top to bottom in columns. For example, if the subject learned the list while afraid but recalled it while sad, you would look along the fear row until it intersected the sadness column where you'd find a score of 69 percent correct recall. Scores in which the learning and recall mood were the same appear along the shaded diagonal. Scores in which the learning mood was the opposite of the recall mood are circled. Interactions that were not measured are indicated by dashed lines. As you can see, the scores were the highest when the learning mood and recall mood were identical and lowest when they were opposites. Intermediate scores were obtained when the emotions and recall environments were closer to each other than the opposites.* (SOURCE: *Bower, 1981, p. 138*)

- According to Plutchik, emotion has five components: a stimulus-event, cognition of that event, an assessment of feeling, a behavior guided by innate mechanisms and based on that assessment, and the function served by the behavior.
- Plutchik has taken the viewpoint that our cognitive abilities have grown and advanced largely to serve emotion.
- Emotions vary in intensity and in their similarity to other emotions. The similarity of emotions can be measured to some degree by experiments such as those that measure mood-dependent memories.

EPILOGUE: THE MUSIC MAN

Psychologists who study emotion know that mood can have a dramatic effect on behavior. The following story illustrates how one man used this knowledge to obtain a desired effect.

In 1949 the great American composer Aaron Copland was asked to write the music for a movie being filmed by director William Wyler. The movie was called The Heiress *and starred Olivia deHaviland and Montgomery Clift. It was based on a novel by Henry James (the brother of psychologist William James) and tells the story of a homely young woman who was courted by a handsome man who was secretly interested only in her fortune.*

At one point in the film the man discovers that the young woman will not inherit her fortune, and so he decides to abandon her. The way in which he abandons her is particularly harsh. He promises to meet her and elope with her, and then he doesn't come.

Copland had to write music to accompany the young woman's hopeful response as she ran to the front door expecting to see her lover each time a carriage went by her

A scene from the motion picture, The Heiress.

*house. Each time it was a false
alarm. Finally, very late at night,
far after the time he had promised
to come, the young woman realizes
what has happened and is broken-
hearted.*

*Copland wrote music that was
romantic and gentle. Then, when the
movie was previewed at a special
screening, he sat in the back of the
theater and watched. The tragic
scene came, the romantic music was
played, and the audience laughed!
Copland was shocked. Here was a
tragic scene, and the audience was
laughing, almost falling in the aisles.*

*Copland realized that he had
created the wrong mood. His music
was romantic and made the audience feel good, while the woman in
the film felt bad. The audience was
not relating to the character emotionally. Instead, safe in pleasant
emotions, the audience was finding
the character's suffering funny.*

*Copland immediately rewrote
the score, making the music harsh
and dissonant, something to jangle
the nerves. It wasn't romantic any
longer; in fact it was disturbing. At
the second screening Copland again
sat in the back and watched the
audience. This time his music had
the proper effect. The viewers felt
nervous and upset, identifying with
the young woman as she felt her
terrible loss. Everyone in the audience was sad except for Copland—
he was smiling.*

Suggestions for Further Reading

1. Ekman, P., & Friesen, W. V. *Unmasking the face.* Englewood Cliffs, N.J.: Prentice-Hall, 1975.
2. Izard, C. E. (ed.). *Emotions in personality and psychopathology.* New York: Plenum, 1979.
3. Plutchik, R. *Emotion: A psychoevolutionary synthesis.* New York: Harper & Row, 1980.

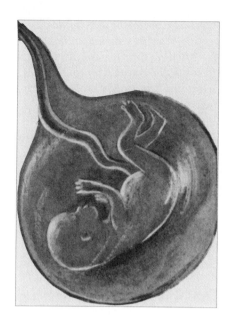

CHAPTER 11
Human Development

UNIT THREE

Development and Individual Differences

CONTENTS

Human Development

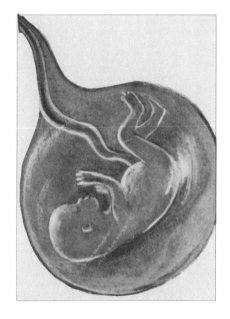

You are aware of being conscious, of residing in your own body, of seeing through your eyes and hearing through your ears. This is self-awareness, the sense that you exist. When did it first develop? When did you become aware that you were alive, that you were you, and that on each passing day when you awoke you would still be you?

You walk into the bathroom and see yourself in a mirror—there you are, it's you all right, as usual. You notice that a smudge of ink has gotten onto your forehead. You wipe it off. You are aware of yourself. You knew that the reflection in the mirror was you; otherwise you wouldn't have been able to make use of the reflection to wipe away the ink. But when do infants become aware of self? When do they realize that what the mirror shows is a reflection of themselves?

In the morning, when you arrive at the child laboratory where you are working as a developmental psychologist, you begin a series of experiments. You place a smudge of red rouge on a five-month-old in-fant's nose and set her before a mirror. She glances at the reflection in the mirror and at objects in the room. She doesn't seem to realize what the reflection is. Later that day you place a smudge of rouge on the nose of a one-year-old child and set him before the mirror. He reaches out and tries to touch the reflection. He smiles. He looks behind the mirror; is he looking for the baby in the reflection? He doesn't seem to realize who the baby with the spot on his nose is (Brooks-Gunn & Lewis, 1975).

Finally you test a 20-month-old child in the same way, placing rouge on her nose and putting her in front of the mirror. She looks at the re-flection, reaches her hand to her face, and rubs the spot on her nose (Amsterdam, 1972). She is aware; she knows that it is her reflection and that she is seeing herself. Some time between the ages of one and two, children become aware of themselves; they become conscious of being living creatures.

In this chapter we'll examine the behavioral repertoire of the

Children develop a sense of self-awareness by about the age of two.

newborn and the effects of genetic heritage and learning on important developmental changes during childhood. We'll study the potential effects of early experiences and learn how human attachments are formed. Then we'll explore cognitive development and the social changes that may be important in childhood. Finally, we'll look at developmental changes during adolescence and adulthood.

Why Psychologists Study Human Development

When should children be expected to walk? How "normal" is it for young children to be strongly attached to their mothers? When do children start to speak, and how much of what is said to them do they understand? How do children acquire a sense of right and wrong? Is adolescence usually a time of stress? Does intelligence decline as adults age?

Through careful experimentation and research, developmental psychologists try to find the answers to these and other questions. Developmental psychology is the study of age-related changes in human behavior during the life span. Developmental psychologists are interested in change over time. Time implies change; if change stops, time has stopped. What was, differs from what is, and what is, differs from what will be. By understanding human development, psychologists know what to expect during different developmental stages, and they learn the parameters of human growth and achievement.

Modern developmental psychology places the greatest emphasis on the years of infancy and childhood, the time when changes are the most apparent. After all, the difference between an infant of two and a child of nine is far greater than that between adults of 52 and 59. Nonetheless, in the last decade interest in adult development has grown rapidly as well.

The Myth of Linear Development

Before we examine developmental psychology more closely, it might be a good idea to end the strong attraction that you probably feel to the concept of linear development. Many people think that human development progresses in a fairly straight line—that is, it proceeds at a steady rate, and each new development is built on all of the developments that came before. But this is not necessarily so. Human development isn't that simple. For instance, when people speak of human development, are they referring to physical change? And, if so, which part of it—the growth of the lymphatic system, the sexual organs, visual acuity, or body size? Or by human development do they mean cognitive development—or intellectual, social, language, emotional, or sexual development?

Of course, human development includes all of these aspects and more. Therefore, development may occur rapidly *and* slowly *and* reach a plateau *and* even appear to reverse, all at the same time depending on which aspects you are considering. Furthermore, some developments appear to be dependent on each other, while others seem to occur in parallel and fairly independently of each other. In a word, human development is complex. Although it is certainly true that human development is a progression, it's not necessarily a smooth and steady one in which every new development is the direct result of an earlier one. Though this is often a difficult reality for students to grasp, there is little appeal from it. A professor of developmental psychology was once asked by a frustrated student whether there weren't some aspect of human development that could be counted on to occur at a nice, simple, fixed rate. After giving it much thought, the professor replied, "Birthdays!"

Development over the Life Span

Developmental psychologists consider the entire life span to be important. The emphasis is still on children, however. At the beginning of the century, research was influenced by the theories of the eminent psychoanalyst Sigmund Freud, who believed that infancy and early childhood were the most important periods in the development of personality.

THE FREUDIAN PERSPECTIVE

In 1908 Sigmund Freud presented a series of lectures in the United States at Clark University. In his lectures, he held up infancy and early childhood, specifically the first six years, as a formative time when many psychological conflicts had to be resolved in order for a healthy personality to develop. Freud believed that children pass through five **psychosexual stages** of development (see Table 11.1), during which physical and psychological satisfaction are centered on erogenous zones. The proper amount of gratification must be received at each stage. If not, fixation may result, with important implications for later development. Freud argued that many serious problems can grow out of a failure to progress properly through the stages, especially the first three, and that such problems may require extensive psychotherapy in later years. (Freud's psychosexual stages will be discussed in more detail in Chapter 13.)

Freud's view of child development as an important predictor of later adult personality helped generate interest in developmental research. During the last few decades, however, there has been growing evidence that, while the first six years of a person's life may be important in determining personality and development, the later years may be just as crucial or even more so—thence developmental psychologists' interest in the entire life span.

Table 11.1 Freud's stages of psychosexual development

AGE	STAGE	COMMENT
0–1 year	Oral	Child obtains greatest gratification through stimulation of lips, gums, and mouth area.
1–3 years	Anal	Child obtains satisfaction by exercising control over anus during elimination and retention.
3–6 years	Phallic	Child obtains greatest satisfaction through stimulation of the genitals.
6–puberty	Latency	Sexual drive becomes dormant and child acquires cultural and social skills.
Puberty–adult	Genital	Heterosexual desire awakens. Healthy adult development takes place.

PSYCHOSOCIAL STAGES
Stages of ego development as formulated
by Erikson, incorporating both sexual
and social aspects.

ERIKSON'S PSYCHOSOCIAL STAGES OF DEVELOPMENT

Erik Erikson, perhaps more than any other researcher, has underlined the importance of the entire life span. As a young student, Erikson worked with Freud, and over the years he has expanded on Freud's ideas. Erikson views human development as a progression through eight **psychosocial stages,** roughly equivalent in time to some of Freud's psychosexual stages (see Table 11.2). Erikson argues that during certain periods in our lives we are faced with opposing conflicts that must be resolved in order for healthy development to occur.

Erikson's view differs from Freud's in three important respects. First, Erikson places much more emphasis on social and cultural forces than Freud did. Freud believed that a child's personality was determined mainly by parents, whereas Erikson places the child in the broader world of parents, friends, family, society, and culture. Second, Erikson does not feel that failure at any particular psychosocial stage will have irreversible consequences. Unlike Freud, he believes that setbacks at any stage can eventually be overcome with proper attention, care, and love. Third, Erikson empha-

Table 11.2 Erikson's psychosocial stages

PERIOD OF TIME	CONFLICT	DESCRIPTION	FREUDIAN STAGES
1. Infancy	Basic trust vs. mistrust	Parents must maintain an adequate environment—supportive, nurturing, and loving—so that the child develops basic trust.	Oral
2. Years 1–3	Autonomy vs. shame or doubt	As the child develops bowel and bladder control, he or she should also develop a healthy attitude toward being independent and somewhat self-sufficient. If the child is made to feel that independent efforts are wrong, then shame and self-doubt develop instead of autonomy.	Anal
3. Years 3–5½	Initiative vs. guilt	The child must discover ways to initiate actions on his or her own. If such initiatives are successful, guilt will be avoided.	Phallic
4. Years 5½–12	Industry vs. inferiority	The child must learn to feel competent, especially when competing with peers. Failure results in feelings of inferiority.	Latency
5. Adolescence	Identity vs. role confusion	A sense of role identity must develop, especially in terms of selecting a vocation and future career.	Genital
6. Early adulthood	Intimacy vs. isolation	The formation of close friendships and relationships with the opposite sex is vital to healthy development.	
7. Middle adulthood	Generativity vs. stagnation	Adults develop useful lives by helping and guiding children. Childless adults must fill this need through adoption or other close relationships with children.	
8. Later adulthood	Ego integrity vs. despair	An adult will eventually review his or her life. A life well spent will result in a sense of well-being and integrity.	

NOTE: For comparison, Freud's psychosexual stages are given on the right.

sizes the life span of an individual, while Freud considered the first six years to be crucial.

In Erikson's view, children face their first major conflict—the establishment of trust rather than mistrust—during their first year. Parents or primary caregivers play the major role in helping them form a sense of basic trust. Not only should parents feed and care for their children, but they should also work to build an affectionate relationship.

After basic trust has been established, Erikson believes that children must develop autonomy in order for healthy ego and personality development to continue. This is the beginning of the second psychosocial conflict—autonomy versus shame or doubt—which Erikson asserts arises between the ages of one and three. Children start developing autonomy when they are taught how to master tasks or do things for themselves. Such accomplishments teach them that they are important and can manipulate their environment. Erikson feels that children who are not encouraged to develop self-confidence may come to doubt themselves or to be ashamed of their inability.

Erik Erikson (1902–   ).

Between the ages of three and five and a half, children who have a sense of basic trust and who feel autonomous or competent may begin to initiate their own activities. At this point the third psychosocial conflict—initiative versus guilt—emerges. According to Erikson, it is important that children be encouraged to initiate activities during this time. Sometimes, of course, the activities they initiate may run counter to parental or social rules of conduct. The best way to handle this problem, Erikson states, is to forbid the inappropriate behavior but in a manner that isn't frightening. When, for example, a five-year-old decides it would be fun to play with delicate stereo equipment, a parent should forbid the activity firmly but also gently, so that the child won't feel guilty for having initiated the behavior in the first place. In this way the child can develop confidence in his or her own planning, without fear that anything initiated may be wrong.

Between the ages of five or six and twelve, the conflict to be resolved is industry versus inferiority. Erikson argues that during this time, children should be encouraged to produce things and to complete the activities they have initiated. Through these efforts, a sense of industry is attained. The conflict between industry and inferiority is especially strong among school children, who are often in competition with each other. Erikson feels that if a child is unsuccessful at this point, feelings of inferiority may result.

The fifth stage occurs during adolescence. During this time, Erikson states, adolescents who have resolved the earlier conflicts will be best able to deal with the next one, identity versus role confusion. "Who am I?" becomes a question of major concern. Adolescents must discover their own world philosophy, ideals, and identity in order to firmly establish a sense of who they are.

During early adulthood, the major conflict is between intimacy and isolation. By intimacy Erikson means marriage and sexual intimacy, as well as social ties. For a young adult to develop healthily, Erikson argues, close bonds must be formed with a spouse, friends, or colleagues.

Erikson considers the major conflict during middle adulthood to be generativity versus stagnation. By generativity he means expanding one's love and concerns beyond the immediate group to include society and future generations. An active parenthood is one way of achieving generativity, though not the only way. Stagnation refers to becoming preoccupied

REFLEXES
An organism's automatic reaction to a stimulus. A reflex is inborn, and depends on the inherited nervous system.

MATURATION
Term used to describe a genetically programmed biological plan of development which is relatively independent of experience.

with one's own material and physical well-being, and having no concern for society or the next generation.

The last stage—ego integrity versus despair—occurs in late adulthood. By this time, Erikson argues, those who have been successful in resolving the earlier psychosocial crises will be able to look back on their lives with satisfaction and a sense of accomplishment. Others, who have lived fruitless lives filled with self-centered pursuits or lost opportunities, may feel despair instead.

Some researchers point out that Erikson's theory agrees with informal observations obtained from many sources; they believe that his theory has much to contribute as a general outline for healthy ego development. Nonetheless, hard scientific proof is not easy to come by because of the difficulty of examining each of Erikson's stages under controlled conditions in a laboratory or by other scientific methods.

Beginnings of Life—Infancy

From the turn of the century until the 1950s, the newborn was considered by many to be a helpless creature who was handed to the world like a lump of clay ready to be molded and shaped. Babies were thought to be totally incompetent and passive. They cried, wet, ate, and slept, they possessed some simple reflexes, and that was it.

However, during the 1960s and 1970s there was a sudden surge of research concerning the capabilities of infants, especially in their role as social beings who initiated interactions and maintained them. This has been referred to as the era of "Oh, look what baby can do" research (Haith & Campos, 1977). Some investigators, having demonstrated that babies actively affect their environments more than had been thought, even described them as "competent individuals." However, now that some of the excitement of this research has worn off, the pendulum appears to be swinging back, and most professors and researchers are reminding their students

Newborns generally weigh between six and nine pounds and are about 20 inches in length.

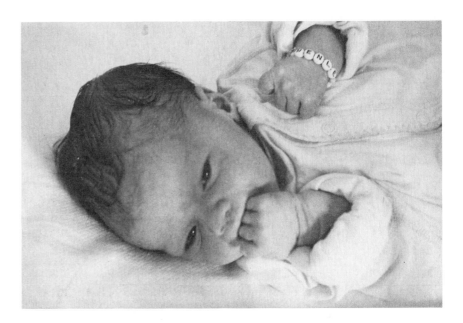

Table 11.3 Typical reflexes in newborns

REFLEX	ELICITING STIMULUS	RESPONSE	DEVELOPMENTAL DURATION
Babinski	Gentle stroke along sole of foot from heel to toe	Toes fan out, big toe flexes.	Disappears by end of 1st year
Babkin	Pressure applied to both palms while baby is lying on back	Eyes close and mouth opens; head returns to center position.	Disappears in 3–4 months
Blink	Flash of light, or puff of air delivered to eyes	Both eyelids close.	Permanent
Diving reflex	Sudden splash of cold water in the face	Heart rate decelerates, blood shunted to brain and heart.	Becomes progressively weaker with age
Knee jerk	Tap on patellar (kneecap) tendon	Knee kicks.	Permanent
Moro reflex	Sudden loss of support	Arms extended, then brought toward each other; lower extremities are extended.	Disappears in about 6 months
Palmar grasp	Rod or finger pressed against infant's palm	The object is grasped.	Disappears in 3–4 months
Rage reflex	Placing hands on sides of alert infant's head and restraining movement; blocking mouth with cheesecloth or other covering for 10 seconds	Infant cries and struggles.	Disappears in 2–4 months
Rooting reflex	Object lightly brushing infant's cheek	Baby turns toward object and attempts to suck.	Disappears in 3–4 months
Sucking reflex	Finger or nipple inserted 2 inches into mouth	Baby sucks rhythmically.	Disappears in 3–4 months
Walking reflex	Holding baby upright and placing soles of feet on hard surface; tipping baby slightly forward	Infant steps forward as if walking.	Disappears in 3–4 months

that although newborns and infants engage in many fascinating behaviors, and are certainly not passive, they are still perhaps the most helpless and dependent offspring to be found in the animal kingdom.

If you are among the many who have not met a newborn; if your first reaction to labor pains is to boil some water; or if you've never thought it odd that in early Hollywood movies the delivery-room nurse always hands the mother a 40-pound "newborn" possessing a crew cut and a full set of teeth, then you are in for some surprises. Real newborn infants (as opposed to the old Hollywood variety) have skin that is soft, dry, and wrinkled. They typically weigh between six and nine pounds and are about 20 inches in length. Their head may seem comically huge in proportion to the rest of the body, making up, as it does, fully one fourth of their length. They have a high forehead and a flat nose, and a body that turns crimson when they cry. And most newborns' eyes are steely blue, even those that will later be brown. Newborns come equipped with a number of **reflexes.** These built-in reflexes, which are independent of any learning or experience, are shown in Table 11.3.

GROWTH AND MATURATION

Many of the age-related changes in behavior observed by developmental psychologists are due in large part to underlying changes in biological development rather than to experience. **Maturation** is the term used to describe such a genetically determined biological plan of development. Human physical growth seems to be mainly a function of maturation and so, to a large extent, does motor development. For instance, approximately 93 percent of all humans will eventually develop a preference for using their

Figure 11.1 *Motor development appears to follow a maturational plan. The onset of different motor abilities at specific (average) ages is based on Mary Shirley's data gathered in 1931. Today, children generally walk at an earlier age.*

right hand. This preference first expresses itself at about the age of two years and becomes firmly ingrained by the age of eight. It appears to be due to genetic arrangement rather than to experience (Hicks & Kinsbourne, 1976). Figure 11.1 describes the maturational plan that a child's motor development appears to follow.

You might argue that a child's first step is also a result of experience with crawling and moving about. This is a type of nature-nurture question.

1. Fetal posture (newborn)

2. Holds chin up (1 month)

3. Holds chest up (2 months)

4. Reaches for object (3 months)

5. Sits when supported (4 months)

6. Sits on lap, grasps object (5 months)

7. Sits in high chair, grasps dangling object (6 months)

8. Sits alone (7 months)

9. Stands with help (8 months)

10. Stands holding furniture (9 months)

11. Crawls (10 months)

12. Walks if led (11 months)

13. Pulls up on furniture (12 months)

14. Climbs stairs (13 months)

15. Stands alone (14 months)

16. Walks alone (15 months)

Do children finally walk because they're physically mature enough, or is experience an extremely important factor along with physical maturity? In 1940 Dennis and Dennis investigated the children of Hopi Indians in an attempt to find the answer. Infants who were being reared in the traditional Hopi manner were placed on cradle boards and bound in such a way that they were unable to move their hands, raise their bodies, or roll in either direction (see Figure 11.2). They were removed from their cradle boards only a few times a day so that their mother could change them. Otherwise they remained on the boards, even while sleeping or being fed. There were also Hopi infants who were being reared without cradle boards, since their parents had adopted "Western" ways. The researchers found that motor development was the same regardless of the method used: All of the infants walked at about 15 months.

Another nature versus nurture investigation was carried out by McGraw, also in 1940, by studying a pair of twins during a toilet-training project. McGraw attempted to train one child to use the toilet from an extremely early age, while the other received no training. After 23 months of practice, the trained twin was finally successful. At the same age, the other twin however, also learned to use the toilet, and after only a few attempts. This experiment demonstrates that children must be maturationally ready before they can learn a particular skill.

Because physical growth and motor development appear to be mainly a function of maturation, it would seem that the environment should have only a small role. Yet environmental factors can have an important bearing on maturational development. For example, although a child's physical growth appears to be biologically determined, nutrition can directly affect growth. With proper nutrition the predetermined biological plan can unfold, allowing the child to reach his or her predetermined physical potential. But without good nutrition, the child's maturation may be severely hindered. Similarly, other environmental experiences may act as "accelerators" or "decelerators" of maturational development.

Look again at Figure 11.1. Mary Shirley observed that the children in her sample walked unaided at an average age of 15 months. Today, children typically walk on their own a few months earlier than this figure indicates. For that matter, children in different countries tend to walk for the first time at different average ages (Hindley, Filliozat, Klackenberg, Nicolet-Meister, & Sand, 1966). How might experience account for these discrepancies in the average ages at which children first walk?

Nutritional differences offer one possible explanation not only of variations between countries but also of the differences over time that have been observed in this country. After all, Shirley's data were taken in 1931 during the Depression. Alternatively, today's accelerated rate may be due to parents who, eager to see their children walk, encourage them to try just as soon as they are maturationally able. On the other hand, parents during the 1930s often had larger families, and they might have been considerably less excited by the first steps of their fourth, fifth, and sixth children and so have encouraged them less. The differences may even be due to the introduction of wall-to-wall carpeting! Perhaps babies who attempted to walk in 1931 found landing on a hardwood floor punishing enough to deter their efforts for a time.

Because of different environmental considerations, such as nutrition, parental attention, and even wall-to-wall carpeting, motor development

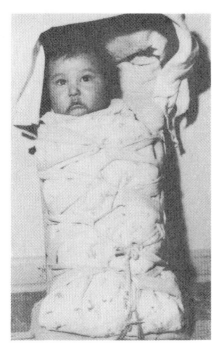

Figure 11.2 *Hopi infant swaddled in a cradle board.*

A child's first steps.

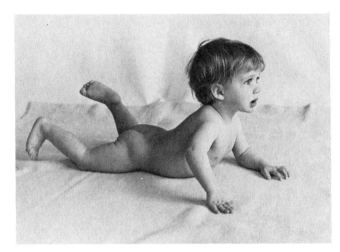 

may occur at a slightly faster or slower rate than we might expect—but only within maturational limits. No matter what kind of nutrition, coaxing, or carpeting is present, a four-month-old is not going to walk unaided.

Individual Differences and Temperament Theories   There is much evidence demonstrating that, even shortly after birth, babies are different from each other. Some cry and fret, some sleep, some are quietly active. Workers on obstetrics wards are familiar with the great range of personalities noticeable within the first few days (Fries, 1954).

Temperament theories are based on the fact that these early personalities or traits are fairly stable over time. In one such theory, put forward by researchers Thomas, Chess, and Birch in 1970, infants were described in terms of "easy" or "difficult" temperaments. The easy infants adapted readily to new situations, were approachable, responded with low or mild intensity, exhibited pleasant moods, and had regular body rhythms. The difficult babies were quite the opposite. Some infants fell in between; they were referred to as "slow-to-warm-up" babies. Other infants were too inconsistent to categorize, exhibiting "mixtures of traits that did not add up to a general characterization" (Thomas, Chess, & Birch, 1970, p. 105).

Among the infants studied, the researchers found that 40 percent were easy, 15 percent slow to warm up, 10 percent difficult, and 35 percent inconsistent. What makes these findings most interesting is that these temperaments are stable over time. An easy child, who didn't cry much over wet diapers at two months of age, was also less likely to fuss when being dressed or undressed at one year of age. Follow-up studies at five and ten years showed continued stability in these traits. Some studies have found that such stable temperaments may even continue into adulthood (Carey & McDevitt, 1978).

Motor Development   Just as individual babies differ from each other, so too do individual rates of motor development. Some infants proceed quickly,

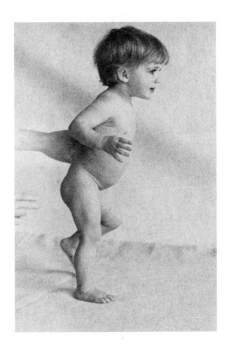
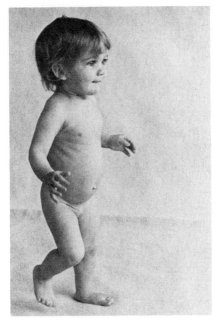
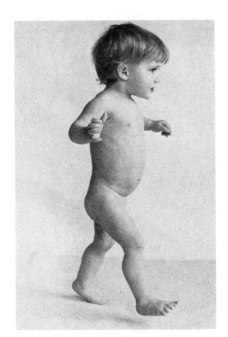

others lag behind. Some develop rapidly in one area and simultaneously are slow in another. Like the tortoise and the hare, some infants may race ahead of their peers only to be equalled or overtaken later.

Parents often place great importance on the speed of their child's physical and motor development. But they should not be too elated or too concerned if their infant is several months ahead of or several months behind the published norms. Sometimes a six-month-old will learn to sit without support and then, from the parents' point of view, develop no further for four or five months. The frustrated parents may wonder why their baby doesn't stand or crawl—surely a prerequisite to walking—only to have the child suddenly stand up and toddle off somewhere after five months of remaining pretty much at the sitting stage.

Neural Development As you might expect, the nervous system of the newborn is relatively immature compared with your own. The readouts from an electroencephalograph (EEG), which, as you'll recall, measures electrical brain activity as waves, may appear to be quite irregular in newborns or even flat. If your EEG were flat, it would typically mean that you were in a deep coma or no longer among the living. But in a newborn a flat EEG doesn't necessarily mean that anything is wrong.

While the differences between adults' and infants' EEG patterns are not always so striking, such differences as are observed are most likely due to the fact that the newborn's nervous system is still growing. Neural dendrites are noticeably immature in newborns. In addition, autopsies of newborns have revealed that the axons of the neurons in the central nervous system, down which neural messages typically travel, are not yet myelinated (Morell & Norton, 1980).

A great deal of the infant's maturational development may be directly tied to a rigid timetable of neural development. For example, it has been observed that infants begin to smile at about the same age the world over, an occurrence that may be directly related to the amount of myelin that

Rhesus monkeys isolated at birth show bizarre behavior patterns once they are older.

the infant possesses (Greenberg, 1977). Some nerve-fiber systems develop myelin rapidly, while others take more time. In fact, some parts of the brain aren't fully myelinated until puberty (Yakolev & Lecours, 1967). Over the last few decades, researchers have been attempting to discover the ages at which basic sensory skills become available to infants.

THE EFFECTS OF EARLY EXPERIENCE

At the University of Wisconsin, different baby rhesus monkeys were socially isolated for the first three, six, and twelve months of their lives. During these times they were kept in small, barren cages and allowed no contact with their mother or any other monkey. These experiments were conducted over a number of years; their intent was to discover the effects of such isolation on later development.

The findings generally demonstrated that three months of isolation produced few long-term deficits (Griffin & Harlow, 1966) but that six months or more of isolation caused severe developmental disturbances. The monkeys in the latter category began to bite themselves. They held onto themselves and rocked back and forth in an autistic way. Their emotions became bizarre, and they made strange facial grimaces. They huddled together and sometimes lashed out in rage or fear. Some of the monkeys isolated for a full year became so withdrawn that they seemed to be little more than "semi-animated vegetables" (Griffin & Harlow, 1966).

In these monkey labs, researchers investigated other important factors related to the effects of early isolation and stimulus deprivation. They discovered that the timing of the isolation was as important as its duration. Monkeys isolated later in life were not as severely affected as those whose isolation began at birth. They also discovered that females seemed to be less affected by early isolation than males (Sackett, Holm, & Landesman-Dwyer, 1975) and that another species of monkey, the pigtail monkey, was not as severely affected by early isolation as was the rhesus (Sackett, Holm, & Ruppenthal, 1976).

This last finding was especially important because the major concern of the researchers was not primarily to discover the effects of early experience on the later development of monkeys, but to generalize their monkey data to human beings. Since different monkey species react to early isolation differently, it can be assumed that humans might also have unique reactions. If this is the case, the data obtained from the rhesus studies may be of only limited value in indicating how such isolation might affect human children.

It would obviously be unethical to attempt such isolation studies with humans. Nonetheless, psychologists have had many opportunities to study children raised in deprived circumstances not of anyone's deliberate making. In 1945 René Spitz examined a number of infants who had been left in a foundling home by mothers too poor to support them. The home was overcrowded, and each caregiver was forced to contend with large numbers of infants at a time. These babies were unable to see their surroundings because the sides of their cribs were draped with white sheets to keep them quiet—the way people drape their canaries at night. The babies were rarely handled. They spent so much time on their backs inside the cribs that small hollows began to develop beneath their bodies in the mattresses. The hollows eventually became so deep that the average one-year-old wasn't able to turn over. The only "toys" they had were their hands and feet (Spitz, 1945).

The infants were found to be developmentally retarded when compared with children in another institution who were receiving care and stimulation. In a two-year follow-up, Spitz noted that many of the children in the original foundling-home study were still developmentally behind, even though conditions at the home had improved dramatically. He concluded that the damage done to the children was probably the result of lack of love and attention from a mother or close personal caregiver (Spitz, 1946). Because of Spitz's discoveries, the use of foundling homes was severely curtailed in the United States and foster programs were begun.

Spitz's research has not gone unchallenged, however. His findings were criticized by a number of researchers because they may have contained some methodological flaws and biases (Pinneau, 1955). Still, his observations give us an indication that such early treatment of young children isn't likely to be beneficial.

Reports of similar circumstances have cited different outcomes. In his book *Children of the Creche* (1973), Dennis described a study, begun in 1959, of infants raised in a Lebanese foundling home in Beirut. There was only one attendant for every ten infants. The infants were rarely handled and were unable to see out of their cribs, since sheets were draped over the sides (sound familiar?). They were swaddled for the first four months of their lives, as is the Near Eastern custom. Because of this, the movement of their arms and legs was severely restricted. These children became developmentally retarded, as did the children Spitz observed. However, children from the Lebanese foundling home who were adopted gained back the ground they had lost during their many years in the institution, and later appeared to be developmentally normal.

Other studies have also indicated that early developmental deficiencies need not necessarily affect later development (Rheingold & Bayley, 1959; Rheingold, 1961). In a study of children in Guatemala, Kagan and Klein (1973) noted that the Guatemalan children generally lived in isolated, poor farm communities and spent the first year of their lives tightly clothed and confined to dark, windowless huts. They had few toys. Adults and siblings talked and played with them only about a third as often as a similar family would have in an American home. Although these children were at first developmentally retarded by our standards, by the time they reached adolescence they had become developmentally equal to American children in a variety of perceptual and cognitive tasks.

Findings such as these demonstrate considerable **plasticity** in children. That is, even given adverse conditions, children appear under some circumstances to be able to bounce back. On the other hand, differential treatment, even within one household, can sometimes have drastic effects on the later development of children, as the following case study indicates.

The Self-fulfilling Prophecy of Mrs. A Mrs. A. had four children. Her husband was in good health, and there was no history of mental retardation in her family. Her first child was healthy and, by all accounts, normal. However, during her second and third pregnancies Mrs. A. came to believe, for reasons that are not known, that the children she was to bear would be retarded. Both the second and the third child were normal at birth and showed no signs of deficiency, but Mrs. A. continued to believe that they

PLASTICITY
The ability of an organism to bounce back from or make up for adverse environmental influences.

were defective. She raised both of these children in relative isolation. She kept them in a bare room and fed them a limited amount of food until the older isolated child, a girl, was six years old. Oddly, Mrs. A. believed that her fourth child would be normal, and she raised that child as she had her first-born, providing warmth, love, and proper nutrition.

The differences between the four children were striking. The second and the third child were seriously developmentally retarded. The oldest of the two, the six-year-old girl, did not speak, and her growth was considerably stunted for her age. In contrast, the first and the fourth child appeared developmentally normal. Mrs. A.'s children were eventually taken from her by the court, and the middle children were last reported to be making some recovery under institutional care (Fletcher, 1974).

Overcoming Adverse Early Experiences As you'll recall, rhesus monkeys raised in total isolation for the first six months of their lives developed bizarre social and emotional behaviors. In 1972, Suomi and Harlow demonstrated that the effects of six months of isolation could be overcome by pairing the abnormal, isolated monkeys with normal monkeys. Previous attempts to pair such isolated animals with normal peers had failed because normal monkeys of the same age tended to overwhelm the helpless and withdrawn isolates. This time, however, the researchers attempted to pair the six-month-old isolates with normal three-month-old rhesus monkeys because younger monkeys were more likely to be sociable without also being aggressive.

In this experiment, four six-month-old male isolates served as "patients," and four normal three-month-old females were the "therapists." Individual "therapy sessions" were arranged between a patient and a therapist for six hours per week. "Group therapy" between more than one patient and more than one therapist was also held. After six months of therapy, the patients and therapists were indistinguishable in their behaviors. As the researchers put it, "The primary finding of this experiment was that monkeys reared in total social isolation for the first six months of life exhibited significant recovery of virtually all behavioral deficits across all testing situations after appropriate therapeutic treatment. Reversal of the isolation syndrome to an equivalent degree over such a range of situations had not been previously achieved or approached via any experimental procedures" (Suomi & Harlow, 1972). In 1973 Harlow and Novak successfully treated rhesus patients that had been isolated for the first 12 months of their lives by placing them with four-month-old therapists.

One of the best-known attempts to overcome early deprivation with human children was the Skeels study begun in the 1930s. Skeels set out to discover whether the debilitating effects of early institutionalization on children could be overcome by placing the children in a better environment, where caregivers could stimulate them and serve as examples of appropriate behaviors. In order to conduct this experiment Skeels arranged to have some of the children in an overcrowded, understaffed orphanage sent to another institution.

The institution that Skeels chose was the Glenwood State School for retarded adult women, where ages ranged from 18 to 50. The two environments were very different from each other. The Glenwood State School was certainly a rich environment compared with the orphanage. At the school, the children were able to engage in one-to-one interaction with adults. These adults, although intellectually deficient compared with average adults, were intellectually superior to the children from the orphanage. The children were placed in open, active wards with the older and relatively brighter inmate women. Both the inmate women and the attendants at the school became very fond of the children placed in their charge. They often played with them, and the different wards liked to compare children to see which ward had the best and brightest.

The average age of the 13 children sent to Glenwood was 19 months; their average IQ was 64.* The average IQ of the 12 children who stayed behind in the orphanage was 87, so Skeels had actually picked the most deficient of the orphans to place in the school. The effects on these orphans of moving to the less deprived environment were striking. The average gain in IQ after only 18 months in the new institution was 29 points.

Skeels was excited by these initial improvements, but he wondered whether they would last. He began a series of follow-up studies, the first of which was conducted 2½ years later. Eleven of the 13 children originally transferred to the Glenwood home had been adopted, and their average IQ was now 101. The two children who had not been adopted were reinstitutionalized and lost their initial gain. The contrast group, 12 children who had not been transferred to Glenwood, had remained institutional wards of the state and now had an average IQ of 66 (an average decrease of 21 points).

In 1966 Skeels again examined these "children," who had now become adults. The differences were stunning. In the experimental group, those raised in the Glenwood State School, he found no deficiencies that he could trace to their early experiences in the orphanage. The differences in terms of occupations and marriage history between the experimental and the contrast group are obvious to anyone viewing the data (see Table 11.4). These findings demonstrate that early deprivation can indeed often be overcome.

It should be added, however, that the Skeels study has been criticized on methodological grounds (Longstreth, 1981). Still, Skeels' study is important because it is one of the few undertaken to determine whether the effects of adverse early experiences could be reversed. As Skeels has said, "It seems obvious that under present-day conditions there are still countless infants born with sound biological constitutions and potentialities for development well within the normal range who will become mentally retarded and noncontributing members of society unless appropriate intervention occurs" (Skeels, 1966).

INFANT ATTACHMENTS

As soon as infants are able to crawl around they tend to follow their mothers or caregivers from room to room. Freud believed that this strong attachment resulted from nursing, during which infants form a pleasure bond with their mother. But research with rhesus monkeys has cast doubt on this speculation (Harlow & Suomi, 1970).

Monkey Love In a series of experiments begun over 20 years ago, Harry Harlow and his colleagues separated rhesus monkeys from their mothers

---

*An average IQ score is 100. Scores below 70 are usually considered to be in the retarded range.

Table 11.4 Comparison of the experimental and contrast groups in the Skeels study—Occupations of subjects and spouses

CASE NO.	SUBJECT'S OCCUPATION	SPOUSE'S OCCUPATION	FEMALE SUBJECT'S OCCUPATION PREVIOUS TO MARRIAGE
EXPERIMENTAL GROUP			
1[a]	Staff sergeant	Dental technician	—
2	Housewife	Laborer	Nurses' aide
3	Housewife	Mechanic	Elementary school teacher
4	Nursing instructor	Unemployed	Registered nurse
5	Housewife	Semi-skilled laborer	No work history
6	Waitress	Mechanic, semi-skilled	Beauty operator
7	Housewife	Flight engineer	Dining room hostess
8	Housewife	Foreman, construction	No work history
9	Domestic service	Unmarried	—
10[a]	Real estate sales	Housewife	—
11[b]	Vocational counselor	Advertising copy writer[b]	—
12	Gift shop sales[c]	Unmarried	—
13	Housewife	Pressman-printer	Office-clerical
CONTRAST GROUP			
14	Institutional inmate	Unmarried	—
15	Dishwasher	Unmarried	—
16	Deceased	—	—
17[a]	Dishwasher	Unmarried	—
18[a]	Institutional inmate	Unmarried	—
19[a]	Compositor and typesetter	Housewife	—
20[a]	Institutional inmate	Unmarried	—
21[a]	Dishwasher	Unmarried	—
22[a]	Floater	Divorced	—
23	Cafeteria (part-time)	Unmarried	—
24[a]	Institutional gardener's assistant	Unmarried	—
25[a]	Institutional inmate	Unmarried	—

SOURCE: Skeels, 1966.   [a]Male.   [b]BA. degree.   [c]Previously had worked as a licensed practical nurse.

SURROGATE MOTHERS
In Harlow's experiments, a substitute mother, often made of wire or cloth, which replaced the real mother in the life of a baby rhesus monkey.

at an early age and placed them with artificial **surrogate mothers** (see Figure 11.3). One surrogate was made of wire; the other was covered with terry cloth and had a more rhesus-looking face. Both "mothers" could be equipped with baby bottles inserted through a hole in the chest, which allowed nursing to take place. Regardless of which mother provided food, the baby rhesus spent as much time as possible cuddling and hugging the cloth mother. Even rhesus monkeys fed only by the wire mother formed strong attachments to the cloth mother and spent most of their time hugging her.

Of course, you might expect such a result because cloth feels better than wire. In this sense "creature comfort" seems to be more important than nursing in the formation of attachments. But Harlow took his experiments further than this. Do you remember those plastic insects called "cooties" that you could buy in the store and assemble (see Figure 11.4)? Harlow discovered that baby rhesus monkeys are generally terrified of cooties. After all, they are about the same size as a baby monkey, and they do look scary. Harlow found that when a baby rhesus was placed in a room with a cootie and a cloth surrogate mother, the infant would run to the mother and cling to her body. It would then relax and become calm; apparently it felt safe. At this point the baby monkey would often begin to use the mother as a safe base of operations from which to explore the environment. Harlow even captured an incident on film in which an infant eventually dared to

Figure 11.3 *The cloth and wire surrogate mothers used by Harlow in his experiments with rhesus monkeys. Even if the only food available was from the wire mother, the infants preferred the cloth mother.*

run up to a cootie, pull off one of its antennae, and run back to the surrogate mother.

Harlow varied the experiment in a number of ways. At one point he placed the cootie between the rhesus and its surrogate cloth mother. The terrified baby ran directly at the cootie, leaped over it, and landed squarely on the surrogate mother where it gradually relaxed and seemed to become secure. This experiment demonstrated the power of the attachment the baby rhesus felt toward the surrogate mother.

Such early attachments in rhesus monkeys are formed quickly and are long-lasting. Baby rhesus monkeys raised with cloth mothers and then separated from them for six months will respond eagerly the instant they are reunited, rushing to the cloth mothers and clinging to them.

Figure 11.4 *The dreaded cootie.*

There may be instinctive components to these attachments. For instance, it may be that an attachment is easier to form with an object that looks like the real mother. But without early experience the attachment won't occur. If a baby rhesus monkey that has been raised without a surrogate mother is placed in a room with one and a fear stimulus such as a cootie, it will not run to the mother but will simply curl up and shake with fear.

Human Attachments   While we must be careful when generalizing from one species to another, it does seem that the attachments that form between human infants and their mothers or primary caregivers are similar to those that form in rhesus monkeys. Human babies also use their mothers as a base of operations from which to explore the environment. Like rhesus babies, human babies and young children are also more likely to explore their immediate surroundings when their mothers are present.

Human infants regularly exhibit a desire to stay near their mothers. This desire, demonstrated by crying and distress when the mother leaves, reaches its peak at about the age of two years. This phenomenon has often been referred to as **separation anxiety.** Between the ages of two and three years, separation anxiety usually decreases, and the child becomes more willing to leave the mother's side and interact with peers and strangers.

Some of the most interesting studies on human attachments during infancy have been conducted by Mary Ainsworth and her colleagues. Ainsworth's studies are superior to most in their scope. They have included a one-year investigation of infant attachments in the home; a 20-minute laboratory test known as the "strange situation," which demonstrates individual differences in the quality of attachment; and an assessment of the variables that determine the maternal quality of infant attachment.

The strange situation was arranged in the following way: A mother and her young child (approximately two years old) would enter the experimental room. The mother would place her child on a small chair surrounded by toys and would then take a seat on the other side of the room. A short time later, a stranger would enter the room, sit quietly for a moment, and then try to engage the child in play. At that point the mother would abruptly leave the room. In a short while, the mother would return and play with the child, and the stranger would leave. Then the mother would exit once more, leaving the child completely alone for three minutes. Then the stranger would return. A few minutes later the mother would return. Everything that happened during those 20-minute tests was recorded through a one-way mirror. As you can see, the organization of the strange situation places the child in a number of circumstances designed to test separation anxiety (see Figure 11.5).

Earlier studies of separation effects had concentrated on how infants cried when abandoned or how they reacted to spending time alone, whereas Ainsworth and her associates were more interested in the infant's reaction to the return of the mother. By using a number of observational techniques, they were able to observe three attachment reactions of differing quality. The most common was called **secure attachment.** Babies exhibiting this response gave their returning mothers a happy greeting and approached them or stayed near them for a time. The second reaction was called **ambivalent attachment.** Infants who responded in this way would approach their mothers, cry to be picked up, and then squirm or fight to get free. The third reaction, **avoidant attachment** (a rather paradoxical term),

Figure 11.5 *Ainsworth used the strange situation to investigate infant attachments. In studies of children aged 2, 2½, and 3, the percentage of those who cried was recorded during different parts of the experiment. Similar patterns emerged, with a general decrease in stress occurring as the child became older.* (SOURCE: *Maccoby & Feldman, 1972, p. 24*)

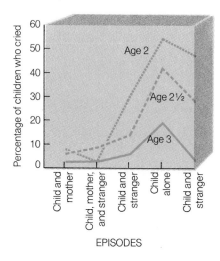

was demonstrated by infants who did not approach their returning mothers or who actively avoided them.

These three kinds of attachment were also observed in the infants monitored at home and appeared to be related to the way in which the mothers reacted to their children (Ainsworth, Bell, & Stayton, 1971). Mothers of babies who reacted ambivalently or showed avoidant attachment typically responded to their infants' cries and demands only when they were in the mood to, and often ignored them at other times. They also appeared to be less sensitive to their infants' requests or needs (Stayton & Ainsworth, 1973; Main, 1975). Ainsworth and her colleagues rated the mothers in terms of accessibility, sensitivity, and cooperation in their daily dealings with their babies. Mothers who rated high also had securely attached babies (Ainsworth, Bell, & Stayton, 1971). These mothers responded rapidly to their infants' cries. Their infants were also more likely to obey verbal commands (Stayton, Hogan, & Ainsworth, 1971).

Ainsworth's impressive studies have not gone completely uncriticized. Some researchers have had reservations about the adequacy of the control methods and the danger of too much subjectivity (Cohen, 1974; Feldman & Ingham, 1975). There have also been a couple of studies that have suggested that, contrary to Ainsworth's hypothesis, infants who exhibit different kinds of attachments may not be behaving differently because of the way their mothers treat them, but rather, the other way around—the mothers may be behaving differently because of the way their infants are acting (Stern, 1971; Gewirtz & Boyd, 1976).

Attachment to Fathers So far in our discussion of attachment, we haven't mentioned fathers. In fact, fathers have been shortchanged, and prior to 1972, most researchers ignored them. Happily, though, fathers have begun to attract attention in the last ten years.

Studies have shown that both the father's presence and absence can affect the personality development of a child (Lynn, 1974). In comparisons of older infants' reactions to mothers, fathers, and strangers, infants have reacted to their fathers more as they do to their mothers than as they do to strangers (Feldman & Ingham, 1975; Kotelchuk, Zelazo, Kagan & Spelke, 1975). (Isn't it nice to know, Dad, that you're not a stranger in your own home?) Similar results have been found in other cultures (Lester, Kotelchuk, Spelke, Sellers, & Klein, 1974). The earliest age at which specific father attachments have been found was eight months (Lamb, 1975).

Interestingly, infants form different kinds of attachments to their father than they do to their mother. In general, infants are more distressed by being separated from their mother (Keller, Montgomery, Moss, Sharp, & Wheeler, 1975). And in frightening laboratory settings, infants are more likely to cling to their mother than their father (Lamb, 1975). What all this probably means is that infants form strong attachments to primary caregivers and slightly weaker attachments to secondary caregivers, and in our culture it is typically the mother's role to be the primary caregiver, while the father takes a lesser part. Of course, there may also be biological reasons for the child to form special attachments with the one who gave birth to him or her—but then again, you have to wonder how an infant would know who that was.

Unfortunately, very few studies have proceeded from the question of *whether* attachments are formed between an infant and his or her father

SEPARATION ANXIETY
Fear of being separated from the caregiver; a form of anxiety that develops in the infant about 10 to 18 months after birth.

SECURE ATTACHMENT
According to Ainsworth, the bond exhibited by infants who approach their mother happily, maintaining an especially close attachment.

AMBIVALENT ATTACHMENT
According to Ainsworth, the bond exhibited by infants who approach their mother happily but then squirm to get free.

AVOIDANT ATTACHMENT
According to Ainsworth, the bond exhibited by infants who actively avoid their mother.

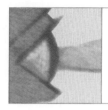

JEAN PIAGET (1896–1980)

Next to Sigmund Freud, Jean Piaget is the most frequently referenced researcher in the psychological literature (Endler, Rushton, & Roediger, 1978). That this should be so is strange in a way, since Piaget was trained as a biologist, not a psychologist. The first paper that Piaget wrote and published was a discussion of a rare part-albino sparrow. At the time he was ten years old. Piaget later became interested in mollusks and wrote over 20 articles on the subject, becoming so well known in the field that he was offered the job of curator of the Mollusk collection at the Geneva museum. He had to turn down the offer because he was still in high school (Leo, 1980).

By the age of 22, Piaget had received a Ph.D. in biology, and he continued to be interested in mollusks. He noticed that when large mollusks were taken from lakes and moved to small ponds, they underwent structural changes because of the reduced wave action in the ponds. He understood this to mean that the mollusks had inherited a structure that was flexible; they would adapt, within limits, to the environment into which they were placed. In other words, the genes in the mollusks not only carried signals for specific biological development, but also signals for biological changes in response to different environmental

experiences. Piaget became curious about whether there were parallels or similarities in our own species.

While observing children responding to intelligence test questions, Piaget noticed that older children seemed to have adapted their thought processes so that they could better deal with the questions. His observations led him to the conclusion that older children, rather than simply knowing more than younger children, actually thought differently about problems. Piaget wondered whether this could be evidence that children's biologically inherited brains flexibly adapted to their environments by altering their underlying thought structures, much as the mollusks had adapted to the ponds. He asked himself how this interplay between biology and experience might develop, and this question led him to investigate cognition and thought processing in human beings. At the age of 24, Piaget began his pioneering studies on the development of intelligence in children. "I was haunted," he once said, "by the idea of discovering a sort of embryology of intelligence" (Leo, 1980, p. 55). By the time he was 30, his work was known throughout Europe and he was acclaimed. However, his theories were slow to gain acceptance in the United States, mainly because of the strong

emphasis American behaviorists place on the environment.

Behaviorists stress that the environment shapes the individual, not heredity. In this view, there are no significant instinctive behaviors or inherited behavioral structures in human beings. Piaget, on the other hand, felt that the development of intelligence and thought was due partly to nature and partly to nurture. In Piaget's view, the maturation of the brain and the nervous system must proceed in conjunction with experience in order for an individual to adapt to the environment. Piaget believed that since humans are genetically similar and share many of the same environmental experiences, they can be expected to exhibit considerable uniformity in their cognitive development. He went on to describe four predictable stages of cognitive development that he argued occur during specific periods in a child's life.

Piaget worked for many decades and contributed greatly to our knowledge. He was undoubtedly one of the most respected psychologists of our time. Yet he did not consider himself a psychologist. Instead, he referred to himself as a genetic epistemologist, that is, a biologist-philosopher who wanted to know how reason and thought developed in human beings.

(they are) to the question of *how* they are formed. Some have suggested that while the mother's role is caregiver, the father's is playmate (Lamb, 1975). The implication of this view is that infants may be more attached to their mother only because of the sex role that society has chosen for her. If, early on, the father took the position of primary caregiver and the mother that of playmate, the attachments formed might be the opposite of what we usually find.

The Developing Child—
Piaget's Stages of Cognitive Development

Cognition refers to the way in which we gain knowledge through perception, memory, and thought processing. Jean Piaget believed that a child's cognitive understanding of the world is *qualitatively* different from an adult's. Children are not simply adults who know less (a quantitative difference), and conversely, adults are not simply knowledgeable children. Adults and older children are capable of thoughts that are, quite literally, beyond the understanding or conceptual abilities of younger children. Even when the thinking of older children is carefully explained and demonstrated, younger children will typically fail to understand the thought processes involved.

In Piaget's view, cognitive development is the combined result of development in the brain and nervous system and of experiences that help the individual adapt to the environment. Piaget argued that cognitive development occurs in stages (see Table 11.5) and that all children follow a similar pattern. However, some individuals develop at a slower pace or fail to complete their development. If you happen to have a child in your home, watching him or her advance through these cognitive stages can afford endless hours of pleasure.

The following handy rules will help you understand Piaget's stages:

1. The ages given in Table 11.5 for each stage are approximate only. A child does not, for example, advance from the sensorimotor to the preoperational stage simply by having a second birthday.
2. All children advance through each stage in the order described; children never skip a stage.
3. Sometimes, while leaving one stage and entering another, a child may exhibit cognitive aspects typical of both stages.
4. An older child or an adult, although at an advanced cognitive stage of development, may at times rely on lower cognitive processes. As a ridiculously exaggerated, but perhaps memorable, example, my very bright grandmother (who was certainly operating with the most advanced stage of cognition) was limited strictly to sensorimotor processes until her first cup of morning coffee!

Jean Piaget (1896–1980).

Table 11.5   Piaget's stages of cognitive development

STAGE	AGE OF OCCURRENCE	CHARACTERISTICS
Sensorimotor	0–2 years	Early: "Out of sight, out of mind" Late: Object permanence begins to emerge
Preoperational	2–7 years	Object permanence fully developed Animistic thinking Egocentrism
Concrete Operations	7–11 years	Conservation Reversibility Decentering
Formal Operations	11 + years	Application of rules to situations that violate principles of reality Hypothetical analysis Systematic and complex deductions Logic of combinations Use of the abstract

The first of Piaget's four stages of cognitive development, the **sensorimotor stage,** is characterized by a lack of fully developed **object permanence.** Object permanence refers to the ability to represent an object, whether or not it is present. Piaget believed that object permanence is necessary before problem solving or thinking can be carried out internally, that is, by using mental symbols or images.

Look around you—do you see a redwood tree? Unless you live in a fairly scenic California setting and are sitting next to a window, you probably don't. But can you mentally represent a redwood tree to yourself, even though one isn't present? You can do this in a number of ways. You can picture a redwood tree in your "mind's eye" (if you know what the tree looks like). Or you can think of the letter symbols REDWOOD TREE. Or you might actually sign a depiction of a redwood tree with your hands. The point is, you can keep any object "permanent," even when it is absent, by using these techniques. Without mental images, symbols, or depictions to represent an object, you would be unable to think of it because you would have no internal way of representing it. In other words, without object permanence, "out of sight, out of mind."

Piaget argued that object permanence is absent during the early part of the sensorimotor stage, and as a result an infant may be unable to think. By the middle of the sensorimotor stage, it is apparent that some thought processing does occur, but object permanence is not fully developed until the end of the sensorimotor stage. Once object permanence is fully developed, the child leaves the sensorimotor stage.

Some of Piaget's most interesting experiments and observations concerned the onset and development of object permanence during the sensorimotor stage. If, during the first four months of the sensorimotor stage, you show infants an object that attracts their attention and then block their view of it with a screen, they will act as if the object had simply vanished. By the middle of the sensorimotor stage, they will try to regain visual contact with an object that has disappeared from view. This attempt may indicate the beginnings of object permanence, since the infant may be searching for the hidden object because it has some internal representation that something was once in view, but is now gone. But even by the middle of the sensorimotor stage, object permanence is not fully developed.

For infants in the Sensorimotor Period, "out of sight" is often "out of mind."

By the end of the sensorimotor stage infants come to a complete understanding of object permanence. For example, a two-year-old child may put his juice glass down on the floor to have both hands free to open a door and, while looking at the door, form a mental image (which requires object permanence) of the door opening and of the juice glass being in the way. At this point, and not before, problem solving can be accomplished by mental combinations, symbols, or images, and it is no longer necessary to depend on the physical existence of an object in order to comprehend it or ways in which it might be manipulated. In the past few years it has also been discovered that great apes—chimpanzees, gorillas, and orangutans—also pass through the sensorimotor stage in a way similar to the human progression (Chevalier-Skolnikoff, 1979). However, once the apes attain object permanence their cognitive development appears to stop, while human cognitive development continues far beyond the capacities of the great apes.

THE PREOPERATIONAL STAGE (2-7 YEARS)

The **preoperational stage** is distinguished from the sensorimotor stage mainly by the continued development and use of internal images and symbols. The development of thought, as represented by the establishment of object permanence, marks the dividing line between the sensorimotor and preoperational stages. This internalized thought may be the precursor of self-awareness. The fact that the great apes, too, develop object permanence may help explain why they share a sense of self-awareness with our species. It may be that when a creature begins thinking to itself by using internal representations of objects (object permanence), it becomes aware that it has a self. That the infants we cited in the chapter Prologue hadn't yet reached this stage may be the reason they didn't know what the mirror was reflecting. Without object permanence, they couldn't engage in the kinds of internal thinking that may be necessary for self-awareness to emerge.

Although there are many similarities between ourselves and the great apes, we are different—perhaps only because our cognitive development continues beyond theirs. As the preoperational stage sets in, the child demonstrates greater and greater use of symbolic functions. Language ability increases dramatically, and imaginative play becomes more apparent as children spend much of their time engaging in make-believe. Another difference of this period is that children can put off imitating another's behavior for some time, implying that they now have a way of symbolically remembering behavior originally observed in a model. All of these actions suggest an internal cognitive mediation between incoming stimuli and later responses.

This stage in a child's cognitive development is called preoperational because the child hasn't acquired the logical operations characteristic of later stages of thought. As children begin to symbolize their environments and develop the ability to internalize objects and events, they develop immature concepts which Piaget called **preconcepts.** For instance, preconceptual children may have a general idea that birds have wings, fly, and are often found in trees, or that cars have wheels, doors, and are found on streets—and yet not be able to distinguish between kinds of birds or kinds of cars. It is common for three-year-olds to refer to every car as Daddy's car or to believe that every Santa Claus they have encountered on a Christmas

SENSORIMOTOR STAGE
According to Piaget, the stage of cognitive development characterized by a lack of object permanence. This stage occurs during the first two years of a child's life.

OBJECT PERMANENCE
Term used by Piaget to refer to the individual's realization that objects continue to exist even though they are no longer visible.

PREOPERATIONAL STAGE
According to Piaget, the stage of cognitive development characterized by object permanence, transductive and syncretic reasoning, animistic thinking, and egocentrism. This stage occurs during the years from two to seven in a child's life.

PRECONCEPT
A Piagetian term describing immature concepts held by children in the preoperational stage.

ANIMISTIC THINKING
The belief that inanimate objects are alive; characteristic of children in Piaget's preoperational stage of development.

EGOCENTRISM
Thought process characteristic of children, in which they view themselves as the reference point in their dealings with the external world. Characteristic of children in Piaget's preoperational stage.

FAILURE TO DECENTER
The inability of preoperational children to comprehend more than one aspect of a problem at a time.

REVERSIBILITY
A Piagetian term describing an ability obtained during the stage of concrete operations. Reversibility is the ability to understand that actions taken on objects if reversed in sequence will return the object to its original state.

CONSERVATION
The principle that quantities such as mass, weight, and volume remain constant regardless of changes in the appearance of these quantities.

CONCRETE OPERATIONS
According to Piaget, the stage of cognitive development characterized by the use of logical operations and rules rather than intuition. This stage occurs between the seventh and eleventh years of a child's life.

Figure 11.6 *The three-mountain problem.*

shopping trip is the one and only Santa. (Of course, as adults you and I know that there is only one Santa and the others are just helpers.)

Animistic thinking is the belief that inanimate objects are alive. Consider the following conversation between Piaget and a preoperational child:

PIAGET: Does the sun move?

CHILD: Yes, when one walks it follows. When one turns around it turns around too. Doesn't it ever follow you too?

PIAGET: Why does it move?

CHILD: Because when one walks, it goes too.

PIAGET: Why does it go?

CHILD: To hear what we say.

PIAGET: Is it alive?

CHILD: Of course, otherwise it wouldn't follow us, it couldn't shine. (Piaget, 1960, p. 215)

In this case the child has attributed life to the sun because it appears to move, which is a quality of most living objects.

In the later part of the preoperational stage, children rely heavily on intuitive rather than logical thinking. That is, they rely more on their senses and imagination than on logic. Piaget also argued that the reasoning of preoperational children is further limited because they tend to be egocentric. **Egocentrism** is self-centeredness. By this Piaget did not mean that children are selfish, but that they generally perceive the world only from their own perspective. Piaget demonstrated this aspect by using the differing-perspectives problem, or, as it is commonly called, the three-mountain problem. In this problem a child is seated in a chair facing a table upon which three mountains are placed (see Figure 11.6). Three other chairs are placed around the table, and a doll is seated in one of these chairs. The child is then instructed to select from a set of drawings what the doll sees. Children seven or eight years old are likely to pick the correct drawing, while preoperational children typically choose the drawing that depicts only what they themselves see.

Preoperational children are limited in other ways as well. One of the most severe limitations is the inability to comprehend more than one aspect of a problem at a time. Piaget referred to this aspect as the **failure to decenter** in order to describe such children's tendency to center exclusively on single aspects of problems. Children who are unable to decenter arrive at solutions that seem more intuitive than logical. For example, a preoperational child presented with two identical glasses of water will realize that they are equally full. But suppose we pour the water from one of the glasses into a dish, while the child watches. He or she will most likely believe, when comparing the dish of water with the remaining glass, that the water in the dish is now less than the water in the glass because it is at a lower level (see Figure 11.7). Of course, you and I know that there is still the same amount. We know that no water has been added or taken away (excluding residue remaining in the glass and evaporating during pouring). We've conserved quantity (one aspect), although the shape of the volume has altered (another aspect). Because we can decenter, we can comprehend more than one aspect at a time. Children in the preoperational stage seem unable to do this.

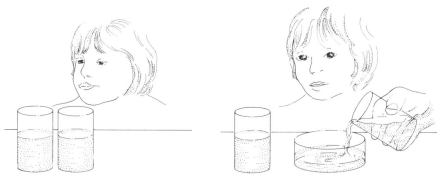

Figure 11.7 *Testing a child for the ability to conserve. (a) The child agrees that glasses A and B contain the same amount of water; (b) water from one of the glasses is poured into a dish. The child doesn't realize that the dish and the remaining glass contain the same amount of water, that is, the child is unable to conserve one aspect (amount) while another aspect (height) changes. Another way to say this is that the child centers his or her attention on only one obvious aspect (height) while an adult would "decenter" and consider all aspects.*

Figure 11.8 *The falling-stick cards represent a temporal, or time, order when placed in the correct sequence. Preoperational children seem unable to comprehend this kind of ordering.*

Another way of solving the problem posed in Figure 11.7 is to imagine that the water from the dish is being poured back into the glass. This action would bring us right back to where we began, proving that the amount of water in the dish was the same as was originally in the glass. The ability to imagine or conceive of doubling back, or reversing what you have just done, is called **reversibility.** Preoperational children have a terrible time with this seemingly simple idea.

In the following example (Phillips, 1969, p. 61), a four-year-old preoperational child is having a little difficulty with reversing. He is asked, "Do you have a brother?" He says, "Yes." Then he is asked, "What's his name?" He replies, "Jim." But when asked, "Does Jim have a brother?", he says, "No."

It also appears that preoperational children don't readily perceive that actions may follow a particular sequence in time. Look at the falling-stick cards shown in Figure 11.8. It would be easy for you or me to arrange them in their correct order, but preoperational children fail to grasp this temporal arrangement. And have you ever asked a class of preschoolers to line up according to height? Good luck! Once you have taught them how to do it, you'll find, moreover, that they haven't mastered the concept of ordering by height, but have simply learned who should be standing behind whom (an effective strategy until someone is absent).

THE STAGE OF CONCRETE OPERATIONS (7-11 YEARS)

Between the ages of seven and eleven, children's thought processes become more competent, flexible, and powerful as they come to understand and apply decentering and reversibility, which we discussed in the previous paragraphs, and **conservation,** which we'll discuss now.

Children are able to conserve when they grasp the fact that quantitative aspects of an object will not change unless something is added or taken away. Children who understand conservation will not be fooled by apparent changes in the amount of water when the water is transferred from a container of one shape to another. They will know that, during these transfers, no water has been added or taken away and, therefore, the amount of water remains the same. It is conserved despite the change in shape.

Piaget stated that the ability to conserve marks the end of the preoperational stage and the beginning of **concrete operations.** The major difference between the preoperational and concrete stages is not that children can no longer be tricked by problems that require conservation, but rather that children are beginning to use logical operations and rules rather than intuition. This change is viewed as a shift from reliance on perception to reliance on logic, and it is a giant leap.

Figure 11.9 outlines the many different kinds of conservation that are acquired during the period of concrete operations. The ages given are approximate and vary with the method employed to test the particular conservation (Baer & Wright, 1974). Piaget used the term **horizontal decalage** to describe the fact that some kinds of conservation are mastered before others. It's fascinating to watch children dealing with conservation tasks before the horizontal decalage is complete. For instance, a child who has grasped one kind of conservation, such as that related to substance, but not a more abstract kind (further along the horizontal decalage), such as that

Figure 11.9 *An example of the many kinds of conservation tasks investigated by Piaget.* (SOURCE: *Lefrancois, 1980, p. 352*)

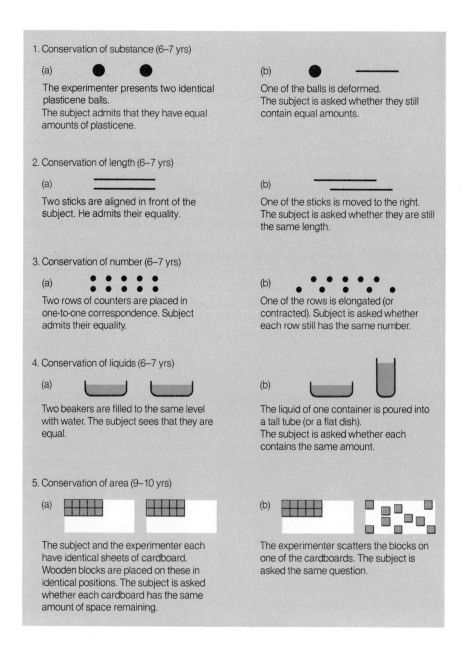

1. Conservation of substance (6–7 yrs)

(a) The experimenter presents two identical plasticene balls.
The subject admits that they have equal amounts of plasticene.

(b) One of the balls is deformed.
The subject is asked whether they still contain equal amounts.

2. Conservation of length (6–7 yrs)

(a) Two sticks are aligned in front of the subject. He admits their equality.

(b) One of the sticks is moved to the right.
The subject is asked whether they are still the same length.

3. Conservation of number (6–7 yrs)

(a) Two rows of counters are placed in one-to-one correspondence. Subject admits their equality.

(b) One of the rows is elongated (or contracted). Subject is asked whether each row still has the same number.

4. Conservation of liquids (6–7 yrs)

(a) Two beakers are filled to the same level with water. The subject sees that they are equal.

(b) The liquid of one container is poured into a tall tube (or a flat dish).
The subject is asked whether each contains the same amount.

5. Conservation of area (9–10 yrs)

(a) The subject and the experimenter each have identical sheets of cardboard. Wooden blocks are placed on these in identical positions. The subject is asked whether each cardboard has the same amount of space remaining.

(b) The experimenter scatters the blocks on one of the cardboards. The subject is asked the same question.

related to weight, may realize that a ball of clay rolled into the shape of a hot dog still has the same *amount* of clay as when it was a ball. But what happens when the child is shown two identical clay balls and watches as they are weighed on a balance scale? The child sees that they weigh the same. Then one of the clay balls is rolled out into a hot dog shape. The child is asked whether the rolled-out clay will still weigh the same as the other ball. Although able to conserve substance, and knowing, therefore, that the *amount* of clay has remained the same despite the change in shape, the child can't yet conserve weight and consequently will not realize that the rolled-out clay will still *weigh* the same.

Operations are logical rules. Preoperational children, as we have seen, do not rely on logic or logical operations in forming their conclusions. Children in the stage of concrete operations are able to use logical rules to deal with problems such as conservation and number concepts. They are limited, however, to the world they have seen. They are not yet able to comprehend the completely hypothetical—to compare what is, with what is not or with what may be.

Ask some children in the concrete operations stage what it would be like if people had tails. You will find that their answers will tend to center on literal descriptions of where the tail would be or how funny it would look; or they might reply that people don't have tails, or that they would use them to hang from trees. The children will stay within the boundaries of what they have actually seen an animal or cartoon character do with a tail. The freedom to imagine beyond the concrete to situations or actions never before seen is limited.

Older children in the stage of formal operations would respond to the same question by freely hypothesizing beyond anything they had ever seen or experienced. They would give you answers such as:

1. Lovers could secretly hold tails under the table.
2. People would leave elevators in a great hurry.
3. Dogs would know when you were happy.

THE STAGE OF FORMAL OPERATIONS (11+ YEARS)

During his years of research, Piaget noted time and again that, unlike children in the concrete operations stage, who are still limited, adolescents and adults are able to apply logical rules to situations that violate principles of reality. During the stage of **formal operations,** individuals acquire the ability to make complex deductions, analyze ways of reasoning, and solve problems by systematically testing hypothetical solutions. In order to make the distinction between concrete and formal operations clearer, let's look in on a game of chess for a moment.

Children in the period of concrete operations are quite able to learn the simple rules of chess. However, they are incapable of playing advanced games because such games require complex hypothetical deductions about all the possible moves that might be made. Children in the period of concrete operations are typically limited to making one move at a time based on what they actually see on the board, rather than thinking four or five moves ahead and imagining all sorts of potential combinations and outcomes. A number of years ago *Time* magazine published an account of "the chess game of the century," a contest between Bobby Fisher and Donald

HORIZONTAL DECALAGE
Term used by Piaget to describe the onset and order of different abilities throughout the concrete and formal operations stages.

FORMAL OPERATIONS
According to Piaget, the stage of cognitive development in which the child becomes capable of the most advanced thinking; including the use of the hypothetical. For most children, this stage begins at about 11 years of age.

Byrne. Chess masters today consider it to be one of the grandest examples of complex and systematic analysis on the chessboard. Bobby Fisher won the game. He was 13 years old at the time! According to Piaget, once a child has entered the stage of formal operations, there are no longer qualitative differences between the child's thought processes and those of an adult many years older. Piaget believed that after the last qualitative leap into formal operations has occurred, any further advances are "mere window dressing."

Adolescents entering the formal operations stage also pass through a horizontal decalage. First, they become capable of dealing with the logic of combinations, which requires the simultaneous manipulation of many factors, either singly or in conjunction with one another. Second, they become able to use abstract concepts in order to make thought more flexible. Third, they become able to deal with the hypothetical as well as the real (Piaget & Inhelder, 1969). According to Piaget, this last step is the most advanced form of cognition, and it defines formal operations thinking.

THE STAGES IN REVIEW — MONOPOLY A LA PIAGET

As a quick review, observe how children's developing cognitive skills become apparent in the way they play a familiar game, monopoly.

SENSORIMOTOR STAGE	Children put houses, hotels, and dice in mouth. Chew on "get out of jail free" card.
PREOPERATIONAL STAGE	Children play "at" monopoly, but intuitively make up their own rules. They can't understand the instructions because they find it difficult to play in turns, conserve amounts (rents owed and money possessed), and generally to comprehend the goals of the game.
CONCRETE OPERATIONS STAGE	Children understand the basic instructions and are able to follow the rules, but they can't deal with hypothetical transactions concerning mortgages, loans, and complex bargains with other players.
FORMAL OPERATIONS STAGE	Children are no longer tied to concrete and tangible rules and are able to engage in the complex hypothetical transactions unique to each game. (Some people call this way of playing cutthroat monopoly, but when I was eight, I called it cheating.)

Cognitive theory has widened the scope of developmental psychology by emphasizing the development of children's active thought processes. As you might imagine, education in Western Europe and North America has been greatly affected by cognitive theory, especially the work of Piaget. At the same time, Piaget's theory has been criticized for placing too much emphasis on the biological development and maturation of underlying cognitive structures, and not enough on the effects of experience and the environment. In support of this contention, some researchers have argued that if the environment is manipulated in certain ways, children can be hurried through the stages of cognitive development faster than Piaget suggested. Or, as Bruner has stated, "Some environments push cognitive growth better, ear-

WHY CHILDREN STOP BELIEVING IN SANTA CLAUS

Since children the world over appear to progress through periods of cognitive development in a specific order, and since each period defines the child's cognitive abilities, parents might be able to understand their children's limitations and abilities better if they considered their children's particular cognitive stage of development. Those who are familiar with Piaget's theory will find many opportunities to observe cognitive advances in their children's thought processes. One researcher, Lawrence Fehr, has examined a particularly familiar example of cognitive development, one that most all of us can relate to through personal experience—namely, why children stop believing in Santa Claus (Fehr, 1976).

Have you ever wondered what kind of thinking is required in order to believe in Santa Claus? Look again at Table 11.5. Why would children in the stage of concrete operations—children capable of conserving—come to doubt Santa's existence?

A child who conserves amount will realize that, for every child in the world to receive at least one gift, the number of toys must equal the number of children. A child who has seen that seven or eight packages just barely fit into the trunk of the car will be perplexed. How can Santa put all of those presents in one sack (or even two or three)? Furthermore, a child engaging in concrete operations, who can understand the temporal sequence of events, will begin to wonder how Santa can visit

Santa and a true believer.

every house in the world on one night. As you can see, even if the mean kid on your block hadn't told you that there was no Santa Claus, you'd probably have deduced it on your own sooner or later.

But what happens when parents try to counter their child's doubts with statements such as, "Santa can do all these things because he has many helpers?" Interestingly, if other adults and peers support the myth and supply such answers, the child may continue to believe. There are many cultures in which wild superstitions are firmly believed by the adults. There is an

important distinction to be made here: The fact that we develop cognitively doesn't necessarily mean that we acquire the ability to distinguish truth from fiction. Thus, the answer to the question "Why do children stop believing in Santa Claus?" is *not* because children develop cognitively; it is rather because the members of the society confess to the myth when a conserving child begins to chip away at it. If peers, parents, and other adults supported the myth and provided answers satisfactory for the child's cognitive level, Santa could be expected to survive the onslaught of concrete operations.

lier, and longer than others . . . it makes a huge difference to the intellectual life of a child simply that he was in school" (1973).

Still, as a description of a very complex matter—the development of thought—Piaget's theory is unequalled. There is no question about what Piaget observed; his observations have been repeatedly confirmed. However, why cognitive development progresses as it does is not as clear. Evidence gathered from investigating the great apes has indicated that cognitive growth, at least during the sensorimotor period, may be closely tied to genetics and biological maturation. It may be that infants and very young children develop cognitively in stages and more uniformly because much of their development is directly tied to neurological maturation, whereas older children and adults develop less in stages and less uniformly because learning and individual experiences come to play a greater role in cognitive processing. Future research may help us to understand more fully the cognitive development of human beings and the respective roles of learning and biology in this development.

The Developing Child—Social Processes

Socialization begins when an infant is treated by others in a way that fosters the development of skills, attitudes, or behaviors deemed appropriate by the society. Some have argued that as soon as a boy baby is wrapped in a blue blanket, or a girl in a pink one, the socialization process has started. Until children are old enough to interact meaningfully with peers, or to enter school, their families are usually the primary agents of socialization. And even after children enter school, their families still function as the central unit in their lives.

THE FAMILY

The social system within a family is usually described by generations and genders and the roles assigned to each (Feiring & Lewis, 1978). Once this initial organization is arranged, psychologists are faced with the incredibly complex task of studying the interactions. How is the child affected by parent-child relationships? How is the husband and wife's relationship affected by the relationships between their children? How does parental behavior affect the child's ability to form peer friendships? The number of possible interactions is extensive, and adding to the complexity is the fact that family relationships often differ between families and across cultures.

Most researchers studying the family take data but are rarely able to organize experiments. As a result, most child-rearing studies are correlational, and cause-effect relationships are very difficult to infer (Bell, 1968). Generally, researchers look for similar patterns of interactions or behavior among many families before drawing general conclusions about family relationships and parenting. Most investigators use questionnaires, interviews, or direct observations. Questionnaires and interviews present problems, however, since parents often recall things as they wish they had been, rather than as they actually were (Robbins, 1963). In their recollections, parents tend to see average offspring as exceptional, or unpopular offspring as widely liked. Also, parents with two or more children often confuse the behaviors of one child with those of another. Direct observation can also present problems, in that parents, children, and other family members usually know they are being watched and they act accordingly. As a result, research into family socialization patterns through observation can be very difficult (Hartup, 1979).

The great bulk of our knowledge in this area is based on descriptive data. Although there have been some laboratory experiments dealing with parent-child interactions in a social context, most work has concentrated on describing the roles of the parents and the child in the socialization process, as well as the roles of other family members.

Parental Roles—On Being Mothers and Fathers   Table 11.6 outlines the tasks of parents and children in the socializing process. As you can see, the parent's job is truly one of "teacher." Of course, parents, too, are products of socialization. They have been taught their obligations within the society, one of which is that they must now pass on their knowledge to their children.

All parents have desires and hopes for their children. The way in which parents achieve these ends can differ greatly from family to family. Researchers do not agree on which of the many child-rearing practices is best. But it is known that parents provide role models for their children and that children rely on their parents to teach them about the world.

When a culture's values and traditions begin to undergo rapid change, it obviously becomes difficult to decide which attitudes and beliefs children should be taught. As one researcher has stated,

> today's children are the first generation to be raised amid doubt about role prescriptions that have long gone unchallenged. This makes their socialization especially difficult. Traditionally, socialization was a process of raising the young to fill major roles in society when the present incumbents vacated them. Yet today we do not know what type of society our children will inherit, nor the roles for which they should be prepared. (Lamb, 1979, p. 941)

Working Mothers   For many years our society favored a household arrangement in which the father worked and the mother was a housewife. Working mothers were considered neglectful of their children if they didn't "have to" work or unfortunate if they did. Obviously, the children would suffer—or would they? These days, many families are finding that both husband and wife must hold full-time jobs in order to make ends meet.

Table 11.6   The tasks of parent and child in the socializing process

PARENTAL AIM OR ACTIVITY	CHILD'S TASK OR ACHIEVEMENT
1. Provision of nurturance and physical care	Acceptance of nurturance (development of trust)
2. Training and channeling of physiological needs in toilet training, weaning, provision of solid foods, etc.	Controlling the expression of biological impulses; learning acceptable channels and times of gratification.
3. Teaching and skill training in language, perceptual skills, physical skills, self-care skills in order to facilitate care, ensure safety, etc.	Learning to recognize objects and cues; language learning; learning to walk, negotiate obstacles, dress, feed self, etc.
4. Orienting the child to her immediate world of kin, neighborhood, community, and society, and to her own feelings.	Developing a cognitive map of one's social world; learning to fit behavior to situational demands.
5. Transmitting cultural and subcultural goals and values and motivating the child to accept them for her own.	Developing a sense of right and wrong; developing goals and criteria for choices; investment of effort for the common good.
6. Promoting interpersonal skills, motives, and modes of feeling and behaving in relation to others.	Learning to take the perspective of another person; responding selectively to the expectations of others.
7. Guiding, correcting, helping the child to formulate her own goals, plan her own activities.	Achieving a measure of self-regulation and criteria for evaluating own performance.

SOURCE: Clausen, 1968, p. 141.

Note: Teaching is a major part of the parent's role. As teachers, parents impart the demands and requirements of the family and society.

Consequently, younger children are often placed in day-care centers or with caregivers while their parents work. Recent findings do not support the contention that such children will necessarily suffer. As measured by achievement on IQ, reading, arithmetic, spelling, and linguistic tests during an eight-year longitudinal study (a study in which the same subjects are repeatedly measured over time), young children of working mothers are not ordinarily adversely affected by their mother's absence (Cherry & Eaton, 1977). In fact, many such children have been found to be superior in cognitive and social development to the children of nonworking mothers. Data obtained from studies of the children of working mothers have suggested that these mothers tend to compensate for their absence by interacting more with their children when they are at home (Hoffman, 1979).

In families where both parents work, the parents obviously model other roles than they do in families where the father is the breadwinner and the mother the homemaker. When both parents work, the father is more likely to become involved in child care. Children from such homes typically display attitudes less tied to sex stereotypes (Hoffman, 1979). This difference is especially notable in the daughters of working mothers, who regard women's roles as more satisfying and women as more competent than do the daughters of nonworking mothers (Broverman, Vogel, Broverman, Clarkson, & Rosenkrantz, 1972). Maternal employment is also likely to function as an incentive to children to set higher occupational or educational goals for themselves (Stein, 1973).

Furthermore, if an employed mother is happy with her job and able to provide for her child's daily needs so that she need not worry about her child's security, she may perform as a parent as well as or better than an unemployed mother. In many cases, unemployed mothers find their homemaking job overly stressful because money problems are more likely to occur in families having only one employed spouse. Finally, and perhaps most importantly, employed mothers tend to encourage their children to be more independent and self-sufficient from an early age (Hock, 1978).

The Father's Changing Role Although fathers are individuals and differ from one another, they have some behavioral patterns in common that have specific effects on their children. By the time children are two, fathers appear to withdraw from their daughters and develop closer ties with their sons. It has been argued that fathers are primarily responsible for initiating sex-differentiating treatment (Lamb, 1977). Two-year-olds generally favor the parent of the same sex, and the father's differential treatment may be responsible for this preference (Lamb, 1977; 1979). Boys raised without fathers are likely to manifest gender-role deficiencies, especially if the father is absent during their infancy (Biller, 1974). Similarly, girls raised without fathers are more likely to show dissatisfaction and maladjustment in the female role and to have problems interacting with males (Hetherington, 1972).

Father's differential treatment of daughters and sons may change as modern trends emphasizing equality of the sexes are adopted to a greater degree. In some psychologists' view, fathers have a very important role to play in the development of "liberated" daughters (Lamb, Owen, & Chase-Lansdale, 1979). However, most fathers still do not approve of their daughters' having nontraditional aspirations regarding achievement and career choice (Lamb, 1979). Perhaps future fathers will be more likely to commu-

nicate to their daughters that such desires aren't unfeminine. Such a change in parental attitudes may eventually relieve many women of any doubts they may have about social or career aspirations.

Divorce and One-Parent Families   Divorce rates in the United States have increased dramatically in the past 20 years. According to current assessments, over 40 percent of marriages among young people will end in divorce. Of the children born in the 1970s, almost 50 percent will spend an average of six years in one-parent households. Nine out of ten of these children will reside with their mothers. Among the children who reside with their fathers, the majority will be of school age (Glick & Norton, 1977).

Divorce should not be viewed as a single event, but rather as a complex series of disorganized transitions requiring considerable adjustment. Since most divorced parents eventually remarry, children often undergo an extended period of transition and disequilibrium during which they must become accustomed to a stepparent and a new environment.

Many children respond to divorce with anger and fear. It is also common for children to feel guilty or in some way responsible for the divorce and

Part of a parent's role is to provide support for his children.

to become withdrawn and depressed (Hetherington, 1979). Most children can adapt to a divorce within a couple of years, but if the crisis is aggravated by additional stress or conflicts, serious developmental disruptions can result. Whether children fare well may depend on their temperament, their past experience, their age, and the support they receive from their parents.

Temperamentally, children labeled as "difficult" (Thomas, Chess, & Birch, 1970) have been found to be more vulnerable to the stress of a divorce than are "easy" children (Graham, Rutter, & George, 1973). It may be that difficult children tend to provoke anger and hostility in their parents, who are already under considerable stress because of the divorce, and that such parental behavior aggravates the situation for the children.

Generally, girls are better able to cope with a divorce than are boys (Tuckman & Regan, 1966). Following a divorce, boys usually have a higher rate of behavior disorders and more problems in relating to others. The reason may be that in most divorces the children "lose" their fathers, and as we have mentioned, boys are usually more attached to their fathers than are girls. The extra difficulties associated with boys may also stem in part from their mother's preconceptions. Mothers who have custody of their sons may expect greater disciplinary problems from them because their fathers are absent, and they may try to forestall such problems by being stricter with them than they are with their daughters. In general, mothers tend to view their sons more negatively after a divorce than they do their daughters (Santrock & Tracy, 1978).

Children may fare well in single-parent families, but the chances of problems increase. Children raised by mothers alone tend to perform more poorly on standardized intelligence and achievement tests, and they generally show cognitive deficits (Biller, 1974). The differences between the scores of these children and those of children from two-parent families can be considerable. As one researcher has reported, children from single-parent families may be two months to a year and a half behind in achievement, and may have IQ scores as much as 14 points lower and grade point averages a full grade less than children from two-parent families (Shinn, 1978). Such intellectual deficits among children from single-parent families are generally found only in children of school age; they are rare in preschoolers (Rees & Palmer, 1970). It has been argued that many of the intellectual problems following divorce may be due to the absence of the father. This assumption must be viewed with caution, however, since it is often difficult to assess the effect that a father's absence is having on a child. Any behavior of the child's that could be attributed to the absence of the father could just as well be attributed to the effects of the mother's economic or emotional distress.

Children's chances of adjusting easily in single-parent families may depend greatly on the community support services available to the parent, such as day-care or financial support. Single parents often find it very helpful to be relieved of the burden of being a parent 24 hours a day, and added financial support may enable them to make ends meet. As Eleanor Maccoby has noted,

> childrearing is something that many people cannot do adequately as single adults functioning in isolation. Single parents need time off from parenting, they need the company of other adults, they need to have other voices joined with theirs in transmitting values and maturity demands to their children. (Maccoby, 1977, p. 17)

Strictly speaking, peers are equals. Nonetheless, children often have play-mates who are three or four years older or younger than they are. Many psychologists therefore consider children who are interacting at about the same behavioral level to be peers, regardless of age (Lewis & Rosenblum, 1975). Even so, explorations of peer relationships usually concentrate on interactions among children of approximately the same age.

Children are individuals, and they don't all behave alike. Nonetheless, certain age-related trends in peer interaction are common to most children. Interaction between peers can begin during the first year of life. While it's hard to imagine eight- or nine-month-olds having friends, infants of this age have been observed, in nurseries and day-care centers, to have definite pref-erences for certain peers (Lee, 1973).

By the age of two, children show some independence from their parents and enjoy interacting with other boys or girls. Still, two-year-olds are much less likely to take advantage of opportunities to interact with peers than are older children (Heathers, 1955). The temperaments of young children may influence their friendships and peer relations for a considerable time. One longitudinal study showed that children who were sociable and friendly at the age of two and a half were likely to be the same way when they were seven (Waldrop & Halverson, 1975).

Between the ages of seven and nine, children generally form close friend-ships with peers of the same sex. This same-sex preference is also appar-ent in children's choices of imaginary playmates (Manosevitz, Prentice, & Wilson, 1973). During this time children begin to rely on their peers as important sources of information, frequently using them as standards by which to measure themselves. They tend to look to their peers as models of behavior and for social reinforcement as often as they look to their own families.

By the age of ten or eleven, peer friendships are very important. If a child's peers profess values and exhibit behaviors that conflict with those espoused by the child's family, challenges to parental authority and serious family arguments may ensue (Elkind, 1971). Generally, though, there is remarkable agreement between a child's peers and family members in terms of accepted values and behaviors (Douvan & Adelson, 1966; Hartup, 1970). This probably happens because children are socialized first of all by

As children grow older, peers become a greater influence.

PUBERTY
The stage of maturation in which the individual becomes physiologically capable of sexual reproduction.

GROWTH SPURT
The time during puberty in which adolescents' growth undergoes a marked acceleration.

their families, and they later choose playmates and friends who hold values similar to those they have been taught.

Peers usually have greater influence over the child's choice of friends and in situations involving challenges to authority, personal or group identity, interpersonal behavior, language fads, and clothing choices (Brittain, 1963). Peers are also more influential in shaping sexual attitudes and behaviors (Vandiver, 1972). Adults, especially parents, are more likely to influence the child's future aspirations, academic choices, and political views (Hyman, 1959). In the majority of cases, though, children's behaviors are the result of influence exerted by both peers and parents (Siman, 1977).

Among six- and seven-year-olds, peer groups tend to be informal and unstructured, but as children grow older their peer groupings sometimes become more organized and formal. The different skills, powers, and abilities of group members become important distinctions. Status ordering based on characteristics such as appearance, pubertal development, athletic skill, academic achievement, or leadership ability is common (Savin-Williams, 1979).

In an effort to be admired and accepted, members of peer groups will attempt as best they can to conform to the standards and values of the group. Conformity to peer group standards generally increases with age, but a great deal depends on the tasks or behaviors demanding conformity. Older children who are certain of their position on an issue are less likely to be influenced by peers than are younger children. In ambiguous situations, however, when children are uncertain of their positions, conformity with peers is more likely with increasing age (Hoving, Hamm, & Galvin, 1969).

Adolescence, Adulthood, and Aging

Behind each maturational change lies the development of essential cells within the brain and body. Every aspect of a child—emotions, skills, and aptitudes—is related either directly or indirectly to body structure. Feelings about body image underlie many social interactions. This is especially true during adolescence, when many obvious physical changes occur.

ADOLESCENCE

Most people know that girls mature earlier than boys, but few people give much thought to the fact that adolescents of the same age may be either completely prepubescent or completely physically mature (see Figure 11.10). Yet the level of physical development can profoundly affect adolescents and their interactions with peers and school. Psychologists need to be aware of physical growth and development and especially of the effect these changes may have on a person's emotions or behavior. In fact, everyone should have a better understanding of the physical changes that take place during adolescence, so as to be able to better understand an adolescent's feelings and behavior.

At the beginning of adolescence a number of physical changes occur. These are maturational changes controlled by genetics and hormones. One change is the development of sexual maturity during a period called **puberty.** At the onset of puberty the testes and ovaries enlarge. During puberty the reproductive system matures, and secondary sexual character-

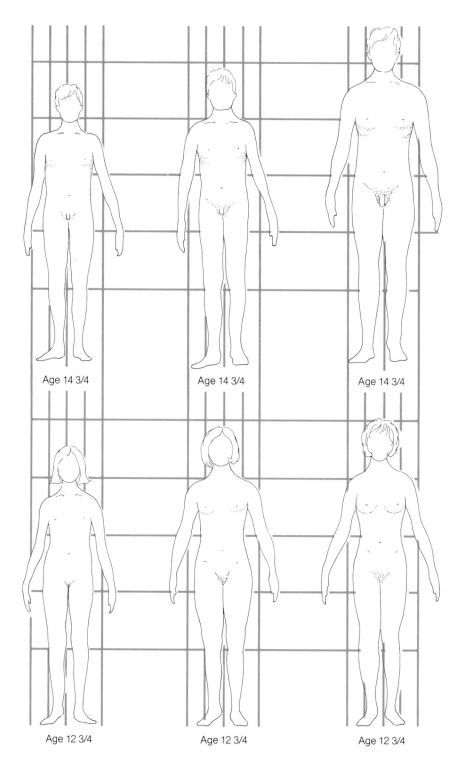

Age 14 3/4   Age 14 3/4   Age 14 3/4

Age 12 3/4   Age 12 3/4   Age 12 3/4

Figure 11.10 *Differing degrees of pubertal development at the same chronological age.* UPPER ROW: *three boys all aged 14.75 years.* LOWER ROW: *three girls all aged 12.75 years.* (SOURCE: *Adapted from Tanner, 1969*)

istics emerge. At this time adolescents' growth undergoes a marked acceleration. Height and weight increase dramatically, and body proportion changes. This occurrence, known as the **growth spurt,** lasts for two to three years and begins in girls about two years earlier than it does in boys (see Figure 11.11). As you can see, the growth rate in centimeters per year declines from birth through age ten in girls and through age twelve in boys.

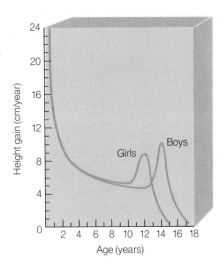

Figure 11.11 *Typical individual growth curves for height in boys and girls. These curves represent the growth of the typical boy and girl at any given instant.* (SOURCE: *Tanner, Whitehouse, & Takaishi, 1966*)

This trend reverses during the growth spurt, when the rate of growth accelerates. During this stage, the legs grow more rapidly than other parts of the body and often give the adolescent a disproportional appearance. It can take a while to become accustomed to a body of new proportions; this may be one of the reasons adolescents occasionally appear clumsy. Boys usually reach their full height between the ages of 18 and 20, while girls reach this plateau between the ages of 16 and 17 (Roche & Davila, 1972). Other common physical changes include the development of acne because of the activity of sebaceous glands beneath the skin, and the vocal changes that embarrass maturing boys by causing their voice suddenly to drop an octave in mid-speech.

As the cognitive skills of adolescents develop, they are confronted for the first time with the overwhelming complexities and abstract qualities of the world. Nothing is simple any more. Religious values, political values, social concepts, and questions about personal identity seem to encompass endless hypothetical possibilities from which the adolescent is expected by parents and society to draw conclusions and adopt a life philosophy. During our adult years we have time to organize and make sense of this confusion. We adopt a philosophy. We take political, social, and moral positions and incorporate them into our identity. In this sense adulthood would have a stability that is not immediately available to the adolescent.

Our culture demands that adolescents handle a number of developmental tasks. Sexual relationships must be faced. Social maturity in dealings with both sexes is expected. One's own masculine or feminine role must be realized and adjusted to one's satisfaction. There must be a coming to terms with one's physical development. Our culture expects adolescents to achieve emotional independence from parents and other adults. Decisions about whether to marry or to have a family become more pressing. Pursuing a career choice is also an essential part of adolescent development. Adolescents are expected to develop a philosophy and moral ideology as well as to achieve socially responsible behavior (Havighurst, 1972).

EARLY ADULTHOOD (18–40)

By the time an individual reaches early adulthood, growth is typically completed, though the potential for greater strength increases during early adulthood and reaches a plateau at about 30 (Troll, 1975). Very few people fulfill their peak strength potential by 30 or at any other time. Between the ages of 20 and 30 a person's strength usually reflects life-style rather than age. Many men and women are stronger than their age-mates because of exercise. On the average, by the time a person reaches 60, there is about a 10 percent loss of muscle strength relative to its peak potential at 30 (Bischof, 1976). But since most people are never at their peak this loss usually goes unnoticed. Thirty-year-olds may also experience a sensory decline resulting in slightly poorer vision and hearing than they had as adolescents, but these differences aren't very significant in their effect on everyday life (Marshall, 1973).

Young adults face many choices and predicaments in our society. There are decisions about sexuality, marriage, children, career, friendships, social and civic interactions, and much more. Furthermore, adults are finding that many social attitudes are changing; for instance, the question whether to marry and have children is less clearcut than it used to be.

Marriage and Parenthood   Today, the structure of relationships between many young adults is markedly different from that existing in their parents' day. Many people are postponing marriage or planning to remain single. In 1960 approximately 6 million single men and women in their thirties stated that they had no intention of marrying (Duberman, 1974). Since that time the number of singles has increased. Many people postpone marriage in order to attend school or pursue a career. Others wait in order to live together out of wedlock in an attempt to know each other better before marriage or as a way of expressing their belief that marriage is an unnecessary ceremony. Also, the pressure to have children is lessening. In the 1940s and 1950s, it was often thought that something must be wrong biologically with one partner or the other if a couple didn't have children. In the more recent past, however, many couples have remained childless by choice, not for biological reasons.

Still, many people anticipate the problems and have children for the joy that they can bring. Such individuals are willing to work at being parents in order to gain the happiness that comes from a healthy interaction between parent and child. These parents succeed in making the transition to parenthood, handling the stress, and obtaining joy and a sense of pride and accomplishment from their parental duties (Clayton, 1975). Different people react differently. In any case it is a good idea to examine in detail what parenthood requires. If the "negative" aspects don't come as a surprise and are accepted as a reasonable trade for the happiness that parenthood can bring, the transition from two to three can be fairly smooth and happy.

Planning for a Career   One of the most important tasks facing young adults is choosing a career. In the last few decades career planning has become a more complex task (Shertzer & Stone, 1976). In the years immediately preceding the Second World War, men had far fewer career choices available to them and women had fewer still.

New fields of specialization are constantly emerging now, and careers have become more accessible than ever before. The reason choices are more difficult now is that, unlike earlier, almost everyone has an opportunity to try his or her hand at almost any career. Gone are the days when only the rich could apply to college, when sons were certain to learn their father's trade, or when careers were determined by chance openings for apprentice-helpers in the neighborhood. People are sometimes overwhelmed by the number of possibilities and are unsure of what they really want to do. Wandering from job to job or career to career is becoming more common. By the time the average person is 35, he or she will have made seven major career changes (Bernard & Fullmer, 1977).

MIDDLE AGE (40–65)

In our culture youth is idolized by the media and the public as a representation of vitality, health, and sexual viability. It's not uncommon for people to report some depression or even weeping on their fortieth birthday, and yet middle age is often the time when the rewards of power, money, and prestige become apparent. Our culture may praise youth, but it's the middle-aged who have the power.

During middle age, most adults become acutely aware that they have less time to live than they have already lived. The attitude of "What will I do

MIDLIFE CRISIS

A sense of panic that may strike individuals during middle age when they realize that the time left to them is limited. This in turn may cause a crisis in which rash behavior becomes more likely as the person attempts to regain lost youth or to gain what he or she feels has been missed.

EMPTY NEST SYNDROME

A syndrome of depression in women believed to occur when grown children leave home.

MUTATION

Any heritable alteration of the genes or chromosomes of an organism.

when I'm grown up," which may have lasted 30 years or more, is replaced by a concern that time is running out or that "There's less time left to make things the way I want them." Such feelings may lead to a **midlife crisis** in which one reevaluates his or her life in the light of this new desperation. During this time any unsatisfactory conditions may no longer be tolerated. Marriages that have lasted 20 years may suddenly dissolve; or the desire to have "one last fling" may result in an extramarital affair that might never have been considered earlier. Social relationships may be drastically altered. Careers may be abandoned. And a fear of illness or death may become so acute that health problems actually arise.

Although the notion of a midlife crisis is popular, most middle-aged adults express attitudes of self-confidence and achievement. Nearly every adult will become anxious, at one time or another, about the approaching prospect of old age or of their children's "leaving the nest." But such realizations needn't precipitate a life crisis.

The Empty Nest   Many studies are being conducted to examine issues that may be faced by women during middle age. Among these issues is the belief that once a woman's children are grown and leave the home she will face the depression of "the empty nest." This belief is founded on the conception of a woman's role as that of mother and caregiver. If this is her role, once the nest is empty it would seem natural for depression to follow.

In a study of 160 middle-aged women, Lillian Rubin investigated the **empty nest syndrome.** All of the women in the study had children who were leaving or who had left home. All had given up jobs for at least ten years following the birth of a child, and a majority were homemakers.

Rubin reported that "except for one, none of these women suffers from the classical symptoms of empty nest syndrome. In fact, just about all of them responded to the departure of the children with a decided sense of relief . . . although a few were ambivalent when the time of departure came close" (Rubin, as cited in Greenberg, 1978, p. 75).

LATER ADULTHOOD (65+)

As people reach their later years, skin loses elasticity, and moisture and wrinkling increase. Bone structure changes; bones become brittle, and older persons may actually get shorter. The body slows down. The kidneys don't filter blood as well, the lungs have reduced capacity, nerves conduct impulses at a slower velocity, the basal metabolic rate decreases, and cardiac output at rest becomes less efficient.

Developmental psychologists who have investigated older individuals have helped undo a number of misconceptions commonly held about the elderly. Their findings have revealed, for instance, that senility is a relatively rare occurrence and not something that happens in the normal course of aging (Arehart-Treichel, 1977), that sexual relationships among the elderly are normal and healthy, that the elderly are not somehow "childlike," that individuals past retirement age still have a great deal to contribute to society, and that illness and old age are not synonymous.

The Quality of Life   As you recall, Erik Erikson feels that during the later years the conflict to be resolved is that between ego integrity and despair.

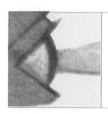

WHY DO WE GROW OLD, AND CAN AGING BE PREVENTED?

Aging is a change we take more or less for granted, since it appears to be common to every living thing. But why does it happen? Why, if you eat properly and obtain the necessary raw materials, doesn't your body reach young adulthood and then, physically, stay there—looking and feeling like the body of a 20-year-old—until you finally succumb to disease or trauma?

One popular theory about this question concerns **mutation**. Mutation may be caused by ultraviolet and X rays, ingested and inhaled chemicals, heat, viruses, and other mutagens. It is thought that as humans live longer, more and more mutations may take place in the genetic codes found in every body cell until they are happening faster than they can be repaired. The process may be like taking a page in a book and substituting random new letters for the original ones: Before long, the whole page ceases to make sense. Genes no longer direct the ''raw materials'' we eat to the right locations. Pigment no longer gets sent to the hair, and the hair appears gray. Skin loses suppleness as skin cells fail to be repaired. Other parts of the body, too, are abandoned bit by bit owing to the growing number of scrambled codes.

Our bodies have never been naturally selected for immortality, only for a life long enough to pass on our genes to the next generation. In fact, longevity in a species has been shown to be well correlated with the number of offspring that species produces for each pregnancy. Elephants and humans, for example, usually give birth to offspring one at a time and are long-lived, while dogs and cats usually have large litters and are relatively short-lived. Longevity, then, may be a way of ensuring that we have enough time to have a significant number of offspring (Begley & Carey, 1981). There may not even be any genes with codes designed to maintain any body part for very long.

Between mutations and accumulating damage (such as progressive hardening of the arteries caused by a build-up of cholesterol), it becomes a race to see which vital body part will break or be interfered with first. This process is called aging.

In the last few years there has been much excitement about the finding that living creatures may be genetically programmed to age and die. At the cellular level, cells seem to be finite in terms of the number of times they can divide. However, cancer cells and sex cells (egg and sperm) appear to be immortal, without limits to their division. Perhaps when egg and sperm fuse at conception they reset the genetic death clock, and perhaps cancer cells reshuffle their genetic information in a similar way (Hayflick, 1980). There are several ways in which aging could be prevented or slowed, and scientists are investigating all of them.

First, it may eventually be possible to replace many of the vital parts that fail with age. Artificial kidneys, hearts, eyes, ears, and joints are being perfected. In this way longevity may be increased.

The second way has to do with the observation that longevity tends to run in families, which has led to speculation that some individuals may be less susceptible to genetic mutation than others. The reasons for such resistance may eventually be discovered and implanted into our children (perhaps before birth).

A third method involves genetic engineering. Genetic engineering may eventually enable us to replace or repair genes in a grown or developed organism. If mutations are responsible for aging, it may be possible to undo such mutations as they occur. The eminent biologist George Sacher told his colleagues, just before his own death at age 63, ''Genetic modifications for increased longevity may be an attainable goal. Eventually, it will be possible . . . to control the rate of accumulation of errors that underlie aging'' (Begley & Carey, 1981, p. 68). Or perhaps there is a way to reset the death clock in body cells. We may be one of the last generations not to live 300 or 400 years.

Finally, there is a fourth method that, unlike the others, is within the reach of us all. Proper diet and exercise have been shown in many cases to help extend life and to improve the quality of life.

Whether we're the last generation to live a lifespan of less than 400 years remains to be seen. But bit by bit, we are making progress toward the elusive goal of a greatly extended life span.

Despite many myths to the contrary, sexual attraction and activity in old age is natural and healthy.

Ego integrity is maintained if one can look back on, and continue to live, a satisfying and fulfilling life. Satisfaction and happiness are subjective matters and difficult to assess. The usual way of gathering data on such questions is to conduct a survey. In one of the largest surveys of its kind, John Flanagan of the American Institute of Research surveyed 2,800 young, middle-aged, and elderly adults (ages 30, 50, and 70) from different parts of the United States. The two most important factors relating to happiness and satisfaction were money and health care. Flanagan stated, "People are coping pretty well, but there certainly is a significant-sized majority, who just don't have the finances and resources to get the food, shelter, and health care they need." He added, "Money isn't the only thing in the world, but it's way ahead of whatever's second" (Flanagan, as cited in Greenberg, 1978, p. 75).

Beyond money and health, other good predictors of the overall quality of life are "work, active recreation, learning, expressing yourself creatively, having close friends, understanding yourself, socializing and (except for the 70-year-olds) close relationship with a spouse" (Flanagan, as cited in Greenberg, 1978, p. 75). Interestingly, the poorest predictors of life quality were having and raising children, relationships with relatives, aiding others, and participating in government.

In general, the more older adults can find satisfaction within a family or social group and the more they can maintain a sense of continuity with the past, the more they are likely to find enjoyment and fulfillment in the later years.

Summary

- Developmental psychology is the study of age-related changes in human behavior during the life span.

- Modern developmental psychology has come to place the greatest emphasis on the years of infancy and childhood. However, in the last decade interest in adult development has grown rapidly as well.

- Many people think that human development progresses in a linear fashion, but this is not necessarily so. Human development includes many aspects, and while some developments seem to be dependent on each other, others seem to occur in parallel and fairly independently of each other.

- Sigmund Freud's view of child development as an important predictor of later adult personality helped generate interest in developmental research.

- Erik Erikson, perhaps more than any other researcher, has underlined the importance of the entire life span.

- In Erikson's view, human development is a progression through eight psychosocial stages, roughly equivalent in time to some of Freud's psychosexual stages.

- Many of the age-related changes in behavior observed by developmental psychologists are due in large part to underlying changes in biological development. Maturation is the term used to describe a genetically determined biological plan of development.

- Physical growth and motor development appear to be mainly a function of maturation. Environmental experiences may act to speed up or slow development, but only within strict maturational limits.

- There is evidence demonstrating that babies are different from each other shortly after birth. Temperament theories are based on the fact that these early personality traits are fairly stable over time.

- Just as individual babies differ from each other, so, too, do individual rates of neural development. The nervous system of the newborn is relatively immature compared to an adult's. A great deal of the infant's maturational development may be directly tied to a rigid timetable of neural development.

- The initial research describing early social deprivation in both monkeys and humans indicated that it had devastating effects on later development. However, some studies have demonstrated considerable plasticity in both monkeys and children in their ability to bounce back from early adverse experiences.

- Experiments on attachments show striking similarities between rhesus monkeys and human beings. Early attachments are formed quickly and are long-lasting. Human infants regularly exhibit a desire to stay near their mothers. In addition, recent research has demonstrated the importance of attachment to fathers.

- Next to Sigmund Freud, Jean Piaget is the most frequently referenced researcher in the psychological literature. Piaget investigated cognitive development in children. In his view, cognitive development occurs in four stages—sensorimotor, preoperational, concrete operational, and formal operational.

- The sensorimotor stage is characterized by a lack of fully developed object permanence. The preoperational stage is characterized by the inability to conserve. The concrete operations stage is characterized by the onset of conservation and logical operations. The formal operations stage is characterized by a growing ability to deal with the hypothetical.

- Socialization begins when an infant is treated by others in a way that fosters the development of skills, attitudes, or behaviors deemed appropriate by society.

- Most researchers studying the family take data but are rarely able to organize experiments. As a result, most child-rearing studies are correlational, and cause-effect relationships are very difficult to infer.

- Researchers have discovered that in general, children are not adversely affected if their mothers work.

- Fathers are primarily responsible for initiating sex-differentiating treatment in their children. Like mothers, fathers play an important socializing role in the development of their children's personalities.

- Divorce should not be viewed as a single event, but rather as a complex series of disorganized transitions requiring considerable adjustment.

- Peers can have an important and lasting influence on a child's social development.

- During adolescence, both physical and cognitive changes can have an important impact on development.

- Young adults face many choices and predicaments in society. They must make decisions about sexuality, marriage, children, career, friendships, social and civic interactions, and more.

- Most middle-aged adults express attitudes of self-confidence and achievement. Researchers have examined a number of phenomena associated with middle adulthood, including midlife crisis, and the empty nest syndrome.

- In general, the more older adults can find satisfaction within a family or social group and the more they can maintain a sense of continuity with the past, the more they are likely to find enjoyment and fulfillment in the later years.

- It may eventually be possible to extend the life span through the use of artificial organs, selective breeding, genetic engineering, a proper diet, and exercise.

EPILOGUE:
ALGEBRA AND FORMAL OPERATIONS

Our knowledge of the development process has many practical applications. School systems, to be effective, must take into account a child's developing cognitive processes. The following is an account of how this development affected my own schooling.

When I was in the eighth grade my cognitive development must have been coming along a little slowly. At the age of 13, before I was far enough into formal operations to deal with abstractions, I had the misfortune of running into algebra. I can remember the previous year, seeing the older kids in the hallway with math books that had covers showing letters being multiplied by numbers. I remember wondering how that was possible. I asked my father if it was hard and he asked me, "How many numbers are there?" I said there must be a zillion. And he said, "Well, how hard can letters be, there are only 26 of them." A solid picture of a small group of finite letters seemed simple enough to deal with, and so I entered algebra class with confidence.

The instructor began by placing an x on the board. It seemed to me that he had passed up a lot of the alphabet and hadn't very far to go, but that was all right. I raised my hand and asked him what "x" was. I wanted something concrete to hang my hat on. He said, "X is an unknown." In my notebook I wrote, "x = ?". I liked that. I decided whenever he used an x I would use a question mark because it would

make everything easier. After a while he wrote a y on the board. I raised my hand and asked what "y" was. He replied that it, too, was an unknown. So I wrote in my notebook, "y = ?". It didn't take Einstein to figure out that if x = ? and y = ?, then x must equal y because they were both question marks. So I raised my hand and volunteered, "Then x = y!" The instructor said, "Well, that can happen sometimes, but it usually doesn't." I don't remember much more about that instructor, but I do remember my friend John who sat next to me in class. He and I spent the rest of that year talking about less confusing things.

The second time I took algebra I think I had the same instructor; at least he looked familiar. This time when he said that x was an unknown and y was an unknown, the meaning was clear to me: They could be anything, equal to each other, or not equal to each other. Gratefully, abstract thinking didn't seem so foreign to me any more. I didn't know it at the time, but I was slowly entering what Piaget called the period of formal operations and was beginning to be able to handle abstract concepts.

Suggestions for Further Reading

1. Adelson, J. (ed.). *Handbook of adolescent psychology.* New York: John Wiley, 1979.
2. Erikson, E. H. *Childhood and society.* New York: Norton, 1963.

3. Maas, H., & Kuypers, J. *From thirty to seventy.* San Francisco: Jossey-Bass, 1974.
4. Osofsky, J. D. (ed.). *Handbook of infant development.* New York: John Wiley, 1980.
5. Rugh, R., & Shettles, L. B. *From conception to birth.* New York: Harper & Row, 1971.
6. Singer, D. G., & Revenson, T. A. *How a child thinks: A Piaget primer.* New York: New American Library, 1978.

CHAPTER 12

Intelligence and Individual Differences

You are working for Thomas Edison in his laboratory at Menlo Park, New Jersey. Your area of expertise is photographic emulsions, and you've been working since early afternoon. It's now 4:00 A.M. You're not alone in the lab, however. A lot of people are working, including the "old man." Edison doesn't sleep much; he catnaps now and then. He likes to keep the lab going 24 hours a day. The building is so large and dingy that it's easy to mistake the time. Still, you enjoy the work and the fact of collaborating with one of the world's foremost intellects, Thomas Edison.

You decide to take a break and get a cup of coffee. You join a man named L. L. Thurstone. He's a mathematician. You ask him what he's doing, since he seems to be working as he sips his coffee.

"The old man's math," he replies.

You nod. "Too busy to do it himself, huh?"

Thurstone looks at you. "Nope, he couldn't do this if he wanted to."

"What do you mean?" you ask. "What kind of math is it?"

"Just algebra," Thurstone says, "but he can't do it. He even has trouble with long division."

"You've got to be kidding me," you say.

Thurstone shakes his head.

"If I were, I wouldn't be working here. I need this job. He needs me."

You think about this for a moment. Then, "Edison must be one of the great geniuses of all time. I'm sure he could do algebra if he wanted to. He just doesn't care to, that's all."

"I've been wondering about that, too," Thurstone says. "And you know? I don't think there is such a thing as intelligence, at least not in any general sense. Watching Edison makes me think that there are many different kinds of intelligence. He's a mechanical genius, for instance; he's great at putting things together. But in other areas he's just not that bright. Believe me, when it comes to mathematical ability, you're probably more intelligent than he is."

In this chapter we'll examine L. L. Thurstone's hypothesis. We'll discuss changes in intelligence and tests that measure intelligence and creativity. We'll look at how such tests are designed. In addition, we'll examine mental retardation, exceptionality, and giftedness.

Why Psychologists Study Intelligence

People within every group or society are aware that some of their members have superior abilities to analyze problems, find solutions, comprehend ideas, and accumulate information. Such people are valued because they can help the society reach its goals. They are considered to be intelligent.

We revere those whose insights, gifts, and knowledge have enabled them to make brilliant deductions or to see things as no one has seen them before. We know their names—Galileo, Einstein, Newton, Michelangelo, Darwin, and Beethoven, to name a few. But why do some people have these abilities, and others not? Are their gifts present at birth, or are they acquired through experience and learning? Can intelligence be taught? Can intellectual potential be found and cultivated in order to prevent its being lost or wasted? Does intelligence change over time, or does it remain stable? Is there a general kind of intelligence, applicable in all situations, or are there many kinds of intelligence, as Thurstone suggested? Psychologists are interested in all of these questions. In fact, intelligence is such an intriguing subject that nearly everyone takes an interest in it.

Defining Intelligence

What is **intelligence**? Is it the ability to do well in school or to figure things out? Is it having the skills to find happiness or knowing when to come in out of the rain? Are the following people intelligent?

The physician who smokes three packs of cigarettes a day?

The Nobel Prize winner whose marriage and personal life are in ruins?

The corporate executive who's worked to reach the top and who's earned a heart attack for the effort?

The brilliant and successful composer who handled his money so poorly that he was always running from his creditors (incidentally, his name was Mozart)?

Examine any of these paradoxes, or consider the lives of your own friends, or even your own life, and it will probably be clear to you that "intelligence" is not easy to define.

The first scientific interest in intelligence and intelligence testing can be traced back to the inheritance theories of Sir Francis Galton. Galton's studies marked not only the beginning of efforts to measure intelligence but also the start of the entire psychological testing movement. The differences between people became an important consideration, especially to anyone interested, like Galton, in positive eugenics (see Chapter 2). After all, distinguishing different traits and measuring inferiority and superiority would be prerequisites for deciding who should be mated with whom.

Although Galton's hopes for a full-fledged eugenics movement were never fulfilled, interest in individual differences and their measurement grew. By the turn of the century the public had come to accept the idea that science could measure psychological differences in order to identify superior and inferior abilities. Clouding serious scientific efforts, however, were the popular nonsensical theories developed by charlatans and pseudoscientists who purported to be able to measure "inherited traits." One such theory was **phrenology,** the study of personality based on the contours of the head. Another was the notion that criminal tendencies were inherited and were directly related to such physical features as a low forehead or shifty eyes. The list of foolish beliefs about inherited characteristics is long. Nonetheless, whether the theory was scientific or pseudoscientific, the emphasis was typically placed on inheritance, with little consideration given to learning or the impact of experience. Consequently, the public came to believe that most behaviors and attributes, including intelligence, were inherited.

Measuring Intelligence—IQ Tests

In 1905, Alfred Binet and Theodore Simon developed the precursor to the modern intelligence test. Its purpose was to determine which Parisian school children would benefit from regular classes and which should receive special education.

Binet established which tasks or questions could be solved easily by children in each of the school grades and which were difficult. Carrying his research further, he developed a concept of **mental age** (MA). For example, a five-year-old child who performed as well on the test as an average six-year-old would be said to have a mental age of six. A ten-year-old who performed only as well as an average five-year-old would be said to have a mental age of five. Binet used the term **chronological age** (CA) to represent the actual age of the child.

A few years later, in order to avoid the fractions that arose when comparing MA and CA, the German psychologist L. Wilhelm Stern developed a formula that yielded a score he called the **intelligence quotient,** or IQ. Stern's formula, MA ÷ CA × 100 = IQ yielded a rough index of how bright or dull any child was in comparison with his or her school peers. In the case of the five-year-old (CA = 60 months) with an MA of 72 months, the IQ is 120, quite sufficient for schoolwork. But the ten-year-old (CA = 120 months) with an MA of 60 months has an IQ of 50, which would be defined as developmentally retarded—not sufficient for school. In 1916 Lewis Terman and his colleagues at Stanford University revised the original Binet-Simon intelligence scale. They incorporated Stern's idea of the IQ. Their revision, known as the Stanford-Binet, became the first of the modern IQ tests. Figure 12.1 depicts the distinction of IQ scores within a normal population.

INTELLIGENCE
A general term for a person's abilities in a wide range of tasks including vocabulary, numbers, problem solving, and concepts. May also include the ability to profit from experience, to learn new pieces of information, and to adjust to new situations.

PHRENOLOGY
A system developed by Franz Joseph Gall for identifying types of people by examining their physical features, especially the configuration of their skulls.

MENTAL AGE
A concept developed by Binet and used to calculate a person's IQ, as in mental age ÷ chronological age × 100 = IQ. The mental age of a person is derived by comparing his or her score with the average scores of others within different specific age groups.

CHRONOLOGICAL AGE
A concept developed by Binet and used to calculate a person's IQ, as in mental age ÷ chronological age × 100 = IQ. The chronological age of a person is his or her actual age.

INTELLIGENCE QUOTIENT
A quotient derived from the formula MA/CA × 100, where MA is mental age and CA is chronological age. The intelligence quotient was devised by psychologist L. Wilhelm Stern and introduced in the United States by Lewis Terman.

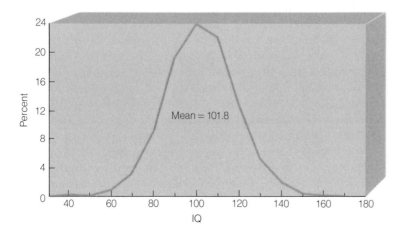

Figure 12.1 *Distribution of IQ scores within the general population.* (SOURCE: *Terman & Merrill, 1973*)

Many IQ tests, such as this Stanford-Binet, are administered to individuals rather than to groups.

TEST VALIDITY

While it is true that we now have IQ (intelligence quotient) tests, intelligence itself has never been adequately defined, and there is some question about the **validity** of these tests. A test is said to be valid if it measures what it claims to measure. Do IQ tests measure intelligence, as most people use the term? Generally, IQ tests measure common skills and abilities, many of which are acquired in school. Consider the areas covered in a widely used intelligence test, the revised Wechsler Adult Intelligence Scale (WAIS-R), shown in Figure 12.2. Does the ability to correctly answer the example questions coincide with most people's understanding of intelligence?

Many people feel, too, that intelligence includes such attributes as creativity, persistent curiosity, and success. IQ tests aren't always good indicators in these areas. For instance, two researchers worked with bright mathematicians whose IQ's were very similar, who were all about the same age, and who all had Ph.D.'s from prestigious universities. These subjects were found to have remarkable differences in creative output, as measured by other mathematicians (Helson & Crutchfield, 1970). IQ tests, then, are not generally a valid measure of this kind of creativity.

In other instances, however, IQ tests have been found to be valid. They are generally able to predict school success with a fairly high degree of certainty—not surprisingly, perhaps, since this is what they were originally designed to do. IQ tests are also sometimes valid for clinical assessments of individuals who have anxiety problems or neurological and perceptual deficiencies.

FACTOR ANALYSIS

Some IQ tests are given individually, one on one, such as the Stanford-Binet or the WAIS-R, while others are given to groups. Some IQ tests are designed to be taken by infants exclusively, or by children, or by adults. All of the IQ tests ask different questions, and although they are all called intelligence tests and they all yield an IQ score, they may measure different abilities. Furthermore, some tests measure the same ability more than once and thereby give that one ability more weight in the final score. The amount of weight or emphasis given to any one ability is known as a **factor load.**

To understand factor loading better, let's look at an example from athletics. Think of Bruce Jenner, who is considered by many to be the world's best all-around athlete because he won the 1976 Olympic decathlon with the highest all-time score, competing in the following ten events:

100-meter dash	javelin (requires running start)
110-meter high hurdles	pole vault (requires running start)
400-meter run	high jump (requires running start)
1,500-meter run	discus
running long jump	shot put

VALIDITY
The capacity of an instrument to measure what it purports to measure.

FACTOR LOAD
The weight or emphasis given to any factor or ability.

The WAIS-R being administered to a subject.

Figure 12.2 *Subtests of the Wechsler Adult Intelligence Scale (WAIS-R, 1981).*

VERBAL SCALE

1. **INFORMATION:** Twenty-nine questions covering a wide range of general knowledge that people have presumably had an opportunity to gain simply by being exposed to the culture.

    EXAMPLE: How many zeros are there in 1 billion?

2. **DIGIT SPAN:** Fourteen groups of from two to nine digits presented orally, one group at a time. After hearing a group, subjects must repeat it from memory. Some exercises require repetition forward, others backward.

3. **VOCABULARY:** Thirty-five vocabulary words of increasing difficulty presented visually and orally. Subjects must define each word.

    EXAMPLE: "What does *parsimony* mean?"

4. **ARITHMETIC:** Fourteen problems similar to those encountered in elementary school. The problems must be solved without paper or pencil.

    EXAMPLE: "How much would three cigars cost if each cigar was $1.80 and the store was offering a 10 percent discount on all purchases?"

5. **COMPREHENSION:** Sixteen questions that ask subjects to indicate the correct thing to do under varied circumstances, what certain proverbs mean, or why certain practices are followed.

    EXAMPLE: "What is meant by 'too many cooks spoil the broth'?"

6. **SIMILARITIES:** Fourteen items requiring that subjects explain the similarity between two things.

    EXAMPLE: "In what way are red and hot alike?" (ANS.: Both can be sensed; both are stimuli.)

PERFORMANCE SCALE

7. **PICTURE COMPLETION:** Twenty pictures. In each picture something is missing. Subjects must identify the missing part.

    EXAMPLE:

8. **PICTURE ARRANGEMENT:** Ten sets of cards. Each set contains cartoon characters performing an action. If the set of cards is placed in the proper sequence, it will depict a sensible story. Subjects must place cards from each set in the proper order.

    EXAMPLE: "Place the cards in the proper sequence so that they depict a sensible story." (ANS. Correct order should be 3, 1, 4, 2.)

Figure 12.2   *continued*

9. BLOCK DESIGN: Nine designs of increasing complexity must be made using four to nine blocks having sides that are white, red, or half white and half red.

    EXAMPLE:

10. OBJECT ASSEMBLY: Subjects are provided with pieces of a puzzle. The pieces are made of hardened cardboard. Subjects must decide what the pieces represent and assemble them correctly.

    EXAMPLE:

11. DIGIT SYMBOL: Nine symbols paired with nine digits are shown. Subjects must then pair the appropriate symbol with the correct digit in a long list of digits. The test is timed. Subjects who forget and have to look back at the pairings take longer to complete the test.

As you can see, one ability is measured more than once, that is, it has a heavy factor load. This ability is running. (Perhaps Bruce Jenner has the best all-around legs.) The idea of trying to balance tests, including IQ tests, for factors, so that each ability would be tested only once, was advocated by L. L. Thurstone in 1938. To accomplish this, Thurstone relied on a technique known as **factor analysis.**

As you learned at the beginning of the chapter, Thurstone was a mathematician who worked in Edison's laboratory, doing the mathematical exercises that Edison seemed completely unable to comprehend. Edison's inability in this area led Thurstone to conclude that, rather than a single quality called general intelligence, there must be many, perhaps unrelated, kinds of intelligence. One of Thurstone's hopes was that it would eventually be possible to distinguish social from nonsocial intelligence, academic from nonacademic intelligence, and mechanical from abstract intelligence.

Since Thurstone's day there have been many such attempts to isolate different kinds of intelligence. One of the most exhaustive efforts was made by J. P. Guilford. Guilford developed a model of intelligence based on his factor analysis of the human intellect. Figure 12.3 shows Guilford's model in three dimensions. Each side of the block represents a major intellectual function. Each function is divided into subfunctions. The total number of interactions possible is 120, since Guilford believed that he had isolated 120 different kinds of intelligence (Guilford, 1967).

Each of these dimensions has a different meaning. "Operations" are the actions taken by a person. "Contents" include the information upon which an operation is performed. "Products" refer to the way in which the information is organized. For instance, a person who is required to recall a series of unrelated numbers is engaging in memory of symbolic units, one of the

FACTOR ANALYSIS
A statistical procedure aimed at discovering the constituent traits within a complex system of personality or intelligence. The method enables the investigator to compute the minimum number of factors required to account for the intercorrelations among the scores on the tests.

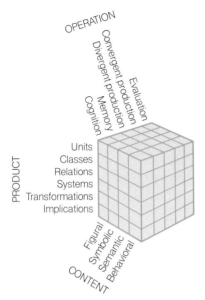

Figure 12.3 *Guilford's model depicting the structure of the intellect.* (SOURCE: *Guilford, 1967, p. 63*)

L. L. Thurstone demonstrating a geometric proposition.

120 factors. In this case the operation is memory, the content is symbolic, and the product is units.

Today, the debate continues over whether there is such a thing as general intelligence or whether, as Thurstone and Guilford have suggested, there are many kinds of intelligence. The answer may lie in between, with "general intelligence" defined as intelligence in a specific area that is applicable in many other instances as well. Of course, since no one has adequately defined intelligence, no one is sure how many kinds of intelligence there may be—a state of affairs that plainly illustrates the difficulty of measuring intelligence.

Although the factor analytic approach has been challenged, there is no doubt that some IQ tests are loaded in favor of particular factors. For instance, I do fairly well on the Stanford-Binet test. This test is heavily loaded in favor of verbal skills, and I enjoy talking and writing. But when I take the WAIS-R, my IQ is 15 points lower. The Wechsler includes many tasks that require hand-eye coordination, and as it turns out, I am a clod with blocks. The point is that both tests give me an IQ score. It would seem that an IQ is an IQ regardless of the test, but as you can see, this is not true.

Whether you are considered intelligent, then, may depend on the test you take. In one study, two researchers went to a suburban Minneapolis school and administered to all of the children in each fifth grade class the 18 most common measures used throughout the United States to determine giftedness (Feldman & Bratton, 1972). Among the 18 measures were high IQ scores, high scholastic grades, high scores on the Primary Mental Abilities Test, and high teacher ratings. Feldman and Bratton labeled the top five students on each measure "gifted."

Reasonably, you might expect that the same few students would have been found to be gifted on each of the 18 measures. Yet no student was in the top five on every measure. More strikingly, 92 percent of all of the students were in the top five on at least one measure! These results indicate that 92 percent of all the children in the fifth grade had the potential of being labeled gifted by a measure popularly used to determine giftedness.

You can imagine the difficulty of developing programs for gifted children without a good definition of giftedness. In fact, one of the major criticisms leveled against programs for the gifted is that giftedness is so hard to define. One caustic and embittered legislator, while debating funding for a program for gifted children, became upset over the inability to define gifted and said, "I define a gifted child as any child who can get through life without my help." Although this is hardly an attitude conducive to creating a program to develop a child's potential, you can understand how the lawmaker came to be frustrated.

Genetic and Environmental Aspects of Intelligence

Your brain, your nervous system, your entire body is constructed according to instructions received from the genes you inherited from your parents. It would seem reasonable that superior genes would provide a child with superior intellectual capacity. And in fact, researchers have discovered that parents with high IQ's tend to have children with high IQ's, while parents with low IQ's tend to have children with low IQ's.

This finding might appear to prove that intelligence is inherited, but does it really? Rich parents tend to have rich children, and parents who like tostados and enchiladas tend to have children who like tostados and enchiladas; it doesn't necessarily follow that these aspects are in the genes. Environment can also play an important role. Perhaps being raised by intelligent parents in a stimulating or intellectual home tends to increase a child's IQ.

BIRTH ORDER AND INTELLIGENCE

In 1896 Galton observed something intriguing about the order in which children were born. He noticed that an exceedingly large number of prominent British scientists were firstborn children. Since Galton's time a number of studies have indicated that firstborn children have a distinct advantage in certain areas of development over other children (Koch, 1955). Firstborns are more articulate and tend to score higher on intelligence tests than children born later. Firstborns also tend to be more reflective, while later children are more impulsive. When dealing with important choices, reflective children tend to examine a number of options and delay decisions so that they can minimize their errors. Impulsive children, on the other hand, are eager to rush to a solution when dealing with problems (Kagan, 1966). Firstborns also appear to have a greater need to achieve (Sampson, 1962) and to perform better academically (Altus, 1967). Firstborns are more likely to attend college (Bayer, 1966). Interestingly, 21 of the first 23 astronauts to travel into space were firstborn children.

The meaning of these birth-order data is not clear. It may have something to do with the size of the family into which children are born. Perhaps firstborns enjoy a more stimulating environment than later children because firstborns have the undivided attention of both parents. Supporting this interpretation is the fact that firstborns develop language rapidly, while twins develop language at a slower rate, and triplets more slowly still (Davis, 1937). Research has shown that twins tend to be shortchanged by their parents because parents don't like to repeat themselves. In other words, a twin is likely to be spoken to less often because parents treat the twins as a unit and do not double their verbal interactions (Lytton, Conway, & Suave, 1977). Since IQ scores reflect verbal skills to a considerable degree, it would not be surprising if firstborns tended to have higher IQ scores than twins—and they do. Furthermore, while firstborns tend to have higher IQ scores than second children, second children also tend to have higher scores than third, third than fourth, and so on (Zajonc & Markus, 1975).

Zajonc and Markus have developed a model of intellectual climate designed to help predict the differences between the average intelligence scores in children from large and small families. In their model the parents are each assigned a value of 30, and the children are assigned a value equal to their chronological age. These values are added and then divided by the number of family members. For example, a firstborn child would enter an intellectual climate equal to 30 (father) + 30 (mother) + 0 (baby) ÷ 3 = 20. A child born to a single parent would be born into an intellectual climate of 30 + 0 ÷ 2 = 15. A second child with a six-year-old brother would be born into a family with an intellectual climate of 30 + 30 + 6 + 0 ÷ 4 = 16½, and so on. With this formula Zajonc and Markus have found close agreement between their values of intellectual climate and the average IQ scores among children in different-size families. It's important to understand that these are only *average* values. There are a number of families in which later children have higher IQ scores or achieve greater success. The Zajonc and Markus formula for intellectual climate is shown in Table 12.1, developed for a family of up to ten children spaced two years apart. In such a large family the intellectual climate actually *increases* for the eighth, ninth, and tenth children. This is because the older siblings are in their late teens by the time these last children arrive and provide a more stimulating intellectual environment.

It's not easy to find a great number of eighth, ninth, and tenth children. However, one very large study conducted in Israel which included 191,933 subjects closely fit the predictions made by the Zajonc-Markus model (Davis, Cahan, & Bashi, 1977). The Israeli researchers found that firstborns scored highest on cognitive and intellectual measures, while second, third, and other subsequent children showed progressively lower scores. However, this trend reversed after the seventh child. Eighth children were found to have higher scores than seventh, ninth higher than eighth, and tenth higher still.

Perhaps parents could overcome these differences if they paid extra attention to their younger children. On the other hand, there may not be great cause for concern, since the differences between firstborns and later children on IQ tests is generally only 3 or 4 points, which, in all practical terms, is not very significant. In addition, the fact that firstborns tend to be more successful may be related to many other factors besides extra parental attention or stimulation. Larger families, for example, are often of lower socioeconomic status, and later children, on the average, are more likely to be at an economic disadvantage than are earlier children in that fewer opportunities can be made available to them. You may find more firstborns among scientists or astronauts simply because, as firstborns, they were given opportunities that those born later were denied. Finally, it should be noted that not all scientists agree that there is a real or significant birth-order effect (Grotevant, Scarr, & Weinberg, 1975). Some studies have

Table 12.1   Zajonc-Markus model of intellectual climate as applied to a large family over an 18-year period with children spaced two years apart.

YEAR OF BIRTH OF CHILD	NUMBER OF CHILDREN	VALUE OF INTELLECTUAL CLIMATE Formula	Result
1964	1	$\dfrac{\text{Mother }(30) + \text{Father }(30) + \text{Baby }(0)}{\text{Number in family }(3)} =$	20.0
1966	2	$\dfrac{\text{Mother }(30) + \text{Father }(30) + \text{2-yr-old }(2) + \text{Baby }(0)}{\text{Number in family }(4)} =$	15.5
1968	3	$66 \div 5$	13.2
1970	4	$72 \div 6$	12.0
1972	5	$80 \div 7$	11.4
1974	6	$90 \div 8$	11.3
1976	7	$102 \div 9$	11.3
1978	8	$116 \div 10$	11.6
1980	9	$132 \div 11$	12.0
1982	10	$150 \div 12$	12.5

reported finding no birth-order effect (McCall & Johnson, 1972). Nonetheless, studies that include large samples of subjects generally support the theory that birth order is related to achievement motivation and IQ test scores (Belmont & Marolla, 1973).

IQ AND RACE

While birth-order data may have pointed to the influence of environmental factors on intelligence, other studies have concerned themselves with the effects of inheritance. A serious controversy developed concerning the heritable aspects of intelligence immediately after the publication of an article in the 1969 *Harvard Educational Review* by Arthur Jensen, a professor of psychology. Jensen suggested that the reason whites were superior to blacks on IQ tests by an average of 15 points was probably related more to genetic variables than to the effects of experience. In other words, Jensen was saying that whites were naturally intellectually superior to blacks. The ensuing debates on radio, TV, and in the press were stormy, usually generating more heat than light. In the middle of all this controversy entered William Shockley, a Nobel prize winner (for coinventing the transistor, not for work related to genetics or psychology), who advocated that blacks be kept from having too many children so that they would not pass on their inferior genes.

Cultural Bias   No one disputes that whites score on an average 15 points higher than blacks on IQ tests. However, this fact does not necessarily mean that Jensen was right. There are other interpretations. The kinds of observations that Jensen made were not new. In 1912 the U.S. Public Health Service gave the then new IQ tests to immigrants arriving in New York. It was discovered that 87 percent of Russians, 83 percent of Jews, 80 percent of Hungarians, and 79 percent of Italians were feebleminded. It didn't matter to the supervisor of the testing, Henry Goddard, that many of the immigrants couldn't speak English. He was convinced that the tests were adequately translated to suit the immigrants. Congress was informed about this "menace of the feebleminded" and responded with immigration quotas favoring, oddly, English-speaking countries. Goddard reported that, thanks to his efforts, many "feebleminded" immigrants had been deported (Goddard, 1917). Immigration quotas still reflect these early biases. Unfortunately, even when translated versions of the intelligence tests were administered to immigrants, a considerable knowledge of American culture was necessary in order to score high. This would mean, not that 79 percent of the Italians tested were feebleminded, but that 79 percent of Italians may have been unaware of the answers to culturally biased questions. Cultural bias may also explain blacks' tendency to score lower on IQ tests. White children may be more likely than black children to be exposed to the kinds of strategies and knowledge required by IQ tests.

Psychologist Sandra Scarr conducted a study in which she gathered data on the IQ scores of black children adopted and raised by white families. Scarr discovered that the younger the black children were at the time of adoption, the closer they came to the white IQ averages (Scarr & Weinberg, 1976). These results strongly suggest that a child's background, experience, and culture will to a great extent influence the child's knowledge and

Arthur Jensen.

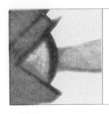

THE HERITABILITY OF INTELLECTUAL CAPACITY

How much of your intellectual capacity is inherited, and how much is the result of environmental experience? This is obviously another nature-nurture question. Psychologists are interested in isolating the factors influencing intelligence, both inherited and acquired. Since intelligence is determined by more than one gene, and since it is also a complex response to the environment, it doesn't follow Mendel's simple laws for the inheritance of traits (see Chapter 2). Nonetheless, psychologists can study the inheritance of human intelligence by examining people who are related to one another. Relatives share many of the same genes. Table 12.2 shows categories of related and unrelated people with a correlation coefficient next to each. These correlations represent the relationship between the IQ scores of pairs of individuals within each category (the scores of two first cousins, of a grandparent and grandchild, etc.).

Let's look at parents and their children to see how the correlations are derived. Each parent and his or her

child are given an IQ test. Then a computation is made that allows these test scores to be compared with each other; each parent's score is compared with his or her own child's score. The more alike these compared scores are, the closer to +1.00 the correlation coefficient will be. A high positive correlation means that the test scores of the parents and their respective children are similar. We can infer from this that, if a parent's IQ is high, his or her child's is likely to be high, or if a parent's IQ is low, his or her child's is likely to be low also. A correlation of zero, or near zero, indicates no relationship between the two scores. A correlation approaching −1.00 indicates an inverse relationship; that is, if one score is high the other will be likely to be low, and vice versa. As you can see, the actual correlation between parents and their children is +.50.

Take a close look at the "children reared apart" category with a coefficient of −.01. The −.01 is very close to a 0 correlation coefficient. This means that children reared

apart *who are not relatives* have IQ scores that are unrelated. If your IQ score is high, what score is Joe Schmitloff from Walton, New York, likely to have? This is a foolish question because your score and his have nothing to do with one another; they are unrelated (0 correlation). Such a 0 correlation would be expected in comparing test scores of unrelated people raised in different environments.

You may wonder why the correlation is −.01 instead of exactly 0. If you flipped a coin a hundred times you would expect 50 heads. But if 51 heads turned up, you wouldn't think the coin was weighted. You would assume it was due to chance. The scores for unrelated people living apart ranged from approximately +.03 to −.03, but averaged out to −.01, which is practically the same as 0. Coefficients are rarely +1.00, 0, or −1.00. They typically fall somewhere in between.[*] As you can see by examining the correlation coefficients in Table 12.2,

[*]For a more detailed discussion of correlation coefficients, see the Statistics Appendix.

thought processing as measured by any particular intelligence test. Different cultures not only teach different things, but also different ways to think about things. As Jerome Kagan once said in reference to two of the best-known IQ tests, "If the Wechsler and Binet Scales were translated into Spanish, Swahili, and Chinese, and given to every 10-year-old child in Latin America, East Africa, and China, the majority would obtain IQ scores in the mentally retarded range" (Kagan, 1973).

Of course, these children wouldn't be mentally retarded in the commonly understood sense of the term, but they would be at a disadvantage until they learned to adapt to our culture. In this case a low IQ score would represent cultural ignorance, not lack of intelligence. Any of us would be at the same disadvantage in another culture.

In a study conducted in Riverside, California, Jane Mercer discovered that a disproportionate number of blacks and Mexican-American children

the more closely related individuals are, the more alike their IQ scores will tend to be. It appears, then, that these similarities are due in part to inheritance.

Table 12.2 Correlations of intelligence test scores

CORRELATIONS BETWEEN INDIVIDUALS	MEDIAN VALUE
UNRELATED PERSONS	
Children reared apart	–.01
Children reared together	+.20
COLLATERALS*	
Second cousins	+.16
First cousins	+.28
Uncle (or aunt) and nephew (or niece)	+.34
Siblings, reared apart	+.46
Siblings, reared together	+.52
Fraternal twins, different sex	+.49
Fraternal twins, same sex	+.56
Identical twins, reared apart	+.75
Identical twins, reared together	+.87
DIRECT LINE	
Grandparent and grandchild	+.30
Parent (as adult) and child	+.50
Parent (as child) and child	+.56

SOURCE: Adapted from Schell, R. E., & Hall, E., 1979. [Originally based on estimates reported in John C. Loehlin, Gardner Lindzey, and J. N. Spuhler. *Race Differences in Intelligence*, San Francisco: W. H. Freeman, 1975; and in Arthur Jensen, "How Much Can We Boost IQ and Scholastic Achievement?" *Harvard Educational Review*, 39 (1969), 49.]

*Descended from the same stock, but different lines.

As you can see, the table includes two kinds of twins, fraternal and identical. Fraternal twins occur when two eggs are fertilized at about the same time, and they are no more genetically alike than siblings. Identical twins occur when a single fertilized egg splits, or fissions, soon after fertilization. As a result, identical twins share the same genetic makeup.

One of the areas of greatest interest is the "twins reared apart" category. It is rare for identical twins to be reared apart, but when they are, they provide an ideal chance to study the IQ's of two people sharing the same genes but having different upbringing and experiences. As you can see from the table, identical twins reared apart have an even higher correlation than siblings reared together. At first glance this result would seem to indicate that inheritance must play an exceedingly large role in the formation of intellectual capacity. However, the "twins reared apart" category is not without problems. The late Cyril Burt, formerly the chairman of psychology at the London College University, did much of the early work in this area. Unfortunately, he became so eager to prove that intellectual capacity was mostly inherited that he faked his data (McAskie, 1978). Other researchers found that identical twins reared apart

have similar IQ's, but their samples were small. "Reared apart" often turned out to mean that they were living next door to one another, or that one was with the father and the other with the mother, and since married couples tend to have similar IQ's the "reared apart" environments may have been quite alike in terms of intellectual stimulation. Furthermore, even when identical twins are separated by state agencies, they may not grow up in radically different surroundings, since some agencies will go out of their way to place such twins in similar environments. Therefore, the "twins reared apart" category may be contaminated (in a research sense). If so, IQ similarities between identical twins reared apart can no longer be sorted in terms of heredity or experience (Schwartz & Schwartz, 1974; Kamin, 1974).

Based on current data many psychologists agree that heredity does play a major role in determining individual differences in intelligence. Just how important, compared with environmental experiences, has yet to be determined.

were being placed in classes for the mentally retarded, based solely on IQ scores. This turned out to be a serious error. The American Association on Mental Deficiency states that "mental retardation refers to significantly subaverage general intellectual functioning [usually an IQ score of less than 70] existing concurrently with deficits in adaptive behavior, and manifested during the developmental period" (Grossman, 1973, p. 11). To test adaptive behavior, Mercer devised a scale. The scale included 28 age-related skills ranging from simple tasks such as feeding or dressing oneself to more complex tasks such as holding a job or being able to shop. Mercer discovered that while all of the Anglo-American children she studied who had IQ scores below 70 failed her adaptive-behavior scale, 90 percent of the blacks and 60 percent of the Chicanos with IQ scores of less than 70 *passed* her test (Mercer, 1971; Mercer, 1972). These data indicate that the black and Chicano children, having been raised in a different culture, were unfamiliar with the

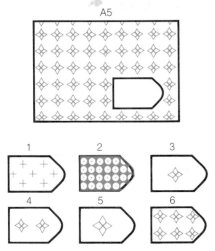

A5

Figure 12.4 *Sample item from the Raven Progressive Matrices Test.*

kinds of words, objects, and strategies required by the questions found on IQ tests. They had low IQ scores, but they were still adapting to their environment.

As a result of Mercer's studies, California passed a law making it illegal to determine that a child is retarded based solely on the results of an IQ test. Other states, too, have passed measures designed to protect children from being mislabeled.

Culture-fair Testing   Any intelligence test that makes use of language is likely to be culturally biased. Consequently, attempts have been made to produce language-free **culture-fair tests** that would be equally difficult for members of any culture. Initial efforts generally relied on pictures and nonverbal instructions, but these still tended to favor some cultures. Children in these cultures were simply more familiar with pictures or the requirements of certain tasks (Vernon, 1965). Still, there are tests that are self-explanatory and do not require pictures of familiar objects. One of the most widely used culture-fair tests is the Raven Progressive Matrices Test. In Figure 12.4 you'll see a sample question from the Raven test. Even without instructions you can understand what is required. In this test, too, however, people from cultures in which fill-in or matching exercises are more common may be more likely to do well than people from other cultures. To date, no one test has been developed that is completely culture-fair.

The Effects of Environmental Stimulation

One way to assess environmental influences on intellectual development is to alter the environment on purpose and observe the effect on IQ scores. Ethically, of course, it's only proper to create a stimulating environment in the hopes of raising IQ scores. In the late 1960s, under the supervision of Rick Heber at the University of Wisconsin, a project was begun to study the effects of intellectual stimulation on children from deprived environments (Garber & Heber, 1973). Let's spend some time examining this project in detail, since it will highlight many of the issues involved in understanding the nature of intelligence.

THE MILWAUKEE PROJECT

In search of a "deprived environment" from which to draw subjects for the study, Heber and his colleagues examined different districts within the city of Milwaukee. One district stood out. Its residents had the lowest median income and lowest level of education in the city. The district also had the highest population density and highest rate of unemployment. One other statistic attracted Heber's attention: Although this district contained only 3 percent of the city's population, it accounted for 33 percent of the children in Milwaukee who had been labeled mentally retarded!

At the beginning of the Milwaukee Project Heber selected 40 newborns from the depressed area of the city he had chosen. The mothers of the infants selected all had IQ's below 80. All of the children in the study were black, and in many cases, the fathers were absent. The 40 newborns were randomly assigned, 20 to an experimental group, and 20 to a control group.

Both the experimental group and the control group were tested an equal number of times throughout the project. An independent testing service was used in order to eliminate possible biases on the part of the project members. In terms of physical or medical variables, there were no observable differences between the two groups.

The experimental group entered a special program. Mothers of the experimental group children received education, vocational rehabilitation, and training in homemaking and child care. The children themselves received personalized enrichment in their home environments for the first three months of their lives, and then their training continued at a special center, five days a week, seven hours a day, until they were ready to begin first grade. The program at the center focused on developing the language and cognitive skills of the experimental group children. The control group children did not receive special education or home-based intervention and enrichment.

By the age of six all of the children in the experimental group were dramatically superior to the children in the control group. This was true on all test measures, especially those dealing with language skills or problem solving. The experimental group had an IQ average of 120.7, as compared with the control group's 87.2.

Interestingly, by the time both groups were ten years old and in fifth grade, the IQ scores of the children in the experimental group had decreased to an average of 105 while the control group's average score held steady at about 85. The children from the experimental group were also having greater disciplinary problems. Although Heber and his colleagues aren't certain why the children from the experimental group lost IQ points and had greater disciplinary problems, they believe that the problem rests with the local school. The children of both groups attended the same school in the poor neighborhood, and the teachers there spent much of their time on custodial and disciplinary tasks rather than academic ones. Furthermore, when academic subjects were introduced, they were geared for the slower students. The brighter children from the experimental group were not given materials suitable for their abilities, and they began to fall back.

The disciplinary problems that plagued the experimental group usually consisted of such teacher complaints as "talking too much" or "talking out of turn." But remember that these children had six years of training in language skills! Finally, during the six years the experimental children spent in the special project center they ate well, receiving three hot, balanced meals a day. Once they left the center and began to attend the local school, many reported going to classes hungry, without breakfast or a hot lunch. As you can see, special institutions are sometimes better equipped to support a child than is the child's home or school.

OTHER EARLY-INTERVENTION PROJECTS

Project Head Start was designed in the 1960s to help disadvantaged preschool children do better in school as they grew older. At first, research results from the Westinghouse Learning Corporation and researchers at Ohio State University indicated that Head Start was making little difference in the long-term intellectual development of its children. However, researchers David P. Weikart and Lawrence J. Schweinhart released an interim report in 1980 on an 18-year study of the progress of 123 children at Perry Elementary School in Ypsilanti, Michigan, which indicates that good-quality preschool education programs do benefit the disadvantaged. The Ypsilanti Project provided 12½ hours a week of education at ages three and four,

CULTURE-FAIR TEST
A test that is supposed to be free of cultural biases, usually constructed so that language differences and other cultural effects are minimized.

plus 90-minute weekly home visits. Children in the enrichment program scored higher on reading, math, and language achievement tests than those in the control group. They also showed fewer antisocial and delinquent tendencies (Williams & King, 1980).

There have been other programs like the Milwaukee Project and the Ypsilanti Project that have been effective. A notable example of institutional enrichment can be found in Israel, where children with a European Jewish heritage have an average IQ of 105 while those with a Middle Eastern Jewish heritage have an average IQ of only 85. Yet when raised on a **kibbutz,** children from both groups have an average IQ of 115.

The most successful projects are those, like the Milwaukee Project, in which home intervention is incorporated. The results of such programs have been very encouraging: By the time participants enter fifth grade, only 1 percent need special education. Among children from similar environments who do not get to participate in home-based early intervention programs, 30 percent usually require special education by the fifth grade ("Vindication of Early," 1977). It has also been discovered that home-based early-intervention programs needn't be extensive in order to be effective. In one program, conducted in Nassau County, New York, an instructor made only two half-hour visits a week for only seven months of the year over a period of two years. He spent time showing the parents participating in the program how best to teach their children at home. The children in this program had initial IQ's in the low 90s, but they are now in school and are averaging IQ's of 107 or 108. In addition, they have consistently demonstrated superior ability on school achievement tests ("Vindication of Early," 1977).

Intellectual Changes over Time

Problems arise when IQ tests are used to measure intellectual changes during the life span. In the 1930s Nancy Bayley developed a test called the Bayley Mental and Motor Scale in order to evaluate infants' intellectual and motor skills. Interestingly, subjects who were measured by the Bayley test when they were nine months of age often had very different IQs when they were retested at five years of age by the Stanford-Binet IQ test. In fact, the correlation between the two IQ scores was zero (Anderson, 1939), indicating that the infants' IQ scores at nine months of age were totally unrelated to their IQ at five years. This result is shown in Table 12.3, along with the

Table 12.3 Correlation between infants' IQ scores at various ages and their scores at five years

AGES	NUMBER OF CHILDREN	TOTAL CORRELATION COEFFICIENT
3 mos. and 5 years	91	.008
6 mos. and 5 years	91	−.065
9 mos. and 5 years	91	−.001
12 mos. and 5 years	91	.055
18 mos. and 5 years	91	.231
24 mos. and 5 years	91	.450

SOURCE: Adapted from Anderson, 1939.

correlations obtained for the infants when they were younger and older. The correlation at nine months was zero because tests given at different ages often measure different abilities. Tests for very young children and infants generally emphasize motor skills, while tests for older children tend to emphasize verbal and cognitive skills. Yet both are said to measure intelligence.

DIFFICULTIES IN MEASURING INTELLECTUAL CHANGE

This problem can be highlighted by considering what appears, at first glance, to be an extraordinary fact. When Koko, the gorilla who learned sign language, whom you met in Chapter 8, was seven years old, she was given the Stanford-Binet IQ test. Her score was 90, an average IQ! Of course, this doesn't mean that Koko is as intelligent as the average human. Rather, the questions younger children are asked on the Stanford-Binet test contain a heavy motor-skill factor loading, and gorillas develop motor skills faster than humans do. A gorilla baby can climb a tree at an age when a human baby is still having trouble crawling. As a result, Koko's MA was inflated on the human test, and her IQ was relatively high. At a later age, when the questions asked will concentrate more on verbal and cognitive skills, Koko will probably fall to an IQ of about 35. This result won't mean a decline in intelligence, but simply that the questions for older children tap different skills, skills that Koko's species does not develop fully. For the same reason, the "intelligence" measured in younger children is usually not well related to the "intelligence" measured in older children. This lack of correlation makes it especially difficult to measure "intellectual" change over time during childhood. As Figure 12.5 shows, IQ scores don't tend to become consistent over time (or "reliable", as psychologists refer to it) until about the age of ten (Bloom, 1964). This means that IQ scores obtained from children younger than ten may not be reliable, that is, they may change considerably as the children grow up.

As far as adults are concerned, psychologists disagree on whether intellectual ability declines or remains stable with age in a population of healthy individuals. Older subjects tend to have lower scores on IQ tests, but then again, they were products of the 1930 school system and not of a modern

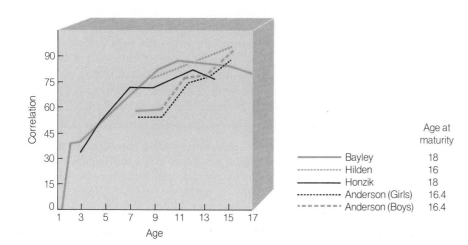

Figure 12.5 *Correlations between children's IQ scores at various ages and their IQ scores at age 18, as cited by several studies.* (SOURCE: *Bloom, 1964*)

LONGITUDINAL STUDY
A research approach that studies
individuals through time, taking measurements at periodic intervals.

one, a fact that may explain some of the observed differences (Kimble & Garmezy, 1968). Furthermore, longitudinal studies, studies that measure people many times over a long period, aren't very helpful in determining age-related changes in intelligence because many older adults grew up during the depression; their lower IQ scores may be due to the long-term effects of malnutrition or poor health rather than age. While some studies have indicated that a gradual decline in intelligence occurs with age, others suggest that no real decline occurs. Some studies have even concluded that intellectual abilities do not decline over time among adults of superior or above-average intelligence but that they lessen noticeably among adults of average or lower intellect (Botwinick, 1967).

Other difficulties also plague research designed to investigate age differences in intellectual development between younger and older adults. Younger adults tend to be faster than older adults on performance tasks such as those found on the Wechsler IQ tests. But does this reflect an intellectual decline or a decline in motor speed? On tasks that require physical quickness, such as block design, object assembly, or digit symbol, 20-year-olds are considerably better than 36-year-olds. This result may be due to differences in reaction time or to the fact that older adults more often value accuracy over speed (Bischof, 1976). The data on intellectual change during adulthood remain complex and unresolved.

TERMAN'S STUDY

In 1921 psychologist Lewis Terman received a grant from New York City to conduct a long-term **longitudinal study** of children with IQ's above 140. Terman selected his 1,528 subjects from grade schools in California. Their average IQ was 150, and 80 of them possessed IQ's of 170 or higher (Terman, 1925). Follow-up studies were conducted in 1922, 1927–28, 1939–40, 1951–52, 1960, 1972, 1977, and 1982.

Since few women were encouraged during the 1920s to seek professions, most of the follow-up studies concerning professional accomplishments concentrated on the approximately 800 men included in the original selection. This is not to say that the Terman women didn't choose professions; many of them did, but there were few professional women in the average general population with whom to compare them. By 1950, at an average age of 40, the men had written and published 67 books, over 1,400 articles, 200 plays and short stories, and had obtained over 150 patents. Seventy-eight of them had received a Ph.D., 48 an M.D., and 85 an LL.B. Seventy-four were university professors, and 47 were listed in *American Men of Science*. As Terman has noted, "nearly all of these numbers are 10 to 30 times as large as would be found for 800 men picked at random" (Terman, 1954).

Among the Terman women there were also some surprises. According to Pauline Sears, who has been reviewing the latest data, the Terman women

> were way ahead of several trends that have only lately become true for the nation as a whole. They were quicker to join the work force. They took longer to marry and have children, and more were childless. A high proportion were in managerial positions; I suspect that because they were bright, they got ahead faster. Their brightness made another intriguing difference: the divorced women among them were happier than most, at least on our measure of satisfaction with their work pattern. Almost all the divorced women worked full time, and

their work was satisfying to them. The same was true of the women who remained single. All of them worked, and they were much happier with their work than most working women are. Their satisfaction wasn't from income, either, but from the work itself. (Goleman, 1980, p. 44)

Pauline Sears' husband, psychologist Robert Sears, is now in charge of overseeing the Terman study. Robert Sears was formerly head of the Psychology Department at Harvard and Dean of Stanford University. He is also one of the 1,528 children in Terman's original study (Goleman, 1980).

The Terman "kids" are now in their seventies and, compared with the average person of that age, they are healthier, happier, and richer, and they have had a far lower incidence of suicide, alcoholism, or divorce. These studies also dispel the myth that genius is next to insanity, since few of the Terman subjects have suffered from serious behavioral disorders compared with the average populace.

A possible reason for high IQ scores' relating to happiness and wealth or to the incidence of alcoholism or divorce may be that the subjects in Terman's study stayed in school (probably because they were good at it, which is what a high IQ would indicate). If you stay in school long enough, and do well, you're likely to obtain an advanced degree. And generally, if you have an advanced degree you'll earn more money. Furthermore, as social psychologists have known for a long time, people who are richer tend to be happier (perhaps that doesn't surprise you). If you are better educated, wealthier, and happier, you can probably afford better medical care, are more aware of how to take good care of yourself, and are probably under less stress. Divorce is also less likely to occur, since happier people get divorced less often. In fact, the major reason for divorce is usually money (not sex), and the Terman "kids," as we have noted, were relatively rich.

Lewis Terman.

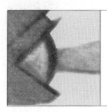

MEETING THE NEEDS OF EXCEPTIONAL PEOPLE

Not all people develop in the same way or at the same rate. And, of course, not all people learn to process information or deal with their environments in the same manner. Some people are extremely adept, like Terman's kids, while others have extreme difficulty. Collectively, those at both extremes are referred to as exceptional. Although the exceptionally gifted and the exceptionally disadvantaged can both benefit from special services designed to meet their unique needs, it is the disadvantaged who are most likely to receive help. This is because our society views the disadvantaged, in contrast to the gifted, as less able to help themselves. Exceptionality may be defined by physical-sensory, social-emotional, or intellectual dimensions. The kinds of aid or services provided for the disadvantaged vary with the nature of the exceptionality.

Physical and Sensory Exceptionality

Among the physical problems that may require special attention are epilepsy, cerebral palsy, various birth defects, injuries due to accident, or physical disorders associated with illness. In each case, the emphasis is twofold. First, it is important to use the available technology to help people overcome as much of their handicap as possible. Second, it is necessary to educate the public to meet their needs. With an epileptic, for example, the technology available includes medication to control seizures and counseling to help the person overcome the doubts, fears, and worries that often accompany the

illness. Public education is a valuable adjunct for teaching people that epilepsy is not a form of mental retardation and that it is not contagious or something that should keep a person from having friends or leading a normal life.

Sensory exceptionality is a term usually applied only to those with visual or auditory dysfunctions. Sightless people usually require special assistance, especially if they must learn braille. On the other hand, many who are legally blind (having vision poorer than 20/200 in both eyes) are able to benefit from magnification devices and books with large print. Surprisingly, among those with sensory handicaps, it is the hearing-impaired who most often experience great academic and social difficulties. Although most people consider sight a more valuable

Exceptional people often need special assistance.

sense than hearing, hearing-impaired people suffer an additional disadvantage beyond their sensory loss— language difficulties. Since auditory feedback is essential for the development of normal spoken language, hearing-impaired children are often unable to learn speech. Those who do learn to vocalize are likely to be troubled by poor pronunciation, pitch, and loudness control. Unfortunately, many uninformed people mistakenly believe that these language problems are a sign of mental incompetence, and they limit their social contact with or totally reject those who are unable to hear or communicate normally.

One of the best ways of helping the hearing-impaired is through a combination of public education and applied technology. The public must be made aware that a hearing loss is not synonymous with a mental deficiency. The hearing-impaired can be integrated into society by means of hearing aids (when possible) and new technological advances such as closed captioned television and type-and-see telephones. At the same time, people who can hear are becoming more familiar with the American Sign Language, and a larger number of hearing-impaired people are learning to lip-read and to vocalize by attending to the feedback from the vibration of their own vocal cords.

Both the visually impaired and the hearing-impaired can usually benefit from, and succeed in, the regular classroom. Nonetheless, some special instruction is often useful.

At the other extreme of physical exceptionality are individuals who are physically gifted. Many societies encourage physical development and athletic achievement, but few are able to enlist the best available technology in order to search out those who have potential talent. In some nations, though, such efforts are greatly stressed. In East Germany, the public is very mindful of the physically gifted, and there is a strong national effort to foster athletic talent.

Social-Emotional Exceptionality

The disadvantaged person within this group is often classified as emotionally disturbed or socially maladjusted. These kinds of behavioral disorders are among the most difficult to categorize. The problems are often unique to the individual. There isn't even a consensus about the prevalence of such disorders. In schools, estimates vary from 2 to 20 percent of all children (Kelly, Bullock, & Dykes, 1977). In many cases it is unclear whether the problem is biogenetically or environmentally induced.

Some children and adults seem to have social-emotional gifts. Their backgrounds would appear to nearly guarantee some kind of serious emotional disorder or social instability, but instead they develop well and seem to thrive on their adversity. Such people are often referred to as **invulnerables** (Pines, 1979). Their existence has led some researchers to believe that it might be possible to prevent others from becoming social-emotional casualties by teaching invulnerability. Some have argued that invulnerability might be taught by helping people experience and conquer a moderate, but not excessive, amount of adversity (Anthony, 1975).

Intellectual Exceptionality

Efforts to aid the intellectually disadvantaged depend greatly on the degree of retardation and its cause.

People with biogenetic disorders such as Down's syndrome are viewed, realistically, as limited in what they can accomplish. However, modern behavior modification techniques, improved medical services, and significant community support have enabled many with biogenetic intellectual dysfunctions to lead more productive and happier lives than was previously thought possible.

The largest group of intellectually retarded is formed by the educable mentally retarded. This group is generally defined by IQ scores ranging from 50 to 69 and by a reduced capacity to function in their environments. Most show no evidence of biogenetic disorders. They represent the greatest concern for the school system. Should they be educated in the regular classroom or separately? Most educable mentally retarded are not obviously different from people of average intelligence, nor do they appear to learn in a qualitatively different way. They do, however, learn at a slower rate and have shorter attention spans (Mercer & Snell, 1977). Whether such children are kept in a regular classroom usually depends on their ability to function there after every step has been taken to help them adjust. Keeping as many exceptional children in the regular classroom as possible is a philosophy known as **mainstreaming**.

It is difficult to meet the needs of the intellectually gifted and the creative because, as we have seen, both groups are hard to identify, and valid ways of measuring high intelligence and creativity have not yet been developed. Ultimately, of course, the quality of help that any exceptional person can expect to receive depends on the public's willingness to support research designed to develop the potential of all exceptional people.

INVULNERABLES
Name given to children who appear to be healthy and able to cope in spite of being reared in highly adverse circumstances.

MAINSTREAMING
The philosophy of keeping as many exceptional children within the regular classroom as possible.

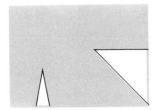

Figure 12.6   *What do you see?*

IQ tests generally are not valid predictors of creativity that exceptional individuals often need.

Creativity

Individual differences in intellectual capacity are not the only characteristics that have attracted interest in recent years. Psychologists are also concerned about the development of **creativity.**

Look at the picture in Figure 12.6 and decide what it is. A fairly common but rather uncreative answer is that it looks like a broken window. But what if someone told you that it was a boat arriving too late to save a drowning witch? That's a more creative response.

One way of defining creativity is by applying the four criteria of **novelty, appropriateness, transcendence of constraints,** and **coalescence of meaning** (Jackson & Messick, 1968). Novel, of course, means new. Something creative should be new. However, spelling *cat* Q-R-S would be new, but it wouldn't be appropriate. Jackson and Messick therefore included appropriateness as a necessary dimension. Something transcends constraints when it goes beyond the traditional. A creative idea may transcend constraints by lending a new perspective to something with which we are all familiar. Finally, the most creative ideas have meanings that coalesce over time. In other words, the depth and value of an extremely creative idea, while often not apparent at first, becomes more obvious as time passes. When Thomas Edison first developed the motion picture projector, many people wondered why the great genius was wasting his time on something that was obviously of little value. It was only after some time that the full value of the invention became apparent.

High creative ability is poorly predicted by IQ tests. Individuals with very similar IQ's often differ considerably in their creativity. This failure of IQ tests to predict creativity was investigated by Guilford and his colleagues in 1957. They felt that IQ tests typically measure a kind of intelligence different from that required for creativity. If you look again at Guilford's model (Figure 12.3) you will see two operations, **convergent productions** and **divergent productions.** Guilford argues that most IQ tests rely heavily on convergent production. When people use convergent production they search their knowledge for all that they can find to help them converge on one correct answer. In divergent production, they use their knowledge to

develop as many solutions to a given problem as possible. Figure 12.7 illustrates the difference between these two thought processes. Guilford has argued that creativity relies more on divergent productions. If Guilford's view is accurate, then the ability to see many solutions to one problem is very different from the ability to develop one correct answer from a store of information.

Some tests have been designed to predict creativity by measuring divergent production. One such test, described by Michael Wallach (1970), employs the concept of ideational fluency. **Ideational fluency** refers to the ability to develop a large number of ideas appropriate to a particular task. To measure ideational fluency, researchers might ask someone to name as many uses as possible for a common object such as a cork or a shoe, or to point out all of the similarities between a train and a tractor. People with high ideational fluency produce many answers (Wallach & Kogan, 1965). Divergent-production tests such as this one are much more accurate in their predictions of creativity than are IQ tests. In a study of almost 500 college students (Wallach & Wing, 1969), ideational fluency was found to be well correlated with creative attainments such as receiving prizes in science contests, publishing original writing, or exhibiting artwork. Like IQ test scores, ideational fluency scores among older children appear to be fairly stable over time (Kogan & Pankove, 1972).

Some Final Thoughts on Individual Differences

Biology is not democratic. Some of us are tall, some of us are short, and some of us are no doubt better designed biologically to develop skills considered to be indicators of intelligence. Inheritance and genes are important. On the other hand, as the Skeels study (see Chapter 11) and the Milwaukee Project have shown, intelligence (or whatever it is that our "intelligence" tests measure) can be dramatically affected by the environment. Intelligence might best be considered to be a complex interaction between genetic heritage and experience. The Terman subjects probably did well in school, and therefore did well on IQ tests which asked academic types of questions, because they inherited excellent brains and nervous systems and also because they were stimulated at home and school to learn and to develop their cognitive and intellectual skills. They were motivated by their success and learned at an early age that they could be successful. Terman discovered that the more stable and academic a home environment his subjects enjoyed, the more likely they were to succeed (Terman, 1954).

Summary

- In 1905 Alfred Binet and Theodore Simon developed the precursor to the modern intelligence test. Its purpose was to determine which Parisian school children should receive special education.
- Binet developed the concept of mental age, or MA. By comparing mental age with chronological age, CA, Binet was able to make comparisons between children. The German psychologist L. Wilhelm Stern developed the formula MA/CA × 100 = IQ, which yielded a rough index of how bright or dull any child was in comparison with school peers.
- While it is true that we now have IQ tests, intelligence itself has never been adequately defined, and there is controversy over whether these tests measure intelligence as most people use the term.

CONVERGENT PRODUCTION ▷
Part of Guilford's model of intelligence. A type of thinking in which an individual attempts to search through his or her knowledge and use all that can be found in order to converge upon one correct answer.

DIVERGENT PRODUCTION ▷
According to Guilford, a type of thinking in which a person searches for multiple ideas or solutions to a problem. Characteristic of the creative thought process.

IDEATIONAL FLUENCY ▷
Term used by Wallach to describe an individual's ability to produce many ideas. Ideational fluency is sometimes used as a measure of creativity and correlates poorly with IQ.

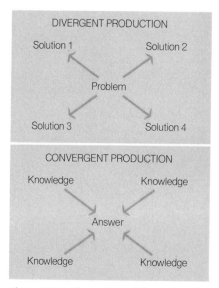

Figure 12.7 *Illustrations of divergent and convergent productions.*

- A test is said to be valid if it measures what it claims to measure. IQ tests have been found to be valid for predicting school performance and for use as a tool in clinical assessment.
- The amount of weight or emphasis given to any one ability as measured on a test is called a factor load. Some IQ tests measure particular factors more than others. For this reason the same individual may score differently on different IQ tests.
- To balance a test for factors so that each ability is tested only once, L. L. Thurstone advocated use of a technique called factor analysis.
- According to Thurstone and other factor analysts, there is not a general ability called intelligence but rather many different kinds of intelligence. The debate over this issue continues today.
- Giftedness has been defined in many different ways. Consequently, whether someone is labeled gifted may depend largely on whether the tests taken emphasized his or her particular abilities.
- In 1896 Sir Francis Galton observed that firstborn children appear to have a distinct advantage in certain areas of development over other children. Firstborns are more articulate, tend to score higher on intelligence tests, and are more reflective than children born later.
- Researchers Zajonc and Markus have developed a model of intellectual climate designed to predict differences in intelligence scores according to birth order. However, not all scientists agree that there is a significant birth-order effect.
- According to researcher Arthur Jensen, the fact that whites average 15 points higher on IQ tests than blacks is mainly the result of genetic variables. According to other arguments, cultural bias on the tests accounts for the discrepancy.
- In one study, Scarr and Weinberg gathered data on the IQ scores of black children adopted by white families. They discovered that the younger the black children were at the time of adoption, the closer they came to white IQ averages.
- The Mercer studies showed that a disproportionate number of blacks and Mexican-American children were being placed in classes for the mentally retarded, based solely on IQ scores. As a result, greater care is being taken to ensure that minorities are not mislabeled owing to cultural bias in the tests.
- Attempts have been made to devise a culture-fair test, one that contains no cultural bias. However, even on tests that do not use language, the advantage will go to people from cultures incorporating any of the aspects required by the test.
- Psychologists have studied the heritability of human intelligence and other characteristics by examining people who are related to one another. Based on current data, many psychologists agree that heredity does play a role in determining individual differences and intelligence. How important it is in comparison with environmental experiences has yet to be determined.
- The Milwaukee Project was conducted to study the effects of environmental stimulation on the intellectual development of children born in deprived circumstances. By the age of six, all of the children in the experimental group of the Milwaukee Project were dramatically superior to the children in the control group.
- The Ypsilanti Project and other home-based early-intervention projects

have generally been successful in raising the intellectual levels of the children who participated.

■ Intellectual changes are difficult to measure over time. Tests measure different skills among subjects of different ages, and as a result reliability is not always high. Psychologists disagree over whether intellectual ability declines or remains stable with age among a population of healthy adults.

■ Lewis Terman conducted a study that surveyed gifted children for over 60 years and is still in progress. The Terman kids are now in their seventies and compared with the average person of that age, they are healthier, happier, and richer, and they have a far lower incidence of suicide, alcoholism, or divorce.

■ Exceptionality may be defined by physical-sensory, social-emotional, or intellectual dimensions. One of the best ways of helping is by combining public education and applied technology.

■ Jackson and Messick have judged creativity by four criteria—novelty, appropriateness, transcendence of constraints, and coalescence of meaning. High creativity is poorly correlated with IQ scores.

■ Some tests have been designed to predict creativity by measuring divergent productions. One such test, described by Michael Wallach, employs the concept of ideational fluency.

■ Intelligence might best be considered to be a complex interaction between genetic heritage and experience.

EPILOGUE: WHAT'S IN A LABEL?

The following is an account of how one individual was inappropriately labeled by an IQ test many years ago and how that mislabeling affected his life.

In the late 1940s, when Gregory Ochoa was a high school student in California, he and his classmates were given an IQ test. Gregory and the other students were told that the results would enable the school to place them in classes commensurate with their skills. It seemed like a fair thing to do; after all, they were all being given the same chance, the same test.

When he looked at the test questions, however, Gregory found that he didn't understand many of the words, and consequently he wasn't sure what he was supposed to do. Spanish was the language spoken in his home, and his English skills were not quite equal to those of most of his classmates. Gregory,

and a few others who were having the same trouble, pointed out their difficulty to the person administering the test. They were told, "Do the best you can."

A few weeks after taking the test, Gregory found himself in a "special" class. Most of the other students in the class also had Spanish surnames. Gregory didn't fully realize what had happened. He never understood the term "educable mentally retarded" which was written on the teacher's letterhead and on the bulletin board in the classroom. All Gregory knew was that his special class didn't do regular school work. Gregory's teacher was sort of a coach, and they played a lot of soccer. Any class member interested in intellectual pursuits, such as going to the school library, was told that such activities were out of bounds.

Gregory soon dropped out of •school. He drifted about and got into trouble. He was sent to a reform school where he received some remedial reading. After reform school he joined the navy. He scored well on the navy tests. They never told him what his IQ was on retesting, but they seemed pleased that a retarded person could do so well. While in the navy Gregory earned high school credits, which eventually enabled him to attend college as a student on probation. His first quarter in college he received all A's. His second quarter he again received all A's, but he was kept on probation. Gregory finally graduated from San Jose City College on the dean's list as an honor student—on probation! *The college was apparently unable to think of him as other than "mentally retarded." By the age of 40, Gregory was an assistant professor at the University of Washington in Seattle, where he taught classes in social casework.*

When asked whether he thinks IQ tests should still be given, Gregory Ochoa said:

I think first of all, one would have to ask why you want to know what this person's intellectual capacity is. Are you using it in order to make sure that every horizon available to him is reached, or are you using it to diminish his opportunities or to prove to him, or to oneself, that Blacks, or Chicanos, or other minorities are inherently inferior to others. I think that is the critical issue— what is it being used for? ("The I.Q. Myth," 1975)

Suggestions for Further Reading

1. Brody, E. B., & Brody, N. *Intelligence: Nature, determinants, and consequences.* New York: Academic Press, 1976.
2. Jensen, A. R. *Genetics and education.* New York: Harper & Row, 1972.
3. Kamin, L. J. *The science and politics of IQ.* Potomac, Maryland: Erlbaum, 1974.
4. Terman, L. M., & Oden, M. H. *The gifted group at midlife.* Palo Alto: Stanford University Press, 1959.
5. Wallach, M., & Wing, C. *The talented student: A validation of the creativity-intelligence distinction.* New York: Holt, Rinehart and Winston, 1969.

CONTENTS

CHAPTER 13

Personality

16 traits

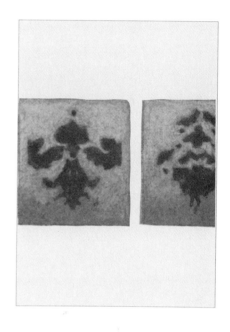

Your psychology professor said that tonight's speaker was one of the grand old men of psychology, so you've come to the meeting at the auditorium out of curiosity. You've heard of Sigmund Freud and B. F. Skinner, but Raymond B. Cattell? Who is this man? What was his contribution to psychology, and what would he be speaking about tonight?

He comes onto the stage—an attractive man in his seventies. He introduces himself and tells you he is a personality theorist. He continues, "In the 1930s my colleagues and I developed a new approach to understanding personality based on a mathematical principle called factor analysis. In fact, much of my training is in mathematics. In one of our early factor analysis experiments we asked raters to describe people that they knew well by checking a list of 171 adjectives such as anxious, friendly, dominating, etc. After much analysis we found that human personality can be broken down into just 16 specific factors. All other aspects are either combinations of these factors or repetitions of these same 16 factors. If you look at the screen up here at the front of the auditorium you can see these 16 factors (shown in Table 13.1).

"How high or low a person rates on any one of these scales is deter-

mined by their answers to a questionnaire, and their answers can tell us some important things. For example, a person who scores very high on factor Q_4 tends to be accident-prone. A low score on Q_1 means you are conservative, and scale Q_3 helps us to predict success in school.

"We once tested two groups of married couples. One hundred of the couples were happily married, while eighty had come to the counseling center because they were on the verge of breaking up. We gave them the personality test and found basically that those who were most compatible were the most like each other. In this case, several personality factors were especially important. Factor A, which implied whether a person was aloof or warm, Factor L, the dimension of trusting vs. suspiciousness, and Factor Q_2 whether you are group dependent or self-sufficient, were important. Persons who were similar on these factors tended to be most stably married. Factor E was also important. Husbands from stable marriages tended to be a little more dominant than their wives, but husbands who were much more dominant than their wives tended to have unstable marriages."

"As you can see, this approach includes the whole human being. I

397

Table 13.1 Cattell's 16 personality factors

FACTOR	DESCRIPTOR	
A	reserved	outgoing
B	less intelligent	more intelligent
C	affected by feelings . .	emotionally stable
E	submissive	dominant
F	serious	happy-go-lucky
G	expedient	conscientious
H	timid	venturesome
I	tough-minded	sensitive
L	trusting	suspicious
M	practical	imaginative
N	forthright	shrewd
O	self-assured	apprehensive
Q_1	conservative	experimenting
Q_2	group dependent . . .	self-sufficient
Q_3	uncontrolled	controlled
Q_4	relaxed	tense

Source: Adapted from the *Administrator's Manual for the 16 PF*, 1979, p. 6.

like to think that someday personality theory will be an exact science. Always remember, the personality of an individual is that which enables us to predict what he will do in a given situation. Mathematically, this is the equation $r = f(ps)$, where p is the personality, s is the stimulus, r is the response, and f is the function. In other words, response is an interaction between personality and the stimulus. I believe that some day all human behavior will be as predictable as the motion of the planets and that to uncover this we must examine all human interaction as it occurs at any given time, using precise mathematical analysis" (Cattell, 1973).

In this chapter we'll examine what personality is and how it is assessed. We'll look at personality from the viewpoint of trait theorists like Cattell and from the viewpoints of psychoanalysts, behaviorists, and humanists. Each position has made an important contribution to our understanding of personality, and each takes a different view of personality.

Why Psychologists Study Personality

Psychology is the study of behavior. If a behavior were likely to occur at any time, it would not be possible to develop a science of psychology. Behavior would be so random that it could not be predicted scientifically. But behavior isn't that way. People are often consistent; they reveal qualities in their behavior that can be relied on. You already know this about yourself, your friends, and your family. You know that some people are almost sure to be shy in a particular circumstance, while others will probably be aggressive, or outgoing and warm. You've learned to count on certain behaviors from certain people. To a psychologist, this means that the behaviors can be predicted, and predictability is the essence of any science.

By assuming that an individual will act in a certain way, we are implying that we know something about that individual's **personality.** Personality is a consistency in a person's behavior that remains stable under varying conditions. In fact, when someone does something inconsistent, we often say, "I was surprised by the change in personality."

Psychologists wonder whether personality is internally or externally governed or, perhaps, controlled by a combination of factors. Is personality shaped by environmental (external) forces? If it is, then it will change drastically if the environment changes drastically. If, on the other hand, personality is subject to internal controls, then altering the environment drastically will have little effect. Psychologists want to find out how stable personalities are and what controls them, so that behavior can be predicted.

How well do you know your own personality? Could you predict how you would behave in various hypothetical circumstances? Is your behavior consistent enough that you know your personality? As you read about personality, you may find yourself wondering what has influenced yours and whether it could easily be changed.

Theories of Personality

To a psychologist, the word *personality* refers to the whole person, not just a part. Personality encompasses intelligence, motivation, emotion, learning, abnormality, cognition, and even social interactions. In describing someone's personality, you might refer to any of these areas. You might say that someone is intelligent, friendly, good humored, and wants to learn. Although these are different aspects of one person, they all add up to a description of personality.

Historically, investigators of personality have attempted to group people into types. This seems a straightforward enough approach. Other sciences began in the same way. Chemistry has classified the elements according to kind, and physics has classified matter and energy according to type. Similarly, personality researchers were interested in grouping people according to their behavioral differences.

Once these personality types had been described, however, researchers began to question what had created the personalities in the first place. There are many theories of personality, each with a different emphasis and explanation of why certain personalities develop. As with all good theories, personality theories should be testable, so that a science of personality can develop. A solid theory of personality would be valuable because it could be used to assess people and guide them toward endeavors to which they would be suited. Certain personalities may be suited for certain kinds of jobs. Other personalities may signal future trouble. Whatever the case, a good theory of personality would help psychologists counsel individuals who seek assistance or information. Haven't you ever wondered whether your personality was right for a particular job, or well-matched with another's in terms of having a successful marriage, business relationship, or friendship? All of us have wondered at one time or another whether we wouldn't benefit from a change in personality. Imagine how useful it would be if personality could be measured so that we could choose the life-styles for which we were best suited and which would enable us to lead the most productive lives. This is the applied goal of all personality theory.

PERSONALITY TYPES

One of the earliest endeavors to categorize people by type of personality was made by the Greek physician Hippocrates (460–377 B. C.). Hippocrates classified personality according to four types, melancholic (sad), phlegmatic (listless and tired), sanguine (content or optimistic), and choleric (easy to anger). With his limited understanding of biology, he believed that these different personality types were caused by one or more of four bodily fluids he called *humors*. A melancholic temperament was the result of too much black bile, a phlegmatic temperament was the result of too much phlegm, a sanguine temperament was the result of too much blood, and a choleric temperament was the result of too much yellow bile.

Among the modern personality type theories is one developed by the American physician William Sheldon that has received considerable attention. In 1940 Sheldon presented a correlation between physique (body type) and personality (Sheldon 1940, 1944). Figure 13.1 illustrates the three physiques—**endomorph, mesomorph,** and **ectomorph.** Sheldon measured subjects according to 7-point scales for each of the three dimensions. For instance, a person who rated 2, 5, and 7 would be low on endomorphy, moderate on mesomorphy, and extremely high on ectomorphy.

Table 13.2 outlines the kinds of personality characteristics that Sheldon felt were correlated with the three body types. But why should different personalities have been found to be associated with different body types? Physique and personality may be correlated simply because of the kinds of experiences different people are exposed to. An overweight person, or endomorph, may find vigorous sports uncomfortable and avoid them. A mesomorph may excel at sports and therefore take part in them frequently. And an ectomorph may learn at an early age that he or she is weaker than the other children, and consequently become fearful and introverted. These correlations may even have been due to biases among observers and raters. Since many people think of fat individuals as jolly, thin individuals as restrained, and muscular individuals as athletic, raters may tend to emphasize these characteristics regardless of subjects' actual behavior (Tyler, 1956). So far, no cause-effect relationship has been established between Sheldon's body types and certain personalities.

Carl Jung (1875–1961), a Swiss psychiatrist and psychoanalyst, developed a personality theory that separated individuals into two types, **introverts** and **extroverts** (Jung, 1933). Introverts are withdrawn and tend to avoid social contact, while extroverts are outgoing and try to interact with people as often as possible. Since interaction with other people is an important dimension of personality, as well as an important part of our lives, whether

Figure 13.1 *Sheldon's body types.*

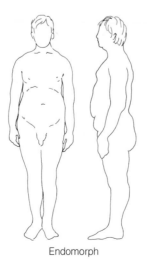 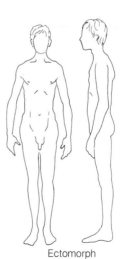 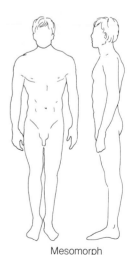

Endomorph   Ectomorph   Mesomorph

Table 13.2 Personalities corresponding to Sheldon's body types

PHYSIQUE	TEMPERAMENT
Endomorphic (soft and round, overdeveloped digestive viscera)	*Viscerotonic* (relaxed, loves to eat, sociable)
Mesomorphic (muscular, rectangular, strong)	*Somatotonic* (energetic, assertive, courageous)
Ectomorphic (long, fragile, large brain and sensitive nervous system)	*Cerebrotonic* (restrained, fearful, introversive, artistic)

we are introverted or extroverted can have a powerful effect on our existence. At one time or another over 80 percent of Americans have considered themselves to be shy, and fully 10 percent (over 20 million Americans) currently feel that they are shy and that their shyness affects the way in which they interact with other people (Zimbardo, 1979).

Categorizing individuals according to type is appealing because it appears so simple and reasonable. Yet it is this simplicity that limits the value of any typing system. People are complex, and they behave in many different ways under different circumstances. Researchers have therefore found it extremely difficult to type individuals. More often, they consider people to have certain traits in lesser or greater degrees.

THE TRAIT APPROACH

Traits are important underlying and enduring qualities of a person. We use trait words all the time in order to describe ourselves and others. Look at the following list of common trait words. Which are most descriptive of your personality?

moody	rigid	pessimistic	unsociable
passive	thoughtful	controlled	even-tempered
sociable	talkative	easygoing	carefree
touchy	aggressive	changeable	optimistic
anxious	sober	reserved	quiet
careful	peaceful	reliable	calm
outgoing	responsive	lively	active
restless	excitable	impulsive	

Although we also sometimes use trait words to explain behavior, in fact they explain nothing. To say that someone is outgoing does not explain why he or she is outgoing. To refer to a behavior pattern as a trait simply argues that this is one behavior pattern that's consistent, and one that can be predictably associated with that individual.

Allport's Trait Theory   One of the best-known advocates of the trait approach was Gordon Allport (1897–1967). Allport recognized that each person has certain consistent aspects, or, as Allport put it, "predispositions to respond to environmental stimuli in certain ways." What might make one person angry might make another person laugh because of the way they are predisposed to respond, or, as you or I might say, because of the personality these people have.

CARDINAL TRAITS
In Allport's theory, an encompassing trait in that almost every act of a person who possesses the trait seems traceable to its influence. Cardinal traits are uncommon, observed in only a few people.

CENTRAL TRAITS
In Allport's theory, behavioral or personality tendencies that are highly characteristic of a given individual and easy to infer. Allport argues that surprisingly few central traits, perhaps five or ten, can give a fairly accurate description of an individual's personality.

SECONDARY TRAITS
In Allport's theory, traits that are not as crucial as central traits for describing personality. Secondary traits are limited in occurrence because they are related to only a few stimuli and a few responses, for instance enjoying going to ballgames as a function of knowing a game is being played nearby.

SURFACE TRAIT
From Cattell's theory of personality, a cluster or group of behaviors that are overt and appear to go together. Inferring the existence of a surface trait makes it possible to classify similar behaviors under one term; for example, constant fighting, yelling, and horrible facial expressions can be categorized under the surface trait term "aggressive."

SOURCE TRAIT
From Cattell's theory of personality. Source traits can only be identified through factor analysis and are more important than surface traits. Cattell argues that personality can be reduced to 16 source traits and that, although surface traits may appear to be more valid to the common-sense observer, source traits have the greater utility for accounting for behavior.

Allport considered traits to be enduring and also general, that is, likely to occur under many different circumstances (Allport, 1937). He recognized that some traits are more enduring and general than others. Consequently, he drew a distinction between **cardinal traits, central traits,** and **secondary traits** (Allport & Odbert, 1936). Cardinal traits are the most general and enduring of all. Allport argued that some individuals have no cardinal traits. For a trait to be cardinal, it must be the overriding factor in a person's life. For example, hatred may have been a cardinal trait of Hitler's, and reverence for every living thing may have been a cardinal trait of Albert Schweitzer's.

Central traits are far more common. They are less enduring and less general than cardinal traits, but they are nonetheless important to us all. According to Allport, central traits are the basic units that make up our personality. Surprisingly few central traits are necessary in order to capture the essence of a person. Allport found that when college students were asked to write a description of a person whom they knew well, they tended to mention on an average only 7.2 central traits (Allport, 1961).

Secondary traits are far less enduring and less general than central traits. In fact, Allport often used the term *attitudes* rather than secondary traits. Examples of secondary traits might be liking to watch old movies, attending baseball games frequently, and putting off work until almost too late.

Allport felt that no two people have exactly the same traits, and as a result, every personality is unique. Still, many people have traits that are similar, and these traits manifest themselves in the way people interact with the environment (see Figure 13.2).

Cattell's Trait Theory Some trait theorists have emphasized the need for statistical analysis, such as factor analysis (see Chapter 12), in order to isolate different traits. After all, you wouldn't expect to find a separate and distinct trait for every trait word in the English language. There would be many overlaps. Raymond Cattell held this view (Cattell, 1950). As you learned in the Chapter Prologue, he was not satisfied with simply classifying traits; he wanted to know how traits were organized and how they were related to one another.

Cattell began his work by examining the visible or apparent portions of a personality. He referred to the obvious traits that we can all see as **surface traits.** He used questionnaires and direct observation to compile data about surface traits from many people. His subsequent statistical analysis turned up certain surface traits that seemed to come in clusters. To Cattell, such groupings indicated a single underlying trait. Cattell referred to these more basic traits as **source traits.** In Figure 13.3 you'll see results from the 16

Figure 13.2 *In Allport's view, traits may be thought of as intervening variables that help relate stimuli and responses that at first may not appear to be related.*

STIMULI	TRAIT	RESPONSES
Meeting a stranger		Dominating, impulsive
Visiting relatives	AGGRESSIVENESS	Assertive, talkative
Working with friends		Controlling, excitable
Dating a friend		Restless, active

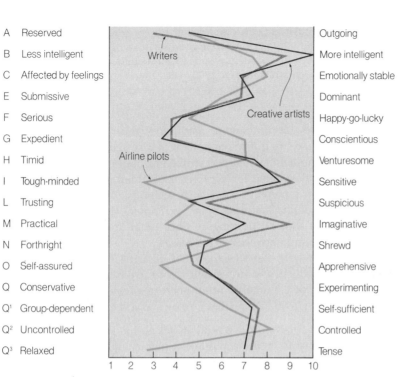

		1	2	3	4	5	6	7	8	9	10	
A	Reserved											Outgoing
B	Less intelligent											More intelligent
C	Affected by feelings											Emotionally stable
E	Submissive											Dominant
F	Serious											Happy-go-lucky
G	Expedient											Conscientious
H	Timid											Venturesome
I	Tough-minded											Sensitive
L	Trusting											Suspicious
M	Practical											Imaginative
N	Forthright											Shrewd
O	Self-assured											Apprehensive
Q	Conservative											Experimenting
Q¹	Group-dependent											Self-sufficient
Q²	Uncontrolled											Controlled
Q³	Relaxed											Tense

Figure 13.3 *The 16PF personality profiles developed by Cattell for three groups of subjects, airline pilots, creative artists, and writers. (*SOURCE: *Adapted from the* Handbook for the 16PF, *1970)*

personality factor questionnaire developed by Cattell (Cattell, Saunders, & Stice, 1950). The questionnaire was given to three groups of subjects, airline pilots, creative artists, and writers. As the results show, members of different professions and different groups of people can sometimes have similar personality profiles. In this case, creative artists and writers have more in common than either group does with airline pilots (Cattell, 1973). Cattell believes that this kind of personality profile can help psychologists predict behavior.

Trait theory has been criticized. It is not yet clear which traits are the most enduring and general. Many personality "traits" may be situationally dependent (Bem & Allen, 1974; Endler & Magnusson, 1976). A person who is dominant in one situation may be submissive in another, and a person who is forthright in one circumstance may be sly in another (Becker, 1960). Trait researchers such as Allport and Cattell recognize this fact. They do not argue that all of human personality can be explained by traits using today's techniques; the immediate situation will always have some effect on behavior. For a science of personality to be broad enough to predict behavior adequately, environmental aspects will have to be considered as well. In this sense, there are probably no strict trait theorists, that is, individuals who see the entire personality as the result of traits alone. As researchers Jackson and Paunonen have humorously pointed out,

Gordon Allport (1897–1967)

> one encounters the term "trait theorist," with all its connotations, in the writings of several authors. Like witches of 300 years ago, there is confidence about their existence, and even possibly their sinister properties, although one is hard pressed to find one in the flesh or even meet someone who has. Similarly, few theorists can be found who take the opposite extreme position that variables associated with the person play no role in behavior. What one can identify are different sets of investigators, some of whom prefer to focus on the stability or continuity of personality across situations, and others who seek to isolate vari-

ables in the environment which, for example, arouse motives. There is a third set, those who argue that it is the person-situation interaction that is of crucial importance (Endler & Magnusson, 1976; Magnusson & Endler, 1977; Mischel, 1977). (Jackson and Paunonen, 1980, p. 523)

THE PSYCHOANALYTIC APPROACH

Sigmund Freud, the founder of *psychoanalytic theory,* derived his system from observations of many patients; it is a system that can be used to predict and explain behavior. Freud studied human personality with the aid of techniques he developed for probing the hidden and unconscious thoughts or desires of his patients. One such technique was the interpretation of dreams by an analysis of their symbolic content (Freud, 1900). Another was the analysis of slips of the tongue, since Freud felt that such slips revealed hidden desires and unconscious processes.

We use the term *psychoanalyst* to describe individuals who have accepted Freud's theory either totally or to a considerable degree. Because Freud's theory of personality attempts to explain most of human behavior (Freud, 1940), it is often considered to be a grand explanatory theory.

The Three-Part Personality Freud relied on his knowledge of biology and social experience to create a model—a picture of personality. In his model the personality is divided into three parts, the **id,** the **ego,** and the **superego** (see Figure 13.4). According to Freud, the id has no objective knowledge of reality. It ruthlessly and relentlessly drives the organism toward pleasure; it is therefore said to follow a **pleasure principle.**

The ego is the part of the personality that must deal with reality if the id's desires are to be met. The ego therefore functions according to a **reality principle.** For instance, the id may insist on possessing all of the money in the bank, but it is the ego that must deal with the safe, the guards, and the other realities of the situation.

On the other hand, we are taught that stealing is wrong, and this is where the superego comes in. Freud considered the superego to be the internal representation of an ideal as expressed in terms of social and traditional values. Since the superego develops as a result of learning or culture, it is obviously not inherited or present at birth.

These hypothetical constructs (id, ego, and superego) were designed to create a picture of the biological (id), psychological (ego), and social (superego) aspects of personality. Freud believed that the dynamics of personality involve a continual conflict between the id, the ego, and the superego (Freud, 1917). He thought that each individual has a certain amount of

Figure 13.4 *Freud's concept of the three-part personality.*

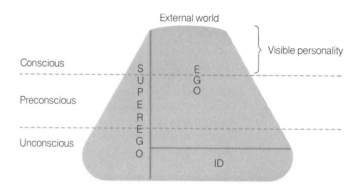

psychological energy, or **libido,** and that conflicts between the three parts of the personality drain this energy. In particular, the instinctive pleasure drive often comes into conflict with the acquired social inhibitions about expressing instinctive desires (Freud, 1905). This antagonism is well illustrated in the classic conflict that Freud called the Oedipus complex.

The Oedipus Complex Oedipus was the Greek king who inadvertently killed his father and married his mother without realizing who they were. Freud believed that all male children developed an **Oedipus complex** and that this complex must be resolved in order for the personality to develop healthily. In Freud's view, the infant boy's id received gratification and pleasure through contact with the mother during nursing. As a result, a **pleasure bond** formed between the infant and the mother.

Within a few years, the boy discovers that he has a rival for his mother's affection, his father. The id then desires the father to be removed or dead so that it can have the mother all to itself. But as the superego emerges, the child learns that it is wrong to kill one's father or wish one's father dead. Furthermore, since the father is so much bigger than the boy it would be dangerous to express this wish in any outright fashion, and so the boy's mind represses the wish—that is, buries it in the unconscious where it is not available for conscious thought or action, but from which it can still influence behavior. In Freud's view, the major determinants of the personality come from this unconscious reservoir of repressed desires and are basically irrational. The major theme of all Freudian psychodynamic personality theory is that people are constantly driven by unreasonable demands resulting from unconscious desires, and that these desires must be uncovered through analysis or resolved before a healthy personality can develop.

Freud said that in order to resolve the Oedipus complex the boy must come to identify with the father. This identification takes place at about the age of six, when the boy resolves to be his father by behaving and acting exactly like him. In this way, Freud argued, the child develops a heterosexual identity as a male and comes to terms with the desire to kill his father and possess his mother. Freud believed that boys who did not take this step may have problems as adults, finding it difficult to relate to men in positions of authority, searching out wives who are like their mothers, and playing basically an infantile role in the marriage. As you can see, Freud felt that the first few years were very powerful determinants of adult personality.

Freud had a different view to describe the development of girls. Since girls, like boys, form a pleasure bond with their mothers (while nursing) rather than with their fathers, girls can't simply follow a mirror image of the Oedipus complex by desiring their mother dead and so on. Instead, Freud argued, girls come to desire their fathers because of what Freud called penis envy. Freud believed that girls feel incomplete when they realize they lack something that boys have; they then become attracted to their father because their father possesses the desired anatomy. Freud called this pattern the **Electra complex** (after the Greek woman Electra, who revenged her father's death by killing her mother). Freud also argued that women, feeling incomplete, could never be as psychologically whole as men and that they were likely to be overly concerned with their physical characteristics and to be narcissistic.

ID
In psychoanalytic theory, the reservoir of instinctive drives, the most inaccesible and primitive portion of the mind.

EGO
In psychoanalytic theory, the part of the personality that regulates the impulses of the id in order to meet the demands of reality and maintain social approval and self-esteem.

SUPEREGO
In psychoanalytic theory, the part of the personality that incorporates parental and social standards of morality.

PLEASURE PRINCIPLE
The psychoanalytic postulate that an organism seeks immediate pleasure and avoids pain. The id functions according to the pleasure principle.

REALITY PRINCIPLE
According to Freud, the principle on which the conscious ego operates as it tries to mediate between the demands of the unconscious id and the realities of the environment.

LIBIDO
To Freud, the psychological energy driving the individual to seek gratification, principally sexual, but also food, comfort, and happiness.

OEDIPUS COMPLEX
A Freudian term representing the sexual attachment of a boy to his mother. This desire is repressed and disguised in various ways. The child expresses jealousy and hatred of the father because the father can have relations with the mother that the son is denied.

PLEASURE BOND
A Freudian term referring to the strong attachment an infant forms for its mother, generally considered to be a result of nursing.

ELECTRA COMPLEX
According to Freud, the female form of the Oedipus complex; the desire of a girl to possess her father sexually.

For this reason and others, Freud liked to use the phrase "Anatomy is destiny." His concepts of women, perhaps more than anything else, got him into trouble with his critics (Horney, 1939).

The Psychoanalytic View of Instincts Freud considered sexual behavior and aggression to be instinctive drives. Throughout the animal kingdom, he argued, aggression helps an animal obtain needed food and territory and sexual behavior maintains species, and as such, both are necessary for survival. In our species, however, these aggressive tendencies and sexual desires run head on into cultural taboos against explicit sexual actions and uncontrolled violence.

Freud believed that this struggle between biological drive and social inhibition produces anxiety, and that the ego throws up defenses in order to control and handle the anxiety effectively. Such defenses may take the form of psychological problems, such as **hysteria.** For example, people who are hysterically blind cannot see even though nothing is physically wrong with their eyes. Freud argued that all hysterias were functional, that is, they served a purpose. In the case of hysterical blindness, there must be something that the ego doesn't want to see and this is its way of dealing with its anxiety.

Psychosexual Stages of Development Freud believed that each person passes through five psychosexual stages as the id, ego, and superego develop. The first three stages—oral, anal, and phallic—involve physical satisfaction and are centered on the erogenous zones. They take place during the first six years of life. The later stages—latency and genital—occur between six years of age and adulthood.

ORAL STAGE (FROM BIRTH TO APPROXIMATELY ONE YEAR OF AGE)   During this time, a child obtains the greatest satisfaction from stimulation of the lips, mouth, tongue, and gums. Freud noted that sucking and chewing are the chief sources of an infant's pleasure.

ANAL STAGE (APPROXIMATELY ONE TO THREE YEARS)   During this time, the child gains the greatest satisfaction from exercising control over the anus during elimination and retention. Freud believed that the anal stage reaches its peak once toilet training is successful.

PHALLIC STAGE (APPROXIMATELY FOUR TO SIX YEARS)   During the phallic stage, the child derives the greatest pleasure from stimulating the genitals. Also, the child comes to identify with the same-sex parent, a critical step toward developing into a healthy, mature adult.

If the transition through these stages doesn't go smoothly, Freud argued, developmental problems can arise. **Fixation** may occur at any stage. For example, if the id doesn't receive enough satisfaction during the oral stage, it may be reluctant to leave that stage until it feels fully satisfied. This kind of *negative fixation* can result, according to Freud, in a manifestation of oral-stage processes later in adult life. Conversely, the id may receive too much satisfaction during the oral stage. If this happens, the id may want to retain oral-stage satisfaction in later life—a condition Freud called *positive fixation.*

As an example of how fixation may manifest itself in later development, consider Winston Churchill, former prime minister of England. He enjoyed eating, he was a fine orator, and he liked cigars—all oral activities. Such behavior in adult life, Freud would argue, might have been the result of positive or negative fixation during the oral stage. Freud believed that such fixation could lead to problems. For example, a child whose id was not satisfied during toilet training because of excessive parental demands might seek satisfaction through undue retention. Freud argued that such *anal retentive* personalities would show signs later in life such as stinginess and selfishness.

Freud considered latency and genital stages to be less important than the first three.

LATENCY STAGE (APPROXIMATELY SIX YEARS TO PUBERTY)   Freud called this the latency stage because he believed that the sexual drive becomes dormant at the age of six and remains so until the onset of puberty. During this time, children are supposedly free of erotic feelings and instead expend their efforts on acquiring cultural and social skills.

GENITAL STAGE (PUBERTY TO ADULTHOOD)   Freud believed that heterosexual desire awakens during this time and that, as long as no strong upsetting fixations have occurred, the child is on his or her way toward a "normal" life.

Contemporaries of Freud   Many prominent psychoanalysts who were students and colleagues of Freud broke with him and developed their own theories when their observations of their patients led them to different conclusions. Carl Jung, for instance, believed that human beings possess two

HYSTERIA
An outdated term once used to describe those with emotional excitability, excessive anxiety, psychogenic sensory or motor disturbances, and psychosomatic disorders.

FIXATION
In psychoanalytic theory, fixation refers to remaining inordinately in a particular psychosexual stage of development because the id has received either too much or too little satisfaction.

Carl Jung (1875–1961)

Alfred Adler (1870–1937)

Otto Rank (1884–1939)

unconscious minds—a personal one, as Freud had claimed, and a species-specific one inherited from our ancestors (Jung, 1936). Jung called the latter concept the **collective unconscious.** He spent much of his life gathering religious and magical artifacts from different cultures and comparing them in order to demonstrate that similar unconscious symbols have played a role in the psychology of our species (Jung, 1955).

Alfred Adler, a Viennese psychiatrist, was one of Freud's colleagues. For Adler, consciousness is the center of personality, quite the opposite of Freud's position (Adler, 1927). Adler believed that most of the problems in human development stem from the discrepancies we observe between our goals in life and our feelings of inferiority. In his view, aggression and the desire to be superior are more important psychological dimensions than sexuality. Furthermore, striving to be superior is instinctive and the absence of such striving will result in a deep-seated **inferiority complex,** a term Adler coined.

Otto Rank, another disciple of Freud's, believed that the trauma of being born plays an important role in later development. He was especially concerned about potential adverse effects. Rank felt that those who suffer from psychological **birth trauma** have not been adequately protected from the overwhelming experience of the world immediately following birth.

The Impact of Psychoanalytic Theory Freud's view of personality development had a powerful influence on the history of psychology. A number of his important concepts have been supported by modern research, including unconscious motivation, the idea that people are often unaware of why they behave as they do. However, it has proved difficult to test many of Freud's ideas by the scientific method (Hook, 1960). To this day, no one has conclusively demonstrated that dreams necessarily mean anything, or that there is any special content hidden in them. Furthermore, many of Freud's ideas have not been well supported. For instance, modern research indicates that the first six years of a person's life, while important and formative, are not as crucial to the development of adult personality as Freud believed. Then again, it must be remembered that Freud's view shouldn't be considered complete just because Freud died. If Freud were alive today, Freudian theory might undergo considerable renovation at the hands of Freud himself.

Whether one agrees with Freud's theory of human personality or not, it is regarded as valuable because it stimulated so much research. Although largely unsupported by scientific data, the theory's full value will remain uncertain until more ways to test it can be devised. In the interim, we owe Freud and his colleagues an historic debt of gratitude for their insights and the impetus they provided research into human personality.

A Psychoanalytic-Behavioral Synthesis American psychology, with its emphasis on the scientific method, has generally rejected psychoanalytic interpretations of personality. However, there have been some interesting attempts to incorporate psychoanalysis and the scientific method. During the late 1940s, John Dollard and Neal Miller at Yale University tried to synthesize psychoanalytic and behavior theory by taking Freud's ideas and translating them into a language and methods of experimental research in behavior and learning theory.

For Dollard and Miller the major factors in personality dynamics were drives, cues, responses, and reinforcement (Dollard & Miller, 1950). They defined drive as a powerful stimulus that forced action. Some drives were considered primary or innate, such as hunger, pain, or thirst. Many others, called secondary drives, were learned through association with primary drives and their reduction. Cues directed behavior and let the organism know when it was appropriate to respond. In this way responses came under the control of different cues. A reinforcer was any event that made it more likely that a response would occur. Anything that reduced a drive could function as a reinforcer.

Dollard and Miller translated Freudian concepts dealing with internalized conflicts and repressions into the terminology of American learning theory. Freud talked about instinctive drives conflicting with social taboos. Dollard and Miller talked about approach tendencies conflicting with avoidance tendencies. In animal experiments, for instance, in which a thirsty cat was given electrified water to drink, the desire to approach the water was in conflict with the desire to avoid the shock, and the conflict led to "experimental neurosis." An animal placed in this situation exhibited anxiety and behavior similar to those suffered by Freud's patients (Masserman, 1943). Dollard and Miller considered repression to be a learned response. In their view, when one learns not to think about an anxiety-producing situation (that is, to repress it), "not thinking" is reinforced because it reduces the drive of fear. Thanks to Dollard and Miller's efforts, attempts to understand personality have become more objective, rigorous, and scientific.

BEHAVIORAL AND SOCIAL LEARNING APPROACHES

Behavioral and social learning theories of personality have developed from the work of the behaviorists, beginning with John B. Watson early in this century (see Chapter 1).

Behavioral Theory   Following in Watson's footsteps, psychologist B. F. Skinner has put forward a view of behavior whose implication is that personality is controlled by processes fundamentally different from those envisioned by trait theorists or psychoanalysts (Skinner, 1953, 1969). Skinner and the behaviorists refuse to consider drives or other internal motivational factors. As you'll recall (see Chapter 1), a fundamental aspect of their position is that anything that is not directly observable, be it a drive or a thought, has no place in an objective science.

Behaviorists believe that conditioning is responsible for the development of personality (see Chapter 6). They argue that complex social interactions and aspects of personality are due to the history of classical and operant conditioning unique to each individual.

In addition, behaviorists do not consider traits to have roots within the person. Instead, they believe that traits are the products of environmental forces and learning. The reason some "traits" seem stable is that the environments in which individuals live are often stable for long periods. Skinner and other behaviorists contend that if the environment is sufficiently manipulated, then aspects of personality that have appeared to endure will disappear and quickly be replaced by others. In this view, then, behavior is controlled by stimulus conditions, and it is not necessary to hypothesize about internal motives, traits, or conflicts.

COLLECTIVE UNCONSCIOUS
Concept proposed by Jung, in which a portion of the unconscious containing certain shared experiences, predispositions, and symbols are inherited and found in all members of a given race or species.

INFERIORITY COMPLEX
A psychoanalytic term coined by Alfred Adler to describe the problems that he believed resulted from the failure to respond to a drive to be superior.

BIRTH TRAUMA
Rank's hypothesis that the birth process has a dramatic and traumatic effect on subsequent human behavior.

Suppose you knocked on someone's door and asked for a contribution to a worthy charity. If the person gave you money would you say that this was evidence of the trait of altruism? Or would you say that underlying motivational factors in the unconscious mind prompted the gift? Both behaviorists and social learning theorists argue that whether a person gives will be determined by the immediate environment and the person's past history of reinforcement for giving. Furthermore, by manipulating the environment it is possible to increase or decrease a person's willingness to give. In fact, you could do several things to increase the amount of money that people gave as you went door to door for charity (Cialdini & Schroeder, 1976; Kleinke, 1977; Bandura, 1969):

1. Dress well, but don't overdo it.
2. Carry identification that officially associates you with the charity.
3. Carry a see-through collection container. In this way the giver can see what kinds of donations have been made and how well you're doing.
   a. Make sure the container is always one-third full. (It will look as if people have been giving but you still have a way to go.)
   b. Remove all pennies. (Donors will believe that other people have been giving bills and silver, their cue to what they should give.)
4. Travel in pairs. (More people will give if more people ask.)
5. Use the phrase "Even a penny will help" when the donor is reluctant. (Very few people will give only a penny, and few will say that they don't have a penny.)

While these arguments seem persuasive, and behavior theory is very popular in the United States—perhaps because of our democratic institutions and desire to view all people as equal at birth—there is evidence of individual differences in personality just after birth, too early for the environment to have had a significant effect. In Chapter 11, we discussed a temperament theory developed by Thomas, Chess, and Birch based on their findings that babies have noticeably different personalities just after birth and that these temperaments are long-lasting. These data argue somewhat against the idea that personality is solely the result of environmental experience. Much more data will have to be compiled before the issue can be resolved.

Social Learning Theory Social learning theorists, such as Albert Bandura, argue that personality is shaped not just by environmental influences on the person, but also by the person's ability to influence the environment (Bandura, 1978). As you learned in Chapter 6, social learning theory states that thinking is an important determinant of behavior. The inclusion of cognitive viewpoints within a behavioral framework has been a relatively recent trend, especially apparent in the work of personality learning theorist J. B. Rotter (Rotter, 1972). Rotter believes that the most important variables in determining personality are the person's expectations concerning future outcomes and the value of different reinforcements that might occur in a particular situation. In other words, a person's behavior depends on what he or she expects the outcome of any particular action to be and what those outcomes are worth. The likelihood of someone's being aggressive when trying to return merchandise to a department store would depend, then, on that individual's expectations regarding how likely aggression is to work.

Rotter doesn't care for the term "trait," preferring instead the term *generalized expectancy.* The implication is that your behavior or "trait" is really the result of your belief that the behavior will serve you well. Moreover, if traits—the stable aspect of a personality—are actually generalized expectancies, then changing the environment and giving you new experiences may lead to behavioral changes and differences in your personality. This potential is not consistent with the connotation of the word *trait*, which is that the qualities of personality are relatively enduring and unchangeable even if the environment should alter drastically.

As you can see, in behavioral and social learning theories the individual's personality is considered to be situationally dependent (Bandura, 1969), while in trait theories and psychoanalytic theories the personality is believed to be stable across many situations and shaped by underlying motivations and predispositional forces.

Actors are able to convince us that they have different traits and personalities when, in fact, they are only responding to direction from an external source. Behaviorists wonder if we aren't all actors.

THE HUMANISTIC APPROACH

The central focus of all humanistic theories of personality is the concept of self. *Self* refers to the individual's own personal internal experiences and subjective evaluations. Humanistic theories are quite varied, but they all share a number of basic themes. They reject the notion that underlying traits or unconscious motivations and conflicts are important forces in the development of personality, arguing instead that human beings are endowed with free will and free choice. Similarly, they reject the idea that environmental forces are the major determinants of personality. Instead, the individual is thought of as an aware human being capable of unique experiences based on his or her own view of the world and the self.

Most humanistic theories stress that people have a positive drive to grow as human beings and to realize their potential to the fullest. Humanistic approaches are sometimes *phenomenonological.* This means that for each of us there is no objective world. There is only our subjective or personal experience of the world, which depends on our self-concept, attitudes, and beliefs. Humanists argue that to understand anyone's personality you must know how he or she perceives the world. We must find a way to "stand in the other person's shoes," even if only for a moment.

Kurt Lewin (1890–1947)

Figure 13.5 *The immediate life space of a child (P) who is looking for an adequate route to obtain candy, and who has two choices: to approach his friend or to approach his mother, both of whom are positive in his view. However, Mother is an impenetrable barrier to getting candy; she will deny him at that moment. The avenue of requesting the friend to buy candy is more open. Therefore, the child is more likely to choose vector 2 than vector 1. Of course, this life space lasts only a brief time and may change considerably depending on new environmental circumstances. It depicts an immediate situation only. Very complex life space drawings can be made. Such drawings facilitate our understanding of what is happening.*

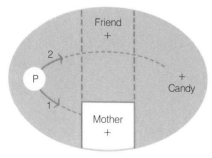

Gordon Allport's Contribution   As you'll recall, Gordon Allport developed a theory of personality based on traits that people share in differing degrees. Additionally, Allport was one of the earliest researchers in personality theory to emphasize the uniqueness of each individual. Another of Allport's ideas was that some aspects of an adult's personality may be maintained independently of the reasons that first created those aspects. Allport referred to this potential as **functional autonomy** (Allport, 1961).

Functional autonomy is probably Allport's most controversial and best-known concept. It means that any activity or behavior may become an end in itself, though it may have begun for different reasons. For example, suppose you wanted to explain what it is in your friend's personality that makes him like to hunt deer. Without considering functional autonomy, you might say that he hunts because he wants to eat. Then, if he continues to hunt even though he has enough food, you might say, in psychoanalytic terms, that he hunts to express an innate aggression. This explanation refers the hunting behavior back to a more primitive motive. Allport's concept of functional autonomy avoids this. Allport might argue that your friend would continue to hunt even if he didn't have a drive such as hunger or aggression, simply because after having hunted often enough he's come to like hunting. In other words, the behavior's function has become autonomous or independent of any earlier motivation or drive.

Oddly, Gordon Allport, a trait theorist, gave impetus to the humanistic view through his idea of functional autonomy, which, applied to personality theory, fits well with the humanist position that behavior can be engaged in for its own sake, separate from any underlying drives, traits, or conditioning.

Kurt Lewin's Field Theory   Kurt Lewin wrote extensively about personality in the 1930s (Lewin, 1935, 1936). He borrowed an idea developed by the physicist Maxwell, who had described force fields such as electric or magnetic fields. At each point within such a field a specific particle might have different influences forcing it in different directions. Some fields are easy to penetrate; others are more difficult. And each field extends only a certain effective distance. Lewin applied this idea to psychology and personality, creating a picture of unique individuals, each with his or her own "self-awareness field."

According to Lewin, each person has a **life space,** a field in which he or she can operate. This space is not a physical setting such as a room through which you can walk or roads down which you can drive, it is a psychological life space (Lewin, 1936). It's a depiction of your own personal world. If you look around you, at your *physical* space, you know that you are living in a nation surrounded by millions of people. You know that you can travel in all three dimensions, and the chief barriers you are likely to confront will be mountains, oceans, or the money needed to cross them. But your psychological life space is different. It includes your friends and relatives, your relationship to them, your ability to get things done in certain ways, and any forces that might inhibit your actions. It includes only a small area in which you typically travel and live, and only a few people with whom you are close. Lewin might say that in terms of your own psychology it would be more reasonable to imagine yourself living on a small island inhabited by only a few people than in a nation of millions. Lewin even drew pictures of psychological life space (see Figure 13.5).

In Lewin's view, people's actions become clearer if you analyze their life space, the choices they face, and the decisions they make. He believed that to understand personality you must understand a person's life space and what it contains at any given time (Lewin, 1935). He referred to this as the *principle of contemporaneity.* Lewin rejected the idea that personality is constant and contains unchanging traits, or that it is a continuation of earlier dynamics and forces. Instead, he argued that personality is always changing in response to what is contained at any given time within the life space. Personality will therefore undergo the greatest change when the life space itself changes owing to the addition of new relationships or to an altered self-perception.

Over the years there have been many experimental attempts to demonstrate the way in which people's life space can be changed by altering their self-perception and their understanding of others and of events. As Lewin suggested, altering self-perception alters the psychological life space—because the life space *is* the individual's self-perception. This humanistic view of personality as a function of a person's current self-perception is stimulating research into the effects of people's self-concept on their personality and behavior (Magnusson, 1980). Carl Rogers, perhaps more than anyone, has conducted extensive research in this area.

Carl Rogers' Self Theory To humanistic psychologist Carl Rogers, a person's unique subjective experience of reality and self is central to any dynamic understanding of personality (Rogers, 1961). Rogers' personality theory is often referred to as a "self" theory because it focuses on the individual's self-perception and personal view of the world. Rogers argues that we develop a self-concept through our experience with the world and our interactions with others, and by listening to what others tell us. We build our own lives, and we are all free to choose for ourselves rather than being at the mercy of learned stimuli or unconscious forces. Rogers stresses that each person is purposeful in his or her behavior and is positively striving to reach self-fulfillment. The major cause of maladjustment is an individual's perception that his or her sense of self is in opposition to personal expectations or goals (Rogers, 1951).

The humanistic approach has been criticized on a number of grounds. First, it has been argued that concentrating on self-perception and subjective assessment does not bring us any closer to explaining the causes of an individual's behavior (Smith, 1950). Second, humanists have been criticized for concentrating too heavily on the individual and ignoring the environmental problems that may be causing discomfort or disharmony. And lastly, humanists have been criticized strongly because their viewpoint has not been demonstrated by rigorous experimentation. There is little evidence, for instance, to support the humanist assertion that human beings are positively striving toward self-fulfillment and possess free will.

Personality Assessment

As mentioned at the beginning of this chapter, we study personality in the hope of providing people with insights into their behavior that will help them lead happier lives. For this reason, psychologists have been very interested in assessing personality and have developed a number of measures and tests for doing so.

FUNCTIONAL AUTONOMY
Allport's theory that an activity originally engaged in as a means to an end frequently acquires an independent function and becomes an end in itself.

LIFE SPACE
Lewin's depiction of an individual and his or her environment as the individual perceives it.

Carl Rogers (1905–   )

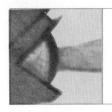
PROMOTING SELF-ACTUALIZATION

The concept of self-actualization is basic to the humanistic understanding of personality. Self-actualization refers to the humanistic perception that people move in the direction of fully developing their personal potential, especially their emotional potential (Maslow, 1954). There is no simple way to have a more creative and fulfilled life. Knowing the qualities of those who have fulfilled their potential or imitating them is no guarantee of realizing one's own potential.

Self-actualization is more a way of life than a final goal. By observing and interviewing many people, humanists have gained some insight into ways to help foster self-actualization (Maslow, 1968).

First, they suggest, you should reject rigidity. If you are dissatisfied with your life as it is now, be willing to accept change. Try to direct your own life. That is, take personal responsibility for your choices rather than depending on others to make them for you. Realize that you are human and that you have faults. Don't expect always to live up to your own ideals or to those of others. By accepting your faults, you can begin to examine them without being afraid of what you might find. You must come to grips with the fact that everyone can't like you, or you will spend your life trying to please others. Although there is nothing wrong with pleasing others, you must first of all be true to yourself.

Become involved with other people and the work that you feel is important. Make a commitment. This will help you to focus on problems outside of yourself. But don't overburden yourself with work. Take time for the pleasures of life. Enjoy the present, and expand it. Plan for the future, but don't live in it.

We often don't know ourselves as well as we think. One way to get better acquainted is to keep a diary of the things you've done during the day and record whether you enjoyed them. You may be doing things out of habit rather than because you enjoy them. By keeping a diary you may discover that some of your activities don't make you happy. If this is the case, then you can actively make an attempt not to do these things any longer. Or you may have been overlooking things you actually enjoy because you forgot how much you liked them at the time.

An avid golf player who kept a journal found that he hated golf and played only because he enjoyed the company of others. He quit golf, but found other ways to be with people. This might seem like a small change, but it made him happier and heightened the quality of his life. Just a few such changes can have an amazing effect. A woman who kept a diary woke up early one morning and decided to take a walk, something she didn't usually do. She might never have taken a walk like that again, because it wasn't her habit, but she later read her diary entry, written immediately after the walk, about how much she had enjoyed it. Now she regularly walks in the morning; she says she feels more restful afterwards and enjoys the day more.

Try keeping such a diary. Write down your feelings as they occur so that you needn't rely on a faulty memory later. The effect is often surprising, and it may enhance the quality of your life.

MEASURING PERSONALITY TRAITS

Trait theorists would like to know which traits predominate and how these traits are likely to influence behavior. Perhaps the best known of the instruments used to measure traits is the Minnesota Multiphasic Personality Inventory (MMPI). Widely used, the MMPI contains roughly 500 phrases to which the subject taking the test may answer "True," "False," or "Cannot say." The phrases tap emotional reactions, psychological symptoms, and beliefs (Hathaway & McKinley, 1940). The following are examples of the kinds of statements made on the MMPI:

There have been times when I've considered killing myself.

I am my own worst enemy.

On the whole I am self-assured.

I find it difficult to fall asleep.

I am happy most of the time.

The MMPI is called a standardized instrument because it has been administered to thousands of people from whom profiles have been obtained. If you were to take the MMPI your profile could be compared with the standards that have already been gathered (Marks & Seeman, 1963). In this way your personality could be assessed in terms of others whose behavior is known and whose personalities have already been examined. Problems can arise with even the best personality gauges, however. Sometimes subjects are unwilling to put down how they really feel, and although the MMPI is considered an objective instrument, one subject's understanding of a statement can be considerably different from another subject's. For example, how would you respond to this sentence:

Sometimes I see things that aren't really there.

You might think to yourself, "This question is asking me whether I have hallucinations, and the answer is definitely no." Or you might think, "This question is asking me whether I see illusions, which is a perfectly normal phenomenon. As a matter of fact, a couple of days ago I was driving down the highway and I thought I saw water on the road up ahead. But when I got there it wasn't there, so I'll check yes." As you can see, a person's subjective interpretation of a statement's intent can lead to different answers.

The MMPI is broken down into ten basic scales. Each measures a different trait (see Table 13.3). In addition, there are three validity (control) scales. The L scale, or lie scale, attempts to spot individuals who are trying to fake a good self-image. People who score high on this scale say that they do a number of commendable daily activities that almost no one engages in, such as never telling a lie or reading for more than an hour a day. The K scale, another control, reflects on how defensive or open the subject is being. The F scale, the third control, tests whether the subject is trying to present an exaggerated impression of his problem. Throughout the MMPI a number of statements are made more than once, with only slightly different wording. Responding differently each time will result in an invalid score. Another scale, the Question scale (?), is a measure of the total number of items put into the "cannot say" category.

Each person's MMPI scores are recorded on a profile (see Figure 13.6). An atlas provided with the MMPI outlines average reactions to situations by people with different profiles. In this way you can be compared with them, and psychologists administering the test might then predict that there is a high probability that your behavior will be similar to that of others who have had a like score.

Research with the MMPI has been extensive; over 100 different studies are published every year. The MMPI can be a valuable instrument if it is used for making general assessments. It is not usually effective for predicting highly specific responses in extraordinary circumstances. But it does indicate the kinds of behavior patterns a person is likely to exhibit.

Other instruments have been designed to measure attitudes and preferences along certain dimensions. The Terman-Miles Masculinity-Femininity test is an example. The Terman-Miles test is a simple paper-and-pencil test that asks adults and adolescents to describe their feelings, beliefs, and likes or dislikes. The test has been standardized so that the responses can be scored as masculine or feminine depending on whether they are like those given by the majority of males or females who were initially measured. A person with a high masculine score is exhibiting the same attitudes, beliefs, and feelings that a majority of men have claimed to exhibit, and a person with a high feminine score is exhibiting the feelings, attitudes, and likes of a majority of females. An **androgynous** score means that the individual was about equal on the masculine and feminine scales.

In general, androgynous individuals have been found to be able to adapt to new situations better than those who score at the more extreme ends of the scales (Bem, 1977). This may be due to their ability to transcend sex-role constraints and engage in a number of different behaviors in many social situations. Some researchers have argued that androgynous individuals have a greater sense of self-worth because their flexibility allows them

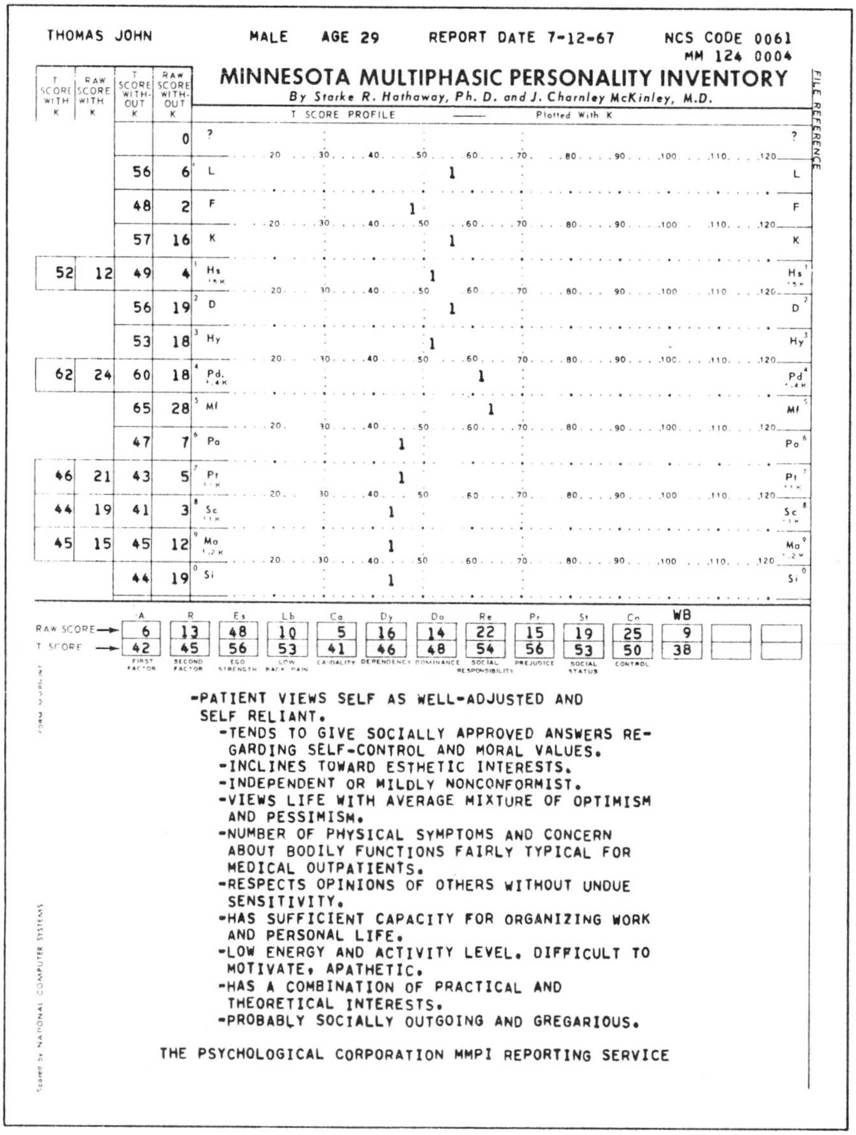

Figure 13.6 *An MMPI profile. This one was scored by a computer. Since the instrument has been standardized, the computer compares the responses against those of a large data bank obtained from the standardized group. Personal biases can then be eliminated on the part of the person administering the profile.* (SOURCE: *Minnesota Multiphasic Personality Inventory Manual, 1970*)

Table 13.3   The MMPI Scales

Validity Scales

1. Lie Scale (L)

A high score on the L scale identifies subjects who have stated they possess socially desirable characteristics and behaviors that are in fact very rare. This happens when subjects attempt to fake a good response and do not provide adequate data.

2. Frequency Scale (F)

A high score on the F scale identifies subjects who have checked items that are rarely marked true except by those who are trying to present an exaggerated impression of their problems or by those who are extremely deviant.

3. Correction Scale (K)

These items reflect how defensive or honest the subject is being. The scale measures attitudes more subtle than those measured by the Lie Scale. A high score indicates that a subject may not be deliberately lying but is keeping a close check on his other true feelings and not being as open as would be desired.

Clinical Scales

1. Hypochondriasis (Hs)

A high score on this scale indicates a subject who is overly concerned with bodily functions in the absence of any real physical illness.

2. Depression (D)

A high score indicates that items have been selected that emphasize pessimism about the future, a sense of helplessness and hopelessness, and a concern with death and suicide.

3. Hysteria (Hy)

These items discriminate those who use physical symptoms to control others and solve their problems or to avoid responsibilities.

4. Psychopathic Deviate (Pd)

A high score indicates that the subject has a disregard for social customs and mores, is unable to benefit from punishing experiences, and lacks emotional commitment to others, particularly in terms of sex and love.

5. Masculinity-Femininity (Mf)

These items identify men who prefer homosexual relations rather than heterosexual ones. Women tend to score low on this scale, and the scale for women cannot be used as a mirror image of the scale for men.

6. Paranoia (Pa)

This scale separates out people who feel that they are being persecuted and victimized by others or who believe undue attention is being paid to them by other people.

7. Psychasthenia (Pt)

A high score indicates the existence of obsessive thoughts, compulsive behaviors, a high degree of fear or guilt, insecurity, and anxiety.

8. Schizophrenia (Sc)

These items identify those who are aloof, remote, and cold, and who may have bizarre emotional feelings, delusions, or hallucinations.

9. Hypomania (Ma)

A high score indicates emotional excitability, hyperactivity, and a tendency to rush from one thing to the next without ever finishing anything.

10. Social Introversion (Si)

These items pinpoint subjects who are withdrawn and who have few social contacts and little interest in being with other people.

to adapt quickly in different situations (Spence, Helmreich, & Stapp, 1975; O'Connor, Mann, & Bardwick, 1978). However, the issue is confused since individuals rated as androgynous on a different measure (the Bem Sex-Role Inventory) were not found to be the highest in self-worth (Jones, Chernovetz, & Hansson, 1978). In one study androgynous males and females were found to get along better with each other than masculine males and feminine females (presumably due to the greater social flexibility of the former) (Ickes & Barnes, 1978). But in another study pretty much the opposite was discovered (Pursell & Banikiotes, 1978). This is often the way things turn out when attempts are made to use assessment instruments to pin down a predictable pattern of behavior. This difficulty aside, the occasional rewards of personality assessment make it worth the effort.

The California F scale is another personality test, and was designed to measure **authoritarianism** (Adorno, Frenkel-Brunswik, Levinson, & Sanford, 1950). It contains statements such as the following:

Murderers should be publicly executed.

A child who is never spanked will eventually lose respect for his parents.

To survive you have to be strong, because it's a dog-eat-dog world.

No respectable woman would give up her virginity before marriage.

To be a strong leader you must have absolute obedience from your followers.

People who agree strongly with these statements receive a high score on authoritarianism. High or low authoritarian scores have been found to correlate with many variables. For instance, an F-scale score can indicate a person's political ideology. In one study, 76 percent of those who scored high on the F scale stated that they were members of the Republican party, and 65 percent who scored low on the F scale stated that they were members of the Democratic party (Leventhal, Jacobs, & Kudirka, 1964).

PREDICTIVE VALIDITY AND RELIABILITY

The results obtained from trait instruments such as the MMPI, the Terman-Miles, and the California F scale are usually considered in the light of a subject's actual behavior. In other words, a correlation is obtained between the subject's behavior and the score. In this way we can say with some confidence that someone who scored high on the social introversion scale of the MMPI is very likely to be withdrawn, shy, and somewhat introverted. Behaviors should reflect scores. If they do, then the instrument is said to have *predictive validity*, that is, it measures what it purports to measure. To determine the predictive validity, sometimes called *criterion validity*, the test score is correlated with predicted behavior patterns. A device that has high predictive validity will yield a score from which accurate predictions about behavior can be made. This is exactly what personality theorists want—instruments that will tell them ahead of time what kind of behavior people with different scores will exhibit. Conversely, if the device indicates behaviors should occur and they don't occur, then the predictive validity is low.

Many personality-assessment instruments have been found to have useful levels of validity. For example, they can often measure and predict a young couple's marital adjustment by assessing the similarity of their needs, the more similar the better the adjustment (Meyer & Pepper, 1977). They can assess the likelihood that someone will graduate from a military training program (Alker & Owen, 1977). These measures aren't accurate all the time, far from it, but they can often help psychologists make predictions with more accuracy than had they not been used.

Unfortunately, assessment instruments don't always work. Quite often they yield an inaccurate description of an individual's personality. There are several reasons for this. One is that people often distort their beliefs, attributes, and attitudes when giving information (Edwards, 1961). What they say they are like and what they are really like may be quite different. Subjects may exaggerate some traits and overlook others. Those who do this are not necessarily trying to lie. Part of the problem may lie with normal, imperfect human memory. For instance, a person who reports feeling anxious most of the time may actually not be, but rather may be remembering occasional moments of anxiety so vividly that anxiety seems an important part of his or her personality. Other people may profess to be honest because this is the way they like to think of themselves, when in fact they cheat on their income taxes, keep extra change when it is given to them, and make up lies to excuse lateness to work.

A trait-measuring device or personality-assessment instrument must be reliable as well as valid. **Reliability** refers to the instrument's consistency. Does the score remain fairly stable over time? As you can imagine, an instrument would not be very valuable if a subject's score changed drastically from day to day. Any measuring device purporting to be disclosing underlying traits should show reliability, since traits by their very nature are considered to be enduring and general. They should be there day after day, month after month, and the instrument should reflect this fact.

PSYCHOANALYTIC PERSONALITY ASSESSMENT

Psychoanalysts have developed measures designed to probe the personality in depth, break through the defenses of the subject, and uncover the hidden unconscious motivations. The subject's early history is the focal point of these investigations, especially the way in which the sexual and aggressive instincts hypothesized by Freud were dealt with.

Historically, the two assessment devices most often used for probing the unconscious have been the Rorschach ink blot test and the Thematic Apperception Test (TAT) (see Figure 13.7). The Rorschach test has become so popular that most students picture psychologists with their ink blots, just as they picture physicians with their stethoscopes.

Both the Rorschach and the TAT are considered to be *projective* tests in that they contain ambiguous stimuli that can be interpreted by subjects in many different ways. The Rorschach consists of ink blots in which a subject can see any number of different things. The TAT contains a series of ambiguous pictures; subjects are asked to make up a story about each. The story should describe what is happening in the picture, but since the picture is so open to interpretation, subjects are free to project onto the picture their own unconscious feelings and desires. Similarly, subjects can project onto an ink blot unconscious images and sensations. The test results are interpreted by a clinician.

Clearly, the clinician is a major factor in this kind of psychoanalytic assessment. In empirical tests of the validity of clinical assessment, clinical judgments have been shown to be often inaccurate and inconsistent. Research has also indicated that a clinician's assessment of a particular person

AUTHORITARIANISM
From personality theory, traits or characteristics manifest in an individual who seeks security in authority and wants a social hierarchy in which everyone has and knows his or her place.

RELIABILITY
The extent to which a test, rating scale, classification system, or other measure is consistent, that is, produces the same results each time it is applied to the same thing in the same way.

Figure 13.7 *Sample items from the TAT and the Rorschach.*

is not generally improved by the use of projective assessment techniques (Golden, 1964; Soskin, 1959). It is not uncommon for different clinicians to view the responses to projective tests quite differently. Some have argued that the problem with projective tests is that they are too projective: Not only is the subject expected to project, but the clinician may also be free to see whatever he or she wants in the score (Goldberg & Werts, 1966).

In general, the view of psychoanalytic assessment among psychologists has been split. On one side of the issue are psychologists who support the tenets of Freudian theory and believe that projective tests are an adequate way to tap unconscious processes. On the other side are psychologists who argue that projective testing as it is now used is invalid and unreliable.

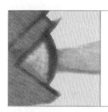

FOCUS ON RESEARCH

PERSONALITY AND VERBAL STYLE

At the University of Maryland a new personality instrument has been developed to supplement standard personality-assessment techniques. Psychiatrist Walter Weintraub based this new assessment method on his discovery that the style and speed of a person's speech can signal important clues to his or her personality. So that a sample of speech can be obtained for analysis, individuals are asked to give a ten-minute improvised speech into a tape recorder (Weintraub, 1981).

During the last two decades Weintraub has studied ten-minute speech samples from almost 250 people. He has concluded that there is a relationship between personality and verbal style, and he has divided speech characteristics into approximately 14 categories. Included in these categories are the rate of speech, the number of times people use references such as "I" or "we," and the way in which people add uncertainty to their statements by qualifying them with phrases such as "kind of" and "I think." Weintraub has also examined what he calls *retractor* words. These are words that in effect cancel what has just been said, such as "but," "however," and "although."

Weintraub has compared his samples of recorded speech gathered from "normal" volunteers with the speech patterns of paranoid, depressed, and impulsive patients

(Franklin, 1981). He has noticed that impulsive patients use many retractors, as though they were trying to undo their impulsive statements. Paranoid patients, by contrast, use many explanatory expressions, beginning many sentences with words such as "because," "since," and "as"—the result, Weintraub believes, of the paranoid's need to rationalize outlandish beliefs.

They come up with fanciful explanations of how the world works and a large part of their conversation is trying to convince people that there really is a plot against them, the mafia really is out to destroy them. . . . These are explanations, and in order to provide explanations you have to use explanatory conjunctions. (Franklin, 1981, p. 235)

Depressed patients are different again. They have speech that is characterized by long pauses, many negative words, and an increased use of "I" and "me," which Weintraub believes reflects their preoccupation with themselves.

Unlike more complex personality-assessment instruments such as the Rorschach or the TAT, a verbal style or syntax analysis can be conducted successfully by someone who has minimal training, since all that is necessary is to count and categorize the kinds of statements and words used. Weintraub points out that his procedure cannot be used alone to assess personality; he believes, though, that it can be a valuable sup-

plement to other personality inventories and measurement instruments.

Analysis of syntax and verbal style has been conducted with children as well. Weintraub has reported that children of five and six years of age exhibit what Jean Piaget referred to as egocentrism (see Chapter 11), using the words "I" and "me" very often and virtually excluding the pronoun "we." After the age of seven, the use of "we" increases greatly while less is heard of "I" and "me." However, as self-conscious adolescence approaches, "I" and "me" again predominate while "we" is used less frequently. As you can see, this kind of analysis may be uncovering some interesting developmental personality changes.

By carefully analyzing speech patterns, we may come to understand why, after simply listening to people talk, we can have hunches about the way in which they will behave. As Weintraub has noted:

We all use syntax to judge people, we just don't know that we do. . . . It should be interesting for people to find out what's at the basis of their hunches—why they say a certain person cannot be trusted or another person appears phony. A lot of it is simply the way we put words together. This [assessment of verbal patterns] is an attempt to deal in a more systematic way with those phenomena that we all deal with every day. (Franklin, 1981, p. 237)

BEHAVIORAL PERSONALITY ASSESSMENT

As you know, the behavioral approach to personality is radically different from that of trait theorists or psychoanalysts. For behaviorists, the assessment of personality is the assessment of behavior, and behavior can be assessed only if it has been carefully defined and directly observed. A be-

CHAPTER 13
PERSONALITY

421

havior is counted or timed—in other words, monitored. In this way a base-line of the behavior in question can be obtained (see Chapter 6). A behavioral assessment of personality includes an examination of the stimuli in the individual's environment and of the behaviors that these stimuli control and reinforce. Attempts to change the individual's personality are made by altering or restructuring the environment. Behaviorists refer to such shaping of the personality as behavior modification. The application of behavioral technology in order to modify personality through therapy will be examined in detail in Chapter 16.

The value and importance of different stimuli in a person's life may be assessed by examining the person's behavior in real situations, by investigating the person's preferences, and by knowing which reinforcers or rewards are most effective and important to the individual. Behaviorists understand that each person is unique and that while some stimuli may be reinforcing for some people, other stimuli may not be.

Behaviorists rely extensively on experimental methods. Because they deal only with the observable aspects of behavior in any given person, they tend to avoid concepts or constructs that rely on internal qualities or motivations such as traits or unconscious desires. Behavioral assessment is often criticized for avoiding what many consider important aspects of personality such as emotion and thought.

HUMANISTIC PERSONALITY ASSESSMENT

The humanistic approach to personality assessment differs greatly from the psychoanalytic, behavioral, or trait approach. Humanists study personality by examining each subject's subjective experience. An individual's private experiences and subjective interpretation are very difficult to assess, but humanists hope to find objective ways of assessing subjective experience. Several specific techniques for studying and uncovering a person's subjective experience have in fact been devised.

Q Sorting   The Q sort is one of the techniques that humanists have developed to examine an individual's subjective experience. A Q sort is conducted by presenting a large number of cards to a subject. Each card shows a different statement. The subject must choose whether the statement is like him or her (Block, 1961). The Q sort cards may contain statements such as the following:

> I am a reasonable person.
>
> Most people like me.
>
> I get frightened easily.
>
> I have a good sense of humor.
>
> I am successful at my work.

By forcing the subject to sort through the cards an impression of the subject's self-image is obtained. The subject is often asked to go through the cards again, only the second time sorting them according to his or her ideal self.

It is possible to obtain a correlation between people's Q sorts and the way in which they are likely to behave. In this way a personality can be objectively appraised based on the individual's subjective self-appraisal (Bem & Funder, 1978).

Interviews   Humanists often use personal interviews to facilitate personality assessment. The interviewer gently explores the other person's self-concept and emotional feelings, trying through empathy to see the world as the subject sees it (Jourard, 1967). The interviewer is careful to avoid interjecting his or her world view and opinions. Carl Rogers has based a client-centered therapy on this technique, which will be discussed in detail in Chapter 16.

In recent years there has been more and more interest in assessing nonverbal cues. Many humanists believe that much about a person's subjective self-appraisal and world view can be learned by examining expressions, posture, gestures, and movement. Some researchers argue that self-concepts such as submissiveness or dominance can be assessed by observing a person's "body language" during the interview.

Humanistic assessment methods have been criticized for their lack of rigor. It has been argued that many clinical assessments derived from the interview method reflect the clinician's subjective appraisals rather than a true understanding of the subject.

In the end, all personality assessment has the common goal of finding out more about the individual, discovering his or her enduring characteristics, and uncovering the forces that have created and maintained them.

Summary

- Personality is the sum total of the ways in which an individual characteristically reacts. Personality refers to the consistency in a person's behavior under varying conditions.
- To a psychologist the word *personality* refers to the whole person, not just a part.
- Historically, investigations of personality have classified people according to certain types. Hippocrates, Sheldon, and Jung are among those who attempted to classify personality in this way.
- Instead of categorizing individuals according to type, modern trait theorists generally believe that people possess certain traits and that they have these traits in lesser or greater degree.
- One of the best-known advocates of the trait approach was Gordon Allport. Allport recognized that some traits were more enduring and general than others, and he drew a distinction between cardinal traits, central traits, and secondary traits.
- Some trait theorists have emphasized the need for statistical analysis in order to isolate traits. Raymond Cattell was one such theorist. Cattell developed the 16PF personality factor questionnaire, which makes use of factor analysis.
- Sigmund Freud was the founder of psychoanalytic theory. Freud divided the personality into three parts, the id, the ego, and the superego. He believed that the dynamics of the personality involve continual conflict between these elements.
- Freud argued that resolving the Oepidus and Electra complexes is important to healthy personality development. He considered sexual behavior and aggression to be instinctive.
- According to Freud, as a person develops, he or she passes through several psychosexual stages. These stages, the oral, anal, phallic, latent and genital, mark important points in the development of healthy personality.

- Many prominent psychoanalysts broke with Freud to develop their own theories of personality. Among them were Jung, Adler, and Rank.
- Researchers Dollard and Miller attempted to integrate Freudian concepts with modern behavioral theory.
- B. F. Skinner and other behaviorists refuse to consider drives or other internal motivational factors in their approach to personality. Instead, they believe that learning and environmental forces impinging upon the organism shape personality.
- Temperament theory argues against the idea that personality is solely the result of environmental experiences.
- Social learning theorists such as Albert Bandura argue that personality is shaped not solely by environmental influences on the person, but also by the person's effect on the environment.
- The focus of all humanistic theories of personality is the concept of self. Self refers to the individual's personal internal experiences and subjective evaluations.
- Gordon Allport's concept of functional autonomy has contributed to the humanistic view of personality development. Functional autonomy means that an activity or behavior may become an end in itself.
- Kurt Lewin emphasized the idea of self by picturing individual life spaces. By life space he meant an individual's personal world at any given moment in time. This depiction can help others understand the motivation and forces operating on a person at a particular time.
- Carl Rogers has developed a humanistic self theory of personality that focuses on the individual's self-perception and personal view of the world.
- Trait theorists are interested in measuring which traits are predominant and how these traits are likely to influence behavior. The best-known instrument for this purpose is the Minnesota Multiphasic Personality Inventory, or MMPI.
- Other instruments, such as the Terman-Miles Masculinity-Femininity test and the California F scale, have been devised to measure attitudes, beliefs, and feelings, as well as to predict behavior.
- Although many personality-assessment instruments have been found to have useful levels of validity, they often fail to yeild an accurate description of an individual's personality.
- Validity refers to an instrument's success in measuring what it claims to measure. Reliability refers to an instrument's consistency.
- Psychoanalysts have developed measures to probe the personality in depth, to break through the defenses of the subject, and to uncover the hidden unconscious motivations. The best-known devices for tapping unconscious aspects of personality are the Rorschach ink blot test and the Thematic Apperception Test (TAT).
- For behaviorists, the assessment of personality is the assessment of behavior. Behaviorists assess personality by examining the stimuli in the individual's environment and the behaviors that these stimuli control and reinforce.
- Humanists assess personality by examining subjects' subjective experiences. They use the Q sorting technique, which forces subjects to choose whether a particular statement applies to them. In this way an impression of a subject's self-image is obtained.
- All personality assessment has the common goal of finding out more about the individual, discovering his or her enduring characteristics, and uncovering the forces that have created and maintained them.

For several years now there has been a growing interest in the extent to which individual biases can influence one person's assessment of another's personality (Jackson & Paunonen, 1980). The following is an account of how one researcher uncovered the biases in the personality of another researcher and how these biases influenced some important research.

In 1976 psychologist Molly Harrower obtained some personality profiles that had been derived from the responses of certain subjects to the Rorschach ink blot test. What made these Rorschach results so interesting was the subjects who had been tested—among them Albert Speer, Hermann Goering, and Rudolf Hess. Next to Adolf Hitler, these men were some of the top leaders of the Nazi Reich. The profiles Harrower had obtained were the results of the Rorschach tests given at the Nuremberg trials in 1946. At that time Gustav Gilbert, a prison psychologist, had been assigned to test the captured Nazi leaders (Maile & Selzer, 1975).

Harrower read in Gilbert's assessments of the Nazis' personalities that they were hostile, violent, concerned with death, needed status, and lacked any real human feeling. Gilbert wrote, "In general, these appear to be individuals who are undeveloped, manipulative, and hostile in their relationships with others" (Maile & Selzer, 1975, p. 278).

There were 16 Nazi files in all. Harrower wondered how much Gilbert's assessment could have been the result of his own personality. After all, he was testing the most hated men on earth. Couldn't that knowledge have influenced his feelings and thoughts?

To test this, Harrower took the Rorschach scores from which Gilbert had derived his assessments and mixed them in with Rorschach scores from normal healthy people. Then she asked a panel of experts in personality assessment to look through all of the scores and to sort normal responses from abnormal ones. Amazingly, none of the experts found anything unusual about any of the test scores (Harrower, 1976).

Gilbert had obviously interpreted the test scores according to his own biases. The test results tell us something about personality, but not about the personality of the Nazi leaders. Instead, they tell us about Gustav Gilbert.

Suggestions for Further Reading

1. Hall, C. S., & Lindzey, G. *Theories of personality* (3rd ed.). New York: Wiley, 1978.

2. Mischel, W. *Introduction to personality* (3rd ed.). New York: Holt, Rinehart, & Winston, 1981.

3. Pervin, L. A. *Current controversies and issues in personality.* New York: Wiley, 1978.

4. Rabin, A., Aronoff, J., Barclay, A., & Aucker, R. (eds.). *Further explorations in personality.* New York: Wiley, 1980.

CHAPTER 14
Coping with Conflict and Stress

UNIT FOUR

Conflict and Adjustment

CONTENTS

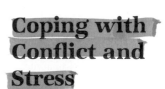

Coping with Conflict and Stress

PROLOGUE

You have been taking part in an experiment with "executive" monkeys. At the beginning of the experiment, rhesus monkeys were divided into two groups and tested two at a time. To begin, two of the monkeys were placed in separate cages; their bodies and heads were held by plastic retainers to limit their movement. Their tails were connected to an electric shock apparatus.

Every 20 seconds both monkeys received a stinging shock to the tail. The first monkey had access to a little control box. This monkey learned that if it pressed the button on the box before 20 seconds had passed, the shock would be postponed another 20 seconds. Whenever it failed to press the button, both it and the other monkey received the shock. However, if the first monkey pressed the button and avoided the shock, both monkeys were spared.

The difference between the monkeys was one of control over the environment. The first monkey could postpone the shock if it pressed the button within 20 seconds. If not, it received a shock. The second monkey had no control. Whether it was shocked or not was, literally, out of its hands. The second monkey sat passively. Sometimes it was

shocked; sometimes it wasn't. It never knew what to expect and could do nothing to influence what was happening to it. By contrast, the first monkey, whimsically known as the executive monkey, was active, working furiously to keep from being shocked. While both monkeys received the same number of shocks, one had to work to avoid them, the other didn't.

After the experiment, all of the monkeys were given a physical examination, and a medical report was prepared. The report indicated that stomach and duodenal ulcers existed. The ulcers were caused by an excess of hydrochloric acid in the stomach that had eaten through the mucosa protection of the stomach lining. It's an extremely painful disorder, and one that is common to many human beings, especially those who are under stress.

You would think that the animals suffering the most stress would be those that were helpless, unable to do anything to avoid the shock. But the results show just the opposite. The executive monkeys had the most ulcers. They were always busy, trying desperately to avoid the shock. They had to maintain a high state of arousal to protect themselves. On the other hand, the passive monkeys in the second

429

group could do nothing, and after a time, they apparently came to accept that fact (Brady, Porter, Conrad, & Mason, 1958).

Think of all the jobs that require action in order to avoid a calamity or a defeat of some sort. Air traffic controllers at airports, city desk editors rushing to meet newspaper deadlines, presidents and diplomats—all must be alert to every possible change and its ramifica-tions. In fact, just about everyone who is struggling daily to make ends meet is under some stress. How much stress can people take?

In this chapter we'll examine conflicts and the stress that can result from them. We'll look at the effects of stress on a person's body and psychology. And, on a positive note, we'll explore ways to reduce stress and cope with conflict.

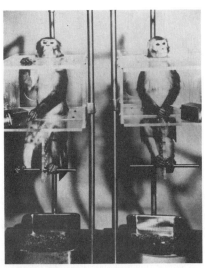

Executive monkeys had to work to avoid shocks.

Why Psychologists Study Conflict and Stress

Conflict is a fact of life that every one of us faces every day. When people face conflict, they must find some way to resolve it. Resolving conflict often requires a physiological reaction; that is, we become aroused and active when facing a conflict. To continue in this state of arousal for any length of time can be stressful. We become nervous, anxious, frightened, worried, concerned, angry, frustrated. In fact, all of these words are so commonly used to describe daily experience that we almost take them for granted.

It is impossible to study the human condition without considering conflict. And since the **stress** produced by conflict can cause psychological and physical disability, it's no wonder that psychologists have been drawn to this area of study. Stress has been called a 20th century disease because it seems that, in the contemporary world, we are surrounded by unique stressors (stimuli that produce stress). George Serban of New York University Medical Center has surveyed over 1,000 individuals to find out what they feel is creating the most stress in their lives. Serban has said of his results that people "are demonstrating unquestionably that the new social and political attitudes and values are inducing serious stress in the majority of our population." People are expressing more worry about violence, crime, drug addiction, changing social and sexual roles, sexual permissiveness, the collapse of authority, and the breakdown of the work ethic (Serban, 1981, p. 328).

However, worry is nothing new and neither is stress. Every century had its stressors and its terrors. The stress caused by crime in the streets pales when compared with the terror of the 13th century's black plague. In earlier centuries, people often died at a young age from famine or diseases such as diphtheria or typhoid. Today, medical science can keep people alive much longer and relatively safe from the great epidemics that once afflicted mankind. What we see now is a greater number of deaths from stress-related diseases such as heart attack, bleeding ulcers, and high blood pressure. The 20th century really is the century of stress, then, in the sense that we are finally living long enough for long-term stress to have an effect. Consequently, psychologists study stress in order to learn how to alleviate it, how to manage it, and how to predict its effects. If we understand conflict and stress, we will be in a better position to cope with them and to reduce their ill effects.

Conflict

Any time you are faced with a choice you are in conflict. Some conflicts are relatively easy to resolve, that is, the choice is clear, and hesitation is brief. But others can be very difficult to handle. As you might imagine, the most stressful conflicts are those that are both difficult to resolve and extremely important. If the conflict represents an important choice, you may spend a great deal of time considering it. You may even become obsessed with it. And if the choices are not clear, you may find yourself vacillating, moving first in one direction and then abruptly changing your mind. Vacillation is likely to make the conflict last longer. Any important, long-lasting conflict that you can't resolve is likely to be stressful. And stress over a long period can be debilitating.

Conflicts are often considered in terms of approach and avoidance. We all want to approach some things, while we want to avoid others. Sometimes, though, our desires to approach and avoid things come in conflict with one another.

Imagine having to choose between two things that you like. At first this might not seem like a conflict. After all, who wouldn't like to choose between several good things? But if you look at the situation for a moment, you can see that a conflict exists. This kind of conflict is known as an **approach-approach conflict** and is one of the easiest to resolve, especially if the choice isn't particularly serious. Perhaps you can't decide whether to go out for Italian food or Chinese food, or maybe you're not sure whether to buy new clothes or a watch. You'd be happy with either choice, but you do have to choose. Sometimes we try to find a way to get both goals eventually. If we go out for a Chinese dinner tonight, perhaps we'll have Italian food next week. But if the conflict is serious, and the goals are definitely exclusive, even an approach-approach conflict can be distressing. Imagine being in love with two people, both of whom you'd like to marry. You can't very well say that you will marry one now and the other later. The choice is mutually exclusive (unless you're extremely creative). Although you may be happy with either, and eventually forget the one you don't marry, the immediate choice can be extremely stressful.

Figure 14.1 depicts an approach-approach conflict. Since both goals are attractive, as you begin to move toward one it becomes easier to continue the approach and leave the other goal behind. In this way the vacillation in an approach-approach conflict is often limited. Once you've made your choice, it's unlikely that you'll reverse your decision. When the scales seem evenly balanced between two goals, we often look for just one thing that may tip the scales and send us rushing toward a resolution.

Sometimes a goal is attractive when you're at a distance, but repulsive when you're close to it. This situation is called an **approach-avoidance conflict.** A neighbor of mine once asked to borrow my 25-foot ladder in order to get a basketball out of a tall tree in his backyard. I asked him how the ball got up there, but he didn't say anything—just sort of mumbled. He put the ladder against a tree limb about 20 feet above the ground so that by climbing to the top he could reach over and knock the basketball loose. As he started up the ladder he entered an approach-avoidance conflict. Getting to the basketball was his goal. It was an attractive goal—viewed from the ground. But the wind was blowing and the ladder was rickety, and he looked a little nervous. The higher he climbed the further away the ground looked. As he reached about 14 feet, he had a look on his face that

CONFLICT
A state in which ambivalent feelings about something or someone cause stress. Conflict is normal when it is temporary and can be resolved; it becomes abnormal when it remains unresolved and results in disablement.

STRESS
A psychological state associated with physiological and hormonal changes caused by conflict, trauma, or other disquieting or disruptive influences.

APPROACH-APPROACH CONFLICT
A conflict in which the individual must choose between two incompatible goals, both of which are desirable.

APPROACH-AVOIDANCE CONFLICT
A conflict in which the goal has both positive and negative factors associated with it.

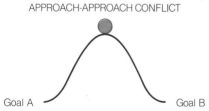

APPROACH-APPROACH CONFLICT

Goal A   Goal B

Figure 14.1 *An approach-approach conflict as depicted by a ball resting on a hill with a goal on either side. The slightest movement in either direction will resolve the conflict.*

said, "My life for a basketball is a rotten trade." At that point he came back down. Oddly, once he was down the goal again appeared attractive. He thought that perhaps he had been wrong and so he started up the ladder again. He was in the approach phase. It wasn't long, though, before he again entered the avoidance phase—at the same rung as before. He came back down, steadied the ladder, looked embarrassed, and tried to go up one more time. At the bottom of the ladder he always wanted to climb, but two thirds of the way up he always wanted to come down. I started to tell him about approach-avoidance conflicts, but he didn't seem interested.

At the time I was having my own approach-avoidance conflict. I really wanted to know how the basketball had gotten up there, but my neighbor obviously didn't want to say. I began to ask, but as the words formed I couldn't bring myself to say them because I had the feeling the answer was an embarrassing one. I started to ask several times but never did. We were busy considering different ways to brace the ladder when my neighbor's eight-year-old son joined us and resolved all conflicts. The boy announced, without being asked, that the basketball was in the tree because his dad had thrown it there accidentally while trying to show him a fancy way to make a basket. My neighbor's face reddened and so, to change the subject, I returned to our discussion of better and better ways to brace the ladder. Then the boy said, very matter-of-fact, "Why don't you just poke the ball loose with the end of the ladder?"*

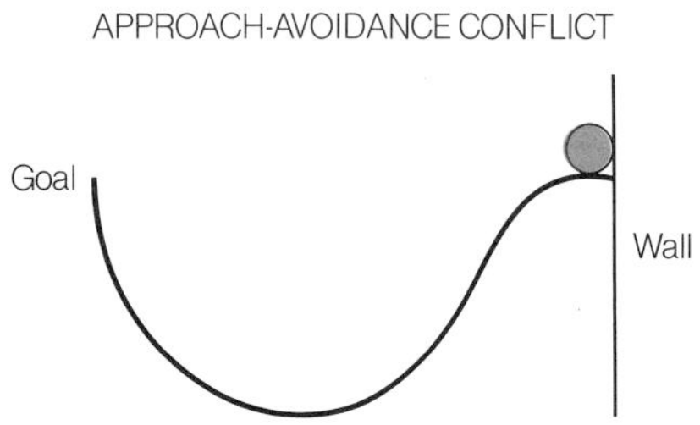

Figure 14.2 illustrates an approach-avoidance conflict. The conflict is usually resolved if the goal is obtained or if the person decides to give it up permanently. If you were to stand in the doorway of an airplane, about to parachute for the first time, you would undoubtedly find yourself in an approach-avoidance conflict. You might want to be a member of the sky-diving club, but at the same time you would have a deep faith that falling 10,000 feet couldn't really be fun. If you committed yourself and jumped, the goal would be obtained and the conflict resolved. Or, if you backed down and refused ever to stand at the doorway again, the conflict would also be resolved.

One of the worst conflicts is the **avoidance-avoidance conflict.** This conflict is the perfect example of "caught between a rock and a hard place," "damned if you do, damned if you don't," or "caught between the devil and the deep blue sea." It's because avoidance-avoidance conflicts can be so awful and memorable that there are so many different cliches to describe them. Figure 14.3 shows an avoidance-avoidance conflict. As you can see, this conflict is certain to cause vacillation. As you approach one goal the desire to avoid it becomes more and more intense, making you want to head the other way. But as you approach the other goal the desire to avoid it becomes more intense, so you turn around and head back. Imagine being trapped in a burning, smoke-filled room on the 11th floor with nowhere to go but out on the ledge. The heat and smoke would be intense, and it would drive you toward the window. But as you began to step out onto the ledge, the fear of falling would become so great that you would want to go back in again. Once back inside, the heat and smoke would force you out again.

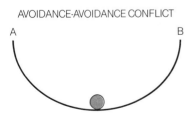

APPROACH-AVOIDANCE CONFLICT

Goal

Wall

Figure 14.2 *An approach-avoidance conflict*

AVOIDANCE-AVOIDANCE CONFLICT

A   B

Figure 14.3 *An avoidance-avoidance conflict*

---

*See Chapter 8 for an explanation of functional fixedness in order to understand how such a *bright* person as myself could make such an *understandable* oversight. Also see "Psychological Defense Mechanisms" later in this chapter for an explanation of why someone would rather make excuses, such as blaming functional fixedness, than admit to being stupid.

Beginning skydivers often find themselves in a double avoidance conflict, afraid to jump and too proud to back down.

This kind of double-avoidance conflict, where life hangs in the balance, is perhaps the worst and most stressful conflict possible. If you have to choose it may mean the end of you, and so you try to stay in the middle. As some have said, when you are forced to make a choice between two evils, choose neither. Of course, if there were a way to choose neither there would be no conflict. In an avoidance-avoidance conflict you must eventually choose.

Figure 14.4 outlines one of the most complex forms of conflict, the **double approach-avoidance conflict.** A double approach-avoidance conflict places a person between two goals, each of which has an approach-avoidance component. For example, "If I take a job now I can make some good money (approach). But to take the job I'll have to leave school, which is something I really don't want to do (avoidance). Then again, I could stay in school, which is what I'd like to do (approach), but then I wouldn't have any money for the things I want (avoidance)." This is different from an approach-approach conflict because if you choose one goal you definitely notice the loss of the other, even though the goal you choose is a desirable one. Most choices that we make have gains and losses attached to them. Consequently, the double approach-avoidance conflict is common. When we resolve this kind of conflict by making a choice, we may still feel that we have given up something. As a result, ambivalence can develop, and stress can continue as we wonder whether our choice was the correct one.

DOUBLE APPROACH-AVOIDANCE CONFLICT

Goal A   Goal B

Figure 14.4 *A double approach-avoidance conflict*

Acute Stress and Chronic Aftermath

The stressors we've discussed so far have all been related to conflict. Sometimes, however, people are plunged unforeseen into acutely stressful situations that are not the result of a conflict. Even though the stressful event may be relatively short-lived, it can be so intense that the memory of it can linger for years, leading to chronic stress. The following are examples of such acute stressors and their psychological aftermath.

In March 1979 there was a nuclear accident at the power plant on Three-Mile Island in Pennsylvania. Later investigation showed that the plant had been very close to a nuclear meltdown. If a meltdown had occurred, nuclear material would have been spewed into the atmosphere by the intense heat, and many thousands of lives might have been lost downwind of the plant.

Throughout the incident the government monitored radiation levels in the nearby area and prepared for evacuation. Some radiation leaked and some was vented on purpose to prevent more serious releases. Now, health agencies are closely monitoring the people who live near Three-Mile Island in order to detect any long-term damage caused by radiation. In studying people living within 55 miles of the reactor, researchers at Pennsylvania State University and at the Department of Health in Pennsylvania have found that the amount of stress suffered is directly related to how close to the reactor people live.

People living closest to the Three Mile Island reactor experienced the most stress.

Peter S. Houts, Robert W. Miller, and their colleagues surveyed over 30,000 people living within 55 miles of the reactor. They found higher levels of stress in 10 to 20 percent of the population within 15 miles of the reactor, while people beyond 20 miles reported much less stress. These findings were derived from people's statements about safety for themselves and their families. The ones who suffered the most stress tended to be younger, well educated, female, married, homeowners, and those with chronic emotional or health problems. Attempts to cope with their distress did not seem to help alleviate their fear. Of course, if it is found later that residents living closer to Three-Mile Island are more likely to become ill, it will be hard to assess whether this susceptibility was due to radiation or to fear induced by living near the reactor. Moreover, since the effects of radiation are thought to be long-lasting or to manifest themselves only many years later, the stress of living in that area continues to be great (Houts, Miller, Tokuhata, & Ham, 1981).

On July 15, 1976, 26 children riding on a school bus were kidnapped in Chowchilla, California. The children, aged between 5 and 14 years, were captives for 27 hours before they were freed. During this time, they were held at gunpoint and buried in an underground truck trailer that had been covered with dirt. Lenore Terr, a psychiatrist at the University of California at San Francisco, has interviewed 23 of the children (Terr, 1981). She finds that now, many years after the kidnapping, a majority of them still have repetitive disturbing dreams about the trauma. Twenty of the children say they are afraid of being kidnapped again and remain vigilant against such a happening. Reassurance by parents has done little to lessen the children's fears, which show up in their attitudes toward normal environmental events which, under usual circumstances, wouldn't cause stress. A nearby motor vehicle, the dark, wind blowing through the house—all cause fear. This stress was found among the children in the entire age range, and no one can guess how long it will continue to be felt.

Over the past few years it has come to light that many Vietnam veterans are suffering severe psychological problems. The Center for Policy Research in New York has concluded an eight-year study for the Veteran's Administration, in which it has found that Vietnam veterans who were involved in significant amounts of combat are far more likely to abuse drugs and alcohol than other veterans and have been arrested more often since returning to civilian life. Over 1,300 veterans were questioned.

All of these veterans are more likely to be suffering from the kinds of symptoms associated with long-term stress, even though the combat has long since ended. These symptoms include dizziness, headaches, memory loss, anxiety, intestinal problems, depression, and nightmares. In addition, many of them have found the readjustment to civilian life extremely difficult.

Clearly, the memories of a traumatic experience can have long-term effects even though the immediate danger has been removed. How long will stress of this sort last? Perhaps as long as the events are remembered.

Is it possible to prepare yourself for acute trauma, to harden yourself psychologically, so that once the event is over the stress won't continue? Perhaps, but if the stress is severe enough even the toughest individuals may suffer. Policemen and firemen working in large cities see disasters from day to day. They become somewhat hardened. But in September of 1979 a tragedy occurred over San Diego that overwhelmed many of these

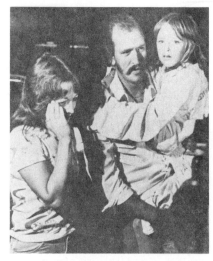

Long after the kidnapping at Chowchilla, the children continued to show the effects of stress.

Vietnam veterans who were in combat experienced the greatest stress once they returned to civilian life.

GENERAL ADAPTATION SYNDROME
Physiologist Hans Selye's description of
the body's physiological-hormonal reaction to stressors. The reaction consists
of three stages, the alarm reaction stage,
the resistance stage, and the exhaustion
stage.

ALARM REACTION STAGE
The first stage of the general adaptation
syndrome, during which cortical hormone levels rise and emotional arousal
and tension increase.

RESISTANCE STAGE
The second stage of the general adaptation syndrome. During this stage,
cortical hormones maintain high levels,
physiological efforts to deal with stress
reach full capacity, and resistance by
means of defense mechanisms and coping strategies intensifies.

EXHAUSTION STAGE
The final stage of the general adaptation
syndrome. During this stage, resistance
to the continuing stress begins to fail.
Brain functioning may be hindered by
metabolic changes; the immune system
becomes much less efficient; and serious
illness or disease becomes likely as the
body begins to break down.

professionals. A Pacific Southwest airliner collided with a small plane and
plunged into a downtown area of San Diego, killing 144 people. The first
police and firemen to arrive on the scene were faced with horrible human
carnage. There was extensive dismemberment among the victims of the
crash, making it more horrifying than most accidents. Different parts of
bodies were found all over lawns, houses, and roads. Some police said they
couldn't even walk down the street without stepping on human tissue.
Many of the officers who helped identify and label the bodies had seen
death before, but afterwards they experienced stress symptoms—nightmares, insomnia, headaches, gastrointestinal problems, memory loss. Some
actually found themselves paralyzed when they attempted to put on the
uniform that they had been wearing the day of the accident. Alan Davidson,
president of the Academy of San Diego Psychologists, said, "This has had an
impact on the human psyche beyond what we can humanly know" ("Crash
Trauma," 1979, p. 61). Police who did not have to deal directly with the
carnage but rather with crowd control or arrests, fared much better. It was
clearly direct contact with the victims that caused the acute stress and left
the memories that resulted in chronic stress.

Twenty-five psychologists in the San Diego area provided free counseling
to all city employees who had worked at the crash site. Nearly 100 sought
treatment, and many of them, perhaps a majority, were veteran police
officers who were haunted by the memories of the horror and hysteria at
the scene of the accident. The first 16 policemen who asked for help felt
degraded for seeking therapy, saying that they felt it was unmanly for
them to be upset by such a thing. Many of them asked the psychologists
to look at videotapes of the scene so that the psychologists would understand that there was a reason for them to be upset. In other words, these
hardened police veterans were surprised at their inability to cope.

To help city employees overcome their stress reaction, psychologists
prescribed active ways in which they could work out their frustration and
anger, such as jogging or target shooting. Behavior modification techniques
were used to help deal with amnesia about the disaster. Davidson has said
that the most successful treatment was simply to provide empathy and
understanding. The clients wanted to hear from the psychologist that they
were normal, but had been put through an abnormal situation (Davidson,
1979). Gentry Harris, a psychiatrist in San Francisco, has said, "It's important to let the person know he's not some kind of screwball. He's still
within the human family. We just need to make people realize that they do
have limitations" ("Crash Trauma," 1979, p. 61).

Reactions to Stress

Conflicts and traumas can cause stress, and stress can lead to illness. But
how does all this come about? How can stress make you ill?

THE BODY'S REACTION

Perhaps more than anyone else, the Canadian physiologist Hans Selye has
examined the body's reaction to stress and stressful situations. Selye calls
the physical reaction to stress the **general adaptation syndrome.** This
syndrome consists of three different stages, the **alarm reaction stage,** the
resistance stage, and the **exhaustion stage** (Selye, 1976).

During the alarm reaction stage, the organism becomes alerted to the stress and the body's resources mobilize to help cope with the stress. Corticoid hormone levels increase as messages from the pituitary to the adrenal cortex trigger the secretion of these hormones. During this time there is emotional arousal and increased tension. The person becomes more sensitive and alert to his or her surroundings. There are attempts to cope, sometimes including defense mechanisms (to be discussed later in this chapter) and attempts to alleviate the stress through direct action. Anxiety persists and tension symptoms of maladjustment such as rash, gastrointestinal upset, hives, and loss of sleep may occur.

During the stage of resistance the stress continues. This stage can be characterized as a "full war effort," whereas the alarm reaction was merely an alert. The attempts at defense have reached full capacity now. The individual must find some way of dealing with the stress in order to prevent complete psychological disintegration. A temporary resistance may be achieved by intensifying the use of defense mechanisms or by taking actions directed at eliminating the stressful situation. During the stage of resistance a person tends to become fixed in his or her pattern of dealing with the stress rather than reevaluating the situation and finding a new way to cope.

Finally, in the stage of exhaustion, all of the person's resources are at an end and the patterns of coping attempted during the stage of resistance begin to collapse. During the stage of exhaustion defensive measures may become inappropriate and exaggerated. Metabolic changes may occur that inhibit normal brain functioning, and eventually a complete psychological disorganization may result. Resistance becomes weaker until, finally, the stress takes its toll as the body begins to break down. The person is exhausted and prone to suffering the diseases that can accompany stress.

Hans Selye was one of the first to research the effects of stress.

Stress and Illness Among the most common early symptoms of chronic stress are headaches from muscle tension, gastrointestinal disturbances, skin rashes and hives, dizziness and fatigue. Chronic stress can also lead to high blood pressure, which is referred to as hypertension. Hypertension in turn can bring on a heart attack, stroke, or kidney failure (Benson, 1975). Chronic stress can also aggravate arthritis, colitis (an inflammation of the large colon), asthma, hypoglycemia, and diabetes. And, as you know from Brady's research with the executive monkeys, sustained stress can lead to ulcers as well. It should be noted, however, that the Brady study has been criticized because the monkey groups were not divided randomly. Instead, the more active monkeys were assigned to the executive group because they were more likely to operate the buttons. Consequently, some have argued that the executive group was predisposed to ulcers. Even so, many other studies have found that the onset of ulcers is well associated with stress (Wolf, 1971). Chronic stress has even been related to cancer and an increased chance of succumbing to contagious diseases.

How can stress be related to so many different kinds of illness? For one thing, stress can have a direct effect on the body's immune system. The immune system's effectiveness can be measured by counting lymphocytes (white blood cells). Lymphocytes are the body's means of attacking and destroying foreign or invading organisms. At the Mt. Sinai School of Medicine in New York researcher Steven J. Schleifer and his colleagues examined the lymphocyte counts in six men who were married to women dying of cancer. The average age of the men was 65. Within ten months the wives of all six men died. The white blood count of these men became lower and lower as the stress continued. According to Schleifer the lymphocyte count was "markedly depressed after bereavement" (Greenberg, 1980, p. 335). It is assumed that lower lymphocyte levels would make people more susceptible to disease. In fact, after the death of a spouse it's not uncommon for the remaining partner to become seriously ill or to die within two years. This higher rate of illness or death is much more common among survivors than among similar individuals of the same age who have not suffered the loss of a loved one (Glick, Weiss, & Parkes, 1974; Parkes, 1972).

Natural killer cells are an important part in each of our immune systems. They help to destroy invading diseases. Researcher Steven Locke randomly selected 117 students at Boston University and evaluated how much stress each suffered by having them complete a stress survey that measured the symptoms they had, such as poor sleep or feelings of anxiety. In addition, Locke asked his subjects how each thought he or she was coping with stress. Then blood samples were drawn from each subject and exposed to human leukemia cells. Locke's aim was to discover how well the natural killer cells in the blood samples could attack the leukemia cells. He found some notable differences between blood samples and something else, too. The ability of the body's immune system to attack effectively did not seem to be directly related to *how much* stress each subject faced but instead to *how well* that person was coping with the stress. In other words, a person who can cope with stress may have a better chance of staying healthy than a person who can't cope. So, the key may be not how much stress you face but how well you handle it. This could explain why two individuals in the same stressful job might show totally different reactions to the stress they face (Locke, Furst, Heisel, & Williams, 1978).

It has also been found that prolonged or intense stress during pregnancy can affect offspring. A number of animal studies and clinical observations have indicated that defects such as cleft palate and hyperactivity may be the result of stress during pregnancy. Rats subjected to stress while pregnant are more likely to give birth to abnormal offspring. It has even been discovered that the experience of stress during pregnancy can affect the expression of genetic traits in the offspring (Jonakait, Bohn, & Black, 1980). Stress, then, can affect the body at an extremely fundamental level.

Measuring Susceptibility to Stress and Illness   Is there any way to measure how much stress you may be facing from day to day? In Table 14.1 you'll see a scale for rating life changes developed by Holmes and Rahe in 1967. Each of these life events is assigned a value, a certain number of stress points. In their study, Holmes and Rahe found that individuals who had more than 300 stress points within the period of one year were two or three times as likely to have illness and other stress-related problems than were individuals who had less stress points.

You should be aware of some things as you read this scale. First, a minor point. A mortgage over $10,000 is not likely to be stressful today compared with 1967. Today you probably couldn't get a doghouse with a mortgage of $10,000. Considering inflation, a mortgage over $30,000 might be a more accurate measure. There are also several major points to keep in mind. First, these data are correlational. You cannot say that they are the direct result of cause and effect. For example, people of lower socioeconomic status (who are also more likely to have poorer health care) lead lives in

Table 14.1 Social-Readjustment Rating Scale

Stress points

RANK	LIFE-EVENT	MEAN VALUE	RANK	LIFE-EVENT	MEAN VALUE
1	Death of spouse	100	23	Son or daughter leaving home	29
2	Divorce	73	24	Trouble with in-laws	29
3	Marital separation	65	25	Outstanding personal achievement	28
4	Jail term	63	26	Wife begins or stops work	26
5	Death of close family member	63	27	Begin or end school	26
6	Personal injury or illness	53	28	Change in living conditions	25
7	Marriage	50	29	Revision of personal habits	24
8	Fired at work	47	30	Trouble with boss	23
9	Marital reconciliation	45	31	Change in work hours or conditions	20
10	Retirement	45	32	Change in residence	20
11	Change in health of family member	44	33	Change in schools	20
12	Pregnancy	40	34	Change in recreation	19
13	Sex difficulties	39	35	Change in church activities	19
14	Gain of new family member	39	36	Change in social activities	18
15	Business readjustment	39	37	Mortgage or loan less than $10,000	17
16	Change in financial state	38	38	Change in sleeping habits	16
17	Death of close friend	37	39	Change in number of family get-togethers	15
18	Change to different line of work	36	40	Change in eating habits	15
19	Change in number of arguments with spouse	35	41	Vacation	13
20	Mortgage over $10,000	31	42	Christmas	12
21	Foreclosure of mortgage or loan	30	43	Minor violations of the law	11
22	Change in responsibilities at work	29			

SOURCE: Holmes and Masuda, 1972, p. 105.

which more changes take place, often due to financial problems. Stressful changes in the lives of such individuals may only be correlated with poor health, not the cause of it. If so, then adding up stress points may not be a valid way to explain future problems. Similarly, the stress points should be used solely as a general guideline. Although the numbers give them the appearance of being highly specific, they aren't; they're only general. For example, it's highly doubtful that one pregnancy, one Christmas, and four vacations would be more stressful than the death of a spouse. So read the table with an open mind.

One interesting detail you may notice while reading the table is that some very nice things seem to be stressful. Among these pleasant events or circumstances are marriage, gaining a new family member, a change in financial state (which could mean for the better as well as for the worse), an outstanding personal achievement, beginning school, family get-togethers, or even a vacation.

Most research dealing with stress and illness begins with an examination of a population suffering from illness; the objective is to determine how much stress that group was under prior to the illness. But this kind of research can be biased in that the researchers often know ahead of time that the people they are dealing with are suffering from stress-related illnesses. When time and funds permit, researchers prefer to conduct *prospective* research, in which they find a healthy population, study the stress patterns, and observe their long-term effect on individuals' health.

The largest study of this kind has been conducted by George E. Vaillant of Harvard University (Vaillant, 1979). He selected 204 men who were in the sophomore class at Harvard from the years 1942 to 1944. For over four decades he kept in touch with 185 of them. During these years Vaillant and

ALPHA

Steady, cautious, depends on own resources, asks little. 25 percent suffered major disorders.

BETA

Bright, spontaneous, orients to present time, not demanding. 26.7 percent suffered major disorders.

GAMMA

Over- or under-cautious, moody, emotional, over- or under-demanding. 77.3 percent suffered major disorders.

Figure 14.5 *The link between personality and stress-related illness.* (SOURCE: *Adapted from Betz & Thomas, 1979*)

others conducted many psychological and physical tests, as well as interviews, with the subjects. Stress predictors included how often they visited a psychiatrist or psychologist, whether they were making poor progress in their job, whether they were dissatisfied with their job, whether their marriage was unhappy, whether they received little vacation or recreation time, and whether they had a poor outlook on life.

The findings of this study generally support the notion that the ability to cope well with stress is likely to result in a healthier person. Of the 59 men in this study who coped well with stress and who had the best mental health, only two became extremely ill or died by the time they were 53 years of age. Of the 48 men who were found to have the worst mental health, 18 became chronically ill or died. The men in this group had shown themselves to be less able to deal with stress. These men all came from very similar backgrounds. Clearly, their ability to cope with stress was directly related to their physical health.

REACTIONS OF DIFFERENT PERSONALITY TYPES

Not surprisingly, people differ in their vulnerability to serious diseases caused by prolonged exposure to stress.

Are you demanding of yourself and others? Do you make a sharp effort every time you deal with something? Do you also tend to be gloomy and sullen? If this pattern fits you, you may be more likely to develop serious stress-related illness than other people. Two researchers at Johns Hopkins Medical School have found evidence that people's temperament is an important factor in disease and premature death caused by stress (Betz & Thomas, 1979).

For over 30 years, Caroline B. Thomas, a cardiologist, has been following the physical and mental well-being of more than 1,300 medical students. While they were attending medical school these students were given thorough mental and physical examinations. Since their graduation they have completed full medical reports and inventories every year. The results show a distinct connection between personality traits and specific stress-related disorders. In collaboration with Barbara Betz, Thomas examined the profiles of these students and others dating back to 1948 and divided them by temperament into three major personalities. The personalities were labeled Alpha, Beta and Gamma.

Alpha personalities rely on themselves, are cautious and unadventurous, steady at what they do, and slow to adapt to new situations. Beta personalities are fun-loving and spontaneous, flexible in new situations, and clever. The Gamma personalities were often the most complex. Gammas tended to be short-tempered, and although often quite intelligent, they expressed a general sense of confusion in their lives. They also tended to be at the extremes, overly cautious at some times, careless at others. Sometimes they looked down on themselves; other times they were tyrannical.

The researchers studied the kinds of serious debilitating illnesses related to stress among the three groups. As you can see in Figure 14.5, while Alpha and Beta personalities suffered about the same number of major disorders, the Gamma personalities were three times more likely to suffer from major illness. The stress-related illnesses included heart attack, severe emotional illness, cancer, high blood pressure, and other serious disorders.

To test their findings, Thomas selected 127 additional students from the classes of 1949 to 1964. By using the records of these students Betz was able to classify them by type of temperament. Following the classification the health of each of these individuals was examined. As in the first study, the Gammas had the highest rate of illness and death. For instance, among the Gammas there had been 13 deaths, while among the Betas there had been none. Betz has said, "Because Gammas are close to their own juices and feelings, they may experience more wear and tear, and more vulnerability to stress and disease" (Seligmann, 1979, p. 40).

Both researchers agree that Gamma types should probably not try to change their personalities, but rather learn to accept how they are—which might help them relax and be less anxious.

ANXIETY

Sometimes you know the exact cause of your stress, and you may even have an idea about how to handle the problem. Much of the time, however, we can't put our finger on the problem when we feel under stress. It may be that over the days and weeks a number of what have been called "little murders" have added up. Little murders include the crunch in the traffic jam, a personal insult from someone, not being appreciated enough on the job, receiving a parking ticket, having to rush to get to work, burning the dinner, having your favorite television show preempted, being two dollars short at the supermarket, spilling ink on your clothes, and sleeping through the alarm. How many irritations like these occur each day, none of them significant by themselves? They can accumulate and create an overall feeling of stress that you can't blame on any one thing. Enough of these little irritations can lead to a general adaptation syndrome.

If we allow ourselves to be subjected to these kinds of stressors often enough, the reaction can last a long time. We can begin to feel fearful about our very existence. This feeling is known as **anxiety**. Anxiety is different from fear. If you are fearful you know what you're afraid of. If you are anxious you may not know what the cause is. Anxiety is not object-related. The American Psychiatric Association has defined anxiety as "apprehension, tension or uneasiness that stems from the anticipation of danger, the source of which is largely unknown or unrecognized."

Anxiety levels are generally found to be higher among those who handle stress poorly. Such people go through the day with a feeling of dread that's just below the surface, a constant tenseness. They're ready for the next insult. Why do some people become anxious when facing little murders, while others remain calm and relaxed? Recent evidence indicates that there may be a biological or genetic difference among those most susceptible to life's little murders.

Many psychologists are beginning to believe that internal conflict is not enough to explain anxiety. Not everyone who is in conflict becomes anxious. A new picture of anxiety is beginning to emerge. Psychological factors are important, but there seems to be a susceptibility that's especially prevalent among those who go on to develop perpetual anxiety.

In an interesting study at the University of Wisconsin, primate expert Stephen Suomi discovered that reactions to stress may be closely related to an individual's biological predisposition. He found that the amount of heart-rate change in a one-month-old monkey who was under stress was a good

ANXIETY
A state of apprehension in which the source is usually not specific as it is in fear. There is a vague but persistent feeling that some future danger is in store, such as punishment or threat to self-esteem. Anxiety typically leads to defensive reactions.

predictor of how the animal would react to stress later in life. In one experiment a tone was sounded in the monkey's cage just prior to a 105-decibel blast of noise. Once the monkeys had learned the tone-noise connection, the amount of heart-rate change during the initial tone correlated well with the amount of stress-related behavior the monkeys showed when they were later separated from their mothers or when they were placed under other kinds of stress months later. Animals that showed sizable changes in heart rate at one month of age were at a later date much more likely to exhibit anxiety responses to stress such as clutching themselves, cowering, or shivering. Suomi also found that monkeys who were blood relatives behaved similarly and that some mothers produced babies that mainly behaved in one particular way toward stress. These findings indicate a possible genetic factor in how we respond to stress and how anxious we become. Of course, this speculation assumes that the information obtained for monkeys also applies to humans ("Anxiety: Fear Grows Up," 1980).

Further evidence of a genetic factor has been gathered by Gregory Carey at Washington University in St. Louis. Carey reports that identical twins are much more likely to react similarly to stress than are fraternal (nonidentical) twins.

Other evidence indicates that there may be biochemical differences among people that influence how they handle stress. Specific brain cells that seek out benzodiazepines have been discovered. Benzodiazepines are tranquilizers such as Valium. The existence of such natural receptors implies that the brain must be manufacturing its own natural Valium, or else why would there be brain cells ready to receive it (see Chapter 2)? This finding indicates that the brain relies on neurochemistry in order to mediate how much anxiety we feel in the face of stress. If it is discovered that people with different levels of anxiety have significantly different brain chemistry, then we might find a biological reason to explain why some people are better able to handle stress than others. In addition, it may eventually be possible to develop totally safe and effective drugs that would enlarge our capacity to endure stress. If such drugs were used judiciously, people could be "tuned" to an optimal level for handling stress without exhausting their psychological and physiological resources.

SUICIDE

In the throes of a conflict, or under intense stress, some people may consider suicide to be a reasonable solution. Many have apparently looked upon suicide as the choice to stop participating in a stressful life. Over the last decade there has been an alarming increase in suicide, especially among adolescents. Among adolescents 15 to 19 suicide is the third-ranking cause of death, just behind accidents and murders. The rate of suicide among the aged is also alarmingly high.

While it's obvious that anyone would be susceptible to the stress associated with a trauma such as a plane crash or a war, it's also true that many of us, even those of us who appear to have everything we need, live in situations that we appraise as stressful. Stress is a highly personal thing, and each individual reacts to it differently. So, some people may suffer severe stress in situations in which others wouldn't experience stress at all or even see the reason for it.

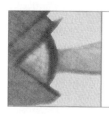

IS THERE A RIGHT TO COMMIT SUICIDE?

A 10,000-word booklet entitled *A Guide to Self-Deliverance* has been published by a London society called Exit—the Society for the Right to Die with Dignity.

The society was formed almost 50 years ago. Its members believe that suicide is acceptable for those who are painfully or incurably ill. Since they believe that suicide is acceptable in certain circumstances, they feel that they are doing a service by providing a pamphlet that describes the simplest, easiest, and least painful ways of committing the act. The pamphlet even gives lethal doses of easy-to-obtain prescription and nonprescription drugs. The *Guide* does counsel, however, against committing suicide for strictly psychological reasons, which they consider may be temporary, or if there is even the remotest chance that a cure might exist.

The announcement of the pamphlet's publication alarmed a great many people. The British Medical As-

sociation expressed fears that the booklet may make people feel that suicide is something to be treated lightly. The Association added, ''There is no reason to assume that a terminally ill patient has no more to contribute or gain in the last months'' (Leo & White, 1980, p. 49). Others feel that the information in the *Guide* may be used to commit homicide or that those who are old or sick may feel under pressure to kill themselves once they have the information and hear that others are using it.

The arguments about the acceptability of suicide among the terminally ill have grown since Jo Roman, an artist in New York, committed a planned suicide in 1980. She was ill, dying of breast cancer. There was no chance that she would survive. She held a party for her relatives and close friends the night she planned to die. They were aware of her intention and knew the reason for the party—it was a farewell gathering. A coffin was provided into

which her friends laid momentoes and things of sentimental value to Ms. Roman. She took an overdose of sleeping pills and died, comforted by the presence of her friends. Her argument was that since she was going to die anyway, she might as well choose the time and the place, and make it at least as happy an occasion as possible.

Planned suicide is a highly emotional issue, and there are outcries on both sides. Some feel that helping suicide in any fashion is a heinous act. Others argue that a prolonged and agonizing death in a hospital surrounded most of the time by strangers and without any control is the last insult and one that should not be borne. Others feel that terminally ill individuals should have the right to die if they want to but that a book such as the *Guide* will change things so that ''committing suicide will no longer be seen as a right. It will fast become a duty'' (Seligmann & Donosky, 1980, p. 77).

Think of stressful times in your life when you were much younger. Suppose you could play the old game of "If I only knew then what I know now." Suppose you could bring your current maturity and knowledge to bear in an earlier stressful situation. Conflicts with parents might seem foolish or needless. Concerns over your complexion or your treatment at the hands of certain classmates might seem trivial. The point of this exercise is to show that people who are under stress may be lacking important information. Their view of their situation may not be the only view. They may see themselves trapped in a horrible conflict with no way out, when anyone else with different knowledge or understanding may not even see a conflict.

Suicide is a final solution, and one from which there can be no return. Many people who have seriously attempted suicide but failed have later found other ways of coping with their stress. Unfortunately, as suicide rates increase, more attention is given to suicide by the media and the public.

As a result, suicide is on the minds of more people and is thought of more often as an alternative.

One interviewer discovered that 65 percent of all college students had at one time or another thought of suicide with sufficient intensity to contemplate the means (Mishara, 1975). Among the adolescents interviewed, 25 percent said that if they took their own lives they would use an automobile to do it. This finding is interesting because of the large number of adolescents who do die in automobile crashes. It makes one wonder how many of these deaths might actually have been suicides. One researcher discovered that automobile fatalities increased by an average of 9.12 percent following the widely publicized suicides of such well-known personalities as Freddie Prinze (Phillips, 1977). Phillips concluded that publicized suicides may "stimulate a wave of imitated suicides, and some of these imitated suicides are distinguished and reported as motor vehicle accidents."

In general, females are more likely to attempt suicide than males, but males are three times more likely to kill themselves (Coleman, 1976). This is probably so because males tend to use means that are immediately lethal, such as shooting or hanging, whereas females tend to favor lethal means that are less violent and take more time, such as poison or gas. In the interim, females are more likely to be rescued or to change their minds and call for help.

Among whites, older people are more likely to commit suicide. Suicides are also more likely to occur among those who are ill, who have recently suffered the loss of a spouse, who have lost their job, or who have had a history of previous suicide attempts. Interestingly, suicides are more likely to occur on holidays and birthdays, probably because these times are emotionally laden and the stresses of an unhappy life become even more apparent then. Among blacks, suicide patterns are quite different. Black suicide is mainly a youthful phenomenon, and occurs equally between males and females (Bush, 1976).

Suicide must always be viewed as a possibility among those who are under considerable stress. One of the goals of psychologists is to be aware of the hazard and to make sure that potential suicides are given a chance to obtain help.

Several signs may warn of a potential suicide. First of all, any attempt at suicide, however mild, or jokes about suicide, however lightly made, must be taken seriously. The individual should be offered help in the form of family support or professional counseling. Among adolescents, an important warning sign is the failure to achieve in school, a sign that should be especially heeded in students who have superior or better-than-average ability. Of those adolescents who have committed suicide because of perceived failure at school, only 11 percent were actually in serious academic trouble (which again serves to show how often stress is in the eye of the beholder) (Jacobs, 1971). Another important sign for members of all age groups is withdrawal from social relationships. Among adolescents, such withdrawal usually occurs because the individual feels unwanted by his or her family (Rosenkrantz, 1978). Rejection by friends and peers can also contribute to withdrawal. Another indication may be the termination or failure of a sexual relationship.

Suicide is common, all too common, and anyone suffering from long-term stress, especially when the exhaustion phase has been reached, may feel that there is nowhere else to turn.

Ways of Coping with Stress

If you stop for a moment and think about some of the conflicts or traumas that we face, you may wonder how we would ever be able to adjust. But there are ways, some of which we turn to almost automatically.

PSYCHOLOGICAL DEFENSE MECHANISMS

Sometimes we're able to handle conflict and stress by using **defense mechanisms.** These are ways of handling information to make it appear more agreeable; we can see a conflict or a trauma in a light that renders it less disturbing. Such defenses are normal and healthy. They help us survive stress. Without them we'd be prey to the full intensity of every conflict or trauma.

The term *defense mechanism* was coined by Sigmund Freud. He argued that it was necessary for individuals to distort reality in some way in order to protect themselves from unacceptable unconscious thoughts and unwanted realities. At first, defense mechanisms may seem to be bad because they twist the truth. But some misrepresentation seems to be necessary for our psychological well-being. In general, psychologists don't consider the use of defense mechanisms to be inappropriate or unhealthy unless they are relied on to an extreme.

Defense mechanisms are descriptions of behavior. They are not explanations. They label and describe a particular action. They do not explain why or how it comes about. The following are among the more commonly discussed defense mechanisms. You will probably recognize a few of them.

Denial   When we use **denial,** we refuse to admit the existence of something that could cause conflict in us. At first you might think of an extreme example such as Aunt Agnes' setting the table for Uncle Henry, even though he's been dead for 12 years. The fact is that denial, in much subtler forms, occurs in all of us from time to time. People who continue to speed even after witnessing a terrible traffic accident are in a sense denying that such a thing could happen to them. A person who gets a bad twinge in a tooth denies that it could be a cavity after the pain subsides. Without the denial, of course, a trip to the dentist is in store (a classic approach-avoidance conflict). Someone who continues to buy on credit or to spend more than is in a checking account is denying that eventually there'll be a deficit of funds. How many times have you decided that you couldn't afford something and then ended up buying it? Didn't you deny the fact that you really didn't have the money? If you hadn't used denial you would have had to face a conflict. As you can imagine, excessive denial of reality can be dangerous.

Rationalization   Vacillating in the face of a conflict is a very uncomfortable experience. No one likes to be in that position long. We all want to have our conflicts resolved, quickly and to our satisfaction. People rationalize for two reasons, (1) to help end a conflict and (2) to help assure themselves that they did, after all, make the right decision.

To rationalize does not mean to act rationally. It means purposely altering your view of a conflict in order to make the decision easier. The most famous example of **rationalization** comes from *Aesop's Fables.* A fox who wanted to eat some grapes found himself under stress because he could not reach them. To relieve his stress, he rationalized the grapes away by saying

DEFENSE MECHANISMS
Reactions to the anxiety caused by conflict that serve to protect and improve the self-image. The mechanisms are not deliberately chosen. They are common to everyone and raise serious problems for adjustment only when they occur excessively and prevent the person from coping realistically with difficulties.

DENIAL
A defense mechanism in which the individual simply denies the existence of the events that have produced the anxiety.

RATIONALIZATION
A defense mechanism in which irrational, impulsive action, or even failure, is justified to others and to oneself by substituting acceptable explanations for the real, but unacceptable, reasons.

that they must have been sour anyhow. This helped relieve the frustration. After all, who wants sour grapes? The opposite of sour grapes is the "sweet lemon." Maybe you own a sweet-lemon car—one you've paid a lot of money for and which is obviously a bomb. It breaks down constantly, but you insist that it's worth owning. In this way you "sweeten" the lemon. Without the rationalization you would be in conflict, having to face the fact that you had spent a great deal of money on something that was not worth it.

We all rationalize from time to time. "I'll start tomorrow." "It's only one test, how much can it matter?" "You can't take it with you." By changing the way we view conflicts through rationalization the conflicts can seem easier to resolve. On the other hand, if we rationalize excessively we may set ourselves up for more severe conflicts later.

Reaction Formation   One of the most stressful kinds of conflicts that we can face pits our desires against what we know to be right. **Reaction formation** is a way of concealing your motives. You react in a way that's the opposite of your true feelings. For instance, a parent who hates his or her child might conceal this unwanted and stressful emotion by behaving in an opposite fashion and being overprotective or overindulgent. Or, a person might be boastful and bellicose in order to hide feelings of inferiority.

Of course, you have to be careful in judging a behavior to be reaction formation. For example, a person who outspokenly hates homosexuals is not necessarily hiding his or her own latent homosexuality, that is, an unconscious desire to be a homosexual. Sometimes this is so, but not always. After all, if you hate dogs, does that make you a latent dog? The point is that in many situations it takes skill and training to detect the use of a defense mechanism. At the same time, not every behavior is proof of the use of a defense mechanism; many behaviors should be taken at face value.

A well-known comedian once told a story about an incident that took place when he was in the third grade. A bully in his class used to beat him up and take his lunch money, so he told his father what was happening. His father said, "Son, all bullies are hiding the fact that they are cowards. Next time, you tell him that." So the next time the boy told the bully, "My dad says all bullies are really cowards." The bully just looked at the boy, turned slowly away—and went straight over to the boy's house and beat up the father.

Projection   **Projection** is a way of attributing our own undesirable thoughts or characteristics to others. Rather than acknowledging these attributes ourselves, we see them in the people around us. People who flirt with other people's spouses might, as a defense against having to face the inappropriateness of their own behavior, incorrectly see as flirtatious any social contact by other people with their own spouse. In this way they excuse their behavior because, after all, "Everyone else is doing it." Projection, then, is a way of believing that other people have our own motives and desires. It allows us to feel free to continue behavior that might otherwise upset us.

Intellectualization   A person may try to become emotionally detached from an upsetting situation by considering the situation in intellectual or abstract terms. **Intellectualization** is often necessary, especially among people who work in highly emotional jobs. For example, a weapons expert who designs thermonuclear bombs would not be able to function if the thought constantly came to mind that the device might eventually burn, kill, and cripple millions of people.

Instead, the expert thinks, "It's a deterrent," or "It's not my decision to use it or not." Similarly, a doctor working on a child cancer ward can't afford to become emotionally involved with every child. Without the intellectual distancing, without treating the children abstractly at least some of the time, it would probably be impossible to function in that setting.

Remember that we all use defense mechanisms in order to make conflict and stress easier to manage. We would probably not be able to get through life without such defenses. Nonetheless, excessive use may create more stress than it alleviates.

DIRECT COPING STRATEGIES

While defense mechanisms may alter your view of the stressors in your life, **direct coping strategies** help you either eliminate the stressor or harden yourself to the little murders that occur every day and the big ones that occur once in a while.

There is no way to avoid stress. But avoiding it may not be necessary. As you'll recall, the amount of stress you face isn't nearly as important as how you deal with it. If you can learn to treat stress in the right way you can defuse it.

Psychologists have concentrated much of their effort on training people to cope directly with their stress. Coping does not always come naturally. It's a skill that must be learned and honed like any other skill. The following suggestions may help you cope with stress.

1. If you find yourself in a conflict, you're probably going to be uncomfortable. No one likes to be uncomfortable. As a result, there is a tendency to get the conflict over with as quickly as possible and to end the discomfort. This can lead to a rushed judgment that may in the long run cause even greater problems—since you might make the wrong choice. One of the best ways to cope with a conflict is to gather as much information as possible. Say to yourself, "All right, I'm uncomfortable and I'll be uncomfortable for a while, but it's more important that I gather information to help me with my choice than to rush to a conclusion I might not be satisfied with." As you gather information, you will usually find that your view of the conflict begins to change and the choice becomes obvious. Suddenly, the conflict will be over because you have enough information to make the right decision.

2. Trust in time. Many stressful events can be very painful. Divorce is a good example. After a divorce many people feel that their lives have been ruined. Even months after a divorce, depression and stress are likely to be severe or even to increase. New stressors must be faced, such as dating again, adjusting to a lower income, or raising children by oneself. It can seem as if the anguish will never end. But, while time may not heal all wounds, it often helps. Mavis Hetherington has found that among divorced couples the stress is often much less two years after the divorce (Hetherington, 1979). In other words, the pain is likely to decrease significantly. People make new friends, form new bonds, and often remarry. This is true not only of divorce, but also of other stressful

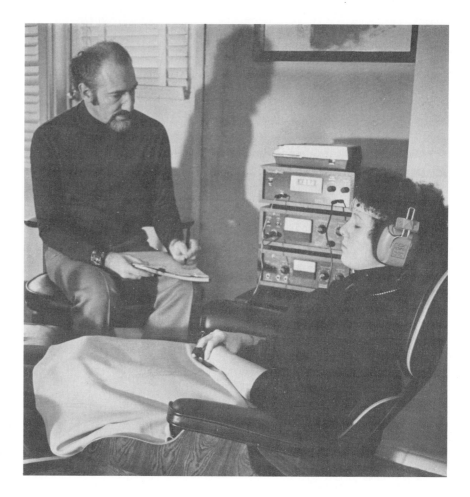
Techniques such as biofeedback have been helpful for training people to relax.

situations. If you find yourself in extreme anguish, feeling that all of your plans are collapsing or that your career is being ruined, trust in time. There is a good possibility that within a year or two after your current world has collapsed you will find yourself in another one that is equally fulfilling.

3. Try not to be alone too much of the time. Maintain friendships and contacts. The lonely and the alone suffer stress more than those who have company. Others can function to distract you by making you interested in things they find exciting. When you're by yourself, you can only keep yourself company, and you tend to discuss issues with yourself. But when you're with others and involved in doing things with them, it's difficult to engage in self-reflection. Often, the good ideas and moods of others can have a relaxing and comforting effect.

4. Think positively and rationally. Keep a sense of humor. Enjoy laughter. If someone doesn't like you, there are other people in the world. If you've planned to be a doctor ever since you were six years old and you didn't make it, it's your own fault for trusting a six-year-old to decide your future. Now that you're an adult, pick again. There are hundreds of other ways to be happy. And remember, not everything is a catastrophe. Not every goal is worth having. In fact, you may have been very lucky that you didn't achieve some of your goals. As Sigmund Freud once said, "Beware of what you really want. You might get it."

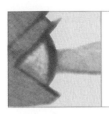

FIGHTING STRESS WITH LAUGHTER

In 1964 Norman Cousins, the editor of *Saturday Review* magazine, was stricken by a disease that caused degeneration of the connective tissue in his body. The disease appeared to be the product of a defect in the immune system. The physicians didn't hold out much hope for his full recovery, telling him that his chances were 1 in 500. Cousins was very frightened, as any of us would be. As the editor of a major magazine, he had lived a life of considerable stress. Although there was little evidence at the time that stress could affect the immune system, Cousins wondered whether the stress he had faced mightn't have contributed to his disease.

He read a book called *The Stress of Life,* in which the author, Hans Selye, asserted that negative emotions associated with stress can disrupt the body's chemistry and cause disease. Although Cousins was not a scientist, he reasoned that if stress could destroy the body, then maybe some kind of antistress could help rebuild it. He thought of all the things in his life that made him forget his problems, made him laugh and relax. For example, Marx Brothers movies always had a

Norman Cousins.

positive effect on him. He'd become immersed in them and forget his troubles. The stress in his life would seem to melt away. With this in mind, Cousins began systematically viewing Marx Brothers movies and other comedies that he enjoyed in an attempt to fight back.

No one knows if that's what cured him, but he beat the odds and recovered. In fact, the more he laughed and the more he enjoyed himself, the more the pain and symptoms disappeared (Cousins, 1979).

Is it possible that Cousins' immune system had been suppressed because of the stress in his life, and that when he systematically relieved the stress through laughter his body was able to fight back? Although the case history of one individual cannot provide a general answer, researchers have begun to study the question. They are examining the health of happy people who laugh easily, enjoy a good joke, and get fun out of life. Early results show that these people are less susceptible to disease and illness.

One exciting finding has been the discovery of receptors on the surface of white blood cells that are specific for endorphin (Berk, 1981) (see Chapter 2). When people feel good, their endorphin levels are often high. It may be that high endorphin levels stimulate the body's immune system.

Who knows? Maybe laughter has more healing power than we ever suspected. There's nothing wrong with apples, of course, but it may be more accurate to say that a Groucho, Harpo, and Chico a day will keep the doctor away.

5. Begin to think of yourself as a relaxed person. Move and speak more slowly. Eat slowly. Take deep breaths; stop from time to time to relax your muscles. Watch how hectic the lives of others seem, and let this remind you to slow down more. Don't schedule your life so that you need to rush from place to place. If you find yourself in a traffic jam, don't think about the future and how the traffic is keeping you from being someplace. Instead, take a deep breath, turn on the radio, listen to the music, and relax. Look at the tense faces and angry expressions of the people around you, and take pleasure in the fact that you are a relaxed person.

SYSTEMATIC RELAXATION
A technique in which deep relaxation
is achieved through the progressive
relaxation of one muscle group at a time,
usually beginning with the feet and legs.
The subject breathes deeply and focuses
attention on each muscle group as it is
relaxed.

You can learn to relax by using special techniques such as **systematic relaxation.** Sit in a comfortable chair and close your eyes. Take deep, slow breaths. Concentrate on a number, any number. Say the number softly to yourself again and again as you breath deeply. Clear your mind of all other thoughts and just concentrate on the number. Begin to relax your muscles starting with your feet and working your way upward. Systematically relax each muscle, one at a time. Feel your feet become heavy and completely relaxed, feel your leg muscles become completely relaxed, and continue the process upward.

If you try this technique for about 15 minutes twice a day, it may have some beneficial effects. It often lowers blood pressure and leaves you feeling much less tense for a number of hours to come. Other techniques that can help individuals relax and cope with stress include biofeedback and meditation (discussed in Chapter 5).

These ideas may seem simple, and in fact, they are. Nonetheless, relying on them can make a powerful difference. Seek counsel and get information before you decide to resolve a conflict. Feel confident that stressful situations often get better with time; be with other people as much as possible; remember that failing to obtain certain goals isn't necessarily a tragedy; and think of yourself as a relaxed person. If you adopt these attitudes you will find that many stressful situations can be overcome.

Most important, remember that stress is not always a bad thing. A small amount of stress may serve to move you to action. Stress is only likely to be detrimental if it is unresolved and long-lasting and, especially, if you are prone to deal poorly with it. In Chinese, the characters for *stress* mean danger, but also opportunity. The Chinese have realized that a small amount of stress can motivate people to take action that will eventually provide them with a good, and for this reason their word for stress has a positive and a negative component.

Summary

- Any time you are faced with a choice you are in conflict. The most stressful conflicts are those that are both difficult to resolve and extremely important.
- Conflicts are often considered in terms of approach or avoidance. In the approach-approach conflict two desired goals compete. In the approach-avoidance conflict a valued goal also has drawbacks associated with it. In the avoidance-avoidance conflict either choice will lead to an aversive situation, and in the double approach-avoidance conflict a person is placed between two goals, each of which has an approach and an avoidance component.
- Sometimes, acutely stressful situations arise that did not derive from a conflict. Even though the stressful event may be of relatively short duration, it can be so intense that the memory of it can linger for years, resulting in chronic stress.
- Stress can lead to illness. Hans Selye has referred to the physical reaction to stress as the general adaptation syndrome. The general adaptation syndrome occurs in three stages. During the alarm reaction stage, the organism becomes alerted to the stress. During the resistance stage, the stress continues and a full war effort is engaged in. During the stage of

exhaustion, all of the person's resources are gone, and the patterns of coping begin to collapse.

■ Chronic stress can lead to high blood pressure, heart attack, stroke, or kidney failure. It can also aggravate arthritis, colitis, asthma, hypoglycemia, and diabetes. Ulcers are also known to be affected by stress.

■ One way of measuring the immune system's effectiveness is by counting lymphocytes (white blood cells). The lymphocyte count is often lower following stressful situations. This finding indicates that stress can have an effect on the immune system at the cellular level.

■ People differ in their vulnerability to serious disease caused by prolonged exposure to stress. Alpha personalities are able to rely on themselves. They are cautious and unadventurous. Beta personalities are fun-loving and spontaneous. Gamma personalities tend to be short-tempered and to express a general sense of confusion about their lives. Research has indicated that Gamma personalities are far more likely to become ill as a result of stress.

■ A new picture of anxiety is beginning to emerge. Psychological factors are important, but there seems to be a susceptibility that's especially prevalent among those who go on to develop anxiety and who, as a result, suffer the effects of stress.

■ Over the last decade there has been an alarming increase in suicide. Although suicide may sometimes seem to be the only way out of a conflict, many people who have made serious attempts at suicide but failed have later found other ways of coping with their stress. Suicide must always be viewed as a possibility among those who are under considerable stress. Such individuals should be offered help in the form of family support or professional counseling.

■ We are sometimes able to handle conflict and stress by using defense mechanisms. The term defense mechanism was coined by Sigmund Freud; it includes the mechanisms of denial, rationalization, reaction formation, projection, and intellectualization.

■ While defense mechanisms may alter your view of the stressors in your life, direct coping strategies help you eliminate the stressor or harden yourself to the stress. Among the direct methods of coping are gathering as much information as possible, trusting in the healing effects of time, keeping a sense of humor, spending time with others, realizing that all goals needn't be obtained, and learning to relax.

EPILOGUE: A FRIEND INDEED

Each person must face conflict and stress in his or her own way. But this does not mean that we must be alone. The following is an account of how one person's stress was eased by another's concern and understanding.

When 14 blacks and women were released from captivity in Iran early in the American Embassy hostage crisis in 1980, Marine Sergeant William Quarles was among them. The Ayatollah Khomeini had decided that all blacks were to be freed. The rest of the Embassy staff stayed behind, to remain in captivity for over a year, during which time no one knew whether they would be released, tried, or executed.

Back in the United States, Sergeant Quarles led a quiet life and generally kept to himself. Then in December, about a month after he had been released, the telephone rang. The man calling was Hank Siegel, a stranger to Quarles. Siegel said, "I know you feel guilty. Don't worry about it—it's normal" ("The Trauma," 1979, p. 59).

Siegel had decided on his own to make the call. He wanted to share with Sergeant Quarles his knowledge of how it feels to leave other captives behind. In 1977, Siegel had been a press officer at the B'Nai B'Rith in Washington, D.C., when the fanatic Hanafi Muslims had held 132 hostages there for over a day and a half. Siegel had been released early because he had recently suffered a heart attack. He had felt terribly guilty when he left the other hostages behind. He thought that since Quarles was a marine sergeant he might feel especially guilty, and he wanted to let Quarles know that this reaction was normal and that he really had no reason to feel guilty. After all, Quarles had had no control of the situation and had done nothing to bring about his release. Afterwards, Siegel was glad he'd decided to call. He said, "Quarles felt a lot better after talking to me."

The empathy and understanding of another had helped, just as it helped the police after the San Diego plane crash. Knowing that we're in a state of stress can, in itself, be stressful. We all need to know that our feelings are acceptable and that others understand.

Suggestions for Further Reading

1. Cousins, N. *Anatomy of an illness as perceived by the patient.* New York: Norton, 1979.
2. Dohrenwend, B. S., & Dohrenwend, B. P. (eds.). *Stressful life events: Their nature and effects.* New York: Wiley, 1974.
3. Levi, L. *Society, stress, and disease.* Oxford: Oxford University Press, 1971.
4. Selye, H. *The stress of life* (2nd ed.). New York: McGraw-Hill, 1976.

CONTENTS

CHAPTER 15

Abnormal Behavior

PROLOGUE

You are sitting with psychologist John Watkins in a jail in Bellingham, Washington. He is interviewing a security guard named Kenneth Bianchi. The police in Bellingham have arrested Bianchi, age 27. They suspect he might be tied to the murders of ten young women in the Los Angeles area from September 1977 through February 1978, the so-called Hillside stranglings. Bianchi was in Los Angeles at the time and also in Bellingham when two similar murders were committed.

John Watkins, who was recommended by the defense attorneys, has put Bianchi under hypnosis. Bianchi's eyes are closed, his head bobs up and down, and he answers questions. Watkins begins to question Bianchi. At one point Watkins asks, "If there is some other part of you that wants to talk to me, I'm here to talk to you."

Up to this time Bianchi had denied any knowledge of the Hillside

stranglings. But now he seems to undergo a change. He laughs and says, "He didn't know what I was doing."

Watkins asks, "Who didn't know?"

Bianchi answers, "Kenneth, Kenneth Bianchi. He didn't know what I was doing. I killed them. I killed them all. He's a fool. He didn't know."

"Who are you?" Watkins asks.

"Steve Walker," he says. "I killed them. I killed them to get him in trouble. He's so stupid he never knew what I was doing."

Under hypnosis Bianchi confessed to the killings. A second personality, a Mr. Hyde type named Steve Walker had appeared and taken credit for the killings that Kenneth Bianchi supposedly knew nothing about. This kind of disorder is known as multiple personality. Within one body there seems to be more than one personality. Some-

453

Kenneth Bianchi, does he possess multiple personalities?

times the personalities are unaware of each other's existence. Was "Steve Walker" a hidden personality with different motivations and drives? Was Kenneth Bianchi suffering from a serious psychological disorder?

Bianchi had many hypnosis sessions with Watkins, and on many occasions Steve Walker appeared, to taunt and laugh at Kenneth, to take credit for the grisly murders, and even to describe in detail each murder as it had occurred. Dr. Watkins administered the Rorschach ink blot test to both Kenneth and Steve. As Kenneth, the responses were normal, but as Steve, they were bizarre and filled with sex and violence. All of the sessions were videotaped.

Back in Los Angeles the videotapes were viewed by five psychiatrists who had been picked by a judge. Two psychiatrists argued that Kenneth was faking. They believed that Watson had cued Kenneth to pretend to have another personality by asking, "If there is some other part of you that wants to talk to me, I'm here to talk to you." One psychiatrist agreed with Watson's interpretation that Kenneth did indeed have a multiple personality. The others couldn't decide whether Kenneth was faking ("Was It Hypnosis," 1980).

On one point, however, the five psychiatrists and psychologist Watson agreed. Kenneth was abnormal. After all, he had apparently strangled 12 women.

In this chapter we will examine mental disorders, the differences between normal and abnormal, how abnormal behaviors are assessed, and the issues that are raised by assessment.

Why Psychologists Study Abnormal Behavior

We are social beings who live in groups called societies; we depend on one another. We have come to trust one another's behavior. Consequently, abnormal or deviant behavior is often viewed as frightening, puzzling, or disruptive. In a humane society, people help each other; the hungry are fed, the homeless are sheltered, the needy are cared for. When people's behavior becomes so aberrant that they are unable to survive on their own, or so deviant that it is harmful to themselves or to others, the members of the society want to help change or prevent the behavior.

Psychology is the study of all behavior, normal and abnormal. Psychologists study abnormal behavior in order to learn more about behavior, and to help those in need.

Defining Abnormality

If researchers are to assess, treat, and possibly prevent **abnormal behavior,** they must have a clear definition of the term. Many students are surprised to discover that the distinction between normal and abnormal is not always clear.

Although people often picture someone who is mentally ill as ranting and raving uncontrollably, such behavior is actually quite rare and at the extreme of what most psychologists consider abnormal. Most abnormality is more subtle than the stereotype of the raving lunatic. For this reason professionals must be careful when assessing behavior; they must keep their own beliefs about what is acceptable from biasing their assessment and leading them to view some behavior as a mental disorder when in fact it isn't. In the Soviet Union the social and political outlook has been greatly influenced by judgments of Soviet psychiatrists and psychologists. Anyone who goes against the party line is generally considered to be mentally or emotionally abnormal and in need of help. As a result, Soviet dissidents are often placed in mental institutions where their so-called abnormal behaviors can be "treated."

While no one in the United States is likely to be judged to have a mental disorder for political reasons, there may be certain biases toward particular groups. For instance, poorer persons are more likely to be labeled psychotic than others (Levy & Rowitz, 1972). Of course, it may well be that the pressures of living at the lower end of the socioeconomic spectrum predispose a person to more serious illness (Kohn, 1973). Conversely, mental disorder may lead to economic loss (Murphy, 1968). But it may also be that evaluators expect poverty and mental illness to go hand in hand, which may bias their judgment and create a self-fulfilling prophecy. The elimination of bias and prejudgment in clinical practice is crucial (Harris, 1981).

How would you define abnormal? The word *abnormal* means "different from the norm or away from normal." In usage, however, the term implies more than just deviating from the norm. Skydiving is certainly a deviation from the norm, in that the average person doesn't do it. In fact, few people do. Statistically, then, those who skydive are "abnormal." But does this mean that they should be helped or stopped from engaging in their sport?

In the clinical sense, for a behavior to be considered abnormal it must not only be different from the norm, but also *maladaptive* or *self-defeating*. Maladaptive means that the behavior interferes with the person's functioning and development, or with the activities of society. A self-defeating behavior is one that will eventually undermine the person's well-being or personal success. Of course, these tests hardly settle the issue. You may have already thought, "Maladaptive or self-defeating by whose standards?" According to this definition, Soviet psychiatrists could consider someone to be abnormal who disagreed vehemently with the Soviet party line, since this behavior would be different and, in terms of what the state deems appropriate, maladaptive and self-defeating for both the individual and society. Whenever we use such terms as maladaptive or self-defeating, we must consider the context. Almost any behavior might be considered normal under the right circumstances. For instance, yelling, shouting, and undressing in front of others, which would be considered abnormal at the public library, would be considered quite normal in a locker room before a football game. Subtle distinctions between normal and abnormal require value judgments and careful assessment. Abnormal behavior is not absolutely distinct from normal; rather, there is a continuum from normal to abnormal.

Models of Psychopathology

In evaluating the abnormal behavior of another, different models may be used to provide an understanding or explanation of the underlying mechanisms that may be contributing to the disorder. As you'll recall, a model

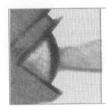

THE LEGAL MODEL: INSANITY AND THE LAW

When Kenneth Bianchi, whom you met in the Prologue, was examined by a panel of psychiatrists, the psychiatrists were unsure whether Bianchi really possessed more than one personality. The psychiatrists' assessment was important to Bianchi's criminal defense, for if it could be proven that he hadn't known right from wrong at the time he committed the murders, he would probably be sent to a mental institution for treatment rather than to prison, where he would probably spend the rest of his life.

Whether the so-called **insane** can be held criminally responsible for their actions is a legal issue, not a psychological one. The legal standards for determining whether someone is insane are often different from those applied by psychiatrists and psychologists. In the middle of the 13th century, madness was defined as a condition in which those afflicted didn't know what they were doing, lacked mind and reason, and were "not far removed from brutes." By the 16th century, the generally accepted definition was more precise: those who couldn't count, couldn't recognize their parents, and couldn't understand profit and loss (Amarilio, 1979). This definition, too, was obviously inadequate, and a modern standard had to be found.

The development of the insanity defense began in England in 1843 when Daniel M'Naghten shot and killed Edward Drummond, the secretary to Robert Peel, then Prime Minister of England. M'Naghten was tried for murder, and in his defense he pleaded insanity. Medical testimony was given that indicated that M'Naghten was driven by strong delusions to commit the murder and that he didn't understand the difference between right and wrong. The jury verdict was not guilty, on the ground of insanity (*M'Naghten's Case,* 1843). The M'Naghten rule is still used as the test for legal insanity in 15 states (Spring, 1979).

The M'Naghten rule has been criticized because only those who appeared *severely* disturbed could be classified as insane under its stringent standard. It is designed to serve the needs of the court rather than to reflect psychological reality. It "does nothing for the person, if he exists, who knows the conduct to be wrong but as a result of mental defect or disease is powerless to control that conduct" (Spring, 1979, p. 26). In many states, therefore, and in the federal court system, further tests of insanity have been developed that attempt to deal with these criticisms (see Table 15.1). However, none of these tests has addressed the most pressing issue, whether insanity should be a defense at all, whether those whom society calls "mad" should be treated differently from others who

ETIOLOGY
The cause of a disease or disorder as determined by psychological or medical diagnosis.

INSANE
Legal term for a mental disorder, implying lack of responsibility for one's acts and an inability to manage one's behavior.

is a depiction or representation that helps you organize your knowledge. There are several different models that may be used to depict the mechanisms that may underlie psychopathology. Different models are often preferred, depending on the professional's training and background. In addition, different therapies or treatments are preferred depending on the approach and the model used. Each model has some value. In some circumstances some models may be more applicable than others. Many mental health professionals rely on more than one model. For example, the vast majority of those who rely on the humanistic-existential model would not deny that abnormal behavior may occasionally be caused by biological dysfunction. Nor is someone who relies heavily on the medical model likely to deny that abnormal behaviors can be learned. Instead, each model helps us understand that abnormal behavior may be the result of many different factors.

THE MEDICAL MODEL

The medical model assumes that the underlying cause, or **etiology,** of a mental disorder is a biological dysfunction. In other words, something has

Table 15.1 Legal standards for determining insanity

TEST	SOURCE AND YEAR	RULE
M'Naghten Rule	*M'Naghten's case* (1843)	Defendant is relieved from criminal responsibility if she either (a) was prevented from knowing the nature and quality of her act by her mental disease or (b) was unable to distinguish between right and wrong.
Irresistible Impulse	*Parsons v. State* (1887)	Used as an adjunct to M'Naghten. Defendant is relieved from criminal responsibility if she meets either of the two criteria above or if she had a mental disease or defect that kept her from controlling her conduct (a so-called "irresistible impulse").
Durham Rule	*Durham v. U.S.* (1954)	"The rule . . . is simply that an accused is not criminally responsible if his unlawful act was the product of mental disease or defect" (*Durham v. United States*, 1954, pp. 874–875).
ALI (Model Penal Code)	American Law Institute (1955)	"A person is not responsible for criminal conduct if at the time of such conduct, as a result of mental disease or defect, he lacked substantial capacity either to appreciate the criminality (or wrongfulness) of his conduct or to conform his conduct to the requirements of the law" (Amarilio, 1979, p. 362).

Note: These tests are listed in order from the most stringent and difficult to prove in court to the least stringent and easiest to prove.

commit crimes. Some have recommended that the insanity defense be abolished (Menninger, 1968; Dershowitz, 1973; Spring, 1979), while others have recommended that it only be considered during the sentencing phase of a trial and not be used to establish guilt or innocence (Stanfiel, 1981).

The state of Washington still follows the M'Naghten rule, the most stringent test of insanity. If Kenneth Bianchi had pleaded innocent by reason of insanity, and had been found guilty, he would have faced the death penalty. Instead, he pleaded guilty to the two murders in Washington and received lengthy terms in prison. If Bianchi had been tried in California, where he had allegedly committed the first series of murders, he might have had a better chance for an insanity verdict, since California recently abandoned the M'Naghten rule for the much more liberal American Law Institute test (again see Table 15.1). This situation illustrates another problem with insanity pleas: Defendants in criminal cases can theoretically be judged both sane and insane, depending on which state or federal court they happen to be in at the time.

gone wrong biologically, owing either to genetics, hormones, biochemical imbalances, trauma, viruses, poisoning, or to any of a host of other events that may disrupt the organism's biology, especially the brain and nervous system. The medical model views abnormal behaviors as symptoms of an underlying disease. Those suffering from mental disorders are referred to as patients, and emphasis is placed on diagnosis and treatment, often incorporating drugs or such other medical therapies as electroshock or psychosurgery.

THE LEARNING MODEL

According to the learning model, abnormal behaviors are acquired in the same way as normal behaviors. That is, they are learned through the processes of classical conditioning, operant conditioning, and social learning. In this case, the behaviors are not considered to be symptoms of an underlying disease, but rather the behaviors themselves are thought to be the problem. Since the person exhibiting the abnormal behavior is not considered medically sick, he or she is referred to as a client, not a patient. The abnormal behaviors are eliminated through retraining and conditioning.

THE PSYCHOANALYTIC MODEL

In the psychoanalytic model, abnormal behaviors are viewed as evidence of unresolved unconscious conflicts between the id, the ego, and the super-ego (see Chapter 13). Treatment usually involves psychoanalysis and a detailed investigation of the desires and conflicts in the unconscious.

THE HUMANISTIC-EXISTENTIAL MODEL

This model depicts abnormal behaviors as the result of a failure to fulfill self-potential. Such failure may occur when people lose contact with their real thoughts and emotions or become isolated from other people; eventually they may view their lives as meaningless and useless. Those who seek therapy are considered to be clients, and their behaviors are considered to result from family and cultural influences and a distorted self-awareness.

Classification and Assessment of Abnormal Behavior

Table 15.2 outlines the incidences of maladjustment in the United States estimated to exist as of 1978. As you can see, the figures in many instances are very large, indicating that great segments of the population may be in need of help. But before treatment can be considered, an assessment must be made in order to determine the nature of the problem. The disorder must also be identified so that it can be adequately explained to others. For this reason, classification systems have been developed that attempt to organize mental disorders systematically.

Although a number of such classification schemes have been developed, to date none has been completely satisfactory. In 1952 the American Psychiatric Association developed the *Diagnostic and Statistical Manual* (DSM), which classified mental disorders according to a format that had been developed by the army during the Second World War. In 1968 the *Diagnostic and Statistical Manual* was modified to bring it into line with classifications used by the World Health Organization. The new manual, known as DSM-II, was used for a number of years, but eventually certain limitations became apparent as new information became available. As a result, a special task force to formulate a revised classification system was assembled in September 1973 under the direction of Robert L. Spitzer, a prominent psychiatrist and clinical diagnostician. By 1977 the work of the task force was complete, and a new classification scheme, **DSM-III,** was presented for extensive testing and field trials. As described in DSM-III,

> a series of field trials was conducted, beginning in 1977 and culminating in a two year NIMH-sponsored [National Institute of Mental Health] field trial from September 1977 to September 1979. In all, 12,667 patients were evaluated by approximately 550 clinicians, 474 of whom were in 212 different facilities, using successive drafts of DSM-III. Critiques of all portions of DSM-III by the field trial participants resulted in numerous changes, as did reviews of case summaries submitted by those participants. Frequently, participants completed questionnaires regarding specific diagnostic issues and their attitudes toward DSM-III and its innovative features. The results indicated that the great majority of participants, regardless of theoretical orientations, had a favorable response to DSM-III.

Table 15.2 Estimated incidence of major maladaptive behavior patterns in the United States in 1978

200,000 reported cases of child abuse

200,000 or more attempted suicides* (26,000 or more individuals dead from suicide)

1,000,000 actively schizophrenic individuals

1,000,000 or more students withdrawing from college each year as a result of emotional problems

2,000,000 individuals suffering from profound depression

6,000,000 or more emotionally disturbed children and teenagers

7,000,000 mentally retarded individuals

10,000,000 individuals reporting alcohol-related problems (1,000,000 individuals being treated for such)

20,000,000 (at least) individuals suffering from neurotic disturbance

53,500,000 individuals suffering from mild to moderate depression

SOURCE: Coleman, Butcher, & Carson, 1980, p. 4. Incidence figures based on Berger (1978), the National Institute of Mental Health (1978), the President's Commission on Mental Health (1978), and Uniform Crime Reports (1978).

*The incidence of suicide attempts may be much higher, given the large number presumed to go unreported.

Perhaps the most important part of the study was the evaluation of diagnostic reliability by having pairs of clinicians make independent diagnostic judgments of several hundred patients. The results, which are presented in an appendix, generally indicate far greater reliability than had previously been obtained with DSM-II. (*Diagnostic and Statistical Manual of Mental Disorders*, 1980, p. 5)

DSM-III was new in a number of ways. It described mental disorders in greater detail and made distinctions between disorders that had previously been unified under one heading. It also provided an evaluation of each individual according to five dimensions or axes. The first three axes are used to assess the immediate condition of the individual (see Table 15.3). The fourth and fifth axes rate the individual's past situation and ability to cope with it. These last two axes are valuable because they include in the description of the disorder the kinds of stressors the individual has been facing in his or her environment, and the skills the person can bring to bear in dealing with the stressors. For example, a particular person may be assessed, in a most general way, along the five axes as follows:

Subject: J. S., Male, age 54

Axis I: Anxiety state; obsessive-compulsive disorder

Axis II: Histrionic

Axis III: Angina pectoris (heart pain); recovering from myocardial infarction (heart attack)

Axis IV: 5-severe; has recently suffered heart attack and is fearful of losing job

Axis V: 4-fair; wishes to return to work but has few close friends

In some cases a particular axis will not apply. For instance, if no personality disorder existed, axis II would not be applicable.

For the next few pages we'll explore the classifications of DSM-III and examine each kind of mental disorder. Examples of the behaviors associ-

Table 15.3 DSM-III classifications

Axis I

1. *Organic mental disorders*

2. *Substance-use disorders*
   Alcohol dependence (alcoholism)

3. *Schizophrenic disorders*
   Disorganized (hebephrenic)
   Catatonic
   Paranoid
   Undifferentiated
   Residual

4. *Paranoid disorders*
   Paranoia
   Shared paranoid disorder
   Acute paranoid disorder

5. *Affective disorders*
   Bipolar disorder
      Mixed
      Manic
      Depressed
   Major depression

6. *Anxiety disorders*
   Phobic disorder (phobic neurosis)
   Anxiety states (anxiety neurosis)
      Generalized anxiety disorder
      Panic disorder
      Obsessive-compulsive disorder
         (obsessive compulsive neurosis)

7. *Somatoform disorders*
   Conversion disorder (hysterical neurosis,
      conversion type)
   Psychogenic pain disorder
   Hypochondriasis (hypochondriacal neurosis)

8. *Dissociative disorders (hysterical neurosis,
      dissociative type)*
   Psychogenic amnesia
   Psychogenic fugue
   Multiple personality

9. *Psychosexual disorders*
   Gender identity disorders
   Paraphilias
   Psychosexual dysfunction

Axis II

Personality disorders
Paranoid
Schizoid
Schizotypal
Histrionic
Narcissistic
Antisocial
Borderline
Avoidant
Dependent
Compulsive
Passive aggressive
Atypical, mixed, or other

Axis III

Any medical or physical disorder that may also be present

Axis IV

A 7-point scale rating the severity of psychological and social factors that may have placed the individual under stress, ranging from 1 (none) to 7 (catastrophe)

Axis V

A 6-point scale rating the individual's recent success in coping with his or her stress, ranging from 1 (superior) to 6 (grossly impaired)

Note: The classifications of AXES I and II are condensed to include only those categories discussed in the text. Older DSM-II classifications are included in parentheses where applicable.

ated with each disorder will be described, and in certain instances case studies will be given.

Before examining these disorders it is valuable to point out once again that mental disorders are usually extremes of normal behaviors. If you feel that some of these disorders fit you a little bit, don't worry. It's not likely to be the first sign that you're on your way toward a mental disorder; it probably just means that you're normal. Everyone has little eccentricities, and these are not considered problems unless they become extreme and interfere with one's life.

In the broadest sense, mental disorders can be segregated into two categories, organic and functional disorders. **Organic disorders** are those in which the cause is physical or strongly suspected to be physical. Neurosyphilis, severe head wounds, and senility are examples of organic disorders that may affect behavior. In each case brain or nerve damage has likely occurred. **Functional disorders** include those in which psychological stressors have traditionally been believed to be the cause of, or a major factor in, the disorder. The term derives from the idea that the disorder exists because it fulfills some function for the patient, that is, it provides an escape from stress. Today, by tradition, many disorders are still called functional even though a physical component or cause is suspected and is highly probable.

Except for the organic disorders, very few of the disorders listed in DSM-III have a known etiology. Many are simply *descriptions* of behavior patterns that have been found to occur in a particular cluster. Therefore, don't assume that because certain behaviors are classified under one label they are necessarily due to the same cause. For example, you should not infer that people who are said to have schizophrenia all have one particular disease. Instead, you should understand that they generally exhibit a similar series or constellation of abnormal behaviors.

It may be difficult at first to realize that many of these disorders are descriptive terms. It's like referring to someone as an accident victim. Accident victims often have a lot in common, such as broken bones, bruises, cuts, concussions. But accidents can happen for all kinds of reasons, and just because two people are labeled accident victims doesn't mean that they are suffering from the same thing. When it comes to illness, we're so used to discussing true diseases that have understood etiologies (such as tuberculosis) that we think a term such as schizophrenia must refer to some particular disease, too. Someday a single cause of schizophrenia may be uncovered, or it may be found that there are many causes. For many of the disorders classified in DSM-III, such a common denominator remains to be discovered.

Anxiety, Somatoform, and Dissociative Disorders

Anxiety, somatoform, and dissociative disorders, along with psychosexual and certain affective disorders, were once classified in DSM-II under the general heading neurosis. The term **neurosis** was first used by Englishman William Cullen in the 18th century. Cullen believed that neurotic disorders were related to defects or deficiencies of the nervous system, and so coined the term neurosis. This definition of neurosis was changed by Sigmund Freud, a neurologist, who argued that neurosis was the result of psychological conflict rather than a defect in the nervous system.

All neurotic disorders were said to share certain characteristics, including feelings of anxiety and inadequacy, avoidance in dealing with problems, and self-defeating behavior that inhibited further growth. In addition, it was argued that neurotic individuals refused to relinquish their behavior patterns despite the fact that they were ineffective and self-defeating. This aspect was known as the **neurotic paradox.**

The team that prepared DSM-III felt that the term neurosis was so all-encompassing that it was of little value. As a result, neurosis was dropped as a description of mental disorder; it was replaced by more specific descriptions. A number of professionals, however, have been upset by this change; they argue that neurosis should be returned to the classification

ORGANIC DISORDER
A severe behavioral disturbance usually requiring hospitalization and resulting from some organic malfunctioning of the body. It is distinguished from functional disorder.

FUNCTIONAL DISORDER
A disorder that has no known organic basis and depend's on experience rather than on structural or organic defects.

NEUROSIS
A broad term once used to describe a wide range of nonpsychotic functional disorders that were characterized by anxiety which the individual attempted to reduce in an unchanging and ineffectual way.

NEUROTIC PARADOX
Refers to a neurotic person's tendency to persist in maladaptive behavior even though it leads to unpleasant consequences.

system because it describes, in their view, some aspects of behavior not clearly expressed in DSM-III. This controversy is mentioned to illustrate the point that any classification scheme should be regarded as a changing system based on compromise and clinical judgment, and not as a rigid doctrine. As our knowledge and experience grow, DSM-III will no doubt be replaced by DSM-IV.

Anxiety disorders are divided into two groups, phobic disorders and anxiety states.

Phobic Disorders   Almost everyone has heard of the word **phobia.** Phobia is more than just a fear, however; it is a specific *unrealistic* fear. Different terms have been used to describe different kinds of phobias. Perhaps you're familiar with some, such as acrophobia (fear of heights), agoraphobia (fear of open spaces), claustrophobia (fear of closed-in spaces), and zoophobia (fear of animals). If you were in a tall building that caught fire and you had to go out onto the ledge of the tenth floor, you'd be bound to feel a little fearful (to say the least). Such behavior is not called a phobic disorder. It's called normal! If you had acrophobia, however, you probably wouldn't be able to go two steps up a ladder, and you would avoid going even to a second floor of a building if you had to be anywhere near a window. People with phobic disorders are well aware that their fear is unrealistic. They are often the first to admit, "This is foolish, but I can't help how I feel."

Most people deal with their phobias by avoiding the thing they are frightened of. Someone with herpetophobia (fear of snakes) would probably go out of his or her way to avoid a job that required working in the country. Treatment is usually required if the phobia begins to interfere seriously with one's life.

In general, phobic disorders are believed to be learned. In Chapter 6 we discussed the case of Little Albert, in which a phobic disorder was produced in the child by associating a rat with a very loud noise. Little Albert eventually came to fear the rat. Similar occurrences have happened outside the laboratory. The following case study illustrates how a phobia can develop as a result of one's experience.

PHOBIC DISORDER: THE CASE OF JUDY R.

Judy R., a 27-year-old college senior, came to the University Counseling Center because of an intense fear of birds. She had been frightened of birds since she was nine years old. She was functioning well socially and academically, but she felt that her phobia was beginning to interfere with her plans to become a teacher. Judy had begun student teaching and several incidents had triggered a severe fear reaction. On four separate occasions she suffered severe and almost incapacitating terror, on a class visit to the bird section of a museum, seeing pictures of birds in textbooks, being offered a feather by a student, and being near a baby chick on animal day.

How Judy became afraid of birds is not completely clear. Before the age of nine, she had a duck and chick as pets. Between the ages of 10 and 15, however, she had a few frightening experiences that may have helped create the phobia.

Once playmates had warned her that there was an owl near her home that attacked people; she once saw her friend's parakeet escape and fly wildly about a room; she was once scared by her brothers with a toy bird; and she had seen Alfred Hitchcock's *The Birds,* in which birds viciously attacked people. But she could not attribute her fear directly to any one of these incidents.

Judy structured her entire life so that she could avoid birds. She selected routes whenever she walked anywhere where there would be minimal foliage and less chance to encounter a bird, even if they took her far out of her way. She would run between her car and entrances to buildings, and she always kept her car windows rolled up to keep birds out. She could not sunbathe, hike, or go on picnics. She didn't dare visit the beach or go to the zoo. She had frequent nightmares about birds and often thought that noises in her house were caused by birds that had somehow gotten in. She was so frightened of birds that she was careful when she backed out of her driveway not to run over or injure a bird for fear that the "word" might get out among the bird community and the birds would get her. She realized that such actions were far beyond the capability of birds and that her fear was irrational, but the thought persisted. (Lassen & McConnell, 1977).

Many phobic disorders, however, do not seem to have one specific cause or beginning. This fact has led some medical researchers to speculate that some phobias may be attributable to changes in brain chemistry. Psychoanalysts, on the other hand, have argued that phobias are symptoms of an underlying conflict and that the phobia cannot be adequately resolved unless the underlying conflict is relieved through psychoanalysis. Still, psychoanalysis has generally not been very effective in treating phobias.

The most commonly used treatments for phobia involve behavior modification and, occasionally, drugs. In Chapter 16 we'll see how Judy R. overcame her phobia through behavior modification.

Anxiety States **Anxiety states** are characterized by a fearful reaction similar to a phobia. As with a phobia, there is intense fear and anxiety. The difference is that the fear or anxiety is not directly related to a particular object. Some researchers have drawn a distinction between the words fear and anxiety, stating that fear is object-related, while anxiety is not.

GENERALIZED ANXIETY DISORDER   Those suffering a **generalized anxiety disorder** are in a relatively continuous state of tension, worry, and dread. Because they fear unforeseen circumstances, they are often unable to make decisions or enjoy life. Because their anxiety is not tied to a specific object, it is often called **free-floating anxiety.** The following case study illustrates this kind of anxiety.

GENERALIZED ANXIETY DISORDER: CASE STUDY

The patient, a thirty-one-year-old mechanic, had been referred for psychotherapy by his physician, whom he had consulted because of dizziness and difficulties in falling asleep. He was quite visibly distressed during the entire initial interview, gulping before he spoke, sweating, and continually fidgeting in his chair. His repeated requests for water to slake a seemingly unquenchable thirst were another indication of this extreme nervousness. Although he first

PHOBIA
Pathological fear of an object or situation. The individual may realize that the fear is irrational but, being unable to control it, avoids the object or situation.

ANXIETY STATES
A group of functional disorders including generalized anxiety disorder, panic disorder, and obsessive-compulsive disorder. All are characterized by heightened anxiety, tension, worry, or fear in the absence of any realistic reason or cause.

GENERALIZED ANXIETY DISORDER
An anxiety state characterized by a relatively constant feeling of dread and tension, without apparent or reasonable cause. Free-floating anxiety is a common complaint.

FREE-FLOATING ANXIETY
A chronic state of foreboding which is unrelated to a specific situation or object but which can be activated by any number of situations and activities.

related his physical concerns, a more general picture of pervasive anxiety soon emerged. He reported that he nearly always felt tense and that "If anything can go wrong, it will." He was apprehensive of possible disasters that could befall him as he worked and interacted with others. He reported a long history of difficulties in interpersonal relationships which had led to his being fired from several jobs. As he put it, "I really like people and try to get along with them, but it seems like I fly off the handle too easily. Little things they do upset me too much. I just can't cope unless everything is going exactly right." (Davison & Neale, 1978, p. 150)

PANIC DISORDER   During an anxiety state a **panic attack** may suddenly overwhelm the person even though he or she can't think of any reason to be frightened. The panic attack can be strong and debilitating. The feeling of terror can be overpowering, almost as if the person were having a heart seizure. Chest pains, heart palpitations, difficulty in breathing, and fainting may occur.

OBSESSIVE-COMPULSIVE DISORDER   One of the most interesting kinds of anxiety states is the **obsessive-compulsive disorder.** In this disorder the anxiety is manifested in a feeling of being forced to go over unwanted thoughts again and again or to engage in certain actions or rituals repetitively, perhaps as a way of coping with anxiety. From time to time all of us have had ideas or thoughts that we couldn't seem to get out of our mind. And sometimes we feel better if we carefully organize our daily activities almost in a ritualistic manner. In the obsessive-compulsive disorder this behavior is taken to the extreme. But it is an ineffective way of coping.

The obsessions and compulsions represent the different properties of the obsessive-compulsive disorder. **Obsessions** continue to enter one's mind unwanted, and the thoughts become impossible to ignore. For example, a person may have the constant obsession that someone is breaking into the house whenever he or she is away. This idea could interfere with life, making every minute away from home uncomfortable because of the persistent thoughts about intruders. Some people are obsessed with thoughts about committing violent acts. The guilt and revulsion that accompany these thoughts only seem to bring them to mind more often, although there is no intention of acting them out. Such obsessions, although never realized, may still result in extremely high levels of anxiety.

Compulsions are ritualistic acts and can take many forms. The need to read every license plate on the highway, the need to wear certain clothes on a certain day, the need to avoid stepping on a crack on the sidewalk, or the need to wash one's hands every 15 minutes are examples of compulsions that can, when carried to extremes, interfere with life.

Although it's possible to have obsessions without engaging in ritualistic acts or to have compulsions without obsessive thoughts, the two often coexist, which is why the disorder is referred to as obsessive-compulsive. In fact, the obsession can often be the cause of the compulsion. The person who is obsessed with the fear that there is a stranger in the house may ritually and compulsively check in all the closets and under all the beds before retiring. An obsessive-compulsive disorder is described in the following case study.

OBSESSIVE-COMPULSIVE DISORDER: THE CASE OF S.K.

S. K. was admitted to a mental hospital at the age of 29. . . . Soon after the patient's admission to the hospital, his wife was asked to give a history of the patient's illness. She reported that he had exhibited a compulsive handwashing for several months but that it became more serious. "He used to wash his hands and keep the water running for 15 minutes at a time. After he had washed them, he would turn off the spigot with his elbow. He had to count and wash and rinse his hands a certain number of times. If he had touched the door or door knob, he would go back and wash his hands again. One time he began to wash his hands at 1 o'clock in the morning. After we moved into our own house, he refused to use the front door or to turn the knob on the door for fear there might be germs. He used to go to the back window and call me to go to the front door and open it for him. He reached the point where he would climb in and out of windows so that he wouldn't have to enter the doors at all." The wife described also the following compulsion: "He also had the idea that when he walked there was something under his shoe. He would stop and look on the sole of his shoe, but there would be nothing there. He also worried as to whether or not his shoe laces were tied. He would pick up his foot and look to make sure. He had to do that a certain number of times before he was absolutely sure they were tied. When he walked down a street, if he kicked a stone he felt that he should put it back in the same place. If he walked on a line, then he would have to walk on all the cracks in the sidewalk." (Kolb, 1973, pp. 427–428)

It is very common for people to have minor obsessions or minor rituals. The point at which such minor manifestations become serious enough to require help is not always clear-cut. As a rule, it's a good idea to seek professional advice any time such behaviors begin to interfere seriously with one's life or functioning.

Why anxiety states occur is not well known. According to the psychoanalytic model, anxiety states result from an unresolved clash between the id, the ego, and the superego.

According to the learning model, anxiety states, like phobic disorders, are learned. Learning theorists argue that there are stimuli that trigger the free-floating anxiety, but these stimuli are not readily apparent (Mowrer, 1947).

According to the humanistic-existential model, both phobic disorders and anxiety states are attributable to a failure to fulfill one's life potential. By this logic society or our own inaccurate self-image creates a sense of terror that can be alleviated by coming to grips with oneself in society.

Researchers using the medical model as a guideline are searching for differences in brain chemistry among those who suffer from anxiety disorders. They believe, for instance, that a panic attack may be due to inappropriate neurotransmitter signals in the brain that warn of great danger when in fact there is none. Of course, even if such biochemical explanations are found to be true it will not necessarily mean that the other approaches are wrong. Underlying conflict, inaccurate self-image, or learning may cause changes in the brain chemistry that bring on an anxiety state. Psychotherapy, counterconditioning techniques, and drugs have all been used to control anxiety states.

Soma means body, and **somatoform disorders** are patterns of behavior in which an individual complains about physical symptoms when no illness can be found. The three major somatoform disorders are conversion disorder, psychogenic pain disorder, and hypochondriasis.

Conversion Disorder   **Conversion disorder** gets its name from the fact that the anxiety and stress faced by the person are converted into physical symptoms. These symptoms may be wide-ranging. For example, people may go blind or become deaf although there's nothing wrong with their eyes or ears. Motor symptoms, too, are not uncommon, such as wobbling, shaking, twitching, and collapse; again, there's nothing physically wrong that should cause these symptoms. Visceral symptoms are also common, such as headache, choking, coughing, and nausea. The visceral symptoms of a conversion disorder can appear very real. Cases of conversion disorder have been known to mimic acute appendicitis, malaria, and tuberculosis, although no organic pathology was present. Cases of pseudopregnancy have even been reported, in which the menstrual cycle ceases, the abdomen swells, and morning sickness begins. No actual pregnancy is involved; the symptoms are the result of the conversion disorder.

The reasons a conversion disorder develops are usually fairly clear. Conversion disorders typically serve the purpose of helping people escape from something they'd rather not do. For example, conversion disorders were very common among pilots during World War II. Pilots who flew night missions often had a conversion disorder of night blindness, while pilots who flew day missions often had other kinds of visual disturbances which caused them to be grounded. Most people who suffer from conversion disorders have at one time or another expressed the wish to become sick to avoid what they had to do. This wish is usually repressed, and when the conversion disorder symptoms begin the sufferer is genuinely unaware that this is not a real physical disease.

Since conversion disorder can mimic so many real illnesses, it's often very difficult for physicians to distinguish it from physical illness. Nonetheless, there are some general guidelines for identifying conversion disorder. In Figure 15.1 you see an example of "glove anesthesia." The entire hand has become paralyzed and immobile, numb all over. If you've ever had novocaine at a dentist's office you know how one side of your lip can be numb while the other side is not. This localized numbness occurs because the nerve beds are laid down lengthwise, not crisscross. Consequently, real neural damage to the hand typically results in paralysis of only one lateral portion (again see Figure 15.1). To a neurologist, glove anesthesia is a dead giveaway of conversion disorder.

About one third of those suffering from conversion disorder express indifference about their symptoms. Instead of being terrified that they can no longer see or that their arm is paralyzed, they often describe their symptoms in a matter-of-fact way, without emotion. It's as though they are relieved to have the symptoms. Often the symptoms are selective. A person who is blind as a result of conversion disorder is not likely to bump into people or objects. Someone who is actually blind and not yet used to it will typically have a number of accidents. Furthermore, the conversion disorder can often be eliminated or altered under hypnosis, and during sleep a

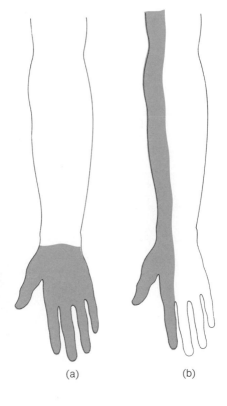

Figure 15.1   *Because of the organization of the human nervous system, a full glove anesthesia (a) without the arm being affected is impossible as a function of only physiological causes. Real nerve damage is more likely to result in a loss of feeling similar to that shown in (b). For this reason, a symptom such as glove anesthesia is an indication of psychological problems.*

(a)   (b)

"paralyzed" limb may be seen to move or a "deaf" sleeper may respond to sounds.

Generally, all of the models of psychopathology view conversion disorder as an unconscious attempt to avoid danger. It has been argued that the right hemisphere of the brain is more likely to use this defense than the left hemisphere. This interesting assertion is derived from the fact that, especially in cases of conversion paralysis such as glove anesthesia, conversion disorder is much more likely to occur on the left side of the body than on the right side (Stern, 1977; Galin, Diamond & Braff, 1977).

Psychogenic Pain Disorder **Psychogenic pain disorder** is characterized by severe and chronic pain in the absence of any known physical cause. The pain is generally located in vital organs, the back, or lower limbs. This ailment should not be confused with migraine or tension headaches, which have an underlying physical cause. People with psychogenic pain disorder tend to use their pain to avoid something unpleasant or to manipulate others and draw attention. They often travel from physician to physician trying to find a cause for their pain. It is generally believed that this disorder is due to learning and the realization that there is an advantage in expressing pain.

Psychogenic pain disorder must be assessed very carefully, since pain is extremely elusive. Just because an underlying physical reason can't be found is no guarantee that there isn't one. Before classifying a complaint as a psychogenic pain disorder, psychologists prefer to see clearly how the person is exploiting the pain. The existence of chronic pain without an apparent cause may not be sufficient reason to make the classification.

Hypochondriasis Hypochondriacs believe themselves to be ill although there is no physical illness present. Unlike those suffering a conversion disorder, hypochondriacs are intensely interested in bodily functions and illness, and will avidly seek medical attention in a search for some dread disease that they are sure is present. **Hypochondriasis** is similar to psychogenic pain disorder in that hypochondriacs use their supposed disability to gain attention, avoid something unpleasant, or feel important. It is a classic sign of hypochondriasis when people become upset at a doctor's reassurances that the tests show no organic pathology and that nothing is wrong. Instead, they hope for some proof that they can hold up to others in order to maintain their maladaptive behavior pattern. Hypochondriacs are different from malingerers in being sincere in their belief. Malingerers knowingly fake a disorder to serve their purposes. Both psychogenic pain disorder and hypochondriasis are difficult to treat because sufferers often leave a physician or psychologist who will not give them attention for their supposed illness in order to seek the services of someone who will. An inveterate hypochondriac is described in the following account.

HYPOCHONDRIASIS: THE CASE OF GRACE H.

Grace H. catalogued in excruciating anatomical detail a full range of symptoms—past, present, and future—to which she was heir. She had "almost" had a series of exotic diseases, had suffered for years from a strange collection of symptoms that fit no known malady in humans, and was about to come down with some-

SOMATOFORM DISORDERS
Patterns of behavior characterized by complaints of physical symptoms in the absence of any real physical illness. Conversion disorder, psychogenic pain disorder, and hypochondriasis are the three main kinds of somatoform disorder.

CONVERSION DISORDER
A somatoform disorder characterized by physical symptoms such as paralysis, blindness, deafness, and loss of sensation. The assumption is that anxiety has been converted into a tangible symptom.

PSYCHOGENIC PAIN DISORDER
A somatoform disorder characterized by severe and chronic pain in the absence of any known physical cause.

HYPOCHONDRIASIS
A somatoform disorder in which there is a persistent and exaggerated concern about diminished health and energy in the absence of demonstable organic pathology.

DISSOCIATIVE DISORDERS
Functional disorders, including psychogenic amnesia, psychogenic fugue, and multiple personality, that are characterized by an attempt to overcome anxiety by dissociating oneself from the core of one's personality.

PSYCHOGENIC AMNESIA
A dissociative disorder involving selective memory loss. The individual forgets, partially or totally, his or her past identity but remembers nonthreatening aspects of life.

FUGUE
From the Latin "to flee." A dissociative disorder in which the individual leaves his or her present situation and establishes a somewhat different mode of existence in another place. Although the former life is blocked from memory, other abilities are unimpaired and the individual appears normal to others.

MULTIPLE PERSONALITY
A rare dissociative disorder in which one person develops two or more distinct personalities, which often vie with each other for consciousness. One personality's memories are usually not accessible to another personality.

thing certain to be nearly fatal. . . . Probably the most startling aspect of the scene was the obvious and absolutely noncontroversial fact that Grace H. looked as healthy as a horse. The fact that she was 72 years old had to be some kind of testimony to her hardiness in the face of plague, pestilence, and, as she viewed it, the perversity of the medical profession. . . . According to the children, Grace's histrionics had been in evidence for at least the last 40 years. The eldest son who was 50 years old, recalled that his mother had been ailing when he was just a child. As he said, "Sometimes when I was in school, I would get worried that mother would be dead by the time I got home. I knew she was sick when I went to school and I was sure it would be all over by the time I got home. I had a hard time concentrating on my school work because I was always worried about her health. . . . " The mother was an artful specialist in hypochondriasis who had practiced all the arts of being sick while staggeringly well. She seemed to be totally free of anxiety until asked about her health and at that point she disintegrated into a mass of nervous energy. (McNeil, 1967, pp. 47–49)

DISSOCIATIVE DISORDERS

Like somatoform disorders, **dissociative disorders** help individuals obtain gratification and simultaneously avoid stress. They also provide a means of denying responsibility for behavior that might otherwise be deemed unacceptable. Individuals with dissociative disorders separate themselves from the core of their personality. The effects of dissociative disorders can be very striking. Psychogenic amnesia, psychogenic fugue, and multiple personality are classified as dissociative disorders.

Psychogenic Amnesia　**Psychogenic amnesia** is a memory loss, either partial or total, that can last for a few hours or many years. Amnesia can be caused by many things, including psychosis, brain damage, and alcoholic delirium. Psychogenic amnesia, however, has no underlying physical cause, and appears to be the result of stress. Individuals suffering from this disorder usually forget personal material such as "Who am I?" together with events and other names associated with personal experience. Rarely would someone with psychogenic amnesia forget the name of his or her country or how to do such things as operate an automobile or read a book.

Psychogenic Fugue　Fugue comes from the Latin word meaning "to flee." A **fugue** is an amnesia in which the sufferer leaves home and surroundings and wanders off. In extreme cases the sufferer may even begin a new life in another city without any recollection of personal events prior to the fugue. Occasionally, the fugue comes to a sudden end and the person is left in a strange city, unable to recall the new identity but again able to remember the original identity. As you can imagine, it would be a little strange to wake up in a different bed and to find out that eight years have passed, you are known by a different name, and you are selling ties in St. Louis! The following case study describes a four-day fugue experienced by a famous American author, Sherwood Anderson.

PSYCHOGENIC FUGUE: THE CASE OF SHERWOOD ANDERSON

Anderson was better known as a paint manufacturer than as a writer in his home town of Elyria, O. He would daydream to escape the boredom of a routine workday and found relaxation in writing short stories. On November 27, 1912, the 36-year-old Anderson suddenly got up from his desk while dictating a letter to his secretary. He stopped in the middle of a sentence, walked out of the room, and was not seen again until four days later, when he was found in a Cleveland drugstore. Anderson was taken to Huron Road Hospital, where experts agreed that he had succumbed to mental strain and was the victim of amnesia. He reportedly told the story of the missing days for the rest of his life, each time with different details. He simply couldn't remember what really happened. (Wallace, Wallechinsky, Wallace, & Wallace, 1980, pp. 434–435)

Multiple Personality In **multiple personality,** more than one personality develops. These personalities rarely appear simultaneously; instead, they seem to vie for consciousness. Often one personality is totally unaware of another. The two most celebrated cases of multiple personality were described in the books *The Three Faces of Eve* and *Sybil.*

MULTIPLE PERSONALITY: THE CASE OF SYBIL DORSETT

Sybil Dorsett was a college graduate and leading what seemed to be a normal healthy existence as a school teacher. In 1954 she began work on a Masters degree at Columbia University. Sybil came to the attention of psychiatrist Cornelia Wilbur because Sybil was having blackouts and periods of amnesia that were becoming progressively longer, and no physical cause for her ailment could be discerned. It was during a therapy session with Dr. Wilbur that there was a sudden and radical change in Sybil's personality. Her voice changed, her manner changed, and she began to act like a little girl; she even threw a temper tantrum. A short time later a third personality emerged, who called herself Vicki. Sybil was unaware of the other personalities, but Vicki knew about them. In the course of several therapy sessions Vicki revealed that throughout her childhood many personalities had been created for Sybil, 16 in all. Some of the personalities were children, some were adults, and some were even male. In Figure 15.2 (color section) you can see different pictures drawn by Sybil as different personalities were in control.

During the therapy Dr. Wilbur discovered that Sybil had been systematically abused and tortured by her schizophrenic mother from as early as the age of three. Apparently, whenever Sybil encountered a situation that she could not handle, a new personality was created to deal with the stress. Over a period of several years Dr. Wilbur worked with all 16 personalities, attempting to solve the problems of each, and eventually integrating them into a 17th and whole personality.

Gordon Bower has suggested that the effects of multiple personality can be understood as an exaggerated form of state-dependent memory (see

Actress Joanne Woodward portraying the personalities of Eve White and Eve Black in the motion picture, The Three Faces of Eve, *a case history of a multiple personality.*

Chapter 7) (Bower, 1981). The multiple personalities that are exhibited are distinctly different from each other in mood and experience. In Bower's view, the memories associated with each personality's experience may be easier to retrieve when that personality is present. As a result, one personality may not be able to gain access to the memory of another personality. You'll recall from the Prologue that, until he became Steve Walker, Kenneth Bianchi claimed to have no knowledge of the murders he had committed. If Bianchi suffered from multiple personality, then he may have had to change mood and become Steve in order to gain access to the memories of the killings.

Dissociative disorders are quite rare, and as a consequence, not much is known about them. Sometimes it's difficult to distinguish a real dissociative disorder from a fabricated one. Individuals who purposely leave their families and take up life in another city may find it easier to pretend that they can't remember anything when they're finally recognized than to admit to what they've done.

Affective Disorders

Affective disorders are classified as **psychoses.** Psychoses are generally considered to be the most severe of psychological disorders. The psychotic person has lost contact with reality, and the personality becomes grossly distorted. In many cases hospitalization is required. Other psychotic disorders that will be discussed later in this chapter include schizophrenic disorders and paranoid disorders.

Affective disorders are disorders of mood and emotion. There are two main kinds, the bipolar disorder and major depression.

BIPOLAR DISORDER

Bipolar disorder (which used to be called *manic-depressive psychosis*) is characterized by drastic changes in mood. All of us are happy some of the time, and sad some of the time, and mood swings are not abnormal in most instances. But in the bipolar affective disorder the mood change is dramatic. People with bipolar disorder may suddenly have feelings of great elation and extreme agitation. They may become very impatient, show poor judgment, and try to initiate a number of endeavors simultaneously. For instance, a person in the midst of the manic phase of bipolar disorder, who owns a small beauty shop, may lease much more space than is necessary, order ten new chairs for customers, hire many new people without a hope of being able to pay them, start a new love affair, and buy round-trip tickets to Mexico for a vacation, all in one day. The entire time this individual would appear excited, agitated, and intent upon doing everything at once, while any reasonable person could see that the entire effort was headed for disaster. Manic behavior is not necessarily a display of happiness. Manic individuals can become outraged at anything that blocks their way. Occasionally they become violent.

At other times the same person may go through periods of intense depression, bordering on suicide. The depressive phase may last for hours or even days. This is what is meant by bipolar disorder—swinging back and forth between two poles, the manic and the depressed. The following case study illustrates this kind of fluctuating behavior.

BIPOLAR DISORDER: THE CASE OF M. M.

M. M. was first admitted to a state hospital at the age of 38, although since childhood she had been characterized by swings of mood, some of which had been so extreme that they had been psychotic in degree. At 17 she suffered from a depression that rendered her unable to work for several months, although she was not hospitalized. At 33, shortly before the birth of her first child, the patient was greatly depressed. For a period of four days she appeared in coma. About a month after the birth of the baby she "became excited" and was entered as a patient in an institution for neurotic and mildly psychotic patients. As she began to improve, she was sent to a shore hotel for a brief vacation. The patient remained at the hotel for one night and on the following day signed a year's lease on an apartment, bought furniture, and became heavily involved in debt. Shortly thereafter Mrs. M. became depressed and returned to the hospital in which she had previously been a patient. . . . In a little less than a year Mrs. M. again became overactive, played her radio until late in the night, smoked excessively, took out insurance on a car that she had not yet bought. Contrary to her usual habits, she swore frequently and loudly, created a disturbance in a club to which she did not belong, and instituted divorce proceedings. On the day prior to her second admission to the hospital, she purchased 57 hats. (Kolb, 1973, p. 376)

This swing back and forth from one extreme to the other is not characteristic of all people with bipolar disorder. Many people show either the manic pattern or the depressed pattern, but not both. These disorders are sometimes referred to as **unipolar.** DSM-III, however, classifies all these types as bipolar disorder: mixed (in which there are mood swings from a manic pole to a depressed pole), depressed (mood swings from a normal pole to a depressed pole), and manic (mood swings from a normal pole to a manic pole). Remember, these changes in mood are extreme, and not to be confused with normal elation and depression. In bipolar disorder, the mood swings are rarely related to external events. This fact has led re-

It is normal for people to have changes of mood, highs and lows.

searchers to believe that there may be important genetic or biological factors directly affecting bipolar disorder. Evidence for this belief comes from a number of sources.

For instance, bipolar disorder has been shown to run in families (see Figure 15.3). At the same time, the biochemical link has been strengthened with the discovery that the element lithium, when given as a drug, has a dramatic effect on bipolar disorder. Lithium is now recognized as an important treatment for that disorder (see Chapter 16).

There is even some fascinating evidence that the cycles of mania and depression may be related to both long-term and short-term biorhythms that have somehow become abnormal. Researchers at the National Institute of Mental Health have examined certain blood metabolites and brain chemicals in "normal" persons during different times throughout the calendar year. Special attention has been paid to the hormone melatonin. The level of melatonin is an indicator of norepinephrine activity in the brain. Norepinephrine is an important neurotransmitter that is known to be related to emotions. It has been found that norepinephrine levels run through a cycle in line with the calendar year, peaking in January and July and hitting lows in May and October. It has also been found that drugs, such as reserpine, that reduce norepinephrine can trigger serious depressions and even suicides (Ellison, 1977). These findings suggest that a drop in norepinephrine might be sufficient to worsen depressive cycles. It's well known that May and October are high suicide months (Goodwin & Wehr, as cited in Greenberg, 1978).

MAJOR DEPRESSION

The term **depression** describes a wide range of emotional lows from sadness to a severe and suicidal state. Each of us has felt unhappy at one time or another, and sadness can be quite natural as long as there is an obvious cause. Major depression, however, is a lasting and continuous state of depression without cause. A mood of unhappiness and apathy prevails. Unlike bipolar disorder, depressed type, major depression is not characterized by continuous mood swings from normal to depressed and back to normal. Depressed persons usually regard themselves in a negative way and blame themselves for things that have gone wrong. They typically experience a decrease in drives such as hunger and sex and an increase in insomnia.

Prolonged depression without apparent cause is common. As many as 55 million people in the United States are estimated to suffer from some form of depression. Those suffering *major* depression generally find little gratification in life. Their favorite activities bore them, and they feel hopeless about the future (Beck, 1972).

In 1962 Harvard psychiatrist Seymour S. Kety began to investigate the possibility of a genetic link in some of these affective disorders. Kety studied 85 adoptees with affective disorder, primarily major depression. These individuals had not been reared by their biological parents at all. Kety reported a significant concentration of depression in the adoptees' *biological* relatives, finding that they were three times more likely to suffer from depression than were members of the adopted families. Among all of the family members in the study, both biological and adopted, there were 18 reported suicides. The fact that 15 of these suicides were among the biological relatives of the depressed group suggests the possibility of a genetic factor in depression and suicide. Kety has said, "There may be a genetic predisposition [to suicide] among those exposed to certain life situations" ("Genetic Depression," 1978, p. 244).

In late November 1981, Lowell Weitkamp of the University of Rochester and Harvey Stancer of the University of Toronto announced that they had isolated genes on a specific site of the sixth chromosome that are associated with the onset of major depression. The researchers emphasized that de-

DEPRESSION
A feeling of sadness and sometimes total apathy. Guilt or the inability to cope with problems, frustration or conflict are often behind the depression. Possibly influenced by chemical imbalances in the brain as well.

Figure 15.3 *This figure outlines the family trees of two families and shows the incidence of psychiatric problems, especially bipolar disorder, for three generations. The oldest generations are at the top of the figure. The numbers represent the individual's age at the time of the study or the person's death. An X indicates that the subject has died. The first generation couple on the left had nine offspring, eight daughters and one son. The third daughter from the left married twice. The grandmother of this family has bipolar disorder and so do three of her living daughters. The first generation couple, on the right, had one daughter, who married the only son of the other first generation couple. In this family the grandfather has bipolar disorder. By following the family tree through different marriages and offspring, the unusually high incidence of mental disorder becomes apparent. (SOURCE: Elliot Gershon, National Institute of Mental Health)*

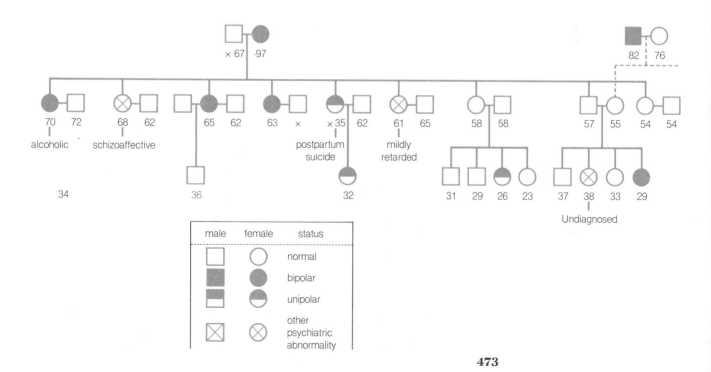

pression is not directly inherited, as eye color is, but rather that the genes pass on a predisposition to develop major depression in response to environmental factors (Weitkamp, Stancer, Persad, Flood, & Guttormsen, 1981). Should this spectacular discovery be replicated by other researchers and proven to be correct, it will no doubt be the foundation upon which future work on the biology of depression will be built (Matthysse & Kidd, 1981).

Further evidence of a biochemical link with depression comes from the work of George Winokur and his colleagues. Winokur knew from previous studies that the drug dexamethasone sets off a glandular reaction that causes the blood level of a substance called cortisol to become suppressed. In depressed persons, however, dexamethasone-induced suppression of cortisol doesn't seem to happen very often. Based on these dexamethasone-suppression tests Winokur and his colleagues were able to distinguish between **endogenous depression,** which seems to develop regardless of life events, and **secondary depression,** which is brought on by a disturbing situation such as the loss of a loved one. In a study of 151 persons, nearly half of those diagnosed as having major depression, probably endogenous, did not show the normal suppression of cortisol when injected with dexamethasone. However, among those with no depression or with secondary depression, not one showed a lack of suppression (Schlesser, Winokur, & Sherman, 1980). Furthermore, nonsuppression, an indication of primary endogenous depression, was found in 75 percent of those diagnosed as having major depression who had close relatives who were also depressed. This finding also points to a possible genetic link. What may have seemed like science fiction only a few years ago is now a reality, a blood test for major depression. Further research has supported Winokur's findings (Carroll, et al., 1981), and researchers are hoping eventually to eliminate endogenous depression through inoculation or drug therapy. Such a discovery could have an immediate impact on many millions of people who are suffering from endogenous depression and who are unable to enjoy the pleasures of life.

Millions of people throughout the world suffer from depression.

Schizophrenic Disorders

Schizophrenia is a serious psychosis affecting as many as a million people in the United States and many millions more throughout the world. One half of all the mental hospital beds in the United States are occupied by persons assessed as schizophrenic (President's Commission on Mental Health, 1978). Although schizophrenia is typically a disorder of young adults, it can occur at any age. Contrary to common belief, schizophrenia does not mean having more than one personality. As you'll recall, multiple personality is a dissociative reaction. Schizophrenia is a split from reality, a complete breakdown of any integrated personality functioning. Emotions become flat and distorted. Thought, language, and behavior become bizarre and disturbed. These bizarre behaviors are commonly accompanied by delusions and hallucinations.

A **delusion** is a strong unrealistic belief that is maintained even though there is ample evidence of its falseness. Schizophrenics who believe that they are Jesus Christ or that the telephone company has wired their brain and is controlling their every movement are exhibiting delusions. Schizophrenics also have **hallucinations,** which, as you'll recall from Chapter 5, are sense perceptions in the absence of appropriate external stimuli. Schizophrenics often see things or hear voices that are not there, and react to them.

The onset of schizophrenia can be gradual or rapid. Gradual onset is usually a bad sign, since such onset is associated with a poor likelihood of recovery. Approximately 25 percent of schizophrenics who are treated undergo remission. A cure is rarely spoken of, since schizophrenia in remission can reoccur.

Figures 15.4 and 15.5 (color section) are paintings drawn by schizophrenics which illustrate the disintegration and reintegration of personality and sensation that often accompany a schizophrenic episode. Note the distortions of perception. The diary entry of a college-age schizophrenic is reproduced in the following case study.

SCHIZOPHRENIA: THE CASE OF DAVID F.

David F. was a young college student who became more and more apprehensive about his future as he neared graduation. He was also concerned about his relationship with his girlfriend, and he had feelings of sexual inadequacy. David began to stay in his room and stopped attending classes almost entirely. He recorded many of his feelings in a diary. The following excerpts were written shortly before he was hospitalized:

Thursday, March 12, 11 a.m. I'm out! I'm through ... boomed out of the tunnel sometime last night and it's raining stars. . . . whooey . . . it's nice out there's time for everything. . . . I can do it I did it and if it happens again I'll do it again twice as hard I got a dexamyl high going and I'm not on dexamyl and I've been up for forty eight or more hours and I'm giddygiddygiddy and I took a test this morning and it was on Voltaire and I kicked him a couple of good ones for being down on Pascal that poor bastard with his shrivelled body and bottomless abysses they're not bottomless!! You get down far enough and it gets thick enough and black enough and then you claw claw claw your way out and pretty soon you're on top again. And I licked it by myself, all alone. . . . I just sat in on one of those weddings of the soul and I tooted tooted . . . I don't care I can use it I can run on it it will be my psychic gasoline now I don't have to sleep sleep all the time to get away with it . . . but if I lose my typewriter? (Bowers, 1965, p. 351)

ENDOGENOUS DEPRESSION
Depression of internal origin, that is, depression without an apparent cause. It is marked by long-term despair and dejection, feelings of apprehension, gloom, and worthlessness. Research points to a possible biochemical and genetic cause.

SECONDARY DEPRESSION
A state of sadness, dejection, or despair brought on by an upsetting or disturbing situation. Depression that has its roots in an environmental cause and can be traced to particular events.

SCHIZOPHRENIA
A term used to describe a number of functional psychoses which are characterized by serious emotional disturbances, withdrawal, inappropriate emotional response or lack of emotional response, hallucinations, and delusions.

DELUSION
A strong belief opposed to reality and maintained in spite of logical persuasion and evidence to the contrary; a symptom of psychosis. There are three main types: delusions of grandeur (the belief that one is an exalted personage), delusions of persecution (the belief that one is being plotted against), and delusions of reference (the belief that chance happenings and conversations concern oneself).

Schizophrenia is classified according to type. Each type is marked by a somewhat different clustering of behaviors or symptoms. There are five major classifications of schizophrenia in DSM-III, the disorganized, the paranoid, the catatonic, the undifferentiated, and the residual.

DISORGANIZED TYPE

Disorganized schizophrenia (formerly called *hebephrenia*) is perhaps the most severe form. It typically occurs at an earlier age than most of the other types. In disorganized schizophrenia the emotions are extremely distorted. Grossly inappropriate silliness and laughter are among the most apparent behaviors. Mannerisms are unusual and bizarre. Obscene behavior, often centered upon sex, is common. The chances for improvement are very slight, and social impairment is extreme.

CATATONIC TYPE

The **catatonic schizophrenic** has alternating periods of intense excitement and extreme withdrawal. In some individuals one or the other of these reactions will predominate. During extreme withdrawal, catatonics will remain very still for hours, sometimes even days. The positions they assume are odd; sometimes an arm is extended, as though they were portraying statues. The limbs show a waxy flexibility. If the patients are moved to another position they may hold the new pose for many hours more. Then there may be an abrupt change, and they enter a period of intense excitement. They may walk about rapidly, carrying on incoherent conversations. Their behavior is uninhibited, wild, and impulsive. They may become violent in this condition. The outlook for the catatonic type is generally better than for the disorganized type.

PARANOID TYPE

The **paranoid schizophrenic** suffers from bizarre delusions and often feels persecuted. Judgment is impaired and unpredictible, and hallucinations are common. Paranoid schizophrenics can be dangerous because they often believe there is a need for self-defense against would-be persecution.

UNDIFFERENTIATED TYPE

In **undifferentiated schizophrenia,** no one type of schizophrenia seems to dominate. There is a rapidly changing mixture of schizophrenic behaviors, delusions, hallucinations, bizarre thoughts, and emotions. Sometimes the undifferentiated type is found in persons who are just becoming schizophrenic and who haven't yet settled on one of the three types previously described. The term undifferentiated is also used to describe schizophrenics during a change from one schizophrenic type to another.

RESIDUAL TYPE

Residual schizophrenia is the term used to describe the subtle indications of schizophrenia that are occasionally observed in those who are recovering from a schizophrenic episode.

CAUSES OF SCHIZOPHRENIA

Recent research into the origin of schizophrenia has concentrated on genetic, biochemical, and physical factors.

Genetic and Environmental Factors Studies of the incidence of schizophrenia among identical and fraternal twins have indicated a possible hereditary component to schizophrenia. For instance, among a large population in Norway it was found that if one identical twin had schizophrenia there was a 38 percent chance that the other would also. However, among fraternal twins there was only a 10 percent chance if one had schizophrenia that the other would (Kringlen, 1967). Similar findings have been obtained in the United States, where it was found that there was a 42 percent chance that if one identical twin had schizophrenia the other would, while there was only a 9 percent chance for a similar result among fraternal twins (Gottesman & Shields, 1972). A case reported at the National Institute of Mental Health even told of schizophrenia in all of the members of a set of identical quadruplets (Rosenthal & Quinn, 1977).

In 1962 Kety and his colleagues began an investigation of the background of 33 schizophrenics in Copenhagen. These 33 schizophrenics had been adopted and raised by foster families. Kety examined the foster parents and the biological parents and blood relatives of the schizophrenics. He found that the incidence of schizophrenia among the *biological* relatives of the 33 schizophrenics was five times greater than among the adopted relatives.

Furthermore, among the biological relatives, the chances of schizophrenia were eight to ten times higher among brothers, sisters, and parents, and only two to three times higher among more distant relatives. This finding indicates that not only is someone with schizophrenia in his or her family more likely to become schizophrenic, but also the likelihood increases in direct proportion to how close the relative is genetically to the offspring (Greenberg, 1980). Still, all schizophrenia can't be considered to be a function of heredity alone, since about half of the biological relatives of the adoptees diagnosed as schizophrenic had absolutely no history of schizophrenia whatsoever. Kety believes that there are two forms of schizophrenia, one genetically caused and the other environmentally caused (Kety, Rosenthal, Wender, Schulsinger, & Jacobsen, 1978). Along this line of thought, some have argued that schizophrenic behaviors are learned as a way of dealing with stress (Laing, 1967). Others have hypothesized that an extreme psychological trauma early in life might predispose someone to become schizophrenic later (Bettelheim, 1955).

It has also been suggested that abnormal interactions between parents and children may eventually create enough stress to lead to a schizophrenic break. Emotionally disturbed parents or extremely destructive marital interactions between parents have been found to correlate with the onset of schizophrenia, but these findings would also be consistent with the heredity hypothesis. Researchers Singer and Wynne have linked schizophrenia with bizarre and deviant patterns of family speech and communication (Singer & Wynne, 1965). Other researchers have argued that these findings were the result of an improper statistical analysis and that, in fact, no relationship between communication deviance and the families of schizophrenics could be found (Woodward & Goldstein, 1977). As you can see, research into the causes of schizophrenia is wide-ranging and complex.

Although there is mounting evidence that schizophrenia is a biochemical, physical, or inherited disorder, this does not preclude the effects of learning and experience. All experience causes a change in the brain. If it did not, the experience would have no effect on behavior. Any time a person learns something, neurochemical changes must occur at the synaptic level. Evidence of synaptic changes and changes in neurotransmitter levels has already been put forward for the processes of habituation and sensitization (see Chapter 6). In this sense an unusual brain chemistry related to schizophrenia may be acquired through learning and experience. Although environmental causes of schizophrenia are being carefully investigated, some recent discoveries have focused attention on biochemical and structural causes.

Biochemical Factors Research into the biochemistry of schizophrenia underwent a revolution in the late 1950s when it was discovered that small amounts of certain chemical agents, once in the body, could produce a number of mental changes (Huxley, 1954). For example, hallucinogenic substances, such as LSD and mescaline, were found to cause a temporary breakdown of the thought process, mental disorganization, and sensory experiences similar to the symptoms of psychosis. Some investigators wondered whether, in the case of schizophrenia, the body wasn't producing its own hallucinogenic substances. My father was a psychiatrist, and in the late 1950s he began experiments with LSD to identify similarities between LSD intoxication and schizophrenia. My mother volunteered to be one of his subjects. Years before the general public had ever heard of LSD, my mother was "dropping acid" under supervised conditions in a laboratory every Thursday. As with most other schizophrenia research conducted at that time, the efforts weren't very fruitful. Thursday night dinners, however, were unique.

To date, no internal hallucinogen similar to LSD has been found to be the cause of schizophrenia. Since the late 1950s our understanding of schizophrenia has grown, and few researchers now think that its mysteries will ever be solved in a simple way.

In the last few years the possibility that some physical or biochemical causes of schizophrenia may be uncovered has grown. If schizophrenia is caused by a biochemical agent or agents, it is believed that they would be related to the neurotransmitters that send nerve impulses across synapses from neuron to neuron in the brain. In the last decade the neurotransmitter dopamine has attracted special interest (Luchins, 1975). This interest in dopamine as a possible causal agent of schizophrenia arose because many of the antipsychotic drugs (drugs used to treat the symptoms of schizophrenia) were known to block dopamine action at the site of the dopamine receptor cell. This effect led researchers to believe that schizophrenia might be caused by an excess of dopamine or that schizophrenics might have too many receptors sensitive to dopamine (Iversen, 1979). This belief is known as the **dopamine hypothesis.** Still, the issue is hotly debated, and inconsistencies with the hypothesis have been found. For example, apomorphine, which boosts the action of dopamine receptors, seems to relieve psychotic symptoms significantly, which is the opposite of what the dopamine hypothesis predicts (Tamminga, Schaffer, Smith, & Davis, 1978). The endorphin system may also play an important role in schizophrenia (see Chapter 2). Naloxone (an endorphin blocking agent) has no effect on schizophrenia when injected alone, but naloxone and dopamine blocking agents injected together have a more powerful effect on schizophrenia than dopamine blocking agents used alone.

Others argue that the most important factor is the relationship between norepinephrine and dopamine. Norepinephrine is a chemical precursor of dopamine, and some have argued that there is a stress-related interaction between the two neurotransmitters affecting the ratio of one to the other (Antelman & Caggiula, 1977).

These neurotransmitters are probably related to schizophrenia in some way. Neurotransmitters such as norepinephrine and dopamine are not found in equal concentrations between the hemispheres. Interestingly, neither is schizophrenia. Schizophrenia appears to be more of a dysfunction of the left hemisphere than of the right (Gur, 1977).

Structural and Anatomical Factors Biochemical hypotheses concerning psychosis are only about three decades old. Before that time, most research centered on the possibility of structural abnormalities in the brains of psychotics. These older studies, some conducted more than 50 years ago, reported enlarged cerebral ventricles (cavities) and other structural problems in the brains of schizophrenics. At that time, the process used for studying brain structure was *pneumoencephalography,* which required that gas or air be injected into the ventricles of the brain so that they could be X-rayed and measured. It was an extremely painful experience to undergo, and although enlarged ventricles were reported in some schizophrenics,

DOPAMINE HYPOTHESIS
The argument that abnormalities in the neurotransmitter dopamine are related to the onset and maintenance of schizophrenic episodes. Either an overabundance of dopamine or the existence of too many dopamine receptors in the brain are deemed responsible.

these findings were dismissed by later researchers as erroneous. It was believed that the injection of gas or air could have artificially enlarged the ventricles and made them appear bigger on X-rays. Modern researchers, however, using computerized axial tomography (CAT) to do more sophisticated X-rays of the brain, have obtained findings that tend to confirm some of the older research. It does indeed appear that among certain kinds of schizophrenics there are enlarged cerebral ventricles as well as other *structural* abnormalities that consistently appear.

Structural abnormalities are often found among chronic (long-term) schizophrenics, but not among those suffering from acute schizophrenia. Daniel R. Weinberger, a psychiatrist at the National Institute of Mental Health, found that approximately two thirds of chronic schizophrenics had some structural abnormalities (Weinberger, Bigelow, Kleinman, Klein, Rosenblatt, & Wyatt, 1980). Further studies indicated that these structural changes were not a result of electric shock treatment or of drug or alcohol use, and they were not connected to how long a person had been in an institution. The structural changes seemed to correlate only with chronic schizophrenia. These findings may help explain why antipsychotic drugs are rarely effective on chronic schizophrenics. Perhaps the chronic and acute forms of schizophrenia have different causes.

Further evidence for the physical and biochemical origin of schizophrenia and other behavioral disorders has been obtained from the PET scan (see Chapter 2). Although the research is in its early stages, striking differences can be seen between the brains of schizophrenics, the brains of bipolar disorder patients, and normal brains (see Figure 15.6, color section).

Paranoid Disorders

In DSM–III, the major paranoid disorders include paranoia, shared paranoid disorder, and acute paranoid disorder.

PARANOIA

Paranoia is a system of delusions that the psychotic individual firmly believes or accepts. The difference between paranoia and paranoid schizophrenia is that in paranoia, hallucinations rarely occur and there is no serious disorganization of the personality. The delusional system usually develops slowly. It is intricate, however, and usually centers on delusions of persecution or of grandeur. For example, paranoid individuals may feel that aliens are trying to take over their mind, or they may believe themselves to be Abraham Lincoln or Joan of Arc. In either case the delusion is severe. Interestingly, the delusions are usually logical, in the sense that if you accept the basic premise the rest of the ideas are consistent. In other words, if you accept that the patient's mind is being controlled by aliens, then the rest of his or her behaviors may seem perfectly reasonable (in that context). One of the most memorable depictions of paranoia in the history of motion pictures was Humphrey Bogart's portrayal of Fred C. Dobbs, a gold prospector, in the film *Treasure of the Sierra Madre.* In the film Dobbs becomes more and more convinced that others are after his share of gold, and he eventually attempts murder in "self-defense."

SHARED PARANOID DISORDER

Shared paranoid disorder is extremely rare. In this disorder one person mimics or takes as his or her own the delusional system of another, who is usually a family member. Shared paranoia is most common among husbands and wives, which would eliminate heredity as the prime cause. Instead, the major factor may be that one partner takes a submissive role to the other's dominant role and in so doing accepts the dominant person's delusional system (Soni & Rockley, 1974).

ACUTE PARANOID DISORDER

Acute paranoid disorder is marked by delusions that are temporary or variable. The delusions lack the logic and systematic organization of paranoia. The condition is often triggered by some immediate stressful situation. Another Bogart film, *The Caine Mutiny*, offers a memorable portrayal of acute paranoid disorder in the person of Captain Queeg. While under wartime stress, Queeg comes to believe that the men around him are disloyal and plotting against him. In one memorable scene, his delusions change somewhat as he calls an emergency 3:00 A.M. meeting in the ward room, where he dishes out a canful of sand, counting the portions to demonstrate how much the can can hold—to discover whether someone else ate any of the officers' strawberries.

Those suffering from acute paranoid disorder generally continue to function in society and to hold jobs, and they rarely seek help or obtain it. Exceedingly jealous spouses and religious zealots may be examples of acute paranoid disorder.

PARANOIA
A functional psychosis characterized by delusions of persecution or grandeur, and extreme suspiciousness. Hallucinations rarely occur and the personality does not undergo the serious disorganization associated with schizophrenia.

SHARED PARANOID DISORDER
A rare psychotic disorder in which one individual's paranoid delusional system is adopted by another, most commonly a spouse.

ACUTE PARANOID DISORDER
A functional psychosis characterized by variable or temporary delusions that generally lack the logic and systematic organization of paranoia.

Humphrey Bogart's portrayal of Captain Queeg in The Caine Mutiny *is an excellent depiction of acute paranoid disorder.*

Some researchers feel that it is not accurate to consider paranoia a separate state from schizophrenia (Meissner, 1978). Paranoia is not always readily distinguishable from paranoid schizophrenia. As a result, many of the causal factors that are associated with schizophrenia are being investigated as possible causes of paranoia as well.

Substance-Use Disorders

The disorders in this category are related to alcohol and drug use.

ALCOHOL DEPENDENCE

Alcohol dependence, or **alcoholism,** is a serious problem. It has been estimated that approximately 10 million adult Americans have abused alcohol and that many of them are alcohol-dependent. Drinking problems generally begin in a similar way for most people and follow a predictible pattern. During the *prealcoholic symptomatic phase,* a person who previously was only a social drinker will begin to use alcohol to alleviate stress or to feel better. Three early warning signs may be apparent during this initial stage. First, the person may consume more alcohol than before. Second, the person may begin to drink first thing in the morning, often as a way of overcoming a hangover from the night before. Third, the person may do something during intoxication that he or she later regrets.

Next comes the *prodromal phase,* in which blackouts may occur. Blackouts refer to the inability to recall, once sober, what happened while intoxicated.

Alcohol dependence is the nation's most serious drug problem.

The *crucial phase* follows the prodromal phase. During the crucial phase, the person may lose control over his or her drinking and may no longer be able voluntarily to avoid alcohol for a significant length of time.

If control is lost during the crucial phase, the *chronic phase* begins. During this definitive phase, alcohol consumption is continuous and compulsive. The person's life deteriorates as the drinking comes to interfere with work, school, social and family life. By this time the person is alcohol-dependent (Jellinek, 1971).

Biogenetic Factors Over the last decade there has been increasing evidence that alcoholism may be related to biological and genetic factors. In 1977 Robert Myers and Christine Melchior discovered that rats that had previously shunned alcohol began to show a distinct preference for it following injections of small amounts of alcohol metabolites into the fluid space of their brains. This result led the researchers to conclude that there might be a chemical cause of alcoholism (Myers & Melchior, 1977).

Other researchers took an interest in the way alcohol metabolites might be handled by the bodies of human alcoholics and nonalcoholics. In one study two researchers examined the children or siblings of alcoholics. They discovered that these relatives had a more intense reaction to alcohol and became more alcoholic than did the matched siblings and children of nonalcoholics who were in a control group (Schuckit & Rayses, 1979).

A genetic link is also suggested by the fact that in the United States, while 9 to 15 percent of men and 2 to 4 percent of women are likely to become alcoholics, the percentages are much higher among those who have alcoholics in their families. Among the latter group, 35 to 45 percent of the men and 12 to 15 percent of the women are likely to become alcoholics. This increased chance of alcoholism among those who have alcoholic family members seems to go back as much as three or four generations (Greenberg, 1980).

University of Iowa researchers have examined youngsters born to alcoholic parents but reared by adoptive parents, and they have found that alcoholism among the youngsters is much greater than would be expected (Cadoret, Cain, & Grove, 1980). The researchers found that other factors, such as psychiatric or alcohol problems in the adoptive family, or inconsistent mothering during infancy, did not predict the rate of alcoholism among the adoptees. These researchers argue that genetics seemed to be more important than anything else. As you can see, these researchers' investigative approach was similar to the one used by Seymour Kety to examine depression and schizophrenia among adoptees.

The Iowa team followed 92 adoptees until they were in their twenties. They found that many of them showed signs of becoming alcoholics by the time they had graduated from high school (Cadoret, Cain, & Grove, 1980).

Besides genetics, other biochemical factors may play a role in alcohol abuse and dependence. As you learned in Chapter 2, Valium and similar tranquilizers fight anxiety by interacting with the neurotransmitter gamma-aminobutyric acid (GABA), which is commonly associated with inhibitory synapses. By studying the brains of anesthetized cats, researchers have found that alcohol, too, increases the action of GABA while not affecting other neurotransmitters. Thus, one of the reasons that alcoholics drink may be to reduce their anxiety by boosting the effect of GABA. In fact, many alcoholics report that they drink in order to escape the stress in their lives.

ALCOHOLISM
Alcohol dependence. A disorder marked by addiction to alcohol and an inability to control drinking behavior.

Unfortunately, long-term alcohol use begins to have the opposite effect; it destroys GABA. Once this occurs the alcoholic may be in a terrible bind. The alcohol that he or she once relied on to quell anxiety no longer seems to work, and more and more alcohol is consumed in the hope of bringing the anxiety under control again (Nestoros, 1980).

Another problem with chronic alcoholism is that heavy use of alcohol can destroy neurons in the brain (Walker, Barnes, Zornetzer, Hunter, & Kubanis, 1980). Although it was once thought that brain-cell death occurred with the ingestion of small amounts of alcohol, it is now known that use must be chronic and long term before neurons are likely to be destroyed. Still, for chronic alcoholics full recovery may be virtually impossible.

Environmental Factors   Alcohol consumption may also be affected by learning, experience, and culture. While the rates of alcoholism in the United States are high, they are low in comparison with the rates in the Soviet Union. Reports from the Russian Research Center at Harvard University conclude that alcoholism in the Soviet Union remains "a true disaster." In population the United States and the Soviet Union are roughly equivalent, and yet there are two Russian alcoholics for every American alcoholic. These differences are probably not the result of Russian versus American genes. Instead, Russians are *taught* to prefer hard liquor. Drinking in the Soviet Union is done for ritual, social, and business purposes (Segal, 1975). There is total permissiveness about drinking, and people are taught that drinking is a competitive and obligatory activity.

OTHER SUBSTANCE-USE DISORDERS*

The DSM-III classification recognizes a number of substance-use disorders. The substances considered are alcohol, barbiturates, opiates, cocaine, amphetamines, phencyclidines, hallucinogens, cannabis, tobacco, and other unspecified substances. Substance-use disorders generally begin for social or psychological reasons. The social reasons include modeling, that is, the subject wishes to imitate others; social pressure to conform; and desire to rebel against social standards. The primary psychological reason is a direct attempt to change one's life through the use of drugs by altering mood or psychological state. There is little evidence that genetic predispositions force people to seek certain drugs.

Once the substances are used, however, a tolerance frequently develops, and higher doses are needed to maintain an effect or to avoid withdrawal. In some cases physical addictions can occur. In cases in which nonaddictive drugs are abused, psychological dependence may develop.

Substance-use disorders are nothing new: In Western culture they can be traced back many centuries. European scholars have recently analyzed an old concoction called Witch's Flying Ointment, which was allegedly used by European witches during the Dark Ages. It turns out to be derived from belladonna alkaloids. Whoever used it must have had quite an experience, since it is an extremely potent hallucinogen (Harper, 1977).

Which substances are likely to be most abused depends very much on their availability. As heroin and other opiates became less available in the

*The effects of psychoactive substances are discussed in Chapter 5, and the treatment of substance-use disorders is covered in Chapter 16.

late 1970s and early 1980s, heroin use dropped drastically in the United States, while the more available amphetamines and cocaine began to be used more extensively.

Substance abuse usually involves more than one substance at a time. Researchers have only recently begun to examine the effects of multidrug use and drug combinations. One study from Yale University reported that out of approximately 1,100 high school students in New Haven, Connecticut, multidrug use was a progressive phenomenon. The drugs most likely to be used in various combinations are alcohol, marijuana, hashish, barbiturates, and heroin (Gould, Berberian, Kasl, Thompson, & Kleber, 1977).

Substance-use disorders can often end in death if not treated. The American Psychiatric Association has reported a survey on drug deaths. Narcotics were most often responsible. The mean age for accidental death was 30, with barbiturate victims slightly older than narcotic victims. Men were more likely to be victims than women. Women, however, were more frequently the victims of analgesics (painkillers) and sedatives. Deaths among whites outnumbered deaths among blacks, except in New York and Washington. Thirteen percent of the victims had received treatment for drug overdose prior to their death (Greenberg, 1978).

Substance abuse may begin quite early, even before high school. Researchers studying a junior high school on Long Island reported that almost one fourth claimed to have used illicit drugs. The drugs most often used were tranquilizers, amphetamines, or sedatives. Drug use appeared to be strongly correlated with family instability, other personal problems, and poor academic performance. Many of the drugs were obtained on prescription from physicians. Over 14 percent of the students took overdoses, half of them intentionally (Anhalt & Klein, 1976).

Since the initial use of a substance that may eventually cause a disorder is based on social and psychological causes, it is hoped that education, especially of the young, will be helpful in eliminating some substance-use disorders. Unfortunately, most studies find that speakers attempting to educate high school students to the dangers of drug abuse have little ability to bring about significant change among the members of their audience (Barresi & Gigliotti, 1975).

Educating adolescents about the dangers of drug abuse can be difficult. Researchers in New York found that junior and senior high school students relied mainly on various school "experts" and former drug users for information about drugs. It appears that such individuals are more likely to be believed than any of the mass media sources available to the students (Dembo, Schmeidler, Babst, & Lipton, 1977).

Substance abuse is not an exclusively urban problem. Small towns have also been absorbed into the national drug culture. Only extremely small towns of less than 2,500 population still report relatively low rates of drug use. Drug use by parents was found to be positively correlated with children's drug use. Although drug use may be somewhat lower in rural areas than it is in urban, on the whole, the similarities are striking (Bowker, 1976).

Psychosexual Disorders

The DSM-III classification of **psychosexual disorders** includes paraphilias, in which potentially harmful or unusual sexual actions become the *primary mode* of arousal, gender identity disorders, and psychosexual dysfunctions.

PSYCHOSEXUAL DISORDERS
Mental disorders, including paraphilias, in which potentially harmful or unusual sexual actions become the primary mode of arousal; gender identity disorders in which there is an inability to resolve a discrepancy between one's anatomical sex and one's gender identity; and psychosexual dysfunctions in which psychological inhibitions interfere with the sex act.

Table 15.4 lists some of these disorders. Transsexualism and gender identity are considered separately in Chapter 18. Homosexuality is also discussed in Chapter 18, and as you can see, it is not included as a psychosexual disorder. In 1973 the American Psychiatric Association and the American Psychological Association determined that homosexuality should not be considered abnormal because it was too prevalent. Also, no particular disorders were associated more with homosexuality than with heterosexuality. As a result, homosexuality is classified simply as an alternative sexual choice and not as a disorder. Still, whether heterosexuality and homosexuality are choices influenced by learning or biochemical factors has not been well determined.

Personality Disorders

Although there are many types of **personality disorders** (see Table 15.5), they all share certain qualities. Individuals with personality disorders are essentially normal and do not exhibit problems associated with psychosis. The most definitive aspect of a personality disorder is that it tends to disrupt social relationships. Individuals with personality disorders seldom feel

Table 15.4   Psychosexual disorders

Gender identity disorders	Major features: inability to resolve a discrepancy between one's anatomical sex and one's gender identity. Often there is a feeling of "being trapped in the wrong-sexed body." A strong and persistent desire to be a member of the opposite sex.
Paraphilias	Unusual or bizarre acts necessary for sexual excitement.
Fetishism	*Must* use or be near certain inanimate objects to achieve sexual excitement, for example shoes, feathers, leather, vibrators.
Transvestism	The practice by heterosexuals of dressing in clothing of the opposite sex for purposes of sexual arousal.
Zoophilia	Preferring animals rather than people as sexual partners, or relying exclusively on animals for sexual arousal.
Pedophilia	The act or fantasy of sexual relations with prepubescent children as a preferred way of sexual arousal.
Exhibitionism	Repeatedly exposing the genitals to unsuspecting strangers as a way of achieving sexual arousal.
Voyeurism	Observing unsuspecting others disrobe or engage in sex as the preferred method of sexual arousal.
Sexual Masochism	Preferring to achieve sexual arousal by being beaten, bound, humiliated, or made to suffer.
Sexual Sadism	Repeatedly inflicting suffering on a nonconsenting partner, or preferring to give pain or suffering, even to a consenting partner, as the primary mode for sexual arousal.
Atypical Paraphilia	A category for other philias not classified, including coprophilia (arousal over feces); frotteurism (rubbing); klismaphilia (arousal caused by enemas); mysophilia (arousal over filth); necrophilia (arousal with corpses); telephone scatalogia (arousal resulting from lewdness—usually obscene telephone calls); and urophilia (arousal over urine).
Psychosexual Dysfunctions	Psychologically caused inhibitions that interfere with any portion of the sex act.

(a)

(b)

Figure 15.2 Some of Sybil's 16 personalities were artists, and their paintings helped Sybil to recover. Each personality had a different artistic style. A painting by "Marcia" (a) depicts a grim self-portrait and highlights Marcia's depressed nature. At center (b) is a painting by an angry, fearful "Peggy." The dark shadow in the foreground represents her sadistic mother. At bottom (c) is a very different painting of a warm home and family environment as depicted by "Mary" who liked to recall her childhood friends.

(c)

Figure 15.4 Louis Wain (1860–1939) was a famous artist who was best known for his witty depictions of cats in human social situations, such as giving a tea party. Fifteen years before his death, Wain suffered a schizophrenic breakdown. The changes in his cat paintings show a fascinating and frightening transition from his former style to one that highlights sensory distortion and turmoil.

(a)

(b)

Figure 15.5 A patient diagnosed as paranoid
schizophrenic was unable to make even a
simple original drawing when asked to do so.
As an aid, a painting from a magazine (a) was
provided. The patient's first attempt to copy (b)
was revealing. The copy showed visual distractions, confusions about language and letters, and lack of color. As therapy progressed,
the patient's recovery was dramatically demonstrated by his improved ability to copy the
original art as shown in (c) and then (d).

(c)

(d)

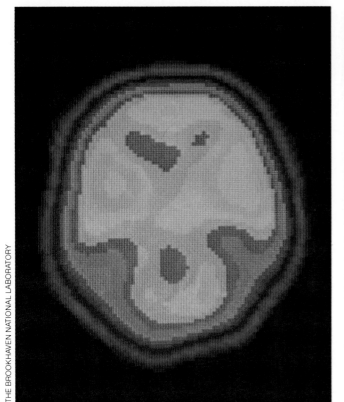

NORMAL

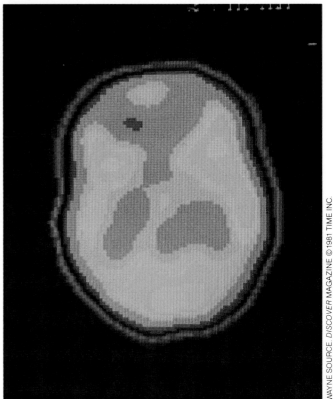

Figure 15.6 Early evidence from the PET scan has revealed intriguing differences between the activity of the brains of patients with bipolar disorder or schizophrenia and that of the normal controls. Six different subjects are shown here. The frontal lobes are at the top of each picture. Red indicates little activity. In scans from those with bipolar/manic type, the right hemisphere appears to be exceedingly active while the left hemisphere is fairly quiet. Schizophrenics generally show a cool, less active frontal lobe. Normal controls show greater activity toward the interior of the brain and exhibit good symmetry in terms of brain activity. With this limited knowledge, can you as a layman identify the scans? Although PET scan diagnosis can be quite complex and is still experimental, it is creating a great deal of interest among researchers.

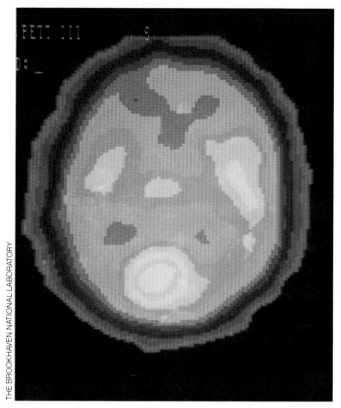

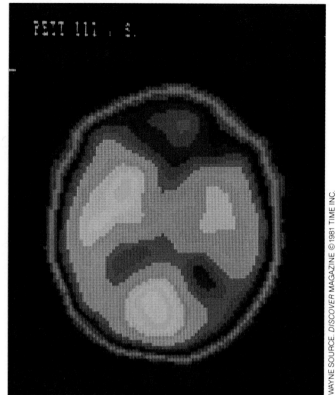

SCHIZOPHRENIC

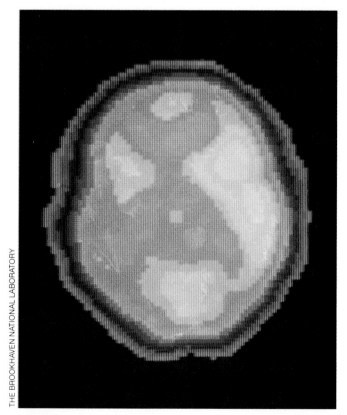

BIPOLAR/MANIC

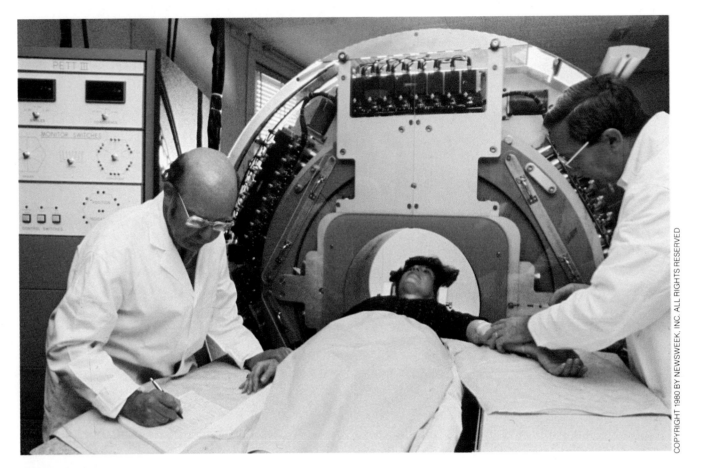

The physician on the right is about to inject a
positron-emitting substance into the patient.
The huge PET scanner into which the patient's
head has been inserted will record cerebral
functioning once the positron-emitting substance reaches the brain. Over 20 technicians
are needed to operate one PET scanner.

Table 15.5 Personality disorders

Paranoid	Major features: a continuous unjustifiable suspiciousness and mistrust of people. Often appears cold or unemotional. Takes offense easily (behavior not due to schizophrenia or paranoid disorder).
Schizoid	Unable to form social relationships, lacks warm or sentimental feelings for others, and is indifferent to praise, criticism, or the feelings of others (behavior not due to schizophrenia or paranoid disorder).
Schizotypal	Strangeness in thought, speech, perception, and behavior, but not severe enough to classify as schizophrenic. Often socially isolated, suspicious, and overly sensitive to criticism.
Histrionic	Behavior is overreactive, intense and overly dramatic to the point of disturbing interpersonal relationships. There is often an over-reaction to minor situations, crying, tantrums. Is seen by others as vain, shallow, dependent, or manipulative.
Narcissistic	Unwarranted sense of self-importance, preoccupation with fantasies of success. Demands attention, often believes he or she is entitled to special treatment. Tends to idolize or devalue others. Lacks empathy.
Antisocial	Continuously violates the rights of others. Was antisocial prior to the age of 15; often fails to hold job or perform adequately on the job. Often lies, fights, steals, and is truant. Usually shows disrespect for the law. Can be engaging for own purposes, manipulative, impulsive. Lacks feelings for others.
Borderline	Unstable mood, behavior, and self-image. Behavior is impulsive and unpredictable. Relationships with others are intense and unstable. Inappropriate and uncontrollable anger. Unable to be alone, long-lasting feelings of boredom or emptiness. Suicidal gestures.
Avoidant	Overly sensitive to rejection or possible humiliation. Avoids relationships unless guaranteed to be accepted uncritically. Low self-esteem. Devastated by the slightest disapproval. Isolated although desires to be with others.
Dependent	Allows others to take over and run his or her life. Lacks self-confidence and cannot function independently. Avoids opportunities to be self-reliant.
Compulsive	Restricted ability to express warmth and affection. Need for perfectionism at the expense of others or at the expense of enjoying life. Insists that others do his or her bidding. Overly devoted to work and productivity at the expense of enjoying life.
Passive-Aggressive	Passively refuses to perform adequately in social relationships at work even though adequate effort is possible. The name for the disorder comes from the belief that the person is passively expressing overt aggression. Often shows procrastination, stubborness, and intentional inefficiency.
Atypical, Mixed, or Other	Category reserved for those who exhibit a disorder not listed above or who have more than one personality disorder.

Note: These are the personality disorders classified in DSM-III. This table only includes descriptions of the most general nature and is completely inadequate for diagnostic purposes. In DSM-III they are described in far more detail.

responsible for the troubles they cause because they generally attribute any problems to bad luck or perceive that the fault is in others. Another marked feature of personality disorders is the maladaptive behavior pattern that persists until those who must deal with the individual finally become exhausted and break off the relationship. Generally, people with personality disorders do poorly in therapy, believing that it is others who are in need of help (Coleman, Butcher, & Carson, 1980). The following is a case study of an antisocial personality, Dan F., a disc jockey at a radio station:

ANTISOCIAL PERSONALITY DISORDER:
THE CASE OF DAN F.

Dan told his friend, a clinical psychologist:

"I can remember the first time in my life when I began to suspect I was a little different from most people. When I was in high school my best friend got leukemia and died and I went to his funeral. Everybody else was crying and feeling sorry for themselves and as they were praying to get him into heaven I suddenly realized that I wasn't feeling anything at all. He was a nice guy but what the hell. That night I thought about it some more and found out that I wouldn't miss my mother and father if they died and that I wasn't too nuts about my brothers and sisters, for that matter. I figured there wasn't anybody I really cared for but, then, I didn't need any of them anyway so I rolled over and went to sleep."

As we discussed his early life he told me he could not recall a time when he was not "doing everybody I could and the easy ones twice." He remembered that when he was 12 years old he had read a pocket book about "con men." It was then he decided it would be his life's work. They were heroes to him and he "fell down laughing" when they took some "mark" for his "bundle." As he said, "There is a sucker born every minute, and I'm glad the birth rate is so high."

One night, a colleague of Dan's committed suicide. . . . My phone started ringing early the next morning with the inevitable question "Why?" The executives at the station called but Dan F. never did. When I did talk to him, he did not mention the suicide. Later, when I brought it to his attention, all he could say was that it was "the way the ball bounces." At the station, however, he was the one who collected money for the deceased and presented it personally to the new widow. As Dan observed, she was really built and had possibilities. (McNeil, 1967, pp. 85, 87)

A good clinician recognizes that these personality disorders are often learned or situational. Some of those who have taken issue with DSM-III are worried that under certain circumstances almost any series of behaviors may be considered deviant depending on who is doing the observation and assessment.

The Assessment of Psychopathology

One of the most difficult problems faced by clinicians is assessment. Errors in assessment can lead to serious misunderstandings and inappropriate treatment. The effectiveness of assessment as it exists in actual practice has been the focus of a number of investigations and controversies.

ASSESSMENT BIAS

One of the most interesting studies dealing with the problems of assessment was conducted several years ago by psychologist David Rosenhan of Stanford University. Rosenhan wondered whether a perfectly sane individual after being hospitalized would be recognized as normal by the staff and discharged. In order to test this hypothesis he obtained the cooperation of eight "patients," actually pseudopatients. Among these eight were a psychology graduate student, three psychologists, a pediatrician, a psychiatrist, a painter, and a housewife. Rosenhan himself was one of the pseudopatients, and with the exception of the hospital administrator and chief psychologist, no one else in the hospital knew that he was checking in as a patient. Twelve hospitals were chosen in five different states on both the East and West coast. Some were old and rundown and some were very new. Some were research hospitals and some weren't. Some had good staff-to-patient ratios and others were very understaffed. Some were private hospitals and others were public.

The pseudopatients' task was to call the hospital for an appointment, arrive, and complain of hearing voices. When asked what the voices said, the patients were instructed to reply that they weren't sure but that they could tell that the voices had said "empty," "hollow," and "thud." Except for alleging the symptoms and using a pseudonym, and in certain cases, claiming a different vocation, every other question asked by the staff during patient intake was answered honestly. All of the pseudopatients behaved in the hospital as they would normally have behaved. When asked by the staff how they felt, they indicated that they no longer had any symptoms and were feeling fine. They politely responded to attendants who requested that they take medication (spitting it out later, however).

Rosenhan had told the pseudopatients that they would have to get by as best they could and convince the staff that they were sane and should be discharged. As Rosenhan said,

David Rosenhan.

> The psychological stresses associated with hospitalization were considerable, and all but one of the pseudopatients desired to be discharged almost immediately after being admitted. They were, therefore, motivated not only to behave sanely, but to be paragons of cooperation. That their behavior was in no way disruptive is confirmed by nursing reports, which have been obtained on most of the patients. These reports uniformly indicated that the patients were "friendly," "cooperative," and "exhibited no abnormal indications" (Rosenhan, 1973, p. 252).

In no case was the sanity of the pseudopatient detected. The condition of seven out of the eight was diagnosed as schizophrenia in remission. The pseudopatients stayed in the hospital from 7 to 52 days, with an average of 19 days. During the first of the hospitalizations, when careful data were kept, 35 out of a total of 118 patients became aware that the pseudopatients were sane. These patients would argue, "You're not crazy. You're a journalist, or a professor. You're checking up on the hospital" (Rosenhan, 1973, p. 252). These patients recognized normality while the hospital staff failed to.

After Rosenhan published his results, one teaching hospital questioned his findings. The staff there argued that such errors were unlikely. Consequently, Rosenhan informed the staff that sometime during the next three months one or perhaps more pseudopatients might attempt to be admitted into that hospital. After admission, they would act sanely. The staff members were asked to try to expose the pseudopatients. The staff carefully examined 193 patients who were admitted for treatment. One member of the staff felt with high confidence that 41 of these patients were pseudopatients. One psychiatrist thought that about 23 were pseudopatients, and another psychiatrist, along with one staff member, agreed that 19 were

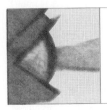

CLASSIFYING MENTAL DISORDERS: IS DSM-III THE ANSWER?

Last century in the United States, Dr. Samuel Cartwright described a ''disease of the mind'' to the Louisiana Medical Association. He called the disease *drapetomania,* from the Greek *drapetes,* which means to run away. He said that drapetomania was the ''insane desire to wander away from home'' and, he argued, this was why slaves ran away—they had this disease of the mind (Chorover, 1979).

As you can see, labeling diseases of the mind without considering social or cultural factors or learning and experience can lead someone to assume that pathology exists when all that really exists is different behavior. Sometimes, as in the case of drapetomania, the behavior is different for a good reason. Critics of DSM-III have likened it to a symphony written by a committee; they argue that the notes are all there, but that the way they are put together reflects the biases in-

herent in such a process. They argue that DSM-III will be a haven for those who feel that their job is to find a label to fit every subjective observation imaginable. Since the underlying causes of these ''pathologies'' are frequently lacking, the DSM-III diagnoses are based on gross descriptions of complex behavior that often appear different to different people (Schacht & Nathan, 1977).

Some professionals have gone so far as to reject all psychological assessment as invalid. For example, Thomas Szasz, a psychiatrist, has written about what he refers to as psychiatric injustice. He argues that psychiatry has been used as a political weapon and that it has eliminated the civil liberties of many people who simply behaved differently by labeling them sick and incarcerating them in hospitals. Szasz argues that in the past those who exhibited abnormal behavior

were labeled witches or warlocks whereas today, they are labeled with psychiatric terms that serve the same purpose, that is, to justify the community in eliminating them from effective participation in the society. In his book *The Myth of Mental Illness* (1961) Szasz writes:

> The term ''mental illness'' is a metaphor. More particularly as this term is used in mental health legislation, ''mental illness'' is not the name of a medical illness or disorder, but is a quasi-medical label whose purpose is to conceal conflict as illness and to justify coercion as treatment. (Szasz, 1961, p. xviii)

This view has been further supported in the conscience of the public by such films as *One Flew over the Cuckoo's Nest,* in which a man is placed in a mental institution simply because he has been disruptive; is forced to take drugs against his will;

probably pseudopatients. At that point Rosenhan admitted that he had never sent anyone to their hospital! Rosenhan concluded that "any diagnostic process that lends itself so readily to massive errors of this sort cannot be a very reliable one" (Rosenhan, 1973, p. 252).

The pseudopatients noticed during their stays that the staff often misinterpreted behavior. Boredom was misinterpreted as nervousness. Anger at being mistreated by an attendant was misinterpreted as berserk behavior caused by pathology. Once a group of patients was sitting outside the cafeteria half an hour before it opened, and a psychiatrist was overheard telling his residents that this was indicative of the oral stage of the patients' syndrome. Apparently it hadn't occurred to the psychiatrist that there was nothing much to do inside a hospital besides eat or wait for lunch.

Rosenhan came to the following conclusion:

> It is clear that we cannot distinguish the sane from the insane in psychiatric hospitals. The hospital itself imposes a special environment in which the meanings of behavior can easily be misunderstood. The consequences to patients hospitalized in such an environment—the powerlessness, depersonalization, segregation, mortification, and self-labeling—seem undoubtedly counter-therapeutic (Rosenhan, 1973, p. 257).

is given shock therapy, supposedly for treatment but really as a clandestine form of discipline; and eventually is given a frontal lobotomy because he has challenged the rule of the ward nurse.

To abandon our system of assessment because errors may occur would be an overreaction, however. In most instances researchers now feel confident that Szasz is in error when he claims that mental illness is a myth. As one researcher said with regard to schizophrenia, although it has been argued that this form of mental illness is a myth, it is a "myth with a genetic basis and a pharmacological treatment" (Valenstein, 1980, p. 321).

Supporters of DSM-III argue that competent clinicians are well aware of the limitations of the classification system. Professionals must be able to communicate with each other, and if DSM-III were not available something less rigorous would take its place. Realistically, no one can expect to eliminate all terminology from psychiatry and psychology. Supporters argue that the DSM-III classifications are on

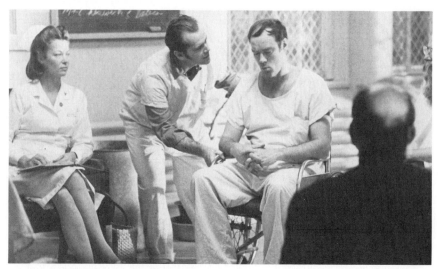

Films such as One Flew Over the Cuckoo's Nest *helped underscore the growing concern people have about providing just and adequate care for the mentally ill.*

the whole quite reliable, that is, different assessors tend to use the same descriptions when confronted with the same cases. Supporters of DSM-III also argue that by carefully describing behavior patterns that have aspects in common, they may be able to identify distinct groups that have a common underlying cause for their disorder.

No doubt, this will not happen for every category, but it may lead to breakthroughs in certain areas.

Since DSM-III has been adopted, and appears to be here to stay—at least until DSM-IV comes along—the general consensus is that it will be a valuable addition so long as its limitations are clearly realized.

Rosenhan replicated his initial study, carried out in 1973, with follow-up studies in 1973, 1974, and 1975. The later studies involved more than ten hospitals (Greenberg, 1981). Rosenhan found essentially the same results.

A number of researchers and clinicians have taken issue with Rosenhan because of his methods and conclusions. For instance, psychologist Max Lewis of the University of Arkansas has stated,

I have some trouble with Rosenhan's study. First of all, subjects did report auditory hallucinations and ask to enter the hospital. Secondly, it is standard operating procedure to keep any admission for a period of observation. Thirdly, I don't have confidence that all pseudopatients presented a "normal" pattern of behavior; they were there to make a point. Fourthly, is it not possible that some of the pseudopatients did exhibit problems worthy of treatment?

Obviously we would all be more comfortable if all the pseudopatients were immediately discovered. But a nineteen day stay is much different from being locked away without a followup. I think Rosenhan has an important point, but the situation doesn't seem so horrible to me as Rosenhan's discussion portrays it (Lewis, 1981).

Since the Rosenhan study DSM-III has been published. Would the more advanced criteria in DSM-III make such misdiagnoses less likely? While

DSM-III may be a considerable improvement over DSM-II, there is still room for making subjective interpretations, for incorrectly classifying normal behaviors as abnormal, and for providing the patient with a label that may have an effect for the rest of his or her life. All assessment must, therefore, be made very carefully and be frequently reviewed.

MISDIAGNOSIS

Sometimes patients are assessed inadequately, and important symptoms are overlooked or ignored. In such cases, it doesn't help much to have well-defined assessment categories, since the patient's difficulties are not being rigorously addressed. Researchers, wondering how often such misdiagnosis is likely to occur, have looked into the problem. One investigation examined 100 psychiatric patients. All of the patients had originally been given an examination at a large psychiatric reception center, to which they had been brought by their families or by the police under mental health warrants. All were to be committed to state mental hospitals after the examination. When they volunteered to be part of the investigation, they were taken to a special clinical research ward instead. There they were given intensive physical and psychological tests. The physicians found that 46 of the 100 patients had medical illnesses that had gone undiagnosed and that were probably the cause of their psychiatric symptoms or had exacerbated them considerably. Another 34 had previously undiagnosed physical illnesses that were not directly related to their psychiatric symptoms.

Sixty-one percent recovered rapidly and their abnormal behavior disappeared once the underlying medical problem was treated. Among the medical problems that had been missed by those who had initially examined the patients were Addison's disease (an inefficiency of adrenaline, which can result in irritability, depression, and emotional instability); arsenic poisoning; Wilson's disease (an inability to metabolize copper properly, which can lead to irritability, depression, emotional instability, and unusual physical symptoms); lead intoxication; vitamin deficiency; and other dietary deficiencies. The number of physical illnesses discovered wasn't surprising, since the patients were mainly from the poorer areas of the city and had not gotten adequate routine medical care (Hall, Stickney, LeCann, & Popkin, 1980). The researchers felt that these 100 patients were generally representative of those who were typically committed to a state mental hospital. They felt that there was a serious failure to properly test incoming psychiatric patients for physical disorders, and that the legal implication of this failure was profound. The medical tests given each patient by the researchers cost an average of only $400. The following case study is illustrative of this problem.

THE ASSESSMENT OF PSYCHOPATHOLOGY: THE CASE OF CAROL T.

Carol T. was born in 1946, but her troubles began in the summer of 1971. One day she felt shaky and her mouth felt a little tight. Then, without warning, she fainted while at work. When she went to see her family doctor, he said she was overtired and gave her Valium. One morning at the end of July, Carol T. felt a strange compulsion for no apparent reason. She went into the bathroom, took a razor, and slashed her wrists. Two days later she was given a psychiatric consultation. She spent one month in a psychiatric hospital and was given thorazine, an antipsychotic drug. Carol then entered psychotherapy. For the next few years she was in and out of mental hospitals and saw many different psychiatrists. She was given electroshock therapy, more antipsychotic drugs, and L-Dopa, a drug to control Parkinson's disease. Still her symptoms got worse. She couldn't tie her shoes, open a jar, comb her hair, or write. She could hardly chew or swallow. She began to limp, she lost her balance, and occasionally fell. Then she had trouble speaking, her voice became higher, and everything became slurred. At that point she was diagnosed as suffering from conversion disorder and transferred to a community mental health center. There, one of the staff doctors just happened to stop in to see her. He took one look at Carol's eyes and recognized the copper-colored rings around her corneas as Kayser-Fleischer rings. These rings are an unmistakable sign of Wilson's disease. They are evidence of the actual buildup of copper in the body. The doctor said, "She was practically a textbook presentation. I think my secretaries could have made the diagnosis" (Roueche, 1980, p. 357). Carol was immediately placed on drugs to help leach the excess copper from her body. She is now fully recovered from the disease that would have cost her her life had the doctor not spotted it.

Functional disorders, as well as organic disorders, are subject to misdiagnosis. One of the most difficult functional disorders to assess is schizophrenia. Although the DSM-III diagnostic criteria are fairly clear, these criteria can sometimes be satisfied by the early onset of disorders other than schizophrenia. For example, disordered and bizarre thinking is not unique to schizophrenia (Harrow & Quinlan, 1977). And, although it's fairly rare, hallucinations can also occur as the result of conversion disorder (Fitzgerald & Wells, 1977). Adding to the problem is the fact that over half of those diagnosed as schizophrenic have learned to fake some of their symptoms and mask some of them in order to help lengthen or shorten their hospital stay (Martin, Hunter, & Moore, 1977). As you can see, diagnostic assessment takes skill, knowledge, and experience. It is anything but simple.

Summary

- The distinction between normal and abnormal behavior is not always a clear one. For this reason professionals must be careful when assessing behavior. For a behavior to be considered abnormal in the clinical sense, it must not only be different from the norm but also be maladaptive or self-defeating.
- In evaluating the abnormal behavior of another, different models may be used in order to arrive at a better understanding of the underlying mechanisms that may be contributing to the disorder. Some models may be more applicable in some circumstances than others.
- The medical model assumes that the underlying cause of a mental disorder is a biological dysfunction. According to the learning model, abnormal behaviors are acquired through conditioning. In the psychoanalytic model, the abnormal behaviors are viewed as evidence of unresolved unconscious conflicts. In the humanistic model, abnormal behaviors are considered to be the result of failure to fulfill self-potential.

- Insanity is a legal term. There are different legal standards for determining whether a defendant in a criminal case is not guilty by reason of insanity.

- In 1980 a new classification scheme, the third edition of the *Diagnostic and Statistical Manual* (DSM-III) was adopted. It provides assessment according to five dimensions or axes. The first three axes assess the immediate condition of the individual, while the fourth and fifth axes classify and assess the individual's past situation and ability to cope with it.

- In the broadest sense, mental disorders can be divided into two categories, organic and functional disorders. Organic disorders are those in which the cause is physical or strongly suspected to be physical. Functional disorders include those in which psychological stressors have traditionally been believed to be the cause of the disorder.

- Anxiety, somatoform, dissociative, affective, and psychosexual disorders were once classified in DSM-II under the general heading neurosis. However, it was felt that the term neurosis was so all-encompassing that it was of little value. It has therefore been discarded.

- Anxiety disorders include phobic disorders, in which an individual suffers from a specific unrealistic fear; anxiety states, which include general anxiety disorder, a relatively continuous state of tension, worry, and dread; a panic disorder, in which a person may suddenly be overwhelmed by panic even though there is no apparent reason to be frightened; and obsessive-compulsive disorder, in which a person is obsessed by an unwanted thought or compulsively engages in actions and repetitive behaviors, perhaps as a way of coping with anxiety.

- Somatoform disorders are patterns of behavior in which an individual claims to have physical symptoms when in fact no illness can be found. Somatoform disorders include conversion disorder, psychogenic pain disorder, and hypochondriasis.

- Dissociative disorders are those in which the person separates himself or herself from the core of his or her personality. Included under dissociative disorders are psychogenic amnesia, which is a memory loss; psychogenic fugue, in which the sufferer leaves home while in a state of amnesia; and multiple personality, in which more than one personality develops.

- Affective disorders, schizophrenic disorders, and paranoid disorders are classified as psychoses. The psychotic person has lost contact with reality, and the personality becomes grossly distorted. In many cases hospitalization is required.

- Affective disorders are disorders of mood and emotion. They include bipolar disorder, in which there may be extreme mood swings from depression to mania, and major depression, a state of severe and utter sadness bordering on suicide.

- Recent evidence has indicated that affective disorder may have a genetic and biological component. Genes that appear to be related to major depression have been isolated on the sixth chromosome. The dexamethasone-suppression test is a blood test that is used to distinguish between endogenous and secondary depression.

- Schizophrenic disorders refer to a complete breakdown of any integrated personality functioning. Emotions become flat and distorted. Thought, language, and behavior become bizarre and disturbed. Delusions and hallucinations often accompany these disturbances. Schizophrenic disorders include the disorganized type, the catatonic type, the paranoid type, the undifferentiated type, and the residual type.

■ Many different causes of schizophrenia have been hypothesized, among them genetic and environmental factors, and biochemical, structural and anatomical factors. There is evidence to support all of these views, indicating that schizophrenia may have many causes.

■ Paranoid disorders refer to a system of delusions that the psychotic individual firmly believes or accepts. Paranoia is different from paranoid schizophrenia because in paranoia, hallucinations rarely occur and there is no serious disorganization of the personality. Paranoid disorders include paranoia, shared paranoid disorder, and acute paranoid disorder.

■ Substance-use disorders refer to any disorder in which a person becomes dependent on an ingested substance that causes behavioral change. Alcoholism is one of the primary substance-use disorders. Recent evidence has found a strong link between alcoholism and heredity.

■ Other substance-use disorders include dependence on barbiturates, cocaine, amphetamines, phencyclidines, hallucinogens, cannabis, tobacco, and other unspecified substances. Which substances are likely to be most abused depends very much on their availability.

■ Psychosexual disorders include categories in which potentially harmful or unusual sexual actions become the primary mode of arousal.

■ Personality disorders are a separate axis in DSM-III. Although there are many different types of personality disorder, they all share certain qualities. Sufferers are essentially normal and do not exhibit the problems associated with psychosis. The most definitive aspect of a personality disorder is that it tends to disrupt social relationships.

■ One of the most difficult problems faced by clinicians is assessment. Errors in assessment can lead to serious misunderstandings and inappropriate treatment. Psychologist David Rosenhan has shown that relatively normal individuals may be assessed in a biased fashion once they have been labeled.

■ Physical diseases may exacerbate behavioral problems, and many behavioral problems may be the result of misdiagnosed or undiagnosed physical ailments.

■ Functional disorders as well as organic disorders are subject to misdiagnosis. Diagnostic assessment takes skill, knowledge, and experience. It is anything but simple.

Searching for the causes and for possible treatments of serious mental disorders is both challenging and frustrating. Every day researchers, working together with their patients, search for answers. The following is a description of one woman, who, desiring to help others, offered to participate in an experiment to test the ideas of a clinical researcher.

Mrs. A. had suffered from bipolar affective disorder for many years. She was now 52 and desperately wanted help. Her affective cycle was about 43 days. During that period, she would swing from manic to normal, to depressed, back to normal, and then once again to manic, completing the cycle. It was at this point in her life that she met Frederick Goodwin, the chief of clinical psychobiology at the National Institute of Mental Health.

Goodwin had observed the daily biological rhythms of a number of persons with affective disorder and had found that they were slightly out of phase with the 24-hour day (Goodwin & Wehr, as cited in Greenberg, 1978). He noticed that a few days before the periodic manic phase began, the sufferers of bipolar disorder would go to bed and wake up somewhat earlier than usual. He wondered whether such a sleep-wake change could be associated with a shift away from depression, and he wanted to conduct an experiment in which he intentionally manipulated the sleep cycle of someone suffering from bipolar disorder. Mrs. A. volunteered.

Goodwin placed Mrs. A. in isolation where she could not see a clock or watch, and created a 22-hour day for her, which he believed might be closer to her own natural rhythm. Mrs. A. was unaware of the day-night cycle outside of the laboratory.

The result was the briefest depression that she had ever experienced. Goodwin then advanced her sleep period six hours on the reasoning that "maybe people (with affective disturbances) were awake when they were supposed to be asleep" (Greenberg, 1978, p. 367). The results were quite dramatic, with an antidepressing effect that lasted for about two weeks before there was a relapse. With another movement of four to six hours there was another two-week improvement. A third advance, which finally placed her a full 18 hours out of phase, did not have an effect.

Goodwin noted that two weeks seemed to be a special time, since that was about how long it took lithium drugs to affect bipolar disorder. Interestingly, it appears that lithium sometimes relieves the symptoms of bipolar disorder and sometimes not. Goodwin has suggested that "maybe there are differences in the effects of drugs in terms of the phase of the illness or time of year." He added, "We have to be very careful, because this sounds at first glance like astrology. But the recognition of cyclicity has been long overdue in the whole variety of human behaviors" (Greenberg, 1978, p. 367).

Goodwin's research is just one of many lines of investigations into bipolar disorder. Although intriguing, whether it leads to an answer to the riddle of bipolar disorder remains to be seen.

Suggestions for Further Reading

1. Coleman, J. C., Butcher, J. N., & Carson, R. C. *Abnormal psychology and modern life* (6th ed.). Glenview, Illinois: Scott Foresman, 1980.
2. Davison, G. C., & Neale, J. M. *Abnormal psychology* (2nd ed.). New York: Wiley, 1978.
3. McNeil, E. B. *The quiet furies.* Englewood Cliffs, N. J.: Prentice-Hall, 1967.
4. Price, R. H., & Lynn, S. J. *Abnormal psychology in the human context.* Homewood, Illinois: The Dorsey Press, 1981.
5. Schreiber, F. R. *Sybil.* Chicago: Regnery, 1973.

CONTENTS

CHAPTER 16

Therapy

PROLOGUE

The year is 1803 and you are a journalist. You are visiting Dr. Johann Christian Reil in Germany, and he is taking you on a tour of a madhouse. He wants you to stay a day or two, observe the improvements, and write about them. Reil, a great believer in the Pinel System, is bringing this humanitarian French reform to Germany. "I have done more than reform the hospital," he says. "I have instituted therapies!"

"What kind of therapies?" you ask.

He replies, "Therapies to shock the patients back to reality," and agrees to show you some of the therapies in practice.

The two of you step through a door into an alleyway leading to a garden on the grounds. Reil continues, "You see, most of these patients have left reality. They prefer their own worlds. It is our job to bring them back to reality, and sometimes we need to shock them to do it. Watch and I'll show you."

At the end of the alley you see an attendant. Next to him is a small cannon, the kind that are loaded with blank charges and used in

ceremonies to fire off salutes. The attendant is peeking around the corner into the garden. Suddenly he pulls back. "Here comes a patient now," he says.

"Good," whispers Reil. "Prepare." As the unsuspecting patient steps into view the cannon is fired. It explodes with a terrific boom. The patient leaps into the air, screams, turns, and looks in horror. He gasps for breath and runs away. "You see," says Reil. "His reaction was normal. For a moment he was normal. Any one of us might have reacted in the same way. Our hope is that he will stay normal for awhile. At best he will not return to his former disease state."

That night you watch more shock therapy. A sleeping patient is grabbed by two attendants, carried out to the garden, and thrown into an icy pond. Another attendant, dressed in a ghost outfit, makes strange sounds while standing on a table at the foot of a patient's bed. The patient awakes, screaming, horrified to see a ghost hovering over him.

The next evening the entire hospital staff participates in an elaborate tableau. Dressed in cos-

tumes and horribly made up, they gather behind a large curtain, props in hand, and freeze in assigned positions. The patients are seated before the curtain, which is abruptly drawn aside. "Tonight," explains Dr. Reil, "they are depicting the resurrection of the dead." One of the staff is being lifted from a coffin, his eyes rolled back. The patients gasp in horror. "A week ago," Reil says, "we did the last judgment. Next week we'll do the yawning gates of hell. We only get this elaborate for the most troublesome cases, though. We want to teach them that it's better to be healthy

than to stay here and be sick. I like to call this method noninjurious torture" (Roueche, 1980).

As you leave the madhouse you think to yourself that your readers will be pleased to know that Dr. Reil and his staff have things well in hand and are doing something to help the patients.

In this chapter we will examine different therapies, including modern drug treatments, electroshock therapy, and psychosurgery. We'll also look at psychotherapies, for instance Freudian psychoanalysis, behavioral therapy, and hypnotherapy.

Why Psychologists Study Therapies

When people suffer from behavioral disorders it's only reasonable that members of society should want to help. As you may have gathered from the Prologue, however, good intentions are not always sufficient. Any help or therapy that is provided should be beneficial. Unproven therapies, despite all the reasoning behind them, may do more harm than good. Psychologists study therapies because rigorous investigation is needed to determine the effectiveness of different therapeutic measures. Once an effective therapy is found, it often furnishes clues to the underlying cause of the disorder. On the other hand, once a therapy has proven to be ineffective, it can be eliminated so that patients no longer need to be subjected to it.

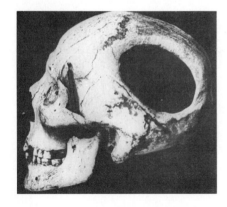

Figure 16.1 *In the primitive procedure of trephining, a hole was cut in the skull, ostensibly to allow evil spirits or devils to escape. The procedure was dangerous, and the chance of hemorrhage and infection was high. Still, trephining occasionally may have relieved pressure on the brain, caused by bleeding or a tumor, and brought about improvement.*

The History of Therapy

Therapeutic attempts to alleviate mental disorders are perhaps as old as humankind. Half a million years ago, Stone Age people applied "medical" techniques to open the skull of patients in distress. The procedure was called **trephining** (see Figure 16.1). An opening was cut in the skull by chipping away at it with a sharp stone tool. Mad thoughts or evil spirits were supposed to escape through this opening. Some trephined skulls show signs of healing around the opening, indicating that the individuals may have survived the procedure and lived for many more years.

Prior to the development and extensive use of the scientific method, it was widely believed that emotional disorders were due to the supernatural—to possessions by spirits, to witchcraft, and to the curses of ancestors. Even today, most primitive societies believe that mental disorders are brought on by supernatural forces (Gillin, 1948).

THE GREEK AND ROMAN ERA
(APPROXIMATELY 400 B.C. TO A.D. 476)

From the time of the Greek physician Hippocrates (460? to 377? B.C.) to the time of another Greek physician, Galen (A.D. 131? to 201?), the Greeks and Romans argued for humane treatment of those with mental disorders. The Greek and Roman countryside was dotted with hundreds of temples, dedicated to the Roman god of medicine and healing, Aesculapius, where people who were troubled could go for rest, sleep, and gentle consultation. At these temples, humane treatment was often combined with attempts by the priests to bring about magical cures.

While these cures weren't particularly effective, the ancient Greeks and Romans did document many disorders and separated them into categories that are still, to some degree, considered valid. For example, the ancients differentiated between acute and chronic disorders, between mania and depression, and they made a distinction between illusions, delusions, and hallucinations. Some of the temple priests even relied on dream interpretation to draw conclusions about their patients (Mora, 1967).

THE MIDDLE AGES (A.D. 476 TO 1453)

When the Roman Empire fell, the rational view of mental disorders was displaced in favor of religious demonology. Those who suffered from mental disorders were suspected of having been invaded by a spirit or a devil. Madness was thought to be the will of God, and therapy for madness was a religious ritual. Psychotics often became the target of religious persecution. Many whose behavior was abnormal were thought to have sold their souls to the devil, and they were burned as witches. These "witches" provided a convenient scapegoat upon which an ignorant society could blame its troubles.

One of the major Christian treatises of the Middle Ages was the *Malleus Maleficarum*, the "witch's hammer." This was a book that described the kinds of signs by which a witch could be identified. These signs closely par-

TREPHINING
An ancient procedure in which the skull was punctured by a sharp instrument so that evil spirits could escape.

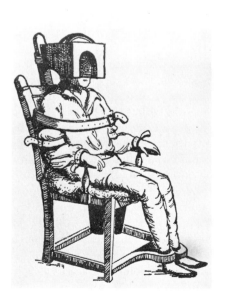

Crude restraining devices were commonly employed in early mental asylums.

allel many of the symptoms of behavioral disorders that are known today. The *Malleus Maleficarum* went through 29 editions, the last published in 1669. By then the Renaissance had established a more humane view of mental disorders.

THE RENAISSANCE (APPROXIMATELY 1400 TO 1600)

During the Renaissance, the writings of the early Greeks and Romans reemerged as a powerful force. The invention of the printing press made it possible to distribute these writings widely. Reading the ancient Greek and Latin texts quickly became the mark of the well educated. In fact, early in the 20th century it was a rare college that did not offer ancient Greek and Latin as part of their curriculum. Gradually, an enlightened view of mental disorder replaced the demonology of the Middle Ages.

AFTER THE RENAISSANCE

The last several centuries have witnessed gradual reform in mental institutions and in mental health care and a growing awareness of possible organic causes of mental disorder as well as of unconscious factors and environmental influences.

Mental Institutions   The asylums built early in the Middle Ages had been designed to hold "suspects" and to protect society from their evil power. During the Renaissance, treatment became more "humane," if only in the sense that people were chained and shackled and treated like animals rather than being systematically tortured or killed. Reform of these institutions did not really begin until the end of the 1700s.

In 1792, shortly after the French Revolution, Philippe Pinel was placed in charge of an asylum for the mad in Paris. After repeated requests, Pinel received permission to try an experiment. Had he failed, he might well have been executed by the new revolutionary government. Believing that the inmates were sick people, not beasts or criminals, Pinel removed their chains and shackles and treated them with kindness and consideration. He placed them in sunny rooms and allowed them to exercise. The noise, the squalor, and the abuse gave way to a more peaceful atmosphere. Pinel's reforms were successful.

Mental institutions continued to be reformed throughout the 18th and 19th centuries. Unfortunately, little was known about helping psychotics and those with other mental disorders. In most institutions, the patients were put together in huge groups. Dorothea Dix (1802–1887) was a devoted reformer who helped establish humane, professionally run hospitals for the emotionally disturbed. Her idea was that patients in institutions should be isolated from one another so that each could have privacy and tranquility. Since then, it has been found that isolating patients in private rooms or cells (still the practice in many institutions, following Dix's lead) is often more harmful than helpful (Foucault, 1965). Good intentions are never enough.

The Era of Psychology   The last person to be publicly murdered by a sanctioned institution for having been a witch died in Switzerland in 1782. As enlightenment spread, the scientific method became the accepted way to advance knowledge, and a new understanding of behavior emerged.

By the mid-1800s, physicians and anatomists began to realize that abnormal behavior could result from damage to the brain or nervous system. It was discovered, for instance, that syphilis was the cause of an organic psychosis known as **general paresis.**

Proponents of organic theory made a sharp break with demonologists in arguing that abnormal behavior was due to underlying physical causes. By implication, rectifying the underlying problem could lead to a cure. In many instances of abnormal behavior, however, problems with the brain or nervous system were not evident. Consequently, additional avenues of interpretation were sought to supplement the organic view.

By the late 1800s a psychological revolution was beginning. Psychiatrists argued that abnormal behavior might be the result of too much stress or unresolved unconscious conflicts. Sigmund Freud, more than anyone else, championed these ideas.

In America, too, interest in understanding mental disorder was growing, owing in part to the publication of Clifford Beers' book *A Mind That Found Itself* (1908). Beers described his own emotional breakdown and recovery. The effect of the book was wide-ranging, and a number of influential Americans began financial and political efforts to develop therapies for those suffering from mental disorders.

The first half of the 1900s saw advances in learning theory and humanistic therapies. Both attempted to explain and treat mental disorders. Then, in the 1950s, medical and biological therapies advanced by great leaps, as certain drugs were found to help control psychotic disturbances and alter mood. Our expanding knowledge of drug and brain chemistry, together with new techniques for examining the brain, indicate that the 1980s may experience another important leap forward in our medical and biological understanding of abnormal behavior and how to treat it.

Today, many people are still treated in hospitals or special institutions for the mentally ill. Although these institutions vary widely, they typically offer a number of therapeutic techniques in response to the needs of individual patients. In the next few pages, we'll be investigating some of these modern therapies.

GENERAL PARESIS
Tertiary (third stage) syphilis, which involves an invasion and severe irreversible damage to the brain. The clinical picture includes tremors, loss of contact with reality, extreme personality deterioration, increasing paralysis, and delirium. The patient may survive many years in this condition.

Somatic Therapies

In 1956 I was nine years old. My father was a staff resident in psychiatry at Brooklyn State Hospital, and we lived on the fourth floor of the staff house on the hospital grounds. From my window I could look out across a narrow road to a large, ugly, four-story brick building. The windows of the building were barred. On the other side of the bars I could see large rooms. These were the wards for psychotics. My parents explained to me that the building was a hospital and that the people inside it were sick. I soon became accustomed to their bizarre behavior. One woman stood by the window most of the day directing an orchestra that didn't exist. Other patients threw themselves on the floor and got into fights. Others stayed in one place and stared straight ahead for hours on end. I became accustomed to these sights. The only thing I didn't get used to was the screaming. From sunrise to sunset and all through the night, there was screaming. I heard screaming laughter, screaming crying, screaming curses, screaming poems, screaming fights. It never ended.

That year my father was drafted into the army, and we left the hospital for a two-year tour of duty in California. In 1959 we returned, but everything was different. The building was still there, the patients were still there, but the screaming was gone. Days would pass by without a single scream from anyone. Attendants seemed to be more busy making beds and serving food than rushing to break up fights. The patients took better care of themselves. They seemed to dress better and to be more sociable with one another. More of them had ground privileges and were out walking about and sitting on the benches.

I didn't know it at the time, but during those two years the first of a series of new antipsychotic drugs, the chlorpromazines, had arrived. The changes I was noticing were due to the effects of these drugs.

Drug treatment is one kind of **somatic therapy,** meaning a therapy that directly interacts with the body and its chemistry. Other kinds include electroshock and psychosurgery.

PSYCHOPHARMACOLOGICAL THERAPY

We will look at four classes of drugs that are used therapeutically: antipsychotic drugs, antidepressants, antimanic drugs, and antianxiety drugs.

Antipsychotic Drugs Today, the most widely used antipsychotic agents are the phenothiazines. They have replaced the chlorpromazines of the 1950s. The **phenothiazines** include such drugs as thorazine, stelazine, compazine, and mellaril. During the 1960s, these drugs were often referred to as the major tranquilizers. Although these drugs do tend to quiet people, the term "tranquilizer" is not as descriptive as "antipsychotic agent" (Denber, 1967) since these drugs, unlike some tranquilizers, also have antipsychotic effects. Often, especially among those with acute psychoses, the drugs help alleviate symptoms, reduce the number of hallucinations, control the severity of delusions, and reduce violent or aggressive behavior. They rarely eliminate the problems totally, and they are not considered cures.

Attempts are currently being made to pinpoint the region in the brain where the antipsychotic drugs have their effect. The procedure is to use antipsychotic drugs that are temporarily radioactive and to trace their route through the brain. The drugs seem to concentrate in areas of the brain that control aspects—language, emotion, sensation—known to be related to psychoses. Still, *why* the antipsychotic drugs have their effect is not clearly understood, although, as you will see, there are some exciting hypotheses.

Antipsychotic drugs vary in their effectiveness. Sometimes they fail to suppress psychotic symptoms, and sometimes their effects last only a short time. Their use is often accompanied by side effects such as a dry mouth or an uncomfortable feeling.

Because the drugs tend to calm patients and make them easier to handle, hospital staff sometimes administer them too freely. Overmedication has become a serious problem in many hospitals and institutions (Zavodnick, 1976). On some wards everyone is medicated, regardless of their condition. This kind of institutional abuse of medication is not therapy; it is a chemical form of crowd control. Critics have contended that drugs are too often used indiscriminately; that psychiatrists, too busy being administrators, scribble out prescriptions without knowing their patients; and that pharmaceutical companies sometimes act as pushers, providing massive numbers of free samples and consultations that always advocate drugs as the primary mode of therapy. In a sense, these critics argue, chemical shackles have taken the place of the old iron ones.

These kinds of abuses are becoming less common, however. For one thing, it has been found that long-term use of antipsychotic medication can cause irreparable damage. In **tardive dyskinesia,** for example, body and facial muscles twitch involuntarily. The effects of tardive dyskinesia are usually permanent, and sometimes the early symptoms are misdiagnosed as part of the mental disorder. In a recent report to the American Psychiatric Association, researchers Rey and Carpenter noted that as many as one fifth of the patients taking antipsychotic drugs are suffering from tardive dyskinesia (Greenberg, 1980). In one experiment antipsychotic drugs were given to healthy monkeys. After a time the drugs were withdrawn and tardive dyskinesia began. This outcome indicates that the tardive dyskinesia is a function of the drugs, and not of the diseases which are being treated (Weiss & Santelli, 1978).

Another reason antipsychotic agents are being used less often than before is that these drugs have been shown to be of little use against the chronic forms of schizophrenia, which is the most prevalent psychotic disorder (see Chapter 15). Furthermore, some have argued that acute schizophrenia may be treated as effectively without drugs as with (Carpenter, McGlashan, & Strauss, 1977; Abruzzi, 1975).

Still, a majority of psychiatric and psychological researchers argue that, used judiciously, antipsychotic drugs make a world of difference. They keep hallucinations and delusions under control so that the patient may benefit from other forms of therapy, and they make it possible for patients to leave the institution and be treated on an outpatient basis (Clark, Gosnell, Shapiro, Huck, & Marbach, 1979).

Antidepressants   **Antidepressants** have sometimes been called mood elevators. There are two main kinds, the tricyclics and the monoamine-oxidase (MAO) inhibitors. Among the tricyclics the best known is probably Elavil, and among the MAO inhibitors the best known is probably Marplan. These drugs are given for depressions that are relatively severe. Their effectiveness in alleviating depression is somewhat variable, and it often takes two to three weeks of continuous use before any of the helpful effects are achieved. Antidepressants are usually more effective against endogenous depression (depression without apparent cause) than against depression that is environmentally induced. Some of these drugs must be monitored carefully because they can be dangerous. For example, MAO inhibitors can be used only in conjunction with strict dietary restrictions in order to prevent possible adverse reactions.

Antimanic Drugs   Perhaps the number one drug success story in the history of psychopharmacology is the use of **lithium carbonate** to treat bipolar disorder. It is sold under a number of trade names such as Lithonate and Lithotabs. Lithium carbonate is often very effective in resolving manic episodes. Against swings toward depression it is less effective, perhaps because depression is a more heterogeneous category. In the case of Ruth H., the drug helped the patient resume a normal life.

SOMATIC THERAPY
Invasive therapeutic intervention that acts directly on the body and its chemistry. Included in this classification are psychopharmacological, electroconvulsive, and psychosurgical procedures.

PHENOTHIAZINES
Antipsychotic drugs, often called the major tranquilizers. These drugs help control and alleviate the symptoms of psychosis.

TARDIVE DYSKINESIA
A severe neuromuscular reaction, possibly due to interference with or depletion of the neurotransmitter acetylcholine, following long-term use or a sudden withdrawal from antipsychotic drugs. The disorder is manifested in the involuntary twitching of body and facial muscles.

ANTIDEPRESSANTS
Drugs used to relieve the symptoms of extreme sadness and withdrawal from life that characterize severe depression. MAO inhibitors and tricyclic drugs are the two main classes of antidepressants.

LITHIUM CARBONATE
A chemical compound that has been found to be effective in controlling the severe mood swings associated with bipolar affective psychosis.

PSYCHOPHARMACOLOGICAL THERAPY: THE CASE OF RUTH H.

For nearly 20 years Ruth H. suffered from bipolar disorder, reaching manic highs and then descending into deep depressions. She had been given antidepressants; she had had psychotherapy and electroshock therapy. Nothing seemed to help. In 1969 she was on the verge of committing suicide when she was given lithium carbonate. She has been able to live normally ever since.

Her bipolar disorder began when she was a child. After college she became an elementary school teacher, but her condition worsened and she had to quit her job. After the birth of her first child she entered a deep depression. The depression was followed by a manic high and thus the pattern began. It was to become a major portion of her life for the next 20 years.

By 1968 her condition had deteriorated; her stable periods came less often. In 1969 she came to the attention of Dr. Ronald Fieve, a psychiatrist who was then developing the new lithium treatment for manic depression. Within a few months Ruth was able to remain stable day after day. She now looks back on those times as bad years. She remembers, "Before I began taking the lithium I'd send out invitations to a party during a manic period and Bob [her husband] would have to cancel it later because I'd be in bed depressed. Now, if I plan a party it will go ahead as scheduled. I know I will be able to function" (Seligmann & Shapiro, 1979, p. 102).

Lithium must be monitored very carefully because it is a dangerous drug. It is highly toxic, and blood tests must be taken to measure the level of toxicity. Monitoring the heart is often advisable as well, since lithium is suspected of causing death in some cases due to cardiovascular blockage (Jaffe, 1977).

Antianxiety Drugs The antianxiety drugs are often referred to as minor tranquilizers. Valium and Librium are among the most commonly known. The minor tranquilizers are not used to treat psychotics. They are used to help individuals with personality problems in which tension or anxiety is a central feature. Among their side effects are drowsiness and lethargy. The minor tranquilizers are toxic and can lead to dependence. Valium has been particularly abused. There has been an alarming number of reports of Valium addiction, in which convulsions occur upon sudden withdrawal of the drug. Many critics argue that these drugs are dispensed like Band-Aids and that our society is too quick to turn to drugs and too drug-dependent. These critics argue that the drugs should be treated with more respect and used judiciously.

As neurologists and psychologists gain a deeper understanding of the brain and nervous system and pharmacologists further their knowledge of the interactions between chemistry and biology, newer and more efficient drug treatments may become available. Research continues. The future of drug therapy is rich with promise and fraught with dangers.

ELECTROCONVULSIVE THERAPY

Electroconvulsive therapy, or electric shock treatment, is a relatively recent refinement of a crude procedure first used in the days when George Washington was president. In the chapter Prologue you met Johann Christian Reil, the German anatomist and neurologist who is credited with the first use of shock therapy. Dr. Reil had some curious ideas about shocking patients back to normality. As you'll recall, these included shooting off cannons behind unsuspecting patients, throwing sleeping patients into icy ponds, and scaring patients by having attendants dress up as ghosts. Today, no one would recommend doing such things. Nonetheless, Reil can be credited with thinking up instant therapy, in which dramatic changes are brought about by a sudden shock or trauma. This idea is the essence of electroconvulsive therapy.

During the 1700s, the American clinician Benjamin Rush (another person with good intentions) practiced a form of shock therapy on his patients. Rush took patients whom he had diagnosed as suffering from mental disorders and made an incision on the back of the neck with a dirty instrument so that an infection would begin. Eventually a large boil would develop. Rush's "shock therapy" involved popping the boil "to excite atomic discharge from the neighborhood of the brain" (Roueche, 1980). By today's standards this is obviously an ineffective and dangerous treatment, not to mention a particularly disgusting one.

By 1890 the development of germ theory provided a new kind of shock therapy. An Austrian neurologist named Julius Wagner von Jauregg injected an extract of tubercle bacillus into a mentally disturbed patient in order to ignite what he thought might be an explosively curative fever. It didn't work. Undaunted, he tried again in 1914, injecting the malaria organism into his patents. This time he noticed a marked improvement. The patients he had treated were suffering from general paresis, and today we know that the sustained fever and sudden buildup of antibodies caused by the injection of the malaria organism may have attacked the syphilis. At that time, however, the reasons for its effect were unknown.

In 1921 the discovery of insulin led to another kind of chemical shock therapy. An Austrian clinician named Manfred Sakel (1900–1957), working in Berlin, began using insulin to induce chemical shock. Most people are familiar with insulin and its treatment for those who have diabetes. Dia-

ELECTROCONVULSIVE THERAPY (ECT) Treatment of mental disorders by passing an electric current through the brain for a certain amount of time, which causes a convulsion, a temporary suspension of breathing, and a coma lasting from 5 to 30 minutes.

During modern ECT procedures, drugs are administered to prevent convulsions.

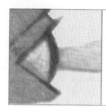

THE DEINSTITUTIONALIZATION OF THE MENTALLY ILL

In Figure 16.2 you can see the inpatient population of state and county mental hospitals in the United States and the changes over the years. The number of inpatients reached a high in 1955, at a little over 550,000, and then decreased dramatically. By 1975 the inpatient population was below 200,000, a decrease of two thirds in 20 years.

The downward trend beginning in about 1956 was due in part to the availability of new antipsychotic drugs that helped control psychotic reactions and enabled patients to be released from the institutions and rehabilitated in their own communities. This emphasis on **deinstitutionalization** increased at the beginning of the Johnson administration in 1964 when the country undertook a massive effort to reform mental health systems. Instead of maintaining large state and county institutions, the intention was to deliver services at community mental health

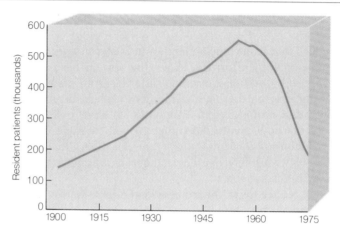

Figure 16.2   *The inpatient population of state and county mental hospitals from the 1950s through the 1970s. In the last 25 years the policies of deinstitutionalization and improved treatment have reduced the inpatient population by two thirds.* (SOURCE: *Bassuk & Gerson, 1978, p. 46*)

centers where patients would be close to their families and homes.

The idea behind the change was a good one. Data were showing that

patients who could live at home and see psychologists or psychiatrists as outpatients were faring much better. Deinstitutionalization also helped improve the institutions for those who had to remain. In the late 1950s, it had not been uncommon for psychiatrists or psychologists to see each patient only 15 minutes per month! Patients were crammed into rooms, many of them lying on floors with no place to go and

---

INSULIN SHOCK THERAPY
A method, infrequently used today, for treating severe psychotic reactions. A coma is created by reducing blood sugar by injecting excessive amounts of insulin.

DEINSTITUTIONALIZATION
The practice, begun in the early 1960s, of placing mental patients in community health centers or treating them on an outpatient basis.

betes occurs when abnormal functioning of the pancreas causes a lack of insulin, which is needed to break down blood sugar. If a healthy individual is injected with a large dose of insulin, the result is disorientation, collapse, sleep, and finally coma. This final stage is known as a hypoglycemic (low blood sugar) coma, since the sugar levels are dangerously low because the body sugars have been broken down by the excess insulin. Sakel was initially interested in using hypoglycemic coma to help morphine addicts get through withdrawal symptoms. Then in 1933 he wondered whether insulin-induced shock would be effective in treating other excited states, especially schizophrenia. In fact, this **insulin shock therapy** has been found by many investigators to be somewhat effective in helping to calm mental patients and reduce psychotic episodes for a few weeks, although no one knows why. Insulin shock therapy is still used in some places, but it can be dangerous. In most cases it has been replaced by electroconvulsive therapy (ECT).

After reading about insulin shock therapy, two Italian clinicians, Ugo Cerletti and Lucio Bini, developed what they believed to be an improve-

not enough staff to attend to them. Now, the drastic overcrowding has been reduced, and psychiatrists and staff can spend more time with individual patients. Many institutions have been carpeted and made more attractive, and offer their patients more adequate facilities.

Deinstitutionalization has been criticized, however (Bassuk & Gerson, 1978). In many instances it has failed because of lack of money and local support. Although the number of patients hospitalized in state and county hospitals has decreased by two thirds since 1955, the rate of admissions has increased 129 percent. This means that the same patients are being admitted and discharged numerous times. The Vietnam war in the late 1960s and the inflation that followed ate away at the financial support required by many community mental health centers. These centers were then unable to maintain the staff necessary to assist the deinstitutionalized patients in their neighborhoods. Many centers saved money by staffing with paraprofessionals instead of professionals, and the quality of care declined (Lewis, 1981). And, all too often, deinstitution-

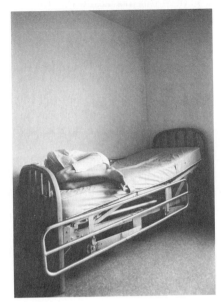

Even today many patients lead lonely, isolated lives in institutions where care is inadequate.

alization meant no care at all. As a result, many patients were discharged to "a lonely existence in hostile communities without adequate care" (Bassuk & Gerson, 1978 p. 46).

The reputation of big mental institutions as inhumane places where people are "warehoused" has helped

gain support for community mental health centers. Yet many patients discharged without adequate preparation end up in flop houses or on the streets, lacking both shelter and food. In pointing out the problems of deinstitutionalization, Bassuk and Gerson have said:

neither the hospital nor the community approach is inherently the more humane. Some 100 years ago the trustees of the Willard Asylum for the Insane in western New York explained the purpose of their new institution. . . . It would be a home "for those people who have neither home nor friends, and who are without the means financially or capacity intellectually to provide for themselves, with intellect shattered, minds darkened, living amid delusions, a constant prey to unrest, haunted by unreal fantasies and wild imagining. They now have in their sore misfortune a safe refuge, kindly care, constant watching, and are as comfortable as their circumstances will allow. This is a result over which every humane and Christian citizen of the state will rejoice." The subsequent failure to maintain and improve institutions with that purpose seems to us to reflect economic, political, administrative and clinical realities rather than any inherent fallacy in the goals themselves. (1978, p. 53)

ment. They called their new treatment *electroshock* and published a paper about it in 1938. It consisted of administering an electric shock to the brain, which caused a convulsion, a kind of epileptic seizure. Cerletti and Bini used their treatment for schizophrenia and reported encouraging results.

Modern researchers have found ECT to be most effective against depression and the depressive lows encountered in bipolar disorder. In the modern procedure, the patient is injected with a muscle-relaxing drug that prevents the convulsions that used to accompany electroshock therapy and that often resulted in broken bones and torn ligaments. An electrode is placed on each temple and, typically, between 80 and 90 volts are passed through the brain for a fraction of a second. During that time, cerebral functioning is halted, short-circuited. About four or five minutes of unconsciousness usually follow. The beneficial results derived are believed to occur because of that brief halting of cerebral functioning. How or why ECT works has never been clearly understood.

Many clinicians feel that ECT is harmless and beneficial if used in the appropriate circumstances. Its use has not gone unchallenged, however. It has been discovered that some long-term memories may be impaired after multiple therapeutic treatments (Costello, 1976). In addition, it has been argued that shocks to other parts of the body may be as effective in treating major depression and depression resulting from bipolar disorder as are shocks to the brain. This effect may indicate that depression can be alleviated by operant conditioning, in that the patient learns not to be depressed because depression is followed by a shock; in this view, the improvement is not due to any particular cessation of cerebral functioning (Costello, 1976).

The effectiveness of ECT is hotly debated. Some researchers, for instance Stuart C. Yudofsky of the New York Psychiatric Institute, predict "a major resurgence in the utilization of ECT in the 1980s" (Yudofsky, 1981, p. 328). Yudofsky cites a number of reasons for this return. First, ECT is becoming a safer and more precise treatment; second, it avoids the dangerous side effects of some currently available drugs; and third, research may eventually explain ECT's effectiveness in treating depression. Other researchers, skeptical about the long-term effectiveness of ECT, are worried about the possibility of permanent memory impairment.

PSYCHOSURGERY

Psychosurgery is "a destruction of some region of the brain in order to alleviate severe, and otherwise intractable, psychiatric disorders" (Valenstein, 1980, p. 12). Brain surgery undertaken to repair damage resulting from strokes or accidents or to treat tumors or spastic disorders is not considered psychosurgery. Similarly, brain surgery performed to prevent epilepsy is not considered psychosurgery because the problem is more neurological than psychological.

The first case of surgical destruction of part of an uninjured brain for the purpose of changing behavior was reported by Gottlieb Burckhardt in 1891. Burckhardt destroyed a portion of the cerebral cortex between the sensory and motor areas in the hope of eliminating the hallucinations of one of his patients. Burckhardt's work was based on some very limited data, and after one of his patients died, he was persuaded by his colleagues to cease experimenting. In 1910 the Russian neurosurgeon Ludwig Puusepp destroyed sections of the brain within the central fissure in three patients with bipolar disorder. He thought the outcomes were very poor and did not justify further attempts.

Frontal Lobotomies In 1935 the Portuguese neurologist Antonio de Êgas Moniz developed the technique that was the real beginning of psychosurgery. He had heard that the destruction of prefrontal areas in the brain of monkeys had had a calming effect on some of the more excitable animals, and he decided that destroying the prefrontal lobes in humans might be a way of controlling dangerous or manic patients. By 1936 Moniz and his colleague Almeida Lima reported encouraging results among their first 20 patients. The operation, called a **frontal lobotomy,** is a rather dramatic and, to some, an indelicate operation. It makes use of a surgical device shaped somewhat like an ice pick, called a leucotome, which is inserted behind the eyeball and pushed or hammered beyond the orbit of the eye until the point punctures the brain. It is then slashed back and forth, destroying many of the white nerve fibers connecting one part of the brain with the other. Moniz first performed this operation on a 63-year-old former prostitute who was suffering from brain syphilis. Two months after the lobotomy, he reported that she was cured. Obviously, this was insufficient time in which to make such a judgment, and, from our modern understanding of medicine, we know that such a surgical procedure could not possibly have cured syphilis (Valenstein, 1980). But Moniz was a highly respected neurologist and his results gained widespread attention, especially in 1944, when he·was partially paralyzed after being shot by one of his lobotomized patients (Valenstein, 1973).

In the 1950s neurosurgeons Walter Freeman and James Watts championed Moniz's methods in the United States. Many hundreds of lobotomies were performed in this country, generally with mixed results. Supporters felt that the operations were valuable but needed to be refined. Opponents felt that physicians were deliberately causing irreparable brain damage and turning "troublesome" patients into more controllable semianimated vegetables.

The technique was accepted, though, for a number of reasons. First, it was practiced by surgeons, a highly respected group. Second, alternatives were lacking or limited. Third, in 1949 the Nobel Prize had been given to Dr. Moniz for his discovery of the frontal lobotomy. Approximately 35,000 such operations have been performed in the United States since 1936.

By 1970, however, interest in psychosurgery was beginning to wane. Effective drug treatments had become available for calming the uncontrollable and for treating mania. Moreover, the overall results from most lobotomy procedures had been disappointing. The majority of the patients either were unchanged or seemed to degenerate afterwards. Finally, a surge of interest in human rights and patient rights arose, emphasizing that the patient must be properly informed before consenting to such a procedure.

The strongest critics argued that psychosurgery should be banned altogether. They pointed out, in addition to the above concerns, that many surgeons admit to having extremely little knowledge about what alterations can be expected in behavior following the surgery (Greenberg, 1977).

Yet in the last few years, psychosurgery is once again attracting attention. Part of the renewed interest stems from the fact that modern psychosurgical techniques are safer and result in less gross physical and intellectual impairment than did the older lobotomy procedures. Also, the area of the brain that is destroyed in modern operations is much smaller and more localized. A psychosurgical operation that has recently become popular is the **cingulotomy.** During a cingulotomy, brain tissue in the area of the cingulate gyrus of the cerebral cortex is destroyed or removed. The surgical procedure is used in the United States on people who suffer severe pain or who have severe psychiatric disorders. A large research team headed by Suzanne Corkin evaluated the neurological and behavioral deficits of 137 cingulotomy patients from one month to ten years after their surgery. Except that some lost the ability to draw as well as they had previously, no other neurological or behavioral deficits could be found (Corkin, 1980).

Modern psychosurgical techniques also include surgery in the areas of the amygdala, thalamus, hypothalamus, and midbrain, as well as surgery on multiple sites at one time. Table 16.1 lists the sites of brain operations and the diagnostic labels given to patients who have had these operations. As you can see, most psychosurgical operations have been done to relieve pain or depression.

PSYCHOSURGERY
Brain surgery for the purpose of altering behavior or alleviating mental disorder.

FRONTAL LOBOTOMY
Psychosurgical procedure, rarely performed today, in which a sharp instrument is inserted through the orbit of the eye and then slashed back and forth in order to separate specific nerve fibers connecting one part of the brain to another.

CINGULOTOMY
A modern psychosurgical procedure in which the cerebral tissue of the cingulate gyrus is destroyed. Often used as a way of controlling chronic pain.

Table 16.1   Diagnoses and sites of psychosurgery conducted in the United States since 1970.

DIAGNOSTIC LABEL[a]	TOTAL NUMBER OF PATIENTS[b]	FRONTAL LOBE PROCEDURE	CINGULUM	AMYGDALA	THALAMUS	HYPOTHALAMUS	MULTIPLE TARGET SITES[c]	MIDBRAIN	BRAIN STIMULATION
Aggression	35			12(34.3%)		4(11.4%)	19(54.3%)		
Neurotic depression	136	9(6.6%)	127(93.4%)						
Psychotic depression[d]	11		11(100.0%)						
Fear and anxiety	4	3(75.0%)	1(25.0%)						
Obsessive-compulsive neurosis	37	9(24.3%)	25(67.6%)				3(8.1%)		
Schizo-affective disorders	7	7(100.0%)							
Schizophrenia and other psychoses	80		32(40.0%)				47(58.8%)		1(1.2%)
Drug addiction and alcoholism	14	1(7.1%)	13(92.9%)						
Pain	379	17(4.5%)	177(46.7%)		120(31.7%)		25(6.6%)	8(2.1%)	32(8.4%)
Psychopathic behavior	6				6(100.0%)				
"Emotional Illness"	9		1(11.1%)				8(88.9%)		
"Agitated states of the aged"	2	2(100.0%)							
Involutional melancholia	1		1(100.0%)						
Epilepsy with psychiatric disorders	45			45(100.0%)					

SOURCE: Valenstein, 1980, p. 103.

Note: For each diagnostic category, the number and percentage of patients are listed according to target of brain surgery. Among the 35 patients labeled aggressive, for example, 12 (or 34.3 percent) underwent surgery in the area of the amygdala. The articles from which this information was drawn are listed in Valenstein, 1977 (Appendix 4). As far as could be determined, only data from patients operated on after 1970 were included.

[a]Labels are those used in the published articles.

[b]In those cases where authors did not provide a quantitative breakdown of their patients, diagnostic labels were assigned in proportion to the average frequency of usage of these labels for psychosurgical patients.

[c]Multiple target sites include the cingulum, amygdala, substantia innominata, and thalamic structure, in different combinations.

[d]Including manic-depressive syndrome.

The Effectiveness of Modern Psychosurgery   A few years ago the National Commission for the Protection of Human Subjects of Biomedical and Behavioral Research and the National Institute of Mental Health conducted a pilot study and a follow-up in order to investigate the effectiveness of psychosurgery. The investigators examined 52 who had undergone psychosurgical operations between 1965 and 1974. The study included eight control subjects who had similar psychiatric illnesses but who had not had the surgical procedures. The patients were evaluated by psychiatrists, psychologists, neurologists, social workers, electroencephalographers, and other experts at the Boston University Medical Center and Boston State Hospital.

The members of the study found that a large majority of patients had received adequate preparation beforehand. They had discussed the risks and benefits with their physician and understood what was likely to happen. It was judged that 27 of the cases (52 percent) improved markedly. No detectable neurological damage or deficit was noted in these 27 cases. The remaining 25 showed less improvement, from slight benefit to, in three cases, definite worsening. No significant neurological damage was attributed to the surgery. Although it had been assumed that depression was most successfully treated by psychosurgery, the follow-up studies showed that a favorable or unfavorable outcome was not associated with a particular mental disorder. It was decided that further investigation into psychosurgery was reasonable and that psychosurgery may in some cases be valuable. Furthermore, the portrayals of postsurgical semianimated vegetables in the popular novel and film *One Flew over the Cuckoo's Nest* (which was sometimes the fate of psychosurgery patients in the 1930s and 1940s owing to the more extensive cutting practiced then) was not found to have a parallel in any of the 52 patients or considered likely to happen with modern psychosurgical techniques (Mirsky & Orzack, 1980).

Psychotherapy

Psychotherapy is any noninvasive psychological technique designed to bring about a positive change in someone's behavior, personality, or adjustment. *Noninvasive* means not directly interacting with the body or its chemistry, such as in somatic therapies, which rely on drugs, surgery, or shock. Although there are many kinds of psychotherapy, they all have certain things in common.

In individual psychotherapy the patient or client interacts directly with the therapist in a personal and trust-inspiring atmosphere. Concerns are discussed and problems can be freely aired. Through interaction and the use of psychotherapeutic techniques the person comes to have a better understanding of himself or herself. With this understanding, and supported by the psychotherapeutic encounter, the person may be better able to adjust to the stress and demands of his or her situation.

The focus varies with the type of psychotherapy. Some therapies emphasize **insight,** that is, the therapist attempts to help the client or patient develop a better understanding of a situation or problem. **Action** therapies usually focus directly on changing a habit or problem that has been troublesome. Some psychotherapies are **directive,** that is, the therapist actually guides the client, giving instructions and advice. Other therapies are **nondirective,** in that primary responsibility for the direction of the therapy is placed on the client's shoulders, and the therapist only helps the client find personal solutions. The emphases of different therapies are shown in Figure 16.3.

PSYCHOANALYSIS

Psychoanalysis is an insight therapy based on the theory and work of Sigmund Freud. There are many variations of psychoanalysis based on work by Freud's contemporaries and predecessors.

In psychoanalysis, abnormal behavior is assumed to be the result of unconscious conflicts. By using special techniques the psychoanalyst hopes to uncover these unconscious conflicts and repressed memories and hence to explain and deal with the motivation behind the abnormal behavior.

The techniques Freud devised for uncovering unconscious conflicts include free association and dream interpretation, which we have touched

PSYCHOTHERAPY
A category of methods for treating psychological disorder. The primary technique is conversation between the patient and the therapist.

INSIGHT THERAPY
Psychotherapy by attempting to uncover the deep causes of the patient's or client's difficulty. The therapist tries to guide the individual to self-understanding.

ACTION THERAPY
Psychotherapy in which the therapist helps the patient or client take direct and immediate action to overcome problems through the use of special techniques.

DIRECTIVE THERAPY
Any approach in which the therapist takes an active role and directs the patient or client to confront problems and life situations.

NONDIRECTIVE THERAPY
A therapeutic technique based on humanistic psychology in which the therapist creates a supportive atmosphere so that clients can work out their own problems.

	DIRECTIVE	NONDIRECTIVE
INSIGHT	Psychoanalysis Gestalt psychology Transactional analysis	Client-centered Existential
ACTION	Rational-emotive therapy Behavior therapy Cognitive restructuring Hypnotherapy	Self-hypnosis

Figure 16.3 *Dimensions of psychotherapy. The term* insight therapy *is generally reserved for therapies whose goal is an in-depth understanding of the individual's self. Although action therapies sometimes help individuals develop insight into their problems, the term* action therapy *refers in general to therapeutic attempts to deal directly and immediately with specific difficulties or current problems.*

upon in earlier chapters. In free association, the patient is to say whatever comes to mind, no matter how ridiculous. Freud believed that unconscious desires were always brewing just below the surface; he argued, therefore, that the first word to come to mind might be closely related to the conflict. In dream interpretation, the patient describes the manifest content of a dream, and works with the analyst to uncover the latent meaning. The idea is that the unconscious thoughts and conflicts will come to the person during sleep but that a psychic censor disguises the conflict in the dream so that it appears in symbolic form and must be analyzed before its real content can be understood.

Freud also looked for points of resistance and analyzed those. By **resistance** he meant that the patient balks at the analyst's attempts to probe certain areas. Freud felt that this reaction was a defense of the unconscious against giving up its secrets; resistance was therefore a sign that the therapist was getting close to the problem.

Analysis of **transference** is another important aspect of Freudian psychoanalysis. The patient often transfers feelings onto the analyst and then behaves as though the analyst were the "rejecting father" or "overbearing mother." In fact, Freud liked to have his patients recline on a couch so that he could sit behind them, thereby removing his physical presence far enough so that the transference became easier. He believed that the analyst could gain insight into patients' thought processes by observing how they began to transfer their feelings from their parent or lover to their analyst.

In its original form Freudian psychoanalysis took a very long time. Freud felt that his therapy sessions should include three to five meetings a week for as long as six years.* At costs of often $70 to $100 an hour, very few people can afford such intensive therapy.

To reduce the expense and the amount of time involved, modern psychoanalysts have developed techniques for shortening the therapy, to perhaps an hour a week for a few years. They have modified Freud's theories and procedures in other ways as well. Neo-Freudians, as these modern analysts are often called, sometimes attach as much importance to cultural, social, and interpersonal factors as to the psychosexual aspects of development that Freud emphasized (see Chapter 13). Many have dispensed with the Freudian couch, and they may explore conscious thoughts and desires as much as unconscious motives. Like Freud, however, neo-Freudians believe that insight into the unconscious processes is the key to resolving mental disorder.

HUMANISTIC-EXISTENTIAL THERAPIES

Freud felt that people were motivated by instinctive urges toward aggression and death. Freud's view of human beings was essentially pessimistic. The humanistic-existential view, on the other hand, is optimistic; human beings are regarded as capable of living rich, fulfilling lives, relatively free of urges toward unhappiness and destruction. The emphasis is on fulfilling potential, or self-actualizing. Great importance is also given to having a sense of belonging, a feeling that you have an important role to play within

---

*In Woody Allen's movie *Sleeper,* Woody is placed in suspended animation for 2,000 years. When he comes to and finds out how long he's been asleep he remarks, "My analyst was a strict Freudian. If I'd been going to him all this time I'd almost be cured now."

the society and that you are not an outsider. Humanistic-existential therapies are considered to be insight therapies.

Client-centered Therapy   Carl Rogers, the humanistic psychologist, is the founder of humanistic **client-centered therapy.** Unlike psychoanalysts, who feel that unconscious motives and drives are the crucial aspects of an individual's personality, Rogers argues that conscious thoughts, feelings, and self-concept are primary. Client-centered therapy is often called non-directive therapy because the therapist refrains from guiding the therapy in any particular direction. The client is considered responsible for his or her therapy and decides the direction in which the therapy will proceed. (Humanists shun the word "patient" because they do not view their clients as sick.)

The client-centered therapist relies on special techniques. First, there is an unconditional positive regard for each client. The client is accepted totally. Second, the therapist attempts to make the therapeutic atmosphere personal and forthright. The therapist doesn't hide behind his or her professional role. Third, the therapist tries to develop genuine empathy for the client.

In nondirective therapy the therapist never advises the client or tells him or her what to do. Instead, the therapist "reflects" the thoughts of the client and the client's feelings by repeating or stating in different words what the client has said or by noting the client's emotional state. The following conversation between a client-centered therapist and a client will give you an impression of this technique.

CLIENT: Sometimes, even when there's no good reason to, I tell lies. I don't know why I do.

THERAPIST: (Remains silent)

CLIENT: I don't know why; it's as though there was some kind of drive or force that makes me do it.

THERAPIST: And how does this make you feel?

CLIENT: It makes me feel bad. I don't like to think of myself as a liar.

THERAPIST: When you tell lies, then, it makes you uncomfortable.

CLIENT: Yes. I feel better when I don't tell lies, when I don't feel the need to.

THERAPIST: There are times when you don't tell lies, and when that happens it makes you feel better?

CLIENT: Yes, I really like it better when I don't, but I don't seem to have any control.

THERAPIST: Then you have no control?

CLIENT: Well, sometimes I can decide what I want to do and then I feel better.

THERAPIST: So sometimes you can control yourself. You can control your life and this makes you feel better.

CLIENT: Yes, I suppose that's the main thing, to learn to control my own life.

THERAPIST: (Does not respond, remains silent)

CLIENT: That's really what I need to do, to control things for myself.

THERAPIST: You want your life to be in your own hands.

RESISTANCE
In psychoanalytic theory, opposition to attempts to bring repressed thoughts into the conscious mind.

TRANSFERENCE
A concept developed by Freud that generally refers to the tendency of a person in therapy to transfer to the therapist perceptions and feelings about other people rather than seeing the therapist as he or she really is.

CLIENT-CENTERED THERAPY
A type of psychotherapy developed by Carl Rogers and based on the belief that the client is responsible for his or her own growth and self-actualization. The therapist creates an atmosphere of acceptance, refrains from directing the client, and reflects back to the client what the client has said.

The therapist in this exchange was unconditionally accepting of the client and avoided interjecting her own thoughts and feelings. Instead, the therapist helped the client understand and reach his feelings and thoughts. This technique of active listening can be valuable in getting to know someone much more intimately.

The aim of humanistic therapy is to expand clients' self-image and self-perception and to help them discover their own solutions to what are, after all, their own problems.

Existential Therapy **Existential therapy** is much like client-centered therapy, except that it emphasizes the idea of free will. Existential therapist Rollo May has argued that people have learned to defer their own responsibility and self-image in favor of society's. They begin to feel like nonentities, lost in society. Existential therapists try to restore people's courage so that they can make choices for themselves and feel in control of the environment rather than the other way around.

Humanistic and existential therapies are so similar that they are often referred to under one heading, humanistic-existential therapy. Both aim at improving a person's self-concept and developing self-acceptance and a belief in one's own ability.

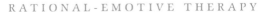

RATIONAL-EMOTIVE THERAPY

Rational-emotive therapy is an action therapy developed by Albert Ellis. Ellis based his therapy on the assumption that people engage in self-defeating behaviors because they hold onto beliefs that are unrealistic or faulty (Ellis, 1962). Rational-emotive therapy focuses on changing these beliefs by getting the client to understand that the faulty beliefs are the problem. For example, a student who, turned down for medical school, is deeply depressed and on the verge of suicide has obviously developed faulty beliefs about the world and his or her situation in it. The faulty belief is that getting into medical school is the only possible way to have a happy and fulfilling life, and that without it there is no point in living. Rational-emotive therapy attacks the faulty belief, examining the emotional beliefs rationally.

Rational-emotive therapy is also a directive therapy. The therapist directly interacts with the client and points out irrational beliefs and values and the way in which they influence the client's thinking. The therapist may even give the client homework to do in order to help overcome the belief systems. The hope is that eventually the client will learn a new belief system that is rational. The following is an example of an exchange between a rational-emotive therapist and a client. The client is a college student who has never been out on a date. Although he wants to, he's too afraid.

CLIENT: She's really nice, and I'd like to ask her out, but I just don't dare.

THERAPIST: What do you think will happen if she turns you down?

CLIENT: Oh, no. I couldn't bear it. It would be awful.

THERAPIST: If she turned you down it would be awful and you couldn't bear it. Isn't that a little strong?

CLIENT: But it *would* make me feel awful if she turned me down.

Albert Ellis, the founder of rational-emotive therapy.

THERAPIST: Why? Does everyone in the world have to like you? If she turns you down isn't there somebody else you could ask out who would be just as good? Even better? Do you expect everyone in the world to like you?

CLIENT: Well, suppose I asked her out and she turned me down and I asked somebody else out and she turned me down, too.

THERAPIST: You've got two people turning you down and you haven't even asked anybody out yet. Suppose only 1 percent of the women in the world liked you, and the other 99 percent didn't like you. What would it be like then?

CLIENT: I suppose it would be pretty awful.

THERAPIST: Why? How long could it take you to ask 100 women out? A couple of weeks? A couple of weeks, and you would have a date. You would finally find someone who liked you. If you liked her you'd be happy. Who cares what the other 99 think?

CLIENT: I don't know. You make it sound all simple.

THERAPIST: Well, it's not that simple, but I think you can make a good beginning by asking her out. Why don't you do that as homework? Go up and ask her out.

CLIENT: I don't know.

THERAPIST: What do you have to lose?

CLIENT: Nothing, I guess.

THERAPIST: That's right, nothing. Everybody doesn't have to like you. As long as they're not throwing rocks at you, it's OK. I know a good politician who says he can tell when he reaches a just solution, because that's when everybody hates him. Think about that. Now, you'll ask her out for homework and you'll record her reactions and how you felt about it and how things went. Right?

CLIENT: Ok, I'll try it, but it might not work.

THERAPIST: And what should you tell yourself if you think it might not work?

CLIENT: That it doesn't matter. That there's more fish in the sea, right?

THERAPIST: Right.

As you can see, this therapy is directive. The therapist is forcefully trying to get the client to see the illogic of his fear, which could lead to a life of isolation. The client needs to understand that the consequences of being rejected are minor and the rewards of tolerating a few rejections for an eventual acceptance could be major.

Rational-emotive therapy follows a particular pattern of therapist-client interaction, as do other therapies. But the pattern isn't rigid. The different psychotherapies don't have a set of strict rules that each therapist must rigidly follow. Therapists are human beings, and they have their own personalities. They may vary their techniques from client to client even though they stay within the philosophical boundaries of a particular therapeutic approach. Observers once recorded Albert Ellis during therapy sessions to see whether he actually used the rational-emotive techniques he claimed to use. The results indicated that he did use these techniques, but also that he varied his approach considerably from client to client based on his own experience (Becker & Rosenfeld, 1976).

(a)

(b)

(c)

(a) *In group therapy situations a number of people join together and share experiences and feelings under the supervision of a therapist.* (b) *In traditional psychoanalysis the patient rests on a couch out of direct view of the analyst.* (c) *Most modern therapists sit face-to-face with their clients.*

GESTALT THERAPY
A form of psychotherapy originated by Perls, who adapted the fundamental concepts of traditional psychoanalysis but placed greater emphasis on the immediacy and importance of the here and now in breaking down the influence of the past. The patient-therapist relationship is more active and democratic than in a traditional psychoanalysis.

PSYCHODRAMA
A specialized technique of psychotherapy developed by J. L. Moreno in which patients act out the roles, situations, and fantasies relevant to their personal problems. Psychodrama is usually conducted in front of a small audience of patients.

SENSITIVITY TRAINING
Group sessions conducted for the purpose of developing personal and interpersonal sensitivity to feelings and needs. The feelings among group members are channeled so that their own self-acceptance and growth are enhanced.

TRANSACTIONAL ANALYSIS
A form of interpersonal therapy based on the interactions of "child," "adult," and "parent" ego states.

GESTALT THERAPY

Frederick (Fritz) Perls developed **Gestalt therapy,** an insight therapy. Gestalt therapy is not directly related to Gestalt psychology, which is concerned with perception. Instead, Gestalt therapy is based heavily on Freudian psychoanalytic ideas. As a technique, however, it differs from the Freudian approach to therapy.

Gestalt means "whole" in German. Fritz Perls felt that an adequate therapy must take into consideration all of the different parts of a person's life. The ultimate goal is to balance and integrate emotion, thought, and action. Through awareness developed during therapy, imbalances in thoughts, actions, and feelings can be checked and a whole personality can be created. The therapy is based on helping the client leave behind unneeded defenses and release pent-up emotions.

Gestalt therapy emphasizes what is happening here and now rather than what happened in the past or what may happen in the future. It focuses on what exists rather than on what is absent, and on what is real rather than on what is fantasy (Korchin, 1976).

This focus on the present brings the client into contact with his or her life, feelings, and thoughts as they really exist. The client is required to speak in the first person and to use the active voice. In this way the client builds a personality centered on himself or herself. For example, the client would be encouraged to say "I am unhappy" (statement from the self) instead of "Anybody could see that it's reasonable that I would be upset" (deferring to others).

Perls often conducted exercises in which clients played out different parts of their personality. In this way they developed awareness about their own feelings, actions, and thoughts. The goal of Gestalt therapy is to enable clients to take responsibility for their own actions and, starting with someone who is fragmented into many social roles and who feels helpless, to reintegrate all aspects of the personality into one whole, functioning person.

GROUP THERAPIES

One of the earliest group approaches was developed by J. L. Moreno, a Viennese psychiatrist who coined the term *group psychotherapy*. **Psychodrama** originated at Vienna's Theatre of Spontaneity in 1921. In psychodrama, an individual may take the role of a family member and portray or act out that person's behavior and feelings. Therapy comes from the release of pent-up emotions and from insights into the way others feel and behave as a result of playing out their roles.

Group therapy was rare before World War II. After World War II and again after the Korean War, the army found that they did not have enough therapists to see all of the soldiers who needed help. Consequently, they decided to try pairing more than one soldier with each therapist. The results were surprising and beneficial. Under the direction of the therapist, members of the therapy group discovered that they often had experiences and insights to share with one another. They were relieved to find that others had similar problems.

Most therapy groups have seven to ten members. Psychiatrists and psychologists frequently see clients individually once a week and also in a group once a week.

Encounter and sensitivity groups help people develop a better understanding of themselves and others.

Sensitivity Training and Encounter Groups During **sensitivity training,** participants learn to become sensitive to the needs and feelings of others and to trust others. For example, a person taking a "blind" walk is blindfolded and led about, having to trust the one who can see not to guide him or her into something that might be injurious. Or participants may extend their bodily awareness by touching others in a platonic way. They may embrace each other as a way of communicating human affection and a bond. In this way sensitivity to others as human beings is heightened and a feeling of belonging to the group is achieved.

In **encounter groups,** individuals confront each other and attempt to break through defenses and false fronts. Sometimes the discussions can be painfully honest and difficult to deal with. A qualified therapist should be present to keep things from getting out of hand, since tearing someone down is much easier than building someone up. The purpose of encounter groups is not to cause psychological injury but to help people encounter themselves by having others challenge their assertions and beliefs.

Transactional Analysis **Transactional analysis,** originated by Eric Berne, is used with groups or couples. The idea behind transactional analysis is described in Berne's popular book *Games People Play* (1964). Berne argues that partners often create unwritten rules that may satisfy their own needs but get in the way of an honest and healthy relationship. Figure 16.4 shows several transactions. Horizontal transactions from A to A, that is, from adult to adult, indicate healthy interactions. In the diagonal transactions, P represents the parent role and C the child role (roles that anyone may adopt). The latter transactions, in which someone takes the parent role and someone takes the child role, may not be healthy interactions. If social interactions are analyzed to find out what kind of a role a person is playing, the rules can be changed to promote mutual satisfaction, and unproductive games can be ended.

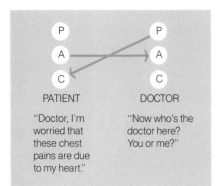

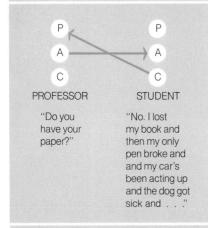

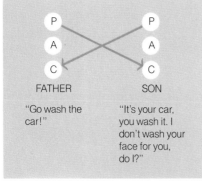

Figure 16.4 *Transactional analysis. Eric Berne describes the interactions shown here as crossed transactions. According to Berne, the personality can express itself as a child, adult, or parent (roughly equivalent to Freud's concept of id, ego, and superego). Healthy transactions are from adult to adult. It's easy to see that the diagonal transactions are likely to create problems.*

BEHAVIOR THERAPY

Behavior therapy relies on learning theory and the principles of conditioning. Behavior therapy is a radical departure from the psychotherapies we have considered to this point. Behavioral therapists are not interested in feelings or dreams for purposes of therapy, but only in observable behaviors and how these behaviors might be changed through conditioning or social learning.

Each therapeutic treatment deals with a specific problem, and terminology such as passive-aggressive personality disorder or somatoform disorder is generally not used, since behaviorists are concerned with observable behavior rather than with constructs such as personality or mental disorder. Behavioral therapies rely on the principles of classical conditioning, operant conditioning, or social learning (described in Chapter 6) or on a combination of all three.

Classical Conditioning Therapy You may recall from Chapter 6 that Little Albert's fear of the rat was created through classical conditioning. Behavioral therapists may make use of a paradigm of this experience called **aversive conditioning.** Aversive conditioning is effective in many situations, for instance, in helping a person stop smoking or drinking.

To treat alcoholism in this fashion, the client may be taken to a laboratory where a bar, similar to a neighborhood bar, has been set up. The taste and smell of the alcohol and the feeling of the surroundings are all reminiscent of the place where the client usually drinks. However, an unconditioned stimulus, an electric shock, is given as the client is drinking. The favorite drink is continually paired with this painful stimulus. After enough pairings, the alcohol begins to elicit an aversive fear.

Aversive conditioning can bring on a very strong response. You might think that a human being, well aware of being in a laboratory under special circumstances, would take up old habits at home, safe in the knowledge that a drink wouldn't be accompanied by an electric shock. Yet this kind of therapy often works. It happened to me once. I like pears. A couple of years ago I was eating a pear and bit right through a large worm. Disgusting, isn't it? To this day I can't eat pears. It doesn't matter that the pears are canned or chopped thoroughly so that I can tell that there's nothing in them. It doesn't matter that I can look carefully and see no worm holes. The aversive conditioning was quite strong. I even hate writing about it.

Unfortunately, the desire to smoke or drink can be so strong that a person may be willing to risk the agony of taking a puff or a sip even after aversive therapy. In this case the conditioned response may quickly be extinguished and the person will end up smoking or drinking once again. Aversive conditioning works often enough, however, to make the attempt worthwhile.

Systematic Desensitization Joseph Wolpe at Temple University has developed what he calls **systematic desensitization.** His therapy is based on the idea of associating a relaxed and tranquil feeling with stimuli that previously caused anxiety. Look at the following hierarchy of fear written by a person who has arachnophobia, an unrealistic fear of spiders. The higher in the hierarchy the item is, the more frightening it is to him.

RATING	HIERARCHY ITEMS
1	Planning a picnic.
10	Hearing about the possibility spiders may be nearby.
20	Hearing someone describe an encounter with a spider.
30	Trying to decide how to make sure no spiders are in the house.
40	Having to do spring cleaning.
50	Thinking that a doctor will make me look at a spider during treatment.
60	Seeing a spider on a wall 20 feet away.
70	Crawling through a cobwebbed attic.
80	Seeing a spider crawl on me.
90	Having a large spider crawl on my face.
100	Falling into a dark pit where hundreds of spiders climb on me and try to crawl into my mouth and ears.

During systematic desensitization, the therapist leads the client through each of the steps in the hierarchy by having him lie down or relax in a chair and think carefully of his fear or even act it out. As he thinks about the first item in the hierarchy he may experience mild anxiety. Eventually he learns to relax while thinking of this item until, whenever he thinks of it, he feels calm and relaxed. Then the next step in the hierarchy is taken and this, too, is associated with relaxation and tranquility. After completing the hierarchy, fear of the object (in this case spiders) decreases, often dramatically.

Operant Behavioral Therapy Therapies based on operant conditioning attempt to end behavior that is inappropriate or to create appropriate behavior that is absent. Table 16.2 outlines the techniques used by operant conditioners in therapy. The following case study describes the effect of operant conditioning in therapy.

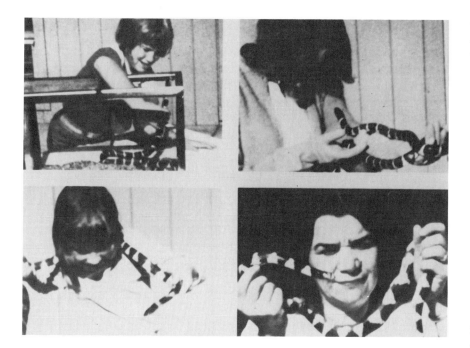

Through modeling and counter-conditioning, Albert Bandura was able to help those with snake phobia overcome their fears.

Table 16.2 Operant techniques used in behavior modification

TECHNIQUE	DESCRIPTION
Positive reinforcement	Providing a reinforcer following an appropriate response.
Negative reinforcement	Removing an aversive stimulus following an appropriate response.
Punishment	Providing an aversive stimulus following an inappropriate response.
Extinction	Removing the reinforcer that is maintaining the inappropriate response.
Positive reinforcement of incompatible response	Reinforcing behavior that is incompatible with the inappropriate response (for example, reinforcing telling the truth, which is incompatible with lying).
Time-out from positive reinforcement	Essentially producing boredom following an inappropriate behavior by removing the opportunity to engage in any reinforcing activities for a brief time (usually a few minutes).
Altering response effort	Structuring the environment in such a way that inappropriate responses are more difficult to make or appropriate responses are easier to make.
Token economy	Providing tokens (generalized secondary reinforcers) for appropriate behaviors. Tokens may later be redeemed for specific reinforcers unique to each person's taste.
Response cost	Imposing fines for inappropriate behavior (often used in conjunction with token economies).
Negative practice	Being forced to repeat an inappropriate behavior (for example, yelling) until it finally becomes aversive to engage in the behavior.

BEHAVIOR THERAPY: THE CASE OF JENNIFER

Jennifer, a five-year-old, had run away from home three times. Each time, she was brought back by either a policeman or a neighbor and was treated kindly and affectionately. Once she was given candy. She had not been treated in any way at home that might make her want to run away. Instead, she seemed to run away for the attention and the affection she found downtown. Downtown was approximately half a mile distant, down a sidewalk that ran along a park and did not cross streets. Jennifer was afraid to cross streets, but that long sidewalk made it easy for her to wander.

A behavior therapy program was set up in which a more important reinforcer, her mother's attention and affection, was provided to Jennifer for staying at home—a behavior that was incompatible with running away. At first the reinforcement was given on a "rich" schedule. Jennifer was reinforced every three minutes by her mother's hugs and praise if she has stayed home. Obviously, Jennifer wouldn't have had time to go anywhere in three minutes.

This schedule of reinforcement could not be maintained indefinitely, however, because it was too difficult for her mother. So, a slightly "leaner" schedule was begun, on which Jennifer was reinforced every five minutes. Then every ten minutes. Later every half hour. It became almost a game with Jennifer, and every half hour she would come running in to let her mother know it was time to hug and kiss.

Eventually the schedule was reduced even more, and the mother rewarded Jennifer only hourly. At that point a variable schedule of reinforcement, rather than a fixed schedule, was put into effect, so that Jennifer would not realize that she could run away and then get back in time for her reward. Her mother reinforced her on the average every two hours, but when the reinforcement would come was unpredictable. Finally the mother needed to reinforce Jennifer only once in the morning and once in the evening. Jennifer never ran away again.

Token economies are another popular means of modifying behavior. This technique uses tokens, such as poker chips, as currency. In institutions for delinquent children and state hospitals, token economies have been found to be effective in controlling and developing behaviors. The tokens function as conditioned reinforcers. They can be given following appropriate behavior or withdrawn following inappropriate behavior. They can be useful both for initiating and for terminating behavior. The tokens can later be traded in for items that are of value. Once behaviors are established, praise and other social reinforcers can take the place of the tokens.

Sometimes **behavioral contracts** are set up between two parties, and each one will agree on a behavior desired by the other. A husband, for example, may promise to play tennis once a week if his wife in return accompanies him bowling.

Behavioral therapies may also be based on social learning principles. In social learning, models are used to demonstrate desired behaviors or responses. Modeling has been found to be a very effective way of producing behavioral changes.

Considering John Watson's denial of the mind as an area of study, behaviorism represented a radical break from other forms of psychology. Nonetheless, many psychologists, especially clinical psychologists, use behavior therapy in conjunction with other forms of psychotherapy. In practice, behavior therapy isn't often used by itself (Farkas, 1980).

Cognitive Behavior Modification **Cognitive behavior modification,** or cognitive restructuring, is a therapeutic treatment in which a client is helped to obtain information about himself or herself through a series of unbiased encounters that make it possible for false beliefs to be disproved. Unlike rational emotive therapy, the client is not persuaded to change behavior but rather to explore, together with the therapist, beliefs, attitudes, and expectations in order to form hypotheses that can be tested. In this way the client can go out and test expectations in an experimental way, and through the experiences can come to a new cognitive understanding of his or her world.

Less difficult tasks are usually assigned first, and more difficult ones later. Occasionally the client's activities for the entire day will be planned moment by moment. These experiments help the client disconfirm erroneous assumptions about the world by testing them.

Cognitive behavior modification seems to be most effective with clients who selectively perceive their world as harmful or dangerous, ignoring any evidence to the contrary; who overgeneralize based on a few limited examples (for instance, because they fail at one thing, they decide they are totally worthless); who magnify unhappy events and blow them out of proportion (for instance, the loss of a job is the end of the world); and who engage in absolutist thinking (always seeing things as black or white, good or bad, never in between) (Hollon & Beck, 1978; Beck, Rush, Shaw & Emery, 1979; Meichenbaum, 1977).

In Table 16.3 are a number of "coping statements" that the client can say and rehearse as a means of restructuring cognitive understanding and bolstering himself or herself against stress. These statements are not simply slogans; their validity has been demonstrated to the client during experimental explorations of each statement in real situations.

TOKEN ECONOMIES
Training, based on operant conditioning, that uses tokens as rewards for certain behaviors. The tokens can be redeemed for special privileges, or primary reinforcers.

BEHAVIORAL CONTRACTS
A technique often used in behavior, group, or family therapy, in which a contract or bargain is struck. The client promises to engage in a certain behavior in return for a particular behavior from another.

COGNITIVE BEHAVIOR MODIFICATION
Behavioral therapeutic technique whereby the client's internal statements are tested in reality in a formal and structured way.

Table 16.3 Coping statements for dealing with stress

Preparing for Stress	What is the task?
	You can work out a way to handle it.
Facing the Stress	You can deal with your fear.
	Being tense is good; it makes you alert.
	Take a deep breath.
	Go one step at a time.
Dealing with Being Overwhelmed	Your fear will rise but you can manage it.
	If you're too frightened, just pause.
	Keep in mind what to do this moment.
Self Statements That Are Reinforcing	It's not as bad as you expected.
	You succeeded!
	You can control your thoughts.

SOURCE: After Meichenbaum, 1977.

HYPNOTHERAPY

Many modern psychotherapists rely on hypnosis for therapeutic intervention. They use **hypnotherapy** in a number of important ways. For instance, it may be used to make a recollection of a past emotion or memory more vivid (Nash, Johnson, & Tipton, 1979). It may also be used to help a patient or client integrate and reorganize past memories or feelings. With sufficient training an individual can engage in self-hypnosis for therapeutic purposes. In such a situation the client can function as his or her own therapist.

Hypnosis has also been beneficial in conjunction with behavior therapy. Some behavior therapists have hypnotized clients during systematic desensitization in order to help the clients relax more deeply and to imagine more vividly the feared object or situation in their hierarchy (Lazarus, 1976).

One of the oldest applications of hypnosis is in pain control. Hypnosis has been used successfully to control pain during major surgery and childbirth. Dentists and plastic surgeons have found it an effective substitute for drugs in carrying out procedures (Kroger, 1977). Hypnosis can even help reduce and control chronic severe pain (Hilgard & Hilgard, 1975).

Physical disorders, especially those associated with anxiety and stress, may also respond to hypnosis. This is especially true of disorders such as dermatitis, asthma, or rash (DePiano & Salzberg, 1979).

Hypnosis has also been effective in the treatment of dissociative disorders such as amnesia, fugue, and multiple personality. Under hypnosis, memories can be recalled more easily, helping the amnesia or fugue state to be overcome or making multiple personalities more accessible. It has been suggested that hypnosis can affect dissociative disorders for two reasons. First, the hypnosis can reduce the anxiety that interferes with memory recall, and second, mood-dependent and other memories become easier to retrieve through the use of the vivid imagery and moods that hypnosis can create.

The Effectiveness of Psychotherapies

Does psychotherapy work? In 1952 H. J. Eysenck assessed the effectiveness of psychoanalytic and nonpsychoanalytic psychotherapy (Eysenck, 1952). Eysenck did an exhaustive review of the literature and examined over 7,000 cases, and his conclusion was that the data failed to prove that psychotherapy of any kind facilitated recovery in patients with abnormal behavior. Eysenck argued that psychotherapy simply took so much time that spontaneous remission eventually occurred. Eysenck found that roughly two thirds of any group of people with behavioral problems will recover or improve markedly within two years whether or not they receive psychotherapy (Eysenck, 1952).

Since that time a number of studies have criticized Eysenck's assumptions, especially his finding that two thirds of any group of people with behavioral problems will improve even without professional help (Bergin, 1971). Still, many researchers contend that the issue has not been settled and that no definitive proof has been presented to show that psychotherapies are effective (Erwin, 1980).

Measuring the effectiveness of psychotherapy tends to be very difficult because the relationship between the client and the therapist is so complex that it's hard to observe what is or is not a beneficial change and whether any change that does take place is due to the therapy (Sacks, Carpenter, & Richmond, 1975). Researchers can make only a few unequivocal statements about psychotherapy. For example, the clients or patients who are most likely to improve are those who are the least maladjusted, have the shortest history of symptoms or of maladaptive behavior when they begin therapy (Shapiro, Struening, Shapiro, & Barten, 1976), are most motivated to change their behavior (Gomes-Schwartz, 1976), and come from the middle or upper class (Derogatis, Yevzeroff, & Wittelsberger, 1975). The therapists who are most likely to have successful results are the most experienced (Brenner & Howard, 1976). Other characteristics of therapists, such as personal adjustment, warmth, empathy, genuineness, or professional status, have not been found to have an obvious or clear relationship to their effectiveness as therapists (Gomes-Schwartz, Hadley, & Strupp, 1978).

Eysenck's argument that psychotherapy and no therapy are equally effective depends on a particular definition of improvement and spontaneous remission. Using different criteria, others have been able to argue that 83 percent of those who receive psychotherapy improve, while only 30 percent who receive no therapy improve (Bergin, 1971). On the other hand, a 30-year follow-up study of over 500 clients who began therapy in childhood found uniformly negative results when that group was compared with a comparable untreated group of children. The researcher suggested that the clients became too dependent on their therapists and came to see themselves as people who always "need help" (McCord, 1977).

One of the most extensive analyses of the effectiveness of psychotherapy was conducted by Mary Smith and Gene Glass in 1977. They devised a statistical method that combined the results of 400 studies that had addressed the question of the effectiveness of psychotherapy. The 400 studies used many different criteria for assessing improvement. Smith and Glass found support for the effectiveness of psychotherapy (see Table 16.4). All of the psychotherapeutic treatments were found to be more effective than nontreatment, with small differences between the therapies. Group therapy was found to be as effective as individual therapy. However, the debate continues.

At best there would be a specific remedy for each form of mental disorder. But this is not generally the case. Therapies are diverse, and sometimes they have limited success. Depending on the circumstances, some

HYPNOTHERAPY
Hypnosis used for therapeutic purposes in cases of pain control or behavior pathology. The method has been used in therapy, dentistry, surgery, and childbirth.

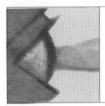

TREATING SUBSTANCE-USE DISORDERS

The therapies for treating substance-use disorders vary greatly depending on the substance that is being abused. In this focus we'll examine three of the most serious disorders (in terms of lives damaged or lost): alcohol dependence, opiate addiction, and nicotine addiction.

Alcohol Dependence (Alcoholism)

The first step in treating alcohol abuse is to detoxify the abuser and take steps toward physical recovery by providing good food and shelter. Detoxification requires a patient's intake of alcohol to be curtailed while the patient is supervised. During this time there may be withdrawal symptoms, which can be mild or severe. In severe cases delirium tremens and convulsions may occur. In modern hospitals and clinics, drugs such as chlordiazepoxide have been found to be helpful in reducing the severity of withdrawal symptoms. Detoxification is only the first step, however. The individual must be taught to take control over the craving for liquor and if necessary to abstain from all drinking.

The drug Antabuse has helped some alcoholics avoid an immediate return to drinking. It creates extreme discomfort following the ingestion of alcohol. Antabuse given without psychotherapy is insufficient, however, since once out of the hospital the patient must self-administer the drug. Antabuse is most effective in keeping the alcohol abuser from drinking for a certain time, during which psychotherapeutic measures can be taken.

Psychotherapy focuses on the individual's need to learn to cope with the problems he or she has been trying to escape and to live without depending on alcohol. Although there is strong genetic evidence that some people have a greater affinity for alcohol than others, it is possible to learn to avoid alcohol altogether regardless of one's inheritance.

Alcoholism may be treated by psychotherapeutic techniques, but the most effective treatment was one begun, and still run, by nonpsychologists. In 1935 Bill W. and Dr. Bob in Akron, Ohio, began an organization known as Alcoholics Anonymous, or AA. Bill W. had recovered from his alcoholism through a spiritual change. He in turn was able to help Dr. Bob stop drinking. The two of them formed a group to help other alcoholics. There are now over 10,000 AA groups with over 1 million members in the United States. AA is a nonprofessional counseling program run by alcoholics for alcoholics. They argue that an alcoholic is an alcoholic for life, and that total abstinence is the only cure. They support each other at group meetings and can call on each other at a moment's notice in time of need. Often, members discuss in front of the group how their lives are now and how their lives were before they stopped drinking. They discuss ways of living without using alcohol. A similar group, Al-Anon, has been established for the families of alcoholics. With modern therapeutic approaches, social support, and good aftercare, overall recovery rates from alcoholism run as high as 75 percent.

Opiate Dependence

The therapeutic treatment for heroin or morphine addiction is similar to the therapeutic techniques for treating alcoholism. Both the physical and psychological dependence must be broken, and the patient must be helped through the withdrawal period.

Before the mid-1960s the standard treatment for opiate dependence was to isolate the patient and slowly lower the opiate dosage until the body was detoxified and no longer dependent on the drug. During this time, withdrawal symptoms occurred that were sometimes quite painful. Only about 10 to 15 percent of those who were detoxified in this way stayed free of the opiate when they were discharged (Stephens & Cottrell, 1972).

In the late 1960s, a new approach was developed by a team at Rocke-

therapies may be more appropriate than others. Often a psychologist uses a combination of therapies and hopes for benefits from each. Such an interdisciplinary approach has raised hopes that psychotherapy will prove to be of greater benefit in the future.

In a very real sense, much therapy is experimental. When it works we sometimes don't know why. It is the job of researchers and psychologists to continue developing therapies and to assess their potential value. In the

feller University in New York. They hoped not only to detoxify the patient but also to remove the craving for heroin that seems to continue even after the withdrawal and detoxification process. The team suggested using a synthetic opiate, methadone, along with the rehabilitation program that included therapy and other procedures. Methadone is related to heroin and is addictive; it satisfies the addict's craving but does not produce psychological impairment (Dole & Nyswander, 1967). To date, however, methadone programs in the United States have succeeded in helping only about 35 percent of heroin addicts to stay free of the drug for at least six years. Those on methadone maintenance often manage to locate sources of additional methadone and become even more addicted, or they find the methadone clinics a suitable social climate for making further drug connections (Stimmel, et al., 1977).

In the last several years, new treatments have been developed that look promising. Clonidine is a nonaddictive drug used primarily to treat high blood pressure. In 1979 Mark S. Gold discovered that clonidine could block and reverse the serious consequences of opiate withdrawal. While kicking the heroin or morphine habit will never be easy, clonidine relieves the pain of withdrawal symptoms. Even more recently, Gold and his colleagues have used a similar drug, lofexidine, which seems to be even more effective, eliminating withdrawal symptoms totally (Gold, 1981).

After withdrawal has been accomplished with the aid of withdrawal-easing agents such as clonidine and lofexidine, opiate blocking agents can be administered. This is called *antagonist therapy*. In this case drugs such as naltrexone (a close cousin of naloxone, discussed in Chapter 2) may be used in therapy to block the effects of any heroin or morphine that may be injected later by the patient (Martin, 1975). Antagonist therapy is often more effective than methadone maintenance (Pierson, et al., 1974). Nonetheless, antagonist therapy is less appealing to addicts than methadone maintenance, and many addicts try to avoid such treatment because they fear they won't be able to return to the opiate if they feel that they need it (Schechter, 1975).

Nicotine Dependence

Stanley Schachter is a well-known social psychologist who has published a series of carefully controlled experiments that demonstrate the addictive power of nicotine. Schachter found that blood nicotine levels correlated well with urinary pH (a measurement of acidity). High levels of acid in the urine caused nicotine levels to fall by washing nicotine from the blood. High levels of acid in the urine also indicated the presence of high levels of stomach and blood acid. Schachter hypothesized that when nicotine was washed from the blood, a craving for a cigarette would develop in a person who had become addicted to nicotine through smoking. In his experiments, he demonstrated that the use of antacids such as Rolaids, Tums, or bi-

carbonate of soda could reduce the craving for cigarettes. Moreover, individuals who smoked cigarettes tended to smoke less when they used antacids to the limit directed on the antacid package. Further studies have shown that the use of antacids can help smokers quit: Their desire for a cigarette is less because the nicotine they are used to is washed from the blood more slowly when acid levels are low, enabling them to withdraw from the nicotine gradually. Schachter also discovered that when an individual is under stress, blood acid and stomach acid levels rise, washing out some nicotine, which may explain why people get the desire for a cigarette when they become nervous (Schachter, 1977; Schachter, Kozlowski & Silverstein, 1977; Silverstein, Kozlowski, & Schachter, 1977; Schachter, Silverstein, & Perlick, 1977).

Following Schachter's experimental reports, other researchers developed a method for reducing nicotine addiction by using various doses of experimental nicotine chewing gum (Schneider, Popek, Jarvik, & Gritz, 1977).

To date the best method for breaking the smoking habit seems to be an all-encompassing one that includes careful record keeping, group pressure, positive reinforcement, rapid smoking (smoking until you feel sick), muscle relaxation, assertiveness training, cancer films, and thought stopping (learning to stop your thoughts each time you think of a cigarette). The success rates have been moderate among volunteer subjects (Trotter, 1978).

meantime, psychotherapy is used by those who feel strongly that it is effective and criticized by those who feel that it has not adequately proven its effectiveness.

Perhaps psychotherapy would be more effective if therapist and client always achieved a rapport. Many therapists have noticed that they are personally more effective with one kind of client than with another. Good therapists are often thought of more as artists than as scientists. The excep-

Table 16.4 Effectiveness of different psychotherapies

TYPE OF THERAPY	MEDIAN TREATED PERSON'S PERCENTILE STATUS IN CONTROL GROUP
Psychoanalytic	72
Transactional analysis	72
Rational-emotive	78
Gestalt	60
Client-centered	74
Systematic desensitization	82
Behavior modification	78

SOURCE: Adapted from Smith & Glass, 1977, p. 756.

Note: The scores represent the median treated person's percentile status as measured against untreated control subjects. If there were no effect, the median treated person's percentile score would be 50. If there were a negative effect, the expected percentile score would be less than 50. As you can see, according to Smith and Glass's study, the average treated person was better off than approximately 75 percent of the untreated controls.

tional ones frequently find it difficult to describe why they are successful or to teach others to do as well as they.

If you should feel that you would like to see a therapist, you can ask your family doctor or psychology professor to make recommendations. Or, you can call your state's psychological association for recommendations. In either case, be an active participant in the decision and work with your doctor, professor, or state association to find a therapist who is right for you.

Summary

■ Therapeutic attempts to alleviate mental disorders are perhaps as old as humankind. Stone Age people resorted to trephining in order to help evil spirits escape the mind.

■ During the Greek and Roman eras treatment of mental disorders was often combined with attempts to bring about magical cures.

■ During the Middle Ages a rational view of mental disorders was replaced by religious demonology.

■ Early reforms of mental institutions followed the French Revolution and continued through the 18th and 19th centuries.

■ By the mid-1800s physicians began to realize that abnormal behavior could result from damage to the brain and nervous system. Today, many people are still treated in hospitals or special institutions for the mentally ill.

■ Somatic therapies directly interact with the body and its chemistry. They include psychopharmacological, electroconvulsive, and psychosurgical procedures.

■ There are four major classes of drugs used in psychopharmacological treatment: antipsychotic drugs, antidepressants, antimanic drugs, and antianxiety drugs.

■ Tardive dyskinesia, an involuntary twitching of the body or facial muscles, can result from long-term use of antipsychotic drugs.

■ Electroconvulsive therapy, a modern shock treatment, is historically related to such earlier forms of shock therapy as the presentation of sudden surprises and insulin shock.

- Psychosurgery is the destruction of a region of the brain for the purpose of alleviating severe psychiatric disorders. The frontal lobotomy, made popular in the 1930s and 1940s, has been replaced by modern psychosurgical techniques that are less invasive and damaging.
- Deinstitutionalization is the practice, begun in 1964, in which mental patients are placed in community mental health centers or seen on an outpatient basis. Because of inadequate funding it has often failed to meet its goals, and patients are often given inadequate care outside of the institution.
- Psychotherapy is a noninvasive psychological therapy designed to bring about a positive change in someone's behavior, personality, or adjustment. Psychotherapy can be divided into therapies that emphasize insight and action therapies that focus directly on changing a habit or problem. Psychotherapies can be further divided into directive therapies in which the therapist guides the client and nondirective therapies in which the client is primarily responsible for the direction of the therapy.
- Psychoanalysis is a therapy based on the work of Sigmund Freud. In psychoanalysis it is assumed that abnormal behavior is the result of unconscious conflicts. The psychoanalyst uses various techniques, including free association and dream interpretation, to uncover these unconscious conflicts.
- In humanistic-existential therapies, people are considered capable of living rich and satisfying lives. The emphasis is on fulfilling one's potential, or self-actualizing.
- Carl Rogers has developed a client-centered therapy in which the therapist refrains from guiding the therapy in any particular direction. Instead, the client is responsible for the direction the therapy takes.
- Existential therapists argue that people must learn to accept responsibility, make choices for themselves, and control their environment rather than the other way around.
- Rational-emotive therapy is an action therapy based on the assumption that people engage in self-defeating behaviors because they hang on to beliefs that are unrealistic or faulty.
- Gestalt therapy is an insight therapy based heavily on Freudian psychoanalytic ideas. The ultimate goal of Gestalt therapy is to balance and integrate emotion, thought, and action. One of the earliest group therapies was psychodrama. Following World War II, group therapy became more popular. It has been found by many therapists to be beneficial.
- During sensitivity training, participants learn to become sensitive to the needs and feelings of others and to trust others.
- In encounter groups, individuals confront each other in an attempt to break through defenses and false fronts.
- Behavior therapy relies on learning theory and the principles of conditioning. Each therapeutic treatment deals with a specific problem. Important behavioral techniques include aversive conditioning, systematic desensitization, operant techniques, token economies, behavioral contracts, and social modeling.
- Cognitive behavior modification is a therapeutic treatment in which the client is helped to obtain information about himself or herself through a series of unbiased encounters that disprove false thoughts and beliefs.
- Modern clinicians use hypnotherapy in a number of important ways. Hypnotherapy can intensify the memory of past emotions and events,

can be used in conjunction with behavior therapy, is useful in controlling pain, and is effective for the treatment of dissociative disorders.

- In treating alcohol and opiate dependence, the user is first detoxified and then given drugs to help alleviate withdrawal symptoms. The treatment may also include antagonistic therapy and psychotherapy.
- Researchers are divided as to whether psychotherapy is effective. Most research indicates that it is effective to a degree.

EPILOGUE: A BIRD IN THE HAND

Psychologists know that therapies can sometimes be very effective in treating and eliminating certain kinds of behavior disorders. In the following account, a phobia is eliminated through behavior therapy.

In Chapter 15 you met Judy R., who had a bird phobia. As you recall, she had come to the counseling center at a university because her unrealistic terror of birds was interfering with her life and her plans to become a teacher. The counselors at the center decided to use behavior therapy to help Judy unlearn her fear of birds.

First, the therapists set up a 35-step hierarchy for systematic desensitization, similar to the hierarchy depicted on page 521. It was decided that Judy would act out the hierarchy rather than just imagine it, since acting something out while learning to be calm is more effective.

A 27-year-old woman, the same age as Judy, served as a model. Judy watched as the model touched bird pictures, the frightening behavior that Judy was to imitate first. The therapy proceeded slowly, with Judy first of all placing her hand on the model's hand and then touching the pictures by herself. A little later, the same procedure was used with feathers.

Then a stuffed bird from a museum was brought in. First the model and Judy looked at the stuffed bird from the distance of several feet, and then they slowly approached it. The model touched

the bird first and then Judy touched it while wearing gloves. Later the gloves were removed. The therapy never moved fast enough to cause Judy much anxiety. Everything was done slowly and gently, and at each step Judy was allowed time to be sure she was calm and comfortable before the next step was taken.

Next, Judy took bird specimens home and kept them in a place where she would see them often. Then came a session in which she was trained to fight off birds, should any happen to fly at her, by waving her arms and shouting. These defensive measures were first modeled for Judy, and then Judy tried them on a group of live pigeons. She dispersed the birds without feeling afraid.

Following this success, Judy went to a live-poultry store and watched the model touch hundreds of small chicks. Next, Judy went to the zoo and spent time at the duck pond, the aviary, and the cages for large birds. Later she was able to go with her model around a bird-populated city mall. Finally, Judy watched the model walk through a large closed aviary at the zoo where people could walk surrounded by hundreds of birds. Judy accompanied the model through the aviary, and then she was able to walk through on her own.

Cognitive restructuring was also employed. Judy was given many factual bits of information about birds that she was able to test on her own by experiencing birds first-hand. For example, Judy was informed that birds almost never fly at people except by accident, a hypothesis she was able to test firsthand on her walk through the aviary.

Before treatment, Judy was unable to get further than about halfway up her hierarchy with a minimum amount of anxiety. After treatment, Judy no longer showed fear of birds (although she admitted that an uncaged eagle might still make her a little nervous). She did not go out of her way to avoid birds. She often drove with her car windows down; she went for walks on the beach and went sunbathing. She even wore a blouse imprinted with vivid pictures of birds. Eventually Judy moved to a new apartment that was on a waterfront populated by seagulls. A follow-up 12 months later showed that the bird phobia had not returned (Lassen & McConnell, 1977).

Suggestions for Further Reading

1. Belkin, G. S. *Contemporary psychotherapies.* Chicago: Rand McNally, 1980.
2. Erickson, M. H., & Rossi, E. *Hypnotherapy: An exploratory casebook.* New York: Irvington, 1979.
3. Garfield, S. L., & Bergin, A. E. (eds.), *Handbook of psychotherapy and behavior change* (2nd ed.). New York: Wiley, 1978.
4. Meichenbaum, D. *Cognitive-behavior modification.* New York: Plenum Press, 1977.
5. Valenstein, E. S. (ed.). *The psychosurgery debate: Scientific, legal, and ethical perspectives.* San Francisco: W. H. Freeman, 1980.

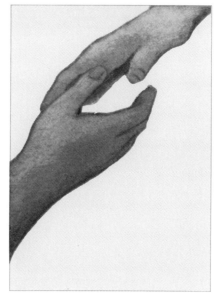

UNIT FIVE

**Relating to
One Another**

CONTENTS

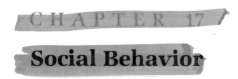

CHAPTER 17

Social Behavior

PROLOGUE

It is the early 1950s and you are a student working with Solomon Asch. Professor Asch is interested in studying conformity, and he's asked you to help him with an experiment. Your job is to collect the data and lead the subjects through the procedure.

After learning what you must do you become worried. The kinds of results you will obtain are obvious to you already. You wish that Professor Asch had designed the experiment with more care. It's definitely not subtle enough.

You begin by having the subject enter a room along with eight other people. These eight people are secretly confederates of yours, but to the subject, they're just other subjects.

Next, you show everyone three comparison lines. Each line is obviously of different length, no doubt about that. Then you show a standard line and place it alongside the comparison lines (see Figure 17.1). You ask all of the subjects which line in the comparison group is the same length as the standard line. The real subject is asked last. All of your confederates have been told

to lie: They pick a line that doesn't match the standard line.

Professor Asch wants to know how the real subject will respond. This is why you are worried about the experiment. The shorter comparison lines are so obviously different that nobody could make a mistake. The subject will either realize that the other eight people are confederates or think they're all crazy. Nobody could possibly agree that the standard line is the same length as the shorter comparison lines.

One by one subjects are led through this procedure, and to your amazement, 75 percent of all subjects go along with the group's lies on at least one occasion (Asch, 1951).

Afterwards you explain the experiment to the subjects and question them. "Could you tell that everyone else was wrong when they said that one of the shorter lines equalled the standard line?"

"Yes," the subjects often reply. "I knew they were wrong."

"Then why did you agree with them?"

"I don't know," the subjects say.

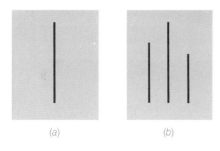

Figure 17.1 *The stimulus cards used in Asch's experiment. The subjects were required to match the standard line on card (a) with the line of the same length on card (b). (After Asch, 1955)*

"I guess I didn't want to rock the boat. I just wanted to go along."

The more you think about the results of Asch's experiment the more disturbed you become. You realize that many people would rather go against the evidence of their own eyes than openly disagree with the unanimous judgment of even a small group of people (Asch, 1951; Wheeler, Deci, Reis, & Zuckerman, 1979).

In this chapter we'll examine many of the ways in which people influence each other. We'll take a look at the factors determining obedience, the effect that groups have on their members, and the way in which our attitudes can be changed by those around us. We'll also study other areas of interest to social psychologists, such as competition and cooperation, conformity, negotiation and bargaining, helping others, moral behavior, and prejudice.

Why Psychologists Study Social Behavior

Except for extremely rare instances, no human being lives in total social isolation. Each of us interacts with others. Social psychology is the study of how people affect the behavior, thoughts, and feelings of others.

If you were told that you had to give up something in your environment, the last thing you or anyone would probably choose to surrender would be the company of others. Most of us would rather live in a cave with other people than in a mansion with no hope of ever seeing another person. Other people are such a common element in our lives that we rarely consider what it would be like without them. They affect us, they shape us, they influence our feelings, attitudes, and thoughts. We, in turn, influence them. Social psychologists study how groups behave and how being a member of a group or society affects individuals.

Social psychology is the study of the effects of groups and social interaction on behavior.

Changing Behavior by Social Means

Two primary forces shaping behavior are the pressure to conform and the desire to obey.

CONFORMITY

As you learned in the Prologue, the tendency to conform can be very strong. Asch demonstrated that we may conform even if it means disavowing the evidence of our own eyes. Still, a degree of **conformity** is important in any society. Without it there would be chaos. The ways in which others expect us to conform are known as **social norms.**

Some social norms are explicit, and may even be spelled out—"No parking," "No smoking in this section," "Shirts and shoes must be worn in this establishment." Other social norms are unspoken and unwritten, but they still influence our behavior. For example, there is probably no functional reason for someone to attend a business meeting dressed in a suit rather than in a sweatshirt, other than the fact that it is an unspoken social norm, and it is expected. There are many unspoken social rules to conform, such as waiting your turn in line, shaking hands when you first meet someone, and not staring at strangers.

Why People Conform   Conformity is common, and people probably have two major reasons for conforming. First, they are often reinforced for conforming. Since childhood we have been reinforced for adopting the "correct" beliefs of our parents, guardians, and teachers. Even as adults, we are often reinforced for acting like others. Because we are reinforced for conforming so often and under so many different circumstances, our conformity tends to generalize to new situations.

The second important force behind conformity may be the result of **social comparison.** We commonly compare ourselves with others, especially those who are like us, as a way of assessing the accuracy of our attitudes, feelings, and beliefs. We like to view ourselves as rational and correct in our views. Consequently, those who rely heavily on social comparison may find it difficult not to change in the direction of conformity (Bleda & Castore, 1973; Fazio, 1979).

Someone who is very different from the other members of a group may make the group feel uncomfortable because he or she will disrupt the group's stable basis for comparison. The group will usually try to force the individual to change. If it fails, the person who is viewed a deviant may be rejected.

Reference Groups   Will a mathematician who hears that most sailors have tatoos want one also? Will you, if you read in an advertisement that all of the "important people" of Norway vacation at a particular resort, want to go there, too? In both cases the pressure to conform is small. Just because a particular group engages in a certain behavior does not necessarily mean that others will want to do the same, or will use that group for purposes of social comparison. Instead, we generally look to people we are like, or wish to be like, in order to make decisions about how we will conform. Social psychologists refer to such groups as **reference groups.** The norms of reference groups tend to be perpetuated because each new member who joins is under pressure to conform and maintain the group's standards.

Although the pressure to conform may be strong, some will struggle against it.

Adolescents feel a special need to conform with their reference group.

Much of the research on conformity grew out of a desire to understand the social forces that had been at work in Nazi Germany. Could you have been a member of the Nazi party? Could you have joined in the mass rallies and the persecutions? The students of Ron Jones' high school history class in California didn't think that they would have gone along with the Nazi movement had they lived in Germany at the time. They believed that they would have resisted. In order to help his class understand more fully the social forces that affected the Nazis, Ron Jones had the class simulate some of the Nazi experience for five days. To his horror, the pretend game became all too real, and a Nazi-like system of beliefs and control took root among his students and throughout the school (Jones, 1978).

What Jones had done to bring this about was quite simple. He began by limiting all answers in class to three words or less. Soon, new nonverbal leaders emerged. A Nazi-like salute was then incorporated, and slogans such as "strength through community" were shouted in unison. Banners were made, new recruits were enlisted from the rest of the school, and mandatory sitting postures were introduced. The group called itself the Third Wave. From Jones' small class the group grew to over 100 members, and membership cards were issued. The better students were often thrown out of class by the others. Once these "deviants" were purged, social comparison helped strengthen conformity.

Jones decided to tell the Third Wave that they were part of a national organization of students who wanted a political change. He emphasized that they were a special group and that they had been selected to help the cause. In this way he reinforced their conformity.

Jones announced that the next day a candidate for president of the United States would announce the formation of the Third Wave. The students were invited to view the occasion on the television monitor in the school auditorium. The following day some 250 students filed into the auditorium wearing their special uniforms and homemade armbands. Muscular student guards stood at the door, while others, enlisted by Jones to help, pretended to be photographers and reporters and circulated among the students. This added charade helped the students believe that they were about to become part of a nationwide movement. The students stood, rank upon rank, tall and proud. As they waited for the announcement, Jones began to show a movie of the Nazi rally at Nuremberg and the history of the Third Reich. The students just stood there, blankly watching what appeared to be an eerie reflection of themselves.

Afterwards Jones explained to the students what had been going on and how they had been manipulated. He predicted that they would never admit to having been part of this madness, to having been manipulated into being such followers. He told the students that they would keep this day and this rally a secret. His prediction appears to be accurate, for few students wish to talk about that time. In five short days seemingly healthy, normal students at Cubberley High School in California had banded together and purged their ranks of "intellectuals," and were ready to follow the orders of a national leader. They had even begun to take pride in relying on coercion and discrimination as means to an unknown end. They may never again have a lesson in history or social psychology of such importance and magnitude.

Look around you. Whom do you admire? What are your reference groups? How have you changed your behavior to conform to their standards? What are their goals, and are these goals that you desire? Of course, most conformity is innocuous. Conforming by wearing a shiny silk blazer when you're part of a bowling league is hardly the same as marching to the cadence of the Third Reich. And yet, as you may have begun to sense, there are similarities. In both cases there is pressure to be part of the group, and to demonstrate appropriate behaviors to new members.

Nazis on trial in Nuremberg, November 25, 1945. Hermann Goering, Rudolf Hess, General von Ribbentrop, and General Kietel are shown in the front row.

OBEDIENCE

While it's possible to get a group of high school students to conform to Nazi-like values and beliefs, it's still a long way from there to the death camps and the murder of millions of people. Or is it? During the Nuremberg trials, in which the Nazi war criminals were brought to account, one phrase was heard so often that it's come to be associated with the German underlings even by people who are not old enough to remember the Second World War. The phrase is, "I was just following orders." As the court records show, this excuse was not well received. The lowest ranking officers, it was conceded, might possibly use such an excuse. But certainly the higher ranking officers had had a choice.

The Milgram Experiment In 1961 social psychologist Stanley Milgram investigated obedience in a study that is now considered a classic. Milgram began by using students from Yale University as subjects and later expanded his research to include a cross section of many people of different ages, occupations, and education.

Stanley Milgram.

Two subjects were ushered into an experimental room and told that they were part of an investigation to test the effects of punishment, in the form of an electric shock, on memory. An experimenter, dressed in a white lab coat, would oversee the experiment. The subjects would draw lots to find out who would be the "learner" and who would be the "teacher." Unknown to the real subject, the other subject, "Mr. Wallace," a gentle-looking, friendly 50-year-old man, was really an actor working for Milgram. The lots were rigged so that the real subject would be assigned the role of teacher.

The teacher was given a sample shock of 45 volts to find out what it would feel like—it stung. The learner was then strapped into the electric chair as the teacher watched. The teacher was taken into an adjacent room and put in front of an array of switches ranging from "Slight shock 15 volts," to "Danger: severe shock, 450 volts." The learner was instructed to repeat a list of words. Every time he made an error, the teacher was to administer a shock, starting with the lowest level and gradually increasing. The actor playing the role of learner-subject had been given a script to follow for each voltage level, since the teacher-subject would be able to hear him from the next room. As the shock level rose, the learner would begin to protest. The stronger the shock, the louder he was to protest. At 75 volts he would moan; at 150 volts he would demand to be released from the chair. At 180 volts he would yell that he could no longer stand the pain. At 300 volts he would protest that he had a heart condition and begin to scream. If the teacher complained at any time, the experimenter would say, "Teacher, you have no other choice; you must go on!" (Milgram, 1963, p. 374). After the 300-volt level it was planned that there would be an ominous silence from the learner's room, as though he were unconscious or even dead. Unknown to the teacher, the learner received no real shocks.

Milgram's aim was to find out how much pressure to obey would be created by the experimenter in the lab coat when he said, "Teacher, you have no other choice; you must go on!" How far would subjects go under these circumstances? Before conducting the experiment, Milgram interviewed 40 psychiatrists, describing the procedure you have just read. He asked them to estimate the behavior of most subjects. The psychiatrists agreed that the majority would not go beyond 150 volts and that perhaps only one tenth of 1 percent, those who were very deviant or sadistic, would go all the way to 450 volts. How far would you have gone?

To everyone's horror, when the experiment was conducted 62 percent of the subject-teachers went all the way to 450 volts! None of them seemed to enjoy it. For example, after delivering 180 volts one subject said,

> He can't stand it! I'm not going to kill that man in there. You hear him hollering? He's hollering. He can't stand it. What if something happens to him? . . . I mean, who is going to take the responsibility if anything happens to that gentleman? (Milgram, 1965a, p. 67)

At that point the experimenter said that he would take responsibility. The subject replied, "All right," and continued delivering shocks.

Of the 38 percent of the subjects who were not willing to go to 450 volts, many went to high levels (see Figure 17.2). All who refused to continue simply walked out of the experiment. Not one of them tried to see how Mr. Wallace was. Interestingly, the personality tests that were administered to the subjects failed to reveal any differences between the subjects who obeyed and those who refused.

Variables Influencing Obedience   Social psychologists have identified at least three variables in this experiment that may help explain the high rate of obedience. First, a legitimate authority, the experimenter, was present and willing to take responsibility. Second, the victim was in another room, and this distance may have lessened the teacher's stress by eliminating the need to see the learner's anguish. Third, the subject-teacher accepted the subordinate role, applying all of the rules ever learned about being a good follower. Perhaps, as social psychologist Philip Zimbardo has suggested, such follower training in public situations begins your first day of school when your teacher tells you, "Stay in your seat no matter what" (Zimbardo, 1979).

It should be stressed that obedience does not only happen under these select conditions. Even if the learner-subject is directly in front of the teacher-subject, the latter may still obey. In a variation of the Milgram experiment the teacher-subject actually had to force the learner's hand down onto an electric shock plate. Obedience under these conditions, though less frequent, was still much higher than anyone had predicted.

By today's standards the Milgram experiment may not be considered ethical because of the stress placed on the subject-teacher. Some of the

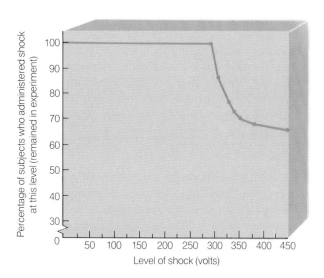

Figure 17.2   *The percentage of subjects who delivered shock at different voltage levels in Milgram's experiment. Approximately two thirds of the subjects continued to 450 volts despite the screaming protests of the learner. No subject discontinued shock before the 300 volt level. (SOURCE: Adapted from Milgram, 1963)*

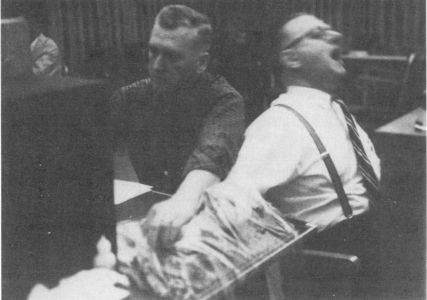

In this variation of the Milgram experiment, a subject-teacher forces the learner's arm onto the electric plate. (Photos © 1965 by Stanley Milgram, from the film Obedience, *distributed by the New York University Film Library.)*

subjects were shaking and weeping as they pressed the 450-volt lever. How do you debrief such a subject after the experiment? Do you say, "Don't feel bad, the learner is only an actor. I just wanted to see if you would electrocute a stranger just because I told you to." No serious aftereffects were observed among the teacher-subjects, but even after a careful debriefing many felt that they had discovered an evil side of themselves. Some of the volunteer experimenters who helped Milgram conduct the research were called to account by university authorities, who asked why they had continued the experiment when they could plainly see that the subject-teachers were under stress. Their frightening answer—"Milgram told us to!"

The Milgram findings are not specific to our society or nation. Similar results have been obtained in many other countries including Germany and Australia (Kilham & Mann, 1974; Mantell, 1971). The same results were even found among three groups of children, aged 7, 11, and 15, who were ordered to shock an innocent victim (Shanab & Yahya, 1977).

In a further variation, information was obtained that demonstrated that Milgram's results were due to the subjects' desire to be obedient rather than to any hidden sadistic pleasure in shocking the learner. Forty-two teenage boys of ages 13 and 14 were asked to take part in an experiment in which they were told they might suffer a 50 percent hearing loss. Following an experimental procedure similar to Milgram's, the researchers found that the subjects were willing to follow orders even though they might cause self-immolation (Martin, Lobb, Chapman, & Spillane, 1976).

CONFORMITY AND OBEDIENCE

As you might imagine, once social psychologists discovered variables that influenced conformity, and variables that influenced obedience, they wanted to see how these variables interrelated.

As an example of research into this area, let's consider another variation of the Milgram experiment. This variation makes use of one learner and three subject-teachers. Only one of the subject-teachers is a real subject, however. Unknown to that individual, the other two subject-teachers, as well as the learner, are actors. In this variation the confederate subject-teachers will disobey. The first of these actors will disobey the experimenter at 150 volts and leave. The second actor will defy the experimenter at 225 volts and leave. The third subject-teacher, the real subject, will then be alone to continue following orders. Under these circumstances, the real subject can use the other two "subjects" for purposes of social comparison. As it turns out, after two actors defy the experimenter only about 12 percent of the subjects will remain and go all the way to 450 volts (see Figure 17.3) (Milgram, 1965b). Conversely, if the two actors both argued for more shock all the way to 450 volts, the real subject was more likely to obey than was the single teacher-subject in the original experiment.

The Jonestown tragedy vividly demonstrated the potential consequences of conformity and blind obedience to authority. In 1978 almost 900 mem-

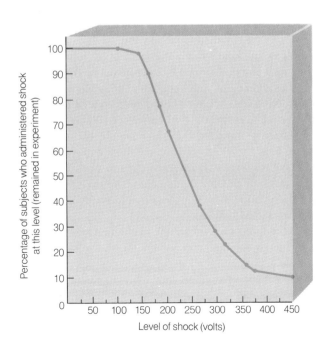

Figure 17.3 *The percentage of subjects who delivered shock at different voltage levels in the repeat of Milgram's experiment when two other subjects disobeyed the researcher's request to shock the learner. The group pressure in this case allowed the subject to discontinue the shocks sooner. Only 10 percent went all the way to 450 volts.* (SOURCE: *Adapted from Milgram, 1965b*)

Aftermath of the tragedy at Jonestown.

bers of the California-based People's Temple died in a ritual mass suicide in Jonestown, Guyana, at the command of their leader Reverend Jim Jones. Jones felt that his communal group was under attack from the outside by forces bent on destroying them. (This outside force was, in reality, nothing more than one congressman, Leo Ryan, who had come to check on people from his district and who was leaving with 14 of them.) After Jones' men had murdered the congressman and several of his party, Jones ordered his followers to kill themselves by taking cyanide. The mass death shocked the world and left people wondering how such a thing could have happened.

Although a few disobeyed Jones and ran into the jungle, most complied. The final tape recordings of Jonestown are horrifying to listen to. The people went to their self-administered deaths crying and screaming for help. Most were not happy to die, which makes their deaths even more incomprehensible.

Now that you have learned something about conformity and obedience, you may begin to appreciate the powerful influences that were in effect that day in Jonestown. The people in Jones' community were followers; they had learned through much practice and training to obey their leader, even carrying out mock suicides. Like Milgram's subject-teachers, many of them cried and were under great stress at the end, but they obeyed. Social comparison certainly had an effect. We would predict that a person surrounded by hundreds of other people committing suicide would be much more likely to do the same. By their actions the people in Jonestown were also complying with reference group norms. Jones' followers had no other group to which they could refer. They were not only completely dependent on the group, they were also isolated in a dense South American jungle, far from their homes.

Would you have been one of the few who escaped? It's easy to feel invulnerable to social forces when they aren't directly working on you. Most people feel that, in all except extreme circumstances, such as a gun to the head, their own internal values and belief systems will override external social forces. But social psychologists are finding that this is in fact a rarity. More often the opposite is true, and social forces turn out to be stronger than our personal values, beliefs, and feelings.

Helping Others

BYSTANDER EFFECT
People's tendency, especially pronounced under crowded conditions, to ignore others who need help or situations that call for action.

People do not always hurt each other or refuse to help someone in need in the way that the subjects in Milgram's experiment did. Sometimes people will go out of their way to help or to prevent another from being hurt. But at other times they will not. Social psychologists feel that the situational forces present at any given moment play a great role in determining whether people will help in an emergency. To test this theory, social psychologists have studied the factors at play during real and "arranged" emergencies. The following incident stimulated great interest in this area of investigation.

In 1964 on Austin Street in Queens, New York, a woman named Kitty Genovese was stabbed to death. It was nighttime when her killer attacked her on the street. She screamed and fought with him. Her screams were so loud that they alerted many people in apartments overlooking the street. Windows lighted up as the occupants awoke and looked outside to see what was happening. Thirty-eight presumably respectable and law-abiding citizens watched as she was stabbed. Their lights scared off the attacker. Kitty lay in the street wounded but still alive. When the people turned off their lights and went back to bed, the attacker struck again. Once again he was scared off by people looking out of their windows, and once again he returned when the lights went out. He stabbed her a third time, killing her. At no time during the entire attack did any of the 38 people call the police or an ambulance! The police were not called until after she had died. Why had these people not helped? They didn't have to fight with the killer. They were safe in their homes and needed only to pick up the telephone. According to the newspapers, this was one more example of unfeeling city people who have no concern for anyone but themselves. But was this the answer?

To shed a little light on what may have happened that night in Austin Street, let's examine an experiment by Darley and Latane conducted in 1968. The subjects were told that they would be taking part in a discussion about the kinds of problems students might face when they are away at college. On the pretext of maintaining anonymity, the students were isolated in separate cubicles; they could not see each other, and they could speak to each other only through an intercom. Each subject was led to believe that he or she would be participating in a discussion group in which there was either one other student, two other students, or five others. Actually, the subject was the only student in the experiment. The other subjects were voices on a tape recorder.

To begin, each student was requested to give a short introductory statement describing himself or herself. During the introduction, one of the pretend students said that he was embarrassed by the fact that he occasionally had epileptic seizures. As the "discussion" got underway, this particular participant began to have what sounded like an epileptic seizure (recorded on the tape beforehand). What would the real subject do? When the subject believed that there was only one other participant and that this other person was having a seizure, the subject was very likely to summon or provide help. However, the more participants that the subject believed were taking part in the discussion, the less likely he or she was to do anything. This tendency is known as the **bystander effect.** The bystander effect may have been responsible for the fact that no one called for help when Kitty Genovese was being stabbed.

One possible reason for the bystander effect. When someone is observed to be in need of help and there are many people around, individuals can come to believe that they need not act, or give aid by placing responsibility to act on other people in the crowd. They may think, for instance, "Someone else will surely help" or "Why should I have to be the one to help?"

What gives rise to the bystander effect? Most people assume that help is more likely to be given when more people see that it is needed, rather than the other way around. But social psychologists have found that the opposite is often true. There appear to be two reasons for the bystander effect: One is **diffusion of responsibility,** and the other is the fear of appearing foolish.

If you are the only one who sees a stranger in distress, and you know that you are the only one, then it is also apparent that if you take no action no help will be forthcoming. This perception places a burden of responsibility on you to act. After all, if you don't, who will? However, if you know that many people besides yourself have seen the person in distress, then it becomes easy to assume that someone else will take action; it is no longer incumbent upon you to do so. Many people watched Kitty Genovese being stabbed and saw that others were watching. There may have been a great diffusion of responsibility, with everyone feeling that someone else would do something. Or the witnesses may have felt that someone else should help and asked themselves, "Why me?" Ironically, had Kitty Genovese been in a more isolated place and been seen by a single witness, there might have been a better chance that the police would have been called or that some action would have been taken.

Have you ever arrived at a bad car accident where there was a large crowd and wondered why it was taking the ambulance so long to arrive? Perhaps you should have been wondering whether anyone had called an ambulance. Everyone may have assumed that someone must have called, or thought that it was someone else's responsibility to call. Think of diffusion of responsibility the next time you see someone in need and there are many witnesses. It may still be incumbent upon you to act, if only to summon help.

The second reason for the bystander effect may be the fear of appearing foolish. Some situations are clearly emergencies; other situations are more ambiguous. In ambiguous situations people are often reluctant to act be-

Because of the bystander effect, this person may receive no help.

cause they are afraid of looking foolish should it turn out that there was no emergency. To test this assertion, two researchers had students fill out a questionnaire in a small room. The researchers weren't really interested in the students' responses to the questionnaire; instead they wanted to see how the students would react to something unusual that began to happen. The room had a small vent. As the students worked on the questionnaire, smoke began to pour through the vent. The smoke came from a smoke generator run by the researchers.

The subjects in this experiment were assigned to one of three conditions. They filled out the questionnaire alone, in the presence of two other subjects, or in the presence of two confederates posing as subjects. In the last case the confederates were told to do nothing when the smoke began to fill the room.

The students who were in the room alone had no reason to fear embarrassment or to interpret the smoke as anything but an emergency. The vast majority of subjects in this condition responded by telling the person in the outer room what was happening. When two other subjects were in the room, the amount of action taken was drastically lessened (see Figure 17.4). As smoke began to filter in, the subjects would look at each other, each examining the others' reactions. For each subject the situation became ambiguous because the others weren't reacting (each of them, of course, was waiting to see whether someone else would react). Not wishing to appear foolish by misinterpreting something as an emergency, many subjects failed to act. In the condition with the two confederates the real subject was even less likely to act because the confederates gave no hint of concern (unlike some participants in the condition that used three real subjects). The confederates made the situation even more ambiguous. Rather than appear foolish by acting in a situation that might not be an emergency, the real subject would sit in the room as it filled with smoke and continue filling out the questionnaire (Latane & Darley, 1968).

In ambiguous situations people are much less likely to help others than

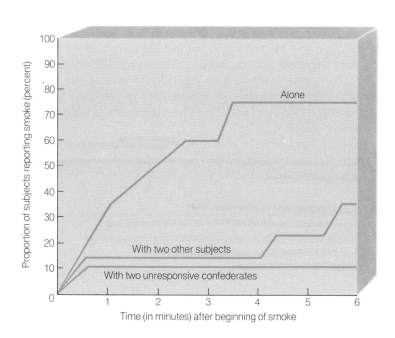

Figure 17.4 *Proportion of subjects who reported smoke in Latane and Darley's 1968 experiment. As you can see, subjects were much more likely to report the smoke if they were alone than if they were with two other subjects or two unresponsive confederates.* (SOURCE: *Adapted from Latane & Darley, 1968, p. 218*)

TASK LOAD
A measure of demand in terms of behavior required per unit of time. In high
task-load conditions there is much to do
and little time in which to do it.

in obvious emergencies (Yakimovich & Saltz, 1971). For example, if an accident victim is seen to be bleeding most people realize that the situation is *not* ambiguous and that help is absolutely required (Shotland & Huston, 1979). It has also been found that people are more likely to help if they are in familiar surroundings than if they are in an unfamiliar location, probably because unfamiliar surroundings heighten the ambiguity (Latane & Darley, 1970).

Other factors may affect the chances that a bystander will lend aid. Researchers Shirlynn Spacapan and Sheldon Cohen conducted an experiment with female students in which **task load** (how busy the subject was) and diffusion of responsibility were measured simultaneously. The women were divided into two groups. The subjects in the first group were required to go into a shopping mall and buy 26 items specified on a list within half an hour. Since this requirement would be relatively easy to carry out and subjects would have time to spare, these subjects were considered the low-task group. The high-task group was required to buy 52 items within half an hour, a task that would take practically the whole time. Members of both groups were sent into the shopping mall during either crowded or uncrowded times.

The results demonstrated that how busy a person is and whether that person stands to lose something by helping may be as important a variable as diffusion of responsibility. In each instance, a "victim" asked the subject to help look for a lost contact lens. In the uncrowded low-task situation, 80 percent of the subjects stopped to look, while in the crowded high-task situation, none did! In the mixed situations, that is, low-task and crowded and high-task and uncrowded, approximately one third of the subjects complied with the request for help (Spacapan & Cohen, 1977).

It has also been found that individuals who maintain their anonymity are less likely to help. In one study, students who wore hoods to hide their faces were found to be less likely to help a fellow student who appeared to have fainted (Solomon & Solomon, 1978). In another study, subjects were asked to shock a woman as part of an experiment. They were told either that the woman was a very nice person or that she was an extremely obnoxious person. In addition, the subjects either wore hoods and garments to disguise themselves or showed themselves and their faces to the woman. The results were that the subjects were only slightly more likely to shock the "obnoxious" woman than the "nice" woman. But if the subjects wore hoods and were able to disguise themselves they gave the woman twice as much shock (Zimbardo, 1979). (The same woman played each role and was not really shocked.)

Latane and Darley have created a bystander intervention model that consists of a five-step process that a person must complete before he or she is likely to give help (Latane & Darley, 1970):

1. The event must be observed.
2. The event must be interpreted as an emergency.
3. The person must accept responsibility for helping.
4. The person has to decide how to help.
5. Action must be taken.

The following example highlights this five-step process of bystander intervention.

On January 13, 1982, a Boeing 737 took off in bad weather from Washington D.C.'s National Airport. Unable to gain altitude, it crashed into the 14th Street bridge, flipped over, and smashed through the ice of the frozen Potomac River. Lenny Skutnik, a Washington office worker, was on his way home when he witnessed the disaster (step 1). As he reached the banks of the river, he observed a rescue helicopter attempting to save drowning victims of the crash (step 2). He noticed that one woman in the water apparently didn't have the strength to hold onto the life preserver dangling from the helicopter. At this point Mr. Skutnik looked around and realized that "she was going to drown if I didn't go get her, because nobody else was going to" (step 3).

The only way to reach her was to swim out to her and help her to safety (step 4). In a truly heroic action Mr. Skutnik plunged into the icy Potomac amid ice chunks and potentially explosive jet fuel, and saved the woman's life (step 5). His empathy and compassion were also a motivating force, as he stated in an interview with NBC news, "It was just in my heart. I just felt really sorry for the girl."

There are three important ways of encouraging people to help others. One, of course, is by studying social psychology. Now that you are aware of these studies you are more likely to inquire whether your help is needed even if it means attracting attention in front of many people who are doing nothing. Helping others can also be fostered by teaching appropriate helping skills. For instance, training seminars in cardiopulmonary resuscitation (CPR) have been very successful in getting people to administer quickly to heart attack victims in order to keep them alive until help arrives. Training in what to do in case of an emergency prepares a person to take action. A third way of encouraging others to help is by reinforcing them for helping and by modeling helping behavior.

Lenny Skutnik, a Washington, D.C. office worker, dove into the frozen Potomac River to save a victim of the airliner crash that occurred on January 13, 1982.

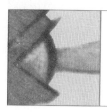

THE DEVELOPMENT OF MORALITY

As you have discovered, some people will conform to the standards of Nazi-like groups, obey orders to harm another, or refuse to help those in need. Other people will not conform or obey, and they willingly give aid. The data presented in this chapter so far have indicated that situational factors determine a person's conformity, obedience, or desire to help. On the other hand, many psychologists believe that morality is not just situationally dependent but is an integral part of an individual's personality. A moral person, they argue, will be less likely to harm another or to refuse to give aid than an amoral person, regardless of the situational factors. During the last two decades, psychologists have examined the development of morals in an effort to learn how subject people's morality is to situational factors.

Morals are the attitudes and beliefs people hold that help them to determine what is right or wrong. Some researchers have come to believe that moral reasoning progresses through a series of stages as the individual is influenced by the reasoning of others. Researcher Lawrence Kohlberg (1963, 1971) has postulated six stages in the development of morality. According to Kohlberg, moral development begins in childhood with an orientation to obey in order to avoid punishment, and it may end with the emergence of concern for reciprocity among individuals and a sense of universal justice.

Kohlberg has devised an assessment tool for determining the stage of moral development an individual has reached. Individuals are presented with a moral dilemma. The reasoning they use to resolve the dilemma indicates

how advanced their moral thinking is. Table 17.1 gives an example of one of these moral dilemmas. For each stage, actual answers have been provided that demonstrate the kinds of reasoning involved. The headings above each set of answers describe, in general terms, the quality of moral reasoning that defines each stage. As you can see, there are no right or wrong answers. Each stage is value-free. A person's position in the stages is determined not by the choice of right or wrong answers according to some value system, but by the kind of moral reasoning used to make the choice.

According to Kohlberg, each stage builds upon the previous stage. More advanced stages of moral thinking reorganize the earlier stages in a way that provides the person with new criteria and perspectives for making moral judgments (Hoffman, 1979). Kohlberg assumes that children begin at the first stage. As they interact with others they may progress through each stage, but they never skip any.

There is no assurance, however, that the most advanced stages will be reached. Kohlberg believes that many individuals never reach the sixth and final stage. In fact, most people do not seem to develop much beyond stage four (Shaver & Strong, 1976). The third and fourth stages are therefore called the conventional level, since they represent the level reached by most adults.

In Kohlberg's view, people advance to a higher stage of moral development by exposure to the moral reasoning of others that is more advanced than their own. This social interaction places a person in a conflict that can be re-

solved only by accepting the more advanced level of moral reasoning.

Psychologist David Rosenhan of Stanford University has used Kohlberg's assessment techniques to measure different individuals' levels of moral thinking. Afterwards he placed these individuals in the role of the teacher-subject in a replication of Stanley Milgram's famous shock experiment which you read about earlier. Even some subjects at Kohlberg's highest moral level, level six, went all the way to 450 volts when shocking the learner. They were, however, less likely to do so than subjects at Kohlberg's stage one (Rosenhan, 1973).

Although Kohlberg's theory presents a well-organized depiction of how moral development may occur, it has been strongly criticized for a number of reasons. Its most serious problem may be that it correlates poorly with moral behavior. Although subject-teachers at level 6 were less likely to shock subject-learners than were those at level 1, whether people will choose to behave in a moral way is often more dependent on the immediate situational and social forces than on their level of moral reasoning. This indicates that fostering high levels of moral reasoning may not bring about more moral behavior (Kurtines & Greif, 1974). It has also been argued that Kohlberg's theory is culturally biased in favor of Western ideas of what is morally "advanced" (Simpson, 1974; Hogan, 1975; Sampson, 1978). Still, Kohlberg's ideas have sparked an interest in how moral values emerge and how they may shape our behavior.

Table 17.1 Presentation of a moral dilemma with answers graded according to Kohlberg's six stages of moral development.

In Europe, a woman was near death from cancer. One drug might save her, a form of radium that a druggist in the same town had recently discovered. The druggist was charging $2,000, ten times what the drug cost him to make. The sick woman's husband, Heinz, went to everyone he knew to borrow the money, but he could only get together about half of what it cost. He told the druggist that his wife was dying and asked him to sell it cheaper or let him pay later. But the druggist said, "No." The husband got desperate and broke into the man's store to steal the drug for his wife. Should the husband have done that? Why?

Preconventional Stages

STAGE 1

Punishment and obedience orientation (physical consequences determine what is good or bad).

Pro He should steal the drug. It isn't really bad to take it. It isn't like he didn't ask to pay for it first. The drug he'd take is only worth $200, he's not really taking a $2,000 drug.

Con He shouldn't steal the drug. It's a big crime. He didn't get permission, he used force and broke and entered. He did a lot of damage, stealing a very expensive drug and breaking up the store, too.

STAGE 2

Instrumental relativist orientation (what satisfies one's own needs is good).

Pro It's all right to steal the drug because she needs it and he wants her to live. It isn't that he wants to steal, but it's the way he has to use to get the drug to save her.

Con He shouldn't steal it. The druggist isn't wrong or bad, he just wants to make a profit. That's what you're in business for, to make money.

Conventional Stages

STAGE 3

Interpersonal concordance or "good boy-nice girl" orientation (what pleases or helps others is good).

Pro He should steal the drug. He was only doing something that was natural for a good husband to do. You can't blame him for doing something out of love for his wife, you'd blame him if he didn't love his wife enough to save her.

Con He shouldn't steal. If his wife dies, he can't be blamed. It isn't because he's heartless or that he doesn't love her enough to do everything that he legally can. The druggist is the selfish or heartless one.

STAGE 4

"Law and order" orientation (maintaining the social order, doing one's duty is good).

Pro You should steal it. If you did nothing you'd be letting your wife die, it's your responsibility if she dies. You have to take it with the idea of paying the druggist.

Con It is a natural thing for Heinz to want to save his wife but it's still always wrong to steal. He still knows he's stealing and taking a valuable drug from the man who made it.

Postconventional Stages

STAGE 5

Social contract-legalistic orientation (values agreed upon by society, including individual rights and rules for consensus, determine what is right).

Pro The law wasn't set up for these circumstances. Taking the drug in this situation isn't really right, but it's justified to do it.

Con You can't completely blame someone for stealing but extreme circumstances don't really justify taking the law into your own hands. You can't have everyone stealing whenever they get desperate. The end may be good, but the ends don't justify the means.

STAGE 6

Universal ethical-principle orientation (what is right is a matter of conscience in accord with universal principles).

Pro This is a situation which forces him to choose between stealing and letting his wife die. In a situation where the choice must be made, it is morally right to steal. He has to act in terms of the principles of preserving and respecting life.

Con Heinz is faced with the decision of whether to consider the other people who need the drug just as badly as his wife. Heinz ought to act not according to his particular feelings toward his wife, but considering the value of all the lives involved.

Description of Kohlberg's stages from Shaver & Strong, 1976. Dilemma and pro and con answers from Rest, 1968.

Coming to Terms with Others

We are only occasionally in a position of lending aid in an emergency. In most social circumstances we meet others on a more equal footing. We may discover that we need each other's help, that we are competitors, or that we must strike a bargain with one another in order to obtain what we want. For this reason, social psychologists have investigated cooperation, competition, bargaining and negotiation, and the factors that are important in each circumstance.

COOPERATION AND COMPETITION

When two or more people work together for their mutual benefit, they are cooperating. Cooperation is a valuable behavior, since societies would not be possible without it. Competition occurs when two or more people vie for a certain goal in which not all can be winners. Competition may be the most successful strategy in one circumstance, and cooperation in another.

Psychologists believe that competition and cooperation are taught by social interaction and that both strategies can be initiated at a very early age. Children are often spontaneously cooperative. But in our society, and in others, individual competition is so often modeled and reinforced that the desire to surpass others sometimes interferes with the need for cooperation. Irrational competition can sometimes spoil the success that cooperation might bring.

In an experiment conducted by M. C. Madsen and his associates, it was discovered that in certain cases cooperation declines as children grow older and that competition may become the most common mode of responding, even when it cannot possibly lead to success. Madsen had children of the same age sit across from each other at opposite ends of a small table (see Figure 17.5). Narrow gutters ran down the length of the table on both sides. The table surface was arched so that a marble placed anywhere on the table would immediately roll into the nearest gutter. A cup was imbedded in the tabletop in front of each child. At the start of the game, a marble was placed in a free-sliding marble holder in the center of the table. The marble holder prevented the marble from running into a gutter. Each child had a string attached to one end of the marble holder. To score, a child needed only to pull the string and cause the marble holder to pass over his or her cup. The marble would then drop into the cup and the child would have succeeded. However, if both children pulled their strings simultaneously, the marble holder would come apart and the marble would roll into the gutter.

Madsen found that cooperation was common among four- and five-year-olds playing this game. The children would usually negotiate and arrange it so that each received about half of the marbles. However, when Madsen tested school children in the second through fifth grades, he found their desire to compete to be so strong that a majority of them failed to obtain a single marble (Madsen, 1971). In a later study, some of the children were so competitive that they argued that it was impossible to get a marble! One child pointed out that success might be possible "if I could play alone" (Kagan & Madsen, 1971, p. 38).

Older children appear to be much more competitive because of their experience and learning. Cross-cultural research supports this supposition. When Madsen examined children from different backgrounds he obtained

Figure 17.5 *Madsen's marble-pull game.* (SOURCE: *Madsen, 1971, p. 367*)

different results. His data indicate that a strong competitive outlook is more likely to develop among older children in urban surroundings. It was observed, for instance that urban Mexican-American and urban Israeli children were more competitive than rural Mexican children or Israeli children raised on a kibbutz (Madsen, 1971; Shapira & Madsen, 1974). American children were generally more competitive regardless of their race, sex, or background, perhaps because competition is so emphasized in American society (Nelson & Madsen, 1969; Madsen & Shapira, 1970).

A more adult version of Madsen's game, known as the Acme-Bolt trucking game, was designed by researchers Deutsch and Krauss in 1960. In Figure 17.6 you can see the layout of the trucking game. To begin, each individual is given a trucking company, either the Acme or the Bolt Company. Each person's job is to move trucks along available routes until the goal is reached. Subjects are given 60¢ for each successful trip to the goal, minus 1¢ for each second it took to complete the trip. You can see that each company has two possible routes: an alternative route, which is long and time-consuming, and the short route, which is a one-lane road. As you might imagine, the best way to play the game is for each person to cooperate with the other and take turns. In this way each can use the shortest route and use it quickly. In most cases this was what happened. Cooperation emerged as the most logical and reasonable way to play the game (Deutsch & Krauss, 1960).

In another variation of the trucking game, Deutsch and Krauss added gates at the positions shown in the figure. The gate on the left was controlled by Acme and the gate on the right by Bolt. The gates could be closed at any time by their respective owners to stop the other player from moving his or her truck along the one-lane road. Two variations of this

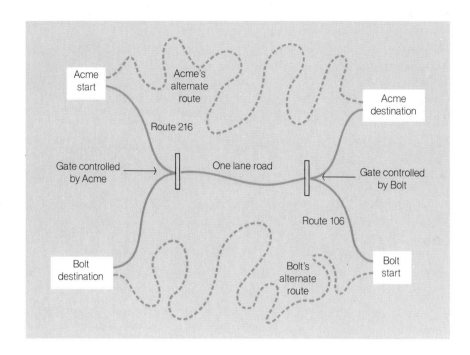

game were played. In one variation, the unilateral-threat condition, only one of the players was given a gate. In the second condition, the bilateral-threat condition, each of the players had gates. Possessing a gate provided the owner with a potential threat. The threat did not exist if the players were willing to trust one another, but if one person wanted to use the gate to accumulate more money than the opponent, he or she could do so. When both people possessed a gate, the danger that one might strike would prompt the other to strike first. Possession of one gate caused losses for both players, and possession of two gates caused the most losses (see Figure 17.7). Players would often slam their gates at the beginning of the session and sit there as each lost money. This research indicates that the chances of cooperation diminish as the ability to threaten one another increases. We needn't travel too far from this sample game to draw parallels between the nuclear arms race and hopes for disarmament. Indeed, if we were to discuss terms such as first-strike capability, implicit threat, lack of cooperation, and the mutual destruction of both sides, you might well assume that someone was weighing the prospects of a potential war between two world powers rather than considering the outcome of the Acme-Bolt trucking game.

BARGAINING AND NEGOTIATION

The ability to bargain and negotiate is extremely important in the conduct of social affairs. How many wars or conflicts, not just among nations, but among families, might have been avoided through careful bargaining or negotiation? The idea behind bargaining is to negotiate a settlement in which both parties to a conflict obtain what each feels is an equitable resolution. Most people agree that it's better to negotiate settlements than to leave a conflict unresolved or to attempt to resolve it by force. Unresolved

PROMOTING COMPETITION AND COOPERATION: THE ROBBERS' CAVE EXPERIMENT

To measure the effects of competition and cooperation, two researchers, C. W. Sherif and M. Sherif, set up a boys' camp in which competition was fostered between two groups of boys. The researchers began by isolating the groups in separate bunkhouses and keeping them apart during the activities of the day. This arrangement continued for a time until the group had developed unified structures. Each group had leaders, and each had given itself a name, the Eagles and the Rattlers. In addition, each had created its own flag. The boys in each group cooperated with other members of their group, and they knew each other mostly by nicknames.

In the second part of the experiment, rivalry was built up between the groups by placing them in a number of competitive events. The Eagles and the Rattlers engaged in a tug-of-war; the Eagles lost and in retaliation took the Rattlers' flag and burned it. This aggression produced more in-group solidarity and greater dislike of members belonging to the other group. Undaunted, the Rattlers countered with

a series of raids on the Eagles' headquarters. In some instances fistfights broke out. During this time a new and aggressive leader emerged among the Eagles, replacing the leader who had led that group during "peacetime."

At this point the researchers wanted to find ways of producing cooperation between the Eagles and the Rattlers. They began by bringing both groups close to each other during meals and such enjoyable activities as watching fireworks. Cooperation between the groups did not result, however. The close proximity simply gave the two groups greater opportunity to engage in conflict. Contact alone, then, was not the answer.

Next the researchers devised ways of forcing the groups to work together in order to achieve a common goal. At one point a truck carrying both groups of boys conveniently "stalled," and the rope that had been used as a tool of contention during tug-of-war became a tool of cooperation as the boys struck onto the idea of tying it to the bumper and pulling the truck to get it started. On another day the truck again con-

veniently "stalled," forcing members of the Eagles and Rattlers to intermingle and, once again, to work together to achieve their common goal. By this time hostility was melting away and an atmosphere of cooperation was developing among all the boys. A number of other cooperative ventures ensued. For example, the boys worked together to repair the water tank that held the camp's water. By the end of the camp experience, the Rattlers rated 36 percent of the Eagles as their friends, and the Eagles rated 23 percent of the Rattlers as their friends. This was a threefold to sixfold increase over previous recordings (Sherif & Sherif, 1956).

Getting two hostile groups to become friends through cooperation to achieve a common goal is not, of course, a new idea. Science fiction authors have envisioned an attack by extraterrestrial beings as the threat that would cause warring nations on earth to band together to defend the planet and, in so doing, to find friendship and peace with one another.

---

conflicts or conflicts resolved by force can often cost both parties much more than they would ever hope to gain. But, as you no doubt know, negotiating an equitable settlement is not always an easy matter.

Have you ever walked into a new-car dealership and tried to strike a bargain? When you do, you may feel at a disadvantage, knowing that the people with whom you are dealing not only have daily experience with this kind of bargaining but also are aware of exactly what a good or a bad bargain is in terms of the profit they will make. In this situation you may feel like the country gentleman who announced, "I've been took!" When asked how he knew, he said, "Because they sold me the car."

Social psychologists have examined the factors that play a role in bargaining and negotiation. For the next few pages, let's look at some of these factors.

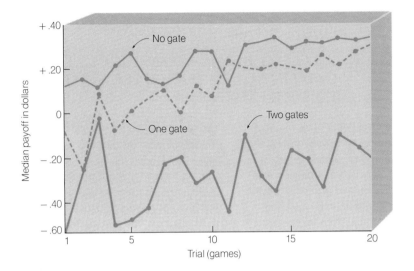

Figure 17.7 *In the Acme-Bolt trucking game, Deutsch and Krauss discovered that cooperation decreased (costing both sides money) as the number of implied threats (the power to stop commerce by using a gate) increased.* (SOURCE: *Deutsch & Krauss, 1960, p. 185*)

Ingratiation **Ingratiation** is a technique in which one person makes another feel grateful for some reason. This technique is sometimes used as a way of obtaining a good settlement for oneself during negotiation. The two most effective ingratiation techniques are flattery and the giving of small favors. Flattery can work if it is engaged in carefully so as not to overdo it, which would make the ploy obvious. People tend to want to help those they like, and they tend to like those who say good things about them (Drachman, Decarufel, & Insko, 1978). It is also possible to ingratiate oneself by doing small favors. A large favor may then be requested in return. Interestingly, people will often return a large favor for a small one. This is the "I lent you a book, now won't you help me move to a new apartment?" effect (Isen & Levin, 1972).

It should be noted that friends often do things for each other without being concerned about how equitable a particular bargain may be. After all, what kind of a friendship would it be if each person kept track of who owes what to whom? A friend may give you sincere compliments, and there's nothing wrong with returning a large favor for a small one. The exchanges that take place in a friendship would not be considered ingratiation. Ingratiation is a tactic by which an individual hopes through certain responses to come out ahead in a bargaining exchange. The car dealer who is extremely friendly, compliments you, and offers to "throw in the extra trim package" is probably not doing so out of friendship.

The Foot-in-the-Door Technique The **foot-in-the-door technique** is a simple strategy. You ask for something very small to begin with, something that seems very reasonable, in order to get the other side to say yes just once. Once they've said yes, there is a better chance that they will agree to something larger later (DeJong, 1979). Sales companies will often request that you accept a free sample or literature about their product before asking you to buy. Perhaps the most famous experiment demonstrating the foot-in-the-door technique was conducted in 1966, when two researchers called people on the phone and asked a few simple questions about the kinds of soaps they used. Most people were willing to spend time discussing the soap they used. In a few days the same researchers called again, but this time they requested that their representatives be allowed into the person's home to conduct an inventory of every product owned, and that this team be allowed to search every single portion of the house, even drawers and cabinets. Unbelievably, 52.8 percent agreed to have their house searched! Other people were then called, but this time the big request was made immediately. Of this second group, only 22.2 percent agreed to have their homes searched (Freedman & Fraser, 1966). Many other studies have found similar results (Baron, 1973; DeJong & Musilli, 1978).

The Door-in-the-Face Technique   In a way the **door-in-the-face technique** is the opposite of the foot-in-the-door technique. If we ask a large favor that is certain to be rejected, and then come back with a request for a smaller favor (the one we wanted in the first place), our request is more likely to be granted (Cialdini, Vincent, Lewis, Catalan, Wheeler, & Darby, 1975).

When offering something for sale there is a danger, of course, that the first offer will so disgust the potential buyer that he or she will leave without ever discussing a counteroffer. For this reason one should be cautious and not appear too adamant about an extremely high price. The effect of this kind of social bargain seems to be based on the buyer's relief at being able to get around the very high and disappointing initial offer. To end up paying $70,000 for a house doesn't feel so bad when you were afraid that you might have to pay $80,000. Sadly, the poorest bargaining technique, although the most honest, is to begin by asking for exactly what you want.

Lowballing   In negotiating it's often better to get someone to agree to a commitment to act before you begin to add specifics that may turn him or her away from the agreement. Refraining from mentioning the high cost of a commitment until the commitment has been made is called **lowballing.** In one experiment students were asked to participate in an experimental course for credit. Only after they had said yes were they informed that the class would meet at 7:00 A.M. In this condition approximately 55 percent of the subjects participated. When, however, students were asked to participate in the experimental class for credit but were told before they made their decision that the class would meet at 7:00 A.M. fewer than 25 percent participated (Cialdini, Cacioppo, Bassett, & Miller, 1978; Pallak, Cook, & Sullivan, 1980).

Car dealers often wait until you have made the commitment to buy before they mention the cost of sales tax, shipping, and dealer preparation. Unscrupulous stores sometimes offer a "great deal" if you hurry right down. When you arrive, however, they inform you that they're sold out of the "great deal" but have some "not-so-great deals" to show you. Such *bait and switch* operations are generally illegal.

The Influence of Groups

In social circumstances, we encounter groups as well as individuals. Psychologists have discovered that groups can affect a person's behavior in special ways. Not only do people rely on groups as a source of comparison and for social norms, but depending on the situation, a group may occasionally deindividuate or polarize its members. Because deindividuation and polarization can strongly influence behavior, social psychologists have been drawn to study these processes.

MORALS
The attitudes and beliefs that people hold that help them to determine what is right or wrong.

INGRATIATION
To purposely bring oneself into the favor or good graces of another, often with flattery, in the hopes of obtaining something of value.

FOOT-IN-THE-DOOR TECHNIQUE
A bargaining technique in which one purposely asks for a very small favor or concession in order to soften up the opposition and set the stage for obtaining a much larger favor.

DOOR-IN-THE-FACE TECHNIQUE
A bargaining technique in which one purposely requests a very large favor or concession that will certainly be refused, in the hopes of increasing the chances of obtaining the smaller favor or concession that's really desired (and which will now seem less unreasonable in comparison with the initial huge request).

LOWBALLING
A negotiation technique in which one purposely omits details of a request that may lessen the chances of compliance until a commitment to comply has been obtained from the other party. Lowballing will generally lead to more compliance.

The process whereby social restraints are weakened, and impulsive and aggressive tendencies released, as the person loses his or her individual identity, usually as the result of being part of a large group or having his or her identity concealed in some way, as by a mask.

DEINDIVIDUATION

We are told from an early age that we are responsible for our actions. Almost no one is likely to walk up to a storefront, smash the window, and loot it just because he or she sees something that's wanted. Similarly, few of us are likely to wait quietly by ourselves until someone passes and then hit that person with a bottle. And not too many of us are likely to go over to the house of someone we don't like, drag that person out to a tree, and hold a lynching. Most of us would assume that anyone doing such things must be socially deviant. But these same behaviors, which few of us would ever dream of doing alone, are more likely to occur if we're part of a group. During blackouts, crowds often engage in looting. During raucous baseball games, people often throw things at the umpires or players. And lynchings are examples of the kinds of behaviors in which mobs may engage.

It seems that the social restraints that are normally placed on us can disappear once we become a member of a group that begins to become aroused or angry. Why should a group have such a restraint-reducing influence? We have words for it, mob mentality, for instance. But mobs are made up of people. Why will people do things in a group that they'd never do when alone? It's not that groups change people in a permanent way. Individuals who've taken part in mob violence often feel ashamed of their behavior when they're alone again.

One reason may be the effects of modeling. When we see many other people engage in a behavior we become more certain that that behavior is appropriate. A second reason may be that a diffusion of responsibility occurs, that is, we can distribute the blame for our actions. After all, "everyone else was doing it, too." A third reason, **deindividuation,** has been suggested (Zimbardo, 1979; Diener, 1980). Deindividuation can occur when we become so caught up in events and in the feelings of the group that we lose our own self-awareness. Once our self-awareness has been reduced we lose track of who we are and what our values are. This in turn causes us to become more impulsive, more sensitive to our present emotional state, and, to some degree, unable to regulate our own behavior. Also, with such reduced self-awareness we are less concerned about what others think of us and what they might do to us. We are more concerned about responding as part of a group.

Reduced self-awareness is not an inevitable part of being a member of a group, but certain conditions can make it more likely. One way is to camouflage the qualities that make us individuals. Taking away a person's individuality compels him or her to conform and blend into the group. Anything that fosters anonymity reduces individuality. Ku Klux Klan members wear hoods, supposedly to conceal their identity, but undoubtedly also to reduce the self-awareness of individuals and make them more amenable to group desires. Concentration on events in the environment rather than on internal thoughts also helps lessen self-awareness. Group unity and a high level of arousal will reduce self-awareness even further.

POLARIZATION

Very often, individuals who enter a group discussion with moderate views will change their views and eventually take a more polarized or extreme position. That is, they will become more conservative or more radical in their approach to a particular issue or decision. Consequently, a group may

Drawing by Booth; © 1977 The New Yorker Magazine, Inc.

Group attitudes may also be altered if they are contradicted by those in power.

reach a more extreme position on an issue than its members might have individually had they decided the issue without group interaction.

In one study researcher Jerald Greenberg asked 200 subjects how they would divide money between two people who had worked at a particular job. They were told that one of the individuals had done a better job than the other, but that they could divide the money as they wished. The average subject's response was that 63.2 percent of the money should go to the one who had done the better job. Some time later the subjects were again asked individually how they would divide the money. The average response the second time was that 64.3 percent should be given to the one who had done the better job, not much different from the first recommendation of 63.2 percent. In another group, the subjects were given the same information and asked individually how they would divide the money. On the average, 64.4 percent of the money was awarded to the person who had done the better job. Then the subjects in this second group were allowed to discuss the situation with four other people. Afterwards individuals were again asked to make a recommendation, and this time the average response was that 76.5 percent of the money should be given to the person who had done the better job (Greenberg, 1979) (see Figure 17.8).

The **polarization effect,** the tendency of members of a group to take a more extreme position than they would as individuals, has been demonstrated many times. The direction of the polarization may be strongly influenced by culture. In cases in which American groups were more likely to polarize in the direction of taking a risk, Chinese groups were more likely to polarize in the direction of caution (Hong, 1978).

There are a number of explanations for the polarization effect. First, when we are among others who share our views we may wish to gain their approval by exemplifying the beliefs and attitudes they hold. To show ourselves worthy of the group's esteem, we may want to be more extreme in ways that the group values. For example, jet fighter pilots admire cool-headedness and lack of emotion in a tough situation. Most nonpilots who agree that coolheadedness is a fine attribute will try to demonstrate it to a degree. They will also express a certain admiration for this behavior. However, should they become fighter pilots and find themselves among many others who agree that coolheadedness and lack of emotion in a tough situation are desirable, each individual may attempt to exemplify these attributes in the extreme in order to obtain the admiration of the group (Pruitt, 1971).

The second reason that groups may tend to polarize is a fairly obvious one. While exchanging information, individuals may make persuasive arguments, and the entire group may shift toward the most convincing of these arguments. A jury furnishes a good example of this kind of polarization effect. Jury members are selected because they are undecided to begin with; potential jurors with extreme views are weeded out. It is up to each side

Figure 17.8 *Subjects in all conditions were asked to divide money between two workers, one who was said to have done a better job. Subjects awarded more money to the better worker after group discussion, which demonstrates the polarizing effect of the group on the judgments of its members. The members shifted toward a more extreme position.* (SOURCE: *After Greenberg, 1979*)

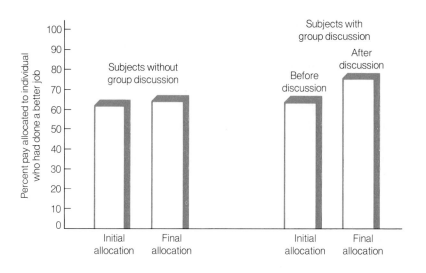

in the courtroom to give persuasive arguments. The jury is expected to become more and more polarized during discussion in the jury room until it reaches a verdict (Kaplan & Schwartz, 1977). We can only hope that juries become polarized because of the convincing arguments presented by the prosecution or the defense and not because of the wish of uncertain jurors to obtain the esteem of those who had already decided one way or the other. Keep the group polarization process in mind. Remember, it is easy to become convinced if many others agree with you. Just because a group takes an extreme position does not necessarily mean that it's a more reasonable position than an individual might take.

The common view that groups tend to reach middle-of-the-road decisions is not altogether inaccurate, however. If all groups became polarized, all governments would become radical or reactionary and all group plans would be extreme. In fact, much of the time this does not happen. Whenever a group includes unified subgroups, each holding opposing views in the group discussion, a typical result is depolarization and compromise (Vinokur & Burnstein, 1978). A case in point is the U.S. Congress, which contains Democrats and Republicans.

LEADERSHIP

Individuals can affect groups of course. Sometimes an extremely influential group member will emerge as a leader. When a person becomes a leader he or she is given the authority of a group and speaks for the group. Throughout history people have wondered about the qualities of leadership and what makes leaders attractive to others. Psychologists have studied leaders and arrived at two very different hypotheses to explain how a leader will emerge.

The first, the **situational-environmental hypothesis,** argues that people are chosen as leaders because they happen to be in the right place at the right time. In other words, if they happen to have certain skills that meet a group's needs at a given moment, they may emerge as leaders (Hollander & Julian, 1970). The situational approach argues that an individual who may be a leader in one set of circumstances may be a follower in different circumstances. In other words, circumstances may arise in which any member of the group may emerge as a leader; it depends on the situation, not the individual.

The other hypothesis, that leaders have particular traits that make them stand apart from other members of their group, is known as the **great-man, great-woman hypothesis.** This idea is not new. The special abilities of leaders have been heralded for centuries. However, these qualities have not been carefully examined until recently. Psychologists have found that one of the most important abilities, one shared by many leaders, is a high degree of verbal skill (Bavelas, Hastorf, Gross, & Kite, 1965). In addition, it has been found that good leaders generally maintain the views of their group. Leaders who wander too far from their group's views tend to be discarded. Aside from these two characteristics, leaders have been found to be very different from one another. Psychologists have not yet been able to uncover specific personalities or an important series of traits that are guaranteed to result in leadership.

POLARIZATION EFFECT
An effect in which members of a group tend to take a more extreme position (more conservative or more daring) than they would have as individuals. Probably the result of social comparison or persuasive group arguments.

SITUATIONAL-ENVIRONMENTAL HYPOTHESIS
The hypothesis that individuals become leaders because of situational or circumstantial forces rather than because of their personality or traits.

GREAT-MAN, GREAT-WOMAN HYPOTHESIS
The hypothesis that individuals become leaders primarily because of the personality or traits they possess.

IN-GROUP
Any group for whom the individual feels a positive regard. A subjective term, depending on one's point of view.

OUT-GROUP
Any group that an individual views in a negative way. A subjective term, depending on one's point of view.

PREJUDICE
Beliefs or judgments made without sufficient evidence and not easily changed by opposing facts or circumstances; preconceived hostile and irrational feelings, opinions, or attitudes about a group or an individual.

DISCRIMINATION
In social psychology, treating people differently on the basis of their race, ethnic group, or class, rather than on their relevant traits. Acts of discrimination are typically premised upon prejudice.

Research has found that both leadership hypotheses have merit and that they often work simultaneously. For example, while certain leaders may emerge owing to circumstances, some individuals, because of their personalities, are more likely to accept and capitalize upon a situational call to leadership than are others (Nydegger, 1975).

Leaders have also been classified according to their abilities to fill certain group needs. One researcher (Bales, 1970) has argued that groups need both task leaders, who are able to get certain jobs done, and social-emotional leaders, who can lift spirits and provide psychological comfort and a sense of well-being to group members. Bales has argued that great leaders combine the best of both task leaders and social-emotional leaders.

Prejudice and Discrimination

We have seen that individuals can affect one another; groups can affect individuals; and individuals may lead groups. In addition, groups can also affect members of other groups. Social psychologists sometimes use the terms **in-group** and **out-group** when discussing the feelings that members of one group may have toward their own group and other groups. Whether a group is considered to be an in-group or an out-group depends on one's perspective. What is an in-group for you may be an out-group for someone else. By definition, a person has a positive regard for in-groups but views out-groups in a negative light. The way in which a person decides which are in-groups and which are out-groups has been of great interest to social psychologists studying prejudice and discrimination. After all, before prejudice can begin it is necessary to identify the in-group and the out-group. As the television character Archie Bunker demonstrated so well, a very prejudiced individual may perceive hundreds of out-groups into which just about every person in existence may be placed.

Prejudice may be defined as learned values and beliefs that may lead an individual to be unfairly biased against members of particular groups. Because of prejudice, people may behave differently toward other groups (out-groups) than they do toward their own (in-group). Different behavior based on prejudice is called **discrimination.**

One of the classic demonstrations of prejudice was set up by Jane Elliott in an experiment she conducted with her third-grade class in Riceville, Iowa. Mrs. Elliott wanted her students to understand something about prejudice. All of the students in her class were white, but their eye color differed. On the first day of the experiment, Mrs. Elliott, who had blue eyes, announced to her class that it was a well-known fact that blue-eyed children were brighter and generally superior to those with brown eyes. There were fewer brown-eyed children in the classroom. It was explained to them that they were inferior and that the blue-eyed children should be respected and considered to be better people. To emphasize their inferiority, the brown-eyed children were forced to sit in the back of the room, to use paper cups instead of the drinking fountain, to stand at the end of the line, and to wear special collars that enabled the blue-eyed students to identify them immediately from a distance or from behind. The blue-eyed students, on the other hand, were given special privileges such as extra time at recess and second helpings at lunch.

Before the first hour had elapsed the effects of discrimination had begun to show on the brown-eyed children. Their schoolwork deteriorated. They

became angry and depressed. They described themselves as sad, stupid, or awful. (You may recall from Chapter 6 that this is not unlike the way in which the black children referred to the black doll in the experiment conducted by Clark and Clark.) In describing the effect on the blue-eyed children the teacher stated, "What had been marvelously cooperative, thoughtful children became nasty, vicious, discriminating little third-graders. . . . it was ghastly" (Zimbardo, 1979, p. 638).

The next day, Mrs. Elliott informed the students that she had made a mistake and that it was really the brown-eyed children who were more intelligent and superior and the blue-eyed children who were inferior. In short order the behaviors of the children switched. The brown-eyed children began to do better at their schoolwork, while the blue-eyed children began to lose their self-confidence.

Feeling prejudice firsthand may be a valuable educational experience for those who, because of their cultural position, are not typically subject to prejudice. The benefits that may be gained from the experience have been demonstrated in an experiment in which children in a third-grade class were assigned randomly to be either green or orange people. They wore colored armbands to show which group they belonged to. At first the orange people were considered superior. They were told that they were cleaner and smarter. The green people were regarded as inferior and were denied many privileges given to the orange people. On the second day the situation was reversed. The effects were similar to those produced in the Elliott study. Each time the group discriminated against felt inferior, lost self-confidence, and did poorly in schoolwork. In this experiment, another class served as a control group and was never exposed to the assignments of orange or green. On the third day, and again after two weeks, students in the control class and students who had gone through the orange and green experiment were asked if they would like to go on a picnic with black children from a nearby school (all of the children in both control and experimental groups were white). On one occasion only 62 percent of the children in the control group agreed, while 96 percent of the children in the group that had experienced prejudice firsthand agreed (Weiner & Wright, 1973).

Both the Elliott and the orange-green experiments show how easily prejudice can be learned. It can be taught by systematically associating other groups with unpleasant stimuli, by rewarding discriminatory behaviors, and by modeling discrimination.

PERSONALITY AND PREJUDICE

While individuals can learn to feel prejudice against a particular group, there is evidence that some people are prejudiced in a much more general way. Like Archie Bunker, these people place just about everyone in out-groups. In 1946 researcher Eugene Hartley, when measuring people's attitudes toward different minority groups, decided to list three minorities that didn't exist, Danerieans, Pirenians, and Walonians. He found that people who identified many out-groups were prejudiced against the made-up groups as well. One generally prejudiced person stated, "I don't know anything about them. Therefore, I would exclude them from my country" (Hartley, 1946).

Perhaps the best-known effort to explain prejudice was made by researchers over 30 years ago (Adorno, Frenkel-Brunswik, Levinson, & Sanford, 1950). Adorno and his colleagues believed that those who were highly prejudiced were likely to have authoritarian personalities. Authoritarian people tend to be submissive and obedient to authority and to reject other groups in a punitive way. They usually see others as either weak or strong. "Either you're with us or against us," in-group or out-group. Adorno felt that individuals became authoritarian because of the harsh and punitive child-rearing practices of their parents (Stephan & Rosenfield, 1978).

To test this hypothesis Adorno and his colleagues developed the California F Scale to measure authoritarianism (see chapter 13). Although the findings are not completely consistent, in general Adorno's hypothesis that those who are extremely authoritarian are more likely to be prejudiced has been supported (Cherry & Byrne, 1976).

OVERCOMING PREJUDICE

There are a number of ways in which to overcome prejudice. Antagonistic groups can be brought into contact with one another. But, as you'll recall from the Rattlers and Eagles study, contact alone is not enough, and it may make matters worse. The groups also need a common goal. For example, racism among members of a baseball team is likely to be remote because all of the players have one goal. They must cooperate with each other to reach this goal, and as a result, they come to think of each other as members of a common in-group.

Prejudice can also be combatted by legislation. Although it is difficult to legislate values, prejudice can be made more or less likely by the structure of the laws in a society. The legal structure in South Africa, for example, makes racial prejudice more likely, since blacks and whites are segregated by law and the persistent economic and political differences between the groups are emphasized. In the United States in the past 20 years, laws such as the Voting Rights Act designed to give minority members equal rights have helped change attitudes and feelings among the population. In 1963 in the South, for example, 61 percent of white parents said that they would not send their children to a school attended by even a few blacks. By 1975 this figure had decreased to 15 percent. Much of the difference was due to a new awareness brought about by legislation (Gallup, 1975).

Finally, through learning, self-esteem may be increased among those who are the victims of prejudice so as to lessen the adverse effects of the prejudice. Concepts such as "Black is beautiful" and "I am somebody" may protect potential victims from some of the detrimental effects of prejudice. Furthermore, all of us who are interested in eliminating prejudice can help by modeling nondiscriminatory behavior and by showing others that we are accepting of the members of potential out-groups. This holds true for sexual discrimination, which is discussed in Chapter 18, as well as for race, age, ethnic, and religious discrimination.

Social Attitudes and Changes in Attitudes

The attitudes that a person has about others can be a powerful influence in social situations. Consequently, psychologists have been drawn to study how social attitudes are formed and how they change. A **social attitude** is a relatively enduring system of feelings, beliefs, and behaviors with respect to a social object. For example, the attitudes you have toward a family member would include your feelings and thoughts about that person and the behaviors toward that person that have been generated by the feelings and thoughts. Knowing how someone thinks or feels about a particular issue makes it easier to predict their behavior (Cialdini, Petty, & Cacioppo, 1981).

FORMING SOCIAL ATTITUDES

As you'll recall from Chapter 6, attitudes may be formed or altered through the process of associative learning. In one study, nationalities such as Swedish or Dutch and names such as Tom and Bill were systematically associated with pleasant or unpleasant words; this association changed people's attitudes toward the nationalities and names (Staats & Staats, 1958).

Instrumental learning can also be important in the formation of attitudes. As children develop, parents typically reinforce or punish the behaviors that stem from the attitudes the children hold. We can all recall a childhood in which adults were there to tell us the attitudes that we should have about stealing other people's property or calling someone a name. Our attitudes and views have been shaped as we have been systematically rewarded for the "right behavior" and punished for anything else.

Social learning through modeling is another important source of attitude acquisition. We often base our attitudes on the behavior of others, even if those others are not trying to transmit their attitudes to us directly. We look to others to help us decide which attitudes are best and appropriate.

Measuring Attitudes Attitudes are often measured by means of questionnaires or scales. Such measurement devices must be used carefully because subtle differences in the meaning of words that appear in them can bias

SOCIAL ATTITUDE
An enduring system of positive or negative evaluations, feelings, and tendencies toward action with respect to a social object.

(a) How do you handle your money? Are you

☐ Generous, or ☐ Stingy

(b) How do you handle your money? Are you

☐ Extravagant, or ☐ Thrifty

Figure 17.9 *An example of how a questionnaire can be biased. Survey questions (a) and (b) appear to ask the same thing, but because of the connotations of the words used, survey (a) will report that people like to spend, while survey (b) will report that they like to save.*

responses. For an extreme example of such bias, examine Figure 17.9. Generally, though, if the questionnaire or scale is worded carefully and used appropriately it can provide much valuable information about attitudes.

Another problem that arises with questionnaires or scales is that people often present attitudes different from their real ones, or they alter their true beliefs, in an attempt to enhance their image in the eyes of the researcher (Braver, Linder, Corwin, & Cialdini, 1977; Schlenker, 1978). When this happens it is difficult to get a true assessment of attitudes. To reduce the incidence of faked attitudes on questionnaires and scales, social psychologists have devised a unique arrangement known as the **bogus pipeline.** In this procedure, the subject is connected to a machine with impressive flashing lights. He or she is told that the machine will monitor physiological responses and will reveal to the experimenter the subject's true opinions whenever the subject supplies an answer about his or her attitudes. A trick is used to help the subject believe in the bogus pipeline. The subject's views on certain questions have been subtly obtained, sometimes days earlier, by coworkers in the experiment. Now the subject is asked to respond to these questions first, so that the experimenter can seem to distinguish the real from the fabricated views. Once the subject is convinced that the machine can detect real opinions, the subject is asked to respond to the questionnaire. It is assumed that the subject will no longer have a reason to fake when answering the attitude questionnaire if the subject believes that the machine will reveal his or her true feelings (Jones & Sigall, 1971).

There is evidence that real attitudes are tapped better by the bogus pipeline technique than by a questionnaire used alone. In one study, for instance, whites expressed a positive attitude toward blacks when asked to answer a standard questionnaire, but expressed more negative attitudes when connected to the bogus pipeline (Jones, Bell, & Aronson, 1972). In another experiment students connected to the bogus pipeline were more likely to confess to having had the answers to a test beforehand than when they were asked on a standardized questionnaire (Quigley-Fernandez & Tedeschi, 1978). The bogus pipeline technique has not always shown positive results, however (Cherry, Byrne, & Mitchell, 1976). It may even be possible that the bogus pipeline causes subjects to "confess" to more negative attitudes than they really have (Gaes, Kalli, & Tedeschi, 1978).

Other approaches designed to reveal a person's real attitudes have been attempted. Real physiological monitors can be used to measure information about the intensity or direction of an emotional or attitudinal response (Mewborn & Rogers, 1979; White & Maltzman, 1978). Such monitors have also been used to measure physiological responses as attitudes undergo change (Cacioppo & Petty, 1979; Kroeber-Riel, 1979), but they are not always very accurate.

Attitudes and Self-Awareness Sometimes subjects aren't certain about their own attitudes, and they may respond to questions about them without carefully monitoring their feelings. The subjects in an experiment were asked about their attitudes toward working particular puzzles. In one condition they described their feelings while seated before a mirror. In the control condition the subjects saw no mirror. The hypothesis stated that while placed before a mirror people will have more self-awareness and that this, in turn, will help them concentrate on their feelings. The experimenters used the subjects' attitudes about how much fun the puzzles would be to predict how long they would play with the puzzles. The attitudes obtained from subjects seated before a mirror predicted much more accurately how long they would play with the puzzles than the attitudes obtained from subjects who were not before the mirror (Pryor, Gibbons, Wicklund, Fazio, & Hood, 1977).

CHANGING ATTITUDES: PERSUASIVE COMMUNICATION

It seems that a day can't go by without someone trying to change our attitudes. All you need to do is turn on a television set, listen to a radio, or look at a billboard to find the attitude changers at work.

Techniques for changing attitudes commonly rely on **persuasive communication.** In persuasive communication we are provided with facts or logical arguments about why we should use a particular product or feel a particular way. These so-called facts or logical arguments are often self-serving and biased. Sometimes these communications will influence our attitudes, sometimes not. The ability of messages from ad agencies, political candidates, or even people we know to affect our attitudes depends on a number of complex interactions.

Characteristics of the Communicator   In general, we tend to trust information from experts (McGinnies & Ward, 1974). Nonetheless, a communicator's intentions can affect our view of his or her credibility. We would normally consider a physician to be an expert on medical matters, but a physician who tells us that cigarettes are good for our health might not be believed once we find out he or she is working for a tobacco company. In such an instance we might regard the communication as biased because of the obvious motives behind the expert's statement (Eagly & Himmelfarb, 1978).

Another important characteristic of the communicator is his or her perceived similarity with the audience. If members of the audience feel that the speaker is similar to them (in socioeconomic class, occupation, appearance, and so on), the speaker will probably be more persuasive. Television commercials capitalize on this, using actors or actresses who look like "someone off the streets," In general, salespersons who are like their customers are more successful at selling the product than even an expert who is perceived to be unlike the customers (Brock, 1965).

During the past few years much evidence has been gathered to show that the information people generate themselves is more powerful in determining attitudes than is information provided by others (Cialdini, Petty, & Cacioppo, 1981). In other words, self-persuasion is most persuasive (Janis & King, 1954). We trust ourselves, but should we? It has been argued that under certain circumstances people can deceive themselves with their own self-persuasion.

In one study, students were asked to write an essay about a particular issue using certain words that were associated with either a pro or an anti position. The students who used the most pro words became more favorable toward the position. Those who used the anti words became less favorable (Eiser & Ross, 1977; Eiser & Pancer, 1979). In a second study, subjects were given essays to read that contained either the pro words or the anti words. But these essays did not affect the subjects' attitudes. In the first study

A procedure for measuring a person's real attitudes and feelings rather than what the person wishes to present. Subjects are lead to believe that a supposed physiological monitor is able to detect their real attitudes and feelings, and that any attempt to hide them will be uncovered.

PERSUASIVE COMMUNICATION
Arguments designed to alter attitudes by appealing to reason by means of logical arguments.

the subjects had used these words in their own essays (self-generated), while in the second study they had read essays in which the words had been used (generated) by others. These studies highlight the greater influence of self-generated arguments.

Characteristics of the Communication   Another important factor in producing attitude change is the form of the message or communication. One kind of communication may be more effective than another depending on the initial view held by the recipient of the message. If the recipient initially opposes the idea that is to be presented, a two-sided argument (in which the speaker clearly presents both sides of the issue) will lower the recipient's resistance to persuasion more effectively than a one-sided argument (in which the speaker presents only the side the recipient opposes). On the other hand, if the recipient initially agrees with the issue, a one-sided argument in favor of the issue will strengthen attitudes toward the issue more effectively than a two-sided argument (Hovland, Lumsdaine, & Sheffield, 1949).

Some communications appeal to the emotions. Cigarette smokers are frightened by stories of lung cancer, a request for funds to feed the hungry is accompanied by photographs of malnourished children, and a message about driver safety is supplemented by an account of an automobile accident. **Emotional appeals** can be very effective in changing attitudes and behavior, but only under certain conditions (Leventhal & Niles, 1965; Simonson & Lundy, 1966). For an emotional appeal to work, the viewers must believe that they can take action that will reduce the stress caused by the emotional appeal, such as giving to the hungry. If action is impossible, viewers tend to deny the emotional appeal or try to ignore it. In addition, viewers who have high self-esteem are more likely to be influenced by emotional appeals (Leventhal, 1970). It may be that those with low self-esteem view themselves as helpless or as under too much stress to be worried about the problems of others. If the recipients of the message feel that they can do nothing, or if they have low self-esteem, a very mild emotional appeal will have a greater effect than a strong one (Janis & Feshbach, 1953).

There are also ways to help people resist attitude change. People who have been taught how to refute arguments that go against their beliefs are less likely to change their beliefs (McGuire, 1964). It's also possible to help people avoid attitude change by forewarning them that the speaker is intent on changing their beliefs (Petty & Cacioppo, 1979).

Simply being exposed to something can alter our attitude in favor of it (Zajonc, 1968). Advertisers, knowing this, attempt to show their products as often as possible. This effect is known as the **mere exposure effect.** It does not hold true for things that have negative outcomes. For example, mere exposure to watching your car being damaged is not likely to make you feel better about it (Swap, 1977). The mere exposure effect does seem to work, however, with objects that are initially disliked but later liked (Bukoff & Elman, 1979). In one clever experiment, researchers took photographs of subjects and of the subjects' friends or lovers. Then, photographs from mirror images of the subjects and the subjects' friends and lovers were made. The photographs were mixed together and the subjects were asked which they felt most favorable toward. When subjects viewed themselves they felt most favorable toward the photograph of the mirror image, but when they viewed friends and lovers they felt most favorable toward the direct photographs (Mita, Dermer, & Knight, 1977). The stimulus doesn't even appear to have to be consciously observed for the mere exposure effect to occur (Wilson, 1979). This may explain why people are more likely to vote for candidates they've seen or been exposed to than for candidates they've not seen, even if they are aware of the issues both candidates support (Grush, 1980).

Characteristics of the Listener   Sometimes people don't give much thought to a particular issue when it is presented, and yet their attitudes change anyway (Miller, Maruyama, Beaber, & Valone, 1976). For example, Miller and his colleagues discovered that listeners were more likely to change their attitudes in favor of a speaker who spoke quickly. However, whether or not a listener has paid careful attention to a particular discussion will affect the endurance of the attitude change. Researchers Petty and Cacioppo have argued that there are two basic routes of persuasion, **central route processing,** in which attitudes are changed while the person is motivated to think carefully about the issue, and **peripheral route processing,** in which attitudes are changed while motivation or ability to think about the issue is very low (Petty & Cacioppo, 1980). An attitude change through the central route (for example after carefully listening to a persuasive argument) is likely to be an enduring change. An attitude change through the peripheral route (for example while noticing that a commercial has a pleasant jingle and nice-looking people) is more likely to be temporary (Cialdini, Levy, Herman, Kozlowski, & Petty, 1976).

One study clearly demonstrated the importance of these two routes of persuasion. Subjects were exposed to a message that contained either two or six arguments in favor of a particular positive position. The messages were given either by a likable or a dislikable person. Half of the subjects were told that they would later be interviewed concerning the issue so that they were motivated to pay attention and to think about it (central route). The other half were told that they would be interviewed on an unrelated issue, and they therefore had little motivation to think about the message (peripheral route). The subjects who expected to be interviewed about the topic showed attitude change that was determined primarily by the number of arguments presented. The attitude change was greater when six rather than two arguments were given. Whether the speaker was likable or dislikable had no effect. Among the subjects who did not expect to be interviewed, the number of arguments (two or six) made little difference in attitude change. The important factor was whether the source, the speaker, was likable or dislikable. Furthermore, a measurement of attitudes taken ten days later showed that the subjects who had expected to be interviewed about the topic (central route) had stable attitude changes, while those whose attitudes had been changed by the peripheral route had shifted back to their premessage attitudes (Chaiken, 1980).

The effect of the recipient's intelligence on his or her susceptibility to persuasion has also been examined. You might expect that it would be more difficult to change the attitudes of an intelligent person. In general, though, there is no reliable relationship between intelligence and a person's ability to resist persuasion (Hovland, Lumsdaine, & Sheffield, 1949). The more intelligent a person is, however, the more likely that a two-sided argument will be effective in creating attitude change rather than a one-sided argument (Miller & Buckhout, 1973).

A person's level of self-esteem has been shown to be an important pre-

EMOTIONAL APPEALS
Arguments designed to alter attitudes by appealing to the emotions through moving visual and verbal messages.

MERE EXPOSURE EFFECT
The effect whereby attitudes become more favorable toward something merely by being opposed to it.

CENTRAL ROUTE PROCESSING
From social-information processing theory, a route of persuasion and attitude change that may occur when a person pays careful attention to a persuasive discussion. Any resulting attitude change is relatively enduring.

PERIPHERAL ROUTE PROCESSING
From social-information processing theory, a route of persuasion and attitude change that may occur even when a person pays little attention to the persuasive message. Any resulting attitude change is usually temporary.

dictor of his or her ability to resist persuasion (Linton & Graham, 1959). Nonetheless, a distinction must be drawn between long-term and short-term self-esteem. Long-term self-esteem refers to the general feelings we have about ourselves over a long period of time, while short-term self-esteem can vary from moment to moment, depending on immediate events. For instance, although you may feel generally good about yourself (your long-term esteem is high) you may call yourself "stupid" if you drop a glass and break it (low short-term self-esteem). By giving subjects tasks in which they were destined to fail, researchers have manipulated short-term self-esteem. Interestingly, the level of short-term self-esteem seems to have a greater effect on the person's ability to resist persuasion than the level of long-term self-esteem. As short-term self esteem lowers, resistance to persuasion decreases (Gollob & Dittes, 1965; Zellner, 1970). Why this should be so is unknown.

COGNITIVE DISSONANCE AND ATTITUDE CHANGE

In the late 1950s Leon Festinger conducted what has become a classic experiment. Subjects were invited to participate in an experiment that was purposely made exceedingly dull. For one hour they were required to move spools on and off of a tray and to rotate pegs quarter turns in a pegboard, always using only one hand. Nothing could have been more boring. The subjects were unaware that they had been assigned to one of two groups. When they were finished they were offered a monetary reward and asked to do a favor. Subjects in the first group were given $1 and then asked to tell the next subject, who was waiting to participate in the experiment, that the experiment had been fun. After taking the dollar and complying with the request, the subjects were asked by an interviewer for their real feelings about the experiment. Subjects in the second group were given $20 as a reward, and they were also asked to tell the next subject that the experiment had been fun. After receiving the money and complying with the request they, too, were asked how they really felt about the experiment. Interestingly, the subjects who had received the $20 reported feeling that the experiment was horribly boring, while the subjects who had received only $1 generally felt that the experiment had been interesting (Festinger & Carlsmith, 1959). Festinger argued that when a person acts in a manner that is inconsistent with his or her real feelings and beliefs, and can find no obvious reason for having done so, **cognitive dissonance** is created. Such dissonance, he argued, must be resolved because it causes an uncomfortable feeling, and the best way to resolve it is to change one's attitudes so that the previous behavior will now appear to be consistent with one's views. In other words, when subjects lied by telling another person that the dull task was really interesting, they behaved in a manner inconsistent with their feelings, and since they had received only $1 for doing this, they were subjected to a high level of cognitive dissonance. The reason the subjects had lied was that they were being obedient to the experimenter. As you'll recall from the Milgram experiments, most people will be obedient. But not knowing why they had lied, the subjects resolved their dissonance by deciding that in fact they had not lied, they had really enjoyed the experiment! By changing their attitudes, they did not have to face the unpleasant feelings of dissonance. Those who received the $20, on the other hand, felt that they had a reason to lie, since they were being well paid to do so; therefore they did not feel much dissonance. As a result, little attitude change occurred in this group (see Figure 17.10). Dissonance effects will

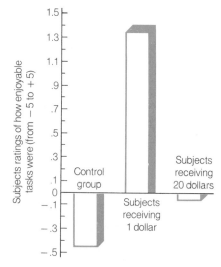

Figure 17.10 *Festinger and Carlsmith's experiment demonstrating the effects of cognitive dissonance. Subjects who lied (told the next subject that the experiment was fun) and received only one dollar reduced their cognitive dissonance by claiming that they had, in fact, liked the experiment. Subjects who lied but received twenty dollars experienced little or no dissonance and claimed to dislike the experiment. A control group, whose members were not requested to lie and who received no money, but who moved spools and turned pegs, really disliked the experiment. (SOURCE: Adapted from Festinger & Carlsmith, 1959, p. 207)*

not occur if people realize that they are being forced to make a choice inconsistent with their feelings or beliefs, or if the actions they take that are inconsistent with their real views have no consequence (Schlenker & Schlenker, 1975).

Attempts to reduce cognitive dissonance will generally cause attitudes to change. For instance, attitudes about whether you will win a wager become much stronger *after* you've placed a bet (Younger, Walker, & Arrowood, 1977). Dissonance theory helps to explain why most people perceive that they have made good decisions after the decisions have been made. The amount of effort or money we have to expend in order to reach a goal or acquire something may be more important in determining how we feel about it than its actual value. For this reason, once a person, or even a nation, makes a commitment or invests in a particular action, it often becomes difficult to convince those responsible that the decision was not a good one and should not be pursued. This is so because they have changed their attitudes to agree with their decision in order to reduce their feelings of dissonance.

One of the best-known experiments that demonstrated this effect was conducted by Aronson and Mills in 1959. These researchers divided female college students into three different groups. In each group the subjects were told that they would be listening to a supposedly exciting taped discussion about sex. The first group was admitted to hear the tape without passing any initiation test. The second group received a mild initiation in which five sex-related words such as *prostitute* or *virgin* had to be read to a male researcher. The third group was given a severe initiation in which subjects had to read a dozen obscene four-letter words and two very explicit sexual passages to a male researcher. After the initiations the subjects did not listen to an exciting discussion concerning sexual behavior as they had been led to believe, but instead to a boring report about animal sexuality that made little sense. After listening to the tape the subjects were asked to rate the value of the discussion. As expected, the more severe the initiation, the more the discussion was valued (Aronson & Mills, 1959). It was argued that those who had gone through the stress of the severe initiation experienced cognitive dissonance when all they received for their efforts was a boring, senseless tape. Rather than feel upset, the subjects altered their perception of the tape and found listening to it to be a valuable experience.

In 1971 dissonance theory was challenged by researchers who argued that dissonance theory results could be explained by people's need to appear consistent to others in terms of their attitudes (Tedeschi, Schlenker, & Bonoma, 1971). That is, the subjects in the cognitive dissonance experiments were not really changing their true attitudes but were reporting that their attitudes had changed so that they would appear consistent in the eyes of others. This view became known as the **impression-management hypothesis.** For example, the impression-management hypothesis argues that the women who went through severe initiation in the experiment just discussed *truly* thought that the tape was boring but they needed to appear consistent in the eyes of others. They asserted that the tape was valuable so that they would not appear foolish for having gone to so much trouble to hear it. In other words, they needed to present attitudes that seemed consistent with their behaviors, although their *real* attitudes had not changed.

To help settle the issue, cognitive dissonance experiments were conducted and the subjects' reactions were obtained through the bogus pipeline procedure. The bogus pipeline procedure indicated that the subjects'

COGNITIVE DISSONANCE
The condition in which one has beliefs or knowledge that are internally inconsistent or that disagree with one's behavior. When such cognitive dissonance arises, the individual is motivated to reduce the dissonance through changes in behavior or cognition.

IMPRESSION-MANAGEMENT HYPOTHESIS
The hypothesis that the results of cognitive dissonance experiments can be explained, not by changes in real attitudes made to reduce dissonance, but rather by a need to appear consistent in the eyes of others.

true attitudes had often not changed in situations in which the subjects in a typical dissonance experiment would normally report an attitude shift (Cialdini, Petty, & Cacioppo, 1981). Although the bogus pipeline procedure may be fallible, the idea of impression management must be considered a possible explanation for cognitive dissonance results until further research helps decide in favor of one hypothesis or the other (Cialdini, Petty & Cacioppo, 1981). The controversy has not yet been resolved to everyone's satisfaction.

Attribution

We are often curious about the personality or motivations of other people. We look for stable traits and underlying motives as a way of understanding others' behavior. We react to people's behavior differently depending on the motives or traits to which we attribute the behavior (Heider, 1958). We engage in **attribution** whenever we try to find the reasons for another's behavior or to understand his or her personality or motivation. In other words, we attribute a person's behavior to certain aspects of his or her personality or environment.

Social psychologists have found that one of the first tasks of attribution is to decide whether the individual's personality is determining the behavior (that is, whether the behavior is being shaped from within) or whether forces in the environment are controlling the behavior (that is, whether the behavior is being shaped from without). We assign blame or give credit depending in part on whether we attribute someone's behavior to internal or external factors. Consider what happened in 1957 when the Soviet Union launched the world's first artificial satellite, the Sputnik. Stunned by this technological achievement, American scientists rushed to match it. Their early attempts to launch rockets failed utterly because they did not know how to build them well. The only people in America who really knew how to build and fly rockets were Nazi scientists captured during World War II. The leading expert was Werner von Braun, who had built the V-2 rocket that had been used against London with such devastating accuracy. Many Americans were dismayed that the U.S. government had to turn to a former Nazi in order to literally get the rocket program off the ground. They argued that we should not entrust the program to a man who had deliberately used his missiles to kill civilians. These people attributed von Braun's behavior in working for the Nazis and being a Nazi to evil personality traits. Other people attributed von Braun's behavior to environmental causes. They argued that von Braun was not responsible, since the Nazis had forced him to build and use the V-2. People who attributed von Braun's behavior to personality traits did not want him to head the missile program while those who attributed his behavior to environmental forces were not opposed to his appointment. In 1960 a film entitled *I Aim at the Stars* cast the German actor Curt Jurgens in the role of von Braun. Its basic premise was that von Braun was internally motivated to explore rocketry and space flight and that his Nazi war effort was attributable to the external forces brought to bear upon him. One caustic movie reviewer, still attributing von Braun's behavior to personality traits, entitled his review of the film, *I Aim at the Stars, but I Hit London.*

One of the most interesting aspects of the attribution process is that it can lead to a biased assessment of others. For instance, we tend to view our own behavior as stemming from situational or environmental forces but the behavior of others as stemming from internal forces (Eisen, 1979). Moreover, people usually find terms for traits to be better descriptions of others than of themselves (Goldberg, 1978).

Psychologists have developed two hypotheses to explain this tendency. The **visual perspective hypothesis** argues that we attribute others' behavior to internal forces and our own to external forces because of our visual perspective. Unless we're standing in front of a mirror, we rarely see ourselves as others see us. But we easily see the environmental forces that impinge upon us from all directions. For this reason, we may be more aware of the environment than we are of ourselves. When dealing with others, however, we tend to see whole people, the way we would see ourselves if we had a mirror. As a result, their "peopleness," with its accompanying traits and personality, may strike us more than the environmental circumstances affecting them. Because of our visual perspective, then, we may consider others to be driven by internal forces and ourselves to be controlled by external forces. This theory may help explain why therapists working with alcoholics have found them to be more willing to take the responsibility for controlling their drinking after they have viewed a videotape showing them intoxicated. By seeing themselves as people, they may attribute more responsibility to internal traits and personality.

The second hypothesis argues that we tend to consider ourselves more than others to be at the mercy of situational forces because we are more acutely aware of our own situation. This idea is known as the **information availability hypothesis.** The more information we obtain about another person, the more likely we are to attribute his or her behavior to environmental factors. Long before social psychologists found evidence for the information availability hypothesis many people in many cultures had demonstrated an understanding of this effect. As an American Indian saying puts it, if you want to know another person, walk a mile in his moccasins. Other cultures have similar sayings. Their import is that you can understand a person better once you really know the forces that impinge upon her. Until then, we will tend to attribute another's behavior to personality traits. In criminal trials, a lawyer will try to bring up as much information as possible about a client's hard life and difficult past. The more information the jury has about the person's situation, the more likely the jury is to attribute the person's action to environmental factors rather than to personality.

Both the visual perspective hypothesis and the information availability hypothesis have been supported by research (Eisen, 1979; Taylor & Fiske, 1978).

Another source of attribution error is the **self-serving bias.** The self-serving bias describes the tendency to attribute behavior that results in a good outcome to internal forces, and behavior that results in a bad outcome to environmental factors (Carver, DeGregorio & Gillis, 1980). In other words, people tend to take responsibility for good results but to attribute bad results to factors beyond their control. The self-serving bias probably occurs because people like to do good things and are at a loss to explain why they occasionally do things that have bad outcomes. The bias probably stems from the belief that we are in control of our behavior all of the time, in which case we must somehow deal with behavior that results in a bad

ATTRIBUTION
The psychosocial process through which we come to believe that certain events or dispositions are responsible for the behavior of ourselves or others.

VISUAL PERSPECTIVE HYPOTHESIS
The hypothesis that explains people's tendency to attribute their own behavior to environmental causes rather than to personality traits as a function of their visual perspective, because they view their surroundings more often than they view their own body.

INFORMATION AVAILABILITY HYPOTHESIS
The hypothesis that explains people's tendency to attribute their own behavior to environmental causes rather than to personality traits as a function of the fact that they have more information about their personal situation and environment and the obvious forces therein, than they have about others.

SELF-SERVING BIAS
An attribution bias describing the fact that people tend to attribute behavior that results in a good outcome to their own personality or traits, and to attribute behavior that results in a bad outcome to the forces or circumstances of the environment.

outcome. The self-serving bias may be a form of rationalization, through which we deny that there are internal forces that lead us to behave in ways we don't like or that we can't control.

To understand our feelings we often look to external sources of information or to the people around us. At other times we search inward for feedback. The latter method is known as **self-directed attention** (Gibbons, Carver, Scheier, & Hormuth, 1979). In one study subjects were shown a series of nude slides. Half of the subjects were told that the slides were not arousing, and the other half were told that the slides were extremely arousing. Furthermore, in each condition subjects were either able to see themselves reflected in the screen between presentations of the slides or not able to see their reflection. As you may recall, evidence has shown that subjects who can see their own reflections tend to focus their attention inward in order to understand their feelings. After the experiment the subjects were asked to rate whether the slides were arousing or not. Those who could see their reflections between slide presentations were not as influenced by having been told beforehand that the slides were or were not arousing. Those who did not see their reflections relied on others to determine their own reactions, and they found the slides arousing or not arousing depending on what they had been told beforehand (Scheier, Carver, & Gibbons, 1979).

Perhaps the most important thing to keep in mind in attempting to attribute motives for another person's behavior is to remain flexible and open to change. Reserve opinion until you know the person well and have seen him or her in many circumstances. As you have learned, limited information can lead to biases and biases in turn can distort further assessments.

Summary

- Social psychology is the study of how people affect the behavior, thoughts, and feelings of others.
- The ways in which others expect us to conform are known as social norms.
- People generally look to reference groups of similar individuals, or of individuals whom they would like to resemble, in order to make decisions about how to conform.
- Researcher Stanley Milgram demonstrated the power of obedience when he found that a majority of people would shock a stranger when they were requested to, even though the stranger appeared to be in pain.
- The tragedy of Jonestown demonstrated the dangers of blind obedience and conformity.
- The situational factors at any given moment play a great role in whether people will help someone in an emergency. In some situations help is less likely to be given the more witnesses there are to the person's distress. This is known as the bystander effect. The bystander effect may be the result of diffusion of responsibility or of the fear of appearing foolish by interpreting an ambiguous situation as an emergency when in fact it is not.
- According to the bystander intervention model, for intervention to occur the event must be observed and interpreted as an emergency, and the

observer must take responsibility for helping decide how to help. All of these requirements must be met before action can be taken.

■ Morals are the attitudes and beliefs that help people determine what is right or wrong. According to researcher Lawrence Kohlberg, moral development begins in childhood and progresses through six stages.

■ Both competition and cooperation are taught by social interaction. In certain instances cooperation declines as children grow older and competition becomes the common mode of responding, even when it cannot possibly lead to success. Cooperation between partners diminishes as the ability to threaten one another increases. Competition can be decreased and cooperation increased if opposing members join forces to work toward a common goal.

■ Bargaining and negotiation are carried out using many different techniques. Among them are ingratiation, the foot-in-the-door technique, the door-in-the-face technique, and lowballing.

■ Individuals are influenced by groups in unique ways. Groups may deindividuate members, or they may lead members to be polarized and to take more extreme positions than they would as individuals.

■ Sometimes an extremely effective group member will emerge as a leader. The great-man, great-woman hypothesis argues that leaders possess special traits. The situational-environmental hypothesis argues that particular situations may arise in which a group member is fortuitously elevated to the position of leader because he or she happens to possess the skills needed at the moment. Research has indicated that both hypotheses may be correct.

■ Prejudice consists of learned values and beliefs that may lead an individual to be unfairly biased toward members of particular out-groups. Different behavior based on prejudice is called discrimination.

■ Individuals with authoritarian personalities tend to be more prejudiced and are especially prone to categorize people as members of in-groups or out-groups.

■ Prejudice may be overcome by education, legislation, increasing the self-esteem of the victims of prejudice, and creating contact between hostile groups as they work together to reach a common goal.

■ A social attitude is a relatively enduring system of feelings, beliefs, and behaviors with respect to a social object. Social attitudes may be formed through the processes of associative learning, instrumental learning, and social learning.

■ Social psychologists typically use questionnaires or scales to measure attitudes. The bogus pipeline procedure is designed to tap the real feelings and attitudes of subjects instead of the pretended feelings or attitudes subjects often report.

■ Individuals tend to assess their own attitudes more accurately and to express more self-awareness when placed in front of a mirror.

■ Techniques for changing attitudes commonly rely on persuasive communication. The characteristics of the communicator can affect the attitudes of the listener. Communicators who are like their audience in socioeconomic class, occupation, or appearance are more persuasive.

■ Self-generated persuasion is more effective than persuasion generated by others.

■ Two-sided arguments are more persuasive on individuals who initially oppose the idea that is presented. One-sided arguments are more persuasive if the recipient initially agrees with the idea.

- Emotional appeals are effective in changing attitudes, and individuals with high self-esteem are more likely to be influenced by emotional appeals.

- People can be helped to resist persuasion by warning them that they are about to be persuaded or by teaching them to refute arguments that go against their beliefs.

- Simply being exposed to something can alter our attitude in favor of it. This is known as the mere exposure effect.

- Central route processing of a message generally leads to a permanent change in attitudes, while peripheral route processing leads to a temporary change.

- When subjects are made to state something that goes against their beliefs and they can see no valid reason for having made the statement, they are placed in cognitive dissonance. It is argued that, to resolve this dissonance, subjects tend to change their attitudes to bring them into line with the statements they have made, or the actions they have taken.

- The impression-management hypothesis argues that cognitive dissonance results can be explained not as changes in real attitudes and beliefs, but rather as professed changes in attitudes and beliefs for the purpose of maintaining an appearance of consistency in the eyes of others.

- We often look for stable traits in others or for the motives behind their behaviors as a way of understanding them. Social psychologists call this attempt attribution. People are generally held accountable for behavior that is attributed to personality or trait variables, and considered blameless for behavior that is attributed to environmental forces. People tend to attribute their own behavior more to environmental forces and the behavior of others more to personality and trait forces.

- The self-serving bias describes people's tendency to attribute behavior that has a good outcome to their own personality traits, and to attribute behavior that has a bad outcome to external forces that are beyond their control.

EPILOGUE: BRAINWASHED

Psychologists know that behavior can be greatly influenced by social processes. The following is an account of how some of these processes influenced the behavior of the victim of a famous crime.

Attorney F. Lee Bailey had his hands full. He had to convince a jury that his client, Patricia Hearst, daughter of publisher Randolph Hearst, was innocent of bank robbery.

In February 1974 Patricia Hearst, then only 19 years old, was kidnapped from her apartment in Berkeley, California. Her kidnappers were members of the Symbionese Liberation Army (SLA), a group of radicals who argued that force was the only way to obtain justice for the poor. Patty was held for ransom. About two months after her kidnapping the Hearst family received a tape in which Patty, who now called herself Tanya, stated that her father was a pig and that she had chosen to stay with the SLA. For almost two years she avoided capture by the FBI. During this time she was involved in at least one bank robbery.

After her capture (rescue?), when she was no longer under threat from the SLA, she continued to espouse the political beliefs of that organization and took credit for her actions. This, perhaps more than anything else, was damaging to her at her trial. Why, the jury wondered, would someone who had been freed from the threat of death by her captors continue to espouse the captors' views if they were really not her own views?

In her defense, Bailey argued that Patty had been brainwashed. He stated that she had gone along with the group's actions in order to reduce her fear. She was made to think up things to say that supported the group's position. She was rewarded by the group for agreeing with them. She may have felt that she could not justify her actions, and had therefore changed her attitudes to conform more to her behavior. She may have been polarized by the group to take a more extreme position. If you consider what you've learned about changing attitudes and group control of behavior, you may see that Patty was in a situation that could force her to change her attitudes and behavior drastically in a way that might continue even after she was freed. Bailey argued that Patty would have to be retrained in a social sense, back to the person that everyone knew. He contended that she had been a victim.

But the jury members attributed Patty's behavior to the traits of her own personality rather than to situational forces, which, as you'll recall, is the way we commonly attribute behavior to others. As a result she was found guilty.

A short time later the tragedy of Jonestown was in the news. Attorney Bailey reflected on the Hearst trial and said that if Jonestown had happened before the trial, Patty would never have been convicted. Perhaps he was right. Jonestown had taught a lesson in social psychology to everyone, a lesson in group compliance and obedience.

Patricia "Tanya" Hearst posing as a member of the SLA. Was she "brainwashed"?

Suggestions for Further Reading

1. Baron, R. A., & Byrne, D. *Social psychology: Understanding human interaction* (3rd ed.). Boston: Allyn & Bacon, 1981.
2. Katz, P. A. (ed.) *Towards the elimination of racism.* Elmsford, N.Y.: Pergamon, 1976
3. Latane, B., & Darley, J. M. *The unresponsive bystander: Why doesn't he help?* New York: Appleton-Century-Crofts, 1970.
4. Milgram, S. *Obedience to authority.* New York: Harper, 1974.
5. Zimbardo, P. G., Ebbesen, E. B., & Maslach, C. *Influencing attitudes and changing behavior* (2nd ed.). Reading, Mass.: Addison-Wesley, 1977.

CONTENTS

C H A P T E R 18

Sexuality, Attraction, and Intimacy

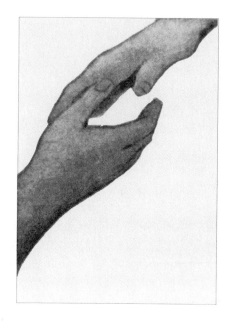

After a long ocean voyage, you've finally arrived at New Guinea, a South Pacific island not far from the Equator. The terrain is dominated by thick jungles and towering green mountains. Although the year is 1935, you feel that modern civilization has barely touched this giant island.

As you arrive at your accommodations in the small town, the young anthropologist you've come so far to see is there to greet you. Her name is Margaret Mead. "I'm glad you're here," she says. "There's so much to show you."

"As you know from my telegraph," you say, "my paper sent me here because they heard you were on to something. By the sound of it, it ought to shake some people up."

"Well, I don't know about that," Mead says, laughing. "But if we're to understand the power of culture and learning on our species, we have to see what's going on outside of Western civilization."

Later you and Mead set off for a distant part of the island. You hadn't counted on the walking. The trails are narrow and slippery. They extend in a precise network into the precipitous mountains. After a time there are no more large villages but

only tiny settlements. This mountain land is barren and infertile. Skinny razor-backed pigs run wild. Shortly, you reach the village of the Arapesh.

The Arapesh turn out to be a very interesting tribe. It's almost immediately apparent that the Arapesh men are not aggressive. "They are taught to help other members of the tribe and to care deeply about others' needs and feelings," Mead tells you. "In temperament, the men of this village behave in ways that Westerners would consider feminine. Among the Arapesh both men and women are nurturing, caring, feeling, and unaggressive."

You leave the Arapesh and journey to the ocean, to the mouth of the Sepik River. You have been thinking about the old Arapesh man's comment when Mead told him where you were going next:

You are going up the Sepik River, where the people are fierce, where they eat men. You are taking some of our boys with you. Go carefully. Do not be misled by your experience among us. We are another kind. They are another kind. So you will find it. (Mead, 1935/ 1963, p. 167)

A long boat ride brings you to the home of the Mundugumor tribe. Here you sense caution and tension among your party as Mead enters the village and the Mundugumor recognize her and come to greet her. In short order you learn that the Mundugumor are a fierce tribe. They are headhunters and cannibals, although they have been under government control for the past three years and have promised not to kill or eat anybody. Both the men and the women are aggressive and dangerous. Both have highly sexed personalities, and both have no hesitation in engaging in forthright sexual behavior. "In this tribe," Mead points out, "the women behave in ways that Westerners would consider masculine. They are tough and strong, and they can be every bit as violent as the men." It's difficult for you to leave your Western ideas behind. It's as though the Arapesh were all feminine and the Mundugumor all masculine.

When you leave the Mundugumor you travel down the Sepik River until you reach the lake, which is so full of vegetation that it looks like black enamel unless the wind stirs it. Alongside the lake is the village of the Tchambuli. Here, sex and temperament roles appear to be reversed. The Tchambuli women are dominant and the men are passive. The men are artists; they paint, dance and make music. The women fish and manufacture trade goods. As Mead notes,

The women's attitude towards the men is one of kindly tolerance and appreciation. They enjoy the games that the men play, they particularly enjoy the theatricals that the men put on for their benefit. (Mead, 1935/1963, p. 255)

The men are emotional and easily embarrassed. The women are the leaders, and the men defer to their authority.

On your return trip to the coast you think about the Arapesh, Mundugumor, and Tchambuli and wonder how they can be so different from the men and women of your culture. As Mead bids you goodbye, she says, "I think you can see now that what we consider natural behavior for men and women may be more a function of culture than of biology. Everyone in Western society should be aware of the people here and of the way in which we acquire our understanding of so-called natural sex roles."

In this chapter we will examine the biological, cognitive, and social-cultural aspects of human sexuality. We will look at biological differences between the brains of men and women, the formation of sex roles and gender identity, and the pressure that society and culture bring to bear in shaping our sexual behavior. We'll also explore love and intimacy, the history of sexual research, and some sexual myths and misunderstandings.

Why Psychologists Study Sexuality, Attraction, and Intimacy

A person's sex greatly influences the relationships, pursuits, choices, and conflicts that he or she will face in life. Because of this, psychologists are interested in every aspect of our sexuality. They want to know how the biological and hormonal aspects of sexuality may affect behavior, how our cognitive understanding of being either male or female shapes our relationships, and how social-cultural influences concerning sexuality can direct our futures and determine our roles in society. Psychologists are also interested in intimacy and love. The reason for their interest was probably best expressed by Harry Harlow in 1958, when he gave the presidential address to the American Psychological Association:

Love is a wondrous state, deep, tender, and reassuring. Because of its intimate and personal nature it is regarded by some as an improper topic for experimental research. But, whatever our personal feelings may be, our assigned mission as psychologists is to analyze all facets of human and animal behavior into their component variables. So far as love or affection is concerned, psychologists have failed in their mission. The little we know about love does not transcend simple observation and the little we write about it has been written better by poets and novelists. (Harlow, 1958, p. 673)

Biological Aspects of Human Sexuality

Anatomy is perhaps the most obvious aspect of a person's sexuality. The basic anatomical differences between males and females are quite apparent, both in terms of primary and secondary sexual characteristics. The penis, scrotum, and testes of the male and the vagina, uterus, and ovaries of the female are **primary sexual characteristics** (see Figure 18.1). **Secondary sexual characteristics** appear at puberty. In girls these include the development of breasts and the widening of the hips, in boys the deepening of the voice and the appearance of facial hair. In both sexes underarm and pubic hair develops. The appearance of secondary sexual characteristics signals that the body is preparing for the capacity to reproduce. This period is reached in males at the time when the first ejaculation of sperm becomes possible and in females when **menarche** (the beginning of menstruation) has occurred. These events usually take place between the ages of 11 and 14, with girls able to reproduce on the average slightly sooner than boys. Healthy males will remain capable of reproduction throughout their lives, and healthy females will be capable until menopause, which signals the end of their regular fertile cycles.

Both the primary and secondary sexual characteristics are closely related to the actions of sex hormones. Hormones are body chemicals carried in the blood that can affect psychological and physiological development (see Chapter 2). The sex glands, called gonads, secrete hormones. The gonads in the female are the ovaries, and in the male they are the testes. The adrenal glands on the adrenal cortex of the kidney are also a source of sex hormones in both sexes. The female hormones are called **estrogens** and the male hormones **androgens.*** It is believed that the secretion of sexual hormones may be directed by the thymus gland (Rebar, Miyake, Low, and Goldstein, 1981), which is located behind the breastbone, and the pituitary gland, which is located at the base of the forebrain. The pituitary itself is controlled by areas of the brain.

A child's genetic sex is determined at conception. If the 23rd pair of chromosomes consists of two X's, then the child will be female. If the 23rd pair of chromosomes is XY, the child will be male. During the development of the embryo, if testosterone (one of the androgens) is present, as usually occurs under the direction of the Y chromosome, male genitals will develop in place of female ones (Money, 1965). In this way genes determine sex indirectly through the action of hormones.

Occasionally a fetus may be exposed to levels of hormones that are higher than normal. For example, young girls have been studied who were

---

*All normal individuals produce both estrogens and androgens. It is the ratio of one substance to the other that affects sexual characteristics.

PRIMARY SEXUAL CHARACTERISTICS
The penis, scrotum, and testes of the male; the vagina, ovaries, and uterus of the female.

SECONDARY SEXUAL CHARACTERISTICS
Physical characteristics that appear in humans around the age of puberty and are sex differentiated but not necessary for sexual reproduction.

MENARCHE
The first occurrence of menstruation.

ESTROGEN
The female sex hormone, produced by the ovaries. Estrogen is responsible for maturation of the female sex organs, secondary sex characteristics, and in some species, sexual behavior.

ANDROGEN
Any male hormone that regulates sexual development. Some androgens are produced by the testes and others by the adrenal cortex.

Figure 18.1 *Primary sexual characteristics of the male (a) and the female (b).*

(a)

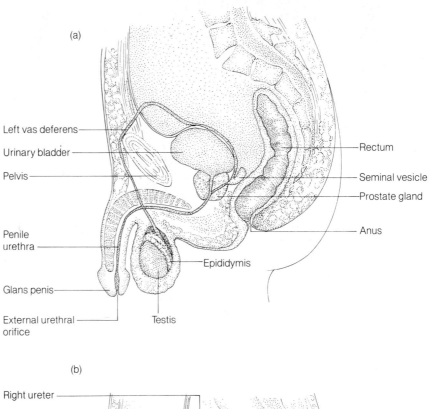

Left vas deferens

Urinary bladder

Pelvis

Penile urethra

Glans penis

External urethral orifice

Rectum

Seminal vesicle

Prostate gland

Anus

Epididymis

Testis

(b)

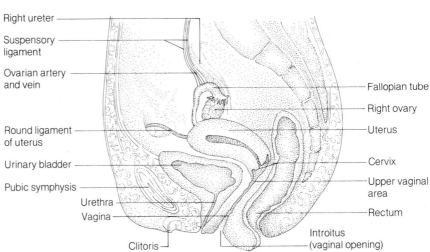

Right ureter

Suspensory ligament

Ovarian artery and vein

Round ligament of uterus

Urinary bladder

Pubic symphysis

Urethra

Vagina

Clitoris

Fallopian tube

Right ovary

Uterus

Cervix

Upper vaginal area

Rectum

Introitus (vaginal opening)

exposed to abnormally large amounts of androgens prior to birth, usually because their mothers needed to be treated with synthetic androgenic hormones during pregnancy. During their preadolescence, these girls played, according to the researchers, in the rough and tumble way more commonly observed among boys, and they were characterized as less culturally feminine than girls usually are (Ehrhardt, 1973). Similarly, two populations of boys ages 6 and 16, whose mothers received large doses of estrogens during pregnancy, were considered by researchers to be less athletic, less assertive, and less aggressive than boys usually are (Yalom, Green & Fisk, 1973).

THE EFFECTS OF HORMONES ON BEHAVIOR

In 1849 the German physiologist Arnold Berthold found that by castrating roosters he could stop the roosters from fighting with one another. When the testicles were transplanted back into the castrated birds they once again began to fight. The transplanted testicles did not make connections with the rooster's nervous system, but rather with the circulatory system. This fact led Berthold and others to assume that something was being carried in the blood that affected behavior.

In 1916 a Canadian physiologist named Frank Lillie presented a paper in which he explained why some genetically normal cows, called free-martins, acted and looked like bulls. Freemartins always have fraternal twin brothers. Lillie speculated that the hormones from the testes of the male twin somehow masculinized the freemartins in the womb.

The first major breakthrough in understanding the effects of hormones on behavior came in 1959 when researchers gave large amounts of testosterone to pregnant guinea pigs (Phoenix, Goy, Gerall, & Young, 1959). The females of the litter were androgynized. They had undifferentiated sex organs (partial organs of both sexes). When these genetic females were three months old their ovaries were removed and more testosterone was injected. These genetically normal females soon began to act like males. They mounted and attempted to copulate with other females, and they tried to dominate the group. The researchers felt that they had changed the sex of the animal's brain.

Modern research has discovered that hormones have a double effect. First, they tend to organize brain structures in a masculinized or a feminized way prior to birth. Second, hormones are active in these structures long after birth, which can lead to more masculine or feminine behavior. Researcher Robert Goy has even caused monkeys to develop in what he describes as an extremely feminine or an extremely masculine direction, measured by their rough and tumble play and their efforts to dominate their group, simply by injecting and maintaining different levels of testosterone prior to birth and again at puberty (Weintraub, 1981).

By injecting radioactive hormones into the brains of animals, researchers have been able to find the main action sites in the brain where hormones have their effect. Both androgens and estrogens tend to concentrate in the cerebral cortex, in the hypothalamus (a portion of the brain implicated in sexual behavior), and also in the amygdala (an area associated with emotion). Although androgens and estrogens concentrate in similar areas of the brain, different receptor sites in these areas attract either one kind of hormone or the other. When female or male hormones take hold at these receptor sites during the prenatal period and just after, they cause nerve cells to grow in the immediate area. Different nerve cells and nerve pathways develop depending on which hormone affects the area of the brain in question (McEwan, 1980).

HORMONES AND GENDER IDENTITY

Although it appears that **gender identity** and sex-role development may be influenced by social factors, the possible contribution of hormones and the way in which they affect behavior must not be overlooked. Researcher Julienne Imperato-McGinley of the Cornell University Medical College has studied 38 boys with a genetic disorder. All of the boys came from the city

GENDER IDENTITY
The sexual orientation, either male or female, with which a person identifies.

of Santo Domingo in the Dominican Republic, where this particular genetic disorder is relatively common. The genetic disorder keeps the male hormone testosterone from being converted into dihydrotestosterone, the hormone required for the formation of male genitals during prenatal development. When the boys who suffer from this disorder are born they look like girls. They are often given girls' names and raised as girls because the parents are unaware that they are boys. But owing to a further secretion of hormones at puberty, the penis, originally thought to be a clitoris, lengthens; the voice deepens; and the boy develops a muscular body. Boys born with this genetic disorder have been socialized to be girls, but after the physical change occurs, they easily adopt the culturally accepted male sex role in terms of identity, occupational desires, and sexual activity. The local Spanish slang terms for this disorder translate roughly to mean "penis-at-12" or "first woman, then man."

Imperato-McGinley has also investigated eight children in the United States who have this genetic disorder. These children were surgically castrated and raised as girls. When they were grown they considered themselves to be women. Nonetheless, they had to take injections to counteract the male hormones that became active at puberty, and five of them had serious psychological problems (Imperato-McGinley, Peterson, Stoller, & Goodwin, 1979).

These data may indicate that the presence of male hormones may predispose individuals to adopt male roles. This possibility might explain why some of those who were forced to remain female have had difficulties. It is also possible, however, that differences between the groups in the two countries are due to environmental forces. As you know from reading about Mead's work in the Prologue, the environment can have a strong influence. For instance, the "girls" in Santo Domingo who became men may have made the transition easily because their environment supported their new role (a couple of parents were even proud to discover that their daughter was really their son). The American "girls" who were surgically forced to become women may be having problems because they are unable to bear children or because they must take hormone injections to maintain their female appearance.

There is further evidence that biological variables may not be the only ones responsible for the development of gender identity. For example, monozygotic (identical) twins share their genetic makeup as well as the same womb. Yet identical twins have been found who clearly would prefer different sexual roles. Investigators Green & Stoller (1971), studying identical eight-year-old twin boys who were anatomically normal, found that one of them unquestionably wanted to be a girl. In another study these same researchers described a pair of identical, anatomically normal, 24-year-old women, one of whom wanted very much to be a man.

Nature-nurture questions are common to the study of sexuality and sex roles. While some have argued that there may be almost no natural male or female human behaviors (Weisstein, 1975), others, such as Imperato-McGinley, believe that hormones and biology greatly affect human behavior.

The Acquisition of Gender Identity and Sex Roles

Your awareness of being a male or a female is a very important determinant of your behavior. But you didn't always know you had a sex. Early in your life you didn't know what it was to be a man or a woman. In order to investigate our cognitive understanding of sexuality and sex roles, psychologists have studied children before they were old enough to grasp the meaning of their sex, and then watched as their gender identity began to form.

GENDER IDENTITY

Children seem to comprehend that they are either boys or girls by about the age of three (Thompson, 1975). Although a two-year-old may tell you she is a girl, she may have a great deal of trouble understanding why she is called a girl or picking out who else is a girl or who is a boy. Three-year-olds are better able to judge who is a boy and who is a girl, but they generally fail to understand **gender constancy,** which refers to the understanding that your own sex will remain constant—"Once a boy, always a boy." Children demonstrate a grasp of gender constancy when they understand that they still remain girls or boys regardless of the clothes they wear or the activities they engage in. A girl who puts on a jersey and plays football does not turn into a boy, and a boy who plays with dolls does not turn into a girl. The formation of gender constancy in children agrees well with Jean Piaget's description of cognitive development (see Chapter 11), since gender constancy is fully developed in children at about the same time that they develop the ability to conserve, approximately six or seven years of age (Emmerich & Goldman, 1972). This connection between Piaget's theory of cognitive development and the formation of gender constancy seems reasonable, because a child who has to deal with a girl playing football or a boy playing dolls must conserve one aspect of that person (his or her sex) as other aspects (choice of clothing or game) appear to switch to what the child may perceive as the behavior of the opposite sex, and it is not until about the age of six or seven that children are able to make such conservations (Marcus & Overton, 1978).

Once boys and girls recognize the invariability of their sex, they are better able to comprehend the social roles culturally deemed appropriate for them. Every organized culture attempts to transmit its beliefs and values

GENDER CONSTANCY
The realization that one's sex is determined by unchanging criteria and is unaffected by one's activities or behavior. It usually develops in children by the age of six or seven.

From a very early age, children engage in behavior that their culture considers appropriate for their sex.

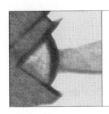

DO MEN AND WOMEN HAVE DIFFERENT BRAINS?

Our sexual feelings and desires, our likes and loves, are controlled by the brain. Many researchers believe that there are important structural differences between the brains of men and women, and that men and women have different abilities or talents because of their different brains.

Close examination has turned up differences in the cerebral cortex of male and female rats. In the female the left hemisphere is thicker than the right and vice versa in the male (Diamond, Johnson, & Ehlert, 1979). If at birth, however, the males are castrated or the females have their ovaries removed, the pattern can be reversed. These structural differences are believed to be the result of hormone action. Further evidence comes from the fact that the amount of male or female hormones administered prenatally can directly affect the width of the cortex of the animal to be born.

Since hormones can affect the cerebral cortex, they may also influence males' and females' thinking. Experiments to measure the ability of male and female rats to run mazes support this suggestion. In general, male rats are better able to run mazes, a task that requires spatial orientation, than are female rats. Similarly, human males are generally superior to females at performing spatial tasks. However, if female rats are exposed to male hormones during a critical period in the womb or immediately after birth, they will be able to run mazes as well as male rats (Beatty, 1979).

Male and female hormones can also affect a rat's ability to learn. Researcher William Beatty taught rats to run to the far end of a box when a light was turned on in order to avoid an electric shock. The females learned faster than the males. However, if the females were given male hormones very early in their development, their ability to learn this particular task lessened and their performance was as poor as the males'. Similarly, if male rats were prevented from being exposed to male hormones before birth and again at puberty, they learned to avoid the light as quickly as females. This outcome is further evidence that hormones can directly influence the development of the brain (Begley & Carey, 1979).

The cerebral cortex of human beings also seems to have sex differences. In men the right hemisphere appears to be more often in control; in women it is the left. Light shined on the left halves of the retinas of both eyes and sound made to the left ear will go to the left hemisphere, while light shined on the right halves of both retinas and sound made to the right ear will go to the right hemisphere. One researcher has found that men are significantly more responsive to light and sound sent to the right hemisphere and that women are more responsive to light and sound sent to the left hemisphere. These findings support the idea that men are more often right-brain dominant, and women are more often left-brain dominant. This theory, if true, may help explain why men tend to be better at geometric mathematics and to have superior spatial skills, and why women tend to have superior verbal ability.

Many researchers have argued that the differences in verbal and mathematical ability that have been observed between men and women are due to social training. For example, girls may not perform as well on math tests because they have been told that they are poor at math, which causes them to become anxious when faced with mathematical problems. Boys may not be as verbal because they are taught to be more physical. However, two psychologists at Johns Hopkins University have come to a different conclusion, at least as far as mathematical ability is concerned. After studying the problem at some length, Camilla Benbow and Julian Stanley stated, "Sex differences in achievement in and attitude toward mathematics result from superior [and natural] male mathematical ability" (Williams & King, 1980, p. 73). Benbow and Stanley examined 9,927 seventh and eighth graders who, up to this point, had had the same exposure to mathematics regardless of sex. They were given the Scholastic Aptitude Test, which includes a mathematical portion. The boys performed significantly better than the girls on the mathematical portion. More than half of the boys scored above 600 out of a possible 800. Not one of the girls scored over 600. The top-scoring boy outranked the top-scoring girl by 190 points. Using attitude questionnaires the researchers found that the girls who were tested liked math as much as the boys did and believed that math would be valuable in their future careers (Benbow & Stanley, 1981).

In opposition, researchers have argued that these kinds of tests alone do not demonstrate in any conclusive way that the superior mathematical ability of males is due to biological or brain differences. Another possibility is that girls are socialized to be afraid of math. In a study of three dozen teenage girls, two groups of girls were given extra lessons to help them increase their math understanding and reduce their anxiety about math. The third group was given no such help. During an eight-week session the girls who were counseled excelled in mathematical ability, showing significant improvement, while the girls who were not counseled showed no improvement (Genshaft & Hirt, 1980).

Finding differences between the brains of men and women or finding that one sex may have inherently superior ability in certain areas in no way argues against the struggle for social equality. Patricia Lund Casserly, a senior research associate at the Educational Testing Service in New Jersey, has argued that whether men are superior at mathematics because of their genetics and biology is not important. She says, "The question of genetic differences doesn't matter to me. The question is, can girls learn math, can girls make fine scientists and engineers? The answer is yes" (Williams & King, 1980, p. 73).

Although superior mathematical ability among men and superior verbal ability among women may be the result of culture, there is, as we have seen, evidence that male and female hormones can cause changes in the brain. Roger Gorski at UCLA has brought about changes in the hypothalamus of rats and the size of clusters of neurons in the hypothalamus by administering hormones soon after the rats were born (see Figure 18.2) (Gordon & Gorski, 1979). Moreover, Imperato-McGinley concluded that the boys she studied in Santo Domingo could adjust to their sudden new male sex roles because their bodies had already been masculinized in the womb by hormones. Imperato-McGinley argued that inside of each "girl's body" was the

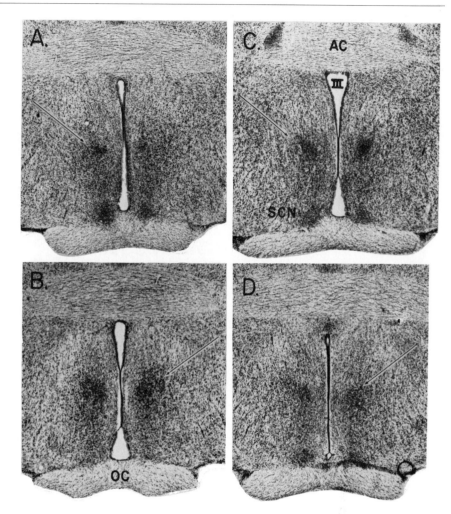

Figure 18.2 *Slides of cell clusters in the hypothalamus of the rat brain. The size of these clusters can be changed by administering hormones soon after birth. (a) Normal female. (b) Normal male. (c) Masculinized female. (d) Castrated male.* (SOURCE: *Dr. Roger A. Gorski, Department of Anatomy, UCLA School of Medicine*)

brain of a boy, made male by the testosterone that was in existence before birth and then activated by another surge of testosterone during the adolescent period.

At this point it is important to reiterate that culture and experience can have profound effects on the development of male or female behaviors in human beings. Although hormones do appear to affect brain structures which in turn may influence behavioral differences between the sexes, the differences are very subtle (Hyde, 1981).

Many women are fine mathematicians and engineers, and many men excel in verbal ability. As researcher Ann Petersen has stated,

A lot of people have been making a lot of political hoopla about our work. They've used it to say that the women's movement will fail, that women are inherently unequal. Our research shows nothing of this sort, of course. There are things that men do better, and things that women do better. It's very important to differentiate between the inferences and the scientific findings. (Weintraub, 1981, p. 20)

to its children. This socialization process helps reinforce and shape behaviors appropriate to particular **sex roles.** Throughout childhood, children are socialized according to what each sex is supposed to do. Sex-role-appropriate behaviors are reinforced by television, books, games, toys, and movies, as well as by the behavior of the people the children observe.

Children engage in socially sex-appropriate behavior even before they are cognitively aware of their gender or its constancy. Children as young as two or three prefer "sex-appropriate" toys and activities. This indicates that parents and society are busy socializing children in appropriate sex-role behavior even before the children are aware of their sex.

From the moment of birth, parents tend to treat boys and girls differently. Although there are few behavioral differences between male and female babies, most parents will describe their daughters as cuter, softer, or more delicate than their sons. Fathers tend to emphasize the beauty and delicacy of their newborn daughters, and the strength and coordination of their newborn sons (Krieger, 1976). Mothers have been reported to be more verbal with their infant daughters (Hetherington & Parke, 1979). However, mothers generally treat boy and girl infants less differently than do fathers. For this reason fathers in our culture may have a greater effect on the early learning of sex roles. This learning of sex roles by the child is called **sex-role typing.**

SEX ROLES

It is believed that a person's gender identity is determined by cognitive as well as social processes. Social learning, cognitive, and psychoanalytic theories all argue that a parent's sexual preference (heterosexual, bisexual, or homosexual) and sex-role modeling (masculine, androgynous, feminine) should have a striking effect on a child's emerging gender identity. Although each theory views the development of gender identity and appropriate sex-role behavior differently, they all agree on this point. Figure 18.3 outlines the development of gender identity in boys according to each theory. In

Figure 18.3 *Development of sex-typed identity in boys according to three major theories of development.* (SOURCE: Kohlberg, 1966)

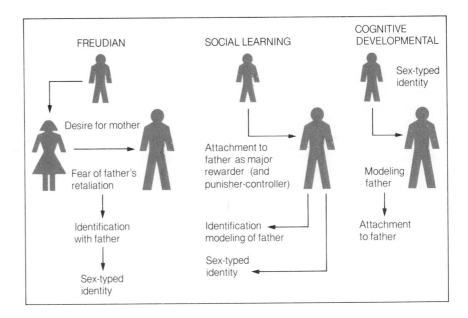

Freudian, or psychoanalytic, theory, the identity with the father results from a drive to avoid retaliation for initially desiring the mother. Once identification with the father is made, the boy adopts the father's ways as his own. According to social learning theory, a boy first becomes attached to his father because his father is the major rewarder and controller in his life. Much evidence indicates that fathers take a special interest in their sons. The boy soon begins to imitate his father, who provides a model of behavior. Once the imitation is well established, the boy forms a male sex-typed identity. According to cognitive theory, in the first phase the boy becomes aware of the concept of "male" and realizes that he is a male. He looks to his father as a model, since his father is also a male. He then imitates his father and becomes attached to him.

Girls may develop in similar ways. Psychoanalytic theory views the girl's sex-role development in terms of the Electra complex. (See Chapter 13.) In cognitive theory, a girl's sex-role development follows the same process as a boy's. Social learning theorists are unsure of how a girl's sex-role development occurs. You might expect that it would be a mirror image of the boy's development, with the mother as the major role model and rewarder-punisher. However, research has indicated that a girl's sex-role development may also be highly influenced by her father (Lamb, 1977, 1979).

As you can see, each theory argues that a parent's sexuality and sex role should affect the child's behavior and gender identity, since in each theory the parent is an important role model. In order to examine this hypothesis, researcher Richard Green conducted a study with 37 children who were being reared either by female homosexuals or by parents who had had sex-change operations and who had adopted the social-sexual roles of the opposite sex. The 37 children studied by Green, 18 males and 19 females, were between 3 and 20 years of age, with an average age of 11.3 years. Twenty-one of the children were being raised by homosexual parents and 16 by transsexual parents. (Most of the children in the latter group were aware that their parent had at one time been a member of the opposite sex.) The study was conducted over a two-year period (Green, 1978).

Green evaluated the younger children by the toys and games that they preferred, their peer preference, the roles they chose during fantasy play, their clothing preferences, and their vocational desires. He also used the Draw-A-Person test in which children usually draw a person of their own sex before drawing a person of the opposite sex. In evaluating the adolescents, Green gathered information about sexual desires and fantasies about sexual partners. He also took data on overt sexual behavior.

With the questionable exception of only one child, all 37 children developed heterosexual preferences and a marked desire to conform to the social-sexual roles provided by their culture. None had homosexual or transsexual fantasies. The adolescents developed desires for the opposite sex. The young children all wanted to play with children of their own sex, which is typical of heterosexual children ages 5 to 11. Boys expressed desires to be doctors, firemen, policemen, engineers, or scientists, and girls wanted to be nurses, teachers, mothers, or housewives (except for one girl who said that when she grew up she wanted to be the Popsicle lady). These findings led Green to surmise that influences outside of the family may be as critical as the parents' influence in the formation of sex roles. Perhaps sex roles are also shaped by peers, school, television, and adult models other than family members or parents.

SEX ROLE
Learned behavior appropriate to one's sex.

SEX-ROLE TYPING
The learning of sex roles by a child.

In Western culture, the majority of people develop heterosexual preferences.

SEXUAL PREFERENCES

One dimension of a sex role is the preference for a particular sexual partner. In our culture the majority of children develop heterosexual preferences. Nonetheless, a large number of people express a homosexual preference, and a still larger number develop a bisexual orientation.

Attempts to uncover hormonal differences between heterosexual and homosexual adults have not proved conclusive (Katchadourian, 1978). In the last 15 to 20 years, social learning and cognitive theories have attempted to deal with this issue. The social learning assumption is that children who are encouraged to display sexual attraction to members of the same sex, or who are encouraged to adopt the social-sexual role of the opposite sex as their own, may eventually express a homosexual preference. Evidence for this assumption has come from other cultures, in which homosexuality has been clearly accepted and in which boys are sometimes specifically trained to grow up to be the lovers of other men. Among the Sakalavas in Madagascar, boys who are considered pretty are raised as girls, and they readily adopt the woman's sex-appropriate role (Green, 1976). The Aleutian Islanders in Alaska also raise handsome boys as girls. The boys' beards are plucked out at puberty, and they are later married to rich men (Westermarck, 1917). These children seem to adapt readily to their assigned sexual roles.

John Money of Johns Hopkins University has studied girls who were chromosomally normal but who were exposed to excessive amounts of androgen during their mothers' pregnancies and developed ambiguous genitals as a result. The girls cognitively accepted the male gender identity. They also accepted the typical male sexual preference for female partners. This acceptance of the male role appears to be cognitive, rather than caused by the hormone, because, as Money noticed, if the mistake in assigned gender role was discovered before the child's third birthday, the child easily accepted the change of gender. But if the error was discovered after the age of three, there were many problems in adjustment. Money has assumed that there may be a special time during the development of gender identity during which the child will be comfortable assuming either sex role. He believes that this period occurs roughly between 18 months and 3 years (Money & Ehrhardt, 1972). After three years of age, though, Money assumes that a child has already begun cognitively to adopt a sex role, and it will be more difficult to change. It may be easier for two-year-olds to change gender identity because they have not yet paid much attention to sex as a marker or statement of who they are. Money has admitted that after the age of three, children may be able to change sex roles and preferences with greater ease if the appropriate relearning techniques are available or if, as was the case with the boys in Santo Domingo, there is ample family and social support. Masters and Johnson (1979) have pointed out that changing sexual preference during adulthood may not be as difficult as one might think.

TRANSSEXUALISM

TRANSSEXUALISM
The most extreme form of gender reversal, in which an individual feels that he or she is really a member of the opposite sex but has been trapped in the wrong-sexed body.

TRANSSEXUAL REASSIGNMENT
A surgical procedure for altering external anatomy and appearance so that the individual resembles the opposite sex.

Transsexualism is the most extreme form of gender identity reversal (Stoller, 1976). Transsexualism is the firmly held belief by an anatomically normal person that he or she is "psychologically" a member of the opposite sex. **Transsexual reassignment** is a medical procedure that anatomically and hormonally enables a person to change sex. At one time as many as 5,000 such operations were performed annually. Approximately 75 percent of sex-change operations have been male to female, since it is a less complex surgical procedure than female to male.

The operation from male to female involves hormonal therapy that eliminates facial hair and creates the curvature of the body more often associated with females (Green & Money, 1969). During the surgical procedure the male genitals are removed and an artificial vagina is surgically built from the remaining skin. Implants are inserted in the breasts to make them larger. In the female-to-male procedure, the breasts are surgically reduced, male hormonal levels are established (which results in the growth of facial hair), and an artificial phallus is surgically added, usually beneath the clitoris. Most of the artificial phalluses were originally designed for men who had lost their genitals in battle or in industrial or vehicular accidents. The phallus can be enlarged with an inflation device.

Unlike the average person who may at one time or another have desired to be a member of the opposite sex, transsexuals have extremely persistent feelings, which they can usually trace back to early childhood. Most transsexuals confess to having always felt as though they were trapped in the wrong-sexed body. Despite the proof that their own bodies give them, transsexuals maintain the belief that they should have been born a member of the opposite sex (Benjamin, 1953). Although some candidates for sex-change operations are psychotic or mentally ill (Finney, Brandsma, Tondow, & LeMaistre, 1975), the large majority of transsexuals are not (Roback, McKee, & Webb, as cited by Davison & Neale, 1978).

The first transsexual operation was accomplished in Europe in 1930. Sex-change operations did not attract worldwide attention, however, until the case of Christine (formerly George) Jorgensen in Copenhagen in 1952.

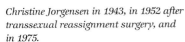
Christine Jorgensen in 1943, in 1952 after transsexual reassignment surgery, and in 1975.

A more modern and personal account of sex change can be found in the book *Conundrum* (1974), written by Jan (formerly James) Morris. One of the best-known transsexuals is tennis celebrity Renée Richards.

Both psychoanalytic and social learning theories agree that transsexualism is directly related to a weak or reversed gender identity. Much of the literature concerning transsexuals contains accounts of young male children praised for dressing in their mother's clothing (Green, 1974). Interestingly, some clinicians have contended that transsexuals may wish to change sex so that *heterosexual* desires can be fulfilled as they gain complete and absolute control over a body of the opposite sex—their own (Davison & Neale, 1978). Whatever the reason, it is generally believed that early childhood experiences play an important role. No hormonal differences have been found between transsexuals and those with normal gender identity.

Often the candidate for transsexual reassignment will be in psychotherapy for one to three years before surgery. This therapy is an attempt to ensure that the transsexual's problems can't be resolved without surgery—since the surgery is irreversible. With careful prescreening and selection, many transsexuals who undergo surgical reassignment remain happy with the change (Hunt & Hampson, 1980).

SEX ROLES AND CULTURE

A mother and her son are driving in a car when an accident occurs. The mother is knocked unconscious and the boy receives a bad laceration on his scalp. They are rushed to a hospital. Doctors work to bring the mother around and also to stop the boy's bleeding. Suddenly a frantic student nurse rushes in and, seeing the child, begins to cry. Another nurse says, "What's wrong?" The student nurse says, "That's my son."

How is this possible? Answer: The student nurse is the boy's father. If you had difficulty with the question, it was probably because you pictured a frantic weeping student nurse as a woman. Perhaps your culture has taught you that "nurse," "frantic," and "weeping" are associated with the woman's role.

With changing times, our perceptions of the behaviors appropriate to sex roles change, too. In our culture just a few decades ago, the use of hair dryers, deodorant, and most jewelry was considered solely the province of women. Then, as cultural attitudes shifted it became acceptable for men to use these items. Different cultures may have different attitudes and beliefs. They may therefore foster different behaviors among their members, as you learned in the Prologue. A culture socializes its new members by encouraging skills, attitudes, or behaviors that the society deems appropriate.

Margaret Mead conducted studies in other cultures that indicated that the socialization process was more important in determining sex roles than were biological variables. This is not to deny that biological variables can be a factor. Consider the assertion that men are generally more aggressive than women. Is this characteristic the result of biology? There does appear to be a biologically determined difference in aggressiveness among primates, but it is only a slight difference. Male chimps and male humans are a little more likely to engage in rough and tumble play than are females. And, if female chimps are given higher levels of the male hormone testosterone, they will become as rough and tumble as the males (Young, Goy, & Phoenix, 1964). This finding implies that the differences in this kind of play between males and females may be due to hormones and therefore constitute a biological difference. But these differences in roughness at play would hardly seem great enough to explain the differences we see between the sexes in terms of the aggression found in our culture. Moreover, in some cultures women are very aggressive, even in comparison with men. The Trobriand Islanders provide a stark example of the differences in aggressive levels between men and women that can be created by culture and social influences. An anthropologist studying the Trobriand Islanders observed that the women, in order to foster their tribe's reputation for virility, would catch a man from another tribe, arouse him to erection, and rape him (Malinowski, 1929). This gang rape was done in an unaffectionate and brutal manner, and was not something that the victim cared to have reoccur. The Trobriand Island women and their tribe were unashamed. In fact, it was common for the rapists to brag about what they had done. Culture obviously has a lot to do with fostering or suppressing aggression. For this reason, many psychologists and anthropologists feel that most of the aggressiveness attributed to males in our culture is due to learning rather than to the biological differences between the sexes.

Many people find it difficult to shake off the idea that it is natural for boys and girls to learn the traditional Western sex roles. If you feel that one way is "natural" or "traditional" while another is not, it may be that your culture has taught you to feel comfortable with the way *you* were raised. Ethel Albert has found many cultures in which women do the heavy work because men are thought to be too weak (Albert, 1963). This cultural assessment of men is generally inaccurate, since the average man is stronger, in terms of the muscle strength required to lift or push objects, than the average woman. Nonetheless, in some of the cultures where women are believed to be stronger than men the women really are stronger because

Whether men and women will be aggressive often depends on culture and experience.

they have been doing heavy work for years, while the men haven't been exercising. In such cultures a man attempting to build his muscles might be considered unmasculine!

Attraction

It would be impossible to fully understand sexuality or intimacy without also investigating attraction between one person and another. Which factors determine who will be our lovers or intimate friends? Psychologists have examined many of the variables that affect our liking and loving of others. In the next section of this chapter we'll look at some of these.

LIKING

All of us know some people whom we especially like. These people have a special significance for us. We look forward to seeing them, we enjoy being with them, and they make our lives happier. And one of the desires that most of us share is the hope that other people will like us.

In general, researchers have found that we tend to like people most who give us the most gratification for the least effort on our own part. If someone is nearby and easy to get along with, if that person fills our needs and makes us laugh, the chances of "falling in like" are much greater than if the person were distant, difficult to get along with, and one who met only a few of our needs. Although this general assessment should hardly surprise you, it is interesting to examine each variable that may affect the probability of liking another. You may find that some of these variables are more important, and that some have a different effect, than you might have imagined.

Closeness   Our relationships with other people depend a great deal on their physical proximity to us. There's a much greater chance that we will like those who live nearby than those who live farther away. In a study in which marriage licenses were examined, it was found that half of those who applied for a license lived within 14 blocks of each other (Koller, 1953). Perhaps your one true love in the world is really your one true love within 14 blocks! In another study, conducted in a college dormitory, students were asked to identify the others in the dormitory whom they especially liked. The person next door was more often liked than the person two doors down the hall. The person two doors away was more liked than someone three doors away, and so on (Priest & Sawyer, 1967). Other studies have found that simply being someone's roommate will foster friendship more often than one might expect (Newcomb, 1961). One of the most striking demonstrations of this proximity effect came to light during research conducted among the students attending the state police training academy in Maryland. Students were asked to identify the members of the class with whom they had become close friends. The researcher was surprised to find that over 44 percent of those identified were those who came either immediately before or immediately after the trainee on the alphabetical list of names used at the academy (Segal, 1974). The explanation for this outcome is that the trainees had been placed in dormitory rooms and assigned seats in the classroom based on alphabetical order. Consequently, those who were close to each other alphabetically were more likely to have contact.

It may have already occurred to you that proximity to another person sometimes leads to dislike as well. If people have dissimilar initial attitudes, then proximity will generally not lead to attraction. The same is true if one of the people involved is annoying. For instance, a stranger who sits close to you in the movie theatre and talks incessantly throughout a film is not likely to become a close friend. And, if strangers stand too close, so that they invade your personal space, you are not likely to care for them. The people in proximity whom we dislike tend to be those who upset or disrupt the enjoyment of our immediate environment (Ebbesen, Kjos, & Konecni, 1976). As a rule, however, closeness leads to liking rather than disliking.

Similarity Once we've had the chance to make the acquaintance of those in our immediate vicinity, whether we will like someone often depends on how similar that person appears to be to ourselves in terms of shared values, attitudes, and beliefs. We also tend to prefer people who are similar to us in age, level of education, status of occupation, and political views (Laumann, 1969).

The fact that likes attract has been documented in many studies. In one study, college students were paired by a computer according to similarity and dissimilarity of attitudes and beliefs. The couples were then sent on a half-hour date to the school cafeteria. When they returned, their attraction for one another was measured by how close they stood together and by a survey taken of their attitudes toward one another. Measures were taken immediately after the date and again several weeks later. Couples with similar attitudes and beliefs were more likely to want to have another date than were couples who were very dissimilar (Byrne, Ervin, & Lamberth, 1970).

A number of reasons have been put forth to help explain why people who are similar to one another are more likely to find each other attractive (Rubin, 1973). First, it feels good to have people agree with us; it gives us confidence in our own opinions and boosts our self-esteem. Second, if other people share our views we immediately feel that we know more about them, and we may feel more comfortable bringing up new topics and less worried that we may start an argument. Third, we are more likely to share activities with people who share our views. We may find it easier to interact with them because they, too, want to go to the church meeting, the political rally, or the film festival. Finally, in order to maintain our self-concept we like to believe that those who share our views are good people, people with whom we should associate.

Under certain circumstances opposites may attract, too. At first, this observation may seem to contradict the research we've been discussing, but "opposites," in this case, doesn't refer to opposite attitudes and beliefs but rather to the fact that each individual may be lacking something that the partner can provide. Psychologists refer to this as sharing complementary needs. For example, if you are a domineering and outgoing person you may be more likely to find someone who is reserved and submissive attractive than someone who is also domineering and outgoing. Some researchers have argued that similarity is most important when a relationship is beginning, but that complementary needs begin to play a more important role as the relationship becomes a long-term one (Kerckhoff & Davis, 1962). Others have argued that similarity remains the most important factor, especially among well-adjusted married couples (Meyer & Pepper, 1977).

Competence We generally prefer someone who is competent. Very few people appreciate incompetence, especially in those on whom we depend. In fact, demonstrating incompetence to people you have just met is a pretty sure way of being disliked. But sometimes people can seem too perfect, too superior. Such people can make us feel inferior, and though we may have a grudging admiration for them, we may not like to be around them. Consequently we may not like them. Nonetheless, if the competent person is not too perfect and seems capable of mistakes, then we are more likely to feel good about that person because he or she will seem more human and, therefore, more like ourselves.

In one experiment, subjects listened to one of four tapes that contained a recording made by a candidate for a quiz contest. Unknown to those who listened, the same person had made each tape. On two of the tapes the contestant was described as extremely intelligent and as very successful in college. On the other two tapes the contestant was said to be of average intelligence and of average ability in school. On one of the tapes in each condition the contestant was overheard to have an accident. He spilled coffee on himself. In the other two tapes there was no accident. In this way all four possibilities, superior-no accident, superior-accident, average-no accident, and average-accident, could be compared. None of the listeners heard more than one tape.

The different groups of listeners were compared as they rated how they felt about the contestant. The best-liked contestant was the superior one who had the accident. Ranked next was the superior contestant who had no accident. Ranked third was the average contestant who had no accident, and ranked fourth was the average contestant who had the accident (Aronson, 1969). The accident had enhanced the likability of the superior contestant and detracted from the likability of the average contestant. In terms of competence, then, the best-liked individuals appear to be those who are competent but who are also human and likely to make occasional mistakes. Because they have proven their competence before, we are likely to forgive them their error because it makes them seem more like us. When a person who is thought of as inferior makes a mistake, we often view the blunder as further evidence of inferiority, which is likely to detract from that individual's appeal.

THEORIES ABOUT LIKING

As you have discovered, many different variables can affect whether we will like someone. Researchers have attempted to integrate these findings into comprehensive theories. The four major theories about liking are the reinforcement theory, the equity theory, the exchange theory, and the gain-loss theory.

Reinforcement Theory   The reinforcement model of liking argues that we come to like or dislike people as a result of our learning. As you learned in Chapter 6, there are three major forms of learning: associative, instrumental, and social. The **reinforcement theory of liking** states that we come to like or dislike other people because of the processes involved in these three modes of learning. Through associative learning we come to like or dislike others because of the experiences and stimuli we associate with them. According to this view, those who are associated with pleasant experiences and attractive attributes will be more liked than those who are associated with unpleasant experiences or unattractive attributes. Of course, reinforcement theory argues that this effect does not just pertain to our likes and dislikes of people, but to our likes and dislikes of almost everything. For example, there are many kinds of sea fish that are edible and taste good, but only those that have attractive names sell well. Few people will purchase a viperfish or a hog sucker. However, rename the same fish silverfin or rock salmon and they will quickly be accepted. Similarly, if we associate new people we meet with things we already like, we are much more likely to accept them and like them.

According to instrumental learning, we like the people who reward us and we dislike the people who punish us. In this view, we are more likely to feel warmth toward someone who provides us with important financial opportunities than we would toward the same person had we interacted with him or her just as often but in a less rewarding situation (Clore & Byrne, 1974; Byrne & Clore, 1970).

REINFORCEMENT THEORY OF LIKING
A social theory of relationships that argues that we like those whom we have been reinforced for liking or whom we associate with pleasurable events or circumstances.

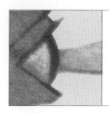

THE POWER OF GOOD LOOKS

An old expression suggests that beauty is only skin deep. This is another way of saying that there is much more to a person than physical appearance and that to discriminate against those who are physically unattractive in favor of those who are attractive is a form of prejudice. Researchers have found, however, that those who are physically attractive are more often liked, not just in a sexual sense, but in most kinds of social situations. To a great degree it seems that many people feel that beauty equals goodness.

In one study, psychologists deliberately left money in a phone booth change return and then watched secretly as the next person came to use the phone. The person in the phone booth was then approached by either an attractive or unattractive individual. This person would ask the subject in the phone booth if he or she had found any money because, as the individual put it, some money may have been left in the change return. Subjects were more likely to

return the money to the attractive individuals (Sroufe, Chaikin, Cook, & Freeman, 1977). This outcome may have occurred because it's more reinforcing to get a smile and a thank you from a beautiful person or because the person who used the phone may have hoped that by returning the change a relationship would begin. Alternatively, the person's good looks may simply have made the person who found the change feel better and, therefore, more likely to give the money back.

In mock trials psychologists have found that juries are more likely to give a less severe sentence to an attractive defendant (Leventhal & Krate, 1977). This is not always the case, however. If the defendant is said to have used his or her good looks while committing the crime, the sentence is more likely to be harsh. It has also been found that attractive, better-dressed panhandlers will make more money than unattractive ones (Kleinke, 1977).

Children learn at a very early age

that physical attractiveness is an important dimension. In one study, three-to six-year-old children were asked to illuminate a slide of either an attractive or an unattractive child. The children were significantly more apt to illuminate the slide of the attractive child (Dion, 1977). By the fifth or sixth grade, attractive children are more successful in influencing and changing the behavior of children of the opposite sex than are unattractive children (Dion & Stein, 1978). And by college, attractive people are more likely to have dating experience and sexual experience than are unattractive people (Curran & Lippold, 1975).

Knowing that you are attractive or unattractive can also affect your personality. One study demonstrated that social skill was positively correlated with physical attractiveness. In this study individuals engaged in telephone conversations and were then rated by their partners, who had not yet seen them, on dimensions of social skill, anxiety, liking, and desirability for future interaction. The more physically

---

EQUITY THEORY
A social theory of relationships that argues that people will try to create fairness in a social relationship so that each person receives as much as he or she contributes.

According to social learning, we are more likely to like those whom we see are liked by others. Because others are modeling the liking of a particular individual we may, especially if we admire the models, be more likely to imitate their behavior by also liking that person. Similarly, it becomes more probable that we will dislike someone whom we see disliked by others whom we admire.

Equity Theory   If simple reinforcement principles were totally in control of whether we like someone, then it might be expected that we would like those who give us the most but take the least. In this kind of relationship we could maximize our reinforcement. But psychologists have observed in actual liking relationships that those we like most are often those we share with. People often say that they feel distressed when they are placed in a situation of social inequity, that is, when they are giving more than they receive or receiving more than they give. The **equity theory** attempts to

attractive an individual was, the higher his or her ratings tended to be. These results probably reflect the fact that unattractive individuals may lack the courage to initiate social interactions or that they have not been approached by others and therefore have failed to obtain the social skills more often demonstrated by attractive individuals (Goldman & Lewis, 1977).

Beauty can also have a radiating effect. In one experiment a film was made of a man walking arm in arm with either an attractive or an unattractive woman. Four different groups observed the films independently. Two groups saw the man with the attractive woman. The first group was told that she was a medical student and the second group that she was a waitress. The third and fourth groups saw the man with an unattractive woman. The third group was told she was a medical student and the fourth group that she was a waitress. All groups were asked to rate the level of happiness and success they believed the *man* possessed. Whether the woman was a waitress or a medical student had some effect on the subjects' ratings of the man. However, in all cases, the man with an attractive woman was rated as significantly more successful and happy than was the same man with the unattractive

woman (Meiners & Sheposh, 1977). It would be interesting to conduct the experiment once again, this time with a woman being filmed with attractive or unattractive men. Perhaps women would value the man's profession more, or perhaps not: What do you think?

It has also been demonstrated that attractive individuals are less likely to be affected by peer pressure. It may be that attractive individuals value their own opinion more than that of others because they have been told that they are themselves valuable. Unattractive individuals are more susceptible to peer pressure because they appear to have a greater desire to be liked and are therefore more likely to comply with group demands (Adams, 1977).

Attractive individuals are not always assessed in a better light. It often depends on which aspect is being evaluated. For instance, people more often perceive attractive people as vain and egotistical and as more likely to have extramarital affairs (Dermer & Thiel, 1975). And, while it is true that physical beauty affects judgments of personality, the reverse is also true. In one experiment 69 males and 58 female undergraduates read either favorable, average, or unfavorable personality descriptions attached to

Is this man attractive?

prerated attractive, average, or unattractive photographs of a female college student. When a picture was accompanied by a favorable description of personality, it was rated higher than it had been without the description, and vice versa (Gross & Crofton, 1977). In this case, what was good was beautiful.

add to the reinforcement theory by describing how people work toward a collective reward system for equitably distributing costs and rewards. According to the equity theory, people learn that what they receive from others should be in proportion to what they have placed in the relationship. Such a system of equity appears to be well established in most cultures. The vast majority of people will agree that if you expect a lot from a relationship then you should expect to put much into it. Many of us feel that when someone does a favor for us, we are in one way or another obliged to return the favor. In this way we can restore equity to the relationship. Even in relationships that others may see as inequitable, the *participants* often feel that there is equity because they have psychologically distorted the exchanges that have been made through the use of defense mechanisms or other psychological means.

The equity theory argues that in romantic relationships or in liking relationships the most successful arrangements are the equitable ones. For

this reason a very attractive man might, perhaps unconsciously, attempt to match himself with a very attractive woman so that he is getting a fair return for his physical attractiveness. Or a wealthy woman might want to trade her money for an intelligent man. In one interesting experiment, researchers discovered that male subjects who were told that they had done poorly on a test were more likely to ask an unattractive woman for a date, while male subjects who were told that they had scored well on a test were more likely to ask out an attractive woman (Kiesler & Baral, 1970). Presumably the subjects' self-worth had been manipulated by the information that they had done either well or poorly, which left them with a greater or lesser amount of "social" currency that could be traded. If, after taking the test, the subject was led to believe that he was intelligent, he may have considered that he could trade his intelligence for an equal amount of beauty.

Exchange Theory The **exchange theory** argues that people will like each other only if, in the social exchange, they both end up with a net profit in terms of what they have put into the relationship. This theory helps explain an attraction between people with opposite needs. In such a situation each person fills the needs of the other and each person feels that there has been a net gain in the exchange, that is, more has been obtained from the relationship than lost (Homans, 1961; Rubin, 1973). Although the exchange theory may clarify the formation and maintenance of liking relationships, it is a very difficult theory to apply because of the difficulty of defining loss or gain in a relationship; these terms are very subjective. Furthermore, the exchange theory is hard-pressed to deal with acts of giving when no return for the action is expected. Such altruistic behavior, engaged in without hope of compensation, would not seem to have any value in the interpersonal marketplace that is described by the exchange theory.

Gain-Loss Theory   The **gain-loss theory** argues that if someone we come to know likes us more and more as time passes, we will generally like that person better than if he or she had liked us from the start. Similarly, we dislike people more whose evaluations of us have become more and more negative with time than people who have always held us in a negative light (Aronson, 1969). It is not known why the gain-loss effect should occur. But a number of explanations have been postulated. One possible reason may be that people tend to ignore things that don't change but to pay particular attention to changes. For this reason, a loss or a gain may seem more important.

Another reason may be that the gain or loss of someone's liking or affection is often attributed to our own behavior. That is, we have either won someone over or driven someone away. If, on the other hand, the person has always liked us or always disliked us, we usually attribute this orientation to the individual's predispositions rather than to anything we have done. If this is true, then gaining someone may enhance our self-esteem, and since the enhancement is associated with that person, it makes him or her more likable. The opposite would be true for someone who initially liked us but over time came to dislike us.

Finally, if someone comes to like us it usually makes us less anxious about them. As we become less anxious, we like them more for reducing our anxiety. Just the opposite would be true for someone who began to dislike us more.

LOVE AND INTIMACY

To say that we love another is, perhaps, to give him or her the most positive evaluation of which we are capable. We talk a great deal about love, but researchers cannot always agree on what we mean by the word. In one sense it is a semantic problem. Love can refer both to the heart-pounding excitement of a first sexual encounter and the gentle affection between two elderly sisters or brothers.

Many people would just as soon not know why couples fall in love. Recently, Senator William Proxmire ridiculed two psychologists who were studying love and had requested an $84,000 federal grant. Proxmire stated, emphatically, "Right at the top of the things we don't want to know is why a man falls in love with a woman." At the same time, though, scientists are finding that, if anything, passionate love and interest in romantic feelings are growing. In the 1960s when college students were asked whether they would marry someone who met all of their needs but whom they didn't love, 24 percent of the women and 60 percent of the men said that they wouldn't. When asked again in 1979, 80 percent of the women and 86 percent of the men said that they wouldn't. Love has apparently become more important than ever. *New York Times* columnist James Reston's response to Senator Proxmire's statement provides a rationale for continuing to study love:

> If the sociologists and psychologists can get even a suggestion of the answer to our patterns of romantic love, marriage, dissolution, divorce—and the children left behind—it could be the best investment of federal money since Mr. Jefferson made the Louisiana Purchase. (Reston, 1975)

Love can be divided into two classifications, passionate love, which is a temporary but intense reaction to another, and conjugal love, which is a long-term relationship based on friendship and mutual respect.

EXCHANGE THEORY
A social theory of relationships that argues that human interactions can best be understood by examining the costs and rewards to each person.

GAIN-LOSS THEORY
A social theory of attraction that argues that we are most attracted to those who have provided us with the greatest net gain and least attracted to those who have caused the greatest net loss.

Passionate Love **Passionate love** is an intense emotional reaction. An individual experiencing it thinks constantly about the person he or she wants to be with, and thinks of that person in the context of love. Passionate love generally leads to an unrealistic evaluation of the love object.

Researchers have argued that there are three criteria that must be met before passionate love can occur (Berscheid & Walster, 1974). First, the person must be exposed by his or her culture to the idea of passionate love. In many cultures the idea of love at first sight or passionate love is uncommon. Instead, marriages are often arranged and love is thought of as something that may develop after many years of companionship. In modern Western culture, the idea of passionate love is not only common, it is thought of as something to be expected. It is heralded in our writing, songs, theater, and television programs. Because of this, a person in our culture not only thinks more about spontaneous and passionate love, but also expects to fall in love, even suddenly.

Second, for passionate love to occur an appropriate person must be present. For most people this refers to an attractive member of the opposite sex. Passionate love and sexual attraction are well associated with one another.

The third important criterion is an emotional arousal that the individual interprets as love. This reaction may take the form of sexual arousal or even of anxiety at meeting the other person. You may think that it wouldn't be easy to make such a misattribution, but consider the following study. Scientists posted observers at two bridges across the Capilano River in British Columbia. One of the bridges was a narrow swinging footbridge that was 230 feet above the rocks. The other bridge was a sturdy low bridge that was wide, made of concrete, and stationary. Men were sent across each bridge and were intercepted by an attractive woman at the other end who pretended to ask for their help in filling out a questionnaire. Using this pretext she gave the men her phone number. A much greater percentage of the men who had crossed the frightening swaying footbridge called her for a date. Presumably, "the men staggered off the bridge with pounding hearts and trembling hands, and seeing a beautiful woman, concluded they must be in love" (Adler & Carey, 1980 p. 89).

Other researchers have argued that all physiological arousal is not qualitatively the same, and that although it is possible, it is not likely that arousing states such as love and hate will be confused. As you'll recall from Chapter 10, Plutchik's theory of emotion argues that love is an emotional state different from any other. Michael Liebowitz of the New York State Psychiatric Institute has agreed with this assessment. He and coworker Donald Klein compared love, and the breakup following a love relationship, to an amphetamine high and the withdrawal symptoms that follow the loss of the drug. The two researchers are searching for specific chemicals in the brain that are associated with being in love. One possible candidate is the chemical phenylethylamine, which is a compound closely related to the amphetamines. In studying people who have a history of love affairs and breakups, the researchers found that following a breakup the subjects often had an unusually strong craving for chocolate. Chocolate is high in phenylethylamine content (Liebowitz & Klein, as cited in Adler & Carey, 1980).

John Money has studied patients who have had various kinds of brain surgery or have suffered from deficiencies in hormones secreted by the pituitary gland. Among both groups of individuals he discovered some who, while being able to experience a wide range of emotion, were unable to feel passionate love. Money has argued that the place to look for the answers to questions about love is within the brain.

Unfortunately, a cultural expectancy, an attractive person, and physical arousal doesn't give us much to go on if we plan to build a long-term relationship or marriage. Countless couples have fallen in love and married quickly only to find later that they were not well suited for each other.

In a survey of over 200 college couples who were dating, and who stated that they were in love, it was found that by the end of two years half of the couples had broken up. At the beginning of their love affair they had felt a strong physical attraction for one another and believed that their futures would be shared together. But by the time two years had passed, half of them stated that they were either bored with the relationship or had found that they did not share similar interests (Hill, Rubin, & Peplau, 1976).

Conjugal Love   Even if we fall passionately in love with someone and our arousal is due to them, it is generally true that although we love that person and stay together, the passion doesn't last, at least not at the same continuous level. The diminishing emotional passion is supplanted by a conjugal relationship. People who have romantic expectations that the sexual passion will remain at a high level usually face disappointment. Psychologist Ellen Bersheid interviewed a large number of undergraduates and asked them what their reaction would be if their passion disappeared from their marriage. More than half said that they would want a divorce. Yet psychologists have found that this disappearance of passion is generally what happens. This may explain, at least to some degree, the high divorce rate in the United States.

Yet **conjugal love** often becomes deeper and more powerful than the initial passionate love. Researchers have found that the most stressful experience the average person will ever face is the death of a spouse (Holmes & Rahe, 1967). Perhaps, more than any other factor, sharing experiences with one another develops conjugal love, or, as it is sometimes called, **companionate love.** Another aspect of conjugal love is the willingness to make sacrifices for one another.

Sexual Myths and Research

Historically there have probably been more myths and misunderstandings about human sexuality than about any other subject. Many people feel that sexual development and sexual behavior are very private matters. It's not uncommon for individuals to become embarrassed when discussing sex. Because of this, the study of sexuality has often lagged behind other areas of investigation or been ignored. Before sexuality had been put to careful study, misunderstandings about sex were common.

EARLY "RESEARCH"

One of the first researchers to write in detail about human sexual behavior was Richard von Krafft-Ebing (1840–1902). He was a professor of psychiatry at the German University of Strasberg. *Psychopathia Sexualis*, his most powerful and frightening work, was first published in 1886 and was

PASSIONATE LOVE
A strong sexual desire for another individual combined with the perception that one is in love. This perception is often the result of misattribution in that heightened physiological arousal for any reason is attributed to love.

CONJUGAL LOVE
A deep and generally abiding love that develops between two people over long periods of time. Associated with a desire to be together, share with one another, and sacrifice for one another.

COMPANIONATE LOVE
See CONJUGAL LOVE.

last reprinted in the 1960s. Krafft-Ebing did little real scientific research, but rather collected a gruesome series of case histories that he used in his book as evidence to support his feelings that human sexual behavior was a collection of disgusting diseases. Krafft-Ebing even argued that **masturbation** was a loathsome disease, often the precursor to lust murder. It has been said that *Psychopathia Sexualis,* probably more than any other book, encouraged disgust and revulsion of sex (Brecher, 1976).

Psychologists now know that masturbation is a normal development in little boys and girls and that it continues to be a normal practice engaged in by a majority of adolescents and adults. Thanks to the efforts of modern sexual researchers, we have been able to break away from the prejudices of the past. We now know, for instance, that it is normal for a sleeping male to have occasional nocturnal emissions of semen (sometimes called wet dreams). In addition, for a male child to have erections prior to puberty is normal. But this kind of information about human sexual development wasn't always apparent to the scientific community. It has come from careful data gathering. Before these data were gathered, misconceptions about sexuality were prevalent, even among professionals.

For example, Samuel Tissot (1728–1797), a Swiss physician, predicted that masturbation would lead to blindness, impotence, acne, and insanity. He fully believed this, even though he never bothered to test his predictions to see whether they really came true after masturbation. In the early 1800s Claude Francois l'Allemand, a French physician, equated wet dreams with gonorrhea, believing that both had the same cause. As a result, he referred to nocturnal emissions as **spermatorrhea** and considered them a serious disorder. Compounding these errors, Charles Drysdale, a physician, described spermatorrhea as a terminal disorder ending with death by a "kind of apoplexy . . . induced by the exhausted state of the brain" (Sussman, 1976, p. 23). These physicians weren't lying, they were making faulty assumptions and false deductions. For instance, Drysdale may have had a dying patient who also had wet dreams, and he may have erroneously linked the two together. At any rate, sex simply wasn't something that people of that time openly discussed. It was a forbidden subject, and little data about human sexual development existed. What "information" did exist was typically concocted by the church or by ignorant physicians who foolishly assumed rules in order to explain antecedent conditions of a sexual nature, and then deduced from these rules false predictions and explanations.

People didn't realize that the predictions were false because no one bothered to check. Sex was often considered disgusting and was associated with such diseases as syphilis. Even as recently as 1900, physicians were so worried about the horrible consequences thought to result from the loss of semen or from sexual stimulation that they openly advocated castration of male children who masturbated and clitoroidectomy (removal of the clitoris) of female children who masturbated. Other physicians recommended severing the nerves to the penis or the cauterization of the genitals with hot irons or glass rods dipped in caustic solutions. Special spermatorrhea rings were made for those who feared arousal or for male children who had erections. As Figure 18.4 shows, an erection would not have been in the best interest of the wearer of such devices (Sussman, 1976). Even Sigmund Freud believed, until the last years of his life, that the loss of 1 ounce of semen could cause the same fatigue as the loss of 40 ounces of blood (Brecher, 1976), which of course is untrue.

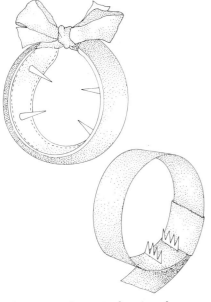

Figure 18.4 *Spermatorrhea rings.* (SOURCE: *Sussman, 1976, p. 60)*

FREUD'S CONTRIBUTION

Just after the turn of the 20th century, attitudes toward human sexual behavior began to change as a result of Freud's writings. Although Freud felt that sexual deviations were symptoms of disease, he took a major step away from Krafft-Ebing by not portraying sexual deviations as disgusting or loathsome. Still, Freud had been educated in the doctrines of Krafft-Ebing, and he clung to many of the old ideas. Freud did not view masturbation as normal, and in one instance he put an adolescent girl on around-the-clock surveillance in order to prevent her from masturbating. But this approach was a significant improvement over the advocacy of clitoroidectomy or cauterization. Furthermore, Freud viewed homosexuality as an immaturity rather than a serious disease. Today, psychologists generally consider homosexuality to be an alternative sexual choice and not an immaturity or a disease.

MODERN RESEARCH

At the end of World War II, Alfred Kinsey, a zoologist and an expert on wasps, published a compendium of human sexual behavior in two volumes, *Sexual Behavior in the Human Male* and *Sexual Behavior in the Human Female.* Included were sexual case histories of over 11,000 men and women. Kinsey taught college in Indiana. Occasionally his students would confide in him and ask questions about human sexual behavior, often in response to his lectures on the sexual behavior of wasps. In an effort to help his students, Kinsey went to the library to search for answers. He found, to his surprise, that very little had been written about human sexual behavior. It was then that Kinsey decided to gather the data for himself.

The Kinsey reports came as a great relief to many people, who discovered that others had the same sexual feelings or behavior that they did. For instance, Kinsey found that more than half of the married women and over two thirds of the married men in his sample had had premarital intercourse. Most of these people had no idea that they were in the majority. Kinsey also discovered that a vast majority of men and women engaged in masturbation. He found that many heterosexual people had homosexual experiences, and vice versa.

Kinsey's data were generally of a survey type. Beginning in the 1960s, psychologists William Masters and Virginia Johnson began a detailed investigation of the human sexual response in the laboratory, something, no doubt, that would have shocked Krafft-Ebing and raised Sigmund Freud's eyebrows. Masters and Johnson's study of human sexuality was published in 1966. It contained detailed descriptions of the volunteer subjects who engaged in sexual behavior to the point of orgasm. Each subject had been monitored by sophisticated physiological devices.

Masters and Johnson discovered that male and female sexual responses were very similar. Both men and women proceed through four stages of sexual arousal. The first is an *excitement phase* that can occur through sexual fantasizing or tactual stimulation. The second is a *plateau phase* during which the genitals become prepared (erection in males, moisture of the vaginal walls in females) for **orgasm.** The *orgasmic phase* follows, in which there are muscular contractions in the genitals of both sexes and ejaculation in the male. Finally, there is a *resolution phase* during which the body returns to its previous state. During the resolution phase men have

William Masters and Virginia Johnson have conducted extensive research into the human sexual response.

a *refractory period* during which a second ejaculation is impossible. Women, however, are often capable of multiple orgasms.

Masters and Johnson have found that orgasms are the same whether created by self-stimulation, fantasy, or intercourse. The fact that fantasy can cause the same arousal as physical stimulation emphasizes the cognitive nature of human sexuality.

Both men and women react to erotic or sexual material. Physiological monitors suggest that men and women are equally aroused by explicit sexual literature (Heiman, 1977).

Masters and Johnson have also developed sex therapy for those who suffer sexual dysfunction of psychological origin (Masters & Johnson, 1970). Most of the therapeutic approaches concentrate on reducing one's worry about sex and encouraging people to center their attention on the pleasure of sex (Heiman, 1979).

Thanks to modern researchers such as Masters and Johnson, who have brought sexual research into the open, we are now better able to separate fact from myth and to gain a fuller understanding of ourselves and others.

Summary

- The most obvious aspect of one's sexuality is anatomical. The primary sexual characteristics are the penis, scrotum, and testes in the male and the vagina, uterus, and ovaries in the female. Secondary sexual characteristics appear at puberty and signal that the body is preparing for the capacity to reproduce.
- The sex glands, called gonads, secrete hormones. Female hormones are called estrogens, male hormones androgens.
- Exposure to excessive amounts of hormones prenatally can affect an organism's sexual behavior. This is especially true of animals lower on the phylogenic scale than humans.

- Men and women appear to have different brains owing to the actions of hormones. The behavioral differences associated with these brain differences are very slight, however.
- Gender identity begins to develop at about the age of two, and it becomes very strong once gender constancy is achieved at about the age of six.
- Through socialization, children learn which sex-role behaviors are appropriate.
- Gender identity appears to be shaped by both cognitive and social processes. Freudian, cognitive, and social learning theories all predict that gender identity is strongly affected by environmental influences. Researcher Richard Green has demonstrated that gender identity may be strongly influenced by environmental forces beyond the immediate family and home.
- Research has not uncovered conclusive evidence that there are hormonal differences between homosexual and heterosexual adults. It is believed that sexual preference is strongly influenced by culture and environment.
- Transsexualism is the most extreme form of gender identity reversal. Transsexual reassignments, together with careful counseling, have been helpful in alleviating stress among some transsexuals.
- Margaret Mead and other researchers have discovered that sex role is strongly determined by culture.
- Researchers have found that we tend to like people most who give us the most gratification for the least effort on our part.
- Our relationships with other people depend a great deal on their physical proximity. Generally, we are more likely to become friends or lovers with those who are physically close to us. We also tend to prefer people who are similar to us in age, level of education, status of occupation, and political views.
- Opposites may attract if the two persons have complementary needs.
- We generally like people who are competent but who show that they are human and capable of mistakes, which makes them seem more like us.
- Physically attractive people are generally better liked than unattractive people.
- Many theories have been developed to explain how people come to like or dislike others. Among the most influential of these theories are the reinforcement theory, the equity theory, the exchange theory, and the gain-loss theory.
- Psychologists have not agreed on a definition of love. Generally, though, they divide love into two categories, passionate love and conjugal love. Passionate love may often be the result of sexual arousal and misattribution of arousal. Conjugal love usually develops after people have spent much time together and have come to share things and sacrifice for one another.
- Historically there have probably been more myths and misunderstandings about human sexuality than about any other subject. Early researchers such as Krafft-Ebing argued that most sexual deviation was the result of disgusting diseases. Until the turn of this century, spermatorrhea (a name for wet dreams) was considered to be a serious disease. It is now known to be a normal sexual occurrence.

- Sigmund Freud helped change ideas by stating that sexual deviations were not disgusting and loathsome diseases.
- Modern researchers such as Kinsey and Masters and Johnson have found normal sexual behavior to encompass a far greater range than earlier researchers had ever dreamed.
- Masters and Johnson have discovered that the male and female sexual response is very similar. Both men and women proceed through four stages of sexual arousal: the excitement phase, the plateau phase, the orgasmic phase, and the resolution phase. Masters and Johnson have developed sex therapy for those who suffer sexual dysfunction of psychological origin.

EPILOGUE:
THE CONQUEST OF SPERMATORRHEA

Psychologists who study human intimacy and sexuality know that they must often overcome ignorance and superstition. The following account describes how a man was driven to find the truth about sexual behavior half a century before Masters and Johnson.

As a young man Havelock Ellis (1859–1939) had read the works of Charles Drysdale, the eminent physician who had described the dread scourge spermatorrhea. Ellis was terrified. He would never masturbate, because he knew it was dangerous, but there was nothing he could do to prevent the nocturnal emissions that he had. He had spermatorrhea—he was a dead man! He wept and prayed, he searched desperately for a cure. Reading medical texts of the day, he was horrified at the gruesome measures suggested by physicians to control spermatorrhea. He planned suicide, but found himself too afraid to attempt it, so he decided to become a monk. After some thought, though, he felt unworthy to become a monk because his problem was sexual. Finally, in an attempt to give the short life remaining to him some meaning, he decided to keep a diary describing his deterioration and death owing to spermatorrhea, and to leave it as a gift to science.

Oddly, as the months came and went, his brain didn't turn to oatmeal. His eyes hadn't even lost their luster, an early symptom predicted by Dr. Drysdale. Slowly, anger came over Ellis as he realized that the books were filled with lies. He had been put through a period of unnecessary fear. It was obvious that the loss of semen during nocturnal emissions did not result in deterioration and death. In that moment, Ellis knew he had a goal in life, to uncover the truth about sexuality. He decided to devote the rest of his days to careful and accurate sexual research.

Although Havelock Ellis is not as well known as Sigmund Freud, his investigation of human sexuality in the early part of this century marked the beginning of modern sexual research. In his books, Studies in the Psychology of Sex, published between 1896 and 1928, Ellis pointed the way for later researchers such as Kinsey and Masters and Johnson. Ellis felt strongly that before anyone can label a sexual behavior deviant, it is necessary to document what normal sexual experiences are. Many of Ellis' findings are still valued. He noted, for instance, that sexual behavior was normal before puberty in both girls and boys, that masturbation was common in both sexes, that homosexuality and heterosexuality were not opposites but occurred in varying degrees, and that women had sexual desires, contrary to the myth advanced by the Victorians. He also found that orgasm is similar in men and women. Ellis stated that male impotence and female frigidity were in most cases caused by psychological problems and that, when it came to perversions, he had found the range of variation within normal limits to be so great that "unusual" sexual behavior was, in fact, commonplace.

Largely as a result of Ellis' work, medical concerns about nocturnal emissions and masturbation came to an end early in this century (Brecher, 1976).

Suggestions for Further Reading

1. Maccoby, E. E., & Jacklin, C. N. *The psychology of sex differences.* Stanford, Calif.: Stanford University Press, 1974.
2. Money, J., & Ehrhardt, A. A. *Man and woman, boy and girl.* Baltimore: Johns Hopkins Press, 1972.
3. Sadock, B. J., Kaplan, H. I., & Freedman, A. M. (eds.), *The sexual experience.* Baltimore: Williams & Wilkins, 1976.
4. Tiefer, L. *Human sexuality.* New York: Harper & Row, 1979.

You are a student in introductory psychology who has developed a healthy respect for what psychology has to offer. You've been impressed with the research methods psychologists use and have decided to conduct a study of your own.

For a long time you have been concerned about television and its possible adverse effects on studies and grades. The children in your family and the children in your friends' families spend a lot of time watching TV. It seems obvious to you that if they watched less, they would do better in school.

The hypothesis you want to test is that students who are heavy TV watchers do not perform as well in their academic studies as students who are light TV watchers.

With the cooperation of a friend, the principal of Tumbleweed Elementary School, and with the permission of the parents involved, you embark on a two-week research project with 50 fourth graders from Tumbleweed. Half of the students are assigned randomly to a group of heavy TV watchers and told to watch 35 hours or more of TV per week, and half are assigned to a group of light TV watchers and told to watch 6 hours or less of TV per week. At the end of two weeks, all students take the same unannounced spelling test consisting of 15 words from a current chapter of their spelling workbook. The results of the spelling test are given in Table A.1. You want to know whether the light watchers did better than the heavies.

Table A.1   Spelling scores of heavy and light TV watchers

HEAVY WATCHERS (35 HOURS OR MORE PER WEEK)						LIGHT WATCHERS (6 HOURS OR LESS PER WEEK)				
11	1	7	4	13		13	10	13	11	13
7	5	2	10	6		15	11	9	14	7
0	15	6	1	7		8	15	14	12	13
9	2	7	0	7		14	11	11	5	8
6	5	8	2	9		13	14	13	5	3

At this point you can't tell for sure. Something must be done with the scores before you can make sense out of them. In this Appendix we will set out strategies and techniques that will help you interpret, understand, and make predictions from research data such as test scores. These strategies and techniques form a very valuable research tool, namely, statistics. So let's apply statistics to your TV watchers' spelling scores.

Descriptive Statistics

Descriptive statistics are used to summarize, organize, describe, boil down, and make sense out of large amounts of data. In Table A.1 you have an incoherent mass of test score data. The scores are disorganized and convey very little information.

FREQUENCY DISTRIBUTIONS AND GRAPHS

One way of organizing the scores to make them more meaningful is to arrange them in a *frequency distribution.*

Richard D. Rees

Table A.2 Frequency distribution of spelling scores of heavy and light TV watchers

HEAVY TV WATCHERS		LIGHT TV WATCHERS	
Spelling Score	Number of Students (Frequency)	Spelling Score	Number of Students (Frequency)
15	1	15	2
14	0	14	4
13	1	13	6
12	0	12	1
11	1	11	4
10	1	10	1
9	2	9	1
8	1	8	2
7	5	7	1
6	3	6	0
5	2	5	2
4	1	4	0
3	0	3	1
2	3	2	0
1	2	1	0
0	2	0	0

Regular Frequency Distribution   In a *regular frequency distribution* each *score value* from highest to lowest is listed once, and beside it, in the frequency column, the number of times that score occurs is written. In examining Table A.2 you can see, for example, that the score of 7 occurred 5 times among the heavy TV watchers.

Grouped Frequency Distribution   If the spread of score values in a distribution is large (for example, a math test with 53 questions on it), then a *grouped frequency distribution* may be used. A grouped frequency distribution condenses the score values into intervals and then shows, in the frequency column, the number of people that received scores falling within each interval (see Table A.3).

To further clarify the arrangement of scores in a frequency distribution, so that you can see at a glance the visual pattern involved, the distribution can be graphed.

Table A.3 Grouped frequency distribution of math scores for 50 students

MATH SCORES IN INTERVALS OF 5	NUMBER OF STUDENTS (FREQUENCY)
50–54	2
45–49	3
40–44	2
35–39	6
30–34	8
25–29	12
20–24	7
15–19	5
10–14	4
5– 9	0
0– 4	1

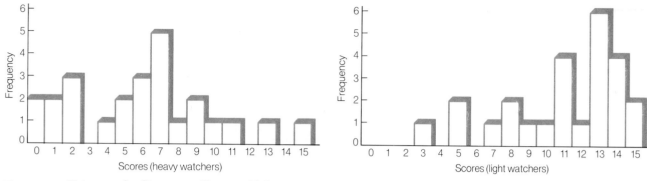

Figure A.1 *Histogram of spelling scores of heavy and light TV watchers.*

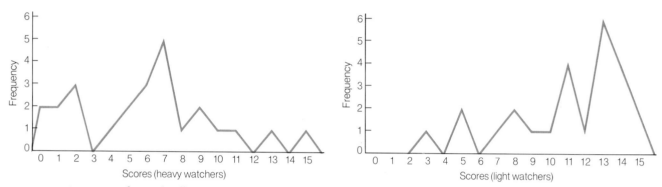

Figure A.2 *Frequency polygon of spelling scores of heavy and light TV watchers.*

Histogram A *histogram* (or *bar graph*) uses a series of vertical bars to show the pattern of scores (see Figure A.1). Notice that the sides of each bar are plotted midway between the scores so that each score falls in the center of the bar.

Frequency Polygon A *frequency polygon* plots the frequencies of the scores as points that are then connected with a straight line. Figure A.2 shows you at a glance that the heavy TV watchers didn't do too well on the spelling test. It certainly conveys more information than the mass of scores in Table A.1.

When large amounts of data (thousands of scores) are plotted, the jagged edges tend to smooth out and the frequency polygon often takes on an identifiable shape. Some of the more commonly observed shapes are (1) a normal *bell-shaped curve* (where the majority of people scored in the middle of the distribution with very few at the extreme high or low ends), (2) a *positively skewed curve* (where most of the people got low scores, with fewer and fewer getting progressively higher ones),* (3) a *negatively skewed curve* (where nearly everyone aced the test), and (4) a *bimodal curve* (where very few people scored in the middle, most either acing the test or bombing it). The curves are shown in Figure A.3.

---

*A positively skewed curve often indicates poor performance, but not always. For example, reaction-time curves are usually positively skewed, indicating that most people have faster reaction times.

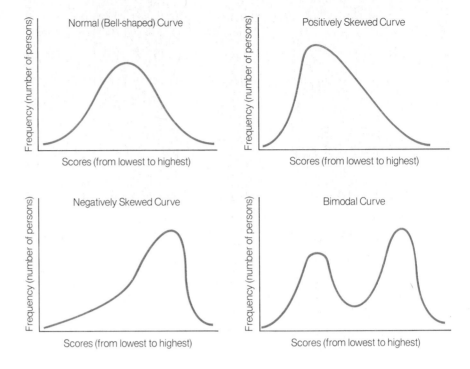

CENTRAL TENDENCY

Another useful descriptive statistic involves measuring the central tendency of a group of scores. *Central tendency* refers to a single number representing the middle or the average of a distribution. There are three measures of central tendency: the mean, the median, and the mode (see Table A.4).

Table A.4   Measures of central tendency of spelling scores for heavy and light TV Watchers

	HEAVY WATCHERS	LIGHT WATCHERS
Mean	$15 + 13 + 11 + 10 + 9 + 9 + 8$ $+ 7 + 7 + 7 + 7 + 7 + 6 + 6 + 6$ $+ 5 + 5 + 4 + 2 + 2 + 2 + 1 + 1$ $+ 0 + 0 = 150$	$15 + 15 + 14 + 14 + 14 + 14 + 13$ $+ 13 + 13 + 13 + 13 + 13 + 12 + 11$ $+ 11 + 11 + 11 + 10 + 9 + 8 + 8$ $+ 7 + 5 + 5 + 3 = 275$
	$\text{Mean} = \dfrac{\text{Sum of scores}}{\text{Number of scores}} = \dfrac{150}{25} = 6$	$\text{Mean} = \dfrac{\text{Sum of scores}}{\text{Number of scores}} = \dfrac{275}{25} = 11$
	Mean = 6	Mean = 11
Median and Mode	15, 13, 11, 10, 9, 9, 8, <u>7</u>, <u>7</u>, <u>7</u>, <u>7</u>, <u>7</u>, ⑥6, 6, 5, 5, 4, 2, 2, 2, 1, 1, 0, 0,	15, 15, 14, <u>14</u>, 14, 14, <u>13</u>, <u>13</u>, <u>13</u>, <u>13</u>, <u>13</u>, <u>13</u>, ⑫11, 11, 11, 11, 10, 9, 8, 8, 7, 5, 5, 3,
	Median = Exact middle score (There are exactly 12 scores on either side of the circled 6.)	Median = Exact middle score (There are exactly 12 scores on either side of the circled 12.)
	Median = 6	Median = 12
	Mode = Most frequently occurring score (There were 5 students who got a score of 7.)	Mode = Most frequently occurring score (There were 5 students who got a score of 13.)
	Mode = 7	Mode = 13

Mean   The *mean* is the arithmetic average and is obtained by adding up all the scores in the distribution and dividing that sum by the total number of scores. The heavy TV watchers' spelling scores add up to 150. Since there were 25 students in this group, we divide 150 by 25 to obtain a mean score of 6. The light TV watchers' scores total 275, which, divided by 25, gives a mean of 11. Out of 15 possible, the light watchers averaged 11 right, and the heavy watchers 6 right. Your hypothesis is looking more plausible all the time, isn't it?

Median   Although the mean is the most commonly used measure of central tendency in statistical analysis, there are times when it is not appropriate to use it (for instance with a highly skewed distribution containing extreme scores). Instead, the *median* is used.

The median is the exact middle of a distribution of scores. Half the scores fall on one side of it and half on the other. There are precise methods for calculating the median, but for our purposes, a convenient way is to list each score from highest to lowest and then count into the center.

Mode   The *mode* is a very crude measure of central tendency. It gives, at best, only a rough estimate of the middle area and is seldom used in statistical analysis. The mode is simply the score in a distribution that occurs more frequently than any other score. For the heavy watchers it is 7, and for the light watchers, 13.

VARIABILITY

Variability refers to the dispersion or scatter of a group of scores. It is concerned with how spread out the scores are. High variability means that the scores are widely separated with much distance between them. Low variability indicates very little spread; the scores are tightly clustered together. Two measures of variability are the range and the standard deviation.

Range   The *range* is obtained by subtracting the lowest from the highest score. The range of spelling scores for the heavy TV watchers is 15 (the scores ranged from 0 to 15). For the light watchers, the range is 12 (from 3 to 15). Although easy to calculate, the range, like the mode, is a crude statistical measure. As you can see, it takes into account only two scores in the distribution, the highest and the lowest.

Standard Deviation   The *standard deviation* (SD) is the most useful measure of variability. It takes into account every score in the distribution. The standard deviation can be thought of as a number representing the average distance of the scores from the mean. The larger the standard deviation, the more spread out the scores. It is calculated by (1) finding the difference between the mean and each score, (2) squaring each of these differences, (3) adding up the squared differences, (4) dividing the sum of the squared differences by the total number of scores (minus one) in the distribution (the average of the squared differences), and (5) taking the square root of the average of the squared differences to obtain the standard deviation.

As you can see in Table A.5, the heavy TV watchers had slightly greater variability on the spelling test than the light watchers. The heavies had a higher range and a larger standard deviation.

Table A.5 Measures of variability of spelling scores for heavy and light TV watchers

	HEAVY WATCHERS			LIGHT WATCHERS		
Range	Range = Highest score minus lowest score			Range = Highest score minus lowest score		
	Range = 15 – 0			Range = 15 – 3		
	Range = 15			Range = 12		

	Scores	Scores minus mean of 6	Scores minus mean, squared	Scores	Scores minus mean of 11	Scores minus mean, squared
	15	9	81	15	4	16
	13	7	49	15	4	16
	11	5	25	14	3	9
	10	4	16	14	3	9
	9	3	9	14	3	9
	9	3	9	14	3	9
	8	2	4	13	2	4
	7	1	1	13	2	4
	7	1	1	13	2	4
	7	1	1	13	2	4
Standard Deviation (SD)	7	1	1	13	2	4
	6	0	0	12	1	1
	6	0	0	11	0	0
	6	0	0	11	0	0
	5	–1	1	11	0	0
	5	–1	1	11	0	0
	4	–2	4	10	–1	1
	2	–4	16	9	–2	4
	2	–4	16	8	–3	9
	2	–4	16	8	–3	9
	1	–5	25	7	–4	16
	1	–5	25	5	–6	36
	0	–6	36	5	–6	36
	0	–6	36	3	–8	64

Sum of scores minus mean, squared	= 374	Sum of scores minus mean, squared	= 268

$$SD = \sqrt{\frac{\text{Sum of (scores minus mean)}^2}{\text{Number of scores minus one}}}$$

$$SD = \sqrt{\frac{374}{25-1}} = \sqrt{15.583} = 3.948$$

Standard deviation = 3.948

$$SD = \sqrt{\frac{\text{Sum of (scores minus mean)}^2}{\text{Number of scores minus one}}}$$

$$SD = \sqrt{\frac{268}{25-1}} = \sqrt{11.167} = 3.342$$

Standard deviation = 3.342

TRANSFORMED SCORES

Sometimes, for purposes of increased clarity or for making comparisons, it is desirable to change or transform scores into new units. Percentiles represent one type of transformed scores, and standard scores are another.

Percentiles   Carol, a subject in the group of light TV watchers, scored 13 correct on the spelling test. Her friend Julie, in the heavy group, got 9 right.

To see how well each girl did in comparison with her own group, we need to transform the scores. A percentile shows the percentage of people in the reference group who scored at or below a certain score. In Carol's reference group (the light watchers), 19 children out of 25 got 13 or fewer words right. Dividing 19 by 25 gives us .76 or 76 percent. Thus, Carol's score of 13 places her at the 76th percentile. Julie's 9 represents the 84th percentile (21 students out of 25 got 9 or less, 21/25 = .84). So Julie with her 9 did better with respect to her group of heavy watchers than Carol with her 13 did with respect to the light watchers.

Standard Scores (Z, T, SAT) *Z scores* are transformed scores that have a mean of 0 and a standard deviation of 1. To obtain a Z score for any raw score in a distribution, simply subtract the mean from the score and divide the result by the standard deviation. Carol's Z score is 0.60 (her score of 13 minus the mean of 11 divided by the standard deviation of 3.341 equals 0.60) in her light TV group. Julie's Z score is 9 minus 6 divided by 3.948 equals 0.76. Again, you can see that Julie with her Z of 0.76 did better with respect to her group than Carol with her Z of 0.60 did with respect to hers, even though Carol's raw score of 13 was higher than Julie's raw score of 9.

Two other standard scores are *T scores,* which have a mean of 50 and a standard deviation of 10, and SAT scores, with a mean of 500 and an SD of 100. To obtain a T score, multiply the Z score by 10 and add 50. Carol's T (10 times 0.60 plus 50) equals 56.1, and Julie's T is 57.6 (10 times 0.76 plus 50). *SAT scores* are obtained by multiplying the T score by 10. Carol's SAT is 56.0 times 10 equals 560, and Julie's is 57.6 times 10 equals 576.

Table A.6 shows transformed scores for Carol with respect to the group of light TV watchers and Julie with respect to the heavy watchers.

Julie's boy friend, Ambitious Andy Angus, who lifts bulls for exercise, watches a lot of TV and doesn't study at all. He got a score of 1 on the spelling test in the heavy watchers group. His Z score is –1.27 (1 minus 6 divided by 3.948). His T score is 37.3 (–1.27 times 10 plus 50), and his SAT is 373.

T scores are easier to interpret for many people because, unlike Z scores, they avoid negative numbers (a Z of –1 is the same as a T of 40). Also, the results of some national exams, such as the *Scholastic Aptitude Test* and the *Graduate Record Exam,* are reported in SAT scores.

THE NORMAL BELL-SHAPED CURVE

Z scores and the standard deviation are related to the normal bell-shaped curve in a fixed and predictable manner. When a frequency polygon is drawn for large numbers of people on certain traits (for instance, intelligence, height, weight, extroversion), the resulting curve is bell-shaped. Because many traits in psychology take this bell shape, the normal curve

Table A.6   Transformed spelling scores

	JULIE (IN HEAVY TV GROUP)	CAROL (IN LIGHT TV GROUP)
Actual Score on Spelling Test	9	13
Percentile	84th	76th
Z Score	+ 0.76	+ 0.60
T Score	57.6	56.0
SAT Score	576	560

is a very useful statistical tool. Since the percentages under the curve never change, by plugging in the standard deviation you can determine the percentage of the people falling above, below, or between certain scores. Look at Figure A.4. Assuming that the mean spelling score on a 25-item test for a *large population* of light TV watchers is 11 with an SD of 3, you can see that about 68 percent of the subjects score between 8 and 14 on the test. Only 13/100 percent (.13 percent) were above a score of 20.

A popular intelligence test (the Wechsler) has a mean IQ of 100 with an SD of 15. As you can see in Figure A.4, about 95 percent of the population have IQ scores between 70 and 130.

Z scores are expressed in standard deviation units, so that a person with a Z score of +3.00 would be 3 standard deviations above the mean and would have outscored over 99 percent of those with scores on that variable. Remember, any score on any test can be converted to a Z score, and by examining the percentages under the curve, you can see at a glance how good that score is.

Inferential Statistics

Whereas descriptive statistics merely describe, organize, and summarize data, inferential statistics are used to make predictions and draw conclusions about populations based on data from a sample.

Figure A.4 *Normal bell-shaped curve showing various scores and percentages under the curve (total area equals 100 percent).*

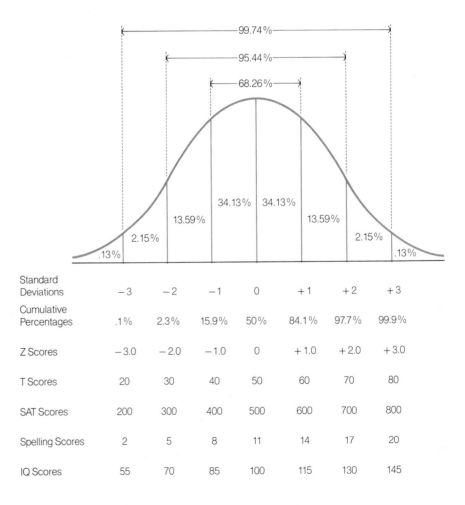

	−3	−2	−1	0	+1	+2	+3
Standard Deviations	−3	−2	−1	0	+1	+2	+3
Cumulative Percentages	.1%	2.3%	15.9%	50%	84.1%	97.7%	99.9%
Z Scores	−3.0	−2.0	−1.0	0	+1.0	+2.0	+3.0
T Scores	20	30	40	50	60	70	80
SAT Scores	200	300	400	500	600	700	800
Spelling Scores	2	5	8	11	14	17	20
IQ Scores	55	70	85	100	115	130	145

The question you want to answer is: Do all fourth graders who are heavy TV watchers really obtain a lower spelling test average (mean) than all fourth graders who are light TV watchers? Your populations of interest, then, are *all* heavy and *all* light TV watchers who are in the fourth grade. However, you couldn't measure them all, so you obtained a sample of each, which is smaller and more manageable and which you *can* measure. If your samples were chosen at random (so that any member of the population had an equal chance of being selected) then they are likely to be representative of the population.

PROBABILITY

Inferential statistics are based on the laws of *probability* or chance. If heavy or light TV watching has no effect at all on spelling scores, then you would expect the mean scores for the two samples (heavy and light) to be about the same; that is, the probability is high that the means will be the same or nearly the same. On the other hand, what are the chances that the heavy watchers sample will average, say, a score of 2 and the light watchers sample will average, say, 14 if TV watching has *no* effect on spelling scores in the population? You wouldn't expect the averages to be so far apart, would you? The probability of such an occurrence is low. If TV watching does not affect spelling scores, then whatever difference showed up between our sample means would be due to chance only and to nothing else.

NULL HYPOTHESIS (RETAIN OR REJECT)

The procedure to follow in inferential statistics is (1) to state the *null hypothesis* (that there is *no* difference between the average scores in the two populations), (2) to draw a sample of the two populations of interest, (3) to find the two sample mean scores, (4) to determine how probable it is that the difference between the two means occurred by chance, and (5) to reject the null hypothesis if the probability is less than 5 percent that the difference could have occurred by chance (the choice of 5 percent is an arbitrary one that psychologists have generally found to be most useful).

In your present study, your null hypothesis is that heavy and light TV watchers will score the same on the spelling test (signifying that TV watching does not affect spelling scores). In your two samples, the heavy watchers and the light watchers scored a mean of 6 and 11, respectively, on the test. Could a mean of 6 in one group and 11 in the other have occurred just by chance if the null hypothesis is true? It could have, but it is not very likely. Using the normal curve and specific inferential statistical testing procedures, we find that the probability that means of 6 and 11 (a difference of 5 points) would occur by chance is less than 5 percent. This is so low that you reject the null hypothesis and conclude that, in the populations, fourth graders who are light TV watchers score better on the spelling test than those who are heavy TV watchers. You have found a significant difference between the means. *Significant* has a specific meaning in statistics. It means that the difference between the sample means could have occurred purely by chance less than five times in a hundred samplings (that is in 5 percent) of the two populations if in fact the two population means are the same (that is, if the null hypothesis is true).

It was not chance that accounted for the heavy group's lower score, it was too much TV. Notice that in rejecting the null hypothesis you are supporting the research hypothesis that you formulated when you began the study. That is, students who are heavy TV watchers do not perform as well in their academic studies as students who are light TV watchers. You could have made an error in drawing this conclusion if that very slim probability (less than five chances in a hundred) actually happened in these samples. But the probability of your having made such an error (known as a Type I error in statistical terminology) is less than 5 percent.

Correlation

Showing that heavy TV watchers score lower on the spelling test than light watchers involved one major statistical procedure, namely, testing for differences between means.

Correlation, another major procedure in statistics, is designed to show relationships between variables. Correlation may be classified as descriptive or inferential depending on how it is used. Instead of setting up an experimental study with two groups of fourth graders assigned to two weeks of heavy or light TV viewing, we could simply select a group of fourth graders, ask them how much TV they watch per week, and give them a spelling test. The correlation or relationship between hours of TV and test scores could then be determined. A trend or a tendency (a correlation) could show up. You might expect that the result would show a strong positive correlation, but it is possible that it could be moderate, weak, or zero. It might even be negative.

CORRELATION COEFFICIENT

The correlation between two variables is expressed as a number known as the correlation coefficient. It can range from 0 to 1 (usually expressed in hundredths, that is, .01, .09, .18, .45, .87, .93, etc.), with higher numbers showing stronger relationships, and it can be positive or negative. A correlation can also be perfect, although perfect correlations rarely occur with psychological data.

POSITIVE, NEGATIVE, PERFECT, AND ZERO CORRELATIONS

A positive correlation means that there is a tendency for the two variables to change together in the same direction. For instance, high school grade point average is positively correlated with college grade point average. That is to say, those who do well in high school tend to do well in college also, and vice versa. Of course, there are exceptions, but the tendency is nevertheless a strong one.

A negative correlation shows that as one variable is increasing, the other is decreasing. The variables change in opposite directions. Absences and grades would likely be negatively correlated. As absences increase, grades go down, and vice versa.

The strongest possible correlation is 1.00 (which can be either a +1.00 or a –1.00), and it is called a perfect correlation. A perfect positive correlation ($+1.00$) means that right down the line each person maintains his or her position from highest to lowest on both variables. The highest person on variable X is also the highest on variable Y and so on, right down the line to the person who is lowest on both variables. There are no exceptions to the pattern. For example, it costs 50¢ for an ice cream cone at the corner ice cream parlor. What is the correlation between money spent for ice cream cones and the number of cones purchased? It is perfect ($+1.00$), isn't it? The person who spends 50¢ gets one cone; whoever spends $1 gets two cones; $10, 20 cones; $50, 100 cones; and so on. You can *predict* exactly a person's "score" on one variable if you know the "score" on the other variable. (If someone spent $20 on ice cream cones, how many did he or she buy? 40! Right.)

Zero correlation means that there is no relationship between the two variables being studied. What would you expect the correlation to be between nose length and IQ for a group of 50 people? It would be zero, or very near to zero, since these two variables are not related.

SCATTER DIAGRAMS

A scatter diagram can show visually the direction and strength of a correlation. The correlation scatter diagrams in Figure A.5 were constructed by plotting a single dot for each person's score on both variables. The closer

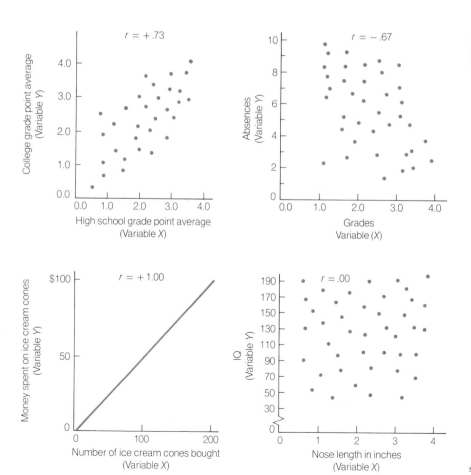

Figure A.5 *Scatter diagrams showing positive, negative, perfect, and zero correlations (r = correlation coefficient).*

Table A.7   Interpreting correlation coefficients

CORRELATION COEFFICIENT (PLUS OR MINUS)	INTERPRETATION
1.00	Perfect relationship
.73 to .99	Very strong relationship
.60 to .72	Strong relationship
.31 to .59	Fairly strong (or moderate) relationship
.16 to .30	Weak relationship
.01 to .15	Very weak relationship
0.00	No relationship

the dots approach a straight line, the higher the correlation; a straight line represents a perfect correlation of + or − 1.00.

Table A.7 shows how different correlation coefficient values are interpreted. Remember, the size of the correlation coefficient shows how strong the relationship is, and the sign (plus or minus) indicates the direction of the relationship (positive meaning that the two variables change together and negative that they vary in opposite directions). A correlation coefficient of −.83, for example, indicates a stronger relationship than does one of +.71, since .83 is a larger value than .71.

CORRELATING TEST SCORES WITH TV VIEWING

Let's take another look at the fourth-grade TV watchers. You want to know whether those who watch TV more tend to score lower on the spelling test. Select 10 fourth graders from Tumbleweed Elementary and find out how many hours per week each watches TV. Also obtain their scores on the spelling test. Table A.8 shows the TV hours and scores, and gives the calculations necessary to obtain the correlation coefficient.

The correlation coefficient of −.72 indicates a strong to very strong relationship between TV watching and spelling scores. The higher-scoring students watch less TV and vice versa. The correlation, however, is not perfect. There are some exceptions to this trend, but the trend is nevertheless striking.

Note that the data in this Appendix were made up and exaggerated to illustrate the statistical concepts. You may now wish to run your own study with real data in order to check your understanding of statistics and to indulge your curiosity about behavior.

CORRELATION AND CAUSATION

Experimental studies, which test the differences between means, help you to draw conclusions about cause and effect relationships, but correlational studies do not establish causation. Just because two variables are correlated does not mean that one causes the other. It may be that when two variables are highly correlated, variable X causes variable Y, or variable Y causes variable X, or X causes Z which in turn causes Y, or W simultaneously causes both X and Y. The correlation coefficient gives us no information about causation. Much TV watching may cause low grades; low grades may

Table A.8 Calculation of correlation coefficient between hours of TV watching and spelling test scores for 10 fourth graders

SUBJECT	HOURS OF TV PER WEEK (VARIABLE X)	VARIABLE X SQUARED (X^2)	SCORE ON 10-WORD SPELLING TEST (VARIABLE Y)	VARIABLE Y SQUARED (Y^2)	VARIABLE X TIMES VARIABLE Y (XY)
1	0	0	10	100	0
2	5	25	8	64	40
3	10	100	9	91	90
4	13	169	2	4	26
5	18	324	6	36	108
6	23	529	5	25	115
7	27	729	3	9	81
8	30	900	0	0	0
9	31	961	7	49	217
10	36	1296	1	1	36
Totals:	193	5033	51	369	713
	Sum of X	Sum of X^2	Sum of Y	Sum of Y^2	Sum of XY
	193	5033	51	369	713

N = Number of subjects = 10

$$r = \frac{N(\text{Sum of } XY) - (\text{Sum of } X)(\text{Sum of } Y)}{\sqrt{N(\text{Sum of } X^2) - (\text{Sum of } X)^2 \; N(\text{Sum of } Y^2) - (\text{Sum of } Y)^2}}$$

$$r = \frac{(10)(713) - (193)(51)}{\sqrt{(10)(5033) - (193)^2 \; (10)(369) - (51)^2}}$$

$$r = \frac{7130 - 9843}{\sqrt{(50330 - 37249)(3690 - 2601)}}$$

$$r = \frac{-2713}{\sqrt{(13081)(1089)}}$$

$$r = \frac{-2713}{\sqrt{14245209}} \qquad r = \frac{-2713}{3774.2825}$$

$$r = -.7188 \text{ or } -.72$$

cause more TV watching; or some other variable (such as increased study time, procrastination, depression, self-concept, intelligence, or social pressure) may be causing both higher grades and less TV or lower grades and more TV.

When birth statistics were examined for a number of European cities several years ago, a high positive correlation was supposed to have been found between the number of babies born per year and the number of storks nesting in the chimneys. Obviously, a hasty assumption about *causation* will lead you to an outdated conclusion. Even your TV-watching fourth graders wouldn't buy that one.

Summary

Psychologists give a lot of tests, conduct all kinds of experiments, and carry out extensive research into many facets of human and animal behavior. The data resulting from all this research must be analyzed, interpreted, summarized, and reported in a meaningful way. By using statistics, researchers can make sense out of the data and can draw valid conclusions about the results of their tests and experiments.

Statistics fall into two main categories: descriptive and inferential. Descriptive statistics are used to summarize, organize, and describe a set of research data, and inferential statistics are used to draw conclusions about populations based on the results obtained from a sample.

Descriptive statistics include frequency distributions (both regular and grouped), graphs (including histograms and frequency polygons), measures of central tendency (mean, median, and mode), measures of variability (the range and the standard deviation), and transformed scores (including percentiles and standard scores).

Although frequency polygons take many shapes (including skewed and bimodal), the most important for use in statistical analysis is the normal bell-shaped curve. The normal curve has a fixed and predictable association with the standard deviation and z scores, permitting direct comparison of the results of many diverse tests and experimental data. The normal curve is also a probability curve which has special applications in conjunction with inferential statistics.

Inferential statistics are based on the laws of probability. The researcher is interested in determining the chances that the results obtained from certain samples represent the true state of affairs in the population. To do this, a null hypothesis (that no difference exists or that observed differences are due only to chance) is stated, and then the null hypothesis is retained or rejected depending on the results of the statistical test employed.

Correlation, another statistical procedure, shows the strength of the relationship between two variables. Correlation coefficients range from 0 to +1.00, or from 0 to –1.00. The higher the correlation coefficient the stronger the relationship. A positive correlation means that the two variables are changing together in the same direction, and a negative correlation shows an inverse relationship (as one variable is getting larger the other is getting smaller and vice versa). Correlation coefficients may be visually displayed in scatter diagrams. Correlation does not imply causation.

A-B-A SINGLE-SUBJECT EXPERIMENTAL   An experimental design in which time is used as a control and only one subject is monitored. The independent variable is given in condition A and withdrawn in condition B. The dependent variable is the subject's behavioral change over time as the independent variable is presented, withdrawn, and finally presented again.

ABNORMAL BEHAVIOR   Behavior that is statistically unusual, considered maladaptive or undesirable by most people, and self-defeating to the person who displays it.

ABSOLUTE THRESHOLD   The minimum intensity a stimulus must have in order to produce a sensation.

ACHIEVING SOCIETY THEORY   David McClelland's theory that nations whose members show the lowest need for achievement also tend to have the lowest gross national product, while nations whose members show the highest need for achievement have the highest gross national product.

ACOUSTIC CODE   From the dual-code theory of memory. Sensory information may be stored directly as sounds.

ACQUIRED REINFORCER   *See* SECONDARY REINFORCER

ACTION POTENTIAL   A localized, rapid change in electrical state that travels across the cell membrane of a neuron at the moment of excitation.

ACTION THERAPY   Psychotherapy in which the therapist helps the patient or client take direct and immediate action to overcome problems through the use of special techniques.

ACTIVATION-SYNTHESIS MODEL   A physiological model of dreaming that argues that the brain synthesizes random neural activity generated during sleep and organizes this activity into a dream.

ACUPUNCTURE   A traditional Chinese therapeutic technique whereby the body is punctured with fine needles. Usually used as an anesthetic or to relieve pain.

ACUTE PARANOID DISORDER   A functional psychosis characterized by variable or temporary delusions that generally lack the logic and systematic organization of paranoia.

ADAPTIVE THEORY   A theory that attempts to explain why we sleep. It argues that for each species a certain amount of waking time is necessary in order to survive. Sleep is seen as nature's way of protecting animals from getting into trouble during the extra time.

ADDITIVE MIXING   The process by which light waves of different hue are mixed or added together. Unlike subtractive mixing, in which colors are absorbed, additive mixing generates more color each time a new light-wave source is added. All wavelengths added together create white light.

ADRENAL GLANDS   Endocrine glands located above the kidneys that secrete the hormones adrenaline, noradrenaline, and steroids. These hormones influence metabolism and the body's reaction to stressful situations.

ADRENALINE   A hormone secreted by the adrenal glands that stimulates the sympathetic nervous system; also called *epinephrine.*

AERIAL PERSPECTIVE   A monocular depth cue. Nearby objects are brighter and sharper than distant objects.

AFFECTIVE DISORDERS   A group of psychotic disorders, including bipolar disorder and major depression, characterized by extremes of mood and emotion.

AFFERENT NERVES   Nerves that carry messages inward to the central nervous system.

AFFORDANCES   The properties of the environment that are relative to any particular organism's perceptual arrangement.

ALARM REACTION STAGE   The first stage of the general adaptation syndrome, during which cortical hormone levels rise and emotional arousal and tension increase.

ALCOHOLISM   Alcohol dependence. A disorder marked by addiction to alcohol and an inability to control drinking behavior.

ALGORITHMS   Mathematical premises. In computer usage, a program that will search for an answer by examining every possibility.

ALPHA WAVES   A pattern of brain waves typical of the relaxed, waking state.

AMES ROOM   A specially designed room that is perceived as rectangular, even though it is not. Objects of the same size placed in different points in the room seem to be totally different in size.

AMINO ACIDS   The basic building blocks of proteins. Some amino acids have been discovered to be neurotransmitters as well. Among these are aspartic acid, glycine, and taurine.

AMPHETAMINES   A group of drugs that excite the central nervous system and suppress appetite, increase heart rate and blood pressure, and alter sleep patterns.

AMPLITUDE   A measurement of the amount of energy carried by a wave, shown in the height of the oscillation.

AMYGDALA   A small bulb at the front of the brain that is associated with emotion. Part of the limbic system.

ANABOLIC   In Hering's opponent-process theory, the building-up phase created within the photoreceptors.

ANDROGEN   Any male hormone that regulates sexual development. Some androgens are produced by the testes and others by the adrenal cortex.

ANDROGYNOUS   From personality theory, referring to those who possess both male and female personality characteristics in terms of their responses to questions or situations.

ANGULAR GYRUS   A portion of the brain in the parietal lobe adjacent to Wernicke's area. The angular gyrus is involved with reading and appears to "translate" the visual word images received by the primary visual cortex into auditory form before passing the information on to Wernicke's area.

ANIMAL MAGNETISM   Term coined by Anton Mesmer to describe the supposed magnetic force that people could exert on each other.

ANTECEDENT CONDITIONS   The set of circumstances existing before an event occurs.

ANTIDEPRESSANTS   Drugs used to relieve the symptoms of extreme sadness and withdrawal from life that characterize severe depression. MAO inhibitors and tricyclic drugs are the two major classes of antidepressants.

ANXIETY   A state of apprehension in which the source is usually not specific as it is in fear. There is a vague but persistent feeling that some future danger is in store, such as punishment or threat to self-esteem. Anxiety typically leads to defensive reactions.

ANXIETY STATES   A group of functional disorders including generalized anxiety disorder, panic disorder, and obsessive-compulsive disorder. All are characterized by heightened anxiety, tension, worry, or fear in the absence of any realistic reason or cause.

APHASIA   The loss of the ability to understand or to use speech, which is usually the result of brain damage.

APPROACH-APPROACH CONFLICT   A conflict in which the individual must choose between two incompatible goals, both of which are desirable.

APPROACH-AVOIDANCE CONFLICT   A conflict in which the goal has both positive and negative factors associated with it.

APPROPRIATENESS   One of the four qualities of creativity defined by Jackson and Messick. Appropriate ideas are those that make sense in context.

ARCUATE FASCICULUS   The bundle of nerve fibers in the brain that connects Wernicke's area with Broca's area.

ASSOCIATION AREAS   The parts of the cerebral cortex, other than the sensory and motor areas, that appear to be linked with language, thinking, and memory.

ASSOCIATIVE LEARNING   Learning that occurs through the association of one stimulus with another. Feelings and attitudes are often shaped by associative experiences.

ATTRIBUTION   The psychosocial process through which we come to believe that certain events or dispositions are responsible for the behavior of ourselves or others.

AUDITORY NERVE   The nerve leading from the cochlea which transmits sound impulses to the brain.

AUTHORITARIANISM   From personality theory, traits or characteristics manifest in an individual who seeks security in authority and wants a social hierarchy in which everyone has and knows his or her place.

AUTOMATIC WRITING   Writing done by the subject during a dissociated hypnotic state but of which the writer is unaware.

AUTONOMIC NERVOUS SYSTEM   The portion of the peripheral nervous system that carries information to and from organs, glands, and organ muscles within the body.

AUTOSOME   Any chromosome that is not a sex chromosome.

AVERSIVE CONDITIONING   An element of behavior therapy whereby unacceptable behavior becomes linked with painful stimuli and is thereafter avoided.

AVOIDANCE-AVOIDANCE CONFLICT   A conflict in which one must choose between two unacceptable goals.

AXON   The long process of a neuron that transmits impulses away from the cell body to the synapse.

BABBLING STAGE   One of the first stages of language development in infants, characterized by inarticulate, meaningless speech sounds.

BABY TALK   The simplification of both vocabulary and individual words. Not to be confused with caretaker speech, which is a more inclusive term.

BEHAVIOR MODIFICATION   A set of procedures for changing

human behavior, especially by using behavior therapy and operant conditioning techniques.

BEHAVIOR THERAPY   A group of techniques based on learning principles used to directly manipulate an individual's behavior in order to promote adaptive while eliminating maladaptive patterns.

BEHAVIORAL CONTRACTS   A technique often used in behavior, group, or family therapy, in which a contract or bargain is struck. The client promises to engage in a certain behavior in return for a particular behavior from another.

BEHAVIORAL THEORY   A view that behavior can be explained as the result of learning and experience and that an understanding of internal events or constructs such as the mind are unneccessary.

BEHAVIORISM   The school of psychology that views learning as the most important aspect of an organism's development. Behaviorists objectively measure behavior and the way in which stimulus-response relationships are formed.

BENZODIAZEPINES   An important class of minor tranquilizers which, since the mid 1950s, have come to replace the more dangerous barbiturates. Usually prescribed by physicians to control anxiety and tension.

BETA ENDORPHIN   A powerful natural neuropeptide. It means "the morphine within" and is so named because it has properties similar to those of heroin and morphine. It is a powerful painkiller and mood elevator.

BINOCULAR CUES   Depth cues that arise only when both eyes are used. Examples include convergence and retinal disparity.

BINOCULAR VISION   Visual perception based on information obtained from the use of two retinas (both eyes) simultaneously. See also RETINAL DISPARITY.

BIOFEEDBACK   A technique of monitoring internal processes such as heart rate, brain waves, or blood pressure in order to enable the subject to gain voluntary control over these processes.

BIOLOGICAL MOTION PERCEPTION   An affordance that may exist in human beings that enables us to easily and quickly make perceptual sense of live objects in motion.

BIPOLAR CELLS   Nerve cells that receive impulses from the rods and cones in the retina and transmit these impulses to the ganglion cells.

BIPOLAR DISORDER   An affective psychosis characterized by severe cyclical mood swings. Its three forms are mixed, manic, and depressed. Formerly called manic-depressive psychosis, bipolar disorder can often be controlled with lithium-based drugs.

BIRTH TRAUMA   Rank's hypothesis that the birth process has a dramatic and traumatic effect on subsequent human behavior.

BLIND SPOT   The region of the retina where the optic nerve attaches and where there are no photoreceptors. Also, the fovea when something is viewed in very dim light.

BLINDSIGHT   The ability to "see" objects in the periphery without being consciously aware of them. Blindsight appears to depend on visual information that is projected to the temporal lobes rather than to the conscious seeing areas in the occipital lobes.

BOGUS PIPELINE   A procedure for measuring a person's real attitudes and feelings rather than what the person wishes to present. Subjects are led to believe that a supposed physiological monitor is able to detect their real attitudes and feelings, and that any attempt to hide them will be uncovered.

BRAIN   The portion of the central nervous system located in the cranium that is responsible for the interpretation of sensory impulses, the coordination and control of bodily activities, and the exercise of emotion and thought.

BRAIN MAPPING   A technique neurosurgeons use to pinpoint the functions of different areas in the brain so that they don't destroy something vital during brain surgery.

BRIGHTNESS CONSTANCY   The perception that objects appear to maintain their brightness independent of the lighting.

BROCA'S APHASIA   A disorder caused by damage to Broca's area. Individuals with this disorder have impaired articulation, labored speech, and difficulty in forming a grammatical sentence, but semantic content is usually clear.

BBROCA'S AREA   An area in the frontal lobe of the cerebral hemisphere that plays an important role in speech production.

BYSTANDER EFFECT   People's tendency, especially pronounced under crowded conditions, to ignore others who need help in situations that call for action.

CAFFEINE   A drug contained in coffee, tea, and kola nuts, which functions as a stimulant and diuretic.

CANALIZATION   The process by which behaviors, due to genetic predisposition, are learned extremely easily, almost inevitably. The more canalized a behavior is, the more difficult it is to change or alter.

CANNON-BARD THEORY OF EMOTION   The theory that environmental stimuli may set off patterns of activity in the hypothalamus and thalamus. These patterns are then relayed to the autonomic and somatic nervous systems, where they trigger the bodily changes associated with emotion, and to the cerebral cortex, where they result in the assessment and feeling of emotion.

CARDINAL TRAITS   In Allport's theory, an encompassing trait in that almost every act of a person who possesses the trait seems traceable to its influence. Cardinal traits are uncommon, observed in only a few people.

CARETAKER SPEECH   A speech pattern used in addressing others who are obviously less competent in their speech than is the speaker. Universally applied, caretaker speech is characterized by short simple sentences, simple vocabulary, a higher-pitched voice, and exaggerated inflections.

CASE STUDY   An intensive study of a single case, with all

available data, test results, and opinions about that individual. Usually done in more depth than studies of groups of individuals.

CATABOLIC   In Hering's opponent-process theory, the tearing-down phase created within the photoreceptors.

CATATONIC SCHIZOPHRENIA   A form of schizophrenia characterized by sudden occasional violence followed by long spells of immobility in which there is a waxy flexibility of body and limbs, loss of motion, and a tendency to remain motionless for hours or days.

CATHARSIS   In psychoanalytic theory, elimination of a complex by bringing it to consciousness and allowing it to express itself. Any emotional release resulting from a buildup of internal tensions.

CAUSE-EFFECT RELATIONSHIP   A relationship whereby one act, of necessity, regularly brings about a particular result.

CENTRAL NERVOUS SYSTEM   The brain and spinal cord. All other neurons compose the peripheral nervous system.

CENTRAL ROUTE PROCESSING   From social-information processing theory, a route of persuasion and attitude change that may occur when a person pays careful attention to a persuasive discussion. Any resulting attitude change is relatively enduring.

CENTRAL SULCUS   A major fissure in the brain, also known as the fissure of Rolando, that separates the frontal from the parietal lobes.

CENTRAL TRAITS   In Allport's theory, behavioral or personality tendencies that are highly characteristic of a given individual and easy to infer. Allport argues that surprisingly few central traits, perhaps five or ten, can give a fairly accurate description of an individual's personality.

CEREBELLUM   A portion of the hindbrain situated just beneath the posterior portion of the cerebrum. Its function is to coordinate muscle tone and fine motor control.

CEREBRAL CORTEX   The extensive outer layer of convoluted gray tissue of the cerebral hemispheres which is largely responsible for higher nervous functions, including intellectual processes; also called the *neocortex.*

CEREBRUM   The large rounded structure of the brain occupying most of the cranial cavity, divided into two cerebral hemispheres by a deep fissure and joined at the bottom by the corpus callosum.

CHROMOSOME   A thread-shaped body contained within the nucleus of a body cell which determines characteristics that will be passed on to the offspring of an organism. Chromosomes carry the genes; humans have 23 pairs of chromosomes.

CHRONOLOGICAL AGE   A concept developed by Binet and used to calculate a person's IQ, as in mental age ÷ chronological age × 100 = IQ. The chronological age of a person is his or her actual age.

CHUNK   Bits of information that can be held in short-term memory. Chunks are not defined by the number of items they contain, such as letters or syllables, but rather by their meaning and organization. One number can be a chunk, but so can an entire sentence if it has a single meaning.

CILIA   Microscopic, hairlike processes extending from a cell surface.

CINGULOTOMY   A modern psychosurgical procedure in which the cerebral tissue of the cingulate gyrus is destroyed. Often used as a way of controlling chronic pain.

CIRCADIAN RHYTHM   A daily 24-hour cycle. Sleep and waking cycles are considered circadian rhythms.

CLASSICAL CONDITIONING   An experimental learning procedure in which a stimulus that normally evokes a given reflex is continually associated with a stimulus that does not usually evoke that reflex, with the result that the latter stimulus will eventually evoke the reflex when presented by itself.

CLIENT-CENTERED THERAPY   A type of psychotherapy developed by Carl Rogers and based on the belief that the client is responsible for his or her own growth and self-actualization. The therapist creates an atmosphere of acceptance, refrains from directing the client, and reflects back to the client what the client has said.

COALESCENCE OF MEANING   A component of creativity as described by Jackson and Messick. The meaning of a creative thought is said to coalesce over time in that it becomes more valuable and powerful with each application.

COCAINE   A habit-forming stimulant that is typically inhaled, and occasionally swallowed, smoked, or injected. It is derived from the leaves of the coca plant and used in medicine as a local anesthetic.

COCHLEA   A spiral tube in the inner ear resembling a snail shell which contains nerve endings essential for hearing.

COGNITION   Mental activity involving thinking, remembering, problem solving, or decision making.

COGNITIVE BEHAVIOR MODIFICATION   Behavioral therapeutic technique whereby the client's internal statements are tested in reality in a formal and structured way.

COGNITIVE DISSONANCE   The condition in which one has beliefs or knowledge that are internally inconsistent with or that disagree with one's behavior. When such cognitive dissonance arises, the individual is motivated to reduce the dissonance through changes in behavior or cognition.

COGNITIVE MAP   A mental representation of one's location in relationship to other locations in a given environment.

COGNITIVE PSYCHOLOGY   The study of behavior as it relates to thinking, remembering, problem solving, or decision making.

COGNITIVE THEORY OF EMOTION   Schachter's theory that emotion stems from one's interpretation of a physiological state occurring under specific circumstances.

COLLECTIVE UNCONSCIOUS   Concept proposed by Jung, in which a portion of the unconscious containing certain shared experiences, predispositions, and symbols are inherited and found in all members of a given race or species.

COLOR BLINDNESS   The inability to see one or more colors. The most common kind of color blindness is red-green color blindness.

COMMUNICATION   The process of making one's thoughts, ideas, desires, or emotions recognizable to another.

COMPANIONATE LOVE   *See* CONJUGAL LOVE.

COMPULSION   A useless, stereotyped, and repetitive act that a person is unable to inhibit.

CONCEPT   An abstract idea based on grouping objects by common properties.

CONDITIONED STIMULUS (CS)   In classical conditioning, a previously neutral stimulus that, through pairing with an unconditioned stimulus, acquires the ability to produce a response.

CONES   Specialized photoreceptor cells in the retina that are primarily responsive to different wavelengths of light and are therefore important in color vision; also associated with high visual acuity.

CONFLICT   A state in which ambivalent feelings about something or someone cause stress. Conflict is normal when it is temporary and can be resolved; it becomes abnormal when it remains unresolved and results in disablement.

CONFORMITY   Action that results from social pressure to comply with social norms. When people conform, they act or behave in correspondence with current customs, rules, or styles.

CONJUGAL LOVE   A deep and generally abiding love that develops between two people over long periods of time. Associated with a desire to be together, share with one another, and sacrifice for one another.

CONSCIOUSNESS   A state of awareness of the external environment and of internal events such as thought.

CONSERVING-ENERGY THEORY   An explanation of why we sleep that argues that sleep is a good way of conserving energy in the face of a sparse food supply. It agrees with the adaptive theory that sleep can be a protective device.

CONSOLIDATION   The strengthening process through which memory traces, or engrams, must go before they can become a fixed part of the long-term memory.

CONTINUITY   A Gestalt principle of perceptual organization stating that points or lines that form straight or gently curving lines when connected will be seen to belong together, and that lines will be seen to follow the smoothest path.

CONTINUOUS REINFORCEMENT   Reinforcing a particular response each time it occurs.

CONTROL   Deliberate arrangement of experimental or research conditions so that observed effects can be directly traced to a known variable or variables.

CONVERGENCE   A binocular depth cue. The eyes tend to turn toward each other in focusing on nearby objects, and tend to focus at infinity when reviewing objects farther away.

CONVERSION DISORDER   A somatoform disorder characterized by physical symptoms such as paralysis, blindness, deafness, and loss of sensation. The assumption is that anxiety has been converted into a tangible symptom.

CONVERGENT PRODUCTION   Part of Guilford's model of intelligence. A type of thinking in which an individual attempts to search through his or her knowledge and use all that can be found in order to converge upon one correct answer.

CORNEA   The transparent outer bulge in the front of the eye through which light waves pass.

CORPUS CALLOSUM   The structure that connects the two cerebral hemispheres to each other. When it is severed the two hemispheres can no longer communicate with each other.

CORRELATION   The relationship between two variables.

COUNTERCONDITIONING   A technique used by behavioral therapists to eliminate unwanted behavior through extinction or punishment, while at the same time promoting the acquisition of a new, more appropriate behavior in place of the old.

CREATIVE PROBLEM SOLVING   Problem solving that requires concepts, thoughts, actions, or an understanding that are not currently in one's repertoire.

CREATIVITY   The ability to originate something new and appropriate by transcending common thought constraints.

CRITICAL DECAY DURATION   From the opponent-process theory of motivation, a time of sufficient length between the onset of an affective A process and its repitition so that no decrease in A process intensity, or increase in B process intensity, is noted.

CRITICAL PERIOD   A specific time period during an organism's development when certain experiences will have an effect, and after which the effect can no longer be obtained through exposure to the experience.

CULTURE-FAIR TEST   A test that is supposed to be free of cultural biases, usually constructed so that language differences and other cultural effects are minimized.

DARK ADAPTED   The process by which the eyes become less sensitive to light in dim illumination.

DEDUCTION   A logical conclusion derived by reasoning from stated premises.

DEEP STRUCTURE   A term used by linguists to describe the meaning that a person who constructs an utterance, such as a sentence, intends to convey.

DEFENSE MECHANISMS   Reactions to the anxiety caused by conflict that serve to protect and improve the self-image. The mechanisms are not deliberately chosen. They are common to everyone and raise serious problems for adjustment only when they occur excessively and prevent the person from coping realistically with difficulties.

DEINDIVIDUATION   The process whereby social restraints are weakened, and impulsive and aggressive tendencies released, as the person loses his or her individual identity, usually as the result of being part of a large group or having his or her identity concealed in some way, as by a mask.

DEINSTITUTIONALIZATION   The practice, begun in the early 1960s, of placing mental patients in community mental health centers or treating them on an outpatient basis.

DELIRIUM TREMENS   A state of delirium resulting from prolonged alcoholism and marked by extreme confusion, vivid hallucinations, and body tremors.

DELTA WAVES   A pattern of brain waves associated with the deepest stages of sleep, often called slow waves because of their relatively low frequency.

DELUSION   A strong belief opposed to reality and maintained in spite of logical persuasion and evidence to the contrary; a symptom of psychosis. There are three main types: delusions of grandeur (the belief that one is an exalted personage), delusions of persecution (the belief that one is being plotted against), and delusions of reference (the belief that chance happenings and conversations concern oneself).

DENDRITES   The short, branched processes of a neuron that receive impulses from other neurons and conduct them toward the cell body.

DENIAL   A defense mechanism in which the individual simply denies the existence of the events that have produced the anxiety.

DEPENDENT VARIABLE   In an experiment, the variable that may change as a result of changes in the independent variable.

DEPOLARIZED   A decrease in the internal negativity of a nerve cell.

DEPRESSANTS   Drugs that can depress or slow the central nervous system. Alcohol and tranquilizers are examples of depressants.

DEPRESSION   A feeling of sadness and sometimes total apathy. Guilt or the inability to cope with problems, frustration or conflict are often behind the depression. Possibly influenced by chemical imbalances in the brain as well.

DEPTH PERCEPTION   Perceptual interpretation of visual cues indicating how far away objects are.

DIENCEPHALON   A division of the forebrain that contains the thalamus and the hypothalamus.

DIFFERENCE THRESHOLD   The minimum change that a stimulus must undergo before the change can be reliably detected; also called *just noticeable difference*.

DIFFUSION OF RESPONSIBILITY   One possible reason for the bystander effect. When someone is observed to be in need of help and there are many people around, individuals can come to believe that they need not act or give aid by placing responsibility to act on other people in the crowd. They may think, for instance, "Someone else will surely help" or "Why should I have to be the one to help?"

DIRECT COPING STRATEGIES   Active rational strategies intended to alleviate stress either by eliminating the stressor or by reducing the psychological effects of stress.

DIRECTIVE THERAPY   Any approach in which the therapist takes an active role and directs the patient or client to confront problems and life situations.

DIRECT-PERCEPTION THEORY   The theory that perceptions are a function of biological organization and innate perceptual mechanisms.

DISCRIMINATION   The ability to recognize the difference between one thing and another. Discriminations are made once an organism responds differently to different stimuli. In social psychology, treating people differently on the basis of their race, ethnic group, or class, rather than on their relevant traits. Acts of discrimination are typically premised upon prejudice.

DISCRIMINATIVE STIMULI   Stimuli in whose presence a response is likely to occur. Discriminative stimuli function as cues enabling us to know when a response is likely to be reinforced.

DISORGANIZED SCHIZOPHRENIA   A severe form of schizophrenia characterized by silliness, absurd behavior, shallowness of feelings, and loss of touch with reality; formerly called hebephrenic schizophrenia.

DISSOCIATION   A separation or splitting off of mental processes often associated with the hypnotic state. Subjects can then perform acts that do not register in their conscious memory, or engage in two behaviors while remembering only one of them.

DISSOCIATIVE DISORDERS   Functional disorders, including psychogenic amnesia, psychogenic fugue, and multiple personality, that are characterized by an attempt to overcome anxiety by dissociating oneself from the core of one's personality.

DIVERGENT PRODUCTION   According to Guilford, a type of thinking in which a person searches for multiple ideas or solutions to a problem. Characteristic of the creative thought process.

DIVINING ROD   A forked branch or stick that allegedly indicates subterranean water or minerals by bending downward when held over the source; also called a *dowsing rod*.

DNA   Deoxyribonucleic acid. A chemical constituent of cell nuclei, consisting of two long chains of alternating phosphate and deoxyribose units twisted into a double helix and joined by bonds between the complementary bases of adenine, thymine, cytosine, and guanine. It is the substance that enables cells to copy themselves.

DOOR-IN-THE-FACE TECHNIQUE   A bargaining technique in which one purposely requests a very large favor or concession that will certainly be refused, in the hopes of increasing the chances of obtaining the smaller favor or concession that's really desired (and which will now seem less unreasonable in comparison with the initial huge request).

DOPAMINE HYPOTHESIS   A proposal that an excess of dopamine or dopamine receptors may be responsible for some forms of schizophrenia.

DOUBLE APPROACH-AVOIDANCE CONFLICT   A situation in which two mutually exclusive goals are desired and in which vascillation occurs because as one goal is approached, the loss of the other becomes more apparent.

DOUBLE-BLIND   A research technique in which neither the subjects nor the experimenters know which subjects have been exposed to the independent variable. It is used for controlling biases that may be introduced by either the subjects or the researchers.

DRIVE   The psychological representation of a need; a complex of internal conditions resulting from the loss of homeostasis and impelling an organism to seek a goal.

DSM-III   The third edition of the *Diagnostic and Statistical Manual,* published by the American Psychiatric Association in 1980. The manual provides clinicians with the most current diagnostic and classification criteria for mental disorders.

DUAL-CODE THEORY   A theory of memory that states that memories contain both sensory and verbal information and that this information is stored directly, without being transformed.

DYNORPHIN   A neuropeptide similar to beta endorphin but which appears to be about 50 times more powerful.

DYSLEXIA   An impairment of reading ability in which letters or words are transposed.

ECTOMORPH   One of Sheldon's three body types. An ectomorph is relatively thin and physically weak. The corresponding temperament is cerebrotonic.

EFFERENT NERVES   Nerves that carry messages outward from the central nervous system.

EGO   In psychoanalytic theory, the part of the personality that regulates the impulses of the id in order to meet the demands of reality and maintain social approval and self-esteem.

EIDETIC IMAGE   The formation and reproduction of accurate mental images of objects not currently present. Possessors of these images are said to have photographic memories.

ELABORATION   Building upon one memory by making many associations with it. Elaborated memories make recall easier because items in the memory can be reached by many different routes.

ELECTRA COMPLEX   According to Freud, the female form of the Oedipus complex; the desire of a girl to possess her father sexually.

ELECTROCONVULSIVE THERAPY (ECT)   Treatment of mania, depression, and schizophrenia by passing an electric current through the brain for a certain amount of time, which causes a convulsion, a temporary suspension of breathing, and a coma lasting from 5 to 30 minutes.

ELECTROENCEPHALOGRAPH (EEG)   An instrument that records the electrical activity of the brain.

ELECTROMAGNETIC SPECTRUM   The entire range of possible wavelengths for light, both visible and invisible (such as X-rays and radio waves).

EMOTION   A complex feeling-state involving conscious experience and internal and overt physical responses that tend to facilitate or inhibit motivated behavior.

EMOTIONAL APPEALS   Arguments designed to alter attitudes by appealing to the emotions through moving visual and verbal messages.

EMOTIONAL CONTRAST   An emotional effect that plays an important part in Solomon's opponent-process theory of motivation. Following any emotional arousal (pleasant or aversive), there is often an opposite emotional state. This contrasting emotional state will last for a time and then diminish or end.

EMPATHY   An insightful awareness and ability to share the emotions, thoughts, and behavior of another person.

ENCODING VARIABILITY   A phenomenon that exists whenever the same information is acquired in different moods, states, or circumstances. Greater encoding variability tends to improve test performance by increasing the chances that the test situation will resemble the study environment.

END BUTTONS   *See* SYNAPTIC KNOBS

ENDOCRINE SYSTEM   A system of ductless glands that pour their secretions directly into the bloodstream. The hormones secreted by the endocrine glands are important regulators of many body activities.

ENDOCRINOLOGISTS   Scientists who study the function and structure of the endocrine system.

ENDOGENOUS DEPRESSION   Depression of internal origin, that is, depression without apparent cause. It is marked by long-term despair and dejection, feelings of apprehension, gloom, and worthlessness. Research points to a possible biochemical genetic cause.

ENDOMORPH   One of Sheldon's three body types. An endomorph is broad or thick in proportion to height, is round and has fairly weak muscles and bones. The corresponding temperament is viscerotonic.

ENGRAM   A lasting trace or impression formed in living tissue responsible for memory.

ENKEPHALIN   A chemical constituent of beta endorphin known to be involved in the brain's pleasure and pain systems.

EPILEPSY   A neural disorder characterized by recurring attacks of motor, sensory, or psychic malfunction with or without unconsciousness or convulsive movements.

EQUILIBRATORY SENSE   The sense that keeps an organism in proper balance.

EQUIPOTENTIALITY   Karl Lashley's argument that memory and learning are not localized in any one particular area of the brain, but rather the entire brain has the potential for handling these functions.

EQUITY THEORY   A social theory of relationships that argues that people will try to create fairness in a social relationship so that each person receives as much as he or she contributes.

ESTROGEN   The female sex hormone, produced by the ovaries. Estrogen is responsible for maturation of the female sex organs, secondary sex characteristics, and in some species, sexual behavior.

ETHOLOGY   The study of human and animal behavior from a biological point of view; characterized by the study of animals in their natural environments.

ETIOLOGY   The cause of a disease or disorder as determined by psychological or medical diagnosis.

EUGENICS   The science concerned with improving animals by controlling hereditary factors.

EVOLUTION   The theory, first proposed by Charles Darwin, that organisms may change in time depending on whether they have characteristics favored by the environment.

EXCHANGE THEORY   A social theory of relationships that argues that human interactions can best be understood by examining the costs and rewards to each person.

EXCITATORY SYNAPSES   Synapses associated with depolarization of the receiving cell once neurotransmitter is secreted. If the receiving cell is a neuron it will become more likely to fire or may even reach action potential.

EXECUTIVE HORMONES   Hormones that order or control the secretion of other hormones.

EXHAUSTION STAGE   The final state of the general adaptation syndrome. During this stage, resistance to the continuing stress begins to fail. Brain functioning may be hindered by metabolic changes; the immune system becomes much less efficient; and serious illness or disease becomes likely as the body begins to break down.

EXISTENTIAL THERAPY   Form of psychotherapy, generally nondirective, derived from the existentialist philosophy that each individual has to choose values and decide on the meaning of his or her own life. The therapist tries to achieve an authentic, spontaneous relationship in order to help the client discover free will and make his or her own choices.

EXOCRINE GLANDS   Glands that secrete fluids through a duct to the outside of the body or to a specific organ.

EXPANSION   An enlargement or extension of initial research efforts.

EXPERIMENT   A test made to demonstrate the validity of a hypothesis or to determine the predictability of a theory. Variables are manipulated and changes are contrasted with a control that has not been exposed to the variables of interest.

EXPLANATION   That which explains an event that has already occurred.

EXTINCTION   The process of eliminating reinforcement in classical and instrumental conditioning, which results in failure to perform the learned response.

EXTROVERT   One of Jung's personality types. A gregarious person who focuses on external events, is not introspective, and likes to be with others.

FACIAL-FEEDBACK THEORY   A theory of emotion put forth by S. S. Tomkins that states that emotions are determined by feedback from our facial expressions, which are innate universal responses to specific events.

FACTOR ANALYSIS   A statistical procedure aimed at discovering the constituent traits within a complex system of personality or intelligence. The method enables the investigator to compute the minimum number of factors required to account for the intercorrelations among the scores on the tests.

FACTOR LOAD   The weight or emphasis given to any factor or ability.

FIXATION   In psychoanalytic theory, fixation refers to remaining inordinately in a particular psychosexual stage of development because the id has received either too much or too little satisfaction.

FIXED-RESPONSE PATTERN   A species specific response pattern that is presumed to have survival value for the organism and is elicited by a sign stimulus or a releaser.

FLASHBULB MEMORY   Term used to describe the vivid impression left on the memory by all of the stimuli associated with a shocking or surprising event.

FOCAL COLORS   Basic colors, described by short, simple words. In English the focal colors are red, green, yellow, blue, brown, purple, orange, pink, gray, white and black.

FOOT-IN-THE-DOOR TECHNIQUE   A bargaining technique in which one purposely asks for a very small favor or concession in order to soften up the opposition and set the stage for obtaining a much larger favor.

FOREBRAIN   The top portion of the brain which includes the thalamus, hypothalamus, corpus callosum, limbic system, and cerebrum.

FOVEA   The area in the center of the retina characterized by great density of cones, and an absence of rods. Images focused on the fovea are seen with highest acuity.

FREE ASSOCIATION   A method used in psychoanalytic therapy in which the patient is to say whatever comes to mind, no matter how trivial, inconsequential, or unrelated to the matter being discussed.

FREE-FLOATING ANXIETY   A chronic state of foreboding that is unrelated to a specific situation or object but that can be activated by any number of situations and activities.

FREQUENCY   The number of cycles per unit of time in a periodic vibration. Determines the pitch of a sound.

FREQUENCY THEORY   A theory of hearing that attempts to explain the reception of sound waves between 20 and 1,000 cycles per second. According to this theory, auditory neurons fire at rates well correlated with the frequency of the sound.

FRONTAL LOBES   The portion of the cerebrum extending from the very front of the cerebrum to the central sulcus. It includes the primary motor association areas, and it is known to be involved with emotion and language.

FRONTAL LOBOTOMY   Psychosurgical procedure, rarely performed today, in which a sharp instrument is inserted through the orbit of the eye and then slashed back and forth in order to separate specific nerve fibers connecting one part of the brain to another.

FRUSTRATION-AGGRESSION HYPOTHESIS   The hypothesis that frustration is the necessary and sufficient condition of aggression and that all aggressive acts are the result of frustration.

FUGUE   From the Latin "to flee." A dissociative disorder in which the individual leaves his or her situation and establishes a somewhat different mode of existence in another place. Although the former life is blocked from memory, other abilities are unimpaired and the individual appears to be normal to others.

FUNCTIONAL AUTONOMY   Allport's theory that an activity originally engaged in as a means to an end frequently acquires an independent function and becomes an end in itself.

FUNCTIONAL DISORDER   A disorder that has no known organic basis and depends on experience rather than on structural or organic defects.

FUNCTIONAL FIXEDNESS   A mental set in which the individual is unable to see beyond an object's customary function to its other possible uses.

FUNCTIONALISM   The school of psychological thought founded by William James which proposed that the function, not the structure, of conscious experience should be studied.

FUNCTION WORDS   Words or word additions that help add meaning to a sentence and are acquired by children generally between the ages of two and a half and five, *In, on, went, are,* and *was* are examples of function words.

GAIN-LOSS THEORY   A social theory of attraction that argues that we are most attracted to those who have provided us with the greatest net gain and least attracted to those who have caused the greatest net loss.

GAMETE   Male or female germ cell (sperm or ovum) containing half the number of chromosomes found in the other cells of the body.

GANGLION CELLS   Nerve cells of the third layer of the retina which receive impulses from rods and cones via the bipolar cells and transmit these impulses to the brain.

GENDER CONSTANCY   The realization that one's sex is determined by unchanging criteria and is unaffected by one's activities or behavior. It usually develops in children by the age of six or seven.

GENDER IDENTITY   The sexual orientation, either male or female, with which a person identifies.

GENERAL ADAPTATION SYNDROME   Physiologist Hans Selye's description of the body's physiological-hormonal reaction to stressors. The reaction consists of three stages, the alarm reaction stage, the resistance stage, and the exhaustion stage.

GENERALIZATION   In operant conditioning, when different stimuli are responded to as though they were the same. In classical conditioning, when stimuli similar to the training stimulus elicit some aspect of the conditioned response.

GENERALIZED ANXIETY DISORDER   An anxiety state characterized by a relatively constant feeling of dread and tension, without apparent or reasonable cause. Free-floating anxiety is a common complaint.

GENERAL PARESIS   Tertiary (third stage) syphilis, which involves an invasion and severe irreversible damage to the brain. The clinical picture includes tremors, loss of contact with reality, extreme personality deterioration, increasing paralysis, and delirium. The patient may survive many years in this deteriorated condition.

GESTALT PSYCHOLOGY   The school of psychological thought that emphasizes that wholes are more than the sum of their parts. Gestalt psychologists study forms and patterns and contend that stimuli are perceived as whole images rather than as parts built into images.

GESTALT THERAPY   A form of psychotherapy originated by Perls, who adapted the fundamental concepts of traditional psychoanalysis but placed greater emphasis on the immediacy and importance of the here and now in breaking down the influence of the past. The patient-therapist relationship is more active and democratic than in traditional psychoanalysis.

GOLGI STAIN   A stain used to make neurons visible for inspection under a microscope. The stain is accepted by about 5 percent of any given group of neurons.

GONADS   The sex glands that regulate sex drive and the physiological changes that accompany physical maturity. These glands are the ovaries in the female and the testes in the male.

GRADED POTENTIAL   All potentials between resting and action potential, usually between -70 and $+30$ millivolts.

GRADIENT OF TEXTURE   A monocular depth cue. Closer objects show greater detail.

GRAMMAR   A set of rules that determine how sounds may be put together to make words and how words may be put together to make sentences.

GREAT-MAN GREAT-WOMAN HYPOTHESIS   The hypothesis that individuals become leaders primarily because of the personality or traits they possess.

GYRI   The prominent rounded and elevated convolutions at the surfaces of the cerebral hemispheres.

HABIT

See OPERANT CHAIN

HABITUATION   A process whereby an organism ceases to respond reflexively to an unconditioned stimulus that is presented repeatedly.

HALLUCINATIONS   A false sense perception for which there is no appropriate external stimulus.

HALLUCINOGENS   Drugs that cause excitation at synapses associated with sense perception. A person taking these drugs may perceive sensations when there is nothing real to see, hear, or feel.

HAWTHORNE EFFECT   A type of bias that may arise when a research subject is aware of being studied, and changes his or her behavior to match perceived expectations.

HEALTHY INSOMNIACS   Individuals who function very well with only three hours of sleep a night or less, and who don't seem to need more than this.

HEIGHT ON A PLANE   A monocular depth cue. Objects higher on a plane are perceived as being farther away.

HEROIN   A highly addictive narcotic drug that is derived from morphine.

HEURISTICS   A method for discovering the correct solution to a problem by exploring the possibilities that seem to offer the most reasonable approach to the goal, rather than *all* possibilities. Heuristics also involves obtaining successive approximations to the correct answer by means of analogies and other search techniques.

HIERARCHY OF MOTIVES   A theory of motivation developed by Abraham Maslow in which more basic needs must be met first before needs of a higher order can come into play.

HIGH-THRESHOLD FIBERS   Cilia in the inner ear that are difficult to bend and respond only to loud noises or sounds.

HIGHWAY HYPNOSIS   An hypnotic state experienced while operating a vehicle—often the result of relaxing too much during a long and boring drive.

HINDBRAIN   The posterior section of the brain which includes the cerebellum, pons, and medulla.

HIPPOCAMPUS   A small area at the back of the telencephalon that is known to be important to the memory process. Part of the limbic system.

HOLOGRAPHIC PHOTOGRAPHY   A method by which a picture can be created through the use of coherent light (light that is reflected in only one direction). Such a picture produces retinal disparity regardless of the viewing angle, and the part of the picture that is seen depends on the viewer's location. The result is an illusion of a real three-dimensional object suspended in space.

HOMEOSTASIS   An internal environment in which such bodily states as blood pressure, blood chemistry, breathing, digestion, temperature, and so on, are kept at levels optimal for the survival of the organism through the creation of drives in the presence of needs.

HORMONES   Secretions of the endocrine glands that specifically affect metabolism and behavior.

HUMANISTIC PSYCHOLOGY   A school of psychology that emphasizes the uniqueness of the individual and the search for self-actualization.

HYPERMNESIC   Unusually exact or vivid memory.

HYPERPOLARIZED   An increase in the internal negativity of a nerve cell.

HYPNOSIS   A state of consciousness characterized by relaxation and suggestibility.

HYPNOTHERAPY   Hypnosis used for therapeutic purposes in cases of pain control or behavior pathology. The method has been used in therapy, dentistry, surgery, and childbirth.

HYPOCHONDRIASIS   A somatoform disorder in which there is a persistent and exaggerated concern about diminished health and energy in the absence of demonstrable organic pathology.

HYPOTHALAMOCENTRIC HYPOTHESIS   Stellar's hypothesis, developed in 1954, that a hunger center responsible for the homeostasis of food intake existed in the hypothalamus.

HYPOTHALAMUS   An elongated structure in the forebrain that appears to control an entire range of autonomic functions, including sleep, body temperature, hunger, and thirst.

HYSTERIA   An outdated term once used to describe those with emotional excitability, excessive anxiety, psychogenic sensory or motor disturbances, and psychosomatic disorders.

ID   In psychoanalytic theory, the reservoir of instinctive drives, the most inaccessible and primitive portion of the mind.

IDEATIONAL FLUENCY   A term used by Wallach to describe an individual's ability to produce many ideas. Ideational fluency is sometimes used as a measure of creativity and correlates poorly with IQ.

ILLUSION   A false perception or misinterpretation of sensory information.

IMAGE AND CUE THEORY   The theory that perceptions are learned by acquiring an understanding of the cues contained within the image that falls on the retina.

IMPRESSION-MANAGEMENT HYPOTHESIS   The hypothesis that the results of cognitive dissonance experiments can be explained, not by changes in real attitudes made to reduce dissonance, but rather by a need to appear consistent in the eyes of others.

IMPRINTING   A term used by ethologists for a species-specific kind of learning that occurs within a limited period of time early in the life of the organism and is relatively unmodifiable thereafter.

IMPULSE INITIATING ZONE   The area at the beginning of an axon that, when sufficiently stimulated, initiates a nerve impulse, or spike.

INCUBATION EFFECT   An effect associated with taking a break during creative problem solving. The individual often returns to the problem with a fresh approach and finds the solution.

INCUS   One of the three small bones in the middle ear; also called the *anvil.*

INDEPENDENT VARIABLE   In an experiment, the variable that is manipulated or treated to see what effect differences in it will have on the variables considered to be dependent on it.

INFERIOR COLLICULI   Small knoblike processes in the midbrain that are primarily involved in relaying and processing auditory information.

INFERIORITY COMPLEX   A psychoanalytic term coined by Alfred Adler to describe the problems that he believed resulted from the failure to respond to a drive to be superior.

INFORMATION AVAILABILITY HYPOTHESIS   The hypothesis that explains people's tendency to attribute their own behavior to environmental causes rather than to personality traits as a function of the fact that they have more information about their personal situation and environment and the obvious forces therein than they have about others.

INGRATIATION   Purposely bringing oneself into the favor or good graces of another, often with flattery, in the hopes of obtaining something of value.

IN-GROUP   Any group for whom the individual feels a positive regard. A subjective term, depending on one's point of view.

INHIBITORY SYNAPSES   A synapse associated with hyperpolarization of the receiving cell once neurotransmitter is secreted. If the receiving cell is a neuron it will become harder to fire.

INNATE   Inborn, hereditary component of a physiological or behavioral trait.

INSANE   Legal term for a mental disorder, implying lack of responsibility for one's acts and an inability to manage one's behavior.

INSIGHT   In problem solving, the sudden perception of relationships leading to a solution. A solution arrived at in this way can be repeated promptly when the same or a similar problem is confronted again.

INSIGHT THERAPY   Psychotherapy by attempting to uncover the deep causes of the patient's or client's difficulty. The therapist tries to guide the individual to self-understanding.

INSOMNIA   Difficulty in going to sleep or in staying asleep for the necessary amount of time.

INSTINCTS   Innate patterns of complex behavior.

INSTRUMENTAL LEARNING   The process by which an organism learns to behave because of the consequences that follow the behavior. The behavior is considered puposeful since it helps the organism to approach pleasant or avoid unpleasant stimuli.

INSULIN SHOCK THERAPY   A method, infrequently used today, for treating severe psychotic reactions. A coma is created by reducing blood sugar by injecting excessive amounts of insulin.

INTELLECTUALIZATION   A defense mechanism in which abstract thinking is used as a means of avoiding emotion by treating emotional material in a coldly intellectual manner.

INTELLIGENCE   A general term for a person's abilities in a wide range of tasks including vocabulary, numbers, problem solving, and concepts. May also include the ability to profit from experience, to learn new pieces of information, and to adjust to new situations.

INTELLIGENCE QUOTIENT   A quotient derived from the formula MA/CA + 100, where MA is mental age and CA is chronological age. The intelligence quotient was devised by psychologist L. Wilhelm Stern and introduced in the United States by Lewis Terman.

INTERFERENCE EFFECTS   Effects that may occur any time stored memories and their associated networks interfere with the storage of new information or the retrieval of old information.

INTERMITTENT SCHEDULE   Reinforcing a particular response, but not each time the response occurs.

INTEROBSERVER RELIABILITY   The degree of disagreement or agreement between two or more observers who simultaneously observe a single event.

INTRINSIC MOTIVATION   A drive to engage in a behavior for its own sake in the absence of any obvious external reward or reinforcer.

INTROSPECTION   The method introduced by structural psychologists that involves the subject's reporting on his or her own conscious experiences.

INTROVERT   One of Jung's personality types. Introverts are socially withdrawn, emotionally reserved, and self-absorbed.

INVULNERABLES   Name given to children who appear to be healthy and able to cope in spite of being reared in highly adverse circumstances.

JAMES-LANGE THEORY OF EMOTION   A classical theory of emotion named for the men who independently proposed it. The theory argues that a stimulus first leads to visceral and motor responses, and that the following awareness of these responses constitutes the experience of the emotion. The theory argues, for instance, that we are sad because we cry rather than that we cry because we are sad.

JET LAG   An uncomfortable feeling caused by the disruption of the sleep-waking cycle that follows an attempt to adjust to a new time zone too quickly. Called jet lag because international travelers often suffer from it.

KARYOTYPE   A photomicrograph of chromosomes in a standard array.

KIBBUTZ   An Israeli farm or collective where children are often reared within groups and receive nurturance and guidance from many different adults and older children.

KINESTHESIS   An inclusive term for the muscle, tendon, and joint senses that yield information about the position and movement of various parts of the body.

LANGUAGE   Any means of communication that uses signs, symbols, or gestures within a grammar and through which novel constructions can be created.

LANGUAGE ACQUISITION DEVICE   An innate biological mechanism that enables humans to acquire and use language. Postulated by Noam Chomsky.

LATENT LEARNING Learning that occurs in the absence of any obvious reinforcement, apparently as a result of just being exposed to stimuli.

LATERALIZED (LATERALIZATION) The degree to which the right and left cerebral hemispheres differ in specific functions.

LAW OF EFFECT Thorndike's principle that responses that are reinforced (rewarded) tend to be repeated, while those that lead to something aversive tend to be eliminated.

LEARNED HELPLESSNESS Giving up even though success is possible because of previous experience with situations in which success was impossible.

LEARNED INDUSTRIOUSNES A technique for overcoming learned helplessness in which one is taught to take responsibility for one's own failures and in which one is exposed to success through a slow shaping process.

LEARNING A relatively permanent change in behavior as a result of experience.

LENS The transparent biconvex structure of the eye which covers the iris and pupil and focuses light rays entering through the pupil to form an image on the retina.

LIBIDO To Freud, the psychological energy driving the individual to seek gratification, principally sexual, but also food, comfort, and happiness.

LIFE SPACE Lewin's depiction of an individual and his or her environment as the individual perceives it.

LIGHT ADAPTED The process by which the eyes become less sensitive to light in bright illumination.

LIMBIC SYSTEM An aggregate of brain structures whose two major components are the amygdala and hippocampus. Some of its major functions include attention, memory, emotion, and motivation.

LINEAR PERSPECTIVE A monocular depth cue. Parallel lines appear to converge in the distance.

LINGUISTIC RELATIVITY Whorf's hypothesis that thought is structured according to the language spoken. Those who speak different languages would have different thinking patterns.

LINGUISTS Those who specialize in and study language.

LINKS From the propositional network theory of memory, links are the pathways between the nodes of the proposition. If two nodes are not directly linked, then recalling the information at one of the nodes will not lead to directly recalling the information at the other node.

LITHIUM CARBONATE A chemical compound that has been found to be effective in controlling the severe mood swings associated with bipolar affective psychosis.

LOCUS OF CONTROL Beliefs or expectations about whether desired outcomes are contingent on one's own behavior (internal locus of control) or on environmental forces (external locus of control).

LONGITUDINAL STUDY A research approach that studies individuals through time, taking measurements at periodic intervals.

LONG-TERM MEMORY Memory with virtually unlimited storage capacity, in which short-term memories may be stored for long periods, even a lifetime.

LOUDNESS A measurement of sound intensity which corresponds to the amplitude of the sound waves.

LOWBALLING A negotiation technique in which one purposely omits details of a request that may lessen the chances of compliance until a commitment to comply has been obtained from the other party. Lowballing will generally lead to more compliance.

LUCID DREAMS Dreams during which the sleeper realizes that he or she is dreaming.

MAINSTREAMING The philosophy of keeping as many exceptional children within the regular classroom as possible.

MALLEUS The largest of the three small bones in the middle ear; also called the *hammer*.

MARFAN'S SYNDROME An inherited disorder associated with elongated fingers and toes and degeneration of connective tissue, the result of a defective gene.

MARIJUANA The dried flowers and leaves of the cannibis variety of hemp.

MASSED PRACTICE Also known as *cramming*. A study method that will not create a spacing effect and is therefore not likely to lead to long-term retention. Material is studied in a single session without any interruption.

MASTURBATION Sexual self-stimulation.

MEANS-END ANALYSIS Problem-solving process in which the difference between the current situation and the desired situation is defined and then a series of steps is taken in order to reduce, and finally eliminate, the difference. Applicable whenever there is a clearly specifiable problem and a clearly specifiable solution.

MEDITATION Deep relaxation brought on by focusing one's attention on a particular sound or image.

MEDULLA The oblong structure at the top of the spinal cord that is responsible for many vital life-support functions, including breathing and heart beat.

MEIOSIS The cell division in sexually reproducing organisms that reduces the number of chromosomes in reproductive cells, leading to the production of gametes.

MEMORY The complex mental function of recalling what has been learned or experienced.

MENARCHE The first occurrence of menstruation.

MENIÉRE'S DISEASE A disease that can destroy the cilia lining the inner ear, causing total and permanent deafness.

MENTAL AGE A concept developed by Binet and used to calculate a person's IQ, as in mental age ÷ chronological age × 100 = IQ. The mental age of a person is derived by comparing his or her score with the average scores of others within different specific age groups.

MENTAL SET   A tendency to continue to use a particular approach or type of solution to a problem based on previous experience or instruction.

MERE EXPOSURE EFFECT   The effect whereby attitudes become more favorable toward something merely by being exposed to it.

MESMERISM   A forerunner of hypnosis. In mesmerism, magnetic forces were called on to relieve pain. Mesmerism was named after Anton Mesmer, who claimed he could cure the ill with magnetism.

MESOMORPH   One of Sheldon's three body types. A mesomorph is characterized by a predominance of muscle and bone, as in an athlete, and is believed to be associated with a somatotonic temperament.

METHOD OF LOCI   A mnemonic technique by which items are more easily remembered by being associated with positions or things along a familiar route.

MICROELECTRODE   An extremely small electric probe capable of monitoring a single cell.

MICROSLEEP   Short snatches of sleep, usually occurring when a person has been sleep-deprived. The person may be totally unaware of having slept, but the EEG will have registered the brain-wave patterns typical of sleep.

MIDBRAIN   The middle section of the brain which contains the inferior and superior colliculi, the structures responsible for processing and relaying visual and auditory information.

MNEMONIC DEVICE   A method for remembering items, or a memory aid.

MNEMONICS   Any device or technique for improving memory.

MODEL   A mathematical, logical, or mechanical replica of a relationship or a system of events so designed that a study of the model can yield some understanding of the real thing. In social learning theory, anyone who demonstrates a behavior that others observe.

MONOAMINES   A group of neurotransmitters that are related because they all contain one amine group (a specific kind of organic molecule). Among these are dopamine, norepinephrine, and serotonin.

MONOCULAR CUES   Cues seen in two dimensions that give rise to a perception of depth. These cues include an object's height on a plane, linear perspective, overlap, relative size, gradient of texture, aerial perspective, and relative motion.

MORALS   The attitudes and beliefs that people hold that help them to determine what is right or wrong.

MOTIVATED FORGETTING   Purposeful forgetting in which memories are suppressed or repressed in order to fulfill unconscious desires to avoid the memories.

MOTOR AREA   An area located in front of the brain's central fissure that controls body movement.

MULTIPLE PERSONALITY   A rare dissociative disorder in which one person develops two or more distinct personalities, which often vie with each other for consciousness. One personality's memories are usually not accessible to another personality.

MYELIN   A white fatty covering on neural fibers that serves to channel impulses along fibers and increase their speed.

NALOXONE   A heroin antagonist. Naloxone binds with and essentially neutralizes heroin. Naloxone has the same effect on morphine and beta endorphin.

NARCOLEPSY   A pathological condition characterized by sudden and uncontrollable lapses into deep sleep.

NARCOTIC   Any drug that dulls the senses, induces sleep, and with prolonged use becomes addictive, for example, heroin, morphine, and codeine.

NATIVIST   One who considers that behavior stems from biological and genetic forces.

NATURAL SELECTION   The process, first suggested by Charles Darwin, by which the individuals of a species that are best adapted to their environment have a better chance of passing on their genes to the next generation than do those that are less well adapted.

NATURALISTIC OBSERVATION   Observations in which researchers refrain from directly interacting with the variable being observed.

NATURE-NURTURE QUESTIONS   Questions relating to the issue of whether inheritance or environment is the primary determinant in development of any behavior.

NEARNESS   A Gestalt principle of perceptual organization stating that things near each other appear to be grouped together.

NEED   A condition whose satisfaction is necessary for the maintenance of homeostasis.

NEED FOR ACHIEVEMENT   A learned motivation, abbreviated n–Ach, described by researcher David McClelland. Those who score high in n–Ach often behave in different ways from those who score low in n–Ach.

NEGATIVE AFTEREFFECTS   Effects brought on by fatigue in visual receptors at higher levels in the visual system. Negative aftereffects, unlike negative afterimages, transfer from one eye to another.

NEGATIVE AFTERIMAGE   An opposite color image that persists after the originally viewed object is removed. It is the result of fatigued color receptors in the retina and lasts briefly.

NEGATIVE REINFORCEMENT   When an organism is reinforced for successfully avoiding or escaping an aversive situation.

NEGATIVE TRANSFER OF LEARNING   The process whereby learning one task makes it harder to learn another.

NEOCORTEX   *See* CEREBRAL CORTEX

NERVES   Bundles of neural fibers that carry impulses from one point in the body to another.

NERVE IMPULSE   The propagation of an electric impulse down the length of a neural axon once a neuron has reached action potential.

NEURONS   Specialized cells that transmit electrical impulses from one part of the body to another.

NEUROPEPTIDES   Extremely small chemical messengers made from short chains of amino acids. Among the neuropeptides are beta endorphin and vasopressin.

NEUROSIS   A broad term once used to describe a wide range of nonpsychotic functional disorders that were characterized by anxiety, which the individual attempted to reduce in an unchanging and ineffectual way.

NEUROTIC PARADOX   Refers to a neurotic person's tendency to persist in maladaptive behavior even though it leads to unpleasant consequences.

NEUROTRANSMITTERS   Chemicals secreted by neurons into the synapse which have an effect on adjacent neurons, muscles, or glands.

NODES   From the propositional network theory of memory, the individual parts of the proposition. Nodes serve as junctions and access points in the memory.

NONDIRECTIVE THERAPY   A therapeutic technique based on humanistic psychology in which the therapist creates a supportive atmosphere so that clients can work out their own problems. A therapy in which the client is primarily responsible for the direction of treatment.

NONVERBAL CUES   Cues other than words, used to assess the emotional state of another. These include facial expressions, body motion, and posture.

NORADRENALINE   A hormone secreted by the adrenal glands that brings about a number of bodily changes, including constriction of the blood vessels near the body's surface. It also causes the adrenal glands to secrete steroids which in turn release sugar so that energy is available for emergency action. Also called *norepinephrine*.

NOVEL CONSTRUCTION   Use of a language and its grammar in order to form new statements to which the originator had not been exposed before. One of the elements defining language.

NOVELTY   A component of creativity described by Jackson and Messick. Creative objects are novel, that is, they are new.

NREM SLEEP   Non-Rem sleep during which no rapid eye movement takes place. Also called *orthodox sleep*.

NUCLEUS   A central body within a living cell that contains the cell's hereditary material and controls its metabolism, growth, and reproduction.

OBSERVER BIAS   An error in observation caused by the expectations of the observer.

OBSESSION   A persistent idea or thought that the individual recognizes as irrational but feels compelled to dwell on.

OBSESSIVE-COMPULSIVE DISORDER   An abnormal reaction characterized by anxiety, persistent unwanted thoughts, and/or the compulsion to repeat ritualistic acts over and over.

OCCIPITAL LOBES   The occipital lobes make up the hind portion of the cerebrum. The primary visual areas are contained within the occipital lobes.

OEDIPUS COMPLEX   A Freudian term representing the sexual attachment of a boy to his mother. This desire is repressed and disguised in various ways. The child expresses jealousy and hatred of the father because the father can have relations with the mother that the son is denied.

OLFACTORY BULB   A mass of cells in the forebrain associated with the sense of smell into which the olfactory nerve fibers enter and form a tract leading farther into the brain.

OLFACTORY EPITHELIUM   Nasal membranes containing receptor cells sensitive to odors.

ONE-WORD STAGE   The universal stage in language development in which children's speech is limited to single words.

OPERANT CHAIN   A series of cues, responses, and reinforcers linked together in such a way that each stimulus consequence reinforces the person's response and cues the next one. Also known as a *habit*.

OPERANT CONDITIONING   B. F. Skinner's term for changes in behavior that occur as a result of stimulus consequences that reinforce or punish emitted responses. These responses are not considered to be purposeful but merely to operate on the environment. They may in turn be shaped by environmental experiences.

OPPONENT-PROCESS THEORY   Hering's theory of color vision in which he argued that photoreceptors function along red-green, blue-yellow, and light-dark continuums and are in opposition to each other.

OPPONENT-PROCESS THEORY OF MOTIVATION   A theory of motivation proposed by Richard Solomon in which it is argued that many acquired motives such as drug addiction, love, affection, social attachment, cravings for sensory and esthetic experiences, skydiving, jogging, sauna bathing, and even self-administered aversive stimuli seem to follow the laws of addiction.

OPTIC NERVE   The bundle of nerve fibers connecting the retina and the brain.

ORGAN OF CORTI   The organ containing hair cells which are hearing receptors. It is located on the basilar membrane in the cochlea.

ORGANIC DISORDER   A severe behavioral disturbance usually requiring hospitalization and resulting from some organic malfunctioning of the body. It is distinguished from functional disorder.

ORGASM   The climax of sexual excitement, normally marked

by ejaculation of semen by the male and muscular spasms of the genitals in both sexes.

ORTHODOX SLEEP   All sleep except REM sleep. It is called orthodox because the EEG pattern is markedly different from the waking state. Also called *NREM sleep*.

OSMOSIS   The diffusion of fluid through a semipermeable membrane, such as that surrounding a living cell, until the concentration of fluid on either side of the membrane is equal.

OUT-GROUP   Any group that an individual views in a negative way. A subjective term, depending on one's point of view.

OVERLAP   A monocular depth cue. Objects that are behind (overlapped by) other objects are farther away.

OVUM   The female reproductive cell of animals; also called an *egg*.

PANIC ATTACK   A sudden overwhelming and debilitating onset of fear characteristic of panic disorder. There is no realistic reason or cause.

PARADOXICAL SLEEP   REM sleep. The EEG pattern closely resembles that of a person who is awake, even though the person is still asleep. Dreaming occurs during this kind of sleep.

PARALLEL ACCESS   A term borrowed from computer terminology and used to describe the fact that we can enter our memories at many different points and locations rather than at only one point as suggested by the trace column theory.

PARANOIA   A functional psychosis characterized by delusions of persecution or grandeur, and extreme suspiciousness. Hallucinations rarely occur and the personality does not undergo the serious disorganization associated with schizophrenia.

PARANOID SCHIZOPHRENIA   A psychosis characterized by elaborate and systematic delusions of persecution or grandeur. Often in the context of a complex delusional system. The disorder is sometimes accompanied by hallucinations, behavior that is consistent with the delusional content, and aggressiveness.

PARASYMPATHETIC NERVOUS SYSTEM   The portion of the autonomic nervous system that is most active during the body's quiescent states.

PARIETAL LOBES   The top portion of the cerebrum extending from the central sulcus to the beginning of the occipital lobes. The parietal lobes contain the primary somatosensory area as well as association, including language, areas.

PARKINSON'S DISEASE   A progressive nervous disease characterized by muscle tremor, slowing of movement, peculiarity of gait and posture, and weakness. It is a direct result of dopamine deficiency and can be treated with a dopamine-like drug, L-dopa.

PASSIONATE LOVE   A strong sexual desire for another individual combined with the perception that one is in love. This perception is often the result of misattribution in that heightened physiological arousal for any reason may be attributed to love.

PCP   A dangerous hallucinogenic drug that can lead to aggressive or psychotic behavior. Also known as *angel dust*.

PERCEPTION   The brain's interpretation of sensation.

PERCEPTUAL CONSTANCIES   The learned perception that an object remains the same in size, shape, and brightness even though the retina conveys a message of a changing size, shape, or brightness.

PERIAQUEDUCTAL GRAY MATTER   A small area within the cerebrum associated with the reception of pain.

PERIPHERAL NERVOUS SYSTEM   The motor and sensory nerves that carry impulses from the sense organs to the central nervous system and from the central nervous system to the muscles and glands of the body.

PERIPHERAL ROUTE PROCESSING   From social-information processing theory, a route of persuasion and attitude change that may occur even when a person pays little attention to the persuasive message. Any resulting attitude change is usually temporary.

PERIPHERAL VISION   All visual experiences outside of the immediate line of sight, that is, other than those derived from light focused on the fovea. The photoreceptor field on the retina surrounding the fovea gives rise to peripheral vision.

PERSONALITY   The organization of relatively enduring characteristics unique to an individual, as revealed by the individual's interaction with his or her environment.

PERSONALITY DISORDERS   Deeply ingrained, habitual, and rigid patterns of behavior or character that severely limit the adaptive potential of the individual but that are often not seen by him or her to be problematic or maladaptive. Sometimes called character disorders.

PERSUASIVE COMMUNICATION   Arguments designed to alter attitudes by appealing to reason by means of logical arguments.

PHENOTHIAZINES   Antipsychotic drugs, often called the major tranquilizers. These drugs help control and alleviate the systems of psychosis.

PHEROMONES   Sexually active substances that, when secreted, attract receptive organisms via olfactory perception.

PHI PHENOMENON   The perception of motion, in particular the illusion of movement in stationary objects achieved by presenting them in quick succession.

PHOBIA   Pathological fear of an object or situation. The individual may realize that the fear is irrational but being unable to control it, avoids the object or situation.

PHONEME   The most basic distinctive sounds in any given language. Phonemes are combined into words.

PHONETIC CONTRACTION   The end of the babbling stage, when infants narrow their use of phonemes mainly to the ones they will be using in the language they will eventually acquire.

PHONETIC EXPANSION   The beginning of the babbling stage, when infants enlarge their repertoire to include more phonemes than they eventually will come to use.

PHONOLOGY   The study of how sounds (phonemes) are put together to make words.

PHOTOGRAPHIC MEMORY   *See* EIDETIC IMAGE

PHRENOLOGY   A system developed by Franz Joseph Gall for identifying types of people by examining their physical features, especially the configuration of their skulls.

PINNA   The visible external portion of the ear.

PITCH   The relative position of a tone in a scale, which is determined by the frequency of the sound. Higher frequencies yield higher pitches.

PITUITARY GLAND   A gland located beneath the hypothalamus that controls many hormonal secretions. It is often called the master gland because it appears to control other glands all over the body.

PLACE-LEARNING   Acquiring an understanding of one's location relative to other locations in an environment through experience with the environment.

PLACE THEORY   The theory of hearing that attempts to explain the reception of sound waves between 4,000 and 20,000 cycles per second. Different frequencies stimulate cilia at different places within the cochlea. High frequencies stimulate cilia near the oval window while low frequencies stimulate cilia farther from the oval window.

PLACEBO   An inert substance often given to control subjects in place of the drug given the subjects in the experimental group

PLEASURE BOND   A Freudian term referring to the strong attachment an infant forms for its mother, generally considered to be a result of nursing.

PLEASURE PRINCIPLE   The psychoanalytic postulate that an organism seeks immediate pleasure and avoids pain. The id functions according to the pleasure principle.

POLARIZATION EFFECT   An effect in which members of a group tend to take a more extreme position (more conservative or more daring) than they would have as individuals. Probably the result of social comparison or persuasive group arguments.

POLYGRAPH   A lie detector. This device measures physiological changes regulated by the autonomic nervous system (heartbeat, blood pressure, galvanic skin response, and breathing rate). The assumption is that deliberate lying will produce detectible physical reactions.

PONS   Part of the brain stem lying just above the medulla and regulating motor messages traveling from the higher brain downward through the pons to the cerebellum. It also regulates sensory information.

POSITIVE REINFORCEMENT   When an organism is reinforced for approaching or obtaining a stimulus.

POSITIVE TRANSFER OF LEARNING   The process whereby learning one task makes it easier to learn another.

POSITRON EMISSION TOMOGRAPHY (PET)   A technique whereby organ functions, especially brain function, can be directly observed. A scanning device monitors the emission of radiation following the injection of a positron-emitting substance that gathers in specific locations determined by ongoing organ functions.

POSITRONS   Atomic particles emitted by certain radioactive substances.

POSTHYPNOTIC SUGGESTION   A suggestion made to a hypnotized subject to perform some task at a particular cue after the hypnotic session is over.

POSTSYNAPTIC SURFACE   The cell surface receiving neurotransmitter secreted into the synapse.

PREDICTION   A deduction made before the fact taking into account antecedent conditions and rules.

PREJUDICE   Beliefs or judgments made without sufficient evidence and not easily changed by opposing facts or circumstances; preconceived hostile and irrational feelings, opinions, or attitudes about a group or an individual.

PRESYNAPTIC SURFACE   The cell surface from which neurotransmitter is secreted into the synapse.

PRIMARY COLORS   The three colors from which all other colors can be made, usually considered to be red, green, and blue.

PRIMARY REINFORCERS   Stimuli that are innately reinforcing, such as food or sleep.

PRIMARY SEXUAL CHARACTERISTICS   The penis, scrotum, and testes of the male; the vagina, ovaries, and uterus of the female.

PROACTIVE INTERFERENCE   When previously learned material interferes with the ability to learn something new.

PROJECTION   A defense mechanism in which the individual attributes his or her own motives or thoughts to others, especially when these motives or thoughts are considered undesirable.

PROPOSITIONAL NETWORK THEORY   The memory theory that states that sensory information and words are transformed into propositions in order to be stored in memory.

PROPOSITIONS   The smallest units of information about which it makes sense to render a judgment of true or false. For example, "red apple" is not a proposition. However, "The apple is red" is a proposition, since the statement is either true or false.

PROSOAGNOSIA   A disorder in which the subject can no longer recognize faces. It is usually accompanied by almost no other neurological or physiological symptoms.

PSEUDO-FORGETTING   Term used to describe the belief that one has forgotten something that was once known when, in fact, the information had never been stored in the first place or had been incorrectly stored.

PSYCHOACTIVE DRUGS   Drugs that alter conscious awareness or perception.

PSYCHOANALYSIS   The school of psychological thought founded by Sigmund Freud which emphasizes the study of unconscious mental processes. Psychoanalysis is also a therapy that seeks to bring unconscious desires into consciousness and make it possible to resolve conflicts usually dating back to early childhood experiences.

PSYCHODRAMA   A specialized technique of psychotherapy developed by J. L. Moreno in which patients act out the roles, situations, and fantasies relevant to their personal problems. Psychodrama is usually conducted in front of a small audience of patients.

PSYCHOEVOLUTIONARY SYNTHESIS OF EMOTIONS   Robert Plutchik's theory that emotions evolved because they function to help a species survive. In his theory, cognitive assessments of stimulus-events may give rise to innate emotional patterns, which in turn motivate behaviors that ultimately have survival value.

PSYCHOGENIC AMNESIA   A dissociative disorder involving selective memory loss. The individual forgets, partially or totally, his or her past identity but remembers unthreatening aspects of life.

PSYCHOGENIC PAIN DISORDER   A somatoform disorder characterized by severe and chronic pain in the absence of any known physical cause.

PSYCHOLOGICAL PRIMARIES   The basic colors in Ewald Hering's opponent-process theory of color vision—red, green, yellow, and blue.

PSYCHOLOGICAL RETICENCE   A common reaction to initial failure. An individual will try to discover what is wrong and look for ways in which to improve performance. After continued failure, psychological reticence may break down, and learned helplessness may begin.

PSYCHOLOGY   The discipline that attempts to describe, explain, and predict the behavior of organisms.

PSYCHOSEXUAL DISORDERS   Mental disorders, including paraphilias, in which potentially harmful or unusual sexual actions become the primary mode of arousal; gender identity disorders in which there is an inability to resolve a discrepancy between one's anatomical sex and one's gender identity; and psychosexual dysfunctions in which psychological inhibitions interfere with the sex act.

PSYCHOSIS   Any of a group of disorders involving extensive and severe psychological disintegration, disruption of all forms of adaptive behavior, and loss of contact with reality. Psychotic individuals may show bizarre motor behavior, extreme emotional states or absence of emotional responsiveness, withdrawal, delusions, hallucinations, and cog-

nitive distortions. Usually leads to institutionalization.

PSYCHOSURGERY   Brain surgery for the purpose of altering behavior or alleviating mental disorder.

PSYCHOTHERAPY   A category of methods for treating psychological disorder. The primary technique is conversation between the patient and the therapist.

PUNISHMENT   A decrease in the strength of an emitted response as a result of an aversive stimulus consequence.

PUPIL   The dark circular aperture in the center of the iris of the eye, which helps regulate the amount of light entering the eye.

RAPID EYE MOVEMENT (REM)   The eyes' rapid back-and-forth movement during sleep. Dreaming is often associated with REM.

RATIONAL EMOTIVE THERAPY   A form of directive therapy associated with Albert Ellis in which the therapeutic goal is the modification of the client's inappropriate cognitions regarding self-concept and relations with others.

RATIONALIZATION   A defense mechanism in which irrational, impulsive action, or even failure, is justified to others and to oneself by substituting acceptable explanations for the real, but unacceptable, reasons.

REACTION FORMATION   A defense mechanism in which the individual exhibits, and at the conscious level believes he or she possesses, feelings opposite to those possessed at the unconscious level.

REALITY PRINCIPLE   According to Freud, the principle on which the conscious ego operates as it tries to mediate between the demands of the unconscious id and the realities of the environment.

REDUCTIONISM   The point of view than an explanation of events at one level is best accomplished by reference to processes at a "lower" or more basic level.

REFERENCE GROUP   A group with which we identify and that we use as our standard of behavior.

REFLEX ARC   The pathway a sensory message travels from a receptor to the spinal cord and back to an effector (the bodily organ that responds to the stimulation) in order to produce a reflex.

REFLEXES   Simple innate responses to an eliciting stimulus.

REHEARSAL   A process by which memories can be held in the short-term memory for relatively long periods. In rehearsal, an item is repeated over and over so that it is not lost. A technique that may eventually result in the storage of items in the long-term memory.

REINFORCEMENT   In operant conditioning, an event that strengthens the response that precedes it.

REINFORCEMENT THEORY OF LIKING   A social theory of relationships that argues that we like those whom we have been reinforced for liking or whom we associate with pleasurable events or circumstances.

RELATIVE MOTION   A monocular depth cue. Objects that are closer appear to move more when the head is moved from side to side.

RELATIVE SIZE   A monocular depth cue. Given objects of identical size, those that are closer appear larger than those that are distant.

RELEASERS   Stimuli that set off a cycle of instinctive behavior. Also known as *sign stimuli.*

RELIABILITY   The extent to which a test, rating scale, classification system, or other measure is consistent, that is, produces the same results each time it is applied to the same thing in the same way.

REM REBOUND   An increase in REM sleep by a person who has been deprived of it.

REPLICATION   Repeating an experiment in order to affirm the reliability of the results.

REPRESSION   A psychological process in which memories and motives are not permitted to enter consciousness but are operative at an unconscious level.

RESIDUAL SCHIZOPHRENIA   A term used to describe subtle indications of schizophrenia observable in an individual who is recovering from schizophrenia or whose schizophrenia is in remission.

RESISTANCE   In psychoanalytic theory, opposition to attempts to bring repressed thoughts into the conscious mind.

RESISTANCE STAGE   The second stage of the general adaptation syndrome. During this stage, cortical hormones maintain high levels, physiological efforts to deal with stress reach full capacity, and resistance by means of defense mechanisms and coping strategies intensifies.

RESTING POTENTIAL   The difference in electrical potential maintained between the outside and inside of a nerve cell, usually about −70 millivolts.

RETICULAR ACTIVATING SYSTEM   A complex network of neurons that monitors the general level of activity in the hindbrain, maintaining a state of arousal.

RETINA   The delicate multilayer, light-sensitive membrane lining the inner eyeball. It consists of layers of ganglion and bipolar cells and photoreceptor cells called rods and cones.

RETINAL DISPARITY   A binocular depth cue. Because the eyes are set apart, objects closer than 25 feet are sensed on significantly different locations on the left and right retinas. At close distances retinal disparity, more than any other cue, gives a strong perception of depth.

RETINEX THEORY   Land's theory of color vision in which color is explained as a function of discrepant light-dark messages sent to the brain by the photoreceptors.

RETRIEVAL CUE   Any stimulus that can help you suddenly gain access to a memory that you had been unable to recall before.

RETRIEVE   To bring material from the long-term memory to the working memory so that it can be examined.

RETROACTIVE INTERFERENCE   When learning something new interferes with the ability to recall previously learned information.

RETROGRADE AMNESIA   An amnesia brought on by a sudden shock or trauma and in which recent events are forgotten. Retrograde amnesia is probably caused by disruption of the consolidation process.

RNA (RIBONUCLEIC ACID)   A constituent of all living cells, consisting of a single-stranded chain of alternating phosphate and sugar units with the bases adenine, guanine, cytosine, and uracil bonded to the sugar. The structure of RNA and the sequences of these bases determine which proteins will be created during protein synthesis.

RODS   Specialized photoreceptor cells in the retina that are primarily responsive to changes in the intensity of light waves and are therefore important in peripheral vision and night vision.

ROUTINE PROBLEM SOLVING   Problem solving that requires concepts, thoughts, actions, and an understanding that are already in one's repertoire.

SAMPLE   A group of subjects who should normally be representative of the population about which an inference is made.

SCHIZOPHRENIA   A term used to describe a number of functional psychoses which are characterized by serious emotional disturbances, withdrawal, inappropriate emotional response or lack of emotional response, hallucinations, and delusions.

SCIENTIFIC METHOD   The principles and processes used to conduct scientific investigations, including hypotheses formation, observation, and experimentation.

SCOTOPHOBIN   A brain protein isolated by Georges Unger from rats that had been trained to avoid the dark. Only a small peptide on the protein is responsible for the effect. The name is derived from the Greek words *skotos,* meaning darkness, and *phobos,* meaning fear.

SECONDARY DEPRESSION   A state of sadness, dejection, or despair brought on by an upsetting or disturbing situation. Depression that has its roots in an environmental cause and can be traced to particular events.

SECONDARY REINFORCER   A reinforcer whose value is learned through association with primary reinforcers or other secondary reinforcers.

SECONDARY SEXUAL CHARACTERISTICS   Physical characteristics that appear in humans around the age of puberty and are sex differentiated but not necessary for sexual reproduction.

SECONDARY TRAITS   In Allport's theory, traits that are not as crucial as central traits for describing personality. Secondary traits are limited in occurrence because they are related to only a few stimuli and a few responses, for instance enjoying going to ballgames as a function of knowing a game is being played nearby.

SELECTIVE BREEDING   A breeding technique by which organisms with select traits or attributes are crossed in order to produce offspring with these traits.

SELF-ACTUALIZATION   Maslow's term for the process of an individual's constant striving to realize full potential.

SELF-DIRECTED ATTENTION   Any attempt or circumstance that increases self-awareness by directing attention inward as a way of finding our true feelings relatively free of external forces or pressures.

SELF-HYPNOSIS   An hypnotic state induced in one's self without the aid of a hypnotist.

SELF-SERVING BIAS   An attribution bias describing the fact that people tend to attribute behavior that results in a good outcome to their own personality or traits, and to attribute behavior that results in a bad outcome to the forces or circumstances of the environment.

SEMANTICS   The study of meaning in language.

SEMICIRCULAR CANALS   Three small liquid-filled canals located in the inner ear containing receptors sensitive to changes in orientation.

SENSITIVE PERIOD   A time during an organism's development when a particular stimulus is likely to have the most effect.

SENSITIVITY TRAINING   Group sessions conducted for the purpose of developing personal and interpersonal sensitivity to feelings and needs. The feelings among group members are channeled so that their own self-acceptance and growth are enhanced.

SENSITIZATION   The proces by which a reflexive response is made stronger and more sensitive to stimuli by pairing the eliciting stimulus with a painful stimulus.

SENSORY DEPRIVATION   See SENSORY ISOLATION

SENSORY ISOLATION   Lack of stimulus input needed for maintaining homeostasis. Prolonged reduction of external stimulation, either in intensity or variety, produces boredom, restlessness, and disturbances of thought processes. Also called SENSORY DEPRIVATION

SENSORY MEMORY   The first stage in the memory process. New information is held in the sensory memory for less than one second and will decay unless it is attended to, that is, encoded and placed in the short-term memory. Also called sensory register.

SERIAL POSITION EFFECT   A phenomenon in verbal learning. Items at the beginning or at the end of a long series are more easily remembered. Items in the middle are the hardest to recall.

SEX CHROMOSOMES   In humans, the chromosomes responsible for determining the sex of a child, the X and Y chromosomes.

SEX ROLE   Learned behavior appropriate to one's sex.

SEX-ROLE TYPING   The learning of sex roles by a child.

SHAPE CONSTANCY   The learned perception that an object remains the same shape, despite the fact that the image it casts on the retina may vary in shape depending on the viewing angle.

SHAPING   A method of modifying behavior by reinforcing successive approximations of the kind of behavior the experimenter desires.

SHARED PARANOID DISORDER   A rare psychotic disorder in which one individual's paranoid delusional system is adopted by another, most commonly a spouse.

SHORT-TERM MEMORY   Memory that has a limited storage capacity and a short duration. It is often called working memory because it must call up items from long-term memory so that the items can be examined. Information encoded from the sensory memory is held in the short-term memory and will decay unless the information is rehearsed or stored in the long-term memory.

SIGN STIMULI   See RELEASERS

SILENT CELLS   Neurons that communicate via graded potentials and that are called silent because they do not create a clicking sound when monitored by an oscilloscope that will register an auditory click when action potential is reached. Silent cells generally communicate over short distances and only with cells in their immediate vicinity.

SIMILARITY   A Gestalt principle of perceptual organization stating that similar things appear to be grouped together.

SIMPLICITY   A Gestalt principle of perceptual organization stating that every stimulus pattern is perceived in such a way that the resulting structure is as simple as possible.

SINGLE-SUBJECT EXPERIMENT   An experiment in which only one subject participates. Time is normally used as the control, that is, the subject's behavior changes over time in relation to the presentation and withdrawal of the independent variable.

SITUATIONAL-ENVIRONMENTAL HYPOTHESIS   The hypothesis that individuals become leaders because of situational or circumstantial forces rather than because of their personality or traits.

SIZE CONSTANCY   The learned perception that an object remains the same size, despite the fact that the size of the image it casts on the retina varies with its distance from the viewer.

SLEEP APNEA   A cessation of breathing during sleep. It may be brief or last for longer periods of time. Brain damage can result if the apnea lasts long enough to create an oxygen deficiency.

SLOW-WAVE SLEEP   The deepest stages of sleep, characterized by an EEG pattern of delta waves.

SOCIAL ATTITUDE   An enduring system of positive or negative evaluations, feelings, and tendencies toward action with respect to a social object.

SOCIAL COMPARISON   Assessing the accuracy of one's own attitudes, feelings, or beliefs by comparing them with those of others.

SOCIAL LEARNING   Learning by observing the actions of others. Also called *vicarious conditioning.*

SOCIAL LEARNING THEORY   A theory developed by Albert Bandura and others that stresses learning by observing and imitating others. Social learning is sometimes called observational learning or vicarious conditioning.

SOCIAL MOTIVATION   Learned motivation states that result from the individual's interaction with his or her social environment or culture.

SOCIAL NORMS   Shared standards of behavior accepted by and expected from group members.

SOCIAL-TEMPORAL THEORY OF MOTIVATION   A theory of motivation put forward by Phillip Zimbardo in which it is argued that an individual's view of time (past, present, or future orientation) can have a profound effect on motivation and behavior.

SOCIOBIOLOGY   A theory of motivation and behavior put forth by zoologist Edward Wilson in 1975 and stating that all human behavior is a function of an inherited biological drive to pass on one's genes. In this sense, morality, love, kindness, aggression, anger, hatred, and all other aspects of human behavior are understood in terms of their functional value for ensuring the survival of one's genes.

SOMA   The cell body.

SOMATIC NERVOUS SYSTEM   The portion of the peripheral nervous system that carries messages inward from the sense organs and outward to the muscles of the skeleton.

SOMATIC THERAPY   Invasive therapeutic intervention that acts directly on the body and its chemistry. Included in this classification are psychopharmacological electroconvulsive, and psychosurgical procedures.

SOMATOFORM DISORDERS   Patterns of behavior characterized by complaints of physical symptoms in the absence of any real physical illness. Conversion disorder, psychogenic pain disorder, and hypochondriasis are the three main kinds of somatoform disorder.

SOMATOSENSORY AREA   An area in the brain located behind the central fissure at the start of the parietal lobe and which controls sensation.

SOURCE TRAIT   From Cattell's theory of personality. Source traits can only be identified through factor analysis and are more important than surface traits. Cattell argues that personality can be reduced to 16 source traits and that, although surface traits may appear to be more valid to the common-sense observer, source traits have the greater utility for accounting for behavior.

SPACED PRACTICE   A study method that creates the spacing

effect. Also known as *distributed practice,* this method requires that studying be accomplished over time with gaps between study sessions. *See* SPACING EFFECT.

SPACING EFFECT   The fact that items are learned better and more easily recalled the greater the amount of time there is between the first and second exposure to the information.

SPECIES-SPECIFIC BEHAVIOR   Inherited behavior characteristics of one species of animal.

SPERM   The male reproductive cell of animals, which fertilizes the ovum to produce a zygote (the cell formed by the union of sperm and ovum).

SPERMATORRHEA   A term coined by the physician Claude l'Allemand based on the erroneous assumption that nocturnal emissions were related to the venereal disease gonorrhea.

SPIKE   A nerve impulse generated by the neuron reaching action potential.

SPINAL CORD   The portion of the central nervous system encased in the backbone and serving as a pathway for the conduction of sensory impulses to and from the brain.

SPONTANEOUS RECOVERY   The brief reoccurrence of a response following extinction.

SPOONERISMS   Unintentional transpositions of sounds in a sentence, as in "people in glass houses shouldn't stow thrones," named for an English clergyman, William A. Spooner (1844–1930), who was well known for such errors.

STAPES   One of the three small bones in the middle ear; also called the *stirrup.*

STATE-DEPENDENT LEARNING   Term used to describe the greater ease with which memories are recalled when one is in the same or a similar mood, state, or location as when the memory was first acquired.

STEROIDS   Any of a number of organic compounds that have a 17-atom carbon ring including some hormones. Cortical steroids (secreted from the adrenal glands) help control the release of sugar stored for use in emergencies.

STIMULANTS   Drugs that can stimulate or excite the central nervous system. Caffeine and amphetamines are examples of stimulants.

STIMULUS   Anything that can be sensed, such as visible light and audible sound.

STIMULUS CONSEQUENCE   Perceived changes in the environment owing to the effects of an emitted response.

STIMULUS CONTROL   From learning theory, the idea that discriminative stimuli come to control the behavior that they cue.

STIMULUS GENERALIZATION   Once a stimulus has come to elicit or cue a response, similar stimuli may also elicit or cue the response, though not usually as effectively.

STIMULUS MOTIVES   Drives or motives that appear to satisfy a need for certain amounts of sensory stimulation.

STREAM OF CONSCIOUSNESS   A term coined by William James

to describe his idea that conscious experience was like a river, always changing and flowing, rather than a permanent fixture.

STRESS   A psychological state associated with physiological and hormonal changes caused by conflict, trauma, or other disquieting or disruptive influences.

STRUCTURALISM   The school of psychological thought founded by Wilhelm Wundt and concerned with reducing experience to its basic parts, determining the laws by which the parts are synthesized, and investigating the structure and content of mental states by introspection.

SUBJECT BIAS   Unwanted changes in a subject's behavior owing to knowledge about the experiment or awareness of being observed.

SUBTRACTIVE MIXING   The mixing of pigments or substances that absorb colors (for instance, red pigments absorb green and blue and reflect red). The more pigments or substances that are mixed the more colors are absorbed, or subtracted, from the original light source.

SUBVOCAL SPEECH   From learning theory, Watson's argument that thinking is really a series of muscular responses.

SULCI   The narrow fissures separating adjacent cerebral convolutions.

SUPEREGO   In psychoanalytic theory, the part of the personality that incorporates parental and social standards of morality.

SUPERIOR COLLICULI   Small knoblike processes in the midbrain that are primarily involved in controlling and regulating eye movement and processing and relaying visual information.

SUPERSTITIOUS LEARNING   Behavior learned simply by virtue of the fact that it happened to be followed by a reinforcer, even though this behavior was not instrumental in obtaining the reinforcement.

SURFACE STRUCTURE   A term used by linguists to denote the grammar structure within which the semantic or deep structure is carried.

SURFACE TRAIT   From Cattell's theory of personality, a cluster or group of behaviors that are overt and appear to go together. Inferring the existence of a surface trait makes it possible to classify similar behaviors under one term; for example, constant fighting, yelling, and horrible facial expressions can be categorized under the surface trait term "aggressive."

SURVEY   A method of collecting data through the use of interviews and questionnaires.

SYMPATHETIC NERVOUS SYSTEM   The portion of the autonomic nervous system that is primarily concerned with emergencies and emotional states.

SYNAPSE   The small space between neurons in which they communicate.

SYNAPTIC KNOBS   The extreme ends of an axon in which neurotransmitter is stored.

SYNTAX   The body of linguistic rules that makes it possible to relate a series of words in a sentence to the underlying meaning of that sentence, that is, the rules governing word order in a language (sentence structure).

SYSTEMATIC DESENSITIZATION   A therapeutic procedure developed by Wolpe in which anxiety-producing stimuli are paired, in a graduated sequence or hierarchy, with a state of physical relaxation until the most difficult situation can be faced without anxiety.

SYSTEMATIC RELAXATION   A technique in which deep relaxation is achieved through the progressive relaxation of one muscle group at a time, usually beginning with the feet and legs. The subject breathes deeply and focuses attention on each muscle group as it is relaxed.

TACTILE SENSORY REPLACEMENT (TSR)   A device to aid the blind. A television camera is connected to a vest worn by the subject. An image is then formed on the viewer's back by means of tactile stimulation. Through practice, the wearer can obtain a perceptual understanding of the visual world.

TARDIVE DYSKINESIA   A severe neuromuscular reaction, possibly due to interference with or depletion of the neurotransmitter acetylcholine, following long-term use or sudden withdrawal from antipsychotic drugs. The disorder is manifested in the involuntary twitching of body and facial muscles.

TASK LOAD   A measure of demand in terms of behavior required per unit of time. In high task load conditions there is much to do and little time in which to do it.

TASTE BUDS   Groups of cells distributed over the tongue that constitute the end organs of the sense of taste.

TELEGRAPHIC SPEECH   Pattern of speech following the two-word stage, in which children rely on a grammar of strict word order to convey their meaning and do not use conjunctions, prepositions, or other function words.

TELENCEPHALON   A division of the forebrain that contains the corpus callosum, the limbic system, and the cerebrum.

TEMPORAL LOBES   The portions of the cerebrum on either side of the head near the temples. The temporal lobes contain the primary auditory areas, as well as association areas. They have to do with emotion, vision, and language.

TESTOSTERONE   The male sex hormone produced by the testes that controls the development of secondary sex characteristics, such as the growth of a beard, and that may influence the sexual activity of the individual.

THALAMUS   Part of the forebrain that relays sensory information and is involved in wakefulness and sleep.

THC   Tetrahydrocannabinol, the active ingredient in marijuana, which causes hallucination in high enough doses.

THEORY   A system of rules or assumptions used to predict or explain phenomena.

THETA WAVES   A pattern of brain waves typically associated with the first stage of sleep.

THINKING   The process that occurs between the sensing of a stimulus and the emergence of an overt response, and that involves the interplay of concepts, symbols, or mediating responses rather than a direct manipulation of environmental objects.

TIP OF THE TONGUE PHENOMENON   The experience of almost being able to recall a certain bit of information. You sense that the information is there, you can almost "feel" it, and yet you cannot grasp it.

TOKEN ECONOMIES   Training, based on operant conditioning, that uses tokens as rewards for certain behaviors. The tokens can be redeemed for special privileges, or primary reinforcers.

TRACE COLUMN   A continuous record of memories analogous to a videotape, put forth by Kurt Koflka in 1935 as an explanation for the way memory functions. Our modern understanding of neural transmission rates in the brain has led us to reject the trace column because it would require neurons to fire much faster than they do.

TRACHEOTOMY   The procedure of cutting into the trachea through the throat. A tube in often inserted through the incision to aid the patient in breathing.

TRAITS   Distinguishing qualities, properties, or attributes of a person that are consistently displayed. According to Allport, a predisposition to respond to many types of stimuli in the same manner.

TRANQUILIZERS   Any of various drugs that are used to pacify.

TRANSACTIONAL ANALYSIS   A form of interpersonal therapy based on the interactions of "child," "adult," and "parent" ego states.

TRANSCENDENCE OF CONSTRAINTS   According to Jackson and Messick, a component of creativity. Creative ideas transcend constraints in that they often shed new light on something familiar.

TRANSFERENCE   A concept developed by Freud that generally refers to the tendency of a person in therapy to transfer to the therapist perceptions and feelings about other people rather than seeing the therapist as he or she really is.

TRANSFORMATIONAL GRAMMAR THEORY   Noam Chomsky's theory of grammar in which he argues that the semantic content of a language is more important than the grammar in helping us to understand how we come to express our meanings or grasp the meanings of others.

TRANSSEXUAL REASSIGNMENT   A surgical procedure for altering external anatomy and appearance so that the individual resembles the opposite sex.

TRANSSEXUALISM   The most extreme form of gender reversal, in which an individual feels that he or she is really a member of the opposite sex but has been trapped in the wrong-sexed body.

TREPHINING   An ancient procedure in which the skull is punctured by a sharp instrument so that evil spirits could escape.

TWO-WORD STAGE   The universal stage of language development in which children's expressions are limited to two-word utterances.

TYMPANIC MEMBRANE   The thin, semitransparent membrane separating the middle ear from the external ear; also called the *eardrum.*

UNCONDITIONED RESPONSE (UR)   Response made to an unconditioned stimulus, as in the case of salivation in response to food.

UNCONDITIONED STIMULUS (US)   The stimulus that normally evokes an unconditioned response, such as the food that originally caused Pavlov's dog to respond with salivation.

UNDIFFERENTIATED SCHIZOPHRENIA   Schizophrenia that cannot be classified as disorganized, catatonic, or paranoid. It is characterized by a complex mixture of delusions, hallucinations, bizarre thinking, and blunted or overreactive emotions. Undifferentiated schizophrenia is often associated with the onset of schizophrenia, when a particular type has not yet been well formed or with the process of changing from one type of schizophrenia to another.

UNIPOLAR   Of, or pertaining to, one pole, a term used to distinguish the manic or depressed type of bipolar disorder from the mixed type, in which the mood vacillates between mania and depression.

VALIDITY   The capacity of an instrument to measure what it purports to measure.

VASOPRESSIN   A neuropeptide known to affect memory. Vasopressin nasal spray has been used clinically to improve memory.

VESTIBULAR SACS   Two baglike structures at the base of the semicircular canals containing receptors for the sense of balance.

VISIBLE SPECTRUM   The range of wavelengths of light visible to the unaided eye.

VISUAL CLIFF   An apparatus constructed to study depth perception in animals and human beings. It consists of a center board resting on a glass table. On one side of the board a checkered surface is visible directly beneath the glass, and on the other side the surface is several feet below the glass, thus giving the impression of a drop-off.

VISUAL CORTEX   An area in the brain located in the occipital lobes through which most visual information is processed.

VISUAL PERSPECTIVE HYPOTHESIS   The hypothesis that explains people's tendency to attribute their own behavior to environmental causes rather than to personality traits as a function of their visual perspective, because they view their surroundings more often then they view their own body.

VOLLEY THEORY   A theory of hearing that attempts to explain the reception of sound waves between 1,000 and 4,000 cycles per second. According to this theory, auditory neurons fire in volleys that are well correlated with the frequency of the sound.

WAVELENGTH   The linear distance from a point on one oscillation of a wave to the corresponding point on the next oscillation of that wave.

WEBER'S LAW   The rule that the larger or stronger a stimulus, the larger the change required for an observer to notice a difference. The smallest difference in intensity between two stimuli that can be reliably detected is a constant fraction of the original stimulus.

WERNICKE'S AREA   An area in the temporal and parietal lobes of the brain associated with speech control.

WERNICKE'S APHASIA   The inability to understand spoken language because of damage to Wernicke's area. Individuals with this disorder generally speak normally in terms of phonetics and grammar content, but their speech is semantically bizarre.

YOGI   One who practices yoga, a Hindu discipline whose aim is to train consciousness to attain a state of perfect spiritual insight and tranquility. Control of bodily functions and mental states is practiced.

YOUNG-HELMHOLTZ THEORY   A theory of color vision that states that there are three basic colors (red, green, and blue) and three types of cones, each of which is receptive to the wavelengths of one of the colors.

Aarons, L. Sleep-assisted instruction. *Psychological Bulletin,* 1976, *83,* 1–40.

Abruzzi, W. Outpatient, non-chemical treatment of psychosis. *Psychotherapy: Theory, Research & Practice,* 1975, *12,* 262–267.

Aceves-Piña, E. O., & Quinn, W. G. Learning in normal and mutant *drosophila* larvae. *Science,* 1979, *206,* 93–96.

Adams, G. R. Physical attractiveness, personality, and social reactions to peer pressure. *Journal of Psychology,* 1977, *96,* 287–296.

Adler, A. *Practice and theory of individual psychology.* New York: Harcourt, Brace & World, 1927.

Adler, J., & Carey, J. The science of love. *Newsweek,* February 25, 1980, pp. 89–90.

Adler, L. L., & Adler, H. E. Ontogeny of observational learning in the dog. *Developmental Psychobiology,* 1977, *10,* 267–271.

Adorno, T. W., Frenkel-Brunswik, E., Levinson, D. J., & Sanford, R. N. *The authoritarian personality.* New York: Harper, 1950.

Ainsworth, M. D. S., Bell, S. M. V., & Stayton, D. J. Individual differences in strange-situation behavior of one year olds. In H. R. Schaffer (Ed.), *The origins of human social relations.* New York: Academic Press, 1971, pp. 17–52.

Albert, E. M. The roles of women: Question of values. In S. M. Farber and K. D. Wilson (Eds.), *The potential of women.* New York: McGraw-Hill, 1963.

Alker, H. A., & Owen, D. W. Biographical, trait, and behavioral-sampling predictions of performance in a stressful life setting. *Journal of Personality and Social Psychology,* 1977, *35,* 717–723.

Allison, T., & Cicchetti, D. V. Sleep in mammals: Ecological and constitutional correlates. *Science,* 1976, *194,* 732–734.

Allport, G. W. *Personality: A psychological interpretation.* New York: Holt, Rinehart & Winston, 1937.

Allport, G. W. *Pattern and growth in personality.* New York: Holt, Rinehart & Winston, 1961.

Allport, G. W., & Odbert, H. S. Trait names: A psycholexical study. *Psychological Monographs,* 1936, *47* (1, whole No. 211).

Altenor, A., Kay, E., & Richter, M. The generality of learned helplessness in the rat. *Learning & Motivation,* 1977, *8,* 54–61.

Altus, W. D. Birth order and its sequelae. *International Journal of Psychiatry,* 1967, *3,* 23–36.

Amarilio, J. D. Insanity—Guilty but mentally ill—Diminished capacity: An aggregate approach to madness. *John Marshall Journal of Practice & Procedure,* 1979, *12,* 351–381.

Amsterdam, B. Mirror self-image reactions before age two. *Developmental Psychobiology,* 1972, *5,* 297–305.

Anand, B. K., & Brobeck, J. R. Localization of a feeding center in the hypothalamus of the rat. *Proceedings of the Society for Experimental Biology and Medicine,* 1951, *77,* 323–324.

Anderson, J. R. *Language, memory, and thought.* Hillsdale, N. J.: Erlbaum, 1976.

Anderson, J. R. *Cognitive psychology and its implications.* San Francisco: W. H. Freeman, 1980.

Anderson, J. R., & Bower, G. H. Configural properties in sentence memory. *Journal of Verbal Learning and Verbal Behavior,* 1972, *11,* 595–605.

Anderson, J. R., & Bower, G. H. *Human associative memory.* Washington, D. C.: Winston, 1973.

Anderson, L. D. The predictive value of infant tests in relation to intelligence at 5 years. *Child Development,* 1939, *10,* 203–212.

Andersson, B. Thirst—and brain control of water balance. *American Scientist,* 1971 *59,* 508–415.

Anhalt, H. S., & Klein, M. Drug abuse in junior high school populations. *American Journal of Drug & Alcohol Abuse,* 1976, *3,* 589–603.

Antelman, S. M., & Caggiula, A. R. Norepinephrine-dopamine interactions and behavior: A new hypothesis of stress-related interactions between brain norepinephrine and dopamine is proposed. *Science,* 1977, *195,* 646–653.

Antelman, S. M., Rowland, N. E., & Fisher, A. E. Stimulation bound ingestive behavior: A view from the tail. *Physiology & Behavior,* 1976, *17,* 743–748.

Anthony, E. J. (Ed.). *Explorations in child psychiatry.* New York: Plenum Press, 1975.

Anxiety: Fear grows up. *Science News,* March 15, 1980, p. 164.

Archer, D. *How to expand your S. I. Q. (social intelligence quotient).* New York: Evans, 1980.

Archer, D., & Akert, R. M. Words and everything else: Verbal and nonverbal cues in social interpretation. *Journal of Personality and Social Psychology,* 1977, *35,* 443–449.

Arehart-Treichel, J. Senility: More than growing old. *Science News,* October 1, 1977, pp. 218–221.

Arehart-Treichel, J. The science of sleep. *Science News,* March 26, 1977, p. 203.

Aronson, E. Some antecedents of interpersonal attraction. In W. J. Arnold & D. Levine (Eds.), *Nebraska symposium on motivation.* Lincoln, Nebraska: University of Nebraska Press, 1969.

Aronson, E., & Mills, J. The effect of severity of initiation on liking for a group. *Journal of Abnormal and Social Psychology,* 1959, *59,* 177–181.

Abnormal and Social Psychology, 1959, *59,* 177–181.

Arvidson, K., & Friberg, U. Human taste—Response and taste bud number in fungiform papillae. *Science,* 1980, *209,* 807–808.

Asch, S. E. Effects of group pressure upon the modification and distortion of judgment. In H. Guetzkow (Ed.), *Groups, leadership, and men.* Pittsburgh: Carnegie, 1951.

Asch, S. E. Opinions and social pressure. *Scientific American,* 1955, *193* (5), 31–35.

Aserinsky, E., & Kleitman, N. Regularly occurring periods of eye motility, and concomitant phenomena, during sleep. *Science,* 1953, *118,* 273–274.

Atkinson, J. W. Studying personality in the context of an advanced motivational psychology. *American Psychologist,* 1981, *36,* 117–128.

Atkinson, K., McWhinney, B., & Stoel, C. *An experiment on the recognition of babbling.* Papers and reports on child language development, Committee on Linguistics, Stanford University, 1970 (No. 1).

Azrin, N. H., & Foxx, R. M. *Toilet training in less than a day.* New York: Simon & Schuster, 1974.

Azrin, N. H., & Holz, W. C. Punishment: In W. K. Honig (Ed.), *Operant behavior.* New York: Appleton-Century Crofts, 1966.

Babor, T. F., Mendelson, J. H., & Kuehnle, J. C. Marihuana and human physical activity. *Psychopharmacology,* 1976, *50,* 11–19.

Bach-Y-Rita, P., Collins, C. C., Saunders, F. A., White, B., & Scadden, L. Vision substitution by tactile image projection. *Nature,* 1969, *221,* 963–964.

Baer, D. M., & Wright, J. C. Developmental psychology. *Annual Review of Psychology,* 1974, *25,* 1–82.

Bales, R. F. *Personality and interpersonal behavior.* New York: Holt, Rinehart & Winston, 1970.

Balster, R. L., & Chait, L. D. The behavioral pharmacology of phencyclidine. *Clinical Toxicology,* 1976, *9,* 513–528.

Bandura, A. Social learning through imitation. In M. R. Jones (Ed.), *Nebraska symposium on motivation: 1962.* Lincoln: University of Nebraska Press, 1962, pp. 211–269.

Bandura, A. Influence of models' reinforcement contingencies on the acquisition of imitative responses. *Journal of Personality and Social Psychology,* 1965, *1,* 589–595.

Bandura, A. *Principles of behavior modification.* New York: Holt, Rinehart, & Winston, 1969.

Bandura, A. *Social learning theory.* Englewood Cliffs, N. J.: Prentice-Hall, 1977.

Bandura, A. The self system in reciprocal determinism. *American Psychologist,* 1978, *33,* 344–358.

Bandura, A., Ross, D., & Ross, S. A. A comparative test of the status envy, social power, and secondary reinforcement theories of identificatory learning. *Journal of Abnormal and Social Psychology,* 1963, *67,* 527–534.

Bandura, A., Ross, D., & Ross, S. A. Imitation of film-mediated aggressive models. *Journal of Abnormal and Social Psychology,* 1963, *66,* 3–11.

Barber, T. X. *Hypnosis: A scientific approach.* New York: Van Nostrand Reinhold, 1969.

Barclay, C. D., Cutting, J. E., & Kozlowski, L. T. Temporal and spatial factors in gait perception that influence gender recognition. *Perception & Psychophysics,* 1978, *23,* 145–152.

Bard, P. The neurohumoral basis of emotional reactions. In C. A. Murchison (Ed.), *Handbook of general experimental psychology.* Worcester, Mass: Clark University Press, 1934.

Baron, R. A. The "foot-in-the-door" phenomenon: Mediating effects of size of first request and sex of requester. *Bulletin of the Psychonomic Society,* 1973, *2,* 113–114.

Barresi, C. M., & Gigliotti, R. J. Are drug education programs effective? *Journal of Drug Education,* 1975, *5,* 301–316.

Bartusiak, M. Beeper man. *Discover,* November 1980, p. 57.

Bassili, J. N. Facial motion in the perception of faces and of emotional expressions. *Journal of Experimental Psychology: Human Perception & Performance,* 1978, *4,* 373–379.

Bassuk, E. L., & Gerson, S. Deinstitutionalization and mental health services. *Scientific American,* 1978, *238,*(2), 46–53.

Bavelas, A., Hastorf, A. H., Gross, A. E., & Kite, W. R. Experiments on the alteration of group structure. *Journal of Experimental Social Psychology,* 1965, *1,* 55–70.

Bayer, A. E. Birth order and college attendance. *Journal of Marriage and the Family,* 1966, *28,* 480–484.

Baylor, D. A., Fuortes, M. G. F., & O'Bryan, P. M. Receptive fields of single cones in the retina of the turtle. *Journal of Physiology,* 1971, *214,* 265–294.

Beach, B. H. Blood, sweat and fears. *Time,* September 8, 1980, p. 44.

Beatty, W. W. Gonadal hormones and sex differences in nonreproductive behaviors in rodents: Organizational and activational influences. *Hormones & Behavior,* 1979, *12,* 112–163.

Beck, A. T. *Depression: Causes and treatment.* Philadelphia: University of Pennsylvania Press, 1972.

Beck, A. T., Rush, A. J., Shaw, B., & Emery, G. *Cognitive therapy of depression: A treatment manual.* New York: Gilford Press, 1979.

Becker, I. M., & Rosenfeld, J. G. Rational emotive therapy—A study of initial therapy sessions of Albert Ellis. *Journal of Clinical Psychology,* 1976, *32,* 872–876.

Becker, W. C. The matching of behavior rating and questionnaire personality factors. *Psychological Bulletin,* 1960, *57,* 201–212.

Beers, C. *A mind that found itself.* New York: Longmans, Green, 1908.

Begley, S., & Carey, J. The sexual brain. *Newsweek,* November 26, 1979, pp. 100–105A.

Begley, S., & Carey, J. Can aging be controlled? *Newsweek,* March 16, 1981, p. 68.

Beiser, A. *Physics* (2nd ed.). Menlo Park, Calif.: Benjamin/Cummings, 1978.

Bell, R. Q. A reinterpretation of the direction of effects in studies of socialization. *Psychological Review,* 1968, *75,* 81–95.

Belmont, L., & Marolla, F. A. Birth order, family size, and intelligence. *Science,* 1973, *182,* 1096–1101.

Bem, D. J., & Allen, A. On predicting some of the people some of the time: The search for cross-situational consistencies in behavior. *Psychological Review,* 1974, *81,* 506–520.

Bem, D. J., & Funder, D. C. Predicting more of the people more of the time: Assessing the personality of situations. *Psychological Review,* 1978, *85,* 485–501.

Bem, S. L. On the utility of alternative procedures for assessing psychological androgyny. *Journal of Consulting and Clinical Psychology,* 1977, *45,* 196–205.

Benbow, C. P., & Stanley, J. C. Mathematical ability—Is sex a factor? *Science,* 1981, *212,* 118.

Benjamin, H. Transvestism and trans-sexualism. *International Journal of Sexology,* 1953, *7,* 12–14.

Benson, H. *The relaxation response.* New York: Morrow, 1975.

Berger, R. J. The sleep and dream cycle. In A. Kales (Ed.), *Sleep: Physiology and pathology.* Philadelphia: Lippincott, 1969, pp. 17–32.

Bergin, A. E. The evaluation of therapeutic outcomes. In A. E. Bergin and S. L. Garfield (Eds.), *Handbook of psychotherapy and behavior change: An empirical analysis.* New York: Wiley, 1971.

Berk, L. S. Personal communication, August 21, 1981.

Berko, J. The child's learning of English morphology, *Word,* 1958, *14,* 150–177.

Berkowitz, L. The concept of aggressive drive: Some additional considerations. In L. Berkowitz (Ed.), *Advances in experimental social psychology* (Vol. 2). New York: Academic Press, 1965.

Berman, H. J., Shulman, A. D., & Marwit, S. J. Comparison of multidimensional decoding of affect from audio, video and audiovideo recordings. *Sociometry,* 1976, *39,* 83–89.

Bernard, H. W., & Fullmer, D. W. *Principles of guidance* (2nd ed.). New York: Crowell Company, 1977.

Berne, E. *Games people play.* New York: Grove Press, 1964.

Berscheid, E., & Walster, E. A little bit about love. In T. L. Huston (Ed.), *Foundations of interpersonal attraction.* New York: Aademic Press, 1974.

Bettelheim, B. *Truants from life: The rehabilitation of emotionally disturbed children.* New York: Free Press, 1955.

Betz, B. J., & Thomas, C. B. Individual temperament as a predictor of health or premature disease. *The Johns Hopkins Medical Journal,* 1979, *144,* 81–89.

The big sleep project. *Science News,* January 5, 1980, p. 8.

Biller, H. B. *Paternal deprivation: Family, school, sexuality, and society.* Lexington, Mass.: Heath, 1974.

Bischof, L. J. *Adult psychology* (2nd ed.). New York: Harper & Row, 1976.

Bishop, P. O. Neurophysiology of binocular single vision and stereopsis. In R. Jung (Ed.), *Handbook of sensory physiology.* Berlin: Springer, 1973, pp. 256–305.

Bitterman, M. E. Thorndike and the problem of animal intelligence. *American Psychologist,* 1969, *24,* 444–453.

Blakemore, C., & Campbell, F. W. Adaptation to spatial stimuli. *Journal of Physiology,* 1968, *200,* 11P–13P.

Blakemore, C., & Cooper, G. F. Development of the brain depends on the visual environment. *Nature,* 1970, *228,* 477–478.

Bleda, P. R., & Castore, C. H. Social comparison, attraction, and choice of a comparison other. *Memory and Cognition,* 1973, *1,* 420–424.

Block, J. *The Q-sort method in personality assessment and psychiatric research.* Springfield, Ill.: Charles C Thomas, 1961.

Bloom, B. S. *Stability and change in human characteristics.* New York: Wiley, 1964.

Blum, K., Briggs, A. H., Feinglass, S. J., Domey, R., & Wallace, J. E. Effects of Delta9 tetrahydrocannabinol on amphetamine-aggregate toxicity in mice. *Current Therapeutic Research,* 1977, *21,* 241–244.

Bogen, J. E., Fisher, E. D., & Vogel, P. J. Cerebral commissurotomy. *Journal of the American Medical Association,* 1965, *194,* 1328–1329.

Bohus, B. Effect of desglycinamide-lysine vasopressin (DG-LVP) on sexually motivated T-maze behavior of the male rat. *Hormones & Behavior,* 1977, *8,* 52–61.

Bolter, A., Heminger, A., Martin, G., & Fry, M. Outpatient clinical experience in a community drug abuse program with phencyclidine abuse. *Clinical Toxicology,* 1976, *9,* 593–600.

Boneau, C. A., & Cuca, J. M. An overview of psychology's human resources. *American Psychologist,* 1974, *29,* 821–840.

Bonnet, M. H., & Webb, W. B. Effect of two experimental sets on sleep structure. *Perceptual and Motor Skills,* 1976, *42,* 343–350.

Booth, D. A. Satiety and appetite are conditioned reactions. *Psychosomatic Medicine,* 1977, *39,* 76–81.

Botwinick, J. *Cognitive processes in maturity and old age.* New York: Springer, 1967.

Boucher, J. D. *Facial behavior and the perception of emotion: Studies of Malays and Temuan Orang Asli.* Paper presented at the Conference of Psychology and Related Disciplines, Kuala Lumpur, 1973.

Bower, G. H. Mood and memory. *American Psychologist,* 1981, *36,* 129–148.

Bower, G. H., Karlin, M. B., & Dueck, A. Comprehension and memory for pictures. *Memory and Cognition,* 1975, *3,* 216–220.

Bowers, K. S. *Hypnosis for the seriously curious.* Monterey, Calif.: Brooks-Cole, 1976.

Bowers, M. The onset of psychosis—a diary account. *Psychiatry,* 1965, *28,* 346–358.

Bowker, L. H. The incidence of drug use and associated factors in two small towns: A community survey. *Bulletin on Narcotics,* 1976, *28,* 17–25.

Brady, J. V., Porter, R. W., Conrad, D. G., & Mason, J. W. Avoidance behavior and the development of gastroduodenal ulcers. *Journal of the Experimental Analysis of Behavior,* 1958, *1,* 69–72.

Braestrup, C., Nielsen, M., Squires, R. F., & Laurberg, S. Benzodiazepine receptor in brain. *Acta Psychiatrica Scandinavica,* 1978, *S274,* 27–32.

Braine, M. D. S. The ontogeny of English phrase structure: The first phase. *Language,* 1963, *39*(1), 1–13.

Brandt, T., Wist, E. R., & Dichgans, J. Foreground and background in dynamic spatial orientation. *Perception & Psychophysics,* 1975, *17,* 497–503.

Braver, S. L., Linder, D. E., Corwin, T. T., & Cialdini, R. B. Some conditions that affect admissions of attitude change. *Journal of Experimental Social Psychology,* 1977, *13,* 565–576.

Brecher, E. M. History of human sexual research and study. In B. J. Sadock, H. I. Kaplan, & A. M. Freedman (Eds.), *The sexual experience.* Baltimore: Williams & Wilkins, 1976, pp. 71–78.

Brenner, D., & Howard, K. Clinical judgment as a function of experience and information. *Journal of Clinical Psychology,* 1976, *32,* 721–728.

Bringmann, W. Wundt's lab: "Humble . . . but functioning." *APA Monitor,* September/October 1979, p. 13.

Brinkman, J., & Kuypers, H. G. J. M. Splitbrain monkeys: Cerebral control of ipsilateral and contralateral arm, hand, and finger movements. *Science,* 1972, *176,* 536–539.

Brittain, C. V. Adolescent choices and parent-peer cross-pressures. *American Sociological Review,* 1963, *28,* 385–391.

Brobeck, J. R., Tepperman, J., & Long, C. N. H. Experimental hypothalamic hyperphagia in the albino rat. *Yale Journal of Biology and Medicine,* 1943, *15,* 831–853.

Brock, T. C. Communicator-recipient similarity and decision change. *Journal of Personality and Social Psychology,* 1965, *1,* 650–654.

Brooks-Gunn, J., & Lewis, M. *Mirror-image stimulation and self-recognition in infancy.* Paper presented at the meeting of the Society for Research in Child Development, Denver, 1975.

Broverman, I. K., Vogel, S. R., Broverman, D. M., Clarkson, F. E., & Rosenkrantz, P. S. Sex-role stereotypes: A current appraisal. *Journal of Social Issues,* 1972, *28*(2), 59–78.

Brown, R., & Kulik, J. Flashbulb memories. *Cognition,* 1977, *5,* 73–99.

Bruner, J. S. *Beyond the information given: Studies in the psychology of knowing.* (J. M. Anglin, Ed.). New York: Norton, 1973.

Buck, R. *Slide-viewing paradigm in the measurement of nonverbal communication.* Paper presented at the meeting of the American Psychological Association, San Francisco, August 1977.

Buckhout, R. Eyewitness testimony. *Scientific American,* 1974, *231*(6), 23–31.

Bugental, D. E., Kaswan, J. W., Love, L. R., & Fox, M. N. Child versus adult perception of evaluative messages in verbal, vocal, and visual channels. *Developmental Psychology,* 1970, 367–375.

Bukoff, A., & Elman, D. Repeated exposure to liked and disliked social stimuli. *Journal of Social Psychology,* 1979, *107,* 133–134.

Burns, K. L. & Beier, E. G. Significance of vocal and visual channels in the decoding of emotional meaning. *Journal of Communication,* 1973, *23,* 118–130.

Bush, J. A. Suicide and Blacks: A conceptual framework. *Suicide and Life-Threatening Behavior,* 1976, *6,* 216–222.

Butter, H. J. *Hyperkinesis—A theoretical and experimental study.* Unpublished doctoral dissertation, University of Ottawa, Ontario, 1974.

Byrne, D., & Clore, G. L. A reinforcement model of evaluative responses. *Personality: An International Journal,* 1970, *1,* 103–128.

Byrne, D., Ervin, C. R., & Lamberth, J. Continuity between the experimental study of attraction and real-life computer dating. *Journal of Personality and Social Psychology,* 1970, *16,* 157–165.

Cacioppo, J. T., & Petty, R. E. Attitudes and cognitive response: An electrophysiological approach. *Journal of Personality and Social Psychology,* 1979, *37,* 2181–2199.

Cadoret, R. J. Cain, C. A., & Grove, W. M. Development of alcoholism in adoptees raised apart from alcoholic biologic relatives. *Archives of General Psychiatry,* 1980, *37,* 561–563.

Calder, N. *The mind of man.* New York: Viking, 1971.

Campos, J. J., Hiatt, S., Ramsay, D., Henderson, C., and Svejda, M. The emergence of fear on the visual cliff. In M. Lewis and L. A. Rosenblum (Eds.), *The development of affect.* New York: Plenum Press, 1978, pp. 149–182.

Cannon, W. B. The James-Lange theory of emotions: A critical examination and an alternative theory. *American Journal of Psychology,* 1927, *39,* 106–124.

Cannon, W. B. *The wisdom of the body.* New York: Norton, 1939.

Caputo, P. *A rumor of war.* New York: Holt, Rinehart & Winston, 1977.

Carey, W. B. & McDevitt, S. C. Stability and change in individual temperament diagnoses from infancy to early childhood. *Journal of the American Academy of Child Psychiatry,* 1978, *17,* 331–337.

Carlson, N. K., Drury, C. G., & Webber, J. A. Discriminability of large weights. *Ergonomics,* 1977, *20,* 87–90.

Carlson, N. R. *Physiology of behavior.* Boston: Allyn and Bacon, 1977.

Carpenter, W. T., McGlashan, T. H., & Strauss, J. S. The treatment of acute schizophrenia without drugs: An investigation of some current assumptions. *American Journal of Psychiatry,* 1977; *134,* 14–20.

Carroll, B. J., Feinberg, M., Greden, J. F., Tarika, J., Albala, A. A., Haskett, R. F., James, N. M., Kronfol, Z., Lohr, N., Steiner, M., de Vigne, J. P., & Young, E. A specific laboratory test for the diagnosis of melancholia. *Archives of General Psychiatry,* 1981, *38,* 15–22.

Cartwright, R. D., Bernick, N., Borowitz, G., & Kling, A. Effect of an erotic movie on the sleep and dreams of young men. *Archives of General Psychiatry,* 1969, *20,* 262–271.

Cartwright, R. D. Problem solving: Waking and dreaming, *Journal of Abnormal Psychology,* 1974, *83,* 451–455.

Carver, C. S., DeGregorio, E., & Gillis, R. Ego-defensive bias in attribution among two categories of observers. *Personality and Social Psychology Bulletin,* 1980, *6,* 44–50.

The Case of Qwerty vs. Maltron. *Time,* January 26, 1981, p. 73.

Cattell, R. B. *Personality: A systematic theoretical and factual study.* New York: McGraw-Hill, 1950.

Cattell, R. B. Personality pinned down. *Psychology Today,* July 1973, pp. 40–46.

Cattell, R. B., Saunders, D. R., & Stice, G. F. *The 16 personality factor questionnaire.* Champaign, Illinois: Institute for Personality and Ability Testing, 1950.

Chaffee, S. H., & McLeod, J. M. *Adolescents, parents, and television violence.* Paper presented at the meeting of the American Psychological Association, Washington, D.C., 1971.

Chaiken, S. Heuristic versus systematic information processing and the use of source versus message cues in persuasion. *Journal of Personality and Social Psychology,* 1980, *39,* 752–766.

Chandler, B. C., & Parsons, O. A. Altered hemispheric functioning under alcohol, *Journal of Studies on Alcohol,* 1977, *38,* 381–391.

Charlesworth, W. R., & Kreutzer, M. A. Facial expression of infants and children. In P. Ekman (Ed.), *Darwin and facial expression.* New York: Academic Press, 1973.

Chase, W. G., & Simon, H. A. The mind's eye in chess. In W. G. Chase (Ed.), *Visual information processing.* New York: Academic Press, 1973.

Cherry, F., & Byrne, D. Authoritarianism. In T. Blass (Ed.), *Personality variables in social behavior.* Hillsdale, N. J.: Erlbaum, 1976.

Cherry, F., Byrne, D., & Mitchell, H. E. Clogs in the bogus pipeline: Demand characteristics and social desirability. *Journal of Research in Personality,* 1976, *10,* 69–75.

Cherry, F. F., & Eaton, E. L. Physical and cognitive development in children of low-income mothers working in the child's early years. *Child Development,* 1977, *48,* 158–166.

Chevalier-Skolnikoff, S. Kids. *Animal Kingdom,* 1979, *82*(3), 11–18.

Chorover, S. L. *From genesis to genocide: The meaning of human nature and the power of behavior control.* Cambridge, Mass.: M.I.T. Press, 1979.

Cialdini, R. B., Cacioppo, J. T., Bassett, R., & Miller, J. A. Low-ball procedure for producing compliance: Commitment then cost. *Journal of Personality and Social Psychology,* 1978, *36,* 463–476.

Cialdini, R. B., Levy, A., Herman, C. P., Kozlowski, L. T., & Petty, R. E. Elastic shifts of opinion: Determinants of direction and durability. *Journal of Personality and Social Psychology,* 1976, *34,* 663–672.

Cialdini, R. B., Petty, R. E., & Cacioppo, J. T. Attitude and attitude change. In M. R. Rosenzweig & L. W. Porter (Eds.), *Annual review of psychology.* Palo Alto, Calif.: Annual Reviews, Inc., 1981.

Cialdini, R. B., & Schroeder, D. A. Increasing compliance by legitimizing paltry contributions: When even a penny helps. *Journal of Personality & Social Psychology,* 1976, *34,* 599–604.

Cialdini, R. B., Vincent, J. E., Lewis, S. K., Catalan, J., Wheeler, D., & Darby, B. L. Reciprocal concessions procedure for inducing compliance: The door-in-the-face technique. *Journal of Personality and Social Psychology,* 1975, *31,* 206–215.

Clark, H. H. Semantics and comprehension. In R. A. Sebeok (Ed.), *Current trends in linguistics* (Vol. 12). The Hague: Mouton, 1974.

Clark, H. H. & Clark, E. V. *Psychology and language: An introduction to psycholinguistics.* New York: Harcourt Brace Jovanovich, 1977.

Clark, K. B., & Clark, M. P. Racial identification and preference in Negro children, In T. M. Newcomb & E. J. Hartley (Eds.), *Readings in social psychology.* New York: Holt, 1947.

Clark, M., Gosnell, M., Shapiro, D., Huck, J., & Marbach, W. D. Drugs and psychiatry: A new era. *Newsweek,* November 12, 1979, pp. 98–104.

Clausen, J. A. Perspectives on childhood socialization, In J. Clausen (Ed.), *Socialization and society.* Boston: Little, Brown, 1968.

652

Clayton, R. R. *The family, marriage, and social change.* Lexington, Mass.: D. C. Heath, 1975.

Cline, V. B., Atzet, J., & Holmes, E. Assessing the validity of verbal and nonverbal cues in accurately judging others. *Comparative Group Studies*, 1972, *3*, 383–394.

Clore, G. L., & Byrne, D. A reinforcement-affect model of attraction. In T. L. Huston (Ed.), *Foundations of interpersonal attraction.* New York: Academic Press, 1974.

Coburn, J. Sterilization regulations: Debate not quelled by HEW document. *Science*, 1974, *183*, 935–939.

Cohen, L. J. The operational definition of human attachment. *Psychological Bulletin*, 1974, *81*, 207–217.

Colby, C. Z., Lanzetta, J. T., & Kleck, R. E. Effects of the expression of pain on autonomic and pain tolerance responses to subject-controlled pain. *Psychophysiology*, 1977, *14*, 537–540.

Coleman, J. C. *Abnormal psychology and modern life* (5th ed.). Glenview, Ill.: Scott Foresman, 1976.

Coleman, J. C., Butcher, J. N., & Carson, R. C. *Abnormal psychology and modern life* (6th ed.). Glenview, Ill.: Scott Foresman, 1980.

Coleman, J. S., Campbell, E. Q., Hobson, C. J., McPartland, J., Mood, A. M., Weinfeld, F. D., & York, R. L. *Equality of educational opportunity.* Report from Office of Education. Washington, D.C.: U.S. Government Printing Office, 1966.

Corkin, S. A prospective study of cingulotomy. In E. S. Valenstein (Ed.), *The psychosurgery debate.* San Francisco: W. H. Freeman, 1980.

Costello, C. G. Electroconvulsive therapy: Is further investigation necessary? *Canadian Psychiatric Association Journal*, 1976, *21*, 61–67.

Cousins, N. *Anatomy of an illness as perceived by the patient.* New York: Norton, 1979.

Crash trauma. *Time*, January 8, 1979, p. 61.

Craske, B. Perception of impossible limb positions induced by tendon vibration. *Science*, 1977, *196*, 71–73.

Crowder, R. F. *Principles of learning and memory.* Hillsdale, N.J.: Erlbaum, 1976.

Curran, J. P., & Lippold, S. The effects of physical attractiveness and attitude similarity on attraction in dating dyads. *Journal of Personality*, 1975, *43*, 528–539.

Cutting, J. E., Proffitt, D. R., & Kozlowski, L. T. A biomechanical invariant for gait perception. *Journal of Experimental Psychology: Human Perception & Performance*, 1978, *4*, 357–372.

Cutting, J. E., & Kozlowski, L. T. Recognizing friends by their walk: Gait perception without familiarity cues. *Bulletin of the Psychonomic Society*, 1977, *9*(5), 353–356.

Cynader, M., & Regan, D. Neurones in cat parastriate cortex sensitive to the direction of motion in three-dimensional space. *Journal of Physiology*, 1978, *274*, 549–569.

Darwin, C. *The expression of the emotions in man and animals.* Chicago: University of Chicago Press, 1967 (Originally published, 1872.)

Davidson, A. D. Coping with stress reactions in rescue workers: A program that worked. *Police Stress*, Spring 1979.

Davis, D. J., Cahan, S., & Bashi, J. Birth order and intellectual development: The confluence model in the light of cross-cultural evidence. *Science*, 1977, *196*, 1470–1472.

Davis, E. A. *The development of linguistic skills in twins, single twins with siblings, and only children from age 5 to 10 years.* Minneapolis: University of Minnesota Press, Institute of Child Welfare Series, No. 14, 1937.

Davison, G. C., & Neale, J. M. *Abnormal psychology* (2nd ed.). New York: Wiley, 1978.

Davitz, J. R. *The language of emotion.* New York: Academic Press, 1969.

Davson, H. (Ed). *The Eye (Vol. 2A): Visual function in man.* New York: Academic Press, 1976.

De Valois, R. L., & De Valois, K. K. Spatial vision. In M. R. Rosenzweig & L. W. Porter (Eds.), *Annual review of psychology.* Palo Alto, Calif.: Annual Reviews, 1980.

de Weid, D., van Wimersma Greidanus, T. B., Bohus, B., Urban, I., & Gispen, W. H. Vasopressin and memory consolidation. *Progress in Brain Research*, 1976, *45*, 181.

deCharms, R. *Personal causation.* New York: Academic Press, 1968.

deCharms, R., & Muir, M. S. Motivation: Social approaches. In M. R. Rosenzweig & L. W. Porter (Eds.), *Annual review of psychology.* Palo Alto, Calif.: Annual Reviews, 1978.

DeJong, W. An examination of self-perception mediation of the foot-in-the-door effect. *Journal of Personality and Social Psychology*, 1979, *37*, 2221–2239.

DeJong, W., & Musilli, L. *Handicapped versus nonhandicapped requestors: The effect of pressure to comply with an initial request on the foot-in-the-door phenomenon.* Paper presented at the Meeting of the Eastern Psychological Association, Washington, D.C., March 1978.

Dembo, R., Schmeidler, J., Babst, D. V., & Lipton, D. S. Drug information source credibility among junior and senior high school youths. *American Journal of Drug & Alcohol Abuse*, 1977, *4*, 43–54.

Dement, W. C. The effect of dream deprivation. *Science*, 1960, *131*, 1705–1707; *132*, 1420–1422.

Denber, H. C. B. Tranquilizers in psychiatry. In A. M. Freedman and H. I. Kaplan (Eds.), *Psychiatry.* Baltimore: Williams & Wilkins, 1967.

Dennis, W. *Children of the creche.* New York: Appleton-Century-Crofts, 1973.

Dennis, W., & Dennis, M. G. The effects of cradling practices upon the onset of walking in Hopi children. *Journal of Genetic Psychology*, 1940, *56*, 77–86.

DePaulo, B. M., Rosenthal, R., Eisenstat, R. A., Finkelstein, S., & Rogers, P. L. Decoding discrepant nonverbal cues. *Journal of Personality and Social Psychology*, 1978, *36*, 313–323.

DePiano, F. A., & Salzberg, H. C. Clinical applications of hypnosis to three psychosomatic disorders. *Psychological Bulletin*, 1979, *86*, 1223–1235.

Deregowski, J. B. Pictorial perception and culture. *Scientific American*, 1972, *227*(5), 82–88.

Dermer, M., & Thiel, D. L. When beauty may fail. *Journal of Personality and Social Psychology*, 1975, *31*, 1168–1176.

Derogatis, L. R., Yevzeroff, H., & Wittelsberger, B. Social class, psychological disorder, and the nature ot the psychopathologic indicator. *Journal of Consulting & Clinical Psychology*, 1975, *43*, 183–191.

Dershowitz, A. Abolishing the insanity defense: The most significant feature of the administration's proposed criminal code. *Criminal Law Bulletin*, 1973, *9*, 435.

Deutsch, M., & Krauss, R. M. The effect of threat upon interpersonal bargaining. *Journal of Abnormal and Social Psychology*, 1960, *61*, 181–189.

deVilliers, J. G., & deVilliers, P. A. A cross-sectional study of the acquisition of grammatical morphemes in child speech. *Journal of Psycholinguistic Research*, 1973, *2*, 267–278.

Dewey, J. *How we think.* Boston: D. C. Heath, 1910.

Diamond, B. Interview regarding Sirhan Sirhan. *Psychology Today*, September 1969, pp. 48–55.

Diamond, M. C., Johnson, R. E., & Ehlert, J. Comparison of cortical thickness in male and female rats: Normal and gonadectomized, young and adult. *Behavioral and Neural Biology*, 1979, *26*, 485–491.

Dichgans, J., & Brandt, T. Visual-vestibular interaction: Effects on self-motion perception and posture control. In R. Held, H. W. Leibowitz, & H. L. Teuber, *Handbook of sensory physiology*. Berlin: Springer, 1978, pp. 755–804.

Diener, E. Deindividuation: The absence of self-awareness and self-regulation in group members. In P. B. Paulus (Ed.), *The psychology of group influence*. Hillsdale, N.J.: Erlbaum, 1980.

Dimond, S. J., Farrington, L., & Johnson, P. Differing emotional response from right and left hemispheres. *Nature*, 1976, *261*, 690–692.

Dion, K. K. The incentive value of physical attractiveness for young children. *Personality & Social Psychology Bulletin*, 1977, *3*, 67–70.

Dion, K. K. & Stein, S. Physical attractiveness and interpersonal influence. *Journal of Experimental Social Psychology*, 1978, *14*, 97–108.

Dole, V. P., & Nyswander, M. The miracle of methadone in the narcotics jungle. *Roche Report*, 1967, *4*, 1–2; 8; 11.

Dollard, J., Doob, L. W., Miller, N. E., Mowrer, O. H., & Sears, R. R. *Frustration and aggression*. New Haven, Conn.: Yale University Press, 1939.

Dollard, J., & Miller, N. E. *Personality and psychotherapy: An analysis in terms of learning, thinking and culture*. New York: McGraw-Hill, 1950.

Doty, R. L., Ford, M., Preti, G., & Huggins, G. R. Changes in the intensity and pleasantness of human vaginal odors during the menstrual cycle. *Science*, 1975, *190*, 1316–1318.

Douvan, E., & Adelson, J. *The adolescent experience*. New York: Wiley, 1966.

Drachman, D., DeCarufel, A., & Insko, C. A. The extra credit effect in interpersonal attraction. *Journal of Experimental Social Psychology*, 1978, *14*, 458–465.

The dream machine. *Discover*, March 1981, p. 56.

Drunk walking. *Science News*, December 10, 1977, p. 393.

Duberman, L. *Marriage and its alternatives*. New York: Praeger, 1974.

Duncker, K. On problem-solving. *Psychological Monographs*, 1945, *58*, No. 270.

Durham v. United States. *Federal 2nd*, 1954, *214*, 862.

Dweck, C. S., & Reppucci, N. D. Learned helplessness and reinforcement responsibility in children. *Journal of Personality and Social Psychology*, 1973, *25*, 109–116.

Eagly, A. H., & Himmelfarb, S. Attitudes and opinions. In M. R. Rosenzweig & L. W. Porter (Eds.), *Annual review of psychology*. Palo Alto, Calif.: Annual Reviews, 1978.

Ebbesen, E. B., Kjos, G. L., & Konecni, V. J. Spatial ecology: Its effects on the choice of friends and enemies. *Journal of Experimental Social Psychology*, 1976, *12*, 505–518.

Ebbinghaus, H. *Memory: A contribution to experimental psychology*. (translated by H. A. Ruger and C. E. Bussenues, 1913). New York: Teachers College, Columbia University, 1885.

Edwards, A. L. Social desirability or acquiescence in the MMPI? A case study with the SD scale. *Journal of Abnormal and Social Psychology*, 1961, *63*, 351–359.

Ehrhardt, A. A. Maternalism in fetal hormonal and related syndromes. In J. Zubin & J. Money (Eds.), *Contemporary sexual behavior*. Baltimore: Johns Hopkins Press, 1973.

Eibl-Eibesfeldt, I. Similarities and differences between cultures in expressive movements. In R. A. Hinde (Ed.), *Nonverbal communication*. Cambridge, England: Cambridge University Press, 1972.

Eisen, S. V. Actor-observer differences in information inferences and causal attribution. *Journal of Personality and Social Psychology*, 1979, *37*, 261–272.

Eisenberger, R., Park, D. C., & Frank, M. Learned industriousness and social reinforcement. *Journal of Personality and Social Psychology*, 1976, *33*, 227–232.

Eiser, J. R., & Pancer, S. M. Attitudinal effects of the use of evaluative biased language. *European Journal of Social Psychology*, 1979, *9*, 39–47.

Eiser, J. R., & Ross, M. Partisan language, immediacy, and attitude change. *European Journal of Social Psychology*, 1977, *7*, 477–489.

Ekman, P. Cross cultural studies of facial expression. In P. Ekman (Ed.), *Darwin and facial expression*. New York: Academic Press, 1973.

Ekman, P., & Friesen, W. V. Detecting deception from the body or face. *Journal of Personality and Social Psychology*, 1974, *29*, 288–298.

Ekman, P., & Oster, H. Facial expressions of emotion. In M. R. Rozenzweig & L. W. Porter (Eds.), *Annual review of psychology* (Vol. 30). Palo Alto, Calif.: Annual Reviews, 1979.

Ekman, P., Sorenson, E. R., & Friesen, W. V. Pan-cultural elements in facial displays of emotion. *Science*, 1969, *164*, 86–88.

Elkind, D. *A sympathetic understanding of the child six to sixteen*. Boston: Allyn and Bacon, 1971.

Ellis, A. *Reason and emotion in psychotherapy*. New York: Lyle Stuart, 1962.

Ellison, G. D. Animal models of psychopathology: The low-norepinephrine and low-serotonin rat. *American Psychologist*, 1977, *32*, 1036–1045.

Emmerich, W., & Goldman, K. S. Boy-girl identity task (technical report). In V. Shipman (Ed.), *Disadvantaged children and their first school experiences* (Technical Report PR-72-20). Educational Testing Service, 1972.

Endler, N. S., & Magnusson, D. Toward an interactional psychology of personality. *Psychological Bulletin*, 1976, *83*, 956–974.

Endler, N. S., Rushton, J. P., & Roediger, H. L. Productivity and scholarly impact (citation of British, Canadian, and U.S. departments of psychology, 1975). *American Psychologist*, 1978, *33*, 1064–1082.

English, H. B. Three cases of the "conditioned fear response." *Journal of Abnormal and Social Psychology*, 1929, *24*, 221–225.

Enroth-Cugell, C., & Robinson, J. G. The contrast sensitivity of retinal ganglion cells of the cat. *Journal of Physiology*, 1966, *187*, 517–552.

Epstein, S., & Fenz, W. D. Steepness of approach and avoidance gradients in humans as a function of experience. *Journal of Experimental Psychology*, 1965, *70*, 1–12.

Eron, L. D. Prescription for reduction of aggression. *American Psychologist*, 1980, *35*, 244–252.

Erwin, E. Psychoanalytic therapy. *American Psychologist*, 1980. *35*, 435–443.

Eysenck, H. J. The effects of psychotherapy: An evaluation. *Journal of Consulting Psychology*, 1952, *16*, 319–324.

Fahlman, S. E. *NETL: A system for representing and using real-world knowledge*. Cambridge, Mass.: M.I.T. Press, 1979.

Fain, G. L., Gold, G. H., & Dowling, J. E. Receptor coupling in the toad retina. *Cold Spring Harbor Symposium Quant. Biology*, 1976, *60*, 547–561.

Fairchild, L., & Erwin, W. M. Physical punishment by parent figures as a model of aggressive behavior in children. *Journal of Genetic Psychology*, 1977, *130*, 279–284.

Farkas, G. M. An ontological analysis of behavior therapy. *American Psychologist*, 1980, *35*, 364–374.

Faust, I. M., Johnson, P. R., & Hirsch, J. Adipose tissue regeneration following lipectomy, *Science,* 1977, *197,* 391–393.

Favreau, O. E., & Corballis, M. C. Negative aftereffects in visual perception. *Scientific American,* 1976, *235*(6), 42–48.

Fazio, R. H. Motives for social comparison: The construction-validation distinction. *Journal of Personality and Social Psychology,* 1979, *37,* 1683–1698.

Fehr, L. A. J. Piaget and S. Claus: Psychology makes strange bedfellows. *Psychological Reports,* 1976, *39,* 740–742.

Feingold, B. F. *Why your child is hyperactive.* New York: Random House, 1974.

Feiring, C., & Lewis, M. The child as a member of the family system. *Behavioral Science,* 1978, *23,* 225–233.

Feldman, D. H., & Bratton, J. C. Relativity and giftedness: Implications for equality of educational opportunity. *Exceptional Children,* 1972, *38,* 491–492.

Feldman, S. S., & Ingham, M. E. Attachment behavior: A validation study in two age groups. *Child Development,* 1975, *46,* 319–330.

Ferster, C. B., & Skinner, B. F. *Schedules of reinforcement.* New York: Appleton-Century-Crofts, 1957.

Festinger, L., & Carlsmith, J. M. Cognitive consequences of forced compliance. *Journal of Abnormal and Social Psychology,* 1959, *58,* 203–210.

Field, J. Coordination of vision and prehension in young infants. *Child Development,* 1977, *48,* 97–103.

Fincher, J. *The brain.* Washington, D.C.: U.S. News Books, 1981.

Finkelstein, N. W., & Ramey, C. T. Learning to control the environment in infancy. *Child Development,* 1977, *48,* 806–819.

Finney, J. C., Brandsma, J. M., Tondow, M., & LeMaistre, G. A study of transsexuals seeking gender reassignment. *American Journal of Psychiatry,* 1975, *132,* 962–964.

Fitzgerald, B. A., & Wells, C. E. Hallucinations as a conversion reaction. *Diseases of the Nervous System,* 1977, *38,* 381–383.

Fitzsimons, J. T. Some historical perspectives in the physiology of thirst. In A. N. Epstein, H. R. Kissileff, & E. Stellar (Eds.), *The neuropsychology of thirst.* Washington D.C.: V. H. Winston, 1973.

Fletcher, J. Attitudes toward defective newborns. *Hastings Center Studies,* 1974, *2,* 21–31.

Foster, G., & Ysseldyke, J. Expectancy and halo effects as a result of artificially induced teacher bias. *Contemporary Educational Psychology,* 1976, *1,* 37–45.

Foucault, M. *Madness and civilization: A history of insanity in the age of reason.* New York: Pantheon, 1965.

Foulkes, D., & Fleisher, S. Mental activity in relaxed wakefulness. *Journal of Abnormal Psychology,* 1975, *84,* 66–75.

Franklin, D. Word windows on personality. *Science News,* October 10, 1981, pp. 235–237.

Freedman, J. L., & Fraser, S. C. Compliance without pressure: The foot-in-the-door technique. *Journal of Personality and Social Psychology,* 1966, *4,* 195–202.

Fredericksen, C. H. Representing logical and semantic structure of knowledge acquired from discourse. *Cognitive Psychology,* 1975, *7,* 371–458.

Freud, S. *Ueber coca.* Vienna: Moritz Perles, 1885. (Translation in Freud, 1974).

Freud, S. The interpretation of dreams. In J. Strachey (Ed.), *The standard edition of the complete psychological works* (vols. 4 and 5). London: Hogarth Press, 1953. (Originally published, 1900).

Freud, S. Three essays on sexuality. In J. Strachey (Ed.), *The standard edition of the complete psychological works* (Vol. 7). London: Hogarth Press, 1953. (Originally published, 1905).

Freud, S. Introductory lectures on psycho-analysis. In J. Strachey (Ed.), *The standard edition of the complete psychological works*

(vols. 15 and 16). London: Hogarth Press, 1963. (Originally published, 1917).

Freud, S. An outline of psychoanalysis. In J. Strachey (Ed.), *The standard edition of the complete psychological works* (vol. 23). London: Hogarth Press, 1964 (Originally published, 1940).

Friedman, M. I., & Stricker, E. M. The physiological psychology of hunger: A physiological perspective. *Psychological Review,* 1976, *83,* 409–431.

Fries, M. E. Some hypotheses on the role of the congenital activity type in personality development. *International Journal of Psychoanalysis,* 1954, *35,* 206–207.

Frisby, J. P. *Seeing.* Oxford, England: Oxford University Press, 1980.

Fromm, E. Age regression with unexpected reappearance of a repressed childhood language. *International Journal of Clinical and Experimental Hypnosis,* 1970, *18,* 79–88.

Furst, B. *Stop forgetting.* Garden City, N.Y.: Garden City Books, 1948.

Gaes, G. G., Kalle, R. J., & Tedeschi, J. T. Impression management in the forced compliance situation. *Journal of Experimental Social Psychology,* 1978, *14,* 493–510.

Galin, D., Diamond, R., & Braff, D. Lateralization of conversion symptoms: More frequent on the left. *American Journal of Psychiatry,* 1977, *134,* 578–580.

Gallup, G. The growing acceptance of racial integration. *San Francisco Chronicle,* October 13, 1975.

Galvan, R. M., Leo, J., & McIntosh, G. Why you do what you do. *Time,* August 1, 1977, pp. 54–63.

Garber, H., & Heber, R. The Milwaukee project: Early intervention as a technique to prevent mental retardation. University of Connecticut Technical Paper, March 1973.

Garcia, J., & Koelling, R. A. Relation of cue to consequence in avoidance learning. *Psychonomic Science,* 1966, *4,* 123–124.

Gardner, R. A., & Gardner, B. T. Teaching sign language to a chimpanzee. *Science,* 1969, *165,* 664–672.

Gatchel, R. J., & Proctor, J. D. Effectiveness of voluntary heart rate control in reducing speech anxiety. *Journal of Consulting and Clinical Psychology,* 1976, *44,* 381–389.

Gazzaniga, M. S. *The bisected brain.* New York: Academic Press, 1970.

Geldard, F. A. Adventures in tactile literacy. *American Psychologist,* 1957, *12,* 115–124.

Genetic basis for narcolepsy. *Science News,* February 11, 1978, p. 86.

'Genetic depression' and 'viral schizophrenia.' *Science News,* October 7, 1978, p. 244.

Genshaft, J. L., & Hirt, M. L. The effectiveness of self-instructional training to enhance math achievement in women. *Cognitive Therapy & Research,* 1980, *4,* 91–97.

Gerner, R. H., Catlin, D. H., Gorelick, D. A., Hui, K. K., & Li, C. H. Beta-endorphin intravenous infusion causes behavioral change in psychiatric inpatients. *Archives of General Psychiatry,* 1980, *37,* 642–647.

Geschwind, N. Specializations of the human brain. *Scientific American,* 1979, *241*(3), 180–199.

Gewirtz, J. L., & Boyd, E. F. Experiments on mother-infant interaction underlying mutual attachment acquisition: The infant conditions the mother. In T. Alloway, L. Krames, & P. Pliner (Eds.), *Attachment behavior: Advances in the study of communication and affect.* New York: Plenum, 1976.

Gibbons, F. X., Carver, C. S., Scheier, M. F., & Hormuth, S. E. Self-focused attention and the placebo effect: Fooling some of the people some of the time. *Journal of Experimental Social Psychology,* 1979, *15,* 263–274.

Gibson, E. J., & Walk, R. D. The "visual cliff." *Scientific American*, 1960, *202*(4), 64–71.

Gibson, J. J. *The perception of the visual world.* Boston: Houghton Mifflin, 1950.

Gibson, J. J. *The ecological approach to visual perception.* Boston: Houghton Mifflin, 1979.

Gillam, B. Geometrical illusions, *Scientific American*, 1980, *242*(1), 102–111.

Gillin, J. Magical fright. *Psychiatry*, 1948, *11*, 387–400.

Glenberg, A. M. Monotonic and nonmonotonic lag effects in paired-associate and recognition memory paradigms. *Journal of Verbal Learning and Verbal Behavior*, 1976, *15*, 1–16.

Glick, I. O., Weiss, R. S., & Parkes, C. M. *The first year of bereavement.* New York: Wiley-Interscience, 1974.

Glick, P. C., & Norton, A. J. Marrying, divorcing and living together in the U.S. today. *Population Bulletin*, 1977, *32*(5), 3–39.

Glickstein, M., & Gibson, A. R. Visual cells in the pons of the brain. *Scientific American*, 1976, *235*(5), 90–98.

Glucksberg, S., & Danks, J. H. Effects of discriminative labels and nonsense labels upon availability of novel function. *Journal of Verbal Learning and Verbal Behavior*, 1968, *7*, 72–76.

Goddard, H. H. Mental tests and the immigrant. *Journal of Delinquency*, 1917, *2*, 243–277.

Godden, D. R., & Baddeley, A. D. Context-dependent memory in two natural environments: On land and underwater. *British Journal of Psychology*, 1975, *66*, 325–331.

Gold, M. S. Lofexidine: Son of clonidine. *Science News*, May 23, 1981, p. 328.

Goldberg, L. W. Differential attribution of trait-descriptive terms to oneself as compared to well-liked, neutral, and disliked others: A psychometric analysis. *Journal of Personality and Social Psychology*, 1978, *36*, 1012–1028.

Goldberg, L. R., & Werts, C. E. The reliability of clinicians' judgments: A multitrait-multimethod approach. *Journal of Consulting Psychology*, 1966, *30*, 199–206.

Golden, M. Some effects of combining psychological tests on clinical inferences. *Journal of Consulting Psychology*, 1964, *28*, 440–446.

Goldin-Meadow, S., & Feldman, H. The development of language-like communication without a language model. *Science*, 1977, *197*, 401–403.

Goldman, W., & Lewis, P. Beautiful is good: Evidence that the physically attractive are more socially skillful. *Journal of Experimental Social Psychology*, 1977, *13*, 125–130.

Goldstein, A., Tachiban, S., Lowney, L. I., Hunkapil, M., & Hood, L. Dynorphin-(1-13), an extremely potent opioid peptide. *Proceedings of the National Academy of Sciences*, 1979, *76*, 6666–6670.

Goleman, D. 1,528 little geniuses and how they grew. *Psychology Today*, February 1980, pp. 28–53.

Gollob, H. F., & Dittes, J. E. Effects of manipulated self-esteem on persuasibility depending on threat and complexity of communication. *Journal of Personality and Social Psychology*, 1965, *2*, 195–201.

Gomes-Schwartz, B. *Effective ingredients in psychotherapy: The roles of exploratory processes, therapist-offered relationship and patient involvement.* PhD. thesis, Nashville, Tenn.: Vanderbilt University, 1976.

Gomes-Schwartz, B., Hadley, S. W., & Strupp, H. H. Individual psychotherapy and behavior therapy. In M. R. Rosenzweig & L. W. Porter (Eds.), *Annual review of psychology.* Palo Alto, California: Annual Reviews, Inc., 1978.

Goodwin, F. K. Human aggression linked to chemical balance. *Science News*, June 3, 1978, p. 356.

Gordon, J. H., & Gorski. R. A. Sexual differentiation of the brain—

Implications for neuroscience. In D. M. Schneider (Ed.), *Reviews of Neuroscience* (vol. 4). New York: Raven Press, 1979.

Got Problems? Listen to Your Heart. *Science News*, June 24, 1978, p. 402.

Gottesman, I. I., & Shields, J. *Schizophrenia and genetics.* New York: Academic Press, 1972.

Gould, L. C., Berberian, R. M., Kasl, S. V., Thompson, W. D., & Kleber, H. D. Sequential patterns of multiple-drug use among high school students. *Archives of General Psychiatry*, 1977, *34*, 216–222.

Graham, P., Rutter, M., & George, S. Temperamental characteristics as predictors of behavior disorders in children. *American Journal of Orthopsychiatry*, 1973, *43*, 328–339.

Greden, J. F., Fontaine, P., Lubetsky, M., & Chamberlin, K. Anxiety and depression associated with caffeinism among psychiatric patients. *American Journal of Psychiatry*, 1978, *135*, 963–966.

Green, R. *Sexual identity conflict in children and adults.* New York: Basic Books, 1974.

Green, R. Atypical sex role behavior during childhood. In B. J. Sadock, H. I. Kaplan, & A. M. Freedman (Eds.), *The sexual experience.* Baltimore: Williams & Wilkins, 1976, pp. 196–205.

Green, R. Sexual identity of 37 children raised by homosexual or transsexual parents. *The American Journal of Psychiatry*, 1978, *135*, 692–697.

Green, R., & Money, J. (Eds.). *Transsexualism and sex reassignment.* Baltimore: Johns Hopkins Press, 1969.

Green, R., & Stoller, R. J. Two monozygotic (identical) twin pairs discordant for gender identity. *Archives of Sexual Behavior*, 1971, *1*, 321–327.

Greenberg, Jerald. Group vs. individual equity judgments: Is there a polarization effect? *Journal of Experimental Social Psychology*, 1979, *15*, 504–512.

Greenberg, J. The brain and emotions. *Science News*, July 30, 1977, pp. 74–75.

Greenberg, J. Psychosurgery at the crossroads. *Science News*, May 14, 1977, pp. 314–315; 317.

Greenberg, J. Adulthood comes of age. *Science News*, July 29, 1978, pp. 74–79.

Greenberg, J. Blind drawings: A new perspective. *Science News*, November 11, 1978, pp. 332–333.

Greenberg, J. Cracking the cycles of depression and mania. *Science News*, November 25, 1978, p. 367.

Greenberg, J. The whos and hows of drug deaths. *Science News*, May 27, 1978, p. 344.

Greenberg, J. Ape talk: More than "Pigeon" English? *Science News*, May 10, 1980, pp. 298–300.

Greenberg, J. Inheriting mental illness: Nature & nurture. *Science News*, January 5, 1980, pp. 10–12.

Greenberg, J. Stressing the immune system. *Science News*, May 24, 1980, p. 335.

Greenberg, J. Underestimating tardive dyskinesia. *Science News*, May 24, 1980, p. 335.

Greenberg, J. An interview with David Rosenhan. *APA Monitor*, June/July 1981, pp. 4–5.

Greenberg, R., & Pearlman, C. Delirium tremens and dreaming. *American Journal of Psychiatry*, 1967, *124*, 133–142.

Greenberg, R., & Pearlman, C. Cutting the REM nerve: An approach to the adaptive role of REM sleep. *Perspectives in Biology and Medicine*, 1974, *17*, 513–521.

Greene, D., Sternberg, B., & Lepper, M. R. Overjustification in a token economy. *Journal of Personality and Social Psychology*, 1976, *34*, 1219–1234.

Gregory, R. L. *The intelligent eye.* New York: McGraw-Hill, 1970.

Grey, A., & Kalsched, D. Oedipus east and west: An exploration via manifest dream content. *Journal of Cross-Cultural Psychology*, 1971, 2, 337–352.

Griffin, G. A., & Harlow, H. F. Effects of three months of total social deprivation on social adjustment and learning in the rhesus monkey. *Child Development*, 1966, 37, 533–547.

Grissom, R. J., Suedfeld, P., & Vernon, J. Memory for verbal material: Effects of sensory deprivation. *Science*, 1962, 138, 429–430.

Gross, A. E., & Crofton, C. What is good is beautiful. *Sociometry*, 1977, 40, 85–90.

Grossman, J. J. (Ed.). *Manual on terminology and classification in mental retardation, 1973 revision*. Washington, D.C.: American Association on Mental Deficiency, 1973.

Grossman, S. P. Neurophysiologic aspects: Extrahypothalamic factors in the regulation of food intake. *Advances in Psychosomatic Medicine*, 1972, 7, 49–72.

Grossman, S. P. Role of the hypothalamus in the regulation of food and water intake. *Psychological Review*, 1975, 82, 200–224.

Grotevant, M. D., Scarr, S., & Weinberg, R. A. *Intellectual development in family constellations with adopted and natural children: A test of the Zajonc and Markus model*. Paper presented at the meeting of the Society for Research in Child Development, New Orleans, March 1975.

Gruber, K. A., Whitaker, J. M., & Buckalew, V. M. Endogenous digitalis-like substance in plasma of volume-expanded dogs. *Nature*, 1980, 287, 743–745.

Gruder, C. L., Cook, T. D., Hennigan, K. M., Flay, B. R., Alessis, C., & Halamaj, J. Empirical tests of the absolute sleeper effect predicted from the discounting cue hypothesis. *Journal of Personality and Social Psychology*, 1978, 36, 1061–1074.

Grush, J. E. The impact of candidate expenditures, regionality, and prior outcomes on the 1976 Democratic Presidential primaries. *Journal of Personality and Social Psychology*, 1980, 38, 337–347.

Guidotti, A., Baraldi, M., Schwartz, J. P., Toffano, G., & Costa, E. Molecular mechanism for the action of benzodiazepines on gabaergic transmission. In P. Krogsgaardlarsen, J. Scheelkruger, & H. Kofod (Eds.), *Gaba-neuro-transmitters*. New York: Academic Press, 1979.

Guilford, J. P. Creative abilities in the arts. *Psychological Review*, 1957, 64, 110–118.

Guilford, J. P. *The nature of human intelligence*. New York: McGraw-Hill, 1967.

Gunn, J., & Robertson, G. Psychopathic personality: A conceptual problem. *Psychological Medicine*, 1976, 6, 631–634.

Gur, R. E. Motoric laterality imbalance in schizophrenia. *Archives of General Psychiatry*, 1977, 34, 33–37.

Haber, R. N. Eidetic images. *Scientific American*, 1969, 220(4), 36–44.

Haith, M. M., & Campos, J. J. Human infancy. In M. R. Rosenzweig & L. W. Porter (Eds.), *Annual review of psychology* (Vol. 28). Palo Alto, Calif.: Annual Reviews, 1977, pp. 251–294.

Hall, C. S., & Domhoff, F. A ubiquitous sex difference in dreams. *Journal of Abnormal and Social Psychology*, 1963, 66, 278–280.

Hall, J. A. Gender effects in decoding nonverbal cues. *Psychological Bulletin*, 1978, 85, 845–857.

Hall, R. C. W., Stickney, S. K., LeCann, A. F., & Popkin, M. K. Physical illness manifesting as psychiatric disease. 2. Analysis of a state-hospital inpatient population. *Archives of General Psychiatry*, 1980, 37, 989–995.

Hanratty, M. A. *Imitation of film-mediated aggression against live and inanimate victims*. Unpublished MA thesis, Vanderbilt University, Nashville, Tennessee, 1969.

Hanratty, M. A., O'Neal, E., & Sulzer, J. L. Effect of frustration upon imitation of aggression. *Journal of Personality and Social Psychology*, 1972, 21, 30–34.

Hardin, G. *Nature and man's fate*. New York: Rinehart, 1959.

Hardyck, C., Petrinovich, L. F., & Goldman, R. D. Left-handedness and cognitive deficit. *Cortex*, 1976, 12, 266–279.

Harlow, H. F. Learning and satiation of response in intrinsically motivated complex puzzle performance in monkeys. *Journal of Comparative and Physiological Psychology*, 1950, 43, 289–294.

Harlow, H. F. The nature of love. *American Psychologist*, 1958, 13, 673–685.

Harlow, H. F., & Novak, M. A. Psychopathological perspectives. *Perspectives in Biology and Medicine*, 1973, 16, 461–478.

Harlow, H. F., & Suomi, S. J. The nature of love—simplified. *American Psychologist*, 1970, 25, 161–168.

Harlow, J. M. Recovery from the passage of an iron bar through the head. *Publ. Mass. Med. Soc.*, 1868, 2, 327.

Harmon, L. D., & Julesz, B. Masking in visual recognition: Effects of two-dimensional filtered noise. *Science*, 1973, 180, 1194–1197.

Harper, C. The witches' flying-ointment. *Folklore*. 1977, 88, 105–106.

Harris, B. Whatever happened to little Albert? *American Psychologist*, 1979, 34, 151–160.

Harris, C. Personal communication, November 1981.

Harrow, M., & Quinlan, D. Is disordered thinking unique to schizophrenia? *Archives of General Psychiatry*, 1977, 34, 15–21.

Harrower, M. Were Hitler's henchmen mad? *Psychology Today*, July 1976, pp. 76–80.

Hartley, E. L. *Problems in prejudice*. New York: Kings Crown, 1946.

Hartup, W. W. Peer interaction and social organization. In P. H. Mussen (Ed.), *Carmichael's manual of child psychology*, (Vol. 1 3rd ed.). New York: Wiley, 1970, pp. 361–456.

Hartup, W. W. The social worlds of childhood. *American Psychologist*, 1979, 34, 944–950.

Hathaway, S. R., & McKinley, J. C. A multiphasic personality schedule (Minnesota): I. Construction of the schedule. *Journal of Psychology*, 1940, 10, 249–254.

Havighurst, R. J. *Developmental tasks and education* (3rd ed.). New York: David McKay, 1972.

Havighurst, R. J. Choosing a middle path for the use of drugs with hyperactive children. *School Review*, 1976, 85, 61–77.

Hayashi, S., & Kimura, T. Sexual behavior of the naive male mouse as affected by the presence of a male and a female performing mating behavior. *Physiology & Behavior*, 1976, 17, 807–810.

Hayes, K. J., & Hayes, C. Imitation in a home-raised chimpanzee. *Journal of Comparative and Physiological Psychology*, 1952, 45, 450–459.

Hayflick, L. The cell biology of human aging. *Scientific American*, 1980, 242(1), 58–65.

Heathers, G. Emotional dependence and independence in nursery school play. *Journal of Genetic Psychology*, 1955, 87, 37–57.

Hebb, D. O. *The organization of behavior*. New York: Wiley, 1949.

Hechinger, N. Seeing without eyes. *Science 81*, March 1981, pp. 38–43.

Heider, F. *The psychology of interpersonal relations*. New York: Wiley, 1958.

Heiman, J. R. A psychophysiological exploration of sexual arousal patterns in females and males. *Psychophysiology*, 1977, 14, 266–274.

Heiman, J. R. Continuing revolutions in sex research. In Z. Rubin & E. B. McNeil, *The psychology of being human*. (Brief update edition). New York: Harper & Row, 1979.

Helson, R., & Crutchfield, R. S. Mathematicians: The creative researcher and the average Ph.D. *Journal of Consulting and Clinical Psychology*, 1970, 34, 250–257.

Hess, E. H. Ethology and developmental psychology. In P. H. Mussen (Ed.), *Carmichael's manual of child psychology* (3rd ed. Vol. 1). New York: Wiley, 1970.

Hetherington, E. M. Effects of father absence on personality development in adolescent daughters. *Developmental Psychology*, 1972, *7*, 313–326.

Hetherington, E. M. Divorce: A child's perspective. *American Psychologist*, 1979, *34*, 851–858.

Hetherington, E. M., & Parke, R. D. *Child psychology: A contemporary viewpoint* (2nd ed.). New York: McGraw-Hill, 1979.

Hicks, R. E. & Kinsbourne, M. On the genesis of human handedness: A review. *Journal of Motor Behavior*, 1976, *8*(4), 257–266.

Hilgard, E. R. *Divided consciousness: Multiple controls in human thought and action.* New York: Wiley-Interscience, 1977.

Hilgard, E. R. Consciousness in contemporary psychology. In M. R. Rosenzweig & L. W. Porter (Eds.), *Annual review of psychology.* Palo Alto, Calif.: Annual Reviews, 1980, pp. 1–26.

Hilgard, E. R., Atkinson, R. L., & Atkinson, R. C. *Introduction to psychology* (7th ed.). New York: Harcourt Brace Jovanovich, 1979.

Hilgard, E. R., & Hilgard, J. R. *Hypnosis in the relief of pain.* Los Altos, Calif.: William Kaufmann, 1975.

Hill, C. T., Rubin, Z., & Peplau, L. A. Breakups before marriage: The end of 103 affairs. *Journal of Social Issues.* 1976, *32*(1), 147–168.

Hinde, R. A. *Animal behaviour.* New York: McGraw-Hill, 1966.

Hindley, C. B., Filliozat, A. M., Klackenberg, G., Nicolet-Meister, D., & Sand, E. A. Differences in age of walking for five European longitudinal samples. *Human Biology*, 1966, *38*, 364–379.

Hiroto, D. S., & Seligman, M. E. P. Generality of learned helplessness in man. *Journal of Personality and Social Psychology*, 1975, *31*, 311–327.

Hobson, J. A., & McCarley, R. W. The brain as a dream state generator: An activation-synthesis hypothesis of the dream process. *The American Journal of Psychiatry*, 1977, *134*, 1335–1348.

Hock, E. Working and nonworking mothers with infants: Perceptions of their careers, their infants' needs, and satisfaction with mothering. *Developmental Psychology*, 1978, *14*, 37–43.

Hodgkin, A. L. Recent work on visual mechanisms. *Proc. R. Soc. Lon Ser. A*, 1971, *326*, v–xx.

Hoffman, L. W. Maternal employment: 1979. *American Psychologist*, 1979, *34*, 859–865.

Hoffman, M. L. Development of moral thought, feeling, and behavior. *American Psychologist*, 1979, *34*, 958–966.

Hogan, R. Theoretical egocentrism and the problem of compliance. *American Psychologist*, 1975, *30*, 533–540.

Hollander, E. P., & Julian J. W. Studies in leader legitimacy, influence, and innovation. In L. Berkowitz (Ed.), *Advances in experimental social psychology* (Vol. 5). New York: Academic Press, 1970.

Hollon, S., & Beck, A. T. Psychotherapy and drug therapy: Comparisons and combinations. In S. L. Garfield & A. E. Bergin (Eds.), *Handbook of psychotherapy and behavior change.* New York: Wiley, 1978.

Holmes, T., & Masuda, M. Psychosomatic syndromes. *Psychology Today*, April 1972, pp. 71–72; 106.

Holmes, T. H. & Rahe, R. H. The social readjustment rating scale. *Journal of Psychosomatic Research*, 1967, *11*, 213–218.

Homans, G. C. *Social behavior: Its elementary forms.* New York: Harcourt, Brace & World, 1961.

Hong, L. K. Risky shift and cautious shift: Some direct evidence on the cultural-value theory. *Social Psychology*, 1978, *41*, 342–346.

Hook, S. (Ed.). *Psychoanalysis, scientific method and philosophy.* New York: Grove, 1960.

Hopson, J. L. Scent and human behavior: Olfaction or fiction? *Science News*, April 28, 1979, pp. 282–283.

Horney, K. *New ways in psychoanalysis.* New York: Norton, 1939.

Hosobuchi, Y., Rossier, J., Bloom, F. E., & Guillemin, R. Stimulation of human periaqueductal gray for pain relief increases immunoreactive β-Endorphin in ventricular fluid. *Science*, 1979, *203*, 279–281.

Houston, J. P., Schneider, N. G., & Jarvik, M. E. Effects of smoking on free recall and organization. *American Journal of Psychiatry*, 1978, *135*, 220–222.

Houts, P. S., Miller, R. W., Tokuhata, G. K., & Ham, K. S. Signs of distress near TMI. *Science News*, March 21, 1981, p. 185.

Hoving, K. L., Hamm, N., & Galvin, P. Social influence as a function of stimulus ambiguity at three age levels. *Developmental Psychology*, 1969, *1*, 631–636.

Hovland, C. I., Lumsdaine, A. A., & Sheffield, F. D. *Experiments on mass communication.* Princeton, N.J.: Princeton University Press, 1949.

Hraba, J., & Grant, G. Black is beautiful: A reexamination of racial preference and identification. *Journal of Personality & Social Psychology*, 1970, *16*, 398–402.

Hubel, D. H. The brain. *Scientific American*, 1979, *241*(3), 44–53.

Hull, C. L. *Principles of behavior.* New York: Appleton-Century-Crofts, 1943.

Hunt, D. D., & Hampson, J. L. Follow-up of 17 biologic male transsexuals after sex-reassignment surgery. *The American Journal of Psychiatry*, 1980, *137*, 432–438.

Huxley, A. *The doors of perception.* New York: Harper & Row, 1954.

Hyde, J. S. How large are cognitive gender differences? *American Psychologist*, 1981, *36*, 892–901.

Hyman, H. M. *Political socialization.* New York: Free Press, 1959.

Ickes, W., & Barnes, R. D. Boys and girls together—and alienated: On enacting stereotyped sex roles in mixed-sex dyads. *Journal of Personality and Social Psychology*, 1978, *36*, 669–683.

Imperato-McGinley, J., Peterson, R. E., Stoller, R., & Goodwin, W. E. Male pseudohermaphroditism secondary to 17 beta-hydroxysteroid dehydrogenase-deficiency: Gender role change with puberty. *Journal of Clinical Endocrinology and Metabolism*, 1979, *49*, 391–395.

The IQ myth. CBS News, 1975.

Isen, A. M., & Levin, P. F. The effect of feeling good on helping: Cookies and kindness. *Journal of Personality and Social Psychology*, 1972, *21*, 384–388.

Iversen, L. L. The chemistry of the brain. *Scientific American*, 1979, *241*(3), 134–149.

Izard, C. *The face of emotion.* New York: Appleton Century Crofts, 1971.

Jackson, D. N., & Paunonen, S. V. Personality structure and assessment. In M. R. Rosenzweig & L. W. Porter (Eds.), *Annual review of psychology.* Palo Alto, Calif.: Annual Reviews, 1980.

Jackson, P. W. & Messick, D. Creativity. In P. London & D. Rosenhan (Eds.), *Foundations of abnormal psychology.* New York: Holt, Rinehart, & Winston, 1968, pp. 226–250.

Jacobs, J. *Adolescent suicide.* New York: Wiley, 1971.

Jacobson, E. I was there. *APA Monitor*, September/October, 1979, p. 13.

Jaffe, C. M. First-degree atrioventricular block during lithium carbonate treatment. *American Journal of Psychiatry*, 1977, *134*, 88–89.

James, W. *The principles of psychology.* New York: Henry Holt and Company, 1890.

Janis, I. L., & Feshbach, S. Effects of fear-arousing communications. *Journal of Abnormal and Social Psychology,* 1953, *48,* 78–92.

Janis, I. L., & King, B. T. The influence of role playing on opinion change. *Journal of Abnormal and Social Psychology,* 1954, *49,* 211–218.

Jellinek, E. M. Phases of alchohol addiction. In G. D. Shean (Ed.), *Studies in abnormal behavior.* Chicago: Rand McNally, 1971.

Jenkins, J. G., & Dallenbach, K. M. Obliviscence during sleep and waking. *American Journal of Psychology,* 1924, *35,* 605–612.

Jensen, A. R. How much can we boost IQ and scholastic achievement? *Harvard Educational Review,* 1969, *39,* 1–123.

Jespersen, O. *Language: Its nature, development, and origin.* London: Allen & Unwin, 1922.

Johansson, G. On theories for visual space perception. *Scandinavian Journal of Psychology,* 1970, *11,* 67–79.

Johansson, G. Visual perception of biological motion and a model for its analysis. *Perception & Psychophysics,* 1973, *14,* 201–211.

Johansson, G. Spatio-temporal differentiation and integration in visual motion perception. *Psychological Research,* 1976, *38,* 379–393.

Johansson, G., von Hofsten, C., & Jansson, G. Event perception. In M. R. Rosenzweig & L. W. Porter (Eds.), *Annual review of psychology.* Palo Alto, Calif.: Annual Reviews, 1980, pp. 27–63.

John, E. R. *Mechanisms of memory.* New York: Academic Press, 1967.

Johnson, L. C., & MacLeod, W. L. Sleep and wake behavior during gradual sleep reduction. *Perceptual & Motor Skills,* 1973, *36,* 87–97.

Johnson, L. C., & Naitoh, P. The operational consequences of sleep deprivation and sleep deficit. *Agardograph,* 1974, *AGARD-AG-193.*

Johnson, O., & Kozma, A. Effects of concurrent verbal and musical tasks on a unimanual skill. *Cortex,* 1977, *13,* 11–16.

Johnson, R. C., & Medinnus, G. R. *Child psychology: Behavior and development* (2nd Ed.). New York: Wiley, 1969.

Jonakait, G. M., Bohn, M. C., & Black, I. B. Maternal glucocorticoid hormones influence neurotransmitter phenotypic expression in embryos. *Science,* 1980, *210,* 551–553.

Jones, E. E., Bell, L., & Aronson, E. The reciprocation of attraction from similar and dissimilar others. In C. McClintock (Ed.), *Experimental social psychology.* New York: Holt, Rinehart & Winston, 1972.

Jones, E. E., & Sigall, H. The bogus pipeline: A new paradigm for measuring affect and attitude. *Psychological Bulletin,* 1971, *76,* 349–364.

Jones, H. S., & Oswald, I. Two cases of healthy insomnia. *Electroencephalography & Clinical Neurophysiology,* 1968, *24,* 378–380.

Jones, R. The third wave. In A. Pines & C. Maslach (Eds.), *Experiencing social psychology.* New York, Knopf, 1978.

Jones, W. H., Chernovetz, M. E. O., & Hansson, R. O. The enigma of androgyny: Differential implications for males and females? *Journal of Consulting and Clinical Psychology,* 1978, *46,* 298–313.

Jordan, H. A. Physiological control of food intake in man. In G. A. Bray et al. (Eds.), *Obesity in perspective* (Vol. 2, DHEW Publication No. NIH 75–708). Washington, D.C.: U.S. Government Printing Office, 1975.

Jourard, S. M. Experimenter-subject dialogue: A paradigm for a humanistic science of psychology. In J. Bugental (Ed.), *Challenges of humanistic psychology.* New York: McGraw-Hill, 1967.

Jung, C. G. *Psychological types.* New York: Harcourt, Brace, & World, 1933.

Jung, C. G. The concept of the collective unconscious. In *Collected works* (vol. 9, Part I). Princeton: Princeton University Press, 1959 (Originally published in 1936).

Jung, C. G. Mandalas. In *Collected works* (Vol. 14). Princeton: Princeton University Press, 1959 (Originally published in 1955).

Kagan, J. Reflection-impulsivity: The generality and dynamics of conceptual tempo. *Journal of Abnormal Psychology,* 1966, *71,* 17–24.

Kagan, J. What is intelligence? *Social Policy,* 1973, *4*(1), 88–94.

Kagan, J. Sexuality: The Human Heritage. PBS: The Thin Edge Series (videotape), 1974.

Kagan, J., & Klein, R. E. Cross-cultural perspectives on early development. *American Psychologist,* 1973, *28,* 947–961.

Kagan, S., & Madsen, M. C. Cooperation and competition of Mexican, Mexican-American, and Anglo-American children of two ages and four instructional sets. *Developmental Psychology,* 1971, *5,* 32–39.

Kales, A., Caldwell, A. B., Preston, T. A., Healey, S., & Kales, J. D. Personality patterns in insomnia: Theoretical implications. *Archives of General Psychiatry,* 1976, *33,* 1128–1134.

Kales, A., Tan, T. L., Kollar, E. J., Naitoh, P., Preston, T. A., & Malmstrom, E. J. Sleep patterns following 205 hr of sleep deprivation. *Psychosomatic Medicine,* 1970, *32,* 189–200.

Kamin, L. J. *The science and politics of IQ.* Potomac, MD.: Erlbaum, 1974.

Kandel, E. R. Small systems of neurons. *Scientific American,* 1979, *241*(3), 66–84.

Kaplan, M. F., & Schwartz, S. (Eds.), *Judgment and decision processes in applied settings.* New York: Academic Press, 1977.

Katchadourian, H. *Human sexuality.* New York: W. W. Norton & Co., 1978.

Kaufman, L., & Rock. I. The moon illusion, I. *Science,* 1962, *136,* 953–961.

Keller, H., Montgomery, B., Moss, J., Sharp, J., & Wheeler, J. *Differential parental effects among one-year-old infants in a stranger and separation situation.* Paper presented at the meeting of the Society for Research in Child Development, Denver, 1975.

Kelly. T. J., Bullock, L. M., & Dykes, M. K. Behavior disorders: Teachers' perceptions. *Exceptional Children,* 1977, *43,* 316–318.

Kennedy, W. A. A follow-up normative study of Negro intelligence and achievement. *Monographs of the Society for Research in Child Development,* 1969, *34* (2, Serial No. 126).

Kerckhoff, A. C., & Davis, K. E. Value consensus and need complementarity in mate selection. *American Sociological Review,* 1962, *27,* 295–303.

Kety, S. S., Rosenthal, D., Wender, P. H. Schulsinger, F., & Jacobsen, B. The biologic and adoptive families of adopted individuals who become schizophrenic: Prevalence of mental illness and other characterisics. In L. C. Wynne, R. L. Cromwell, & S. Matthysse (Eds.), *The nature of schizophrenia: New approaches to research and treatment.* New York: Wiley, 1978.

Kiesler, S., & Baral, R. The search for a romantic partner: The effects of self-esteem and physical attractiveness on romantic behavior. In K. Gergen & D. Marlowe (Eds.), *Personality and social behavior.* Reading, Mass.: Addison-Wesley, 1970.

Kilham, W., & Mann, L. Level of destructive obedience as a function of transmitter and executant roles in the Milgram obedience paradigm. *Journal of Personality and Social Psychology,* 1974, *29,* 696–702.

Kimble, G. A., & Garmezy, N. *Principles of general psychology* (3rd ed.). New York: Ronald Press, 1968.

Kintsch, W. *The representation of meaning in memory.* Hillsdale, N.J.: Erlbaum, 1974.

Kleinke, C. L. Effects of dress on compliance to requests in a field setting. *Journal of Social Psychology*, 1977, *101*, 223–224.

Kline, M. V. The dynamics of hypnotically induced antisocial behavior. *Journal of Psychology*, 1958, *45*, 239–245.

Koch, H. L. The relation of certain family constellation characteristics and the attitudes of children toward adults. *Child Development*, 1955, *26*, 13–40.

Koffka, K. *Principles of gestalt psychology.* New York: Harcourt, 1935.

Kohlberg, L. Development of children's orientation towards a moral order. II. Sequence in the development of moral thoughts. *Vita humana*, 1963, *6*, 11–36.

Kohlberg, L. From is to ought: How to commit the naturalistic fallacy and get away with it in the study of moral development. In T. Mischel (Ed.), *Cognitive development and genetic epistemology.* New York: Academic Press, 1971.

Kohlberg, L. Moral stages and moralization: The cognitive-developmental approach. In T. Lickona (Ed.), *Moral development and behavior: Theory, research and social issues.* New York: Holt, Rinehart & Winston, 1976.

Köhler, W. Gestaltprobleme und Anfange einer Gestalttheorie. *Jahresbericht u. d. ges. Physiol.*, 1925, *3*, 512–539. (Translated in Ellis, W. D. *A source book of gestalt psychology.* New York: Harcourt, Brace & World, 1938.)

Köhler, W. *The mentality of apes.* London: Routledge & Kegan Paul, 1927.

Kohn, M. L. Social class and schizophrenia: A critical review and a reformulation. *Schizophrenia Bulletin*, 1973, No. 7, 60–79.

Kolb, L. C. *Modern clinical psychiatry* (8th ed.). Philadelphia: Saunders, 1973.

Koller, M. R. Residential and occupational propinquity. In R. F. Winch & R. McGinnis (Eds.), *Marriage and the family.* New York: Holt, Rinehart & Winston, 1953.

Konopasky, R. J., & Telegdy, G. A. Conformity in the rat: A leader's selection of door color versus a learned door-color discrimination. *Perceptual & Motor Skills*, 1977, *44*, 31–37.

Korchin, S. J. *Modern clinical psychology.* New York: Basic Books, 1976.

Kotelchuk, M., Zelazo, P., Kagan, J., & Spelke, E. Infant reaction to parental separation when left with familiar and unfamiliar adults. *Journal of Genetic Psychology*, 1975, *126*, 255–262.

Krauss, R. M. & Glucksberg, S. Social and nonsocial speech. *Scientific American*, 1977, *236*(2), 100–105.

Krieger, W. G. Infant influences and the parent sex by child sex interaction in the socialization process. *JSAS Catalogue of Selected Documents in Psychology*, 1976, *6*(1), 36 (Ms. No. 1234).

Kringlen, E. *Heredity and environment in the functional psychosis: An epidemiological-clinical twin study.* Oslo: Universitsforlaget, 1967.

Kripke, D. F. & Simons, R. N. Average sleep, insomnia, and sleeping pill use. *Sleep Research*, 1976, *5*, 110.

Kroeber-Riel, W. Activation research: Psychobiological approaches in consumer research. *Journal of Consumer Research*, 1979, *5*, 240–250.

Kroger, W. S. *Clinical and experimental hypnosis* (2nd ed.). Philadelphia: Lippincott, 1977.

Kurtines, W., & Greif, E. B. The development of moral thought: Review and evaluation of Kohlberg's approach. *Psychological Bulletin*, 1974, *81*, 453–470.

Kogan, N., & Pankove, E. Creative ability over a five-year span. *Child Development*, 1972, *43*, 427–442.

LaBerge, S. P. Lucid dreaming. *Psychology Today*, January 1981, pp. 48–57.

Ladd, G. T. *Elements of physiological psychology.* New York: Scribner's, 1887.

Laing, R. D. Schizophrenic split. *Time*, February 3, 1967, p. 56.

Laird, J. D. Self-attribution of emotion: The effects of expressive behavior on the quality of emotional experience. *Journal of Personality and Social Psychology*, 1974, *29*, 475–486.

Lamb, M. E. *Infants, fathers, and mothers: Interaction at 8 months of age in the home and in the laboratory.* Paper presented at the meeting of the Eastern Psychological Association, New York, 1975.

Lamb, M. E. The development of parental preferences in the first two years of life. *Sex Roles*, 1977, *3*, 495–497.

Lamb, M. E. Paternal influences and the father's role. *American Psychologist*, 1979, *34*, 938–943.

Lamb, M. E., Owen, M. T., & Chase-Lansdale, L. The father-daughter relationship: Past, present, and future. In C. B. Kopp & M. Kirkpatrick (Eds.), *Becoming female.* New York: Plenum Press, 1979.

Lamb, T. D., & Simon, E. J. The relation between intercellular coupling and electrical noise in turtle photoreceptors. *Journal of Physiology*, 1976, *263*, 257–286.

Land, E. H. The retinex theory of color vision. *Scientific American*, 1977, *237*(6), 108–128.

Landis, D. A scan for mental illness. *Discover*, October 1980, pp. 26–28.

Lange, C. G., & James, W. *The emotions.* Baltimore: Williams & Wilkins, 1922.

Lange-Eichbaum, W. *The problem of genius.* New York: Macmillan, 1932.

Langone, J. Girth of a nation. *Discover*, February 1981, pp. 56–60.

Lanzetta, J. T., Cartwright-Smith, J., & Kleck, R. E. Effects of nonverbal dissimulation on emotional experience and autonomic arousal. *Journal of Personality and Social Psychology*, 1976, *33*, 354–370.

Lashley, K. S. In search of the engram. In *Symposium of the Society for Experimental Biology*, Vol. 4. New York: Cambridge University Press, 1950.

Lassen, M. K., & McConnell, S. C. Treatment of a severe bird phobia by participant modeling. *Journal of Behavior Therapy & Experimental Psychiatry*, 1977, *8*, 165–168.

Latane, B., & Darley, J. M. Group inhibition of bystander intervention in emergencies. *Journal of Personality and Social Psychology*, 1968, *10*, 215–221.

Latane, B., & Darley, J. M. *The unresponsive bystander: Why doesn't he help?* New York: Appleton-Century-Crofts, 1970.

Laumann, E. O. Friends of urban men: An assessment of accuracy in reporting their socioeconomic attributes, mutual choice, and attitude agreement. *Sociometry*, 1969, *32*, 54–69.

Lazarus, A. A. *Multimodal behavior therapy.* New York: Springer, 1976.

Le Vine, R. *Dreams and deeds: Achievement motivation in Nigeria.* Chicago: University of Chicago Press, 1966.

Leavitt, H. J., & Schlosberg, H. The retention of verbal and motor skills. *Journal of Experimental Psychology*, 1944, *34*, 404–417.

Lee, C. L. *Social encounters of infants: The beginnings of popularity.* Paper presented at the meeting of the International Society for the Study of Behavioral Development, Ann Arbor, Mich., August 1973.

Leff, D. N. Brain chemistry may influence feelings, behavior. *Smithsonian*, June 1978, pp. 64–70.

Lefrancois, G. R. *Of children.* Belmont, Calif.: Wadsworth, 1980.

Legros, J. J., Gilot, P., Seron, X., Claessens, J., Adam, A., Moeglen, J. M., Audibert, A., & Berchier, P. Influence of vasopressin on learning and memory. *The Lancet*, 1978, *I*(8054), 41–42.

Lenneberg, E. H. The natural history of language. In F. Smith & G. A. Miller (Eds.), *The genesis of language*. Cambridge, Mass.: M. I. T. Press, 1966.

Lenneberg, E. H. *Biological foundations of language*. New York: Wiley, 1967.

Leo, J. From mollusks to moppets. *Time*, September 29, 1980, p. 55.

Leo, J. Memory: The unreliable witness. *Time*, January 5, 1981, p. 89.

Leo, J., & White, A. How to commit suicide. *Time*, July 7, 1980, p. 49.

Lepper, M. R., Greene, D., & Nisbett, R. E. Undermining children's intrinsic interest with extrinsic reward: A test of the "overjustification" hypothesis. *Journal of Personality and Social Psychology*, 1973, *28*, 129–137.

Lester, B. M., Kotelchuk, M., Spelke, E., Sellers, M. J., & Klein, R. E. Separation protest in Guatemalan infants: Cross-cultural and cognitive findings. *Developmental Psychology*, 1974, *10*, 79–85.

Leventhal, G., & Krate, R. Physical attractiveness and severity of sentencing. *Psychological Reports*, 1977, *40*, 315–318.

Leventhal, H. Findings and theory in the study of fear communications. In L. Berkowitz (Ed.), *Advances in experimental social psychology* (Vol. 5). New York: Academic Press, 1970.

Leventhal, H., Jacobs, R. L., & Kudirka, N. Z. Authoritarianism, ideology, and political candidate choice. *Journal of Abnormal and Social Psychology*, 1964, *69*, 539–549.

Leventhal, H., & Niles, P. Persistence of influence for varying durations of exposure to threat stimuli. *Psychological Reports*, 1965, *16*, 223–233.

Levine, J. D., Gordon, N. C., & Fields, H. L. The mechanism of placebo analgesia. *The Lancet*, 1978, *II*(8091), 654–657.

Levy, J., & Reid, M. Variations in writing posture and cerebral organization. *Science*, 1976, *194*, 337–339.

Levy, L., & Rowitz, L. *The ecology of mental disorders*. New York: Behavioral Publications, 1972.

Lewin, K. *A dynamic theory of personality*. New York: McGraw-Hill, 1935.

Lewin, K. *Principles of topological psychology*. New York: McGraw-Hill, 1936.

Lewin, R. The shadowy world of blindsight. *Science 81*, March 1981, p. 42.

Lewis, M., & Rosenblum, L. A. (Eds.). *Friendship and peer relations*. New York: Wiley, 1975.

Lewis, Max. Personal communication, November 1981.

Lieberman, P., Crelin, E. S., & Klatt, D. H. Phonetic ability and related anatomy of the newborn and adult human, Neanderthal man, and the chimpanzee. *American Anthropologist*, 1972, *74*, 287–307.

Liebert, R. M., Poulos, R. W., & Marmor, G. S. *Developmental psychology*. Englewood Cliffs, N. J.: Prentice-Hall, 1977.

Linton, H., & Graham, E. Personality correlates of persuasibility. In C. I. Hovland & I. L. Janis (Eds.), *Personality and Persuasibility*. New Haven, Conn.: Yale University Press, 1959.

Lippitt, R., Polansky, N., & Rosen, S. The dynamics of power. *Human Relations*, 1952, *5*, 37–64.

Locke, S. E., Furst, M. W., Heisel, J. S., & Williams, R. M. *The influences of stress on the immune response*. Paper presented at the annual meeting of the American Psychosomatic Society, Washington, D.C., April 1978.

Loftus, E. F., & Loftus, G. R. On the permanence of stored information in the human brain. *American Psychologist*, 1980, *35*, 409–420.

Longstreth, L. E. Revisiting Skeels' final study: A critique. *Developmental Psychology*, 1981, *17*, 620–625.

Loop, M. S., & Bruce, L. L. Cat color vision: The effect of stimulus size. *Science*, 1978, *199*, 1221–1222.

Lorenz, K. Z. Uber die Bildung des Instinkbegriffes. *Naturwissenschaften*, 1937, *25*, 289–300, 307–318, 324–331.

Lorenz, K. Z. Die angeborenen Formen möglicher Erfahrung. *Z. Tierpsychologie*, 1943, *5*, 235–409.

Luchins, A. S. Mechanization in problem solving. *Psychological Monographs*, 1942, *54*, No. 248.

Lucins, D. The dopamine hypothesis of schizophrenia: A critical analysis. *Neuropsychobiology*, 1975, *1*, 365–378.

Luisada, P. V., & Brown, B. I. Clinical management of the phencyclidine psychosis. *Clinical Toxicology*, 1976, *9*, 539–545.

Luria, A. R. *The mind of a mnemonist*. New York: Basic Books, Inc., 1968.

Lykken, D. T. *A tremor in the blood: Uses and abuses of the lie detector*. New York: McGraw-Hill, 1981.

Lynn, D. B. *The father: His role in child development*. Monterey, Calif.: Brooks/Cole, 1974.

Lytton, H., Conway, D., & Suave, R. The impact of twinship on parent-child interaction. *Journal of Personality and Social Psychology*, 1977, *35*, 97–107.

Maccoby, E. E. *Current changes in the family, and their impact upon the socialization of children*. Paper presented at the meeting of the American Sociological Association, Chicago, September 1977.

Maccoby, E. E., & Feldman, S. S. Mother attachment and stranger reactions in the third year of life. *Monographs of the Society for Research in Child Development*, 1972, *37*(no. 1), 1–86.

MacLeod, D. I. A. Visual sensitivity. In M. R. Rosenzweig, & L. W. Porter (Eds.), *Annual review of psychology*. Palo Alto, California: Annual Reviews, Inc., 1978, pp. 613–645.

MacNichol, E. F. Three pigment color vision. *Scientific American*, 1964, *211*(6), 48–64.

Madigan, S. A. Intraserial repetition and coding processes in free recall. *Journal of Verbal Learning and Verbal Behavior*, 1969, *8*, 828–835.

Madsen, M. C. Developmental and cross-cultural differences in the cooperative and competitive behavior of young children. *Journal of Cross-Cultural Psychology*, 1971, *2*, 365–371.

Madsen, M. C., & Shapira, A. Cooperative and competitive behavior of urban Afro-American, Anglo-American, Mexican-American, and Mexican village children. *Developmental Psychology*, 1970, *3*, 16–20.

Magnusson, D. (Ed.). *The situation: An interactional perspective*. Hillsdale, N. J.: Erlbaum, 1980.

Magnusson, D., & Endler, N. S. Interactional psychology: Present status and future prospects. In D. Magnusson & N. S. Endler (Eds.), *Personality at the crossroads*. New York: Wiley-Erlbaum, 1977.

Maier, N. R. F. Reasoning in humans: II. The solution of a problem and its appearance in consciousness. *Journal of Comparative Psychology*, 1931, *12*, 181–194.

Maile, F. R., & Selzer, M. *The Nuremberg mind: The psychology of the Nazi leaders*. New York: New York Times Book Co., 1975.

Main, M. *Mother-avoiding babies*. Paper presented at the meeting of the Society for Research in Child Development, Denver, 1975.

Malinowski, B. *The sexual life of savages*. New York: Harcourt, Brace and World, 1929.

Manchester, W. *The glory and the dream*. Boston: Little, Brown, 1974.

Manosevitz, M., Prentice, N. M., & Wilson, F. Individual and family correlates of imaginary companions in preschool children. *Developmental Psychology*, 1973, *8*, 72–79.

Mantel, D. M. The potential for violence in Germany. *Journal of Social Issues*, 1971, *27*(4), 101–112.

Marcus, D. E., & Overton, W. F. The development of cognitive gender constancy and sex role preferences. *Child Development,* 1978, *49,* 434–444.

Margules, D. L. Beta-endorphin and endoloxone—Hormones of the autonomic nervous system for the conservation or expenditure of bodily resources and energy in anticipation of famine or feast. *Neuroscience and Biobehavioral Reviews,* 1979, *3,* 155-162.

Marks, P. A., & Seeman, W. *Actuarial description of abnormal personality.* Baltimore: Williams & Wilkins, 1963.

Marr, D. Early processing of visual information. *Philos. Trans. R. Soc. London Ser. B,* 1976, *275,* 483–524.

Marshall, W. A. The body. In R. R. Sears & S. S. Feldman (Eds.), *The seven ages of man.* Los Altos, Calif.: William Kaufmann, 1973.

Martin, J., Lobb, B., Chapman, G. C., & Spillane, R. Obedience under conditions demanding self-immolation. *Human Relations,* 1976, *29,* 345–356.

Martin, P. J., Hunter, M. L., & Moore, J. E. Pulling the wool: Impression-management among hospitalized schizophrenics. *Research Communications in Psychology, Psychiatry & Behavior,* 1977, *2,* 21–26.

Martin, W. R. Realistic goals for antagonist therapy. *American Journal of Drug & Alcohol Abuse,* 1975, *2,* 353–356.

Martino, E., Seo, H., Lernmark, A., & Refetoff, S. Ontogenetic patterns of thyrotropin-releasing hormone-like material in rat hypothalamus, pancreas, and retina—selective effect of light deprivation. *Proceedings of the National Academy of Sciences—Biological Sciences,* 1980, *77,* 4345–4348.

Marx, M. H., & Hillix, W. *Systems and theories in psychology.* New York: McGraw-Hill, 1963.

Masland, R. H., & Mills, J. W. Choline accumulation by photoreceptor cells of the rabbit retina. *Proceedings of the National Academy of Sciences,* 1980, *77*(3), 1671–1675.

Maslow, A. H. *Motivation and personality.* New York: Harper & Row, 1954.

Maslow, A. H. *Toward a psychology of being* (2nd ed.). New York: Van Nostrand, 1968.

Masserman, J. H. *Behavior and neuroses.* Chicago: Chicago University Press, 1943.

Masters, W. H., & Johnson, V. E. *Human sexual response.* Boston: Little, Brown, 1966.

Masters, W. H., & Johnson, V. E. *Human sexual inadequacy.* Boston: Little, Brown, 1970.

Masters, W. H., & Johnson, V. E. *Homosexuality in perspective.* Boston: Little, Brown, 1979.

Matthysse, S., & Kidd, K. K. Evidence of HLA linkage in depressive disorders. *New England Journal of Medicine,* 1981, *305,* 1340.

Mazur, A., & Rosa, E. An empirical test of McClelland's "achieving society" theory. *Social Forces,* 1977, *55,* 769–774.

McAskie, M. Carelessness or fraud in Sir Cyril Burt's kinship data? *American Psychologist,* 1978, *33,* 496–498.

McCall, J. N., & Johnson, O. G. The independence of intelligence from family size and birth order. *Journal of Genetic Psychology,* 1972, *121,* 207–213.

McClearn, G. E. Genetic influences on behavior and development. In P. H. Mussen (Ed.), *Carmichael's manual of child psychology* (Vol. 1, 3rd ed.). New York: Wiley, 1970.

McClelland, D. C., Davis, W. N., Kalin, R., & Wanner, E. *The drinking man.* New York: Free Press, 1972.

McConnell, J. V. *Understanding human behavior* (2nd ed.). New York: Holt, Rinehart, & Winston, 1977.

McCord, J. Thirty year followup: Counseling fails. *Science News,* November 26, 1977, p. 357.

McDonald, M. C. The dream debate. *Science News,* June 13, 1981,

pp. 378–380.

McEwen, B. S. Binding and metabolism of sex steroids by the hypothalamic-pituitary unit: Physiological implications. *Annual Review of Physiology,* 1980, *42,* 97–110.

McGinnies, E., & Ward, C. D. Personality as a function of source credibility and locus of control: Five cross-cultural experiments. *Journal of Personality,* 1974, *42,* 360–371.

McGraw, M. B. Neural maturation as exemplified in achievement of bladder control. *Journal of Paediatrics,* 1940, *16,* 580–590.

McGuire, W. J. Inducing resistance to persuasion: Some contemporary approaches. *Advances in Experimental Social Psychology,* 1964, *1,* 192–229.

McKee, S. P., McCann, J. J. & Benton, J. L. Color vision from rod and long-wave cone interactions: Conditions in which rods contribute to multicolored images. *Vision Research,* 1977, *17,* 175–185.

McNeil, E. B. *The quiet furies.* Englewood Cliffs, N. J.: Prentice-Hall, 1967.

Mead, M. *Sex and temperament in three primitive societies.* New York: William Morrow, 1963. (Originally published, 1935).

Meddis, R. On the function of sleep. *Animal Behaviour,* 1975, *23,* 676–691.

Meddis, R., Pearson, A. J. D., & Langford, G. An extreme case of healthy insomnia. *Electroencephalography and Clinical Neurophysiology,* 1973, *35,* 213–221.

Meichenbaum, D. *Cognitive-behavior modification: An integrative approach.* New York: Plenum Press, 1977.

Meiners, M. L., & Sheposh, J. P. Beauty or brains: Which image for your mate? *Personality & Social Psychology Bulletin,* 1977, *3,* 262–265.

Meissner, W. W. *The paranoid process.* New York: Jason Aronson, 1978.

Menninger, K. *The crime of punishment.* New York: Viking, Compass, 1968.

Mercer, C. D., & Snell, M. E. *Learning theory research in mental retardation: Implications for teaching.* Columbus, Ohio: Charles E. Merrill, 1977.

Mercer, J. R. Sociocultural factors in labeling mental retardates. *The Peabody Journal of Education,* 1971, *48,* 188–203.

Mercer, J. R. IQ: The lethal label. *Psychology Today,* September 1972, pp. 44–47; 95–97.

Mesulam, M. M., & Geschwind, N. Possible role of neocortex and its limbic connections in process of attention and schizophrenia. *Journal of Psychiatric Research,* 1978, *14,* 249–259.

Mewborn, C. R., & Rogers, R. W. Effects of threatening and reassuring components of fear appeals on physiological and verbal measures of emotion and attitudes. *Journal of Experimental Social Psychology,* 1979, *15,* 242–253.

Meyer, J. P., & Pepper, S. Need compatibility and marital adjustment in young married couples. *Journal of Personality and Social Psychology,* 1977, *35,* 331–342.

Michael, R. P., & Bonsall, R. W. Peri-ovulatory synchronisation of behaviour in male and female rhesus monkeys. *Nature,* 1977, *265,* 463–465.

Michael, R. P., & Zumpe, D. Potency in male rhesus monkeys: Effects of continuously receptive females. *Science,* 1978, *200,* 451–453.

Middlemist, R. D., Knowles, E. S., & Matter, C. F. Personal space invasions in the lavatory: Suggestive evidence for arousal. *Journal of Personality and Social Psychology,* 1976, *33,* 541–546.

Milgram, S. Behavioral study of obedience. *Journal of Abnormal and Social Psychology,* 1963, *67,* 371–378.

Milgram, S. Some conditions of obedience and disobedience to authority. *Human Relations,* 1965a, *18,* 57–76.

Milgram, S. Liberating effects of group pressure. *Journal of Personality and Social Psychology*, 1965b, *1*, 127–134.

Miller, G. A. The magical number seven, plus or minus two: Some limits on our capacity for processing information. *Psychological Review*, 1956, *63*, 81–97.

Miller, G. A., & Buckhout, R. *Psychology: The science of mental life*. New York: Harper & Row, 1973.

Miller, L., Cornett, T., & Brightwell, D. Marijuana and memory impairment: The effect of retrieval cues on free recall. *Pharmacology, Biochemistry, & Behavior*, 1976, *5*, 639–643.

Miller, N., Maruyama, G., Beaber, R. J., & Valone, K. Speed of speech and persuasion. *Journal of Personality and Social Psychology*, 1976, *34*, 615–624.

Miller, N. E. Obituary, Walter R. Miles (1885–1978). *American Psychologist*, 1980, *35*, 595–596.

Miller, R. L., Brickman, P., & Bolen, D. Attribution versus persuasion as a means for modifying behavior. *Journal of Personality and Social Psychology*, 1975, *31*, 430–441.

Mirsky, A. F., & Orzack, M. H. Two retrospective studies of psychosurgery. In E. S. Valenstein (Ed.), *The Psychosurgery Debate*. San Francisco: W. H. Freeman, 1980.

Mischel, W. On the future of personality measurement. *American Psychologist*, 1977, *32*, 246–254.

Mishara, B. L. The extent of adolescent suicidality. *Psychiatric Opinion*, 1975, *12*, 32–37.

Mita, T. H., Dermer, M., & Knight, J. Reversed facial images and the mere-exposure hypothesis. *Journal of Personality and Social Psychology*, 1977, *35*, 597–601.

M'Naghten's Case. *English Reports*, 1843, *8*, 718.

Moffitt, A. R. Consonant cue perception by twenty- to twenty-four-week-old infants. *Child Development*, 1971, *42*, 717–731.

Money, J. Influence of hormones on sexual behavior. *Annual Review of Medicine*, 1965, *16*, 67–82.

Money, J., & Ehrhardt, A. A. *Man and woman, boy and girl*. Baltimore: Johns Hopkins, 1972.

A monkey blueprint for sexual boredom. *Science News*, May 6, 1978, p. 294.

Mora, G. History of psychiatry. In A. M. Freedman and H. I. Kaplan (Eds.), *Psychiatry*. Baltimore: Williams & Wilkins, 1967.

Morden, B., Mitchell, G., & Dement, W. C. Selective REM sleep deprivation and compensation phenomena in the rat. *Brain Research*, 1967, *5*, 339–349.

Morell, P., & Norton, W. T. Myelin. *Scientific American*, 1980, *242*(5), 88–118.

Moskowitz, B. A. The acquisition of language. *Scientific American*, 1978, *239*(5), 92–108.

Mowrer, O. H. On the dual nature of learning—a reinterpretation of "conditioning" and "problem-solving." *Harvard Educational Review*, 1947, *17*, 102–148.

Murphy, H. B. Cultural factors in the genesis of schizophrenia. In D. Rosenthal & S. S. Kety (Eds.), *The transmission of schizophrenia*. Elmsford, N. Y.: Pergamon Press, 1968.

Musick, P. L. *Interdisciplinary study of creativity and behavior: Special child development*. Paper presented at the meeting of the American Psychological Association, San Francisco, August 1977.

Myers, R. D., & Melchior, C. L. Alcohol drinking: Abnormal intake caused by tetrahydropapaveroline in the brain. *Science*, 1977, *196*, 554–556.

Nash, M. R., Johnson, L. S., & Tipton, R. D. Hypnotic age regression and the occurrence of transitional object relationships. *Journal of Abnormal Psychology*, 1979, *88*, 547–554.

Nauta, W. J. H., & Feirtag, M. The organization of the brain. *Scientific American*, 1979, *241*(3), 88–111.

Neisser, U. *Cognitive psychology*. New York: Appleton-Century-Crofts, 1967.

Nelson, L., & Madsen, M. C. Cooperation and competition in four-year-olds as a function of reward contingency and subculture. *Developmental Psychology*, 1969, *1*, 340–344.

Nestoros, H. N. Ethanol specifically potentiates GABA-mediated neurotransmission in feline cerebral cortex. *Science*, 1980, *209*, 708–710.

Newcomb, T. M. *The acquaintance process*. New York: Holt, Rinehart & Winston, 1961.

Newell, A., & Simon, H. *Human problem solving*. Englewood Cliffs, N. J.: Prentice-Hall, 1972.

Newport, E. Personal communication, June 1979.

Nickerson, R. S., & Adams, M. J. Long-term memory for a common object. *Cognitive Psychology*, 1979, *11*, 287–307.

Nisbett, R. E. Determinants of food intake in obesity. *Science*, 1968, *159*, 1254–1255.

Norman, D. A., & Rumelhart, D. E. *Explorations in cognition*. San Francisco: W. H. Freeman, 1975.

Nova, "A touch of sensitivity." Public Broadcasting System, 1980.

Novin, D. Visceral mechanisms in the control of food intake. In D. Novin, W. Wyrwicka, & G. A. Bray (Eds.), *Hunger: Basic mechanisms and clinical implications*. New York: Raven Press, 1976.

Nunnally, J. C., Duchnowski, A. J., & Parker, R. K. Association of neutral objects with rewards: Effect on verbal evaluation, reward expectancy, and selective attention. *Journal of Personality and Social Psychology*, 1965, *1*, 270–274.

Nydegger, R. V. Information processing complexity and leadership status. *Journal of Experimental Social Psychology*, 1975, *11*, 317–328.

O'Connor, K., Mann, D. W., & Bardwick, J. M. Androgyny and self-esteem in the upper-middle class: A replication of Spence. *Journal of Consulting and Clinical Psychology*, 1978, *46*, 1168–1169.

Oke, A., Keller, R., Mefford, I., & Adams, R. N. Lateralization of norepinephrine in human thalamus. *Science*, 1978, *200*, 1411–1413.

Olds, J. Pleasure centers in the brain. *Scientific American*, 1956, *195*(4), 105–116.

Olds, M. E., & Forbes, J. L. The central basis of motivation: Intracranial self-stimulation studies. In M. R. Rosenzweig & L. W. Porter (Eds.), *Annual review of psychology*. Palo Alto, Calif.: Annual Reviews, 1981.

Olfactory synchrony of menstrual cycles. *Science News*, July 2, 1977, p. 5.

Oliveros, J. C., Jandali, M. K., Timsit-Berthier, M., Remy, R., Benghezal, A., Audibert, A., & Moeglen, J. M. Vasopressin in amnesia. *The Lancet*, 1978, *I*(8054), 42.

Orne, M. T., & Evans, F. J. Social control in the psychological experiment: Antisocial behavior and hypnosis. *Journal of Personality and Social Psychology*, 1965, *1*, 189–200.

Ostberg, O. Circadian rhythms of food intake and oral temperature in "morning" and "evening" groups of individuals. *Ergonomics*, 1973, *16*, 203–209.

Overton, D. A. State-dependent learning produced by alcohol and its relevance to alcoholism. In B. Kissin & H. Begleiter (Eds.), *Physiology and behavior* (Vol. 2). New York: Plenum Press, 1972.

Packard, V. *The people shapers*. Boston: Little, Brown, 1977.

Paillard, J., & Beaubaton, D. Triggered and guided components of visual reaching. Their dissociation in split-brain studies. In M.

Shahami (Ed.), *Motor systems: Neuropsychology and muscle mechanisms.* Amsterdam: Elsevier, 1976, pp. 333–347.

Paivio, A. *Imagery and verbal processes.* New York: Holt, Rinehart, & Winston, 1971.

Pallak, M. S., Cook, D. A., & Sullivan, J. J. Commitment and energy conservation. *Applied Social Psychology Ann.,* 1980, *1,* 235–253.

Pappenheimer, J. R. The sleep factor. *Scientific American,* 1976, *235*(2), 24–29.

Parkes, C. M. *Bereavement.* New York: International Universities Press, 1972.

Parsons v. State. *Southern Reporter,* 1887, *2,* 866.

Patrick, G. T. W., & Gilbert, J. A. On the effects of loss of sleep. *Psychological Review,* 1896, *3,* 469–483.

Patterson, F. *Creative and abstract uses of language: A gorilla case study.* Paper presented at the meeting of the Western Psychological Association, San Diego, April 1979.

Pavlov, I. P. *Conditioned reflexes.* New York: Oxford University Press, 1927.

Pelham, W. E. Withdrawal of a stimulant drug and concurrent behavioral intervention in the treatment of a hyperactive child. *Behavior Therapy,* 1977, *8,* 473–479.

Penfield, W. Consciousness, memory, and man's conditioned reflexes. In K. Pribram (Ed.), *On the biology of learning.* New York: Harcourt, Brace & World, 1969.

Penfield, W., & Roberts, L. *Speech and brain mechanisms.* Princeton: Princeton University Press, 1959.

Penn, R. D., & Hagins, W. A. Kinetics of the photocurrent of retinal rods. *Biophysical Journal,* 1972, *12,* 1073–1094.

Perry, R. B. *The thought and character of William James* (Vol. 1), 1926.

Perry, R. B. *The thought and character of William James* (Vol. 2), 1936.

Peterson, J. M. Left-handedness: Differences between student artists and scientists. *Perceptual & Motor Skills,* 1979, *48,* 961–962.

Petty, R. E., & Cacioppo, J. T. Effects of forewarning of persuasive intent and involvement on cognitive responses and persuasion. *Personality and Social Psychology Bulletin,* 1979, *5,* 173–176.

Petty, R. E., & Cacioppo, J. T. *Attitudes and persuasion. Classic and contemporary approaches.* Dubuque: Wm. C. Brown, 1980.

Phillips, D. P. Motor vehicle fatalities increase just after publicized suicide stories. *Science,* 1977, *196,* 1464–1465.

Phillips, J. L. *The origins of intellect: Piaget's theory.* San Francisco: W. H. Freeman, 1969.

Phoenix, C. H., Goy, R. W., Gerall, A. A., & Young, W. C. Organizing action of prenatally administered testosterone propionate on the tissues mediating mating behavior in the female guinea pig. *Endocrinology,* 1959, *65,* 369–382.

Piaget, J. *The origins of intelligence in children.* New York: International Universities Press, 1952.

Piaget, J. *The child's conception of the world.* London: Routledge, 1960.

Piaget, J., & Inhelder, B. *The psychology of the child.* (H. Weaver, trans.). New York: Basic Books, 1969. (Originally published 1967).

Pierson, P. S., et. al. Naloxone in the treatment of the young heroin abuser. *American Journal of Drug & Alcohol Abuse,* 1974, *1,* 243–252.

Pihl, R. O., & Parkes, M. Hair element content in learning disabled children. *Science,* 1977, *198,* 204–206.

Pines, M. Superkids. *Psychology Today,* January 1979, pp. 53–63.

Pinneau, S. R. The infantile disorders of hospitalism and anaclitic depression. *Psychological Bulletin,* 1955, *52,* 429–452.

Pirsig, R. M. *Zen and the art of motorcycle maintenance: An inquiry into values.* New York: Morrow, 1974.

Plutchik, R. A language for the emotions. *Psychology Today,* February 1980, pp. 68–78.

Polansky, N., Lippitt, R., & Redl, F. An investigation of behavioral contagion in groups. *Human Relations,* 1950, *3,* 319–348.

Pomeranz, B., Cheng, R., & Law, P. Acupuncture reduces electrophysiological and behavioral responses to noxious stimuli: Pituitary is implicated. *Experimental Neurology,* 1977, *54,* 172–178.

Postman, L., & Rau, L. Retention as a function of the method of measurement. *University of California Publications in Psychology,* 1957, *8*(3).

President's Commission on Mental Health. *Report to the president.* Washington, D. C.: U. S. Government Printing Office, 1978.

Presti, D., & Pettigrew, J. D. Ferromagnetic coupling to muscle receptors as a basis for geomagnetic field sensitivity in animals. *Nature,* 1980, *285,* 99–101.

Priest, R. F., & Sawyer, J. Proximity and peership: Bases of balance in interpersonal attraction. *American Journal of Sociology,* 1967, *72,* 633–649.

Pruitt, D. G. Conclusions: Toward an understanding of choice shifts in group discussion. *Journal of Personality and Social Psychology,* 1971, *20,* 495–510.

Pryor, J. B., Gibbons, F. X., Wicklund, R. A., Fazio, R. H., & Hood, R. Self-focused attention and self-report validity. *Journal of Personality,* 1977, *45,* 513–527.

Pursell, S. A., & Banikiotes, P. G. Androgyny and initial interpersonal attraction. *Personality and Social Psychology Bulletin,* 1978, *4,* 235–239.

Quigley-Fernandez, B., & Tedeschi, J. T. The bogus pipeline as lie detector: Two validity studies. *Journal of Personality and Social Psychology,* 1978, *36,* 247–256.

Rader, N. *The behavior of pre-crawling infants on the visual cliff with locomotor aids.* Paper presented at the meeting of the Western Psychological Association, San Diego, April 1979.

Raviola, E. Intercellular junctions in the outer plexiform layer of the retina. *Investigative Ophthalmology,* 1976, *15,* 881–895.

Ray, E., & Herskowitz, M. Kidnap at Chowchilla. *Ladies Home Journal,* November 1976, pp. 114–115.

Razran, G. The observable unconscious and the inferable conscious in current Soviet psychophysiology. *Psychological Review,* 1961, *68,* 81–147.

Rebar, R. W., Miyake, A., Low, T. L. K., & Goldstein, A. L. Thymosin stimulates secretion of Luteinizing hormone-releasing factor. *Science,* 1981, *214,* 669–671.

Redican, W. K. Facial expression in nonhuman primates. In L. A. Rosenblum (Ed.), *Primate behavior* (Vol. 4). New York: Academic Press, 1975.

Rees, A. H., & Palmer, F. H. Factors related to change in mental test performance. *Developmental Psychology Monograph,* 1970, *3,* 1–57.

Regan, D., & Cynader, M. Neurons in area 18 of cat visual cortex selectively sensitive to changing size: Nonlinear interactions between responses to two edges. *Vision Research,* 1979, *19,* 699–711.

Rest, J. *Developmental hierarchy in preference and comprehension of moral judgment.* Unpublished doctoral dissertation, University of Chicago, 1968.

Reston, J. Proxmire on love. *New York Times,* March 14, 1975.

Rheingold, H. L. The effect of environmental stimulation upon social and exploratory behavior in the human infant. In B. M. Foss (Ed.), *Determinants of infant behavior* (Vol. 1). New York: Wiley, 1961, pp. 143–177.

Rheingold, H. L., & Bayley, N. The later effects of an experimental modification of mothering. *Child Development,* 1959, *30,* 363–372.

Ripps, H., Shakib, M., & MacDonald, E. D. Peroxidase uptake by photoreceptor terminals of the skate retina. *Journal of Cell Biology,* 1976, *70,* 86–96.

Robbins, L. C. The accuracy of parental recall of aspects of child development and of child rearing practice. *Journal of Abnormal and Social Psychology,* 1963, *66,* 261–270.

Roche, A. F., & Davila, G. H. Late adolescent growth in stature. *Pediatrics,* 1972, *50,* 874–880.

Rodin, J. Current status of the internal-external hypothesis for obesity: What went wrong? *American Psychologist,* 1981, *36,* 361–372.

Rodin, J., & Slowchower, J. Fat chance for a favor: Obese-normal differences in compliance and incidental learning. *Journal of Personality and Social Psychology,* 1976, *29,* 557–565.

Roethlisberger, F. J. & Dickson, W. J. *Management and the worker.* Cambridge, Mass.: Harvard University Press, 1940.

Rogers, C. R. *Client-centered therapy: Its current practice, implications, and theory.* Boston: Houghton Mifflin, 1951.

Rogers, C. R. *On becoming a person.* Boston: Houghton Mifflin, 1961.

Rosch, E. On the internal structure of perceptual and semantic categories. In T. E. Moore (Ed.), *Cognitive development and the acquisition of language.* New York: Academic Press, 1973.

Rosch, E. Human categorization. In N. Warren (Ed.), *Advances in cross-cultural psychology* (Vol. I). London: Academic Press, 1977.

Rosen, D. H. Suicide survivors: Psychotherapeutic implications of egocide. *Suicide: A Quarterly Journal of Life-Threatening Behavior,* 1976, *6,* 209–215.

Rosenhan, D. L. On being sane in insane places. *Science,* 1973, *179,* 250–258.

Rosenhan, D. L. Moral development. CRM McGraw-Hill Films, 1973.

Rosenkrantz, A. L. A note on adolescent suicide: Incidence, dynamics and some suggestions for treatment. *Adolescence,* 1978, *13,* 209–214.

Rosenthal, D., & Quinn, O. W. Quadruplet hallucinations: Phenotypic variations of a schizophrenic genotype. *Archives of General Psychiatry,* 1977, *34,* 817–827.

Roth, S., & Bootzin, R. R. Effects of experimentally induced expectancies of external control: An investigation of learned helplessness. *Journal of Personality and Social Psychology,* 1974, *29,* 253–264.

Rotter, J. B. Beliefs, social attitudes, and behavior: A social learning analysis. In J. B. Rotter, J. E. Chance, & E. J. Phares (Eds.), *Applications of a social learning theory of personality.* New York: Holt, Rinehart & Winston, 1972.

Roueché, B. *The medical detectives.* New York: Truman Talley Books, 1980.

Rubenstein, R., & Newman, R. The living out of "future" experiences under hypnosis. *Science,* 1954, *119,* 472–473.

Rubin, Z. *Liking and loving: An invitation to social psychology.* New York: Holt, Rinehart & Winston, 1973.

Ruch, J. C. Self-hypnosis: The result of heterohypnosis or vice versa? *International Journal of Clinical and Experimental Hypnosis,* 1975, *23,* 282–304.

Rucker, R. Who makes math marvelous, turns magic satin smooth, tends the looking-glass garden, and can make a winner of anyone who plays his games? *Science 81,* July/August 1981, pp. 33–37.

Rundus, D. Analysis of rehearsal processes in free recall. *Journal of Experimental Psychology,* 1971, *89,* 63–77.

Sachs, J., & Truswell, L. Comprehension of two-word instructions by children in the one-word stage. *Journal of Child Language,* 1978, *5,* 17–24.

Sackeim, H. A., Gur, R. C., & Saucy, M. C. Emotions are expressed more intensely on the left side of the face. *Science,* 1978, *202,* 434–436.

Sackett, G. P., Holm, R. A., & Landesman-Dwyer, S. Vulnerability for abnormal development: Pregnancy outcomes and sex differences in macaque monkeys. In N. R. Ellis (Ed.), *Aberrant development in infancy.* New York: Erlbaum, 1975, pp. 59–76.

Sackett, G. P., Holm, R. A., & Ruppenthal, G. C. Social isolation rearing: Species differences in behavior of macaque monkeys. *Developmental Psychology,* 1976, *12,* 283–288.

Sacks, M., Carpenter, W. T., & Richmond, M. B. Psychotherapy in hospitalized research patients. *Archives of General Psychiatry,* 1975, *32,* 581–585.

Sampson, E. E. Birth order, need achievement, and conformity. *Journal of Abnormal and Social Psychology,* 1962, *64,* 155–159.

Sampson, E. E. Scientific paradigms and social values: Wanted—A scientific revolution. *Journal of Personality and Social Psychology,* 1978, *36,* 1332–1343.

Sandman, C. A., George, J. M., Nolan, J. D., Van Riezen, H., & Kastin, A. J. Enhancement of attention in man with ACTH/MSH 4-10. *Physiology and Behavior,* 1975, *15,* 427–431.

Santrock, J. W., & Tracy, R. L. Effects of children's family structure status on the development of stereotypes by teachers. *Journal of Educational Psychology,* 1978, *70,* 754–757.

Sarbin, T. R. Contributions to role-taking theory: I. Hypnotic behavior. *Psychological Review,* 1950, *57,* 255–270.

Sarbin, T. R., & Coe, W. C. *Hypnosis: A social psychological analysis of influence communication.* New York: Holt, Rinehart & Winston, 1972.

Savage-Rumbaugh, E. S., Rumbaugh, D. M., & Boysen, S. Symbolic communication between two chimpanzees. *Science,* 1978, *201,* 641–644.

Savin-Williams, R. C. Dominance hierarchies in groups of early adolescents. *Child Development,* 1979, *50,* 923–935.

Savitsky, J. C., Rogers, R. W., Izard, C. E., & Liebert, R. M. Role of frustration and anger in the imitation of filmed aggression against a human victim. *Psychological Reports,* 1971, *29,* 807–810.

Scarr, S., & Weinberg, R. A. IQ test performance of black children adopted by white families. *American Psychologist,* 1976, *31,* 726–739.

Schacht, T., & Nathan, P. E. But is it good for the psychologists? *American Psychologist,* 1977, *21,* 1017–1025.

Schachter, S. Studies of the interaction of psychological and pharmacological determinants of smoking: 1. Nicotine regulation in heavy and light smokers. *Journal of Experimental Psychology: General,* 1977, *106,* 5–12.

Schachter, S., & Gross, L. P. Manipulated time and eating behavior. *Journal of Personality and Social Psychology,* 1968, *10,* 98–106.

Schachter, S., Kozlowski, L. T., & Silverstein, B. Studies of the interaction of psychological and pharmacological determinants of smoking: 2. Effects of urinary pH on cigarette smoking. *Journal of Experimental Psychology: General,* 1977, *106,* 13–19.

Schachter, S., Silverstein, B., & Perlick, D. Studies of the interaction of psychological and pharmacological determinants of smoking: 5. Psychological and pharmacological explanations of smoking under stress. *Journal of Experimental Psychology: General,* 1977, *106,* 31–40.

Schachter, S., & Singer, J. E. Cognitive, social, and physiological determinants of emotional state. *Psychological Review,* 1962, *69,* 379–399.

Schechter, A. Clinical use of naltrexone: EN1639(a): Pt. 2. Experience for the first fifty patients in a New York City treatment clinic. *American Journal of Drug & Alcohol Abuse,* 1975, *2,* 433–442.

Scheier, M. F., Carver, C. S., & Gibbons, F. X. Self-directed attention, awareness of bodily states, and suggestibility. *Journal of Personality and Social Psychology,* 1979, *37,* 1576–1588.

Schell, R. E., & Hall, E. *Developmental psychology today* (3rd ed.). New York: Random House, 1979.

Schlenker, B. R. Attitudes as actions: Social identity theory and consumer research. *Advances in Consumer Research,* 1978, *5,* 352–359.

Schlenker, B. R., & Schlenker, P. A. Reactions following counterattitudinal behavior which produces positive consequences. *Journal of Personality and Social Psychology,* 1975, *31,* 962–971.

Schlesser, M. A., Winokur, G., & Sherman, B. M. Hypothalamic-pituitary-adrenal axis activity in depressive illness: Its relationship to classification. *Archives of General Psychiatry,* 1980, *37,* 737–743.

Schmidt-Kessen, W., & Kendel, K. Influence of room temperature on night sleep in man. *Research in Experimental Medicine,* 1973, *160,* 220–233.

Schmitt, M. Influences of hepatic portal receptors on hypothalamic feeding and satiety centers. *American Journal of Physiology,* 1973, *225,* 1089–1095.

Schneider, N. G., Popek, P., Jarvik, M. E., & Gritz, E. R. The use of nicotine gum during cessation of smoking. *American Journal of Psychiatry,* 1977, *134,* 439–440.

Schrag, P., & Divoky, D. *The myth of the hyperactive child and other means of child control.* New York: Pantheon, 1975.

Schuckit, M. A., & Rayses, V. Ethanol ingestion: Differences in blood-acetaldehyde concentrations in relatives of alcoholics and controls. *Science,* 1979, *203,* 54–55.

Schwartz, H. Abraham Lincoln and cardiac decompensation: A preliminary report. *Western Journal of Medicine,* 1978, *128*(2), 174–177.

Schwartz, M., & Schwartz, J. Evidence against a genetical component to performance on IQ tests. *Nature,* 1974, *248,* 84–85.

Seeing stars. *Time Magazine,* July 3, 1978, p. 85.

Segal, B. M. Drinking and alcoholism in Russia. *Psychiatric Opinion,* 1975, *12,* 21–29.

Segal, M. W. Alphabet and attraction: An unobtrusive measure of the effect of propinquity in a field setting. *Journal of Personality and Social Psychology,* 1974, *30,* 654–657.

Seligman, M. E. P. On the generality of the laws of learning. *Psychological Review,* 1970, *77,* 406–418.

Seligman, M. E. P. *Helplessness.* San Francisco: W. H. Freeman, 1975.

Seligmann, J. Temperamental ills. *Newsweek,* August 13, 1979, p. 40.

Seligmann, J., & Donosky, L. A manual on how to commit suicide. *Newsweek,* April 7, 1980, p. 77.

Seligmann, J., & Shapiro, D. Saved by lithium. *Newsweek,* November 12, 1979, p. 102.

Selye, H. *The stress of life* (2nd ed.). New York: McGraw-Hill, 1976.

Serban, G. Stress: A sign of the times. *Science News,* May 23, 1981, p. 328.

Shanab, M. E., & Yahya, K. A. A behavioral study of obedience in children. *Journal of Personality and Social Psychology,* 1977, *35,* 530–536.

Shapira, A., & Madsen, M. C. Between- and within-group cooperation and competition among kibbutz and nonkibbutz children. *Developmental Psychology,* 1974, *10,* 140–145.

Shapiro, A. K., Struening, E., Shapiro, E., & Barten, H. Prognostic correlates of psychotherapy in psychiatric outpatients. *American Journal of Psychiatry,* 1976, *133,* 802–808.

Shapiro, J. G. Variability and usefulness of facial and body cues. *Comparative Group Studies,* 1972, *3,* 437–442.

Shaver, J. P., & Strong, W. *Facing value decisions: Rationale-building for teachers.* Belmont, Calif.: Wadsworth, 1976.

Sheldon, W. H. *The varieties of human physique: An introduction to constitutional psychology.* New York: Harper, 1940.

Sheldon, W. H. Constitutional factors in personality. In J. McV. Hunt (Ed.), *Personality and the behavior disorders.* New York: Ronald Press, 1944.

Sherif, M., & Sherif, C. W. *An outline of social psychology* (2nd ed.). New York: Harper & Row, 1956.

Shertzer, B., & Stone, S. C. *Fundamentals of guidance* (3rd ed.). Boston: Houghton Mifflin, 1976.

Shiffrin, R. M., & Atkinson, R. C. Storage and retrieval processes in long-term memory. *Psychological Review,* 1969, *76,* 179–193.

Shinn, M. Father absence and children's cognitive development. *Psychological Bulletin,* 1978, *85,* 295–324.

Shirley, M. M. The first two years. *A study of twenty-five babies* (Vol. 1). *Postural and locomotor development.* Minneapolis: University of Minnesota Press, 1931.

Shotland, R. L., & Huston, T. L. Emergencies: What are they and do they influence bystanders to intervene? *Journal of Personality and Social Psychology,* 1979, *37,* 1822–1834.

Silberner, J. Another day, another hormone mediator. *Science News,* July 12, 1980, p. 24.

'Silent' cells: Quiet revolution in brain science. *Science News,* July 9, 1977, pp. 20–21.

Silveira, J. *Incubation: The effect of interruption timing and length on problem solution and quality of problem processing.* Unpublished doctoral dissertation, University of Oregon, 1971.

Silverstein, B., Kozlowski, L. T., & Schachter, S. Studies of the interaction of psychological and pharmacological determinants of smoking: 3. Social life, cigarette smoking, and urinary pH. *Journal of Experimental Psychology: General,* 1977, *106,* 20–23.

Siman, M. L. Application of a new model of peer group influence to naturally existing adolescent friendship groups. *Child Development,* 1977, *48,* 270–274.

Simonson, N. R., & Lundy, R. M. The effectiveness of persuasive communication presented under conditions of irrelevant fear. *Journal of Communication,* 1966, *16,* 32–37.

Simpson, E. L. Moral development research: A case study of scientific cultural bias. *Human Development,* 1974, *17,* 81–106.

Singer, M. T., & Wynne, L. C. Thought disorder and family relations of schizophrenics. *Archives of General Psychiatry,* 1965, *12,* 187–212.

Sinnott, E. W., Dunn, L. C., & Dobzhansky, T. *Principles of genetics.* New York: McGraw-Hill, 1958.

Skeels, H. M. Updegraff, R., Wellman, B. L., & Williams, H. M. A study of environmental stimulation: An orphanage preschool project. *University of Iowa Studies in Child Welfare,* 1938, *15,* No. 4.

Skeels, H. M. Adult status of children with contrasting early life experiences. *Monographs of the Society for Research in Child Development,* 1966, *31,* (3, Serial No. 105).

Skinner, B. F. *Walden two.* London: Macmillan, 1948.

Skinner, B. F. *Science and human behavior.* New York: Macmillan, 1953.

Skinner, B. F. *Contingencies of reinforcement: A theoretical analysis.* New York: Appleton-Century-Crofts, 1969.

Skinner, B. F. *Beyond freedom and dignity.* New York: Knopf, 1971.

Slobin, D. I. The acquisition of Russian as a native language. In F. Smith & G. Miller (Eds.), *The genesis of language.* Cambridge, Mass.: M. I. T. Press, 1966, pp. 129–148.

Slobin, D. I. Universals of grammatical development in children. In G. B. Flores d'Arcams & W. J. M. Levelt (Eds.), *Advances in psycholinguistics.* New York: American Elsevier, 1970.

666

Smith, M. B. The phenomenological approach in personality theory: Some critical remarks. *Journal of Abnormal and Social Psychology,* 1950, *45,* 516–522.

Smith, M. L., & Glass, G. V. Meta-analysis of psychotherapy outcome studies. *American Psychologist,* 1977, *32,* 752–760.

Smith, S. M., Brown, H. O., Toman, J. E. P., & Goodman, L. S. The lack of cerebral effects of d-Tubercurarine. *Anesthesiology,* 1947, *8,* 1–14.

Smith, S. M., Glenberg, A., & Bjork, R. A. Environmental context and human memory. *Memory and Cognition,* 1978, *6,* 342–353.

Snyder, C. R., Shenkel, R. J., & Lowery, C. R. Acceptance of personality interpretations: The "Barnum effect" and beyond. *Journal of Consulting & Clinical Psychology,* 1977, *45,* 104–114.

Snyder, S. H. Amphetamine psychosis: A "model" schizophrenia mediated by catecholamines. *American Journal of Psychiatry,* 1973, *130,* 61–67.

Solomon, H., & Solomon, L. Z. *Effects of anonymity on helping in emergency situations.* Paper presented at the meeting of the Eastern Psychological Association, Washington, D.C., March 1978.

Solomon, R. L. The opponent-process theory of acquired motivation: The costs of pleasure and the benefits of pain. *American Psychologist,* 1980, *35,* 691–712.

Soni, S. D., & Rockley, G. J. Socio-clinical substrates of folie à deux. *British Journal of Psychiatry,* 1974, *125,* 230–235.

Soskin, W. F. Influence of four types of data on diagnostic conceptualization in psychological testing. *Journal of Abnormal and Social Psychology,* 1959, *58,* 69–78.

Spacapan, S., & Cohen, S. *Density, task load, and helping: Interpreting the aftereffects of stress.* Paper presented at the meeting of the American Psychological Association, San Francisco, August 1977.

Spalding, D. A. Instinct, with original observations on young animals. *Macmillan's Magazine,* 1873, *27,* 282–293. Reprinted in *British Journal of Animal Behaviour,* 1954, *2,* 2–11.

Spence, J. T., Helmreich, R., & Stapp, J. Ratings of self and peers on sex role attributes and their relation to self-esteem and conceptions of masculinity and feminity. *Journal of Personality and Social Psychology,* 1975, *32,* 29–39.

Sperling, G. The information available in brief visual presentations. *Psychological Monographs,* 1960, *74,* (11, Whole No. 498).

Spiegel, T. A. Caloric regulation of food intake in man. *Journal of Comparative and Physiological Psychology,* 1973, *84,* 24–37.

Spitz, R. A. Hospitalism: An inquiry into the genesis of psychiatric conditions in early childhood. *Psychoanalytic Study of the Child,* 1945, *1,* 53–74.

Spitz, R. A. Hospitalism: A follow-up report on investigation described in Volume I, 1945. *Psychoanalytic Study of the Child,* 1946, *2,* 113–117.

Spitzer, R. L. (Ed.). *Diagnostic and statistical manual of mental disorders.* Washington, D.C.: American Psychiatric Association, 1980.

Spring, R. L. The end of insanity. *Washburn Law Journal,* 1979, *19,* 23–37.

Sroufe, R., Chaikin, A., Cook, R., & Freeman, V. The effects of physical attractiveness on honesty: A socially desirable response. *Personality & Social Psychology Bulletin,* 1977, *3,* 59–62.

Staats, A. W., & Staats, C. K. Attitudes established by classical conditioning. *Journal of Abnormal and Social Psychology,* 1958, *57,* 37–40.

Stanfiel, J. D. The questionable sanity of the insanity defense. *Barrister,* Spring 1981, pp. 19–20; 48–51.

Starr, M. D. An opponent-process theory of motivation: VI. Time and intensity variables in the development of separation-induced distress calling in ducklings. *Journal of Experimental Psychology: Animal Behavior Processes,* 1978, *4,* 338–355.

Stayton, D. J., & Ainsworth, M. D. S. Individual differences in infant responses to brief, everyday separations as related to other infant and maternal behaviors. *Developmental Psychology,* 1973, *9,* 226–235.

Stayton, D. J., Hogan, R., & Ainsworth, M. D. S. Infant obedience and maternal behavior: The origins of socialization reconsidered. *Child Development,* 1971, *42,* 1057–1069.

Stein, A. H. The effects of maternal employment and educational attainment on the sex-typed attributes of college females. *Social Behavior and Personality,* 1973, *1,* 111–114.

Stellar, E. The physiology of motivation. *Psychological Review,* 1954, *61,* 5–22.

Stephan, W. G., & Rosenfield, D. Effects of desegregation on racial attitudes. *Journal of Personality and Social Psychology,* 1978, *36,* 795–804.

Stephens, R., & Cottrell, E. A follow-up study of 200 narcotic addicts committed for treatment under the narcotic addict rehabilitation act. *British Journal of Addiction,* 1972, *67,* 45–53.

Stern, D. A micro-analysis of mother-infant interaction: Behavior regulating social contact between a mother and her 3½-month-old twins. *Journal of the American Academy of Child Psychiatry,* 1971, *10,* 501–517.

Stern, D. B. Handedness and the lateral distribution of conversion reactions. *Journal of Nervous & Mental Disease,* 1977, *164,* 122–128.

Stevens, C. F. The neuron. *Scientific American,* 1979, *241*(3), 54–65.

Stimmel, B., Goldberg, J., Rotkopf, E., & Cohen, M. Ability to remain abstinent after methadone detoxification. *Journal of the American Medical Association,* 1977, *237,* 1216–1220.

Stoller, R. J. Gender identity. In B. J. Sadock, H. I. Kaplan & A. M. Freedman (Eds.), *The sexual experience.* Baltimore: Williams & Wilkins, 1976.

Straus, E., & Yalow, R. S. Cholecystokinin in the brain of obese and nonobese mice. *Science,* 1979, *203,* 68–69.

Sulloway, F. J. *Freud: Biologist of the mind.* New York: Basic Books, 1979.

Suomi, S. J., Harlow, H. F., & McKinney, W. T. Monkey psychiatrists. *American Journal of Psychiatry,* 1972, *128,* 927–932.

Sussman, N. Sex and sexuality in history. In B. J. Sadock, H. I. Kaplan & A. M. Freedman (Eds.), *The sexual experience.* Baltimore: Williams & Wilkins, 1976.

Swap, W. C. Interpersonal attraction and repeated exposure to rewarders and punishers. *Personality and Social Psychology Bulletin,* 1977, *3,* 248–251.

Szasz, T. S. *The myth of mental illness: Foundations of a theory of personal conduct.* New York: Harper & Row, 1961.

Szucko, J. J., & Kleinmuntz, B. Statistical versus clinical lie detection. *American Psychologist,* 1981, *36,* 488–496.

Tamminga, C. A., Schaffer, M. H., Smith, R. C., & Davis, J. M. Schizophrenic symptoms improve with apomorphine. *Science,* 1978, *200,* 567–568.

Tanner, J. M. Growth and endocrinology in the adolescent. In L. I. Gardner (Ed.), *Endocrine and genetic diseases of childhood.* Philadelphia: Saunders, 1969.

Tanner, J. M., Whitehouse, R. H., & Takaishi, M. Standards from birth to maturity for height, weight, height velocity and weight velocity: British children, 1965. *Archives of Disease in Childhood,* 1966, *41,* 454–471; 613–635.

Tate, D. F., Galvan, L., & Ungar, G. Isolation and identification of two learning-induced brain peptides. *Pharmacology, Biochemistry, & Behavior*, 1976, *5*(4), 441–448.

Taub, J. M., & Berger, R. J. Altered sleep duration and sleep period time displacements: Effects on performance in habitual long sleepers. *Physiology & Behavior*, 1976, *16*, 177–184.

Tauber, E. S. Phylogeny of sleep. In E. D. Weitzman (Ed.), *Advances in sleep research I.* New York: Spectrum, 1974, pp. 133–172.

Taussig, H. B. "Death" from lightning and the possibility of living again. *American Scientist*, 1969, *57*, 306–316.

Taylor, S. E., & Fiske, S. T. Salience, attention, and attribution: Top of the head phenomena. In L. Berkowitz (Ed.), *Advances in experimental social psychology* (Vol. 11). New York: Academic Press, 1978.

Teborg, R. H. *Dissipation of functional fixedness by means of conceptual grouping tasks.* Unpublished doctoral dissertation, Michigan State University, 1968.

Tedeschi, J. T., Schlenker, B. R., & Bonoma, T. V. Cognitive dissonance: Private ratiocination or public spectacle? *American Psychologist*, 1971, *26*, 685–695.

Terman, L. M. Mental and physical traits of a thousand gifted children. In L. M. Terman (Ed.), *Genetic studies of genius.* Stanford, Calif.: Stanford University Press, 1925.

Terman, L. M. Scientists and nonscientists in a group of 800 gifted men. *Psychological Monographs*, 1954, *68*(7), 1–44.

Terman, L. M., & Merrill, M. A. *Stanford-Binet Intelligence Scale* (2nd revision). Boston: Houghton Mifflin, 1937.

Ter-Pogossian, M. M., Raichle, M. E., & Sobel, B. E. Positron-emission tomography. *Scientific American*, 1980, *243*(4), 170–181.

Terr, L. C. Psychic trauma in children: Observations following the Chowchilla school-bus kidnapping. *The American Journal of Psychiatry*, 1981, *138*, 14–19.

Terrace, H. S. *Nim.* New York: Knopf, 1979.

Thomas, A., Chess, S., & Birch, H. G. The origin of personality. *Scientific American*, 1970, *223*(2), 102–109.

Thompson, S. K. Gender labels and early sex-role development. *Child Development*, 1975, *46*, 339–347.

Thomsen, D. E. Compassed about biologically. *Science News*, April 26, 1980, p. 267.

Thorndike, E. L. Animal intelligence: An experimental study of the associative processes in animals. *Psychological Monographs*, 1898, *2*, (Whole No. 8).

Thorndike, E. L. *The elements of psychology.* New York: Seiler, 1905.

Thorndike, E. L. *Animal intelligence: Experimental studies.* New York: Macmillan, 1911.

Thurstone, L. L. Primary mental abilities. *Psychometric Monographs*, 1938, *1*.

Tolman, E. C., Ritchie, B. F., & Kalish, D. Studies in spatial learning. I. Orientation and the short-cut. *Journal of Experimental Psychology*, 1946, *36*, 13–24.

Tomkins, S. S. *Affect, imagery, consciousness, the positive affects* (Vol. 1). New York: Springer, 1962.

Tomkins, S. S. *Affect, imagery, consciousness, the negative affects* (Vol. 2). New York: Springer, 1963.

The trauma of captivity. *Time*, December 24, 1979. p. 59.

Troll, L. E. *Early and middle adulthood.* Monterey, Calif.: Brooks/Cole, 1975.

Trotter, R. J. Fifty ways to quit your smoking. *Science News*, January 7, 1978, p. 9.

Tryon, R. C. Genetic differences in maze learning in rats. *Yearbook of the National Society for Studies in Education*, 1940, *39*, 111–119.

Tsitoura, P. D., Martin, C. E., Harman, S. M., & Gregerman, R. I. The relationship of testosterone to sexual activity in aged men. *Clinical Research*, 1979, *27*, A452.

Tuckman, J., & Regan, R. A. Intactness of the home and behavioral problems in children. *Journal of Child Psychology and Psychiatry*, 1966, *7*, 225–233.

Tulving, E. Cue-dependent forgetting. *American Scientist*, 1974, *62*, 74–82.

Tune, G. S. Sleep and wakefulness in 509 normal human adults. *British Journal of Medical Psychology*, 1969, *42*, 75–79.

Turnbull, C. M. Some observations regarding the experiences and behavior of the Bambuti Pygmies. *American Journal of Psychology*, 1961, *74*, 304–308.

Turvey, M. T., & Shaw, R. E. The primacy of perceiving: An ecological reformulation of perception for understanding memory. In L. G. Nilsson (Ed.), *Perspectives on memory research.* Hillsdale, N.J.: Erlbaum, 1979, pp. 167–222.

Tyler, L. E. *The psychology of human differences.* New York: Appleton, 1956.

Ungar, G., Desiderio, D. M., & Parr, W. Isolation, identification and synthesis of a specific-behaviour-inducing brain peptide. *Nature*, 1972, *238*, 198–202.

Ungar, G., Galvan, L., & Clark, R. H. Chemical transfer of learned fear. *Nature*, 1968, *217*, 1259–1261.

Urbina, S., & Grey, A. Cultural and sex differences in the sex distribution of dream characters. *Journal of Cross-Cultural Psychology*, 1975, *6*, 358–364.

Vaillant, G. E. Natural history of male psychologic health: Effects of mental health on physical health. *New England Journal of Medicine*, 1979, *301*, 1249–1254.

Valenstein, E. S. *Brain control: A critical examination of brain stimulation and psychosurgery.* New York: Wiley, 1973.

Valenstein, E. S. In A. Wauquier & E. T. Rolls (Eds.), *Brain stimulation reward.* Amsterdam: North Holland, 1976.

Valenstein, E. S. Causes and treatments of mental disorders. In E. S. Valenstein (Ed.), *The psychosurgery debate.* San Francisco: W. H. Freeman, 1980.

Valenstein, E. S. Historical perspective. In E. S. Valenstein (Ed.), *The psychosurgery debate.* San Francisco: W. H. Freeman, 1980.

Valenstein, E. S. Who receives psychosurgery? In E. S. Valenstein (Ed.), *The psychosurgery debate.* San Francisco: W. H. Freeman, 1980.

Valins, S. Cognitive effects of false heart-rate feedback. *Journal of Personality and Social Psychology*, 1966, *4*, 400–408.

Vanderweele, D. A., & Sanderson, J. D. Peripheral gluco-sensitive satiety in the rabbit and the rat. In D. Novin, W. Wyrwicka, & G. A. Bray (Eds.), *Hunger: Basic mechanisms and clinical implications.* New York: Raven Press, 1976.

Vandiver, R. *Sources and interrelation of premarital sexual standards and general liberality conservatism,* Unpublished doctoral dissertation, Southern Illinois University, 1972.

Vernon, P. E. Ability factors and environmental influences. *American Psychologist*, 1965, *20*, 723–733.

Vindication of early childhood programs. *Science News*, March 5, 1977, p. 151.

Vinokur, A., & Burnstein, E. Depolarization of attitudes in groups. *Journal of Personality and Social Psychology.* 1978, *36*, 872–885.

Vogel, G. W. A review of REM sleep deprivation. *Archives of General Psychiatry*, 1975, *32*, 749–761.

von Hofsten, C., & Lindhagen, K. Observations on the development

668

of reaching for moving objects. *Journal of Experimental Child Psychology*, 1979, *28*, 158–173.

Waid, W. M., Orne, E. C., Cook, M. R., & Orne, M. T. Meprobamate reduces accuracy of physiological detection of deception. *Science*, 1981, *212*, 71–73.

Waldrop, M. F., & Halverson, C. F. Intensive and extensive peer behavior: Longitudinal and cross-sectional analyses, *Child Development*, 1975, *46*, 19–26.

Walker, D. W., Barnes, D. E., Zornetzer, S. F., Hunter, B. E., & Kubanis, P. Neuronal loss in hippocampus induced by prolonged ethanol consumption in rats. *Science*, 1980, *209*, 711–712.

Wallace, I., Wallechinsky, D., Wallace, A., & Wallace, S. *The book of lists #2*. New York: Bantam Books, 1980.

Wallach, M. A. Creativity. In P. H. Mussen (Ed.), *Carmichael's manual of child psychology* (3rd ed.). New York: Wiley, 1970, pp. 1211–1272.

Wallach, M. A., & Kogan, N. *Modes of thinking in young children: A study of the creativity-intelligence distinction*. New York: Holt, Rinehart & Winston, 1965.

Wallach, M. A., & Wing, C. W. *The talented student: A validation of the creativity-intelligence distinction*. New York: Holt, Rinehart & Winston, 1969.

Walters, G. C., & Grusec, J. E. *Punishment*. San Francisco: W. H. Freeman, 1977.

Wanner, H. E. *On remembering, forgetting, and understanding sentences: A study of the deep structure hypothesis*. Unpublished doctoral dissertation, Harvard University, 1968.

Was it hypnosis or hype? *Time Magazine*, January 14, 1980, p. 50.

Washburn, S. L., & Hamburg, D. A. The study of primate behavior. In I. DeVore (Ed.), *Primate behavior: Field studies of monkeys and apes*. New York: Holt, Rinehart & Winston, 1965.

Watson, J. B. Psychology as the behaviorist views it. *Psychological Review*, 1913, *20*, 158–177.

Watson, J. B. *Psychology from the standpoint of a behaviorist* (3rd ed.). Philadelphia: Lippincott, 1929.

Watson, J. B. *Behaviorism*. New York: Norton, 1930.

Watson, J. B., & Rayner, R. Conditioned emotional reactions. *Journal of Experimental Psychology*, 1920, *3*, 1–14.

Watson, J. S., & Ramey, C. T. *Reactions to responsive contingent stimulation in early infancy*. Paper presented at the biennial meeting of the Society for Research in Child Development, Santa Monica, Calif.: March, 1969.

Watson, J. S., & Ramey, C. T. Reactions to response-contingent stimulation in early infancy. *Merrill-Palmer Quarterly*, 1972, *18*, 219–227.

Webb, W. B. Sleep as an adaptive response. *Perceptual & Motor Skills*, 1974, *38*, 1023–1027.

Webb, W. B. *Sleep the gentle tyrant*. Englewood Cliffs, N.J.: Prentice-Hall, 1975.

Webb, W. B., & Agnew, H. W. Jr. Sleep: Effects of a restricted regime. *Science*, 1965, *150*, 1745–1747.

Webb, W. B., & Cartwright, R. D. Sleep and dreams. In M. R. Rosenzweig & L. W. Porter (Eds.), *Annual review of psychology*. Palo Alto, Calif.: Annual Reviews, 1978, pp. 223–252.

Weinberger, D. R., Bigelow, L. B., Kleinman, J. E., Klein, S. T., Rosenblatt, J. E., & Wyatt, R. J. Cerebral ventricular enlargement in chronic schizophrenia. *Archives of General Psychiatry*, 1980, *37*, 11–13.

Weiner, M. J., & Wright, F. E. Effects of undergoing arbitrary discrimination upon subsequent attitudes toward a minority group. *Journal of Applied Social Psychology*, 1973, *3*, 94–102.

Weingartner, H., Gold, P., Bullenger, J. C., Smallberg, S. A., Summers, R., Rubinow, D. R., Post, R. M., & Goodwin, F. K. Effects of vasopressin on human memory functions. *Science*, 1981, *211*, 601–603.

Weintraub, P. Wired for sound. *Discover*, December 1980, pp. 50–51.

Weintraub, P. The brain: His and hers. *Discover*, April 1981, pp. 15–20.

Weintraub, W. *Verbal behavior: Adaptation and psychopathology*. New York: Springer, 1981.

Weir, R. H. Some questions on the child's learning of phonology. In F. Smith & G. Miller (Eds.), *The genesis of language*. Cambridge, Mass.: M.I.T. Press, 1966, pp. 153–168.

Weiss, B., & Santelli, S. Dyskinesias evoked in monkeys by weekly administration of haloperidol. *Science*, 1978, *200*, 799–801.

Weisstein, N. Psychology constructs the female. In I. S. Cohen (Ed.), *Perspectives on psychology*. New York: Praeger, 1975, pp. 318–331.

Weitkamp, L. R., Stancer, H. C., Persad, E., Flood, C., & Guttormsen, S. Depressive disorders and HLA: A gene on chromosome 6 that can affect behavior. *New England Journal of Medicine*, 1981, *305*, 1301–1306.

Weitzenhoffer, A. M., & Hilgard, E. R. *The Stanford Hypnotic Susceptibility Scale, form C*. Palo Alto, Calif.: Consulting Psychologists Press, 1962.

Wertheimer, M. Experimentelle Studien über das Schen von Bewegunen. *Zool. Psychol.*, 1912, *61*, 121–165.

Wertheimer, M. Psycho-motor coordination of auditory-visual space at birth. *Science*, 1961, *134*, 1692.

Westermarck, E. *The origin and development of the moral ideas*. London: Macmillan, 1917.

Wetli, C. V., & Wright, R. K. Death caused by recreational cocaine use. *Journal of the American Medical Association*, 1979, *241*, 2519–2522.

Whalen, C. K., & Henker, B. Psychostimulants and children: A review and analysis. *Psychological Bulletin*, 1976, *83*, 1113–1130.

Wheeler, L., Deci, L., Reis, H., & Zuckerman, M. *Interpersonal influence* (2nd ed.) Boston: Allyn & Bacon, 1978.

White, B. W., Saunders, F. A., Scadden, L., Bach-Y-Rita, P., & Collins, C. C. Seeing with the skin. *Perception and Psychophysics*, 1970, *7*, 23–27.

White, G. L., & Maltzman, I. Pupillary activity while listening to verbal pasages. *Journal of Research in Personality*, 1978, *12*, 361–369.

Whorf, B. L. *Language, thought, and reality*. Cambridge, Mass.: M.I.T. Press, 1956.

Wickelgren, W. A. The long and the short of memory. *Psychological Bulletin*, 1973, *80*, 425–438.

Wickelgren, W. A. Human learning and memory. In M. R. Rosenzweig & L. W. Porter (Eds.), *Annual review of psychology*. Palo Alto, Calif.: Annual Reviews, 1981, pp. 21–52.

Williams, D. A., & King, P. Do males have a math gene? *Newsweek*, December 15, 1980, p. 72.

Williams, D. A., & King, P. It really is a head start. *Newsweek*, December 22, 1980, p. 54.

Wilson, W. R. Feeling more than we can know: Exposure effects without learning. *Journal of Personality and Social Psychology*, 1979, *37*, 811–821.

Witelson, S. F. Sex and the single hemisphere: Specialization of the right hemisphere for spatial processing. *Science*, 1976, *193*, 425–427.

Wolf, S. Psychosocial influences in gastrointestinal function. In L. Levi (Ed.), *The psychosocial environment and psychosomatic disease* (Vol. 1). London: Oxford University Press, 1971.

Wong, S. C. P., & Frost, B. J. Subjective motion and acceleration induced by the movement of the observer's entire visual field. *Perception & Psychophysics*, 1978, *24*, 115–120.

Woodward, J. A., & Goldstein, M. J. Communication deviance in the families of schizophrenics: A comment on the misuse of analysis of covariance. *Science*, 1977, *197*, 1096–1097.

Wooley, S. E. Physiologic versus cognitive factors in short-term food regulation in the obese and nonobese. *Psychosomatic Medicine*, 1972, *34*, 62.

Wortman, C. B., & Brehm, J. W. Responses to uncontrollable outcomes: An integration of reactance theory and the learned helplessness model. *Advances in Experimental Social Psychology*, 1975, *8*, 277–336.

Wulbert, M., & Dries, R. The relative efficacy of methylphenidate (Ritalin) and behavior-modification techniques in the treatment of a hyperactive child. *Journal of Applied Behavior Analysis*, 1977, *10*, 21–31.

Yakimovich, D., & Saltz, E. Helping behavior: The cry for help. *Psychonomic Science*, 1971, *23*, 427–428.

Yakolev, P. I., & Lecours, A. R. The myelogenetic cycles of regional maturation in the brain. In A. Minkowski (Ed.), *Regional development of the brain in early life*. Oxford: Blackwell, 1967.

Yaksh, T. L., & Myers, R. D. Neurohumoral substance released from hypothalamus of the monkey during hunger and satiety. *American Journal of Physiology*, 1972, *222*, 503–515.

Yalom, I. D., Green, R., & Fisk, N. Prenatal exposure to female hormones: Effect on psychosexual development in boys. *Archives of General Psychiatry*, 1973, *28*, 554–561.

Yerkes, R. M., & Dodson, J. D. The relation of strength of stimulus to rapidity of habit formation. *Journal of Comparative Neurology and Psychology*, 1908, *18*, 459–482.

Young, W. C., Goy, R. W., & Phoenix, C. H. Hormones and sexual behavior. *Science*, 1964, *143*, 212–218.

Younger, J. C., Walker, L., & Arrowood, A. J. Postdecision dissonance at the fair. *Personality and Social Psychology Bulletin*, 1977, *3*, 284–287.

Yudofsky, S. C. ECT: Shocking depression. *Science News*, May 23, 1981, p. 328.

Zajonc, R. Attitudinal effects of mere exposure. *Journal of Personality and Social Psychology*, 1968, *9*, 1–27.

Zajonc, R. B., & Markus, G. B. Birth order and intellectual development. *Psychological Review*, 1975, *82*, 74–88.

Zavodnick, S. Suggestions for a rational approach to the chemotherapy of schizophrenia. *Diseases of the Nervous System*, 1976, *37*, 671–675.

Zellner, M. Self-esteem, reception, and influenceability. *Journal of Personality and Social Psychology* 1970, *15*, 87–93.

Zimbardo, P. G. *Psychology and life* (10th ed.). Glenview, Ill.: Scott Foresman, 1979.

Zimbardo, P. G. *The hidden power of our time sense: Promoting poverty and sexless successes*. Paper presented at the meeting of the Western Psychological Association, Los Angeles, April 1981.

Zimbardo, P. G., Haney, C., Banks, W. C., & Jaffe, D. A pirandellian prison. *The New York Times Magazine*, April 8, 1973, pp. 38–60.

Zimmerman, W. B. Sleep mentation and auditory awakening thresholds. *Psychophysiology*, 1970, *6*, 540–549.

Zuckerman, M., DeFrank, R. S., Hall, J. A., & Rosenthal, R. Accuracy of nonverbal communication as determinant of interpersonal expectancy effects. *Environmental Psychology & Nonverbal Behavior*, 1978, *2*, 206–214.

Zukin, S. R., & Zukin, R. S. Specific phencyclidine-3 binding in rat central nervous system. *Proceedings of the National Academy of Sciences*, 1979, *10*, 5372–5376.

Zylman, R. Drinking-driving and fatal crashes: A new perspective. *Journal of Alcohol & Drug Education*, 1975, *21*, 1–10.

Stice, G. F., 403
Stickney, S. K., 492
Stimmel, B., 527
Stoel, C., 248
Stoller, R., 584
Stoller, R. J., 67, 584, 591
Stone, S. C., 363
Straus, E., 275
Strauss, J. S., 505
Stricker, E. M., 276
Strong, W., 550–551
Struening, E., 525
Strupp, H. H., 525
Sullivan, J. J., 557
Sulloway, F. J., 13
Sulzer, J. L., 21
Summers, R., 211
Suave, R., 379
Suedfeld, P., 221
Sultan, 233–234
Suomi, S. J., 338–339, 441
Sussman, N., 68, 604
Svejda, M., 122
Swap, W. C., 568
Szasz, T. S., 490–491
Szucko, J. J., 305

Tachiban, S., 61
Takaishi, M., 362
Tamminga, C. A., 479
Tan, T. L., 143
Tanner, J. M., 361–362
Tate, D. F., 213
Taub, J. M., 146
Tauber, E. S., 139
Taussig, H. B., 297
Taylor, S. E., 573
Teborg, R. H., 244
Tedeschi, J. T., 566, 571
Telegdy, G. A., 193
Tepperman, J., 273
Terman, L. M., 373, 388–390, 393
Ter-Pogossian, M. M., 51
Terr, L. C., 435
Terrace, H. S., 263
Thiel, D. L., 599
Thomas, A., 334, 358, 410
Thomas, C. B., 440–441
Thompson, B., 317
Thompson, W. D., 485
Thompson, S. K., 585
Thomsen, D. E., 99
Thorndike, E. L., 180
Thurstone, L. L., 371–372, 377
Timsit-Berthier, M., 211
Tipton, R. D., 524
Tissot, S., 604
Titchener, E. B., 9
Toffano, G., 160
Tokuhata, G. K., 435
Tolman, E. C., 198
Toman, J. E. P., 236

Tomkins, S. S., 314
Tondow, M., 591
Tracy, R. L., 358
Troll, L. E., 362
Trotter, R. J., 527
Truswell, L., 251
Tryon, R. C., 67
Tsitoura, P. D., 278
Tuckman, J., 358
Tulving, E., 220
Tune, G. S., 141
Turnbull, C. M., 103
Turvey, M. T., 127
Tyler, L. E., 400

Ungar, G., 212–213
Updegraff, R., 69
Urban, I., 211
Urbina, S., 149

Vaillant, G. E., 439
Valenstein, E. S., 275–276, 491, 510–512
Valins, S., 299–300, 307
Valone, K., 569
Van Riezen, H., 219
van Wimersma Greidanus. T. B., 211
Vanderweele, D. A., 276
Vandiver, R., 360
Verbeek, G., 112
Vernon, J., 221
Vernon, P. E., 384
Vincent, J. E., 557
Vinokur, A., 561
Vogel, G. W., 144
Vogel, P. J., 53
Vogel, S. R., 356
von Braun, V., 572
von Hofsten, C., 119–120, 127, 129–130
von Jauregg, J. W., 507

Waid, W. M., 305
Waldrop, M. F., 359
Walk, R. D., 121
Walker, D. W., 484
Walker, L., 571
Wallace, A., 469
Wallace, I., 469
Wallace, J. E., 163
Wallace, S., 469
Wallach, M. A., 393
Wallechinsky, D., 469
Walster, E., 602
Walters, G. C., 186
Wanner, E., 286
Wanner, H. E., 214
Ward, C. D., 567
Warrington, E., 120
Washburn, S. L., 66
Washoe, 260–261, 263
Watkins, J., 453–454
Watson, J. B., 10–12, 136, 176–178, 235–236, 409, 523

Watson, J. S., 284
Watts, J., 511
Webb, W. B., 137–139, 141–143
Webber, J. A., 75
Weber, E., 75
Weikart, D. P., 385
Weinberg, R. A., 69, 380–381
Weinberger, D. R., 480
Weiner, M. J., 564
Weinfeld, F. D., 285
Weingartner, H., 211
Weintraub, P., 92–93, 583, 587
Weintraub, W., 421
Weir, R. H., 248
Weiskrantz, L., 120
Weiss, B., 505
Weiss, R. S., 438
Weisstein, N., 584
Weitkamp, L. R., 473–474
Weitzenhoffer, A. M., 153
Wellman, B. L., 69
Wells, C. E., 493
Wender, P. H., 478
Wernicke, C., 264
Wertheimer, Max, 12
Wertheimer, Michael, 122
Werts, C. E., 420
Westermarck, E., 590
Wetli, C. V., 159
Wheeler, D., 557
Wheeler, J., 343
Wheeler, L., 536
Whitaker, J. M., 62
White, A., 443
White, B., 129
White, B. W., 129
White, G. L., 566
Whitehouse, R. H., 362
Whitman, C., 50–52, 305
Whorf, B. L., 246–247
Winter, D., 286
Wickelgren, W. A., 216
Wicklund, R. A., 567
Wilber, C., 469
Williams, D. A., 386, 586–587
Williams, H. M., 69
Williams, R. M., 438
Wilson, E., 280, 281
Wilson, F., 359
Wilson, W. R., 569
Wing, C. W., 393
Winokur, G., 474
Wist, E. R., 119
Witelson, S. F., 57
Wittelsberger, B., 525
Wolf, S., 437
Wolpe, J., 520
Wong, S. C. P., 119
Woodward, J. A., 478
Wooley, S. E., 274
Wortman, C. B., 285
Wright, F. E., 564

---

*Italicized page numbers that appear in this index refer to pages on which a running glossary definition of the particular subject can be found.

682

683

Page 180, Figure 6.5. From "Thorndike and the Problem of Animal Intelligence," by M. E. Bitterman. In *American Psychologist,* 1969, *24,* 444–453. Copyright 1969 by the American Psychological Association. Reprinted by permission of the publisher and author.

Page 192. Reprinted from NEBRASKA SYMPOSIUM ON MOTIVATION, 1962, Marshall R. Jones, Editor. Copyright © 1962 by the University of Nebraska Press.

Page 206, Figure 7.4. From "Retention as a Function of the Method of Measurement," by L. Postman & L. Rau. In *University of California Publications in Psychology,* 1957, *8* (3). Reprinted by permission of the University of California Press.

Page 209, Table 7.2. Excerpt from STOP FORGETTING by Bruno Furst. Copyright 1948, 1949 by Bruno Furst. Reprinted by permission of Doubleday & Company, Inc.

Page 222, Figure 7.12. From "Long-term Memory for a Common Object," by R. S. Nickerson & M. J. Adams. In *Cognitive Psychology,* 1979, *11,* 287–307. Reprinted by permission of Academic Press, Inc., and the author.

Page 224, Figure 7.14. From COGNITIVE PSYCHOLOGY AND ITS IMPLICATIONS by John R. Anderson. W. H. Freeman and Company. Copyright © 1980.

Page 226, Figure 7.15. Adapted from "Mood and Memory," by G. H. Bower. In *American Psychologist,* 1981, *36,* 129–148. Copyright 1981 by the American Psychological Association. Reprinted by permission of the publisher and author.

Page 245. Excerpt from pp. 279–280 in ZEN AND THE ART OF MOTORCYCLE MAINTE-NANCE by Robert M. Pirsig. Copyright © 1974 by Robert M. Pirsig. By permission of William Morrow & Company and The Bodley Head.

Page 252, Figure 8.7. From "The Acquisition of Language," by Breyne Arlene Moskowitz. Copyright © 1978 by Scientific American, Inc. All rights reserved.

Page 254, Table 8.2. From PSYCHOLOGY AND LANGUAGE by Herbert H. and Eve V. Clark, © 1977 by Harcourt Brace Jovanovich, Inc. Reprinted by permission of the publisher.

Page 254, Figure 8.8. From WORD, Fig. 1, p. 154, 1958. By permission of Johnson Reprint Corporation.

Page 292, Figure 9.7. From "Steepness of Approach and Avoidance Gradients in Humans as a Function of Experience. In *Journal of Experimental Psychology,* 1965, *70,* 1–12. Copyright 1965 by the American Psychological Association. Reprinted by permission of the publisher and author.

Page 293–294, Figure 9.8, 9.9, Table 9.1. From "The Opponent-Process Theory of Acquired Motivation," by Richard L. Solomon. In *American Psychologist,* 1980, *35,* 691–712. Copyright 1980 by the American Psychological Association. Reprinted by permission of the publisher and author.

Pages 316, 318, Figures 10.10 and 10.12, Table 10.2. From "A Language for the Emotions," by Robert Plutchik. In *Psychology Today,* February 1980. Reprinted from PSYCHOLOGY TODAY MAGAZINE. Copyright © 1980 Ziff-Davis Publishing Company.

Page 340, Table 11.4. From "Adult Status of Children with Contrasting Life Experiences," by H. M. Skeels. In *Monographs of the Society for Research in Child Development,* 1966, *31,* (3, Serial No. 105). © The Society for Research in Child Development, Inc.

Page 342, Figure 11.5. From "Mother Attachment and Stranger Reactions in the Third Year of Life," by E. E. Maccoby & S. S. Feldman. In *Monographs of the Society for Research in Child Development,* 1972, 37, (No. 1). © The Society for Research in Child Development, Inc.

Page 350, Figure 11.9. From OF CHILDREN, AN INTRODUCTION TO CHILD DEVELOP-MENT, Third Edition, by Guy R. Lefrancois. © 1980 by Wadsworth, Inc. Reprinted by permission of Wadsworth Publishing Company, Belmont, California 94002.

Page 355, Table 11.6. From *Socialization and Society,* by J. Clausen. Boston: Little, Brown, 1968. Reprinted by permission of J. Clausen.

Page 361, Figure 11.10. Adapted from Tanner, J. M.: Growth and endocrinology of the adolescent. In Gardner, L. I.: *Endocrine and Genetic Diseases of Childhood.* 2nd edition. Philadelphia, W. B. Saunders Company, 1975.

Page 362, Figure 11.11. From "Standards from Birth to Maturity for Height, Weight, Height Velocity, and Weight Velocity," by J. M. Tanner, R. H. Whitehouse, & M. Takaishi. In *Archives of Disease in Childhood,* 1966, *41,* 454–635. Reprinted by permission of the publisher and Dr. J. M. Tanner.

Page 373, Figure 12.1. From Terman, L. M., and Merrill, M. A., Stanford-Binet Intelligence Scale. Manual for the Third Revision Form L-M © 1973. Reproduced with permission from The Riverside Publishing Company.

Page 378, Figure 12.3. From *The Nature of Human Intelligence,* by J. P. Guilford. New York: McGraw-Hill, 1967. Reprinted by permission of the publisher.

Page 383, Table 12.1. From *Developmental Psychology Today* by R. E. Schell & E. Hall. New York: Random House, Inc., 1979. Reprinted by permission of the publisher.

Page 384, Figure 12.4. Item A5 from STANDARD PROGRESSIVE MATRICES by J. C. Raven. Reprinted by permission of J. C. Raven Limited.

Page 387, Figure 12.5. From *Stability and Change in Human Characteristics* by B. S. Bloom. New York: John Wiley & Sons, 1964. Reprinted by permission of the publisher.

CHAPTER 1
7 The Bettmann Archive; **8, 9, 10,** Brown Brothers; **12** United Press International; **13** The Bettmann Archive; **14** © Ted Polumbaum; **20** Jean-Claude Lejeune, Stock, Boston.

CHAPTER 2
40 Y. Jan, Department of Physiology, School of Medicine, University of California, San Francisco; **50** United Press International; **63** Dr. Fred Hecht, The Genetics Center of Southwest Biomedical Research Institute; **64** Jill Freedman, Archive Pictures, Inc.; **66** Peter Vandermark, Stock, Boston.

CHAPTER 3
85 John Dworetzky; **98** United Press International.

CHAPTER 4
107 (top) Stephen S. Cooper, (bottom) H. Morgan, Stock, Boston; **110** The Museum of Modern Art Film Archives; **116, 117** The Ames Room is an exhibit at the Exploratorium, a participatory museum of science and human perception located in San Francisco, California; photographs by Baron Wollman; **121** Albert Fenn, Life Magazine © Time Inc.; **127** © Hubertos Kanus, Photo Researchers, Inc.; **129** Black Star; **133** New York Times Pictures.

CHAPTER 5
138, 147 Photographs courtesy of Dr. William C. Dement and Dr. Theodore L. Baker, Sleep Disorders Research Center, Stanford University School of Medicine. **139** The Bettmann Archive; **150** Courtesy of the Detroit Institute of Arts, Gift of Mr. and Mrs. Bert L. Smokler and Mr. and Mrs. Lawrence A. Fleischman. **152** The Bettmann Archive; **155** Mimi Forsyth, Monkmeyer Press Photo Service; **157** Bruce Coleman, Inc.; **159** Courtesy Peter N. Wih, M.D.; **162** Misha Erwitt, Magnum.

CHAPTER 6
171 Thomas McAvoy, Life Magazine © 1955 Time Inc.; **178** Courtesy of Dr. Ben Harris, from J. B. Watson's *Experimental Investigation of Babies* (1919). **182** Yale Joel, Life Magazine © 1950 Time Inc.; **185** © Guy Gillette, Photo Researchers, Inc.; **188** Elliott Erwitt, Magnum; **191** Misha Erwitt, Magnum; **192** Wide World Photos; **193** Eliot Elisofon, Life Magazine © 1958 Time Inc.; **194** Courtesy of Albert Bandura, Stanford.

CHAPTER 7
204 The Bettmann Archive; **209** Wide World Photos; **216** Burt Glinn, Magnum; **218** Tim Carlson, Stock, Boston; **227** (left) Cary Wolinsky, Stock, Boston, (right) © Robert A. Isaacs 1978, Photo Researchers, Inc.

CHAPTER 8
234 From *The Mentality of Apes* by Wolfgang Kohler. Permission granted by Routledge & Kegan Paul, Ltd., London, England, 1982. **239** Geoffrey Gove, Photo Researchers, Inc.; **251** Jean-Claude Lejeune, Stock, Boston; **255** © Alice Kandell, Photo Researchers, Inc.; **257** Ivan Massar, Black Star; **260** Paul Fusco, Magnum; **268** Wide World Photos.

CHAPTER 9
273 Dr. Neal E. Miller; **277** (left) Ira Kirschenbaum, Stock, Boston; (right) © Margot Granitsas, Photo Researchers, Inc.; **288** University of Wisconsin Primate Laboratory; **289** © Arthur Tress, Photo Researchers, Inc.; **291** © Hans Namuth, Photo Researchers, Inc.; **295** © Rebuffat, Photo Researchers, Inc.

CHAPTER 10
302 Terry Evans, Magnum; **303/306** Mary Ellen Mark, Archive Pictures, Inc.; **305** © Bruce Roberts, Photo Researchers, Inc.; **312** Reproduced by special permission from *Pictures of Facial Affect* by Dr. Wallace Friesen and Dr. Paul Ekman. Copyright 1976, published by Consulting Psychologists Press, Inc., Palo Alto, Ca. 94306. **313** Dane Archer and Robin M. Akert, "Words and Everything Else: Verbal and Nonverbal Cues in Social Interpretation. *Journal of Personality and Social Psychology,* 1977, 35:443–449. **315** (top row, left) Joseph A. Kovacs, Stock, Boston, (top row, right) Clif Garboden, Stock, Boston, (bottom row, left) Peter Vandermark, Stock, Boston, (bottom row, right) David Powers, Stock, Boston; **320** Culver Pictures, Inc.

CHAPTER 11
326 George Zimbel, Monkmeyer Press Photo Service; **329** United Press International; **330** © Fritz Henle, Photo Researchers, Inc.; **333** Colvin, Monkmeyer Press Photo Service; **334–335** © Gerry Cranham, Photo Researchers, Inc.; **336, 341** University of Wisconsin Primate

Laboratory; **345** Yves DeBraine, Black Star; **346** George Zimbel, Monkmeyer Press Photo Service; **353** James R. Holland, Stock, Boston; **357** Shirley Zeiberg, Taurus; **358** Kagan, Monkmeyer Press Photo Service; **359** © Jeanne Tifft, Photo Researchers; **366** Ginger Chih, © Peter Arnold, Inc.

C H A P T E R 12
374 Mimi Forsyth, Monkmeyer Press Photo Service; **375** Courtesy The Psychological Corporation; **378** Wide World Photos; **381** Christopher Springman, Black Star; **389** News and Publication Service, Stanford University; **390** Susie Fitzhugh, Stock, Boston; **392** Jean-Claude Lejeune, Stock, Boston.

C H A P T E R 13
403 United Press International; **406** Historical Pictures Service, Inc., Chicago; **408** (top) © George Gerster, Black Star, (middle) United Press International, (bottom) Brown Brothers; **411** Culver Pictures, Inc.; **412** Wide World Photos; **413** The Bettmann Archive.

C H A P T E R 14
430 Walter Reed Army Institute of Research, Department of the Army; **432** Peter Southwick, Stock, Boston; **434** United Press International; **435** (top) Wide World Photos, (bottom) Owen Franken, Stock, Boston; **437** United Press International; **448** © Ray Ellis, Photo Researchers, Inc.; **449** Waring Abbott, Black Star.

C H A P T E R 15
454 United Press International; **470** Culver Pictures, Inc.; **472** Mike Mazzaschi, Stock, Boston; **474** Peter Vandermark, Stock, Boston; **477** Michael Weisbrot, Stock, Boston; **481** Culver Pictures, Inc.; **482** Sybil Shelton, Peter Arnold, Inc.; **489** News and Publication Service, Stanford University; **491** Culver Pictures, Inc.

C H A P T E R 16
500, 501 The Bettmann Archive, Inc.; **507** Paul Fusco, Magnum; **509** Burk Uzzle, Magnum; **516** United Press International; **517** John Dworetzky; **519** George Zimbel, Monkmeyer Press Photo Service; **521** Courtesy Albert Bandura, Stanford.

C H A P T E R 17
536 Ginger Chih, © Peter Arnold, Inc.; **539** United Press International; **538** © Eric Kroll, Taurus; **537** Ellis Herwig, Stock, Boston; **540** Eric Kroll; **544** United Press International; **546** © Jan Lukas, Photo Researchers, Inc.; **549** United Press International; **563** © Bruce Roberts, Photo Researchers, Inc.; **577** Owen D. B., Black Star.

C H A P T E R 18
585 © Suzanne Szasz, Photo Researchers, Inc.; **590** Erika Stone, © Peter Arnold, Inc.; **592** United Press International; **593** Ellis Herwig, Stock, Boston; **595** (upper left) Stern, Hamburg 1, Black Star, (upper right) © 1978 Ed Lettau, Photo Researchers, Inc., (lower) Rene Burri, Magnum; **599** The Bettmann Archive; **600** © Hella Hammid, Photo Researchers, Inc.; **605** Robert J. Levin, Black Star.